AMERICAN CONSTITUTIONAL LAW: POWER AND POLITICS

Volume II

Civil Rights and Liberties

Gregg Ivers
American University

Houghton Mifflin Company Boston • New York

Editor in Chief: Jean L. Woy
Sponsoring Editor: Mary Dougherty
Development Editor: Katherine Meisenheimer
Editorial Assistant: Tonya Lobato
Senior Project Editor: Tracy Patruno
Manufacturing Manager: Florence Cadran
Marketing Manager: Nicola Poser

Cover image: *Optimistic over anti-segregation,* © Bettmann/CORBIS

Printed in the U.S.A.

Library of Congress Control Number: 00-133890

ISBN: 0-395-88987-1

1 2 3 4 5 6 7 8 9 - CRS - 05 04 03 02 01

For my family,
past, present, and future

Contents

Preface

Each semester when I teach Constitutional Law and Civil Liberties, I always tell my undergraduates that no one is going to learn anything, including myself, if we cannot make the subject come alive. And what makes the study of the Constitution fun is the human drama behind the cases that have resulted in many of the landmark decisions by the United States Supreme Court. In *American Constitutional Law,* I have emphasized the relationship between law and society, with a special focus on the people and organized interests that turned their personal disputes with the law into cases of monumental importance that resulted in constitutional change.

How the Book Is Organized

Like most professors, I have a certain point of view about the subjects I teach and write about. One point I want my students to understand is that the Constitution was not handed to the American people as God is said to have handed Moses the Ten Commandments on Mount Sinai. The Constitution was the result of an intense political battle between bitterly divided foes over how to organize the nation's social and economic life, how to distribute political power to govern a new nation, and how to secure individual rights while maintaining an orderly society. In the introductory chapter, I explain the theoretical and political roots of the Framers' decisions on these issues. I also introduce in Chapter 1 the concept of law as an instrument of social and political change, and describe the important role that organized interests play in the litigation process.

In Chapter 2, I offer an in-depth discussion of constitutional theory and why it matters. Here, I do not follow the path of some of my colleagues in emphasizing the attitudinal model of judicial behavior, or focus solely on modes of judicial review or emphasize the Court's decision-making process independent of concurrent social and political forces. Instead, I take the student through various theories of constitutional interpretation and explain the choices that the justices and the parties involved in litigation face in trying to articulate and defend what they believe the Constitution means. While I offer a balanced discussion of the strengths and weaknesses of different approaches to interpreting the Constitution, I also want the student to understand that constitutional theory has its roots in what Justice Oliver Wendell Holmes Jr. called the "felt necessities" of our time. In other words, the societal arrangements that law protects do not just exist; they are the product of political choices. I emphasize this theme beyond this one chapter on constitutional interpretation to give it prominent weight throughout the casebook.

Volume II is subtitled *Civil Rights and Liberties,* and the themes I explore include the relationship between liberty and authority, the evolution of civil rights and liberties over time, and the important role that organized interests have played in shaping the meaning of constitutional rights.

Although the emphasis in Volume II is on the substantive meaning of the Bill of Rights, I also infuse constitutional development with commentary on the social and political dynamics of the era. Supreme Court justices, like everybody else, are products of their time. How a justice in the late 1800s, for example, understood the application of the Fourteenth Amendment's equal protection and due process guarantees against encroachments of state power on the rights and liberties of individual citizens had a great deal to do with the revolution wrought in American society by the Civil War, the emancipation of African Americans, and the purpose of Reconstruction in reforging the bonds of union. Likewise, how a justice felt about the power of Congress and the states to suppress political dissent in the 1950s was colored by the "cold war" between the United States and the Soviet Union (now Russia). The same is certainly true for modern issues such as privacy and technology, equality between the sexes, and the role of religion in society: the world the justices face in twenty-first-century America is very different from the one their predecessors faced in 1791.

Features of the Book

Each chapter begins with an opening story that is designed to illustrate the complexities involved in that particular area of constitutional law and how the law affects the lives of ordinary American citizens. I then offer an essay that leads students into the cases and, from that point forward, interweave commentary and narrative with excerpts from Supreme Court opinions. In almost every case, I include concurring and dissenting opinions so that students can see the range of views among the justices on important constitutional questions. Each case excerpt is preceded by a headnote that emphasizes the social and political dimension of the litigation and, when appropriate, the role of organized interests. Starting with Chapter 2, each chapter includes several SIDEBARs, short pieces that highlight the human origins and real-world consequences of particularly critical cases. I also include suggested readings at the end of each chapter to assist students writing research papers or who simply want to know more about the subject.

Houghton Mifflin will provide instructors and students comprehensive support for *American Constitutional Law.* The award-winning CD-ROM *The Supreme Court's Greatest Hits* is available with new copies of the text. This CD contains more than seventy hours of Supreme Court oral arguments and opinion pronouncements from fifty of the most important cases decided in the last forty years. Cases on the CD that are excerpted in the text are marked with a CD icon; this cross-referencing will help students easily locate the multimedia resources that correspond to their assigned readings.

There is also a Web site (accessible via the College Division homepage at http://college.hmco.com) that will provide hypothetical problems to use in conjunction with each chapter; ACE self-tests that students can use to test their comprehension of the readings; a Guide to Legal Reports and Periodicals to help students with their research; and links to organizations that frequently participate in Supreme Court litigation. Each year, Houghton Mifflin will publish an annual supplement to *American Constitutional Law* online to keep instructors and students abreast of the Court's most recent decisions and other related developments.

Acknowledgments

I never had the slightest illusion I could undertake this book without research support and assistance from my students, who remain a teacher's greatest resource. I would like to thank the following students for all their hard work: Dan Weiss, Kristen Eastlick, Chris Donovan, Erika Schlachter, Eric Eikenberg, Mari Strydom, Meredith Mecca, Scott Shoreman, Kyle Cruley, Kim Horn, Meg Streff, Kristen Murray, Nicole Goodrich, Kara Ruzicka, Carey Ng, Jennie Tucker, Jarrett Alexander, Erin Ackerman, Reuben Ackerman, Gina Connell, Jay Liotta, Stephanie Lenner, Michelle Moyer, Dominique Fanizza, Danielle White, Shannon Thornton, and Jeremy Gauld. Several other students helped make my life easier in many other ways, and they, too, deserve thanks: Lisa Loftin, Amy Hannah, Allison Viscardi, Michael Wilkosz, Sarah Simmons, Bridget McGuire, Fred Turner, Chris Canavan, Tim Titus, Jon Liebman, Damon Manetta, Shawn Bates, Kim Nelson, Meg Scully, Carla Cerino, Melanie Auerbach, Maura Harris, Stacey Farber, and Cori Roth. These are all special people who are destined for great things. It was a privilege to work with all of you.

Scott Diener, Bruce Field, John Reteneller, Scott Stephenson, and Jim Verhoff are not political scientists, but they are great friends and always a necessary source of laughter, error correction, and support. Jon Kaplan and Scott Aronson, two great friends and talented musicians, were my partners in Available Jones, one of Washington's great bar and party bands. Thanks for helping me not think about the Constitution while we were cranking out the hits! And you're welcome for learning that drummers rule.

My colleagues at American University have provided support, advice, and inspiration along the way, and a special group deserves my thanks: Ron Shaiko, Diane Singerman, Saul Newman, Joe Soss, Karen O'Connor, Bill LeoGrande, David Rosenbloom, Richard Bennett, Christine DeGregorio, and Jim Thurber. I am especially grateful for the support of my former Dean in the School of Public Affairs, Neil Kerwin, who has always encouraged me to pursue my interests on my own terms. I also appreciate the support of my current Dean, Walter Broadnax, who gave me the time I needed to bring this casebook to fruition.

Several colleagues from other colleges and universities provided first-rate criticism and suggestions during the development of this casebook. These reviewers helped me articulate my own ideas, even if they did not necessarily agree with them. Thanks to: Vanessa A. Baird, University of Colorado at Boulder; Shala Mills Bannister, Fort Hays State University; Mike Caldwell, University of Illinois at Urbana–Champaign; Robert A. Carp, University of Houston; Stanley Eugene Clark, California State University, Bakersfield; Gus Cochran, Agnes Scott College; Deirdre M. Condit, Virginia Commonwealth University; John P. Forren, Miami University; Stacia Haynie, Louisiana State University; John C. Kilwein, West Virginia University; William Lasser, Clemson University; Susan Lawrence, Rutgers University, New Brunswick; Jeffrey Segal, State University of New York at Stony Brook; Reggie Sheehan, Michigan State University; Shannon Smithey, University of Pittsburgh; Neil Snortland, University of Arkansas at Little Rock; and James S. Todd, University of Arizona.

Three people deserve a special mention all of their own: Sarah Becker, who agreed to work with me her senior year in college on this project when it was still getting off the ground. You gave me the gift of your maturity, intelligence, and persistence. Thank you for believing in me. Michael Palermo, who has shared his endless smile with my family for almost ten years, thank you for the gifts you have given all of us, and especially my children. David Kaib has been much more than my graduate assistant for the past three years. He has been quite literally, my lifeline, without whom this book never would have seen the light of day. Dave read every word of this casebook, from the photo captions to the opinions, tracked down every missing citation and, in the spirit of full disclosure, saved me from screwing up on a daily basis. He is "Uncle Dave" to my children, and, in the eyes of my wife, a candidate for sainthood. As my son, Max, once told a playmate in the sandbox, "Uncle Dave is my dad's assistant. My dad's a professor and when he doesn't know what to do he calls Uncle Dave and Uncle Dave fixes it. He's one of my best friends."

Former Sponsoring Editor Melissa Mashburn is many things—witty, charming, endlessly optimistic, persistent, and a first-rate connoisseur of barbecue and donuts—but most of all endlessly supportive and marvelously inspirational. Melissa gave me the confidence to move forward with this casebook. After I reached the initial wall, Melissa told me, "Don't worry! I'm going to get you a great development editor! Just wait! You'll love her!" And, lo and behold, Katherine Meisenheimer came along, and sure enough, whipped this project into shape and kept me going, offering just the perfect blend of support, encouragement, and "that's great, Gregg, but when am I going to see Chapter 5" reminders that every author needs. Faced with Katherine's powerful intelligence and acute sense of purpose, I was left with little choice but to listen to this amazing woman. Nancy Benjamin managed the production process with ease and skill. Beth Morel turned frequently unintelligible prose bearing only a remote kinship to the English language into coherent sentences. Martha Friedman took my less-than-specific ideas for photographs and illustrations and managed to find exactly what I wanted. Jean Woy, Editor-in-Chief, is legendary in political science publishing circles, and after working with her on *American Constitutional Law,* I understand why. I also want to thank Mary Dougherty, my Sponsoring Editor, for her support and enthusiasm. Finally, thanks to Nicola Poser, Marketing Manager, and the Houghton Mifflin sales representatives for believing in and selling my book.

For Janet, still sweet and lovely after all these years, and Max, who makes every day a fun day, and Claire, the wonderwaif of Maplewood Park, you make me feel all right, and that is better than I can say

AMERICAN CONSTITUTIONAL LAW: POWER AND POLITICS

Volume II

Civil Rights and Liberties

Law and Constitutional Structure

A student preparing to study American constitutional law for the first time usually experiences a mix of emotions. First, the big, fat casebook—like this one—that goes with the course immediately suggests to the student that a lot of reading will be involved, inviting fear. Professors think that reading is a good thing. In fact, some even take pride in believing that their constitutional law course will require students to read more than any other course the student ever takes. Second, after flipping through this clean, unhighlighted, new casebook, the student notices that phrases such as *ipso facto, ex post facto, subpoena duces tecum, in toto,* and *stare decisis* appear—repeatedly—throughout the opinions, leaving him or her to wonder in just what language constitutional law is taught. Third, as if this newly discovered need to brush up on Latin is not enough to cause anguish, the student then discovers that familiar topics such as congressional committees, majority leaders, cabinet secretaries, and political parties have been replaced by obscure subjects: appellants filing writs of *certiorari, amici curiae* briefs, jurisdictional claims, and equitable remedies. The result? Bewilderment, confusion or maybe a little of each!

So, is it possible for the uninitiated student to learn about constitutional law and, as only a professor could dare ask, love it at the same time?

Indeed it is, for constitutional law is about far more than dry legal rules and their application to what seem like distant abstract disputes. Constitutional law is about how the most critical and important questions involving government power, social and political organization, and individual rights evolved from disputes between citizens and their government—or between and among the different branches and levels of government—into legal rules. Concurrent with this theme is the other critical component in understanding American constitutional law: how the Supreme Court has interpreted the United States Constitution and what the Court's interpretations mean for the relationship between law and society. This casebook has two purposes: (1) to help you understand the social and political context of modern American constitutional law and (2) to encourage you to think about the Court not only as an institution that creates constitutional doctrine based on iron-clad rules of legal jurisprudence but also as one whose decisions are intertwined with social and political forces.

Students of the Court and the Constitution need to know more than just the chronological development of constitutional law. This casebook includes materials that tell you who the clients were in these cases and how they were selected; the role organized interests play in the dynamics of the litigation process; the historical and social context in which particularly controversial cases were decided; and how the Court's decisions affect the real world. The Court most often has the last word on what the Constitution means. But after the Court hands down an opinion, responsibility shifts to government agencies, large corporations, small businesses, college admissions directors, farmers, police departments, and public schools, to name just a few of the people and institutions that must apply judicial decisions to everyday life.

Law as Constitutional Foundation

Constitutional law is more than just a body of rules that organize our social and political institutions, protect individual rights, and establish government power. Law serves as the "connective tissue" that binds the structure, substance, and culture of American constitutionalism together.[1] Law is the foundation upon which government and social organization rests. Think for a moment about the use of the adjective *constitutional* to describe the rule of law. The Constitution created our current government structure and established, in principle, the balance between liberty and authority. But the decision of the Framers to create a written constitution also represented the decision to create, or *constitute,* a government. Although the American model of government is often described as representative and democratic, it is above all a constitutional government because it depends on the consent of the governed for its legitimacy. A government that derives its authority from sources other than the people is not, under this definition, properly constituted.

Our Constitution, then, creates the legal structure for our political institutions. The decision of the Framers to create a political system in which the legislature, the executive branch, and the courts served independent purposes and were accountable to different societal interests reflected a *political theory* about the possibilities and limits of popular government. That government should represent the wishes and aspirations of the people held out the more optimistic side of the Framers. That the sources of political power and the motives that drove its exercise were, in the view of James Madison, a pernicious threat to the operation of representative democracy represented their own experience with popular government. "The accumulation of all powers, legislative, executive, and judiciary, in the same hands," wrote Madison in *Federalist* 47, "whether of one, a few, or many, and whether hereditary, self-appointed, or elective, may justly be pronounced the very definition of tyranny."[2]

Here, well before Alexander Hamilton's more explicit description of judicial power in *Federalist* 78, Madison also hints of the important functional role the courts will have in the American form of constitutional government. To defend his model of popular government based on the separation of powers, Madison drew heavily from the French philosopher Baron de Montesquieu's classic 1784 work of political theory, *The Spirit of the Laws.* Noting Montesquieu's argument on behalf of an independent judicial branch in an otherwise elected popular government, Madison wrote that "he did not mean that these departments ought to have no partial agency in, or no control over, the acts of each other. [W]here the whole power of one department is exercised by the same hands which possess the whole power of another department, the fundamental principles of a free constitution are subverted."[3]

Madison, and the Framers in general, believed that a proper constitutional structure was necessary to limit government power and protect individual rights. In a perfect world no constitution would be needed because no government would be necessary to organize and channel social and political currents. But, as Madison wrote in *Federalist* 51, his most famous defense of the new constitutional order: "In framing a government which is to be administered by men over men, the great difficulty lies in this: you must first enable the government to control the governed; and in the next place oblige it to control itself. A dependence on the people is, no doubt, the primary control on the government; but experience has taught mankind the necessity of auxiliary precautions."[4] What were—and remain—those "auxiliary precautions" of which Madison spoke? A constitutional government that called for separation of powers, checks and balances, federalism, and protections for individual rights against reckless majority rule.

In 1789 the nation ratified its new Constitution and with it "A New Order for the Ages," or *Novus Ordo Seclorum,* the Latin phrase embossed on the great seal of the United States. These core principles of American constitutionalism remain vibrant and timeless. But, as you will see over the course of this book, the transformation of those principles into constitutional law has created new issues and questions that continue to confront the participants in our constitutional system. The next section examines the basic structure of the Constitution, the government it created, and the political theory underlying American popular government.

Constitutional Structure

In *Federalist* 1, Alexander Hamilton made clear that nothing less than the survival of the United States as a democratic republic was at stake in the ratification process over the new Constitution. Indeed, in the first paragraph of the first of eighty-five papers that he, Madison, and John Jay, writing under the pseudonym of *Publius,* Latin for "Public Man," Hamilton implored the nation to consider the historical significance of the Constitution's ratification. "The subject speaks its own importance; comprehending in its consequences nothing less than the existence of the UNION," Hamilton wrote, "[f]or it has been frequently remarked that it seems to have been reserved to the people of this country, by their conduct and example, to decide the important question, *whether societies of men are really capable of good government through reflection and choice, or whether they are forever destined to depend for their political constitutions on accident and force.*"[5]

Could popular government, rooted in consent—a word mentioned no less than forty-eight times in the *Federalist Papers*—and dependent upon the power of reason rather than the power of force survive the factional disputes that would be inevitable among a people characterized by social, economic, religious, and political differences? For *Publius,* the answer was yes if the nation was willing to embrace a constitution that created a strong national government, separated and divided the sources of government power, gave each branch of government partial control over the other, allowed states to retain jurisdiction over matters of law and public policy closest to the people, and kept tyrannical majorities from usurping individual rights.

Here, let us remember that the Constitution is much more than a suggestion box for good government. It is the foundation for the rule of law. Even early opponents of the Constitution could agree with the assessment of one Boston newspaper, not long after the Constitution's ratification, that "that which is not regulated by law must depend on the arbitrary will of the rulers, which would put an end to civil society."[6] The Constitution is also *public* law in that it creates the rules that govern the relationship between our public institutions and the people. All laws made by our legal and political institutions must be consistent with its meaning. What the Constitution means or, better phrased, *should* mean, is open to debate. How and where to ascribe meaning to the Constitution, what it means from generation to generation, and who should have ultimate authority in constitutional interpretation are questions that have been at the center of constitutional litigation since the establishment of the Republic.

Creating the constitutional structure of public law was the problem that confronted the state representatives to the Constitutional Convention held in Philadelphia during the summer of 1787. Consensus existed among the delegates over the inadequacies of the Articles of Confederation, but opinion over the extent to which the Articles should be revised was far from settled. When the Constitution was completed and presented to the public later that September, its language reflected the textual ambiguities that are an essential feature in the art of political compromise. Convention delegates and numerous others involved in the drafting of the Constitution held widely divergent views on what it was supposed to mean. Several delegates left the convention confused over the meaning of key sections of the Constitution even after it was completed. Some of the more prominent Framers, including Madison and Hamilton, changed their original views on the Constitution's meaning during their lifetimes. Notable opponents of ratification, such as George Mason, who refused to sign the Constitution and actively campaigned against its ratification, later became more hopeful of its possibilities. If the Framers resolved their political differences through textual ambiguities and, in some cases, deliberate exclusion, should it come as any great surprise that subsequent generations continue to disagree over what the Constitution means?[7]

The Constitution that emerged from the convention in September 1787 created a legal and political structure radically different from the Articles of Confederation. No nation had ever devised a constitutional framework that centralized power in an elected national government to the extent the United States Constitution did. No nation had created an elaborate federal structure to protect the domain of state governments from national intrusion. No nation had ever developed such an imaginative and complex series of constitutional safeguards against the improper use of institutional power. No nation steeped in the culture and language of popular rule had ever created a judicial branch unaccountable to electoral will to declare acts and laws of political majorities unconstitutional. And, in the Bill of Rights, no nation had ever deemed civil and political liberties so fundamental that their protection was not dependent on the sentiments and prejudices of popular

George Washington presiding over the Constitutional Convention in 1787.
Bettmann/CORBIS.

majorities. That women, African Americans, Native Americans, and poor whites were not, in different degrees, the beneficiaries of the Constitution's majestic promises raised troublesome questions then—and even now—about the democratic intentions of the constitutional Framers. We will deal with these important issues throughout this casebook. For now, let us consider the four major and interlocking components of our constitutional structure: national government, separation of powers, federalism, and civil and constitutional rights.

National Government

Complaints directed at the Constitution's decided emphasis on national power by the Anti-Federalists, as the various opponents of ratification were better known, were quite legitimate if we consider how the new constitutional structure altered the sources and distribution of government power established by the Articles of Confederation. In place of the loose, lateral framework that characterized the Articles, one in which the states retained their primacy, the Constitution delegated supreme legislative, executive, and judicial authority to the national government. Moreover, the Constitution provided comprehensive and specific powers to each branch that the Articles did not. Among the most dramatic changes that illustrated the Constitution's emphasis on national power were the following:

- Congress, in Article I, now had the exclusive power to regulate interstate commerce; to authorize and collect taxes; to create federal courts and establish their jurisdiction; and the general authority to make all laws necessary and proper to exercise its legislative responsibilities. Throughout this volume you will see how, since the early nineteenth century, the Court's interpretation of the Necessary and Proper Clause, the Commerce Clause, and the power of Congress to tax and spend has been instrumental in the expansion of legislative power at the national level.

- The executive branch, created by Article II, now consisted of a single, elected president, and not, as some Anti-Federalists had wanted, a plural council. Article II also delegated to the president the power to make judicial and cabinet appointments. In language that first appeared to be an afterthought but has proven to be critical in the constitutional expansion of executive power, Article II reserved to the president the power to faithfully execute the laws of the United States. This book also explores how the growth of presidential power based on the "implied powers" of the executive has been enormous and extraordinarily consequential for the balance of constitutional power.
- Concurrent with the exercise of the judicial power by the Supreme Court, the sole court created by Article III of the Constitution, was the implied power of judicial review. Judicial review remains controversial for this reason alone. However, the Court's use of judicial review to advance dramatic new concepts of government power and individual rights, often in the face of popular opposition, has generated additional controversy.
- Article VI made all laws and treaties enacted under the "Authority of the United States . . . the supreme Law of the Land," and bound the state governments to the laws created under national power. Disagreement continues, however, over the scope of power retained by the states in areas such as commercial and police power regulation.

Criticism of the Constitution, which came in a series of written responses to the *Federalist Papers,* was swift and severe. *Brutus,* the pseudonym of one of most vociferous and articulate Anti-Federalists, charged:

> This government is to possess absolute and uncontroulable power, legislative, executive and judicial, with respect to every object to which it extends, for by the last clause of section 8th, article 1st, it is declared 'that the Congress shall have power to make all laws which shall be necessary and proper for carrying into execution the foregoing powers, and all other powers vested by this constitution, in the government of the United States; or in any department or office thereof.' And by the 6th article, it is declared 'that this constitution, and the laws of the United States . . . shall be the supreme law of the land; and the judges in every state shall be bound thereby, any thing in the constitution, or law of any state to the contrary notwithstanding.'
>
> This government then, so far as it extends, is a complete one, and not a confederation. It [has] . . . absolute and perfect powers to make and execute all laws, to appoint all officers, institute courts, declare offences, and annex penalties, with respect to every object to which it extends, as any other in the world. So far therefore as its powers reach, all ideas of confederation are given up and lost. It is true this government is limited to certain objects, or to speak more properly, some small degree of power is still left to the states, but a little attention to the powers vested in the general government, will convince every candid man, that if it is capable of being executed, all that is reserved for the individual states must very soon be annihilated, except so far as they are barely necessary to the organization of the general government.[8]

Although several influential opponents of the Constitution acknowledged the need for a more efficient and cohesive national government, they never anticipated the wholesale transfer of legal and political power from the states to the national level.[9] But the inherent contradiction of the Anti-Federalists' desires to retain the advantages of a small, state-centered republic while granting to the national government the necessary power to forge and maintain the bonds of union left the Constitution's opponents vulnerable to the scornful criticism of *Publius:*

> For the absurdity must continually stare us in the face of confiding to a government the direction of the most essential national interests, without daring to trust it to the authorities which are indispensable to their proper and efficient management. Let us not attempt to reconcile contradictions, but firmly embrace a rational alternative.[10]

Publius had a powerful point here, "given the Anti-Federalists' own desire for a Union government powerful enough to secure common interests, especially defense."[11] By itself *Publius*'s argument that the proposed

THE

FEDERALIST:

ADDRESSED TO THE

PEOPLE OF THE STATE OF NEW-YORK.

NUMBER I.

Introduction.

AFTER an unequivocal experience of the inefficacy of the ſubſiſting federal government, you are called upon to deliberate on a new conſtitution for the United States of America. The ſubject ſpeaks its own importance; comprehending in its conſequences, nothing leſs than the exiſtence of the UNION, the ſafety and welfare of the parts of which it is compoſed, the fate of an empire, in many reſpects, the moſt intereſting in the world. It has been frequently remarked, that it ſeems to have been reſerved to the people of this country, by their conduct and example, to decide the important queſtion, whether ſocieties of men are really capable or not, of eſtabliſhing good government from reflection and choice, or whether they are forever deſtined to depend, for their political conſtitutions, on accident and force. If there be any truth in the remark, the criſis, at which we are arrived, may with propriety be regarded as the æra in which

A that

The Federalist Papers, *written by Alexander Hamilton, John Jay, and James Madison in support of the ratification of the Constitution, originally were published in New York City newspapers from October 1787 to August 1788.*
North Wind Picture Archives.

Constitution at least presented the kind of "rational alternative" to the Articles of Confederation was one that the Anti-Federalists could not answer. They were unable to reconcile their own wants and aspirations into a new governmental structure.[12] National power as the thread that would bind the states into a union became the baseline for the Federalists' argument on behalf of the Constitution. *Publius* said as much in *Federalist* 44, where he commented that without strong and substantive national power, "the whole Constitution would be a dead letter."[13]

Here, it is important to understand that what the opponents of the Constitution, such as *Brutus,* feared from national power—that, for example, the scheme of representation proposed for Congress would result in a "heterogeneous" and chaotic composition of interests—the Federalists viewed as its great strength.[14] To secure the political and economic stability of a large, commercial republic and protect the rights of its citizens from unreasonable majority rule, Madison believed the Constitution had to quell three major threats. The first was disunion, the second was the "mischiefs of faction," and the third was the threat to the rights and liberties of individuals and political minorities regardless of whether those threats came from majorities or other minorities.[15] Madison's solution was to establish first a strong, vibrant national government, complete with the appropriate powers to allow the branches to pursue their respective ends. Such "energetic" government, *Publius* confessed, would need constitutional constraints to promote both the "public good and private rights." Separation of powers, as you will see, became the most important of those constraints.

Separation of Powers

Before the Federalists could turn their attention to how the Constitution's positive features would attract virtuous leaders dedicated to the promotion of good government, they had to persuade the public that it was, above all, a safe government. In *Federalist* 47, Madison conceded the point that the "accumulation" of all legislative, executive and judicial power in a single branch of government could "*justly* be pronounced the very definition of tyranny." To sooth the suspicions of the Constitution's opponents, Madison asserted his agreement with their "objection" that governments that fail to adhere to the principle of separation of powers *do* endanger the liberties of the people.

> One of the principal objections inculcated by the more respectable adversaries to the Constitution is its supposed

violation of the *political maxim that the legislative, executive, and judiciary departments ought to be separate and distinct. In the structure of the federal government no regard, it is said, seems to have been paid to this essential precaution in favor of liberty.*[16]

Madison makes two fundamental points here in defense of the constitutional arrangement of the separation of powers. The first is that Madison admits as "truth" the notion that the accumulation of all powers in the "same hands" is the "very definition" of tyranny. With that truth established, Madison states that the "maxim" deduced from it is that separation of powers is necessary to protect a constitutional government. If the Constitution really accumulates or tends to accumulate power in the same hands, then "no further arguments would be necessary to inspire a universal reprobation of the system."[17]

A steadfast belief in limited government based on separation of powers also reinforced the commitment of the Framers to the rule of law. Because the Constitution announces the division of legislative, executive, and judicial functions among the three branches, each is required to exercise its respective power by what one of the most influential Enlightenment philosophers on the Framers, John Locke, referred to as "declared Laws."[18] Rule by "declared," or public, law, constrained the abilities of the three branches to act against their enumerated, limited powers. Laws enacted and enforced under popular government were known in advance and thus generally applicable to all cases in which such laws applied. Rule by law is possible without a government formed on the separation of powers principle. But the conception of separation of powers, as applied to our constitutional structure, *requires* government by the rule of law. The Constitution, because it is "declared" law that defines the duties and limits of its various powers, meets this requirement.[19]

Separation of powers, designed to quell the concerns of the public and allow it to guard against the false exercise of government power, could not function without each branch having the constitutional means to resist the potential intrusions of another. Of course, the Constitution creates three separate branches of the national government, each with distinct powers and responsibilities, and divides levels of government power along a federal structure, allowing state and local governments to retain appropriate legal jurisdiction and political power. These lines of division, however, are not strict. The constitutional structure outlined by the Framers can be more accurately described as one in which separate government institutions share in the exercise of their responsibilities. Each branch, as Madison states in *Federalist* 51, "should have a will of its own." But the constitutional structure envisioned by *Publius* also included an interest of each branch in the operation of another. As Madison argued:

> [T]he great security against a gradual concentration of the several powers in the same department consists in giving to those who administer each department the necessary constitutional means and personal motives to resist encroachments of the others.
>
> The provision for [each branch's] defense must in this, as in all other cases, be made commensurate to the danger of attack. *Ambition must be made to counteract ambition. The interest of the man must be connected to the constitutional rights of the place.*[20]

The assignment of different powers to different branches is intended to do more than just prevent the rise of a zealous national government. A major objective of the Framers was to promote equilibrium among the branches. That meant paying as much attention to the "balances" component of the "checks and balances" principle as to the "checks." For *Publius,* the degree to which one branch can check the actions of another depends on the nature of the power exercised. The "constitutional rights" of each branch must have enough substantive power to attract worthwhile occupants, who, in turn, must have the personal and public motive to both exercise and defend its powers.

Notice here how *Publius* uses a circular path of reasoning to create an interdependent relationship between strong national government and separation of powers. "Energetic" national government is essential to preserve the Union. Separation of powers creates an institutional safeguard against oppressive, tyrannical government. Checks and balances ensure that each branch, while having a "will of its own," remains bound by law to its constitutional powers. Finally, only strong, coequal branches will have the personal and public incentives to defend their constitutional prerogatives.

How and where does the Constitution put this principle into practice? Here are a few examples:

- Article I provides Congress the power to declare war, but the president, in Article II, is made commander in chief of the armed forces.
- Article III creates the Supreme Court and vests it with jurisdiction over all cases arising under "law and equity." Article I leaves to Congress the power to create inferior courts. Congress is also given the power to establish the jurisdiction of the lower courts by Article III. Congress also decides how much money the federal judiciary receives each year to operate. Who appoints judges to the federal courts? The president. Who confirms them? The Senate.
- Article II says nothing about the president's power to make laws, but the president's constitutional responsibility to address the state of the union and recommend measures "he shall judge necessary and expedient" gives the office a considerable role in the congressional lawmaking function that is for Congress.
- Article II places the power to veto legislation in the hands of the president, but Congress, in Article I, has the power to override presidential vetoes with the support of two-thirds majorities of each chamber.

Difficult questions emerge from these examples. Does Article I allow Congress to create a "legislative veto" over rules made by administrative agencies it created to carry out federal law? Does the Constitution permit one branch of government to delegate its power to another? For example, may Congress delegate to agencies under the control of the judicial branch the power to create and enforce sentencing guidelines for federal judges? Suppose majorities in both the House and Senate believe that the Supreme Court has erred on a major constitutional question, such as one that involves abortion rights, school prayer, or affirmative action. Does the Exceptions and Regulations Clause of Article III, which leaves to Congress the responsibility to establish federal court jurisdiction, mean that it has the right to remove the Court's authority to hear cases involving those issues? Or does congressional authority to establish federal court jurisdiction mean something more general and less intrusive as it applies to courts' core functions?

These are hard questions, indeed. They are not just tough for students encountering constitutional law for the first time but, as you will see, for the Supreme Court as well.

Federalism

Madison's conception of separation of powers was not the only departure from the established principles of popular government. The Constitution, *Publius* argued, created a republic that was a mixture of national and federal principles. Federalism, as we understand its most basic form, creates a multilevel government that permits the national and various state governments to operate in parallel fashion. But, as James Monroe, who later served as the nation's fifth president, wrote in opposition to the Constitution's proposed federal structure:

> To mark the precise point at which the powers of the general government shall cease, and that from whence those of the states shall commence, to poise them in such manner as to prevent either destroying the other, will require the utmost force of human wisdom and ingenuity. No possible ground of variance or even interference should be left, for there would the conflict commence, that might prove fatal to both.[21]

Monroe's complaint was that the Constitution avoided the specific assignment of power along federal lines. He is on solid ground here, for the character of the Constitution, as Madison claimed in *Federalist* 39, was "mixed," a combination of national and federal principles. "The proposed Constitution," Madison wrote, "therefore is in strictness neither a national nor federal constitution; but a composition of both. In its foundation, it is federal, not national; in the sources from which the ordinary powers of the Government are drawn, it is partly federal and partly national; in the operation of these powers, it is national not federal."[22]

It is difficult to know even now, as it was during the founding period, how these generalities apply to specific problems that arise between the forces of state and national power. However, the "new" federal structure that Madison envisioned undoubtedly represented a dramatic departure from the "old" federalism of the Articles of Confederation. Madison might not have been clear about the line separating national from state responsibilities, but he did confess that the federal structure proposed in the Constitution left the states in a subordinate position to the national government. For the Constitution's supporters, a confederate structure in which the states retained sovereign power against the national government was out of the question. The failure of the Articles, as Madison reminded the "adversaries" of the Constitution, assured that much:

> The difference between a federal and national government, as it relates to the *operation of government,* is by the adversaries of the plan of the convention supposed to consist in this, that in the former the powers operate on the political bodies composing the Confederacy in their political capacities; in the latter, on the individual citizens composing the nation in their individual capacities. On trying the Constitution by this criterion, it falls under the *national* not the *federal* character; though perhaps not so completely as has been understood.[23]

Federalism, like the separation of powers, was essential to the equilibrium that Madison believed was the basis for the Constitution's success. Placing power where it did not belong, whether on the national or state level, could doom the Constitution. This concern is similar to Madison's in *Federalist* 51, where he emphasized the need to diffuse the sources of unrest in the administration of government by "supplying" each branch of the national government with "opposite and rival interests."[24] Federalism allows the national and state governments to retain control over their respective spheres of influence. States retain explicit constitutional guarantees for the right to exist and to administer their respective governments. Those guarantees include the following:

- The Tenth Amendment, which states that "the powers not delegated to the United States by the Constitution, nor prohibited by it to the states, are reserved to the states respectively, or to the people." Remember the phrase "powers not delegated to the United States" as you encounter the Court's opinions on federal structure. Supporters of more state independence from federal rules and judicial decisions have pointed to those words as supportive of their position. Are they?
- Article V requires that all proposed amendments to the Constitution must be ratified, upon approval of two-thirds of the Senate and the House of Representatives, by three-fourths of the states. Although this process gives the states the ultimate power to amend the Constitution, the Framers' decision to create a nonunanimous decision rule represented a "mixed" approach somewhere between supreme national power—congressional approval only—and state supremacy—a unanimous rule would permit one state to determine ratification or rejection. In whose favor does the balance of constitutional power over the Constitution tip, the national government or the states?

In the end, the Constitution's federal structure emphasizes the need for union through national government. Several other key constitutional provisions support the national character of the federal structure. Article IV, for example, requires each state to give "Full Faith and Credit" to the public laws of another state. It also affords citizens of other states the "Privileges and Immunities" provided to its own and empowers the United States to "guarantee" each state a republican form of government.

THE FUGITIVE SLAVE LAW IN OPERATION.

Article IV, Section 2, of the Constitution originally permitted slave owners to capture fugitive slaves who had escaped into free states. This provision was later nullified by the Thirteenth Amendment, ratified in 1865.

North Wind Picture Archives.

Despite the national features of the federal structure created by the Constitution, the states have continued to press for more power and independence. On more than one occasion, the states have prevailed in their efforts to retain control over matters that have ranged from civil rights protection to gun control to commercial regulation. Federalism continues to remain a vibrant constitutional principle.

Civil and Constitutional Rights

Most Americans believe the chief purpose of the Constitution is to protect the fundamental rights of individuals and minorities from harsh majority rule. Thus it is remarkable to learn that the proposal for a bill of rights in the Constitutional Convention was considered and rejected with little more than a snap of the fingers. Debate over the inclusion of a bill of rights was limited to the morning of September 12, 1787, less than a week before the convention completed the Constitution and adjourned. Each state present when the proposal for the Bill of Rights was submitted to the floor of the convention, including Virginia, which counted James Madison, Thomas Jefferson, George Washington, and George Mason among its more famous residents, voted against the document. What little debate took place centered on George Mason's comments that he wished the Constitution "had been prefaced with a bill of rights. It would give great quiet to the people." Mason added that the convention could put together a bill of rights in no time; it would simply adopt the language of the eight states that had bills of rights of their own.[25]

The issue that concerned Mason, and later the Anti-Federalist writers in their subsequent fight against ratification, was the potential of the national government to use its "supreme" power to declare certain rights, such as freedom of speech and religion, that were included in various state constitutions as incompatible with national objectives. To the Constitution's opponents, the broad powers granted to Congress under the Necessary and Proper Clause, and to the national government more generally under the Supremacy Clause, did nothing to guarantee that state constitutions would be respected. If the states were no longer sovereign, but now political subdivisions of the national government with limited rights and powers, some constitutional assurance was needed, as the Anti-Federalist tract written by the *Federal Farmer* claimed, to ensure the "people [that they] may never lose their liberties by construction" of the new government.[26] *Aristocrotis* put the matter in even more direct terms:

> [T]his Constitution is much better and gives more scope to the rulers than they [might] safely take if there was no constitution at all; for then the people might contend that the power was inherent in them; and that they had made some implied reserves in the original grant; but now they cannot, for every thing is expressly given away to government in this plan. No one [could stop Congress] unless we had a bill of rights to which we might appeal; and under which we might contend against any assumption of undue power and appeal to the judicial branch of the government to protect us by their judgements.[27]

Even upon submission of the Constitution to the states for ratification, the Federalists refused to concede that the absence of a bill of rights posed a potential problem in the protection of individual rights and liberties. Hamilton, in *Federalist* 84, wrote that the Constitution itself was, "in every rational sense, and to every useful purpose, A BILL OF RIGHTS." Furthermore, wrote Hamilton:

> I go further, and affirm that bills of rights, in the sense and in the extent in which they are contended for, are not only unnecessary in the proposed constitution, but would even be dangerous. They would contain various exceptions to powers which are not granted; and on this very account, would afford a colourable pretext to claim more than were granted. For why declare that things shall not be done which there is no power to do? Why for instance, should it be said, that the liberty of the press shall not be restrained, when no power is given by which restrictions may be imposed?[28]

Hamilton's last point here exemplifies the Federalists' initial position against the Bill of Rights. Because the Constitution vested each branch of government with no more than its textually defined power, all other rights and liberties were, therefore, reserved by the people and, where appropriate, the states. The Constitution permitted the government to exercise only those powers expressly granted in the text. James Wilson, a Federalist proponent of the Constitution who had considerable influence on the ideas of *Publius,* summarized this position in language somewhat less argumentative than Hamilton's in *Federalist* 84:

> [T]he congressional power is to be collected, not from tacit implication, but from the positive grant expressed in the instrument of the union. Thus, it would have been superfluous and absurd to have stipulated with a federal body of our own creation, that we should enjoy those privileges of which we are not divested, either by the intention or the act that has brought the body into existence.

To admit the need for a bill of rights, wrote Wilson, "would imply that whatever is not expressed [in the Constitution] was given, which is not the principle of the proposed Constitution."[29]

Wilson and Hamilton also pressed a second point, one that was more utilitarian than structural, on the question of whether a bill of rights was necessary. Could a bill of rights competently enumerate all the rights of man? What about the "natural rights" that people retained under the principles of "natural law?"[30] Does the failure of the constitutional text to enumerate "natural rights" mean that the government has seized them, or at least subjugated them to political order? No bill of rights could provide all the rights the people retained under constitutional government, especially one whose existence depended on the sovereignty of the people. Under the proposed American constitutional structure, the Federalists maintained, the people could lose their rights in only two ways: either by their own choosing (consent) or through the illegitimate exercise of government power (tyranny). Because of the enumerated, limited nature of government power under the Constitution, the people are not disposed to return their rights. The Constitution's structural design, as *Publius* made clear throughout the *Federalist Papers,* prevented the formation of tyrannical government.

What is wrong with this argument, at least from the perspective of the Constitution's opponents? First, although the Constitution does enumerate specific grants of power to all three branches, it offers no insight as to what the "necessary and proper" exercise of congressional power might be. Such latent, broad power vested in the national government was, to the Anti-Federalists, a sleeping giant. Even now, the constitutional definition of this clause, as well as other provisions of Article I such as the Commerce Clause, continues to evolve. The Supreme Court often becomes the arbiter of these intra- and intergovernmental disputes over what powers belong to which levels and branches of American government.

Second, the Constitution does, in fact, include several provisions that pertain to the concerns of the Anti-Federalists, such as the writ of *habeas corpus,* included in Article I, and the prohibition against religious oaths to hold public office, included in Article IV. Their inclusion in the original Constitution contradicted the Federalists' position that it was a self-executing bill of rights. Nothing in the Constitution permitted the government to suspend writs of *habeas corpus,* compel religious obedience to serve as a public official, or, perhaps most obvious, declare that the criminally accused were entitled to a trial by jury, included in Article III.

Such rights, the Anti-Federalists contended, were assumed even before the Constitutional Convention began. If their inclusion in the Constitution was simply to reinforce their importance, then the Federalists had just made the Anti-Federalists' point for them: Bills of rights are essential tools in the moral and civic education of a free people. Points such as these, hammered home in the opposition pamphlets and articles of such Anti-Federalists as *Brutus,* George Mason, and the *Federal Farmer,* gradually took hold among a public skeptical of Hamilton's position that constitutional silences equaled individual rights and liberties retained by the people. Wasn't a nation willing to experiment with a radical new constitutional structure and the political institutions it created entitled to know whether the most basic rights were independent of legislative control and political whim? Wrote the *Federal Farmer:*

> We do not by declarations change the nature of things, or create new truths, but we give existence, or at least establish in the minds of the people truths and principles which they might never otherwise have thought of, or soon forgot. If a nation means its systems, religious or political shall have duration, it ought to recognize the leading principles of them in the front page of every family book.[31]

James Madison recognized that ratification would be a much smoother process if the Constitution's proponents promised to consider the inclusion of a bill of rights upon approval of the original document. It is also fair to say that Madison was not unsympathetic to the Anti-Federalists' objections over the Constitution's lack of a bill of rights. Over time, Madison, prodded by his friend Thomas Jefferson, became a firm proponent of a bill of rights. He agreed with Jefferson that "a bill of rights is what the people are entitled to against every government on earth, general or particular, and what no just government should refuse, or rest on inference."[32] Perhaps a bill of rights would contribute to the public education of the people and reassure them that the Constitution did more than just authorize what the national government was allowed to do: By attaching an absolute negative on the exercise of government power, as the command throughout the First Amendment that "Congress shall make no law . . . abridging the freedom of speech," a bill of rights would declare what government could not do to its people.

In the process the inclusion of a bill of rights further reinforced the institutional safeguards created by the original Constitution and strengthened the rights of individuals and minorities against the possibilities of foolish, oppressive, and expedient government rule. In return for ratification of the original Constitution, Madison agreed to introduce a bill of rights in the opening session of the First Congress. In December 1791, Rhode Island became the final state to ratify the ten amendments written largely by Madison. He received considerable conceptual and intellectual guidance from fellow Virginians Thomas Jefferson and George Mason, who authored the Virginia constitution's Declaration of Rights in 1776.

In light of this historical backdrop, it might seem strange that the modern construction and application of the majestic promises contained in the Bill of Rights has been a twentieth-century phenomenon, and a rather late one at that. Our perception of the Supreme Court's counter-majoritarian role in defending fundamental rights from the clutches of powerful political majorities is a development that dates from the Great Depression. Prior to the 1930s the Court decided only a handful of cases involving claims brought under the Bill of Rights. You will see throughout both volumes of this casebook that as the Court began to assert its authority over the Bill of Rights, aggrieved individuals and institutions redirected their resources toward the legal resolution of problems once thought to be the province of the political branches of government. Seen in this light, law is much more than our constitutional foundation. Law, in the form of litigation, is also an instrument of social and political reform.

Legal Instrumentalism and Constitutional Development

The other prominent theme of this casebook is the importance of litigation, or the resolution of legal conflicts through the judicial process, in constitutional development. The litigation process attracts organizations that represent public and private interests; elite law firms; and various government actors, such as the Department of Justice, states attorneys general, and public defenders. Political scientist Richard C. Cortner, writing in 1968, noted that great constitutional cases do not arrive on the "Supreme Court's doorsteps like orphans in the night."[33] He was right. In the cases and materials presented in this casebook, note how often the Court's resolution of landmark cases began with the deliberate decision of an interest group, a public interest law firm, a trade association, or an elite private firm to use a particular case to challenge the legal status quo. Public law litigation, because it deals with constitutional provisions, federal statutes, or state laws that raise federal constitutional questions, is about much more than the resolution of an individual claim or grievance. In a single judicial stroke, the Court can affect the lives of people on a national scale and redraw the boundaries in which our political institutions make public policy.

The American constitutional arrangement offers multiple points of access to organized interests and individuals seeking to influence the various branches of government. Organized influence in the political process is something we all learn in American government. Often, in the same course, we are also taught to consider the courts, and the judicial process more generally, as the neutral and independent branch of government where legal, not political, disputes are resolved. Judges should make decisions in accordance with what a law or constitutional provision means. They should not introduce their biases, personal experience, or other nonlegal factors into the decision-making calculus. Judicial appointments should be based on merit, not politics; competence, not ideological leanings; and so on.

But the fact is that judges are people, not computers, whose constitutional vision is the sum of a constellation of values rooted in their life experience, their education, their professional socialization, and numerous other factors more difficult to pin down. The process of judicial selection and confirmation is a political one, with the president, who is the figurative leader of a political party, in the position to nominate someone who can extend the interests of the executive branch in the courts. Presidents, however, are not always successful. Sometimes they guess wrong. Other times their nominees are rejected, forcing them to turn to someone less controversial. In truth, judicial appointments represent a mixture of politics and merit.[34]

Whatever the case, one is hard-pressed to escape the conclusion that the courts, and the Supreme Court in particular, are an integral part of the American political process. Former Justice William Brennan, who served on the Court from 1956 to 1990, acknowledged the partisan nature of constitutional litigation in *NAACP* v. *Button* (1963), an important case involving freedom of association. Brennan wrote in *Button* that litigation is "a form of political expression, [which] may well be the sole practicable avenue open to a minority to petition for redress of grievances."[35] Litigants before the Supreme Court that have failed to secure redress for their constitutional grievances in the elected branches of government have included corporations and labor unions, slaveholders and abolitionists, abortion rights advocates and pro-life opponents, civil rights organizations and state governments opposing their claims, newspapers and public officials, and religious activists and civil libertarians. This list is far from exhaustive. Litigation, as you will discover, is a powerful tool of political advocacy and, in some cases, social reform.

Law as constitutional foundation. Law as constitutional structure. Law and litigation as instruments of social and political reform. These three themes serve as the collective undercurrent for our approach to the study of constitutional law. Rules are important. The Court's most important decisions affecting our constitutional order are all included here. But you will also see how the development and adjudication of constitutional law occurs within a set of social and political processes. As such, litigation affects society as a whole.

FOR FURTHER READING

Ackerman, Bruce. *We the People: Foundations.* Cambridge, Mass.: Harvard University Press, 1991.

———. *We The People: Transformations.* Cambridge, Mass.: Harvard University Press, 1998.

Bowen, Catherine Drinker. *Miracle at Philadelphia.* New York: Little, Brown and Co., 1986.

Epstein, David F. *The Political Theory of the Federalist.* Chicago: University of Chicago Press, 1984.

Hall, Kermit L. *The Magic Mirror: Law in American History.* New York: Oxford University Press, 1989.

Hamilton, Alexander, John Jay, and James Madison. *The Federalist Papers.* Clinton Rossiter, ed. New York: Mentor Books, 1961.

Horwitz, Morton. *The Transformation of American Law, 1780–1860.* Cambridge, Mass.: Harvard University Press, 1977.

———. *The Transformation of American Law, 1870–1960.* New York: Oxford University Press, 1994.

Irons, Peter. *A People's History of the Supreme Court.* New York: Viking, 1999.

Kammen, Michael. *A Machine That Would Go of Itself: The Constitution in American Culture.* New York: Vintage Books, 1987.

O'Brien, David. *Storm Center: The Supreme Court in American Politics.* New York: W. W. Norton, 1993.

Rakove, Jack N. *Original Meanings: Politics and Ideas in the Making of the Constitution.* New York: Alfred A. Knopf, 1997.

Rosenberg, Gerald. *The Hollow Hope.* Chicago: University of Chicago Press, 1991.

Storing, Herbert J. *What the AntiFederalists Were For.* Chicago: University of Chicago Press, 1981.

Vose, Clement E. *Caucasians Only: The Supreme Court, the NAACP, and the Restrictive Covenant Cases.* Berkeley: University of California Press, 1959.

Wills, Garry. *A Necessary Evil: A History of American Distrust of Government.* New York: Simon & Schuster, 1999.

Wood, Gordon S. *The Creation of the American Republic, 1776–1787.* Chapel Hill: University of North Carolina Press, 1969.

2 Interpreting the Constitution

When the Beatles released their second album, *With the Beatles,* in late 1963, William Mann, the classical music critic for the London newspaper, the *Times,* referred to songwriters John Lennon and Paul McCartney as "the outstanding English composers of 1963." Enamored in particular with the melodic and harmonic structure of one Lennon-McCartney composition, "Not a Second Time," Mann congratulated the songwriters for their use of "Aeolian cadences" and noted that the song featured the same chord progression that ended Mahler's "Song of the Earth." Curious that a classical musicologist could find such sophisticated musical technique in a self-professed primitive rock 'n' roll song, John Lennon remarked years later that "it was just chords like any other chords. To this day, I have no idea what Aeolian cadences are. They sound like exotic birds."[1]

Musicians are not alone in having others outside the walls of their creative process take it upon themselves to assign to their words and ideas an intent that, in their own minds, never existed. From almost the moment the Constitution was ratified, each subsequent generation of Americans has argued over the document's meaning and application. The range of opinions, whether of scholars or Supreme Court justices, on what the clauses and provisions of the Constitution mean, how it divides and allocates power among the branches of government, and the limits it creates on the exercise of government power over individual rights is so wide that one unfamiliar with this debate would be stunned to discover that almost all of its participants claim to speak on behalf of the Framers' intent.

The debate over the Constitution's meaning is remarkable for the emphasis it places on original meaning, intent, and historical context. But the idea that it is possible to recover and discern the Constitution's "true" meaning obscures the larger point of this enterprise: the need for participants in this debate—judges, lawyers, scholars, and so on—to find a "usable past" to defend their interpretation of the Constitution.[2] The emphasis on historical and theoretical precision sometimes leads us to forget that the Constitution was the work of statesmen and politicians, not philosophers and theorists.[3] Still, the Framers were more than just political pragmatists in search of a constitutional structure to defend their social, economic, and political preferences. They also had clear moral goals that they believed the Constitution's republican form of government could best promote.[4]

The purpose of this chapter is to explore the various approaches and theories to interpreting the Constitution. Since even those who believe that the Constitution means and requires different things agree that the Constitution is the authoritative source of law in the United States, the Court's decisions must have legitimacy. Because the Supreme Court is so often the last word on what the Constitution means, constitutional theory is often bound together with the process of judicial review. For constitutional adjudication to have power and resonance, the Court must explain how and why it has reached its decision. Its decisions cannot stand if they are viewed as nothing more than raw exercises in political power. Even if the justices, regardless of their assertions to the contrary, cannot help but infuse their constitutional philosophies with their own policy preferences, those choices must bear some relationship to the more general, abstract principles of the Constitution.

What should judges emphasize in interpreting the Constitution? Some theories suggest that the Court should minimize the role of judicial review and allow legislatures and other democratic institutions wide latitude in their policy choices. Other theories suggest that the Court must remain aware of the prevailing social and political sentiments and interpret the Constitution in light of modern societal norms. Still, two broad and interrelated sets of ideas are pervasive throughout all constitutional theories. One is that theories of constitutional interpretation often differ about the certainty of the constitutional text's meaning and the appropriate methods for discovering its meaning. The second involves beliefs about the allocation of institutional responsibilities and roles between the courts and the elected branches of government.[5]

"As a matter of fact, I have read the Constitution, and, frankly, I don't get it."

Keep in mind as well another important question that pervades the debate over constitutional interpretation as you think through the ideas presented in this chapter: Is it possible to separate constitutional theory from the outcomes it produces? How the Court decides, for example, to interpret the power of Congress to regulate interstate commerce will do more than just address an important theoretical question about the separation of powers. It will mean that Congress will have more or less power to regulate the environment or the sale and ownership of handguns. The same is true for the Free Speech Clause of the First Amendment. The Court's decision to interpret free speech rights broadly will, on a much more specific level, affect our rights to engage in public protest, our rights to use the public schools for religious purposes, and the rights of homeowners to place objectionable signs on their lawns. In sum, the enterprise of constitutional interpretation has real consequences for our public institutions and the lives of the most common of citizens. With this background in mind, consider whether it is possible to separate the rules that should govern constitutional interpretation from their real-world consequences.

Methods and Approaches

The categorization of complex, sometimes overlapping ideas in an effort to emphasize differences in approaches and methods to constitutional interpretation is hard to avoid. Although text, intent, and structure often provide the basic foundation for theories of constitutional interpretation, the emphasis of one factor over another results in a particular approach being labeled as interpretivist or noninterpretivist; literalist or indeterminist; activist or strict constructionist; traditionalist or postmodernist; and so on. Some scholars discount the effort to root constitutional interpretation in legal theories and instead insist that judicial behavior is an expression of ideological and policy-based values. Supreme Court outcomes can and should be understood as reflective of strategic choices made by the justices to advance these interests.[6]

The discussion here resists the lure of seeing constitutional interpretation as the result of mutually exclusive legal and nonlegal influences. It is true that a "system of interpretation that disregards the constitutional text cannot deserve support."[7] That said, legal theories have risen, fallen, and risen again that have emphasized different blends of legal, political, social, and economic considerations, largely because of the persuasiveness, or lack thereof, of the principles used to justify them.

Categorization, despite its risks and drawbacks, does have certain advantages. We have created three broad categories that draw the sharpest distinctions between competing approaches to constitutional interpretation: legal formalism, alternatives to formalism, and natural law. On the most general level, the differences between these approaches are greater than their similarities. A clear view of these visible differences will allow you to see the different weight accorded to constitutional text, Framers' intent, and other sources used to support different theories of constitutional interpretation. But also note the differences that exist within a particular school of thought as well as the similarities between what superficially appear to be separate categories.

We will return to summarize and synthesize the questions and problems generated by this discussion after we examine these three categories.

Legal Formalism

Legal formalism rests largely on the assumption that the Constitution can be understood as having a specific and true meaning. The sole task of those charged with interpreting the Constitution is to uncover the historical intent of its creators. Judges should not take it upon themselves to decide what the Constitution *should* mean, but instead uncover the facts and historical intent that informs the language of the Constitution. To suggest that the Constitution does not impart clear commands risks putting judges in the position of "creating" and not "discovering" constitutional values. Personal biases must be constrained in favor of a neutral approach to constitutional interpretation. If the Constitution no longer stands apart from politics, then it becomes just another instrument for the advancement of a social and political agenda.

Perhaps the most stark and dramatic expression of legal formalism is found in the interpretive method called *originalism*. Advocates of originalism (or, as it is also called, *original intent*), argue that the Constitution (and the Bill of Rights) must be interpreted in a manner consistent with those who wrote and ratified it. Originalists claim that judges who favor approaches inconsistent with the intent of the Framers are legislators in disguise, creating and bending the law to suit their own version of the Constitution.

Originalism has always been part of the debate over constitutional interpretation, but the publication of former U.S. Court of Appeals judge Robert H. Bork's *The Tempting of America* in 1990 gave the issue a renewed prominence.[8] For reasons that were as much about politics as they were about ideas, *The Tempting of America* created quite a stir. In 1987 the Senate defeated Judge Bork's nomination to replace Justice Lewis F. Powell, a far more moderate jurist, on the Supreme Court. Judge Bork was defeated, in part, because his views were considered eccentric in light of contemporary constitutional values. But what tipped the scales against Bork was the powerful and unparalleled media campaign on the part of civil rights and civil liberties groups to defeat his nomination. Washington, D.C., advocacy groups such as People for the American Way, the NAACP, the National Organization for Women, and the Alliance for Justice succeeded in painting Bork's views as hostile to women, racial minorities, First Amendment freedoms, and the rights of criminal defendants.[9] They produced television commercials, including a memorable one featuring Gregory Peck, an actor famous for his portrayal of Abraham Lincoln, reducing the complexity of Bork's views to cartoonlike snapshots. Negative ads appeared in newspapers around the country. These strategies were continually updated and refined in light of constant public opinion polls to gauge their success.[10]

Bork was also hurt by charges that he was a Trojan horse for the conservative political agenda of the Reagan administration. This charge stemmed from the similarities between the constitutional philosophy of Judge Bork and Edwin Meese, who served as attorney general under President Ronald Reagan from 1985 to 1988. In a 1985 address to the American Bar Association, Attorney General Meese called for the Court to return to "a jurisprudence of original intention." He stated in no uncertain terms that several of the Court's recent and more well-known decisions involving abortion rights, school prayer, affirmative action, federalism, and criminal due process were wrong as matters of constitutional law.[11]

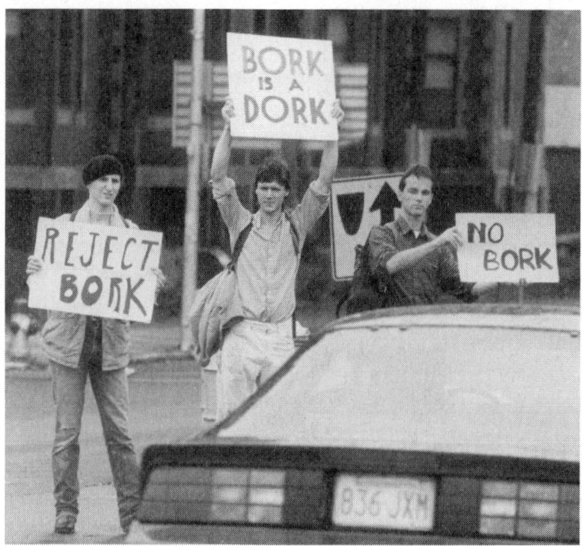

Robert Bork's nomination to the Supreme Court in 1987 drew opposition in the streets as well as in the corridors of power in Washington, D.C.
AP/Wide World Photos.

During the Reagan presidency (1981–1989), the Department of Justice, with full support from the White House, urged the Supreme Court to overrule several of these cases, which together painted over the broad canvas of American constitutional law. As strange as it was for a sitting attorney general to question the worth of the Court's constitutional jurisprudence in full public view, even more unusual was the response that Meese's comments generated from a sitting justice, William J. Brennan. In a public address to the Georgetown Law School in Washington, D.C., Justice Brennan replied that it was "arrogant to pretend that from our vantage we can gauge accurately the intent of the Framers. . . . *Those who would restrict claims of right to the values of 1789 specifically articulated in the Constitution, turn a blind eye to social progress and eschew adaptation of overarching principles to changes of social circumstances.*"[12] Justice Brennan was often cited by originalists as the evil spirit behind the modern Court's entrance into policy questions properly left with political branches, explained in part his candid response to Attorney General Meese's remarks.[13]

Caught in the crossfire of this political firestorm was Judge Bork. Although he continued to insist that his support for originalism bore no relationship to his own personal views, and defended his theories as "apolitical" and based on "neutral legal principles," his opponents continued to attack Bork and attack him hard. By the end more than three hundred organized interests were on record as opposing Bork's nomination to the Court, a standing army with resources that far exceeded his supporters, including his White House patrons.[14] Bork was unable to explain how originalism stood apart from the conservative political agenda and unwilling to retract his criticism of Supreme Court cases such as *Brown* v. *Board of Education* (1954), the landmark school desegregation case, and *Roe* v. *Wade* (1973), which established a legal right to abortion. He was defeated in his nomination to serve on the Court by a Senate vote of 58–42.[15]

Judge Bork used *The Tempting of America* to explain originalism outside the political vortex of his confirmation hearings. Originalism, wrote Judge Bork, "is the only method that can preserve the Constitution, the separation of powers, and the liberties of the people." To the claim that the original intent of the Constitution's Framers is unknowable, Judge Bork writes that the sources for discerning their original intent are "abundant." These include the *Federalist Papers* and the collected Anti-Federalist commentaries; congressional debates; early, seminal Supreme Court decisions such as *Marbury* v. *Madison* (1803); and authoritative judicial commentaries such as Justice Joseph Story's (1812–1845) *Commentaries on the Constitution of the United States* (1833). Concluded Judge Bork, "About much of the Constitution, therefore, we know a good deal; about other parts less; and, in a few cases, very little or nothing."[16]

On those rare occasions when a judge cannot make out a constitutional provision, "the judge should refrain from working. A provision whose meaning cannot be ascertained is precisely like a provision that is written in Sanskrit or is obliterated past deciphering by an ink blot. No judge is entitled to interpret an ink blot on the grounds that there might be something under it." Adherence to neutral principles, defined as the Framers' choices and not the judge's, absolves a judge from making unguided value judgments better left to the political branches. Originalism "is capable of supplying neutrality in all three respects—in deriving, defining, and applying principle."[17]

Criticism of originalism comes from several angles. The most obvious question comes first: Who were the "Framers" and how do we know they were of one mind? Few dispute the intellectual force that Thomas Jefferson brought to the constitutional design of American government and his oceanic influence over what later became the First Amendment. But Jefferson was in Paris during the four-year period when the Constitution and the Bill of Rights were written and ratified. Moreover, in correspondence with James Madison, Jefferson, while pleased with the basic constitutional structure of the government, was disturbed at "the omission of a bill of rights," a defect he insisted must be remedied before the Constitution could be complete.[18] John Adams, who succeeded George Washington as president and was another monumental figure in the founding of the Republic, was in London serving the nation as an emissary to Great Britain while Jefferson was in Paris. Should the ideas of these two pivotal figures be dismissed because of their absence during the Constitutional Convention and ratification period?

Should George Mason, a prominent Virginian who attended the convention and vigorously debated its provisions, but refused to sign the Constitution because the delegates failed to include a bill of rights, which he proposed, be considered a Framer? If not for the decision of the Federalists, especially James Madison, to agree to the submission of a Bill of Rights during the First Congress, the Constitution may have never been ratified. Do we include the Anti-Federalist pamphleteers as Framers, since the final version of the Constitution would have been far different without them? Originalism, despite its promises, provides no clear answer to the larger question of who framed the Constitution and whether consensus existed among those so designated as Framers.

Moreover, it is important to remember that the historical materials favored by originalists were also manipulated to serve the partisan political agendas of the Framers and, later, its ratifiers. Those who would rely upon convention records should be "warn[ed] that there are problems with most of them and that some have been compromised—perhaps fatally—by the editorial interventions of hirelings and partisans. . . . To recover original intent from these records may be an impossible . . . assignment."[19] For example, James Madison's notes and commentaries on the Constitutional Convention, although reliable, are incomplete. Madison also did not permit the release of his notes in full form until after his death. Thus the American public did not have Madison's notes on the convention or his other constitutional commentaries until 1840. Problems such as these raise the question of whether an incomplete and sometimes unreliable historical record compromise the originalist enterprise beyond repair.

Second, is originalism a truly "value free," or "neutral" approach to constitutional interpretation? Bork admits the Constitution embodies partisan political values but argues that because those choices were "made long ago by those who designed and enacted the Constitution" they form the starting point of discussions of its meaning.[20] Judges should honor the Framers' choices, not disturb them. One critic has argued that Bork's claim is an assertion on behalf of originalism, not a defense of it:

> On this view, the original understanding is binding because the original understanding was that the original understanding is binding. The historical claim itself is debatable. The breadth of the words of the Constitution invites the view that its meaning is capable of change over time. There is evidence that the framers did not believe that their original understanding would control the future. But we should put that point to one side. Bork's claim is that the binding character of the original understanding is settled by the original understanding. This is not an argument at all; it is circular, or a rallying cry. To those who believe it is necessary to defend the view that the original understanding is binding, it cannot be persuasive.[21]

In other words, originalism treats the limits on government power and protections for individual rights created by the Constitution as prepolitical and presocial. These conditions are not a product of law, but a reflection of "nature." Originalists argue that no substantive defense or theoretical justification is necessary to explain the Constitution because the Constitution explains itself. This viewpoint raises two important questions: Is it possible to interpret the Constitution without taking into account the social and political context of law and litigation? Is it possible to interpret the admittedly abstract and vague provisions of the Constitution in neutral fashion?

Third, critics of originalism claim that it understates and misreads the Framers' intent. Indeed, the Constitution is quite specific in some parts—no one, for example, can dispute the constitutional requirement that one must be thirty-five years old to serve as president or that Congress possesses the sole power to establish the "Post Office and post Roads." It is, however, also ill-defined, open-ended, abstract, and anything but self-evident in its meaning and application. For courts to interpret the freedom of speech guarantee in an age of instantaneous communication through the Internet; criminal due-process rights in light of modern, wholly unimagined electronic and computerized surveillance and evasion techniques; or the nature of interstate commerce without going beyond the text assumes that constitutional choices are self-evident. Constitutional scholar H. Jefferson Powell describes this problem well:

> It is commonly assumed that the "interpretive intention" of the Constitution's framers was that the Constitution would be construed in accordance with what future interpreters could gather of the framers' own purposes, expectations, and intentions. Inquiry shows that assumption to be incorrect. Of the numerous . . . options that were available in the framers' day. . . none corresponds to the modern notion of [originalism]. . . . In defending their claim that the "original understanding at Philadelphia" should control constitutional interpretation, modern intentionalists usually argue that other interpretive strategies undermine or even deny the possibility of subjectivity and consistency in constitutional law. Critics of this position typically respond with a battery of practical and theoretical objections to the attempt to construe the nation's fundamental law in accord with historical reconstructions of the purposes of the framers. There may well be grounds to support either of these positions. This debate cannot be resolved, however, and should not be affected, by the claim or assumption that modern [original] intentionalism was the original presupposition of American constitutional discourse. Such a claim is historically mistaken.[22]

Wallace v. *Jaffree*

472 U.S. 38 (1985)

In 1978 the Alabama legislature enacted a law requiring elementary school teachers to establish a moment of silence before school started for student meditation, reflection, or prayer. In 1981 Alabama enacted another law that gave teachers the discretion to provide a one-minute period of silence for meditation or "voluntary" prayer. A year later the legislature passed another law, this time giving "any teacher or professor . . . in any public educational institution within the state of Alabama" the right to lead "willing students" in specifically worded prayer that expressly recognized "God . . . Creator and Supreme Judge of the World."

The 1981 law eventually reached the Supreme Court after Ishmael Jaffree, a legal services lawyer, challenged its constitutionality on behalf of his three children in the Mobile school system. Jaffree was raised a Baptist, although later became an agnostic in college. His wife, Mozelle, was a devout Bahai, but she agreed with her husband that religious practices had no place in public schools. Jaffree had tried to settle with school authorities outside of court. Support, however, from Alabama's political establishment for the prayer laws was overwhelming, thus making any chance to resolve the issue impossible.

The Court, 6-3, struck down the 1981 law (the 1978 and 1982 laws were invalidated in lower courts and not appealed). *Wallace* was notable not only for raising the school prayer issue almost twenty years to the day that such practices were declared unconstitutional but also for Justice Rehnquist's dissent. In a thirty-page dissent that demonstrated remarkable historical range and facility, Justice Rehnquist offered a powerful critique of the Court's religion decisions. His reliance on Framers' intent and historical sources offers an excellent example of the originalist approach to constitutional interpretation.

▼▲▼

JUSTICE REHNQUIST, dissenting.

Thirty-eight years ago this Court, in *Everson* v. *Board of Education,* 330 U.S. 1 (1947), summarized its exegesis of the Establishment Clause doctrine thus:

> In the words of Jefferson, the clause against establishment of religion by law was intended to erect "a wall of separation between church and State."

This language from *Reynolds,* a case involving the Free Exercise Clause of the First Amendment, rather than the Establishment Clause, quoted from Thomas Jefferson's letter to the Danbury Baptist Association the phrase

> I contemplate with sovereign reverence that act of the whole American people which declared that their legislature should "make no law respecting an establishment of religion, or prohibiting the free exercise thereof," thus building a wall of separation between church and State.

It is impossible to build sound constitutional doctrine upon a mistaken understanding of constitutional history, but unfortunately the Establishment Clause has been expressly freighted with Jefferson's misleading metaphor for nearly 40 years. Thomas Jefferson was, of course, in France at the time the constitutional Amendments known as the Bill of Rights were passed by Congress and ratified by the States. His letter to the Danbury Baptist Association was a short note of courtesy, written 14 years after the Amendments were passed by Congress. He would seem to any detached observer as a less than ideal source of contemporary history as to the meaning of the Religion Clauses of the First Amendment.

Jefferson's fellow Virginian, James Madison, with whom he was joined in the battle for the enactment of the Virginia Statute of Religious Liberty of 1786, did play as large a part as anyone in the drafting of the Bill of Rights. He had two advantages over Jefferson in this regard: he was present in the United States, and he was a leading Member of the First Congress. But when we turn to the record of the proceedings in the First Congress leading up to the adoption of the Establishment Clause of the Constitution, including Madison's significant contributions thereto, we see a far different picture of its purpose than the highly simplified "wall of separation between church and State." . . .

On the basis of the record of these proceedings in the House of Representatives, James Madison was undoubtedly the most important architect among the Members of the House of the Amendments which became the Bill of Rights, but it was James Madison speaking as an advocate of sensible legislative compromise, not as an advocate of incorporating the Virginia Statute of Religious Liberty into the United States Constitution. During the ratification debate in the Virginia Convention, Madison had actually opposed the idea of any Bill of Rights. His sponsorship of the Amendments in the House was obviously not that of a zealous believer in the necessity of the Religion Clauses, but of one who felt it might do some good, could do no harm, and would satisfy those who had ratified the Constitution on the condition that Congress propose a Bill of Rights. His original language "nor shall any national religion be established" obviously does not conform to the "wall of separation" between church and State idea which latter-day commentators have ascribed to him. His explanation on the floor of the meaning of his language—"that Congress should not establish a religion, and enforce the legal observation of it by law"—is of the same ilk. When he replied to Huntington in the debate over the proposal which came from the Select Committee of the House, he urged that the language "no religion shall be established by law" should be amended by inserting the word "national" in front of the word "religion."

It seems indisputable from these glimpses of Madison's thinking, as reflected by actions on the floor of the House in 1789, that he saw the Amendment as designed to prohibit the establishment of a national religion, and perhaps to prevent discrimination among sects. He did not see it as requiring neutrality on the part of government between religion and irreligion. Thus the Court's opinion in *Everson*—while correct in bracketing Madison and Jefferson together in their exertions in their home State leading to the enactment of the Virginia Statute of Religious Liberty—is totally incorrect in suggesting that Madison carried these views onto the floor of the United States House of Representatives when he proposed the language which would ultimately become the Bill of Rights. . . .

The actions of the First Congress, which reenacted the Northwest Ordinance for the governance of the Northwest Territory in 1789, confirm the view that Congress did not mean that the Government should be neutral between religion and irreligion. The House of Representatives took up the Northwest Ordinance on the same day as Madison introduced his proposed amendments which became the Bill of Rights; while at that time the Federal Government was, of course, not bound by draft amendments to the Constitution which had not yet been proposed by Congress, say nothing of ratified by the States, it seems highly unlikely that the House of Representatives would simultaneously consider proposed amendments to the Constitution and enact an important piece of territorial legislation which conflicted with the intent of those proposals. The Northwest Ordinance, 1 Stat. 50, reenacted the Northwest Ordinance of 1787 and provided that "[r]eligion, morality, and knowledge, being necessary to good government and the happiness of mankind, schools and the means of education shall forever be encouraged." . . .

It would seem from this [and other] evidence [discussed by Justice Rehnquist in his dissent, omitted here] that the Establishment Clause of the First Amendment had acquired a well-accepted meaning: it forbade establishment of a national religion, and forbade preference among religious sects or denominations. Indeed, the first American dictionary defined the word "establishment" as "the act of establishing, founding, ratifying or ordaining," such as in "[t]he episcopal form of religion, so called, in England." The Establishment Clause did not require government neutrality between religion and irreligion, nor did it prohibit the Federal Government from providing nondiscriminatory aid to religion. There is simply no historical

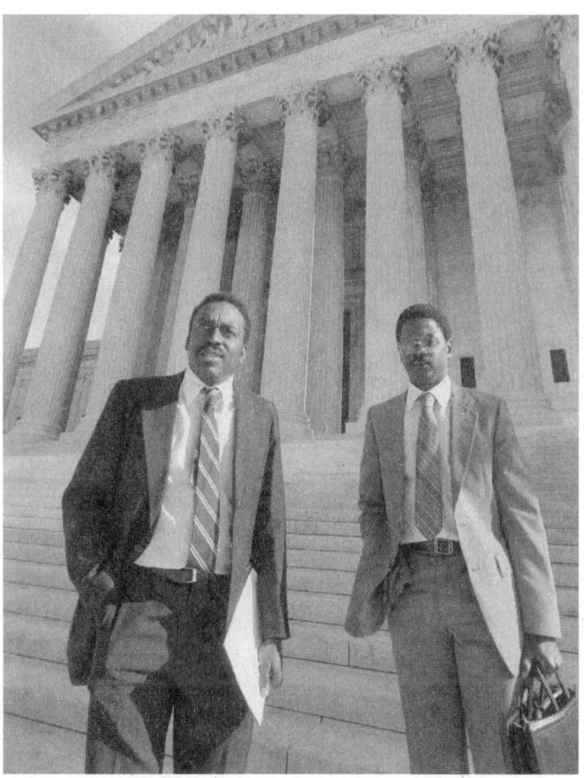

Ishmael Jaffree, left, who challenged Alabama's school prayer law in the early 1980s, with his attorney, Ronnie L. Williams, on the steps of the U.S. Supreme Court.
AP/Wide World Photos.

foundation for the proposition that the Framers intended to build the "wall of separation" that was constitutionalized in *Everson.*

Notwithstanding the absence of a historical basis for this theory of rigid separation, the wall idea might well have served as a useful, albeit misguided, analytical concept, had it led this Court to unified and principled results in Establishment Clause cases. The opposite, unfortunately, has been true; in the 38 years since *Everson,* our Establishment Clause cases have been neither principled nor unified. Our recent opinions, many of them hopelessly divided pluralities, have with embarrassing candor conceded that the "wall of separation" is merely a "blurred, indistinct, and variable barrier," which "is not wholly accurate" and can only be "dimly perceived."

Whether due to its lack of historical support or its practical unworkability, the *Everson* "wall" has proved all but useless as a guide to sound constitutional adjudication. It illustrates only too well the wisdom of Benjamin Cardozo's observation that "[m]etaphors in law are to be narrowly watched, for starting as devices to liberate thought, they end often by enslaving it."

But the greatest injury of the "wall" notion is its mischievous diversion of judges from the actual intentions of the drafters of the Bill of Rights. The "crucible of litigation" is well adapted to adjudicating factual disputes on the basis of testimony presented in court, but no amount of repetition of historical errors in judicial opinions can make the errors true. The "wall of separation between church and State" is a metaphor based on bad history, a metaphor which has proved useless as a guide to judging. It should be frankly and explicitly abandoned. . . .

The true meaning of the Establishment Clause can only be seen in its history. As drafters of our Bill of Rights, the Framers inscribed the principles that control today. Any deviation from their intentions frustrates the permanence of that Charter, and will only lead to the type of unprincipled decisionmaking that has plagued our Establishment Clause cases since *Everson.*

The Framers intended the Establishment Clause to prohibit the designation of any church as a "national" one. The Clause was also designed to stop the Federal Government from asserting a preference for one religious denomination or sect over others. Given the "incorporation" of the Establishment Clause as against the States via the Fourteenth Amendment in *Everson,* States are prohibited as well from establishing a religion or discriminating between sects. As its history abundantly shows, however, nothing in the Establishment Clause requires government to be strictly neutral between religion and irreligion, nor does that Clause prohibit Congress or the States from pursuing legitimate secular ends through nondiscriminatory sectarian means. . . .

It would come as much of a shock to those who drafted the Bill of Rights as it will to a large number of thoughtful Americans today to learn that the Constitution, as construed by the majority, prohibits the Alabama Legislature from "endorsing" prayer. George Washington himself, at the request of the very Congress which passed the Bill of Rights, proclaimed a day of "public thanksgiving and prayer, to be observed by acknowledging with grateful hearts the many and signal favors of Almighty God." History must judge whether it was the Father of his Country in 1789, or a majority of the Court today, which has strayed from the meaning of the Establishment Clause.

Legal formalism also finds a visible and prominent place in *literalism.* Constitutional literalists, like originalists, argue that the Constitution, as written, settles the need to go beyond the text to understand its meaning. Literalism and originalism also share similarities in their acceptance, but fundamental distrust, of judicial review. Each approach emphasizes the need for courts to defer to the laws created by democratic majorities—especially when the Constitution is silent on a particular question or when dealing with one of its more open-ended clauses. Judges that stray from the text of the Constitution and the intent of the Framers, properly understood, have granted themselves a license to impose their own values through judicial review.

Literalism and originalism do share the trait of legal authoritarianism, or a belief that judicial choices are self-evident, but their similarities end there.[23] It is far more difficult to tie literalism to a specific set of political outcomes than to do so with originalism. Another important difference between the two approaches is the role that each assigns to the Court to use judicial review to defend the clear and absolute commands of the Constitution. No individual better exemplifies the literalist approach to constitutional interpretation and its differences with originalism than former Supreme Court justice Hugo L. Black.

A giant of twentieth-century American law and jurisprudence, Justice Black served on the Supreme Court for thirty-four years (1937–1971), under five chief justices and six U.S. presidents. Prior to his appointment by President Franklin D. Roosevelt, Justice Black represented Alabama in the U.S. Senate, where he developed a justified reputation as one of the staunchest supporters of the New Deal. Unlike most justices when they come to the Court, Justice Black arrived almost fully formed in his approach to constitutional interpretation. He believed that courts should not interfere with the right of Congress and the state legislatures to regulate the nation's economic and business affairs unless a clear violation of due process had occurred. His most succinct description of this view is captured in his opinion for the Court in *Ferguson* v. *Skrupa* (1963) in which he wrote, "[w]e refuse to sit as a 'super-legislature to weigh the wisdom of legislation.' Whether the legislature takes for its textbook Adam Smith, Herbert Spencer, Lord Keynes, or some other is no concern of ours."[24]

Justice Black also adhered to a rigid conception of the separation of powers, rejecting even the slightest suggestion that one branch had the power to assume the functions of another. *Youngstown Sheet & Tube Co.* v. *Sawyer* (1952), which involved President Harry S Truman's famous effort to seize the nation's steel mills, provided "the setting for the most clear-cut expression" of Justice Black's constitutional literalism outside the context of the Bill of Rights.[25] President Truman invoked his presidential authority to end a strike at the nation's steel mills and force production to assure a steady supply of materials to the armed forces at the height of the Korean War. In the *Youngstown* opinion, which halted President Truman's action, note the emphasis that Justice Black places on the formal construction of the separation of powers:

> In the framework of our Constitution, the President's power to see that the laws are faithfully executed refutes the idea that he is to be a lawmaker. The Constitution limits his functions in the lawmaking process to the recommending of laws he thinks wise and the vetoing of laws he thinks bad. *And the Constitution is neither silent nor equivocal about who shall make the laws which the President is to execute. The first section of [Article I] says that "All legislative Powers herein granted shall be vested in a Congress of the United States. . . .* It is said that other Presidents without congressional authority have taken possession of private business enterprises in order to settle labor disputes. But even if this is true, Congress has not thereby lost its exclusive constitutional authority to make laws necessary and proper to carry out the powers vested by the Constitution.[26]

But where Justice Black receives the most attention for his constitutional literalism is for his position on the First Amendment. Here, Justice Black took the phrase "Congress shall make no law . . ." as it applied to all the guarantees of the First Amendment—speech, press, assembly, and religious freedom—at its word. No plausible argument was possible in defense of a law that touched upon the guarantees of the First Amendment. Historical evidence to the contrary—and there is much—did not dissuade Justice Black from his position that the Framers intended for the absolute protection of the First Amendment to apply absolutely.[27] Otherwise, Black claimed, they would have used different phrasing. Justice Black's own words capture his position on the First Amendment best:

> My view is, without deviation, without exception, without any if's, but's, or whereases, that freedom of speech means that government shall not do anything to people . . . either for the views they have or the views they express or the words they speak or write. Some people would have you believe that this is a very radical position, and maybe it is. But all I am doing is following what to me is the clear wording of the First Amendment. . . .
>
> As I have said innumerable times before I simply believe that "Congress shall make no law" means Congress shall make no law . . . abridging freedom of speech or the press.[28]

Note here the difference in how Justice Black's literalism and Judge Bork's originalism interpret the freedom-of-speech guarantee. Justice Black, with his emphasis on the absolute phrasing of the First Amendment, believed the originalist interpretation of the First Amendment—that it protects little more than political speech—was simply wrong. In Justice Black's view, obscenity is protected without the need to weigh or balance "competing" government interests, libel and slander laws are unconstitutional per se, and political speech that advocates the violent overthrow of the government is beyond the power of majorities to control. Originalists, on the other hand, reach the opposite conclusion based on their historical understanding of the First Amendment, not its linguistic commands.[29]

Although literalism and originalism in constitutional interpretation have their differences, each adheres to the fundamental tenets of legal formalism. Constitutional interpretation does not require one to go beyond the Constitution because its clauses and provisions define themselves. To wander in search of legal and theoretical sources "outside" the Constitution is to risk the imposition of value judgments that compromise the authority and integrity of its majestic commands. Our discussion of originalism and literalism has questioned whether either approach provides a sufficient baseline from which to interpret the Constitution. But what are the alternatives, and are they any better?

Alternatives to Formalism

Formalism dominated the Court's approach to constitutional interpretation from the founding period until the early part of the twentieth century, when the first serious challenge emerged to this long-held consensus in American law and jurisprudence. Parallel to the larger "progressive" movement underfoot in American politics, legal scholars, jurists, and social scientists began to question the legal foundation upon which the current economic, social, and political arrangements rested. Unlike formalists, who stressed the predetermined nature of legal rights, *legal realists* argued that law was the creation of a political process, one in which ever-changing social and economic forces competed for control of the public interest. Existing law reflected the triumph of private interests that used the legislative process to assert their place in the social and political order, not "discoveries" of the Framers' intent or rights self-evident in the "natural" law. Law determined the social order; it did not reflect a natural or predetermined state of affairs and thus could not have a meaning independent of the environment in which it was created.[30]

Legal realism, because of its association with the Progressive Era and the challenge to the status quo, attracted some of the most prominent intellectuals in American public life. Several of the most influential Progressive writers offered perspectives outside the law. Individuals such as Robert Hale, Morris Cohen, John Dewey, Thorstein Veblen, William James, and Jane Addams, none of whom was a lawyer, influenced the idea championed by the legal realists of law as instrumental in nature. Legal realists questioned several orthodox assumptions about the organization and distribution of social, economic, and political power in American society. They argued that law not only created the status quo but also could and should be used to change it.

Front and center in the legal realist movement were two of the most eminent figures in the history of American law, Oliver Wendell Holmes Jr. and Louis D. Brandeis. Their association with legal realism added luster to its strength as a counterpoint to formalism. Although scholars consider Holmes (1902–1932) and Brandeis (1916–1939) among the greatest justices to serve on the Supreme Court, each had left an indelible mark on American constitutional development before entering what, for each man, was the final stage of his career. In 1881, Holmes, while still in private practice, published *The Common Law,* which rejected the natural law tradition. Holmes argued in the clearest and most comprehensive terms to date that law reflected the deliberate choices made by people in response to perceived social and economic needs.[31] Holmes's central thesis, that law embodied policy preferences and that such preferences should be allowed to stand in absence of a clear constitutional mistake on the part of the legislature, had little influence on the Court but reverberated throughout some of the nation's most elite law schools. Harvard, Yale, and Columbia embraced Holmes's legal theories and a subsequent generation of legal scholars, advocates, and judges, including Brandeis and, later, Felix Frankfurter (1939–1962), absorbed Holmes's often-quoted lesson that "[t]he life of the law has not been logic: it has been experience."[32]

Because law, in addition to being a product of experience, was a social creation, Holmes believed that the Constitution permitted legislatures to make laws designed to meet evolving societal challenges. Such laws were entitled to a presumption of constitutionality unless a legislature could demonstrate no reasonable relationship of a law to its body's policy objectives. Holmes believed that using natural rights theories to reject legal change "w[as] simply [a] 'pontifical or imperial way of forbidding discussion.' Policy was no longer derivable from customary norms but was a coercive imposition of the state."[33]

Holmes did not share the reform-minded goals of the Progressives. If legislatures had chosen not to respond to the economic consequences of industrialization and other social crises that pervaded American life in the late nineteenth and early twentieth centuries, he would not have insisted that courts do their work for them. Brandeis, however, was a true believer in the Progressive cause. Before he joined the Court, Brandeis was the most famous "public interest" lawyer in America, having labored on behalf of reform causes almost his entire career. Unlike Holmes, who believed that legislatures should be permitted to experiment free from judicial supervision as part of the democratic nature of American politics, Brandeis believed that judges should evaluate the reasonableness of legislation through an assessment of the "facts" that formed the basis of legislation. Brandeis advocated a jurisprudence that enabled judges to differentiate between reform-minded legislation and laws that simply reflected the struggles between powerful private interests, the more classic Madisonian vision to which Holmes subscribed.

Brandeis's experience in pushing public interest legislation through state legislatures had "taught him that what appeared to be a reasonable piece of legislation might be no more than a giveaway to vested interests."[34] Although Holmes offered the first comprehensive argument for legal realism, Brandeis introduced "sociological jurisprudence" to American law. Brandeis believed that facts should preface legislative purpose and that courts should weigh the impact that laws would have on social betterment. Holmes recognized law's dynamic qualities and insisted that they should be allowed to flourish independent of a mythical attachment to a natural order. But Brandeis believed that legislatures and courts should use their knowledge of modern social science to improve the world, an approach he first brought to the Court's attention with stunning success in *Muller v. Oregon* (1908).[35]

Muller involved a challenge to a maximum-work-hour law for women who worked in commercial laundries. Brandeis submitted a brief of about one hundred pages, only two of which dealt with questions of law. The rest consisted of evidence collected from around the country on the public health consequences for women and their families who worked longer than ten hours per day in such demanding conditions. So impressed was the Court that it directly referred to the "very copious" body of information provided by Brandeis as the basis for its decision. The "Brandeis Brief" became a model for subsequent generations of reform-minded lawyers attacking a wide range of established government practices, from racial discrimination to public education expenditures.

Although Holmes and Brandeis are often grouped as twins in discussions of legal realism's place in American law, other than their mutual disdain for formalism and natural law, they held very different conceptions of law's potential to transform the conditions of American life. Holmes's skepticism of law as the protector of "natural" truths formed the basis for his views. Brandeis, on the other hand, believed that law and litigation could be positive forces in altering the balance of social and economic power between worker and owner, dissident and majority, and rich and poor.

SIDEBAR

OLIVER WENDELL HOLMES JR. AND THE COMMON LAW

Perhaps the most revered figure in the history of American law, Oliver Wendell Holmes Jr. enjoyed a remarkable legal career, one that began as the Civil War came to a close and ended shortly after Franklin Roosevelt won his first presidential campaign in 1932. A Harvard law graduate, Holmes spent only a limited part of his career in private practice. His intellectual gifts were evident as far back as his freshman year in college, and he impressed many of his college professors as a literary stylist. Indeed, Holmes's judicial opinions are remembered as much for their well-crafted language as for their legal thought.

But the importance of Holmes's contribution to the development of legal theory is unmistakable. His opinions in *Schenck* v. *United States* (1919) and *Abrams* v. *United States* (1919) established the "clear and present danger" test and the "marketplace of ideas" concept, which together established the constitutional baseline for the boundaries of modern free speech law. In addition, Holmes argued that legislatures should be free to experiment with solutions to social and economic problems without judicial interference, but he placed tight reigns on their ability to interfere with more "fundamental" rights, such as freedom of speech, religion, and assembly.

Oliver Wendell Holmes enjoying an afternoon in the garden—with, of course, a little reading.
Courtesy of the Harvard University Archives.

The Common Law

The object of this book is to present a general view of the Common Law. To accomplish the task, other tools are needed besides logic. It is something to show that the consistency of a system requires a particular result, but it is not all. The life of the law has not been logic: it has been experience. The felt necessities of the time, the prevalent moral and political theories, intuitions of public policy, avowed or unconscious, even the prejudices which judges share with their fellow-men, have had a good deal more to do than the syllogism in determining the rules by which men should be governed. The law embodies the story of a nation's development through many centuries, and it cannot be dealt with as if it contained only the axioms and corollaries of a book of mathematics. In order to know what it is, we must know what it has been, and what it tends to become. We must alternately consult history and existing theories of legislation. But the most difficult labor will be to understand the combination of the two into new products at every stage. The substance of the law at any given time pretty nearly corresponds, so far as it goes, with what is then understood to be convenient; but its form and machinery, and the degree to which it is able to work out desired results, depend very much upon its past.

In Massachusetts today, while, on the one hand, there are a great many rules which are quite sufficiently accounted for by their manifest good sense, on the other, there are some which can only be understood by reference to the infancy of procedure among the German tribes, or to the social condition of Rome under the Decemvirs.

I shall use the history of our law so far as it is necessary to explain a conception or to interpret a rule, but no further. In doing so there are two errors equally to be avoided both by writer and reader. One is that of supposing, because an idea seems very familiar and natural to us, that it has always been so. Many things which we take for granted have had to be laboriously fought out or thought out in past times. The other mistake is the opposite one of asking too much of history. We start with man full grown. It may be assumed that the earliest barbarian whose practices are to be considered had a good many of the same feelings and passions as ourselves.

Legal realism came to dominate the Court's jurisprudence immediately after the Constitutional Revolution of 1937, a term often used to describe the Court's sudden rejection of formalism. But legal realism, while an influence in the modern Court's approach to constitutional interpretation, soon came in for harsh criticism. Even constitutional theorists who acknowledged that the Court makes social and political value choices when it interprets the Constitution suggested that a more principled, less political justification was required to defend the Court's decisions. Accordingly, in the first major challenge to legal realism in the post–New Deal era, Herbert Wechsler argued that the Court must make its decisions based on *neutral principles* of law, not on contextual or policy-based considerations.[36]

Wechsler's conception of neutral principles differed from the formalist model in several crucial aspects. Wechsler did not contest the proposition that the Constitution authorized judicial review. Nor did he dispute the central contention of the legal realists that constitutional interpretation and the exercise of judicial review required the Court to make value choices. But Wechsler argued that constitutional interpretation should not be rooted in a contextual, case-specific examination of a particular set of facts. Instead, constitutional interpretation should be a neutral principle of law that applied equally to all parties. To illustrate his point, Wechsler argued that the Court should have decided the historic *Brown* case on freedom of association grounds, not under the Equal Protection Clause. The National Association for the Advancement of Colored People, which represented the African American families in *Brown,* not only argued that mandated school segregation fostered unequal educational opportunities for blacks, created a racial stigma, and lessened their future economic opportunities but also introduced social science data to support these arguments.[37]

Wechsler argued that the Court should have ruled that school segregation violated the freedom-of-association rights of African American students to attend the schools of their choice. Wechsler believed the Court had interpreted the Fourteenth Amendment to favor African Americans based on their disadvantaged position in public education, a decision that amounted to a partisan choice. Freedom of association was a "race neutral" principle applicable in such cases that avoided the "sociological jurisprudence" of the actual *Brown* decision. Wechsler commented that segregation laws penalized whites and African Americans to an equal degree because members of both races were denied the lawful opportunity to free association based on race.

Putting aside for the moment the unusual notion that racial segregation harmed whites and African Americans to an equal degree, are neutral principles really possible in American constitutional law? In some ways, Wechsler could not have picked a worse case to use as the basis for his neutral-principles argument. Segregation was a condition created by a political system steeped in racial prejudice, one that excluded African Americans from meaningful participation and representation until the mid-1960s. It was not a condition of nature. Segregation was precisely the sort of problem pointed out by the legal realists.

Still, Wechsler's effort to offer an alternative to legal realism was an important contribution to constitutional theory. Neutral principles, as an idea, was an attempt to reconcile the consequences of the Constitutional Revolution of 1937 with the position of legal formalists that the Constitution should have a meaning independent of what the justices think it should mean at a given point in time.[38] The same concerns that motivated Wechsler were also evident in the subsequent contribution of another exceptionally influential theorist, John Hart Ely, who, in *Democracy and Distrust* (1981), argued that courts should refrain from using their power to create rights through the "open textured" clauses of the Constitution. Ely claimed the Court in the post–New Deal era had done just that. Instead, the Court should limit judicial review to laws that prevented the political process from functioning in a fair and open manner. Ely agreed with critics of legal formalism that a "clause bound" approach to constitutional interpretation was impossible, but he was also suspicious of grandiose legal theories that granted excessive power to the courts to "discover" the Constitution's fundamental values.

Ely laid out three specific instances when the courts should strike down laws: (1) when laws violated specific substantive constitutional guarantees (e.g., free speech, criminal due-process protections); (2) when laws operated to disadvantage "discrete and insular" minorities in the political process (e.g., voting rights, political participation); and (3) when laws created procedural obstacles that created unreasonable barriers to political and social reform through the political process. Courts should defer to the political process in disputes involving the open-ended provisions of the Constitution. Ely believed that such cases presented dangerous vehicles for the courts to impose their value choices on the general population, a practice he believed had no defense in constitutional theory.[39]

Constitutional scholars and political scientists have found much to admire in Ely's studied and ambitious effort to construct a generally applicable theory of judicial review. But critics have pointed out that his ideas offer little guidance on how to interpret the substance of the Constitution. *Democracy and Distrust* denied one of the central lessons of the legal realist movement: that constitutional choices involve moral and substantive value choices, not just determinations of procedural fairness. For example, a court's conclusion that the political process is "malfunctioning," to use Ely's term, calls for a value choice.[40] Moreover, Ely believes that courts have the obligation to strike down legislation that violates free speech or religious rights, but he notes that the content of those rights is not necessarily defined by text of the Constitution.[41] Thus, is it really possible for the courts to avoid discretionary value choices even when they confront the "specific" clauses of the Constitution? Chief among those flaws is the need to use substantive values. Ely relies on the very "value-oriented" approach that he seeks, through a process-based theory, to avoid.[42]

Process-oriented approaches to constitutional law emphasize the need to understand the limits and possibilities of judicial review in the American system of government rather than the value choices made by the courts. Perhaps, then, it is only natural that a resurgence of *rights-oriented* theories has emerged to challenge the central premises of the process-oriented *and* originalist approaches. Rights-oriented theories of constitutional interpretation place a decided emphasis on the value choices involved in constitutional interpretation, with judicial review, viewed here as a means to accomplish particular policy goals, given secondary attention. Although such theories have their historical antecedent in legal realism, modern rights-oriented theories are much more concerned with questions involving, for example, affirmative action, abortion rights, obscenity, and sexual privacy—questions that never concerned Holmes, Brandeis, and the Progressives influenced by them.

For some time, rights-oriented theories of constitutional interpretation were developed in support of liberal political objectives that stood little chance of success in the political branches. Scholars such as Ronald Dworkin and Laurence Tribe argued that the courts were best suited to make principled decisions about the substance and scope of protected rights, in contrast to the "interest based" outcomes that were characteristic of the push and pull of legislative politics.[43] Guided by reason and unaccountable to the political impulses of majorities, the courts should use their special position and special competence to examine the moral and political components of rights-based claims. The courts should make decisions that best enforce the abstract principles of the Constitution, which include concepts such as human dignity, equality, and fairness.

More so than any other liberal rights-oriented scholar, Dworkin has argued for sweeping judicial power to determine the rights inherent in these constitutional concepts on the assumption that the Supreme Court, and by extension the lower federal courts, is a "forum of principle."[44] On first glance Dworkin's approach might appear to give judges the broad discretion to create any suitable "concept" of constitutional theory. But he does insist that the courts are constrained by legal norms, including the Constitution, judicial precedent, and common law principles. In the end, however, Dworkin, indicative of most rights-oriented constitutional theorists, offers little institutional assurance to constrain judicial discretion. His hope is that judges will make the correct moral choices.

Recent conservative constitutional theorists have used the language of rights, rather than appeals to originalism, to mount provocative challenges to legal scholars in search of liberal political outcomes. Two major tenets of liberal theories of rights have come under close scrutiny. The first is the belief that the right to make individual choices is more important than the moral consequences of what those choices entail; the second is the idea that majorities should not make moral judgments about whether certain choices are better than others.[45] For example, the law should not allow the majority's conceptions of abortion, gay rights, or obscenity to interfere with an individual's basic right to lead an independent life. Majorities usually do a pretty good job of protecting their own rights and interests, but individuals looked down upon for their political or religious views, their sexual orientation, or their interest in sexually explicit materials have to fight much harder for their legal rights. Rights theories should be concerned with the protection of minorities who cannot protect themselves.

Conservative rights theorists do not suggest that constitutional interpretation should or can be value neutral. Instead, they argue that rights and their purpose in the larger moral universe should be considered in another fashion. Rights should be assigned based on whether their exercise allows individuals to do or accomplish something that is good. Rights are a means to achieve some productive or useful moral end. Rights should recognize that some choices are morally superior to others. Constitutional law should not treat a woman's decision to choose an abortion over childbirth as morally indistinguishable; churches and religious individuals should, in some cases, receive preferential treatment over atheists and skeptics; and homosexual love weighs differently in the minds of the public than heterosexual love, thus raising different questions about the value of extending legal recognition to same-sex marriages. For their constitutional status, rights depend on the consequences that permitting such choices will have on the moral and political fabric of society.

Conservative and liberal constitutional theorists might want very different things from the law, but these rights-oriented approaches to constitutional law share certain similarities. Interpretive principles and the substance of rights receive a heavy and unapologetic injection of moral and political philosophy. When making their decisions, judges should not attempt to reconcile rights claims with the Framers' intent or similar fixed poles in the legal universe, but should consider the moral sensibilities of communities as well as the individual. Constitutional interpretation should take place at a very abstract level that allows for an open, evolving dialogue over the substance and range of rights and power. Judicial discretion to define and impose value choices is not an inherent evil. One is hard-pressed to find such a deliberative discussion over the future direction of our constitutional culture unattractive. But do rights-oriented theories provide a better and more defensible theory of constitutional interpretation and judicial power than any of the other theories discussed thus far?

Furman v. *Georgia*

408 U.S. 238 (1972)

Disturbed by patterns of racial discrimination and arbitrariness in capital sentencing, as well as a general sense that society had evolved to the point where it no longer considered capital punishment constitutional, the National Association for the Advancement of Colored People Legal Defense Fund (LDF) and the American Civil Liberties Union (ACLU) joined forces in the mid-1960s to develop a litigation campaign to end the death penalty. Encouragement for the LDF's and the ACLU's legal efforts came from a dissent issued by Justice Arthur Goldberg from the Supreme Court's denial of *certiorari* in a 1963 case, *Rudolph* v. *Alabama,* in which the defendant was sentenced to death for rape. Goldberg believed that the Court should have taken the case to consider whether "evolving standards of decency" had made the death penalty no longer consistent with the Eighth Amendment's prohibition on cruel and unusual punishments.

The LDF targeted death-penalty appeals all over the country that would highlight various objections to capital punishment. By 1971 the Court had agreed to consolidate three capital cases out of Georgia and Texas and decide them together. Of the three only *Furman* involved murder; the other two were rape cases.

By a 5-4 vote, the Court invalidated the death penalty as violative of the Eighth Amendment ban on cruel and unusual punishment. Each justice in the majority, however, wrote a separate decision to explain his objection to the death penalty as it was currently administered in the United States. Only two justices, William Brennan and Thurgood Marshall, believed that the death penalty was unconstitutional under any circumstance. The three other justices cited due-process concerns and racial discrimination as their reasons for holding the death penalty unconstitutional.

Justice Brennan's opinion offers an excellent counterpoint to the originalism of Justice Rehnquist's *Wallace* dissent. Compared with Rehnquist, Justice Brennan believes that history is far less exact and the Framers' far more ambiguous about their intentions.

▼▲▼

MR. JUSTICE BRENNAN, concurring.

We have very little evidence of the Framers' intent in including the Cruel and Unusual Punishments Clause. . . .

[Little] evidence of the Framers' intent appears from the debates in the First Congress on the adoption of the Bill of Rights. As the Court noted in *Weems* v. *United States* (1910), the Cruel and Unusual Punishments Clause "received very little debate." The extent of the discussion, by two opponents of the Clause in the House of Representatives, was this:

> Mr. SMITH, of South Carolina, objected to the words "nor cruel and unusual punishments," the import of them being too indefinite.
>
> Mr. LIVERMORE.—The [Eighth Amendment] seems to express a great deal of humanity, on which account I have no objection to it; but as it seems to have no meaning in it, I do not think it necessary. . . . No cruel and unusual punishment is to be inflicted; it is sometimes necessary to hang a man, villains often deserve whipping, and perhaps having their ears cut off; but are we in future to be prevented from inflicting these punishments because they are cruel? If a more lenient mode of correcting vice and deterring others from the commission of it could be invented, it would be very prudent in the Legislature to adopt it; but until we have some security that this will be done, we ought not to be restrained from making necessary laws by any declaration of this kind.
>
> The question was put on the [Eighth Amendment], and it was agreed to by a considerable majority.

Several conclusions thus emerge from the history of the adoption of the Clause. We know that the Framers' concern was directed specifically at the exercise of legislative power. They included in the Bill of Rights a prohibition upon "cruel and unusual punishments" precisely because the legislature would otherwise have had the unfettered power to prescribe punishments for crimes. Yet we cannot now know exactly what the Framers thought "cruel and unusual punishments" were. Certainly they intended to ban torturous punishments, but the available evidence does not support the further conclusion that only torturous punishments were to be outlawed. As Livermore's comments demonstrate, the Framers were well aware that the reach of the Clause was not limited to the proscription of unspeakable atrocities. Nor did they intend simply to forbid punishments considered "cruel and unusual" at the time. The "import" of the Clause is, indeed, "indefinite," and for good reason. . . .

In short, this Court [has] adopted the Framers' view of the Clause as a "constitutional check" to ensure that, "when we come to punishments, no latitude ought to be

left, nor dependence put on the virtue of representatives." That, indeed, is the only view consonant with our constitutional form of government. . . .

Judicial enforcement of the Clause, then, cannot be evaded by invoking the obvious truth that legislatures have the power to prescribe punishments for crimes. That is precisely the reason the Clause appears in the Bill of Rights. The difficulty arises, rather, in formulating the "legal principles to be applied by the courts" when a legislatively prescribed punishment is challenged as "cruel and unusual." In formulating those constitutional principles, we must avoid the insertion of "judicial conception[s] of . . . wisdom or propriety," yet we must not, in the guise of "judicial restraint," abdicate our fundamental responsibility to enforce the Bill of Rights. Were we to do so, the "constitution would indeed be as easy of application as it would be deficient in efficacy and power. Its general principles would have little value and be converted by precedent into impotent and lifeless formulas. Rights declared in words might be lost in reality." The Cruel and Unusual Punishments Clause would become, in short, "little more than good advice." . . .

> Ours would indeed be a simple task were we required merely to measure a challenged punishment against those that history has long condemned. That narrow and unwarranted view of the Clause, however, was left behind with the 19th century. Our task today is more complex. We know "that the words of the [Clause] are not precise, and that their scope is not static." We know, therefore, that the Clause "must draw its meaning from the evolving standards of decency that mark the progress of a maturing society." That knowledge, of course, is but the beginning of the inquiry.

In *Trop* v. *Dulles* (1958) it was said that "[t]he question is whether [a] penalty subjects the individual to a fate forbidden by the principle of civilized treatment guaranteed by the [Clause]." It was also said that a challenged punishment must be examined "in light of the basic prohibition against inhuman treatment" embodied in the Clause. It was said, finally, that:

> The basic concept underlying the [Clause] is nothing less than the dignity of man. While the State has the power to punish, the [Clause] stands to assure that this power be exercised within the limits of civilized standards.

At bottom, then, the Cruel and Unusual Punishments Clause prohibits the infliction of uncivilized and inhuman punishments. The State, even as it punishes, must treat its members with respect for their intrinsic worth as human beings. A punishment is "cruel and unusual," therefore, if it does not comport with human dignity.

This formulation, of course, does not, of itself, yield principles for assessing the constitutional validity of particular punishments. Nevertheless, even though "[t]his Court has had little occasion to give precise content to the [Clause]," *ibid.*, there are principles recognized in our cases and inherent in the Clause sufficient to permit a judicial determination whether a challenged punishment comports with human dignity. . . .

More than the presence of pain, however, is comprehended in the judgment that the extreme severity of a punishment makes it degrading to the dignity of human beings. The barbaric punishments condemned by history, "punishments which inflict torture, such as the rack, the thumbscrew, the iron boot, the stretching of limbs and the like," are, of course, "attended with acute pain and suffering." When we consider why they have been condemned, however, we realize that the pain involved is not the only reason. The true significance of these punishments is that they treat members of the human race as nonhumans, as objects to be toyed with and discarded. They are thus inconsistent with the fundamental premise of the Clause that even the vilest criminal remains a human being possessed of common human dignity.

In determining whether a punishment comports with human dignity, we are aided also by a second principle inherent in the Clause—that the State must not arbitrarily inflict a severe punishment. This principle derives from the notion that the State does not respect human dignity when, without reason, it inflicts upon some people a severe punishment that it does not inflict upon others. Indeed, the very words "cruel and unusual punishments" imply condemnation of the arbitrary infliction of severe punishments. . . .

A third principle inherent in the Clause is that a severe punishment must not be unacceptable to contemporary society. Rejection by society, of course, is a strong indication that a severe punishment does not comport with human dignity.

The question under this principle, then, is whether there are objective indicators from which a court can conclude that contemporary society considers a severe punishment unacceptable. Accordingly, the judicial task is to review the history of a challenged punishment and to examine society's present practices with respect to its use. Legislative authorization, of course, does not establish acceptance. The acceptability of a severe punishment is measured not by its availability, for it might become so offensive to society as never to be inflicted, but by its use.

The final principle inherent in the Clause is that a severe punishment must not be excessive. A punishment is excessive under this principle if it is unnecessary: the infliction of a severe punishment by the State cannot comport with human dignity when it is nothing more than the pointless infliction of suffering. If there is a significantly less severe punishment adequate to achieve the purposes for which the punishment is inflicted, the punishment inflicted is unnecessary, and therefore excessive. . . .

Since the Bill of Rights was adopted, this Court has adjudged only three punishments to be within the prohibition of the Clause. *Weems* v. *United States,* (1910) (12 years in chains at hard and painful labor); *Trop* v. *Dulles,* (1958) (expatriation); *Robinson* v. *California,* (1962) (imprisonment for narcotics addiction). Each punishment, of course, was degrading to human dignity, but of none could it be said conclusively that it was fatally offensive under one or the other of the principles. Rather, these "cruel and unusual punishments" seriously implicated several of the principles, and it was the application of the principles in combination that supported the judgment. That, indeed, is not surprising. The function of these principles, after all, is simply to provide means by which a court can determine whether a challenged punishment comports with human dignity. They are, therefore, interrelated, and, in most cases, it will be their convergence that will justify the conclusion that a punishment is "cruel and unusual." The test, then, will ordinarily be a cumulative one: if a punishment is unusually severe, if there is a strong probability that it is inflicted arbitrarily, if it is substantially rejected by contemporary society, and if there is no reason to believe that it serves any penal purpose more effectively than some less severe punishment, then the continued infliction of that punishment violates the command of the Clause that the State may not inflict inhuman and uncivilized punishments upon those convicted of crimes. . . .

In comparison to all other punishments today, then, the deliberate extinguishment of human life by the State is uniquely degrading to human dignity. I would not hesitate to hold, on that ground alone, that death is today a "cruel and unusual" punishment, were it not that death is a punishment of longstanding usage and acceptance in this country. I therefore turn to the second principle—that the State may not arbitrarily inflict an unusually severe punishment. . . .

[Justice Brennan then provided an analysis of the infrequency of executions in the United States in the twentieth century, concluding that the odds of execution for capital crimes was so remote as to make such punishment arbitrary and "freakish."]

There is, then, no substantial reason to believe that the punishment of death, as currently administered, is necessary for the protection of society. The only other purpose suggested, one that is independent of protection for society, is retribution. Shortly stated, retribution in this context means that criminals are put to death because they deserve it. . . .

In sum, the punishment of death is inconsistent with [the] four principles [described here]: death is an unusually severe and degrading punishment; there is a strong probability that it is inflicted arbitrarily; its rejection by contemporary society is virtually total; and there is no reason to believe that it serves any penal purpose more effectively than the less severe punishment of imprisonment. The function of these principles is to enable a court to determine whether a punishment comports with human dignity. Death, quite simply, does not.

Natural Law

Our discussion thus far leaves us with two certainties. First, the Constitution creates certain rights and freedoms that deserve protection from the exercise of "naked" majoritarian preferences. That is, majorities must have solid grounds for treating certain individuals or groups within society differently, other than for reasons of raw political power.[46] Today, the rational basis of practices such as slavery, Jim Crow, sex-based discrimination, zoning restrictions designed to disadvantage unpopular religious movements, or the exploitation of child labor is difficult to understand. We have come to associate these practices with prejudice and greed, not public value. Conservative and liberals, legal formalists and their critics, and constitutional theorists who see the Constitution and the legal culture in very different terms agree in far more cases than not that laws must, at minimum, further some rational public objective. Indeed, much of the intricate design of the Constitution is premised on the rationale that the governmental branches possess the power to veto public policies that do not serve interests beyond those of powerful, self-interested majorities. Second, and obvious by now, is that constitutional scholars cannot agree on what the Constitution means; how to enforce its substantive and procedural provisions; and who, or which branch of government, should possess the preeminent power to undertake these responsibilities.

Do certainties, then, exist in constitutional interpretation and the exercise of judicial power? If we accept the premises of *natural law and natural rights* theorists, that certain rights exist independent of those established by artificial legal rules, then the answer is yes. Natural law theories presuppose certain unalienable truths about individuals and the rights they retain when they enter civil and political society. If the phrase "unalienable truths" sounds familiar, it should. Thomas Jefferson alluded to the natural rights tradition in the Declaration of Independence, writing that "the Laws of Nature and of Nature's God" endowed men with "certain unalienable rights," among which were "Life, Liberty and the Pursuit of Happiness." Historian Forrest McDonald has noted that the American colonies' invocation of natural law as the basis for rebellion made the British constitution irrelevant. American independence largely owes its intellectual justification to the decision of the revolution's leaders "to go outside the forms and norms of English law" and claim their rights on the basis of natural law.[47] On an abstract level natural law has great appeal, for it posits that universal truths, absolute in their moral goodness, exist outside the relativist framework of *positive law,* or the legal rules that society chooses to create. Natural law theorists contend that laws enacted by civil societies, even if done through open and democratic processes, are invalid if they violate these universal principles. Edward Corwin, whose work in the early twentieth century was quite influential in how political scientists thought about the relationship between law and society, wrote that the Constitution was conceived against the "higher" background of natural law and deserved an appropriate place in constitutional adjudication.[48]

But the application of natural law theories to the Constitution raises serious problems. Political scientist Benjamin F. Wright, in an early appraisal of the use of natural law as a source of interpretive principles, noted:

> [N]atural law has had as its content whatever the individual in question desired to advocate. This has varied from a defense of theocracy to a defense of the complete separation of church and state, from revolutionary rights in 1776 to liberty of contract in recent judicial opinions, from the advocacy of universal adult suffrage to a defense of rigid limitations upon the voting power . . . from the advocacy of the inalienable right to succession to the assertion of the natural law of national supremacy, from the right of majority rule to the rights of vested interests.[49]

Wright wrote in 1931 but neglected to mention that natural law principles were prominent in three of the Court's less luminous nineteenth-century opinions. In all three cases the Court rejected individual rights claims on grounds now thoroughly discredited in modern constitutional law: *Dred Scott* v. *Sandford* (1857), in which the Court ruled that African Americans were bound by the laws of nature to their status as property;[50] *Bradwell* v. *Illinois* (1873), where the Court held that state law could bar women from becoming lawyers on the grounds that "the civil law, as well as nature herself, has always recognized a wide difference in the respective spheres and destinies of man and woman. . . . The paramount destiny and mission of women are to fulfill the noble and benign offices of wife and mother [because] this is the law of the Creator";[51] and *Plessy* v. *Ferguson* (1896), in which the Court upheld state-enforced racial segregation as a legitimate exercise of "the established usages, customs and traditions of the people."[52] To enfold this latter phrase into natural law theories of rights creates an unstoppable double helix of constitutional possibilities, as "custom and tradition" are malleable terms that can mean almost anything, depending upon whose customs and traditions are in question. Garry Wills is succinct on this point, noting that "[r]unning men out of town on a rail is as much an American tradition as declaring unalienable rights."[53]

In modern times natural law principles have been used to defend and attack abortion rights, affirmative action, conscientious objector status, capital punishment, the minimum wage, gun control, gay rights, and the rights of terminally ill or comatose patients.[54] This ambiguity leads one to ask what should be an obvious question: If natural law recognizes the existence of universal rights that can be derived from moral absolutes, why have legal scholars, philosophers, theologians, and constitutional scholars been unable to agree on what those universal rights are? One reason is that almost no one agrees on the sources of natural rights. Do natural rights have a divine origin as Jefferson's rhetoric in the Declaration of Independence suggests? Are they derived from the ancient Greek philosophers? If so, how were the Greeks able to distinguish natural from positive rights? Another reason for the lack of agreement on the specifics of universal rights is that although the constitutional founders were certainly influenced by natural rights theories, we have no indication that the founders intended a place for such theories in the Constitution. John Hart Ely has noted that because revolutionaries are unlikely to have positive law on their side, appeals to natural law and natural rights, or whatever will help justify their cause, are inevitable.[55]

The Constitution quite clearly is the product of legal positivism. It is also intended to govern. References, explicit or otherwise, to natural law are absent from the Constitution. Given the abstract nature and uncertain origins of natural law, is it unreasonable to conclude that the enactment of the Constitution and the Bill of Rights, the two most enduring acts of written legal positivism in Western civilization, reflect the Framers' deliberate refutation of such theories? On the other hand, are natural law theories implicit in some of the other approaches to constitutional interpretation discussed thus far? What similarities and differences do you see when natural law theories are compared with other theories of constitutional interpretation?

Griswold v. *Connecticut*

381 U.S. 479 (1965)

Estelle Griswold served as the executive director of the Connecticut office of Planned Parenthood. An advocate of low-cost access to birth control and other materials to assist in family planning, Griswold spent more than twenty years attempting to overturn an 1879 Connecticut law prohibiting such services before the Supreme Court agreed to hear her case.

In 1961, Griswold, along with physician C. Lee Buxton, opened a family-planning clinic in New Haven fully expecting—and hoping—to be arrested. Their wish was quickly granted, and Griswold and Buxton were charged with violating the 1879 law. A legal team, led by Yale law professor Thomas Emerson, had been assembled to defend Griswold and Buxton. The lawyers rooted their argument in the "liberty" component of the Due Process Clause of the Fourteenth Amendment, claiming that the clause was broad enough to encompass a right to privacy that permitted married couples to receive information about birth control and use it.

The Court, 7-2, struck down the Connecticut law, agreeing with Griswold's lawyers that it violated a marital right of privacy protected by the Constitution. Griswold prompted several strong opinions, with two of the most notable being Justice Arthur Goldberg's concurrence and Justice Hugo Black's dissent. Goldberg alludes to the idea that certain rights and liberties exist outside the constitutional text. Black offers a classic statement of his literalist approach to constitutional interpretation, including a pointed criticism of Goldberg's opinion as founded in a "mysterious and uncertain natural law" concept.

▼▲▼

MR. JUSTICE GOLDBERG, with whom THE CHIEF JUSTICE and MR. JUSTICE BRENNAN join, concurring.

I agree with the Court that Connecticut's birth control law unconstitutionally intrudes upon the right of marital privacy, and I join in its opinion and judgment. Although I have not accepted the view that "due process," as used in the Fourteenth Amendment, incorporates all of the first eight Amendments, I do agree that the concept of liberty protects those personal rights that are fundamental, and is not confined to the specific terms of the Bill of Rights. My conclusion that the concept of liberty is not so restricted, and that it embraces the right of marital privacy, though that right is not mentioned explicitly in the Constitution, is supported both by numerous decisions of this Court, referred to in the Court's opinion, and by the language and history of the Ninth Amendment. In reaching the conclusion that the right of marital privacy is protected as being within the protected penumbra of specific guarantees of the Bill of Rights, the Court refers to the Ninth Amendment. I add these words to emphasize the relevance of that Amendment to the Court's holding. . . .

The language and history of the Ninth Amendment reveal that the Framers of the Constitution believed that there are additional fundamental rights, protected from governmental infringement, which exist alongside those fundamental rights specifically mentioned in the first eight constitutional amendments. The Ninth Amendment reads, "The enumeration in the Constitution, of certain rights, shall not be construed to deny or disparage others retained by the people." The Amendment is almost entirely the work of James Madison. It was introduced in Congress by him, and passed the House and Senate with little or no debate and virtually no change in language. It was proffered to quiet expressed fears that a bill of specifically enumerated rights could not be sufficiently broad to cover all essential rights, and that the specific mention of certain rights would be interpreted as a denial that others were protected. . . .

While this Court has had little occasion to interpret the Ninth Amendment, "[i]t cannot be presumed that any clause in the constitution is intended to be without effect," *Marbury* v. *Madison* (1803). In interpreting the Constitution, "real effect should be given to all the words it uses." The Ninth Amendment to the Constitution may be regarded by some as a recent discovery, and may be forgotten by others, but, since 1791, it has been a basic part of the Constitution which we are sworn to uphold. To hold that a right so basic and fundamental and so deep-rooted in our society as the right of privacy in marriage may be infringed because that right is not guaranteed in so many words by the first eight amendments to the Constitution is to ignore the Ninth Amendment, and to give it no effect whatsoever. Moreover, a judicial construction that this fundamental right is not protected by the Constitution because it is not mentioned in explicit terms by one of the first eight amendments or elsewhere in the Constitution would violate the Ninth Amendment, which specifically states that "[t]he enumeration in the Constitution, of certain rights, shall not be *construed* to deny or disparage others retained by the people." . . .

In determining which rights are fundamental, judges are not left at large to decide cases in light of their personal and private notions. Rather, they must look to the "traditions and [collective] conscience of our people" to determine whether a principle is "so rooted [there] . . . as to be ranked as fundamental." . . .

Although the Constitution does not speak in so many words of the right of privacy in marriage, I cannot believe that it offers these fundamental rights no protection. The fact that no particular provision of the Constitution explicitly forbids the State from disrupting the traditional relation of the family—a relation as old and as fundamental as our entire civilization—surely does not show that the Government was meant to have the power to do so. Rather, as the Ninth Amendment expressly recognizes, there are fundamental personal rights such as this one, which are protected from abridgment by the Government, though not specifically mentioned in the Constitution. . . .

In sum, I believe that the right of privacy in the marital relation is fundamental and basic—a personal right "retained by the people" within the meaning of the Ninth Amendment. Connecticut cannot constitutionally abridge this fundamental right, which is protected by the Fourteenth Amendment from infringement by the States. I agree with the Court that petitioners' convictions must therefore be reversed.

MR. JUSTICE BLACK, with whom MR. JUSTICE STEWART joins, dissenting.

In order that there may be no room at all to doubt why I vote as I do, I feel constrained to add that the law is every bit as offensive to me as it is to my Brethren of the majority and my Brothers HARLAN, WHITE and GOLDBERG, who, reciting reasons why it is offensive to them, hold it unconstitutional. There is no single one of the graphic and eloquent strictures and criticisms fired at the policy of this Connecticut law either by the Court's opinion or by those of my concurring Brethren to which I cannot subscribe—except their conclusion that the evil qualities they see in the law make it unconstitutional. . . .

One of the most effective ways of diluting or expanding a constitutionally guaranteed right is to substitute for the crucial word or words of a constitutional guarantee another word or words, more or less flexible and more or less restricted in meaning. This fact is well illustrated by the use of the term "right of privacy" as a comprehensive substitute for the Fourth Amendment's guarantee against "unreasonable searches and seizures." "Privacy" is a broad, abstract and ambiguous concept which can easily be shrunken in meaning but which can also, on the other hand, easily be interpreted as a constitutional ban against many things other than searches and seizures. I have expressed the view many times that First Amendment freedoms, for example, have suffered from a failure of the courts to stick to the simple language of the First Amendment in construing it, instead of invoking multitudes of words substituted for those the Framers used. For these reasons, I get nowhere in this case by talk about a constitutional "right of privacy" as an emanation from one or more constitutional provisions. I like my privacy as well as the next one, but I am nevertheless compelled to admit that government has a right to invade it unless prohibited by some specific constitutional provision. For these reasons, I cannot agree with the Court's judgment and the reasons it gives for holding this Connecticut law unconstitutional. . . .

My Brother GOLDBERG has adopted the recent discovery that the Ninth Amendment as well as the Due Process Clause can be used by this Court as authority to strike down all state legislation which this Court thinks violates "fundamental principles of liberty and justice," or is contrary to the "traditions and [collective] conscience of our people." He also states, without proof satisfactory to me, that, in making decisions on this basis, judges will not consider "their personal and private notions." One may ask

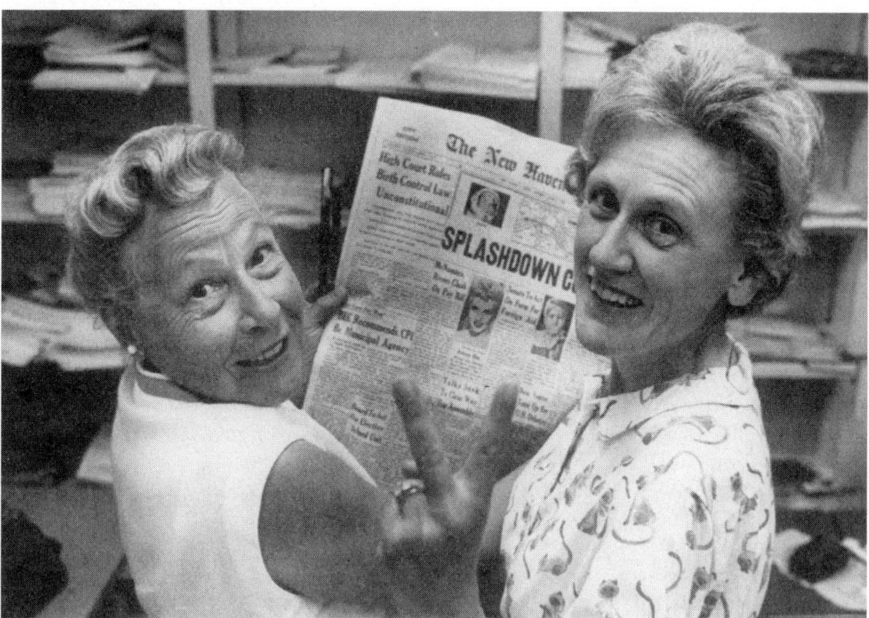

Estelle Griswold, left, and Mrs. Ernest Jahncke, president of the Planned Parenthood League of Connecticut, are all smiles as they read about the Supreme Court's decision striking down Connecticut's anti–birth control law.
UPI/Bettmann–CORBIS.

how they can avoid considering them. Our Court certainly has no machinery with which to take a Gallup Poll. And the scientific miracles of this age have not yet produced a gadget which the Court can use to determine what traditions are rooted in the "[collective] conscience of our people." . . .

I realize that many good and able men have eloquently spoken and written, sometimes in rhapsodical strains, about the duty of this Court to keep the Constitution in tune with the times. The idea is that the Constitution must be changed from time to time, and that this Court is charged with a duty to make those changes. For myself, I must, with all deference, reject that philosophy. The Constitution makers knew the need for change, and provided for it. Amendments suggested by the people's elected representatives can be submitted to the people or their selected agents for ratification. That method of change was good for our Fathers, and, being somewhat old-fashioned, I must add it is good enough for me. And so I cannot rely on the Due Process Clause or the Ninth Amendment or any mysterious and uncertain natural law concept as a reason for striking down this state law. The Due Process Clause, with an "arbitrary and capricious" or "shocking to the conscience" formula, was liberally used by this Court to strike down economic legislation in the early decades of this century, threatening, many people thought, the tranquility and stability of the Nation. That formula, based on subjective considerations of "natural justice," is no less dangerous when used to enforce this Court's views about personal rights than those about economic rights. I had thought that we had laid that formula, as a means for striking down state legislation, to rest once and for all in cases such as *West Coast Hotel Co.* v. *Parrish* (1937).

In Search of Constitutional Meaning

Do not be disappointed as we leave this chapter without a clear answer to the question posed at the outset: How should we interpret the Constitution? Does that mean we have no preference in how you choose to think about constitutional interpretation and the other questions it raises? Not at all. We have deliberately offered a diverse palette of theoretical choices that have their intellectual roots in the law-based theories of how the courts—and the other branches of government as well—should approach constitutional interpretation. Although disputing the notion that social and political forces influence constitutional law and litigation—whether from the vantage point of the justices, elected officials, or aggrieved individuals in search of their rights and liberties—makes little sense, we believe that thinking about the Constitution in law-based terms is important. The cases, narrative commentaries, and Court's opinions that make up this casebook include threads of all the approaches discussed here. The purpose of this chapter has been twofold: to provide you with the tools to understand the sources of the justices' approaches to constitutional interpretation and to encourage you to develop a theoretical rationale of your own to assist in the explanation and defense of the constitutional choices you will make.

Notice that phrases or descriptions of judicial review and constitutional interpretation that you might have encountered before, such as judicial activism, judicial restraint, the "living Constitution," and strict construction, are absent from this chapter. This omission is no accident. Our concern here is with the substance of constitutional interpretation because the search for constitutional values is part of a larger debate over which societal values deserve protection. To reduce this complex enterprise to a handful of simplistic and often inaccurate descriptions of how the Court interprets the Constitution is to forget, as one prominent legal scholar has summarized it, that "much of what looks like a difference in approach is really a disagreement over substantive goals."[56] Consider these two questions as you go forward: Does any singular, universal theory of constitutional interpretation best capture the spirit and intent of the Constitution? Is it possible to create a theoretical approach to constitutional interpretation independent of the substantive values that one understands the Constitution to protect?

FOR FURTHER READING

Amar, Akhil Reed. *The Bill of Rights: Creation and Reconstruction.* New Haven, Conn.: Yale University Press, 1998.

Bickel, Alexander. *The Least Dangerous Branch.* New Haven, Conn.: Yale University Press, 1962.

Black, Hugo L. *A Constitutional Faith.* New York: Alfred A. Knopf, 1969.

Bork, Robert H. *The Tempting of America.* New York: The Free Press, 1990.

Brigham, John. *The Constitution of Interests.* New York: New York University Press, 1996.

Bronner, Ethan. *Battle for Justice.* New York: W. W. Norton, 1989.

Dworkin, Ronald. *Law's Empire.* Cambridge, Mass.: Harvard University Press, 1986.

Ely, John Hart. *Democracy and Distrust.* Cambridge, Mass.: Harvard University Press, 1980.

Garvey, John H. *What Are Freedoms For?* Cambridge, Mass.: Harvard University Press, 1996.

Kahn, Ronald. *The Supreme Court and Constitutional Theory, 1953–1993.* Lawrence: University Press of Kansas, 1994.

Levy, Leonard W. *The Emergence of a Free Press.* New York: Oxford University Press, 1985.

———. *Original Intent and the Framers' Constitution.* New York: Oxford University Press, 1988.

McDonald, Forrest. *Novus Ordo Seclorum: The Intellectual Origins of the Constitution.* Lawrence: University Press of Kansas, 1985.

Savage, David G. *Turning Right: The Making of the Rehnquist Supreme Court.* New York: John Wiley & Sons, 1992.

Scalia, Antonin. *A Matter of Interpretation: Federal Courts and the Law.* Princeton, N.J.: Princeton University Press, 1997.

Segal, Jeffrey A. and Harold J. Spaeth. *The Supreme Court and the Attitudinal Model.* New York: Cambridge University Press, 1993.

Simon, James F. *The Center Holds: The Power Struggle inside the Rehnquist Court.* New York: Simon & Schuster, 1995.

Strum, Phillipa. *Louis D. Brandeis: Justice for the People.* New York: Schoken, 1984.

Sunstein, Cass R. *One Case at a Time: Judicial Minimalism and the Supreme Court.* Cambridge, Mass.: Harvard University Press, 1993.

Tushnet, Mark. *Taking the Constitution Away from the Courts.* Princeton, N.J.: Princeton University Press, 1999.

Walker, Samuel. *The Rights Revolution: Rights and Community in Modern America.* New York: Oxford University Press, 1998.

Wright, Benjamin F. *American Interpretations of Natural Law.* Cambridge, Mass.: Harvard University Press, 1931.

Yarbrough, Tinsley E. *Mr. Justice Black and His Critics.* Durham, N.C.: Duke University Press, 1988.

The Rights Revolution in American Constitutional Law

Buchanan County, Virginia, is home to United Coal Company, one of the largest privately owned coal companies in the United States. The only incorporated town in Buchanan County is Grundy. With a population of less than two thousand, Grundy also serves as the county's main commercial center and county seat. And it was in this small coal-mining town that Roger Keith Coleman, who worked in a drift mine a few miles from Grundy, was convicted of raping and murdering nineteen-year-old Wanda Fay Thompson McCoy. Violence was not unknown in Buchanan County. In 1980, the year before McCoy was killed, Buchanan County reported seven murders, which gave it a murder rate twice that of the entire state of Virginia. But McCoy's murder was particularly gruesome. She had been stabbed twice in the chest, and her neck had been slashed so deeply that her head was nearly severed from the rest of her body.[1]

Wanda's younger sister, Patricia, was married to Roger Coleman. Just after midnight on March 11, 1981, Peggy Thompson Stiltner, the oldest of the Thompson sisters, drove to Patricia and Roger's house to tell them about Wanda's murder. Patricia and Roger had been sleeping, but dressed quickly and headed over to Wanda's house to comfort her grieving husband, Brad, and the rest of the Thompson family. Within hours, Roger Coleman became a suspect. On April 13, the Virginia state police indicted Coleman for rape and capital murder, for which, if convicted, he could receive either life in prison or the death penalty. A few days later, Nicholas Persin, a Buchanan County judge, appointed two attorneys with little criminal trial experience to represent Coleman. For almost a year, Roger Coleman languished in jail, as Judge Persin had ordered him held without bond.

On March 15, 1982, Judge Persin began jury selection in the state's case against Roger Coleman. Of the forty-nine prospective jurors questioned by the judge, twenty-four admitted that they had heard, read, or talked about Wanda's murder. Fourteen potential jurors admitted that they had formed an opinion on Coleman's guilt and were excused. Other prospective jurors were excused because they opposed the death penalty. By 6:30 that evening, Judge Persin found twelve jurors he believed could give Coleman a fair hearing. The next morning the trial began. From the beginning, the defense attorneys were overmatched by state prosecutors. Coleman's lawyers made no effort to challenge the state's presentation of scientific evidence, which consisted of blood and hair samples that matched the defendant's own, but offered no conclusive evidence that they indeed were Coleman's. Nor did Coleman's lawyers raise questions about the state's failure to perform scientific tests that could have narrowed the range of population having a certain blood type. The police found no fingerprints matching Coleman's inside or outside the house, a factor that received no attention from the defense lawyers. The state offered one witness, Roger Matney, who claimed Coleman made a jailhouse confession to him while they shared a cell shortly after Coleman's arrest. Defense lawyers did not challenge the prosecution witness's background, which included four prior convictions for felonies in Virginia and one in Kentucky. They also failed to raise the fact that Matney was facing new charges for beating and threatening to kill a fellow inmate who refused to have sex with him.

Three days later, Judge Persin sent the jury to deliberate the state's case against Coleman. Within five hours, including an hour and a half for dinner, the jury returned its verdict: Roger Keith Coleman was guilty of rape and capital murder. After a short sentencing hearing on March 19, the jury sentenced Coleman to death. Judge Persin did not believe that the state's largely circumstantial case created the absolute certainty that Virginia law required to impose the death penalty, and asked Coleman to offer a written statement on the jury's decision. In clear and concise handwriting, Coleman told Judge Persin:

> . . . I see very little difference between two life sentences and the death penalty. . . . Considering all that I've already lost I have very little left that matters to me to lose. There's no way I can fear the death penalty, I can't live in the future. I can only continue as I do now, live one day at a time and take whatever comes to me the best way I can.

Judge Persin believed that Coleman had not offered him anything that would allow him to set the jury's verdict aside. Despite his misgivings about the death penalty, Judge Persin, sitting before a courtroom packed with the Thompson, McCoy, and Coleman families, announced that Roger Coleman would receive the death penalty for the murder of Wanda Thompson McCoy. He closed with the words "May God have mercy on your soul."

University of Virginia law students became aware of Coleman's case through a prison reform group, who brought it to their attention shortly after he was sentenced to death. They read the transcript of the trial, and were stunned at the incompetence of Coleman's attorneys. After their initial research, the UVA students referred the case to the prestigious Washington, D.C., law firm Arnold & Porter. The firm identified what it believed were several other serious problems with Coleman's trial: Jurors who opposed the death penalty had been improperly excluded; the state had failed to provide Coleman's attorneys with key documents that might have weakened the prosecution's case; and the trial should have been moved out of Buchanan County to a less prejudicial venue. But the issue Arnold & Porter attorneys ultimately presented in the greatest detail was that Roger Coleman had been denied his Sixth Amendment right to the effective assistance of counsel.* Coleman's new lawyers decided to file suit with the Virginia courts, seeking a writ of habeas corpus on the grounds that their client had not received his federal constitutional rights to a fair trial.

Judge Glyn Phillips denied Coleman's request for a new trial, and signed an appropriate order dated September 4, 1986. Because the judge had heard Coleman's arguments in neighboring Dickinson County, the order had to be mailed to the Buchanan County courthouse. It arrived on September 9 and was entered into the record the same day. Coleman's lawyers had thirty days to file an appeal. On October 6, Johnny Farmer, a local lawyer retained by Arnold & Porter to handle Coleman's court appearances, mailed the notice of appeal. Since Farmer did not send the appeal through certified mail, it was entered on the day it was received, October 7. The Virginia Supreme Court agreed with the prosecution that the thirty-day period began when Judge Phillips signed the order denying Coleman's original request for a new trial. October 4 was a Saturday, and under Virginia law that extended the thirty-day period to Monday, October 6. Farmer's appeal arrived one day late. Any relief that Coleman might receive would now have to be delivered by a federal court.

Over the next four years, two federal courts dismissed Coleman's request for a writ of habeas corpus, leaving only one other option: the U.S. Supreme Court. But on June 24, 1991, the Court ended Roger Coleman's chance of leaving death row, ruling 6 to 3 that permitting a federal court to consider the constitutional defects raised by Coleman's lawyers would give inadequate weight to "the respect that federal courts owe the States and the States' procedural rules." *Coleman* v. *Thompson* (1991) was not, for the Court's majority, a case about the substance of Coleman's claims. The first line of Sandra Day O'Connor's opinion read: "This is a case about fed-

*The firm had once been known as Arnold, Fortas & Porter. Abe Fortas, then in private practive, was the lawyer appointed by the United States Supreme Court to represent Clarence Earl Gideon in the landmark case of *Gideon* v. *Wainwright* (1963), which established the right to counsel in criminal cases involving felony offenses (see Chapter 8). President Lyndon Johnson later appointed Fortas to the Court, where he served from 1965 to 1969.

eralism." In dissent, Justice Harry A. Blackmun countered, "One searches in vain for any mention of . . . Coleman's right to a criminal proceeding free from constitutional defect or his interest in finding a forum for his constitutional challenge to his conviction and sentence of death."[2] On May 20, 1992, Roger Coleman was executed by the state of Virginia.

For the Court's majority, Coleman's case was about the federal structure and the limits on national power to interfere with state prerogatives. For the Court's dissenters, the case was about the obligation of the federal courts to protect the constitutional rights of a criminal defendant who may not have received the full benefits of due process in a state proceeding. In many ways, Roger Keith Coleman's odyssey through the maze of the American criminal justice system brings to light several of the larger questions posed by the Bill of Rights since its ratification in 1791. Was the primary purpose of the Bill of Rights *structural,* that is, to protect the power of the states to establish rights and liberties free from federal interference? Or was the Bill of Rights *substantive* in scope, protecting universal rights for all citizens, regardless of where they lived or what their state constitutions said? And what about the subsequent ratification of the Fourteenth Amendment, enacted after the Civil War? Do the provisions of Section 1 of the Fourteenth Amendment—which bar the states from making or enforcing any law abridging the privileges and immunities of citizens of the United States, denying to any person life, liberty, or property without due process of law, and denying any person the equal protection of the law—make the Bill of Rights applicable against the states?

Over time, Supreme Court justices, constitutional scholars, and organized interests active in constitutional litigation have advanced several theories to explain the structural and substantive meaning of the Bill of Rights. These different approaches to understanding the Bill of Rights have not been without controversy. Indeed, the persistent comparison of what the Framers of the original Bill of Rights meant, particularly James Madison, with what the key architects of the Fourteenth Amendment believed the Bill of Rights should mean after the Civil War offers an example of how reasonable people can interpret text, history, and constitutional structure in radically different terms. The purpose of this chapter is to explore how the Court first understood the Bill of Rights and later how that meaning was transformed by the Fourteenth Amendment. This chapter will also give important consideration to the role that organized interests have played in driving much of the litigation that resulted in the "rights revolution" of the late twentieth century.

Early Interpretation of the Bill of Rights

Referring to James Madison as the "father" of the Bill of Rights, as many scholars have done, contains more than just a touch of irony. Initially, Madison did not support the position of the Anti-Federalists that a bill of rights was necessary to protect the states and their citizens from the tyranny of the national government. Madison found some merit in the argument of Federalists such as John Adams, Alexander Hamilton, and James Wilson that a formal declaration of rights was unnecessary, since the Constitution established a national government of limited and enumerated power. In *Federalist* 84, Hamilton argued that specifying the rights reserved to the people might result in a narrow rather than generous interpretation of their substance. A bill of rights, wrote Hamilton, "would contain various exceptions to powers which are not granted; and, on this very

"The way I see it, the Constitution cuts both ways. The First Amendment gives you the right to say what you want, but the Second Amendment gives me the right to shoot you for it."

account, would afford a colorable pretext to claim more than were granted."[3] Madison, in correspondence with Thomas Jefferson (with whom he would remain allied throughout the remainder of his political career), expressed concern that the courts might interpret a bill of rights without sufficient "latitude."[4]

Steady correspondence with Jefferson and mounting distrust of the grandiose nationalist ambitions of Hamilton, his *Federalist Papers* coauthor, gradually led Madison to embrace Anti-Federalist sentiment during the ratification debates for a bill of rights. In December 1787, Jefferson had written Madison to tell him that he approved of the Constitution, with one exception:

> . . . I will now add what I do not like. First, the omission of a bill of rights providing clearly & without the aid of sophisms for freedom of religion, freedom of the press, protection against standing armies, restriction against monopolies, the eternal & unremitting force of the habeas corpus laws, and trials by jury in all matters . . . . Let me add that a bill of rights is what the people are entitled to against every government on earth, general or particular, & what no just government should refuse, or rest on inference.[5]

Ever the politician, Jefferson, writing from Paris in February 1788, just as the ratification process had heated up, also told Madison:

> I am glad to hear that the new constitution is received with favor. I sincerely wish that the 9 first conventions may receive, & the 4. last reject it. The former will secure it finally; while the latter will oblige them to offer a declaration of rights in order to complete the union. We shall thus have all it's [sic] good, and cure it's [sic] principal defect.[6]

By late 1788, Madison embraced the idea of a bill of rights, and agreed to introduce a series of articles during the First Congress, which met in March 1789. Madison's bill of rights was intended to cure the Constitution's omission of those rights and liberties now taken for granted as fundamental: freedom of speech, press, religion, assembly, due process in criminal proceedings, and other protections against unwarranted government intrusion into personal privacy and property. Madison introduced seventeen separate articles, ten of which were approved and became the Bill of Rights. But the article that Madison considered his most important, the fourteenth, was rejected by the Senate. Keenly aware that state legislatures, far more so than Congress, were likely to reflect the immediate passions of popular majorities, Madison attempted to include restrictions on state power in his proposed Bill of Rights. In a speech before the First Congress, Madison said:

> But I do confess that I do conceive, that in a Government modified like this of the United States, the great danger lies rather in the abuse of the community than in a legislative body. The prescriptions in favor of liberty ought to be leveled against the quarter where the greatest danger lies, namely, that which possesses the highest prerogative of power. But this is not found in either the executive or the legislative departments of Government, but in the body of the people, operating by the majority against the minority.[7]

Madison specifically included "equal rights of conscience," "speech," "press," and criminal jury trials for protection against state intrusion. "If there was any reason to restrain the Government of the United States from infringing upon these essential rights," said Madison, "it was equally necessary that they should be secured against the State Governments." The Senate did not agree with Madison, and his proposal died there. Legal scholar Akhil Reed Amar has argued that Article IV of the Constitution, which obligates the states to maintain a republican form of government, a guarantee enforceable by Congress, could be understood to protect freedom of speech, press, and many of the other rights in the Bill of Rights. But Madison's conception of the Bill of Rights would not come into focus until the ratification of the Fourteenth Amendment after the Civil War. By then, forces hostile to Reconstruction, which by the 1870s included the Court, soon succeeded in advancing an interpretation of the Bill of Rights that was primarily structural and not substantive. This was so even though many constitutional scholars have mounted an impressive array of evidence demonstrating that this understanding of the Fourteenth Amendment flew in the face of its supporters.[8] The idea that the Bill of Rights limited only the power of the national government to intrude on fundamental freedoms lasted until the late 1920s, when the Court slowly began the process of applying the Bill of Rights to the states through the Fourteenth Amendment. Until then, the Court followed the structural interpretation of the Bill of Rights offered by Chief Justice John Marshall in *Barron* v. *Baltimore* (1833).

Barron v. Baltimore

32 U.S. 243 (1833)

By the early 1800s, Baltimore had become one of the busiest port cities on the eastern seaboard. John Barron and John Craig had built up a small fortune as the co-owners of a busy wharf on the Baltimore harbor. The secret to their success was the deep water surrounding their wharf, which allowed Barron and Craig to accommodate some of the biggest ships coming into Baltimore. To encourage greater commercial activity in the city, Baltimore began paving its streets, building dams, and making improvements to its drainage system. Changes to the city's infrastructure resulted in new water flow patterns, which brought new sand and sludge into Barron and Craig's wharf, and their business suffered immeasurably.

By 1822, Barron and Craig were fed up with the city's action and sued Baltimore in local court for compensation for their economic losses, basing their argument on the Takings Clause of the Fifth Amendment. Barron and Craig claimed that the provision of the clause prohibiting Congress from depriving "any person of life, liberty, or property, without due process of law; nor shall private property be taken for public use, without just compensation" also bound state and local governments. They asked for $20,000, and were awarded $4,500. A Maryland appeals court reversed the lower court.

Before the Court, Barron's lawyer emphasized the economic deprivation that his client had suffered as a result of the city's action. All that the justices were interested in hearing was whether the Fifth Amendment applied to the states. So unimpressed were the justices with Barron's argument that the Fifth Amendment did apply to the states that they chose not to hear the arguments of Baltimore's lawyer, Roger B. Taney. In 1836, Taney succeeded Marshall as chief justice of the United States Supreme Court.

The Court's decision was unanimous. Chief Justice Marshall delivered the opinion of the Court. Justice Baldwin did not participate.

▼▲▼

Mr. Chief Justice Marshall delivered the opinion of the Court.

The question thus presented is, we think, of great importance, but not of much difficulty. The Constitution was ordained and established by the people of the United States for themselves, for their own government, and not for the government of the individual States. Each State established a constitution for itself, and in that constitution provided such limitations and restrictions on the powers of its particular government as its judgment dictated. The people of the United States framed such a government for the United States as they supposed best adapted to their situation and best calculated to promote their interests. The powers they conferred on this government were to be exercised by itself, and the limitations on power, if expressed in general terms, are naturally, and we think necessarily, applicable to the government created by the instrument. They are limitations of power granted in the instrument itself, not of distinct governments framed by different persons and for different purposes.

If these propositions be correct, the fifth amendment must be understood as restraining the power of the General Government, not as applicable to the States. In their several Constitutions, they have imposed such restrictions on their respective governments, as their own wisdom suggested, such as they deemed most proper for themselves. It is a subject on which they judge exclusively, and with which others interfere no further than they are supposed to have a common interest. . . .

Had the people of the several States, or any of them, required changes in their Constitutions, had they required additional safeguards to liberty from the apprehended encroachments of their particular governments, the remedy was in their own hands, and could have been applied by themselves. A convention could have been assembled by the discontented State, and the required improvements could have been made by itself. The unwieldy and cumbrous machinery of procuring a recommendation from two-thirds of Congress and the assent of three-fourths of their sister States could never have occurred to any human being as a mode of doing that which might be effected by the State itself. Had the framers of these amendments intended them to be limitations on the powers of the State governments, they would have imitated the framers of the original Constitution, and have expressed that intention. Had Congress engaged in the extraordinary occupation of improving the Constitutions of the several States by affording the people additional protection from the exercise of power by their own governments in matters which concerned themselves alone, they would have declared this purpose in plain and intelligible language.

But it is universally understood, it is a part of the history of the day, that the great revolution which established the Constitution of the United States was not effected without immense opposition. Serious fears were extensively entertained that those powers which the patriot statesmen who then watched over the interests of our country deemed essential to union, and to the attainment of those invaluable objects for which union was sought, might be exercised in a manner dangerous to liberty. In almost every convention by which the Constitution was adopted, amendments to guard against the abuse of power were recommended. These amendments demanded security against the apprehended encroachments of the General Government—not against those of the local governments. In compliance with a sentiment thus generally expressed, to quiet fears thus extensively entertained, amendments were proposed by the required majority in Congress and adopted by the States. These amendments contain no expression indicating an intention to apply them to the State governments. This court cannot so apply them.

We are of opinion that the provision in the Fifth Amendment to the Constitution declaring that private property shall not be taken for public use without just compensation is intended solely as a limitation on the exercise of power by the Government of the United States, and is not applicable to the legislation of the States. We are therefore of opinion that there is no repugnancy between the several acts of the general assembly of Maryland, given in evidence by the defendants at the trial of this cause, in the court of that State, and the Constitution of the United States. This court, therefore, has no jurisdiction of the cause, and it is dismissed.

Marshall's opinion is a straightforward defense of the structural view of the Bill of Rights. In *Barron*, the Court could have held that the rights in the Bill of Rights were fundamental liberties to which any citizen was entitled and that no government was permitted to abridge. Or the Court could have invoked the Supremacy Clause of Article VI, thus making any state law infringing on the Bill of Rights without force. But Chief Justice Marshall, a Federalist and nationalist to the core, instead handed states' rights advocates a major victory by holding that only Congress was bound by the Bill of Rights. Marshall understood full well that his decision in *Barron* meant that states were free to restrict as well as protect such fundamental freedoms as speech, press, assembly, and, ironically for a Federalist, property rights.

Legal scholar Michael Kent Curtis has pointed out that William Lloyd Garrison had started the abolitionist newspaper the *Liberator* in 1831, the same year that Nat Turner led a rebellion of slaves that resulted in the massacre of a plantation family. Prior to the Civil War, every Southern state viewed abolitionist writings as sedition. *Barron* left slave-holding states in the position to ban their publication and distribution without having to worry about whether or not law restricting political dissent violated the First Amendment.[9] Beyond the slavery question, *Barron* also meant that states were free to impose restraints on the freedom of speech, press, religion, and assembly, and disregard the procedural rights of criminal defendants. Before the Fourteenth Amendment and the Court's subsequent nationalization of these fundamental freedoms, the Bill of Rights belonged to the states and not to the people as citizens of the United States.

Ironically, many state courts, even after *Barron*, believed that the Bill of Rights restricted the power of the states to interfere with fundamental freedoms. For example, the Georgia supreme court, in 1846, ruled that the Second Amendment prohibited the state legislature from banning the carrying of weapons, and several other state supreme courts ruled that the due process guarantees of the Fifth and Sixth Amendments bound state criminal and civil action. But perhaps the most ardent supporters of the Bill of Rights as conferring national citizenship and universal rights were abolitionists. Long before the Civil War, the abolitionist movement, which drew a disproportionate share of its support from early feminist activists such as Elizabeth Cady Stanton and Lucretia Mott, argued that permitting states to define the rights of citizens of the United States was wholly incompatible with the idea of free and equal citizenship. The abolitionist legacy became the Fourteenth Amendment, enacted in 1868 as the cornerstone of Reconstruction.

From Structure to Substance: The Fourteenth Amendment and the Bill of Rights

The Republican Party was born out the sectional conflict between the North and South that became increasingly protracted after 1830 and ultimately resulted in the Civil War. Perhaps the defining event that triggered Northern Democrats to leave their party was the passage of the Kansas-Nebraska Act of 1854, which permitted the territories of Kansas and Nebraska to enter the Union as either free or slave states. The law was wildly unpopular in the North, so much so that only seven of the fifty-four Northern Democrats in the House of Representatives who voted for the law won reelection. Until then, many Northern Democrats opposed to slavery agreed with the position of Illinois Representative Stephen A. Douglas, who argued that the Constitution neither required nor prohibited slavery in the states. But as Southern Democrats began to shift their defense of slavery away from Douglas's "popular sovereignty" theory to one that insisted that slave holders had constitutional rights to own slaves based on their status as property, Republicans garnered support by campaigning against slavery as morally wrong. Initially, Republicans hoped to destroy slavery in the South through federal patronage and by encouraging abolitionists to circulate anti-slavery literature. The South's response was to tighten restrictions on free speech, assembly, and press in the states. Since the Bill of Rights was still seen as a structural defense on behalf of states' rights, Northern Republicans had little leverage to use federal power against the South.[10]

The Civil War revolutionized the Republican cause. By December 1865, when the Thirty-ninth Congress convened to consider the readmission of the Southern states into the Union, the Republican Party had made the abolition of slavery its unifying creed. President Abraham Lincoln's decision to emancipate the slaves in 1863 had been the turning point in the Republicans' effort to save the Union. The party was divided in how to achieve the legal protection for the civil and political rights of blacks, with Radical Republicans urging the immediate and full enfranchisement of blacks, including special programs designed to promote literacy, education, and economic advancement. Other Republicans were more cautious about the Radicals' agenda for Reconstruction and black voting rights, believing that reforging the bonds of Union with the defeated Southern states took priority. But the Republican Party was united on the crucial issue to emerge during this period: the need to make the protections afforded by the Constitution and the Bill of Rights applicable to citizens in the states. Accordingly, Republicans in the Thirty-ninth Congress understood the guarantees in the Bill of Rights to restrain the power of the states. They also believed the Thirteenth Amendment, which abolished slavery and involuntary servitude, authorized Congress to pass laws securing the rights of blacks. Indeed, the Civil Rights Act of 1866, which extended to "colored" persons the same rights as "white citizens" to make contracts and have them enforced in court, was one such law.[11]

Still, Republicans believed that an additional constitutional amendment was needed to offset lingering uncertainty that Congress possessed the power to enact laws protecting the civil rights of all Americans. By the time Congress passed the Fourteenth Amendment in June 1866, any doubt that one of the principal aims of Reconstruction was to remedy the deficiencies of the structural theory of the Bill of Rights had vanished. Section 1, stating that "All persons born or naturalized in the United States, and subject to the jurisdiction thereof, are citizens of the United States and of the State wherein they reside," made national citizenship superior to state citizenship. But the most important clauses in Section 1 came later. The Republican leadership that drafted and steered the Fourteenth Amendment to passage left no doubt that its provisions reading, "No State shall make or enforce any law which shall abridge the privileges or immunities of citizens of the United States; nor shall any State deprive any person of life, liberty, or property, without due process of law; nor deny to any person within its jurisdiction the equal protection of the laws," were intended to make the Bill of Rights binding upon the states. Thaddeus Stevens, a Radical Republican from Pennsylvania and leading spokesperson for the Fourteenth Amendment, summarized its purpose this way:

> I can hardly believe that any person can be found who will not admit that every one of these provisions is just. They are all asserted, in some form or other, in our DECLARATION or organic law. But the Constitution limits only the action of Congress, and is not a limitation on the States. This amendment supplies that defect, and allows Congress to correct the unjust legislation of the States, so far that the law which operates upon one man shall operate equally upon all.[12]

John A. Bingham, a congressman from Ohio and the primary author of the Fourteenth Amendment, made clear from the start that Section 1 was designed "to protect by national law the privileges and immunities of all the citizens of the Republic and the inborn rights of every person within its jurisdiction whenever the same shall be abridged or denied by the unconstitutional acts of any State."[13] Bingham continued to articulate this theory of the Fourteenth Amendment even after the states completed its ratification in 1868. In an 1871 House floor speech, Bingham responded to further inquiries about the Fourteenth Amendment's intent, noting that he believed it overruled *Barron* v. *Baltimore* and linked "the privileges and immunities of the citizens of the United States" with the Bill of Rights:

> [T]he privileges and immunities of citizens of the United States, as contradistinguished from citizens of a State, are chiefly defined in the first eight amendments to the Constitution of the United States. . . . These eight articles I have shown never were limitations upon the power of the States, until made so by the fourteenth amendment.[14]

Akhil Reed Amar has noted that over thirty Republican representatives and senators in the Thirty-eighth and Thirty-ninth Congresses voiced similar sentiments to those of Stevens and Bingham. Not a single one believed *Barron* was intended to survive the ratification of the Fourteenth Amendment, or spoke up to deny that the primary purpose of the Privileges or Immunities Clause was to apply the Bill of Rights to the states. The nation's leading newspapers, such as the *New York Times* and the *New York Herald,* knew that Bingham was the primary author of the Fourteenth Amendment and paid particular attention to his speeches and comments on its meaning.[15] Nonetheless, the Court, caught up in the mounting opposition to Reconstruction, soon abandoned the intent of the Fourteenth Amendment's framers, and the structural interpretation of the Bill of Rights soon reemerged. The notion of whether the Bill of Rights was meant to apply to the states later became a major point of contention among scholars, lawyers, politicians, and Supreme Court justices. For the Thirty-ninth Congress, however, the transformation of the Bill of Rights by the Fourteenth Amendment was not controversial at all.[16]

The Judicial Nullification of the Privileges or Immunities Clause: The *Slaughterhouse Cases*

In 1871, a lower federal court ruled that the Bill of Rights applied to the states through the Privileges or Immunities Clause of the Fourteenth Amendment. In *United States* v. *Hall* (1871), Judge William B. Woods, who later served on the Court (1880–1887), upheld the conviction of several men who were convicted of conspiring to deprive others of their constitutional rights to freedom of speech and assembly. The defendants claimed the federal government had no jurisdiction to prosecute them because the First Amendment did not apply to the states. Writing for a unanimous panel on the Fifth Circuit Court of Appeals, Woods wrote:

> By the original constitution citizenship in the United States was a consequence of citizenship in a state. By this [privileges and immunities] clause this order of things is reversed. . . . What are the privileges and immunities of citizens of the United States here referred to? They are undoubtedly those which may be denominated fundamental. . . . Among these we are safe in including those which in the constitution are expressly secured to the people, either as against the action of federal or state government. Included in these are the right of freedom of speech, and the right to peaceably assemble. We think, therefore, that the right of freedom of speech, and the other rights enumerated in the first eight [amendments] to the constitution of the United States, are the privileges and immunities of citizens of the United States.[17]

Several other courts and federal prosecutors around this time also believed the Fourteenth Amendment made the Bill of Rights applicable to the states.[18] One sitting Supreme Court justice, Joseph P. Bradley, even wrote Judge Woods to express his agreement with his *Hall* opinion.[19] But, two years after Judge Woods decided *Hall,* the Court, in the *Slaughterhouse Cases* (1873), offered a very constricted interpretation of the Fourteenth Amendment. By then, Northern enthusiasm for Reconstruction had ebbed, even among Republicans who had steadfastly supported the Fourteenth Amendment. The Court's opinion in the *Slaughterhouse Cases* certainly reflected the changing tenor of the times.

The *Slaughterhouse Cases* (*The Butchers' Benevolent Association of New Orleans v. The Crescent City Live-Stock Landing and Slaughter-House Company*)

83 U.S. 36 (1873)

In 1869, the Louisiana legislature created the Crescent City Live-Stock Landing and Slaughter-House Company and granted it an exclusive twenty-five-year franchise over the slaughter of all livestock in its largest and oldest city, New Orleans, located on the Mississippi River near the Gulf Coast. The state claimed that the law, which also covered the parishes around New Orleans, was necessary to contain the further pollution of the Mississippi. After the Civil War, southern Louisiana had experienced an outbreak of cholera and other diseases, a development that the state believed was directly related to the region's slaughterhouse industries.

Smaller butchers did not see the law as a civic-minded response to a public health and environmental crisis. They saw it as a political payoff to well-connected and powerful financial backers of state legislators. Worse, the butchers had to contend with the effects of monopoly. They were forced to pay exorbitant prices to use the Crescent City slaughterhouse, and their own profits suffered for it. Quite simply, the butchers believed the state had deprived them of their now constitutionally protected right under the Fourteenth Amendment to earn a living without undue state interference. To bolster their financial and political power, the independent butchers created their own trade group, the Butchers' Benevolent Association, and filed suit against Crescent City to have the monopoly overturned. They lost in the state courts before the Supreme Court agreed to hear the case.

The Court's decision was 5 to 4. Justice Miller delivered the opinion of the Court. Justices Bradley, Field, and Swayne filed separate dissents.

▼▲▼

MR. JUSTICE MILLER delivered the opinion of the Court.

The power here exercised by the legislature of Louisiana is, in its essential nature, one which has been, up to the present period in the constitutional history of this country, always conceded to belong to the States; however it may *now* be questioned in some of its details. . . .

This power is, and must be from its very nature, incapable of any very exact definition or limitation. Upon it depends the security of social order, the life and health of the citizen, the comfort of an existence in a thickly populated community, the enjoyment of private social life, and the beneficial use of property. . . .

The regulation of the place and manner of conducting the slaughtering of animals, and the business of butchering within a city, and the inspection of the animals to be killed for meat, and of the meat afterwards, are among the most necessary and frequent exercises of this power. It is not, therefore, needed that we should seek for a comprehensive definition, but rather look for the proper source of its exercise. . . .

It may, therefore, be considered as established that the authority of the legislature of Louisiana to pass the present statute is ample unless some restraint in the exercise of that power be found in the constitution of that State or in the amendments to the Constitution of the United States, adopted since the date of the decisions we have already cited.

The plaintiffs in error, accepting this issue, allege that the statute is a violation of the Constitution of the United States in these several particulars:

- That it creates an involuntary servitude forbidden by the thirteenth article of amendment;
- That it abridges the privileges and immunities of citizens of the United States;
- That it denies to the plaintiffs the equal protection of the laws; and,
- That it deprives them of their property without due process of law, contrary to the provisions of the first section of the fourteenth article of amendment.

This court is thus called upon for the first time to give construction to these articles.

The most cursory glance at these articles discloses a unity of purpose, when taken in connection with the history of the times, which cannot fail to have an important bearing on any question of doubt concerning their true meaning. Nor can such doubts, when any reasonably exist, be safely and rationally solved without a reference to that history, for in it is found the occasion and the necessity for recurring again to the great source of power in this country, the people of the States, for additional guarantees of human rights; additional powers to the Federal government; additional restraints upon those of the States.

Fortunately, that history is fresh within the memory of us all, and its leading features, as they bear upon the matter before us, free from doubt.

The institution of African slavery, as it existed in about half the States of the Union, and the contests pervading the public mind for many years between those who desired its curtailment and ultimate extinction and those who desired additional safeguards for its security and perpetuation, culminated in the effort, on the part of most of the States in which slavery existed, to separate from the Federal government and to resist its authority. This constituted the war of the rebellion, and whatever auxiliary causes may have contributed to bring about this war, undoubtedly the overshadowing and efficient cause was African slavery. . . .

These circumstances, whatever of falsehood or misconception may have been mingled with their presentation, forced upon the statesmen who had conducted the Federal government in safety through the crisis of the rebellion, and who supposed that, by the thirteenth article of amendment, they had secured the result of their labors, the conviction that something more was necessary in the way of constitutional protection to the unfortunate race who had suffered so much. They accordingly passed through Congress the proposition for the fourteenth amendment, and they declined to treat as restored to their full participation in the government of the Union the States which had been in insurrection until they ratified that article by a formal vote of their legislative bodies.

Before we proceed to examine more critically the provisions of this amendment, on which the plaintiffs in error rely, let us complete and dismiss the history of the recent amendments, as that history relates to the general purpose which pervades them all. A few years' experience satisfied the thoughtful men who had been the authors of the other two amendments that, notwithstanding the restraints of those articles on the States and the laws passed under the additional powers granted to Congress, these were inadequate for the protection of life, liberty, and property, without which freedom to the slave was no boon. They were in all those States denied the right of suffrage. The laws were administered by the white man alone. It was urged that a race of men distinctively marked, as was the negro, living in the midst of another and dominant race, could never be fully secured in their person and their property without the right of suffrage. . . .

We repeat, then, in the light of this recapitulation of events, almost too recent to be called history, but which are familiar to us all, and on the most casual examination of the language of these amendments, no one can fail to be impressed with the one pervading purpose found in them all, lying at the foundation of each, and without which none of them would have been even suggested; we mean the freedom of the slave race, the security and firm establishment of that freedom, and the protection of the newly made freeman and citizen from the oppressions of those who had formerly exercised unlimited dominion over him. It is true that only the fifteenth amendment, in terms, mentions the negro by speaking of his color and his slavery. But it is just as true that each of the other articles was addressed to the grievances of that race, and designed to remedy them as the fifteenth.

We do not say that no one else but the negro can share in this protection. Both the language and spirit of these articles are to have their fair and just weight in any question of construction. Undoubtedly while negro slavery alone was in the mind of the Congress which proposed the thirteenth article, it forbids any other kind of slavery, now or hereafter. . . . But what we do say, and what we wish to be understood, is that, in any fair and just construction of any section or phrase of these amendments, it is necessary to look to the purpose which we have said was the pervading spirit of them all, the evil which they were designed to remedy, and the process of continued addition to the Constitution, until that purpose was supposed to be accomplished as far as constitutional law can accomplish it. . . .

The next observation is more important in view of the arguments of counsel in the present case. It is that the distinction between citizenship of the United States and citizenship of a State is clearly recognized and established. Not only may a man be a citizen of the United States without being a citizen of a State, but an important element is necessary to convert the former into the latter. He must reside within the State to make him a citizen of it, but it is only necessary that he should be born or naturalized in the United States to be a citizen of the Union.

It is quite clear, then, that there is a citizenship of the United States, and a citizenship of a State, which are distinct from each other, and which depend upon different characteristics or circumstances in the individual.

We think this distinction and its explicit recognition in this amendment of great weight in this argument, because the next paragraph of this same section, which is the one mainly relied on by the plaintiffs in error, speaks only of privileges and immunities of citizens of the United States, and does not speak of those of citizens of the several States. The argument, however, in favor of the plaintiffs rests wholly on the assumption that the citizenship is the same, and the privileges and immunities guaranteed by the clause are the same.

The language is, "No State shall make or enforce any law which shall abridge the privileges or immunities of citizens of *the United States*." It is a little remarkable, if this clause was intended as a protection to the citizen of a State against the legislative power of his own State, that the word citizen of the State should be left out when it is so carefully used, and used in contradistinction to citizens of the United States, in the very sentence which precedes it. It is too clear for argument that the change in phraseology was adopted understandingly and with a purpose.

Of the privileges and immunities of the citizen of the United States, and of the privileges and immunities of the citizen of the State, and what they respectively are, we will presently consider; but we wish to state here that it is only the former which are placed by this clause under the protection of the Federal Constitution, and that the latter, whatever they may be, are not intended to have any additional protection by this paragraph of the amendment. . . .

The argument has not been much pressed in these cases that the defendant's charter deprives the plaintiffs of their property without due process of law, or that it denies to them the equal protection of the law. The first of these paragraphs has been in the Constitution since the adoption of the fifth amendment, as a restraint upon the Federal power. It is also to be found in some form of expression in the constitutions of nearly all the States, as a restraint upon the power of the States. This law, then, has practically been the same as it now is during the existence of the government, except so far as the present amendment may place the restraining power over the States in this matter in the hands of the Federal government.

We are not without judicial interpretation, therefore, both State and National, of the meaning of this clause. And it is sufficient to say that under no construction of that provision that we have ever seen, or any that we deem admissible, can the restraint imposed by the State of Louisiana upon the exercise of their trade by the butchers of New Orleans be held to be a deprivation of property within the meaning of that provision.

"Nor shall any State deny to any person within its jurisdiction the equal protection of the laws." In the light of the history of these amendments, and the pervading purpose of them, which we have already discussed, it is not difficult to give a meaning to this clause. The existence of laws in the States where the newly emancipated negroes resided, which discriminated with gross injustice and hardship against them as a class, was the evil to be remedied by this clause, and by it such laws are forbidden.

If, however, the States did not conform their laws to its requirements, then by the fifth section of the article of amendment Congress was authorized to enforce it by suitable legislation. We doubt very much whether any action of a State not directed by way of discrimination against the negroes as a class, or on account of their race, will ever be held to come within the purview of this provision. It is so clearly a provision for that race and that emergency that a strong case would be necessary for its application to any other. But as it is a State that is to be dealt with, and not alone the validity of its laws, we may safely leave that matter until Congress shall have exercised its power, or some case of State oppression, by denial of equal justice in its courts, shall have claimed a decision at our hands. We find no such case in the one before us, and do not deem it necessary to go over the argument again, as it may have relation to this particular clause of the amendment.

In the early history of the organization of the government, its statesmen seem to have divided on the line which should separate the powers of the National government from those of the State governments, and though this line has never been very well defined in public opinion, such a division has continued from that day to this.

[W]e do not see in [the Thirteenth, Fourteenth and Fifteenth] Amendments any purpose to destroy the main features of the general system. Under the pressure of all the excited feeling growing out of the war, our statesmen have still believed that the existence of the State with powers for domestic and local government, including the regulation of civil rights, the rights of person and of property, was essential to the perfect working of our complex form of government, though they have thought proper to impose additional limitations on the States, and to confer additional power on that of the Nation.

But whatever fluctuations may be seen in the history of public opinion on this subject during the period of our national existence, we think it will be found that this court, so far as its functions required, has always held with a steady and an even hand the balance between State and Federal power, and we trust that such may continue to be the history of its relation to that subject so long as it shall have duties to perform which demand of it a construction of the Constitution or of any of its parts.

Mr. Justice Field, dissenting.

I am unable to agree with the majority of the court in these cases, and will proceed to state the reasons of my dissent from their judgment.

The act of Louisiana presents the naked case, unaccompanied by any public considerations, where a right to pursue a lawful and necessary calling, previously enjoyed by every citizen, and in connection with which a thousand persons were daily employed, is taken away and vested exclusively for twenty-five years, for an extensive district and a large population, in a single corporation, or its exercise is for that period restricted to the establishments of the corporation, and there allowed only upon onerous conditions. . . .

The question presented is, therefore, one of the gravest importance not merely to the parties here, but to the whole country. It is nothing less than the question whether the recent amendments to the Federal Constitution protect the citizens of the United States against the deprivation of their common rights by State legislation. In my judgment, the fourteenth amendment does afford such protection, and was so intended by the Congress which framed and the States which adopted it.

The counsel for the plaintiffs in error have contended with great force that the act in question is also inhibited by the thirteenth amendment.

That amendment prohibits slavery and involuntary servitude, except as a punishment for crime, but I have not supposed it was susceptible of a construction which would cover the enactment in question. I have been so accustomed to regard it as intended to meet that form of slavery which had previously prevailed in this country, and to which the recent civil war owed its existence, that I was not prepared, nor am I yet, to give to it the extent and force ascribed by counsel. Still it is evidence that the language of the amendment is not used in a restrictive sense. It is not confined to African slavery alone. It is general and universal in its application. Slavery of white men as well as of black men is prohibited, and not merely slavery in the strict sense of the term, but involuntary servitude in every form. . . .

It is not necessary, however, as I have said, to rest my objections to the act in question upon the terms and meaning of the thirteenth amendment. The provisions of the fourteenth amendment, which is properly a supplement to the thirteenth, cover, in my judgment, the case before us, and inhibit any legislation which confers special and exclusive privileges like these under consideration. The amendment was adopted to obviate objections which had been raised and pressed with great force to the validity of the Civil Rights Act, and to place the common rights of American citizens under the protection of the National government. It first declares that, "all persons born or naturalized in the United States, and subject to the jurisdiction thereof, are citizens of the United States and of the State wherein they reside." It then declares that, "no State shall make or enforce any law which shall abridge the privileges or immunities of citizens of the United States, nor shall any State deprive any person of life, liberty, or property, without due process of law, nor deny to any person within its jurisdiction the equal protection of the laws."

The first clause of the fourteenth amendment changes this whole subject, and removes it from the region of discussion and doubt. It recognizes in express terms, if it does not create, citizens of the United States, and it makes their citizenship dependent upon the place of their birth, or the fact of their adoption, and not upon the constitution or laws of any State or the condition of their ancestry. A citizen of a State is now only a citizen of the United States residing in that State. The fundamental rights, privileges, and immunities which belong to him as a free man and a free citizen now belong to him as a citizen of the United States, and are not dependent upon his citizenship of any State. The exercise of these rights and privileges, and the degree of enjoyment received from such exercise, are always more or less affected by the condition and the local institutions of the State, or city, or town where he resides. They are thus affected in a State by the wisdom of its laws, the ability of its officers, the efficiency of its magistrates, the education and morals of its people, and by many other considerations. This is a result which follows from the constitution of society, and can never be avoided, but in no other way can they be affected by the action of the State, or by the residence of the citizen therein. They do not derive their existence from its legislation, and cannot be destroyed by its power.

The terms "privileges" and "immunities" are not new in the amendment; they were in the Constitution before the amendment was adopted. They are found in the second section of the fourth article, which declares that "the citizens of each State shall be entitled to all privileges and immunities of citizens in the several States," and they have been the subject of frequent consideration in judicial decisions.

The privileges and immunities designated are those which of right belong to the citizens of all free governments. Clearly among these must be placed the right to pursue a lawful employment in a lawful manner, without other restraint than such as equally affects all persons. . . .

[G]rants of exclusive privileges, such as is made by the act in question, are opposed to the whole theory of free government, and it requires no aid from any bill of rights to render them void. That only is a free government, in the American sense of the term, under which the inalienable right of every citizen to pursue his happiness is unrestrained, except by just, equal, and impartial laws.

I am authorized by the CHIEF JUSTICE, MR. JUSTICE SWAYNE, and MR. JUSTICE BRADLEY to state that they concur with me in this dissenting opinion.

MR. JUSTICE BRADLEY, also dissenting.

First. Is it one of the rights and privileges of a citizen of the United States to pursue such civil employment as he may choose to adopt, subject to such reasonable regulations as may be prescribed by law?

Secondly. Is a monopoly, or exclusive right, given to one person to the exclusion of all others, to keep slaughterhouses, in a district of nearly twelve hundred square miles, for the supply of meat for a large city, a reasonable regulation of that employment which the legislature has a right to impose? . . .

In my view, a law which prohibits a large class of citizens from adopting a lawful employment, or from following a lawful employment previously adopted, does deprive them of liberty as well as property, without due process of law. Their right of choice is a portion of their liberty; their occupation is their property. Such a law also deprives those citizens of the equal protection of the laws, contrary to the last clause of the section.

The constitutional question is distinctly raised in these cases; the constitutional right is expressly claimed; it was violated by State law, which was sustained by the State court, and we are called upon in a legitimate and proper way to afford redress. Our jurisdiction and our duty are plain and imperative.

It is futile to argue that none but persons of the African race are intended to be benefited by this amendment. They may have been the primary cause of the amendment, but its language is general, embracing all citizens, and I think it was purposely so expressed.

The mischief to be remedied was not merely slavery and its incidents and consequences, but that spirit of insubordination and disloyalty to the National government which had troubled the country for so many years in some of the States, and that intolerance of free speech and free discussion which often rendered life and property insecure, and led to much unequal legislation. The amendment was an attempt to give voice to the strong National yearning for that time and that condition of things, in which American citizenship should be a sure guaranty of safety, and in which every citizen of the United States might stand erect on every portion of its soil, in the full enjoyment of every right and privilege belonging to a freeman, without fear of violence or molestation.

▼▲▼

The *Slaughterhouse Cases* left an indelible mark upon constitutional law and development, one that affected the course of the interpretation and application of the Fourteenth Amendment for generations to come. How so? First, Justice Miller found that "the most cursory" glance at the Civil War Amendments revealed a "unity of purpose, when taken in connection with the history of the times." That purpose was to protect the rights of African Americans from their former oppressors.[20] Such a construction of the Fourteenth Amendment set aside the argument of whether it was intended to protect the "fundamental" rights of all citizens, without regard to race, from state legislative intrusion. Justice Miller said that the Privileges or Immunities Clause protected only a narrow band of rights and privileges secured by the Constitution, such as the right to protection on the high seas and the right to interstate travel, since these were requisites of national citizenship. Fundamental rights of the nature associated with protection from the national government were not transferable to the states.

Second, the Court used the *Slaughterhouse Cases* to affirm its 1833 decision in *Barron* v. *Baltimore*. The Court refused the chance to embrace the Fourteenth Amendment as an instrument intended to extend the protections of the Bill of Rights to the states. Justice Miller's construction of the Privileges or Immunities Clause clearly runs counter to the intent of John Bingham, Thaddeus Stevens, and the other key Republicans who dominated the proceedings over the Fourteenth Amendment. They believed that the Privileges or Immunities Clause embraced the fundamental rights of *national* citizenship in the Bill of Rights that the states could not abridge. Seen in this light, Justice Miller inverted the entire design of the Fourteenth Amendment.[21]

It is also difficult to square the Court's simultaneous nullification of the Privileges or Immunities Clause and affirmation of *Barron* with its conclusion that the Fourteenth Amendment was, above all, intended to extend the Constitution's protections to African Americans. In Justice Miller's opinion, the Fourteenth Amendment did not require the states to respect core constitutional guarantees as conditions of national citizenship. Applied to the Equal Protection Clause, this interpretation left no constraints on the states to create a new, albeit "separate," standard of citizenship for blacks. The Fourteenth Amendment, as Justice Miller wrote, had "nothing to do" with state enforcement of the Constitution's fundamental rights guarantees. If that was true, as Justice Stephen Field wrote in dissent, then the

Fourteenth Amendment was a "vain and idle enactment, which accomplished nothing and most unnecessarily excited Congress and the people upon its passage."[22]

The Court's narrow interpretation of the Fourteenth Amendment in the *Slaughterhouse Cases* laid the groundwork for a series of decisions that devastated all the possibilities that Reconstruction might have held for African-American equality.[23] Two cases stand out. In *United States* v. *Cruikshank* (1876), a case born out of the Colfax massacre in Louisiana, the bloodiest race-motivated killing and lynching spree of the Reconstruction era, the Court held that the responsibility for prosecuting criminal acts rested with state and local authorities, not the national government.[24] This decision, rooted in the Court's pre–Civil War conception of federalism, rendered the Enforcement Act of 1870, designed to provide federal remedies for conspiracies intended to deprive individuals of their civil rights, without force. The Court said, in effect, that the Fourteenth Amendment did not confer upon Congress, the language of Section 5 aside, the power to protect blacks or provide legal remedies for constitutional violations as citizens of their respective states.

In the *Civil Rights Cases* (1883) (see Chapter 11), the Court, in a decision that consolidated four separate challenges to the Civil Rights Act of 1875, ruled that Congress had no power under the Fourteenth Amendment to enforce the Equal Protection Clause outside of direct state action. The law prohibited racial discrimination in public accommodations. Justice Bradley, dissenting in the *Slaughterhouse Cases,* had written that "the mischief to be remedied" by the Fourteenth Amendment "was not merely slavery and its . . . consequences; but that spirit of insubordination and disloyalty . . . and (allow) every citizen . . . the full enjoyment of every right and privilege belonging to a freedman, without fear of violence or molestation."[25] Ten years later, now writing for the *Civil Rights Cases* majority, Bradley held that the Fourteenth Amendment did not confer upon Congress the power to "create a code of municipal law for the regulation of private rights."[26]

Discrimination might well be wrong, offered Justice Bradley, but it is a "private wrong," one which the government is powerless to eradicate. The Fourteenth Amendment provides a guarantee against wrongful acts "sanctioned in some way by the State." It does not, however, prohibit the exercise of such acts when carried out in private. Justice Bradley, who had argued in his dissent in the *Slaughterhouse Cases* that the Fourteenth Amendment was foremost a constitutional provision to protect African Americans, had completely reversed himself. Although the *Slaughterhouse Cases* and the *Civil Rights Cases* differ in one key aspect—state action versus private action—a concurrent theme runs through both cases: The responsibility for securing the civil rights of individuals belonged to the states, not the national government.

The line of logic from the *Slaughterhouse Cases* through *Cruikshank* to the *Civil Rights Cases* should make clear that the Court, by the late 1870s, had decided to ignore the original expectations of the Republican sponsors of the Fourteenth Amendment that the federal courts would enforce the Bill of Rights against the states.[27] Here was the Court's response to the Fourteenth Amendment nationalists:

- The Privileges or Immunities Clause does not recognize universal national citizenship or extend any of the Bill of Rights to the states. Responsibility for the substantive content of fundamental rights and their enforcement belongs to the states. (*Slaughterhouse Cases*)
- The Fourteenth Amendment does not authorize the national government to enforce congressional laws intended to protect the civil rights of African Americans. The protection of citizens in the states is the business of state and local government. (*Cruikshank*)
- Section 5 of the Fourteenth Amendment, which gives Congress the power to enforce the Privileges or Immunities, Due Process, and Equal Protection Clauses, does not confer upon African Americans the right to use public accommodations. Such rights are *private* in nature. (*Civil Rights Cases*)

The Court's decisions in *Cruikshank* and the *Civil Rights Cases* paralleled the collapse of Reconstruction and the "redemption" of the Southern states by white supremacists.[28] In 1877, President Rutherford B. Hayes reached an agreement with Southern Democrats to withdraw federal troops from the South, a decision that Hayes knew would open the door for white supremacists to seize power in their respective states. Hayes had lost the popular vote in the November 1876 election. To take office he needed the electoral votes of the Southern states. Hayes agreed to appoint Southern Democrats to his cabinet, extend financial aid to the South, and establish a policy of federal noninterference in Southern affairs. These promises did win him the electoral votes in several disputed outcomes in Southern states during the 1876 presidential election. Most tellingly, the compromise reached in February 1877, which tilted the election in Hayes's favor, demonstrated that blacks were no longer important to Republicans. "The negro," the *Nation* magazine editorialized, "will disappear from the field of national politics. Henceforth, the nation, as a nation, will have nothing more to do with him."[29]

Ironically, the justices' decision to avert their eyes to the Fourteenth Amendment's primary purpose after the *Slaughterhouse Cases* did not mean that the Court had returned the greatly expanded jurisdiction it now enjoyed over the states. The Court now chose to employ its authority over the states to strike down economic regulation that interfered with "liberty of contract," a doctrine that emerged as the core value of the Due Process Clause of the Fourteenth Amendment. By the late 1890s, the Court had validated the social and political subordination of blacks in *Plessy* v. *Ferguson* (1896) (see Chapter 11) and enshrined the economic values of the Gilded Age into constitutional law in *Allgeyer* v. *Louisiana* (1897) (see Volume 1, Chapter 9). Both decisions cast a long shadow over American constitutional development for several more decades.

The Privileges and Immunities Clause was not the only provision of the Fourteenth Amendment to emerge stillborn from the Court during the demise of Reconstruction. In *Hurtado* v. *California* (1884), the Court ruled that the Due Process Clause did not make the Fifth Amendment's guarantees of criminal indictment by a grand jury applicable to the states. Justice John Harlan I, who dissented from the Court's majority holding in the *Civil Rights Cases,* also dissented in *Hurtado*. His unequivocal view that the Fourteenth Amendment made the Bill of Rights applicable to the states, a position also known as the *doctrine of total incorporation,* is considered by many scholars one the finest legal opinions on the subject.*

Hurtado v. *California*

110 U.S. 516 (1884)

Joseph Hurtado was no stranger to the saloons and barroom brawls of Sacramento, California. After Hurtado learned that his wife, Susie, was having an affair with his good friend, Jose Antonio Estaurado, he often shrieked, wept, and tore his hair out when he discussed his difficulties with friends. When Hurtado finally confronted Estaurado in front of the Bank Exchange Saloon about the affair, his friend confessed, telling Hurtado, "I am the meat and you are the knife, kill me if you like." Instead, Hurtado told Estaurado to leave Sacramento, and Estaurado agreed to the demand as soon as he earned enough money. In no time, however, Estaurado was back pursuing Susie Hurtado. In February 1882, Hurtado finally lost his temper and shot Estaurado in broad daylight.

Hurtado was charged with murder, an offense punishable by death in California. Nonetheless, California did not use a grand jury system to bring indictments against criminal defendants. All that prosecutors were required to do was to show judges sufficient information that a crime had been committed. Hurtado claimed that the state's waiver of the grand jury system denied him the due process of law guaranteed by the Fifth Amendment, which requires the federal government to present all criminal indictments to grand juries, made applicable to the states through the Fourteenth Amendment.

After two California courts rejected Hurtado's pleas, the Supreme Court agreed to hear, for the first time, whether the Due Process Clause made provisions of the Bill of Rights applicable to the states.

The Court's decision was 7 to 1. Justice Matthews delivered the opinion of the Court. Justice Harlan dissented. Justice Field did not participate.

MR. JUSTICE MATTHEWS delivered the opinion of the Court.

The proposition of law we are asked to affirm is that an indictment or presentment by a grand jury, as known to

*Justice John Harlan I served on the Supreme Court from 1877–1911. His tenure was remarkable both for the intellectual force of his opinions and his personal journey from proponent of slavery in his native Kentucky before the Civil War to the Court's staunchest defender of the civil rights of blacks. Justice Harlan I also dissented in *Plessy,* writing the famous phrase, "The Constitution is color-blind and neither knows nor tolerates distinctions among its citizens." His grandson, Justice John Harlan II, served on the Court from 1955 to 1971. Scholars commonly refer to the first Justice Harlan as (I) and the second as (II). That convention will be used here when it is necessary to identify them.

the common law of England, is essential to that "due process of law," when applied to prosecutions for felonies, which is secured and guaranteed by this provision of the Constitution of the United States, and which, accordingly, it is forbidden to the States respectively to dispense with in the administration of criminal law.

The question is one of grave and serious import, affecting both private and public rights and interests of great magnitude, and involves a consideration of what additional restrictions upon the legislative policy of the States has been imposed by the Fourteenth Amendment to the Constitution of the United States. . . .

According to a recognized canon of interpretation especially applicable to formal and solemn instruments of constitutional law, we are forbidden to assume, without clear reason to the contrary, that any part of this most important amendment is superfluous. The natural and obvious inference is that, in the sense of the Constitution, "due process of law" was not meant or intended to include . . . the institution and procedure of a grand jury in any case. The conclusion is equally irresistible that, when the same phrase was employed in the Fourteenth Amendment to restrain the action of the States, it was used in the same sense and with no greater extent, and that, if in the adoption of that amendment it had been part of its purpose to perpetuate the institution of the grand jury in all the States, it would have embodied, as did the Fifth Amendment, express declarations to that effect. Due process of law in the latter refers to that law of the land which derives its authority from the legislative powers conferred upon Congress by the Constitution of the United States, exercised within the limits therein prescribed and interpreted according to the principles of the common law. In the Fourteenth Amendment, by parity of reason, it refers to that law of the land in each State which derives its authority from the inherent and reserved powers of the State, exerted within the limits of those fundamental principles of liberty and justice which lie at the base of all our civil and political institutions, and the greatest security for which resides in the right of the people to make their own laws, and alter them at their pleasure. . . .

But it is not to be supposed that these legislative powers are absolute and despotic, and that the amendment prescribing due process of law is too vague and indefinite to operate as a practical restraint. It is not every act, legislative in form, that is law. Law is something more than mere will exerted as an act of power. It must be not a special rule for a particular person or a particular case, but, in the language of Mr. Webster, in his familiar definition, "the general law, a law which hears before it condemns, which proceeds upon inquiry and renders judgment only after trial," so that "every citizen shall hold his life, liberty, property and immunities under the protection of the general rules which govern society," and thus excluding, as not due process of law, acts of attainder, bills of pains and penalties, acts of confiscation, acts reversing judgments, and acts directly transferring one man's estate to another, legislative judgments and decrees, and other similar special, partial and arbitrary exertions of power under the forms of legislation. Arbitrary power, enforcing its edicts to the injury of the persons and property of its subjects, is not law, whether manifested as the decree of a personal monarch or of an impersonal multitude. And the limitations imposed by our constitutional law upon the action of the governments, both State and national, are essential to the preservation of public and private rights, notwithstanding the representative character of our political institutions. The enforcement of these limitations by judicial process is the device of self-governing communities to protect the rights of individuals and minorities, as well against the power of numbers as against the violence of public agents transcending the limits of lawful authority, even when acting in the name and wielding the force of the government. . . .

It follows that any legal proceeding enforced by public authority, whether sanctioned by age and custom, or newly devised in the discretion of the legislative power, in furtherance of the general public good, which regards and preserves these principles of liberty and justice, must be held to be due process of law. . . .

Tried by these principles, we are unable to say that the substitution for a presentment or indictment by a grand jury of the proceeding by information, after examination and commitment by a magistrate, certifying to the probable guilt of the defendant, with the right on his part to the aid of counsel, and to the cross-examination of the witnesses produced for the prosecution, is not due process of law. It is, as we have seen, an ancient proceeding at common law, which might include every case of an offence of less grade than a felony, except misprision of treason, and in every circumstance of its administration, as authorized by the statute of California, it carefully considers and guards the substantial interest of the prisoner. It is merely a preliminary proceeding, and can result in no final judgment except as the consequence of a regular judicial trial, conducted precisely as in cases of indictments. . . .

For these reasons, finding no error therein, the judgment of the Supreme Court of California is

Affirmed.

MR. JUSTICE HARLAN, dissenting.

"Due process of law," within the meaning of the national Constitution, does not import one thing with reference to the powers of the States and another with reference to the powers of the general government. If particular proceedings conducted under the authority of the general government, and involving life, are prohibited because not constituting that due process of law required by the Fifth Amendment of the Constitution of the United States, similar proceedings, conducted under the authority of a State, must be deemed illegal as not being due process of law within the meaning of the Fourteenth Amendment. What, then, is the meaning of the words "due process of law" in the latter amendment? . . .

My brethren concede that there are principles of liberty and justice lying at the foundation of our civil and political institutions which no State can violate consistently with that due process of law required by the Fourteenth Amendment in proceedings involving life, liberty, or property. Some of these principles are enumerated in the opinion of the court. But, for reasons which do not impress my mind as satisfactory, they exclude from that enumeration the exemption from prosecution, by information, for a public offence involving life. . . .

[I]t results from the doctrines of the opinion—if I do not misapprehend its scope—that the clause of the Fourteenth Amendment forbidding the deprivation of life or liberty without due process of law would not be violated by a State regulation, dispensing with petit juries in criminal cases and permitting a person charged with a crime involving life to be tried before a single judge, or even a justice of the peace, upon a rule to show cause why he should not be hanged. I do no injustice to my brethren by this illustration of the principles of the opinion. It is difficult, in my judgment, to overestimate the value of the petit jury system in this country. A sagacious statesman and jurist has well said that it was "the best guardian of both public and private liberty which has been hitherto devised by the ingenuity of man," and that "liberty can never be insecure in that country in which the trial of all crimes is by the jury." Mr. Madison observed that, while trial by jury could not be considered as a natural right, but one resulting from the social compact, yet it was "as essential to secure the liberty of the people as any one of the preexistent rights of nature. . . ."

It seems to me that too much stress is put upon the fact that the framers of the Constitution made express provision for the security of those rights which, at common law, were protected by the requirement of due process of law, and, in addition, declared, generally that no person shall "be deprived of life, liberty or property without due process of law." The rights for the security of which these express provisions were made were of a character so essential to the safety of the people that it was deemed wise to avoid the possibility that Congress, in regulating the processes of law, would impair or destroy them. Hence their specific enumeration in the earlier amendments of the Constitution, in connection with the general requirement of due process of law, the latter itself being broad enough to cover every right of life, liberty or property secured by the settled usages and modes of proceeding existing under the common and statute law of England at the time our government was founded.

When the Fourteenth Amendment was adopted, all the States of the Union, some in terms, all substantially, declared, in their constitutions, that no person shall be deprived of life, liberty, or property, otherwise than "by the judgment of his peers, or the law of the land," or "without due process of law." When that Amendment was adopted, the constitution of each State, with few exceptions, contained, and still contains, a Bill of Rights enumerating the rights of life, liberty and property which cannot be impaired or destroyed by the legislative department. . . . Now it is a fact of momentous interest in this discussion that, when the Fourteenth Amendment was submitted and adopted, the Bill of Rights and the constitutions of twenty-seven States expressly forbade criminal prosecutions, by information, for capital cases; while, in the remaining ten States, they were impliedly forbidden by a general clause declaring that no person should be deprived of life otherwise than by "the judgment of his peers or the law of the land," or "without due process of law. It may be safely affirmed that, when that Amendment was adopted, a criminal prosecution, by information, for a crime involving life was not permitted in any one of the States composing the Union. So that the court, in this case, while conceding that the requirement of due process of law protects the fundamental principles of liberty and justice, adjudges, in effect, that an immunity or right, recognized at the common law to be essential to personal security, jealously guarded by our national Constitution against violation by any tribunal or body exercising authority under the general government, and expressly or impliedly recognized, when the Fourteenth Amendment was adopted in the Bill of Rights or Constitution of every State in the Union, is, yet, not a fundamental principle in governments established, as those of the States of the Union are, to secure to the citizen liberty and justice, and, therefore, is not involved in that due process of law required in proceedings conducted under the sanction of

a State. My sense of duty constrains me to dissent from this interpretation of the supreme law of the land.

▼▲▼

Clearly, *Hurtado* buried any possibility that the Court would follow John Bingham's design for the Fourteenth Amendment. By ruling that the Due Process Clause did not make the Fifth Amendment applicable to the states, the Court completed the mutation of the Fourteenth Amendment, complementing the restrictive interpretation that it had given the Privileges and Immunities Clause in the *Slaughterhouse Cases* and the Equal Protection Clause in the *Civil Rights Cases*. The return to *Barron* and the structural understanding of the Bill of Rights was now complete. In only one case over approximately the next forty years, *Chicago, Burlington & Quincy Railroad* v. *Chicago* (1897), did the Court apply any of the provisions of the Bill of Rights to the states. But *Chicago Railroad* was about the protection of property rights against the eminent domain power of government, not about equality of citizenship, First Amendment freedoms, or any of the other fundamental freedoms in the Bill of Rights.[30] By this time, the Court was firmly on the side of the nation's proprietary and business interests and decided *Chicago Railroad* as a liberty of contract case, not as a case about the incorporation of the Bill of Rights.

As we have discussed, a complex array of social, economic, and political forces led the Court to ignore the intent of the Fourteenth Amendment and substitute its own conception of federalism for the vision of the Thirty-ninth Congress. No explanation of the Court's decisions on the Bill of Rights between the *Slaughterhouse Cases* and *Gitlow* v. *New York* (1925), the first case in which the Court applied a provision of the Bill of Rights outside the context of economic regulation to the states, can be found in the historical materials leading up to the Fourteenth Amendment's passage.[31] The mystery, then, is not whether the Fourteenth Amendment was intended to apply the Bill of Rights to the states. The more compelling question is why the Court chose for so long to ignore what the Thirty-ninth Congress, with no objection, believed the Fourteenth Amendment was designed to do.

Nonetheless, many constitutional scholars have remained skeptical of the view that the Fourteenth Amendment was intended to make the Bill of Rights applicable to the states. Such opposition rests on three major premises. First, opponents of this view note that the Fourteenth Amendment was approved in a highly partisan atmosphere. Passed by margins of 120 to 32 in the House and 33 to 11 in the Senate, the Fourteenth Amendment was supported universally by Republicans and opposed universally by Democrats. President Andrew Johnson, who opposed congressional Reconstruction, argued that since only twenty-five of the nation's thirty-six states were represented in Congress—the Confederate states had not yet been readmitted to the Union—the Fourteenth Amendment lacked the necessary approval of two-thirds of Congress as required by Article V. Other critics have noted that the Southern states were given no choice but to ratify the Fourteenth Amendment, as such action was required for their readmission into the Union. Such circumstances call into question the legitimacy of the Fourteenth Amendment as an exercise in constitutional reform.[32]

Second, some scholars have argued that Bingham, Stevens, and other prominent supporters of the Fourteenth Amendment offered no clear explanation for its relationship to the Bill of Rights. Was the Privileges and Immunities Clause simply a shorthand term for the Bill of Rights, or was its intent less ambitious? If the Republican leadership had intended to transform the Bill of Rights through the Fourteenth Amendment, suggest other critics, opposition would have been much more vocal than it was. Silence on the part of Republicans in Congress can be interpreted as something far different from uniform support for the total incorporation view. It can also be understood, as some scholars have suggested, as not taking seriously Bingham's view that the Fourteenth Amendment, and specifically the Privileges and Immunities Clause, was intended to bind the states to the Bill of Rights.[33]

Moreover, many Republicans supported passage of the Fourteenth Amendment for reasons other than to protect the rights of the newly freed slaves. Section 2 of the amendment greatly expanded congressional power to determine voting rights by punishing all states that refused to extend the franchise to male inhabitants over the age of twenty-one. Section 3 punished the Confederate states by stripping the right to vote from any person who had supported insurrection or rebellion against the United States. In fact, many Republicans were extremely skeptical about extending the full equal protection of the law to African Americans, especially the right to vote. Radical Republicans originally had demanded a provision in the Fourteenth Amendment securing the right to vote for blacks, but such a proposal was defeated in committee and never reached the full Congress. Instead, Section 2 left to the states the decision of whether or not to extend the franchise to African Americans. Some scholars have interpreted the complexity of issues bound up in the Fourteenth Amendment to mean that the application of the Bill of Rights to the states was not its major premise. Rather, the chief purpose of the Fourteenth Amendment was to secure the Northern victory in the Civil War and reconstruct the bonds of union on Northern terms. The Privileges and Immunities Clause, as understood by critics of total incorporation, embodied a narrow anti-discrimination principle that required states to treat citizens from other states equally under their own laws and little else.[34]

Third, critics of total incorporation also argue that a principled commitment to federalism makes any complete application of the Bill of Rights to the states impossible. The Framers of the 1787 Constitution would never have sanctioned an amendment that authorized the federal courts to possess such sweeping power over matters properly belonging to the states. In our remaining chapters, we will see how important the limitations established by the Bill of Rights on congressional power were during the formative years of the Republic. Many of the most ardent supporters of the Bill of Rights believed that states were better suited to protect the rights and liberties of their citizens through their own constitutions. Few contest the notion that the Fourteenth Amendment was necessary as an instrument to protect against secession and to establish a guarantee of national citizenship. However, critics of total incorporation argue that it was never intended to compromise federalism to the point where states were little more than functionaries under the control of an expansive national government.[35]

Organized Interests and the Nationalization of the Bill of Rights

After *Hurtado,* Justice John Harlan I persisted in his campaign to bring the guarantees of the Bill of Rights to the states. In *Maxwell* v. *Dow* (1900), Harlan I returned to the Privileges and Immunities Clause nullified by the *Slaughterhouse Cases.* In *Maxwell,* the Court, 8 to 1, ruled that under state law criminal defendants in non-capital cases were not entitled to grand jury hearings and twelve-person juries. The Utah constitution secured neither right, and the Court held that "[t]rial by jury has never been affirmed to be a necessary requisite of due process of law."[36] Dissenting, Harlan I wrote:

> Suppose the State of Utah should amend its constitution and make the Mormon religion the established religion of the State, to be supported by taxation on all the people of Utah. . . . If such an amendment were alleged to be invalid under the National Constitution, could not [today's opinion] be cited as showing that the right to the free exercise of religion was not a privilege of a "citizen of the United States" protected within the meaning of the Fourteenth Amendment?"[37]

Eight years later, Harlan I wrote perhaps his most celebrated opinion on the incorporation question. Dissenting in *Twining* v. *New Jersey,* Harlan I wrote that criminal defendants were protected by the Due Process Clause from self-incrimination. The Fifth Amendment states that "No person . . . shall be compelled in any criminal case to be a witness against himself." Harlan described the privilege against self-incrimination as an English common-law privilege that existed prior to ratification of the Constitution. Harlan also wrote that "real, genuine freedom could not exist in any country" that abridged the privilege against self-incrimination. This privilege, wrote Harlan, ranked "among the essential, fundamental principles of the English common law."[38] Recognizing that an appeal to the intent of the framers of the Fourteenth Amendment was futile, Harlan I turned to English common-law principles, which still held considerable sway among nineteenth-century lawyers and judges, to justify the incorporation of the Bill of Rights.[39] Although he was the sole dissenter in *Twining,* Harlan I was not speaking to an audience of one. Soon, the Court would begin the process of incorporation.

The Legal Mobilization of the Bill of Rights

In 1917, Roger Baldwin formed the Civil Liberties Bureau (CLB) of the American Union against Militarism, a pacifist organization that opposed the entry of the United States into World War I. The CLB's initial concern, defending conscientious objectors to the draft, soon branched out to free speech, as Congress began

Norman Thomas, a founding member of the ACLU, being pelted with eggs by an angry crowd as he attempted to speak in Jersey City, New Jersey, June 1938.
AP/Wide World Photos

passing laws to limit the rights of political dissidents after America entered the war. The CLB soon created an independent organization, the National Civil Liberties Bureau (NCLB), to specialize in such matters. By 1920, the NCLB had been reorganized and renamed the American Civil Liberties Union (ACLU), with Baldwin remaining as its executive director and driving force. Other groups that later became important forces in the expansion of the Bill of Rights, such as the American Jewish Congress (1916), the Anti-Defamation League of B'nai B'rith (1913), the American Jewish Committee (1906), and the National Association for the Advancement of Colored People (NAACP) (1909), had already formed. But these groups were designed to serve particular constituencies: Jews, African Americans, and other racial, religious, and ethnic minorities then denied equal rights under law. The ACLU was unique in that it was designed to protect the principle of free speech, regardless of who was doing the speaking. Indeed, the ACLU butted heads with the NAACP in one of its first efforts to defend the universal free speech principle when it decided to defend the right of the Ku Klux Klan to convene in a public meeting hall after Boston's mayor had banned the organization.*[40]

*The ACLU and the NAACP have since remained closely allied on most major civil rights and liberties issues. But on occasion, they still sometimes disagree on the limits of racist speech. The ACLU has also been in some very public disagreements with the major American Jewish organizations on free speech limits. The most famous of these disputes involved the ACLU's decision to defend the right of a Nazi group, the National Socialist Party of America (NSWP), to march in Skokie, Illinois, a predominantly Jewish suburb on the north shore of Chicago. In the late 1970s, one of every six residents in Skokie was either a survivor of or related to a survivor of the Holocaust. The ACLU's decision to defend the Nazis resulted in a staggering loss in membership, and alienated many of its long-time Jewish supporters. The best account of the group politics involved in the ACLU's decision to defend the right of the Nazis to march in Skokie can be found in Philippa Strum, *When the Nazis Came to Skokie* (Lawrence: University Press of Kansas, 1999). By the mid-1980s, the ACLU had recovered its membership and was in better financial health than ever. It received an unexpected boost in 1988, when vice-president George Bush, running against Massachusetts governor Michael Dukakis for president, painted his opponent as a "card-carrying member of the ACLU," which, in fact, was true. Whether amused or angered by Bush's remarks, new members joined the ACLU in droves and old members called the organization to demand their "card." By 1990, the ACLU's membership reached 275,000, exceeding its pre-Skokie levels. By 2000, ACLU membership stood at approximately 300,000.

Benjamin Gitlow, right, preparing to address the 1928 Socialist Party Convention at Madison Square Garden in New York City.
© Bettmann/CORBIS

The ACLU's decision to enter *Gitlow* v. *New York* (1925) was far less controversial within the civil liberties community. World War I had taken a tremendous toll on the free speech rights of political dissidents, and the Russian Revolution of 1917, which resulted in the formation of the Soviet Union, sent shivers not only through the United States government, but state legislatures as well. The response from government at all levels was to clamp down further on free speech rights, particularly as they involved labor organizing and sympathy for socialist and Communist political doctrines. The ACLU did not, in *Gitlow,* prevail on the free speech question. But it did accomplish a much more long-term victory: the application of the Free Speech Clause to the states through the Fourteenth Amendment.

Gitlow v. *New York*

268 U.S. 652 (1925)

Born on December 21, 1891, to poverty-stricken Russian-Jewish immigrants, Benjamin Gitlow grew up immersed in radical politics. By his eighteenth birthday, fresh out of high school, Gitlow had joined the Socialist Party. After dabbling in law for a few years, Gitlow turned full time to furthering the cause of socialist revolution in the United States, the Russian Revolution having had a tremendous impact on his political consciousness. In 1918, the year after the Bolsheviks had seized power in Russia, Gitlow won a seat in the New York legislature on the Socialist Party ticket. Around this same time, Gitlow had joined forces with the more radical element of the Socialist Party to publish *Revolutionary Age*. This newspaper advocated the destruction of the parliamentary state and its replacement with a "new state of organized producers, which will deprive the bourgeoisie of political power, and function as a revolutionary dictatorship of the proletariat."[41]

If this rhetoric sounds a bit dated now, it was serious business in the days following the Russian Revolution. In 1919, Gitlow was arrested under the New York Criminal Anarchy Act of 1902, which made it illegal for any person to write, advocate, advise, or teach the duty, necessity, or propriety of criminal anarchism. The law was actually a response to the assassination of President William McKinley by a reputed anarchist in 1901, not a reaction to the Russian Revolution. It was an effective tool against political dissent nonetheless, and in February 1920 Benjamin Gitlow was convicted of violating the 1902 act.

Clarence Darrow, the nation's most famous civil liberties lawyer, had initially represented Gitlow, but his appeal was handled by the ACLU. Baldwin persuaded Walter Pollak, a well-known New York corporate lawyer active in civil liberties causes, to represent Gitlow in his appeal to the Supreme Court. Pollak emphasized that Gitlow's conviction did not stem from any direct action he had taken against the government, but from the mere advocacy of radical ideas. More importantly, Pollak argued in his brief that the Due Process Clause of the Fourteenth Amendment incorporated the guarantees of the First Amendment and made them binding on the states.

Pollak's argument was risky. The Court's staunchest free speech advocates, Justices Louis Brandeis and Oliver Wendell Holmes, adamantly opposed the Court's use of the Due Process Clause to protect a "liberty of contract" that had made it nearly impossible for the states to regulate the economy in the public interest. There was some concern within the ACLU that arguing for the application of the First Amendment to the states might offer the Court's economic conservatives further justification for their views. After internal deliberation, the ACLU agreed that Pollak should make the incorporation argument.

The Court's decision was 7 to 2. Justice Sanford delivered the opinion of the Court. Justice Holmes, joined by Justice Brandeis, dissented.

▼▲▼

MR. JUSTICE SANFORD delivered the opinion of the Court.

The sole contention here is, essentially, that as there was no evidence of any concrete result flowing from the publication of the Manifesto or of circumstances showing the likelihood of such result, the statute as construed and applied by the trial court penalizes the mere utterance, as such, of "doctrine" having no quality of incitement, without regard either to the circumstances of its utterance or to the likelihood of unlawful sequences, and that, as the exercise of the right of free expression with relation to government is only punishable "in circumstances involving likelihood of substantive evil," the statute contravenes the due process clause of the Fourteenth Amendment. The argument in support of this contention rests primarily upon the following propositions: 1st, that the "liberty" protected by the Fourteenth Amendment includes the liberty of speech and of the press, and 2nd, that while liberty of expression "is not absolute," it may be restrained "only in circumstances where its exercise bears a causal relation with some substantive evil, consummated, attempted or likely," and as the statute "takes no account of circumstances," it unduly restrains this liberty and is therefore unconstitutional.

The precise question presented, and the only question which we can consider under this writ of error, then is whether the statute, as construed and applied in this case by the state courts, deprived the defendant of his liberty of expression in violation of the due process clause of the Fourteenth Amendment.

The statute does not penalize the utterance or publication of abstract "doctrine" or academic discussion having no quality of incitement to any concrete action. It is not aimed against mere historical or philosophical essays. It does not restrain the advocacy of changes in the form of government by constitutional and lawful means. What it prohibits is language advocating, advising or teaching the overthrow of organized government by unlawful means. . . .

The Manifesto, plainly, is neither the statement of abstract doctrine nor, as suggested by counsel, mere prediction that industrial disturbances and revolutionary mass strikes will result spontaneously in an inevitable process of evolution in the economic system. It advocates and urges in fervent language mass action which shall progressively foment industrial disturbances and, through political mass strikes and revolutionary mass action, overthrow and destroy organized parliamentary government. . . .

For present purposes, we may and do assume that freedom of speech and of the press which are protected by the First Amendment from abridgment by Congress are among the fundamental personal rights and "liberties" protected by the due process clause of the Fourteenth Amendment from impairment by the States. . . .

It is a fundamental principle, long established, that the freedom of speech and of the press which is secured by the Constitution does not confer an absolute right to speak or publish, without responsibility, whatever one may choose, or an unrestricted and unbridled license that gives immunity for every possible use of language and prevents the punishment of those who abuse this freedom. Reasonably limited, it was said by Story in the passage cited, this freedom is an inestimable privilege in a free government; without such limitation, it might become the scourge of the republic.

That a State in the exercise of its police power may punish those who abuse this freedom by utterances inimical to the public welfare, tending to corrupt public morals, incite to crime, or disturb the public peace, is not open to question. . . .

We cannot hold that the present statute is an arbitrary or unreasonable exercise of the police power of the State unwarrantably infringing the freedom of speech or press, and we must and do sustain its constitutionality. . . .

This being so, it may be applied to every utterance—not too trivial to be beneath the notice of the law—which is of such a character and used with such intent and purpose as to bring it within the prohibition of the statute. . . . In other words, when the legislative body has determined generally, in the constitutional exercise of its discretion, that utterances of a certain kind involve such danger of substantive evil that they may be punished, the question whether any specific utterance coming within the prohibited class is likely, in and of itself, to bring about the substantive evil is not open to consideration. It is sufficient that the statute itself be constitutional and that the use of the language comes within its prohibition. . . .

And finding, for the reasons stated, that the statute is not, in itself, unconstitutional, and that it has not been applied in the present case in derogation of any constitutional right, the judgment of the Court of Appeals is

Affirmed.

MR. JUSTICE HOLMES, dissenting.

MR. JUSTICE BRANDEIS and I are of opinion that this judgment should be reversed. The general principle of free speech, it seems to me, must be taken to be included in the Fourteenth Amendment, in view of the scope that has been given to the word "liberty" as there used, although perhaps it may be accepted with a somewhat larger latitude of interpretation than is allowed to Congress by the sweeping language that governs or ought to govern the laws of the United States. . . .

It is said that this manifesto was more than a theory, that it was an incitement. Every idea is an incitement. It offers itself for belief, and, if believed, it is acted on unless some other belief outweighs it or some failure of energy stifles the movement at its birth. The only difference between the expression of an opinion and an incitement in the narrower sense is the speaker's enthusiasm for the result. Eloquence may set fire to reason. But whatever may be thought of the redundant discourse before us, it had no chance of starting a present conflagration. If, in the long run, the beliefs expressed in proletarian dictatorship are destined to be accepted by the dominant forces of the community, the only meaning of free speech is that they should be given their chance and have their way.

If the publication of this document had been laid as an attempt to induce an uprising against government at once, and not at some indefinite time in the future, it would have presented a different question. The object would have been one with which the law might deal, subject to the doubt whether there was any danger that the publication could produce any result, or in other words, whether it was not futile and too remote from possible consequences. But the indictment alleges the publication, and nothing more.

The Court's conclusion that freedom of speech and press were "among the fundamental personal rights and 'liberties' protected by the due process clause of the Fourteenth Amendment from impairment by the States" came from nowhere. Justice Sandford offered no historical or analytical basis for the application of the First Amendment to the states, other than it seemed to make sense. Dissenting, Justice Holmes wrote that the "general principle of free speech, it seems to me, must be taken to be included in the Fourteenth Amendment, in view of the scope that has been given to the word 'liberty' as there used, although perhaps it may be accepted with a somewhat larger latitude of interpretaton than is allowed to Congress by the sweeping language that governs, or ought to govern, the laws of the United States."[42] Surprisingly, Holmes, one of the most scholarly of justices ever to serve on the Court, did not turn to John Bingham's floor speeches in the Thirty-ninth Congress or any of the Reconstruction-era debates on the Fourteenth Amendment for his conclusion. Like Sandford, Holmes believed that it just seemed to make sense that such a fundamental right as free speech should receive protection from state as well as federal encroachment.

Nonetheless, the Court had opened the door for the application of the Bill of Rights to the states through the Fourteenth Amendment, and lawyers, litigants, and groups once hesitant to appeal their cases to the Court were now prepared to move forward. Six years later, in *Near* v. *Minnesota* (1931) (see Chapter 5), the Court declared that a state law prohibiting newspapers from publishing material that was "lewd" or "obscene" was an unconstitutional prior restraint on press freedom protected by the First Amendment. The Court reached this conclusion by applying the First Amendment through the Due Process Clause of the Fourteenth Amendment.[43]

Earlier that term, the Court, in *Stromberg* v. *California* (1931), struck down a state law outlawing the display of a "red flag, banner or badge . . . as a sign, symbol or emblem of opposition to organized government."[44] A nineteen-year-old camp counselor named Yetta Stromberg worked at a Communist summer camp for children, and every morning she led her young campers in raising and saluting the Soviet flag. After her arrest, the ACLU joined forces with a Communist-front organization called the International Labor Defense (ILD) to defend Stromberg's free speech rights all the way to the United States Supreme Court. In *Near,* the ACLU had been involved in the early stages of the litigation, but participated as *amicus curiae* by the time it reached the Court. In its *amicus* brief, the ACLU argued that the Fourteenth Amendment made the Free Press Clause applicable to the states. Near and Stromberg personified the universal commitment of the ACLU to freedom of speech and press. In *Stromberg,* the ACLU worked with and defended a Communist; in *Near,* the ACLU defended the free speech rights of an anti-Catholic, anti-Jewish, and racist newspaper publisher. A year later, in *Powell* v. *Alabama* (see Chapter 9), brought by an unusual coalition of the ACLU, ILD, and the NAACP, the Court ruled that capital defendants in state proceedings were entitled to representation if they could not afford an attorney under the Sixth Amendment, made applicable to the states through the Fourteenth Amendment.[45]

Not until *Palko* v. *Connecticut* (1937), however, did the Court attempt to explain the basis for its gradual incorporation of the Bill of Rights to the states through the Fourteenth Amendment. In contrast to the arguments in Justice Harlan I's dissenting opinions in *Hurtado* and *Twining,* which advocated the *total incorporation* of the Bill of Rights to the states, Justice Benjamin Cardozo's majority opinion in *Palko* suggested an alternative that scholars often call the *doctrine of selective incorporation.* What is the difference?

Palko v. *Connecticut*

302 U.S. 319 (1937)

In the wee hours of September 30, 1935, two Bridgeport, Connecticut, police officers observed a young man named Frank Palko carrying a cheap radio. Earlier, at about midnight, two young men had smashed the window of a downtown music store and made off with two radios that matched the description of the one Palko was carrying. When confronted by the police, Palko shot and killed them both. A month later, Palko was arrested in Buffalo, New York, and, in possession of a gun, a blackjack, and a large sum of money, confessed to Buffalo police about the Bridgeport murders. A trial judge later threw out the confession, which left the jury in the position to consider only second-degree murder, since premeditation was no longer in evidence. Connecticut prosecutors alleged that the trial judge had made serious errors in jury instruction that harmed the prosecution's case, chiefly that the state had to demonstrate that Palko had left his apartment with the intent to murder. The Connecticut Supreme Court of Errors reversed the lower court opinion, ruling that the trial judge's jury instructions severely prejudiced the prosecution's case. The court ruled that Frank Palko could stand trial again on first-degree murder charges.

Palko's lawyers argued that the Connecticut appeals court ruling violated the Fifth Amendment's guarantee against double jeopardy, made applicable to the states through the Fourteenth Amendment.

The Court's decision was 8 to 1. Justice Cardozo delivered the opinion of the Court. Justice Butler dissented.

▼▲▼

Mr. Justice Cardozo delivered the opinion of the Court.

The Fifth Amendment provides, among other things, that no person shall be held to answer for a capital or otherwise infamous crime unless on presentment or indictment of a grand jury. This court has held that, in prosecutions by a state, presentment or indictment by a grand jury may give way to informations at the instance of a public officer. The Fifth Amendment provides also that no person shall be compelled in any criminal case to be a witness against himself. This court has said that, in prosecutions by a state, the exemption will fail if the state elects to end it. The Sixth Amendment calls for a jury trial in criminal cases, and the Seventh for a jury trial in civil cases at common law where the value in controversy shall exceed twenty dollars. This court has ruled that consistently with those amendments trial by jury may be modified by a state or abolished altogether. . . .

On the other hand, the due process clause of the Fourteenth Amendment may make it unlawful for a state to

abridge by its statutes the freedom of speech which the First Amendment safeguards against encroachment by the Congress, or the like freedom of the press, or the free exercise of religion, or the right of peaceable assembly, without which speech would be unduly trammeled, or the right of one accused of crime to the benefit of counsel. In these and other situations, immunities that are valid as against the federal government by force of the specific pledges of particular amendments have been found to be implicit in the concept of ordered liberty, and thus, through the Fourteenth Amendment, become valid as against the states.

The line of division may seem to be wavering and broken if there is a hasty catalogue of the cases on the one side and the other. Reflection and analysis will induce a different view. There emerges the perception of a rationalizing principle which gives to discrete instances a proper order and coherence. The right to trial by jury and the immunity from prosecution except as the result of an indictment may have value and importance. Even so, they are not of the very essence of a scheme of ordered liberty. To abolish them is not to violate a "principle of justice so rooted in the traditions and conscience of our people as to be ranked as fundamental." Few would be so narrow or provincial as to maintain that a fair and enlightened system of justice would be impossible without them. What is true of jury trials and indictments is true also, as the cases show, of the immunity from compulsory self-incrimination. This too might be lost, and justice still be done. Indeed, today, as in the past, there are students of our penal system who look upon the immunity as a mischief, rather than a benefit, and who would limit its scope, or destroy it altogether. No doubt there would remain the need to give protection against torture, physical or mental. Justice, however, would not perish if the accused were subject to a duty to respond to orderly inquiry. The exclusion of these immunities and privileges from the privileges and immunities protected against the action of the states has not been arbitrary or casual. It has been dictated by a study and appreciation of the meaning, the essential implications, of liberty itself.

We reach a different plane of social and moral values when we pass to the privileges and immunities that have been taken over from the earlier articles of the federal bill of rights and brought within the Fourteenth Amendment by a process of absorption. These, in their origin, were effective against the federal government alone. If the Fourteenth Amendment has absorbed them, the process of absorption has had its source in the belief that neither liberty nor Justice would exist if they were sacrificed. This is true, for illustration, of freedom of thought, and speech. Of that freedom one may say that it is the matrix, the indispensable condition, of nearly every other form of freedom. With rare aberrations, a pervasive recognition of that truth can be traced in our history, political and legal. So it has come about that the domain of liberty, withdrawn by the Fourteenth Amendment from encroachment by the states, has been enlarged by latter-day judgments to include liberty of the mind as well as liberty of action. The extension became, indeed, a logical imperative when once it was recognized, as long ago it was, that liberty is something more than exemption from physical restraint, and that, even in the field of substantive rights and duties, the legislative judgment, if oppressive and arbitrary, may be overridden by the courts. Fundamental too in the concept of due process, and so in that of liberty, is the thought that condemnation shall be rendered only after trial. The hearing, moreover, must be a real one, not a sham or a pretense. For that reason, ignorant defendants in a capital case were held to have been condemned unlawfully when in truth, though not in form, they were refused the aid of counsel. The decision did not turn upon the fact that the benefit of counsel would have been guaranteed to the defendants by the provisions of the Sixth Amendment if they had been prosecuted in a federal court. The decision turned upon the fact that, in the particular situation laid before us in the evidence, the benefit of counsel was essential to the substance of a hearing.

Our survey of the cases serves, we think, to justify the statement that the dividing line between them, if not unfaltering throughout its course, has been true for the most part to a unifying principle. On which side of the line the case made out by the appellant has appropriate location must be the next inquiry, and the final one. Is that kind of double jeopardy to which the statute has subjected him a hardship so acute and shocking that our polity will not endure it? Does it violate those "fundamental principles of liberty and justice which lie at the base of all our civil and political institutions"? The answer surely must be "no." What the answer would have to be if the state were permitted after a trial free from error to try the accused over again or to bring another case against him, we have no occasion to consider. We deal with the statute before us, and no other. The state is not attempting to wear the accused out by a multitude of cases with accumulated trials. It asks no more than this, that the case against him shall go on until there shall be a trial free from the corrosion of substantial legal error. This is not cruelty at all, nor even vexation in any immoderate degree. If the trial had been infected with error adverse to the accused, there might have been review at his instance, and as often as necessary to purge the vicious taint. A reciprocal privilege, subject at all times to the discretion of the presiding judge, has now been granted to the state. There is here no seismic innovation. The edifice of justice stands, its symmetry, to many, greater than before. . . .

The judgment is
Affirmed.

By *Palko,* the Court had embraced the New Deal of Franklin Roosevelt and rejected the idea that states could not regulate economic rights to promote the public interest. Justice Cardozo's discussion of the "fundamental" nature of freedom of speech and press suggested that some rights and liberties under the Constitution should receive "preferred" treatment, while others fell within the greater purview of the state to regulate. A year later, in *United States* v. *Carolene Products* (1938), Chief Justice Harlan Fiske Stone, in a footnote that certainly ranks as the most influential one or two in the Court's history,[46] wrote that, "There may be a narrower scope for operation of the presumption of constitutionality, when legislation appears on its face to be within a specific prohibition of the Constitution, such as those of the first ten amendments, which are held *equally specific when held to be embraced within the Fourteenth.*" Stone also wrote: "It is not necessary to consider now" whether the Court should review "with more exacting scrutiny" laws that restrict access to the political process, discriminated against "discreet and insular minorities," or targeted racial, religious, or ethnic minorities for unequal treatment.[47]

Coming on the heels of the Constitutional Revolution of 1937, the point that marked the transformation of the Court from the protector of property and contract rights to the guardian of the Bill of Rights, many interest groups viewed Stone's footnote in *Carolene Products* as further encouragement to use litigation to press their causes that had been unsuccessful in the legislative process. By 1940, the Jehovah's Witnesses, which had launched a legal battle in the mid-1930s to challenge anti-proselytizing laws and other measures designed to limit their religious activities in public, had succeeded in having the Court, in *Cantwell* v. *Connecticut* (1940), strike down a state law under the Free Exercise Clause of the First Amendment.[48] Shortly afterward, an obscure New Jersey fraternal order, the Junior Order of United Auto Mechanics, backed by the American Jewish Congress and the ACLU, decided to challenge a local law permitting religious schools to receive public assistance for bus transportation. The Court did not rule that such assistance was unconstitutional, but it did hold, in *Everson* v. *Board of Education* (1947) (see Chapter 6), that the Establishment Clause was applicable to the states. On a parallel course was the NAACP, which was busy bringing lawsuits in state and federal courts around the nation, challenging the "separate but equal" interpretation of the Fourteenth Amendment. In *Shelley* v. *Kraemer* (1948) (see Chapter 11), the NAACP, backed by *amicus* briefs from the ACLU and the major Jewish organizations, succeeded in persuading the Court to strike down racially restrictive real estate covenants.[49] The NAACP's litigation campaign culminated six years later in *Brown* v. *Board of Education* (1954) (see Chapter 11), in which the Court ruled that racial segregation in the public schools violated the Equal Protection Clause of the Fourteenth Amendment, setting the stage for the coming revolution in American race relations.[50]

In the cases bringing the guarantees of the First Amendment and other provisions of the Bill of Rights to the states after *Palko* (see Table 3.1), the Court, in theory, was clearly following the selective incorporation model of Justice Cardozo. But Cardozo's case-by-case approach was not enough for Justice Hugo Black. Like Justice Harlan I, Black believed that the Fourteenth Amendment applied the Bill of Rights to the states in full. In *Adamson* v. *California* (1947), Black revisited the origins of the Fourteenth Amendment, taking the Court to task for incorporating many of the guarantees of the Bill of Rights without offering any analysis of its history or intent. Juxtaposed against Black's dissent was Justice Felix Frankfurter's concurring opinion defending Cardozo's model of selective incorporation. For Frankfurter, the key issue was whether a state had violated an individual's right to *fundamental fairness,* the cornerstone of what the Due Process Clause was designed to protect. *Adamson,* as you will see in many other cases in this volume, was not the first time these two giants of the Court went head-to-head on a great issue in constitutional law, nor would it be the last.[51]

TABLE 3.1 Cases Incorporating the Bill of Rights Through the Due Process Clause of the Fourteenth Amendment

Constitutional Provision	Case and Year
FIRST AMENDMENT	
Freedom of speech	*Gitlow* v. *New York* (1925)
Freedom of the press	*Near* v. *Minnesota* (1931)
Freedom of assembly	*De Jonge* v. *Oregon* (1937)
Free exercise of religion	*Cantwell* v. *Connecticut* (1940)
Establishment clause	*Everson* v. *Board of Education* (1947)
SECOND AMENDMENT	
Right to bear arms	Not incorporated
THIRD AMENDMENT	
Freedom from quartering of troops in peacetime	Not incorporated
FOURTH AMENDMENT	
Unreasonable search and seizure	*Wolf* v. *Colorado* (1949)
Exclusionary rule	*Mapp* v. *Ohio* (1961)
FIFTH AMENDMENT	
Grand jury clause	Not incorporated
Self-incrimination clause	*Malloy* v. *Hogan* (1964)
Double jeopardy clause	*Benton* v. *Maryland* (1969)
SIXTH AMENDMENT	
Right to a public trial	*In re Oliver* (1948)
Notice clause	*Cole* v. *Arkansas* (1948)
Right to counsel	*Gideon* v. *Wainwright* (1963)/*Argersinger* v. *Hamlin* (1972)
Confrontation clause	*Pointer* v. *Texas* (1965)
Right to impartial jury	*Parker* v. *Gladden* (1966)
Right to a speedy trial	*Klopfer* v. *North Carolina* (1967)
Compulsory process clause	*Washington* v. *Texas* (1967)
Right to jury trial (criminal cases)	*Duncan* v. *Louisiana* (1968)
SEVENTH AMENDMENT	
Right to jury trial (civil cases)	Not incorporated
EIGHTH AMENDMENT	
Ban on cruel and unusual punishments	*Robinson* v. *California* (1962)
Ban on excessive bail	*Schilb* v. *Kuebel* (1971)
Ban on excessive fines	Not incorporated

Note: In *Griswold* v. *Connecticut* (1965), a majority of justices agreed that several provisions of the Bill of Rights (First, Third, Fourth, and Fifth Amendments) created a right to privacy. Although some justices believed the Ninth Amendment created a right to privacy, a majority did not.

Adamson v. *California*

332 U.S. 46 (1947)

After Dewey Adamson was arrested for the first-degree murder of Stella Blauvelt, a sixty-four-year-old widow who had lived in Los Angeles, his lawyers decided that, in view of his criminal record, he should not take the stand. True, Adamson's criminal record predated Blauvelt's murder by twenty years, and involved robbery and burglary in Missouri. But this was 1944, and Adamson was a black man accused of murdering a white woman and stealing her jewelry. If Adamson testified on his own behalf, the prosecution could bring in his criminal record to challenge his credibility. That would certainly not sit well with a jury that consisted of eleven women and one man, all of whom were white.[52]

Under the California constitution, prosecutors were permitted to comment on a witness's refusal to testify in his or her own behalf. Los Angeles County deputy district attorney Ernest Roll made the best of his opportunity and attacked Adamson's refusal to testify with abandon, telling the jury that "it would take about twenty or fifty horses to keep someone off the stand if he was not afraid. He does not tell you. No. . . . I am going to make this one statement to you: Counsel asked to find this defendant not guilty. But does the Defendant get on the stand and say, under oath, 'I am not guilty'? Not one word from him, and not one word from a single witness. I leave the case in your hands."

Adamson was convicted of first-degree murder and robbery, and later sentenced to death. His lawyers appealed his conviction to the California Supreme Court, claiming that the prosecution's closing statement was the equivalent of having Adamson testify against himself. The California Supreme Court, citing *Twining* v. *New Jersey,* affirmed Adamson's conviction, ruling that the Fifth Amendment's guarantees against self-incrimination did not apply to the state's comment practice.

The Court's decision was 5 to 4. Justice Reed delivered the opinion of the Court. Justice Frankfurter wrote a concurring opinion. Justice Black, joined by Justice Douglas, dissented. Justice Murphy, joined by Justice Rutledge, also dissented.

▼▲▼

Mr. Justice Reed delivered the opinion of the Court.

[A]ppellant urges that the provision of the Fifth Amendment that no person "shall be compelled in any criminal case to be a witness against himself" is a fundamental national privilege or immunity protected against state abridgment by the Fourteenth Amendment or a privilege or immunity secured, through the Fourteenth Amendment, against deprivation by state action because it is a personal right, enumerated in the federal Bill of Rights. . . .

It is settled law that the clause of the Fifth Amendment, protecting a person against being compelled to be a witness against himself, is not made effective by the Fourteenth Amendment as a protection against state action on the ground that freedom from testimonial compulsion is a right of national citizenship, or because it is a personal privilege or immunity secured by the Federal Constitution as one of the rights of man that are listed in the Bill of Rights. . . .

For a state to require testimony from an accused is not necessarily a breach of a state's obligation to give a fair trial. Therefore, we must examine the effect of the California law applied in this trial to see whether the comment on failure to testify violates the protection against state action that the due process clause does grant to an accused. The due process clause forbids compulsion to testify by fear of hurt, torture or exhaustion. It forbids any other type of coercion that falls within the scope of due process. California follows Anglo-American legal tradition in excusing defendants in criminal prosecutions from compulsory testimony. That is a matter of legal policy, and not because of the requirements of due process under the Fourteenth Amendment. So our inquiry is directed not at the broad question of the constitutionality of compulsory testimony from the accused under the due process clause, but to the constitutionality of the provision of the California law that permits comment upon his failure to testify. . . .

Generally, comment on the failure of an accused to testify is forbidden in American jurisdictions. California . . . is one of a few states that permit limited comment upon a defendant's failure to testify. That permission is narrow. The California law . . . authorizes comment by court and counsel upon the "failure of the defendant to explain or to deny by his testimony any evidence or facts in the case against him." This does not involve any presumption, rebuttable or irrebuttable, either of guilt or of the truth of any fact, that is offered in evidence. It allows inferences to be drawn from proven facts. Because of this clause, the court can direct the jury's attention to whatever evidence there may be that a defendant could deny and the prosecution can argue as to inferences that may be drawn from the accused's failure to testify. There is here no lack of power in the trial court to adjudge, and no denial of a hearing. California has prescribed a method for advising the jury in the search for truth. However sound may be the legislative conclusion that an accused should not be compelled in any criminal case to be a witness against himself, we see no reason why comment should not be made upon his silence. It seems quite natural that, when a defendant has opportunity to deny or explain facts and determines not to do so, the prosecution should bring out the strength of the evidence by commenting upon defendant's failure to explain or deny it. The prosecution evidence may be of facts that may be beyond the knowledge of the accused. If so, his failure to testify would have little, if any, weight. But the facts may be such as are necessarily in the knowledge of the accused. In that case, a failure to explain would point to an inability to explain. . . .

It is true that, if comment were forbidden, an accused in this situation could remain silent and avoid evidence of former crimes and comment upon his failure to testify. We are of the view, however, that a state may control such a situation in accordance with its own ideas of the most efficient administration of criminal justice. The purpose of due process is not to protect an accused against a proper conviction, but against an unfair conviction. When evidence is before a jury that threatens conviction, it does not seem unfair to require him to choose between leaving the adverse evidence unexplained and subjecting himself to impeachment through disclosure of former crimes. Indeed, this is a dilemma with which any defendant may be faced. If facts adverse to the defendant are proven by the prosecution, there may be no way to explain them favorably to the accused except by a witness who may be vulnerable to impeachment on cross-examination. The defendant must then decide whether or not to use such a witness. The fact that the witness may also be the defendant makes the choice more difficult, but a denial of due process does not emerge from the circumstances.

Affirmed.

MR. JUSTICE FRANKFURTER, concurring.

Between the incorporation of the Fourteenth Amendment into the Constitution and the beginning of the present membership of the Court—a period of seventy years—the scope of that Amendment was passed upon by forty-three judges. Of all these judges, only one, who may respectfully be called an eccentric exception, ever indicated the belief that the Fourteenth Amendment was a shorthand summary of the first eight Amendments theretofore limiting only the Federal Government, and that due process incorporated those eight Amendments as restrictions upon the powers of the States. Among these judges were not only those who would have to be included among the greatest in the history of the Court, but—it is especially relevant to note—they included those whose services in the cause of human rights and the spirit of freedom are the most conspicuous in our history. . . . [T]hey were also judges mindful of the relation of our federal system to a progressively democratic society, and therefore duly regardful of the scope of authority that was left to the States even after the Civil War. And so they did not find that the Fourteenth Amendment, concerned as it was with matters fundamental to the pursuit of justice, fastened upon the States procedural arrangements which, in the language of Mr. Justice Cardozo, only those who are "narrow or provincial" would deem essential to "a fair and enlightened system of justice." To suggest that it is inconsistent with a truly free society to begin prosecutions without an indictment, to try petty civil cases without the paraphernalia of a common law jury, to take into consideration that one who has full opportunity to make a defense remains silent is, in de Tocqueville's phrase, to confound the familiar with the necessary. . . .

Indeed, the suggestion that the Fourteenth Amendment incorporates the first eight Amendments as such is not unambiguously urged. Even the boldest innovator would shrink from suggesting to more than half the States that they may no longer initiate prosecutions without indictment by grand jury, or that, thereafter, all the States of the Union must furnish a jury of twelve for every case involving a claim above twenty dollars. There is suggested merely a selective incorporation of the first eight Amendments into the Fourteenth Amendment. Some are in and some are out, but we are left in the dark as to which are in and which are out. Nor are we given the calculus for determining which go in and which stay out. If the basis of selection is merely that those provisions of the first eight Amendments are incorporated which commend themselves to individual justices as indispensable to the dignity and happiness of a free man, we are thrown back to a merely subjective test. The protection against unreasonable search and seizure might have primacy for one judge, while trial by a jury of twelve for every claim above twenty dollars might appear to another as an ultimate need in a free society. In the history of thought, "natural law" has a much longer and much better founded meaning and justification than such subjective selection of the first eight Amendments for incorporation into the Fourteenth. If all that is meant is that due process contains within itself certain minimal standards which are "of the very essence of a scheme of ordered liberty," putting upon this Court the duty of applying these standards from time to time, then we have merely arrived at the insight which our predecessors long ago expressed. . . .

It may not be amiss to restate the pervasive function of the Fourteenth Amendment in exacting from the States observance of basic liberties. The Amendment neither comprehends the specific provisions by which the founders deemed it appropriate to restrict the federal government nor is it confined to them. The Due Process Clause of the Fourteenth Amendment has an independent potency, precisely as does the Due Process Clause of the Fifth Amendment in relation to the Federal Government. It ought not to require argument to reject the notion that due process of law meant one thing in the Fifth Amendment and another in the Fourteenth. The Fifth Amendment specifically prohibits prosecution of an "infamous crime" except upon indictment; it forbids double jeopardy; it bars compelling a person to be a witness against himself in any criminal case; it precludes deprivation of "life, liberty, or property, without due process of law. . . ." Are Madison and his contemporaries in the framing of the Bill of Rights to be charged with writing into it a meaningless clause? To consider "due process of law" as merely a shorthand statement of other specific clauses in the same amendment is to attribute to the authors and proponents of this Amendment ignorance of, or indifference to, a historic conception which was one of the great instruments in the arsenal of constitutional freedom which the Bill of Rights was to protect and strengthen.

JUSTICE BLACK, with whom JUSTICE DOUGLAS joins, dissenting.

My study of the historical events that culminated in the Fourteenth Amendment, and the expressions of those who sponsored and favored, as well as those who opposed, its submission and passage persuades me that one of the chief objects that the provisions of the Amendment's first section, separately and as a whole, were intended to accomplish was to make the Bill of Rights, applicable to the states. With full knowledge of the import of the *Barron* decision, the framers and backers of the Fourteenth Amendment proclaimed its purpose to be to overturn the constitutional rule that case had announced. This historical purpose has never received full consideration or exposition in any opinion of this Court interpreting the Amendment. . . .

[T]he Court . . . again today declines . . . to appraise the relevant historical evidence of the intended scope of the first section of the Amendment. Instead, it relied upon previous cases, none of which had analyzed the evidence showing that one purpose of those who framed, advocated, and adopted the Amendment had been to make the Bill of Rights applicable to the States. None of the cases relied upon by the Court today made such an analysis. . . .

I cannot consider the Bill of Rights to be an outworn 18th Century "strait jacket," . . . Its provisions may be thought outdated abstractions by some. And it is true that they were designed to meet ancient evils. But they are the same kind of human evils that have emerged from century to century wherever excessive power is sought by the few at the expense of the many. In my judgment, the people of no nation can lose their liberty so long as a Bill of Rights like ours survives and its basic purposes are conscientiously interpreted, enforced and respected so as to afford continuous protection against old, as well as new, devices and practices which might thwart those purposes. I fear to see the consequences of the Court's practice of substituting its own concepts of decency and fundamental justice for the language of the Bill of Rights as its point of departure in interpreting and enforcing that Bill of Rights. If the choice must be between the selective process of the *Palko* decision, applying some of the Bill of Rights to the States, or the *Twining* rule, applying none of them, I would choose the *Palko* selective process. But, rather than accept either of these choices, I would follow what I believe was the original purpose of the Fourteenth Amendment—to extend to all the people of the nation the complete protection of the Bill of Rights. To hold that this Court can determine what, if any, provisions of the Bill of Rights will be enforced, and, if so, to what degree, is to frustrate the great design of a written Constitution.

MR. JUSTICE MURPHY, with whom MR. JUSTICE RUTLEDGE concurs, dissenting.

While in substantial agreement with the views of MR. JUSTICE BLACK, I have one reservation and one addition to make.

I agree that the specific guarantees of the Bill of Rights should be carried over intact into the first section of the Fourteenth Amendment. But I am not prepared to say that the latter is entirely and necessarily limited by the Bill of Rights. Occasions may arise where a proceeding falls so far short of conforming to fundamental standards of procedure as to warrant constitutional condemnation in terms

of a lack of due process despite the absence of a specific provision in the Bill of Rights.

That point, however, need not be pursued here, inasmuch as the Fifth Amendment is explicit in its provision that no person shall be compelled in any criminal case to be a witness against himself. That provision, as MR. JUSTICE BLACK demonstrates, is a constituent part of the Fourteenth Amendment.

Justice Black's position on total incorporation differed from Harlan I's in one important respect. Whereas Harlan I called for the incorporation of the entire Bill of Rights to the states through the Fourteenth Amendment, Black considered the Ninth and Tenth Amendments federalism provisions and thus not applicable beyond their structural boundaries.[53] Black's position also differed from that of his dissenting colleagues in *Adamson,* Justices Murphy and Rutledge, who believed that the Fourteenth Amendment also incorporated other "fundamental" rights not specifically set out in the Bill of Rights. As we saw in Chapter 2, Black's dissenting opinion in *Griswold* v. *Connecticut* (1965) made clear his rejection of the idea that the Bill of Rights protected rights not enumerated in the text. After *Adamson,* the Court continued to apply the Bill of Rights to the states on a selected basis. Although the Court never again returned to a serious discussion of the history and intent of the Framers of the Fourteenth Amendment, by the late 1960s it had incorporated almost the entire Bill of Rights to the states. Black, much more so than Frankfurter and Cardozo, had emerged triumphant on the Fourteenth Amendment in practice, if not in theory. Moreover, the Court had also quietly incorporated the Equal Protection Clause of the Fourteenth Amendment into the Fifth Amendment (which contains no equal protection clause), ruling that Congress could not deny to persons in their capacity as citizens of the United States rights to which they were entitled in the states.

After the Rights Revolution

Organized interests played a crucial role in bringing several of the key cases that resulted in the application of the provisions of the Bill of Rights to the states, and also in encouraging the Court to adopt a much more expansive view of civil rights and liberties. During the 1960s and 1970s, groups such as the ACLU, the American Jewish Congress, Americans United for Separation of Church and State, the NAACP, the National Organization for Women, and Planned Parenthood brought dozens of cases that dramatically expanded the constitutional rights of American citizens. The "rights revolution" in American constitutional law, as many scholars have described the period from the New Deal through early 1980s, painted across the broad canvas of civil rights and liberties, and dramatically altered the relationship between minority rights and majority power under the American Constitution. Moreover, Congress continued to build upon the principles of the New Deal by expanding federal authority to regulate the environment, institute stringent occupational safety and health rules, and expand the legal rights of employees under federal civil rights law.[54] The landmark cases that resulted in these dramatic changes in the Bill of Rights and other areas involving civil rights and liberties and the role that organized interests played in this process are discussed in later chapters in this volume.

The nationalization and expansion of the guarantees of the Bill of Rights has not been without controversy. While some scholars continue to challenge the notion that the Fourteenth Amendment incorporates the Bill of Rights to the states, most of the contemporary debate has concerned the Court's interpretation of the substantive rights and liberties guaranteed to individuals. In response to the success that liberal organizations had in using litigation to transform the Bill of Rights during the 1940s, 1950s, and 1960s, a number of conservative groups expanded their advocacy strategies to include litigation and founded public interest law firms of their own. Since the early 1980s, groups such as the American Center for Law and Justice, the Beckett Fund, the Center for Individual Rights, National Right to Life Committee, the Pacific Legal Foundation, and the Washington Legal Foundation have turned to the courts with great success.[55] At the cusp of the new millennium, Supreme Court litigation politics is more complex, group driven, and ideologically diverse than ever before. The remainder of this volume will provide you with a window into the social and political dynamics that drive the current debate over the meaning and application of the Bill of Rights.

FOR FURTHER READING

Amar, Akhil Reed. *The Bill of Rights: Creation and Reconstruction*. New Haven, Conn.: Yale University Press, 1998.

Berger, Raoul. *Government by Judiciary: The Transformation of the Fourteenth Amendment*. Cambridge, Mass.: Harvard University Press, 1977.

Casper, Jonathan D. *Lawyers before the Warren Court*. Urbana, Ill.: University of Illinois Press, 1973.

Cortner, Richard C. *The Supreme Court and the Second Bill of Rights*. Madison: University of Wisconsin Press, 1981.

Curtis, Michael Kent. *No State Shall Abridge: The Fourteenth Amendment and the Bill of Rights*. Durham, N.C.: Duke University Press, 1990.

Epp, Charles. *The Rights Revolution: Lawyers, Activists, and Supreme Courts in Comparative Perspective*. Chicago: University of Chicago Press, 1998.

Fairman, Charles. "Does the Fourteenth Amendment Incorporate the Bill of Rights?" *Stanford Law Review* 2 (1949): 5.

Glendon, Mary Ann. *Rights Talk*. New York: Free Press, 1991.

Hickok, Eugene W., ed. *The Bill of Rights: Original Meaning and Current Understanding*. Charlottesville: University Press of Virginia, 1991.

Kyvig, David E. *Explicit and Authentic Acts: Amending the U.S. Constitution, 1776–1995*. Lawrence: University Press of Kansas, 1995.

Maltz, Eric M. *Civil Rights, the Constitution, and Congress, 1863–1869*. Lawrence: University Press of Kansas, 1990.

Nelson, Michael. *The Fourteenth Amendment: From Political Principle to Judicial Doctrine*. Cambridge, Mass.: Harvard University Press, 1988.

McCann, Michael W. *Rights at Work*. Chicago: University of Chicago Press, 1994.

Powe, Lucas A. Jr. *The Warren Court and American Politics*. Cambridge, Mass.: Harvard University Press, 2000.

Scheingold, Stuart A. *The Politics of Rights*. New Haven, Conn.: Yale University Press, 1974.

tenBroek, Jacobus. *The Antislavery Origins of the Fourteenth Amendment*. Berkeley: University of California Press, 1951.

Vose, Clement E. *Constitutional Change: Amendment Politics and Supreme Court Litigation Since 1900*. Lexington, Mass.: Lexington Books, 1972.

Walker, Samuel. *The Rights Revolution: Rights and Community in Modern America*. New York: Oxford University Press, 1998.

Freedom of Speech, Assembly, and Association

By late 1965, Americans no longer had to wonder if President Lyndon Johnson's decision to commit United States armed forces to Vietnam had crossed the threshold from military assistance to full-fledged war. Film footage on the evening news programs—remember, these were the days before around-the-clock cable and Internet news updates—brought home the bombing in graphic detail. For the first time, the American public was watching a war on television as it unfolded, with all its bloody carnage. A sizable number of Americans began to question openly whether the United States had any business taking sides in the civil war of a faraway and unfamiliar nation. In early November, the United States had reported its highest weekly death toll since 1961, when the nation had entered the battlefield in Vietnam. Over one thousand military personnel had now been lost to combat. With 170,000 soldiers stationed in Vietnam by the end of December and more on the way, the death toll was only going to increase. Ultimately, approximately 58,000 American soldiers were reported dead or missing-in-action by the time the United States left Vietnam in 1975.[1]

As the war in Vietnam intensified, so did public protest against it at home. Americans were now taking to the streets to express their disdain for the Johnson administration's policies. On college campuses, some students staged draft-card burnings to symbolize their opposition to the war; professors canceled their regular classes to stage "teach-ins" about United States policy toward Vietnam; and antiwar speakers began making public appearances to encourage students to take action against the war. Protesters also came to Washington, D.C., to stage antiwar demonstrations on the Mall. The nation's capital had always drawn protesters, from slavery abolitionists in the early 1800s to the nation's army of unemployed during the Great Depression of the 1930s. What made the emerging protest movement against the Vietnam War so unusual was that it comprised, at least initially, the nation's white, well-educated middle-class. Just such an assembly gathered for the first major anti-Vietnam demonstration in Washington in November 1965. Over 25,000 people, drawn from 140 different groups, many with religious affiliations, gathered on the Mall to encourage a peaceful end to the Vietnam War. Compared to the increasingly confrontational and, at times, violent demonstrations that characterized anti-Vietnam sentiment by the late 1960s, the 1965 march was peaceful, relaxed, and polite.[2]

Among the protesters were John Tinker and Christopher Eckhardt, both teenagers who attended high school in Des Moines, Iowa. Both boys' parents were active in local peace and social justice causes, and had arranged, through the American Friends Service Committee (a Quaker-sponsored group) and the Women's International League for Peace, for buses for approximately fifty Iowans to travel to the November 1965 march. On the trip back to Des Moines, Tinker and Eckhardt decided they needed to express, in peaceful fashion, their opposition to the Vietnam War. About twenty-five high school and college students and their parents met at the Eckhardts' home over an early December weekend to discuss plans for a protest, and a consensus soon emerged:

The students would wear black arm bands adorned by a white peace symbol to their classes.

Local high school administrators soon learned of the impending protest, and made clear that they would consider any student wearing an arm band to be in violation of school policies banning such "disruptions" of the normal school day. Upon hearing the school announce its "zero-tolerance" policy toward the anti-Vietnam arm bands, one student responded: "What a joke! Only last year we were all asked to wear black arm bands to mourn the loss of school spirit at basketball games. Even a black coffin was marched through the halls! Nobody was afraid of that disrupting the educational process." Students at Des Moines high schools heard countless warnings from teachers and administrators that wearing the arm bands would be treated as a violation of school policy. No consequences were announced, but the assumption was that any punishment would involve a mild suspension. Physical violence also loomed from students who supported the Vietnam War. During a Friday afternoon gym class, Christopher Eckhardt went through his exercises watching his classmates glare at him while shouting, "Beat the Vietcong." His teachers and the school's coaches made it known that they could not be held responsible for what angry students might do to their classmates who demonstrated such a "lack of patriotism."

On December 16 and 17, 1965, somewhere between twenty-five and fifty students wore black arm bands adorned with the peace symbol to school. Some removed their arm bands after other students threatened them, some went unreported by teachers who decided that the students were entitled to their say, and some were sent to the principal's office and, subsequently, home. In the end, only five students were disciplined for wearing their arm bands. A week later, the Iowa Civil Liberties Union (ICLU), an affiliate of the national ACLU, approached the students about challenging their suspensions as an abridgement of their right to freedom of speech under the First Amendment. Christopher Eckhardt, John Tinker, and his younger sister, Mary Beth, a thirteen-year-old eighth grader who wore a black arm band to her middle school, agreed to serve as plaintiffs in what became a landmark constitutional decision. Four years later, the United States Supreme Court, in *Tinker* v. *Des Moines* (1969), vindicated their right to wear their arm bands to school as "symbolic" speech protected by the First Amendment. Writing for the Court, Justice Abe Fortas held that, "First Amendment rights, applied in light of the special characteristics of the school environment, are available to teachers and students. It can hardly be argued that either students or teachers shed their constitutional rights at the schoolhouse gate. This has been the unmistakable holding of this Court for almost fifty years."[3]

By the time the Court decided *Tinker,* Christopher Eckhardt and John Tinker were in college, and Mary Beth Tinker was a high school senior living in St. Louis, where her father's work in the Methodist Church had taken them shortly after the lawsuit was underway. But their victory in the Supreme Court had an impact far beyond their right to wear arm bands to school in December 1965. Dan Johnston, the ICLU attorney who argued *Tinker* before the Court, later commented that the "Arm band Case . . . opened the public schools and colleges to antiwar organizing . . . and was a major factor in bringing the Vietnam War to an end."[4] In fairness, *Tinker* may not have had a direct relationship in leading the United States to withdraw from Vietnam. But the decision did offer a powerful lesson of what happens when social and political forces combine to challenge the legal status quo, and the key role that organized interests can play in driving the dynamics of constitutional litigation.

This chapter will examine the struggles over the meaning of free speech under the First Amendment. Most certainly, constitutional law is not immune from the social and political context in which it develops. Accordingly, the rights of Americans to believe and say what they want, to take their case to the streets, and to challenge some of the most fundamentally held beliefs about their nation's founding principles have undergone constant change since the ratification of the First Amendment in 1791. Beginning in the early 1920s, organized interests began to assume a central role in standing up for the rights of political dissenters. How groups have helped to transform the Free Speech Clause from one that protects "pure speech" to one that insulates a broad range of "expressive activities" from government suppression is another major theme of this chapter.

Did the Framers Believe in Free Speech?

Is this even a fair question? Constitutional historians and other scholars of the Founding period are in general agreement that the Framers did support the idea of freedom of speech. However, they diverge on the degree to which individuals were permitted to challenge the dominant social, political, and, in some cases, religious sentiments of the day free from government retribution. Contemporary discussion of freedom of speech often assumes that the libertarian tradition stems from the late 1700s, especially after the American colonies declared their independence from Great Britain, and was embodied by the ratification of the First Amendment in 1791. In truth, freedom of speech, as the term is understood now, was relatively unknown in America until the Founding period. Until then, freedom of speech was a parliamentary right allowing legislators to speak or debate in their official capacities without punishment. Freedom of speech as an individual right did not develop until later, and only after the newly established American states were secure enough to accept differences of opinion among their fellow citizens. In 1776, Pennsylvania inserted a provision protecting freedom of speech into its state Declaration of Rights, making it the only state to have such protection before the First Amendment was ratified fifteen years later.[5]

The First Amendment did not, however, secure an unfettered national right to freedom of speech. As discussed in Chapter 3, the Bill of Rights spoke as much to the structural concerns of the Framers about the distribution of power between the national government and the states as it did the substance and scope of the rights and liberties it secured. So, while Congress could not abridge the freedom of speech, it was not uncommon for states to limit political dissent, just as they limited freedom of the press and freedom of religion. Indeed, one of the distinct features of the American federal structure was that it allowed the states, free from congressional control, to tailor their laws to the tastes and prejudices of local communities. Although modern free speech law is dominated by a libertarian philosophy strongly protective of unpopular expression, the First Amendment initially offered greater protection to political majorities in the states than it did to individuals professing unorthodox views. Truthful speech was certainly protected, and truth was generally understood as conformity to majority opinion.[6]

A major turning point in the meaning of free speech came in 1798, when Congress enacted the Alien and Sedition Acts. By punishing any "false, scandalous, and malicious" commentary against the national government, Congress stepped across both the structural and substantive barriers of the First Amendment by placing a content-based restriction on freedom of expression. As discussed in greater detail in Chapter 5, the Sedition Act was motivated by the Federalists' desire to silence the Jeffersonian Republicans, who had become increasingly vocal in their criticism of Federalist President John Adams and his policies abroad. So unpopular was the Sedition Act in the states that voters rallied to the polls in 1800 to turn out Adams and replace him with Thomas Jefferson. Ironically, Jefferson had never opposed the law of seditious libel, which permitted state governments to punish individual citizens for political dissent. His views on freedom of speech and press, although certainly more libertarian than many of his contemporaries, were consistent with the generally accepted notion that personal liberty did not extend to "criminal acts" against the government.[7]

The Sedition Act expired in 1801, was not renewed, and Congress never again passed a law making *general* criticism of the government a crime. Although Jefferson believed the Sedition Act was unconstitutional and later pardoned anyone convicted under the law, he continued to support the selective prosecution of political opponents under state seditious libel laws. In an 1804 letter to Abigail Adams, the wife of President Adams, Jefferson wrote that the unconstitutionality of the Sedition Act did not "remove all restraint from the overwhelming torrent of slander which is confounding all vice and virtue, all truth and falsehood in the U.S. The power to do that is fully possessed by the several state legislatures. . . . While we deny that Congress ha[s] a right to control the freedom of the press, we have ever asserted the right of the states, and their exclusive right to do so."[8]

Conversely, James Madison, who had been Jefferson's key political ally since the ratification period of the Constitution, was much more unnerved by the nation's experience with the Sedition Act than was Jefferson. Along with several other important writers of the early 1800s, Madison became part of a small but influential circle of thinkers advocating a more libertarian conception of freedom of speech. Granted, the states did not drop their seditious libel laws immediately, nor did they wholly discount the embedded notion that government should have some control over speech that encouraged criminal conduct or flouted societal norms of decency. Here, as elsewhere in early American constitutional theory, Madison's voice rose above the rest. For Madison, free speech became much more than a rhetorical flourish. Free thought and exchange became essential to the health of democratic institutions and the principle of self-government. Again, Madison's early commitment to what later became known as the *marketplace model* of free speech—that government should stand back and allow "government by discussion" to flourish, with ideas rising or falling on their own merits—was not without constraints.[9] But, the absolute phrasing of the First Amendment notwithstanding, no one in Madison's generation believed that all expression was necessarily speech that deserved legal protection, or that even "pure" speech—speech that consisted solely of words and not conduct—should receive absolute protection by law. In this sense, the Court's modern understanding of protection for political speech, as we shall see later in this chapter, is consistent with that of Madison and his more libertarian-minded contemporaries of the early Republic.

While the views of Madison and his contemporaries are certainly essential to understanding the baseline conception of the free speech guarantee, the historical record is only so useful in helping us understand how the meaning of the First Amendment has developed over time. During the nineteenth century, several theories of free speech began to emerge from law professors, jurists, and others who believed that the free flow of ideas and information allowed individuals to progress and realize their full potential. Political scientist Mark Graber has noted that many of these early free speech theorists, consistent with their economic libertarianism, also endorsed a minimal role for government in regulating commercial conduct and private property. This libertarian conservatism constituted the first major movement to bring protection for free speech beyond the narrow definition of politics to include virtually any idea that promoted self-fulfillment.[10] Legal protection for such a theory, however, did not follow.

In the early 1900s, libertarian theory advanced again, this time under the auspices of the nation's emergent Progressive movement. Rather than view broad rights of freedom of expression in the strictly individual sense, progressive libertarian thought stressed the contribution that free speech could make to social and public affairs. Consistent with the skepticism voiced by Oliver Wendell Holmes Jr. in *The Common Law* (1881) (see Chapter 2) toward legal formalism, which emphasized tradition in legal understanding, the progressives encouraged a philosophy of free speech that went beyond the social and cultural confines of previous generations. The most influential voice among these new libertarians was that of Zechariah Chafee, who believed that any modern system of freedom of expression must derive from contemporary social and political conditions. Changing circumstances altered the terms for open discussion, and neither the structural nor the substantive protections offered by the Framers' First Amendment were sufficient for the modern era.[11] Chafee's libertarian philosophy was enormously influential on the Court's two earliest defenders of modern free speech principles, Oliver Wendell Holmes and Louis Brandeis, both of whom ultimately abandoned their early support for government suppression of political dissent in favor of an expansive libertarianism. Holmes and Brandeis, although guided by very different concerns, offered an early blueprint for the Court's eventual embrace of a more decidedly libertarian approach to free speech in the 1960s.

These two strains of libertarian free speech theory that emerged in the late nineteenth and early twentieth centuries have proven especially resilient in the Court's modern construction of First Amendment free speech doctrine. Today, debate over whether to shield sexually explicit materials, hate speech, and other controversial expression from government control often turns on whether the material or speech in question is considered socially or politically valuable and thus deserving of constitutional protection. This *instrumental* theory of free speech stands in contrast to the libertarian approach, popular among groups like the ACLU, which comes as close as anyone ever has to defending an *absolutist* theory of free speech. The absolutist approach endorses the intrinsic value of free speech, unrelated to any purpose other than to affirm individual liberty in a democratic society. Throughout the cases and materials in this chapter, you will have plenty of opportunities to see the synthesis of history and theory that has guided the Court's approach to the free speech guarantee.

War at Home, Enemies Abroad: Establishing the Early Limits on Political Dissent

On February 26, 1917, a German submarine patrolling the Atlantic Ocean in search of British and American merchant boats sank the luxury liner *Laconia,* killing two American passengers. This was no accident. From the outset of World War I (1914–1918), pausing only for a brief interlude in late 1916 and early 1917, the German Navy had made commercial ships military targets of its vastly superior fleet of submarines, or "U-boats" as they were known. The Germans had decided to resume attacks on ships carrying commercial goods because they believed such a strategy would bring the British, French, and Italian economies to their knees, forcing surrender. But the attack on the *Laconia,* coupled with a German U-boat attack on three American commercial ships two weeks later, led President Woodrow Wilson to ask Congress on April 2 to declare war on Germany. Less than a week later, the United States was formally at war with Germany, Austria-Hungary, Turkey, and Bulgaria.

Until then, President Wilson had no desire to enter the United States in World War I, which most Americans viewed as a large-scale European civil war. The German U-boat campaign against British merchant vessels in 1915 had been brought to a close after Wilson warned that he would enlist the United States Navy to protect commercial travel on the high seas. Beyond this passing threat, Wilson, high-minded and academic by nature, continued to press for a negotiated solution to the war. Moreover, Americans had demonstrated little enthusiasm to enter World War I, a sentiment that was especially strong among the European ethnic groups that had immigrated to the United States in the late 1800s and early 1900s. Smaller peace groups, many of which were affiliated with churches and humanist societies, voiced their opposition to America's entry into the war and encouraged young men to resist the call to arms. At home, Wilson considered the Socialist Party a greater threat to American domestic tranquility than the German Kaiser because of the party's increasingly visible role in labor organizing and criticism of American business practices.[12]

Nonetheless, once the Wilson administration entered World War I, it did so with full force. In May 1917, Congress enacted its first military conscription law since the Civil War to bolster America's standing army, which stood at approximately 110,000. In contrast, the British and French had already lost nearly 2 million men to combat by the time the United States sent its first troops to Europe in June 1917. To force obedience to the draft, Congress enacted the Espionage Act of 1917, which made it illegal to "interfere with the operation or success of the military or naval forces of the United States . . . [that] will cause or attempt to cause insubordination, disloyalty, mutiny, or refusal of duty in the military or naval forces of the United States, or shall wilfully obstruct the recruiting or enlistment services of the United States." Congress clearly intended to quash any criticism of the government's wartime policies by drafting a law that so broadly threatened critics and potential draft resisters. Said Attorney General Thomas Gregory: "May God have mercy on them [draft resisters], for they need expect none from an outraged people and an avenging government." Even after President Wilson presented his case for American entrance in World War I, draft-eligible men had not hurried down to local military recruiting centers, and the war's opponents had become even more vocal. Military officers were reporting that those men who reported for induction did so reluctantly, many of whom claimed health or religious exemptions. By November 1918, when World War I ended, government authorities had classified over 330,000 American men as draft evaders, just over 10 percent of those who reported for duty.[13]

Initial efforts to prosecute dissenters under the Espionage Act proved less than successful, as government lawyers frequently encountered judges and juries who were unwilling to convict individuals they believed were not involved in any conspiracy, but who were simply expressing their beliefs and opinions on America's role in World War I. Congress responded by passing the Sedition Act of 1918, which made illegal "any disloyal . . . scurrilous, abusive language intended to bring the form of government of the United States . . . into contempt, scorn . . . or disrepute." As discussed earlier in this chapter, sedition laws have a longer and more ignoble history than many Americans like to admit, but what made the 1918 law different from its predecessors was the zeal with which federal prosecutors went after political dissenters during and after World War I. No doubt, the Russian Revolution of 1917 and the support it received from the fledgling American labor movement simply added to the government's decision to crack down on dissenters. Such was the environment when the Court, in *Schenck* v. *United States* (1919), handed down its first-ever decision on the meaning of the Free Speech Clause of the First Amendment.

Schenck v. *United States*

249 U.S. 47 (1919)

On August 13, 1917, members of the Socialist Party in Philadelphia gathered in a small building near Independence Hall, the birthplace of the American Constitution, for their monthly meeting. Their main order of business was to discuss publicizing the Socialist Party's opposition to the military draft instituted by Congress in May 1917. As was common during World War I, local newspapers published the names of men who had been drafted and had passed their physical examinations. These were the men whom Charles J. Schenck wanted to reach. Party members quickly agreed on language for a leaflet denouncing the draft and discouraging registration. Brandishing the bold headline "LONG LIVE THE CONSTITUTION OF THE UNITED STATES," the leaflet said that "A conscript is little better than a convict. He is deprived of his liberty and of his right to think and act as a free man." Continuing, the leaflet implored readers "not [to] submit to intimidation. Exercise your rights of free speech, peaceful assemblage and petitioning the government for a redress of grievances. Come to the headquarters of the Socialist Party, 1326 Arch Street, and sign a petition to Congress for the repeal of the Conscription Act."

Federal agents arrived at Socialist Party headquarters before any potential draft resisters did. Schenck and four other members of the executive committee were charged, under the Espionage Act of 1917, with conspiring to "obstruct the recruiting and enlistment services of the United States." A federal district court dismissed the charges against three executive committee members, but found Schenck and another party official, Elizabeth Baer, guilty. Schenck and Baer appealed directly to the Supreme Court. By the time the justices heard their case in January 1919, World War I was over and the draft had been shelved.[14]

The Court's decision was unanimous. Justice Holmes delivered the opinion of the Court.

MR. JUSTICE HOLMES delivered the opinion of the Court.

The document in question, upon its first printed side, recited the first section of the Thirteenth Amendment, said that the idea embodied in it was violated by the Conscription Act, and that a conscript is little better than a convict. In impassioned language, it intimated that conscription was despotism in its worst form, and a monstrous wrong against humanity in the interest of Wall Street's chosen few. It said "Do not submit to intimidation," but in form, at least, confined itself to peaceful measures such as a petition for the repeal of the act. The other and later printed side of the sheet was headed "Assert Your Rights." It stated reasons for alleging that anyone violated the Constitution when he refused to recognize "your right to assert your opposition to the draft," and went on, "If you do not assert and support your rights, you are helping to deny or disparage rights which it is the solemn duty of all citizens and residents of the United States to retain." It described the arguments on the other side as coming from cunning politicians and a mercenary capitalist press, and even silent consent to the conscription law as helping to support an infamous conspiracy. It denied the power to send our citizens away to foreign shores to shoot up the people of other lands, and added that words could not express the condemnation such cold-blooded ruthlessness deserves, &c., &c., winding up, "You must do your share to maintain, support and uphold the rights of the people of this country." Of course, the document would not have been sent unless it had been intended to have some effect, and we do not see what effect it could be expected to have upon persons subject to the draft except to influence them to obstruct the carrying of it out. The defendants do not deny that the jury might find against them on this point.

But it is said, suppose that that was the tendency of this circular, it is protected by the First Amendment to the Constitution. Two of the strongest expressions are said to be quoted respectively from well known public men. It

well may be that the prohibition of laws abridging the freedom of speech is not confined to previous restraints, although to prevent them may have been the main purpose. . . . We admit that, in many places and in ordinary times, the defendants, in saying all that was said in the circular, would have been within their constitutional rights. But the character of every act depends upon the circumstances in which it is done. The most stringent protection of free speech would not protect a man in falsely shouting fire in a theatre and causing a panic. It does not even protect a man from an injunction against uttering words that may have all the effect of force. The question in every case is whether the words used are used in such circumstances and are of such a nature as to create a clear and present danger that they will bring about the substantive evils that Congress has a right to prevent. It is a question of proximity and degree. When a nation is at war, many things that might be said in time of peace are such a hindrance to its effort that their utterance will not be endured so long as men fight, and that no Court could regard them as protected by any constitutional right. It seems to be admitted that, if an actual obstruction of the recruiting service were proved, liability for words that produced that effect might be enforced. The statute of 1917, in § 4, punishes conspiracies to obstruct, as well as actual obstruction. If the act (speaking, or circulating a paper), its tendency, and the intent with which it is done are the same, we perceive no ground for saying that success alone warrants making the act a crime. . . . But, as the right to free speech was not referred to specially, we have thought fit to add a few words.

Judgments affirmed.

▼▲▼

For his introduction of the *clear and present danger* test ("whether the words used are used in such circumstances and are of such a nature as to create a clear and present danger that they will bring about the substantive evils that Congress has a right to prevent"), supported by a succinct metaphor to explain its application ("[t]he most stringent protection of free speech would not protect a man in falsely shouting fire in a theatre"), *Schenck* is one of Justice Holmes's most famous opinions. But unlike his equally famous, though dissenting, opinions, in *Lochner* v. *New York* (1905) (Volume I, Chapter 9) and *Abrams* v. *United States* (1919), discussed next, *Schenck* has not held up well over time. Indeed, many First Amendment scholars argue that Holmes's "clear and present" danger test, while an admirable turn of phrase, instilled in the government far too much power to punish speech that it did not like. Charles Schenck was not punished because his call to resist the draft actually obstructed the conscription process. Rather, Holmes sustained his conviction because his words were thought to have a *tendency* to produce that effect. A clear and present danger suggests immediacy, or, in Holmes's words, a "question of proximity and degree." A *bad tendency,* on the other hand, offers no such timetable.[15]

A few days after *Schenck,* the Court announced two more unanimous decisions affirming the convictions of political dissenters. In *Frohwerk* v. *United States* (1919), the Court upheld the conviction of an editorial writer for a German-language newspaper, the *Staats Zeitung,* who had written several pieces critical of America's intervention in World War I. Although Holmes noted that Frohwerk had condemned antidraft riots in Oklahoma and violence elsewhere toward the American government, he nonetheless concluded that conspiracies begin by "words of persuasion."[16] Nowhere in *Frohwerk* did Holmes mention the clear and present danger test; it was simply enough that this foreign-language paper with a tiny circulation "might" kindle the flame of unlawful action.

The Court's hostility to political dissenters was further borne out in *Debs* v. *United States* (1919), in which Holmes upheld the government's prosecution of the well-known American labor leader Eugene Debs. As the founder of the Socialist Party of America, Debs had also run for president four times between 1900 and 1920.[17] Debs first came to national attention in the 1890s, when he led strikes against the Great Northern Railroad and the Pullman Palace Car Company. These strikes were well-received by laborers across the country and did much to encourage America's growing unionization movement in the 1910s and 1920s. In *In re Debs* (1895), the Court upheld a criminal contempt conviction against Debs for his refusal to end the Pullman strike, which had attracted support from other unions around the country.[18] With railroad travel brought to a standstill, the Department of Justice, invoking the federal government's power to regulate interstate commerce, responded to pleas from railroad executives and ordered an end to the strike.[19]

Debs went to prison a Democrat and came out a socialist. He spent the remainder of his life promoting workers' rights and campaigning against global conflict. He delivered the speech that earned him his second trip to the Court in Canton, Ohio. Speaking to a large assembly, Debs said that "the master class has always declared the war and the subject class has always fought the battles [and] furnish[ed] the corpses. . . . You need to know that you are fit for something better than slavery and cannon fodder." Holmes sustained Debs's conviction, and again relied on the bad tendency test, concluding that the "one purpose of the speech, whether incidental or not does not matter, was to oppose not only war in general but this war. . . . [I]ts natural and intended effect would be to obstruct recruiting."[20] In 1920, Debs garnered 915,000 votes for president while serving his prison term.[21]

Debs is notable for the negative mark it left on the Court's First Amendment jurisprudence and for the crisis of conscience it appeared to arouse in Justice Holmes. Although Holmes sent Debs to prison without apparent reservation, the case led him to doubt the premises of his thoughts on free speech. Why Holmes converted so suddenly remains a mystery. Some scholars have suggested that Holmes was stung by the criticism he received from men he considered his intellectual equals, such as the First Amendment scholar Zechariah Chafee, whose libertarian approach to free speech would weigh greatly on the justice's future such opinions.[22] Then there is Holmes's own well-known distrust of legal absolutes, an intellectual trait that shaped the legal realist movement of which he was a prominent member. As First Amendment scholar Rodney Smolla has commented: "In the course of a few short months, [Holmes] underwent a spectacular conversion experience. It was if some angel of free speech had appeared to Holmes in the night."[23]

In *Abrams* v. *United States*, the next major protest case decided by the Court, Holmes penned one of his truly great dissents, introducing the metaphor of the "marketplace of ideas" into the modern lexicon of free speech thought.[24] Ironically, the Court's majority opinion, which Holmes heavily criticized, was drawn directly from the bad tendency analysis of his *Frohwerk* and *Debs* opinions.

Abrams v. *United States*

250 U.S. 616 (1919)

By the turn of the twentieth century, the Lower East Side of Manhattan in New York City was home to thousands of Russian Jews who had come to America to escape the anti-Semitism and frequent murderous rampages of the czarist government in their mother country. Openly sympathetic to the Bolshevik revolutionaries who came to power in October 1917 with their new Communist regime, many Russian Jews worked diligently, but secretly, to promote a socialist revolution in United States. They were often openly critical of the United States war effort, and especially President Wilson's decision to send 7,500 troops to eastern Russia, a decision they viewed as an intimidation of the Bolshevik government.

On August 22, 1918, anyone walking down Second Avenue near Eighth Street in lower Manhattan in the early evening would have noticed leaflets cascading from the rooftops. The leaflets were printed in English and Yiddish, and featured the headline "THE HYPOCRISY OF THE UNITED STATES AND HER ALLIES." Concerned citizens brought copies of the leaflets to the police, who conducted house-to-house searches in the area, but found no suspects for the leaflets' disbursement.

The next morning, however, police received a tip, leading them to the American Hat Company, where Hyman Rosansky worked as a hat presser. Rosansky, an admitted radical, told police that a man named Hyman Lychowsky had given him the leaflets and told him to throw them out the windows. That evening, Rosansky was scheduled to meet Lychowsky and several others to receive more leaflets. Police and military personnel staked out the exchange, and subsequently arrested Jacob Abrams, Hyman Lychowsky, Samuel Lipman, Jacob Schwartz, and Mollie Steimer for violating the Sedition Act of 1918. The *New York World* described all five detained Russians as "long-haired anarchists."

The English version of the leaflet exhorted "workers of America, workers of Germany" to be "AWAKE!" to their government's efforts to bring down the Russian Revolution, which gave birth to the Soviet Union. But the Yiddish version said, "Workers, Wake Up!" and appealed to men and women toiling in the munitions factories "producing bullets, bayonets, cannon, to murder not only the Germans, but also your dearest, best, who are in Russia and are fighting for freedom." The Yiddish leaflet also counseled workers, "Workers, our reply to the barbaric intervention has to be a general strike!" There was only one problem with this strategy. In 1918, factories in lower Manhattan were making clothes, shoes, buttons, and hats—not guns. A federal district court nonetheless found Abrams and his colleagues—except Joseph Schwartz, who had died in prison the night before the trial began—guilty of violating federal law.[25]

The Court's decision was 7 to 2. Justice Clarke delivered the opinion of the Court. Justice Holmes, joined by Justice Brandeis, dissented.

▼▲▼

MR. JUSTICE CLARKE delivered the opinion of the Court.

. . . [I]t is argued, somewhat faintly, that the acts charged against the defendants were not unlawful because within the protection of that freedom of speech and of the press which is guaranteed by the First Amendment to the Constitution of the United States, and that the entire Espionage Act is unconstitutional because in conflict with that Amendment. . . .

It will not do to say, as is now argued, that the only intent of these defendants was to prevent injury to the Russian cause. Men must be held to have intended, and to be accountable for, the effects which their acts were likely to produce. Even if their primary purpose and intent was to aid the cause of the Russian Revolution, the plan of action which they adopted necessarily involved, before it could be realized, defeat of the war program of the United States, for the obvious effect of this appeal, if it should become effective, as they hoped it might, would be to persuade persons of character such as those whom they regarded themselves as addressing, not to aid government loans, and not to work in ammunition factories where their work would produce "bullets, bayonets, cannon" and other munitions of war the use of which would cause the "murder" of Germans and Russians. . . .

This is not an attempt to bring about a change of administration by candid discussion, for, no matter what may have incited the outbreak on the part of the defendant anarchists, the manifest purpose of such a publication was to create an attempt to defeat the war plans of the Government of the United States by bringing upon the country the paralysis of a general strike, thereby arresting the production of all munitions and other things essential to the conduct of the war. . . .

That the interpretation we have put upon these articles, circulated in the greatest port of our land, from which great numbers of soldiers were at the time taking ship daily, and in which great quantities of war supplies of every kind were at the time being manufactured for transportation overseas, is not only the fair interpretation of them, but that it is the meaning which their authors consciously intended should be conveyed by them to others is further shown by the additional writings found in the meeting place of the defendant group and on the person of one of them. . . .

These excerpts sufficiently show that, while the immediate occasion for this particular outbreak of lawlessness on the part of the defendant alien anarchists may have been resentment caused by our Government's sending troops into Russia as a strategic operation against the Germans on the eastern battle front, yet the plain purpose of their propaganda was to excite, at the supreme crisis of the war, disaffection, sedition, riots, and, as they hoped, revolution, in this country for the purpose of embarrassing, and, if possible, defeating the military plans of the Government in Europe. A technical distinction may perhaps be taken between disloyal and abusive language applied to the *form* of our government or language intended to bring the *form* of our government into contempt and disrepute, and language of like character and intended to produce like results directed against the President and Congress, the agencies through which that form of government must function in time of war. But it is not necessary to a decision of this case to consider whether such distinction is vital or merely formal, for the language of these circulars was obviously intended to provoke and to encourage resistance to the United States in the war, as the third count runs, and the defendants, in terms, plainly urged and advocated a resort to a general strike of workers in ammunition factories for the purpose of curtailing the production of ordnance and munitions necessary and essential to the prosecution of the war as is charged in the fourth count. Thus, it is clear not only that some evidence, but that much persuasive evidence, was before the jury tending to prove that the defendants were guilty as charged in both the third and fourth counts of the indictment, and, under the long established rule of law hereinbefore stated, the judgment of the District Court must be

Affirmed.

MR. JUSTICE HOLMES dissenting.

I never have seen any reason to doubt that the questions of law that alone were before this Court in the cases of *Schenck, Frohwerk* and *Debs,* were rightly decided. I do not doubt for a moment that, by the same reasoning that would justify punishing persuasion to murder, the United States constitutionally may punish speech that produces or is intended to produce a clear and imminent danger that it will bring about forthwith certain substantive evils that the United States constitutionally may seek to prevent. The power undoubtedly is greater in time of war than in time of peace, because war opens dangers that do not exist at other times.

But, as against dangers peculiar to war, as against others, the principle of the right to free speech is always the same. It is only the present danger of immediate evil or an intent to bring it about that warrants Congress in setting a limit to the expression of opinion where private rights are not concerned. Congress certainly cannot forbid all effort to change the mind of the country. Now nobody can suppose that the surreptitious publishing of a silly leaflet by an unknown man, without more, would present any immediate danger that its opinions would hinder the success of the government arms or have any appreciable tendency to do so. Publishing those opinions for the very purpose of obstructing, however, might indicate a greater danger, and, at any rate, would have the quality of an attempt. So I assume that the second leaflet, if published for the purposes alleged in the fourth count, might be punishable. But it seems pretty clear to me that nothing less than that would bring these papers within the scope of this law. An actual intent in the sense that I have explained is necessary to constitute an attempt, where a further act of the same individual is required to complete the substantive crime. . . . It is necessary where the success of the attempt depends upon others because, if that intent is not present, the actor's aim may be accomplished without bringing about the evils sought to be checked. An intent to prevent interference with the revolution in Russia might have been satisfied without any hindrance to carrying on the war in which we were engaged.

I do not see how anyone can find the intent required by the statute in any of the defendants' words. The second leaflet is the only one that affords even a foundation for the charge, and there, without invoking the hatred of German militarism expressed in the former one, it is evident from the beginning to the end that the only object of the paper is to help Russia and stop American intervention there against the popular government—not to impede the United States in the war that it was carrying on. To say that two phrases, taken literally, might import a suggestion of conduct that would have interference with the war as an indirect and probably undesired effect seems to me by no means enough to show an attempt to produce that effect. . . .

In this case, sentences of twenty years' imprisonment have been imposed for the publishing of two leaflets that I believe the defendants had as much right to publish as the Government has to publish the Constitution of the United States now vainly invoked by them. Even if I am technically wrong, and enough can be squeezed from these poor and puny anonymities to turn the color of legal litmus paper, I will add, even if what I think the necessary intent were shown, the most nominal punishment seems to me all that possibly could be inflicted, unless the defendants are to be made to suffer not for what the indictment alleges, but for the creed that they avow—a creed that I believe to be the creed of ignorance and immaturity when honestly held, as I see no reason to doubt that it was held here, but which, although made the subject of examination at the trial, no one has a right even to consider in dealing with the charges before the Court.

Persecution for the expression of opinions seems to me perfectly logical. If you have no doubt of your premises or your power, and want a certain result with all your heart, you naturally express your wishes in law, and sweep away all opposition. To allow opposition by speech seems to indicate that you think the speech impotent, as when a man says that he has squared the circle, or that you do not care wholeheartedly for the result, or that you doubt either your power or your premises. But when men have realized that time has upset many fighting faiths, they may come to believe even more than they believe the very foundations of their own conduct that the ultimate good desired is better reached by free trade in ideas—that the best test of truth is the power of the thought to get itself accepted in the competition of the market, and that truth is the only ground upon which their wishes safely can be carried out. That, at any rate, is the theory of our Constitution. It is an experiment, as all life is an experiment. Every year, if not every day, we have to wager our salvation upon some prophecy based upon imperfect knowledge. While that experiment is part of our system, I think that we should be eternally vigilant against attempts to check the expression of opinions that we loathe and believe to be fraught with death, unless they so imminently threaten immediate interference with the lawful and pressing purposes of the law that an immediate check is required to save the country. I wholly disagree with the argument of the Government that the First Amendment left the common law as to seditious libel in force. History seems to me against the notion. I had conceived that the United States, through many years, had shown its repentance for the Sedition Act of 1798, by repaying fines that it imposed. Only the emergency that makes it immediately dangerous to leave the correction of evil counsels to time warrants making any exception to the sweeping command, "Congress shall make no law . . . abridging the freedom of speech." Of course, I am speaking only of expressions of opinion and exhortations, which were all that were uttered here, but I regret that I cannot put into more impressive words my belief that, in their conviction upon this indictment, the defendants were deprived of their rights under the Constitution of the United States.

MR. JUSTICE BRANDEIS concurs with the foregoing opinion.

Holmes had another opportunity to refine his approach to free speech in *Gitlow* v. *New York* (1925), discussed in Chapter 3. Now hopelessly distanced from the Court's hard-line approach to speech considered seditious, Holmes wrote that, "[I]f in the long run the beliefs expressed in proletarian dictatorship are destined to be accepted by the dominant forces of the community, the only meaning of free speech is that they should be given their chance and have their way."[26] Two years later, in *Whitney* v. *California* (1927), Justice Louis Brandeis underscored Holmes's more expansive approach to free speech by suggesting that conduct, not belief, become the trip wire of the clear and present danger test. But with the nation firmly ensconced in the First Red Scare, free speech was not exactly in a renaissance period. As discussed in Chapter 3, the repressive climate for free speech and press during World War I and the 1920s led Roger Baldwin to form the American Civil Liberties Union. *Gitlow* and *Whitney*, in fact, were argued by Samuel Pollak, a prominent New York lawyer recruited by the ACLU.

During the 1920s, Congress devoted considerable energy to investigating potential sources of "foreign" unrest in the American labor movement, particularly among unskilled workers, who comprised the fastest growing segment of unionized workers. Concerned by the social and economic dislocation touched off by the Great Depression, which began in 1929, the American government actively encouraged "internal security" measures to control potential sources of unrest. With the parallel rise of fascist ideologies in Western Europe and, most ominous and threatening of all, the ascension of Nazi Germany, Congress began to turn its investigative powers to what it perceived were internal threats to America's security at home. Fearful that the Russian Revolution of 1917 would encourage similar workers' revolts at home, American law enforcement agencies at the state and federal levels launched routine raids on labor unions. For the first time, unions had begun to wield genuine economic and political clout in their negotiations with the industrial corporations for whom they worked. Thousands of individuals, a great number of whom were recent European immigrants, were arrested on suspicion of harboring sympathies for foreign ideologies such as anarchism, Communism, and socialism, and supporting the violent overthrow of the American government.[27]

Around the same time, Congress supported this effort by opening investigations of its own into "subversive elements" in the American labor movement. Later, Adolf Hitler's rise to power in Nazi Germany made anti-Semitism in that country no longer a prominent cultural strain but a requirement of political faith. And the Soviet revolution in Russia quickly collapsed into the authoritarian control of Joseph Stalin. These two political upheavals abroad caused Congress to expand the scope of its investigation to question the political beliefs and associational ties of American citizens whose national origin now made their patriotism suspect. What began as an effort to root out potential threats to domestic security in a time when the world was entering one of the darkest periods in modern history soon dissipated into a series of congressional inquisitions. The Second Red Scare would ruin the lives of thousands of innocent American citizens and plunge the nation into a era of unprecedented political repression.

"I Have Here in My Hand . . .": Congress Confronts the Red Scare

In May 1930, Representative Hamilton Fish (R-N.Y.) introduced a proposal to form a temporary committee to investigate Communist Party activities and domestic subversion. By a vote of 210 to 18, Congress established the House Special Committee to Investigate Communist Activities in the United States. Representative Fish assured his colleagues that the committee was not intended to "interfere with any group except the Communists in the United States." After another member suggested during debate on the resolution that Congress ought to spend its time figuring out ways to combat the social and economic ills brought about by the Great Depression, Fish responded that the deportation of "alien Communists" would create job opportunities for honest, loyal, but unemployed Americans.[28]

After six months of investigation, Fish's committee produced a report that credited the Communist Party with around 12,000 dues-paying members and 500,000 more sympathizers. In January 1934, Representative Samuel Dickstein (D-N.Y.) succeeded in forming a Special Committee on Un-American Activities. Chaired by Representative. John W. McCormack (D-Mass.), the committee focused less on domestic Communism and more on Nazi sympathizers. A year later, the Dickstein-McCormack committee submitted a report that yielded little new information, other than to document that a handful of pro-Nazi organizations existed in the United States.

Congress soon enacted two laws designed to counteract such activities. The first required foreign agents distributing information and propaganda in the United States to register with the American government. The other authorized Congress to use its subpoena power in investigations undertaken outside of Washington, D.C. Representative Martin Dies Jr. (D-Tex.), an outspoken anti-Communist, fervent opponent of the New Deal, and an open anti-Semite, was undaunted by the apparent lack of congressional power to outlaw foreign ideologies that exhibited no genuine threat to domestic tranquility. In August 1938, Dickstein and Dies succeeded in forming another special committee to investigate "subversive and un-American propaganda." Previous committees had limited their mandates to Communism and Nazi sympathizers; the Dies resolution, a modified form of an earlier, unsuccessful resolution introduced by Dickstein, expanded its investigative scope to include all "subversive" activities, a category so broad that it was impossible to discern its limits. Enamored with the possibilities that a congressional investigation offered to elevate his own national political profile, Dies subpoenaed hundreds of individuals with alleged ties to Nazi and Communist causes before his committee within the first month of its existence.

The Dies Committee continued to press ahead with its investigations, but the entrance of the United States into World War II in December 1941 swept congressional inquiries into domestic subversion off the front pages. After World War II ended in August 1945, Congress evidenced no real desire to renew the Dies Committee's special standing. That is, until Representative John E. Rankin (D-Miss.), an outspoken anti-Communist, as well as a racist and an anti-Semite, defied the House leadership and persisted in his efforts to make the House Committee on Un-American Activities (HUAC) a permanent, standing committee. His concern was not with Nazi and fascist ideologies, but with Communist infiltration into American government, the media, and other powerful industries. After his initial resolution failed, Rankin insisted on a roll call vote. Fearful that opposition to HUAC would brand them as Communist sympathizers, a solid majority voted to create permanent status for HUAC.[29] Thus were sown the seeds for what later became known as "McCarthyism," a period that one historian has described as "one of the most severe episodes of political repression the United States ever experienced."[30]

McCarthyism took its name from Senator Joseph McCarthy (D-Wisc.), who dominated the post–World War II Red Scare more so than any other individual. McCarthy did not emerge as a visible leader in the congressional inquiries into the American Communist movement until well after HUAC had launched its investigation into alleged Communist influence in the United States Department of State. In need of a reelection issue to shore up a faltering campaign, McCarthy gave a speech in February 1950 before a Wheeling, West Virginia, women's club that ranks as one of the great moments in American political theatre. After decrying Communist influence in American government, McCarthy reached in his pocket, held up a piece of paper, and charged that it contained a list of 205 "card carrying" Communists who worked in the State Department. In fact, McCarthy had no such list, but that was secondary to the possibility that, to a public fearful of Soviet-inspired threats to American domestic security, one could exist.[31]

For the next two years, McCarthy used the Senate Permanent Investigations Subcommittee as his springboard to accuse countless high government officials, including President Harry S Truman and Secretary of State Dean Acheson, of either direct involvement with or providing unwitting assistance to Communist infiltrators. Historian William L. O'Neill has commented that McCarthy soon discovered, "to his own amazement, that he could say almost anything with impunity. Millions of people, frightened and confused by Cold War reverses, were prepared to swallow any charge McCarthy made, however ridiculous. They did not care if he had any evidence himself and were singularly unmoved by evidence to the contrary."[32] For his personal style and unbridled aggressiveness, Joseph McCarthy remains the best-remembered self-appointed Communist investigator of the period that bears his name. Scholars have never been able to pinpoint the exact number of writers, professors, and government officials who lost their jobs during the McCarthy Era. The best estimates place the figure at around 20,000, the vast majority of whom had done nothing to suggest subversion.[33] And no figure comes close to capturing the number of people who found their reputations irreparably damaged as a result of being considered a Communist sympathizer.

It was against these social and political forces that the Court again took up the question of the free speech rights of "subversive" speakers. In *Dennis v. United States* (1951), the Court confronted a First Amendment challenge to the Smith Act, a 1940 law passed by Congress that made it illegal to teach or advocate the overthrow of the United States government by force or violence. Although the defendants in *Dennis* did not engage in any violent behavior, they did teach what the Smith Act banned. The Court ruled that such teachings posed an "imminent and probable" danger to public order that justified their suppression, an opinion from which only Justices Black and Douglas dissented.[34]

Dennis v. United States

341 U.S. 494 (1951)

After World War II ended in August 1945, the United States and the Soviet Union settled into the Cold War, in which espionage, propaganda, and careful control of political dissent on both sides became standard fare. But in June 1950, North Korea, a Soviet ally, invaded South Korea, which was allied with the United States. American soldiers joined the United Nations forces already stationed there to "police" the truce between North and South Korea. Soon, Communist China sent forces into the area, overwhelming the American troops that had managed to push the North Koreans out of South Korean territory. The Korean War, clearly a proxy fight between the Soviet Union and the United States, suddenly made the Cold War radiantly hot.

So it was with the invasion as a backdrop that Eugene Dennis and eleven other American Communists were arrested under the Smith Act for conspiring to "teach and advocate the overthrow and destruction of the government of the United States by force and violence." Dennis's offense was to circulate, in the United States, material reprinting the writings of Karl Marx, Vladimir Lenin, and Joseph Stalin. The United States Department of Justice prosecuted Dennis and his comrades based on these materials alone and not on anything original they had said or written. The defendants were convicted by a federal district court and sentenced to five years in prison.

Dennis was argued in the Supreme Court on the same day that morning newspapers reported major Chinese advances into South Korea, pushing American forces further back from the North Korean border.

The Court's decision was 6 to 2. Chief Justice Vinson delivered the opinion of the Court. Justices Black and Douglas each wrote dissenting opinions. Justice Clark, who had participated in the prosecution of Dennis and the other defendants, did not take part in the case.

Mr. Chief Justice Vinson announced the judgment of the Court and an opinion in which Mr. Justice Reed, Mr. Justice Burton, and Mr. Justice Minton join.

The obvious purpose of the statute is to protect existing Government not from change by peaceable, lawful and constitutional means, but from change by violence, revolution and terrorism. That it is within the power of the Congress to protect the Government of the United States from armed rebellion is a proposition which requires little discussion. Whatever theoretical merit there may be to the argument that there is a "right" to rebellion against dictatorial governments is without force where the existing structure of the government provides for peaceful and orderly change. We reject any principle of governmental helplessness in the face of preparation for revolution, which principle, carried to its logical conclusion, must lead to anarchy. No one could conceive that it is not within the

power of Congress to prohibit acts intended to overthrow the Government by force and violence. The question with which we are concerned here is not whether Congress has such power, but whether the means which it has employed conflict with the First and Fifth Amendments to the Constitution. . . .

One of the bases for the contention that the means which Congress has employed are invalid takes the form of an attack on the face of the statute on the grounds that, by its terms, it prohibits academic discussion of the merits of Marxism-Leninism, that it stifles ideas and is contrary to all concepts of a free speech and a free press. Although we do not agree that the language itself has that significance, we must bear in mind that it is the duty of the federal courts to interpret federal legislation in a manner not inconsistent with the demands of the Constitution. . . .

The very language of the Smith Act negates the interpretation which petitioners would have us impose on that Act. It is directed at advocacy, not discussion. Thus, the trial judge properly charged the jury that they could not convict if they found that petitioners did "no more than pursue peaceful studies and discussions or teaching and advocacy in the realm of ideas." . . . Congress did not intend to eradicate the free discussion of political theories, to destroy the traditional rights of Americans to discuss and evaluate ideas without fear of governmental sanction. Rather Congress was concerned with the very kind of activity in which the evidence showed these petitioners engaged.

But although the statute is not directed at the hypothetical cases which petitioners have conjured, its application in this case has resulted in convictions for the teaching and advocacy of the overthrow of the Government by force and violence, which, even though coupled with the intent to accomplish that overthrow, contains an element of speech. For this reason, we must pay special heed to the demands of the First Amendment marking out the boundaries of speech. . . .

No important case involving free speech was decided by this Court prior to *Schenck* v. *United States* (1919). Indeed, the summary treatment accorded an argument based upon an individual's claim that the First Amendment protected certain utterances indicates that the Court at earlier dates placed no unique emphasis upon that right. It was not until the classic dictum of Justice Holmes in the *Schenck* case that speech *per se* received that emphasis in a majority opinion. . . .

In several later cases involving convictions under the Criminal Espionage Act, the nub of the evidence the Court held sufficient to meet the "clear and present danger" test enunciated in *Schenck* was as follows: *Frohwerk* v. *United States* (1919)—publication of twelve newspaper articles attacking the war; *Debs* v. *United States* (1919)—one speech attacking United States' participation in the war; *Abrams* v. *United States* (1919)—circulation of copies of two different socialist circulars attacking the war; *Schaefer* v. *United States* (1920)—publication of a German language newspaper with allegedly false articles, critical of capitalism and the war; *Pierce* v. *United States* (1920)—circulation of copies of a four-page pamphlet written by a clergyman, attacking the purposes of the war and United States' participation therein. Justice Holmes wrote the opinions for a unanimous Court in *Schenck, Frohwerk* and *Debs.* He and Justice Brandeis dissented in *Abrams, Schaefer* and *Pierce.* The basis of these dissents was that, because of the protection which the First Amendment gives to speech, the evidence in each case was insufficient to show that the defendants had created the requisite danger under *Schenck.* But these dissents did not mark a change of principle. The dissenters doubted only the probable effectiveness of the puny efforts toward subversion. . . .

The rule we deduce from these cases is that, where an offense is specified by a statute in nonspeech or nonpress terms, a conviction relying upon speech or press as evidence of violation may be sustained only when the speech or publication created a "clear and present danger" of attempting or accomplishing the prohibited crime, *e.g.,* interference with enlistment. The dissents, we repeat, in emphasizing the value of speech, were addressed to the argument of the sufficiency of the evidence. . . .

[Since *Whitney* and *Gitlow*] there is little doubt that subsequent opinions have inclined toward the Holmes-Brandeis rationale. . . . But . . . neither Justice Holmes nor Justice Brandeis ever envisioned that a shorthand phrase should be crystallized into a rigid rule to be applied inflexibly without regard to the circumstances of each case. Speech is not an absolute, above and beyond control by the legislature when its judgment, subject to review here, is that certain kinds of speech are so undesirable as to warrant criminal sanction. Nothing is more certain in modern society than the principle that there are no absolutes, that a name, a phrase, a standard has meaning only when associated with the considerations which gave birth to the nomenclature. To those who would paralyze our Government in the face of impending threat by encasing it in a semantic straitjacket we must reply that all concepts are relative.

In this case, we are squarely presented with the application of the "clear and present danger" test, and must decide what that phrase imports. We first note that many of the cases in which this Court has reversed convictions by use of this or similar tests have been based on the fact that the interest which the State was attempting to protect was itself too insubstantial to warrant restriction of speech. . . . Overthrow of the Government by force and violence is certainly a substantial enough interest for the Government to limit speech. Indeed, this is the ultimate value of any society, for if a society cannot protect its very structure from armed internal attack, it must follow that no subordinate value can be protected. If, then, this interest may be protected, the literal problem which is presented is what has been meant by the use of the phrase "clear and present danger" of the utterances bringing about the evil within the power of Congress to punish.

Obviously, the words cannot mean that, before the Government may act, it must wait until the putsch is about to be executed, the plans have been laid and the signal is awaited. If Government is aware that a group aiming at its overthrow is attempting to indoctrinate its members and to commit them to a course whereby they will strike when the leaders feel the circumstances permit, action by the Government is required. The argument that there is no need for Government to concern itself, for Government is strong, it possesses ample powers to put down a rebellion, it may defeat the revolution with ease needs no answer. For that is not the question. Certainly an attempt to overthrow the Government by force, even though doomed from the outset because of inadequate numbers or power of the revolutionists, is a sufficient evil for Congress to prevent. The damage which such attempts create both physically and politically to a nation makes it impossible to measure the validity in terms of the probability of success, or the immediacy of a successful attempt. In the instant case, the trial judge charged the jury that they could not convict unless they found that petitioners intended to overthrow the Government "as speedily as circumstances would permit." This does not mean, and could not properly mean, that they would not strike until there was certainty of success. What was meant was that the revolutionists would strike when they thought the time was ripe. We must therefore reject the contention that success or probability of success is the criterion.

The situation with which Justices Holmes and Brandeis were concerned in *Gitlow* was a comparatively isolated event, bearing little relation in their minds to any substantial threat to the safety of the community. . . . They were not confronted with any situation comparable to the instant one—the development of an apparatus designed and dedicated to the overthrow of the Government, in the context of world crisis after crisis. . . .

[W]e are in accord with the court below, which affirmed the trial court's finding that the requisite danger existed. The mere fact that, from the period 1945 to 1948, petitioners' activities did not result in an attempt to overthrow the Government by force and violence is, of course, no answer to the fact that there was a group that was ready to make the attempt. The formation by petitioners of such a highly organized conspiracy, with rigidly disciplined members subject to call when the leaders, these petitioners, felt that the time had come for action, coupled with the inflammable nature of world conditions, similar uprisings in other countries, and the touch-and-go nature of our relations with countries with whom petitioners were in the very least ideologically attuned, convince us that their convictions were justified on this score. And this analysis disposes of the contention that a conspiracy to advocate, as distinguished from the advocacy itself, cannot be constitutionally restrained, because it comprises only the preparation. It is the existence of the conspiracy which creates the danger. If the ingredients of the reaction are present, we cannot bind the Government to wait until the catalyst is added. . . .

We hold that . . . the Smith Act do[es] not inherently, or as construed or applied in the instant case, violate the First Amendment and other provisions of the Bill of Rights, or the First and Fifth Amendments because of indefiniteness. Petitioners intended to overthrow the Government of the United States as speedily as the circumstances would permit. Their conspiracy to organize the Communist Party and to teach and advocate the overthrow of the Government of the United States by force and violence created a "clear and present danger" of an attempt to overthrow the Government by force and violence. They were properly and constitutionally convicted for violation of the Smith Act. The judgments of conviction are

Affirmed.

Mr. Justice Frankfurter, concurring in affirmance of the judgment.

Few questions of comparable import have come before this Court in recent years. The appellants maintain that they have a right to advocate a political theory, so long, at least, as their advocacy does not create an immediate danger of obvious magnitude to the very existence of our present scheme of society. On the other hand, the Government asserts the right to safeguard the security of the Nation by such a measure as the Smith Act. Our judgment is thus solicited on a conflict of interests of the utmost concern to the wellbeing of the country. This conflict of interests cannot be resolved by a dogmatic preference for one or the other, nor by a sonorous formula which is, in fact, only a euphemistic disguise for an unresolved conflict. If adjudication is to be a rational process, we cannot escape a candid examination of the conflicting claims with full recognition that both are supported by weighty title-deeds. . . .

Primary responsibility for adjusting the interests which compete in the situation before us of necessity belongs to the Congress. The nature of the power to be exercised by this Court has been delineated in decisions not charged with the emotional appeal of situations such as that now before us. We are to set aside the judgment of those whose duty it is to legislate only if there is no reasonable basis for it. . . .

A generation ago, this distribution of responsibility would not have been questioned. But, in recent decisions, we have made explicit what has long been implicitly recognized. In reviewing statutes which restrict freedoms protected by the First Amendment, we have emphasized the close relation which those freedoms bear to maintenance of a free society. Some members of the Court—and at times a majority—have done more. They have suggested that our function in reviewing statutes restricting freedom of expression differs sharply from our normal duty in sitting in judgment on legislation. . . .

Free-speech cases are not an exception to the principle that we are not legislators, that direct policymaking is not our province. How best to reconcile competing interests is the business of legislatures, and the balance they strike is a judgment not to be displaced by ours, but to be respected unless outside the pale of fair judgment. . . .

Not every type of speech occupies the same position on the scale of values. There is no substantial public interest in permitting certain kinds of utterances, "the lewd and obscene, the profane, the libelous, and the insulting or "fighting" words—those which, by their very utterance, inflict injury or tend to incite an immediate breach of the peace," *Chaplinsky* v. *New Hampshire* (1942). We have frequently indicated that the interest in protecting speech depends on the circumstances of the occasion. It is pertinent to the decision before us to consider where on the scale of values we have in the past placed the type of speech now claiming constitutional immunity.

The defendants have been convicted of conspiring to organize a party of persons who advocate the overthrow of the Government by force and violence. The jury has found that the object of the conspiracy is advocacy as "a rule or principle of action," "by language reasonably and ordinarily calculated to incite persons to such action," and with the intent to cause the overthrow "as speedily as circumstances would permit."

On any scale of values which we have hitherto recognized, speech of this sort ranks low. . . .

Civil liberties draw, at best, only limited strength from legal guaranties. Preoccupation by our people with the constitutionality, instead of with the wisdom, of legislation or of executive action is preoccupation with a false value. Even those who would most freely use the judicial brake on the democratic process by invalidating legislation that goes deeply against their grain, acknowledge, at least by paying lip service, that constitutionality does not exact a sense of proportion or the sanity of humor or an absence of fear. Focusing attention on constitutionality tends to make constitutionality synonymous with wisdom. When legislation touches freedom of thought and freedom of speech, such a tendency is a formidable enemy of the free spirit. Much that should be rejected as illiberal, because repressive and envenoming, may well be not unconstitutional. The ultimate reliance for the deepest needs of civilization must be found outside their vindication in courts of law; apart from all else, judges, howsoever they may conscientiously seek to discipline themselves against it, unconsciously are too apt to be moved by the deep undercurrents of public feeling. A persistent, positive translation of the liberating faith into the feelings and thoughts and actions of men and women is the real protection against attempts to strait-jacket the human mind. Such temptations will have their way, if fear and hatred are not exorcized. The mark of a truly civilized man is confidence in the strength and security derived from the inquiring mind. We may be grateful for such honest comforts as it supports, but we must be unafraid of its incertitudes. Without open minds, there can be no open society. And if society be not open, the spirit of man is mutilated, and becomes enslaved.

MR. JUSTICE BLACK, dissenting.

At the outset, I want to emphasize what the crime involved in this case is, and what it is not. These petitioners were not charged with an attempt to overthrow the Government. They were not charged with overt acts of any kind designed to overthrow the Government. They were not even charged with saying anything or writing anything designed to overthrow the Government. The charge was that they agreed to assemble and to talk and publish certain ideas at a later date: the indictment is that they conspired to organize the Communist Party and to use speech or newspapers and other publications in the future to teach and advocate the forcible overthrow of the Government. No matter how it is worded, this is a virulent form of prior censorship of speech and press, which I believe the First Amendment forbids. I would hold [Section] 3 of the Smith Act authorizing this prior restraint unconstitutional on its face and as applied.

But let us assume, contrary to all constitutional ideas of fair criminal procedure, that petitioners, although not indicted for the crime of actual advocacy, may be punished for it. Even on this radical assumption, the other opinions in this case show that the only way to affirm these convictions is to repudiate directly or indirectly the established "clear and present danger" rule. This the Court does in a way which greatly restricts the protections afforded by the First Amendment. The opinions for affirmance indicate that the chief reason for jettisoning the rule is the expressed fear that advocacy of Communist doctrine endangers the safety of the Republic. Undoubtedly a governmental policy of unfettered communication of ideas does entail dangers. To the Founders of this Nation, however, the benefits derived from free expression were worth the risk. They embodied this philosophy in the First Amendment's command that "Congress shall make no law . . . abridging the freedom of speech, or of the press. . . ." I have always believed that the First Amendment is the keystone of our Government, that the freedoms it guarantees provide the best insurance against destruction of all freedom. At least as to speech in the realm of public matters, I believe that the "clear and present danger" test does not "mark the furthermost constitutional boundaries of protected expression," but does "no more than recognize a minimum compulsion of the Bill of Rights." . . .

So long as this Court exercises the power of judicial review of legislation, I cannot agree that the First Amendment permits us to sustain laws suppressing freedom of speech and press on the basis of Congress' or our own notions of mere "reasonableness." Such a doctrine waters down the First Amendment so that it amounts to little more than an admonition to Congress. The Amendment as so construed is not likely to protect any but those "safe" or orthodox views which rarely need its protection. . . .

Public opinion being what it now is, few will protest the conviction of these Communist petitioners. There is hope, however, that, in calmer times, when present pressures, passions and fears subside, this or some later Court will restore the First Amendment liberties to the high preferred place where they belong in a free society.

MR. JUSTICE DOUGLAS, dissenting.

There was a time in England when the concept of constructive treason flourished. Men were punished not for raising a hand against the king, but for thinking murderous thoughts about him. The Framers of the Constitution were alive to that abuse, and took steps to see that the practice would not flourish here. Treason was defined to require overt acts—the evolution of a plot against the country into an actual project. The present case is not one of treason. But the analogy is close when the illegality is made to turn on intent, not on the nature of the act. We then start probing men's minds for motive and purpose; they become entangled in the law not for what they did, but *for what they thought;* they get convicted not for what they said, but for the purpose with which they said it.

Intent, of course, often makes the difference in the law. An act otherwise excusable or carrying minor penalties may grow to an abhorrent thing if the evil intent is present. We deal here, however, not with ordinary acts, but with speech, to which the Constitution has given a special sanction.

The vice of treating speech as the equivalent of overt acts of a treasonable or seditious character is emphasized by a concurring opinion, which, by invoking the law of conspiracy, makes speech do service for deeds which are dangerous to society. The doctrine of conspiracy has served divers and oppressive purposes, and, in its broad reach, can be made to do great evil. But never until today has anyone seriously thought that the ancient law of conspiracy could constitutionally be used to turn speech into seditious conduct. Yet that is precisely what is suggested. I repeat that we deal here with speech alone, not with speech plus acts of sabotage or unlawful conduct. Not a single seditious act is charged in the indictment. To make a lawful speech unlawful because two men conceive it is to raise the law of conspiracy to appalling proportions. That course is to make a radical break with the past and to violate one of the cardinal principles of our constitutional scheme.

Free speech has occupied an exalted position because of the high service it has given our society. Its protection is essential to the very existence of a democracy. The airing of ideas releases pressures which otherwise might become destructive. When ideas compete in the market for acceptance, full and free discussion exposes the false, and they gain few adherents. Full and free discussion even of ideas we hate encourages the testing of our own prejudices and preconceptions. Full and free discussion keeps a society from becoming stagnant and unprepared for the stresses and strains that work to tear all civilizations apart. . . .

There comes a time when even speech loses its constitutional immunity. Speech innocuous one year may at another time fan such destructive flames that it must be halted in the interests of the safety of the Republic. That is the meaning of the clear and present danger test. When conditions are so critical that there will be no time to avoid the evil that the speech threatens, it is time to call a halt. Otherwise, free speech which is the strength of the Nation will be the cause of its destruction.

Yet free speech is the rule, not the exception. The restraint to be constitutional must be based on more than fear, on more than passionate opposition against the speech, on more than a revolted dislike for its contents. There must be some immediate injury to society that is likely if speech is allowed. . . .

How it can be said that there is a clear and present danger that [Communist] advocacy will succeed is, therefore, a mystery. Some nations less resilient than the United States, where illiteracy is high and where democratic traditions are only budding, might have to take drastic steps and jail these men for merely speaking their creed. But in America, they are miserable merchants of unwanted ideas; their wares remain unsold. The fact that their ideas are abhorrent does not make them powerful.

Dennis sent a clear signal that the Court was very much a partner in the American government's larger effort to contain domestic Communist influence. By upholding the Smith Act, the Court cleared the way for the attorney general to deport foreign-born members of the Communist Party. University and even high school administrators were free to fire teachers who were suspected of teaching or advocating the overthrow of the government. The ACLU, which condemned *Dennis* as the "worst single blow to civil liberties in all our history," privately asked the Justice Department to limit its prosecutions of suspected Communists to those against whom it had concrete evidence of conspiratorial activity. The attorney general declined the ACLU's invitation. Anti-Communist activity increased in the states, with "loyalty oaths" emerging as the most common instrument to ensure internal security. By 1954, thirty-nine states required government employees, labor organizers, political candidates, and teachers to pledge their allegiance to the United States and swear that they were not members of the Communist Party.[35]

That same year, however, McCarthy was ultimately undone by his own personal and political excesses, his downfall played out before millions of Americans in the first congressional investigation into Communist activity broadcast on national television, the Army-McCarthy hearings. Called to investigate possible Soviet espionage in the United States Army, the hearings were really an opportunity for McCarthy to showboat before an unprecedented American television audience. This time, however, the public was put off by his intemperate behavior, his rude treatment of witnesses and his Senate colleagues, and his baseless smears against people unconnected to the matter under investigation. Public support for the Wisconsin senator fell through the floor after the Army-McCarthy hearings, as did his Senate colleagues' tolerance for his boorish behavior. In December 1954, by a 67–22 margin, his colleagues voted to censure him for conduct unbecoming a member of the Senate. He served out the remainder of his term. Hobbled by health problems, personal disgrace, and alcoholism, he died in May 1957.[36]

A month after McCarthy's death, the Court handed down two major decisions indicating that distance from the worst excesses of the early 1950s Cold War period had given the justices a different perspective on the free speech rights of Communists and other political dissenters. In *Watkins v. United States* (1957) (see Volume I, Chapter 4), the Court, 6 to 1, overturned the contempt of Congress conviction of John T. Watkins, a labor organizer for the United Automobile Workers (UAW) and self-professed one-time Communist, for refusing to answer questions about the political activities of others. In a pointed rebuke to HUAC, the Court held that congressional investigative power, while certainly broad, did not confer "power to expose for the sake of exposure where the predominant result can be only an invasion of the private rights of individuals."[37]

In *Yates v. United States* (1957), the Court severely curtailed the scope of the Smith Act by holding that teaching "abstract doctrine" did not fall within the law's prohibition on advocacy and encouraging the direct incitement of illegal conduct.[38] By throwing out the conviction of fourteen individuals convicted of publishing and disseminating Communist materials and engaging in other organizing activities, the justices took a giant step forward from *Dennis*. Shortly after *Yates*, the Court also invalidated a California law requiring churches to administer loyalty oaths to their members to retain their tax exemptions. Although the Court did not reach the broader question of loyalty oaths beyond the religious context, *First Unitarian Church of Los Angeles v. County of Los Angeles* (1958) certainly placed their constitutionality in doubt.[39]

Predictably, anti-Communist senators moved against the Court, introducing a series of bills intended to overturn the Court's "Red Monday" decisions, the nickname given to *Watkins* and *Yates* by their detractors. Ironically, Chief Justice Earl Warren, while governor of California, strongly supported the state's loyalty oath program and signed a state sedition law modeled on the Smith Act.

No sooner had civil liberties groups congratulated themselves on the 1957 decisions curtailing federal power to punish Communists—the ACLU had submitted *amicus* briefs in *Yates* and *Watkins* and helped steer them through the appeals process—than did the Court renew HUAC's Communist hunting license. In *Barenblatt* v. *United States* (1959), Justice John Harlan wrote that the importance of the government's interest in domestic security must be balanced against the purpose of the free speech rights in question. Justice Hugo Black, whose own literal approach to the First Amendment led him to conclude that all "speech, writings, thoughts and public assemblies" were protected against government censorship, strongly criticized Harlan's approach to this case. Of Harlan's balancing approach, Black wrote that it left "all persons to guess just what the law really means to cover, and fear of a wrong guess inevitably leads people to forego the very rights the Constitution sought to protect above all others."[40]

By the mid-1960s, the Court was no longer an ally in the Cold War campaign to root out domestic subversion by stripping Americans of their First Amendment right to dissent from the political mainstream of the United States government. Since the late 1950s, the Court had substantially broadened its interpretation of the First Amendment on matters involving public protests, press, religion, and assembly. Having been a central player in the litigation involving the expansion of these other First Amendment rights, the ACLU decided the time was right for the Court to revisit the vitality of the "clear and present" danger and "balancing" tests that had dominated its approach to the rights of political dissenters since *Schenck*. Consistent with its long-held philosophy of defending the principle and not the substance of free speech, the ACLU agreed, in *Brandenburg* v. *Ohio*, to represent a Ku Klux Klan chapter that had been prosecuted under a law enacted shortly after World War I to contain foreign purveyors of Communism, socialism, and other threatening ideologies.

Brandenburg v. *Ohio*

395 U.S. 444 (1969)

Claiming that if "our President, our Congress, our Supreme Court, continues to suppress the white, Caucasian race, it's possible that there might have to be some revengance [*sic*] taken," Charles Brandenburg, the Ohio leader of the Knights of the Ku Klux Klan, warned that he and his men stood ready to defend America against a takeover by blacks and Jews. Not that anyone asked him, but Brandenburg also offered the opinion that "personally, I believe the nigger should be returned to Africa, the Jew returned to Israel." Unfortunately for Brandenburg, only twelve Klansmen had turned out for his rally.

Always publicity conscious, Brandenburg had invited a Cincinnati television crew to film his gathering. Ohio authorities prosecuted Brandenburg under a 1919 criminal syndicalism law making it illegal to "advocate . . . the duty, necessity, or propriety of crime, sabotage, violence, or unlawful methods of terrorism," and for "voluntarily" assembling with any such group to promote such aims. Originally intended to apply to Communist and other "foreign" ideologies that had surfaced in America during and after World War I, the law was now being used to prosecute the Klan for their racist, anti-Semitic *views*. Nowhere in the state's prosecution did it accuse Brandenburg of violent action against African Americans or Jews.

The Court's opinion was unanimous, and was delivered *per curiam*. Justices Black and Douglas, each a stalwart opponent of the "clear and present" danger test favored by the Court since *Schenck*, concurred.

▼▲▼

PER CURIAM.

The appellant, a leader of a Ku Klux Klan group, was convicted under the Ohio Criminal Syndicalism statute for "advocat[ing] . . . the duty, necessity, or propriety of crime, sabotage, violence, or unlawful methods of terrorism as a means of accomplishing industrial or political reform" and for "voluntarily assembl[ing] with any society, group, or assemblage of persons formed to teach or advocate the doctrines of criminal syndicalism." . . .

[Recent decisions of the Court] have fashioned the principle that the constitutional guarantees of free speech and free press do not permit a State to forbid or proscribe advocacy of the use of force or of law violation except where such advocacy is directed to inciting or producing imminent lawless action and is likely to incite or produce such action. As we said in *Noto* v. *United States* (1961), "the mere abstract teaching . . . of the moral propriety or even moral necessity for a resort to force and violence is not the same as preparing a group for violent action and steeling it to such action." A statute which fails to draw this distinction impermissibly intrudes upon the freedoms guaranteed by the First and Fourteenth Amendments. It sweeps within its condemnation speech which our Constitution has immunized from governmental control.

Measured by this test, Ohio's Criminal Syndicalism Act cannot be sustained. The Act punishes persons who "advocate or teach the duty, necessity, or propriety" of violence "as a means of accomplishing industrial or political reform"; or who publish or circulate or display any book or paper containing such advocacy; or who "justify" the commission of violent acts "with intent to exemplify, spread or advocate the propriety of the doctrines of criminal syndicalism"; or who "voluntarily assemble" with a group formed "to teach or advocate the doctrines of criminal syndicalism." Neither the indictment nor the trial judge's instructions to the jury in any way refined the statute's bald definition of the crime in terms of mere advocacy not distinguished from incitement to imminent lawless action.

Accordingly, we are here confronted with a statute which, by its own words and as applied, purports to punish mere advocacy and to forbid, on pain of criminal punishment, assembly with others merely to advocate the described type of action. Such a statute falls within the condemnation of the First and Fourteenth Amendments. The contrary teaching of *Whitney* v. *California* cannot be supported, and that decision is therefore overruled.

Reversed.

MR. JUSTICE BLACK, concurring.

I agree with the views expressed by MR. JUSTICE DOUGLAS in his concurring opinion in this case that the "clear and present danger" doctrine should have no place in the interpretation of the First Amendment. I join the Court's opinion, which, as I understand it, simply cites *Dennis* v. *United States* (1951), but does not indicate any agreement on the Court's part with the "clear and present danger" doctrine on which *Dennis* purported to rely.

MR. JUSTICE DOUGLAS, concurring.

I see no place in the regime of the First Amendment for any "clear and present danger" test, whether strict and tight, as some would make it, or free-wheeling, as the Court in *Dennis* rephrased it.

When one reads the opinions closely and sees when and how the "clear and present danger" test has been applied, great misgivings are aroused. First, the threats were often loud, but always puny, and made serious only by judges so wedded to the *status quo* that critical analysis made them nervous. Second, the test was so twisted and perverted in *Dennis* as to make the trial of those teachers of Marxism an all-out political trial which was part and parcel of the cold war that has eroded substantial parts of the First Amendment.

Action is often a method of expression, and within the protection of the First Amendment.

Suppose one tears up his own copy of the Constitution in eloquent protest to a decision of this Court. May he be indicted?

Suppose one rips his own Bible to shreds to celebrate his departure from one "faith" and his embrace of atheism. May he be indicted? . . .

The line between what is permissible and not subject to control and what may be made impermissible and subject to regulation is the line between ideas and overt acts.

The example usually given by those who would punish speech is the case of one who falsely shouts fire in a crowded theatre.

This is, however, a classic case where speech is brigaded with action. They are indeed inseparable, and a prosecution can be launched for the overt acts actually caused. Apart from rare instances of that kind, speech is, I think, immune from prosecution. Certainly there is no constitutional line between advocacy of abstract ideas, as in *Yates*, and advocacy of political action, as in *Scales*. The quality of advocacy turns on the depth of the conviction, and government has no power to invade that sanctuary of belief and conscience.

▼▲▼

By arguing that the appropriate test for free speech was whether the speech actually led to *imminent lawlessness*, the Court, in *Brandenburg*, abandoned the *clear and present danger* test created in *Schenck*. Of note was the Court's decision to overrule a 1927 ACLU case, *Whitney* v. *California*, which held that states could punish speech that promoted a *bad tendency*. Now, fifty years later, the ACLU had come full circle, winning with the same theory of free speech with which it had defended Charlotte Whitney during the First Red Scare—that advocacy could not be punished, even if it supported the necessity of violent action. Although the Smith Act has never been overturned by the Court or stricken by Congress, *Brandenburg* effectively set aside the 1940 law. Today, imminent lawlessness remains the threshold for restricting the *political* content of speech.

Protests, Pickets, and Demonstrations

At some point during college, if not in high school, you have probably taken a literature course requiring you to read short stories or novels that are heavy with symbolic meaning. A classic of American literature, *The Adventures of Huckleberry Finn,* by Mark Twain, is rarely taught or discussed without referring to the symbolic meaning of the Mississippi River or the relationship between Jim, the runaway slave, and Huck, the novel's white protagonist. Was the Mississippi River merely an avenue for adventure, or symbolic of Huck's rejection of formal education and religion? Was the river a metaphor for freedom and Twain's antislavery views? Did Twain's use of racial epithets symbolize his contempt for the racist mind? How, for example, would you interpret this passage, spoken by a drunken Pap, Huck's father:

> There was a free nigger there from Ohio. . . . They said he was a p'fessor in college, and could talk all kinds of languages, and knowed everything. And that ain't the wust. They said he could vote when he was at home.

Does Pap's statement illustrate the hypocrisy of many whites by displaying their own ignorance while acting superior to blacks? Or does Pap's (and most every other character's) freewheeling use of the racial epithet "nigger" reinforce the widely held view by whites in the pre–Civil War South that blacks lacked humanity and were not real people with genuine feelings? Some literary scholars have argued that Twain's novel, set in the 1840s pre–Civil War South, is one the most powerful antiracist statements ever made by an American author. Conversely, many high schools across the United States have banned *The Adventures of Huckleberry Finn* because of Twain's choice of language and their uncertainty over Twain's true motives in the novel. And what meaning did the great writer attach to his work? "My works are like water," said Twain. "The works of the great masters are like wine. But everyone drinks water."[41]

Assigning Value to Gestures: Symbolic Speech

Although words can convey a message far deeper than their surface-level meaning, the Court does not treat such speech as a literary critic would. Public protests, parades, demonstrations, and even clothing all have expressive qualities, and the Court has chosen to identify and, in most cases, protect such communication as *symbolic speech.* But the Court has also drawn firm lines between what it considers disruptive behavior and symbolic speech protected by the First Amendment. And while the Court has generally held that *time, place, and manner* restrictions may not bear any relationship to the substance of the expressive conduct, consider whether the justices have heeded to this rule when they have upheld restrictions on symbolic speech.

Until 1931, the Court had never formally defined symbolic speech or ruled whether it was protected by the First Amendment. That year, the justices ruled in *Stromberg* v. *California* (discussed in Chapter 3) that a California law banning the display of a "red flag, banner or badge . . . as a sign, symbol or emblem of opposition to organized government" violated the First Amendment. Important as well in *Stromberg* was the role of the ACLU, which brought the first successful argument on the symbolic nature of nonverbal speech to the Court. Having ruled that not all speech deserving constitutional protection necessarily had to be spoken, the Court was soon confronted with another question that involved the right to refrain from speaking when compelled to do so by the government. Silence can be interpreted in many ways—from a quiet statement of personal conscience to outright defiance. In the early 1940s, the Court heard two important cases that involved the right of Jehovah's Witnesses not to participate in the mandatory flag salute and pledge of allegiance during the public school day. *West Virginia Board of Education* v. *Barnette* (1943), decided during World War II, offers an early opportunity to see how the Court placed the principle of individual liberty above political expediency in a time of crisis.

West Virginia Board of Education v. *Barnette*

319 U.S. 624 (1943)

Few groups in American history have done more to expand the definition of freedom of speech, assembly, and religion under the First Amendment than the Jehovah's

Witnesses. Despite constant harassment by the communities in which they lived and frequent criminal prosecution for their incessant public proselytizing, the Witnesses brought twenty-three cases before the Supreme Court between 1938 and 1946, and were victorious in fifteen of them. The Witnesses challenged laws restricting both their right to engage in door-to-door solicitation and broadcast their religious messages from car-mounted loudspeakers. By 1940, the Witnesses secured a major victory when the Court, in *Cantwell* v. *Connecticut*, ruled that municipalities could not target religious groups for discriminatory treatment in laws that applied to the general population. *Cantwell* brought the Free Exercise Clause of the First Amendment to the states, and substantially broadened the justices' thinking about the rights of religious minorities more generally. *Cantwell* and the litigation strategy of the Witnesses during this period are discussed in greater detail in Chapter 6.

But the same year the Court decided *Cantwell*, the justices dealt the Witnesses a crushing blow when they held that mandatory flag salute laws in the public schools were not unconstitutional under the Free Speech Clause. The flag salute laws had originated as a way for the public schools to "socialize" immigrants in American values. After World War II began in Europe in 1939, public school authorities increasingly viewed the flag salute laws as an instrument to promote patriotism. Anyone refusing to comply was viewed with great suspicion. In *Minersville School District* v. *Gobitis* (1940), the Court upheld a small Pennsylvania town's mandatory flag salute law, even though lower court records detailed the violence directed against Witness schoolchildren who did not comply. Ironically, the flag salute law challenged in *Gobitis*—as did virtually all the other state flag salute laws—required students to extend their right arm straight out, with their palm open—the signature salute of Adolf Hitler's Third Reich in Nazi Germany.

In 1942, the West Virginia Board of Education adopted a mandatory flag salute. Students who refused to comply were considered insubordinate and expelled. Although the Parent Teachers Association (PTA), the Boy and Girl Scouts, and several other civic clubs objected to the "Hitler-like" stiff-arm salute, the West Virginia authorities left the salute relatively unmodified. Students were required to recite: "I pledge allegiance to the Flag of the United States of America and to the Republic for which it stands; one Nation, indivisible, with liberty and justice for all." Walter Barnette agreed to challenge the law on behalf of himself and his school-age children.

The Court's decision was 6 to 3. Justice Jackson delivered the opinion of the Court. Justices Black and Douglas filed a joint concurring opinion. Justice Murphy also filed a concurring opinion. Justice Frankfurter, who wrote the Court's opinion in *Gobitis*, offered one of the most visceral and personal dissents of his twenty-three-year career on the Court.

MR. JUSTICE JACKSON delivered the opinion of the Court.

The freedom asserted by these appellees does not bring them into collision with rights asserted by any other individual. It is such conflicts which most frequently require intervention of the State to determine where the rights of one end and those of another begin. But the refusal of these persons to participate in the ceremony does not interfere with or deny rights of others to do so. Nor is there any question in this case that their behavior is peaceable and orderly. The sole conflict is between authority and rights of the individual. The State asserts power to condition access to public education on making a prescribed sign and profession and at the same time to coerce attendance by punishing both parent and child. The latter stand on a right of self-determination in matters that touch individual opinion and personal attitude.

As the present CHIEF JUSTICE said in dissent in the *Gobitis* case, the State may "require teaching by instruction and study of all in our history and in the structure and organization of our government, including the guaranties of civil liberty, which tend to inspire patriotism and love of country." Here, however, we are dealing with a compulsion of students to declare a belief. They are not merely made acquainted with the flag salute so that they may be informed as to what it is or even what it means. The issue here is whether this slow and easily neglected route to aroused loyalties constitutionally may be short-cut by substituting a compulsory salute and slogan. . . .

There is no doubt that, in connection with the pledges, the flag salute is a form of utterance. Symbolism is a primitive but effective way of communicating ideas. The use of an emblem or flag to symbolize some system, idea, institution, or personality is a short-cut from mind to mind. Causes and nations, political parties, lodges, and ecclesiastical groups seek to knit the loyalty of their followings to a flag or banner, a color or design. The State announces rank, function, and authority through crowns and maces, uniforms and black robes; the church speaks through the

Cross, the Crucifix, the altar and shrine, and clerical raiment. Symbols of State often convey political ideas, just as religious symbols come to convey theological ones. Associated with many of these symbols are appropriate gestures of acceptance or respect: a salute, a bowed or bared head, a bended knee. A person gets from a symbol the meaning he puts into it, and what is one man's comfort and inspiration is another's jest and scorn.

Over a decade ago, Chief Justice Hughes led this Court in holding that the display of a red flag as a symbol of opposition by peaceful and legal means to organized government was protected by the free speech guaranties of the Constitution, *Stromberg* v. *California* (1931). Here, it is the State that employs a flag as a symbol of adherence to government as presently organized. It requires the individual to communicate by word and sign his acceptance of the political ideas it thus bespeaks. Objection to this form of communication, when coerced, is an old one, well known to the framers of the Bill of Rights.

It is also to be noted that the compulsory flag salute and pledge requires affirmation of a belief and an attitude of mind. It is not clear whether the regulation contemplates that pupils forego any contrary convictions of their own and become unwilling converts to the prescribed ceremony, or whether it will be acceptable if they simulate assent by words without belief, and by a gesture barren of meaning. It is now a commonplace that censorship or suppression of expression of opinion is tolerated by our Constitution only when the expression presents a clear and present danger of action of a kind the State is empowered to prevent and punish. It would seem that involuntary affirmation could be commanded only on even more immediate and urgent grounds than silence. But here, the power of compulsion is invoked without any allegation that remaining passive during a flag salute ritual creates a clear and present danger that would justify an effort even to muffle expression. To sustain the compulsory flag salute, we are required to say that a Bill of Rights which guards the individual's right to speak his own mind left it open to public authorities to compel him to utter what is not in his mind.

Whether the First Amendment to the Constitution will permit officials to order observance of ritual of this nature does not depend upon whether as a voluntary exercise we would think it to be good, bad or merely innocuous. Any credo of nationalism is likely to include what some disapprove or to omit what others think essential, and to give off different overtones as it takes on different accents or interpretations. If official power exists to coerce acceptance of any patriotic creed, what it shall contain cannot be decided by courts, but must be largely discretionary with the ordaining authority, whose power to prescribe would no doubt include power to amend. Hence, validity of the asserted power to force an American citizen publicly to profess any statement of belief, or to engage in any ceremony of assent to one, presents questions of power that must be considered independently of any idea we may have as to the utility of the ceremony in question.

Nor does the issue, as we see it, turn on one's possession of particular religious views or the sincerity with which they are held. While religion supplies appellees' motive for enduring the discomforts of making the issue in this case, many citizens who do not share these religious views hold such a compulsory rite to infringe constitutional liberty of the individual. It is not necessary to inquire whether nonconformist beliefs will exempt from the duty to salute unless we first find power to make the salute a legal duty.

We examine, rather than assume existence of, this power, and, against this broader definition of issues in this case, reexamine specific grounds assigned for the *Gobitis* decision.

1. It was said that the flag salute controversy confronted the Court with "the problem which Lincoln cast in memorable dilemma: 'Must a government of necessity be too strong for the liberties of its people, or too weak to maintain its own existence?', and that the answer must be in favor of strength." . . .

It may be doubted whether Mr. Lincoln would have thought that the strength of government to maintain itself would be impressively vindicated by our confirming power of the State to expel a handful of children from school. Such oversimplification, so handy in political debate, often lacks the precision necessary to postulates of judicial reasoning. If validly applied to this problem, the utterance cited would resolve every issue of power in favor of those in authority, and would require us to override every liberty thought to weaken or delay execution of their policies. . . .

2. It was also considered in the *Gobitis* case that functions of educational officers in States, counties and school districts were such that to interfere with their authority "would in effect make us the school board for the country."

The Fourteenth Amendment, as now applied to the States, protects the citizen against the State itself and all of its creatures—Boards of Education not excepted. These have, of course, important, delicate, and highly discretionary functions, but none that they may not perform within the limits of the Bill of Rights. That they are educating the young for citizenship is reason for scrupulous protection of Constitutional freedoms of the individual, if we are not to strangle the free mind at its source and teach youth to discount important principles of our government as mere platitudes. . . .

3. The *Gobitis* opinion reasoned that this is a field "where courts possess no marked, and certainly no controlling, competence," that it is committed to the legislatures, as well as the courts, to guard cherished liberties, and that it is constitutionally appropriate to "fight out the wise use of legislative authority in the forum of public opinion and before legislative assemblies, rather than to transfer such a contest to the judicial arena," since all the "effective means of inducing political changes are left free."

The very purpose of a Bill of Rights was to withdraw certain subjects from the vicissitudes of political controversy, to place them beyond the reach of majorities and officials, and to establish them as legal principles to be applied by the courts. One's right to life, liberty, and property, to free speech, a free press, freedom of worship and assembly, and other fundamental rights may not be submitted to vote; they depend on the outcome of no elections.

In weighing arguments of the parties, it is important to distinguish between the due process clause of the Fourteenth Amendment as an instrument for transmitting the principles of the First Amendment and those cases in which it is applied for its own sake. The test of legislation which collides with the Fourteenth Amendment, because it also collides with the principles of the First, is much more definite than the test when only the Fourteenth is involved. Much of the vagueness of the due process clause disappears when the specific prohibitions of the First become its standard. The right of a State to regulate, for example, a public utility may well include, so far as the due process test is concerned, power to impose all of the restrictions which a legislature may have a "rational basis" for adopting. But freedoms of speech and of press, of assembly, and of worship may not be infringed on such slender grounds. They are susceptible of restriction only to prevent grave and immediate danger to interests which the State may lawfully protect. It is important to note that, while it is the Fourteenth Amendment which bears directly upon the State, it is the more specific limiting principles of the First Amendment that finally govern this case.

Nor does our duty to apply the Bill of Rights to assertions of official authority depend upon our possession of marked competence in the field where the invasion of rights occurs. True, the task of translating the majestic generalities of the Bill of Rights, conceived as part of the pattern of liberal government in the eighteenth century, into concrete restraints on officials dealing with the problems of the twentieth century, is one to disturb self-confidence. These principles grew in soil which also produced a philosophy that the individual was the center of society, that his liberty was attainable through mere absence of governmental restraints, and that government should be entrusted with few controls, and only the mildest supervision over men's affairs. We must transplant these rights to a soil in which the *laissez-faire* concept or principle of noninterference has withered, at least as to economic affairs, and social advancements are increasingly sought through closer integration of society and through expanded and strengthened governmental controls. These changed conditions often deprive precedents of reliability, and cast us more than we would choose upon our own judgment. But we act in these matters not by authority of our competence, but by force of our commissions. We cannot, because of modest estimates of our competence in such specialties as public education, withhold the judgment that history authenticates as the function of this Court when liberty is infringed.

4. Lastly, and this is the very heart of the *Gobitis* opinion, it reasons that "National unity is the basis of national security," that the authorities have "the right to select appropriate means for its attainment," and hence reaches the conclusion that such compulsory measures toward "national unity" are constitutional. Upon the verity of this assumption depends our answer in this case.

National unity, as an end which officials may foster by persuasion and example, is not in question. The problem is whether, under our Constitution, compulsion as here employed is a permissible means for its achievement.

Struggles to coerce uniformity of sentiment in support of some end thought essential to their time and country have been waged by many good, as well as by evil, men. Nationalism is a relatively recent phenomenon, but, at other times and places, the ends have been racial or territorial security, support of a dynasty or regime, and particular plans for saving souls. As first and moderate methods to attain unity have failed, those bent on its accomplishment must resort to an ever-increasing severity. As governmental pressure toward unity becomes greater, so strife becomes more bitter as to whose unity it shall be. Probably no deeper division of our people could proceed from any provocation than from finding it necessary to choose what doctrine and whose program public educational officials shall compel youth to unite in embracing. . . . Those who begin coercive elimination of dissent soon find themselves exterminating dissenters. Compulsory unification of opinion achieves only the unanimity of the graveyard.

It seems trite but necessary to say that the First Amendment to our Constitution was designed to avoid these ends by avoiding these beginnings. There is no mysticism in the American concept of the State or of the nature or origin of its authority. We set up government by consent of the governed, and the Bill of Rights denies those in power any legal opportunity to coerce that consent. Authority here is to be controlled by public opinion, not public opinion by authority.

The case is made difficult not because the principles of its decision are obscure, but because the flag involved is our own. Nevertheless, we apply the limitations of the Constitution with no fear that freedom to be intellectually and spiritually diverse or even contrary will disintegrate the social organization. To believe that patriotism will not flourish if patriotic ceremonies are voluntary and spontaneous, instead of a compulsory routine, is to make an unflattering estimate of the appeal of our institutions to free minds. We can have intellectual individualism and the rich cultural diversities that we owe to exceptional minds only at the price of occasional eccentricity and abnormal attitudes. When they are so harmless to others or to the State as those we deal with here, the price is not too great. But freedom to differ is not limited to things that do not matter much. That would be a mere shadow of freedom. The test of its substance is the right to differ as to things that touch the heart of the existing order.

If there is any fixed star in our constitutional constellation, it is that no official, high or petty, can prescribe what shall be orthodox in politics, nationalism, religion, or other matters of opinion, or force citizens to confess by word or act their faith therein. If there are any circumstances which permit an exception, they do not now occur to us.

Affirmed.

MR. JUSTICE ROBERTS and MR. JUSTICE REED adhere to the views expressed by the Court in *Minersville School District* v. *Gobitis* and are of the opinion that the judgment below should be reversed.

MR. JUSTICE MURPHY, concurring.

The right of freedom of thought and of religion, as guaranteed by the Constitution against State action, includes both the right to speak freely and the right to refrain from speaking at all, except insofar as essential operations of government may require it for the preservation of an orderly society—as in the case of compulsion to give evidence in court. Without wishing to disparage the purposes and intentions of those who hope to inculcate sentiments of loyalty and patriotism by requiring a declaration of allegiance as a feature of public education, or unduly belittle the benefits that may accrue therefrom, I am impelled to conclude that such a requirement is not essential to the maintenance of effective government and orderly society. To many, it is deeply distasteful to join in a public chorus of affirmation of private belief. By some, including the members of this sect, it is apparently regarded as incompatible with a primary religious obligation, and therefore a restriction on religious freedom. Official compulsion to affirm what is contrary to one's religious beliefs is the antithesis of freedom of worship which, it is well to recall, was achieved in this country only after what Jefferson characterized as the "severest contests in which I have ever been engaged." . . .

Any spark of love for country which may be generated in a child or his associates by forcing him to make what is to him an empty gesture and recite words wrung from him contrary to his religious beliefs is overshadowed by the desirability of preserving freedom of conscience to the full. It is in that freedom and the example of persuasion, not in force and compulsion, that the real unity of America lies.

MR. JUSTICE FRANKFURTER, dissenting.

One who belongs to the most vilified and persecuted minority in history is not likely to be insensible to the freedoms guaranteed by our Constitution. Were my purely personal attitude relevant, I should wholeheartedly associate myself with the general libertarian views in the Court's opinion, representing, as they do, the thought and action of a lifetime. But, as judges, we are neither Jew nor Gentile, neither Catholic nor agnostic. We owe equal attachment to the Constitution, and are equally bound by our judicial obligations whether we derive our citizenship from the earliest or the latest immigrants to these shores. As a member of this Court, I am not justified in writing my private notions of policy into the Constitution, no matter how deeply I may cherish them or how mischievous I may deem their disregard. The duty of a judge who must decide which of two claims before the Court shall prevail, that of a State to enact and enforce laws within its general competence or that of an individual to refuse obedience because of the demands of his conscience, is not that of the ordinary person. It can never be emphasized too much that one's own opinion about the wisdom or evil of a law should be excluded altogether when one is doing one's duty on the bench. The only opinion of our own even looking in that direction that is material is our opinion whether legislators could, in reason, have enacted such a law. In the light of all the circumstances, including the history of this question in this Court, it would require more daring than I possess to deny that reasonable legislators could have taken the action which is before us for review. Most unwillingly, therefore, I must differ from my brethren with regard to legislation like this. I cannot bring my mind to believe that the "liberty" secured by the Due Process Clause gives this Court authority to deny to the State of West Virginia the attainment of that which we all recognize as a legitimate legislative end, namely, the promotion of good citizenship, by employment of the means here chosen. . . .

Under our constitutional system, the legislature is charged solely with civil concerns of society. If the avowed or intrinsic legislative purpose is either to promote or to discourage some religious community or creed, it is clearly within the constitutional restrictions imposed on legislatures, and cannot stand. But it by no means follows that legislative power is wanting whenever a general nondiscriminatory civil regulation, in fact, touches conscientious scruples or religious beliefs of an individual or a group. Regard for such scruples or beliefs undoubtedly presents one of the most reasonable claims for the exertion of legislative accommodation. It is, of course, beyond our power to rewrite the State's requirement by providing exemptions for those who do not wish to participate in the flag salute or by making some other accommodations to meet their scruples. That wisdom might suggest the making of such accommodations, and that school administration would not find it too difficult to make them, and yet maintain the ceremony for those not refusing to conform, is outside our province to suggest. Tact, respect, and generosity toward variant views will always commend themselves to those charged with the duties of legislation so as to achieve a maximum of good will and to require a minimum of unwilling submission to a general law. But the real question is, who is to make such accommodations, the courts or the legislature? . . .

That which to the majority may seem essential for the welfare of the state may offend the consciences of a minority. But, so long as no inroads are made upon the actual exercise of religion by the minority, to deny the political power of the majority to enact laws concerned with civil matters, simply because they may offend the consciences of a minority, really means that the consciences of a minority are more sacred and more enshrined in the Constitution than the consciences of a majority.

We are told that symbolism is a dramatic but primitive way of communicating ideas. Symbolism is inescapable. Even the most sophisticated live by symbols. But it is not for this Court to make psychological judgments as to the effectiveness of a particular symbol in inculcating concededly indispensable feelings, particularly if the state happens to see fit to utilize the symbol that represents our heritage and our hopes. And surely only flippancy could be responsible for the suggestion that constitutional validity of a requirement to salute our flag implies equal validity of a requirement to salute a dictator. The significance of a symbol lies in what it represents. To reject the swastika does not imply rejection of the Cross. And so it bears repetition to say that it mocks reason and denies our whole history to find in the allowance of a requirement to salute our flag on fitting occasions the seeds of sanction for obeisance to a leader. To deny the power to employ educational symbols is to say that the state's educational system may not stimulate the imagination because this may lead to unwise stimulation.

The right of West Virginia to utilize the flag salute as part of its educational process is denied because, so it is argued, it cannot be justified as a means of meeting a "clear and present danger" to national unity. In passing, it deserves to be noted that the four cases which unanimously sustained the power of states to utilize such an educational measure arose and were all decided before the present World War. But to measure the state's power to make such regulations as are here resisted by the imminence of national danger is wholly to misconceive the origin and purpose of the concept of "clear and present danger." To apply such a test is for the Court to assume, however unwittingly, a legislative responsibility that does not belong to it. To talk about "clear and present danger" as the touchstone of allowable educational policy by the states whenever school curricula may impinge upon the boundaries of individual conscience is to take a felicitous phrase out of the context of the particular situation where it arose and for which it was adapted. . . .

The flag salute exercise has no kinship whatever to the [religious] oath tests so odious in history. For the oath test was one of the instruments for suppressing heretical beliefs. Saluting the flag suppresses no belief, nor curbs it. Children and their parents may believe what they please, avow their belief and practice it. It is not even remotely suggested that the requirement for saluting the flag involves the slightest restriction against the fullest opportunity on the part both of the children and of their parents to disavow, as publicly as they choose to do so, the meaning that others attach to the gesture of salute. All channels of affirmative free expression are open to both children and parents. Had we before us any act of the state putting the slightest curbs upon such free expression, I should not lag behind any member of this Court in striking down such an invasion of the right to freedom of thought and freedom of speech protected by the Constitution. . . .

In the past, this Court has from time to time set its views of policy against that embodied in legislation by finding laws in conflict with what was called the "spirit of the Constitution." Such undefined destructive power was not conferred on this Court by the Constitution. Before a duly enacted law can be judicially nullified, it must be forbidden by some explicit restriction upon political authority in the Constitution. Equally inadmissible is the claim to strike down legislation because, to us as individuals, it seems opposed to the "plan and purpose" of the Constitution. That is too tempting a basis for finding in one's personal views the purposes of the Founders. . . .

Of course, patriotism cannot be enforced by the flag salute. But neither can the liberal spirit be enforced by judicial invalidation of illiberal legislation. Our constant preoccupation with the constitutionality of legislation, rather than with its wisdom, tends to preoccupation of the American mind with a false value. The tendency of focussing attention on constitutionality is to make constitutionality synonymous with wisdom, to regard a law as all right if it is constitutional. Such an attitude is a great enemy of liberalism. Particularly in legislation affecting freedom of thought and freedom of speech, much which should offend a free-spirited society is constitutional. Reliance for the most precious interests of civilization, therefore, must be found outside of their vindication in courts of law. Only a persistent positive translation of the faith of a free society into the convictions and habits and action of a community is the ultimate reliance against unabated temptations to fetter the human spirit.

▼▲▼

By holding that the government could not compel an individual to affirm a repugnant belief, the Court, in *Barnette,* added a crucial element to the mix of political expression receiving First Amendment protection. In *Gobitis,* the Court, much like it had in *Schenck,* was caught up in a nationalist fervor as America prepared to go to war against the Japanese empire and Nazi Germany. *Barnette* was decided about eighteen months after the United States had entered World War II. The justices, all of whom by this time had been appointed by President Franklin D. Roosevelt, were well-positioned among the corridors of power in Washington, D.C. They were privy to the mounting evidence of Hitler's "Final Solution" to exterminate the Jews of Europe and anyone else undesirable to the Nazi regime, including homosexuals, "gypsies," and Jehovah's Witnesses. Thus, when Justice Jackson wrote, "Those who begin coercive elimination of dissent soon find themselves exterminating dissenters. Compulsory unification of opinion achieves only the unanimity of the graveyard," the message was clear: A free nation had to tolerate dissenters, or soon they take on the characteristics of the totalitarian regimes they had pledged to defeat.

In contrast to the NAACP's litigation campaign to dismantle racial segregation, in place by the time *Barnette* was decided (see Chapter 11), or the American Jewish Congress's attempt in the late 1940s to challenge government support for religion (see Chapter 6), the ACLU had no such grand plan to expand the constitutional boundaries of free speech. Nonetheless, over the next thirty years, the ACLU was involved in nearly every critical free speech case decided by the Supreme Court during a time when the First Amendment was undergoing a dramatic expansion. By the 1960s, the ACLU had firmly embraced the absolutist notion of free speech, and was eager to assert this principle in cases involving anti–Vietnam War dissenters. As discussed earlier, antiwar protests had become increasingly commonplace by the 1960s, but they had largely been confined to peaceful demonstrations, speeches, "teach-ins," and other constitutionally permissible uses of public space, or what the Court has called the *traditional public forum.*

It was one thing to give a speech against Vietnam on the town hall steps or organize a rally of tens of thousands on the Mall in Washington. It was something else entirely when young men called to military service decided to stage the ultimate protest by burning their draft cards in public. Restrictions on political speech were governed by *Brandenburg.* Conduct, on the other hand, was subject to a different analysis. In 1965, the ACLU had represented a Vietnam draftee named David Miller who burned his draft card on the front steps of an induction center in New York City, despite knowing full well that a six-week-old law prohibited such an act. ACLU lawyers argued that Miller's conduct was protected symbolic speech, but the New York courts disagreed, and the Supreme Court declined to grant review.[42] Three years later, however, the Court agreed to decide whether burning a draft card in defiance of a federal law to the contrary violated the First

Amendment. Representing the defendants in *United States* v. *O'Brien* (1968) was the Massachusetts affiliate of the ACLU, which, invoking *Stromberg* and *Barnette,* again argued that draft-card burning was protected by the First Amendment.

United States v. *O'Brien*

391 U.S. 367 (1968)

On March 31, 1966, David O'Brien and three friends, all of whom described themselves as pacifists and conscientious objectors to the Vietnam War, burned their draft cards on the steps of a South Boston courthouse. Their demonstration was well attended by the media, and it also drew a vocal opposition from the war's supporters, who mounted a brief assault on the draft-card burners before they were ushered to safety by FBI agents on the scene.

O'Brien was prosecuted under the federal selective service law, which made the destruction or mutilation of draft cards a criminal offense.

The Court's decision was 7 to 1. Chief Justice Warren delivered the opinion of the Court. Justice Harlan wrote a concurring opinion. Justice Douglas dissented. Justice Marshall did not participate.

▼▲▼

MR. CHIEF JUSTICE WARREN delivered the opinion of the Court.

O'Brien first argues that the 1965 Amendment is unconstitutional as applied to him because his act of burning his registration certificate was protected "symbolic speech" within the First Amendment. His argument is that the freedom of expression which the First Amendment guarantees includes all modes of "communication of ideas by conduct," and that his conduct is within this definition because he did it in "demonstration against the war and against the draft."

We cannot accept the view that an apparently limitless variety of conduct can be labeled "speech" whenever the person engaging in the conduct intends thereby to express an idea. However, even on the assumption that the alleged communicative element in O'Brien's conduct is sufficient to bring into play the First Amendment, it does not necessarily follow that the destruction of a registration certificate is constitutionally protected activity. This Court has held that, when "speech" and "nonspeech" elements are combined in the same course of conduct, a sufficiently important governmental interest in regulating the nonspeech element can justify incidental limitations on First Amendment freedoms. To characterize the quality of the governmental interest which must appear, the Court has employed a variety of descriptive terms: compelling; substantial; subordinating; paramount; cogent; strong. Whatever imprecision inheres in these terms, we think it clear that a government regulation is sufficiently justified if it is within the constitutional power of the Government; if it furthers an important or substantial governmental interest; if the governmental interest is unrelated to the suppression of free expression, and if the incidental restriction on alleged First Amendment freedoms is no greater than is essential to the furtherance of that interest. We find that the 1965 Amendment to § 12(b)(3) of the Universal Military Training and Service Act meets all of these requirements, and consequently that O'Brien can be constitutionally convicted for violating it.

The constitutional power of Congress to raise and support armies and to make all laws necessary and proper to that end is broad and sweeping. The power of Congress to classify and conscript manpower for military service is beyond question. Pursuant to this power, Congress may establish a system of registration for individuals liable for training and service, and may require such individuals, within reason, to cooperate in the registration system. The issuance of certificates indicating the registration and eligibility classification of individuals is a legitimate and substantial administrative aid in the functioning of this system. . . .

O'Brien's argument to the contrary is necessarily premised upon his unrealistic characterization of Selective Service certificates. He essentially adopts the position that such certificates are so many pieces of paper designed to notify registrants of their registration or classification, to be retained or tossed in the wastebasket according to the convenience or taste of the registrant. Once the registrant has received notification, according to this view, there is no reason for him to retain the certificates. O'Brien notes that most of the information on a registration certificate serves no notification purpose at all; the registrant hardly needs to be told his address and physical characteristics. We agree that the registration certificate contains much information of which the registrant needs no notification. This circumstance, however, does not lead to the conclusion that the certificate serves no purpose, but that, like the classification certificate, it serves purposes in addition to initial notification. Many of these purposes would be defeated by the certificates' destruction or mutilation. Among these are:

1. The registration certificate serves as proof that the individual described thereon has registered for the draft. The classification certificate shows the eligibility classification of a named but undescribed individual. Voluntarily displaying the two certificates is an easy and painless way for a young man to dispel a question as to whether he might be delinquent in his Selective Service obligations. Correspondingly, the availability of the certificates for such display relieves the Selective Service System of the administrative burden it would otherwise have in verifying the registration and classification of all suspected delinquents. Further, since both certificates are in the nature of "receipts" attesting that the registrant has done what the law requires, it is in the interest of the just and efficient administration of the system that they be continually available, in the event, for example, of a mix-up in the registrant's file. Additionally, in a time of national crisis, reasonable availability to each registrant of the two small cards assures a rapid and uncomplicated means for determining his fitness for immediate induction, no matter how distant in our mobile society he may be from his local board.
2. The information supplied on the certificates facilitates communication between registrants and local boards, simplifying the system and benefiting all concerned. To begin with, each certificate bears the address of the registrant's local board, an item unlikely to be committed to memory. Further, each card bears the registrant's Selective Service number, and a registrant who has his number readily available so that he can communicate it to his local board when he supplies or requests information can make simpler the board's task in locating his file. Finally, a registrant's inquiry, particularly through a local board other than his own, concerning his eligibility status is frequently answerable simply on the basis of his classification certificate; whereas, if the certificate were not reasonably available and the registrant were uncertain of his classification, the task of answering his questions would be considerably complicated.
3. Both certificates carry continual reminders that the registrant must notify his local board of any change of address, and other specified changes in his status. The smooth functioning of the system requires that local boards be continually aware of the status and whereabouts of registrants, and the destruction of certificates deprives the system of a potentially useful notice device.
4. The regulatory scheme involving Selective Service certificates includes clearly valid prohibitions against the alteration, forgery, or similar deceptive misuse of certificates. The destruction or mutilation of certificates obviously increases the difficulty of detecting and tracing abuses such as these. Further, a mutilated certificate might itself be used for deceptive purposes.

The many functions performed by Selective Service certificates establish beyond doubt that Congress has a legitimate and substantial interest in preventing their wanton and unrestrained destruction and assuring their continuing availability by punishing people who knowingly and willfully destroy or mutilate them. And we are unpersuaded that the preexistence of the nonpossession regulations in any way negates this interest. . . .

We think it apparent that the continuing availability to each registrant of his Selective Service certificates substantially furthers the smooth and proper functioning of the system that Congress has established to raise armies. We think it also apparent that the Nation has a vital interest in having a system for raising armies that functions with maximum efficiency and is capable of easily and quickly responding to continually changing circumstances. For these reasons, the Government has a substantial interest in assuring the continuing availability of issued Selective Service certificates.

It is equally clear that the 1965 Amendment specifically protects this substantial governmental interest. We perceive no alternative means that would more precisely and narrowly assure the continuing availability of issued Selective Service certificates than a law which prohibits their willful mutilation or destruction. The 1965 Amendment prohibits such conduct and does nothing more. In other words, both the governmental interest and the operation of the 1965 Amendment are limited to the noncommunicative aspect of O'Brien's conduct. . . .

In conclusion, we find that, because of the Government's substantial interest in assuring the continuing availability of issued Selective Service certificates, because amended § 462(b) is an appropriately narrow means of protecting this interest and condemns only the independent noncommunicative impact of conduct within its reach, and because the noncommunicative impact of O'Brien's act of burning his registration certificate frustrated the Government's interest, a sufficient governmental interest has been shown to justify O'Brien's conviction. . . .

O'Brien finally argues that the 1965 Amendment is unconstitutional as enacted because what he calls the "purpose" of Congress was "to suppress freedom of speech." We reject this argument because under settled principles the purpose of Congress, as O'Brien uses that term, is not a basis for declaring this legislation unconstitutional. . . .

Inquiries into congressional motives or purposes are a hazardous matter. When the issue is simply the interpretation of legislation, the Court will look to statements by legislators for guidance as to the purpose of the legislature, because the benefit to sound decisionmaking in this circumstance is thought sufficient to risk the possibility of misreading Congress' purpose. It is entirely a different matter when we are asked to void a statute that is, under well settled criteria, constitutional on its face, on the basis of what fewer than a handful of Congressmen said about it. What motivates one legislator to make a speech about a statute is not necessarily what motivates scores of others to enact it, and the stakes are sufficiently high for us to eschew guesswork. We decline to void essentially on the ground that it is unwise legislation which Congress had the undoubted power to enact and which could be reenacted in its exact form if the same or another legislator made a "wiser" speech about it.

We think it not amiss, in passing, to comment upon O'Brien's legislative purpose argument. There was little floor debate on this legislation in either House. Only Senator Thurmond commented on its substantive features in the Senate. After his brief statement, and without any additional substantive comments, the bill, H.R. 10306, passed the Senate. In the House debate only two Congressmen addressed themselves to the Amendment—Congressmen Rivers and Bray. The bill was passed after their statements without any further debate by a vote of 393 to 1. It is principally on the basis of the statements by these three Congressmen that O'Brien makes his congressional "purpose" argument. We note that, if we were to examine legislative purpose in the instant case, we would be obliged to consider not only these statements, but also the more authoritative reports of the Senate and House Armed Services Committees. . . . While both reports make clear a concern with the "defiant" destruction of so-called "draft cards" and with "open" encouragement to others to destroy their cards, both reports also indicate that this concern stemmed from an apprehension that unrestrained destruction of cards would disrupt the smooth functioning of the Selective Service System.

MR. JUSTICE DOUGLAS, dissenting.

The Court states that the constitutional power of Congress to raise and support armies is "broad and sweeping," and that Congress' power "to classify and conscript manpower for military service is 'beyond question.'" This is undoubtedly true in times when, by declaration of Congress, the Nation is in a state of war. The underlying and basic problem in this case, however, is whether conscription is permissible in the absence of a declaration of war. That question has not been briefed nor was it presented in oral argument; but it is, I submit, a question upon which the litigants and the country are entitled to a ruling. . . . [T]his Court has never ruled on the question. It is time that we made a ruling.

Note that Chief Justice Warren barely mentions the First Amendment issue, focusing instead on the interest of Congress in managing the "smooth and efficient operation" of the draft system. Despite several statements from members of Congress vowing to punish "open defiance" of the draft law, Warren also declined to address the motive behind the enactment of the anti–draft card burning provision, concluding that "[I]nquiries into congressional motives or purposes are a hazardous matter." The ACLU had attached a separate appendix to its brief documenting what it believed was the law's true purpose—to stamp out political dissent. But with the exception of Justice Douglas, no justice agreed with the ACLU's argument. That the Court saw burning a draft card as different from other symbolic speech was evident during oral argument, when Chief Justice Warren engaged in the following exchange with ACLU lawyer Marvin Karpatkin:

> *Warren:* Suppose a soldier over in Vietnam, in front of a large crowd of soldiers, broke his weapon and said it was a protest against the War and the foreign policy of the Government. Would that be symbolic speech?
>
> *Karpatkin:* Mr. Chief Justice, I don't know whether that would or wouldn't be symbolic speech.
>
> *Warren:* Well, we have to go a little farther than just this particular case, do we not?
>
> *Karpatkin:* We certainly do not argue, as the Government in its brief suggests, that under our theory anything which communicates is protected, and that anything which communicates an idea is protected. We don't argue that the dumping of garbage is protected, or that political assassination is protected, or that any other of the fanciful notions which the Government seems to charge us with, is protected.

Also of interest in *O'Brien* is how the Court's two self-described First Amendment absolutists, Douglas and Black, had begun to diverge on free speech questions that involved symbolic speech, protests, and other forms of expressive conduct. Since *Barnette,* Douglas had voted consistently to uphold such claims as protected by the First Amendment. Black now argued that the absolute protection afforded by the First Amendment to ideas communicated through verbal speech did not necessarily extend into the public realm. In *Tinker,* decided the year after *O'Brien,* Black rejected the argument that the First Amendment protected the right of students to wear their arm bands to school. That same year, Black dissented again in an important free speech case brought by the ACLU involving expressive conduct, *Street* v. *New York* (1969). James Street had burned the American flag on a New York City street corner and his case involved a challenge to a state law making it illegal "publicly [to] mutilate, deface, defile, or defy, trample upon, or cast contempt upon either by words or act [any flag of the United States]." By a 5 to 4 margin, the Court concluded that James Street had been convicted because of what he had said during his deed: "We don't need no damn flag."[43] Street had burned the flag as a response to the assassination of Martin Luther King Jr. in April 1968.

Five years later, the Court upheld another First Amendment claim brought by the ACLU involving a flag desecration law. In *Spence* v. *Washington* (1974), the Court overturned the conviction of a college student in Washington State who had displayed an American flag with a peace symbol in the window of his dorm room. The Court noted that compared to the more violent demonstrations that regularly inflamed the nation's streets and college campuses, this protest was relatively tame and "restrained."[44] *Spence* put to rest, for the moment, the question of whether defacing the American flag was protected expression under the First Amendment. Fifteen years later, the Court, in a time of peace and prosperity, returned to a question that had been left open since *Street:* Was *burning* the American flag, as opposed to condemning or handling it inappropriately, protected symbolic speech? The question produced one of the Court's most controversial and emotionally charged opinions since *Barnette.*

Texas v. *Johnson*

491 U.S. 397 (1989)

Outside the Republican Party convention hall in 1984, Gregory Lee Johnson was leading a denunciation of both Ronald Reagan's administration's policies and those of several large corporations based in Dallas, where the convention was being held. Earlier in the day, Johnson had marched through downtown streets with other protesters, some of whom had spray-painted buildings and destroyed potted plants. Johnson was not among the protesters engaging in such criminal activity. He did, however, take an American flag that had been stripped from a flagpole by another protestor, place it on the ground, and, while others chanted, "America, the red, white and blue, we spit on you," lit the flag on fire.

Johnson was charged with violating a Texas law that made it illegal to "desecrate a venerated object," defined as a public monument, a place of worship or burial, or a state or national flag. Under the law, to desecrate meant to "deface, damage, or otherwise physically mistreat in a way that the actor knows will seriously offend one or more persons likely to observe or discover his action." Johnson's conviction was reversed by the Texas Court of Criminal Appeals, which held that flag burning was symbolic speech protected by the First Amendment.

The Court's decision was 5 to 4. Justice Brennan delivered the opinion of the Court. Justice Kennedy filed a concurring opinion. Chief Justice Rehnquist wrote a dissenting opinion, which was joined by Justices O'Connor and White. Justice Stevens dissented, and his dissent is particularly noteworthy. Normally among the most liberal members of the Court on freedom of speech issues, Stevens was, however, the only member of the Court with wartime experience, having served in World War II.

JUSTICE BRENNAN delivered the opinion of the Court.

Johnson was convicted of flag desecration for burning the flag, rather than for uttering insulting words. This fact somewhat complicates our consideration of his conviction under the First Amendment. We must first determine whether Johnson's burning of the flag constituted expressive conduct, permitting him to invoke the First Amendment in challenging his conviction. If his conduct was

expressive, we next decide whether the State's regulation is related to the suppression of free expression. If the State's regulation is not related to expression, then the less stringent standard we announced in *United States* v. *O'Brien* for regulations of noncommunicative conduct controls. If it is, then we are outside of *O'Brien*'s test, and we must ask whether this interest justifies Johnson's conviction under a more demanding standard. A third possibility is that the State's asserted interest is simply not implicated on these facts, and, in that event, the interest drops out of the picture.

The First Amendment literally forbids the abridgment only of "speech," but we have long recognized that its protection does not end at the spoken or written word. While we have rejected "the view that an apparently limitless variety of conduct can be labeled 'speech' whenever the person engaging in the conduct intends thereby to express an idea," we have acknowledged that conduct may be "sufficiently imbued with elements of communication to fall within the scope of the First and Fourteenth Amendments." . . .

Especially pertinent to this case are our decisions recognizing the communicative nature of conduct relating to flags. Attaching a peace sign to the flag, refusing to salute the flag, and displaying a red flag, we have held, all may find shelter under the First Amendment. That we have had little difficulty identifying an expressive element in conduct relating to flags should not be surprising. The very purpose of a national flag is to serve as a symbol of our country. . . . Pregnant with expressive content, the flag as readily signifies this Nation as does the combination of letters found in "America."

We have not automatically concluded, however, that any action taken with respect to our flag is expressive. Instead, in characterizing such action for First Amendment purposes, we have considered the context in which it occurred. . . .

The State of Texas conceded for purposes of its oral argument in this case that Johnson's conduct was expressive conduct, and this concession seems to us as prudent as was Washington's in *Spence*. Johnson burned an American flag as part—indeed, as the culmination—of a political demonstration that coincided with the convening of the Republican Party and its renomination of Ronald Reagan for President. The expressive, overtly political nature of this conduct was both intentional and overwhelmingly apparent. At his trial, Johnson explained his reasons for burning the flag as follows: "The American Flag was burned as Ronald Reagan was being renominated as President. And a more powerful statement of symbolic speech, whether you agree with it or not, couldn't have been made at that time. It's quite a just position [juxtaposition]. We had new patriotism and no patriotism." In these circumstances, Johnson's burning of the flag was conduct "sufficiently imbued with elements of communication" to implicate the First Amendment.

The government generally has a freer hand in restricting expressive conduct than it has in restricting the written or spoken word. . . . It is, in short, not simply the verbal or nonverbal nature of the expression, but the governmental interest at stake, that helps to determine whether a restriction on that expression is valid.

Thus, although we have recognized that, where "'speech' and 'nonspeech' elements are combined in the same course of conduct, a sufficiently important governmental interest in regulating the nonspeech element can justify incidental limitations on First Amendment freedoms," we have limited the applicability of *O'Brien*'s relatively lenient standard to those cases in which "the governmental interest is unrelated to the suppression of free expression." In stating, moreover, that *O'Brien*'s test "in the last analysis is little, if any, different from the standard applied to time, place, or manner restrictions," we have highlighted the requirement that the governmental interest in question be unconnected to expression in order to come under *O'Brien*'s less demanding rule.

In order to decide whether *O'Brien*'s test applies here, therefore, we must decide whether Texas has asserted an interest in support of Johnson's conviction that is unrelated to the suppression of expression. If we find that an interest asserted by the State is simply not implicated on the facts before us, we need not ask whether *O'Brien*'s test applies. The State offers two separate interests to justify this conviction: preventing breaches of the peace and preserving the flag as a symbol of nationhood and national unity. We hold that the first interest is not implicated on this record, and that the second is related to the suppression of expression.

Texas claims that its interest in preventing breaches of the peace justifies Johnson's conviction for flag desecration. However, no disturbance of the peace actually occurred or threatened to occur because of Johnson's burning of the flag. Although the State stresses the disruptive behavior of the protestors during their march toward City Hall, it admits that "no actual breach of the peace occurred at the time of the flagburning or in response to the flagburning." The State's emphasis on the protestors' disorderly actions prior to arriving at City Hall is not only somewhat surprising, given that no charges were brought on the basis of this conduct, but it also fails to show that a disturbance of the peace was a likely reaction to Johnson's conduct. The only evidence offered by the State at trial to show the reaction to Johnson's actions was the testimony of several persons who had been seriously offended by the flag burning.

The State's position, therefore, amounts to a claim that an audience that takes serious offense at particular expression is necessarily likely to disturb the peace, and that the expression may be prohibited on this basis. Our precedents do not countenance such a presumption. . . .

Thus, we have not permitted the government to assume that every expression of a provocative idea will incite a riot, but have instead required careful consideration of the actual circumstances surrounding such expression, asking whether the expression "is directed to inciting or producing imminent lawless action and is likely to incite or produce such action," *Brandenburg* v. *Ohio* (1969). To accept Texas' arguments that it need only demonstrate "the potential for a breach of the peace," and that every flag burning necessarily possesses that potential, would be to eviscerate our holding in *Brandenburg*. This we decline to do.

Nor does Johnson's expressive conduct fall within that small class of "fighting words" that are "likely to provoke the average person to retaliation, and thereby cause a breach of the peace." No reasonable onlooker would have regarded Johnson's generalized expression of dissatisfaction with the policies of the Federal Government as a direct personal insult or an invitation to exchange fisticuffs. We thus conclude that the State's interest in maintaining order is not implicated on these facts. The State need not worry that our holding will disable it from preserving the peace. We do not suggest that the First Amendment forbids a State to prevent "imminent lawless action." And, in fact, Texas already has a statute specifically prohibiting breaches of the peace, which tends to confirm that Texas need not punish this flag desecration in order to keep the peace. . . .

It remains to consider whether the State's interest in preserving the flag as a symbol of nationhood and national unity justifies Johnson's conviction. . . .

Whether Johnson's treatment of the flag violated Texas law thus depended on the likely communicative impact of his expressive conduct. . . .

Texas argues that its interest in preserving the flag as a symbol of nationhood and national unity survives this close analysis. Quoting extensively from the writings of this Court chronicling the flag's historic and symbolic role in our society, the State emphasizes the "'special place'" reserved for the flag in our Nation. The State's argument is not that it has an interest simply in maintaining the flag as a symbol of *something,* no matter what it symbolizes; indeed, if that were the State's position, it would be difficult to see how that interest is endangered by highly symbolic conduct such as Johnson's. Rather, the State's claim is that it has an interest in preserving the flag as a symbol of *nationhood* and *national unity,* a symbol with a determinate range of meanings. According to Texas, if one physically treats the flag in a way that would tend to cast doubt on either the idea that nationhood and national unity are the flag's referents or that national unity actually exists, the message conveyed thereby is a harmful one, and therefore may be prohibited.

If there is a bedrock principle underlying the First Amendment, it is that the government may not prohibit the expression of an idea simply because society finds the idea itself offensive or disagreeable.

We have not recognized an exception to this principle even where our flag has been involved. . . .

In short, nothing in our precedents suggests that a State may foster its own view of the flag by prohibiting expressive conduct relating to it. To bring its argument outside our precedents, Texas attempts to convince us that, even if its interest in preserving the flag's symbolic role does not allow it to prohibit words or some expressive conduct critical of the flag, it does permit it to forbid the outright destruction of the flag. The State's argument cannot depend here on the distinction between written or spoken words and nonverbal conduct. That distinction, we have shown, is of no moment where the nonverbal conduct is expressive, as it is here, and where the regulation of that conduct is related to expression, as it is here. . . .

Texas' focus on the precise nature of Johnson's expression, moreover, misses the point of our prior decisions: their enduring lesson, that the government may not prohibit expression simply because it disagrees with its message, is not dependent on the particular mode in which one chooses to express an idea. If we were to hold that a State may forbid flag burning wherever it is likely to endanger the flag's symbolic role, but allow it wherever burning a flag promotes that role—as where, for example, a person ceremoniously burns a dirty flag—we would be saying that when it comes to impairing the flag's physical integrity, the flag itself may be used as a symbol—as a substitute for the written or spoken word or a "short cut from mind to mind"—only in one direction. We would be permitting a State to "prescribe what shall be orthodox" by saying that one may burn the flag to convey one's attitude toward it and its referents only if one does not endanger the flag's representation of nationhood and national unity. . . .

There is . . . no indication—either in the text of the Constitution or in our cases interpreting it—that a separate juridical category exists for the American flag alone. Indeed, we would not be surprised to learn that the persons who framed our Constitution and wrote the Amendment that we now construe were not known for their reverence for the Union Jack. The First Amendment does not guarantee that other concepts virtually sacred to our Nation as a whole—such as the principle that discrimination on the basis of race is odious and destructive—will go unquestioned in the marketplace of ideas. We decline, therefore, to create for the flag an exception to the joust of principles protected by the First Amendment.

It is not the State's ends, but its means, to which we object. It cannot be gainsaid that there is a special place reserved for the flag in this Nation, and thus we do not doubt that the government has a legitimate interest in making efforts to "preserv[e] the national flag as an unalloyed symbol of our country." We reject the suggestion, urged at oral argument by counsel for Johnson, that the government lacks "any state interest whatsoever" in regulating the manner in which the flag may be displayed. Congress has, for example, enacted precatory regulations describing the proper treatment of the flag, and we cast no doubt on the legitimacy of its interest in making such recommendations. . . .

We are fortified in today's conclusion by our conviction that forbidding criminal punishment for conduct such as Johnson's will not endanger the special role played by our flag or the feelings it inspires. To paraphrase Justice Holmes, we submit that nobody can suppose that this one gesture of an unknown man will change our Nation's attitude towards its flag. Indeed, Texas' argument that the burning of an American flag "'is an act having a high likelihood to cause a breach of the peace,'" and its statute's implicit assumption that physical mistreatment of the flag will lead to "serious offense," tend to confirm that the flag's special role is not in danger; if it were, no one would riot or take offense because a flag had been burned.

We are tempted to say, in fact, that the flag's deservedly cherished place in our community will be strengthened, not weakened, by our holding today. Our decision is a reaffirmation of the principles of freedom and inclusiveness that the flag best reflects, and of the conviction that our toleration of criticism such as Johnson's is a sign and source of our strength. Indeed, one of the proudest images of our flag, the one immortalized in our own national anthem, is of the bombardment it survived at Fort McHenry. It is the Nation's resilience, not its rigidity, that Texas sees reflected in the flag—and it is that resilience that we reassert today. . . .

Johnson was convicted for engaging in expressive conduct. The State's interest in preventing breaches of the peace does not support his conviction, because Johnson's conduct did not threaten to disturb the peace. Nor does the State's interest in preserving the flag as a symbol of nationhood and national unity justify his criminal conviction for engaging in political expression. The judgment of the Texas Court of Criminal Appeals is therefore

Affirmed.

CHIEF JUSTICE REHNQUIST, with whom JUSTICE WHITE and JUSTICE O'CONNOR join, dissenting.

In holding this Texas statute unconstitutional, the Court ignores Justice Holmes' familiar aphorism that "a page of history is worth a volume of logic." For more than 200 years, the American flag has occupied a unique position as the symbol of our Nation, a uniqueness that justifies a governmental prohibition against flag burning in the way respondent Johnson did here. . . .

Here it may . . . be said that the public burning of the American flag by Johnson was no essential part of any exposition of ideas, and at the same time it had a tendency to incite a breach of the peace. Johnson was free to make any verbal denunciation of the flag that he wished; indeed, he was free to burn the flag in private. He could publicly burn other symbols of the Government or effigies of political leaders. He did lead a march through the streets of Dallas, and conducted a rally in front of the Dallas City Hall. He engaged in a "die-in" to protest nuclear weapons. He shouted out various slogans during the march, including: "Reagan, Mondale which will it be? Either one means World War III"; "Ronald Reagan, killer of the hour, Perfect example of U.S. power"; and "red, white and blue, we spit on you, you stand for plunder, you will go under." For none of these acts was he arrested or prosecuted; it was only when he proceeded to burn publicly an American flag stolen from its rightful owner that he violated the Texas statute. . . .

The result of the Texas statute is obviously to deny one in Johnson's frame of mind one of many means of "symbolic speech." Far from being a case of "one picture being worth a thousand words," flag burning is the equivalent of an inarticulate grunt or roar that, it seems fair to say, is most likely to be indulged in not to express any particular idea, but to antagonize others. . . . The Texas statute deprived Johnson of only one rather inarticulate symbolic form of protest—a form of protest that was profoundly offensive to many—and left him with a full panoply of other symbols and every conceivable form of verbal expression to express his deep disapproval of national policy. Thus, in no way can it be said that Texas is punishing him because his hearers—or any other group of people—were profoundly opposed to the message that he sought to convey. Such opposition is no proper basis for restricting speech or expression under the First Amendment. It was Johnson's use of this particular symbol, and not the idea that he sought to convey by it or by his many other expressions, for which he was punished. . . .

The Court concludes its opinion with a regrettably patronizing civics lecture, presumably addressed to the Members of both Houses of Congress, the members of the 48 state legislatures that enacted prohibitions against flag burning, and the troops fighting under that flag in Vietnam who objected to its being burned: "The way to preserve the flag's special role is not to punish those who feel differently about these matters. It is to persuade them that they are wrong."

The Court's role as the final expositor of the Constitution is well established, but its role as a platonic guardian admonishing those responsible to public opinion as if they were truant schoolchildren has no similar place in our system of government. The cry of "no taxation without representation" animated those who revolted against the English Crown to found our Nation—the idea that those who submitted to government should have some say as to what kind of laws would be passed. Surely one of the high purposes of a democratic society is to legislate against conduct that is regarded as evil and profoundly offensive to the majority of people—whether it be murder, embezzlement, pollution, or flag burning. . . .

Uncritical extension of constitutional protection to the burning of the flag risks the frustration of the very purpose for which organized governments are instituted. The Court decides that the American flag is just another symbol, about which not only must opinions pro and con be tolerated, but for which the most minimal public respect may not be enjoined. The government may conscript men into the Armed Forces where they must fight and perhaps die for the flag, but the government may not prohibit the public burning of the banner under which they fight. I would uphold the Texas statute as applied in this case.

JUSTICE STEVENS, dissenting.

A country's flag is a symbol of more than "nationhood and national unity." It also signifies the ideas that characterize the society that has chosen that emblem as well as the special history that has animated the growth and power of those ideas. . . . The message conveyed by some flags—the swastika, for example—may survive long after it has outlived its usefulness as a symbol of regimented unity in a particular nation.

So it is with the American flag. It is more than a proud symbol of the courage, the determination, and the gifts of nature that transformed 13 fledgling Colonies into a world power. It is a symbol of freedom, of equal opportunity, of religious tolerance, and of goodwill for other peoples who share our aspirations. The symbol carries its message to dissidents both at home and abroad who may have no interest at all in our national unity or survival.

The value of the flag as a symbol cannot be measured. Even so, I have no doubt that the interest in preserving that value for the future is both significant and legitimate. Conceivably, that value will be enhanced by the Court's conclusion that our national commitment to free expression is so strong that even the United States, as ultimate guarantor of that freedom, is without power to prohibit the desecration of its unique symbol. But I am unpersuaded. The creation of a federal right to post bulletin boards and graffiti on the Washington Monument might enlarge the market for free expression, but at a cost I would not pay. Similarly, in my considered judgment, sanctioning the public desecration of the flag will tarnish its value—both for those who cherish the ideas for which it waves and for those who desire to don the robes of martyrdom by burning it. That tarnish is not justified by the trivial burden on free expression occasioned by requiring that an available, alternative mode of expression—including uttering words critical of the flag—be employed. . . .

The ideas of liberty and equality have been an irresistible force in motivating leaders like Patrick Henry, Susan B. Anthony, and Abraham Lincoln, schoolteachers like Nathan Hale and Booker T. Washington, the Philippine Scouts who fought at Bataan, and the soldiers who scaled the bluff at Omaha Beach. If those ideas are worth fighting for—and our history demonstrates that they are—it cannot be true that the flag that uniquely symbolizes their power is not itself worthy of protection from unnecessary desecration.

I respectfully dissent.

Predictably, *Johnson* elicited an immediate response from Capitol Hill. The House passed a unanimous resolution condemning the decision, and the Senate also passed a similar nonbinding measure over only three "no" votes. Senator Robert Dole (R-Kans.), a decorated World War II veteran, introduced a constitutional amendment proposing to overturn *Johnson*. In an interesting generational twist, opposition in the Senate to the amendment was led by Senator Bob Kerrey (D-Neb.), who earned the Medal of Honor during his service in Vietnam. Dole and Kerrey both suffered horrible and life-altering injuries—Dole lost the use of his right arm and Kerrey had his right leg removed after combat-related injuries. Ultimately, the Dole proposal fell sixteen votes short of the necessary two-thirds majority required to send a constitutional amendment to the states for ratification. Congress did, however, enact legislation that attempted to satisfy the defects the Court found in the Texas law in *Johnson*. By the same 5 to 4 majority, the Court, in *United States* v. *Eichman* (1990), declared the Federal Flag Protection Act unconstitutional. From 1990 to 2000, fewer than five incidents involving the burning of the American flag were reported in the United States, suggesting that flag burning no longer incited the intended reaction.[45]

Abortion Politics and the First Amendment

During the 1970s and 1980s, right-to-life organizations mounted a vigorous campaign in legislatures and courtrooms across the nation to restrict the Court's landmark 1973 decision, *Roe* v. *Wade*, which established a constitutional right to abortion. As pro-life and pro-choice groups battled over the moral and legal issues involved in the abortion debate, another closely related constitutional issue was heating up on a different burner. Rather than confining protests against the Court's abortion decisions to traditional public places, right-to-life groups began to hold demonstrations in front of abortion clinics. These protests often resulted in violence, as increasing numbers of pro-life demonstrators were arrested for verbally and physically abusing patients and staff seeking access to abortion facilities. In 1992, the Court affirmed a woman's right to abortion in *Planned Parenthood* v. *Casey*, a case in which pro-choice and pro-life groups had explicitly asked the justices to resolve the constitutional question one way or the other (see Chapter 10). After *Casey*, clinic violence increased, and many states responded by passing laws designed to protect safe access to medical facilities providing abortions.[46]

Common features of these state laws included floating and fixed "buffer zones," which regulated how closely protesters could come to individuals entering and leaving clinics; bans on "observable images," such as aborted fetuses, on picket signs; and prohibitions on "sidewalk counseling," as the practice of distributing literature to women discouraging abortion is sometimes called. The American Center for Law and Justice (ACLJ) is a conservative public interest group that formed in the late 1980s to counter the ACLU on numerous fronts involving constitutional rights. With the backing of the ACLJ, individuals and groups in the pro-life movement filed several lawsuits in the 1990s challenging these laws on First Amendment grounds. Defending the access-to-clinic laws were groups such as Planned Parenthood, the National Organization for Women Legal Defense Fund, and the ACLU. As will be discussed in Chapter 10, since *Roe* the ACLU, through its Reproductive Freedom Project, has carried on much of the litigation attacking abortion restrictions in the states. Many pro-life advocates accused the ACLU of setting aside its historic commitment to the principle of absolute protection for free speech in favor of protecting abortion rights.

The group politics behind the Court's decisions on state and federal laws guaranteeing access to abortion clinics, as well as the violence that encouraged their enactment, are discussed in the accompanying SIDEBAR to *Hill* v. *Colorado* (2000). *Hill* involved a challenge brought by the ACLJ against a Colorado law establishing limits on protests staged near abortion clinics. *Hill* offers a good example of how the Court's decisions may have important consequences for many groups beyond those with an interest in the immediate facts of a case.

Hill v. *Colorado*

530 U.S. 703 (2000)

In 1993, Colorado enacted a law prohibiting any person within one hundred feet of any health care facility from "knowingly approaching" another person to hand them a leaflet or handbill, or to engage in oral protest or "sidewalk counseling." By using the phrase "any health care facility," the Colorado legislature obscured the real purpose of the law, which was to shield women entering abortion facilities from potentially abusive confrontations with pro-life demonstrators. Demonstrators were permitted to come within eight feet of any person entering or leaving a health care facility; they simply could not advance beyond that point without the individual's consent.

The Colorado courts ruled that the law did not violate the First Amendment. Critical to their conclusion was legislative testimony from supporters and opponents of the law that demonstrations in front of abortion clinics impeded access of individuals to the clinics.. Beginning in the late 1980s, escort patrols were commonly employed to secure the safety of doctors, patients, and staff using abortion facilities, after several people reported incidents of violent threats made against them. Also undisputed in the legislative record was the emotional intensity of the antiabortion demonstrations.

The Court's decision was 6 to 3. Justice Stevens delivered the opinion of the Court. Justice Souter concurred, and was joined by Justices Breyer, Ginsburg, and O'Connor. Justice Scalia, joined by Justice Thomas, dissented. Justice Kennedy also dissented.

▼▲▼

JUSTICE STEVENS delivered the opinion of the Court.

Before confronting the question whether the Colorado statute reflects an acceptable balance between the constitutionally protected rights of law-abiding speakers and the interests of unwilling listeners, it is appropriate to examine the competing interests at stake. A brief review of both sides of the dispute reveals that each has legitimate and important concerns.

The First Amendment interests of petitioners are clear and undisputed. As a preface to their legal challenge, petitioners emphasize three propositions. First, they accurately explain that the areas protected by the statute encompass all the public ways within 100 feet of every entrance to every health care facility everywhere in the State of Colorado. There is no disagreement on this point, even though the legislative history makes it clear that its enactment was primarily motivated by activities in the vicinity of abortion clinics. Second, they correctly state that their leafleting, sign displays, and oral communications are protected by the First Amendment. The fact that the messages conveyed by those communications may be offensive to their recipients does not deprive them of constitutional protection. Third, the public sidewalks, streets, and ways affected by the statute are "quintessential" public forums for free speech. Finally, although there is debate about the magnitude of the statutory impediment to their ability to communicate effectively with persons in the regulated zones, that ability, particularly the ability to distribute leaflets, is unquestionably lessened by this statute.

On the other hand, petitioners do not challenge the legitimacy of the state interests that the statute is intended to serve. It is a traditional exercise of the States' "police powers to protect the health and safety of their citizens." That interest may justify a special focus on unimpeded access to health care facilities and the avoidance of potential trauma to patients associated with confrontational protests. Moreover, as with every exercise of a State's police powers, rules that provide specific guidance to enforcement authorities serve the interest in evenhanded application of the law. Whether or not those interests justify the particular regulation at issue, they are unquestionably legitimate.

It is also important when conducting this interest analysis to recognize the significant difference between state restrictions on a speaker's right to address a willing audience and those that protect listeners from unwanted communication. This statute deals only with the latter.

The right to free speech, of course, includes the right to attempt to persuade others to change their views, and may not be curtailed simply because the speaker's message may be offensive to his audience. But the protection afforded to offensive messages does not always embrace offensive speech that is so intrusive that the unwilling audience cannot avoid it. Indeed, "[i]t may not be the content of the speech, as much as the deliberate 'verbal or visual assault,' that justifies proscription." Even in a public forum, one of the reasons we tolerate a protester's right to wear a jacket expressing his opposition to government policy in vulgar language is because offended viewers can "effectively avoid further bombardment of their sensibilities simply by averting their eyes."

The unwilling listener's interest in avoiding unwanted communication has been repeatedly identified in our cases. It is an aspect of the broader "right to be let alone" that one of our wisest Justices characterized as "the most comprehensive of rights and the right most valued by civilized men." The right to avoid unwelcome speech has special force in the privacy of the home, and its immediate surroundings, but can also be protected in confrontational settings. Thus, this comment on the right to free passage in going to and from work applies equally—or perhaps with greater force—to access to a medical facility. . . .

We have . . . recognized that the "right to persuade" discussed in that case is protected by the First Amendment, as well as by federal statutes. Yet we have continued to maintain that "no one has a right to press even 'good' ideas on an unwilling recipient." None of our decisions has minimized the enduring importance of "the right to be free" from persistent "importunity, following and dogging" after an offer to communicate has been declined. While the freedom to communicate is substantial, "the right of every person 'to be let alone' must be placed in the scales with the right of others to communicate." It is that right, as well as the right of "passage without obstruction," that the Colorado statute legitimately seeks to protect. The restrictions imposed by the Colorado statute only apply to communications that interfere with these rights rather than those that involve willing listeners. . . .

First, [the Colorado statute] is not a "regulation of speech." Rather, it is a regulation of the places where some speech may occur. Second, it was not adopted "because of disagreement with the message it conveys." This conclusion is supported not just by the Colorado courts' interpretation of legislative history, but more importantly by the State Supreme Court's unequivocal holding that the statute's "restrictions apply equally to all demonstrators, regardless of viewpoint, and the statutory language makes no reference to the content of the speech." Third, the State's interests in protecting access and privacy, and providing the police with clear guidelines, are unrelated to the content of the demonstrators' speech. As we have repeatedly explained, government regulation of expressive activity is "content neutral" if it is justified without reference to the content of regulated speech. . . .

It is common in the law to examine the content of a communication to determine the speaker's purpose. Whether a particular statement constitutes a threat, blackmail, an agreement to fix prices, a copyright violation, a public offering of securities, or an offer to sell goods often depends on the precise content of the statement. We have never held, or suggested, that it is improper to look at the content of an oral or written statement in order to determine whether a rule of law applies to a course of conduct. With respect to the conduct that is the focus of the Colorado statute, it is unlikely that there would often be any need to know exactly what words were spoken in order to determine whether "sidewalk counselors" are engaging in "oral protest, education, or counseling" rather than pure social or random conversation.

Theoretically, of course, cases may arise in which it is necessary to review the content of the statements made by a person approaching within eight feet of an unwilling listener to determine whether the approach is covered by the statute. But that review need be no more extensive than a determination of whether a general prohibition of "picketing" or "demonstrating" applies to innocuous speech. The regulation of such expressive activities, by definition, does not cover social, random, or other everyday communications. . . .

The Colorado statute . . . places no restrictions on—and clearly does not prohibit—either a particular viewpoint or any subject matter that may be discussed by a speaker. Rather, it simply establishes a minor place restriction on an extremely broad category of communications with unwilling listeners. Instead of drawing distinctions based on the subject that the approaching speaker may wish to address, the statute applies equally to used car salesmen, animal rights activists, fundraisers, environmentalists, and missionaries. Each can attempt to educate unwilling listeners on any subject, but without consent may not approach within eight feet to do so.

With respect to oral statements, the distance certainly can make it more difficult for a speaker to be heard, particularly if the level of background noise is high and other speakers are competing for the pedestrian's attention. Notably, the statute places no limitation on the number of speakers or the noise level, including the use of amplification equipment, although we have upheld such restrictions in past cases. More significantly, this statute does not suffer from the failings that compelled us to reject the "floating buffer zone" in *Schenck* [v. *Pro-Choice* (1997)]. Unlike the 15-foot zone in *Schenck,* this 8-foot zone allows the speaker to communicate at a "normal conversational distance." Additionally, the statute allows the speaker to remain in one place, and other individuals can pass within eight feet of the protester without causing the protester to violate the statute. Finally, here there is a "knowing" requirement that protects speakers "who thought they were keeping pace with the targeted individual" at the proscribed distance from inadvertently violating the statute. . . .

The burden on the ability to distribute handbills is more serious because it seems possible that an 8-foot interval could hinder the ability of a leafletter to deliver handbills to some unwilling recipients. The statute does not, however, prevent a leafleteer from simply standing near the path of oncoming pedestrians and proffering his or her material, which the pedestrians can easily accept. And, as in all leafletting situations, pedestrians continue to be free to decline the tender. In *Heffron* v. *International Soc. for Krishna Consciousness, Inc.* (1981), we upheld a state fair regulation that required a religious organization desiring to distribute literature to conduct that activity only at an assigned location—in that case booths. As in this case, the regulation primarily burdened the distributors' ability to communicate with unwilling readers. We concluded our opinion by emphasizing that the First Amendment protects the right of every citizen to "'reach the minds of willing listeners and to do so there must be opportunity to win their attention.'"

The Colorado statute adequately protects those rights.

Finally, in determining whether a statute is narrowly tailored, we have noted that "[w]e must, of course, take account of the place to which the regulations apply in determining whether these restrictions burden more speech than necessary." States and municipalities plainly have a substantial interest in controlling the activity around certain public and private places. For example, we have recognized the special governmental interests surrounding schools, courthouses, polling places, and private homes. Additionally, we previously have noted the unique concerns that surround health care facilities. . . .

Persons who are attempting to enter health care facilities—for any purpose—are often in particularly vulnerable physical and emotional conditions. The State of Colorado has responded to its substantial and legitimate interest in protecting these persons from unwanted encounters, confrontations, and even assaults by enacting an exceedingly modest restriction on the speakers' ability to approach. . . .

Finally, the 8-foot restriction occurs only within 100 feet of a health care facility—the place where the restriction is most needed. The restriction interferes far less with a speaker's ability to communicate than did the total ban on picketing on the sidewalk outside a residence, the restriction of leafletting at a fairground to a booth, or the "silence" often required outside a hospital. Special problems that may arise where clinics have particularly wide entrances or are situated within multipurpose office buildings may be worked out as the statute is applied. . . .

Finally, petitioners argue that [the law's] consent requirement is invalid because it imposes an unconstitutional "prior restraint" on speech. We rejected this argument previously in *Schenck* . . . and *Madsen*. Moreover, the restrictions in this case raise an even lesser prior restraint concern than those at issue in *Schenck* and *Madsen* where particular speakers were at times completely banned within certain zones. Under this statute, absolutely no channel of communication is foreclosed. No speaker is silenced. And no message is prohibited. Petitioners are simply wrong when they assert that "[t]he statute compels speakers to obtain consent to speak and it authorizes private citizens to deny petitioners' requests to engage in expressive activities." To the contrary, this statute does not provide for a "heckler's veto" but rather allows every speaker to engage freely in any expressive activity communicating all messages and viewpoints subject only to the narrow place requirement imbedded within the "approach" restriction.

Furthermore, our concerns about "prior restraints" relate to restrictions imposed by official censorship. The regulations in this case, however, only apply if the pedestrian does not consent to the approach. Private citizens have always retained the power to decide for themselves what they wish to read, and within limits, what oral messages they want to consider. This statute simply empowers private citizens entering a health care facility with the ability to prevent a speaker, who is within eight feet and advancing, from communicating a message they do not wish to hear. Further, the statute does not authorize the pedestrian to affect any other activity at any other location or relating to any other person. These restrictions thus do not constitute an unlawful prior restraint.

The judgment of the Colorado Supreme Court is affirmed.

It is so ordered.

JUSTICE SOUTER, with whom JUSTICE O'CONNOR, JUSTICE GINSBURG, and JUSTICE BREYER join, concurring.

Concern about employing the power of the State to suppress discussion of a subject or a point of view is not, however, raised in the same way when a law addresses not the content of speech but the circumstances of its delivery. The right to express unpopular views does not necessarily immunize a speaker from liability for resorting to otherwise impermissible behavior meant to shock members of the speaker's audience, or to guarantee their attention. Unless regulation limited to the details of a speaker's delivery results in removing a subject or viewpoint from effective discourse (or otherwise fails to advance a significant public interest in a way narrowly fitted to that objective), a reasonable restriction intended to affect only the time, place, or manner of speaking is perfectly valid.

It is important to recognize that the validity of punishing some expressive conduct, and the permissibility of a time, place, or manner restriction, does not depend on showing that the particular behavior or mode of delivery has no association with a particular subject or opinion. Draft card burners disapprove of the draft, and abortion protesters believe abortion is morally wrong. There is always a correlation with subject and viewpoint when the law regulates conduct that has become the signature of one side of a controversy. But that does not mean that every regulation of such distinctive behavior is content based as First Amendment doctrine employs that term. The correct rule, rather, is captured in the formulation that a restriction is content based only if it is imposed because of the content of the speech, and not because of offensive behavior identified with its delivery.

Since this point is as elementary as anything in traditional speech doctrine, it would only be natural to suppose that today's disagreement between the Court and the dissenting Justices must turn on unusual difficulty in evaluating the facts of this case. But it does not. The facts overwhelmingly demonstrate the validity of [the law] as a content-neutral regulation imposed solely to regulate the manner in which speakers may conduct themselves within 100 feet of the entrance of a health care facility.

No one disputes the substantiality of the government's interest in protecting people already tense or distressed in anticipation of medical attention (whether an abortion or some other procedure) from the unwanted intrusion of close personal importunity by strangers. The issues dividing the Court, then, go to the content neutrality of the regulation, its fit with the interest to be served by it, and the availability of other means of expressing the desired message (however offensive it may be even without physically close communication). . . .

This is not to say that enforcement of the approach restriction will have no effect on speech; of course it will make some difference. The effect of speech is a product of ideas and circumstances, and time, place, and manner are circumstances. The question is simply whether the ostensible reason for regulating the circumstances is really something about the ideas. Here, the evidence indicates that the ostensible reason is the true reason. The fact that speech by a stationary speaker is untouched by this statute shows that the reason for its restriction on approaches goes to the approaches, not to the content of the speech of those approaching. What is prohibited is a close encounter when the person addressed does not want to get close. So, the intended recipient can stay far enough away to prevent the whispered argument, mitigate some of the physical shock of the shouted denunciation, and avoid the unwanted handbill. But the content of the message will survive on any sign readable at eight feet and in any statement audible from that slight distance. . . .

JUSTICE SCALIA, with whom JUSTICE THOMAS joins, dissenting.

The Court today concludes that a regulation requiring speakers on the public thoroughfares bordering medical facilities to speak from a distance of eight feet is "not a 'regulation of speech,'" but "a regulation of the places where some speech may occur," and that a regulation directed to only certain categories of speech (protest, education, and counseling) is not "content-based." For these reasons, it says, the regulation is immune from the exacting scrutiny we apply to content-based suppression of speech in the public forum. The Court then determines that the regulation survives the less rigorous scrutiny afforded content-neutral time, place, and manner restrictions because it is narrowly tailored to serve a government interest—protection of citizens' "right to be let alone"—that has explicitly been disclaimed by the State, probably for the reason that, as a basis for suppressing peaceful private expression, it is patently incompatible with the guarantees of the First Amendment.

None of these remarkable conclusions should come as a surprise. What is before us, after all, is a speech regulation directed against the opponents of abortion, and it therefore enjoys the benefit of the "ad hoc nullification machine" that the Court has set in motion to push aside whatever doctrines of constitutional law stand in the way of that highly favored practice. Having deprived abortion opponents of the political right to persuade the electorate that abortion should be restricted by law, the Court today continues and expands its assault upon their individual right to persuade women contemplating abortion that what they are doing is wrong. Because, like the rest of our abortion jurisprudence, today's decision is in stark contradiction of the constitutional principles we apply in all other contexts, I dissent. . . .

[I]t blinks reality to regard this statute, in its application to oral communications, as anything other than a content-based restriction upon speech in the public forum. As such, it must survive that stringent mode of constitutional analysis our cases refer to as "strict scrutiny," which requires that the restriction be narrowly tailored to serve a compelling state interest. Since the Court does not even attempt to support the regulation under this standard, I shall discuss it only briefly. Suffice it to say that if protecting people from unwelcome communications (the governmental interest the Court posits) is a compelling state interest, the First Amendment is a dead letter. And if (as I shall discuss at greater length below) forbidding peaceful, nonthreatening, but uninvited speech from a distance closer than eight feet is a "narrowly tailored" means of preventing the obstruction of entrance to medical facilities (the governmental interest the State asserts) narrow tailoring must refer not to the standards of Versace, but to those of Omar the tentmaker. . . .

As the Court explains, under our precedents even a content-neutral, time, place, and manner restriction must be narrowly tailored to advance a significant state interest, and must leave open ample alternative means of communication. It cannot be sustained if it "burden[s] substantially more speech than is necessary to further the government's legitimate interests."

. . . [W]hat *is* the significant interest the State seeks to advance? Here there appears to be a bit of a disagreement between the State of Colorado (which should know) and the Court (which is eager to speculate). Colorado has identified in the text of the statute itself the interest it sought to advance: to ensure that the State's citizens may "obtain medical counseling and treatment in an unobstructed manner" by "preventing the willful obstruction of a person's access to medical counseling and treatment at a health care facility." In its brief here, the State repeatedly confirms the interest squarely identified in the statute under review. The Court nevertheless concludes that the Colorado provision is narrowly tailored to serve . . . *the State's interest in protecting its citizens' rights to be let alone from unwanted speech.*

Indeed, the situation is even more bizarre than that. The interest that the Court makes the linchpin of its analysis was not only unasserted by the State; it is not only completely *different* from the interest that the statute specifically sets forth; it was explicitly *disclaimed* by the State in its brief before this Court, and characterized as a "straw interest" *petitioners* served up in the hope of discrediting the State's case. We may thus add to the lengthening list of "firsts" generated by this Court's relentlessly proabortion jurisprudence, the first case in which, in order to sustain a statute, the Court has relied upon a governmental interest not only unasserted by the State, but positively repudiated. . . .

. . . [T]he 8-foot buffer zone attaches to every person on the public way or sidewalk within 100 feet of the entrance of a medical facility, regardless of whether that person is seeking to enter or exit the facility. In fact, the State acknowledged at oral argument that the buffer zone would attach to any person within 100 feet of the entrance door of a skyscraper in which a single doctor occupied an office on the 18th floor. And even with respect to those who *are* seeking to enter or exit the facilities, the statute does not protect them only from speech that is so intimidating or threatening as to impede access. Rather, it covers *all* unconsented-to approaches for the purpose of oral protest, education, or counseling (including those made for the purpose of the most peaceful appeals) and, perhaps even more significantly, *every* approach made for the purposes of leafletting or handbilling, which we have never considered, standing alone, obstructive or unduly intrusive. The sweep of this prohibition is breathtaking. . . .

The burdens this law imposes upon the right to speak are substantial, despite an attempt to minimize them that is not even embarrassed to make the suggestion that they might actually "assist . . . the speakers' efforts to communicate their messages." The Court displays a willful ignorance of the type and nature of communication affected by the statute's restrictions. It seriously asserts, for example, that the 8-foot zone allows a speaker to communicate at a "normal conversational distance." I have certainly held conversations at a distance of eight feet seated in the quiet of my chambers, but I have never walked along the public sidewalk—and have not seen others do so—"conversing" at an 8-foot remove. The suggestion is absurd. So is the suggestion that the opponents of abortion can take comfort in the fact that the statute "places no limitation on the number of speakers or the noise level, including the use of amplification equipment." That is good enough, I suppose, for "protesting"; but the Court must know that most of the "counseling" and "educating" likely to take place outside a health care facility cannot be done at a distance and at a high-decibel level. The availability of a powerful amplification system will be of little help to the woman who hopes to forge, in the last moments before another of her sex is to have an abortion, a bond of concern and intimacy that might enable her to persuade the woman to change her mind and heart. The counselor may wish to walk alongside and to say, sympathetically and as softly as the circumstances allow, something like: "My dear, I know what you are going through. I've been through it myself. You're not alone and you do not have to do this. There are other alternatives. Will you let me help you? May I show you a picture of what your child looks like at this stage of her human development?" The Court would have us believe that this can be done effectively—yea, perhaps even *more* effectively—by shouting through a bullhorn at a distance of eight feet. . . .

Does the deck seem stacked? You bet. As I have suggested throughout this opinion, today's decision is not an isolated distortion of our traditional constitutional principles, but is one of many aggressively proabortion novelties announced by the Court in recent years. Today's distortions, however, are particularly blatant. Restrictive views of the First Amendment that have been in dissent since the 1930's suddenly find themselves in the majority. "Uninhibited, robust, and wide open" debate is replaced by the power of the state to protect an unheard-of "right to be let alone" on the public streets. I dissent.

SIDEBAR

HILL V. COLORADO

Reconciling Rights in Conflict

For Dr. David Gunn, the morning of March 10, 1993, began like any other when pulled his car into the parking lot of the Pensacola Women's Medical Services Clinic, one of two such facilities that performed abortions in this broad swath of the Florida panhandle. Pro-life demonstrators surrounded the clinic, waving signs that featured enlarged photographs of aborted fetuses, quoting Bible verses, and naming Gunn as a murderer who would one day burn in hell. Such protests had become part of Gunn's daily routine, and, while bothering him at first—Gunn also regularly received threats at home—he had learned to ignore them. As Gunn walked toward the back door entrance into the clinic, Michael Griffin, a regular participant in the pro-life demonstrations at Gunn's clinic, walked up behind him and shot Gunn from point-blank range three times in the back. Upon arrest, Griffin proudly admitted shooting Gunn, claiming that he was acting in God's name.

Gunn's murder was not the first time abortion clinic–related violence had surfaced in Pensacola, a coastal city of 55,000 with a curious mix of military retirees, seasonal residents from the Midwest and Northeast, and a thriving gay community. On Christmas Day 1984, all three abortion clinics were firebombed. Like Michael Griffin, the bombers claimed that were acting on God's wishes, describing the act as "a gift for Jesus on his birthday." Although abortion clinics had been bombed, burned, vandalized, and broken into in many other parts of the country, the publicity surrounding the Pensacola bombings, the swift prosecution and punishment of the perpetrators, and the successful struggle to reopen two of the three clinics drew national attention. Soon, Pensacola became a magnet for pro-life demonstrators, especially the more extreme fringes of the movement that supported violence to end abortion.

This violent faction within the pro-life movement acted again in July 1994, when Paul Hill fired his twelve-gauge shotgun at Dr. John B. Britton and his seventy-four-year-old escort, retired Air Force lieutenant colonel James H. Barrett, killing them both as they walked into the Pensacola Ladies Center. Hill, however, refused to plead guilty to murder charges, instead arguing that the double murder of Britton and Barrett was "justifiable homicide." Hill circulated a petition to pro-life groups encouraging them to support his argument. But pro-life groups such as the National Right to Life Committee (NRLC), the American Center for Law and Justice (ACLJ), Concerned Women for America (CWA), and the United States Catholic Conference (USCC) would have nothing to do with Hill's defense. In response, Cardinal John J. O'Connor, head of the Archdiocese of New York and then America's best-known Catholic priest, said: "If anyone has an urge to kill an abortionist, let him kill me, instead. That's about as clearly as I can renounce such madness." In the end, only thirty-two people signed Hill's "justifiable homicide" petition.

Hill became the first person prosecuted under the new congressional Freedom of Access to Clinics Entrances Act (FACE), which had been introduced two weeks after Gunn was murdered in March 1993.

FACE was enacted by solid majorities in the House and Senate. President Bill Clinton, the nation's first pro-choice chief executive in twelve years, signed the law in 1994. Modeled on state laws such as the one challenged in *Hill,* FACE made blocking access to abortion clinics or engaging in face-to-face intimidation of anyone entering or leaving a clinic a federal crime. The year before, the Court ruled in *Bray* v. *Alexandria Women's Health Clinic* (1993) that the Ku Klux Klan Act of 1871, a Reconstruction-era law designed to permit federal prosecution of anyone "conspiring" to deprive a citizen of the right to travel, did not apply to abortion clinic protesters. FACE nationalized civil rights protection for women and professional staff entering and leaving abortion clinics. Another feature that FACE shared with state clinic-access laws was a provision authorizing the courts to issue injunctions banning demonstrators from coming within certain distances of abortion clinics. Injunctions could not be issued unless the court had some evidence that violence was likely or that abortion clinics had been the target of criminal activity.

In *Madsen* v. *Women's Health Center* (1994), the Court ruled that courts could issue injunctions under such circumstances. *Madsen* had been brought by Operation Rescue, a pro-life group that favored civil disobedience but stopped short of endorsing violence. Three years later, the Court affirmed *Madsen* against a challenge brought by the ACLJ in *Schenck* v. *Pro-Choice Network of Western New York* (1997). Operation Rescue, the ACLJ, and the National Right-to-Life Committee, while representing different strains of the pro-life movement, continued to argue that the "buffer zones" prominently featured in the clinic-access laws deprived demonstrators of their free speech rights. Interestingly, the ACLU, which had lobbied on behalf of FACE when it was being debated in Congress, maintained that First Amendment arguments were not relevant when it came to preventing the physical and emotional harassment of women seeking to exercise a protected constitutional right—in this case, the right to abortion.

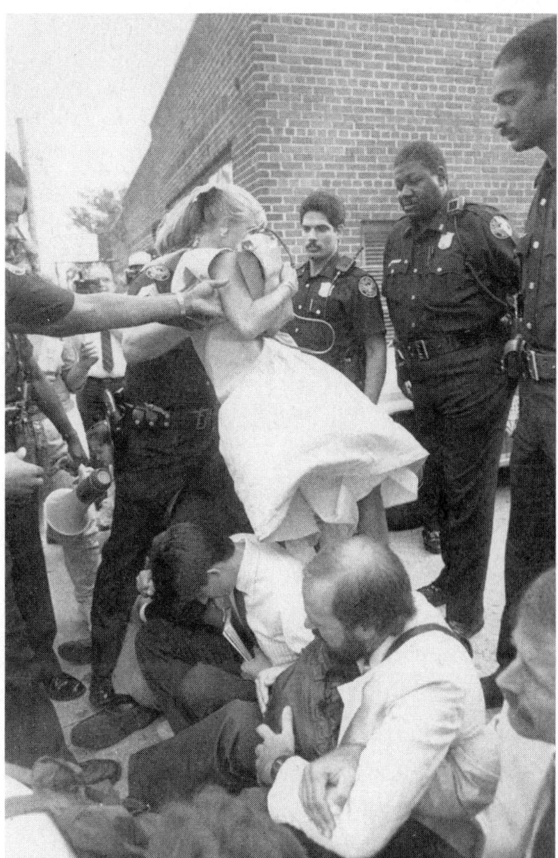

Police assist a woman seeking access to an abortion clinic past a "sit-in" of pro-life demonstrators.
© Bettmann/CORBIS.

The Court has also upheld the application of other federal laws to restrain clinic protests. In *National Organization for Women* v. *Scheidler* (1994), the Court upheld the use of the federal Rackeeter Influenced and Corrupt Organizations Act (RICO) by a federal court to ban the Pro-Life Action League from directing protest activities at abortion clinics. NOW, supported by *amicus* briefs from Planned Parenthood, several pro-choice religious organizations, the ACLU, and the Clinton administration, argued that RICO, which had been enacted to give federal prosecutors an effective tool against organized crime, should apply to any group conspiring to drive out a business by unlawful means. The ACLJ represented Joseph Scheidler, a pro-life activist who had disrupted several abortion clinics in suburban Chicago.

Although the Court has firmly ruled that women, their escorts, and health care professionals have a legal right to enter abortion clinics free from physical intimidation and constraints, cases such as *Hill* demonstrate that pro-life demonstrators are determined to press the argument that such laws violate their First Amendment rights. Many pro-life demonstrators liken their cause to the civil rights movement of the early 1960s, which often employed sit-ins and other forms of civil disobedience to protest laws mandating racial segregation. Civil liberties groups were firmly on the side of the civil rights movement, claiming that a broad interpretation of First Amendment rights was essential to encourage social and political change within the democratic process. Pro-life groups claim that clinic-access laws are denying them the same opportunity. Is there a double standard at work in the First Amendment, or does the problem posed by clinic-related violence call for a different understanding of free speech rights?

References

Blanchard, Dallas A. *Religious Violence and Abortion: The Gideon Project*. Gainesville: University of Florida Press, 1993.

Craig, Barbara, and David O'Brien. *Abortion in American Politics*. Chatham, N.J.: Chatham House, 1995.

O'Connor, Karen. *No Neutral Ground: Abortion Politics in an Age of Absolutes*. Boulder, Colo.: Westview Press, 1996.

"That's Disgusting!" Yes, But Is It Unconstitutional? Free Speech Beyond Political Borders

As discussed earlier in this chapter, the Court has developed different levels of constitutional protection for speech based on how it categorizes that speech. Political speech receives the greatest protection under the First Amendment, with government infringement justified only if the speech crosses the threshold of imminent lawlessness. Nonpolitical speech having literary, artistic, and scientific value is also fully protected under the Court's modern First Amendment doctrine. But speech considered offensive, whether it comes in the form of profanity, nude dancing, or "fighting words," is not always entitled to constitutional protection because, in the Court's analysis, such speech is often unrelated to the core values of the First Amendment. Some protection, however, is better than no protection, which is where speech and expression considered obscene and libelous fall in the Court's hierarchy of protected speech.

Assigning different levels of constitutional protection to speech that nonetheless has expressive value to the speaker is a curious development. Certainly, the notion that some speech is political and other speech is not is a conclusion that deserves some discussion on its own. A neo-Nazi has as much right to circulate a newsletter calling for white supremacist rule as a civil rights group has to call for racial and religious harmony. But do neo-Nazis have the right to broadcast racial epithets over the radio airwaves? Could a county-owned cable company refuse to permit neo-Nazis the right to broadcast a television program on a public access channel? Suppose a member of the Ku Klux Klan showed up in a courtroom wearing a white hood and robe to watch a trial involving a civil rights case brought by an African American against a white friend of the Klansman. Could the judge require the Klansman to leave the courtroom because his wardrobe was *potentially* disruptive? Or because it was offensive?

In truth, the expressed idea—the speech—in each scenario has a political cast to it. After you read the cases and materials in this section, you will discover that prevailing First Amendment doctrine would treat some of this speech as fully protected (probably the Klansman in the courtroom, although a judge could require the hood to be removed if no other hats or headwear were permitted); some of it as less protected (probably neo-Nazi access to the radio airwaves); and some of it not protected at all (the cable access channel could probably tell the neo-Nazis no). It is hard to dispute, however, that all this speech has deeply political meaning to the speakers. What, then, establishes the constitutional dividing line—the line that protects certain speech and limits other speech by devaluing its content? Because many legal scholars attach great significance to concepts like "neutrality," "the marketplace of ideas," and "judicial detachment" when it comes to free speech, it is sometimes tempting to forget that the core values of the First Amendment have never been self-executing. Deciding what the First Amendment should mean, both in form and in substance, has been a process of constant evolution. It is also a process steeped in politics. Our earlier discussion of the rights of political dissenters during World War I offers an early example of the importance of politics in determining the boundaries of protected speech. Since then, social and political forces have changed the meaning of abstract concepts like equality, personal freedom, and public morality. As society has changed, so has the meaning of the First Amendment.[47]

Public Decency

Recall that in *Brandenburg* v. *Ohio* the Court viewed the right of the Ku Klux Klan to hold a public meeting as a "core" First Amendment value and struck down a state law prohibiting "anti-patriotic" groups from promoting their beliefs. The Klan, it is fair to say, is widely considered an offensive organization. Three years later, the Court ruled in *Cohen* v. *California* (1971) that Paul Cohen, a young man opposed to the Vietnam War, was fully within his First Amendment rights to wear a jacket that said, "Fuck the Draft" in a Los Angeles courtroom. The Court noted that Cohen's behavior was in poor taste, but it emphasized that public expression could not be limited to only those words and phrases considered unobjectionable by the majority. Wrote Justice John Harlan:

> How is one to distinguish this from any other offensive word? Surely the State has no right to cleanse public debate to the point where it is grammatically palatable to the most squeamish among us. Yet no readily ascertainable general principle exists for stopping short of that result were we to affirm the judgment below. For, while the particular four-letter word being litigated here is perhaps more distasteful than others of its genre, it is nevertheless often true that one man's vulgarity is another's lyric.[48]

That said, why does the Court consider the right of political satirists to use profanity in their monologues broadcast on the radio less protected than either the Klan's right to meet in public or Paul Cohen's right to wear his jacket, and in some cases not protected at all? *Federal Communications Commission* v. *Pacifica Foundation* (1978) offers a good opportunity to consider how the Court treats different types of offensive speech. *Pacifica* also demonstrates that the forum in which speech takes place also matters in determining whether speech is constitutionally protected.

Federal Communications Commission v. *Pacifica Foundation*

438 U.S. 726 (1978)

Founded in 1946 by pacifist Frank Hill, the Pacifica Foundation is a small, nonprofit radio network featuring left-wing political and cultural programming. Based in Berkeley, California, and operating five radio stations around the country, Pacifica provides news and commentary to sixty other affiliates nationwide. Pacifica is well known for pushing the limits of the decency requirements of the Federal Communications Commission, the government agency responsible for regulating the nation's radio and television airwaves. During the 1950s, Pacifica was one of the few outlets for the blossoming counterculture that would come to the fore in the 1960s. Poets, musicians, storytellers, and political dissidents have always found a home in Pacifica.

But no story better illustrates Pacifica's sense of "anything goes" than its decision to broadcast the "Filthy Dirty Words" monologue by comedian George Carlin. In the early afternoon of October 30, 1973, Pacifica's New York station played the monologue. No one contested the profane content of Carlin's monologue. After a few satiric comments about literary double standards in modern culture, Carlin moved to the heart of the monologue, noting there were "seven words you couldn't say on the public, ah, airwaves, um, the ones you definitely wouldn't say, ever . . . shit, piss, fuck, cunt, cocksucker, motherfucker, and tits." Carlin then used these words in and out of their profane context to illustrate his central point: that the words had no meaning beyond that which people wanted to give them. Audience laughter could be heard in the background.

John R. Douglas, a national board member of Morality in Media, a conservative "watchdog" group, was driving with his fifteen-year-old son when he heard the monologue on his car radio. Six days later, Douglas wrote the FCC to complain about it, noting that while he could understand the "record's being sold for private use, I certainly cannot understand the broadcast of [the] same over the air that, supposedly, you control."

The FCC investigated the complaint and agreed that Carlin's monologue was "patently offensive." Pacifica, which received no other complaints about the broadcast, was not punished, but it was warned that a similar infraction in the future could cause it to lose its license. Pacifica appealed, and ultimately won a favorable ruling in federal appeals court.

The Court's decision was 5 to 4. Justice Stevens delivered the judgment of the Court. Only two justices, Burger and Rehnquist, joined his opinion. Justice Powell, joined by Justice Blackmun, wrote a concurring opinion. Justices Brennan, Marshall, Stewart, and White dissented.

MR. JUSTICE STEVENS delivered the opinion of the Court . . . in which THE CHIEF JUSTICE and MR. JUSTICE REHNQUIST joined [in part].

This case requires that we decide whether the Federal Communications Commission has any power to regulate a radio broadcast that is indecent but not obscene. . . .

The words of the Carlin monologue are unquestionably "speech" within the meaning of the First Amendment. It is equally clear that the Commission's objections to the broadcast were based in part on its content. The order must therefore fall if, as Pacifica argues, the First Amendment prohibits all governmental regulation that depends on the content of speech. Our past cases demonstrate, however, that no such absolute rule is mandated by the Constitution. . . .

[Several] distinctions based on content have been approved in the years since *Schenck*. The government may forbid speech calculated to provoke a fight. It may pay heed to the "'common sense differences' between commercial speech and other varieties." It may treat libels against private citizens more severely than libels against public officials. Obscenity may be wholly prohibited. And, only two Terms ago, we refused to hold that a "statutory classification is unconstitutional because it is based on the content of communication protected by the First Amendment."

The question in this case is whether a broadcast of patently offensive words dealing with sex and excretion may be regulated because of its content. Obscene materials have been denied the protection of the First Amendment because their content is so offensive to contemporary moral standards. But the fact that society may find speech offensive is not a sufficient reason for suppressing it. Indeed, if it is the speaker's opinion that gives offense, that consequence is a reason for according it constitutional protection. For it is a central tenet of the First Amendment that the government must remain neutral in the marketplace of ideas. If there were any reason to believe that the Commission's characterization of the Carlin monologue as offensive could be traced to its political content—or even to the fact that it satirized contemporary attitudes about four-letter words—First Amendment protection might be required. But that is simply not this case. These words offend for the same reasons that obscenity offends. Their place in the hierarchy of First Amendment values was aptly sketched by Mr. Justice Murphy when he said: "[S]uch utterances are no essential part of any exposition of ideas, and are of such slight social value as a step to truth that any benefit that may be derived from them is clearly outweighed by the social interest in order and morality," *Chaplinsky* v. *New Hampshire*.

Although these words ordinarily lack literary, political, or scientific value, they are not entirely outside the protection of the First Amendment. Some uses of even the most offensive words are unquestionably protected. Indeed, we may assume . . . that this monologue would be protected in other contexts. Nonetheless, the constitutional protection accorded to a communication containing such patently offensive sexual and excretory language need not be the same in every context. It is a characteristic of speech such as this that both its capacity to offend and its "social value," to use Mr. Justice Murphy's term, vary with the circumstances. Words that are commonplace in one setting are shocking in another. To paraphrase Mr. Justice Harlan, one occasion's lyric is another's vulgarity.

In this case, it is undisputed that the content of Pacifica's broadcast was "vulgar," "offensive," and "shocking." Because content of that character is not entitled to absolute constitutional protection under all circumstances, we must consider its context in order to determine whether the Commission's action was constitutionally permissible.

We have long recognized that each medium of expression presents special First Amendment problems. And of all forms of communication, it is broadcasting that has received the most limited First Amendment protection.

Thus, although other speakers cannot be licensed except under laws that carefully define and narrow official discretion, a broadcaster may be deprived of his license and his forum if the Commission decides that such an action would serve "the public interest, convenience, and necessity." Similarly, although the First Amendment protects newspaper publishers from being required to print the replies of those whom they criticize, it affords no such protection to broadcasters; on the contrary, they must give free time to the victims of their criticism.

The reasons for these distinctions are complex, but two have relevance to the present case. First, the broadcast media have established a uniquely pervasive presence in the lives of all Americans. Patently offensive, indecent material presented over the airwaves confronts the citizen not only in public, but also in the privacy of the home, where the individual's right to be left alone plainly outweighs the First Amendment rights of an intruder. Because the broadcast audience is constantly tuning in and out, prior warnings cannot completely protect the listener or viewer from unexpected program content. To say that one may avoid further offense by turning off the radio when he hears indecent language is like saying that the remedy for an assault is to run away after the first blow. One may hang up on an indecent phone call, but that option does not give the caller a constitutional immunity or avoid a harm that has already taken place.

Second, broadcasting is uniquely accessible to children, even those too young to read. Although Cohen's written message might have been incomprehensible to a first grader, Pacifica's broadcast could have enlarged a child's vocabulary in an instant. Other forms of offensive expression may be withheld from the young without restricting the expression at its source. Bookstores and motion picture theaters, for example, may be prohibited from making indecent material available to children. . . . The ease with which children may obtain access to broadcast material . . . amply justif[ies] special treatment of indecent broadcasting.

It is appropriate, in conclusion, to emphasize the narrowness of our holding. This case does not involve a two-way radio conversation between a cab driver and a dispatcher, or a telecast of an Elizabethan comedy. We have not decided that an occasional expletive in either setting would justify any sanction or, indeed, that this broadcast would justify a criminal prosecution. The Commission's decision rested entirely on a nuisance rationale under which context is all-important. The concept requires consideration of a host of variables. The time of day was emphasized by the Commission. The content of the program in which the language is used will also affect the composition of the audience, and differences between radio, television, and perhaps closed-circuit transmissions, may also be relevant. As Mr. Justice Sutherland wrote, a "nuisance may be merely a right thing in the wrong place,—like a pig in the parlor instead of the barnyard." We simply hold that, when the Commission finds that a pig has entered the parlor, the exercise of its regulatory power does not depend on proof that the pig is obscene.

The judgment of the Court of Appeals is reversed.

It is so ordered.

MR. JUSTICE BRENNAN, with whom MR. JUSTICE MARSHALL joins, dissenting.

Without question, the privacy interests of an individual in his home are substantial, and deserving of significant protection. In finding these interests sufficient to justify the content regulation of protected speech, however, the Court commits two errors. First, it misconceives the nature of the privacy interests involved where an individual voluntarily chooses to admit radio communications into his home. Second, it ignores the constitutionally protected interests of both those who wish to transmit and those who desire to receive broadcasts that many—including the FCC and this Court—might find offensive. . . .

Even if an individual who voluntarily opens his home to radio communications retains privacy interests of sufficient moment to justify a ban on protected speech if those interests are "invaded in an essentially intolerable manner," the very fact that those interests are threatened only by a radio broadcast precludes any intolerable invasion of privacy; for unlike other intrusive modes of communication, such as sound trucks, "[t]he radio can be turned off,"—and with a minimum of effort. . . .

Because the Carlin monologue is obviously not an erotic appeal to the prurient interests of children, the Court, for the first time, allows the government to prevent minors from gaining access to materials that are not obscene, and are therefore protected, as to them. It thus ignores our recent admonition that "[s]peech that is neither obscene as to youths nor subject to some other legitimate proscription cannot be suppressed solely to protect the young from ideas or images that a legislative body thinks unsuitable for them." The Court's refusal to follow its own pronouncements is especially lamentable, since it has the anomalous subsidiary effect, at least in the radio context at issue here, of making completely unavailable to adults material which may not constitutionally be kept even from children. . . .

Today's decision will thus have its greatest impact on broadcasters desiring to reach, and listening audiences composed of, persons who do not share the Court's view as to which words or expressions are acceptable and who, for a variety of reasons, including a conscious desire to flout majoritarian conventions, express themselves using words that may be regarded as offensive by those from different socio-economic backgrounds. In this context, the Court's decision may be seen for what, in the broader perspective, it really is: another of the dominant culture's inevitable efforts to force those groups who do not share its mores to conform to its way of thinking, acting, and speaking.

Pacifica, in response to an FCC inquiry about its broadcast of Carlin's satire on "'the words you couldn't say on the public . . . airways,'" explained that "Carlin is not mouthing obscenities, he is merely using words to satirize as harmless and essentially silly our attitudes towards those words." In confirming Carlin's prescience as a social commentator by the result it reaches today, the Court evinces an attitude toward the "seven dirty words" that many others besides Mr. Carlin and Pacifica might describe as "silly." Whether today's decision will similarly prove "harmless" remains to be seen. One can only hope that it will.

▼▲▼

The Authors League of America, the Motion Picture Association of America, and the Writers Guild filed separate *amicus* briefs in *Pacifica*. Each organization's brief carried a common theme: They pointed to the negative effect that upholding the FCC's ban on "indecent" speech would have for the artistic license of writers, broadcasters, actors, commentators, or anyone else who used the public airwaves to communicate controversial material. Note how the Court did not contest the right of George Carlin to perform his material in a concert setting or sell recordings featuring the "seven dirty words" monologue in stores. Critical to the Court's approach to "indecent" speech in *Pacifica* was the fact that it occurred over the public airwaves, which were much more indiscriminate in their reach into the privacy of a home or car. How does Justice Stevens's opinion in *Pacifica* compare with Justice Harlan's conclusion in *Cohen* v. *California*?

As discussed earlier, political speech takes on modes of expression that go beyond simply speaking and writing. The Court has upheld such conduct as fully protected by the Constitution, assuming that it satisfies time, place, and manner criteria. Likewise, offensive speech takes on many forms as well. But again, the problem arises of assigning political value to expressive conduct that is nonetheless considered offensive and banishing conduct less directed toward public affairs that is nonetheless expressive. Flag burning is a good example of the Court's willingness to protect political expression that is offensive. No such protection exists, as we shall see, for nude dancing and other forms of live "adult entertainment" open to the public, even though the Court has acknowledged that such conduct is expressive.

Semi-nude and erotic dancing have long graced the stages and theatres of the United States, and are considered by many high-minded art forms. But while the Court has ruled that nudity in public performances having literary qualities is protected expression, nude dancing in bars and nightclubs is not. In *Barnes* v. *Glen Theatre, Inc.* (1991), a 5–4 Court held that an Indiana indecency law prohibiting public nudity applied to establishments featuring nude dancing. Justice Sandra Day O'Connor held that the Indiana law was "substantially related" to protecting order and public morality, and "unrelated to the suppression of expression." Key in O'Connor's analysis was her decision to classify topless dancers working in the Kitty Kat Lounge and Glen Theatre in South Bend as appearing nude in public, thus bringing them within the scope of the state's indecency law. Is there a difference, however, in appearing nude in public, and dancing nude in a public place restricted to paying adults? In your mind, is nude dancing indoors any more or less offensive than permitting outdoor flag burning or a march by the Ku Klux Klan outdoors?

The Court confronted a slightly different but constitutionally distinct question involving the right of communities to limit nude dancing in *Erie* v. *Pap's A.M.* (2000). In *Barnes*, the Indiana law was not written specifically to ban nude dancing; it was a general public decency law designed to curb immoral public behavior. In *Pap's A.M.*, the question was whether a law specifically directed toward the suppression of nude dancing violated the First Amendment.

Erie v. *Pap's A.M.*

529 U.S. 277 (2000)

In September 1994, Erie, Pennsylvania, enacted a law making it a criminal offense to appear in public in a "state of nudity." Erie had not experienced any problems with its citizens walking around in public nude, but it did have several nightclubs that featured semi-nude and nude dancing. Nick Panos, who owned and operated the Kandyland nightclub, refused to comply with the law's requirement that dancers wear G-strings and pasties to cover their genitals and nipples. Panos challenged the law as unconstitutional, claiming that nude dancing was protected by the First Amendment. Ultimately, the Pennsylvania Supreme Court agreed with Panos, who responded by placing the sign "First Amendment Headquarters" on the marquee outside his nightclub.

The nudity law had been approved by four of Erie's six city council members. Each council member who voted for the law made it clear that it was not directed toward any other kind of "public nudity" than the kind found in Kandyland and a handful of other strip clubs that operated in Erie. Said one lawmaker: "We're not talking about nudity. We're not talking about the theater or art. . . . We're talking about what is indecent and immoral." Another lawmaker contrasted nude dancing in nightclubs with his personal recollection of nude swimming by high school students in the school's pool, noting that such nudity was not "indecent," but simply "nudity." What ultimately persuaded the Pennsylvania Supreme Court to strike the law down was its exclusive focus on nude dancing found in strip clubs such as Kandyland.

To avoid a review on the First Amendment issue in the Supreme Court, Panos temporarily closed down Kandyland, arguing that being out of business made the case moot.

The Court divided 6 to 3, but did so along several lines. Five justices agreed with Justice O'Connor's opinion reversing the Pennsylvania Supreme Court, but only three justices agreed with her analysis. Justice Scalia, joined by Justice Thomas, filed a concurring opinion. Justice Souter filed an opinion concurring in part and dissenting in part. Justice Stevens, joined by Justice Ginsburg, also dissented.

▼▲▼

JUSTICE O'CONNOR announced the judgment of the Court and delivered the opinion of the Court with respect to Parts I and II, and an opinion with respect to Parts III and IV, in which THE CHIEF JUSTICE, JUSTICE KENNEDY, and JUSTICE BREYER join.

I

[Omitted]

II

[Omitted]

III

Being "in a state of nudity" is not an inherently expressive condition. . . . [H]owever, nude dancing of the type at issue here is expressive conduct, although we think that it falls only within the outer ambit of the First Amendment's protection, *Barnes* v. *Glen Theatre Inc.* (1991). . . .

To determine what level of scrutiny applies to the ordinance at issue here, we must decide "whether the State's regulation is related to the suppression of expression," *Texas* v. *Johnson* (1989); see also *United States* v. *O'Brien* (1968). If the governmental purpose in enacting the regulation is unrelated to the suppression of expression, then the regulation need only satisfy the "less stringent" standard from *O'Brien* for evaluating restrictions on symbolic speech. If the government interest is related to the content of the expression, however, then the regulation falls outside the scope of the *O'Brien* test and must be justified under a more demanding standard. . . .

The city of Erie argues that the ordinance is a content-neutral restriction that is reviewable under *O'Brien* because the ordinance bans conduct, not speech; specifically, public nudity. Respondent counters that the ordinance targets nude dancing and, as such, is aimed specifically at suppressing expression, making the ordinance a content-based restriction that must be subjected to strict scrutiny.

The ordinance here, like the statute in *Barnes*, is on its face a general prohibition on public nudity. By its terms, the ordinance regulates conduct alone. It does not target nudity that contains an erotic message; rather, it bans all public nudity, regardless of whether that nudity is accompanied by expressive activity. And like the statute in *Barnes*, the Erie ordinance replaces and updates provisions of an "Indecency and Immorality" ordinance that has been on the books since 1866, predating the prevalence of nude dancing establishments such as Kandyland. . . .

[T]his case is similar to *O'Brien*. O'Brien burned his draft registration card as a public statement of his antiwar views, and he was convicted under a statute making it a crime to knowingly mutilate or destroy such a card. This Court rejected his claim that the statute violated his First Amendment rights, reasoning that the law punished him for the "noncommunicative impact of his conduct, and for nothing else." In other words, the Government regulation prohibiting the destruction of draft cards was aimed at maintaining the integrity of the Selective Service System and not at suppressing the message of draft resistance that O'Brien sought to convey by burning his draft card. So too here, the ordinance prohibiting public nudity is aimed at combating crime and other negative secondary effects caused by the presence of adult entertainment establishments like Kandyland and not at suppressing the erotic message conveyed by this type of nude dancing. Put another way, the ordinance does not attempt to regulate the primary effects of the expression, *i.e.*, the effect on the audience of watching nude erotic dancing, but rather the secondary effects, such as the impacts on public health, safety, and welfare, which we have previously recognized are "caused by the presence of even one such" establishment. . . .

Respondent's argument that the ordinance is "aimed" at suppressing expression through a ban on nude dancing—an argument that respondent supports by pointing to statements by the city attorney that the public nudity ban was not intended to apply to "legitimate" theater productions—is really an argument that the city council also had an illicit motive in enacting the ordinance. As we have said before, however, this Court will not strike down an otherwise constitutional statute on the basis of an alleged illicit motive. In light of the Pennsylvania court's determination that one purpose of the ordinance is to combat harmful secondary effects, the ban on public nudity here is no different from the ban on burning draft registration cards in *O'Brien,* where the Government sought to prevent the means of the expression and not the expression of antiwar sentiment itself. . . .

Even if we had not already rejected the view that a ban on public nudity is necessarily related to the suppression of the erotic message of nude dancing, we would do so now because the premise of such a view is flawed. The State's interest in preventing harmful secondary effects is not related to the suppression of expression. In trying to control the secondary effects of nude dancing, the ordinance seeks to deter crime and the other deleterious effects caused by the presence of such an establishment in the neighborhood. In *Clark* v. *Community for Creative Non-Violence* (1984), we held that a National Park Service regulation prohibiting camping in certain parks did not violate the First Amendment when applied to prohibit demonstrators from sleeping in Lafayette Park and the Mall in Washington, D.C., in connection with a demonstration intended to call attention to the plight of the homeless. . . . [T]he Court concluded that the Government interest in conserving park property was unrelated to the demonstrators' message about homelessness. So, while the demonstrators were allowed to erect "symbolic tent cities," they were not allowed to sleep overnight in those tents. Even though the regulation may have directly limited the expressive element involved in actually sleeping in the park, the regulation was nonetheless content neutral.

Similarly, even if Erie's public nudity ban has some minimal effect on the erotic message by muting that portion of the expression that occurs when the last stitch is dropped, the dancers at Kandyland and other such establishments are free to perform wearing pasties and G-strings. Any effect on the overall expression is *de minimis*. . . .

Even if the city thought that nude dancing at clubs like Kandyland constituted a particularly problematic instance of public nudity, the regulation is still properly evaluated as a content-neutral restriction because the interest in combating the secondary effects associated with those clubs is unrelated to the suppression of the erotic message conveyed by nude dancing. We conclude that Erie's asserted interest in combating the negative secondary effects associated with adult entertainment establishments like Kandyland is unrelated to the suppression of the erotic message conveyed by nude dancing. The ordinance prohibiting public nudity is therefore valid if it satisfies the four-factor test from *O'Brien* for evaluating restrictions on symbolic speech.

IV

Applying that standard here, we conclude that Erie's ordinance is justified under *O'Brien*. The first factor of the *O'Brien* test is whether the government regulation is within the constitutional power of the government to enact. Here, Erie's efforts to protect public health and safety are clearly within the city's police powers. The second factor is whether the regulation furthers an important or substantial government interest. The asserted interests of regulating conduct through a public nudity ban and of combating the harmful secondary effects associated with nude dancing are undeniably important. And in terms of demonstrating that such secondary effects pose a threat, the city need not "conduct new studies or produce evidence independent of that already generated by other cities" to demonstrate the problem of secondary effects, "so long as whatever evidence the city relies upon is reasonably believed to be relevant to the problem that the city addresses." Because the nude dancing at Kandyland is of the same character as the adult entertainment at issue in *Renton, Young* v. *American Mini Theatres, Inc.* (1976) . . . , it was reasonable for Erie to conclude that such nude dancing was likely to produce the same secondary effects. . . .

Finally, it is worth repeating that Erie's ordinance is on its face a content neutral restriction that regulates conduct, not First Amendment expression. And the government should have sufficient leeway to justify such a law based on secondary effects. On this point, *O'Brien* is especially instructive. The Court there did not require evidence that the integrity of the Selective Service System would be jeopardized by the knowing destruction or mutilation of draft cards. It simply reviewed the Government's various administrative interests in issuing the cards, and then concluded that "Congress has a legitimate and substantial interest in preventing their wanton and unrestrained destruction and assuring their continuing availability by punishing people who knowingly and willfully destroy or mutilate them." There was no study documenting instances of draft card mutilation or the actual effect of such mutilation on the Government's asserted efficiency interests. But the Court permitted Congress to take official notice, as it were, that draft card destruction would jeopardize the system. The fact that this sort of leeway is appropriate in a case involving conduct says nothing whatsoever about its appropriateness in a case involving actual regulation of First Amendment expression. As we have said, so long as the regulation is unrelated to the suppression of expression, "[t]he government generally has a freer hand in restricting expressive conduct than it has in restricting the written or spoken word," *Texas* v. *Johnson*. . . .

As to the second point—whether the regulation furthers the government interest—it is evident that, since crime and other public health and safety problems are caused by the presence of nude dancing establishments like Kandyland, a ban on such nude dancing would further Erie's interest in preventing such secondary effects. To be sure, requiring dancers to wear pasties and G-strings may not greatly reduce these secondary effects, but *O'Brien* requires only that the regulation further the interest in combating such effects. Even though the dissent questions the wisdom of Erie's chosen remedy, the "'city must be allowed a reasonable opportunity to experiment with solutions to admittedly serious problems.'" It also may be true that a pasties and G-string requirement would not be as effective as, for example, a requirement that the dancers be fully clothed, but the city must balance its efforts to address the problem with the requirement that the restriction be no greater than necessary to further the city's interest.

The ordinance also satisfies *O'Brien*'s third factor, that the government interest is unrelated to the suppression of free expression. The fourth and final *O'Brien* factor—that the restriction is no greater than is essential to the furtherance of the government interest—is satisfied as well. The ordinance regulates conduct, and any incidental impact on the expressive element of nude dancing is *de minimis*. The requirement that dancers wear pasties and G-strings is a minimal restriction in furtherance of the asserted government interests, and the restriction leaves ample capacity to convey the dancer's erotic message. . . .

We hold, therefore, that Erie's ordinance is a content-neutral regulation that is valid under *O'Brien*. Accordingly, the judgment of the Pennsylvania Supreme Court is reversed, and the case is remanded for further proceedings not inconsistent with this opinion.

It is so ordered.

JUSTICE STEVENS, with whom JUSTICE GINSBURG joins, dissenting.

Far more important than the question whether nude dancing is entitled to the protection of the First Amendment are the dramatic changes in legal doctrine that the Court endorses today. Until now, the "secondary effects" of commercial enterprises featuring indecent entertainment have justified only the regulation of their location. For the first time, the Court has now held that such effects may justify the total suppression of protected speech. Indeed, the plurality opinion concludes that admittedly trivial advancements of a State's interests may provide the basis for censorship. The Court's commendable attempt to replace the fractured decision in *Barnes* v. *Glen Theatre, Inc.* (1991), with a single coherent rationale is strikingly unsuccessful; it is supported neither by precedent nor by persuasive reasoning. . . .

Correct analysis of the issue in this case should begin with the proposition that nude dancing is a species of expressive conduct that is protected by the First Amendment. . . . [N]ude dancing fits well within a broad, cultural tradition recognized as expressive in nature and entitled to First Amendment protection. The nudity of the dancer is both a component of the protected expression and the specific target of the ordinance. It is pure sophistry to reason from the premise that the regulation of the nudity component of nude dancing is unrelated to the message conveyed by nude dancers. Indeed, both the text of the ordinance and the reasoning in the Court's opinion make it pellucidly clear that the city of Erie has prohibited nude dancing *"precisely because of its communicative attributes," Barnes*. . . .

The four city council members who approved the measure (of the six total council members) each stated his or her view that the ordinance was aimed specifically at nude adult entertainment, and not at more mainstream forms of entertainment that include total nudity, nor even at nudity in general. One lawmaker observed: "We're not talking about nudity. We're not talking about the theater or art. . . . We're talking about what is indecent and immoral. . . . We're not prohibiting nudity, we're prohibiting nudity when it's used in a lewd and immoral fashion." Though not quite as succinct, the other council members expressed similar convictions. For example, one member illustrated his understanding of the aim of the law by contrasting it with his recollection about high school students swimming in the nude in the school's pool. The ordinance was not intended to cover those incidents of nudity: "But what I'm getting at is [the swimming] wasn't indecent, it wasn't an immoral thing, and yet there was nudity." The same lawmaker then disfavorably compared the nude swimming incident to the activities that occur in "some of these clubs" that exist in Erie—clubs that would be covered by the law. Though such comments could be consistent with an interest in a general prohibition of nudity, the complete absence of commentary on that broader interest, and the council members' exclusive focus on adult entertainment, is evidence of the ordinance's aim. In my view, we need not strain to find consistency with more general purposes when the most natural reading of the record reflects a near obsessive preoccupation with a single target of the law. . . .

It is clear beyond a shadow of a doubt that the Erie ordinance was a response to a more specific concern than nudity in general, namely, nude dancing of the sort found in Kandyland. Given that the Court has not even tried to defend the ordinance's total ban on the ground that its censorship of protected speech might be justified by an overriding state interest, it should conclude that the ordinance is patently invalid. . . .

I respectfully dissent.

Hate Speech

In April 1940, Walter Chaplinsky, a Jehovah's Witness, had been preaching in the open air of the Rochester, New Hampshire, town square when a mob, enraged by his statements, gathered and began to assault him. He was arrested under a state law that prohibited using "any offensive, derisive, or annoying word to any other person who is lawfully in the street." Irate, Chaplinsky demanded to know from the officer on the scene why it was he being arrested and not his attackers. After the officer told him to "shut up," Chaplinsky returned the volley, calling him a "fascist" and a "God damned racketeer." The Witnesses took up Chaplinsky's legal defense, and succeeded in appealing his case to the Supreme Court. But the justices were no more enamored of Chaplinsky's behavior than the lower courts had been. A unanimous Court, in *Chaplinsky v. New Hampshire* (1942), concluded that the First Amendment permitted a *fighting words* exception, which it defined as a "face-to-face" exchange "plainly likely to cause a breach of the peace by the addressee." Walter Chaplinsky then went to jail for six months.[49]

Since *Chaplinsky,* the Court has rarely turned to the fighting words exception to justify government restraints on public speech. A splendid example of just how narrow the Court considers the fighting words exception came in *National Socialist Workers Party v. Village of Skokie* (1977), in which it vacated a lower Illinois court's decision upholding a municipal ordinance banning the public display of the Nazi swastika. The Court did not reach the merits of the case. But, in ordering a new trial, the justices' *per curiam* opinion made very clear that Skokie, Illinois, a small Chicago suburb with the nation's highest per capita population of Holocaust survivors, could not restrain the right of an American Nazi group to march in its public streets. Recall our discussion in Chapter 3 of the ACLU's role in defending the free speech rights of the Nazis and the subsequent fallout that decision created for the group's membership and reputation.[50]

The Nazis-in-Skokie episode introduced a new phrase into the lexicon of American freedom of expression: "hate speech." Certainly, their hatred of Jews, not a desire to educate the public or criticize public policy, is what prompted the Nazis to choose Skokie as their demonstration site. Put in different terms, the Nazis' march was a carefully calibrated effort to select a particular audience and taunt them through peaceful means, or through what political scientist Donald Alexander Downs has called "targeted racial vilification."[51] Although the Nazis ultimately received clearance to march in Skokie after several more rounds in the courts, they never actually marched, instead staging a small, poorly attended demonstration in downtown Chicago.

A direct outgrowth of the battle over the rights of the Nazis to march in Skokie was the subsequent introduction of "hate crimes" laws. These laws took two forms. The first involved penalty enhancement for bias-motivated crimes; the second involved specific prohibitions on particular viewpoints considered fighting words when uttered. Leading the way in this novel approach to punishing and deterring hate-motivated conduct was the Anti-Defamation League of B'nai B'rith, which had been among the groups to file suit seeking an injunction against the Nazis' right to march in Skokie. For many people, however, hate crimes laws raised serious constitutional questions. In the case of penalty-enhancement laws, they appeared to punish the thoughts that went into conduct; as for the laws based on the fighting words exception, they left unprotected particular viewpoints. These complex legal and political considerations came together in *R.A.V.* v. *City of St. Paul* (1992).

R.A.V. v. *City of St. Paul*

505 U.S. 377 (1992)

Public cross burnings are synonymous with the Ku Klux Klan, the white supremacist group that formed during Reconstruction to intimidate African Americans from asserting their newly won civil rights. Congress soon clamped down on the Klan and by the late 1870s the organization ceased to exist. However, in 1915, William J. Simmons, a Spanish-American War veteran–turned preacher–turned salesman, convinced fifteen friends to make the trip with him from Atlanta to nearby Stone Mountain, Georgia. On Thanksgiving Eve, Simmons and his new fraternity brothers built a twenty-foot cross from cheap pine boards, recited a hastily drafted oath, lit a match, and the Ku Klux Klan of the twentieth century was born. And so by the early 1920s, the Klan had reorganized in the South as an "invisible" empire to enforce the laws of racial segregation. The Klan also added Catholics and Jews, who had arrived from Europe by the millions during the late 1800s and early 1900s, to their list of enemies.

The Klan has waxed and waned since its high point in 1926, when 40,000 hooded Klansmen from all over the country marched down Pennsylvania Avenue in Washington, D.C., thus exploding the myth that the Klan was purely a Southern phenomenon. Although current estimates place Klan membership nationwide at less than 5,000, the burning cross remains a powerful symbol because of its historical context. Although the modern Klan claims that cross burning is a symbol of white Christian pride, most Americans, particularly religious and racial minorities, do not share that view. Whether Robert A. Viktora, a seventeen-year-old high school dropout who lived in St. Paul, Minnesota, had any historical appreciation of cross burning is not clear. But if Viktora and his three friends, who placed an eighteen-inch-high cross in the yard of Russell and Laura Jones and their five children, thought they were playing some kind of joke, they severely underestimated the resolve of this African American family to stand up against what it viewed as an overt racist act.

Rather than prosecute Viktora under a criminal trespass, arson, or vandalism law, the St. Paul district attorney's office decided to charge him under its new "hate speech" ordinance. The law stated, in part: "Whoever places on public or private property a symbol, object, appellation, characterization or graffiti, including but not limited to, a burning cross or Nazi swastika, which one knows or has reasonable grounds to know arouses anger, alarm or resentment in others on the basis of race, color, creed, religion, or gender, commits disorderly conduct. . . ."

The accompanying SIDEBAR offers an in-depth examination of the group politics behind the *R.A.V.* case and alternative legal strategies for dealing with hate speech.

The Court was unanimous in finding the St. Paul law unconstitutional, but split several ways on the law's constitutional defects. Justice Scalia's opinion was joined by five other justices. Justices Blackmun, Stevens, and White filed concurring opinions.

▼▲▼

JUSTICE SCALIA delivered the opinion of the Court.

The First Amendment generally prevents government from proscribing speech, or even expressive conduct, because of disapproval of the ideas expressed. Content-based

regulations are presumptively invalid. From 1791 to the present, however, our society, like other free but civilized societies, has permitted restrictions upon the content of speech in a few limited areas, which are "of such slight social value as a step to truth that any benefit that may be derived from them is clearly outweighed by the social interest in order and morality," *Chaplinsky* v. *New Hampshire* (1942). We have recognized that "the freedom of speech" referred to by the First Amendment does not include a freedom to disregard these traditional limitations. Our decisions since the 1960's have narrowed the scope of the traditional categorical exceptions for defamation, and for obscenity, but a limited categorical approach has remained an important part of our First Amendment jurisprudence.

We have sometimes said that these categories of expression are "not within the area of constitutionally protected speech," or that the "protection of the First Amendment does not extend" to them. Such statements must be taken in context, however, and are no more literally true than is the occasionally repeated shorthand characterizing obscenity "as not being speech at all." What they mean is that these areas of speech can, consistently with the First Amendment, be regulated *because of their constitutionally proscribable content* (obscenity, defamation, etc.)—not that they are categories of speech entirely invisible to the Constitution, so that they may be made the vehicles for content discrimination unrelated to their distinctively proscribable content. Thus, the government may proscribe libel; but it may not make the further content discrimination of proscribing *only* libel critical of the government. . . .

The proposition that a particular instance of speech can be proscribable on the basis of one feature (*e.g.*, obscenity) but not on the basis of another (*e.g.*, opposition to the city government) is commonplace, and has found application in many contexts. We have long held, for example, that nonverbal expressive activity can be banned because of the action it entails, but not because of the ideas it expresses—so that burning a flag in violation of an ordinance against outdoor fires could be punishable, whereas burning a flag in violation of an ordinance against dishonoring the flag is not. Similarly, we have upheld reasonable "time, place, or manner" restrictions, but only if they are "justified without reference to the content of the regulated speech." And just as the power to proscribe particular speech on the basis of a non-content element (*e.g.*, noise) does not entail the power to proscribe the same speech on the basis of a content element, so also the power to proscribe it on the basis of one content element (*e.g.*, obscenity) does not entail the power to proscribe it on the basis of *other* content elements.

In other words, the exclusion of "fighting words" from the scope of the First Amendment simply means that, for purposes of that Amendment, the unprotected features of the words are, despite their verbal character, essentially a "nonspeech" element of communication. Fighting words are thus analogous to a noisy sound truck: each is, as Justice Frankfurter recognized, a "mode of speech," both can be used to convey an idea; but neither has, in and of itself, a claim upon the First Amendment. As with the sound truck, however, so also with fighting words: the government may not regulate use based on hostility or favoritism—towards the underlying message expressed. . . .

Even the prohibition against content discrimination that we assert the First Amendment requires is not absolute. It applies differently in the context of proscribable speech than in the area of fully protected speech. The rationale of the general prohibition, after all, is that content discrimination "rais[es] the specter that the Government may effectively drive certain ideas or viewpoints from the marketplace." But content discrimination among various instances of a class of proscribable speech often does not pose this threat.

When the basis for the content discrimination consists entirely of the very reason the entire class of speech at issue is proscribable, no significant danger of idea or viewpoint discrimination exists. Such a reason, having been adjudged neutral enough to support exclusion of the entire class of speech from First Amendment protection, is also neutral enough to form the basis of distinction within the class. To illustrate: a State might choose to prohibit only that obscenity which is the most patently offensive *in its prurience—i.e.*, that which involves the most lascivious displays of sexual activity. But it may not prohibit, for example, only that obscenity which includes offensive *political* messages. . . .

Another valid basis for according differential treatment to even a content-defined subclass of proscribable speech is that the subclass happens to be associated with particular "secondary effects" of the speech, so that the regulation is "*justified* without reference to the content of the . . . speech." A State could, for example, permit all obscene live performances except those involving minors. Moreover, since words can in some circumstances violate laws directed not against speech. but against conduct (a law against treason, for example, is violated by telling the enemy the nation's defense secrets), a particular content-based subcategory of a proscribable class of speech can be swept up incidentally within the reach of a statute directed at conduct, rather than speech. Thus, for example, sexually derogatory "fighting words," among other words, may produce a violation of Title VII's general prohibition against sexual discrimination in employment practices. Where the government does not target conduct on the basis of its expressive content, acts are not shielded from regulation merely because they express a discriminatory idea or philosophy. . . .

Applying these principles to the St. Paul ordinance, we conclude that, even as narrowly construed by the Minnesota Supreme Court, the ordinance is facially unconstitutional. Although the phrase in the ordinance, "arouses anger, alarm or resentment in others," has been limited by the Minnesota Supreme Court's construction to reach only those symbols or displays that amount to "fighting words," the remaining, unmodified terms make clear that the ordinance applies only to "fighting words" that insult, or provoke violence, "on the basis of race, color, creed, religion or gender." Displays containing abusive invective, no matter how vicious or severe, are permissible unless they are addressed to one of the specified disfavored topics. Those who wish to use "fighting words" in connection with other ideas—to express hostility, for example, on the basis of political affiliation, union membership, or homosexuality—are not covered. The First Amendment does not permit St. Paul to impose special prohibitions on those speakers who express views on disfavored subjects.

In its practical operation, moreover, the ordinance goes even beyond mere content discrimination to actual viewpoint discrimination. Displays containing some words—odious racial epithets, for example—would be prohibited to proponents of all views. But "fighting words" that do not themselves invoke race, color, creed, religion, or gender—aspersions upon a person's mother, for example—would seemingly be usable *ad libitum* in the placards of those arguing *in favor* of racial, color, etc. tolerance and equality, but could not be used by that speaker's opponents. One could hold up a sign saying, for example, that all "anti-Catholic bigots" are misbegotten; but not that all "papists" are, for that would insult and provoke violence "on the basis of religion." St. Paul has no such authority to license one side of a debate to fight freestyle, while requiring the other to follow Marquis of Queensbury Rules.

What we have here, it must be emphasized, is not a prohibition of fighting words that are directed at certain persons or groups (which would be *facially* valid if it met the requirements of the Equal Protection Clause); but rather, a prohibition of fighting words that contain (as the Minnesota Supreme Court repeatedly emphasized) messages of "bias-motivated" hatred and, in particular, as applied to this case, messages "based on virulent notions of racial supremacy." One must wholeheartedly agree with the Minnesota Supreme Court that "[i]t is the responsibility, even the obligation, of diverse communities to confront such notions in whatever form they appear," but the manner of that confrontation cannot consist of selective limitations upon speech. St. Paul's brief asserts that a general "fighting words" law would not meet the city's needs, because only a content-specific measure can communicate to minority groups that the "group hatred" aspect of such speech "is not condoned by the majority." The point of the First Amendment is that majority preferences must be expressed in some fashion other than silencing speech on the basis of its content. . . .

Finally, St. Paul and its *amici* defend the conclusion of the Minnesota Supreme Court that, even if the ordinance regulates expression based on hostility towards its protected ideological content, this discrimination is nonetheless justified because it is narrowly tailored to serve compelling state interests. Specifically, they assert that the ordinance helps to ensure the basic human rights of members of groups that have historically been subjected to discrimination, including the right of such group members to live in peace where they wish. We do not doubt that these interests are compelling, and that the ordinance can be said to promote them. But the "danger of censorship" presented by a facially neutral statute requires that weapon be employed only where it is "necessary to serve the asserted [compelling] interest." The existence of adequate content-neutral alternatives thus "undercut[s] significantly" any defense of such a statute, casting considerable doubt on the government's protestations that "the asserted justification is in fact an accurate description of the purpose and effect of the law." The dispositive question in this case, therefore, is whether content discrimination is reasonably necessary to achieve St. Paul's compelling interests; it plainly is not. An ordinance not limited to the favored topics, for example, would have precisely the same beneficial effect. In fact, the only interest distinctively served by the content limitation is that of displaying the city council's special hostility towards the particular biases thus singled out. That is precisely what the First Amendment forbids. The politicians of St. Paul are entitled to express that hostility—but not through the means of imposing unique limitations upon speakers who (however benightedly) disagree.

Let there be no mistake about our belief that burning a cross in someone's front yard is reprehensible. But St. Paul has sufficient means at its disposal to prevent such behavior without adding the First Amendment to the fire.

The judgment of the Minnesota Supreme Court is reversed, and the case is remanded for proceedings not inconsistent with this opinion.

JUSTICE WHITE, with whom JUSTICE BLACKMUN and JUSTICE O'CONNOR join, and with whom JUSTICE STEVENS joins . . . concurring in the judgment.

I agree with the majority that the judgment of the Minnesota Supreme Court should be reversed. However, our agreement ends there.

[I]n the present case, the majority casts aside long-established First Amendment doctrine without the benefit of briefing and adopts an untried theory. This is hardly a judicious way of proceeding, and the Court's reasoning in reaching its result is transparently wrong.

This Court's decisions have plainly stated that expression falling within certain limited categories so lacks the values the First Amendment was designed to protect that the Constitution affords no protection to that expression. . . .

Thus, as the majority concedes, this Court has long held certain discrete categories of expression to be proscribable on the basis of their content. For instance, the Court has held that the individual who falsely shouts "fire" in a crowded theatre may not claim the protection of the First Amendment. The Court has concluded that neither child pornography nor obscenity is protected by the First Amendment. And the Court has observed that, "[l]eaving aside the special considerations when public officials [and public figures] are the target, a libelous publication is not protected by the Constitution."

All of these categories are content-based. But the Court has held that the First Amendment does not apply to them, because their expressive content is worthless or of *de minimis* value to society. We have not departed from this principle. . . .

Today, however, the Court announces that earlier Courts did not mean their repeated statements that certain categories of expression are "not within the area of constitutionally protected speech." The present Court submits that such clear statements "must be taken in context," and are not "literally true."

To the contrary, those statements meant precisely what they said: the categorical approach is a firmly entrenched part of our First Amendment jurisprudence. . . .

. . . [T]he majority holds that the First Amendment protects those narrow categories of expression long held to be undeserving of First Amendment protection—at least to the extent that lawmakers may not regulate some fighting words more strictly than others because of their content. The Court announces that such content-based distinctions violate the First Amendment because "the government may not regulate use based on hostility—or favoritism—towards the underlying message expressed." Should the government want to criminalize certain fighting words, the Court now requires it to criminalize all fighting words.

It is inconsistent to hold that the government may proscribe an entire category of speech because the content of that speech is evil, but that the government may not treat a subset of that category differently without violating the First Amendment; the content of the subset is, by definition, worthless and undeserving of constitutional protection.

The majority's observation that fighting words are "quite expressive indeed," is no answer. Fighting words are not a means of exchanging views, rallying supporters, or registering a protest; they are directed against individuals to provoke violence or to inflict injury. Therefore, a ban on all fighting words or on a subset of the fighting words category would restrict only the social evil of hate speech, without creating the danger of driving viewpoints from the marketplace.

Therefore, the Court's insistence on inventing its brand of First Amendment underinclusiveness puzzles me. The overbreadth doctrine has the redeeming virtue of attempting to avoid the chilling of protected expression, but the Court's new "underbreadth" creation serves no desirable function. Instead, it permits, indeed invites, the continuation of expressive conduct that, in this case, is evil and worthless in First Amendment terms, until the city of St. Paul cures the underbreadth by adding to its ordinance a catch-all phrase such as "and all other fighting words that may constitutionally be subject to this ordinance."

Any contribution of this holding to First Amendment jurisprudence is surely a negative one, since it necessarily signals that expressions of violence, such as the message of intimidation and racial hatred conveyed by burning a cross on someone's lawn, are of sufficient value to outweigh the social interest in order and morality that has traditionally placed such fighting words outside the First Amendment. Indeed, by characterizing fighting words as a form of "debate," the majority legitimates hate speech as a form of public discussion.

Furthermore, the Court obscures the line between speech that could be regulated freely on the basis of content (*i.e.,* the narrow categories of expression falling outside the First Amendment) and that which could be regulated on the basis of content only upon a showing of a compelling state interest (*i.e.,* all remaining expression). By placing fighting words, which the Court has long held to be valueless, on at least equal constitutional footing with political discourse and other forms of speech that we have deemed to have the greatest social value, the majority devalues the latter category.

JUSTICE STEVENS, with whom JUSTICE WHITE and JUSTICE BLACKMUN join . . . concurring in the judgment.

Conduct that creates special risks or causes special harms may be prohibited by special rules. Lighting a fire near an ammunition dump or a gasoline storage tank is especially dangerous; such behavior may be punished more severely than burning trash in a vacant lot. Threatening someone because of her race or religious beliefs may cause particularly severe trauma or touch off a riot, and threatening a high public official may cause substantial social disruption; such threats may be punished more severely than threats against someone based on, say, his support of a particular athletic team. There are legitimate, reasonable, and neutral justifications for such special rules.

This case involves the constitutionality of one such ordinance. Because the regulated conduct has some communicative content—a message of racial, religious or gender hostility—the ordinance raises two quite different First Amendment questions. Is the ordinance "overbroad" because it prohibits too much speech? If not, is it "underbroad" because it does not prohibit enough speech? . . .

Unlike the Court, I do not believe that all content-based regulations are equally infirm and presumptively invalid; unlike JUSTICE WHITE, I do not believe that fighting words are wholly unprotected by the First Amendment. To the contrary, I believe our decisions establish a more complex and subtle analysis, one that considers the content and context of the regulated speech, and the nature and scope of the restriction on speech. Applying this analysis and assuming *arguendo* (as the Court does) that the St. Paul ordinance is not overbroad, I conclude that such a selective, subject matter regulation on proscribable speech is constitutional.

Not all content-based regulations are alike; our decisions clearly recognize that some content-based restrictions raise more constitutional questions than others. Although the Court's analysis of content-based regulations cannot be reduced to a simple formula, we have considered a number of factors in determining the validity of such regulations. . . .

The St. Paul ordinance is evenhanded. In a battle between advocates of tolerance and advocates of intolerance, the ordinance does not prevent either side from hurling fighting words at the other on the basis of their conflicting ideas, but it does bar *both* sides from hurling such words on the basis of the target's "race, color, creed, religion or gender." To extend the Court's pugilistic metaphor, the St. Paul ordinance simply bans punches "below the belt"—*by either party*. It does not, therefore, favor one side of any debate.

Finally, it is noteworthy that the St. Paul ordinance is, as construed by the Court today, quite narrow. The St. Paul ordinance does not ban all "hate speech," nor does it ban, say, all cross-burnings or all swastika displays. Rather, it only bans a subcategory of the already narrow category of fighting words. Such a limited ordinance leaves open and protected a vast range of expression on the subjects of racial, religious, and gender equality. As construed by the Court today, the ordinance certainly does not "'raise the specter that the Government may effectively drive certain ideas or viewpoints from the marketplace.'" Petitioner is free to burn a cross to announce a rally or to express his views about racial supremacy, he may do so on private property or public land, at day or at night, so long as the burning is not so threatening and so directed at an individual as to, "by its very [execution,] inflict injury." Such a limited proscription scarcely offends the First Amendment.

In sum, the St. Paul ordinance (as construed by the Court) regulates expressive activity that is wholly proscribable, and does so not on the basis of viewpoint, but rather in recognition of the different harms caused by such activity. Taken together, these several considerations persuade me that the St. Paul ordinance is not an unconstitutional content-based regulation of speech. Thus, were the ordinance not overbroad, I would vote to uphold it.

Many scholars considered Justice Scalia's opinion in *R.A.V.* the most resolute statement of absolutist free speech principles in recent memory. By holding that St. Paul could not categorize objectionable viewpoints as fighting words, Scalia was well within the Court's approach to the First Amendment since *Brandenburg*. But Scalia's analysis went an additional major step, one that called into question the vitality of the fighting words exception. Concluding that the fighting words exception involved a "nonspeech element of communication," Scalia held that government could not even ban specific viewpoints within a category of *unprotected* speech. In their concurring opinions, Justices Stevens and White strongly criticized Scalia's analysis. They each claimed that certain categories of speech had traditionally been less protected under the First Amendment, such as the "indecent" speech at issue in *Pacifica*, or not protected at all, such as obscenity, and thus not beyond the power of government to regulate. Which of the opinions in *R.A.V.* do you believe are more consistent with a proper understanding of the First Amendment?

SIDEBAR

R.A.V. v. City of St. Paul

Making Hate Crime Pay

Late one morning in March 1961, approximately 190 high school and college African American students marched toward the state house grounds in Columbia, South Carolina. They were, by all accounts, well dressed and orderly. Carrying signs bearing such messages as "I am proud to be a Negro" and "Down with segregation," they were guided by law enforcement officers through the capitol area and told that they could continue their demonstration as long as they remained peaceful. As the African American students continued to march toward the area secured for them, somewhere between two and three hundred onlookers, all of whom were white, had gathered to watch the proceedings. Although no words were exchanged between the black demonstrators and the white audience, and car and pedestrian traffic continued unimpeded, the police suddenly told the students they had fifteen minutes to disperse in a peaceful fashion or they would be arrested. Shortly afterward, Columbia police arrested the students under a state "breach of peace" law, claiming they had become boisterous and unruly. White witnesses, whose opinions were the only ones that mattered in the pre–civil rights era South, later testified that all the African American students had done was to sing some religious hymns and "The Star-Spangled Banner."

The NAACP brought suit against South Carolina, arguing that the law violated the demonstrators' First Amendment rights to freedom of speech and assembly. An 8–1 Supreme Court agreed, holding that the Constitution "does not permit a State to make criminal the peaceful expression of unpopular views." Inviting dispute and disagreement, held the Court, were core values of the First Amendment.

Edwards v. *South Carolina* (1963) was a major victory for the civil rights movement, which, in the early 1960s, had made grass-roots public protests the central element of its strategy to secure the constitutional rights of African Americans. Almost thirty years later, in *R.A.V.*, the NAACP filed an *amicus* brief supporting the St. Paul hate crimes ordinance. So did the Anti-Defamation League of B'nai B'rith, which had strongly supported the rights of civil rights demonstrators during the 1960s. Another liberal civil liberties organization, People for the American Way, also filed a brief defending the St. Paul ordinance. These groups all believed that the St. Paul law, while not without its problems, had met the criteria of the Court's 1942 decision, *Chaplinsky* v. *New Hampshire,* which established the "fighting words" exception to the First Amendment. Simply put, the Court ruled that it was not unconstitutional to punish speech that was intended to provoke a violent response. Burning a cross or displaying a Nazi swastika had no purpose other than to antagonize African Americans and Jews. These groups were clearly torn by their commitment to civil rights protection for minorities—indeed, such was the founding purpose of the NAACP and the ADL—and their understanding of the historic connection between free speech rights and equality.

A major reason that the NAACP, the ADL, People for the American Way, and other groups representing Asian Americans and gays and lesbians supported the St. Paul ordinance was because they believed a

Supreme Court decision striking it down would jeopardize "enhancement laws" that increased penalties for bias-motivated criminal conduct. In 1981, the ADL developed the first model hate crimes law that increased punishments for bias-motivated crimes, which were defined as attacks on institutions or individual assaults that were motivated by race, religion, color, national origin, sexual orientation, or gender. By the early 1990s, over thirty-five states had adopted hate crimes laws, although not all included the provisions on sexual orientation. By 2000, Congress had hate crimes laws on the books, as did forty-two states and the District of Columbia. The year after *R.A.V.*, the Court upheld penalty-enhancement laws against a First Amendment challenge brought by the Wisconsin affiliate of the ACLU. In *Wisconsin* v. *Mitchell* (1993), a unanimous Court rejected the argument that penalty-enhancement laws punished people for their personal prejudices and biases. Instead, the justices viewed such laws as similar to civil rights laws banning discrimination in employment, public accommodations, and education. It was one thing not to like somebody, but another thing entirely to affect public policy by acting on those prejudices.

Ku Klux Klansmen hoist the burning cross during a rally in Pulaski, Tennessee. This small southern town, located near the Alabama border, was the birthplace of the Klan, which formed shortly after the Civil War.
William Campbell/TimePix

But perhaps the most innovative and effective tactic to emerge in the battle against bias-motivated crime has been the use of civil lawsuits to deprive extremist groups of their financial resources. This approach was pioneered by the Southern Poverty Law Center (SPLC), which was founded in 1971 by Morris Dees, a lawyer who headed a successful publishing company, and by Joe Levin, his law partner. Their decision to open a public interest law firm to combat racial discrimination was not well received by their fellow white Alabamians, who were already miffed with Dees for his successful lawsuit in 1969 forcing the Montgomery YMCA to end its racially discriminatory policies. Rather than comply with desegregation rulings affecting public accommodations, Montgomery closed all its public parks and pools and secretly began supporting the YMCA's recreational programs. When Dees found out, he filed suit claiming that Montgomery had vested the YMCA with a "municipal character," which now made it subject to federal civil rights laws. Federal district court judge Frank Johnson, who was reviled by the segregationist establishment throughout the South for his rulings mandating compliance with the Supreme Court's decisions expanding civil rights for African Americans, ruled in favor of Dees.

During the 1970s and early 1980s, the SPLC won several important victories against the Ku Klux Klan, various paramilitary groups, and other extremist organizations engaged in terrorist campaigns against minorities. For example, in 1981 the SPLC represented several Vietnamese immigrants forced out of fishing in the Galveston Bay of Texas by Klansmen who had burned their fishing boat. Here, the SPLC successfully persuaded a court to shut down the Klan's paramilitary training bases. This decision ended the Klan's campaign in the region by depriving them of their training resources. But the case that brought national attention to the SPLC was Dees's decision in 1988 to file a wrongful death lawsuit against two of the most powerful leaders in the Aryan Resistance Movement, Tom and John Metzger, for the murder of a young Ethiopian immigrant named Mulugeta Seraw.

On November 12, 1988, several members of a Portland, Oregon, skinhead group, East Side White Pride, abducted Seraw right off the street and proceeded to beat him to death with a baseball bat. The attackers were arrested, successfully prosecuted, and received extensive prison sentences. Further investigation by local law enforcement revealed that the Portland skinhead group had strong ties to the Metzger family, long a powerful presence in the extremist movement. Tom Metzger, a former grand dragon of the California Knights of the Ku Klux Klan, once ran the White Aryan Resistance from his home in San Diego. His son, John Metzger, was then the leader of the Aryan Youth Movement, the recruitment arm of his father's organization. A former skinhead, David Mazzella, had provided the Los Angeles office of the Anti-Defamation League with crucial information linking his former organization to Metzger. Mazzella, in fact, had presided over an East Side White Pride meeting the night Seraw was murdered, encouraging skinhead members to commit acts of racial violence. Mazzella later testified against the Metzgers at their trial.

Based on extensive evidence that the ADL had collected, Dees went forward with the wrongful death suit. He carefully explained how the Metzgers, through their sponsorship of the East Side White Pride group, were actually responsible for the death of Mulugeta Seraw. This civil suit against the Metzgers was not intended to establish their criminal guilt, but, quite literally, to bankrupt them by proving their responsibility for Seraw's murder. Dees asked the jury to send a message that Portland would not tolerate such violent racial extremism by returning a substantial damage award to the Seraw family.

The Portland jury awarded Seraw's family $5 million in punitive damages against Tom Metzger, $4 million against John Metzger, $3 million against the White Aryan Resistance, and $500,000 against the skinheads who actually killed Seraw. The Oregon Court of Appeals rejected the Metzgers' effort to have the $12.5 million judgment overturned. The Supreme Court, in *Metzger* v. *Berhanu* (1994), refused to grant *certiorari*. The ADL and the SPLC, which worked closely together on *Berhanu,* knew going into the trial that the Metzgers were in no immediate position to pay the full judgment against them. But the verdict required the White Aryan Resistance to sell their assets to satisfy the judgment, and effectively ended the reign of one of the nation's most powerful extremist networks.

In July 1998, the SPLC obtained a $37.8 million judgment against the Christian Knights of the Ku Klux Klan and several individuals for their roles in setting fire to the Macedonia Baptist Church in South Carolina, which was burned to the ground in June 1995. The jury award was the largest ever directed toward an extremist group in the United States. Although civil litigation cannot quiet the racist messages of hate groups, the legal strategies of the SPLC and other civil rights groups have certainly made any bias-motivated conduct prohibitively expensive.

References

Cleary, Edward J. *Beyond the Burning Cross: A Landmark Case of Race, Censorship, and the First Amendment.* New York: Random House, 1994.

Dees, Morris. *Hate on Trial: The Case Against America's Most Dangerous Neo-Nazi.* New York: Villard Books, 1993.

Obscenity

In 1864, an alarmed postmaster general of the United States reported that "great numbers" of provocative photographs and "lewd" books were being mailed to Union troops during the Civil War. Apparently, seminude photographs of women were among the most popular uses of this new technology. In 1865, Congress enacted legislation making the shipping of any "obscene book, pamphlet, picture, print or other publication of vulgar and indecent character" through the United States mail a federal crime. By 1873, a former dry goods clerk from New York, Anthony Comstock, had developed a national reputation as a tireless crusader against obscenity as the secretary of the New York Society for the Suppression of Vice. Leading members of Congress invited him to Washington to help draft national legislation prohibiting the sale and distribution of obscene materials through the mail. A savvy public relations man, Comstock arrived in the nation's capital with a large cloth bag stuffed with "indecent" books and articles. He was given a private office in the Capitol, where he displayed the "unsuitable" materials that he believed should not be available to the public. Comstock's tactics proved quite effective. That same year, Congress enacted a comprehensive anti-obscenity law that broadened the 1865 law's coverage, and added a provision that banned sending any "article or thing, designed or intended for the prevention of conception or procuring of abortion."[52] The law also enabled Comstock, who had been named a special unpaid agent of the Post Office, to walk into any post office and search any mail that he believed might contain obscene materials.[53]

The Comstock Law's true objective, according to its author, was to protect impressionable young minds from corruption. Since the American courts had not heard any obscenity cases, lawmakers turned to the British common law system for guidance, drawing upon *Regina* v. *Hicklin* (1868) to justify the legal suppression of materials with sexual themes. According to *Hicklin,* any literary value a publication might have was irrelevant if the courts concluded that it might have an immoral influence on younger readers. Some courts concluded that "obscene" passages, in the hands of a skilled literary stylist, actually enhanced the power of a book to "deprave and corrupt."[54] Comstock also targeted the early creators of "pulp" fiction—the fat, cheap novels, often laced with sexual themes, that brought pleasure reading to the masses. Comstock referred to such books as "devil-traps."[55]

Within six months, Comstock claimed to have seized almost 250,000 obscene pictures, drawings, slides, and books. He continued his morals crusade until the late 1910s, when he passed away, but his cause endured. By then, even the major New York publishing houses were intimidated by government agents and private groups determined to root out indecency. During the 1920s, books by D. H. Lawrence (*Women in Love*), Theodore Dreiser (*The Genius*), and James Joyce (*Ulysses*) were withdrawn by their publishers and future copies destroyed for fear that their "erotic" passages would result in prosecution under the Comstock Law. *Ulysses,* still considered a classic in Irish literature, was treated most harshly. In 1920, the publishers of a small literary magazine were successfully prosecuted for publishing excerpts of Joyce's novel. No American publisher went near *Ulysses* for eleven years, until Random House, a new entrant into the New York publishing world, decided to contract with a French publisher for distribution of the novel in the United States. When boxes containing French translations of *Ulysses* arrived in New York, customs officials seized them and Random House was off to court.[56] In 1934, a federal appeals court agreed with the publisher, which was supported by the ACLU and several literary guilds, that the material in question must be viewed as a whole, not in selected parts, when deciding if it fell under the definition of an obscenity prohibition.[57]

American courts did not apply the *Hicklin* rule with any real force after *Ulysses* cleared the tentacles of the Comstock Law. In 1952, the United States Supreme Court opened up a whole new debate on the boundaries of obscenity law when it struck down a New York law that banned the showing of the film *The Miracle* on the grounds that it was sacrilegious. By ruling that movies were a protected form of First Amendment expression, the Court said that moviemakers, their sponsors, and their audiences, not government boards, would now decide the content of their films. Perhaps not coincidentally, the pornographic film industry, although firmly underground, began to grow in the 1950s. Around the same time, Congress convened hearings on the nation's "pornography industry." Although pornography has no precise legal definition, it is most commonly understood as referring to written or photographic material deliberately intended to excite or arouse one sexually. In 1957, the Court was drawn into the obscenity standards debate by a small-time pornographer whose first major business venture involved, ironically enough, defying the informal ban on *Ulysses*.

Roth v. *United States*

354 U.S. 476 (1957)

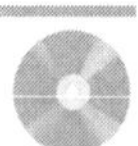

Samuel Roth was born into an Orthodox Jewish community in Austria in 1894 and came to America with his family when he was nine years old. From an early age, Roth demonstrated an entrepreneurial spirit. By the time he was thirty, Roth had already gained notoriety in fashionable New York publishing circles for publishing erotic literature, including James Joyce's *Ulysses,* when nobody else would. Usually, Roth pirated his materials and published them without permission, which left the authors unable to earn royalties. Over the next twenty-five years, Roth became a literary outlaw, going to jail on numerous occasions. Ironically, his first trip to jail came courtesy of the Committee of the Federation of Hungarian Jews in America. This group was upset over Joyce's portrayal of a Jewish character in *Ulysses,* so the committee went after Roth to punish him for fostering anti-Semitism. After his first prison term, Roth returned his attention to erotic literature, sending copies of books such as *Fanny Hill,* which was banned in many states, through the mail, using the name of the noted New York publishing house Alfred A. Knopf as the return addressee. In 1936, federal prosecutors sent Sam Roth back to jail for trafficking in obscenity. While Roth served his time, his wife, Pauline, ran the family business.

By the early 1950s, Roth was back in business in New York City, shipping magazines and books such as *Photo and Body, Good Times,* and *American Aphrodite* through the mail to legions of loyal customers. In 1955, Roth was called before a congressional committee investigating obscenity in the United States to explain his business. Roth responded that he was simply giving the people what they wanted, and there was no shortage of paying customers who wanted to look at nude photographs of men and women. By modern standards, Roth's publications were tame: In *Good Times,* for example, men and women's genitalia were airbrushed out by staff artists. Before the committee, however, Roth never stood a chance. Psychiatrists offered testimony about the harmful long-range impact of pornography on young boys, and attributed the increasing availability of "obscene" materials to the breakdown of American social institutions.[58]

Roth was ultimately found guilty of breaking federal obscenity laws and again sentenced to federal prison, this time for five years.

The Court's decision was 6 to 3. Justice Brennan delivered the opinion of the Court. Chief Justice Warren filed a concurring opinion. Justice Harlan concurred and dissented in part. Justice Black, joined by Justice Douglas, dissented.

▼▲▼

MR. JUSTICE BRENNAN delivered the opinion of the Court.

The . . . question is whether obscenity is utterance within the area of protected speech and press. Although this is the first time the question has been squarely presented to this Court, either under the First Amendment or under the Fourteenth Amendment, expressions found in numerous opinions indicate that this Court has always assumed that obscenity is not protected by the freedoms of speech and press. . . .

The protection given speech and press was fashioned to assure unfettered interchange of ideas for the bringing about of political and social changes desired by the people. . . .

All ideas having even the slightest redeeming social importance—unorthodox ideas, controversial ideas, even ideas hateful to the prevailing climate of opinion—have the full protection of the guaranties, unless excludable because they encroach upon the limited area of more important interests. But implicit in the history of the First Amendment is the rejection of obscenity as utterly without redeeming social importance. This rejection for that reason is mirrored in the universal judgment that obscenity should be restrained, reflected in the international agreement of over 50 nations, in the obscenity laws of all of the 48 States, and in the 20 obscenity laws enacted by the Congress from 1842 to 1956. . . . We hold that obscenity is not within the area of constitutionally protected speech or press.

It is strenuously urged that these obscenity statutes offend the constitutional guaranties because they punish incitation to impure sexual *thoughts,* not shown to be related to any overt antisocial conduct which is or may be incited in the persons stimulated to such *thoughts*. . . .

However, sex and obscenity are not synonymous. Obscene material is material which deals with sex in a manner appealing to prurient interest. The portrayal of sex, *e.g.,* in art, literature and scientific works, is not itself sufficient reason to deny material the constitutional protection of freedom of speech and press. Sex, a great and mysterious motive force in human life, has indisputably been a subject of absorbing interest to mankind through the ages; it is one of the vital problems of human interest and public concern. . . .

The early leading standard of obscenity allowed material to be judged merely by the effect of an isolated excerpt upon particularly susceptible persons. Some American courts adopted this standard, but later decisions have rejected it and substituted this test: whether, to the average person, applying contemporary community standards, the dominant theme of the material, taken as a whole, appeals to prurient interest. The *Hicklin* test, judging obscenity by the effect of isolated passages upon the most susceptible persons, might well encompass material legitimately treating with sex, and so it must be rejected as unconstitutionally restrictive of the freedoms of speech and press. On the other hand, the substituted standard provides safeguards adequate to withstand the charge of constitutional infirmity. . . .

The judgments are
Affirmed.

MR. JUSTICE HARLAN, concurring in part and dissenting in part.

I regret not to be able to join the Court's opinion. I cannot do so, because I find lurking beneath its disarming generalizations a number of problems which . . . leave me with serious misgivings as to the future effect of today's decisions. . . .

In final analysis, the problem presented by these cases is how far, and on what terms, the state and federal governments have power to punish individuals for disseminating books considered to be undesirable because of their nature or supposed deleterious effect upon human conduct. Proceeding from the premise that "no issue is presented in either case, concerning the obscenity of the material involved," the Court finds the "dispositive question" to be "whether obscenity is utterance within the area of protected speech and press," and then holds that "obscenity" is not so protected, because it is "utterly without redeeming social importance." This sweeping formula appears to me to beg the very question before us. The Court seems to assume that "obscenity" is a peculiar *genus* of "speech and press," which is as distinct, recognizable, and classifiable as poison ivy is among other plants. On this basis, the *constitutional* question before us simply becomes, as the Court says, whether "obscenity," as an abstraction, is protected by the First and Fourteenth Amendments, and the question whether a *particular* book may be suppressed becomes a mere matter of classification, of "fact," to be entrusted to a factfinder and insulated from independent constitutional judgment. But surely the problem cannot be solved in such a generalized fashion. Every communication has an individuality and "value" of its own. The suppression of a particular writing or other tangible form of expression is, therefore, an *individual* matter, and in the nature of things every such suppression raises an individual constitutional problem, in which a reviewing court must determine for *itself* whether the attacked expression is suppressable within constitutional standards. Since those standards do not readily lend themselves to generalized definitions, the constitutional problem, in the last analysis, becomes one of particularized judgments which appellate courts must make for themselves. . . .

The Federal Government has, for example, power to restrict seditious speech directed against it, because that Government certainly has the substantive authority to protect itself against revolution. But, in dealing with obscenity, we are faced with the converse situation, for the interests which obscenity statutes purportedly protect are primarily entrusted to the care not of the Federal Government, but of the States. Congress has no substantive power over sexual morality. Such powers as the Federal Government has in this field are but incidental to its other powers, here, the postal power, and are not of the same nature as those possessed by the States, which bear direct responsibility for the protection of the local moral fabric. . . .

Not only is the federal interest in protecting the Nation against pornography attenuated, but the dangers of federal censorship in this field are far greater than anything the States may do. It has often been said that one of the great strengths of our federal system is that we have, in the forty-eight States, forty-eight experimental social laboratories. . . .

Different States will have different attitudes toward the same work of literature. The same book which is freely read in one State might be classed as obscene in another. And it seems to me that no overwhelming danger to our freedom to experiment and to gratify our tastes in literature is likely to result from the suppression of a borderline book in one of the States so long as there is no uniform nationwide suppression of the book, and so long as other States are free to experiment with the same or bolder books. . . .

It is no answer to say, as the Court does, that obscenity is not protected speech. The point is that this statute, as here construed, defines obscenity so widely that it encompasses matters which might very well be protected speech. I do not think that the federal statute can be constitutionally construed to reach other than what the Government has termed as "hard-core" pornography. Nor do I think the statute can fairly be read as directed only at *persons* who are engaged in the business of catering to the prurient minded, even though their wares fall short of hard-core pornography. Such a statute would raise constitutional questions of a different order. That being so, and since, in my opinion, the material here involved cannot be said to be hard-core pornography, I would reverse this case with instructions to dismiss the indictment.

MR. JUSTICE DOUGLAS, with whom MR. JUSTICE BLACK concurs, dissenting.

The test of obscenity the Court endorses today gives the censor free range over a vast domain. To allow the State to step in and punish mere speech or publication that the judge or the jury thinks has an undesirable impact on thoughts, but that is not shown to be a part of unlawful action, is drastically to curtail the First Amendment. . . .

If we were certain that impurity of sexual thoughts impelled to action, we would be on less dangerous ground in punishing the distributors of this sex literature. But it is by no means clear that obscene literature, as so defined, is a significant factor in influencing substantial deviations from the community standards. . . .

The absence of dependable information on the effect of obscene literature on human conduct should make us wary. It should put us on the side of protecting society's interest in literature, except and unless it can be said that the particular publication has an impact on action that the government can control. . . .

Freedom of expression can be suppressed if, and to the extent that, it is so closely brigaded with illegal action as to be an inseparable part of it. As a people, we cannot afford to relax that standard. For the test that suppresses a cheap tract today can suppress a literary gem tomorrow. All it need do is to incite a lascivious thought or arouse a lustful desire. The list of books that judges or juries can place in that category is endless.

I would give the broad sweep of the First Amendment full support. I have the same confidence in the ability of our people to reject noxious literature as I have in their capacity to sort out the true from the false in theology, economics, politics, or any other field.

Justice Brennan's opinion in *Roth* attempted to accomplish two goals—to define obscenity and to develop a judicial standard to analyze whether sexually explicit material met that definition. He did not succeed on either count. Phrases such as "average person," "community standards," and "prurient interests" offered no meaningful contours, since they offered such wide variation in any potential application. Moreover, Brennan's conclusion that "obscenity is not within the area of constitutionally protected speech" suggested that a bright line could be drawn distinguishing sexual speech and expression from all other speech, when in fact sex and politics, as subjects, are often difficult to separate. Certainly, in the contemporary context, many important political issues involve sexual issues or themes: the legal rights accorded to homosexuals, abortion and contraception, the legalization of prostitution, sex education in public schools, AIDS research, sexual content in movies, television, and music, and, as shall be discussed later in this chapter, public funding for controversial art with sexual themes.[59] That bright line, as Justice Brennan later confessed in subsequent obscenity cases, was simply a function of social convention and political choices, and did not spring from any clear principle flowing from the First Amendment.

While America underwent a sexual revolution in the 1960s, with sexuality and sex roles more openly discussed than ever before, the Court spent the decade searching in vain for some improvement on Brennan's formulation in *Roth*. Unable to agree on what obscenity was—Justice Potter Stewart's classic quip in *Jacobellis* v. *Ohio* (1964), "I know it when I see it," captured the Court's approach better than any formal legal definition—the Court slogged through dozens of cases involving state prosecutions and almost always reversed them. Although the Court contained obscenity at the margins (prohibiting the sale of sexually explicit magazines to minors, for example), by the late 1960s the justices had become exasperated. In *Stanley* v. *Georgia* (1969), the Court ruled that a state could not prosecute an individual for possessing obscene materials in the home. In another often quoted line from the Court's adventures into obscenity regulation, Justice Marshall wrote: "If the First Amendment means anything, it means that a State has no business telling a man, sitting alone in his own house, what books he may read or what films he may watch."[60] *Stanley* exemplified the Court's frustration with *Roth*. Although obscene materials were not entitled to the protection of the First Amendment, the justices nonetheless refused to authorize a criminal sanction for possession of sexually explicit matter even though it transgressed *Roth*'s constitutional threshold.

In sum, from 1967 to 1971, the Court reversed thirty-one obscenity convictions, while at the same time widening the protection afforded to sexual speech and expression under the First Amendment.[61] In 1968, President Lyndon Johnson had appointed the President's Commission on Obscenity and Pornography to study the impact that easier access to and public interest in sexually explicit materials was having on society. Two years later, the commission recommended the repeal of all obscenity laws prohibiting the distribution of sexually oriented material and encouraged a wide-scale public education program. But President Richard Nixon, elected in 1968 (Johnson did not run for reelection), had promised during his campaign to "crack down on pornographers" and "remove smut from the streets." Appropriately enough, Nixon ignored the Johnson commission's report and encouraged Congress and the states to enact tough anti-pornography measures. Although the states had been constrained by *Roth*'s holding that obscenity was judged according to national community standards, Nixon and many other conservative critics of the Court argued that states and localities should have the right to customize their obscenity laws to state and local standards. *Miller* v. *California* (1973) brought these legal and political disagreements over obscenity law to the Court, which decided to revisit Justice Brennan's opinion in *Roth*.

Miller v. *California*

413 U.S. 15 (1973)

Marvin Miller was a career pornographer who was looking to catch a break in the burgeoning "adult entertainment" industry in southern California in the early 1970s. Miller decided to blanket the Los Angeles metropolitan area with mail brochures advertising his products, which included books called "Intercourse," "Man-Woman," "Sex Orgies Illustrated," and "An Illustrated History of Pornography." Also available was a film entitled "Marital Intercourse." Miller's mailing arrived unsolicited in a Newport Beach restaurant, where the manager and his elderly mother opened the unmarked package to find Miller's brochure, complete with explicit sexual photos. Miller was arrested and convicted under California obscenity law.

The Court's decision was 5 to 4. Chief Justice Burger delivered the opinion of the Court. Justice Douglas dissented. Justice Brennan also dissented, and was joined by Justices Stewart and Marshall.

Mr. Chief Justice Burger delivered the opinion of the Court.

This is one of a group of "obscenity-pornography" cases being reviewed by the Court in a reexamination of standards enunciated in earlier cases involving what Mr. Justice Harlan called "the intractable obscenity problem.". . .

Apart from the initial formulation in the *Roth* case, no majority of the Court has at any given time been able to agree on a standard to determine what constitutes obscene, pornographic material subject to regulation under the States' police power. We have seen "a variety of views among the members of the Court unmatched in any other course of constitutional adjudication." This is not remarkable, for in the area of freedom of speech and press the courts must always remain sensitive to any infringement on genuinely serious literary, artistic, political, or scientific expression. This is an area in which there are few eternal verities. . . .

This much has been categorically settled by the Court, that obscene material is unprotected by the First Amendment. We acknowledge, however, the inherent dangers of undertaking to regulate any form of expression. State statutes designed to regulate obscene materials must be carefully limited. As a result, we now confine the permissible scope of such regulation to works which depict or describe sexual conduct. That conduct must be specifically defined by the applicable state law, as written or authoritatively construed. A state offense must also be limited to works which, taken as a whole, appeal to the prurient interest in sex, which portray sexual conduct in a patently offensive way, and which, taken as a whole, do not have serious literary, artistic, political, or scientific value.

The basic guidelines for the trier of fact must be:

(a) whether "the average person, applying contemporary community standards" would find that the work, taken as a whole, appeals to the prurient interest; (b) whether the work depicts or describes, in a patently offensive way, sexual conduct specifically defined by the applicable state law; and (c) whether the work, taken as a whole, lacks serious literary, artistic, political, or scientific value. We do not adopt as a constitutional standard the "utterly without redeeming social value" test; that concept has never commanded the adherence of more than three Justices at one time. If a state law that regulates obscene material is thus limited, as written or construed, the First Amendment values applicable to the States through the Fourteenth Amendment are adequately protected by the ultimate power of appellate courts to conduct an independent review of constitutional claims when necessary.

We emphasize that it is not our function to propose regulatory schemes for the States. That must await their concrete legislative efforts. It is possible, however, to give a few plain examples of what a state statute could define for regulation under part (b) of the standard announced in this opinion.

a. Patently offensive representations or descriptions of ultimate sexual acts, normal or perverted, actual or simulated.
b. Patently offensive representations or descriptions of masturbation, excretory functions, and lewd exhibition of the genitals.

Sex and nudity may not be exploited without limit by films or pictures exhibited or sold in places of public accommodation any more than live sex and nudity can be exhibited or sold without limit in such public places. At a minimum, prurient, patently offensive depiction or description of sexual conduct must have serious literary, artistic, political, or scientific value to merit First Amendment protection. . . .

Mr. Justice Brennan has abandoned his former position and now maintains that no formulation of this Court, the Congress, or the States can adequately distinguish obscene material unprotected by the First Amendment from protected expression, *Paris Adult Theatre I* v. *Slaton* (1973). Paradoxically, Mr. Justice Brennan indicates that suppression of unprotected obscene material is permissible to avoid exposure to unconsenting adults, as in this case, and to juveniles, although he gives no indication of how the division between protected and nonprotected materials may be drawn with greater precision for these purposes than for regulation of commercial exposure to consenting adults only. Nor does he indicate where in the Constitution he finds the authority to distinguish between a willing "adult" one month past the state law age of majority and a willing "juvenile" one month younger.

Under the holdings announced today, no one will be subject to prosecution for the sale or exposure of obscene materials unless these materials depict or describe patently offensive "hard core" sexual conduct specifically defined by the regulating state law, as written or construed. We are satisfied that these specific prerequisites will provide fair notice to a dealer in such materials that his public and commercial activities may bring prosecution. If the inability to define regulated materials with ultimate, god-like precision altogether removes the power of the States or the Congress to regulate, then "hard core" pornography may be exposed without limit to the juvenile, the passerby, and the consenting adult alike. . . .

It is certainly true that the absence, since *Roth,* of a single majority view of this Court as to proper standards for testing obscenity has placed a strain on both state and federal courts. But today, for the first time since *Roth* was decided in 1957, a majority of this Court has agreed on concrete guidelines to isolate "hard core" pornography from expression protected by the First Amendment. Now we may . . . attempt to provide positive guidance to federal and state courts alike.

This may not be an easy road, free from difficulty. But no amount of "fatigue" should lead us to adopt a convenient "institutional" rationale—an absolutist, "anything goes" view of the First Amendment—because it will lighten our burdens. "Such an abnegation of judicial supervision in this field would be inconsistent with our duty to uphold the constitutional guarantees." Nor should we remedy "tension between state and federal courts" by arbitrarily depriving the States of a power reserved to them under the Constitution, a power which they have enjoyed and exercised continuously from before the adoption of the First Amendment to this day. . . .

Under a National Constitution, fundamental First Amendment limitations on the powers of the States do not vary from community to community, but this does not mean that there are, or should or can be, fixed, uniform national standards of precisely what appeals to the "prurient interest" or is "patently offensive." These are essentially questions of fact, and our Nation is simply too big and too diverse for this Court to reasonably expect that such standards could be articulated for all 50 States in a single formulation, even assuming the prerequisite consensus exists. When triers of fact are asked to decide whether "the average person, applying contemporary community standards" would consider certain materials "prurient," it would be unrealistic to require that the answer be based on some abstract formulation. The adversary system, with lay jurors as the usual ultimate factfinders in criminal prosecutions, has historically permitted triers of fact to draw on the standards of their community, guided always by limiting instructions on the law. To require a State to structure obscenity proceedings around evidence of a *national* "community standard" would be an exercise in futility. . . .

It is neither realistic nor constitutionally sound to read the First Amendment as requiring that the people of Maine or Mississippi accept public depiction of conduct found tolerable in Las Vegas, or New York City. People in different States vary in their tastes and attitudes, and this diversity is not to be strangled by the absolutism of imposed uniformity. . . . [T]he primary concern with requiring a jury to apply the standard of "the average person, applying contemporary community standards" is to be certain that, so far as material is not aimed at a deviant group, it will be judged by its impact on an average person, rather than a particularly susceptible or sensitive person—or indeed a totally insensitive one. We hold that the requirement that the jury evaluate the materials with reference to "contemporary standards of the State of California" serves this protective purpose and is constitutionally adequate.

The dissenting Justices sound the alarm of repression. But, in our view, to equate the free and robust exchange of ideas and political debate with commercial exploitation of obscene material demeans the grand conception of the First Amendment and its high purposes in the historic struggle for freedom. It is a "misuse of the great guarantees of free speech and free press. . . ." The First Amendment protects works which, taken as a whole, have serious literary, artistic, political, or scientific value, regardless of whether the government or a majority of the people approve of the ideas these works represent. . . . But the public portrayal of hard-core sexual conduct for its own sake, and for the ensuing commercial gain, is a different matter. . . .

In sum, we (a) reaffirm the *Roth* holding that obscene material is not protected by the First Amendment; (b) hold that such material can be regulated by the States, subject to the specific safeguards enunciated above, without a showing that the material is "utterly without redeeming social value"; and (c) hold that obscenity is to be determined by applying "contemporary community standards." The judgment of the Appellate Department of the Superior Court, Orange County, California, is vacated and the case remanded to that court for further proceedings not inconsistent with the First Amendment standards established by this opinion.

Vacated and remanded.

MR. JUSTICE DOUGLAS, dissenting.

Today we leave open the way for California to send a man to prison for distributing brochures that advertise books and a movie under freshly written standards defining obscenity which until today's decision were never the part of any law. . . .

Today the Court retreats from the earlier formulations of the constitutional test and undertakes to make new definitions. This effort, like the earlier ones, is earnest and well intentioned. The difficulty is that we do not deal with constitutional terms, since "obscenity" is not mentioned in the Constitution or Bill of Rights. And the First Amendment makes no such exception from "the press" which it undertakes to protect nor, as I have said on other occasions, is an exception necessarily implied, for there was no recognized exception to the free press at the time the Bill of Rights was adopted which treated "obscene" publications differently from other types of papers, magazines, and books. So there are no constitutional guidelines for deciding what is and what is not "obscene." The Court is at large because we deal with tastes and standards of literature. What shocks me may be sustenance for my neighbor. What causes one person to boil up in rage over one pamphlet or movie may reflect only his neurosis, not shared by others. We deal here with a regime of censorship which, if adopted, should be done by constitutional amendment after full debate by the people.

Obscenity cases usually generate tremendous emotional outbursts. They have no business being in the courts. If a constitutional amendment authorized censorship, the censor would probably be an administrative agency. Then criminal prosecutions could follow as, if, and when publishers defied the censor and sold their literature. Under that regime, a publisher would know when he was on dangerous ground. Under the present regime—whether the old standards or the new ones are used—the criminal law becomes a trap. A brand new test would put a publisher behind bars under a new law improvised by the courts after the publication. . . .

The idea that the First Amendment permits government to ban publications that are "offensive" to some people puts an ominous gloss on freedom of the press. That test would make it possible to ban any paper or any journal or magazine in some benighted place. The First Amendment was designed "to invite dispute," to induce "a condition of unrest," to "create dissatisfaction with conditions as they are," and even to stir "people to anger." The idea that the First Amendment permits punishment for ideas that are "offensive" to the particular judge or jury sitting in judgment is astounding. No greater leveler of speech or literature has ever been designed. To give the power to the censor, as we do today, is to make a sharp and radical break with the traditions of a free society. The First Amendment was not fashioned as a vehicle for dispensing tranquilizers to the people. Its prime function was to keep debate open to "offensive" as well as to "staid" people. The tendency throughout history has been to subdue the individual and to exalt the power of government. The use of the standard "offensive" gives authority to government that cuts the very vitals out of the First Amendment. As is intimated by the Court's opinion, the materials before us may be garbage. But so is much of what is said in political campaigns, in the daily press, on TV, or over the radio. By reason of the First Amendment—and solely because of it—speakers and publishers have not been threatened or subdued because their thoughts and ideas may be "offensive" to some. . . .

We deal with highly emotional, not rational, questions. To many, the Song of Solomon is obscene. I do not think we, the judges, were ever given the constitutional power to make definitions of obscenity. If it is to be defined, let the people debate and decide by a constitutional amendment what they want to ban as obscene and what standards they want the legislatures and the courts to apply. Perhaps the people will decide that the path towards a mature, integrated society requires that all ideas competing for acceptance must have no censor. Perhaps they will decide otherwise. Whatever the choice, the courts will have some guidelines. Now we have none except our own predilections.

MR. JUSTICE BRENNAN, with whom MR. JUSTICE STEWART and MR. JUSTICE MARSHALL join, dissenting.*

This case requires the Court to confront once again the vexing problem of reconciling state efforts to suppress sexually oriented expression with the protections of the First Amendment, as applied to the States through the Fourteenth Amendment. No other aspect of the First Amendment has, in recent years, demanded so substantial a commitment of our time, generated such disharmony of views, and remained so resistant to the formulation of stable and manageable standards. I am convinced that the approach initiated 16 years ago in *Roth* v. *United States* (1957), and culminating in the Court's decision today, cannot bring stability to this area of the law without jeopardizing fundamental First Amendment values, and I have concluded that the time has come to make a significant departure from that approach. . . .

Our experience with the *Roth* approach has certainly taught us that the outright suppression of obscenity cannot be reconciled with the fundamental principles of the First and Fourteenth Amendments. For we have failed to formulate a standard that sharply distinguishes protected from unprotected speech, and out of necessity, we have resorted to the *Redrup* approach, which resolves cases as between the parties, but offers only the most obscure guidance to legislation, adjudication by other courts, and primary conduct. By disposing of cases through summary reversal or denial of *certiorari,* we have deliberately and effectively obscured the rationale underlying the decisions. It comes as no surprise that judicial attempts to follow our lead conscientiously have often ended in hopeless confusion.

Of course, the vagueness problem would be largely of our own creation if it stemmed primarily from our failure to reach a consensus on any one standard. But, after 16 years of experimentation and debate, I am reluctantly forced to the conclusion that none of the available formulas, including the one announced today, can reduce the vagueness to a tolerable level while at the same time striking an acceptable balance between the protections of the First and Fourteenth Amendments, on the one hand, and, on the other, the asserted state interest in regulating the dissemination of certain sexually oriented materials. Any effort to draw a constitutionally acceptable boundary on state power must resort to such indefinite concepts as "prurient interest," "patent offensiveness," "serious literary value," and the like. The meaning of these concepts necessarily varies with the experience, outlook, and even idiosyncrasies of the person defining them. Although we have assumed that obscenity does exist and that we "know it when [we] see it," we are manifestly unable to describe it in advance except by reference to concepts so elusive that they fail to distinguish clearly between protected and unprotected speech. . . .

The vagueness of the standards in the obscenity area produces a number of separate problems, and any improvement must rest on an understanding that the problems are to some extent distinct. First, a vague statute fails to provide adequate notice to persons who are engaged in the type of conduct that the statute could be thought to proscribe. The Due Process Clause of the Fourteenth Amendment requires that all criminal laws pro-

*Justice Brennan's dissent is excerpted from *Paris Adult Cinema I* v. *Slaton* (1973), decided the same day as *Miller.*

vide fair notice of "what the State commands or forbids." In the service of this general principle, we have repeatedly held that the definition of obscenity must provide adequate notice of exactly what is prohibited from dissemination. While various tests have been upheld under the Due Process Clause, I have grave doubts that any of those tests could be sustained today. For I know of no satisfactory answer to the assertion by Mr. Justice Black, "after the fourteen separate opinions handed down" in the trilogy of cases decided in 1966, that "no person, not even the most learned judge, much less a layman, is capable of knowing in advance of an ultimate decision in his particular case by this Court whether certain material comes within the area of "obscenity." . . .

Our experience since *Roth* requires us not only to abandon the effort to pick out obscene materials on a case-by-case basis, but also to reconsider a fundamental postulate of *Roth:* that there exists a definable class of sexually oriented expression that may be totally suppressed by the Federal and State Governments. Assuming that such a class of expression does, in fact, exist, I am forced to conclude that the concept of "obscenity" cannot be defined with sufficient specificity and clarity to provide fair notice to persons who create and distribute sexually oriented materials, to prevent substantial erosion of protected speech as a byproduct of the attempt to suppress unprotected speech, and to avoid very costly institutional harms. Given these inevitable side effects of state efforts to suppress what is assumed to be *unprotected* speech, we must scrutinize with care the state interest that is asserted to justify the suppression. For, in the absence of some very substantial interest in suppressing such speech, we can hardly condone the ill effects that seem to flow inevitably from the effort. . . .

[W]e have assumed—incorrectly, as experience has proved—that obscenity could be separated from other sexually oriented expression without significant costs either to the First Amendment or to the judicial machinery charged with the task of safeguarding First Amendment freedoms. [But] we have no occasion in *Roth* to probe the asserted state interest in curtailing unprotected, sexually oriented speech. Yet, as we have increasingly come to appreciate the vagueness of the concept of obscenity, we have begun to recognize and articulate the state interests at stake. . . .

[I]n *Stanley,* we rejected as "wholly inconsistent with the philosophy of the First Amendment," the notion that there is a legitimate state concern in the "control [of] the moral content of a person's thoughts," and we held that a State "cannot constitutionally premise legislation on the desirability of controlling a person's private thoughts." That is not to say, of course, that a State must remain utterly indifferent to—and take no action bearing on—the morality of the community. The traditional description of state police power does embrace the regulation of morals as well as the health, safety, and general welfare of the citizenry. And much legislation—compulsory public education laws, civil rights laws, even the abolition of capital punishment—is grounded, at least in part, on a concern with the morality of the community. But the State's interest in regulating morality by suppressing obscenity, while often asserted, remains essentially unfocused and ill-defined. And, since the attempt to curtail unprotected speech necessarily spills over into the area of protected speech, the effort to serve this speculative interest through the suppression of obscene material must tread heavily on rights protected by the First Amendment. . . .

If, as the Court today assumes, "a state legislature may . . . act on the . . . assumption that commerce in obscene books, or public exhibitions focused on obscene conduct, have a tendency to exert a corrupting and debasing impact leading to antisocial behavior," then it is hard to see how state-ordered regimentation of our minds can ever be forestalled. For if a State, in an effort to maintain or create a particular moral tone, may prescribe what its citizens cannot read or cannot see, then it would seem to follow that in pursuit of that same objective a State could decree that its citizens must read certain books or must view certain films. However laudable its goal—and that is obviously a question on which reasonable minds may differ—the State cannot proceed by means that violate the Constitution. . . .

In short, while I cannot say that the interests of the State—apart from the question of juveniles and unconsenting adults—are trivial or nonexistent, I am compelled to conclude that these interests cannot justify the substantial damage to constitutional rights and to this Nation's judicial machinery that inevitably results from state efforts to bar the distribution even of unprotected material to consenting adults. I would hold, therefore, that, at least in the absence of distribution to juveniles or obtrusive exposure to unconsenting adults, the First and Fourteenth Amendments prohibit the State and Federal Governments from attempting wholly to suppress sexually oriented materials on the basis of their allegedly "obscene" contents. Nothing in this approach precludes those governments from taking action to serve what may be strong and legitimate interests through regulation of the manner of distribution of sexually oriented material.

Miller highlighted the fractured thinking among the justices over how to deal with obscenity. Justices Brennan, Douglas, Marshall, and Stewart were clearly uncomfortable with the Court acting as a national standards board for sexually expressive speech, and believed that the appropriate solution was simply to let consenting adults decide for themselves what they wanted to read or watch. On the other hand, Chief Justice Burger believed that states and localities ought to have more discretion in applying their own community standards to questions of whether sexually explicit materials challenged as offensive were "patently offensive." Marvin Miller's lawyer, Burton Marks, had told the justices during oral argument that "probably no member of [the] Court [had] engaged in either the prosecution or the defense of an obscenity case where you are required to deal with the various rules of law and procedure which have been set forth by the Court concerning the handling of such a case. And therefore it's somewhat equivalent, as my wife used to say, 'You can understand that I have a lot of pain when I have a child, but you'll never experience it.' There is a lot of pain in the trial and trying to work out the rules which have been established by this Court." Marks then told the justices that they should overrule *Roth,* since any effort to define obscenity at any level, national, state, or local, was doomed to failure.

In contrast, the Orange County prosecutors defending the California obscenity law argued that communities had the right to decide for themselves when publishers had "crossed the line" from the indecent to the obscene. During oral argument, Chief Justice Burger, who wrote the Court's majority opinion, acknowledged the difficulty of defining obscenity, much less applying "contemporary community standards" to determine when sexually explicit material met that standard:

> *Burger:* Well, there's quite a difference between saying that we aren't bound by the standards of 1791 than saying that the standard is outdated if it's based on some sort of survey made in 1965. I get it that you're suggesting that this has to be kept up to date on a month-by-month basis, to see what people are thinking just lately.
>
> *Prosecutor:* I think that is true, Mr. Chief Justice, that because of—
>
> *Burger:* Then you've set out an impossible task for yourself, haven't you?

Although the Court did tighten the legal standards on obscenity by giving state and local authorities more power to ban sexually explicit materials lacking in "serious" literary, artistic, political, or scientific value, *Miller* did nothing to discourage what legal scholar Nadine Strossen calls the "business of sex."[62] On the same day it decided *Miller,* the Court, in *Paris Adult Theatre I* v. *Slaton,* upheld a conviction under a Georgia law brought against a movie theatre proprietor for showing an obscene film.[63] Still, live sexual entertainment, such as telephone sex services, strip clubs, and other erotic venues, flourished during the 1970s and continued to do so into the 1980s. On occasion, the Court upheld state and local laws against First Amendment challenges that involved "zoning out" adult bookstores, prohibitions on unsolicited mailings of sexual material, or nude dancing establishments.[64] But these decisions did not reach the core issue that concerned many cultural conservatives and, interestingly, several high-profile feminists traditionally aligned with liberal organizations on most civil rights and liberties issues—the proliferation of increasingly hard-core sexually explicit materials.

Cultural conservatives argued for a sterner application of *Miller*. They supported that position based on an *originalist* approach to the First Amendment, claiming that the Framers never intended to protect graphic sexual expression. In the early 1980s, law professors Andrea Dworkin and Catherine MacKinnon took an altogether different route. They successfully lobbied the city of Indianapolis to treat the sale, distribution, and possession of sexually explicit materials considered "degrading to women" as forms of sex discrimination prohibited by civil rights law.[65] A federal appeals court, however, struck down the law as unconstitutional, concluding that the remedy for the perceived social harm wrought by pornography was public education through countervailing speech.[66]

In 1985, responding to continuing pressure from cultural conservatives and anti-pornography feminists, United States Attorney General Edwin Meese formed a national commission to investigate the scope of the nation's ever-growing "adult entertainment" industry, and the social harm that such entertainment caused women and other victims. When the Meese Commission released its final report in 1986, many critics pointed out that it failed to offer a workable definition of obscenity. By defining obscenity as "material [that] is predominantly sexually explicit and intended primarily for purpose of sexual arousal," the Meese Commission had virtually guaranteed that any state law employing such a vague definition would be found unconstitutional.[67]

The Meese Commission was successful in encouraging states to adopt more stringent laws banning the sale, distribution, and possession of child pornography. Earlier, the Court, in *New York* v. *Ferber* (1982), had ruled that no constitutional right existed under the First Amendment to sell sexually explicit materials involving minors. In 1990, the Court confronted another problematic issue involving child pornography. Almost no one defended the manufacture, sale, and distribution of sexually explicit materials involving minors. But laws concerning possession raised a different question, as those laws involved government power to reach into the home, triggering privacy concerns among civil liberties groups. Conservative groups, on the other hand, argued that no First Amendment values were implicated by criminalizing the possession of child pornography. Recalling Justice Holmes's *Schenck* opinion, child pornography was precisely the "societal evil" that state legislatures had the right to prevent. Such was the issue in *Osborne* v. *Ohio* (1990).

Osborne v. *Ohio*

495 U.S. 103 (1990)

Clyde Osborne was convicted of violating an Ohio law that made it illegal to "possess or view any material or performance that shows a minor who is not the person's child or [ward] in a state of nudity." After obtaining a search warrant, Columbus police found four photographs of "adolescent-age" boys in sexually explicit positions. Osborne was convicted and sentenced to six months in prison.

Lawyers affiliated with a local ACLU chapter represented Osborne. They contended that the Ohio law was overly broad and thus unconstitutional. They also argued that the general nature of the language threatened to sweep under the law's prohibition many images and photographs of children that were not pornographic, such as photographs of children bathing, swimming, or playing without their clothes. No groups filed *amicus* briefs on behalf of Osborne, an unusual circumstance in a First Amendment free speech case when important principles were allegedly at stake. In contrast, a dozen state attorneys general filed briefs urging the Court to uphold Osborne's conviction, as they had similar laws that would be ripe for attack if the Ohio law was found unconstitutional.

The Court's decision was 6 to 3. Justice White delivered the opinion of the Court. Justice Brennan, joined by Justices Marshall and Stevens, dissented. Recall that White had been part of a unanimous Court in *Stanley* v. *Georgia* (1969), upholding the right to possess obscene materials involving adults in the privacy of one's home.

▼▲▼

JUSTICE WHITE delivered the opinion of the Court.

The threshold question in this case is whether Ohio may constitutionally proscribe the possession and viewing of child pornography or whether, as Osborne argues, our decision in *Stanley* v. *Georgia* (1969) compels the contrary result. In *Stanley,* we struck down a Georgia law outlawing the private possession of obscene material. We recognized that the statute impinged upon Stanley's right to receive information in the privacy of his home, and we found Georgia's justifications for its law inadequate.

Stanley should not be read too broadly. We have previously noted that *Stanley* was a narrow holding, and, since the decision in that case, the value of permitting child pornography has been characterized as "exceedingly modest, if not *de minimis*." But assuming, for the sake of argument, that Osborne has a First Amendment interest in viewing and possessing child pornography, we nonetheless find this case distinct from *Stanley* because the interests underlying child pornography prohibitions far exceed the interests justifying the Georgia law at issue in *Stanley*. . . .

The difference here is obvious: the State does not rely on a paternalistic interest in regulating Osborne's mind. Rather, Ohio has enacted [the law] in order to protect the victims of child pornography; it hopes to destroy a market for the exploitative use of children. . . .

It is also surely reasonable for the State to conclude that it will decrease the production of child pornography if it penalizes those who possess and view the product, thereby decreasing demand. In *New York* v. *Ferber* (1982), where we upheld a New York statute outlawing the distribution of child pornography, we found a similar argument persuasive: "[t]he advertising and selling of child pornography provide an economic motive for, and are thus an integral part of, the production of such materials, an activity illegal throughout the Nation. . . . It rarely has been suggested that the constitutional freedom for speech and press extends its immunity to speech or writing used as an integral part of conduct in violation of a valid criminal statute."

Osborne contends that the State should use other measures, besides penalizing possession, to dry up the child pornography market. Osborne points out that, in *Stanley,* we rejected Georgia's argument that its prohibition on obscenity possession was a necessary incident to its proscription on obscenity distribution. This holding, however, must be viewed in light of the weak interests asserted by the State in that case. *Stanley* itself emphasized that we did not "mean to express any opinion on statutes making criminal possession of other types of printed, filmed, or recorded materials. . . . In such cases, compelling reasons may exist for overriding the right of the individual to possess those materials."

Given the importance of the State's interest in protecting the victims of child pornography, we cannot fault Ohio for attempting to stamp out this vice at all levels in the distribution chain. According to the State, since the time of our decision in *Ferber,* much of the child pornography market has been driven underground; as a result, it is now difficult, if not impossible, to solve the child pornography problem by only attacking production and distribution. Indeed, 19 States have found it necessary to proscribe the possession of this material. . . .

Given the gravity of the State's interests in this context, we find that Ohio may constitutionally proscribe the possession and viewing of child pornography. . . .

The Ohio statute, on its face, purports to prohibit the possession of "nude" photographs of minors. We have stated that depictions of nudity, without more, constitute protected expression. Relying on this observation, Osborne argues that the statute, as written, is substantially overbroad. We are sceptical of this claim because, in light of the statute's exemptions and "proper purposes" provisions, the statute may not be substantially overbroad under our cases. However that may be, Osborne's overbreadth challenge, in any event, fails because the statute, as construed by the Ohio Supreme Court on Osborne's direct appeal, plainly survives overbreadth scrutiny. Under the Ohio Supreme Court reading, the statute prohibits "the possession or viewing of material or performance of a minor who is in a state of nudity, where such nudity constitutes a lewd exhibition or involves a graphic focus on the genitals, and where the person depicted is neither the child nor the ward of the person charged." By limiting the statute's operation in this manner, the Ohio Supreme Court avoided penalizing persons for viewing or possessing innocuous photographs of naked children.

Justice Brennan, with whom Justice Marshall and Justice Stevens join, dissenting.

In my view, the state law, even as construed authoritatively by the Ohio Supreme Court, is still fatally overbroad, and our decision in *Stanley* v. *Georgia* (1969) prevents the State from criminalizing appellant's possession of the photographs at issue in this case. I therefore respectfully dissent.

Indeed, the broad definition of nudity in the Ohio statutory scheme means that "child pornography" could include any photograph depicting a "lewd exhibition" of even a small portion of a minor's buttocks or any part of the female breast below the nipple. Pictures of topless bathers at a Mediterranean beach, of teenagers in revealing dresses, and even of toddlers romping unclothed, all might be prohibited. Furthermore, the Ohio law forbids not only depictions of nudity *per se,* but also depictions of the buttocks, breast, or pubic area with less than a "full, opaque covering." Thus, pictures of fashion models wearing semitransparent clothing might be illegal, as might a photograph depicting a fully clad male that nevertheless captured his genitals "in a discernibly turgid state." The Ohio statute thus sweeps in many types of materials that are not "child pornography" as we used that term in *Ferber,* but rather that enjoy full First Amendment protection.

It might be objected that many of these depictions of nudity do not amount to "lewd exhibitions." But in the absence of *any* authoritative definition of that phrase by the Ohio Supreme Court, we cannot predict which ones. Many would characterize a photograph of a seductive fashion model or alluringly posed adolescent on a topless European beach as "lewd," although such pictures indisputably enjoy constitutional protection. Indeed, some might think that *any* nudity, especially that involving a minor, is by definition "lewd," yet this Court has clearly established that nudity is not excluded automatically from the scope of the First Amendment. The Court today is unable even to hazard a guess as to what a "lewd exhibition" might mean; it is forced to rely entirely on an inapposite case—*Ferber*—that simply did not discuss, let alone decide, the central issue here. . . .

The Ohio Supreme Court also added a "graphic focus" element to the nudity definition. This phrase, a stranger to obscenity regulation, suffers from the same vagueness difficulty as "lewd exhibition." Although the Ohio Supreme Court failed to elaborate what a "graphic focus" might be, the test appears to involve nothing more than a subjective estimation of the centrality or prominence of the genitals in a picture or other representation. Not only is this factor dependent on the perspective and idiosyncrasies of the observer, it also is unconnected to whether the material at issue merits constitutional protection. Simple nudity, no matter how prominent or "graphic," is within the bounds of the First Amendment. Michelangelo's "David" might be said to have a "graphic focus" on the genitals, for it plainly portrays them in a manner unavoidable to even a casual observer. Similarly, a painting of a partially clad girl could be said to involve a "graphic focus," depending on the picture's lighting and emphasis, as could the depictions of nude children on the friezes that adorn our Courtroom. Even a photograph of a child running naked on the beach or playing in the bathtub might run afoul of the law, depending on the focus and camera angle.

In sum, the "lewd exhibition" and "graphic focus" tests are too vague to serve as any workable limit. Because the statute, even as construed authoritatively by the Ohio Supreme Court, is impermissibly overbroad, I would hold that appellant cannot be retried under it.

At bottom, the Court today is so disquieted by the possible exploitation of children in the *production* of the pornography that it is willing to tolerate the imposition of criminal penalties for simple *possession*. While I share the majority's concerns, I do not believe that it has struck the proper balance between the First Amendment and the State's interests, especially in light of the other means available to Ohio to protect children from exploitation and the State's failure to demonstrate a causal link between a ban on possession of child pornography and a decrease in its production. "The existence of the State's power to prevent the distribution of obscene matter"—and of child pornography—"does not mean that there can be no constitutional barrier to any form of practical exercise of that power." . . .

When speech is eloquent and the ideas expressed lofty, it is easy to find restrictions on them invalid. But were the First Amendment limited to such discourse, our freedom would be sterile indeed. Mr. Osborne's pictures may be distasteful, but the Constitution guarantees both his right to possess them privately and his right to avoid punishment under an overbroad law. I respectfully dissent.

The Meese Commission's report had concluded that "child pornography is often used as part of a method of seducing child victims. A child who is reluctant to engage in sexual activity with an adult or to pose for sexually explicit photos can sometimes be convinced by viewing other children having 'fun' participating in the activity."[68] The Court's opinion, which emphasized the alleged link between child abuse and the sale and possession of sexually explicit materials involving children, was consistent with the position of various *amici* and the Meese Commission. Indeed, Justice White even cited the Meese Commission's report as an authority on the subject. Although the *Osborne* dissenters may well have had a point in noting the potential reach of the law's sweeping language, it was clear that a majority of the Court focused instead on the social evil of child pornography.

Beyond child pornography, regulating sexually explicit materials involving adults has remained a much more elusive task. Although the Court has upheld some restrictions on where and how "adult entertainment" establishments can conduct their businesses, *Miller* has not curbed the wide range of hard-core sexually oriented material available to the public. For example, while *Paris Adult Theatre I* had held that states could ban public movie theatres from showing "obscene" films, in the 1980s and 1990s producers of sexually explicit films turned their attention away from theatres to the booming home video rental market. But the VCR was not the only technological innovation that changed the way that sexually explicit materials reached the private consumer. Rapidly unfolding changes in computer technology during the 1990s made communication and information sharing more immediate and intimate than ever before, requiring legislatures and courts to decide novel questions of law and policy with no clear precedent in existing media.

In *United States* v. *Playboy Entertainment Group* (2000), for example, the Court invalidated a provision of the federal Telecommunications Act of 1996 that limited the broadcasting of sexually explicit adult programming to pay-cable channels from 10 P.M. to 6 A.M. Congress had required cable operators to scramble or block out sexually oriented programming during the day to shield children from accidental access. By a 5 to 4 majority, the Court ruled that the law was not narrowly tailored and violated the First Amendment rights of adults who wanted to view sexually oriented pay programming during other times.[69] Clearly, technological innovation has made regulation even more constitutionally problematic than it was during the days before cable television and the Internet.

On the New Frontier: The Internet as a Marketplace of Ideas

In 1957, in response to the Soviet Union's successful launch of the Sputnik satellite, the Pentagon created the Advanced Research Projects Agency (ARPA) to develop science and high-technology applications to serve the military. Foremost on ARPA's agenda was the development of a computer network capable of switching systems in the event that parts of the system were damaged. In 1969, ARPA created a computer network called ARPNET, which permitted computer systems around the world to "talk" to each other. Five years later, ARPA unveiled the Transmission Control Protocol/Internet Protocol (TCP/IP), which, by 1983, had become the standard communication language for all ARPNET traffic. Colleges and universities, regional computer networks, businesses, and the National Science Foundation began to adapt their computing systems to the ARPNET protocol. However, by 1991 ARPNET had been abandoned in favor of the World Wide Web, a vast connection of international computing networks featuring astounding graphics capabilities. Around the same time, powerful personal computers were introduced with telecommunications capabilities, allowing anyone with a phone line to link to the Internet.

By 1995, the National Science Foundation introduced the Backbone Network Service, which connected "supercomputing centers" around the world and routed computer traffic through the World Wide Web. That same year, the Web became the most heavily trafficked network in the world, as on-line and dial-up servers began providing Web access. Because the Internet remained essentially a government-subsidized project, for-profit users could pay a nominal fee to register their businesses on the Web. Not-for-profit users, designated by their .edu or .org domain address, still had free access to the Web.

By the late 1990s, the Internet had completely revolutionized the way that Americans communicated with each other and the rest of the world. Businesses soon discovered they could advertise, sell, and deliver their products to customers who preferred the ease of "e-commerce" to fighting the masses at the malls. Researchers found they could place their information in the public domain for colleagues and students to access for use in their own work. Indeed, it is probably difficult for the contemporary college student to imagine undertaking a research project without access to the Web. How fast has the Internet grown since the mid-1990s? In 1993, 130 sites existed on the Web. By 1996, that figure had increased to approximately 300,000; in June 2000, *over 17 million* sites existed on the Web![70]

As the Internet grew in the late 1990s, the atmosphere on-line resembled a high-technology version of the lawless Wild West of the 1800s. Quite literally, anyone with access to the Internet could say or display anything they wanted. While such open, unfettered exchange and the ability to communicate with other people around the world in real time was certainly exciting, such easy access meant that individuals navigating the Web could encounter sexually explicit, racist, or other offensive materials just by entering a seemingly benign keyword into a search engine. Naturally, questions soon arose over whether government regulation was necessary to police the Internet. Because political speech enjoys nearly absolute protection under the First Amendment, efforts by some civil rights organizations, such as the Anti-Defamation League of B'nai B'rith and the Southern Poverty Law Center, to monitor "hate speech" on the Web focused on getting Internet service providers to provide warnings to users who "hit" on such sites. Sexually explicit materials were also much easier to access on the Web than through conventional commercial outlets. To forestall government regulation, many Internet providers of sexually explicit images agreed to warn users of their site's content. But concern that such self-policing would not work prompted Congress to enact the Communications Decency Act (CDA) of 1996.

In *Sable Communications* v. *Federal Communications Commission* (1989), the Court ruled that a 1988 amendment to the Communications Act of 1934 permitting the FCC to ban "indecent" telephone conversations and messages was unconstitutional, but a provision of the same law punishing "obscene" telephone speech was not.[71] The target of the 1988 law was the nation's growing "dial-a-porn" industry, which enticed customers with sexual conversation for a fee billed directly to their credit cards. But unlike the law at issue in *Sable Communications,* which dealt with an area long within FCC jurisdiction, the CDA represented a journey into unknown territory. Was the Internet a broadcast medium and thus within federal regulatory power? Or was the Internet more akin to print journalism and entitled to full First Amendment protection? Such was the issue in *Reno* v. *American Civil Liberties Union* (1997).

Reno v. *American Civil Liberties Union*

521 U.S. 844 (1997)

On the same day President Clinton signed the Communications Decency Act (CDA) of 1996 into law, the American Civil Liberties Union, representing over twenty plaintiffs, filed suit challenging its constitutionality in federal district court. The ACLU contended that the CDA's provisions banning "indecent" or "patently offensive" speech that could be transmitted to minors on the Internet violated the First Amendment. Three weeks later, the American Library Association filed suit against the Department of Justice asking to have the CDA declared unconstitutional. The two lawsuits were consolidated, but the lawyers from the ACLU and the ALA worked together throughout the litigation. The diversity of the organizations wanting the CDA declared unconstitutional was simply amazing, ranging from small technology groups to some of the biggest names in the on-line services field, including America Online, Apple Computer, Microsoft, Prodigy, and CompuServe. Literary and journalistic groups, such as the American Booksellers Association, American Association of Publishers, Editors and Writers, and the Society for Professional Journalists, participated in the suit, as did public advocacy groups such as Human Rights Watch, Planned Parenthood, and the ACLU's Stop Prisoner Rape project. All these groups believed that the CDA's "anti-porn" provisions were far too broad and risked placing socially valuable speech outside the protection of the First Amendment.

A lower court declared the CDA unconstitutional, and the Department of Justice appealed. Congress, fully expecting a constitutional challenge to the CDA, inserted a provision accelerating review to the Court. An indication of congressional misgivings about the law's constitutionality was evident when only eight Senators and seventeen members of the House agreed to sign a joint *amicus* brief submitted on their behalf in support of the Justice Department.

The Court's judgment was unanimous in finding the challenged provisions of the CDA unconstitutional. Justice Stevens delivered the opinion of the Court. Justice O'Connor, joined by Chief Justice Rehnquist, dissented in part.

Justice Stevens delivered the opinion of the Court.

At issue is the constitutionality of two statutory provisions enacted to protect minors from "indecent" and "patently offensive" communications on the Internet. Notwithstanding the legitimacy and importance of the congressional goal of protecting children from harmful materials, we agree with the three-judge District Court that the statute abridges "the freedom of speech" protected by the First Amendment. . . .

In *Federal Communications Commission* v. *Pacifica Foundation* (1978), we upheld a declaratory order of the Federal Communications Commission, holding that the broadcast of a recording of a 12-minute monologue entitled "Filthy Words" that had previously been delivered to a live audience "could have been the subject of administrative sanctions." The Commission had found that the repetitive use of certain words referring to excretory or sexual activities or organs "in an afternoon broadcast when children are in the audience was patently offensive," and concluded that the monologue was indecent "as broadcast." The respondent did not quarrel with the finding that the afternoon broadcast was patently offensive, but contended that it was not "indecent" within the meaning of the relevant statutes because it contained no prurient appeal. After rejecting respondent's statutory arguments, we confronted its two constitutional arguments: (1) that the Commission's construction of its authority to ban indecent speech was so broad that its order had to be set aside even if the broadcast at issue was unprotected; and (2) that, since the recording was not obscene, the First Amendment forbade any abridgement of the right to broadcast it on the radio.

In the portion of the lead opinion not joined by Justices Powell and Blackmun, the plurality stated that the First Amendment does not prohibit all governmental regulation that depends on the content of speech. Accordingly, the availability of constitutional protection for a vulgar and offensive monologue that was not obscene depended on the context of the broadcast. Relying on the premise that "of all forms of communication" broadcasting had received the most limited First Amendment protection, the Court concluded that the ease with which children may obtain access to broadcasts, "coupled with the concerns recognized in *Ginsberg*," justified special treatment of indecent broadcasting.

. . . [T]here are significant differences between the order upheld in *Pacifica* and the CDA. First, the order in *Pacifica*, issued by an agency that had been regulating radio stations for decades, targeted a specific broadcast that represented a rather dramatic departure from traditional program content in order to designate when—rather than whether—it would be permissible to air such a program in that particular medium. The CDA's broad categorical prohibitions are not limited to particular times and are not dependent on any evaluation by an agency familiar with the unique characteristics of the Internet. Second, unlike the CDA, the Commission's declaratory order was not punitive; we expressly refused to decide whether the indecent broadcast "would justify a criminal prosecution." Finally, the Commission's order applied to a medium which as a matter of history had "received the most limited First Amendment protection," in large part because warnings could not adequately protect the listener from unexpected program content. The Internet, however, has no comparable history. Moreover, the District Court found that the risk of encountering indecent material by accident is remote because a series of affirmative steps is required to access specific material.

In *Renton* v. *Playtime Theatres* (1986), we upheld a zoning ordinance that kept adult movie theatres out of residential neighborhoods. The ordinance was aimed, not at the content of the films shown in the theaters, but rather at the "secondary effects"—such as crime and deteriorating property values—that these theaters fostered: "'It is th[e] secondary effect which these zoning ordinances attempt to avoid, not the dissemination of "offensive" speech.'" According to the Government, the CDA is constitutional because it constitutes a sort of "cyberzoning" on the Internet. But the CDA applies broadly to the entire universe of cyberspace. And the purpose of the CDA is to protect children from the primary effects of "indecent" and "patently offensive" speech, rather than any "secondary" effect of such speech. Thus, the CDA is a content-based blanket restriction on speech, and, as such, cannot be "properly analyzed as a form of time, place, and manner regulation." These precedents, then, surely do not require us to uphold the CDA and are fully consistent with the application of the most stringent review of its provisions. . . .

[S]ome of our [previous] cases have recognized special justification for regulation of broadcast media that are not applicable to other speakers. Those factors are not present in cyberspace. Neither before nor after the enactment of the CDA have the vast democratic fora of the Internet been subject to the type of government supervision and regulation that has attended the broadcast industry. Moreover, the Internet is not as "invasive" as radio or television. [In most instances], "[a]lmost all sexually explicit images are preceded by warnings as to the content," and the "'odds are slim' that a user would come across a sexually explicit site by accident." . . .

Finally, unlike the conditions that prevailed when Congress first authorized regulation of the broadcast spectrum, the Internet can hardly be considered a "scarce" expressive commodity. It provides relatively unlimited, low-cost capacity for communication of all kinds. The Government estimates that "[a]s many as 40 million people use the Internet today, and that figure is expected to grow to 200 million by 1999." This dynamic, multifaceted category of communication includes not only traditional print and news services, but also audio, video, and still images, as well as interactive, real-time dialogue. Through the use of chat rooms, any person with a phone line can become a town crier with a voice that resonates farther than it could from any soapbox. Through the use of Web pages, mail exploders, and newsgroups, the same individual can become a pamphleteer. As the District Court found, "the content on the Internet is as diverse as human thought." We agree with its conclusion that our cases provide no basis for qualifying the level of First Amendment scrutiny that should be applied to this medium.

Regardless of whether the CDA is so vague that it violates the Fifth Amendment, the many ambiguities concerning the scope of its coverage render it problematic for purposes of the First Amendment. For instance, each of the two parts of the CDA uses a different linguistic form. The first uses the word "indecent," while the second speaks of material that, "in context, depicts or describes, in terms patently offensive as measured by contemporary community standards, sexual or excretory activities or organs." Given the absence of a definition of either term, this difference in language will provoke uncertainty among speakers about how the two standards relate to each other and just what they mean. Could a speaker confidently assume that a serious discussion about birth control practices, homosexuality, the First Amendment issues raised by the Appendix to our *Pacifica* opinion, or the consequences of prison rape would not violate the CDA? This uncertainty undermines the likelihood that the CDA has been carefully tailored to the congressional goal of protecting minors from potentially harmful materials.

The vagueness of the CDA is a matter of special concern for two reasons. First, the CDA is a content-based regulation of speech. The vagueness of such a regulation raises special First Amendment concerns because of its obvious chilling effect on free speech. Second, the CDA is a criminal statute. In addition to the opprobrium and stigma of a criminal conviction, the CDA threatens violators with penalties including up to two years in prison for each act of violation. The severity of criminal sanctions may well cause speakers to remain silent rather than communicate even arguably unlawful words, ideas, and images. . . .

We are persuaded that the CDA lacks the precision that the First Amendment requires when a statute regulates the content of speech. In order to deny minors access to potentially harmful speech, the CDA effectively suppresses a large amount of speech that adults have a constitutional right to receive and to address to one another. That burden on adult speech is unacceptable if less restrictive alternatives would be at least as effective in achieving the legitimate purpose that the statute was enacted to serve.

In evaluating the free speech rights of adults, we have made it perfectly clear that "[s]exual expression which is indecent but not obscene is protected by the First Amendment." Indeed, *Pacifica* itself admonished that "the fact that society may find speech offensive is not a sufficient reason for suppressing it." . . .

In arguing that the CDA does not so diminish adult communication, the Government relies on the incorrect factual premise that prohibiting a transmission whenever it is known that one of its recipients is a minor would not interfere with adult-to-adult communication. The findings of the District Court make clear that this premise is untenable. Given the size of the potential audience for most messages, in the absence of a viable age verification process, the sender must be charged with knowing that one or more minors will likely view it. Knowledge that, for instance, one or more members of a 100-person chat group will be minor—and therefore that it would be a crime to send the group an indecent message—would surely burden communication among adults.

The District Court found that at the time of trial existing technology did not include any effective method for a sender to prevent minors from obtaining access to its communications on the Internet without also denying access to adults. The Court found no effective way to determine the age of a user who is accessing material through e-mail, mail exploders, newsgroups, or chat rooms. As a practical matter, the Court also found that it would be prohibitively expensive for noncommercial—as well as some commercial—speakers who have Web sites to verify that their users are adults. These limitations must inevitably curtail a significant amount of adult communication on the Internet. . . .

The breadth of the CDA's coverage is wholly unprecedented. Unlike the regulatio[n] upheld in . . . *Pacifica,* the scope of the CDA is not limited to commercial speech or commercial entities. Its open-ended prohibitions embrace all nonprofit entities and individuals posting indecent messages or displaying them on their own computers in the presence of minors. The general, undefined terms "indecent" and "patently offensive" cover large amounts of nonpornographic material with serious educational or other value. Moreover, the "community standards" criterion as applied to the Internet means that any communication available to a nationwide audience will be judged by the standards of the community most likely to be offended by the message. The regulated subject matter includes any of the seven "dirty words" used in the *Pacifica* monologue, the use of which the Government's expert acknowledged could constitute a felony. It may also extend to discussions about prison rape or safe sexual practices, artistic images that include nude subjects, and arguably the card catalogue of the Carnegie Library.

For the purposes of our decision, we need neither accept nor reject the Government's submission that the First Amendment does not forbid a blanket prohibition on all "indecent" and "patently offensive" messages communicated to a 17-year-old—no matter how much value the message may contain and regardless of potential approval. It is at least clear that the strength of the Government's interest in protecting minors is not equally strong throughout the coverage of this broad statute. Under the CDA, a parent allowing her 17-year-old to use the family computer to obtain information on the Internet that she, in her parental judgment, deems appropriate could face a lengthy prison term. Similarly, a parent who sent his 17-year-old college freshman information on birth control via e-mail could be incarcerated even though neither he, his child, nor anyone in their home community, found the material "indecent" or "patently offensive," if the college town's community thought otherwise.

The breadth of this content-based restriction of speech imposes an especially heavy burden on the Government to explain why a less restrictive provision would not be as effective as the CDA. It has not done so. The arguments in this Court have referred to possible alternatives such as requiring that indecent material be "tagged" in a way that facilitates parental control of material coming into their homes, making exceptions for messages with artistic or educational value, providing some tolerance for parental choice, and regulating some portions of the Internet—

such as commercial Web sites—differently than others, such as chat rooms. Particularly in the light of the absence of any detailed findings by the Congress, or even hearings addressing the special problems of the CDA, we are persuaded that the CDA is not narrowly tailored if that requirement has any meaning at all. . . .

The record demonstrates that the growth of the Internet has been and continues to be phenomenal. As a matter of constitutional tradition, in the absence of evidence to the contrary, we presume that governmental regulation of the content of speech is more likely to interfere with the free exchange of ideas than to encourage it. The interest in encouraging freedom of expression in a democratic society outweighs any theoretical but unproven benefit of censorship.

For the foregoing reasons, the judgment of the district court is affirmed.

It is so ordered.

JUSTICE O'CONNOR, with whom THE CHIEF JUSTICE joins, concurring in the judgment in part and dissenting in part.

I write separately to explain why I view the Communications Decency Act of 1996 (CDA) as little more than an attempt by Congress to create "adult zones" on the Internet. Our precedent indicates that the creation of such zones can be constitutionally sound. Despite the soundness of its purpose, however, portions of the CDA are unconstitutional because they stray from the blueprint our prior cases have developed for constructing a "zoning law" that passes constitutional muster. . . .

The creation of "adult zones" is by no means a novel concept. States have long denied minors access to certain establishments frequented by adults. States have also denied minors access to speech deemed to be "harmful to minors." The Court has previously sustained such zoning laws, but only if they respect the First Amendment rights of adults and minors. That is to say, a zoning law is valid if (i) it does not unduly restrict adult access to the material; and (ii) minors have no First Amendment right to read or view the banned material. As applied to the Internet as it exists in 1997, the "display" provision and some applications of the "indecency transmission" and "specific person" provisions fail to adhere to the first of these limiting principles by restricting adults' access to protected materials in certain circumstances. Unlike the Court, however, I would invalidate the provisions only in those circumstances . . .

Cyberspace differs from the physical world in another basic way: Cyberspace is malleable. Thus, it is possible to construct barriers in cyberspace and use them to screen for identity, making cyberspace more like the physical world and, consequently, more amenable to zoning laws. This transformation of cyberspace is already underway. Internet speakers (users who post material on the Internet) have begun to zone cyberspace itself through the use of "gateway" technology. Such technology requires Internet users to enter information about themselves—perhaps an adult identification number or a credit card number—before they can access certain areas of cyberspace, much like a bouncer checks a person's driver's license before admitting him to a nightclub. Internet users who access information have not attempted to zone cyberspace itself, but have tried to limit their own power to access information in cyberspace, much as a parent controls what her children watch on television by installing a lock box. This user-based zoning is accomplished through the use of screening software (such as Cyber Patrol or SurfWatch) or browsers with screening capabilities, both of which search addresses and text for keywords that are associated with "adult" sites and, if the user wishes, blocks access to such sites. The Platform for Internet Content Selection (PICS) project is designed to facilitate user-based zoning by encouraging Internet speakers to rate the content of their speech using codes recognized by all screening programs.

Although the prospects for the eventual zoning of the Internet appear promising, I agree with the Court that we must evaluate the constitutionality of the CDA as it applies to the Internet as it exists today. Given the present state of cyberspace, I agree with the Court that the "display" provision cannot pass muster. Until gateway technology is available throughout cyberspace, and it is not in 1997, a speaker cannot be reasonably assured that the speech he displays will reach only adults because it is impossible to confine speech to an "adult zone." Thus, the only way for a speaker to avoid liability under the CDA is to refrain completely from using indecent speech. But this forced silence impinges on the First Amendment right of adults to make and obtain this speech and, for all intents and purposes, "reduce[s] the adult population [on the Internet] to reading only what is fit for children." As a result, the "display" provision cannot withstand scrutiny.

The "indecency transmission" and "specific person" provisions present a closer issue, for they are not unconstitutional in all of their applications. As discussed above, the "indecency transmission" provision makes it a crime to transmit knowingly an indecent message to a person the sender knows is under 18 years of age. The "specific person" provision proscribes the same conduct, although it does not as explicitly require the sender to know that the intended recipient of his indecent message is a minor. Appellant urges the Court to construe the provision to impose such a knowledge requirement.

So construed, both provisions are constitutional as applied to a conversation involving only an adult and one or more minors—*e.g.*, when an adult speaker sends an e-mail knowing the addressee is a minor, or when an adult and minor converse by themselves or with other minors in a chat room. In this context, these provisions are no different from the law we sustained in *Ginsberg*. Restricting what the adult may say to the minors in no way restricts the adult's ability to communicate with other adults. He is not prevented from speaking indecently to other adults in a chat room (because there are no other adults participating in the conversation) and he remains free to send indecent e-mails to other adults. The relevant universe contains only one adult, and the adult in that universe has the power to refrain from using indecent speech and consequently to keep all such speech within the room in an "adult" zone. . . .

[T]he constitutionality of the CDA as a zoning law hinges on the extent to which it substantially interferes with the First Amendment rights of adults. Because the rights of adults are infringed only by the "display" provision and by the "indecency transmission" and "specific person" provisions as applied to communications involving more than one adult, I would invalidate the CDA only to that extent. Insofar as the "indecency transmission" and "specific person" provisions prohibit the use of indecent speech in communications between an adult and one or more minors, however, they can and should be sustained. The Court reaches a contrary conclusion, and from that holding I respectfully dissent.

ACLU lawyers argued in their brief that the Internet was analogous to print, and thus entitled to the same protection afforded to speech under the *Miller* test. In *Reno,* the justices clearly agreed with the numerous civil liberties, cultural, and news organizations filing *amicus* briefs in the case that the Internet should be left alone to encourage the free exchange of ideas. No doubt, future issues involving government regulation and the Internet will come up, but for now *Reno* has answered the fundamental question over the constitutional status of cyberspace.

Does the Piper Call the Tune? Public Funds and Artistic Freedom

In 1965, Congress established the National Endowment for the Arts (NEA) to promote support for the arts by providing federal funding to individuals and groups across a wide range of artistic endeavors. The NEA was not the federal government's first project to provide support to artists. During the 1930s, President Franklin D. Roosevelt created the Works Progress Administration (WPA), which may well have touched more individual lives than any other New Deal agency. The WPA was a work-relief program that guaranteed a sustenance income to any man willing to build highways, clean parks, paint abandoned buildings, or engage in any public works improvement program. Later, an effort was made to include women by providing work in sewing and household services, nursery schools, general recreation, elderly care, and, later, light manual labor. Although women earned far less than men and were deemed fit only for "women's work," for a federal jobs program to include women was, in those days, a controversial proposition. Even more controversial was the WPA's decision to fund artistic programs, since artists were largely considered society's rebels. Federal relief coordinator Harry Hopkins responded to criticism of federal support for artists by saying, "Hell! They've got to eat just like other people." By 1935, the WPA's funding for the arts included the Federal Music Project, the Federal Theater Project, and the Federal Writers' Project, programs continued by the NEA and the National Endowment for the Humanities (NEH) after the WPA disbanded.[72]

Almost all of the WPA's arts funding went to politically safe endeavors, such as youth symphonies, public murals, local theatre productions, and literacy programs. On occasion, though, artists attempted to fuse their work with social and political commentary on the most important issues of the day, such as labor organizing, the widespread poverty created by the Great Depression, and the quiet havoc that sexually transmitted diseases were wreaking on the poor. Also touchy for many Southern segregationists in Congress was the WPA's decision to fund African American art and theatre productions, including renditions of the classics, Shakespeare, and other European literary giants. By the late 1930s, the WPA's arts projects had not transformed the cultural landscape of America, but the organization did bring art, music, theatre, and literature to more people than ever before.

Between 1965 and 2000, the NEA has awarded approximately $3.3 billion in grants, almost all of the monies directed to artists well within the cultural mainstream. In 1989, however, the NEA emerged from relative obscurity when two artistically provocative projects it had funded attracted national attention. The Institute of Contemporary Art, housed at the University of Pennsylvania, used $30,000 of a visual arts grant to fund a retrospective by photographer Robert Mapplethorpe titled "The Perfect Moment," which carried a homoerotic theme. Many members of Congress considered Mapplethorpe's work pornographic and demanded to know how such a project could receive federal support. Around the same time, Andres Serrano's exhibit, "Piss Christ," which featured a photograph of a crucifix dipped in urine, drew an equally condemnatory response from Congress. Serrano had received a $15,000 grant from an NEA-funded arts group.

Shortly after the flap over the Mapplethorpe and Serrano exhibits, Congress amended the federal law governing the NEA to prohibit the agency from funding art projects that promoted, disseminated, or produced depictions of "sadomasochism, homoeroticism and sexual exploitation of children or individuals engaged in sex acts." A federal district court declared the law unconstitutional after the ACLU brought suit against it. But in 1990, Congress adopted a new provision that required the NEA to consider "general standards of decency and respect for the diverse beliefs and values of the American public" in making awards to grantees.

Of course, as our earlier discussion makes clear, such a standard could not apply to private expression, even that which includes intense and often offensive sexual themes. But the issue in *National Endowment for the Arts v. Finley* (1998) was not government regulation of sexually laced or "sacrilegious" art underwritten by private donors displayed in a privately owned gallery. Rather, the issue was whether the NEA could now require artists to meet decency standards in order to receive federal funding.

National Endowment for the Arts v. Finley

524 U.S. 569 (1998)

On June 30, 1990, Karen Finley, John Fleck, Holly Hughes, and Tim Miller received some unsettling and unexpected news. Although their grant applications had been approved by the NEA's peer review panels, agency chairman John Frohnmayer ruled that each artist had included "obscene" subject matter in the work. Undoubtedly, Frohnmayer's decision was fueled by the highly charged partisan atmosphere that had surrounded the NEA since the Mapplethorpe and "Piss Christ" controversies the year before. Dubbed the "NEA 4" by their supporters, Finley, Fleck, Hughes, and Miller, supported by the ACLU and the Center for Individual Rights, sued the NEA, claiming the "decency" clause in the arts agency's funding policies violated the First Amendment.

Finley, a performance artist who smeared her nude body in warm chocolate to symbolize violative acts against women's bodies, quickly emerged as the most outspoken of the four. The "chocolate-smearing" performance, as her critics called it, was only one small part of a performance called "We Keep Our Victims Ready." However, for the NEA's critics, Finley's "art" was precisely the sort of material that it believed the government had no business funding.

A federal district court agreed with the performance artists and directed the NEA to devise a settlement. In 1993, the artists received a $252,000 damage award. The artists had their grants reinstated and each received a punitive damage award in the amount of $6,000. The rest went to lawyers' fees and court costs. A divided federal appeals panel affirmed.

The Court's decision was 8 to 1. Justice O'Connor delivered the opinion of the Court. Justice Scalia filed a concurring opinion. Justice Souter dissented.

JUSTICE O'CONNOR delivered the opinion of the Court.

Respondents argue that the provision is a [perfect] example of viewpoint discrimination because it rejects any artistic speech that either fails to respect mainstream values or offends standards of decency. The premise of respondents' claim is that § 954(d)(1) constrains the

agency's ability to fund certain categories of artistic expression. The NEA, however, reads the provision as merely hortatory, and contends that it stops well short of an absolute restriction. Section 954(d)(1) adds "considerations" to the grant-making process; it does not preclude awards to projects that might be deemed "indecent" or "disrespectful," nor place conditions on grants, or even specify that those factors must be given any particular weight in reviewing an application. Indeed, the agency asserts that it has adequately implemented § 954(d)(1) merely by ensuring the representation of various backgrounds and points of view on the advisory panels that analyze grant applications. We do not decide whether the NEA's view—that the formulation of diverse advisory panels is sufficient to comply with Congress' command—is in fact a reasonable reading of the statute. It is clear, however, that the text of § 954(d)(1) imposes no categorical requirement. The advisory language stands in sharp contrast to congressional efforts to prohibit the funding of certain classes of speech. When Congress has in fact intended to affirmatively constrain the NEA's grant-making authority, it has done so in no uncertain terms. . . .

That § 954(d)(1) admonishes the NEA merely to take "decency and respect" into consideration, and that the legislation was aimed at reforming procedures rather than precluding speech, undercut respondents' argument that the provision inevitably will be utilized as a tool for invidious viewpoint discrimination. In cases where we have struck down legislation as facially unconstitutional, the dangers were both more evident and more substantial. In *R.A.V. v. St. Paul* (1992), for example, we invalidated on its face a municipal ordinance that defined as a criminal offense the placement of a symbol on public or private property "'which one knows or has reasonable grounds to know arouses anger, alarm, or resentment in others on the basis of race, color, creed, religion, or gender.'" That provision set forth a clear penalty, proscribed views on particular "disfavored subjects," and suppressed "distinctive idea[s], conveyed by a distinctive message."

In contrast, the "decency and respect" criteria do not silence speakers by expressly "threaten[ing] censorship of ideas." Thus, we do not perceive a realistic danger that § 954(d)(1) will compromise First Amendment values. As respondents' own arguments demonstrate, the considerations that the provision introduces, by their nature, do not engender the kind of directed viewpoint discrimination that would prompt this Court to invalidate a statute on its face. Respondents assert, for example, that "[o]ne would be hard-pressed to find two people in the United States who could agree on what the 'diverse beliefs and values of the American public' are, much less on whether a particular work of art 'respects' them"; and they claim that "'[d]ecency' is likely to mean something very different to a septuagenarian in Tuscaloosa and a teenager in Las Vegas." The NEA likewise views the considerations enumerated in § 954(d)(1) as susceptible to multiple interpretations. Accordingly, the provision does not introduce considerations that, in practice, would effectively preclude or punish the expression of particular views. Indeed, one could hardly anticipate how "decency" or "respect" would bear on grant applications in categories such as funding for symphony orchestras. . . .

Respondent's reliance on our decision in *Rosenberger v. Rector and Visitors of Univ. of Va.* (1995) is therefore misplaced. In *Rosenberger,* a public university declined to authorize disbursements from its Student Activities Fund to finance the printing of a Christian student newspaper. We held that by subsidizing the Student Activities Fund, the University had created a limited public forum, from which it impermissibly excluded all publications with religious editorial viewpoints. Although the scarcity of NEA funding does not distinguish this case from *Rosenberger,* the competitive process according to which the grants are allocated does. In the context of arts funding, in contrast to many other subsidies, the Government does not indiscriminately "encourage a diversity of views from private speakers." The NEA's mandate is to make aesthetic judgments, and the inherently content-based "excellence" threshold for NEA support sets it apart from the subsidy at issue in Rosenberger—which was available to all student organizations that were "'related to the educational purpose of the University,'" and from comparably objective decisions on allocating public benefits, such as access to a school auditorium or a municipal theater, or the second class mailing privileges available to "'all newspapers and other periodical publications.'"

Finally, although the First Amendment certainly has application in the subsidy context, we note that the Government may allocate competitive funding according to criteria that would be impermissible were direct regulation of speech or a criminal penalty at stake. So long as legislation does not infringe on other constitutionally protected rights, Congress has wide latitude to set spending priorities. In the 1990 Amendments that incorporated § 954(d)(1), Congress modified the declaration of purpose in the NEA's enabling act to provide that arts funding should "contribute to public support and confidence in the use of taxpayer funds," and that "[p]ublic funds . . .

must ultimately serve public purposes the Congress defines." § 951(5). And as we held in *Rust,* Congress may "selectively fund a program to encourage certain activities it believes to be in the public interest, without at the same time funding an alternative program which seeks to deal with the problem in another way." In doing so, "the Government has not discriminated on the basis of viewpoint; it has merely chosen to fund one activity to the exclusion of the other." . . .

In the context of selective subsidies, it is not always feasible for Congress to legislate with clarity. Indeed, if this statute is unconstitutionally vague, then so too are all government programs awarding scholarships and grants on the basis of subjective criteria such as "excellence." . . .

Section 954(d)(1) merely adds some imprecise considerations to an already subjective selection process. It does not, on its face, impermissibly infringe on First or Fifth Amendment rights. Accordingly, the judgment of the Court of Appeals is reversed and the case is remanded for further proceedings consistent with this opinion.

It is so ordered.

JUSTICE SOUTER, dissenting.

The decency and respect proviso mandates viewpoint-based decisions in the disbursement of government subsidies, and the Government has wholly failed to explain why the statute should be afforded an exemption from the fundamental rule of the First Amendment that viewpoint discrimination in the exercise of public authority over expressive activity is unconstitutional. The Court's conclusions that the proviso is not viewpoint based, that it is not a regulation, and that the NEA may permissibly engage in viewpoint-based discrimination, are all patently mistaken. Nor may the question raised be answered in the Government's favor on the assumption that some constitutional applications of the statute are enough to satisfy the demand of facial constitutionality, leaving claims of the proviso's obvious invalidity to be dealt with later in response to challenges of specific applications of the discriminatory standards. This assumption is irreconcilable with our long standing and sensible doctrine of facial overbreadth, applicable to claims brought under the First Amendment's speech clause. I respectfully dissent.

"If there is a bedrock principle underlying the First Amendment, it is that the government may not prohibit the expression of an idea simply because society finds the idea itself offensive or disagreeable," *Texas* v. *Johnson* (1989). . . . Because this principle applies not only to affirmative suppression of speech, but also to disqualification for government favors, Congress is generally not permitted to pivot discrimination against otherwise protected speech on the offensiveness or unacceptability of the views it expresses, *Rosenberger* v. *Rector and Visitors of Univ. of Va.* (1995) (public university's student activities funds may not be disbursed on viewpoint-based terms); *Lamb's Chapel* v. *Center Moriches Union Free School Dist.* (1993) (after-hours access to public school property may not be withheld on the basis of viewpoint). . . .

It goes without saying that artistic expression lies within this First Amendment protection. The constitutional protection of artistic works turns not on the political significance that may be attributable to such productions, though they may indeed comment on the political, but simply on their expressive character, which falls within a spectrum of protected "speech" extending outward from the core of overtly political declarations. Put differently, art is entitled to full protection because our "cultural life," just like our native politics, "rests upon [the] ideal" of governmental viewpoint neutrality. When called upon to vindicate this ideal, we characteristically begin by asking "whether the government has adopted a regulation of speech because of disagreement with the message it conveys. The government's purpose is the controlling consideration." The answer in this case is damning. One need do nothing more than read the text of the statute to conclude that Congress's purpose in imposing the decency and respect criteria was to prevent the funding of art that conveys an offensive message; the decency and respect provision on its face is quintessentially viewpoint based, and quotations from the Congressional Record merely confirm the obvious legislative purpose. In the words of a cosponsor of the bill that enacted the proviso, "[w]orks which deeply offend the sensibilities of significant portions of the public ought not to be supported with public funds." Another supporter of the bill observed that "the Endowment's support for artists like Robert Mapplethorpe and Andre[s] Serrano has offended and angered many citizens," behooving "Congress . . . to listen to these complaints about the NEA and make sure that exhibits like [these] are not funded again." Indeed, if there were any question at all about what Congress had in mind, a definitive answer comes in the succinctly accurate remark of the proviso's author, that the bill "add[s] to the criteria of artistic excellence and artistic merit, a shell, a screen, a viewpoint that must be constantly taken into account."

In the face of such clear legislative purpose, so plainly expressed, the Court has its work cut out for it in seeking a constitutional reading of the statute. . . .

A . . . basic strand in the Court's treatment of today's question in effect assumes that whether or not the statute mandates viewpoint discrimination, there is no constitutional issue here because government art subsidies fall within a zone of activity free from First Amendment restraints. The Government calls attention to the roles of government-as-speaker and government-as-buyer, in which the government is of course entitled to engage in viewpoint discrimination: if the Food and Drug Administration launches an advertising campaign on the subject of smoking, it may condemn the habit without also having to show a cowboy taking a puff on the opposite page; and if the Secretary of Defense wishes to buy a portrait to decorate the Pentagon, he is free to prefer George Washington over George the Third. . . .

Our most thorough statement of these principles is found in the recent case of *Rosenberger* v. *Rector and Visitors of Univ. of Va.* (1995), which held that the University of Virginia could not discriminate on viewpoint in underwriting the speech of student-run publications. We recognized that the government may act on the basis of viewpoint "when the State is the speaker" or when the state "disburses public funds to private entities to convey a governmental message." But we explained that the government may not act on viewpoint when it "does not itself speak or subsidize transmittal of a message it favors but instead expends funds to encourage a diversity of views from private speakers." When the government acts as patron, subsidizing the expression of others, it may not prefer one lawfully stated view over another.

Rosenberger controls here. The NEA, like the student activities fund in *Rosenberger,* is a subsidy scheme created to encourage expression of a diversity of views from private speakers. Congress brought the NEA into being to help all Americans "achieve a better understanding of the past, a better analysis of the present, and a better view of the future." The NEA's purpose is to "support new ideas" and "to help create and sustain . . . a climate encouraging freedom of thought, imagination, and inquiry." Given this congressional choice to sustain freedom of expression, *Rosenberger* teaches that the First Amendment forbids decisions based on viewpoint popularity. So long as Congress chooses to subsidize expressive endeavors at large, it has no business requiring the NEA to turn down funding applications of artists and exhibitors who devote their "freedom of thought, imagination, and inquiry" to defying our tastes, our beliefs, or our values. . . .

The question of who has the burden to justify a categorical exemption has never been explicitly addressed by this Court, despite our recognition of the speaker and buyer categories in the past. The answer is nonetheless obvious in a recent statement by the Court synthesizing a host of cases on viewpoint discrimination. "The First Amendment presumptively places this sort of discrimination beyond the power of the government." Because it takes something to defeat a presumption, the burden is necessarily on the Government to justify a new exception to the fundamental rules that give life to the First Amendment. It is up to the Government to explain why a sphere of governmental participation in the arts (unique or not) should be treated as outside traditional First Amendment limits. The Government has not carried this burden here, or even squarely faced it.

The NEA 4 received support from several prominent names in American art and literature, including the American Association of University Professors, the Association of American Museums, and the Rockefeller Foundation. All of these groups believed that anyone whose work was tied to government funding—professors, researchers, public museums, and so on—could be subject to regulation if the 1990 law were upheld. Note, however, that the Court treats the law as little more than a guideline for the NEA to use in awarding grants. Peer review panels are still free to award grants to whomever they wish as long as they take the "decency" standard into account. Given the NEA's exceedingly small budget—its funding represents less than one one-hundredth of 1 percent of the federal budget—the controversy involving artists denied funding in the early 1990s was never about "wasting taxpayers' dollars" on subsidizing pornographic art. Rather, the battle over the NEA, which survived several attempts during the 1990s by conservatives in Congress to abolish it, was about politics. The furor over the NEA 4 has subsided, but the important constitutional questions raised by *Finley,* namely, whether or not the government can regulate the content of publicly funded expression beyond "indecent" art, still linger.

Freedom of Association

Writing in 1830, Alexis de Tocqueville, the astute French observer of social and political conditions in the early Republic, noted that Americans were "forever forming associations" to advance their interests. These organizational ties were not just formed to advance the causes of politics and industry, but to promote any conceivable interest capable of uniting two or more minds. Associations, Tocqueville noted, ranged from the "religious, moral, serious, futile" to the "very general and very limited, immensely large and very minute."[73] The right of people to come together for common purposes was an extension of their need to do so in a democratic society in which individuals were responsible for bettering themselves. Associational freedom certainly does have an instrumental relationship to carrying out other fundamental rights, such as freedom of speech, press, and assembly. Such freedom is also critical in helping individuals develop the power necessary to make their voices heard among the cacophony of interests pushing and pulling the institutions of American democracy.

Freedom of association extends beyond those rights to which it bears a close relationship. Such freedom is necessary to maintain personal and intimate relationships, which certainly require no constitutional justification. Associational freedom also permits individuals to realize personal fulfillment that is unconnected to love by joining groups formed around the promotion of charitable activities, hobbies, spiritual interests, self-help, recreation, promoting career opportunities, and so on. Here, associational freedom is less instrumental in nature and more intrinsic, that is, it involves those things done because we enjoy coming together with like-minded people with whom we can enjoy our common interests. Sometimes it is easier and more fun to do things with other people than it is to do them alone.[74]

At what point, however, does associational freedom give way to other important, often competing claims enjoying a prominent place in our system of constitutional values? Although the Constitution says nothing about associational freedom, the Court has relied upon its instrumental qualities to conclude that such a right is protected by the First Amendment. As discussed earlier in this chapter, the Court has repeatedly upheld the right of individuals to come together to discuss politics, watch sexually explicit films, or indulge their racism against government efforts seeking to outlaw such conduct. Such expressive conduct is intimately linked to associational freedom, and the Court has never questioned whether individuals have the right to come together to exercise their rights set out in the Constitution.[75] What happens when associations more general and less expressive in nature decide to exclude persons on the basis of race, sex, color, political belief, religious affiliation, or sexual orientation? Does the government's interest in combating discrimination outweigh the value of associational freedom for its own sake? How the Court resolved these questions in *Roberts* v. *United States Jaycees* (1984) has framed contemporary discussion on the tension inherent in these questions.[76]

In 1920, the United States Jaycees was founded by the United States Chamber of Commerce to serve as its junior partner. The Jaycees were open to men between the ages of eighteen to thirty-five, and its objective was to pursue "such educational and charitable purposes as will promote and foster the growth and development of young men's civic organizations in the United States." Another goal was to provide young men "with opportunity for personal development and achievement and an avenue for intelligent participation . . . in the affairs of their community, state and nation, and to develop true friendship and understanding among young men of all nations."

In 1974 and 1975, the Minneapolis and St. Paul chapters of the Jaycees began admitting women as regular members, a decision that conflicted directly with national policy. After several warnings from the national office, the president of the Jaycees informed the Minnesota chapters in December 1978 that the Board of Directors was prepared to take up the question of their expulsion. Shortly afterward, the two chapters filed a sex discrimination complaint with the Minnesota Department of Human Rights, claiming that the policy of the national office violated the Minnesota Human Rights Act. The law made it a discriminatory practice "to deny [to] any person the full and equal enjoyment of the goods, services, facilities, privileges, advantages, and accommodations of a place of public accommodation because of race, color, creed, religion, disability, national origin or sex." The Jaycees contended that it was not a public accommodation, but a private association free to select its own members and thus not covered by the Minnesota law. By the time the case went to trial, the Jaycees had approximately 295,000 members with 7,400 local chapters affiliated with 51 state organizations. The Jaycees' national staff worked closely with state and local organizations to promote community programs and business skills, and offered numerous incentives to individual members in the form of cash gifts and prizes.

Writing for a unanimous Court, Justice William Brennan concluded that the Jaycees were not a private association exempt from the Minnesota civil rights law. In reversing a federal appeals court, Brennan wrote that private organizations retain their associational rights when their core activities are exercised in conjunction with First Amendment freedoms, such as religion or expressive speech, or when the organization possesses the characteristics of an intimate club, such as small size, selectivity, and seclusion from the general public. The Court held that the Jaycees fell into neither category of these constitutionally protected organizations. *Roberts* attracted *amicus* briefs from the ACLU and the NAACP Legal Defense Fund that argued that the Jaycees were not an "intimate" or "expressive" association entitled to exemption from the Minnesota civil rights law. Another point raised in their briefs was the importance of the Jaycees in promoting business opportunities for its members. By discriminating against women, the Jaycees were also denying professional women the same opportunity to develop contacts and network as men had. Within the next four years, the justices extended *Roberts* to include all-male "dining clubs" catering to business professionals. In *New York State Club Association, Inc. v. City of New York* (1988), the Court held that such clubs were designed to further commerce, and upheld a New York City law written to ban discrimination in just such places.[77]

Two recent cases involving the rights of organizations to refuse the membership of individuals who want to participate in the group have taken the question of the associational freedom into a different and more controversial realm. In *Hurley v. Irish-American Gay, Lesbian and Bisexual Group of Boston* (1995) and *Boy Scouts of America v. Dale* (2000), the Court confronted demands from gays and lesbians who wanted to take part in the associational life of groups that in turn did not want them to participate because of their sexual orientation. This outright exclusion by two associations claiming that they were private makes these different cases from *Roberts*, which involved a dispute between the national and local levels of the Jaycees *after* the Minneapolis and St. Paul chapters agreed to admit women as full members.

Hurley v. Irish-American Gay, Lesbian, and Bisexual Group of Boston

515 U.S. 557 (1995)

On March 17, 1776, Revolutionary forces, under the command of General George Washington, captured key military installations in South Boston and drove British and Loyalist troops out. Historians have claimed that Washington reportedly drew on the earlier tradition of using "St. Patrick" as the response to "Boston," the password used in the colonial lines on what became known in Massachusetts as Evacuation Day. Although the courts did not officially designate March 17 as Evacuation Day until 1938, public celebrations were held every year under the sponsorship of the city of Boston, and featured parades, songs, and fireworks.

In 1947, Mayor James Michael Curley ended formal sponsorship of the March 17 parade, transferring responsibility for the St. Patrick's Day–Evacuation Day parade to the South Boston Allied War Veterans Council. Every year since then, the Veterans Council has applied for and received a permit to conduct the parade, which is an enormously popular event, drawing more than 20,000 marchers and 1 million observers. Through 1992, Boston permitted the Veterans Council to use the city's seal and printing services to publicize the parade and also provided funding assistance. That was the year that the Irish-American Gay, Lesbian, and Bisexual Group of Boston (GLIB) asked the Veterans Council for permission to take part in the parade to express their solidarity and pride with the other descendants of Irish immigrants. GLIB was denied permission, but successfully obtained a state court order permitting it to march in the 1992 parade. GLIB participated that year among the 10,000 other marchers without incident.

GLIB applied to march in the 1993 parade, and was denied permission by the Veterans Council's president, John J. "Wacko" Hurley. This time, GLIB, represented by the Gay and Lesbian Advocates and Defenders, sued under a state public accommodations law prohibiting "any distinction, discrimination or restriction on account of . . . sexual orientation . . . relative to the admission of any person to, or treatment in any place of public accommodation, resort or amusement." A Massachusetts state trial court ruled that the law applied to the March 17 parade because it accepted or solicited the patronage of the general public.

The Council also permitted groups to march without submitting an application and did not generally inquire into the points of view of the marchers taking part in the parade. The Supreme Judicial Court of Massachusetts concluded that a great diversity of themes characterized the parade, and concluded there was no basis to exclude GLIB.

The Court's decision was unanimous. Justice Souter delivered the opinion of the Court.

Ironically, the Lambda Legal Defense and Education Fund and the ACLU joined forces after *Hurley* to defeat the petition of an anti–gay rights organization that wanted to march in a San Diego gay pride parade sponsored by area gay and lesbian groups. Parade organizers had rejected the application of Normal People to march in the event because of their message, a reason the Court said in *Hurley* was firmly protected by the First Amendment.

▼▲▼

JUSTICE SOUTER delivered the opinion of the Court.

The issue in this case is whether Massachusetts may require private citizens who organize a parade to include among the marchers a group imparting a message the organizers do not wish to convey. We hold that such a mandate violates the First Amendment. . . .

If there were no reason for a group of people to march from here to there except to reach a destination, they could make the trip without expressing any message beyond the fact of the march itself. Some people might call such a procession a parade, but it would not be much of one. . . . Hence, we use the word "parade" to indicate marchers who are making some sort of collective point, not just to each other but to bystanders along the way. Indeed a parade's dependence on watchers is so extreme that nowadays, as with Bishop Berkeley's celebrated tree, "if a parade or demonstration receives no media coverage, it may as well not have happened." Parades are thus a form of expression, not just motion, and the inherent expressiveness of marching to make a point explains our cases involving protest marches. . . . [I]n *Edwards* v. *South Carolina* (1963), where petitioners had joined in a march of protest and pride, carrying placards and singing The Star-Spangled Banner, we held that the activities "reflect an exercise of these basic constitutional rights in their most pristine and classic form."

The protected expression that inheres in a parade is not limited to its banners and songs, however, for the Constitution looks beyond written or spoken words as mediums of expression. Noting that "[s]ymbolism is a primitive but effective way of communicating ideas," *West Virginia Bd. of Ed.* v. *Barnette* (1943), our cases have recognized that the First Amendment shields such acts as saluting a flag (and refusing to do so), wearing an arm band to protest a war, *Tinker* v. *Des Moines Independent Community School Dist.* (1969), displaying a red flag, *Stromberg* v. *California* (1931), and even "[m]arching, walking or parading" in uniforms displaying the swastika, *National Socialist Party of America* v. *Skokie* (1977). As some of these examples show, a narrow, succinctly articulable message is not a condition of constitutional protection, which if confined to expressions conveying a "particularized message," would never reach the unquestionably shielded painting of Jackson Pollock, music of Arnold Schoenberg, or Jabberwocky verse of Lewis Carroll.

Not many marches, then, are beyond the realm of expressive parades, and the South Boston celebration is not one of them. Spectators line the streets; people march in costumes and uniforms, carrying flags and banners with all sorts of messages (*e.g.*, "England get out of Ireland," "Say no to drugs"); marching bands and pipers play, floats are pulled along, and the whole show is broadcast over Boston television. To be sure, we agree with the state courts that in spite of excluding some applicants, the Council is rather lenient in admitting participants. But a private speaker does not forfeit constitutional protection simply by combining multifarious voices, or by failing to edit their themes to isolate an exact message as the exclusive subject matter of the speech. Nor, under our precedent, does First Amendment protection require a speaker to generate, as an original matter, each item featured in the communication. . . . For that matter, the presentation of an edited compilation of speech generated by other persons is a staple of most newspapers' opinion pages, which, of course, fall squarely within the core of First Amendment security, as does even the simple selection of a paid noncommercial advertisement for inclusion in a daily paper. The selection of contingents to make a parade is entitled to similar protection.

Respondents' participation as a unit in the parade was equally expressive. GLIB was formed for the very purpose of marching in it, as the trial court found, in order to celebrate its members' identity as openly gay, lesbian, and bisexual descendants of the Irish immigrants, to show that there are such individuals in the community, and to support the like men and women who sought to march in the New York parade. The organization distributed a fact sheet describing the members' intentions, and the record otherwise corroborates the expressive nature of GLIB's participation. In 1993, members of GLIB marched behind a shamrock-strewn banner with the simple inscription "Irish American Gay, Lesbian and Bisexual Group of Boston." GLIB understandably seeks to communicate its ideas as part of the existing parade, rather than staging one of its own. . . .

After the Civil War, the Commonwealth of Massachusetts was the first State to . . . ensure access to public accommodations regardless of race. In prohibiting discrimination "in any licensed inn, in any public place of amusement, public conveyance or public meeting," the original statute already expanded upon the common law, which had not conferred any right of access to places of public amusement. As with many public accommodations statutes across the Nation, the legislature continued to broaden the scope of legislation, to the point that the law today prohibits discrimination on the basis of "race, color, religious creed, national origin, sex, sexual orientation . . . , deafness, blindness or any physical or mental disability or ancestry" in "the admission of any person to, or treatment in any place of public accommodation, resort or amusement." Provisions like these are well within the State's usual power to enact when a legislature has reason to believe that a given group is the target of discrimination, and they do not, as a general matter, violate the First or Fourteenth Amendments. Nor is this statute unusual in any obvious way, since it does not, on its face, target speech or discriminate on the basis of its content, the focal point of its prohibition being rather on the act of discriminating against individuals in the provision of publicly available goods, privileges, and services on the proscribed grounds.

In the case before us, however, the Massachusetts law has been applied in a peculiar way. Its enforcement does not address any dispute about the participation of openly gay, lesbian, or bisexual individuals in various units admitted to the parade. The petitioners disclaim any intent to exclude homosexuals as such, and no individual member of GLIB claims to have been excluded from parading as a member of any group that the Council has approved to march. Instead, the disagreement goes to the admission of GLIB as its own parade unit carrying its own banner. Since every participating unit affects the message conveyed by the private organizers, the state courts' application of the statute produced an order essentially requiring petitioners to alter the expressive content of their parade. Although the state courts spoke of the parade as a place of public accommodation, once the expressive character of both the parade and the marching GLIB contingent is understood, it becomes apparent that the state courts' application of the statute had the effect of declaring the sponsors' speech itself to be the public accommodation. Under this approach any contingent of protected individuals with a message would have the right to participate in petitioners' speech, so that the communication produced by the private organizers would be shaped by all those protected by the law who wished to join in with some expressive demonstration of their own. But this use of the State's power violates the fundamental rule of protection under the First Amendment, that a speaker has the autonomy to choose the content of his own message. . . .

Petitioners' claim to the benefit of this principle of autonomy to control one's own speech is as sound as the South Boston parade is expressive. Rather like a composer, the Council selects the expressive units of the parade from potential participants, and though the score may not produce a particularized message, each contingent's expression in the Council's eyes comports with what merits celebration on that day. Even if this view gives the Council credit for a more considered judgment than it actively made, the Council clearly decided to exclude a message it did not like from the communication it chose to make, and that is enough to invoke its right as a private speaker to shape its expression by speaking on one subject while remaining silent on another. The message it disfavored is not difficult to identify. Although GLIB's point (like the Council's) is not wholly articulate, a contingent marching behind the organization's banner would at least bear witness to the fact that some Irish are gay, lesbian, or bisexual, and the presence of the organized marchers would suggest their view that people of their sexual orientations have as much claim to unqualified social acceptance as heterosexuals and indeed as members of parade units organized around other identifying characteristics. The parade's organizers may not believe these facts about Irish sexuality to be so, or they may object to unqualified social acceptance of gays and lesbians or have some other reason for wishing to keep GLIB's message out of the parade. But whatever the reason, it boils down to the choice of a speaker not to propound a particular point of view, and that choice is presumed to lie beyond the government's power to control. . . .

The [Massachusetts law] is a piece of protective legislation that announces no purpose beyond the object both expressed and apparent in its provisions, which is to prevent any denial of access to (or discriminatory treatment in) public accommodations on proscribed grounds, including sexual orientation. On its face, the object of the law is to ensure by statute for gays and lesbians desiring to make use of public accommodations what the old common law promised to any member of the public wanting a meal at the inn, that accepting the usual terms of service, they will not be turned away merely on the proprietor's exercise of personal preference. When the law is applied to expressive activity in the way it was done here, its apparent object is simply to require speakers to modify the content of their expression to whatever extent beneficiaries of the law choose to alter it with messages of their own. But in the absence of some further, legitimate end, this object is merely to allow exactly what the general rule of speaker's autonomy forbids.

It might, of course, have been argued that a broader objective is apparent: that the ultimate point of forbidding acts of discrimination toward certain classes is to produce a society free of the corresponding biases. Requiring access to a speaker's message would thus be not an end in itself, but a means to produce speakers free of the biases, whose expressive conduct would be at least neutral toward the particular classes, obviating any future need for correction. But if this indeed is the point of applying the state law to expressive conduct, it is a decidedly fatal objective. Having availed itself of the public thoroughfares "for purposes of assembly [and] communicating thoughts between citizens," the Council is engaged in a use of the streets that has "from ancient times, been a part of the privileges, immunities, rights, and liberties of citizens." Our tradition of free speech commands that a speaker who takes to the street corner to express his views in this way should be free from interference by the State based on the content of what he says. The very idea that a noncommercial speech restriction be used to produce thoughts and statements acceptable to some groups or, indeed, all people, grates on the First Amendment, for it amounts to nothing less than a proposal to limit speech in the service of orthodox expression. The Speech Clause has no more certain antithesis. While the law is free to promote all sorts of conduct in place of harmful behavior, it is not free to interfere with speech for no better reason than promoting an approved message or discouraging a disfavored one, however enlightened either purpose may strike the government. . . .

New York State Club Association is also instructive by the contrast it provides. There, we turned back a facial challenge to a state antidiscrimination statute on the assumption that the expressive associational character of a dining club with over 400 members could be sufficiently attenuated to permit application of the law even to such a private organization, but we also recognized that the State did not prohibit exclusion of those whose views were at odds with positions espoused by the general club memberships. In other words, although the association provided public benefits to which a State could ensure equal access, it was also engaged in expressive activity; compelled access to the benefit, which was upheld, did not trespass on the organization's message itself. If we were to analyze this case strictly along those lines, GLIB would lose. Assuming the parade to be large enough and a source of benefits (apart from its expression) that would generally justify a mandated access provision, GLIB could nonetheless be refused admission as an expressive contingent with its own message just as readily as a private club could exclude an applicant whose manifest views were at odds with a position taken by the club's existing members.

Our holding today rests not on any particular view about the Council's message, but on the Nation's commitment to protect freedom of speech. Disapproval of a private speaker's statement does not legitimize use of the Commonwealth's power to compel the speaker to alter the message by including one more acceptable to others. Accordingly, the judgment of the Supreme Judicial Court is reversed, and the case remanded for proceedings not inconsistent with this opinion.

It is so ordered.

Boy Scouts of America v. *Dale*

530 U.S. 640 (2000)

The facts and background of this case are set out in the accompanying SIDEBAR.

The Court's decision was 5 to 4. Chief Justice Rehnquist delivered the opinion of the Court. Justice Stevens filed a dissenting opinion, which was joined by Justices Souter, Ginsburg, and Breyer. Justice Souter, joined by Justices Ginsburg and Breyer, filed a separate dissenting opinion.

CHIEF JUSTICE REHNQUIST delivered the opinion of the Court.

To determine whether a group is protected by the First Amendment's expressive associational right, we must determine whether the group engages in "expressive association." The First Amendment's protection of expressive association is not reserved for advocacy groups. But to come within its ambit, a group must engage in some form of expression, whether it be public or private. . . .

[T]he general mission of the Boy Scouts is clear: "[T]o instill values in young people." The Boy Scouts seeks to instill these values by having its adult leaders spend time with the youth members, instructing and engaging them in activities like camping, archery, and fishing. During the time spent with the youth members, the scoutmasters and assistant scoutmasters inculcate them with the Boy Scouts' values—both expressly and by example. It seems indisputable that an association that seeks to transmit such a system of values engages in expressive activity.

Given that the Boy Scouts engages in expressive activity, we must determine whether the forced inclusion of Dale as an assistant scoutmaster would significantly affect the Boy Scouts' ability to advocate public or private viewpoints. This inquiry necessarily requires us first to explore, to a limited extent, the nature of the Boy Scouts' view of homosexuality.

The values the Boy Scouts seeks to instill are "based on" those listed in the Scout Oath and Law. The Boy Scouts explains that the Scout Oath and Law provide "a positive moral code for living; they are a list of 'do's' rather than 'don'ts.'" The Boy Scouts asserts that homosexual conduct is inconsistent with the values embodied in the Scout Oath and Law, particularly with the values represented by the terms "morally straight" and "clean."

Obviously, the Scout Oath and Law do not expressly mention sexuality or sexual orientation. And the terms "morally straight" and "clean" are by no means self-defining. Different people would attribute to those terms very different meanings. For example, some people may believe that engaging in homosexual conduct is not at odds with being "morally straight" and "clean." And others may believe that engaging in homosexual conduct is contrary to being "morally straight" and "clean." The Boy Scouts says it falls within the latter category. . . .

The Boy Scouts asserts that it "teach[es] that homosexual conduct is not morally straight," and that it does "not want to promote homosexual conduct as a legitimate form of behavior." We accept the Boy Scouts' assertion. We need not inquire further to determine the nature of the Boy Scouts' expression with respect to homosexuality. But because the record before us contains written evidence of the Boy Scouts' viewpoint, we look to it as instructive, if only on the question of the sincerity of the professed beliefs.

A 1978 position statement to the Boy Scouts' Executive Committee . . . expresses the Boy Scouts' "official position" with regard to "homosexuality and Scouting":

> The Boy Scouts of America is a private, membership organization and leadership therein is a privilege and not a right. We do not believe that homosexuality and leadership in Scouting are appropriate. We will continue to select only those who in our judgment meet our standards and qualifications for leadership.

Thus, at least as of 1978—the year James Dale entered Scouting—the official position of the Boy Scouts was that avowed homosexuals were not to be Scout leaders.

A position statement promulgated by the Boy Scouts in 1991 (after Dale's membership was revoked but before this litigation was filed) also supports its current view: "We believe that homosexual conduct is inconsistent with the requirement in the Scout Oath that a Scout be morally straight and in the Scout Law that a Scout be clean in word and deed, and that homosexuals do not provide a desirable role model for Scouts."

This position statement was redrafted numerous times but its core message remained consistent. For example, a 1993 position statement, the most recent in the record, reads, in part: "The Boy Scouts of America has always reflected the expectations that Scouting families have had for the organization. We do not believe that homosexuals provide a role model consistent with these expectations. Accordingly, we do not allow for the registration of avowed homosexuals as members or as leaders of the BSA."

We must . . . determine whether Dale's presence as an assistant scoutmaster would significantly burden the Boy Scouts' desire to not "promote homosexual conduct as a legitimate form of behavior." As we give deference to an association's assertions regarding the nature of its expression, we must also give deference to an association's view of what would impair its expression. That is not to say that an expressive association can erect a shield against antidiscrimination laws simply by asserting that mere acceptance of a member from a particular group would impair its message. But here Dale, by his own admission, is one of a group of gay Scouts who have "become leaders in their community and are open and honest about their sexual orientation." Dale was the copresident of a gay and lesbian organization at college and remains a gay rights activist. Dale's presence in the Boy Scouts would, at the very least, force the organization to send a message, both to the youth members and the world, that the Boy Scouts accepts homosexual conduct as a legitimate form of behavior.

Hurley is illustrative on this point. There we considered whether the application of Massachusetts' public accommodations law to require the organizers of a private St. Patrick's Day parade to include among the marchers an Irish-American gay, lesbian, and bisexual group, GLIB, violated the parade organizers' First Amendment rights. We noted that the parade organizers did not wish to exclude the GLIB members because of their sexual orientations, but because they wanted to march behind a GLIB banner. . . .

Here, we have found that the Boy Scouts believes that homosexual conduct is inconsistent with the values it seeks to instill in its youth members; it will not "promote homosexual conduct as a legitimate form of behavior." As the presence of GLIB in Boston's St. Patrick's Day parade would have interfered with the parade organizers' choice not to propound a particular point of view, the presence of Dale as an assistant scoutmaster would just as surely interfere with the Boy Scout's choice not to propound a point of view contrary to its beliefs. . . .

[T]he Boy Scouts is an expressive association and [we conclude] that the forced inclusion of Dale would significantly affect its expression. . . . [and] we [now] inquire whether the application of New Jersey's public accommodations law to require that the Boy Scouts accept Dale as an assistant scoutmaster runs afoul of the Scouts' freedom of expressive association. We conclude that it does.

State public accommodations laws were originally enacted to prevent discrimination in traditional places of public accommodation—like inns and trains. Over time, the public accommodations laws have expanded to cover more places. New Jersey's statutory definition of "'[a] place of public accommodation'" is extremely broad. The term is said to "include, but not be limited to," a list of over 50 types of places. Many on the list are what one would expect to be places where the public is invited. For example, the statute includes as places of public accommodation taverns, restaurants, retail shops, and public libraries. But the statute also includes places that often may not carry with them open invitations to the public, like summer camps and roof gardens. In this case, the New Jersey Supreme Court went a step further and applied its public accommodations law to a private entity without even attempting to tie the term "place" to a physical location. As the definition of "public accommodation" has expanded from clearly commercial entities, such as restaurants, bars, and hotels, to membership organizations such as the Boy Scouts, the potential for conflict between state public accommodations laws and the First Amendment rights of organizations has increased.

We recognized in cases such as *Roberts* . . . that States have a compelling interest in eliminating discrimination against women in public accommodations. But in each of these cases we went on to conclude that the enforcement of these statutes would not materially interfere with the ideas that the organization sought to express. . . .

In *Hurley,* we applied traditional First Amendment analysis to hold that the application of the Massachusetts public accommodations law to a parade violated the First Amendment rights of the parade organizers. Although we did not explicitly deem the parade in *Hurley* an expressive association, the analysis we applied there is similar to the analysis we apply here. We have already concluded that a state requirement that the Boy Scouts retain Dale as an assistant scoutmaster would significantly burden the organization's right to oppose or disfavor homosexual conduct. The state interests embodied in New Jersey's public accommodations law do not justify such a severe intrusion on the Boy Scouts' rights to freedom of expressive association. That being the case, we hold that the First Amendment prohibits the State from imposing such a requirement through the application of its public accommodations law.

Justice Stevens's dissent makes much of its observation that the public perception of homosexuality in this country has changed. Indeed, it appears that homosexuality has gained greater societal acceptance. But this is scarcely an argument for denying First Amendment protection to those who refuse to accept these views. The First Amendment protects expression, be it of the popular variety or not. And the fact that an idea may be embraced and advocated by increasing numbers of people is all the more reason to protect the First Amendment rights of those who wish to voice a different view. . . .

We are not, as we must not be, guided by our views of whether the Boy Scouts' teachings with respect to homosexual conduct are right or wrong; public or judicial disapproval of a tenet of an organization's expression does not justify the State's effort to compel the organization to accept members where such acceptance would derogate from the organization's expressive message. . . .

The judgment of the New Jersey Supreme Court is reversed, and the cause remanded for further proceedings not inconsistent with this opinion.

It is so ordered.

Justice Stevens, with whom Justice Souter, Justice Ginsburg, and Justice Breyer join, dissenting.

In this case, Boy Scouts of America contends that it teaches the young boys who are Scouts that homosexuality is immoral. Consequently, it argues, it would violate its right to associate to force it to admit homosexuals as members, as doing so would be at odds with its own shared goals and values. This contention, quite plainly, requires us to look at what, exactly, are the values that BSA actually teaches.

To bolster its claim that its shared goals include teaching that homosexuality is wrong, BSA directs our attention to two terms appearing in the Scout Oath and Law. The first is the phrase "morally straight," which appears in the Oath ("On my honor I will do my best . . . To keep myself . . . morally straight"); the second term is the word "clean," which appears in a list of 12 characteristics together comprising the Scout Law. . . .

It is plain as the light of day that neither one of these principles—"morally straight" and "clean"—says the slightest thing about homosexuality. Indeed, neither term in the Boy Scouts' Law and Oath expresses any position whatsoever on sexual matters.

BSA's published guidance on that topic underscores this point. Scouts, for example, are directed to receive their sex education at home or in school, but not from the organization: "Your parents or guardian or a sex education teacher should give you the facts about sex that you must know." To be sure, Scouts are not forbidden from asking their Scoutmaster about issues of a sexual nature, but Scoutmasters are, literally, the last person Scouts are encouraged to ask: "If you have questions about growing up, about relationships, sex, or making good decisions, ask. Talk with your parents, religious leaders, teachers, or Scoutmaster." Moreover, Scoutmasters are specifically directed to steer curious adolescents to other sources of information. . . .

In light of BSA's self-proclaimed ecumenism, furthermore, it is even more difficult to discern any shared goals or common moral stance on homosexuality. Insofar as religious matters are concerned, BSA's bylaws state that it is "absolutely nonsectarian in its attitude toward . . . religious training." "The BSA does not define what constitutes duty to God or the practice of religion. This is the responsibility of parents and religious leaders." In fact, many diverse religious organizations sponsor local Boy Scout troops. Because a number of religious groups do not view homosexuality as immoral or wrong and reject discrimination against homosexuals, it is exceedingly difficult to believe that BSA nonetheless adopts a single particular religious or moral philosophy when it comes to sexual orientation. This is especially so in light of the fact that Scouts are advised to seek guidance on sexual matters from their religious leaders (and Scoutmasters are told to refer Scouts to them); BSA surely is aware that some religions do not teach that homosexuality is wrong. . . .

BSA [has] never [taken] any clear and unequivocal position on homosexuality. Though the 1991 and 1992 policies state one interpretation of "morally straight" and "clean," the group's published definitions appearing in the Boy Scout and Scoutmaster Handbooks take quite another view. And BSA's broad religious tolerance combined with its declaration that sexual matters are not its "proper area" render its views on the issue equivocal at best and incoherent at worst. We have never held, however, that a group can throw together any mixture of contradictory positions and then invoke the right to associate to defend any one of those views. At a minimum, a group seeking to prevail over an antidiscrimination law must adhere to a clear and unequivocal view. . . .

. . . [O]ther than a single sentence, BSA fails to show that it ever taught Scouts that homosexuality is not "morally straight" or "clean," or that such a view was part of the group's collective efforts to foster a belief. Furthermore, BSA's policy statements fail to establish any clear, consistent, and unequivocal position on homosexuality. Nor did BSA have any reason to think Dale's sexual *conduct,* as opposed to his orientation, was contrary to the group's values. . . .

BSA's claim finds no support in our cases. We have recognized "a right to associate for the purpose of engaging in those activities protected by the First Amendment—speech, assembly, petition for the redress of grievances, and the exercise of religion." And we have acknowledged that "when the State interferes with individuals' selection of those with whom they wish to join in a common endeavor, freedom of association . . . may be implicated." But "[t]he right to associate for expressive purposes is not . . . absolute"; rather, "the nature and degree of constitutional protection afforded freedom of association may vary depending on the extent to which . . . the constitutionally protected liberty is at stake in a given case." Indeed, the right to associate does not mean "that in every setting in which individuals exercise some discrimination in choosing associates, their selective process of inclusion and exclusion is protected by the Constitution." For example, we have routinely and easily rejected assertions of this right by expressive organizations with discriminatory membership policies, such as private schools, law firms, and labor organizations. In fact, until today, we have never once found a claimed right to associate in the selection of members to prevail in the face of a State's antidiscrimination law. To the contrary, we have squarely held that a State's antidiscrimination law does not violate a group's right to associate simply because the law conflicts with that group's exclusionary membership policy. . . .

Several principles are made perfectly clear by *Roberts* v. *Jaycees* (1984). . . . First, to prevail on a claim of expressive association in the face of a State's antidiscrimination law, it is not enough simply to engage in *some kind* of expressive activity. Both the Jaycees and the Rotary Club engaged in expressive activity protected by the First Amendment, yet that fact was not dispositive. Second, it is not enough to adopt an openly avowed exclusionary membership policy. Both the Jaycees and the Rotary Club did that as well. Third, it is not sufficient merely to articulate *some* connection between the group's expressive activities and its exclusionary policy. The Rotary Club, for

BOY SCOUTS OF AMERICA V. DALE

To Be Morally Straight

Like many other eight-year-old boys, James Dale could not wait to attend his first Cub Scout meeting and discover all the excitement that awaited him. He looked forward to the campfires, the overnight trips, learning the skills, and developing the courage and character to one day become a Boy Scout. The Cub Scouts were an important part of Dale's childhood, and he relished every minute of his involvement with scouting. After entering the Boy Scouts when he turned twelve, Dale became an Eagle Scout, an honor reached by only 2 percent of all scouts. By the time he reached the age of eighteen, the maximum age a scout can be, Dale had earned over thirty merit badges and been named into the Boy Scouts of America (BSA) honorary society, the Order of the Arrow. He continued to serve as an Assistant Scoutmaster, the adult program for scout leaders, until he received a letter from the Boy Scouts asking him to sever his relationship with the program.

Dale was stunned. Why would the Boy Scouts ask him, a dedicated and highly respected scout, to leave the program? When Dale asked for an explanation, Boy Scout officers told him that the organization forbids membership to homosexuals. How did they know? Dale wondered. Yes, he was gay, but he had never discussed his sexual orientation with anyone in the Boy Scouts. Then something clicked. Since arriving at Rutgers University, Dale had been involved with the campus student group, the Rutgers Lesbian/Gay Alliance, and eventually become its co-president. During a campus conference on the psychological and physical health needs of gay teenagers, a reporter from the *Newark Star-Ledger* asked him how he had gotten involved with the Lesbian/Gay Alliance. Dale responded: "I was looking for a role model, someone who was gay and accepting of me." Dale never mentioned the Boy Scouts or any other aspect of his personal life.

Nonetheless, someone from the Boy Scouts Monmouth Council, the New Jersey branch that sponsored Dale's troop, had seen the *Newark Star-Ledger* article and ordered the Eagle Scout's expulsion. Dale inquired further, and, five months later, an attorney from the Boy Scouts told him that the organization did not admit "avowed homosexuals." When Dale asked where the Boy Scouts charter mentioned anything about disqualifying gay men, lawyers responded that homosexuality was inconsistent with the Boy Scout Oath. The Oath states:

> On my honor I will do my best
> To do my duty to God and my country and to obey the Scout Law;
> To help other people at all times;
> To keep myself physically strong, mentally awake, and morally straight.

Dale was told that keeping one's self "morally straight" did not include homosexuality, "avowed" or otherwise. Such an interpretation was not one that Dale had ever heard anyone give to the morally straight clause of the Boy Scout Oath. The Scout Handbook states that a Scout should "[r]espect and defend the right of all people. Your relationships with others should be honest and open. Be clean in your speech and actions, and faithful in your religious beliefs." Dale also believed that several other points in the Scout Law contradicted excluding homosexuals. The fourth point in the Scout Law says that a "Scout is friendly. . . . He seeks to understand others. He respects those with ideas and customs that are different from his own. . . . Every person is an individual with his or her own ideas and ways of doing things. To be a real friend you must accept people as they are, show interest in them, and respect their differences." Convinced that the Boy Scouts had no right to exclude him from membership, Dale filed suit under a New Jersey civil rights law that banned sexual orientation discrimination by public accommodations.

The Lambda Legal Defense and Education Fund assisted Dale with his lawsuit, working with local counsel in New Jersey. Although a trial court ruled that the Boy Scouts organization is not subject to the state law because it was not a "public accommodation," in March 1998 the New Jersey Supreme Court ultimately found that the Scouts were subject to the law. The court noted that the BSA is a federally chartered corporation with 5 million members, including 1 million youth members and 420,000 adult members in its scouting program. Citing the Boy Scouts charter, which states that the purpose of the program was to "provide an educational program for boys and young adults to build character, to train in the responsibilities of participating citizenship, and to develop personal fitness," the court concluded the Boys Scouts of America was a public accommodation and thus bound by the New Jersey law. The court also noted that public schools, government organizations, churches, synagogues, mosques, and civic groups sponsor Scout troops.

New Jersey was not the first legal battleground over the membership policies of the Boy Scouts. A month before, the California Supreme Court, in *Curran* v. *Mt. Diablo Council of the Boys Scouts of America* (1998), rejected a similar argument brought by Lambda and the ACLU on behalf of Tim Curran, a gay Eagle Scout who had originally challenged the BSA's membership policies in 1981. The court concluded that the BSA was not a business establishment and thus was permitted to choose its membership. That

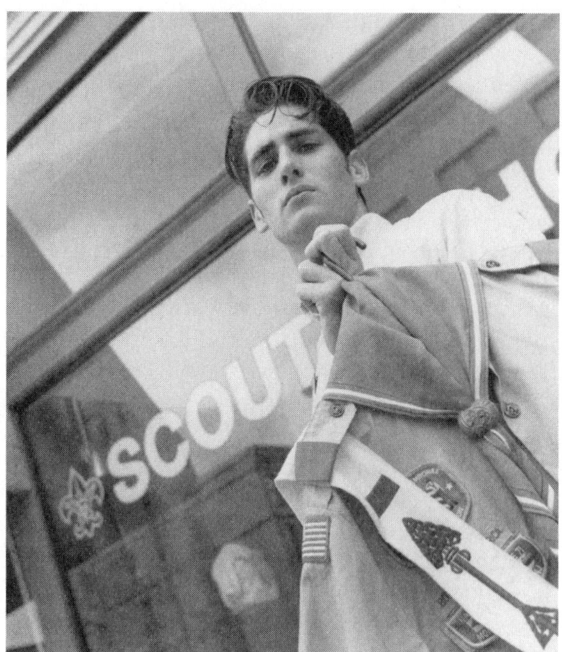

James Dale, expelled from the Boy Scouts for his homosexuality, holding his uniform.
© Marc Geller

reasoning enabled the BSA to withstand a lawsuit brought under the California civil rights law by the ACLU on behalf of two agnostic boys who were denied membership. In *Randall* v. *Boy Scouts of America, Orange County Council* (1998). Michael and William Randall refused to take the Oath pledging allegiance to God and were expelled. Ironically, their expulsion came just after the Orange County Council had awarded each unanimously with their Eagle badges.

Shortly after the *Curran* and *Randall* decisions, Levi Strauss, headquartered in San Francisco, and the United Way of San Francisco withdrew their funding for state and local scouting programs that discriminated on the basis of sexual orientation. Separately, the Orange County Council of the BSA signed an agreement with the United Way of Orange County stating that it would not require any Boy Scout to take part in a religious activity. That agreement permitted the Orange County Council to keep the $750,000 it received from the United Way. These responses, however, were atypical of United Way chapters across the nation: Fewer than a dozen of approximately fourteen hundred United Way chapters withdrew their funding for the BSA.

After the Court's decision in *Dale,* several major American corporations that had long funded the BSA, including Chase Manhattan Corp., the global financial concern, and Knight-Ridder, a major communications company, withdrew hundreds of thousands of dollars in financial support. But several other prominent BSA supporters, including American Airlines and General Electric, decided to continue their contributions, claiming that withdrawing their support would hurt too many young men who had benefited so greatly from scouting. Indeed, many companies were torn between their own commitment to diversity, including their own corporate internal policies prohibiting discrimination on the basis of sexual orientation, and the exclusionary policy of the BSA.

Several state and local governments reacted in similar fashion. Within months after *Dale,* Chicago, San Francisco, and San Jose, California, told local scout troops that they could no longer use their parks and schools for meetings and activities. The Connecticut state government issued a directive banning employees from designating charitable contributions to the Scouts run by state associations. Some municipalities, such as Miami Beach, permitted local scout troops to continue using their facilities, but required them to sign a nondiscrimination clause or pay facilities fees commonly waived for other civic and nonprofit groups. Some public schools, such as those in Miami-Dade County, postponed BSA recruiting drives.

James Dale was thirty-one years old when the Supreme Court finally ruled that the BSA could exclude and expel members based on their sexual orientation. By then, he was living in New York City and working for a media concern that dealt with health issues among gay men. Dale was resigned to the fact that he could never again participate in scouting programs. The BSA's response to the Court decision was to say that it "respects the rights of people and groups who hold values that differ from those encompassed in the Scout Oath and Law, and the BSA makes no effort to deny the rights of those whose views differ to hold their attitudes or opinions." No doubt that public fallout will continue over *Dale,* reflecting the continuing and evolving debate over the right to equal treatment versus the right to freedom of association.

example, justified its male-only membership policy by pointing to the "'aspect of fellowship . . . that is enjoyed by the [exclusively] male membership'" and by claiming that only with an exclusively male membership could it "operate effectively" in foreign countries. Rather, in *Jaycees,* we asked whether Minnesota's Human Rights Law requiring the admission of women "impose[d] any *serious burdens*" on the group's "collective effort on behalf of [its] *shared goals.*" . . .

The evidence before this Court makes it exceptionally clear that BSA has, at most, simply adopted an exclusionary membership policy and has no shared goal of disapproving of homosexuality. BSA's mission statement and federal charter say nothing on the matter; its official membership policy is silent; its Scout Oath and Law—and accompanying definitions—are devoid of any view on the topic; its guidance for Scouts and Scoutmasters on sexuality declare that such matters are "not construed to be Scouting's proper area," but are the province of a Scout's parents and pastor; and BSA's posture respecting religion tolerates a wide variety of views on the issue of homosexuality. Moreover, there is simply no evidence that BSA otherwise teaches anything in this area, or that it instructs Scouts on matters involving homosexuality in ways not conveyed in the Boy Scout or Scoutmaster Handbooks. In short, Boy Scouts of America is simply silent on homosexuality. There is no shared goal or collective effort to foster a belief about homosexuality at all—let alone one that is significantly burdened by admitting homosexuals. . . .

[T]he majority insists that we must "give deference to an association's assertions regarding the nature of its expression" and "we must also give deference to an association's view of what would impair its expression." So long as the record "contains written evidence" to support a group's bare assertion, "[w]e need not inquire further." Once the organization "asserts" that it engages in particular expression, "[w]e cannot doubt" the truth of that assertion.

This is an astounding view of the law. I am unaware of any previous instance in which our analysis of the scope of a constitutional right was determined by looking at what a litigant asserts in his or her brief and inquiring no further. It is even more astonishing in the First Amendment area, because, as the majority itself acknowledges, "we are obligated to independently review the factual record." It is an odd form of independent review that consists of deferring entirely to whatever a litigant claims. But the majority insists that our inquiry must be "limited," because "it is not the role of the courts to reject a group's expressed values because they disagree with those values or find them internally inconsistent." . . .

Even if BSA's right to associate argument fails, it nonetheless might have a First Amendment right to refrain from including debate and dialogue about homosexuality as part of its mission to instill values in Scouts. It can, for example, advise Scouts who are entering adulthood and have questions about sex to talk "with your parents, religious leaders, teachers, or Scoutmaster," and, in turn, it can direct Scoutmasters who are asked such questions "not undertake to instruct Scouts, in any formalized manner, in the subject of sex and family life" because "it is not construed to be Scouting's proper area." Dale's right to advocate certain beliefs in a public forum or in a private debate does not include a right to advocate these ideas when he is working as a Scoutmaster. And BSA cannot be compelled to include a message about homosexuality among the values it actually chooses to teach its Scouts, if it would prefer to remain silent on that subject. . . .

BSA has not contended, nor does the record support, that Dale had ever advocated a view on homosexuality to his troop before his membership was revoked. Accordingly, BSA's revocation could only have been based on an assumption that he would do so in the future. . . .

Dale's inclusion in the Boy Scouts is nothing like the case in *Hurley*. His participation sends no cognizable message to the Scouts or to the world. Unlike GLIB, Dale did not carry a banner or a sign; he did not distribute any fact sheet; and he expressed no intent to send any message. If there is any kind of message being sent, then, it is by the mere act of joining the Boy Scouts. Such an act does not constitute an instance of symbolic speech under the First Amendment. . . .

Over the years, BSA has generously welcomed over 87 million young Americans into its ranks. In 1992 over one million adults were active BSA members. The notion that an organization of that size and enormous prestige implicitly endorses the views that each of those adults may express in a non-Scouting context is simply mind boggling. . . . It is . . . farfetched to assert that Dale's open declaration of his homosexuality, reported in a local newspaper, will effectively force BSA to send a message to anyone simply because it allows Dale to be an Assistant Scoutmaster. For an Olympic gold medal winner or a Wimbledon tennis champion, being "openly gay" perhaps communicates a message—for example, that openness about one's sexual orientation is more virtuous than concealment; that a homosexual person can be a capable and virtuous person who should be judged like anyone else; and that homosexuality is not immoral—but it certainly does not follow that they necessarily send a message on behalf of the organizations that sponsor the activities in which they excel. The fact that such persons participate in these organizations is not usually construed to convey a message on behalf of those organizations any more than does the inclusion of women, African-Americans, religious minorities, or any other discrete group. Surely the organizations are not forced by antidiscrimination laws to take any position on the legitimacy of any individual's private beliefs or private conduct. . . .

Unfavorable opinions about homosexuals "have ancient roots," *Bowers* v. *Hardwick* (1986). Like equally atavistic opinions about certain racial groups, those roots have been nourished by sectarian doctrine. Over the years, however, interactions with real people, rather than mere adherence to traditional ways of thinking about members of unfamiliar classes, have modified those opinions. A few examples: The American Psychiatric Association's and the American Psychological Association's removal of "homosexuality" from their lists of mental disorders; a move toward greater understanding within some religious communities . . . Justice Blackmun's classic [dissenting] opinion in *Bowers* . . . and New Jersey's enactment of the provision at issue in this case. . . .

That such prejudices are still prevalent and that they have caused serious and tangible harm to countless members of the class New Jersey seeks to protect are established matters of fact that neither the Boy Scouts nor the Court disputes. That harm can only be aggravated by the creation of a constitutional shield for a policy that is itself the product of a habitual way of thinking about strangers. . . .

If we would guide by the light of reason, we must let our minds be bold. I respectfully dissent.

JUSTICE SOUTER, with whom JUSTICE GINSBURG and JUSTICE BREYER join, dissenting.

The right of expressive association does not, of course, turn on the popularity of the views advanced by a group that claims protection. Whether the group appears to this Court to be in the vanguard or rearguard of social thinking is irrelevant to the group's rights. I conclude that BSA has not made out an expressive association claim, therefore, not because of what BSA may espouse, but because of its failure to make sexual orientation the subject of any unequivocal advocacy, using the channels it customarily employs to state its message. As JUSTICE STEVENS explains, no group can claim a right of expressive association without identifying a clear position to be advocated over time in an unequivocal way. To require less, and to allow exemption from a public accommodations statute based on any individual's difference from an alleged group ideal, however expressed and however inconsistently claimed, would convert the right of expressive association into an easy trump of any antidiscrimination law.

If, on the other hand, an expressive association claim has met the conditions JUSTICE STEVENS describes as necessary, there may well be circumstances in which the antidiscrimination law must yield, as he says. It is certainly possible for an individual to become so identified with a position as to epitomize it publicly. When that position is at odds with a group's advocated position, applying an antidiscrimination statute to require the group's acceptance of the individual in a position of group leadership could so modify or muddle or frustrate the group's advocacy as to violate the expressive associational right. While it is not our business here to rule on any such hypothetical, it is at least clear that our estimate of the progressive character of the group's position will be irrelevant to the First Amendment analysis if such a case comes to us for decision.

FOR FURTHER READING

Cleary, Edward J. *Beyond the Burning Cross*. New York: Random House, 1994.

Curtis, Michael Kent. *Free Speech, "The People's Darling Privilege."* Durham, N.C.: Duke University Press, 2000.

Emerson, Thomas. *The System of Free Expression*. New York: Random House, 1970.

Fish, Stanley. *There's No Such Thing as Free Speech*. New York: Oxford University Press, 1994.

Goldstein, Robert Justin. *Saving Old Glory: The History of the American Flag Desecration Controversy*. Boulder, Colo.: Westview Press, 1996.

Graber, Mark A. *Transforming Free Speech: The Ambiguous Legacy of Civil Libertarianism*. Berkeley: University of California Press, 1991.

Greenawalt, Kent. *Fighting Words: Individuals, Communities, and Liberties of Speech*. Princeton, N.J.: Princeton University Press, 1995.

Gutmann, Amy. *Freedom of Association*. Princeton, N.J.: Princeton University Press, 1998.

Jacobs, James, and Kimberly Potter. *Hate Crimes: Criminal Law and Identity Politics*. New York: Oxford University Press, 1998.

Johnson, John W. *The Struggle for Student Rights: Tinker v. Des Moines and the 1960s*. Lawrence: University Press of Kansas, 1997.

Kalven, Harry, Jr. *A Worthy Tradition*. New York: Harper & Row, 1988.

O'Neill, Robert M. *Free Speech in the College Community*. Bloomington: Indiana University Press, 1997.

Papke, Daniel. *The Pullman Case: The Clash of Labor and Capital in Industrial America*. Lawrence: University Press of Kansas, 1999.

Smolla, Rodney A. *Free Speech in an Open Society*. New York: Alfred A. Knopf, 1992.

Strossen, Nadine. *Defending Pornography*. New York: Scribner's, 1995.

Strum, Philippa. *When the Nazis Came to Skokie: Freedom for Speech We Hate*. Lawrence: University Press of Kansas, 1999.

Sunstein, Cass R. *Democracy and the Problem of Free Speech*. New York: Free Press, 1995.

Freedom of the Press

If everything had gone according to plan, subscribers to the *Progressive* magazine would have opened their mailboxes in March 1979 to see freelance writer Howard Morland's article: "The H-Bomb Secret: How We Got It, Why We're Telling It." For quite some time, the *Progressive*'s editors had wanted to publish an article that challenged what they viewed as the American government's unnecessary obsession with secrecy. What better way to shatter the myth that secrecy served national security than by publishing an article explaining in terms understandable to anyone the basics of how to design a thermonuclear weapon? Morland himself had no scientific training, and knew only as much about nuclear weapons as he had learned while writing his article. By reading some decent, high school–level physics textbooks and unclassified government documents, interviewing Department of Energy employees, and visiting nuclear production facilities open to the public, Morland demonstrated that, with a little effort, anyone could pierce the veil of secrecy surrounding atomic weapons.[1]

Morland submitted the first draft of his article in January 1979. *Progressive* editors sent copies of the article to several nuclear experts for comments on its accuracy. Without telling the magazine, one recipient of Moorland's article forwarded a copy to the Department of Energy. Within days, the federal government ordered the *Progressive* to kill Morland's article. The editors refused to back down, claiming that a fundamental principle involving "what kind of information was being withheld that might help people formulate informed judgments on such vital questions as environmental risks, occupational health and safety threats, nuclear proliferation and the continuing arms race, and the astronomical costs of the nuclear weapons program" was at stake in the article's publication. Not surprisingly, the government viewed Morland's article as a threat to national security, and took the *Progressive* to federal court to block its publication.

In court, the government offered several witnesses to support its position that Morland's article posed a "grave threat to the peace and security of the world." The secretaries of defense, state, and energy under President Jimmy Carter stated without reservation that if the *Progressive* were allowed to publish the article many people who had no business having thermonuclear weapons would have easy access to them. Erwin Knoll, the *Progressive*'s editor-in-chief, responded that, by publishing Morland's article, the magazine was taking steps to enhance American national security. Said Knoll: "I am totally convinced that publication of the article will be of substantial benefit to the United States because it will demonstrate that this country's security does not lie in an oppressive and ineffective system of secrecy and classification but in open, honest, and informed public debate about issues which the people must decide."

Judge Robert Warren agreed with the government's position, and issued an injunction preventing the *Progressive* from publishing its April edition containing Morland's article. Conceding that Patrick Henry had a point when he said, "Give me liberty or give me death," Judge Warren nonetheless concluded that, in the short run anyway, "one cannot enjoy freedom of speech, freedom to worship or freedom of the press unless one first enjoys the freedom to live." The judge agreed with the *Progressive* that Morland's article was not a "do-it-yourself" guide to building an atomic weapon, as the government had argued. But Warren was convinced that Morland's article could provide an unnecessary assist to a smaller nation in search of a thermonuclear device. And such a weapon in the hands of the enemies of America and its allies could spell unthinkable disaster. "Faced with a stark choice between upholding the right to continued life and the right to freedom of the press," wrote Warren, "most jurists would have no difficulty in opting for the chance to continue to breathe and function as they work to achieve perfect freedom of expression."

Shortly after the *Progressive* appealed Judge Warren's decision to the Seventh Circuit Court of Appeals, a San Francisco computer programmer named Charles Hansen wrote a letter to Illinois senator Charles Percy containing virtually all of the same material as Morland's article. Hansen sent copies of his letter to two college newspapers, the Berkeley, California–based *Daily Californian* and the *Madison Press Connection,* in Madison, Wisconsin. The Department of Justice successfully persuaded a federal district court in San Francisco to issue a temporary restraining order halting the *Daily Californian* from publishing Hansen's letter to Percy. But the *Madison Press Connection* distributed eight thousand copies of Hansen's letter before the government could obtain an injunction. By then, the Justice Department gave up, recognizing that it could not prevent every newspaper in the country that wanted to print Hansen's letter from doing so. The government asked the courts hearing the *Progressive's* case and considering the injunction against Hansen in California to vacate the appeal, since the letter had already gone public, making requests for any further prior restraints pointless. Judge Warren's ruling against the *Progressive,* however, remains good law.

Imagine if Howard Morland's article had landed on the desks of the *Progressive's* editors today. How long would it take for the magazine to post the piece on its Web site? Could the government obtain an injunction barring its publication before the article circulated to the public? Even if a government employee intercepted a copy of the article as it was being checked for accuracy by nuclear experts, has technological innovation rendered obsolete the 1979 confrontation between the *Progressive* and the U.S. government? How have the Internet, cellular technology, and high-speed fiber-optic cable networks linking millions of computer users worldwide in real time changed the relationship between the news media and the government? Does the absolute language of the Press Clause preclude any government regulation of the news media? May the news media release any material they want, or must information entering the public domain be true?

Other important questions confront the freedom of press guarantee beyond the matter of prior restraint. May reporters, writers, or news organizations be held accountable for defaming their subjects? What happens when freedom of the press conflicts with other important constitutional rights, such as the right to a fair trial? In both cases, the Court must often decide whether the First Amendment provides the news media with special privileges that ordinary citizen-speakers generally do not possess.

Freedom of the Press in the Minds of the Framers

The notion that colonial America was a bastion of freedom where anyone could voice an opinion on anything or practice religion free from government persecution or community antagonism is, as historian Leonard Levy has commented, "a sentimental hallucination that ignores history."[2] Each settlement tended to harbor orthodox views on religion, politics, and just about any other matter of social significance. Dissenters were not tolerated; indeed, their expulsion from communities where their opinions were considered heretical or dangerous was quite common. To the extent that colonial America welcomed the diversity of religious and political opinion, it did so in "closed enclaves . . . where one could generally settle with his co-believers in safety and comfort and exercise the right of oppression."[3]

The legal instrument used to enforce the conformity of opinion was the law of *seditious libel,* which had been adopted from the English common law tradition. Sedition laws in the colonies punished persons for publishing or writing material that was considered dangerous, offensive, or otherwise improper. These prohibitions were so broad that just about any undesirable opinion could fall within their limitations. By the early 1700s, the American colonies had lifted nearly all prior restraints on the press, a development that followed the decision of the British Parliament in 1694 not to renew its system of requiring publishers to obtain a government license to operate. The licensing system in England allowed government officials to control the content of material that circulated to the public, thus making the free exchange of opinion or criticism of the government impossible. Indeed, John Milton's *Areopagitica—A Speech for the Liberty of Unlicensed Printing,* published in 1644 and considered one the great defenses of modern free speech principles, emerged out of the long and bitter battle between writers, editors, publishers, and the British government.

But Milton never questioned the right of the government to punish anyone who published material that was considered libelous, nor did most opponents of prior restraint in seventeenth- and eighteenth-century England and colonial America. And since seditious libel was a common law crime, the power rested with judges to define the alleged offense, giving the state a powerful weapon with which to intimidate potential dissidents. Prior to the American Revolution, the judiciary in America was no friend to those who dared to challenge prevailing opinion. Juries were generally not permitted to consider anything other than whether or not the accused had published the material in question. Truth served as no defense, since the harm prohibited by seditious libel laws was simply whether someone had their feelings hurt or their self-esteem lowered by the offending matter.[4]

An early signal that freedom of the press in America might take a different turn from its British common law origins came in 1735, when John Peter Zenger, who published the *New York Weekly Journal,* was acquitted of seditious libel against William Cosby, the royal governor of New York. The *Weekly Journal* published editorials mercilessly critical of the Cosby administration, leading the governor to burn four copies of the paper before a crowd in a New York City town square. Soon, Zenger was arrested and charged with seditious libel. Since the only question before the jury was whether Zenger was "guilty" of publishing the articles critical of Cosby, most observers assumed the verdict was a foregone conclusion. But what most people did not know was that Zenger's supporters had secured the services of Andrew Hamilton, the most famous trial lawyer in the American colonies. His presence elicited "oohs" and "ahhs" from the audience in attendance at Zenger's trial. Hamilton never contested whether Zenger published the material in question, relying solely on his summation to persuade the jury that "truth" should be considered a legitimate defense in libel trials. Said Hamilton:

> Men who injure and oppress the people under their administration provoke them to cry out and complain; and then make that very complaint the foundation for new oppressions and prosecutions. . . . Gentlemen of the jury, . . . it is not the cause of a poor printer, nor of New York alone, which you are now trying. No! It may in its consequences affect every freeman that lives under a British government on the main of America. It is the best cause. It is the cause of liberty; and I make no doubt but your upright conduct this day will not only entitle you to the love and esteem of your fellow citizens, but every man who prefers freedom to a life of slavery will bless you and honor you, as men who have baffled the attempt of tyranny.[5]

Zenger was acquitted, and word soon spread throughout the colonies that a jury had refused to convict a publisher for libel based on "truth" as a defense. Libertarians on both sides of the Atlantic viewed Zenger's acquittal as a great leap forward in securing more comprehensive protection for press freedom and political discourse. Nevertheless, the *Zenger* case, while arousing public opinion to the dubious nature of seditious libel laws, had no appreciable impact on freedom of the press in New York or anywhere else. Newspapers continued to criticize the British government and their colonial rulers in the colonies at their peril. The law of seditious libel remained intact, and, by the Revolution, the *Zenger* case had become a distant memory from another era. Not even the most passionate advocates of freedom of expression questioned the power of government to punish seditious speech.[6] In drafting the Virginia constitution in 1776, Thomas Jefferson wrote that freedom of religion "shall not be held to justify any seditious preaching or conversation against the authority of the civil government." Jefferson later drafted a treason law punishing anyone who "by any word" or deed defended the cause of Great Britain. Upon ratification of the First Amendment, the United States continued to embrace the British common law definition of freedom of the press offered by Sir William Blackstone, the great British legal scholar whose *Commentaries on the Laws of England* (1765–1769) were enormously influential among American judges and lawyers:

> Where blasphemous, immoral, treasonable . . . seditious or scandalous libels are punished by the English law . . . the liberty of the press, properly understood, is by no means infringed or violated. The liberty of the press is indeed essential to the nature of a free state; but this consists in laying no previous restraints upon publications, and not in freedom from censure from criminal matter when published. Every freeman has an undoubted right to lay what sentiments he pleases before the public: to forbid this is to destroy the freedom of the press: but if he publishes what is improper, mischievous or illegal, he must take the consequences of his own temerity. . . . To punish (as the law does at present) any dangerous or offensive writings, which, when published, shall on a fair and impartial trial be adjudged of a pernicious tendency, is necessary for the preservation of peace and good order, a government and religion, the only solid foundations of civil liberty.[7]

Unfortunately for libel defendants, Blackstone believed that judges, not juries, should decide sedition charges, and truth was not considered an admissible defense.[8] Free press libertarians continued to argue that the courts, by heeding to Blackstone's common law standard, were blind to what, in modern terms, might be described as the Catch-22 of libel law: the greater the truth, the greater the libel. The very purpose of a free press was to allow writers to publish what the government did not want the public to hear. But, by denying truth as a defense and permitting only judges to determine guilt or innocence, state sedition laws discouraged newspapers and pamphleteers from circulating material critical of the government.

James Madison, the primary architect of the First Amendment, saw no contradiction between the absolute language of the free press guarantee and the Blackstonian principles that guided its understanding. During the ratification debates over the Constitution and the Bill of Rights that took place between 1787 and 1791, Madison offered no dissent to suggestions by prominent Federalists and Anti-Federalists that absolute restrictions on government power to interfere with press freedoms were undesirable. By 1791, the Press Clause had come to mean that Congress was barred from passing any law placing a prior restraint on the right of the press to publish. But this prohibition was understood as jurisdictional and not substantive in nature. In other words, the First Amendment established no substantive guarantees on behalf of free speech, press, religion, or association. Responsibility for determining the scope of what we now consider our First Amendment freedoms remained with the states, which were now guaranteed protection from federal interference.[9]

In 1798, Congress enacted the Sedition Act, a measure that was designed to intimidate opponents of the Federalist majorities in the House and Senate and Federalist President John Adams. The law authorized the federal government to prosecute anyone who uttered or published any "false, scandalous, and malicious" statements against the government. The Sedition Act was passed in conjunction with the Alien Act, which authorized the president to deport "all such aliens as he shall judge dangerous to the peace and safety of the United States." Both laws were intended as pure punishment against the Jeffersonian Republicans, who had supported the French Revolution much to the consternation of such fierce Federalist partisans as Alexander Hamilton and John Adams. After the Federalists swept the 1798 congressional elections, they immediately sought to punish Jefferson's French allies through the Alien Act and silence their domestic critics with the Sedition Act.

Political scientist Peter Irons has commented that the Sedition Act sent Federalist prosecutors on "a witch-hunt that rivaled those of colonial Salem and the more recent McCarthy era."[10] Between 1798 and 1800, when the Sedition Act expired, over two dozen Republicans and other Federalist opponents were prosecuted for seditious libel, about half of whom were jailed. A Vermont congressman was convicted under the Sedition Act for writing a constituent that Adams had an "unbounded thirst for ridiculous pomp, foolish adulation and selfish avarice." A Pennsylvania militia captain was tried for treason for leading an armed revolt against federal tax collectors. By the presidential election of 1800, the American public had seen enough of the Sedition Act's consequences and turned Adams out of office, replacing him with Thomas Jefferson. Republicans won majorities in both houses of Congress as well.

The harrowing experience of the Sedition Act persuaded libertarians such as Madison and Jefferson to abandon Blackstone's definition of freedom of the press and argue for the right to publish without fear of retribution. Madison, in particular, rejected the British common law model as one "that can never be admitted to be the American idea of [freedom of the press]" because the threat of criminal punishment for "seditious" speech carried the same effect as a rule of prior restraint. Wrote Madison: "It would seem a mockery to say that no laws shall be passed preventing publications from being made but that laws might be passed for punishing them in case they should be made."[11] By the early 1800s, First Amendment libertarians had constructed the foundation of what is now the familiar but then truly novel idea of a free press. And that, in the words of George Hay, a prominent Republican critic of the Sedition Act, meant that anyone should have the "sanctuary of the press . . . even if he condemns the principle of republican institutions."[12]

Libertarian theory was slow to catch up with American law on seditious libel. Many states left their libel laws in place even after the Sedition Act expired. Congress, well into the twentieth century, continued to enact laws prohibiting the advocacy of "disloyal," "abusive," and "contemptuous" ideas that threatened the integrity of the United States government. These laws, as discussed in Chapter 4, were primarily an outgrowth of perceived national emergencies and wartime crises, and were directed toward the sorts of "injurious acts" that free press libertarians believed were permissible exceptions to the scope of protected expression under the First Amendment. Still, freedom of the press flourished after the expiration of the Sedition Act as never before, with newspapers, cartoonists, and pamphleteers assuming an increasingly aggressive edge throughout the nineteenth century and into the early twentieth century. Federal and state prosecutors were increasingly reluctant to enforce seditious libel laws, knowing that juries were unlikely to return guilty verdicts against individuals charged with criticizing the government.[13] After the Sedition Act, Congress never again passed a law making *general* criticism of the government a crime. This gradual merging of libertarian theory and law did not mean, however, that a firm constitutional standard existed defining freedom of the press. The U.S. Supreme Court did not rule on either the First Amendment's limits on prior restraint until the 1930s, or the protection afforded to the news media to criticize private citizens and public officials without fear of retribution until the 1960s.

Prior Restraint: Censorship or Public Interest?

Prior restraint is not a concept unique to the rights of the news media or the crusading freelance reporter to publish controversial material. In *Schenck* v. *United States* (1919), *Abrams* v. *United States* (1919), and *Debs* v. *United States* (1919) (see Chapter 4), the Court upheld the convictions of individuals accused of violating the federal Espionage Act of 1917, which prohibited anyone from interfering with or conspiring to disrupt the military draft after America's entrance into World War I. The Court, in *Schaefer* v. *United States* (1920), also upheld the constitutionality of the Sedition Act of 1918, which made it illegal to say or publish anything intended to cause contempt and scorn for the United States, interfere with defense production, or advocate any such conduct. By authorizing prior restraints on political speech considered threatening to the government's national security interests, the Court left uncertain the constitutional status of the Sedition Act of 1798. The Court did not, in the World War I cases, confront the 1798 law, focusing instead on the obstruction of the draft and the war effort. Justices Holmes and Brandeis's decision to back away from prior restraints after *Schenck* was based in part on their assumption that Congress's unwillingness to enact a law as general as the one of 1798 meant that the original sedition law and any subsequent ones placing prior restraints on speech and press were unconstitutional.[14]

In *Near* v. *Minnesota* (1931), the Court confronted its first major opportunity to rule upon the constitutionality of a prior restraint outside the context of national security. In addition to writing the no prior restraint rule into American constitutional law for the first time, the Court held that states were bound by the Due Process Clause of the Fourteenth Amendment to respect the emerging guarantees of the Press Clause. In *Gitlow* v. *New York* (see Chapter 3), the Court upheld the conviction of socialist Benjamin Gitlow under a state sedition law, ruling that he had no First Amendment right to distribute approximately 16,000 copies of his "Left Wing Manifesto." The Court agreed with Gitlow's contention that the First Amendment protected the free speech and press rights of individuals from state law, but did not find that his cause was among those that deserved such protection. In *Near,* note that Chief Justice Hughes makes sure to emphasize that the right to publish does not release the press from criminal and civil responsibility for libel. Blackstone's shadow continued to lurk over the First Amendment for another thirty years, until the Court announced its historic decision in *New York Times v. Sullivan* (1964), effectively immunizing the press from libel lawsuits by public officials.

Near v. Minnesota

283 U.S. 697 (1931)

During the early 1900s, Minneapolis was considered a wide-open town brimming with gambling joints, slot machines, and houses of prostitution. If you could not buy off the mayor or the cops, you could not enter the liquor and gambling rackets. With such activity rampant, the payoffs were obvious to everyone—including the newspapers, respectable and otherwise, of Minneapolis and its sister city across the Mississippi River, St. Paul.[15]

By the mid-1920s, the cozy group of gangsters, politicians, and cops that ran the Twin Cities of Minneapolis and St. Paul had enough of one newspaper in particular, the *Saturday Press.* The *Press* was sensationalistic, crude, openly anti-Semitic, anti-Catholic, anti-organized labor, anti–African American, and, to the city establishment's great annoyance, mercilessly critical of its corrupt ways. In 1925, the Minnesota legislature passed a public nuisance law designed to silence the critics of politicians everywhere. The law made any person guilty of a nuisance who "engaged in the business of regularly or customarily producing, publishing or circulating, having in possession, selling or giving away, (a) an obscene, lewd and lascivious newspaper, magazine, or other periodical, or (b) a malicious, scandalous and defamatory newspaper." Jay Near, the editor of the *Saturday Press,* was prosecuted and later convicted under the state nuisance law. His appeals in state courts failed, and his newspaper was shut down. Just as it appeared that Near was headed for jail, media magnate Robert McCormick, owner of the *Chicago Tribune,* who shared the Minneapolis newspaperman's affection for liberals, Jews, blacks and so on, agreed to take up his case. For more on the litigation history of *Near,* see the accompanying SIDEBAR.

The Court's decision was 5 to 4. Chief Justice Hughes delivered the opinion of the Court. Justice Pierce Butler dissented, and was joined by Justices Van Devanter, McReynolds, and Sutherland.

MR. CHIEF JUSTICE HUGHES delivered the opinion of the Court.

This statute, for the suppression as a public nuisance of a newspaper or periodical, is unusual, if not unique, and raises questions of grave importance transcending the local interests involved in the particular action. It is no longer open to doubt that the liberty of the press, and of speech, is within the liberty safeguarded by the due process clause of the Fourteenth Amendment from invasion by state action. It was found impossible to conclude that this essential personal liberty of the citizen was left unprotected by the general guaranty of fundamental rights of person and property. In maintaining this guaranty, the authority of the State to enact laws to promote the health, safety, morals and general welfare of its people is necessarily admitted. The limits of this sovereign power must always be determined with appropriate regard to the particular subject of its exercise. Thus, while recognizing the broad discretion of the legislature in fixing rates to be charged by those undertaking a public service, this Court has decided that the owner cannot constitutionally be deprived of his right to a fair return, because that is deemed to be of the essence of ownership. So, while liberty of contract is not an absolute right, and the wide field of activity in the making of contracts is subject to legislative supervision, this Court has held that the power of the State stops short of interference with what are deemed to be certain indispensable requirements of the liberty assured, notably with respect to the fixing of prices and wages. Liberty of speech, and of the press, is also not an absolute right, and the State may punish its abuse. Liberty, in each of its phases, has its history and connotation, and, in the present instance, the inquiry is as to the historic conception of the liberty of the press and whether the statute under review violates the essential attributes of that liberty. . . .

First. The statute is not aimed at the redress of individual or private wrongs. Remedies for libel remain available and unaffected. The statute, said the state court, "is not directed at threatened libel, but at an existing business which, generally speaking, involves more than libel." It is aimed at the distribution of scandalous matter as "detrimental to public morals and to the general welfare," tending "to disturb the peace of the community" and "to provoke assaults and the commission of crime." In order to obtain an injunction to suppress the future publication of the newspaper or periodical, it is not necessary to prove the falsity of the charges that have been made in the publication condemned. In the present action, there was no allegation that the matter published was not true. It is alleged, and the statute requires the allegation, that the publication was "malicious." But, as in prosecutions for libel, there is no requirement of proof by the State of malice in fact, as distinguished from malice inferred from the mere publication of the defamatory matter. The judgment in this case proceeded upon the mere proof of publication. The statute permits the defense not of the truth alone, but only that the truth was published with good motives and for justifiable ends. It is apparent that, under the statute, the publication is to be regarded as defamatory if it injures reputation, and that it is scandalous if it circulates charges of reprehensible conduct, whether criminal or otherwise, and the publication is thus deemed to invite public reprobation and to constitute a public scandal. . . .

Second. The statute is directed not simply at the circulation of scandalous and defamatory statements with regard to private citizens, but at the continued publication by newspapers and periodicals of charges against public officers of corruption, malfeasance in office, or serious neglect of duty. Such charges, by their very nature, create a public scandal. They are scandalous and defamatory within the meaning of the statute, which has its normal operation in relation to publications dealing prominently and chiefly with the alleged derelictions of public officers.

Third. The object of the statute is not punishment, in the ordinary sense, but suppression of the offending newspaper or periodical. The reason for the enactment, as the state court has said, is that prosecutions to enforce penal statutes for libel do not result in "efficient repression or suppression of the evils of scandal." Describing the business of publication as a public nuisance does not obscure the substance of the proceeding which the statute authorizes. It is the continued publication of scandalous and defamatory matter that constitutes the business and the declared nuisance. In the case of public officers, it is the reiteration of charges of official misconduct, and the fact that the newspaper or periodical is principally devoted to that purpose, that exposes it to suppression. . . .

This suppression is accomplished by enjoining publication, and that restraint is the object and effect of the statute.

Fourth. The statute not only operates to suppress the offending newspaper or periodical, but to put the publisher under an effective censorship. When a newspaper or periodical is found to be "malicious, scandalous, and defamatory," and is suppressed as such, resumption of publication is punishable as a contempt of court by fine or imprisonment. Thus, where a newspaper or periodical has been suppressed because of the circulation of charges against public officers of official misconduct, it would seem to be clear that the renewal of the publication of such charges would constitute a contempt, and that the judgment would lay a permanent restraint upon the publisher, to escape which he must satisfy the court as to the character of a new publication. . . .

If we cut through mere details of procedure, the operation and effect of the statute, in substance, is that public authorities may bring the owner or publisher of a newspaper or periodical before a judge upon a charge of conducting a business of publishing scandalous and defamatory matter—in particular, that the matter consists of charges against public officers of official dereliction—and, unless the owner or publisher is able and disposed to bring competent evidence to satisfy the judge that the charges are true and are published with good motives and for justifiable ends, his newspaper or periodical is suppressed and further publication is made punishable as a contempt. This is of the essence of censorship.

The question is whether a statute authorizing such proceedings in restraint of publication is consistent with the conception of the liberty of the press as historically conceived and guaranteed. In determining the extent of the constitutional protection, it has been generally, if not universally, considered that it is the chief purpose of the guaranty to prevent previous restraints upon publication. . . .

But it is recognized that punishment for the abuse of the liberty accorded to the press is essential to the protection of the public, and that the common law rules that subject the libeler to responsibility for the public offense, as well as for the private injury, are not abolished by the protection extended in our constitutions. The law of criminal libel rests upon that secure foundation. There is also the conceded authority of courts to punish for contempt when publications directly tend to prevent the proper discharge of judicial functions. In the present case, we have no occasion to inquire as to the permissible scope of subsequent

SIDEBAR

NEAR V. MINNESOTA

"The Paper That Refused to Stay Gagged"

Back in Northampton, Massachusetts, Howard Guilford was known as a con man of the first rank. He specialized in winning the friendships of the politicians and public figures who sometimes operated outside the law. Then Guilford would threaten to expose their unsavory dealings to the public unless he was paid a handsome sum. And usually they paid. Jay Near had gotten his start in Fort Atkinson, Iowa, where he built a reputation as a journalistic scavenger, preying on the sins and seamy sides of famous people and publishing them without fear or favor. Around the same time, Guilford and Near each independently decided to broaden the market for their outrageous brand of journalism. In the early 1910s, each man set his sights on Minneapolis.

By 1916, Guilford and Near had found each other. Guilford published the *Twin City Reporter,* which specialized in reporting on the sexual escapades and alleged corruption of St. Paul and Minneapolis's economic and political elite. Near came to work for Guilford in 1916, and the two quickly became soul mates. Headlines such as "Smooth Minneapolis Doctor with Woman in St. Paul Hotel" graced the front pages of the *Twin City Reporter* on a regular basis. Racial and religious minorities were described in such pejorative terms as "yids," "bohunks," and "spades." Guilford and Near even identified the Salvation Army as a corrupt and dangerous institution. But their favorite targets were politicians and prominent businessmen. They had no trouble finding out what famous person had been caught in a compromising position by regularly slipping local police cash under the table to dish the dirt. By 1917, Guilford and Near had tired of the *Reporter*. Guilford sold his interest in the paper and Near moved to California.

Ten years later, Guilford, out of the newspaper business and unable to earn a decent living, and Near, back from California, ran into each other on a Minneapolis street. Near suggested to Guilford that they renew their partnership and publish a weekly newspaper, but this time under one condition: no sex, just corruption. With no shortage of corruption, Guilford agreed and, in September 1927, the *Saturday Weekly Press* was born. After the police learned that the *Press* was about to publish a story about police protection for a local gambling and prostitution house, organized crime figures ordered Guilford and Near killed. The *Press* decided not to publish that story, but it did report the threat on their lives. The next day, Guilford was shot, but recovered to write the following story: "I headed into the city on September 26, ran across three Jews in a Chevrolet; stopped a lot of lead and won a bed for myself in St. Barnabas Hospital for six weeks. Wherefore, I have withdrawn all allegiance to anything with a hook nose that eats herring."

The *Press* published an article laced with anti-Semitic broadsides about the police's unwillingness to respond to the threat of an allegedly Jewish organized crime figure, Mose Barnett, against the owner of a small dry-cleaning business, who was also Jewish. Despite the irony of defending a Jewish businessman from an alleged Jewish gangster, Minneapolis district attorney Floyd B. Olson decided to prosecute Jay Near under the state's public nuisance law. A county judge agreed that the *Press* was a public nuisance, and issued a temporary restraining order shutting down the paper. The Minnesota Supreme Court affirmed.

Down and desperate, Near contacted the American Civil Liberties Union (ACLU), which had been founded by Roger Baldwin in 1920 to defend political dissidents and other unpopular speakers. By now, Guilford had bailed out, tired of the constant run-ins with authorities. Baldwin, without knowing much about Near, decided to commit $150 to defend the *Press*. The ACLU released the following statement describing the consequences of the Minneapolis law: "Heretofore the only control of the press has been by prosecution for criminal or libelous matter after the offense. We see in this new device for previous restraint of publication a menace to the whole principle of freedom of the press." Despite Baldwin's support, Near appealed to other potential supporters. When *Chicago Tribune* publisher Robert Rutherford McCormick weighed in with an offer to support Near, the Minneapolis newspaperman jumped for joy. "The Colonel," as McCormick was also known—he sometimes paraded through the *Tribune* newsroom in full military regalia—shared Near's politics. "If the Ku Klux Klan had a brief life in Illinois, it undoubtedly prospered while it lived because of the *Tribune*'s aid," said Oswald Villard, the editor and publisher of the liberal magazine the *Nation*. McCormick threw his money behind Near's case, convinced that the *Saturday Press* had some literary merit. Besides, McCormick believed Near's charges against Mose Barnett.

McCormick's lawyers soon replaced the ACLU, whose sympathies for Communists, radicals, and other "sordid" characters were not to Near's taste. They argued Near's case in the subsequent hearing to decide whether to lift the temporary restraining order against the *Saturday Press*. Near soon figured out that McCormick's attorneys were angling for an appeal to the U.S. Supreme Court, a strategy that did not sit well with him. He wanted his newspaper back in print as soon as possible and had no interest in high-minded constitutional questions. But Weymouth Kirkland, the lead attorney now representing Near, knew that the key to this case was to persuade the Court that prior restraint held out a much more dangerous precedent that permitting newspapers like the *Saturday Press* to publish scandalous material. Kirkland argued that any potential punishment should come *afterward*, not beforehand. "So long as men do evil," Kirkland told the justices during oral argument, "so long will newspapers publish defamation."

After the Court struck down the public nuisance law, Jay Near's name as the smalltime scandal sheet monger who heralded a new era for freedom of the press appeared nowhere in the national news media. A year after the Court's decision, Near, with Guilford back on board, had the *Saturday Press* up and running, with the caption "The Paper That Refused to Stay Gagged" appearing on the front page. In September 1934, reputed gangsters shot Guilford in broad daylight in an exclusive section of Minneapolis. By this time, Guilford and Near had parted ways again. Still, Near had a soft spot for his former partner, commenting, "Howard was undoubtedly killed by assassins, and I think the killers were hired by communists." Two years after Guilford's murder, Near died of natural causes in a Minneapolis hospital. Neither man merited much attention in the obituary columns of the local papers, but the legacy of Guilford and Near lives on in newsrooms and publishing houses everywhere.

Reference

Friendly, Fred W. *Minnesota Rag: The Dramatic Story of the Landmark Supreme Court Case That Gave New Meaning to Freedom of the Press*. New York: Random House, 1981.

punishment. For whatever wrong the appellant has committed or may commit by his publications the State appropriately affords both public and private redress by its libel laws. As has been noted, the statute in question does not deal with punishments; it provides for no punishment, except in case of contempt for violation of the court's order, but for suppression and injunction, that is, for restraint upon publication.

The objection has also been made that the principle as to immunity from previous restraint is stated too broadly, if every such restraint is deemed to be prohibited. That is undoubtedly true; the protection even as to previous restraint is not absolutely unlimited. But the limitation has been recognized only in exceptional cases: "When a nation is at war, many things that might be said in time of peace are such a hindrance to its effort that their utterance will not be endured so long as men fight, and that no Court could regard them as protected by any constitutional right," *Schenck* v. *United States* (1919). No one would question but that a government might prevent actual obstruction to its recruiting service or the publication of the sailing dates of transports or the number and location of troops. On similar grounds, the primary requirements of decency may be enforced against obscene publications. The security of the community life may be protected against incitements to acts of violence and the overthrow by force of orderly government. . . . These limitations are not applicable here. . . .

The fact that, for approximately one hundred and fifty years, there has been almost an entire absence of attempts to impose previous restraints upon publications relating to the malfeasance of public officers is significant of the deep-seated conviction that such restraints would violate constitutional right. Public officers, whose character and conduct remain open to debate and free discussion in the press, find their remedies for false accusations in actions under libel laws providing for redress and punishment, and not in proceedings to restrain the publication of newspapers and periodicals. The general principle that the constitutional guaranty of the liberty of the press gives immunity from previous restraints has been approved in many decisions under the provisions of state constitutions.

The importance of this immunity has not lessened. While reckless assaults upon public men, and efforts to bring obloquy upon those who are endeavoring faithfully to discharge official duties, exert a baleful influence and deserve the severest condemnation in public opinion, it cannot be said that this abuse is greater, and it is believed to be less, than that which characterized the period in which our institutions took shape. Meanwhile, the administration of government has become more complex, the opportunities for malfeasance and corruption have multiplied, crime has grown to most serious proportions, and the danger of its protection by unfaithful officials and of the impairment of the fundamental security of life and property by criminal alliances and official neglect, emphasizes the primary need of a vigilant and courageous press, especially in great cities. The fact that the liberty of the press may be abused by miscreant purveyors of scandal does not make any the less necessary the immunity of the press from previous restraint in dealing with official misconduct. Subsequent punishment for such abuses as may exist is the appropriate remedy consistent with constitutional privilege. . . .

Nor can it be said that the constitutional freedom from previous restraint is lost because charges are made of derelictions which constitute crimes. With the multiplying provisions of penal codes, and of municipal charters and ordinances carrying penal sanctions, the conduct of public officers is very largely within the purview of criminal statutes. The freedom of the press from previous restraint has never been regarded as limited to such animadversions as lay outside the range of penal enactments. Historically, there is no such limitation; it is inconsistent with the reason which underlies the privilege, as the privilege so limited would be of slight value for the purposes for which it came to be established.

The statute in question cannot be justified by reason of the fact that the publisher is permitted to show, before injunction issues, that the matter published is true and is published with good motives and for justifiable ends. If such a statute, authorizing suppression and injunction on such a basis, is constitutionally valid, it would be equally permissible for the legislature to provide that at any time the publisher of any newspaper could be brought before a court, or even an administrative officer (as the constitutional protection may not be regarded as resting on mere procedural details) and required to produce proof of the truth of his publication, or of what he intended to publish, and of his motives, or stand enjoined. If this can be done, the legislature may provide machinery for determining in the complete exercise of its discretion what are justifiable ends, and restrain publication accordingly. And it would be but a step to a complete system of censorship. . . .

Equally unavailing is the insistence that the statute is designed to prevent the circulation of scandal which tends to disturb the public peace and to provoke assaults and the commission of crime. Charges of reprehensible conduct, and in particular of official malfeasance, unquestionably create a public scandal, but the theory of the constitutional guaranty is that even a more serious public evil would be caused by authority to prevent publication. . . . There is nothing new in the fact that charges of reprehensible conduct may create resentment and the disposition to resort to violent means of redress, but this well understood tendency did not alter the determination to protect the press against censorship and restraint upon publication. . . . The danger of violent reactions becomes greater with effective organization of defiant groups resenting exposure, and if this consideration warranted legislative interference with the initial freedom of publication, the constitutional protection would be reduced to a mere form of words.

For these reasons we hold the statute . . . to be an infringement of the liberty of the press guaranteed by the Fourteenth Amendment. We should add that this decision rests upon the operation and effect of the statute, without regard to the question of the truth of the charges contained in the particular periodical. The fact that the public officers named in this case, and those associated with the charges of official dereliction, may be deemed to be impeccable cannot affect the conclusion that the statute imposes an unconstitutional restraint upon publication.

Judgment reversed.

MR. JUSTICE BUTLER, dissenting.

The Minnesota statute does not operate as a *previous* restraint on publication within the proper meaning of that phrase. It does not authorize administrative control in advance such as was formerly exercised by the licensers and censors but prescribes a remedy to be enforced by a suit in equity. In this case, there was previous publication made in the course of the business of regularly producing malicious, scandalous and defamatory periodicals. The business and publications unquestionably constitute an abuse of the right of free press. The statute denounces the things done as a nuisance on the ground, as stated by the state supreme court, that they threaten morals, peace and good order. There is no question of the power of the State to denounce such transgressions. The restraint authorized is only in respect of continuing to do what has been duly adjudged to constitute a nuisance. . . .

There is nothing in the statute purporting to prohibit publications that have not been adjudged to constitute a nuisance. It is fanciful to suggest similarity between the granting or enforcement of the decree authorized by this statute to prevent *further* publication of malicious, scandalous and defamatory articles and the *previous* restraint upon the press by licensers as referred to by Blackstone and described in the history of the times to which he alludes.

It is well known . . . that existing libel laws are inadequate effectively to suppress evils resulting from the kind of business and publications that are shown in this case. The doctrine that measures such as the one before us are invalid because they operate as previous restraints to infringe freedom of press exposes the peace and good order of every community and the business and private affairs of every individual to the constant and protracted false and malicious assaults of any insolvent publisher who may have purpose and sufficient capacity to contrive and put into effect a scheme or program for oppression, blackmail or extortion. The judgment should be affirmed.

▼▲▼

After *Near,* the Court struck down several types of laws imposing either direct or indirect prior restraints on the press. From the 1930s until the late 1960s, the Court ruled that state laws imposing taxes on newspapers were unconstitutional when their impact was to limit circulation; found local ordinances controlling or prohibiting outright the distribution of handbills and pamphlets an unconstitutional form of censorship; and made clear that the Press Clause, as much as the Free Exercise Clause, protected the rights of religious groups to distribute materials in public places.[16] These cases, however, did not require the Court to return to the constitutionality of prior restraints on information that possibly compromised national security, an exception that Chief Justices Hughes hinted in *Near* was permissible under the Press Clause. *New York Times Co.* v. *United States* (1971), a landmark decision affecting both executive power in times of crisis and the right of the news media to publish information the government wanted withheld, forced the Court to revisit when, if ever, national security justified a prior restraint.

The events setting *New York Times* in motion actually began in 1964, when President Johnson sought and received congressional authorization to increase American military involvement in Vietnam to warlike levels without asking for a formal declaration of war. The Gulf of Tonkin Resolution, which did not have the force of law, authorized the "President . . . to take all necessary steps, including the use of armed force, to assist any member or protocol state of the Southeast Asia Collective Defense Treaty requesting defense of its freedom." Antiwar activists brought suit on several occasions in the late 1960s and early 1970s asking the Court to declare the American presence in Vietnam unconstitutional because of the absence of a congressional war declaration. The Court refused to consider these requests on the grounds that the relationship between Congress and president in the conduct of war was a political question.[17]

By the late 1960s, domestic support for American involvement in Vietnam began to deteriorate. This was due in large part to the widening gap between what Americans were reading in their newspapers and seeing on the nightly television news and the government's continued insistence on the war's success. To restore public confidence in the war effort, Secretary of Defense Robert McNamara commissioned the Rand Corporation, a nongovernmental research organization, to collect top-secret government materials related to the war and to produce a comprehensive analysis of American involvement in Vietnam. McNamara had expressed his own private doubts about the war; he believed, however, that the report would vindicate the government's position. But the forty-seven-volume report, referred to by government officials as the Pentagon Papers, proved so critical of America's war effort that plans for its eventual public release were immediately cancelled.

The Pentagon Papers, in the words of Pulitzer Prize–winning journalist Sanford J. Ungar, "illustrated the Orwellian vocabulary of Vietnam policymaking, a bizarre combination of frontier talk and show business jargon" used to discuss the business of war. Such language troubled several members of the Vietnam History Task Force, created by McNamara without the knowledge of President Johnson, to study further America's worsening position in the war. Said one member: "To talk about the use of bombing as if it were an orchestral score—you know, heavy on the brass, a bit of tympani, and that sort of thing—when you're talking about the use of napalm and high explosives and terrible devices . . . was very dangerous."[18]

Only fifteen copies of the Pentagon Papers were distributed to McNamara and other high-level officials involved with the Vietnam War. Embarrassed by their contents, Pentagon officials gave the Pentagon Papers a "top-secret-sensitive" classification to ensure that no one within the government would have access to make them public. This strategy enabled the Pentagon Papers to remain secret for almost four years. But in March 1971, after months of careful negotiation, Daniel Ellsberg, one of the lead authors on the project, agreed to provide copies of the Papers to a *New York Times* reporter who once served as the paper's Vietnam correspondent. After his work on the Pentagon Papers, Ellsberg's opposition to America's involvement in the war intensified to the point that he viewed his decision to release all but the final four volumes of the report as a way to help stop "the bombing and killing."[19]

The *New York Times,* after debating the legal and journalistic issues involved in publishing classified government materials, began running excerpts from the Pentagon Papers in June 1971. By this time, Ellsberg had also made copies of the Papers available to the *Washington Post.* Two days after the *New York Times* ran its first installment, the Nixon administration requested a federal court to enjoin both newspapers from publishing further excerpts. The lower court refused, but an appeals court granted President Nixon's request. On June 25, the Court agreed to hear the Pentagon Papers and set arguments for the next day. In the interim, the Court upheld the appeals court's decision to enjoin publication of the Pentagon Papers until it ruled on the case.

Within a week, the Court announced its historic ruling in *New York Times Co.* v. *United States,* holding that the president possessed no inherent power to order the prior restraint of the Pentagon Papers from publication by either the *New York Times* or the *Washington Post.*[20] So divided was the Court that the justices were left to issue an unsigned, *per curiam* opinion on behalf of the majority and issue individual concurring opinions. The Court's three dissenters wrote separate opinions as well. Only two justices, Black and Douglas, believed that such government-imposed restrictions were always unconstitutional. The remaining justices who signed the Court's opinion concluded that the president possessed the power to quash the dissemination of information whose publication could cause irreparable damage to national security. Congressional authorization and the individual merits of the government's claim, however, bolstered the constitutionality of such action.[21]

In dissent, Justice John Harlan suggested the Court had been "irresponsibly feverish in dealing" with the Pentagon Papers case. Does Harlan have a point? Suppose that Ellsberg had given the Pentagon Papers to a small, radical antiwar publication instead of two titans of the mainstream American news media, whose respective editors deliberated the propriety of publishing the papers for months before they finally went ahead. Do you believe the Court might have ruled in favor of the government?

New York Times Co. v. *United States*

403 U.S. 670 (1971)

The Pentagon Papers controversy was not the first time the *New York Times* had come into a direct conflict with the American government over the national security implications of publishing sensitive material.[22] In late March and early April 1961, Tad Szulc, a *Times* reporter, learned that the Central Intelligence Agency, with the full support of President John F. Kennedy, had been training Cuban exiles in Guatemala to invade Cuba and topple the revolutionary government of Fidel Castro. The exile army had been led to believe that they would receive the full backing of American land and sea forces when they landed at the Bay of Pigs in Cuba. Ultimately, the Kennedy administration refused to commit American forces and the invasion was a spectacular failure. Castro had learned of the invasion well in advance, and Cuban forces were waiting for the arrival of their former countrymen. The nearly twelve hundred exiles that made landing were captured and over one hundred were killed.

Between the time when Szulc told his editors at the *Times* about the Bay of Pigs operation and the actual invasion in mid-April, high-level officials in the Kennedy administration pressured *Times* editors not to publish the story. Separately, a *Washington Post* reporter had submitted a lengthy article on CIA activities involving the Cuban exile community to the *New Republic*, a then-liberal magazine. Gilbert Harrison, the editor of the *New Republic,* sent the piece to Arthur Schlesinger, a White House aide, to confirm its accuracy. After receiving the article, Schlesinger called Harrison immediately and asked him "on the highest authority of the government not to publish it." Neither the *Times* nor the *New Republic* ran their CIA stories. The Bay of Pigs, a disaster as much for the press as for the Kennedy administration, marked a turning point in the willingness of the news media to submit to future government requests to withhold information from the public on national security grounds. The Pentagon Papers crystallized the more adversarial relationship that soon emerged between the press and the government during the Vietnam War.

The Court's *per curiam* decision was 6 to 3. Justices Black, Douglas, Brennan, Stewart, White, and Marshall filed concurring opinions. Chief Justice Burger and Justices Harlan and Blackmun dissented.

PER CURIAM.

We granted certiorari in these cases in which the United States seeks to enjoin the New York Times and the Washington Post from publishing the contents of a classified study entitled "History of U.S. Decision-Making Process on Viet Nam Policy." [The Pentagon Papers]

"Any system of prior restraints of expression comes to this Court bearing a heavy presumption against its constitutional validity," *Bantam Books, Inc.* v. *Sullivan* (1963); *Near* v. *Minnesota* (1931). The Government "thus carries a heavy burden of showing justification for the imposition of such a restraint," *Organization for a Better Austin* v. *Keefe* (1971). The District Court for the Southern District of New York, in the *New York Times* case, and the District Court for the District of Columbia and the Court of Appeals for the District of Columbia Circuit, in the *Washington Post* case, held that the Government had not met that burden. We agree.

The judgment of the Court of Appeals for the District of Columbia Circuit is therefore affirmed. The order of the Court of Appeals for the Second Circuit is reversed, and the case is remanded with directions to enter a judgment affirming the judgment of the District Court for the Southern District of New York. The stays entered June 25, 1971, by the Court are vacated. The judgments shall issue forthwith.

So ordered.

MR. JUSTICE BLACK, with whom MR. JUSTICE DOUGLAS joins, concurring.

I adhere to the view that the Government's case against the *Washington Post* should have been dismissed, and that the injunction against the *New York Times* should have been vacated without oral argument when the cases were first presented to this Court. I believe that every moment's continuance of the injunctions against these newspapers amounts to a flagrant, indefensible, and continuing violation of the First Amendment. . . . In my view, it is unfortunate that some of my Brethren are apparently willing to hold that the publication of news may sometimes be enjoined. Such a holding would make a shambles of the First Amendment.

Our Government was launched in 1789 with the adoption of the Constitution. The Bill of Rights, including the First Amendment, followed in 1791. Now, for the first time in the 182 years since the founding of the Republic, the federal courts are asked to hold that the First Amendment does not mean what it says, but rather means that the Government can halt the publication of current news of vital importance to the people of this country.

In seeking injunctions against these newspapers, and in its presentation to the Court, the Executive Branch seems to have forgotten the essential purpose and history of the First Amendment. When the Constitution was adopted, many people strongly opposed it because the document contained no Bill of Rights to safeguard certain basic freedoms. They especially feared that the new powers granted to a central government might be interpreted to permit the government to curtail freedom of religion, press, assembly, and speech. In response to an overwhelming public clamor, James Madison offered a series of amendments to satisfy citizens that these great liberties would remain safe and beyond the power of government to abridge. Madison proposed what later became the First Amendment in three parts, two of which are set out below, and one of which proclaimed: "The people shall not be deprived or abridged of their right to speak, to write, or to publish their sentiments, *and the freedom of the press, as one of the great bulwarks of liberty, shall be inviolable.*" The amendments were offered to curtail and restrict the general powers granted to the Executive, Legislative, and Judicial Branches two years before in the original Constitution. The Bill of Rights changed the original Constitution into a new charter under which no branch of government could abridge the people's freedoms of press, speech, religion, and assembly. Yet the Solicitor General argues and some members of the Court appear to agree that the general powers of the Government adopted in the original Constitution should be interpreted to limit and restrict the specific and emphatic guarantees of the Bill of Rights adopted later. I can imagine no greater perversion of history. Madison and the other Framers of the First Amendment, able men that they were, wrote in language they earnestly believed could never be misunderstood: "Congress shall make no law . . . abridging the freedom . . . of the press. . . ." Both the history and language of the First Amendment support the view that the press must be left free to publish news, whatever the source, without censorship, injunctions, or prior restraints.

In the First Amendment, the Founding Fathers gave the free press the protection it must have to fulfill its essential role in our democracy. The press was to serve the governed, not the governors. The Government's power to censor the press was abolished so that the press would remain forever free to censure the Government. The press was protected so that it could bare the secrets of government and inform the people. Only a free and unrestrained press can effectively expose deception in government. And paramount among the responsibilities of a free press is the duty to prevent any part of the government from deceiving the people and sending them off to distant lands to die of foreign fevers and foreign shot and shell. In my view, far from deserving condemnation for their courageous reporting, the *New York Times*, the *Washington Post*, and other newspapers should be commended for serving the purpose that the Founding Fathers saw so clearly. In revealing the workings of government that led to the Vietnam war, the newspapers nobly did precisely that which the Founders hoped and trusted they would do. . . .

In other words, we are asked to hold that, despite the First Amendment's emphatic command, the Executive Branch, the Congress, and the Judiciary can make laws enjoining publication of current news and abridging freedom of the press in the name of "national security." The Government does not even attempt to rely on any act of Congress. Instead, it makes the bold and dangerously far-reaching contention that the courts should take it upon themselves to "make" a law abridging freedom of the press in the name of equity, presidential power and national security, even when the representatives of the people in Congress have adhered to the command of the First Amendment and refused to make such a law. To find that the President has "inherent power" to halt the publication of news by resort to the courts would wipe out the First Amendment and destroy the fundamental liberty and security of the very people the Government hopes to make "secure." No one can read the history of the adoption of the First Amendment without being convinced beyond any doubt that it was injunctions like those sought here that Madison and his collaborators intended to outlaw in this Nation for all time.

The word "security" is a broad, vague generality whose contours should not be invoked to abrogate the fundamental law embodied in the First Amendment. The guarding of military and diplomatic secrets at the expense of informed representative government provides no real security for our Republic. The Framers of the First Amendment, fully aware of both the need to defend a new nation and the abuses of the English and Colonial governments, sought to give this new society strength and security by providing that freedom of speech, press, religion, and assembly should not be abridged.

MR. JUSTICE DOUGLAS, with whom MR. JUSTICE BLACK joins, concurring.

. . . The Government says that it has inherent powers to go into court and obtain an injunction to protect the national interest, which, in this case, is alleged to be national security. . . .

The dominant purpose of the First Amendment was to prohibit the widespread practice of governmental suppression of embarrassing information. It is common knowledge that the First Amendment was adopted against the widespread use of the common law of seditious libel to punish the dissemination of material that is embarrassing to the powers-that-be. Z. Chafee, *Free Speech in the United States* (1941). The present cases will, I think, go down in history as the most dramatic illustration of that principle. A debate of large proportions goes on in the Nation over our posture in Vietnam. That debate antedated the disclosure of the contents of the present documents. The latter are highly relevant to the debate in progress. Secrecy in government is fundamentally antidemocratic, perpetuating bureaucratic errors. Open debate and discussion of public issues are vital to our national health. On public questions, there should be "uninhibited, robust, and wide-open" debate. . . .

MR. JUSTICE BRENNAN, concurring.

I write separately in these cases only to emphasize what should be apparent: that our judgments in the present cases may not be taken to indicate the propriety, in the future, of issuing temporary stays and restraining orders to block the publication of material sought to be suppressed by the Government. So far as I can determine, never before has the United States sought to enjoin a newspaper from publishing information in its possession. The relative novelty of the questions presented, the necessary haste with which decisions were reached, the magnitude of the interests asserted, and the fact that all the parties have concentrated their arguments upon the question whether permanent restraints were proper may have justified at least some of the restraints heretofore imposed in these cases. Certainly it is difficult to fault the several courts below for seeking to assure that the issues here involved were preserved for ultimate review by this Court. But even if it be assumed that some of the interim restraints were proper in the two cases before us, that assumption has no bearing upon the propriety of similar judicial action in the future. To begin with, there has now been ample time for reflection and judgment; whatever values there may be in the preservation of novel questions for appellate review may not support any restraints in the future. More important, the First Amendment stands as an absolute bar to the imposition of judicial restraints in circumstances of the kind presented by these cases. . . .

MR. JUSTICE STEWART, with whom MR. JUSTICE WHITE joins, concurring.

In the governmental structure created by our Constitution, the Executive is endowed with enormous power in the two related areas of national defense and international relations. This power, largely unchecked by the Legislative and Judicial branches, has been pressed to the very hilt since the advent of the nuclear missile age. For better or for worse, the simple fact is that a President of the United States possesses vastly greater constitutional independence in these two vital areas of power than does, say, a prime minister of a country with a parliamentary form of government.

In the absence of the governmental checks and balances present in other areas of our national life, the only effective restraint upon executive policy and power in the areas of national defense and international affairs may lie in an enlightened citizenry—in an informed and critical public opinion which alone can here protect the values of democratic government. For this reason, it is perhaps here that a press that is alert, aware, and free most vitally serves the basic purpose of the First Amendment. For, without an informed and free press, there cannot be an enlightened people.

Yet it is elementary that the successful conduct of international diplomacy and the maintenance of an effective national defense require both confidentiality and secrecy. Other nations can hardly deal with this Nation in an atmosphere of mutual trust unless they can be assured that their confidences will be kept. And, within our own executive departments, the development of considered and intelligent international policies would be impossible if those charged with their formulation could not communicate with each other freely, frankly, and in confidence. In the area of basic national defense, the frequent need for absolute secrecy is, of course, self-evident.

I think there can be but one answer to this dilemma, if dilemma it be. The responsibility must be where the power is. If the Constitution gives the Executive a large degree of unshared power in the conduct of foreign affairs and the maintenance of our national defense, then, under the Constitution, the Executive must have the largely unshared duty to determine and preserve the degree of internal security necessary to exercise that power successfully. It is an awesome responsibility, requiring judgment and wisdom of a high order. I should suppose that moral, political, and practical considerations would dictate that a very first principle of that wisdom would be an insistence upon avoiding secrecy for its own sake. For when everything is classified, then nothing is classified, and the system becomes one to be disregarded by the cynical or the careless, and to be manipulated by those intent on self-protection or self-promotion. I should suppose, in short, that the hallmark of a truly effective internal security system would be the maximum possible disclosure, recognizing that secrecy can best be preserved only when credibility is truly maintained. But, be that as it may, it is clear to me that it is the constitutional duty of the Executive—as a matter of sovereign prerogative, and not as a matter of law as the courts know law—through the promulgation and enforcement of executive regulations, to protect the confidentiality necessary to carry out its responsibilities in the fields of international relations and national defense.

This is not to say that Congress and the courts have no role to play. Undoubtedly, Congress has the power to enact specific and appropriate criminal laws to protect government property and preserve government secrets. Congress has passed such laws, and several of them are of very colorable relevance to the apparent circumstances of these cases. And if a criminal prosecution is instituted, it will be the responsibility of the courts to decide the applicability of the criminal law under which the charge is brought. Moreover, if Congress should pass a specific law authorizing civil proceedings in this field, the courts would likewise have the duty to decide the constitutionality of such a law, as well as its applicability to the facts proved.

But in the cases before us, we are asked neither to construe specific regulations nor to apply specific laws. We are asked, instead, to perform a function that the Constitution gave to the Executive, not the Judiciary. We are asked, quite simply, to prevent the publication by two newspapers of material that the Executive Branch insists should not, in the national interest, be published. I am convinced that the Executive is correct with respect to some of the documents involved. But I cannot say that disclosure of any of them will surely result in direct, immediate, and irreparable damage to our Nation or its people. That being so, there can under the First Amendment be but one judicial resolution of the issues before us. . . .

Mr. Justice White, with whom Mr. Justice Stewart joins, concurring.

I concur in today's judgments, but only because of the concededly extraordinary protection against prior restraints enjoyed by the press under our constitutional system. I do not say that in no circumstances would the First Amendment permit an injunction against publishing information about government plans or operations. Nor, after examining the materials the Government characterizes as the most sensitive and destructive, can I deny that revelation of these documents will do substantial damage to public interests. Indeed, I am confident that their disclosure will have that result. But I nevertheless agree that the United States has not satisfied the very heavy burden that it must meet to warrant an injunction against publication in these cases, at least in the absence of express and appropriately limited congressional authorization for prior restraints in circumstances such as these.

The Government's position is simply stated: the responsibility of the Executive for the conduct of the foreign affairs and for the security of the Nation is so basic that the President is entitled to an injunction against publication of a newspaper story whenever he can convince a court that the information to be revealed threatens "grave and irreparable" injury to the public interest; and the injunction should issue whether or not the material to be published is classified, whether or not publication would be lawful under relevant criminal statutes enacted by Congress, and regardless of the circumstances by which the newspaper came into possession of the information. At least in the absence of legislation by Congress, based on its own investigations and findings, I am quite unable to agree that the inherent powers of the Executive and the courts reach so far as to authorize remedies having such sweeping potential for inhibiting publications by the press. Much of the difficulty inheres in the "grave and irreparable danger" standard suggested by the United States. If the United States were to have judgment under such a standard in these cases, our decision would be of little guidance to other courts in other cases, for the material at issue here would not be available from the Court's opinion or from public records, nor would it be published by the press. Indeed, even today, where we hold that the United States has not met its burden, the material remains sealed in court records and it is properly not discussed in today's opinions. Moreover, because the material poses substantial dangers to national interests, and because of the hazards of criminal sanctions, a responsible press may choose never to publish the more sensitive materials. To sustain the Government in these cases would start the courts down a long and hazardous road that I am not willing to travel, at least without congressional guidance and direction.

It is not easy to reject the proposition urged by the United States, and to deny relief on its good faith claims in these cases that publication will work serious damage to the country. But that discomfiture is considerably dispelled by the infrequency of prior-restraint cases. Normally, publication will occur and the damage be done before the Government has either opportunity or grounds for suppression. So here, publication has already begun, and a substantial part of the threatened damage has already occurred. The fact of a massive breakdown in security is known, access to the documents by many unauthorized people is undeniable, and the efficacy of equitable relief against these or other newspapers to avert anticipated damage is doubtful, at best.

MR. JUSTICE MARSHALL, concurring.

The Government contends that the only issue in these cases is whether, in a suit by the United States, "the First Amendment bars a court from prohibiting a newspaper from publishing material whose disclosure would pose a 'grave and immediate danger to the security of the United States.'" With all due respect, I believe the ultimate issue in these cases is even more basic than the one posed by the Solicitor General. The issue is whether this Court or the Congress has the power to make law. The problem here is whether, in these particular cases, the Executive Branch has authority to invoke the equity jurisdiction of the courts to protect what it believes to be the national interest. The Government argues that, in addition to the inherent power of any government to protect itself, the President's power to conduct foreign affairs and his position as Commander in Chief give him authority to impose censorship on the press to protect his ability to deal effectively with foreign nations and to conduct the military affairs of the country. Of course, it is beyond cavil that the President has broad powers by virtue of his primary responsibility for the conduct of our foreign affairs and his position as Commander in Chief. And, in some situations, it may be that, under whatever inherent powers the Government may have, as well as the implicit authority derived from the President's mandate to conduct foreign affairs and to act as Commander in Chief, there is a basis for the invocation of the equity jurisdiction of this Court as an aid to prevent the publication of material damaging to "national security," however that term may be defined.

It would, however, be utterly inconsistent with the concept of separation of powers for this Court to use its power of contempt to prevent behavior that Congress has specifically declined to prohibit. There would be a similar damage to the basic concept of these co-equal branches of Government if, when the Executive Branch has adequate authority granted by Congress to protect "national security," it can choose, instead, to invoke the contempt power of a court to enjoin the threatened conduct. The Constitution provides that Congress shall make laws, the President execute laws, and courts interpret laws, *Youngstown Sheet & Tube Co.* v. *Sawyer* (1952). It did not provide for government by injunction in which the courts and the Executive Branch can "make law" without regard to the action of Congress. It may be more convenient for the Executive Branch if it need only convince a judge to prohibit conduct, rather than ask the Congress to pass a law, and it may be more convenient to enforce a contempt order than to seek a criminal conviction in a jury trial. Moreover, it may be considered politically wise to get a court to share the responsibility for arresting those who the Executive Branch has probable cause to believe are violating the law. But convenience and political considerations of the moment do not justify a basic departure from the principles of our system of government.

MR. JUSTICE HARLAN, with whom THE CHIEF JUSTICE and MR. JUSTICE BLACKMUN join, dissenting.

These cases forcefully call to mind the wise admonition of MR. JUSTICE HOLMES. . . .

> Great cases, like hard cases, make bad law. For great cases are called great not by reason of their real importance in shaping the law of the future, but because of some accident of immediate overwhelming interest which appeals to the feelings and distorts the judgment. These immediate interests exercise a kind of hydraulic pressure which makes what previously was clear seem doubtful, and before which even well settled principles of law will bend.

With all respect, I consider that the Court has been almost irresponsibly feverish in dealing with these cases.

This frenzied train of events took place in the name of the presumption against prior restraints created by the First Amendment. Due regard for the extraordinarily important and difficult questions involved in these litigations should have led the Court to shun such a precipitate timetable. In order to decide the merits of these cases properly, some or all of the following questions should have been faced:

1. Whether the Attorney General is authorized to bring these suits in the name of the United States.

2. Whether the First Amendment permits the federal courts to enjoin publication of stories which would present a serious threat to national security.
3. Whether the threat to publish highly secret documents is of itself a sufficient implication of national security to justify an injunction on the theory that, regardless of the contents of the documents, harm enough results simply from the demonstration of such a breach of secrecy.
4. Whether the unauthorized disclosure of any of these particular documents would seriously impair the national security.
5. What weight should be given to the opinion of high officers in the Executive Branch of the Government with respect to questions 3 and 4.
6. Whether the newspapers are entitled to retain and use the documents notwithstanding the seemingly uncontested facts that the documents, or the originals of which they are duplicates, were purloined from the Government's possession, and that the newspapers received them with knowledge that they had been feloniously acquired.
7. Whether the threatened harm to the national security or the Government's possessory interest in the documents justifies the issuance of an injunction against publication in light of—
   a. The strong First Amendment policy against prior restraints on publication;
   b. The doctrine against enjoining conduct in violation of criminal statutes; and
   c. The extent to which the materials at issue have apparently already been otherwise disseminated.

These are difficult questions of fact, of law, and of judgment; the potential consequences of erroneous decision are enormous. The time which has been available to us, to the lower courts, and to the parties has been wholly inadequate for giving these cases the kind of consideration they deserve. It is a reflection on the stability of the judicial process that these great issues—as important as any that have arisen during my time on the Court—should have been decided under the pressures engendered by the torrent of publicity that has attended these litigations from their inception.

Forced as I am to reach the merits of these cases, I dissent from the opinion and judgments of the Court. Within the severe limitations imposed by the time constraints under which I have been required to operate, I can only state my reasons in telescoped form, even though, in different circumstances, I would have felt constrained to deal with the cases in the fuller sweep indicated above. . . .

In a speech on the floor of the House of Representatives, Chief Justice John Marshall, then a member of that body, stated [in 1800]: "The President is the sole organ of the nation in its external relations, and its sole representative with foreign nations." From that time, shortly after the founding of the Nation, to this, there has been no substantial challenge to this description of the scope of executive power.

From this constitutional primacy in the field of foreign affairs, it seems to me that certain conclusions necessarily follow. Some of these were stated concisely by President Washington, declining the request of the House of Representatives for the papers leading up to the negotiation of the Jay Treaty:

> The nature of foreign negotiations requires caution, and their success must often depend on secrecy; and even when brought to a conclusion, a full disclosure of all the measures, demands, or eventual concessions which may have been proposed or contemplated would be extremely impolitic; for this might have a pernicious influence on future negotiations, or produce immediate inconveniences, perhaps danger and mischief, in relation to other powers.

. . . Pending further hearings in each case conducted under the appropriate ground rules, I would continue the restraints on publication. I cannot believe that the doctrine prohibiting prior restraints reaches to the point of preventing courts from maintaining the *status quo* long enough to act responsibly in matters of such national importance as those involved here.

Mr. Justice Blackmun, dissenting.

. . . The First Amendment . . . is only one part of an entire Constitution. Article II of the great document vests in the Executive Branch primary power over the conduct of foreign affairs, and places in that branch the responsibility for the Nation's safety. Each provision of the Constitution is important, and I cannot subscribe to a doctrine of unlimited absolutism for the First Amendment at the cost of downgrading other provisions. First Amendment absolutism has never commanded a majority of this Court, *Near* v. *Minnesota* (1931) and *Schenck* v. *United States* (1919). What is needed here is a weighing, upon properly developed standards, of the broad right of the press to print and of the very narrow right of the Government to prevent. Such standards are not yet developed. The parties here are in disagreement as to what those standards should be. But even the newspapers concede that there are situations where restraint is in order and is constitutional. . . .

It may well be that, if these cases were allowed to develop as they should be developed, and to be tried as lawyers should try them and as courts should hear them, free of pressure and panic and sensationalism, other light would be shed on the situation, and contrary considerations, for me, might prevail. But that is not the present posture of the litigation. . . .

I hope that damage has not already been done. If, however, damage has been done, and if, with the Court's action today, these newspapers proceed to publish the critical documents and there results therefrom "the death of soldiers, the destruction of alliances, the greatly increased difficulty of negotiation with our enemies, the inability of our diplomats to negotiate," to which list I might add the factors of prolongation of the war and of further delay in the freeing of United States prisoners, then the Nation's people will know where the responsibility for these sad consequences rests.

By the time the Pentagon Papers were published, public opposition to the Vietnam War had increased to the point where such opinion now reflected the dominant mood of Congress. Put off by what it believed was an intentional campaign of deceit and lies by the Nixon administration with regard to American involvement in Vietnam, Congress, for the first time in the post–World War II era, reclaimed its constitutional role in the conduct and management of war.[23] In 1973, large majorities in both houses of Congress, over the veto of President Nixon, passed the War Powers Resolution, which requires the president to consult Congress when possible before committing American forces to imminent hostilities. The resolution also requires the president to inform Congress within forty-eight hours of sending American military forces into hostilities of the purpose and intent of his order. Finally, it authorizes Congress, after a period of sixty days, to recall armed forces in the absence of an additional resolution approving the president's stated mission, or pass a declaration of war. Scholars, journalists, and government officials have since questioned the effectiveness of the War Powers Resolution, but there is little doubt that *New York Times Co.* v. *United States* directly contributed to its passage and intensified the news media's determination not to be used as a conduit for American foreign policy.

Prior Restraint After *New York Times*

Although the justices, in *New York Times*, did not declare prior restraints on the news media unconstitutional per se, their ruling has prevented any similar showdowns since then. But the Court has dealt with the issue of prior restraint on the press in other contexts. In *Hazelwood* v. *Kuhlmeier* (1988), a 5–3 Court upheld the right of a suburban St. Louis high school principal to pull several pages of material discussing teen pregnancy, divorce, and other sensitive family issues from the school newspaper over the objection of its student editors.[24] The principal explained his decision was motivated by the privacy of the students and families, who, in his own words, "were described in such a way that the readers could tell who they were."[25] Rejecting the principal's action as the equivalent of a governmental prior restraint, the Court relied upon the special circumstances in which it had traditionally considered the free speech rights of students in public school settings. In fact, the Court did not even broach the prior restraint issues raised in *New York Times*. *Hazelwood* was, for the Court, a case in which a public school's interest in the privacy rights of its students and their families justified what it referred to as "editorial control" by school administrators. Although it generated a considerable amount of attention after the Court decided to hear the case, *Hazelwood* has had virtually no impact beyond the public schools, where it continues to have an important bearing.

In *Alexander* v. *United States* (1993), the Court revisited the prior restraint issue in a context wholly different from any of its previous such cases. A sharply divided Court disagreed over whether certain provisions of the federal Rackeeter-Influenced and Corrupt Organizations Act (RICO), which permits the federal government to compel the forfeiture of any asset believed to have been acquired illegally, amounted to an unconstitutional abridgement of free speech and press rights.

Alexander v. *United States*

509 U.S. 544 (1993)

In 1970, Congress enacted RICO, giving federal prosecutors their most effective federal statute yet with which to target organized crime. Previous federal laws had proven ineffective against organized crime, in large part because they targeted only the individuals involved in criminal activity, rather than the criminal enterprise itself. On occasion, the Federal Bureau of Investigation made a dramatic arrest of a high-ranking organized crime figure, but criminal syndicates were able to flourish by hiding most of their assets in legitimate businesses. RICO authorized prosecutors to do much more than arrest, imprison, and fine criminal offenders; the law required the forfeiture of any property obtained through a criminal enterprise. In 1984, Congress amended RICO to include possessing or trafficking in obscenity as a criminal enterprise.

In 1985, Attorney General Edwin Meese established a special commission to investigate pornography in the United States. The Meese Commission was little more than a public relations effort to trumpet the Reagan administration's opposition to what it viewed as lax pornography laws and judicial standards to punish offenders in the "adult entertainment" trade. Civil liberties groups, particularly the ACLU, lambasted the Meese Commission's efforts, and derided the attorney general as the leader of a petty campaign to impose Victorian morality standards on a country that no longer wanted them. The ACLU, along with Public Citizen, a liberal public interest group founded by the consumer advocate Ralph Nader, filed suit to require the commission to open its records to the public before its reports were officially released. Ultimately, the Meese Commission suffered under the weight of its own intentions. Its final report to Congress was laced with explicit descriptions of sexual conduct, skirting close to the constitutional definition of obscenity.

What the Reagan administration could not accomplish through the Meese Commission it could with the 1984 RICO amendments. In 1989, the Justice Department successfully prosecuted Ferris J. Alexander under the obscenity provision of RICO, which resulted in fines and penalties of over $100,000 and the forfeiture of his "adult entertainment" businesses, including over $9 million in inventory. Alexander contested the seizure of several magazines and videos as an unconstitutional prior restraint, since they were taken not because of their content, but because their sale had contributed to the financial coffers of a criminal enterprise. The lower federal courts rejected Alexander's contention.

The Court's decision was 5 to 4. Chief Justice Rehnquist delivered the opinion of the Court. Justice Kennedy, joined by Justices Blackmun, Souter, and Stevens, dissented.

▼▲▼

Chief Justice Rehnquist delivered the opinion of the Court.

Petitioner first contends that the forfeiture in this case, which effectively shut down his adult entertainment business, constituted an unconstitutional prior restraint on speech, rather than a permissible criminal punishment. According to petitioner, forfeiture of expressive materials and the assets of businesses engaged in expressive activity, when predicated solely upon previous obscenity violations, operates as a prior restraint because it prohibits future presumptively protected expression in retaliation for prior unprotected speech. Practically speaking, petitioner argues, the effect of the RICO forfeiture order here was no different from the injunction prohibiting the publication of expressive material found to be a prior restraint in *Near* v. *Minnesota ex rel. Olson* (1931). As petitioner puts it, the forfeiture order imposed a complete *ban* on his future expression because of previous unprotected speech. We disagree. By lumping the forfeiture imposed in this case after a full criminal trial with an injunction enjoining future speech, petitioner stretches the term "prior restraint" well beyond the limits established by our cases. To accept petitioner's argument would virtually obliterate the distinction, solidly grounded in our cases, between prior restraints and subsequent punishments.

The term prior restraint is used "to describe administrative and judicial orders *forbidding* certain communications when issued in advance of the time that such communications are to occur." Temporary restraining orders and permanent injunctions—*i.e.*, court orders that actually forbid speech activities—are classic examples of prior restraints. This understanding of what constitutes a prior restraint is borne out by our cases, even those on which petitioner relies. In *Near* . . . we invalidated a court order that perpetually enjoined the named party, who had published a newspaper containing articles found to violate a state nuisance statute, from producing any future "malicious, scandalous and defamatory" publication. *Near,* therefore, involved a true restraint on future speech—a permanent injunction. . . .

By contrast, the RICO forfeiture order in this case does not *forbid* petitioner from engaging in any expressive activities in the future, nor does it require him to obtain prior approval for any expressive activities. It only deprives him of specific assets that were found to be related to his previous racketeering violations. Assuming, of course, that he has sufficient untainted assets to open new stores, restock his inventory, and hire staff, petitioner can go back into the adult entertainment business tomorrow, and sell as many sexually explicit magazines and videotapes as he likes, without any risk of being held in contempt for violating a court order. . . . He is perfectly free to open an adult bookstore or otherwise engage in the production and distribution of erotic materials; he just cannot finance these enterprises with assets derived from his prior racketeering offenses.

The constitutional infirmity in nearly all of our prior restraint cases involving obscene material, including those on which petitioner and the dissent rely, was that Government had seized or otherwise restrained materials suspected of being obscene without a prior judicial determination that they were, in fact, so. In this case, however, the assets in question were not ordered forfeited because they were believed to be obscene, but because they were directly related to petitioner's past racketeering violations. The RICO forfeiture statute calls for the forfeiture of assets because of the financial role they play in the operation of the racketeering enterprise. The statute is oblivious to the expressive or nonexpressive nature of the assets forfeited; books, sports cars, narcotics, and cash are all forfeitable alike under RICO. Indeed, a contrary scheme would be disastrous from a policy standpoint, enabling racketeers to evade forfeiture by investing the proceeds of their crimes in businesses engaging in expressive activity. . . .

[P]etitioner's proposed definition of the term "prior restraint" would undermine the time-honored distinction between barring speech in the future and penalizing past speech. The doctrine of prior restraint originated in the common law of England, where prior restraints of the press were not permitted, but punishment after publication was. This very limited application of the principle of freedom of speech was held inconsistent with our First Amendment as long ago. . . . While we may have given a broader definition to the term "prior restraint" than was given to it in English common law, our decisions have steadfastly presented the distinction between prior restraints and subsequent punishments. Though petitioner tries to dismiss this distinction as "neither meaningful nor useful," we think it is critical to our First Amendment jurisprudence. Because we have interpreted the First Amendment as providing greater protection from prior restraints than from subsequent punishments, it is important for us to delineate with some precision the defining characteristics of a prior restraint. To hold that the forfeiture order in this case constituted a prior restraint would have the exact opposite effect: it would blur the line separating prior restraints from subsequent punishments to such a degree that it would be impossible to determine with any certainty whether a particular measure is a prior restraint or not. . . .

Petitioner's real complaint is not that the RICO statute is overbroad, but that applying RICO's forfeiture provisions to businesses dealing in expressive materials may have an improper "chilling" effect on free expression by deterring others from engaging in protected speech. No doubt the monetarily large forfeiture in this case may induce cautious booksellers to practice self-censorship and remove marginally protected materials from their shelves out of fear that those materials could be found obscene, and thus subject them to forfeiture. . . .

For these reasons, we hold that RICO's forfeiture provisions, as applied in this case, did not violate the First Amendment, but that the Court of Appeals should have considered whether they resulted in an "excessive" penalty within the meaning of the Eighth Amendment's Excessive Fines Clause. Accordingly, we vacate the judgment of the Court of Appeals and remand the case for further proceedings consistent with this opinion.

It is so ordered.

Justice Kennedy, with whom Justice Blackmun, Justice Stevens, and Justice Souter join . . . dissenting.

The Court today embraces a rule that would find no affront to the First Amendment in the Government's destruction of a book and film business and its entire inventory of legitimate expression as punishment for a single past speech offense. Until now, I had thought one could browse through any book or film store in the United States without fear that the proprietor had chosen each item to avoid risk to the whole inventory and indeed to the business itself. This ominous, onerous threat undermines free speech and press principles essential to our personal freedom.

Obscenity laws would not work unless an offender could be arrested and imprisoned despite the resulting chill on his own further speech. But, at least before today, we have understood state action directed at protected books or other expressive works themselves to raise distinct constitutional concerns. The Court's decision is a grave repudiation of First Amendment principles, and, with respect, I dissent. . . .

The fundamental defect in the majority's reasoning is a failure to recognize that the forfeiture here cannot be equated with traditional punishments such as fines and jail terms. Noting that petitioner does not challenge either the 6-year jail sentence or the $100,000 fine imposed against him as punishment for his RICO convictions, the majority ponders why RICO's forfeiture penalty should be any different. The answer is that RICO's forfeiture penalties are different from traditional punishments by Congress' own design as well as in their First Amendment consequences.

The majority tries to occupy the high ground by assuming the role of the defender of the doctrine of prior restraint. It warns that we disparage the doctrine if we reason from it. But as an analysis of our prior restraint cases reveals, our application of the First Amendment has adjusted to meet new threats to speech. The First Amendment is a rule of substantive protection, not an artifice of categories. The admitted design and the overt purpose of the forfeiture in this case are to destroy an entire speech business and all its protected titles, thus depriving the public of access to lawful expression. This is restraint in more than theory. It is censorship all too real. . . .

Although we consider today a new method of government control with unmistakable dangers of official censorship, the majority concludes that First Amendment freedoms are not endangered because forfeiture follows a lawful conviction for obscenity offenses. But this explanation does not suffice. The rights of free speech and press in their broad and legitimate sphere cannot be defeated by the simple expedient of punishing after in lieu of censoring before. This is so because, in some instances, the operation and effect of a particular enforcement scheme, though not in the form of a traditional prior restraint, may be to raise the same concerns which inform all of our prior restraint cases: the evils of state censorship and the unacceptable chilling of protected speech. . . .

In a society committed to freedom of thought, inquiry, and discussion without interference or guidance from the state, public confidence in the institutions devoted to the dissemination of written matter and films is essential. That confidence erodes if it is perceived that speakers and the press are vulnerable for all of their expression based on some errant expression in the past. Independence of speech and press can be just as compromised by the threat of official intervention as by the fact of it. Though perhaps not in the form of a classic prior restraint, the application of the forfeiture statute here bears its censorial cast. . . .

Given the Court's principal holding, I can interpose no objection to remanding the case for further consideration under the Eighth Amendment. But it is unnecessary to reach the Eighth Amendment question. The Court's failure to reverse this flagrant violation of the right of free speech and expression is a deplorable abandonment of fundamental First Amendment principles. I dissent from the judgment and from the opinion of the Court.

Remember that in *New York Times* only two justices, Black and Douglas, believed that prior restraint was always and under any condition unconstitutional. The other four justices who voted against the lower court's injunction holding up the publication of the Pentagon Papers believed that, under extraordinary circumstances, the government could prohibit the publication of certain materials. *Alexander* offers a much different scenario from *New York Times*, which involved exactly the type of prior restraint rejected by the Framers—prohibiting the publication of material that placed the government in an unfavorable light. The issues raised by *Alexander* foreshadow another difficult question with which the Court has grappled in determining the boundaries of press freedom under the First Amendment: Does the right of the news media to publish or broadcast information ever give way to other competing government interests?

What Does the Public Have the Right to Know?

The no prior restraint rule makes clear that the baseline definition of freedom of the press means the right to publish information and opinions without government approval. But does a virtually absolute right to publish or broadcast just about anything mean that the public always has a right to receive what the news media wants it to know? Moreover, does freedom of the press mean that journalists are entitled to greater privileges in gathering and reporting information than citizens at large? These are the questions considered in this section.

Fair Trials and a Free Press

The Sixth Amendment guarantees a criminal defendant "the right to a speedy and public trial . . . by an impartial jury in the State and district wherein the crime shall have been committed." The Framers' concern with criminal due process has its roots in the Star Chamber trials for seditious libel that flourished in England during the 1600s. The very idea that an individual could be arrested and tried in secret was repulsive to the Framers, who believed that jury trials were an essential form of popular control in a democratic society. Some Anti-Federalists expressed concern during the ratification debates that the Constitution did not adequately protect trial by jury in civil cases, even though Article III specified that the "trial of all crimes, except in cases of impeachment, shall be by jury." Jury trials, claimed the *Federal Farmer,* "are the means by which the people are let into the knowledge of public affairs—are enabled to stand as the guardians of each other's rights, and to restrain, by regular and extreme measures, those who otherwise might infringe upon them."[26]

The Court, beginning in the early 1940s, has been called upon to weigh a criminal defendant's right to a public trial against the right of the press to report and broadcast the more sensationalistic—and perhaps newsworthy—aspects of the crime before the trial has even started. The Court once frowned upon media intrusiveness into the trial process as inherently prejudicial toward the accused. In *Estes* v. *Texas* (1965), the Court barred the admission of television cameras into a courtroom on the *probability* that their presence would compromise the fair trial rights of a criminal defendant.[27] Now, that has changed. The media circus that accompanied the murder trial of former-football-star-turned-actor O. J. Simpson in the mid-1990s spurred the rise in popularity of Court TV, the cable channel that broadcasts trials and commentary twenty-four hours a day. Now, the important question of whether courtrooms and cameras make an unconstitutional mix is no longer as controversial. Still, the Court, which has resisted televising its oral arguments, continues to permit judges considerable discretion to balance the Court's interest in fair and open trials with the right of the press to report those trials' proceedings.[28]

Journalists are fond of saying that the public has "a right to know" when their news-gathering techniques and judgment in reporting are questioned. *New York Times* v. *United States* made clear that the public *does not* have a constitutional right to know everything the news media might want to report. Similarly, the Court's decisions attempting to balance the right to a fair trial with free press rights have demonstrated that the First Amendment is neither a sword nor a shield for the news media. In *Sheppard* v. *Maxwell* (1966), the Court found itself drawn into what was the most spectacular and widely reported murder trial of the still-fledgling television news era.

Sheppard v. *Maxwell*

384 U.S. 333 (1966)

Early on the morning of July 4, 1954, Sam Sheppard was startled awake by the sounds of his wife's screams. After entertaining some friends the evening before in his lakefront Cleveland home, Sheppard, a wealthy thirty-year-old physician, had fallen asleep on the couch. Just after midnight, their guests departed and Marilyn Sheppard went upstairs to bed. Now, racing up the stairs, Sheppard entered his bedroom, where he saw a "form" standing over his bed. After attempting to subdue the "form," Sheppard was knocked unconscious. The next thing Sheppard remembered was waking up in the bedroom to find his wife dead. Then, Sheppard heard some loud noises outside, and he rushed down the stairs to find "a man with bushy hair" rustling through some trees. Sheppard chased the alleged intruder down to the beach and tackled him from behind. After a second struggle with the "form" again left Sheppard unconscious, he awoke to find himself partially immersed in the waters of Lake Erie. Dazed and confused, Sheppard staggered back to his home and called for help.[29]

Police arrived to find Marilyn Sheppard's half-naked body lying in a pool of blood, her face smashed to a pulp. Downstairs, Sheppard's medical bag had been ransacked and the contents of his desk emptied out and thrown all over the room. But Sam Sheppard was not home when the police arrived. Sheppard's two brothers had come over and taken him to the hospital that the three of them jointly owned. Later, a canvas bag was found at Sheppard's house containing his watch, a fraternity ring, and keys, leading reporters and police to speculate that Sheppard had faked a robbery to conceal the fact that he had murdered his wife. After a subsequent disclosure that Sheppard had been involved in a lengthy sexual affair with his lab assistant, all eyes bore down on the young doctor as the primary suspect.

Sheppard was arrested and charged with his wife's murder. His trial began in October before Judge Edward Blythin, who was up for reelection in November. To win favor with the news media, Blythin permitted reporters and photographers special access into his courtroom, which had taken on a circuslike atmosphere. Prosecutors took full advantage of the judge's obvious bias against the defendant, emphasizing the circumstantial aspects of the case—no sand in Sheppard's clothes after a beach struggle or evidence of a break-in—to compensate for the fact that police had found no murder weapon.

Before the trial, Judge Blythin had done nothing to stop the media's assault on Sam Sheppard's innocence. The day of the evening Sheppard was arrested a front-page editorial appeared in a Cleveland paper demanding, "Why Isn't Sam Sheppard in Jail?" All the local papers published the names and addresses of the jurors called to serve in the Sheppard trial, and no effort was later made to shield jurors from the flow of unfavorable publicity directed toward the defendant. Famed New York gossip columnist Walter Winchell broadcast an allegation on his television and radio programs that a New York woman under arrest for robbery had borne Sheppard a child while his "mistress." Later, during the trial, Judge Blythin remarked to one reporter that "Sheppard [was] guilty as hell," and continually overruled the defense team's objections at every turn.

The jury, which was not sequestered in spite of all the publicity surrounding the Sheppard case and permitted to place outside calls without monitoring or reporting, returned a guilty verdict of murder in the second degree after four days. Seven years later, in November 1961, a twenty-nine-year-old lawyer named F. Lee Bailey took Sheppard's case. Bailey filed appeal after appeal to have Sheppard's conviction thrown out based on the adverse publicity before his case. After close to two and a half years of getting nowhere, Bailey bumped into the Cleveland reporter Dorothy Kilgallen, to whom Judge Blythin had made his "guilty as hell" remark. Bailey filed a habeas corpus petition in federal district court and got Sheppard released on bail on the grounds that his trial fell below "minimum requirements for due process." A federal appeals court reversed, and the Court agreed to hear Bailey's appeal for a writ of *certiorari*.

Sam Sheppard's case later served as the inspiration for the popular 1960s television program *The Fugitive*, in which the lead character, Dr. Richard Kimble, flees authorities after evidence points to him as the suspect in his wife's murder.

The Court's decision was 8 to 1. Justice Clark delivered the opinion of the Court. Justice Black dissented.

▼▲▼

MR. JUSTICE CLARK delivered the opinion of the Court.

The principle that justice cannot survive behind walls of silence has long been reflected in the "Anglo-American distrust for secret trials," *In re Oliver* (1948). A responsible press has always been regarded as the handmaiden of effective judicial administration, especially in the criminal field. Its function in this regard is documented by an impressive record of service over several centuries. The press does not simply publish information about trials, but guards against the miscarriage of justice by subjecting the police, prosecutors, and judicial processes to extensive public scrutiny and criticism. This Court has, therefore, been unwilling to place any direct limitations on the freedom traditionally exercised by the news media for "[w]hat transpires in the courtroom is public property." . . .

But the Court has also pointed out that "[l]egal trials are not like elections, to be won through the use of the meeting-hall, the radio, and the newspaper." And the Court has insisted that no one be punished for a crime without "a charge fairly made and fairly tried in a public tribunal free of prejudice, passion, excitement, and tyrannical power." . . .

The undeviating rule of this Court was expressed by Mr. Justice Holmes over half a century ago . . . : "The theory of our system is that the conclusions to be reached in a case will be induced only by evidence and argument in open court, and not by any outside influence, whether of private talk or public print." Moreover, "the burden of showing essential unfairness . . . as a demonstrable reality," need not be undertaken when television has exposed the community "repeatedly and in depth to the spectacle of [the accused] personally confessing in detail to the crimes with which he was later to be charged." In *Turner* v. *Louisiana* (1965), two key witnesses were deputy sheriffs who doubled as jury shepherds during the trial. The deputies swore that they had not talked to the jurors about the case, but the Court nonetheless held that, "even if it could be assumed that the deputies never did discuss the case directly with any members of the jury, it would be blinking reality not to recognize the extreme prejudice inherent in this continual association. . . ."

Only last Term, in *Estes* v. *Texas* (1965), we set aside a conviction despite the absence of any showing of prejudice. We said there: "It is true that, in most cases involving claims of due process deprivations, we require a showing of identifiable prejudice to the accused. Nevertheless, at times, a procedure employed by the State involves such a probability that prejudice will result that it is deemed inherently lacking in due process." . . .

It is clear that the totality of circumstances in this case also warrants such an approach. Unlike Estes, Sheppard was not granted a change of venue to a locale away from where the publicity originated; nor was his jury sequestered. The Estes jury saw none of the television broadcasts from the courtroom. On the contrary, the Sheppard jurors were subjected to newspaper, radio, and television coverage of the trial while not taking part in the proceedings. They were allowed to go their separate ways outside of the courtroom, without adequate directions not to read or listen to anything concerning the case. . . . At intervals during the trial, the judge simply repeated his "suggestions" and "requests" that the jurors not expose themselves to comment upon the case. Moreover, the jurors were thrust into the role of celebrities by the judge's failure to insulate them from reporters and photographers. The numerous pictures of the jurors, with their addresses, which appeared in the newspapers before and during the trial itself exposed them to expressions of opinion from both cranks and friends. The fact that anonymous letters had been received by prospective jurors should have made the judge aware that this publicity seriously threatened the jurors' privacy.

The press coverage of the Estes trial was not nearly as massive and pervasive as the attention given by the Cleveland newspapers and broadcasting stations to Sheppard's prosecution. Sheppard stood indicted for the murder of his wife; the State was demanding the death penalty. For months, the virulent publicity about Sheppard and the murder had made the case notorious. Charges and countercharges were aired in the news media besides those for which Sheppard was called to trial. In addition, only three months before trial, Sheppard was examined for more than five hours without counsel during a three-day inquest which ended in a public brawl. The inquest was televised live from a high school gymnasium seating hundreds of people. Furthermore, the trial began two weeks before a hotly contested election at which both Chief Prosecutor Mahon and Judge Blythin were candidates for judgeships.

While we cannot say that Sheppard was denied due process by the judge's refusal to take precautions against the influence of pretrial publicity alone, the court's later rulings must be considered against the setting in which the trial was held. In light of this background, we believe that the arrangements made by the judge with the news media caused Sheppard to be deprived of that "judicial serenity and calm to which [he] was entitled." The fact is that bedlam reigned at the courthouse during the trial, and newsmen took over practically the entire courtroom, hounding most of the participants in the trial, especially Sheppard. . . .

There can be no question about the nature of the publicity which surrounded Sheppard's trial. . . . Indeed, every court that has considered this case, save the court that tried it, has deplored the manner in which the news media inflamed and prejudiced the public.

Much of the material printed or broadcast during the trial was never heard from the witness stand, such as the charges that Sheppard had purposely impeded the murder investigation, and must be guilty, since he had hired a prominent criminal lawyer; that Sheppard was a perjurer; that he had sexual relations with numerous women; that his slain wife had characterized him as a "Jekyll-Hyde"; that he was "a bare-faced liar" because of his testimony as to police treatment; and, finally, that a woman convict claimed Sheppard to be the father of her illegitimate child. As the trial progressed, the newspapers summarized and interpreted the evidence, devoting particular attention to the material that incriminated Sheppard, and often drew unwarranted inferences from testimony. At one point, a front-page picture of Mrs. Sheppard's blood-stained pillow was published after being "doctored" to show more clearly an alleged imprint of a surgical instrument.

Nor is there doubt that this deluge of publicity reached at least some of the jury. On the only occasion that the jury was queried, two jurors admitted in open court to hearing the highly inflammatory charge that a prison inmate claimed Sheppard as the father of her illegitimate child. Despite the extent and nature of the publicity to which the jury was exposed during trial, the judge refused defense counsel's other requests that the jurors be asked whether they had read or heard specific prejudicial comment about the case, including the incidents we have previously summarized. In these circumstances, we can assume that some of this material reached members of the jury. . . .

The carnival atmosphere at trial could easily have been avoided, since the courtroom and courthouse premises are subject to the control of the court. As we stressed in *Estes*, the presence of the press at judicial proceedings must be limited when it is apparent that the accused might otherwise be prejudiced or disadvantaged. Bearing in mind the massive pretrial publicity, the judge should have adopted stricter rules governing the use of the courtroom by newsmen, as Sheppard's counsel requested. The number of reporters in the courtroom itself could have been limited at the first sign that their presence would disrupt the trial. They certainly should not have been placed inside the bar. Furthermore, the judge should have more closely regulated the conduct of newsmen in the courtroom. For instance, the judge belatedly asked them not to handle and photograph trial exhibits lying on the counsel table during recesses.

Secondly, the court should have insulated the witnesses. All of the newspapers and radio stations apparently interviewed prospective witnesses at will, and in many instances disclosed their testimony. . . .

Thirdly, the court should have made some effort to control the release of leads, information, and gossip to the press by police officers, witnesses, and the counsel for both sides. Much of the information thus disclosed was inaccurate, leading to groundless rumors and confusion. . . .

More specifically, the trial court might well have proscribed extrajudicial statements by any lawyer, party, witness, or court official which divulged prejudicial matters, such as the refusal of Sheppard to submit to interrogation or take any lie detector tests; any statement made by Sheppard to officials; the identity of prospective witnesses or their probable testimony; any belief in guilt or innocence; or like statements concerning the merits of the case. . . . Being advised of the great public interest in the case, the mass coverage of the press, and the potential prejudicial impact of publicity, the court could also have requested the appropriate city and county officials to promulgate a regulation with respect to dissemination of information about the case by their employees. In addition, reporters who wrote or broadcast prejudicial stories could have been warned as to the impropriety of publishing material not introduced in the proceedings. The judge was put on notice of such events by defense counsel's complaint about the WHK broadcast on the second day of trial. In this manner, Sheppard's right to a trial free from outside interference would have been given added protection without corresponding curtailment of the news media. Had the judge, the other officers of the court, and the police placed the interest of justice first, the news media would have soon learned to be content with the task of reporting the case as it unfolded in the courtroom—not pieced together from extrajudicial statements. . . .

Since the state trial judge did not fulfill his duty to protect Sheppard from the inherently prejudicial publicity which saturated the community and to control disruptive influences in the courtroom, we must reverse the denial of the habeas petition. The case is remanded to the District Court with instructions to issue the writ and order that Sheppard be released from custody unless the State puts him to its charges again within a reasonable time.

▼▲▼

Sheppard's second trial in 1966 did not attract nearly as much attention as his 1954 trial, and local prosecutors were no match for Bailey, who, after this case, became the most famous, successful, and expensive criminal defense lawyer in the country.[30] Bailey was able to get the coroner in the original Sheppard prosecution, Samuel Gerber, to confess that he had never found the "surgical knife" that prosecutors claimed Sheppard had used to bludgeon his wife. Jurors took only twelve hours to find Sheppard not guilty. After his release from prison, Sheppard set out to prove his innocence. The last years of his life, however, were tragic. Unable to return to his medical practice, he became a professional wrestler under the name "Killer Sheppard," working only sporadically before dying of alcoholism at age 45. His son, Sam Reese Sheppard, who as a child had slept in the next room apparently undisturbed while his mother was murdered, continued the effort to exonerate his father. In 1997, the younger Sheppard provided DNA evidence to prosecutors linking Richard Eberling, a local handyman later jailed in Virginia for murder, to Marilyn Sheppard's murder.

If an uncontrolled press poses a threat to the right of criminal defendants to receive a fair trial, does it follow that judges may prevent them from reporting actual trial proceedings by issuing a "gag order"? Fresh from the lessons of *Sheppard* and distrustful of the growing impact of television on the public's appetite for criminal justice as performance art, the American Bar Association, in 1968, issued guidelines to judges and lawyers on how to safeguard the rights of criminal suspects while upholding the rights of the news media. By 1970, Nebraska was one of many states to adopt the ABA guidelines and modified them to conform to local practices. Publishers and editors from around the state reached an agreement with the state bar association that they would not report a suspect's previous criminal record, whether the suspect had confessed to a crime, or speculate on the suspect's guilt or innocence. Still, many journalists chafed at what they considered a *de facto* prior restraint on their right to communicate freely to the public. They continued to report what they wanted, much to the consternation of judges and criminal defense lawyers. Nebraska's conflict between the press and legal community was not unusual, but the gruesome events of an October evening in Sutherland, a small farming community, highlighted this variation of the right to a fair trial versus the rights of a free press debate for the entire nation.

Nebraska Press Association v. *Stuart*

427 U.S. 539 (1976)

Erwin Charles Simants, an unemployed laborer with an IQ of 75, walked into the home of his brother-in-law, William Boggs, on the evening of October 18, 1970, took his .22 caliber rifle, and headed toward the home of James Henry Kellie. There, he found ten-year-old Florence Kellie all alone, raped her, and later put a bullet through her forehead. Family members standing outside heard Florence scream, and as they came in Simants gunned them down one by one, sparing no one, neither the oldest member of the family, Florence's sixty-six-year-old grandfather, James Henry, nor her five-year-old brother, Daniel. Not even the police were prepared for the massacre in Sutherland, especially the revelation that some of the victims had been sexually assaulted after they were killed.[31]

Word about the murders spread throughout the Sutherland community and beyond before Simants was apprehended by police and arrested the following morning. In the early morning hours reporters had already arrived from larger cities of Omaha and Lincoln, small towns from around the state, and out of state from as far away as Denver. They camped in front of the Kellie house and waited for authorities to bring the bodies out. Police, prosecutors, and various reporters soon got into shouting matches over the refusal of state authorities to provide the press with any information. Adding to the mayhem, a television helicopter hovered, waiting to catch any glimpse of a dead body or picture of the crime scene. Frustrated and tired, a few policemen leaked tidbits of information to the news media. By 2 A.M., less than five hours after the murders, the Associated Press ran a story claiming that Simants was the chief suspect. By 7 A.M., the AP reported that Simants had confessed to his father. That information, it was later learned, came from a conversation that an ambulance driver claimed to have overheard between Simants and his father. Television stations had begun running stories that Simants had "tearfully" confessed to his father. For the moment, Sutherland had become ground zero in the first major post-*Sheppard* conflict between free trial and free press rights.

Mass murderer Erwin Simants being taken into custody after surrendering to police.

After some sparring in the lower courts, a Nebraska trial judge ordered the media gagged from reporting several specific aspects of the Simants proceeding, including Simants' confession and its contents, anything that Simants may have told anyone else, and the names of the victims of the alleged sexual assaults and what had taken place during the assaults. Later the Nebraska Supreme Court narrowed Judge Hugh Stuart's ruling, prohibiting the press from reporting the confession and its contents and any other facts "strongly implicative" of the accused. The Nebraska Press Association, on the advice of the Reporters Committee for Freedom of the Press, a Washington, D.C.–based legal defense and education group, appealed to the U.S. Supreme Court. Meanwhile, Simants's case went forward. After Simants pleaded not guilty by reason of insanity, a jury from the Sutherland community found him guilty of first-degree murder, and Judge Stuart later sentenced him to death. After the trial, several jurors admitted that they had heard all the grisly details of the Kellie family massacre, including the allegations that Simants had sexually assaulted his victims after they were dead.

The Court's decision was unanimous. Chief Justice Burger delivered the opinion of the Court. Justice Brennan, joined by Justices Stewart and Marshall, wrote a concurring opinion. Justice Stevens also concurred.

The Nebraska Supreme Court later reversed Simants's conviction on the grounds that adverse publicity had rendered a fair trial impossible. After a new trial, Simants was found not guilty by reason of insanity, and sentenced to life in a mental institution.

▼▲▼

MR. CHIEF JUSTICE BURGER delivered the opinion of the Court.

The problems presented by this case are almost as old as the Republic. Neither in the Constitution nor in contemporaneous writings do we find that the conflict between these two important rights was anticipated, yet it is inconceivable that the authors of the Constitution were unaware of the potential conflicts between the right to an unbiased jury and the guarantee of freedom of the press. The unusually able lawyers who helped write the Constitution and later drafted the Bill of Rights were familiar with the historic episode in which John Adams defended British soldiers charged with homicide for firing into a crowd of Boston demonstrators; they were intimately familiar with the clash of the adversary system and the part that passions of the populace sometimes play in influencing potential jurors. They did not address themselves directly to the situation presented by this case; their chief concern was the need for freedom of expression in the political arena and the dialogue in ideas. But they recognized that there were risks to private rights from an unfettered press. . . .

The trial of Aaron Burr in 1807 presented Mr. Chief Justice Marshall, presiding as a trial judge, with acute problems in selecting an unbiased jury. Few people in the area of Virginia from which jurors were drawn had not formed some opinions concerning Mr. Burr or the case, from newspaper accounts and heightened discussion both private and public. The Chief Justice conducted a searching *voir dire* of the two panels eventually called, and rendered a substantial opinion on the purposes of *voir dire* and the standards to be applied. Burr was acquitted, so there was no occasion for appellate review to examine the problem of prejudicial pretrial publicity. Mr. Chief Justice Marshall's careful *voir dire* inquiry into the matter of possible bias makes clear that the problem is not a new one.

The speed of communication and the pervasiveness of the modern news media have exacerbated these problems. . . .

In practice, of course, even the most ideal guidelines [between lawyers and the news media] are subjected to powerful strains when a case such as Simants' arises, with reporters from many parts of the country on the scene. Reporters from distant places are unlikely to consider themselves bound by local standards. They report to editors outside the area covered by the guidelines, and their editors are likely to be guided only by their own standards. To contemplate how a state court can control acts of a newspaper or broadcaster outside its jurisdiction, even though the newspapers and broadcasts reach the very community from which jurors are to be selected, suggests something of the practical difficulties of managing such guidelines. . . .

In *Sheppard* v. *Maxwell* (1966), the Court focused sharply on the impact of pretrial publicity and a trial court's duty to protect the defendant's constitutional right to a fair trial. With only Mr. Justice Black dissenting, and he without opinion, the Court ordered a new trial for the petitioner, even though the first trial had occurred 12 years before. Beyond doubt, the press had shown no responsible concern for the constitutional guarantee of a fair trial; the community from which the jury was drawn had been inundated by publicity hostile to the defendant. . . .

Cases such as these are relatively rare, and we have held in other cases that trials have been fair in spite of widespread publicity . . .

. . . [But] pretrial publicity—even pervasive, adverse publicity—does not inevitably lead to an unfair trial. The capacity of the jury eventually impaneled to decide the case fairly is influenced by the tone and extent of the publicity, which is in part, and often in large part, shaped by what attorneys, police, and other officials do to precipitate news coverage. The trial judge has a major responsibility. What the judge says about a case, in or out of the courtroom, is likely to appear in newspapers and broadcasts. More important, the measures a judge takes or fails to take to mitigate the effects of pretrial publicity—the measures described in *Sheppard*—may well determine whether the defendant receives a trial consistent with the requirements of due process. That this responsibility has not always been properly discharged is apparent from the decisions just reviewed. . . .

[Chief Justice Burger then summarized the Court's prior decisions on prior restraint.]

The thread running through all these cases is that prior restraints on speech and publication are the most serious and the least tolerable infringement on First Amendment rights. A criminal penalty or a judgment in a defamation case is subject to the whole panoply of protections afforded by deferring the impact of the judgment until all avenues of appellate review have been exhausted. Only after judgment has become final, correct or otherwise, does the law's sanction become fully operative.

A prior restraint, by contrast and by definition, has an immediate and irreversible sanction. If it can be said that a threat of criminal or civil sanctions after publication "chills" speech, prior restraint "freezes" it at least for the time.

The damage can be particularly great when the prior restraint falls upon the communication of news and commentary on current events. Truthful reports of public judicial proceedings have been afforded special protection against subsequent punishment. . . .

The authors of the Bill of Rights did not undertake to assign priorities as between First Amendment and Sixth Amendment rights, ranking one as superior to the other. In this case, the petitioners would have us declare the right of an accused subordinate to their right to publish in all circumstances. But if the authors of these guarantees, fully aware of the potential conflicts between them, were unwilling or unable to resolve the issue by assigning to one priority over the other, it is not for us to rewrite the Constitution by undertaking what they declined to do. It is unnecessary, after nearly two centuries, to establish a priority applicable in all circumstances. Yet it is nonetheless clear that the barriers to prior restraint remain high unless we are to abandon what the Court has said for nearly a quarter of our national existence and implied throughout all of it. The history of even wartime suspension of categorical guarantees, such as habeas corpus or the right to trial by civilian courts, cautions against suspending explicit guarantees. . . .

Our review of the pretrial record persuades us that the trial judge was justified in concluding that there would be intense and pervasive pretrial publicity concerning this case. He could also reasonably conclude, based on common human experience, that publicity might impair the defendant's right to a fair trial. He did not purport to say more, for he found only "a clear and present danger that pretrial publicity *could* impinge upon the defendant's right to a fair trial." (Emphasis added.) His conclusion as to the impact of such publicity on prospective jurors was, of necessity, speculative, dealing as he was with factors unknown and unknowable. . . .

Finally, we note that the events disclosed by the record took place in a community of 850 people. It is reasonable to assume that, without any news accounts being printed or broadcast, rumors would travel swiftly by word of mouth. One can only speculate on the accuracy of such reports, given the generative propensities of rumors; they could well be more damaging than reasonably accurate news accounts. But plainly a whole community cannot be restrained from discussing a subject intimately affecting life within it.

Given these practical problems, it is far from clear that prior restraint on publication would have protected Simants' rights. . . .

Of necessity, our holding is confined to the record before us. But our conclusion is not simply a result of assessing the adequacy of the showing made in this case; it results in part from the problems inherent in meeting the heavy burden of demonstrating, in advance of trial, that without prior restraint a fair trial will be denied. The practical problems of managing and enforcing restrictive orders will always be present. In this sense, the record now before us is illustrative, rather than exceptional. It is significant that, when this Court has reversed a state conviction because of prejudicial publicity, it has carefully noted that some course of action short of prior restraint would have made a critical difference. However difficult it may be, we need not rule out the possibility of showing the kind of threat to fair trial rights that would possess the requisite degree of certainty to justify restraint. This Court has frequently denied that First Amendment rights are absolute and has consistently rejected the proposition that a prior restraint can never be employed.

Our analysis ends as it began, with a confrontation between prior restraint imposed to protect one vital constitutional guarantee and the explicit command of another that the freedom to speak and publish shall not be abridged. We reaffirm that the guarantees of freedom of expression are not an absolute prohibition under all circumstances, but the barriers to prior restraint remain high, and the presumption against its use continues intact. We hold that, with respect to the order entered in this case prohibiting reporting or commentary on judicial proceedings held in public, the barriers have not been overcome; to the extent that this order restrained publication of such material, it is clearly invalid. To the extent that it prohibited publication based on information gained from other sources, we conclude that the heavy burden imposed as a condition to securing a prior restraint was not met, and the judgment of the Nebraska Supreme Court is therefore

Reversed.

MR. JUSTICE BRENNAN, with whom MR. JUSTICE STEWART and MR. JUSTICE MARSHALL join, concurring in the judgment.

No one can seriously doubt . . . that uninhibited prejudicial pretrial publicity may destroy the fairness of a criminal trial, and the past decade has witnessed substantial debate, colloquially known as the Free Press/Fair Trial controversy, concerning this interface of First and Sixth Amendment rights. In effect, we are now told by respondents that the two rights can no longer coexist when the press possesses and seeks to publish "confessions or admissions against interest" and other information "strongly implicative" of a criminal defendant as the perpetrator of a crime, and that one or the other right must therefore be subordinated. I disagree. Settled case law concerning the impropriety and constitutional invalidity of prior restraints on the press compels the conclusion that there can be no prohibition on the publication by the press of any information pertaining to pending judicial proceedings or the operation of the criminal justice system, no matter how shabby the means by which the information is obtained. This does not imply, however, any subordination of Sixth Amendment rights, for an accused's right to a fair trial may be adequately assured through methods that do not infringe First Amendment values. . . .

I unreservedly agree with Mr. Justice Black that "free speech and fair trials are two of the most cherished policies of our civilization, and it would be a trying task to choose between them." But I would reject the notion that a choice is necessary, that there is an inherent conflict that cannot be resolved without essentially abrogating one right or the other. To hold that courts cannot impose any prior restraints on the reporting of or commentary upon information revealed in open court proceedings, disclosed in public documents, or divulged by other sources with respect to the criminal justice system is not, I must emphasize, to countenance the sacrifice of precious Sixth Amendment rights on the altar of the First Amendment. For although there may in some instances be tension between uninhibited and robust reporting by the press and fair trials for criminal defendants, judges possess adequate tools short of injunctions against reporting for relieving that tension. To be sure, these alternatives may require greater sensitivity and effort on the part of judges conducting criminal trials than would the stifling of publicity through the simple expedient of issuing a restrictive order on the press; but that sensitivity and effort is required in order to ensure the full enjoyment and proper accommodation of both First and Sixth Amendment rights.

Voluntary codes such as the Nebraska Bar-Press Guidelines are a commendable acknowledgment by the media that constitutional prerogatives bring enormous responsibilities, and I would encourage continuation of such voluntary cooperative efforts between the bar and the media. However, the press may be arrogant, tyrannical, abusive, and sensationalist, just as it may be incisive, probing, and informative. But at least in the context of prior restraints on publication, the decision of what, when, and how to publish is for editors, not judges. Every restrictive order imposed on the press in this case was accordingly an unconstitutional prior restraint on the freedom of the press.

Chief Justice Burger's opinion makes clear that the Court considered Judge Stuart's gag order a heavy-handed form of prior restraint on freedom of the press. During the Court's conference on *Nebraska Press Association*, Burger had noted that "prior restraints may in some cases be permissible," but such was not the case here. The Court, Burger said, "decided this case when we decided the *Pentagon Papers* case." Even justices committed to a less absolutist view of free speech and press rights, such as Justices Blackmun and Rehnquist, could not justify a prior restraint on "what has occurred in open court."[32] What made *Nebraska Press Association* a far different case from *New York Times* was that it involved information already in the hands of the public, not information being withheld by the government. However distasteful the Court found the prospect of inflammatory pretrial publicity in Sam Sheppard's trial, *Nebraska Press Association* makes clear that a prior restraint on the rights of the news media to disseminate information is far more repugnant. Since *Nebraska Press Association*, the Court has invalidated laws prohibiting the press from reporting the names of rape victims and other such prior restraints involving judicial proceedings.[33]

Do Reporters Have More First Amendment Rights Than Anybody Else?

Prior restraints such as those in the *Pentagon Papers* case and *Nebraska Press Association* deal with the outer limits of the press under the First Amendment to *report* what they know to the public. But the Court has also decided several important cases that raise the question of whether the First Amendment affords the news media rights above and beyond ordinary persons to *gather* news. No privilege is more zealously guarded among journalists than the right to protect the confidentiality of their news sources, even when that means running afoul of government demands to reveal those sources' names or produce information in connection with a criminal investigation or trial proceeding. Likewise, journalists have also asserted that the Press Clause permits them access to sources and information off-limits to the general public. In *Branzburg* v. *Hayes* (1972) and *Houchins* v. *KQED, Inc.* (1978), the Court rejected the arguments of two journalists that the First Amendment entitled them special rights unavailable to the general public.

Branzburg v. *Hayes*

408 U.S. 665 (1972)

Paul Branzburg, a reporter for the *Louisville Courier-Journal*, had written an extensive investigative article on how marijuana was processed into a much more potent drug, hashish. In writing the story, Branzburg had cultivated the confidence of several drug producers and street dealers, based on his promise of confidentiality. One drug producer told Branzburg he was cooperating with the reporter "to make the narcs mad." A judge later ordered Branzburg to appear before a grand jury hearing a drug case and identify his sources. Branzburg refused, and was cited for contempt of court. An appeal to have the contempt order set aside on the grounds that a reporter's right to protect his sources is protected by the First Amendment was denied.

Two other reporters, Paul Pappas and Earl Caldwell, brought separate lawsuits after they were subpoenaed by federal grand juries to discuss their news stories that appeared in the late 1960s and early 1970s on the Black Panthers and other African American groups, which were considered "militant" by government authorities.

The Court's decision was 5 to 4. Justice White delivered the opinion of the Court. Justice Powell wrote a concurring opinion. Justice Stewart, joined by Justices Brennan and Marshall, dissented. Justice Douglas also dissented.

Opinion of the Court by MR. JUSTICE WHITE, announced by THE CHIEF JUSTICE.

The issue in these cases is whether requiring newsmen to appear and testify before state or federal grand juries abridges the freedom of speech and press guaranteed by the First Amendment. We hold that it does not. . . .

We do not question the significance of free speech, press, or assembly to the country's welfare. Nor is it suggested that news gathering does not qualify for First Amendment protection; without some protection for seeking out the news, freedom of the press could be eviscerated. But these cases involve no intrusions upon speech or assembly, no prior restraint or restriction on what the press may publish, and no express or implied command that the press publish what it prefers to withhold. No exaction or tax for the privilege of publishing, and no penalty, civil or criminal, related to the content of published material is at issue here. The use of confidential sources by the press is not forbidden or restricted; reporters remain free to seek news from any source by means within the law. No attempt is made to require the press to publish its sources of information or indiscriminately to disclose them on request.

The sole issue before us is the obligation of reporters to respond to grand jury subpoenas as other citizens do, and to answer questions relevant to an investigation into the commission of crime. Citizens generally are not constitutionally immune from grand jury subpoenas, and neither the First Amendment nor any other constitutional provision protects the average citizen from disclosing to a grand jury information that he has received in confidence. The claim is, however, that reporters are exempt from these obligations because, if forced to respond to subpoenas and identify their sources or disclose other confidences, their informants will refuse or be reluctant to furnish newsworthy information in the future. This asserted burden on news gathering is said to make compelled testimony from newsmen constitutionally suspect, and to require a privileged position for them.

It is clear that the First Amendment does not invalidate every incidental burdening of the press that may result from the enforcement of civil or criminal statutes of general applicability. . . .

The prevailing view is that the press is not free to publish with impunity everything and anything it desires to publish. Although it may deter or regulate what is said or published, the press may not circulate knowing or reckless falsehoods damaging to private reputation without subjecting itself to liability for damages, including punitive damages, or even criminal prosecution. A newspaper or a journalist may also be punished for contempt of court, in appropriate circumstances.

It has generally been held that the First Amendment does not guarantee the press a constitutional right of special access to information not available to the public generally. [F]or example, the Court sustained the Government's refusal to validate passports to Cuba even though that restriction "render[ed] less than wholly free the flow of information concerning that country." . . .

Despite the fact that news gathering may be hampered, the press is regularly excluded from grand jury proceedings, our own conferences, the meetings of other official bodies gathered in executive session, and the meetings of private organizations. Newsmen have no constitutional right of access to the scenes of crime or disaster when the general public is excluded, and they may be prohibited from attending or publishing information about trials if such restrictions are necessary to assure a defendant a fair trial before an impartial tribunal. In *Sheppard* v. *Maxwell* (1966), for example, the Court reversed a state court conviction where the trial court failed to adopt "stricter rules governing the use of the courtroom by newsmen, as Sheppard's counsel requested," neglected to insulate witnesses from the press, and made no "effort to control the release of leads, information, and gossip to the press by police officers, witnesses, and the counsel for both sides." . . .

The prevailing constitutional view of the newsman's privilege is very much rooted in the ancient role of the grand jury that has the dual function of determining if there is probable cause to believe that a crime has been committed and of protecting citizens against unfounded criminal prosecutions. Grand jury proceedings are constitutionally mandated for the institution of federal criminal prosecutions for capital or other serious crimes, and "its constitutional prerogatives are rooted in long centuries of Anglo-American history." The Fifth Amendment provides that "[n]o person shall be held to answer for a capital, or otherwise infamous crime, unless on a presentment or indictment of a Grand Jury." The adoption of the grand jury "in our Constitution as the sole method for preferring charges in serious criminal cases shows the high place it held as an instrument of justice." Although state systems of criminal procedure differ greatly among themselves, the grand jury is similarly guaranteed by many state constitutions and plays an important role in fair and effective law enforcement in the overwhelming majority of the States. Because its task is to inquire into the existence of possible criminal conduct and to return only well founded indictments, its investigative powers are necessarily broad. . . .

The preference for anonymity of those confidential informants involved in actual criminal conduct is presumably a product of their desire to escape criminal prosecution, and this preference, while understandable, is hardly deserving of constitutional protection. It would be frivolous to assert—and no one does in these cases—that the First Amendment, in the interest of securing news or otherwise, confers a license on either the reporter or his news sources to violate valid criminal laws. Although stealing documents or private wiretapping could provide newsworthy information, neither reporter nor source is immune from conviction for such conduct, whatever the impact on the flow of news. Neither is immune, on First Amendment grounds, from testifying against the other, before the grand jury or at a criminal trial. The Amendment does not reach so far as to override the interest of the public in ensuring that neither reporter nor source is invading the rights of other citizens through reprehensible conduct forbidden to all other persons. . . . Thus, we cannot seriously entertain the notion that the First Amendment protects a newsman's agreement to conceal the criminal conduct of his source, or evidence thereof, on the theory that it is better to write about crime than to do something about it. Insofar as any reporter in these cases undertook not to reveal or testify about the crime he witnessed, his claim of privilege under the First Amendment presents no substantial question. The crimes of news sources are no less reprehensible and threatening to the public interest when witnessed by a reporter than when they are not. . . .

[T]he privilege claimed is that of the reporter, not the informant, and that, if the authorities independently identify the informant, neither his own reluctance to testify nor the objection of the newsman would shield him from grand jury inquiry, whatever the impact on the flow of news or on his future usefulness as a secret source of information. More important, it is obvious that agreements to conceal information relevant to commission of crime have very little to recommend them from the standpoint of public policy. . . .

Of course, the press has the right to abide by its agreement not to publish all the information it has, but the right to withhold news is not equivalent to a First Amendment exemption from the ordinary duty of all other citizens to furnish relevant information to a grand jury performing an important public function. Private restraints on the flow of information are not so favored by the First Amendment that they override all other public interests. . . .

We are admonished that refusal to provide a First Amendment reporter's privilege will undermine the freedom of the press to collect and disseminate news. But this is not the lesson history teaches us. As noted previously, the common law recognized no such privilege, and the constitutional argument was not even asserted until 1958. From the beginning of our country the press has operated without constitutional protection for press informants, and the press has flourished. The existing constitutional rules have not been a serious obstacle to either the development or retention of confidential news sources by the press.

It is said that currently press subpoenas have multiplied, that mutual distrust and tension between press and officialdom have increased, that reporting styles have changed, and that there is now more need for confidential sources, particularly where the press seeks news about minority cultural and political groups or dissident organizations suspicious of the law and public officials. These developments, even if true, are treacherous grounds for a far-reaching interpretation of the First Amendment fastening a nationwide rule on courts, grand juries, and prosecuting officials everywhere. The obligation to testify in response to grand jury subpoenas will not threaten these sources not involved with criminal conduct and without information relevant to grand jury investigations, and we cannot hold that the Constitution places the sources in these two categories either above the law or beyond its reach. . . .

We are unwilling to embark the judiciary on a long and difficult journey to such an uncertain destination. The administration of a constitutional newsman's privilege would present practical and conceptual difficulties of a high order. Sooner or later, it would be necessary to define those categories of newsmen who qualified for the privilege, a questionable procedure in light of the traditional doctrine that liberty of the press is the right of the lonely pamphleteer who uses carbon paper or a mimeograph just as much as of the large metropolitan publisher who utilizes the latest photocomposition methods. . . . The informative function asserted by representatives of the organized press in the present cases is also performed by lecturers, political pollsters, novelists, academic researchers, and dramatists. Almost any author may quite accurately assert that he is contributing to the flow of information to the public, that he relies on confidential sources of information, and that these sources will be silenced if he is forced to make disclosures before a grand jury. . . .

[N]ews gathering is not without its First Amendment protections, and grand jury investigations, if instituted or conducted other than in good faith, would pose wholly different issues for resolution under the First Amendment. Official harassment of the press undertaken not for purposes of law enforcement, but to disrupt a reporter's relationship with his news sources would have no justification. Grand juries are subject to judicial control and subpoenas to motions to quash. We do not expect courts will forget that grand juries must operate within the limits of the First Amendment as well as the Fifth. . . .

The decision . . . in *Branzburg* v. *Hayes* . . . must be affirmed.

MR. JUSTICE STEWART, with whom MR. JUSTICE BRENNAN and MR. JUSTICE MARSHALL join, dissenting.

The Court's crabbed view of the First Amendment reflects a disturbing insensitivity to the critical role of an independent press in our society. The question whether a reporter has a constitutional right to a confidential relationship with his source is of first impression here, but the principles that should guide our decision are as basic as any to be found in the Constitution. . . . [T]he Court in these cases holds that a newsman has no First Amendment right to protect his sources when called before a grand jury. The Court thus invites state and federal authorities to undermine the historic independence of the press by attempting to annex the journalistic profession as an investigative arm of government. Not only will this decision impair performance of the press' constitutionally protected functions, but it will, I am convinced, in the long run harm, rather than help, the administration of justice. . . .

The right to gather news implies, in turn, a right to a confidential relationship between a reporter and his source. This proposition follows as a matter of simple logic once three factual predicates are recognized: (1) newsmen require informants to gather news; (2) confidentiality—the promise or understanding that names or certain aspects of communications will be kept off the record—is essential to the creation and maintenance of a newsgathering relationship with informants; and (3) an unbridled subpoena power—the absence of a constitutional right protecting, in any way, a confidential relationship from compulsory process—will either deter source from divulging information or deter reporters from gathering and publishing information.

It is obvious that informants are necessary to the newsgathering process as we know it today. If it is to perform its constitutional mission, the press must do far more than merely print public statements or publish prepared handouts. Familiarity with the people and circumstances involved in the myriad background activities that result in the final product called "news" is vital to complete and responsible journalism, unless the press is to be a captive mouthpiece of "newsmakers."

Houchins v. *KQED, Inc.*

438 U.S. 1 (1978)

On March 31, 1975, KQED, a television station serving the San Francisco Bay area, learned that an African American inmate had committed suicide in the Little Greystone wing of the Alameda County jail. Based on reports it had received from psychiatrists and other prison professionals on the poor conditions in Little Greystone, KQED requested permission to take photographs of the facility. KQED wanted to investigate whether prison conditions were responsible for the inmate's death, as their sources had told station reporters. The county sheriff refused to grant a KQED news team access to Little Greystone, which prompted the local chapter of the NAACP to file suit under federal civil rights law demanding access to the facility. The NAACP claimed that television coverage of the conditions in the cells and facilities was the most effective way of informing the public of squalid prison conditions. Indeed, something must not have been quite right in Little Greystone; one psychiatrist who met with KQED reporters was fired after the broadcast.

In response, the local sheriff agreed to start holding monthly tours of the Alameda jail open to the public and the news media, but forbade reporters from entering the Little Greystone wing, home to the prison's most violent offenders. But the sheriff also banned cameras and sound equipment and refused to permit visitors to conduct interviews with inmates. The NAACP contested this policy, claiming that by prohibiting media access to information the sheriff was denying the community at large from entering into the public debate about local prison conditions. Ultimately, a federal district court judge agreed with the NAACP that the sheriff's policy violated KQED's constitutional right to enter the jail and record information for broadcast to the public. The Ninth Circuit Court of Appeals affirmed.

The Court's decision was 4 to 3. Chief Justice Burger delivered the plurality opinion of the Court, which was joined by Justices Rehnquist and White. Justice Stewart filed an opinion concurring in the judgment. Justice Stevens, joined by Justices Brennan and Powell, dissented. Justices Blackmun and Marshall did not participate.

MR. CHIEF JUSTICE BURGER announced the judgment of the Court and delivered an opinion, in which MR. JUSTICE WHITE and MR. JUSTICE REHNQUIST joined.

The question presented is whether the news media have a constitutional right of access to a county jail, over and above that of other persons, to interview inmates and make sound recordings, films, and photographs for publication and broadcasting by newspapers, radio, and television.

[KQED] assert[s] that the right recognized by the Court of Appeals flows logically from our decisions construing the First Amendment. They argue that there is a constitutionally guaranteed right to gather news under . . . *Branzburg* v. *Hayes* (1972). From the right to gather news and the right to receive information, they argue for an implied special right of access to government-controlled sources of information. This right, they contend, compels access as a constitutional matter. [KQED] contend[s] that public access to penal institutions is necessary to prevent officials from concealing prison conditions from the voters and impairing the public's right to discuss and criticize the prison system and its administration.

We can agree with many of the respondents' generalized assertions; conditions in jails and prisons are clearly matters "of great public importance." Penal facilities are public institutions which require large amounts of public funds, and their mission is crucial in our criminal justice system. Each person placed in prison becomes, in effect, a ward of the state for whom society assumes broad responsibility. It is equally true that, with greater information, the public can more intelligently form opinions about prison conditions. Beyond question, the role of the media is important; acting as the "eyes and ears" of the public, they can be a powerful and constructive force, contributing to remedial action in the conduct of public business. They have served that function since the beginning of the Republic, but, like all other components of our society, media representatives are subject to limits.

The media are not a substitute for or an adjunct of government and, like the courts, they are "ill-equipped" to deal with problems of prison administration. We must not confuse the role of the media with that of government; each has special, crucial functions, each complementing—and sometimes conflicting with—the other.

The public importance of conditions in penal facilities and the media's role of providing information afford no basis for reading into the Constitution a right of the public or the media to enter these institutions, with camera equipment, and take moving and still pictures of inmates for broadcast purposes. This Court has never intimated a First Amendment guarantee of a right of access to all sources of information within government control. Nor does the rationale of the decisions upon which respondents rely lead to the implication of such a right. . . .

Branzburg v. *Hayes* offers [little] support for the respondents' position. Its observation, in dictum, that "news gathering is not without its First Amendment protections," in no sense implied a constitutional right of access to news sources. That observation must be read in context; it was in response to the contention that forcing a reporter to disclose to a grand jury information received in confidence would violate the First Amendment by deterring news sources from communicating information. There is an undoubted right to gather news "from any source by means within the law," but that affords no basis for the claim that the First Amendment compels others—private persons or government to supply information.

That the Court assumed in *Branzburg* that there is no First Amendment right of access to information is manifest from its statements that "the First Amendment does not guarantee the press a constitutional right of special access to information not available to the public generally," and that "[n]ewsmen have no constitutional right of access to the scenes of crime or disaster when the general public is excluded." . . .

[KQED's] argument is flawed . . . because it invites the Court to involve itself in what is clearly a legislative task which the Constitution has left to the political processes. Whether the government should open penal institutions in the manner sought by respondents is a question of policy which a legislative body might appropriately resolve one way or the other. . . .

There is no discernible basis for a constitutional duty to disclose, or for standards governing disclosure of or access to information. Because the Constitution affords no guidelines, absent statutory standards, hundreds of judges would, under the Court of Appeals' approach, be at large to fashion *ad hoc* standards, in individual cases, according to their own ideas of what seems "desirable" or "expedient." We, therefore, reject the Court of Appeals' conclusory assertion that the public and the media have a First Amendment right to government information regarding the conditions of jails and their inmates and presumably all other public facilities such as hospitals and mental institutions. . . .

Neither the First Amendment nor the Fourteenth Amendment mandates a right of access to government information or sources of information within the government's control. Under our holdings, . . . until the political branches decree otherwise, as they are free to do, the media have no special right of access to the Alameda County Jail different from or greater than that accorded the public generally.

The judgment of the Court of Appeals is reversed, and the case is remanded for further proceedings.

Reversed and remanded.

MR. JUSTICE STEWART, concurring in the judgment.

I agree that the preliminary injunction issued against the petitioner was unwarranted, and therefore concur in the judgment. In my view, however, KQED was entitled to injunctive relief of more limited scope.

The First and Fourteenth Amendments do not guarantee the public a right of access to information generated or controlled by government, nor do they guarantee the press any basic right of access superior to that of the public generally. The Constitution does no more than assure the public and the press equal access once government has opened its doors. Accordingly, I agree substantially with what the opinion of THE CHIEF JUSTICE has to say on that score.

We part company, however, in applying these abstractions to the facts of this case. Whereas he appears to view "equal access" as meaning access that is identical in all respects, I believe that the concept of equal access must be accorded more flexibility in order to accommodate the practical distinctions between the press and the general public.

When on assignment, a journalist does not tour a jail simply for his own edification. He is there to gather information to be passed on to others, and his mission is protected by the Constitution for very specific reasons. "Enlightened choice by an informed citizenry is the basic ideal upon which an open society is premised. . . ," *Branzburg* v. *Hayes* (1972). Our society depends heavily on the press for that enlightenment. . . .

That the First Amendment speaks separately of freedom of speech and freedom of the press is no constitutional accident, but an acknowledgment of the critical role played by the press in American society. The Constitution requires sensitivity to that role, and to the special needs of the press in performing it effectively. A person touring Santa Rita jail can grasp its reality with his own eyes and ears. But if a television reporter is to convey the jail's sights and sounds to those who cannot personally visit the place, he must use cameras and sound equipment. In short, terms of access that are reasonably imposed on individual members of the public may, if they impede effective reporting without sufficient justification, be unreasonable as applied to journalists who are there to convey to the general public what the visitors see.

Under these principles, KQED was clearly entitled to some form of preliminary injunctive relief. At the time of the District Court's decision, members of the public were permitted to visit most parts of the Santa Rita jail, and the First and Fourteenth Amendments required the Sheriff to give members of the press effective access to the same areas. The Sheriff evidently assumed that he could fulfill this obligation simply by allowing.reporters to sign up for tours on the same terms as the public. I think he was mistaken in this assumption, as a matter of constitutional law. . . .

In two respects, however, the District Court's preliminary injunction was overbroad. It ordered the Sheriff to permit reporters into the Little Greystone facility and it required him to let them interview randomly encountered inmates. In both these respects, the injunction gave the press access to areas and sources of information from which persons on the public tours had been excluded, and thus enlarged the scope of what the Sheriff and Supervisors had opened to public view. The District Court erred in concluding that the First and Fourteenth Amendments compelled this broader access for the press.

MR. JUSTICE STEVENS, with whom MR. JUSTICE BRENNAN and MR. JUSTICE POWELL join, dissenting.

KQED, Inc., has televised a number of programs about prison conditions and prison inmates, and its reporters have been granted access to various correctional facilities in the San Francisco Bay area, including San Quentin State Prison, Soledad Prison, and the San Francisco County Jails at San Bruno and San Francisco, to prepare program material. They have taken their cameras and recording equipment inside the walls of those institutions and interviewed inmates. No disturbances or other problems have occurred on those occasions.

KQED has also reported newsworthy events involving the Alameda County Jail in Santa Rita, including a 1972 newscast reporting a decision of the United States District Court finding that the "shocking and debasing conditions which prevailed [at Santa Rita] constituted cruel and unusual punishment for man or beast as a matter of law." . . .

Here . . . the restrictions on access to the inner portions of the Santa Rita jail that existed on the date this litigation commenced concealed from the general public the conditions of confinement within the facility. The question is whether petitioner's policies, which cut off the flow of information at its source, abridged the public's right to be informed about those conditions.

The answer to that question does not depend upon the degree of public disclosure which should attend the operation of most governmental activity. Such matters involve questions of policy which generally must be resolved by the political branches of government. Moreover, there are unquestionably occasions when governmental activity may properly be carried on in complete secrecy. For example, the public and the press are commonly excluded from "grand jury proceedings, our own conferences, [and] the meetings of other official bodies gathered in executive session. . . ," *Branzburg* v. *Hayes* (1972). In addition, some functions of government—essential to the protection of the public and indeed our country's vital interests—necessarily require a large measure of secrecy, subject to appropriate legislative oversight. . . .

In this case, the record demonstrates that both the public and the press had been consistently denied any access to the inner portions of the Santa Rita jail, that there had been excessive censorship of inmate correspondence, and that there was no valid justification for these broad restraints on the flow of information. An affirmative answer to the question whether respondents established a likelihood of prevailing on the merits did not depend, in final analysis, on any right of the press to special treatment beyond that accorded the public at large. Rather, the probable existence of a constitutional violation rested upon the special importance of allowing a democratic community access to knowledge about how its servants were treating some of its members who have been com-

mitted to their custody. An official prison policy of concealing such knowledge from the public by arbitrarily cutting off the flow of information at its source abridges the freedom of speech and of the press protected by the First and Fourteenth Amendments to the Constitution.

Houchins was a close case; indeed, Chief Justice Burger's plurality opinion began as a dissent, with Stevens originally assigned to write the Court's plurality opinion on behalf of himself, Brennan, Powell, and Stewart. But Stevens's conclusion that the news media had a broad right of access under the First Amendment proved too much for Stewart, who had earlier written his colleagues, "The First Amendment does not give [the press] access superior to that of the general public. [T]here is no such thing as a constitutional right to know." Had the sheriff decided not to open the Alameda jail for limited public tours, Stewart argued that he would have had no special obligation to provide access to the press. Burger summarized the majority's view in his second draft opinion, which now included Stewart: "As a legislator, I would vote for a reasonably orderly access to prisons, etc., by media, because it would be useful. But that is not the issue. The question is whether special access rights are *constitutionally compelled*." The answer, said Burger, was no.[34]

Decisions subsequent to *Branzburg* and *KQED* make clear that the Court does not subscribe to the news media's view that the First Amendment provides legal immunity for journalistic endeavors and affords the press a special right of access to information not available to the general public. In *Zurcher* v. *Stanford Daily* (1978), the Court ruled that a college newspaper had no First Amendment defense against the police making an unannounced search of its newsroom to comb through its records and files for material relevant to a criminal investigation. Newsrooms around the country reacted with great dismay to *Zurcher.* Many began concealing records that might implicate their sources in ongoing investigative stories or previously published or broadcast material. So unpopular was *Zurcher* with the public that Congress, in 1980, passed the Privacy Protection Act, which prohibited searches of journalists for documentary materials except in cases of unusual circumstances. Those circumstances include the following situations: (1) the prevention of death or injury to another person; (2) the protection of documents from destruction; (3) a subpoena has been ineffective in securing the requested materials; and (4) the journalist is suspected of criminal behavior. States are also permitted to enact laws allowing reporters to protect their sources and granting special rights to the news media to acquire information not available to the general public.

Congress has also enacted legislation affording the broader public the right to retrieve federal records, thus bypassing the Court's position that access to government information is not necessarily a constitutional right. The most well-known of such federal laws is the Freedom of Information Act (FOIA). Enacted in 1966 and amended several times since then, the FOIA has enabled journalists, scholars, political dissidents, and ordinary Americans to retrieve records involving previously closed matters, including any records kept on themselves.[35]

Libel

Libertarian theory in the early 1800s openly questioned the constitutionality of seditious libel laws. After the American Revolution, state libel laws distinguished between "truth" and "facts," which were permissible defenses, and "falsehoods," which were punishable under criminal law. Similar distinctions in libel law were also drawn between statements made with "good motives" and those motivated by "criminal intent." These distinctions were gradually phased out during the nineteenth century, as they were perceived as unhelpful to juries now charged with determining the guilt or innocence of persons charged with libel. Indeed, James Madison believed the theory of "malice," or the idea that certain statements were knowingly false and defamatory, as a spear in the heart of the freedom of the press. Criminal punishment for "malice" was a powerful and subjective tool of the government to silence its critics, who, Madison concluded, tended to excite unfavorable sentiments in their comments.[36]

Libel law did not, however, follow the libertarian model preferred by Madison and other early-nineteenth-century advocates of broad free speech and press rights. By the early 1960s, most states still followed the common law of libel that had developed after the demise of the Sedition Act of 1798. Three principles formed the basis of libel law during this period. First, a statement considered defamatory was presumed false. This placed the burden of proof in libel trials on the publisher, and truth was—and remains—difficult to prove. Second, it did not matter whether a falsehood was published intentionally or negligently. All that mattered was whether the information was false. Finally, the injured party did not have to demonstrate *actual* harm to his or her reputation. Harm was presumed to exist from publication. Combined, the force of these three rules meant that libel defendants had to prove the absolute accuracy of what they said or they would lose.[37]

New York Times v. *Sullivan* (1964) completely revolutionized libel law. For the first time, the Court forged a constitutional definition of libel by drawing upon the common law rules that had sought to balance freedom of the press with the right of individuals against defamation. Before *Sullivan,* the Court had only scuffled with libel law, upholding in *Beauharnais* v. *Illinois* (1952) a state law mandating penalties for words or photos depicting the "depravity, criminality, unchastity, or lack of virtue of a class of citizens, or any race, color or creed." *Beauharnais* involved a criminal penalty against a private citizen for group libel. But Justice William Douglas, dissenting, perceptively noted the implications the Court's decision might have for individuals who chose to denounce public officials, the very basis of the civil libel action in *Sullivan*. Wrote Douglas: "Today, a white man stands convicted for protesting in unseemly language against our decisions invalidating restrictive covenants. Tomorrow a Negro will be hauled before a court for denouncing lynch law in heated terms. . . . Intemperate speech is a distinctive characteristic of man. Hot-heads blow off and release destructive energy in the process."[38] *Sullivan,* however, chartered a much different course.

New York Times v. *Sullivan*

376 U.S. 254 (1964)

In February 1960, four African American college students entered the Woolworth's department store in downtown Greensboro, N.C., quietly took a seat at the lunch counter reserved for whites only, and politely requested service. They were refused service and subsequently arrested for violating a state segregation law. But word of their courageous action spread throughout the Deep South. Soon, other African American and occasionally white students followed suit, thus giving birth to the "sit-ins" that later became an extremely effective tactic of the civil rights movement. Dr. Martin Luther King Jr. publicly endorsed the student sit-in movement, which only served further to infuriate white segregationist politicians. In early March, Alabama officials arrested King on trumped-up felony tax evasion charges, the first such arrest in Alabama history. By jailing King, Alabama demonstrated that it was not afraid to strike at the heart of the civil rights movement's leadership.

In response, civil rights leaders set up a separate committee in New York City to raise funds to fight the legal battles of King and several others who had been arrested and jailed by Southern law enforcement. In late March, the committee put together an advertisement entitled "Heed Their Rising Voices," which described Southern hostility toward the civil rights movement. The ad was signed by over fifty people, including entertainers, professional athletes, and political activists, and endorsed by nineteen ministers from the Deep South.

In 1960, the *New York Times* had a circulation of 650,000. Only 394 of those newspapers were delivered to Alabama. Ray Jenkins, the city editor of the *Alabama Journal,* Montgomery's evening paper, saw the "Heed Their Rising Voices" advertisement. He noticed there were several small errors in fact throughout the advertisement, and wrote a story the same day pointing out these errors. Word of the ad later passed to City Commissioner L. B. Sullivan, who believed that it wrongly implicated him and the Montgomery police in "grave misconduct." Sullivan sent a letter to the *New York Times* demanding a "full and fair retraction of the entire false and defamatory matter." Lawyers for the newspaper asked Sullivan to point out how the advertisement defamed him, since the commissioner was never mentioned. Sullivan did not reply to the *Times;* instead, he filed a $500,000 libel suit against the newspaper in state court. Under Alabama law, a public official could not recover monetary damages for libel unless he or she first asked for a retraction and did not receive one. Moreover, Sullivan named as co-defendants four of the ministers, all from Alabama, who had signed the advertisement.

Federal judicial procedure permits a case involving a civil action to be heard in federal court if the parties are from different states. Lawyers for Sullivan believed that by bringing the Alabama ministers into the lawsuit, the *New York Times* would have to try the case in state court, a much friendlier venue for a local public official involved in a libel action against both black ministers and a Northern newspaper sympathetic to the civil rights movement. Governor John Patterson also filed a libel suit against the *New York Times* and the same black ministers, even though the *Times* had published a retraction for any unfounded charges the advertisement might have made against him. By the time the *Sullivan* and *Patterson* cases went to trial, the defendants faced possible damage awards of $3,000,000.[39]

The jury awarded Sullivan $500,000. The Alabama Supreme Court unanimously upheld Sullivan's libel award. The *Times* and the ministers, Ralph D. Abernathy, Fred Shuttlesworth, S. S. Seay Sr., and Joseph E. Lowry, had only one option left to avoid paying the damages to Sullivan: to appeal to the United States Supreme Court.

The Court's decision was unanimous. Justice Brennan delivered the opinion of the Court. Justices Black and Goldberg wrote separate concurring opinions, both of which were joined by Justice Douglas.

▼▲▼

MR. JUSTICE BRENNAN delivered the opinion of the Court.

We are required in this case to determine for the first time the extent to which the constitutional protections for speech and press limit a State's power to award damages in a libel action brought by a public official against critics of his official conduct. . . .

We reverse the judgment. We hold that the rule of law applied by the Alabama courts is constitutionally deficient for failure to provide the safeguards for freedom of speech and of the press that are required by the First and Fourteenth Amendments in a libel action brought by a public official against critics of his official conduct. We further hold that, under the proper safeguards, the evidence presented in this case is constitutionally insufficient to support the judgment for respondent.

The . . . contention is that the constitutional guarantees of freedom of speech and of the press are inapplicable here, at least so far as the *Times* is concerned, because the allegedly libelous statements were published as part of a paid, "commercial" advertisement. . . .

The publication here was not a "commercial" advertisement. . . . It communicated information, expressed opinion, recited grievances, protested claimed abuses, and sought financial support on behalf of a movement whose existence and objectives are matters of the highest public interest and concern. That the *Times* was paid for publishing the advertisement is as immaterial in this connection as is the fact that newspapers and books are sold. Any other conclusion would discourage newspapers from carrying "editorial advertisements" of this type, and so might shut off an important outlet for the promulgation of information and ideas by persons who do not themselves have access to publishing facilities—who wish to exercise their freedom of speech even though they are not members of the press. The effect would be to shackle the First Amendment in its attempt to secure "the widest possible dissemination of information from diverse and antagonistic sources." To avoid placing such a handicap upon the freedoms of expression, we hold that, if the allegedly libelous statements would otherwise be constitutionally protected from the present judgment, they do not forfeit that protection because they were published in the form of a paid advertisement.

Under Alabama law, as applied in this case, a publication is "libelous *per se*" if the words "tend to injure a person . . . in his reputation" or to "bring [him] into public contempt"; the trial court stated that the standard was met if the words are such as to "injure him in his public office, or impute misconduct to him in his office, or want of official integrity, or want of fidelity to a public trust. . . ." The jury must find that the words were published "of and concerning" the plaintiff, but, where the plaintiff is a public official, his place in the governmental hierarchy is sufficient evidence to support a finding that his reputation has been affected by statements that reflect upon the agency of which he is in charge. Once "libel *per se*" has been established, the defendant has no defense as to stated facts unless he can persuade the jury that they were true in all their particulars. His privilege of "fair comment" for expressions of opinion depends on the truth of the facts upon which the comment is based. Unless he can discharge the burden of proving truth, general damages are presumed, and may be awarded without proof of pecuniary injury. A showing of actual malice is apparently a prerequisite to recovery of punitive damages, and the defendant may, in any event, forestall a punitive award by a retraction meeting the statutory requirements. Good motives and belief in truth do not negate an inference of malice, but are relevant only in mitigation of punitive damages if the jury chooses to accord them weight.

The question before us is whether this rule of liability, as applied to an action brought by a public official against critics of his official conduct, abridges the freedom of speech and of the press that is guaranteed by the First and Fourteenth Amendments.

Respondent relies heavily, as did the Alabama courts, on statements of this Court to the effect that the Constitution does not protect libelous publications. Those statements do not foreclose our inquiry here. None of the cases sustained the use of libel laws to impose sanctions upon expression critical of the official conduct of public officials. . . . Like insurrection, contempt, advocacy of unlawful acts, breach of the peace, obscenity, solicitation of legal business, and the various other formulae for the repression of expression that have been challenged in this Court, libel can claim no talismanic immunity from constitutional limitations. It must be measured by standards that satisfy the First Amendment. . . .

[W]e consider this case against the background of a profound national commitment to the principle that debate on public issues should be uninhibited, robust, and wide-open, and that it may well include vehement, caustic, and sometimes unpleasantly sharp attacks on government and public officials. The present advertisement, as an expression of grievance and protest on one of the major public issues of our time, would seem clearly to qualify for the constitutional protection. The question is whether it forfeits that protection by the falsity of some of its factual statements and by its alleged defamation of respondent.

Authoritative interpretations of the First Amendment guarantees have consistently refused to recognize an exception for any test of truth—whether administered by judges, juries, or administrative officials—and especially one that puts the burden of proving truth on the speaker. The constitutional protection does not turn upon "the truth, popularity, or social utility of the ideas and beliefs which are offered." As Madison said, "Some degree of abuse is inseparable from the proper use of every thing, and in no instance is this more true than in that of the press." . . .

Injury to official reputation affords no more warrant for repressing speech that would otherwise be free than does factual error. Where judicial officers are involved, this Court has held that concern for the dignity and reputation of the courts does not justify the punishment as criminal contempt of criticism of the judge or his decision. This is true even though the utterance contains "half-truths" and "misinformation." Such repression can be justified, if at all, only by a clear and present danger of the obstruction of justice. If judges are to be treated as "men of fortitude, able to thrive in a hardy climate," surely the same must be true of other government officials, such as elected city commissioners. Criticism of their official conduct does not lose its constitutional protection merely because it is effective criticism, and hence diminishes their official reputations.

If neither factual error nor defamatory content suffices to remove the constitutional shield from criticism of official conduct, the combination of the two elements is no less inadequate. This is the lesson to be drawn from the great controversy over the Sedition Act of 1798, which first crystallized a national awareness of the central meaning of the First Amendment. . . . The Act allowed the defendant the defense of truth, and provided that the jury were to be judges both of the law and the facts. Despite these qualifications, the Act was vigorously condemned as unconstitutional in an attack joined in by Jefferson and Madison. In the famous Virginia Resolutions of 1798, the General Assembly of Virginia resolved that . . . [The Sedition Act] exercises . . . a power not delegated by the Constitution, but, on the contrary, expressly and positively forbidden by one of the amendments thereto—a power which, more than any other, ought to produce universal alarm because it is leveled against the right of freely examining public characters and measures, and of free communication among the people thereon, which has ever been justly deemed the only effectual guardian of every other right. . . . The right of free public discussion of the stewardship of public officials was thus, in Madison's view, a fundamental principle of the American form of government.

Although the Sedition Act was never tested in this Court, the attack upon its validity has carried the day in the court of history. Fines levied in its prosecution were repaid by Act of Congress on the ground that it was unconstitutional. . . . Jefferson, as President, pardoned those who had been convicted and sentenced under the Act and remitted their fines, stating:

> I discharged every person under punishment or prosecution under the sedition law because I considered, and now consider, that law to be a nullity, as absolute and as palpable as if Congress had ordered us to fall down and worship a golden image. . . .

A rule compelling the critic of official conduct to guarantee the truth of all his factual assertions—and to do so on pain of libel judgments virtually unlimited in amount—leads to . . . "self-censorship." Allowance of the defense of truth, with the burden of proving it on the defendant, does not mean that only false speech will be deterred. Even courts accepting this defense as an adequate safeguard have recognized the difficulties of adducing legal proofs that the alleged libel was true in all its factual particulars. Under such a rule, would-be critics of official conduct may be deterred from voicing their criticism, even though it is believed to be true and even though it is, in fact, true, because of doubt whether it can be proved in court or fear of the expense of having to do so. . . . The rule thus dampens the vigor and limits the variety of public debate. It is inconsistent with the First and Fourteenth Amendments. The constitutional guarantees require, we think, a federal rule that prohibits a public official from recovering damages for a defamatory falsehood relating to his official conduct unless he proves that the statement was made with "actual malice"—that is, with knowledge that it was false or with reckless disregard of whether it was false or not. . . .

Such a privilege for criticism of official conduct is appropriately analogous to the protection accorded a public official when he is sued for libel by a private citizen. . . . The States accord the same immunity to statements of their highest officers, although some differentiate their lesser officials and qualify the privilege they enjoy. But all hold that all officials are protected unless actual malice can be proved. The reason for the official privilege is said to be that the threat of damage suits would otherwise "inhibit the fearless, vigorous, and effective administration of policies of government" and "dampen the ardor of all but the most resolute, or the most irresponsible, in the unflinching discharge of their duties." Analogous considerations support the privilege for the citizen-critic of government. It is as much his duty to criticize as it is the official's duty to administer. As Madison said, "the censorial power is in the people over the Government, and not in the Government over the people." It would give public servants an unjustified preference over the public they serve, if critics of official conduct did not have a fair equivalent of the immunity granted to the officials themselves.

We conclude that such a privilege is required by the First and Fourteenth Amendments.

We hold today that the Constitution delimits a State's power to award damages for libel in actions brought by public officials against critics of their official conduct. Since this is such an action, the rule requiring proof of actual malice is applicable. While Alabama law apparently requires proof of actual malice for an award of punitive damages, where general damages are concerned malice is "presumed." Such a presumption is inconsistent with the federal rule. . . . Since the trial judge did not instruct the jury to differentiate between general and punitive damages, it may be that the verdict was wholly an award of one or the other. But it is impossible to know, in view of the general verdict returned. Because of this uncertainty, the judgment must be reversed and the case remanded.

Since respondent may seek a new trial, we deem that considerations of effective judicial administration require us to review the evidence in the present record to determine whether it could constitutionally support a judgment for respondent. This Court's duty is not limited to the elaboration of constitutional principles; we must also in proper cases review the evidence to make certain that those principles have been constitutionally applied. . . .

Applying these standards, we consider that the proof presented to show actual malice lacks the convincing clarity which the constitutional standard demands, and hence that it would not constitutionally sustain the judgment for respondent under the proper rule of law. The case of the individual petitioners requires little discussion. Even assuming that they could constitutionally be found to have authorized the use of their names on the advertisement, there was no evidence whatever that they were aware of any erroneous statements or were in any way reckless in that regard. The judgment against them is thus without constitutional support.

As to the *Times*, we similarly conclude that the facts do not support a finding of actual malice. The statement by the *Times'* Secretary that, apart from the padlocking allegation, he thought the advertisement was "substantially correct," affords no constitutional warrant for the Alabama Supreme Court's conclusion that it was a "cavalier ignoring of the falsity of the advertisement [from which] the jury could not have but been impressed with the bad faith of the *Times*, and its maliciousness inferable therefrom." The statement does not indicate malice at the time of the publication; even if the advertisement was not "substantially correct"—although respondent's own proofs tend to show that it was—that opinion was at least a reasonable one, and there was no evidence to impeach the witness' good faith in holding it. The *Times'* failure to retract upon respondent's demand, although it later retracted upon the demand of Governor Patterson, is likewise not adequate evidence of malice for constitutional purposes. . . .

Finally, there is evidence that the *Times* published the advertisement without checking its accuracy against the news stories in the *Times'* own files. The mere presence of the stories in the files does not, of course, establish that the *Times* "knew" the advertisement was false, since the state of mind required for actual malice would have to be brought home to the persons in the *Times'* organization having responsibility for the publication of the advertisement. With respect to the failure of those persons to make the check, the record shows that they relied upon their knowledge of the good reputation of many of those whose names were listed as sponsors of the advertisement, and upon the letter from A. Philip Randolph, known to them as a responsible individual, certifying that the use of the names was authorized. There was testimony that the persons handling the advertisement saw nothing in it that would render it unacceptable under the *Times'* policy of rejecting advertisements containing "attacks of a personal character"; their failure to reject it on this ground was not unreasonable. We think the evidence against the *Times* supports, at most, a finding of negligence in failing to discover the misstatements, and is constitutionally insufficient to show the recklessness that is required for a finding of actual malice.

The judgment of the Supreme Court of Alabama is reversed, and the case is remanded to that court for further proceedings not inconsistent with this opinion.

Mr. Justice Black, with whom Mr. Justice Douglas joins, concurring.

I concur in reversing this half-million-dollar judgment against the New York Times Company and the four individual defendants. In reversing, the Court holds that "the Constitution delimits a State's power to award damages for libel in actions brought by public officials against critics of their official conduct."

I base my vote to reverse on the belief that the First and Fourteenth Amendments not merely "delimit" a State's power to award damages to "public officials against critics of their official conduct," but completely prohibit a State from exercising such a power. The Court goes on to hold that a State can subject such critics to damages if "actual malice" can be proved against them. "Malice," even as defined by the Court, is an elusive, abstract concept, hard to prove and hard to disprove. The requirement that malice be proved provides, at best, an evanescent protection for the right critically to discuss public affairs, and certainly does not measure up to the sturdy safeguard embodied in the First Amendment. Unlike the Court, therefore, I vote to reverse exclusively on the ground that the *Times* and the individual defendants had an absolute, unconditional constitutional right to publish in the *Times* advertisement their criticisms of the Montgomery agencies and officials. . . .

The half-million-dollar verdict does give dramatic proof, however, that state libel laws threaten the very existence of an American press virile enough to publish unpopular views on public affairs and bold enough to criticize the conduct of public officials. The factual background of this case emphasizes the imminence and enormity of that threat. One of the acute and highly emotional issues in this country arises out of efforts of many people, even including some public officials, to continue state-commanded segregation of races in the public schools and other public places despite our several holdings that such a state practice is forbidden by the Fourteenth Amendment. Montgomery is one of the localities in which widespread hostility to desegregation has been manifested. This hostility has sometimes extended itself to persons who favor desegregation, particularly to so-called "outside agitators," a term which can be made to fit papers like the *Times,* which is published in New York. The scarcity of testimony to show that Commissioner Sullivan suffered any actual damages at all suggests that these feelings of hostility had at least as much to do with rendition of this half-million-dollar verdict as did an appraisal of damages. Viewed realistically, this record lends support to an inference that, instead of being damaged, Commissioner Sullivan's political, social, and financial prestige has likely been enhanced by the *Times'* publication. . . .

In my opinion, the Federal Constitution has dealt with this deadly danger to the press in the only way possible without leaving the free press open to destruction—by granting the press an absolute immunity for criticism of the way public officials do their public duty. Stopgap measures like those the Court adopts are, in my judgment, not enough. . . .

We would, I think, more faithfully interpret the First Amendment by holding that, at the very least, it leaves the people and the press free to criticize officials and discuss public affairs with impunity. This Nation of ours elects many of its important officials; so do the States, the municipalities, the counties, and even many precincts. These officials are responsible to the people for the way they perform their duties. While our Court has held that some kinds of speech and writings, such as "obscenity," and "fighting words," are not expression within the protection of the First Amendment, freedom to discuss public affairs and public officials is unquestionably, as the Court today holds, the kind of speech the First Amendment was primarily designed to keep within the area of free discussion. To punish the exercise of this right to discuss public affairs or to penalize it through libel judgments is to abridge or shut off discussion of the very kind most needed. This Nation, I suspect, can live in peace without libel suits based on public discussions of public affairs and public officials. But I doubt that a country can live in freedom where its people can be made to suffer physically or financially for criticizing their government, its actions, or its officials.

Justice Brennan touched upon the Sedition Act of 1798, but stopped short of declaring the law unconstitutional. However, by referring to President Jefferson's decisions to repay the fines levied against violators of the law, and approvingly citing the dissents of Justices Holmes and Brandeis in *Abrams,* Brennan made clear that the very concept of seditious libel violated the First Amendment. And although Brennan did not go far enough for the Court's First Amendment absolutists—Black and Douglas wanted the Court to rule that any libel law chilled the free and open exchange of ideas—the "actual malice" standard established near absolute protection for the news media against libel suits by public officials.

Sullivan is rightly considered one the most important decisions the Court has ever handed down on freedom of expression. But Brennan's opinion also handed the civil rights movement a timely and critical victory. Had the Court upheld Commissioner Sullivan's verdict, Governor Patterson and the nearly one dozen other Alabama public officials who had filed libel suits against the *Times* and ministers Abernathy, Shuttlesworth, Seay, and Lowry would have been able to collect nearly $2.5 million in additional damage awards. In plain terms, the civil rights movement did not have $3 million to donate to the coffers of white segregationists. Before the Court overturned the *Sullivan* verdict, Abernathy, Shuttlesworth, and Lowry had their cars seized and sold at public auctions to satisfy their share of any potential damage award. Lowry's car was bought by a member of his church in Mobile for $800. The man then sold it to the minister's wife for a dollar. Shuttlesworth and Abernathy did not fare as well; they never saw their old cars again. So fearful was Lowry that the state would come after his personal property, including his home, that he left his Mobile pulpit for a church in Cincinnati. Alabama reaped a less than substantial payoff from the auction—less than $2,500.[40] The money, however, was not the point. Showing the African American community who was boss was the Alabama government's motive. Harassment against blacks assumed many forms in the Deep South, and libel law was just another tool in the arsenal of white supremacists. *Sullivan* neutered what was previously a very effective weapon against the civil rights movement. The role of race in the *Sullivan* case is discussed in the accompanying SIDEBAR.

The Limits of Actual Malice: Public and Private Figures

Three years later, the Court addressed one of the major questions left unanswered by Justice Brennan's opinion in *Sullivan:* Did the virtual immunity created by the Court for the news media against libel suits by public officials extend to public figures? In two cases, *Associated Press* v. *Walker* (1967) and *Curtis Publishing Co.* v. *Butts* (1967), a sharply divided Court ruled that libel actions brought by public figures, that is, persons who operate in the public arena but hold no public office, were subject to the "actual malice" standard.[41] *Associated Press* concerned a lawsuit brought by a retired army general, Edwin A. Walker, who claimed the news service falsely reported that he encouraged white students at the University of Mississippi to attack federal marshals assigned to protect James Meredith, the first African American student admitted to the university. Walker, who had presided over federal troops assigned to protect the nine African American students who integrated Central High School in Little Rock, Arkansas, during the 1958 school year (see *Cooper* v. *Aaron* [1958] in Chapter 11), claimed that the eyewitness's statements published by the Associated Press were libelous. Writing for a 5 to 4 majority, Justice John Harlan ruled that Walker was a public figure and thus subject to the "actual malice" standard. In *Butts,* Harlan, again writing for a 5 to 4 majority, upheld a libel award against the *Saturday Evening Post*. The *Post* had run an article, "The Story of a College Football Fix," alleging that the athletic director of the University of Georgia, Wally Butts, had conspired to throw a football game by giving his team's plays and "secret" information to the University of Alabama. Paul "Bear" Bryant, then one of the most famous figures in college or professional sports, coached the Alabama football team.

A jury determined that the *Post* had not met the standards of professional reporting before running the story and awarded Butts $480,000. Harlan agreed with the *Post* that Butts was a public figure and should have to pursue his libel action under the *Sullivan* standard, but agreed with Butts that the magazine had been guilty of "highly unreasonable conduct constituting an extreme departure from the standards of investigative reporting."[42] The upshot of *Associated Press* and *Butts* was that

NEW YORK TIMES V. SULLIVAN

Through the Prism of Race

To hear L. B. Sullivan and Governor John Patterson tell it, the factual errors that ran in the "Heed Their Rising Voices" advertisement in the *New York Times* must have been the first time that either man had come under criticism for his handling of civil rights protesters. On the contrary, the *Montgomery Advertiser,* the *Birmingham Age-Herald,* and, outside Alabama, the *Atlanta Constitution,* the *Nashville Tennessean,* and the *Louisville Courier-Journal* regularly criticized political figures for their treatment of the civil rights movement, authorizing the police to use excessive force to thwart peaceful protests, and failing to rein in lynch mobs determined to secure their own perverted sense of justice. Granted, the major Southern newspapers did not necessarily line up behind the goals of the civil rights movement. Conversely, many accepted the Court's most far-reaching civil rights decision prior to the 1960s, *Brown* v. *Board of Education* (1954), and encouraged everyone to work together to bring about a peaceful transition in this exceedingly sensitive area of race relations. Such notable figures in the Southern press as Ralph McGill, editor of the *Atlanta Constitution,* and Hodding Carter Jr., editor of the *Delta-Democrat Times* in Greenville, Mississippi, regularly hounded government officials on everything from their personal behavior in public to their unwillingness to address the economic and educational deficiencies of the South to their reactionary attitudes on racial equality. No Southern public official had ever sued a white journalist or the white-owned newspapers before *Sullivan*. Only when Southern segregationists realized that state libel law packed a powerful potential punch against the African American civil rights movement did they demand their reputations rightfully restored.

Journalist Taylor Branch, in his Pulitzer Prize–winning book on the early days of the civil rights movement, *Parting the Waters: America in the King Years 1954–1963,* observed that the *Sullivan* case confronted the American courts with a delicate political dilemma, with the "unbearable sensitivities of race" pushing the judges into almost surreal extremes of irony. By the time *Sullivan* reached the Supreme Court, the justices avoided the racial undercurrent of the case by focusing on the Alabama libel law and the legal standard that should govern defamation cases. An entire new standard of news reporting and commentary emerged based on a paid advertisement that mentioned no government official by name, involved not a single reporter, and never passed under an editor's scrutiny. Only in the segregated South could African Americans be punished for making allegedly false and libelous statements against an unnamed white government official.

Sensitive to its image among potential Alabama jurors and judges as a "Northern agitator" supportive of the civil rights movement, the *New York Times* hired a Birmingham firm, Beddow, Embry & Beddow, to handle the *Sullivan* case. The firm was respected for its legal work, but not its choice of clientele: On many occasions, Beddow had defended blacks charged with crimes, which was not something that most whites approved of in the pre–civil rights era South. The four black ministers named as defendants by Sullivan had hired separate lawyers, Fred Gray, Vernon Z. Crawford, and S. S. Seay Jr., all of whom were black, to represent them, and this produced a curious but perfectly normal entry into the trial transcripts. The white attorneys all received the honorific "Mr." before their last names. The black attorneys were referred to as "Lawyer" Gray, "Lawyer Crawford," and "Lawyer Seay." Even when they were lawyers and not criminal defendants, African Americans could not stand as equals to their white counterparts in an Alabama courtroom.

Calvin Whitesell, an attorney for L. B. Sullivan, began the prosecution's case by reading the "Heed Their Rising Voices" advertisement, pronouncing the word "Negro" as something closer to "nigger." Vernon Crawford objected strenuously to Whitesell's pronunciation. Later, Crawford, Whitesell, and the trial judge spent quite some time discussing the proper pronunciation of "Negro" before Whitesell could continue his case. Judge Walter Jones, whose father fought in the Civil War and carried the truce flag from Robert E. Lee to Ulysses S. Grant at Appomattox, asked Whitesell if he was pronouncing "Negro" in an inappropriate way. Whitesell responded that he was pronouncing the word as he had all his life. Judge Jones, who collected Confederate memorabilia and participated in Civil War enactments, permitted Whitesell to say "nigra," a term not unfamiliar to white Southerners. Whatever problems Whitesell had with phonics did not seem to bother the gallery, some of whom were decked out in Confederate Army uniforms.

THE NEW YORK TIMES, TUESDAY, MARCH 29, 1960. L

"The growing movement of peaceful mass demonstrations by Negroes is something new in the South, something understandable.... Let Congress heed their rising voices, for they will be heard."

—New York Times editorial Saturday, March 19, 1960

Heed Their Rising Voices

As the whole world knows by now, thousands of Southern Negro students are engaged in widespread non-violent demonstrations in positive affirmation of the right to live in human dignity as guaranteed by the U. S. Constitution and the Bill of Rights. In their efforts to uphold these guarantees, they are being met by an unprecedented wave of terror by those who would deny and negate that document which the whole world looks upon as setting the pattern for modern freedom....

In Orangeburg, South Carolina, when 400 students peacefully sought to buy doughnuts and coffee at lunch counters in the business district, they were forcibly ejected, tear-gassed, soaked to the skin in freezing weather with fire hoses, arrested en masse and herded into an open barbed-wire stockade to stand for hours in the bitter cold.

In Montgomery, Alabama, after students sang "My Country, 'Tis of Thee" on the State Capitol steps, their leaders were expelled from school, and truckloads of police armed with shotguns and tear-gas ringed the Alabama State College Campus. When the entire student body protested to state authorities by refusing to re-register, their dining hall was padlocked in an attempt to starve them into submission.

In Tallahassee, Atlanta, Nashville, Savannah, Greensboro, Memphis, Richmond, Charlotte, and a host of other cities in the South, young American teenagers, in face of the entire weight of official state apparatus and police power, have boldly stepped forth as protagonists of democracy. Their courage and amazing restraint have inspired millions and given a new dignity to the cause of freedom.

Small wonder that the Southern violators of the Constitution fear this new, non-violent brand of freedom fighter . . . even as they fear the upswelling right-to-vote movement. Small wonder that they are determined to destroy the one man who, more than any other, symbolizes the new spirit now sweeping the South—the Rev. Dr. Martin Luther King, Jr., world-famous leader of the Montgomery Bus Protest. For it is his doctrine of non-violence which has inspired and guided the students in their widening wave of sit-ins; and it this same Dr. King who founded and is president of the Southern Christian Leadership Conference—the organization which is spearheading the surging right-to-vote movement. Under Dr. King's direction the Leadership Conference conducts Student Workshops and Seminars in the philosophy and technique of non-violent resistance.

Again and again the Southern violators have answered Dr. King's peaceful protests with intimidation and violence. They have bombed his home almost killing his wife and child. They have assaulted his person. They have arrested him seven times—for "speeding," "loitering" and similar "offenses." And now they have charged him with "perjury"—a *felony* under which they could imprison him for *ten years.* Obviously, their real purpose is to remove him physically as the leader to whom the students and millions of others—look for guidance and support, and thereby to intimidate *all* leaders who may rise in the South. Their strategy is to behead this affirmative movement, and thus to demoralize Negro Americans and weaken their will to struggle. The defense of Martin Luther King, spiritual leader of the student sit-in movement, clearly, therefore, is an integral part of the total struggle for freedom in the South.

Decent-minded Americans cannot help but applaud the creative daring of the students and the quiet heroism of Dr. King. But this is one of those moments in the stormy history of Freedom when men and women of good will must do more than applaud the rising-to-glory of others. The America whose good name hangs in the balance before a watchful world, the America whose heritage of Liberty these Southern Upholders of the Constitution are defending, is *our* America as well as theirs . . .

We must heed their rising voices—yes—but we must add our own.

We must extend ourselves above and beyond moral support and render the material help so urgently needed by those who are taking the risks, facing jail, and even death in a glorious re-affirmation of our Constitution and its Bill of Rights.

We urge you to join hands with our fellow Americans in the South by supporting, with your dollars, this Combined Appeal for all three needs—the defense of Martin Luther King—the support of the embattled students—and the struggle for the right-to-vote.

Your Help Is Urgently Needed . . . NOW!!

Stella Adler
Raymond Pace Alexander
Harry Van Arsdale
Harry Belafonte
Julie Belafonte
Dr. Algernon Black
Marc Blitztein
William Branch
Marlon Brando
Mrs. Ralph Bunche
Diahann Carroll
Dr. Alan Knight Chalmers
Richard Coe
Nat King Cole
Cheryl Crawford
Dorothy Dandridge
Ossie Davis
Sammy Davis, Jr.
Ruby Dee
Dr. Philip Elliott
Dr. Harry Emerson Fosdick
Anthony Franciosa
Lorraine Hansbury
Rev. Donald Harrington
Nat Hentoff
James Hicks
Mary Hinkson
Van Heflin
Langston Hughes
Morris Iushewitz
Mahalia Jackson
Mordecai Johnson
John Killens
Eartha Kitt
Rabbi Edward Klein
Hope Lange
John Lewis
Viveca Lindfors
Carl Murphy
Don Murray
John Murray
A. J. Muste
Frederick O'Neal
L. Joseph Overton
Clarence Pickett
Shad Polier
Sidney Poitier
A. Philip Randolph
John Raitt
Elmer Rice
Jackie Robinson
Mrs. Eleanor Roosevelt
Bayard Rustin
Robert Ryan
Maureen Stapleton
Frank Silvera
Hope Stevens
George Tabori
Rev. Gardner C. Taylor
Norman Thomas
Kenneth Tynan
Charles White
Shelley Winters
Max Youngstein

We in the south who are struggling daily for dignity and freedom warmly endorse this appeal

Rev. Ralph D. Abernathy (*Montgomery, Ala.*)
Rev. Fred L. Shuttlesworth (*Birmingham, Ala.*)
Rev. Kelley Miller Smith (*Nashville, Tenn.*)
Rev. W. A. Dennis (*Chattanooga, Tenn.*)
Rev. C. K. Steele (*Tallahassee, Fla.*)
Rev. Matthew D. McCollom (*Orangeburg, S. C.*)
Rev. William Holmes Borders (*Atlanta, Ga.*)
Rev. Douglas Moore (*Durham, N. C.*)
Rev. Wyatt Tee Walker (*Petersburg, Va.*)
Rev. Walter L. Hamilton (*Norfolk, Va.*)
I. S. Levy (*Columbia, S. C.*)
Rev. Martin Luther King, Sr. (*Atlanta, Ga.*)
Rev. Henry C. Bunton (*Memphis, Tenn.*)
Rev. S. S. Seay, Sr. (*Montgomery, Ala.*)
Rev. Samuel W. Williams (*Atlanta, Ga.*)
Rev. A. L. Davis (*New Orleans, La.*)
Mrs. Katie E. Whickham (*New Orleans, La.*)
Rev. W. H. Hall (*Hattiesburg, Miss.*)
Rev. J. E. Lowery (*Mobile, Ala.*)
Rev. T. J. Jemison (*Baton Rouge, La.*)

Please mail this coupon TODAY

Committee To Defend Martin Luther King and The Struggle For Freedom In The South
312 West 125th Street, New York 27, N. Y. UNiversity 6-1700

I am enclosing my contribution of $______ for the work of the Committee.

Name ______ (PLEASE PRINT)
Address ______
City ______ Zone ____ State ______

☐ I want to help ☐ Please send further information

Please make checks payable to:
Committee To Defend Martin Luther King

COMMITTEE TO DEFEND MARTIN LUTHER KING AND THE STRUGGLE FOR FREEDOM IN THE SOUTH
312 West 125th Street, New York 27, N. Y. UNiversity 6-1700

Chairmen: A. Philip Randolph, Dr. Gardner C. Taylor; *Chairmen of Cultural Division:* Harry Belafonte, Sidney Poitier; *Treasurer:* Nat King Cole; *Executive Director:* Bayard Rustin; *Chairmen of Church Division:* Father George B. Ford, Rev. Harry Emerson Fosdick, Rev. Thomas Kilgore, Jr., Rabbi Edward E. Klein; *Chairman of Labor Division:* Morris Iushewitz

During the trial, Sullivan was never able to point out any specific reference about him or any other Alabama public official in the *Times* advertisement. Instead, he maintained that several sentences in the sixth paragraph, including

> Again and again the Southern violators have answered Dr. King's peaceful protests with intimidation and

violence. They have bombed his home almost killing his wife and child. They have assaulted his person. . . .

strongly implicated him, since Sullivan, as city commissioner, supervised the Montgomery police. Sullivan may well have felt implicated, but he offered a curious explanation to Crawford and T. Eric Embry, a lawyer for the *Times*, when they cross-examined him. Crawford asked Sullivan if he "considered your police force to be Southern law violators?" Sullivan responded, "I certainly do not." Crawford then asked him, "Then, Mr. Sullivan, do you consider yourself as Police Commissioner a Southern law violator." Sullivan bristled again and said, "I don't consider myself a violator period, Southern or otherwise." Apparently, Sullivan did not realize that by stating for the record that he was not a "Southern law violator" he had made it difficult to explain how the advertisement could have implicated him. This point was lost on the jury.

Sullivan also testified that the ad diminished his "ability and integrity." That comment prompted the following exchange between Embry and Sullivan:

Embry: "Have you ever been ridiculed? Do you feel ill at ease walking about the streets of Montgomery?"

Sullivan: "I haven't had anyone come up to me personally and say they held me in ridicule because of the ad."

Embry: "Have you been shunned by anyone in a public place or at the house of a friend or in any restaurant?"

Sullivan: "I don't recall."

So again, even though Sullivan testified that he had not suffered any meaningful injury to his reputation or standing in the community after the *Times* published "Heed Their Rising Voices," the very fact that a white man had claimed libel was enough "evidence" for the jury. Just two hours and twenty minutes after the jury had received the judge's instructions, twelve white men decided that the *Times* advertisement, which carried not a single name of an Alabama public official, had libeled Commissioner Sullivan. Race disappeared from the record once the Court agreed to hear *Sullivan*. But during the summer of 1960, race was everywhere and nowhere in that Montgomery courtroom, just like it was in the rest of Southern society.

References

Branch, Taylor. *Parting the Waters: America During the King Years 1954–1963*. New York: Simon & Schuster, 1988.

Egerton, John. *Speak Now Against the Day. The Generation Before the Civil Rights Movement in the South*. New York: Alfred A. Knopf, 1994.

Lewis, Anthony. *Make No Law: The Sullivan Case and the First Amendment*. New York: Random House, 1991.

public figures were now considered no different under libel law than public officials. It was also clear that the Court, having divided 5–4 on this matter, was struggling with the fine-tuning of the modern law of libel that it created in *Sullivan*. These struggles between the justices were readily apparent in *Gertz* v. *Welch* (1974), which asked the Court to decide whether a private figure had to demonstrate "actual malice" in order to demonstrate libel.

Gertz v. *Welch*

418 U.S. 323 (1974)

Home from a busy day of shopping, Mary Giampietro opened a pamphlet that someone had handed to her as she was rushing from one store to another. Enclosed was an excerpt from an article entitled, "Frame-Up, Richard Nuccio and the War on Police," which had been published in the magazine *American Opinion*, sponsored by the John Birch society. As Giampietro thumbed through the article, she did a double take when she saw a picture of Elmer Gertz, a prominent Chicago attorney for whom her husband worked. Below was the caption, "Elmer Gertz of Red Guild Harasses Nuccio." Giampietro passed the pamphlet along to Gertz, who quickly figured out what motivated the *American Opinion* article. Seven months before, in August 1968, Gertz had represented the family of Ronald Nelson in a civil suit against Nuccio, a Chicago police officer found guilty of murder in the shooting of his client. The article accused Gertz of active involvement in "the Communist War on Police," a national conspiracy aimed at destroying local police "so that Communists can pose their totalitarian dictatorship." Gertz was also accused of "carefully orchestrating" a campaign to frame Nuccio for Nelson's murder.[43]

If Alan Stang, who had written the *American Opinion* article, or the John Birch Society, an organization so far off the map of American conservatism that it once accused President Dwight Eisenhower, a Republican, of being a "conscious agent of the Communist conspiracy," thought that Gertz would turn the other cheek, neither one had done his homework. Gertz promptly filed suit in federal court against the John Birch Society's corporate backer, Robert Welch, Inc., alleging that Stang's article was not protected by the *Sullivan* standard. Additional background on this modest Chicago lawyer's decision to take on the John Birch Society is set out in the accompanying SIDEBAR.

The Court's decision was 5 to 4. Justice Powell delivered the opinion of the Court. Justice Blackmun filed a concurring opinion. Justices Brennan, Burger, Douglas, and White each filed separate dissents.

▼▲▼

MR. JUSTICE POWELL delivered the opinion of the Court.

The principal issue in this case is whether a newspaper or broadcaster that publishes defamatory falsehoods about an individual who is neither a public official nor a public figure may claim a constitutional privilege against liability for the injury inflicted by those statements. . . .

We begin with the common ground. Under the First Amendment, there is no such thing as a false idea. However pernicious an opinion may seem, we depend for its correction not on the conscience of judges and juries, but on the competition of other ideas. But there is no constitutional value in false statements of fact. Neither the intentional lie nor the careless error materially advances society's interest in "uninhibited, robust and wide-open" debate on public issues, *New York Times Co.* v. *Sullivan* (1964). They belong to that category of utterances which "are no essential part of any exposition of ideas, and are of such slight social value as a step to truth that any benefit that may be derived from them is clearly outweighed by the social interest in order and morality," *Chaplinsky* v. *New Hampshire* (1942).

Although the erroneous statement of fact is not worthy of constitutional protection, it is nevertheless inevitable in free debate. . . . And punishment of error runs the risk of inducing a cautious and restrictive exercise of the constitutionally guaranteed freedoms of speech and press. Our decisions recognize that a rule of strict liability that compels a publisher or broadcaster to guarantee the accuracy of his factual assertions may lead to intolerable self-censorship. . . . The First Amendment requires that we protect some falsehood in order to protect speech that matters.

The need to avoid self-censorship by the news media is, however, not the only societal value at issue. If it were, this Court would have embraced long ago the view that publishers and broadcasters enjoy an unconditional and indefeasible immunity from liability for defamation. Such a rule would, indeed, obviate the fear that the prospect of civil liability for injurious falsehood might dissuade a timorous press from the effective exercise of First Amendment freedoms. Yet absolute protection for the communications media requires a total sacrifice of the competing value served by the law of defamation.

The legitimate state interest underlying the law of libel is the compensation of individuals for the harm inflicted on them by defamatory falsehood. We would not lightly require the State to abandon this purpose, for . . . the individual's right to the protection of his own good name. . . .

Some tension necessarily exists between the need for a vigorous and uninhibited press and the legitimate interest in redressing wrongful injury. . . . In our continuing effort to define the proper accommodation between these competing concerns, we have been especially anxious to assure to the freedoms of speech and press that "breathing space" essential to their fruitful exercise. To that end, this Court has extended a measure of strategic protection to defamatory falsehood.

The *New York Times* [v. *Sullivan*] standard defines the level of constitutional protection appropriate to the context of defamation of a public person. Those who, by reason of the notoriety of their achievements or the vigor and success with which they seek the public's attention, are properly classed as public figures and those who hold governmental office may recover for injury to reputation only on clear and convincing proof that the defamatory falsehood was made with knowledge of its falsity or with reckless disregard for the truth. This standard administers an extremely powerful antidote to the inducement to media self-censorship of the common law rule of strict liability for libel and slander. And it exacts a correspondingly high price from the victims of defamatory falsehood. Plainly, many deserving plaintiffs, including some intentionally subjected to injury, will be unable to surmount the barrier of the *New York Times* test. Despite this substantial abridgment of the state law right to compensation for wrongful hurt to one's reputation, the Court has concluded that the protection of the *New York Times* privilege should be available to publishers and broadcasters of defamatory falsehood concerning public officials and public figures. We think that these decisions are correct, but we do not find their holdings justified solely by reference to the interest of the press and broadcast media in immunity from liability. Rather, we believe that the *New York Times* rule states an accommodation between this concern and the limited state interest present in the context of libel actions brought by public persons. For the reasons stated below, we conclude that the state interest in compensating injury to the reputation of private individuals requires that a different rule should obtain with respect to them.

Theoretically, of course, the balance between the needs of the press and the individual's claim to compensation for wrongful injury might be struck on a case-by-case basis. . . . But this approach would lead to unpredictable results and uncertain expectations, and it could render our duty to supervise the lower courts unmanageable. Because an *ad hoc* resolution of the competing interests at stake in each particular case is not feasible, we must lay down broad rules of general application: such rules necessarily treat alike various cases involving differences as well as similarities. Thus, it is often true that not all of the considerations which justify adoption of a given rule will obtain in each particular case decided under its authority.

With that caveat, we have no difficulty in distinguishing among defamation plaintiffs. The first remedy of any victim of defamation is self-help—using available opportunities to contradict the lie or correct the error, and thereby to minimize its adverse impact on reputation. Public officials and public figures usually enjoy significantly greater access to the channels of effective communication, and hence have a more realistic opportunity to counteract false statements than private individuals normally enjoy. Private individuals are therefore more vulnerable to injury, and the state interest in protecting them is correspondingly greater.

More important than the likelihood that private individuals will lack effective opportunities for rebuttal, there is a compelling normative consideration underlying the distinction between public and private defamation plaintiffs. An individual who decides to seek governmental office must accept certain necessary consequences of that involvement in public affairs. He runs the risk of closer public scrutiny than might otherwise be the case. And society's interest in the officers of government is not strictly limited to the formal discharge of official duties. . . .

Those classed as public figures stand in a similar position. Hypothetically, it may be possible for someone to become a public figure through no purposeful action of his own, but the instances of truly involuntary public figures must be exceedingly rare. For the most part, those who attain this status have assumed roles of especial prominence in the affairs of society. Some occupy positions of such persuasive power and influence that they are deemed public figures for all purposes. More commonly, those classed as public figures have thrust themselves to the forefront of particular public controversies in order to influence the resolution of the issues involved. In either event, they invite attention and comment.

No such assumption is justified with respect to a private individual. He has not accepted public office or assumed an "influential role in ordering society." He has relinquished no part of his interest in the protection of his own good name, and consequently he has a more compelling call on the courts for redress of injury inflicted by defamatory falsehood. Thus, private individuals are not only more vulnerable to injury than public officials and public figures; they are also more deserving of recovery.

For these reasons, we conclude that the States should retain substantial latitude in their efforts to enforce a legal remedy for defamatory falsehood injurious to the reputation of a private individual. The extension of the *New York Times* test . . . would abridge this legitimate state interest to a degree that we find unacceptable. And it would occasion the additional difficulty of forcing state and federal judges to decide on an *ad hoc* basis which publications address issues of "general or public interest" and which do not. . . . We doubt the wisdom of committing this task to the conscience of judges. . . . The "public or general interest" test for determining the applicability of the *New York Times* standard to private defamation actions inadequately serves both of the competing values at stake. On the one hand, a private individual whose reputation is injured by defamatory falsehood that does concern an issue of public or general interest has no recourse unless he can meet the rigorous requirements of *New York Times*. This is true despite the factors that distinguish the state interest in compensating private individuals from the analogous interest involved in the context of public persons. On the other hand, a publisher or broadcaster of a defamatory error which a court deems unrelated to an issue of public or general interest may be held liable in damages even if it took every reasonable precaution to ensure the accuracy of its assertions. . . .

We hold that, so long as they do not impose liability without fault, the States may define for themselves the appropriate standard of liability for a publisher or broadcaster of defamatory falsehood injurious to a private individual. This approach provides a more equitable boundary between the competing concerns involved here. It recognizes the strength of the legitimate state interest in compensating private individuals for wrongful injury to reputation, yet shields the press and broadcast media from the rigors of strict liability for defamation. . . . Our inquiry would involve considerations somewhat different from those discussed above if a State purported to condition civil liability on a factual misstatement whose content did not warn a reasonably prudent editor or broadcaster of its defamatory potential. . . .

Our accommodation of the competing values at stake in defamation suits by private individuals allows the States to impose liability on the publisher or broadcaster of defamatory falsehood on a less demanding showing than that required by *New York Times*. This conclusion is not based on a belief that the considerations which prompted the adoption of the *New York Times* privilege for defamation of public officials and its extension to public figures are wholly inapplicable to the context of private individuals. Rather, we endorse this approach in recognition of the strong and legitimate state interest in compensating private individuals for injury to reputation. But this countervailing state interest extends no further than compensation for actual injury. For the reasons stated below, we hold that the States may not permit recovery of presumed or punitive damages, at least when liability is not based on a showing of knowledge of falsity or reckless disregard for the truth. . . .

Notwithstanding our refusal to extend the *New York Times* privilege to defamation of private individuals, respondent contends that we should affirm the judgment below on the ground that petitioner is either a public official or a public figure. There is little basis for the former assertion. Several years prior to the present incident, petitioner had served briefly on housing committees appointed by the mayor of Chicago, but, at the time of publication, he had never held any remunerative governmental position. Respondent admits this, but argues that petitioner's appearance at the coroner's inquest rendered him a "*de facto* public official." Our cases recognize no such concept. Respondent's suggestion would sweep all lawyers under the *New York Times* rule as officers of the court, and distort the plain meaning of the "public official" category beyond all recognition. We decline to follow it.

Respondent's characterization of petitioner as a public figure raises a different question. That designation may rest on either of two alternative bases. In some instances an individual may achieve such pervasive fame or notoriety that he becomes a public figure for all purposes and in all contexts. More commonly, an individual voluntarily injects himself or is drawn into a particular public controversy, and thereby becomes a public figure for a limited range of issues. In either case, such persons assume special prominence in the resolution of public questions.

Petitioner has long been active in community and professional affairs. He has served as an officer of local civic groups and of various professional organizations, and he has published several books and articles on legal subjects. Although petitioner was consequently well known in some circles, he had achieved no general fame or notoriety in the community. None of the prospective jurors called at the trial had ever heard of petitioner prior to this litigation, and respondent offered no proof that this response was atypical of the local population. We would not lightly assume that a citizen's participation in community and professional affairs rendered him a public figure for all purposes. Absent clear evidence of general fame or notoriety in the community, and pervasive involvement in the affairs of society, an individual should not be deemed a public personality for all aspects of his life. It is preferable to reduce the public figure question to a more meaningful context by looking to the nature and extent of an individual's participation in the particular controversy giving rise to the defamation.

In this context, it is plain that petitioner was not a public figure. He played a minimal role at the coroner's inquest, and his participation related solely to his representation of a private client. He took no part in the criminal prosecution of Officer Nuccio. Moreover, he never discussed either the criminal or civil litigation with the press, and was never quoted as having done so. He plainly did not thrust himself into the vortex of this public issue, nor did he engage the public's attention in an attempt to influence its outcome. We are persuaded that the trial court did not err in refusing to characterize petitioner as a public figure for the purpose of this litigation.

We therefore conclude that the *New York Times* standard is inapplicable to this case, and that the trial court erred in entering judgment for respondent. Because the jury was allowed to impose liability without fault and was permitted to presume damages without proof of injury, a new trial is necessary. We reverse and remand for further proceedings in accord with this opinion.

It is so ordered.

MR. JUSTICE BLACKMUN, concurring.

The Court today refuses to apply *New York Times* to the private individual, as contrasted with the public official and the public figure. . . . It thereby fixes the outer boundary of the *New York Times* doctrine, and says that, beyond that boundary, a State is free to define for itself the appropriate standard of media liability so long as it does not impose liability without fault. . . . I sense some illogic in this.

The Court, however, seeks today to strike a balance between competing values where necessarily uncertain assumptions about human behavior color the result. Although the Court's opinion in the present case . . . now conditions a libel action by a private person upon a showing of negligence, as contrasted with a showing of willful or reckless disregard, I am willing to join, and do join, the Court's opinion and its judgment. . . .

By removing the specters of presumed and punitive damages in the absence of *New York Times* malice, the Court eliminates significant and powerful motives for self-censorship that otherwise are present in the traditional libel action. By so doing, the Court leaves what should prove to be sufficient and adequate breathing space for a vigorous press. What the Court has done, I believe, will have little, if any, practical effect on the functioning of responsible journalism.

MR. JUSTICE BRENNAN, dissenting.

I agree with the conclusion . . . that, at the time of publication of respondent's article, petitioner could not properly have been viewed as either a "public official" or "public figure"; instead, respondent's article, dealing with an alleged conspiracy to discredit local police forces, concerned petitioner's purported involvement in "an event of public or general interest," *Roosenbloom* v. *Metromedia, Inc.* (1971). I cannot agree, however, that free and robust debate—so essential to the proper functioning of our system of government—is permitted adequate "breathing space," when, as the Court holds, the States may impose all but strict liability for defamation if the defamed party is a private person and "the substance of the defamatory statement 'makes substantial danger to reputation apparent.'" I adhere to my view [previously] expressed . . . that we strike the proper accommodation between avoidance of media self-censorship and protection of individual reputations only when we require States to apply the *New York Times Co.* v. *Sullivan* (1964) "knowing or reckless falsity" standard in civil libel actions concerning media reports of the involvement of private individuals in events of public or general interest. . . .

Although acknowledging that First Amendment values are of no less significance when media reports concern private persons' involvement in matters of public concern, the Court refuses to provide, in such cases, the same level of constitutional protection that has been afforded the media in the context of defamation of public persons. The accommodation that this Court has established between free speech and libel laws in cases involving public officials and public figures—that defamatory falsehood be shown by clear and convincing evidence to have been published with knowledge of falsity or with reckless disregard of truth—is not apt, the Court holds, because the private individual does not have the same degree of access to the media to rebut defamatory comments as does the public person, and he has not voluntarily exposed himself to public scrutiny.

While these arguments are forcefully and eloquently presented, I cannot accept them. . . .

Since petitioner failed, after having been given a full and fair opportunity, to prove that respondent published the disputed article with knowledge of its falsity or with reckless disregard of the truth, I would affirm the judgment of the Court of Appeals.

Gertz's own comments about his case are instructive for understanding how the Court has subsequently determined whether an individual is a public or private figure when bringing a libel lawsuit. "Time and place," as Gertz observed, are the key factors in how the Court has shaped the definition of who qualifies as a public figure. For example, in *Time, Inc.* v. *Firestone* (1976), the Court ruled that Mary Alice Firestone, the ex-wife of the heir to the tire company fortune, was not a public figure, even though she had gone through a very public divorce that dragged on for seventeen months. *Time*, the weekly news magazine, had published a short notice on the divorce between Mary Alice and her husband, Russell Firestone, and referred to their "extramarital adven-

SIDEBAR

GERTZ V. WELCH

A Right to One's Reputation

Elmer Gertz was sixty-one years old when he learned, courtesy of the John Birch Society in March 1969, that he was a "Communist-fronter," a disciple of V. I. Lenin, and hell-bent on destroying the Chicago police department. Alan Stang's article in *American Opinion* offered no dates, no names, and no sources for the accusations against Gertz. All that Stang had to go on for Gertz's "treasonous" ways was his membership in the "Communist" National Lawyer's Guild. Needless to say, Stang's accusations came as quite a surprise to this Chicago-born and bred lawyer. During a career that extended back to the early 1930s, when he worked for $15 a week for the politically connected law firm of McInerny, Epstein & Arvey, Gertz had always been interested in politics and public affairs. After fourteen years, Gertz decided to start his own law practice. Over time, he became active in such groups as the American Jewish Congress, the National Lawyer's Guild, and various fair-housing organizations. He enjoyed a solid reputation among his peers, but by no definition had Gertz developed a taste for celebrity.

In the early 1950s, Gertz stumbled upon his first encounter with national fame when he succeeded the legendary civil liberties lawyer Clarence Darrow as Nathan Leopold's attorney. Leopold, along with Richard Loeb, had been sentenced to life imprisonment for the "thrill-killing" of Bobby Franks, a fourteen-year-old high school student. Leopold and Loeb were teenagers themselves when they bashed Franks's skull four times with a chisel. Darrow was able to persuade the sentencing judge that Leopold and Loeb killed Franks "as they might kill a spider or a fly, for the experience. They killed him because they were made that way." Loeb was later slashed to death in prison, but Leopold became a model inmate. In 1958, Illinois governor Adlai Stevenson commuted Leopold's sentence to time served after Gertz persuaded state authorities that his client was fully rehabilitated. In 1964, Gertz joined the legal team defending Jack Ruby, who had been convicted of killing Lee Harvey Oswald, President John F. Kennedy's assassin. On November 23, 1963, Ruby, a local nightclub owner, shot Oswald as he was being escorted through a Dallas police station. Ruby's alleged connections to organized crime set off numerous conspiracy theories concerning Kennedy's assassination, and Gertz later succeeded in persuading an appeals court to overturn his client's conviction on the grounds that the publicity surrounding his first trial tainted the jury's verdict. And, in a case that many legal scholars believed marked his greatest contribution to the legal system, Gertz won a decision before the Supreme Court, *Witherspoon* v. *Illinois* (1968), holding that excluding potential jurors in capital cases because they opposed the death penalty was unconstitutional.

Gertz's experience in the Leopold and Ruby cases left him clear about what it meant to be a public figure. By 1968, few people outside the legal profession knew of Elmer Gertz. His lawsuit against the John Birch Society illustrated the importance of time and place in the ability to bring a libel action. Gertz was clearly a public figure when he represented Nathan Leopold—"I couldn't go anywhere in Chicago without being instantly recognized. People would stop me on the streets and say, How's your client getting along?"—but that was before the *Sullivan* decision. So was the Ruby case. Then, in Gertz's own words he "receded into being an ordinary lawyer." Juries had no idea who he was when he argued before them. After reading Stang's article, Gertz thought about all the other people that the John Birch Society had attacked, such as Eisenhower and Chief Justice Earl Warren. Enough was enough, thought Gertz, "Somebody ought to call a halt to that kind of thing . . . I nominated myself to do the job."

Gertz, working closely with Wayne Giampietro, zeroed in on Stang's comment at the end of his article in which he claimed to have conducted "extensive research" into the Nuccio case. At trial, Giampietro's questioning of Stang and the *American Opinion*'s editor, Scott Stanley, revealed that little research had gone into the article. Stanley admitted that he had no personal knowledge of any facts in the case, had never heard of Gertz before Stang handed him the article, and made no effort to confirm any of Stang's claims. Had Stang done any research into Gertz's history, he would have learned that the Chicago lawyer had never been associated with any Communist organizations. But perhaps the most damaging witness to the John Birch Society's defense was Michael Kachigan, the lawyer who represented Officer Nuccio. Kachigan testified that Gertz had a "very good" professional reputation and that loyalty to the United States was "excellent." Far worse news for the defendants came when Kachigan was asked if he had ever heard of Alan Stang. "I don't believe so," he responded.

Elmer Gertz, center, shown here with one of his most famous clients, Nathan Leopold, far right, the "thrill killer" whom his earlier lawyer, Clarence Darrow, was able to save from execution during his original 1924 trial by pleading the insanity defense. Gertz represented Leopold in his successful appeal for parole in the late 1950s.
Chicago Tribune photo

James A. Boyle, the Birch Society's attorney, conceded during his closing statement that Stang "wasn't right in all respects in this case" and that Gertz was not a Communist. Based on that admission, the trial judge concluded that under Illinois law Gertz had been libeled, and directed the jury to award damages. The jury awarded Gertz $50,000. In a strange turn of events, the trial judge, who had determined before the trial that Gertz was not a public figure, changed his mind and decided that Gertz met the *Sullivan* standard. "By representing the victim's family in litigation brought against the policeman," wrote the judge, "Gertz thrust himself into the vortex of this important public controversy." The judge agreed that Stang was negligent—the libel standard under Illinois law—but had not acted with actual malice. Gertz asked the Eighth Circuit Court of Appeals to reverse the trial judge's decision. Writing for the appeals court, John Paul Stevens, who was appointed to the Supreme Court three years later by President Gerald Ford, agreed with the trial judge that Stang and Stanley had not been guilty of actual malice. Later, Gertz attended a dinner hosted by the governor of Illinois in honor of Stevens's elevation to the Supreme Court. When Gertz asked Stevens why he ruled against him, the future justice replied that he believed that was how the Court was going to rule.

Elmer Gertz practiced law until his death in April 2000. Of all the cases and causes in which he had been involved over the course of a sixty-year career, his successful lawsuit against the John Birch Society remained his proudest moment. He opposed restrictions on obscenity and fought efforts to censor controversial books, but never wavered from his belief that the news media should be held to a higher rather than lesser standard in libel cases. "I'm no longer a person, I'm a legal landmark," Gertz liked to tell law students after the Court's decision. True enough, but even legal landmarks, as Gertz successfully argued, deserve a right to their reputation.

References

Irons, Peter. *The Courage of Their Convictions*. New York: Free Press, 1988, pp. 333–354.

Janega, Janice, and Maurice Possley, "Civil Rights Champion, Defender of Underdog," *Chicago Tribune*, April 28, 2000, pp. 1, 23.

Knappman, Edward A., ed. *Great American Trials: From Salem Witchcraft to Rodney King*. Detroit: Visible Ink Press, 1994, pp. 307–311.

tures on both sides" as one of the reasons for the couple's marital woes. Asserting that the trial judge considered testimony about her alleged adultery as "unreliable," Mary Alice Firestone sued *Time* for libel after the magazine refused to print a retraction. *Time* claimed that Mary Alice Firestone was a public figure under the *Sullivan* standard. The Court, 5–3, affirmed the Florida State Supreme Court's decision upholding a $100,000 judgment against *Time*. Refining the Court's ruling in *Gertz*, Justice Rehnquist wrote:

> Dissolution of a marriage through judicial proceedings is not the sort of "public controversy" referred to in *Gertz*, even though the marital difficulties of extremely wealthy individuals may be of interest to some portion of the reading public. Nor did respondent freely choose to publicize issues as to the propriety of her married life. She was compelled to go to court by the State in order to obtain legal release from the bonds of matrimony. We have said that in such an instance "[r]esort to the judicial process . . . is no more voluntary in a realistic sense than that of the defendant called upon to defend his interests in court." Her actions, both in instituting the litigation and in its conduct, were quite different from those of General Walker in [*Associated Press* v.] *Curtis Publishing Co*. She assumed no "special prominence in the resolution of public questions." We hold respondent was not a "public figure" for the purpose of determining the constitutional protection afforded petitioner's report of the factual and legal basis for her divorce. . . . For similar reasons we likewise reject petitioner's claim for automatic extension of the *New York Times* privilege to all reports of judicial proceedings.[44]

Gertz and *Firestone* have not made it easier for public figures to bring successful libel lawsuits. Nor did they reduce the range accorded to the news media in *Sullivan* to engage in robust and critical discussion of matters touching public concern. These two cases did, however, ease the burden on *private* figures who believed they had been defamed according to the standards of state law. A major point of contention between the *Gertz* and *Firestone* majorities and the dissenters was the apparent double standard that now existed under the Court's line of libel cases since *Sullivan*. Public officials and public figures had to demonstrate actual malice according to the Court's interpretation of the First Amendment, but private figures were not required to meet a federal constitutional standard, just the standards defined by state law. Often, state law required nothing more than a showing that the alleged libel contained false information or injured a person's reputation. Indeed, that is the standard that Elmer Gertz and Mary Alice Firestone were permitted to meet in their libel actions. Has the Court, in fact, established an unfair double standard in libel lawsuits involving public and private figures that cannot be squared with the First Amendment?

Fact, Fiction, and Opinion: When Does the *Sullivan* Standard Apply?

Gertz and *Firestone* also clarified another principle that continues to animate the Court's approach to libel law since *Sullivan*. Any allegation of "emotional distress" by a public official or public figure caused by the publication of offensive material, even if the publisher's motive was intentional, is flatly inconsistent with the Court's modern understanding of freedom of the press. Private figures, on the other hand, may still prevail under an emotional distress claim caused by the invasion of privacy.[45] Emotional distress has its roots in the British common law tradition, and is designed to protect individuals against reckless behavior by the press and other public speakers. Indeed, Louis Brandeis's famous 1890 article, "The Right to Privacy," which has served as an important intellectual undercurrent in the development of the Court's modern approach to the law of personal and sexual privacy (see Chapter 10) and the right against unreasonable searches and seizures (see Chapter 7), was an effort to limit the rights of the press to publish material about the lives of private figures.[46]

In *Hustler Magazine* v. *Falwell* (1988), the Court confronted the thin line between the protection afforded to private citizens under the emotional distress claim and the First Amendment rights of the news media to publish outrageous commentary about public figures. Much more than the future livelihood of the nation's political cartoonists was at stake in *Falwell*. At the time, this case involved two well-known public figures whom people either loved or hated. When the case reached the Court, it was clear that the decision was going to turn on whether Jerry Falwell, one of America's best-known religious broadcasters, had, in the context of time and place, suffered emotional distress at the hands of Larry Flynt, one of America's best-known pornographic magazine publishers.

Hustler Magazine v. *Falwell*

485 U.S. 46 (1988)

No one can say if Larry Flynt harbored dreams of becoming a First Amendment martyr during his childhood days as a moonshine runner in the coal towns of northern Kentucky. But from the first day that Flynt published his crudely pornographic magazine, *Hustler*, it was clear that he was on a collision course with the First Amendment. Flynt's decision to base his magazine in Cincinnati, Ohio, put him in confrontation with some of the nation's most restrictive obscenity laws and a particularly zealous antipornography group, the Center for Decency Through Law, headed by Charles Keating. Keating was a successful businessman of impeccable conservative credentials who went head-to-head with Flynt throughout the 1970s. On more than one occasion, Keating successfully shut *Hustler* down. In the late 1980s, Keating again emerged as a public figure, this time as a Phoenix banker found guilty of attempting to unduly influence several members of Congress and lying to federal regulators over a scam to bilk millions of dollars from depositors through his savings and loan companies.

Flynt relished his fights with Cincinnati authorities, which only served to increase his notoriety and *Hustler*'s circulation. Every time Flynt was knocked down, he got right back up, and *Hustler*'s content—the sex, the political commentary, and the humor—grew more and more brash. In November 1983, *Hustler*, under Flynt's direction, published a parody of an advertisement for Campari vermouth featuring the nationally known religious broadcaster Jerry Falwell. Falwell also headed the Moral Majority, a conservative Christian group active in politics and public affairs. The real Campari ads, which carried a not-so-subtle sexual theme, featured interviews with celebrities discussing their "first time" with the liqueur. In the *Hustler* parody, Falwell was depicted in a mock interview discussing his "first time" with Campari, which took place in an outhouse during a sexual encounter with his mother. At the bottom of the page was a brief and barely noticeable disclaimer, "Ad parody—not to be taken seriously."

Falwell sued Flynt for emotional distress and asked for $45 million in damages. During his trial, Falwell's attorney asked him to address each allegation made by the advertisement:

"Have you ever taken alcoholic beverages before going into the pulpit to deliver your message?" asked Falwell's attorney.

"Never at any time," responded Falwell.

Over a vigorous defense objection, Falwell was permitted to answer the question of whether "specifically, did you and your mother ever commit incest?"

"Absolutely not," responded Falwell. "It is the most hurtful, damaging, despicable, low-type personal attack that I can imagine one human being . . . inflict[ing] upon another."

By allowing Falwell to answer the question of whether he committed incest with his mother, the judge treated the advertisement's portrayal as having an air of seriousness. *Hustler*'s entire defense had been based on the idea that the allegations in the ad were so preposterous that no one could take them seriously. When it came time for Flynt to testify, he did so in the wheelchair to which he had been confined since an assassin attempted to take his life in 1978. Said Flynt, "If I really wanted to hurt Reverend Falwell, I would do a serious article on the inside . . . if you really want to hurt someone . . . you put down things that are believable. You don't put down things that are totally unbelievable."[47]

The jury rejected Falwell's libel suit, agreeing with *Hustler* that the Campari ad did not offer any content meant to be taken as fact. But, in a stunning and unprecedented verdict, the jury awarded Falwell $200,000 in actual and punitive damages, concluding that the televangelist had suffered emotional distress. Flynt appealed to the United States Supreme Court.

The Court's decision was unanimous. Justice Kennedy did not participate.

▼▲▼

CHIEF JUSTICE REHNQUIST delivered the opinion of the Court.

This case presents us with a novel question involving First Amendment limitations upon a State's authority to protect its citizens from the intentional infliction of emotional distress. We must decide whether a public figure may recover damages for emotional harm caused by the publication of an ad parody offensive to him, and doubtless gross and repugnant in the eyes of most. Respondent would have us find that a State's interest in protecting public figures from emotional distress is sufficient to deny First Amendment protection to speech that is patently offensive and is intended to inflict emotional injury, even when that speech could not reasonably have been interpreted as stating actual facts about the public figure involved. This we decline to do.

At the heart of the First Amendment is the recognition of the fundamental importance of the free flow of ideas and opinions on matters of public interest and concern. . . . We have therefore been particularly vigilant to ensure that individual expressions of ideas remain free from governmentally imposed sanctions. The First Amendment recognizes no such thing as a "false" idea. . . .

The sort of robust political debate encouraged by the First Amendment is bound to produce speech that is critical of those who hold public office or those public figures who are "intimately involved in the resolution of important public questions or, by reason of their fame, shape events in areas of concern to society at large." Justice Frankfurter put it succinctly. . . . when he said that "[o]ne of the prerogatives of American citizenship is the right to criticize public men and measures." Such criticism, inevitably, will not always be reasoned or moderate; public figures as well as public officials will be subject to "vehement, caustic, and sometimes unpleasantly sharp attacks." . . .

Of course, this does not mean that any speech about a public figure is immune from sanction in the form of damages. Since *New York Times Co.* v. *Sullivan* (1964), we have consistently ruled that a public figure may hold a speaker liable for the damage to reputation caused by publication of a defamatory falsehood, but only if the statement was made "with knowledge that it was false or with reckless disregard of whether it was false or not." False statements of fact are particularly valueless; they interfere with the truthseeking function of the marketplace of ideas, and they cause damage to an individual's reputation that cannot easily be repaired by counterspeech, however persuasive or effective. But even though falsehoods have little value in and of themselves, they are "nevertheless inevitable in free debate," and a rule that would impose strict liability on a publisher for false factual assertions would have an undoubted "chilling" effect on speech relating to public figures that does have constitutional value. "Freedoms of expression require breathing space." This breathing space is provided by a constitutional rule that allows public figures to recover for libel or defamation only when they can prove both that the statement was false and that the statement was made with the requisite level of culpability.

Respondent argues, however, that a different standard should apply in this case because, here, the State seeks to prevent not reputational damage, but the severe emotional distress suffered by the person who is the subject of an offensive publication. In respondent's view, . . . so long as the utterance was intended to inflict emotional distress, was outrageous, and did in fact inflict serious emotional distress, it is of no constitutional import whether the statement was a fact or an opinion, or whether it was true or false. It is the intent to cause injury that is the gravamen of the tort, and the State's interest in preventing emotional harm simply outweighs whatever interest a speaker may have in speech of this type.

Generally speaking, the law does not regard the intent to inflict emotional distress as one which should receive much solicitude, and it is quite understandable that most, if not all, jurisdictions have chosen to make it civilly culpable where the conduct in question is sufficiently "outrageous." But in the world of debate about public affairs, many things done with motives that are less than admirable are protected by the First Amendment. . . . [W]hile such a bad motive may be deemed controlling for purposes of tort liability in other areas of the law, we think the First Amendment prohibits such a result in the area of public debate about public figures.

Were we to hold otherwise, there can be little doubt that political cartoonists and satirists would be subjected to damages awards without any showing that their work falsely defamed its subject. *Webster's* defines a caricature as "the deliberately distorted picturing or imitating of a person, literary style, etc. by exaggerating features or mannerisms for satirical effect." The appeal of the political cartoon or caricature is often based on exploitation of unfortunate physical traits or politically embarrassing events—an exploitation often calculated to injure the feelings of the subject of the portrayal. The art of the cartoonist is often not reasoned or evenhanded, but slashing and one-sided. One cartoonist expressed the nature of the art in these words: "The political cartoon is a weapon of attack, of scorn and ridicule and satire; it is least effective when it tries to pat some politician on the back. It is usually as welcome as a bee sting, and is always controversial in some quarters."

Several famous examples of this type of intentionally injurious speech were drawn by Thomas Nast, probably the greatest American cartoonist to date, who was associated for many years during the post–Civil War era with *Harper's Weekly*. In the pages of that publication Nast conducted a graphic vendetta against William M. "Boss" Tweed and his corrupt associates in New York City's "Tweed Ring." It has been described by one historian of the subject as "a sustained attack which in its passion and effectiveness stands alone in the history of American graphic art. . . ."

Despite their sometimes caustic nature, from the early cartoon portraying George Washington as an ass down to the present day, graphic depictions and satirical cartoons have played a prominent role in public and political debate. Nast's castigation of the Tweed Ring, Walt McDougall's characterization of Presidential candidate James G. Blaine's banquet with the millionaires at Delmonico's as "The Royal Feast of Belshazzar," and numerous other efforts have undoubtedly had an effect on the course and outcome of contemporaneous debate. Lincoln's tall, gangling posture, Teddy Roosevelt's glasses and teeth, and Franklin D. Roosevelt's jutting jaw and cigarette holder have been memorialized by political cartoons with an effect that could not have been obtained by the photographer or the portrait artist. From the viewpoint of history, it is clear that our political discourse would have been considerably poorer without them.

Respondent contends, however, that the caricature in question here was so "outrageous" as to distinguish it from more traditional political cartoons. There is no doubt that the caricature of respondent and his mother published in *Hustler* is at best a distant cousin of the political cartoons described above, and a rather poor relation at that. If it were possible by laying down a principled standard to separate the one from the other, public discourse would probably suffer little or no harm. But we doubt that there is any such standard, and we are quite sure that the pejorative description "outrageous" does not supply one. "Outrageousness" in the area of political and social discourse has an inherent subjectiveness about it which would allow a jury to impose liability on the basis of the jurors' tastes or views, or perhaps on the basis of their dislike of a particular expression. An "outrageousness" standard thus runs afoul of our longstanding refusal to allow damages to be awarded because the speech in question may have an adverse emotional impact on the audience. . . .

We conclude that public figures and public officials may not recover for the tort of intentional infliction of emotional distress by reason of publications such as the one here at issue without showing, in addition, that the publication contains a false statement of fact which was made with "actual malice," *i.e.*, with knowledge that the statement was false or with reckless disregard as to whether or not it was true. This is not merely a "blind application" of the *New York Times* standard, it reflects our considered judgment that such a standard is necessary to give adequate "breathing space" to the freedoms protected by the First Amendment. . . .

Reversed.

In addition to clarifying further the definition of a public figure, Chief Justice Rehnquist's opinion in *Falwell* affirmed that "on issues of public concern, the match between the First Amendment and the tort of intentional infliction of emotional distress is no contest; the First Amendment always wins."[48]

The First Amendment does not, however, always win when it comes to the right of the news media to publish opinion and commentary about public figures that has little basis in fact or whose accuracy is open to question. In *Milkovich v. Lorain Journal Co.* (1990), the Court confronted the question of whether statements of opinion, as opposed to statements of fact, could ever be considered defamatory. Since World II, the American courts had worked from the common law assumption that opinions were not actionable under libel law since truth could not be easily determined. A libel action brought by an Ohio high school wrestling coach against a local newspaper, which had published an opinion column accusing the coach of inciting a brawl between his team and its opponent after a match, and then lying about it before an administrative hearing. A state court rejected *Milkovich*'s libel claim, ruling that Theodore Diadiun's column was constitutionally protected opinion. A 7–2 Court, with Chief Justice Rehnquist writing for the majority, ruled, however, that the First Amendment provided no special protection to statements of opinions in defamation cases. Simply prefacing a sentence with, "I believe," or "In my opinion," before calling someone a liar did not protect a speaker from liability for false statements. Rehnquist concluded that the First Amendment did not create a "wholesale defamation exemption for anything that might be labeled opinion."[49]

Falwell and *Milkovich* established constitutional guidelines on the news media's right to publish opinion and commentary on public figures. A question left open by these cases was whether information presented as fact after an admission from the publisher that an article or story contained fabricated quotes or additional embellishments was protected by the First Amendment. Did the *New York Times* standard extend to such cases? This was precisely the issue in the carefully watched, high-profile case of *Masson v. New Yorker* (1991).

Masson v. New Yorker

501 U.S. 496 (1991)

Jeffrey Masson had never struck anyone who had ever worked with him as the shy, retiring type. A Harvard-trained scholar, Masson taught Sanskrit and Indian studies at the University of Toronto. Masson spent eight years of his nine years there training to become a psychoanalyst. Through his professional activities, Mason met Dr. Kurt Eissler, head of the Sigmund Freud Archives in London, and Anna Freud, Sigmund Freud's daughter and a respected psychoanalyst in her own right. Supremely self-confident and extremely ambitious, Masson persuaded Eissler and Freud to hire him to serve as the project director of the Freud archives. In 1980, Masson assumed his new post, but became quickly disillusioned with Freudian psychology. A year later, Masson presented a paper critical of Freud at a professional meeting. Eissler and Freud promptly released him from his contract.

Shortly after Masson's departure from the Freud archives, Janet Malcolm, a writer for the *New Yorker* magazine, called Masson to inquire about a full-length feature story about his relationship with Eissler and Freud, his work with the archives, his disillusion with Freudian psychology, and so on. Masson jumped at the chance, recognizing that a profile in the *New Yorker,* considered by many writers, reporters, critics, and cartoonists as the finest magazine in American journalism, would be great publicity. Malcolm had a reputation among her peers as a skillful interviewer who was quite adept at getting her subjects to reveal themselves. Masson, perhaps, revealed a little too much of himself, as Malcolm's two-part profile, which ran in December 1983, portrayed him as someone infatuated with his own abilities, sexually promiscuous, and a professional opportunist with a penchant for self-promotion. Malcolm's article was extremely well received and later expanded into a 1985 book, *In the Freud Archives*.

The article infuriated Masson. He claimed that Malcolm had fabricated quotes left and right and pulled apart many other quotes to distort beyond repair the accuracy of what Masson said in his interviews. After Masson filed a libel suit in federal court based on the fabricated quotations attributed to him, Malcolm was required to produce transcripts and recordings of her interview notes. In most cases, Malcolm's quotes were correct, but in at least five instances long passages that Malcolm had attributed to Masson could not be drawn from the recorded interviews or her notes. These included a comment that Masson had referred to himself as an "intellectual gigolo." According to Malcolm, Masson said that, had he remained at the Freud archives, he would have turned it into a "center of scholarship, but it would also have been a place of sex, women, and fun." Malcolm admitted that some the quotes published in her article, such as the one above, had been drawn from memory.

A federal district court entered a summary judgment on behalf of Malcolm, holding that the alleged fabricated quotes did not amount to actual malice under the *New York Times* v. *Sullivan* standard. The Ninth Circuit Court of Appeals affirmed.

The Court's decision was 7 to 2. Justice Kennedy delivered the opinion of the Court. Justice White, joined by Justice Scalia, wrote a separate opinion concurring in part and dissenting in part.

▼▲▼

JUSTICE KENNEDY delivered the opinion of the Court.

The First Amendment protects authors and journalists who write about public figures by requiring a plaintiff to prove that the defamatory statements were made with what we have called "actual malice," a term of art denoting deliberate or reckless falsification. We consider in this opinion whether the attributed quotations had the degree of falsity required to prove this state of mind, so that the public figure can defeat a motion for summary judgment and proceed to a trial on the merits of the defamation claim. . . .

The First Amendment limits [state] libel law in various respects. When, as here, the plaintiff is a public figure, he cannot recover unless he proves by clear and convincing evidence that the defendant published the defamatory statement with actual malice, *i.e.*, with "knowledge that it was false or with reckless disregard of whether it was false or not," *New York Times Co.* v. *Sullivan* (1964). Mere negligence does not suffice. Rather, the plaintiff must demonstrate that the author "in fact entertained serious doubts as to the truth of his publication," or acted with a "high degree of awareness of . . . probable falsity." Actual malice under the *New York Times* standard should not be confused with the concept of malice as an evil intent or a motive arising from spite or ill-will. We have used the term actual malice as a shorthand to describe the First Amendment protections for speech injurious to reputation, and we continue to do so here. But the term can confuse as well as enlighten. In this respect, the phrase may be an unfortunate one. In place of the term actual malice, it is better practice that jury instructions refer to publication of a statement with knowledge of falsity or reckless disregard as to truth or falsity. This definitional principle must be remembered in the case before us.

In general, quotation marks around a passage indicate to the reader that the passage reproduces the speaker's words verbatim. They inform the reader that he or she is reading the statement of the speaker, not a paraphrase or other indirect interpretation by an author. By providing this information, quotations add authority to the statement and credibility to the author's work. Quotations allow the reader to form his or her own conclusions, and to assess the conclusions of the author, instead of relying entirely upon the author's characterization of her subject.

A fabricated quotation may injure reputation in at least two senses, either giving rise to a conceivable claim of defamation. First, the quotation might injure because it attributes an untrue factual assertion to the speaker. An example would be a fabricated quotation of a public official admitting he had been convicted of a serious crime when in fact he had not.

Second, regardless of the truth or falsity of the factual matters asserted within the quoted statement, the attribution may result in injury to reputation because the manner of expression or even the fact that the statement was made indicates a negative personal trait or an attitude the speaker does not hold. John Lennon once was quoted as saying of the Beatles, "We're more popular than Jesus Christ now. . . ." [O]ne need not determine whether petitioner is or is not the greatest analyst who ever lived in order to determine that it might have injured his reputation to be reported as having so proclaimed. . . .

The work at issue here . . . as with much journalistic writing, provides the reader no clue that the quotations are being used as a rhetorical device or to paraphrase the speaker's actual statements. To the contrary, the work purports to be nonfiction, the result of numerous interviews. At least a trier of fact could so conclude. The work contains lengthy quotations attributed to petitioner, and neither Malcolm nor her publishers indicate to the reader that the quotations are anything but the reproduction of actual conversations. Further, the work was published in *The New Yorker,* a magazine which at the relevant time seemed to enjoy a reputation for scrupulous factual accuracy. These factors would, or at least could, lead a reader to take the quotations at face value. A defendant may be able to argue to the jury that quotations should be viewed by the reader as nonliteral or reconstructions, but we conclude that a trier of fact in this case could find that the reasonable reader would understand the quotations to be nearly verbatim reports of statements made by the subject.

The constitutional question we must consider here is whether, in the framework of a summary judgment motion, the evidence suffices to show that respondents acted with the requisite knowledge of falsity or reckless disregard as to truth or falsity. This inquiry, in turn, requires us to consider the concept of falsity, for we cannot discuss the standards for knowledge or reckless disregard without some understanding of the acts required for liability. We must consider whether the requisite falsity inheres in the attribution of words to the petitioner which he did not speak.

In some sense, any alteration of a verbatim quotation is false. But writers and reporters, by necessity, alter what people say, at the very least to eliminate grammatical and syntactical infelicities. If every alteration constituted the falsity required to prove actual malice, the practice of journalism, which the First Amendment standard is designed to protect, would require a radical change, one inconsistent with our precedents and First Amendment principles. . . .

We reject the idea that any alteration beyond correction of grammar or syntax by itself proves falsity in the sense relevant to determining actual malice under the First Amendment. An interviewer who writes from notes often will engage in the task of attempting a reconstruction of the speaker's statement. That author would, we may assume, act with knowledge that, at times, she has attributed to her subject words other than those actually used. Under petitioner's proposed standard, an author in this situation would lack First Amendment protection if she reported as quotations the substance of a subject's derogatory statements about himself.

Even if a journalist has tape recorded the spoken statement of a public figure, the full and exact statement will be reported in only rare circumstances. The existence of both a speaker and a reporter; the translation between two media, speech and the printed word; the addition of punctuation; and the practical necessity to edit and make intelligible a speaker's perhaps rambling comments, all make it misleading to suggest that a quotation will be reconstructed with complete accuracy. The use or absence of punctuation may distort a speaker's meaning, for example, where that meaning turns upon a speaker's emphasis of a particular word. In other cases, if a speaker makes an obvious misstatement, for example by unconscious substitution of one name for another, a journalist might alter the speaker's words but preserve his intended meaning. And conversely, an exact quotation out of context can distort meaning, although the speaker did use each reported word. . . .

We conclude that a deliberate alteration of the words uttered by a plaintiff does not equate with knowledge of falsity for purposes of *New York Times* and *Gertz* v. *Welch,* unless the alteration results in a material change in the meaning conveyed by the statement. The use of quotations to attribute words not in fact spoken bears in a most important way on that inquiry, but it is not dispositive in every case.

Deliberate or reckless falsification that comprises actual malice turns upon words and punctuation only because words and punctuation express meaning. Meaning is the life of language. And, for the reasons we have given, quotations may be a devastating instrument for conveying false meaning. In the case under consideration, readers of *In the Freud Archives* may have found Malcolm's portrait of petitioner especially damning because so much of it appeared to be a self-portrait, told by petitioner in his own words. And if the alterations of petitioner's words gave a different meaning to the statements, bearing upon their defamatory character, then the device of quotations might well be critical in finding the words actionable. . . .

We apply these principles to the case before us. . . . So we must assume, except where otherwise evidenced by the transcripts of the tape recordings, that petitioner is correct in denying that he made the statements attributed to him by Malcolm, and that Malcolm reported with knowledge or reckless disregard of the differences between what petitioner said and what was quoted.

First, many of the challenged passages resemble quotations that appear on the tapes, except for the addition or alteration of certain phrases, giving rise to a reasonable inference that the statements have been altered. Second, Malcolm had the tapes in her possession, and was not working under a tight deadline. Unlike a case involving hot news, Malcolm cannot complain that she lacked the practical ability to compare the tapes with her work in progress. Third, Malcolm represented to the editor-in-chief of *The New Yorker* that all the quotations were from the tape recordings. Fourth, Malcolm's explanations of the time and place of unrecorded conversations during which petitioner allegedly made some of the quoted statements have not been consistent in all respects. Fifth, petitioner suggests that the progression from typewritten notes, to manuscript, then to galleys provides further evidence of intentional alteration. Malcolm contests petitioner's allegations, and only a trial on the merits will resolve the factual dispute. But at this stage, the evidence creates a jury question whether Malcolm published the statements with knowledge or reckless disregard of the alterations. . . .

The judgment of the Court of Appeals is reversed, and the case is remanded for further proceedings consistent with this opinion.

Kennedy's opinion concluding that Malcolm's sloppy reporting did not amount to actual malice under the *New York Times* standard should not be interpreted as vindication for journalists to present risk-free fabricated quotes about their subjects. During the trial phase of *Masson,* Malcolm had continually denied that she deliberately altered the meaning of the psychoanalyst's quotes or shaped the content of her interviews with Masson to fit a particular agenda. The Court's decision to vacate the trial court verdict against Masson and order a new trial suggested that the justices were not convinced of Malcolm's innocence. Ultimately, after two more trials, a jury decided that Malcolm had not committed actual malice in her *New Yorker* articles.

Libel law has undergone a seismic shift since *New York Times* v. *Sullivan*. In cases involving public officials and public figures, the First Amendment now serves as the centerpiece of litigation, replacing state sedition and defamation law. However, the Court has not cordoned off the news media behind the First Amendment when private figures allege libel, defamation, or emotional distress. *New York Times* has not disturbed state law permitting a private figure to recover damages by showing negligence on the part of the press. Moreover, a private figure is not required to demonstrate that he or she has been libeled under most state privacy laws. Emotional distress, for example, has nothing to do with whether a published statement is true or false, but whether the reported information has any bearing on the public interest. The complexities of modern libel law are bound to continue to occupy the courts, as the Internet and other forms of computer technology have made access to the public much easier than it was in 1964, both to criticize and defend one's reputation.

FOR FURTHER READING

Adler, Renata. *Reckless Disregard*. New York: Alfred A. Knopf, 1986.

Cooper, Cynthia. *Mockery of Justice: The True Story of the Sheppard Murder*. Boston: Northeastern University Press, 1995.

Forer, Louis A. *A Chilling Effect: The Mounting Threat of Libel and Invasion of Privacy Actions to the First Amendment*. New York: Norton, 1987.

Friendly, Fred W. *Minnesota Rag: The Dramatic Story of the Landmark Supreme Court Case That Gave New Meaning to Freedom of the Press*. New York: Random House, 1981.

Halberstam, David. *The Powers That Be*. New York: Alfred A. Knopf, 1979.

Levy, Leonard. *The Emergence of a Free Press*. New York: Oxford University Press, 1985.

Lewis, Anthony. *Make No Law: The Sullivan Case and the First Amendment*. New York: Random House, 1991.

Slotnick, Eliot, and Jennifer A. Segal. *Television News and the Supreme Court*. New York: Cambridge University Press, 1998.

Smolla, Rodney A. *Jerry Falwell v. Larry Flynt*. New York: St. Martin's Press, 1988.

———. *Free Speech in an Open Society*. New York: Alfred A. Knopf, 1992.

Tedford, Thomas L. *Freedom of Speech in the United States,* 3d ed. State College, Penn.: Strata Publishing, 1997.

Ungar, Sanford J. *The Papers & the Papers: An Account of the Legal and Political Battle over the Pentagon Papers*. New York: Columbia University Press, 1972.

Walker, Samuel. *In Defense of American Liberties*. New York: Oxford University Press, 1990.

6 Freedom of Religion

In 1925, Clarence Darrow and William Jennings Bryan engaged in a historic confrontation in a Dayton, Tennessee, courtroom over the meaning of the Bible and its place in American public education. Just before they were to begin, Bryan told a throng of assembled supporters that his presence was more than just a personal effort to save "the Christian Church from those who are trying to destroy her faith."[1] With charm and charisma pouring from the shadow where he stood, Bryan announced that his involvement in the case of *Tennessee v. Scopes* resulted from an equally disturbing possibility: Can a minority use the courts to force its ideas upon schools in particular and society in general? Majorities, Bryan insisted, acted with the natural self-restraint that the Constitution required. If the "godless" were indeed a majority, then by all means elect them. And if they were not, was it fair to have the courts impose their will on an unwelcoming citizenry through a constitutional command?

To Bryan, of course, the answer was no. To Clarence Darrow, the famous American Civil Liberties Union lawyer who defended teacher John Scopes, the question was not whether a political minority should have the power to force its will upon everybody else. Instead, it was whether a religious majority had a constitutional right to compel others to believe things they did not believe, and enshrine those beliefs in the law. Darrow understood that many religious believers rejected Darwin's theory of evolution as the explanation of the origin of mankind. But he also pointed out that the Biblical account of creation had its share of skeptics, many of whom were religious as well as secular. Putting Bryan, a self-professed "expert on religion," on the stand, Darrow asked him if he accepted the literal account of the Bible. "I am more interested in the Rock of Ages than in the age of rocks," responded Bryan. Did that mean he believed that Moses really parted the Red Sea, or that a whale swallowed Jonah the prophet? "Of course," Bryan responded.[2]

The jury ultimately found John Scopes guilty of violating Tennessee's law prohibiting any public school from teaching "any theory that denies the story of the divine creation of man as taught in the Bible, and to teach instead that man has descended from a lower order of animals." But the judge imposed only a $100 fine, a decision the Tennessee Supreme Court reversed, ruling that such a decision belonged to the jury. In the long run, Darrow's relentless cross-examination overwhelmed Bryan, making him look like a prisoner of superstition rather than a man of his times. Two weeks after the *Scopes* trial ended, Bryan collapsed and died of a heart attack, taking much of the steam out of the Fundamentalist movement. Only two more states, Arkansas and Mississippi, enacted anti-evolution laws, while the rest stopped enforcing their anti-evolution laws.[3] Forty years later, the United States Supreme Court, in *Epperson v. Arkansas* (1968), declared such laws unconstitutional under the Establishment Clause of the First Amendment. Almost twenty years after *Epperson,* the Court struck down an effort by Louisiana to require "equal time" for teaching Biblical creation in public schools that taught evolution.[4]

The *Scopes* trial is, of course, one of the best known in American history, bringing together two larger-than-

Clarence Darrow, the nation's most famous civil liberties lawyer in the early twentieth century, arguing his case during the 1925 Scopes "Monkey" trial.
UPI Bettmann/CORBIS

life personalities in William Jennings Bryan and Clarence Darrow. It produced an atmosphere that resembled more a carnival than a sober inquiry into law and justice. But it did offer a powerful illustration of the tensions that have always simmered and often boiled over between America's original roots in Protestant Christianity and the demands of religious minorities to freedom of belief and equal treatment under law. John Scopes, the twenty-four-year-old biology teacher who agreed to violate the Tennessee anti-evolution law so that the ACLU could challenge it in court, probably had no idea that the combustible mix of issues involved in his case—religious establishment, free speech, and religious free exercise—would soon find a permanent place on the Court's docket.

This chapter examines the twin principles of the separation of church and state and the right to free exercise of religion. Together these principles form the constitutional guarantee of religious freedom. First, we will examine some of the Framers' concerns when they drafted the Establishment and Free Exercise Clauses of the First Amendment. Second, we will see how religious freedom unfolded in the early Republic. Finally, we will discuss the group dynamics that have shaped the litigation responsible for the Supreme Court's contemporary understanding of the Religion Clauses.

Heavenly Statecraft: The Constitution and Religion

In *Church of the Holy Trinity* v. *United States* (1892), the Supreme Court ruled that a federal law prohibiting American citizens from entering into contracts with aliens to encourage their immigration to the United

States violated the Establishment Clause. By the late 1800s, Catholics, Jews, and Buddhists had begun to alter the religious demographics of the United States. Congress responded in turn with laws discouraging immigration and, in some cases, placing specific quotas on or banning outright the entrance of Irish, Italians, European Jews, Japanese, and Chinese into the United States. Congress justified the law challenged in *Holy Trinity* as necessary to stem the tide of cheap immigrant workers that threatened to unsettle the American labor market. Here, though, the Holy Trinity Church was not attempting to acquire cheap labor to build railroads or dig foundations for the great buildings going up in American cities. An English citizen had contracted with the church to serve as its pastor and rector, and the church argued that the law could not be understood to prohibit Christian ministers from entering the United States to serve God. A unanimous Court agreed with Holy Trinity, noting in its opinion that the United States was "a Christian nation."[5]

The Constitution, however, does not mention God, Christianity, or anything else even remotely connected with any one church or particular religion. The only references the Constitution makes to religion actually constrain government power to act on behalf of or against religion. Article IV states that "no religious Test shall ever be required as a Qualification to any Office or public Trust under the United States." The Test Oath Clause "depriv[ed] the government of one of its most potent weapons of religious discrimination."[6] The Framers held many different conceptions of what religious liberty meant, and those differences emerged with great force during the debate over the language of the Religion Clauses. But none of the delegates to the Constitutional Convention contested the Test Oath Clause; few Americans during the period leading up to the ratification of the Constitution believed the federal government should have any power over religion.[7]

Likewise, the First Amendment provides an explicit constraint on the federal government's power to interfere with religious liberty. Historian Thomas Curry notes that the states would have been unable to reach agreement on a single definition of religious liberty, but, as with the Test Oath Clause, they agreed that Congress should have no power to meddle in the affairs of religion.[8] Beyond a consensus that Congress and, by extension, the federal government, should steer clear of religion, Americans, including several key Framers of the First Amendment, held wildly varying conceptions of the proper relationship between church and state. To some, establishment of religion meant placing state authority behind a single religion (*preferential* establishment), taxing citizens to support its churches and ministerial functions, and allowing a single religious denomination to maintain control over state and local political arrangements. But it was completely acceptable to permit "multiple establishments" of religion (*nonpreferential* establishment), or state laws that respected and assisted religion generally. Many Americans, however, disagreed with both preferential and nonpreferential forms of religious establishment, believing that neither the federal government nor the states should support religion on any level. Yet, almost all Americans understood freedom of religion as most Protestant Christian reformers had defined it over the years: the freedom to follow one's conscience to the truth of Christ.[9]

So was it wrong for the Court, in *Holy Trinity,* to conclude that America was "a Christian nation"? By the turn of the twentieth century, Protestant Christianity still reigned supreme as the nation's de facto religion, despite the great wave of Catholic and Jewish immigration to the United States that had begun soon after the Civil War. Less than 5 percent of Americans at this time identified themselves as belonging to a non-Christian faith; well over three fourths considered themselves Protestant. The nation's schools, civic institutions, and its politics were all steeped in the language and values of Protestant Christianity. Very few people, including Catholics, felt the need or had the political leverage to challenge the way things were.[10] Seen in this light, the United States was indeed a Christian nation and, even with greater religious diversity outside of Christianity than ever before, remains one today.

To conclude that America is a Christian nation because most Americans are Christian, however, gives short shrift to the complexity of social, religious, and political forces that have driven the development of church-state relations in the United States. Moreover, such a conclusion ignores the great care that the Framers took to extend religious liberty to groups beyond the Protestant majority. Certainly, Catholics, Jews, Mormons, and other "peculiar" and "foreign" religions, from the colonial period until the mid–nineteenth century, were denied civil and political rights, such as the right to hold office and the right to vote. More generally, they were viewed as something less than American by many Protestants. But the right of persons to worship according to the dictates of their conscience was protected. Only in cases when religious conduct breached the civil peace were state governments permitted to limit liberty of conscience. In sum, the Constitution did not require American citizens to believe in God, to profess faith in Christianity, or to support any religion, including their own, with taxes.

Of course, most Americans did believe in God and profess faith in Christianity when the Constitution was ratified, leading some scholars to argue that the First Amendment was designed to do little more than protect the diverse and flourishing arrangement of Protestant religious life. Any benefit that flowed to Jews, Catholics, Turks, and other non-Protestant or non-Christian religions was purely incidental.[11] One such incidental benefit, however, was religious tolerance, an attitude that ultimately blossomed into an equal respect for the religious liberty of non-Protestant religions. The Framers and their generation generally did not consider Jews, Catholics, Mormons, and others outside the "Cope of Heaven" the equals of Protestants, but they also recognized that establishing an official religion was a recipe for civil strife.[12] James Madison, in *Federalist* 51, acknowledged as much when he wrote, "In a free government, the security for civil rights must be the same as for religious rights. It consists in the one case in the multiplicity of interests, and in the other, in the multiplicity of sects."[13] The First Amendment thus can be understood to embody articles of faith and articles of peace.

Religious Disestablishment

Was there something contradictory about the First Amendment's clear intent to prohibit the establishment of a national religion and yet at the same time to permit continued state support for religion? By contemporary standards, yes. By the standards emerging in the late 1700s and early 1800s, the answer is less clear. In 1776, only four colonies, Rhode Island, Pennsylvania, Delaware, and New Jersey, had never supported the establishment of religion in any form. New York, Massachusetts, Connecticut, and New Hampshire, on the other hand, practiced what was then a uniquely American model of religious establishment: Civil authority in the states protected and supported multiple churches. Respect for multiple establishments of religion was in marked contrast to the European model with which most Americans were familiar, such as the Anglican Church, the officially established church of Great Britain. Only the Southern colonies, Georgia, Virginia, North Carolina, South Carolina, and Maryland, had an established religion in the European sense, with the Anglican Church of England receiving the backing of their colonial governments.[14]

After the Revolution, religious freedom in the United States began to move toward complete disestablishment. New York repudiated all establishments of religion in 1777, resolving a long dispute between the Anglican Church and all other religions over whether the state recognized a single establishment or multiple establishments of religion. The New England states permitting multiple churches to receive state support resisted disestablishment until well into the early nineteenth century. In 1833, Massachusetts voted to repeal its state constitutional provision establishing religion, beginning the process of disestablishment throughout the region. In the Southern states, the European model collapsed entirely, with North Carolina, in 1776, banning all establishments of religion in its new constitution. Georgia, Maryland, and South Carolina each eliminated the supremacy of the Anglican Church in their new state constitutions; by 1810, these three states had withdrawn all legal and financial support for multiple establishments of religion. South Carolina even guaranteed the free exercise of religion for Jews and Catholics.[15] By far the most dramatic disestablishment of religion in the early Republic, however, came in Virginia, the home to the First Amendment's two key architects, James Madison and Thomas Jefferson.

In 1779, Jefferson introduced into the Virginia legislature his Bill Establishing Religious Freedom, which prohibited the government from compelling any person "to frequent or support any religious worship, place or ministry whatsoever." Although Jefferson certainly respected the rights of persons to follow their conscience free from government's corrupting influence, he was just as leery—perhaps more so—of an established religion's potential disruptive impact on the secular state. Historians have pointed out that Jefferson made his case for disestablishment, and later a "wall of separation" separating church and state, by using language claiming to free religion in order to help religion.[16] In this sense, Jefferson's arguments are close to those of Roger Williams, the New England preacher who carried the torch of religious liberty in colonial Rhode Island. In 1644, Williams had used the "wall of separation" metaphor to argue against the enforced uniformity of religious belief, writing that government support for an established religion offered the "greatest occasion of civill Warre."[17] Jefferson, in his famous 1802 letter to the Danbury Connecticut Baptist Association, wrote: "I contemplate with sovereign reverence the act of the whole American people which declared that their legislature should 'make no law respecting an establishment of religion, or prohibiting the free exercise thereof,' thus building a wall of separation between church and state."

Whether Jefferson was motivated primarily to help religion or to protect government from what he believed were the failed lessons of past experiments with support for established churches is a question that continues to draw the attention of scholars. But no one questions the tremendous influence that his Virginia bill on behalf of religious freedom had on Madison's equally important statement on church-state relations, the *Memorial and Remonstrance Against Religious Assessments.* Madison wrote the *Memorial and Remonstrance* in response to a countermeasure introduced by Patrick Henry in 1779 that would have permitted a general assessment against Virginia citizens to support teachers in all Protestant churches. Sensing that Baptists, Methodists, and Presbyterians would soon rise up against what had been the preeminent position of the Episcopal Church in Virginia, Madison organized a massive drive to defeat the Assessment Bill in 1785. The *Memorial and Remonstrance,* in which Madison wrote that "the same authority which can force a citizen to contribute three pence only of his property for the support of any one establishment, may force him to conform to any other establishment in all cases," soon became a classic statement of religious freedom in the United States.[18] In 1786, the Virginia legislature enacted Jefferson's Bill Establishing Religious Freedom.

Madison and Jefferson's writings on religious freedom, their prominence in the battle to disestablish religion in Virginia, and their outsized role in crafting the Religion Clauses of the First Amendment have all featured prominently in the Supreme Court's understanding of the constitutional boundaries of church-state relations. Historian Garry Wills has suggested that Madison, more so than Jefferson, was more "absolute, effective and consistent" in his articulation of disestablishment, which he viewed as the precursor to the separation of church and state. The Court's twentieth-century decisions striking down state-sponsored prayer in the public schools, banning religious tests to hold public office, permitting nonreligious conscientious objection to military service, and prohibiting, until recently, direct subsidies for parochial schools and religious witnessing would have been welcomed by Madison or Jefferson. Both men embraced a vision of religious liberty that went beyond mere "toleration" for less favored religions to one that embraced the equal standing of all religious denominations with special status for none.[19]

Or so *some* scholars have argued. Arguments against the separation principle advanced by Madison and Jefferson range from those insisting that neither Virginian ever intended to divorce religion completely from state support to those claiming that the First Amendment offered nothing more than a release of federal control over religion with no accompanying substantive definition of religious freedom.[20] Constitutional scholars sympathetic to Madison and Jefferson as firm church-state separationists have argued that the history surrounding the adoption of the Establishment Clause permits no clear generalization of what was meant by an establishment of religion, other than state support for a single church.[21] Moreover, the disestablishment of religion in the United States was not accompanied by the withering of Protestant values in education and civic life. Religion was also an important moral force in early reform movements in American politics, such as temperance, equal rights for women, and the abolition of slavery.[22]

Today, Americans continue to debate the role of religion in public life. The intent of the Framers is invoked to justify both support for and opposition to prayer in public schools, government aid to parochial schools and social services provided by religious institutions, and the rights of religious ideas to command a place in making public policy. The same themes that occupied the minds of Americans during the formative period of religious disestablishment—religious purity, civic peace, toleration, equality of standing, and religion as a moral compass in a secular state—continue to find a prominent place in the Court's decisions on the Establishment Clause.

Religious Free Exercise

Religious disestablishment created a more conducive environment for what many in the Founding generation valued most of all: the free exercise of religion. As discussed above, the right to follow one's conscience during the battle for religious disestablishment in the states meant the pursuit of a Protestant path that ultimately led to the truth of Christ. The Free Exercise Clause was not, as early-nineteenth-century constitutional scholar and Supreme Court Justice Joseph Story observed, intended to advance or encourage the practice of non-Christian religions such as Judaism.[23] Indeed, even after the ratification of the First Amendment, restrictions on minority religions abounded in the states. These ranged from bans on non-Protestants, non-Christians, atheists, and persons who did not believe in an afterlife from holding office to criminal laws requiring all persons to observe the Christian Sabbath.[24]

Such harsh examples of the narrowness of the free exercise guarantee during the early Republic were, however, offset by examples of Protestant goodwill and fellowship to religious minorities. In 1790, George Washington, in a letter answering an inquiry from a Newport, Rhode Island, Jewish congregation about their status in America, wrote

> All possess alike liberty of conscience and immunities of citizenship. It is now no more that toleration is spoken of, as if it was by the indulgence of one class of people, that another enjoyed the exercise of their inherent natural rights. For happily the government of the United States, which gives to bigotry no sanction, to persecution no assistance, requires only that they who live under its protection should demean themselves as good citizens, in giving it all occasions their effectual support.[25]

Similarly, Thomas Jefferson, who did not find much to like in orthodox Protestant Christianity, Judaism, or Catholicism, nonetheless believed that government should stay out of the way when it came to the right of individuals to exercise their religious faith. Only when religious "principles break out into overt acts against peace & good order" was it permissible for government to interfere with the exercise of conscience.[26] Many constitutional scholars have argued that Jefferson's description of religious free exercise ultimately carried the day as religious life in the United States took on a much more plural character. Religious minorities certainly did not carry the same presumptions to equality under the Free Exercise Clause as did the Protestant majority. But the need to promote civic peace and protect religious liberty in principle eventually led the states to loosen their restrictions on the ability of religious minorities to participate fully in civic life and follow completely the dictates of their conscience.[27]

The notion that the Free Exercise Clause is designed to protect religious minorities is a popular one that enjoys broad support among constitutional scholars.[28] True, religious minorities have, especially in the twentieth century, successfully invoked the Free Exercise Clause to protect themselves against laws and practices denying them their basic right to worship as they please. But what sometimes remains unspoken is that religious minorities have had to fight harder and longer to obtain equal standing in the brotherhood of American religion. Even then, minority religions do not always fare well in the courts. Since 1878, when the Court, in *Reynolds* v. *United States,* upheld the conviction of a Mormon under a federal law banning polygamy, religious minorities have rarely emerged victorious under the Free Exercise Clause. Those that have won protection for the right to exercise their beliefs have been smaller, less mainstream Christian denominations, such as Jehovah's Witnesses and Seventh-day Adventists. Not one single non-Christian religion, however, has *ever* won a free exercise case in the Supreme Court.

Religion scholar Eric Mazur has argued that religious minorities stand the best chance of winning protection for their religious practices the closer they are to Protestant Christianity. Certainly, religious minorities have received protection for the right to engage in their religious practices. But oftentimes those practices falling outside Jefferson's acceptable boundaries of "peace & good order" are less likely to receive protection. And, as the Court's free exercise decisions clearly demonstrate, religious "principles breaking into overt acts" against the civil order are many circles removed from Protestant Christianity.[29] Like the Establishment Clause, the Free Exercise Clause derives its original meaning from the concerns of those who sought to reconcile the competing demands of Congregationalists, Episcopalians, Baptists, Methodists, Presbyterians, Anglicans, Quakers, and other Protestant denominations for equal treatment under law. At no time in colonial America or during the formative years of the nation was Judaism, Buddhism, Islam, or anything other than a Christian religion ever established. The Court's decisions involving the Establishment and Free Exercise Clauses are still informed in part by America's deep roots in the Protestant Christian tradition.

In 1835, Alexis de Tocqueville observed that "there is no other country in the world where the Christian religion retains a greater influence over the souls of men than in America," emphasizing the bond between Protestant Christianity and American public life that came together "in one undivided current."[30] Tocqueville wrote during the time that America was a much less religiously plural nation than it would become by the late nineteenth and early twentieth centuries. Entering the twenty-first century, America is more religiously diverse than ever before. Accordingly, the concepts of separation of church and state and religious free exercise during the early Republic are not necessarily responsive to the demands of religious minorities today. Moreover, the historical materials available to derive the intent of the Religion Clauses are not always sufficient to the questions brought about by two centuries of change in the social and political status of religious minorities. As we shall see, attempting to link history to principle, balance religious freedom with the needs of the secular state, and satisfy the vast array of religious groups that have mobilized to protect their place in the constitutional order is not an easy task.

The Supreme Court and the Establishment Clause

The Court's decisions defining the constitutional boundaries involving the separation of church and state have touched upon numerous aspects of American public and private life. Here, we focus on the three major areas of Establishment Clause litigation: government funding for parochial education; equal treatment for religious speech by public institutions; and religion and the public schools. But first we discuss the foundation of modern Establishment Clause law and litigation.

Establishing the Separation Principle: Early Cases

In the late 1920s, a group of taxpayers challenged a Louisiana law that authorized the state to provide free textbooks to students in religious schools. *Cochran* v. *Louisiana* (1930) was not the first time the Supreme Court had heard a challenge to a public program that aided religion.[31] In *Bradfield* v. *Roberts* (1899), the Court upheld a federal expenditure to a Roman Catholic hospital, ruling that public support for free medical care for the poor was a secular policy that advanced no religious purpose.[32] The Court followed that approach in *Cochran,* unanimously holding that such an expenditure of tax funds advanced a legitimate secular welfare objective intended to benefit children, not aid churches that supported parochial schools. The idea that certain forms of public assistance to parochial schools were permissible as long as they were *indirect* would have quite an influence on the Court's first major Establishment Clause decision, *Everson* v. *Board of Education* (1947).

Everson began when a small fraternal group called the Junior Order of United American Mechanics (JOUAM) decided to challenge a 1941 New Jersey law permitting the expenditure of public funds to subsidize bus transportation for school-age children to "any schoolhouse," including parochial schools. The law enjoyed widespread support among New Jersey citizens, who submitted program-supporting petitions that totaled approximately 500,000 signatures. Such popular support did not deter several religious, educational, and civil liberties groups, such as the New Jersey Taxpayers Association, the League of Women Voters, representatives of numerous Protestant churches, and the state chapter of the ACLU, from lobbying against the bus subsidies program. The motives of JOUAM were somewhat different from these other groups, as it consisted of Protestant members that did not want to aid the Roman Catholic Church. In New Jersey, Catholic schools received over 95 percent of the funds provided to private schools under the law.

JOUAM, concerned that *Cochran* acted as a barrier to an Establishment Clause challenge under the federal Constitution, decided to file suit in state court, claiming that the bus law violated the New Jersey constitution. The New Jersey Supreme Court struck down the law, but the state's Court of Errors and Appeals reversed. Along the way, the ACLU had offered litigation support for JOUAM, filing an *amicus* brief and working with the lead attorneys on strategy and tactics. Encouraged by the ACLU, JOUAM decided to attack the New Jersey law as unconstitutional under the Establishment Clause. It hoped that the Court would use *Everson* to complete the nationalization of the Religion Clauses. In *Cantwell* v. *Connecticut* (1940), the Court, in striking down a state law prohibiting public proselytizing, had ruled that the Free Exercise Clause applied to the states through the Fourteenth Amendment. Assembling an impressive coalition of religious and civic groups, including the Baptist Conference Committee on Public Relations, the Seventh-day Adventists, and local teachers' unions, to support its appeal with *amicus* briefs, JOUAM persuaded the Court to decide the constitutionality of the New Jersey bus law.

Everson v. *Board of Education*

330 U.S. 1 (1947)

Arch Everson, who lived in Ewing Township, a suburb of Trenton, had been active in JOUAM for years, and was happy to serve as the plaintiff in the landmark Establishment Clause case bearing his name. Like many Protestant parents with children in the public schools, Everson strongly opposed the idea of public subsidies for parochial school students. Wary of growing Catholic power in New Jersey politics, Protestant fraternal groups, mainline churches, and teachers' unions kept a careful watch on legislative initiatives that included parochial schools as beneficiaries. They viewed efforts such as the New Jersey bus law, and Ewing's separate program authorizing local reimbursement to all parents of parochial school students for out-of-pocket costs associated with their transportation, as transparent ploys to garner Catholic votes.

Everson brought to light sharp differences within the Court over the meaning of the Establishment Clause, igniting a debate over the proper balance between respect for religious pluralism and the nation's deep roots in the Protestant Christian tradition. Ironically, *Everson* involved a Protestant-led challenge to a law benefiting Catholic schools. In 1947, the public schools were still very much steeped in the Protestant tradition, as they had been since Horace Mann, the great nineteenth-century educator, put forth the idea of a "common school" system in the early 1800s. Prayer, Bible reading, and other religious practices were quite common in the public schools, and most Protestants had no objection to them. But public aid to parochial education was another matter. Opponents of such aid argued that it drained resources from the public schools and amounted to a tax to support Roman Catholic instruction.

The Court's decision was 5 to 4. Justice Black delivered the opinion of the Court. Justice Jackson, joined by Justice Frankfurter, dissented. Justice Rutledge wrote a separate dissent, which Justices Frankfurter, Jackson, and Burton joined.

▼▲▼

MR. JUSTICE BLACK delivered the opinion of the Court.

The only contention here is that the state statute and the resolution, insofar as they authorized reimbursement to parents of children attending parochial schools, violate the Federal Constitution in these two respects, which to some extent overlap. *First.* They authorize the State to take by taxation the private property of some and bestow it upon others to be used for their own private purposes. This, it is alleged, violates the due process clause of the Fourteenth Amendment. *Second.* The statute and the resolution forced inhabitants to pay taxes to help support and maintain schools which are dedicated to, and which regularly teach, the Catholic Faith. This is alleged to be a use of state power to support church schools contrary to the prohibition of the First Amendment which the Fourteenth Amendment made applicable to the states. . . .

It is much too late to argue that legislation intended to facilitate the opportunity of children to get a secular education serves no public purpose. The same thing is no less true of legislation to reimburse needy parents, or all parents, for payment of the fares of their children so that they can ride in public busses to and from schools, rather than run the risk of traffic and other hazards incident to walking or "hitchhiking." Nor does it follow that a law has a private, rather than a public, purpose because it provides that tax-raised funds will be paid to reimburse individuals on account of money spent by them in a way which furthers a public program. . . .

Whether this New Jersey law is one respecting an "establishment of religion" requires an understanding of the meaning of that language, particularly with respect to the imposition of taxes. Once again, therefore, it is not inappropriate briefly to review the background and environment of the period in which that constitutional language was fashioned and adopted.

A large proportion of the early settlers of this country came here from Europe to escape the bondage of laws which compelled them to support and attend government-favored churches. The centuries immediately before and contemporaneous with the colonization of America had been filled with turmoil, civil strife and persecutions, generated in large part by established sects determined to maintain their absolute political and religious supremacy. With the power of government supporting them, at various times and places, Catholics had persecuted Protestants, Protestants had persecuted Catholics, Protestant sects had persecuted other Protestant sects, Catholics of one shade of belief had persecuted Catholics of another shade of belief, and all of these had from time to time persecuted Jews. In efforts to force loyalty to whatever religious group happened to be on top and in league with the government of a particular time and place, men and women had been fined, cast in jail, cruelly tortured, and killed. Among the offenses for which these punishments had been inflicted were such things as speaking disrespectfully of the views of ministers of government-established churches, non-attendance at those churches, expressions of nonbelief in their doctrines, and failure to pay taxes and tithes to support them.

These practices of the old world were transplanted to, and began to thrive in, the soil of the new America. The very charters granted by the English Crown to the individuals and companies designated to make the laws which would control the destinies of the colonials authorized these individuals and companies to erect religious establishments which all, whether believers or nonbelievers, would be required to support and attend. An exercise of this authority was accompanied by a repetition of many of the old-world practices and persecutions. Catholics found themselves hounded and proscribed because of their faith; Quakers who followed their conscience went to jail; Baptists were peculiarly obnoxious to certain dominant Protestant sects; men and women of varied faiths who happened to be in a minority in a particular locality were persecuted because they steadfastly persisted in worshipping God only as their own consciences dictated. And all of these dissenters were compelled to pay tithes and taxes to support government-sponsored churches whose ministers preached inflammatory sermons designed to strengthen and consolidate the established faith by generating a burning hatred against dissenters.

These practices became so commonplace as to shock the freedom-loving colonials into a feeling of abhorrence. The imposition of taxes to pay ministers' salaries and to build and maintain churches and church property aroused their indignation. It was these feelings which found expression in the First Amendment. No one locality and no one group throughout the Colonies can rightly be given entire credit for having aroused the sentiment that culminated in adoption of the Bill of Rights' provisions embracing religious liberty. But Virginia, where the established church had achieved a dominant influence in political affairs and where many excesses attracted wide public attention, provided a great stimulus and able leadership for the movement. The people there, as elsewhere, reached the conviction that individual religious liberty could be achieved best under a government which was stripped of all power to tax, to support, or otherwise to assist any or all religions, or to interfere with the beliefs of any religious individual or group.

The movement toward this end reached its dramatic climax in Virginia in 1785–86 when the Virginia legislative body was about to renew Virginia's tax levy for the support of the established church. Thomas Jefferson and James Madison led the fight against this tax. Madison wrote his great Memorial and Remonstrance against the law. In it, he eloquently argued that a true religion did not need the support of law; that no person, either believer or nonbeliever, should be taxed to support a religious institution of any kind; that the best interest of a society required that the minds of men always be wholly free, and that cruel persecutions were the inevitable result of government-established religions. Madison's Remonstrance received strong support throughout Virginia, and the Assembly postponed consideration of the proposed tax measure until its next session. When the proposal came up for consideration at that session, it not only died in committee, but the Assembly enacted the famous "Virginia Bill for Religious Liberty" originally written by Thomas Jefferson. . . .

This Court has previously recognized that the provisions of the First Amendment, in the drafting and adoption of which Madison and Jefferson played such leading roles, had the same objective, and were intended to provide the same protection against governmental intrusion on religious liberty as the Virginia statute. Prior to the adoption of the Fourteenth Amendment, the First Amendment did not apply as a restraint against the states. Most of them did soon provide similar constitutional protections for religious liberty. But some states persisted for about half a century in imposing restraints upon the free exercise of religion and in discriminating against particular religious groups. In recent years, so far as the provision against the establishment of a religion is concerned, the question has most frequently arisen in connection with proposed state aid to church schools and efforts to carry on religious teachings in the public schools in accordance with the tenets of a particular sect. . . .

The meaning and scope of the First Amendment, preventing establishment of religion or prohibiting the free exercise thereof, in the light of its history and the evils it was designed forever to suppress, have been several times elaborated by the decisions of this Court prior to the application of the First Amendment to the states by the Fourteenth. The broad meaning given the Amendment by these earlier cases has been accepted by this Court in its decisions concerning an individual's religious freedom rendered since the Fourteenth Amendment was interpreted to make the prohibitions of the First applicable to state action abridging religious freedom. There is every reason to give the same application and broad interpretation to the "establishment of religion" clause. . . .

The "establishment of religion" clause of the First Amendment means at least this: neither a state nor the Federal Government can set up a church. Neither can pass laws which aid one religion, aid all religions, or prefer one religion over another. Neither can force nor influence a person to go to or to remain away from church against his will or force him to profess a belief or disbelief in any religion. No person can be punished for entertaining or professing religious beliefs or disbeliefs, for church attendance or non-attendance. No tax in any amount, large or small, can be levied to support any religious activities or institutions, whatever they may be called, or whatever form they may adopt to teach or practice religion. Neither a state nor the Federal Government can, openly or secretly, participate in the affairs of any religious organizations or groups, and vice versa. In the words of Jefferson, the clause against establishment of religion by law was intended to erect "a wall of separation between church and State."

We must consider the New Jersey statute in accordance with the foregoing limitations imposed by the First Amendment. But we must not strike that state statute down if it is within the State's constitutional power, even though it approaches the verge of that power. New Jersey cannot, consistently with the "establishment of religion" clause of the First Amendment, contribute tax-raised funds to the support of an institution which teaches the tenets and faith of any church. On the other hand, other language of the amendment commands that New Jersey cannot hamper its citizens in the free exercise of their own religion. Consequently, it cannot exclude individual Catholics, Lutherans, Mohammedans, Baptists, Jews, Methodists, Nonbelievers, Presbyterians, or the members of any other faith, *because of their faith, or lack of it,* from receiving the benefits of public welfare legislation. While we do not mean to intimate that a state could not provide transportation only to children attending public schools, we must be careful, in protecting the citizens of New Jersey against state-established churches, to be sure that we do not inadvertently prohibit New Jersey from extending its general state law benefits to all its citizens without regard to their religious belief.

Measured by these standards, we cannot say that the First Amendment prohibits New Jersey from spending tax-raised funds to pay the bus fares of parochial school pupils as a part of a general program under which it pays the fares of pupils attending public and other schools. It is undoubtedly true that children are helped to get to church schools. There is even a possibility that some of the children might not be sent to the church schools if the parents were compelled to pay their children's bus fares out of their own pockets when transportation to a public school would have been paid for by the State. The same possibility exists where the state requires a local transit company to provide reduced fares to school children, including those attending parochial schools, or where a municipally owned transportation system undertakes to carry all school children free of charge. Moreover, state-paid policemen, detailed to protect children going to and from church schools from the very real hazards of traffic, would serve much the same purpose and accomplish much the same result as state provisions intended to guarantee free transportation of a kind which the state deems to be best for the school children's welfare. And parents might refuse to risk their children to the serious danger of traffic accidents going to and from parochial schools the approaches to which were not protected by policemen. Similarly, parents might be reluctant to permit their children to attend schools which the state had cut off from such general government services as ordinary police and fire protection, connections for sewage disposal, public highways and sidewalks. Of course, cutting off church schools from these services so separate and so indisputably marked off from the religious function would make it far more difficult for the schools to operate. But such is obviously not the purpose of the First Amendment. That Amendment requires the state to be a neutral in its relations with groups of religious believers and nonbelievers; it does not require the state to be their adversary. State power is no more to be used so as to handicap religions than it is to favor them. . . .

The First Amendment has erected a wall between church and state. That wall must be kept high and impregnable. We could not approve the slightest breach. New Jersey has not breached it here.

Affirmed.

MR. JUSTICE JACKSON, dissenting.

I find myself, contrary to first impressions, unable to join in this decision. I have a sympathy, though it is not ideological, with Catholic citizens who are compelled by law to pay taxes for public schools, and also feel constrained by conscience and discipline to support other schools for their own children. Such relief to them as this case involves is not, in itself, a serious burden to taxpayers, and I had assumed it to be as little serious in principle. Study of this case convinces me otherwise. The Court's opinion marshals every argument in favor of state aid, and puts the case in its most favorable light, but much of its reasoning confirms my conclusions that there are no good grounds upon which to support the present legislation. In fact, the undertones of the opinion, advocating complete and uncompromising separation of Church from State, seem utterly discordant with its conclusion, yielding support to their commingling in educational matters. The case which irresistibly comes to mind as the most fitting precedent is that of Julia who, according to Byron's reports, "whispering 'I will ne'er consent,'—consented.". . .

It is no exaggeration to say that the whole historic conflict in temporal policy between the Catholic Church and non-Catholics comes to a focus in their respective school policies. The Roman Catholic Church, counseled by experience in many ages and many lands and with all sorts and conditions of men, takes what, from the viewpoint of its own progress and the success of its mission, is a wise estimate of the importance of education to religion. It does not leave the individual to pick up religion by chance. It relies on early and indelible indoctrination in the faith and order of the Church by the word and example of persons consecrated to the task.

Our public school, if not a product of Protestantism, at least is more consistent with it than with the Catholic culture and scheme of values. It is a relatively recent development, dating from about 1840. It is organized on the premise that secular education can be isolated from all religious teaching, so that the school can inculcate all needed temporal knowledge and also maintain a strict and lofty neutrality as to religion. The assumption is that, after the individual has been instructed in worldly wisdom, he will be better fitted to choose his religion. Whether such a disjunction is possible, and, if possible, whether it is wise, are questions I need not try to answer.

I should be surprised if any Catholic would deny that the parochial school is a vital, if not the most vital, part of the Roman Catholic Church. If put to the choice, that venerable institution, I should expect, would forego its whole service for mature persons before it would give up education of the young, and it would be a wise choice. Its growth and cohesion, discipline and loyalty, spring from its schools. Catholic education is the rock on which the whole structure rests, and to render tax aid to its Church school is indistinguishable to me from rendering the same aid to the Church itself. . . .

It seems to me that the basic fallacy in the Court's reasoning, which accounts for its failure to apply the principles it avows, is in ignoring the essentially religious test by which beneficiaries of this expenditure are selected. A policeman protects a Catholic, of course, but not because he is a Catholic; it is because he is a man, and a member of our society. The fireman protects the Church school but not because it is a Church school; it is because it is property, part of the assets of our society. Neither the fireman nor the policeman has to ask before he renders aid, "is this man or building identified with the Catholic Church?" But, before these school authorities draw a check to reimburse for a student's fare, they must ask just that question, and, if the school is a Catholic one, they may render aid because it is such, while if it is of any other faith or is run for profit, the help must be withheld. To consider the converse of the Court's reasoning will best disclose its fallacy. That there is no parallel between police and fire protection and this plan of reimbursement is apparent from the incongruity of the limitation of this Act if applied to police and fire service. Could we sustain an Act that said the police shall protect pupils on the way to or from public schools and Catholic schools, but not while going to and coming from other schools, and firemen shall extinguish a blaze in public or Catholic school buildings, but shall not put out a blaze in Protestant Church schools or private schools operated for profit? That is the true analogy to the case we have before us, and I should think it pretty plain that such a scheme would not be valid.

The Court's holding is that this taxpayer has no grievance, because the state has decided to make the reimbursement a public purpose, and therefore we are bound to regard it as such. I agree that this Court has left, and always should leave, to each state great latitude in deciding for itself, in the light of its own conditions, what shall be public purposes in its scheme of things. It may socialize utilities and economic enterprises and make taxpayers' business out of what conventionally had been private business. It may make public business of individual welfare, health, education, entertainment or security. But it cannot make public business of religious worship or instruction, or of attendance at religious institutions of any character.

MR. JUSTICE FRANKFURTER joins in this opinion.

MR. JUSTICE RUTLEDGE, with whom MR. JUSTICE FRANKFURTER, MR. JUSTICE JACKSON, and MR. JUSTICE BURTON agree, dissenting.

Not simply an established church, but any law respecting an establishment of religion, is forbidden. The Amendment was broadly, but not loosely, phrased. It is the compact and exact summation of its author's views formed during his long struggle for religious freedom. In Madison's own words characterizing Jefferson's Bill for Establishing Religious Freedom, the guaranty he put in our national charter, like the bill he piloted through the Virginia Assembly, was "a Model of technical precision, and perspicuous brevity." Madison could not have confused "church" and "religion," or "an established church" and "an establishment of religion."

The Amendment's purpose was not to strike merely at the official establishment of a single sect, creed or religion, outlawing only a formal relation such as had prevailed in England and some of the colonies. Necessarily, it was to uproot all such relationships. But the object was broader than separating church and state in this narrow sense. It was to create a complete and permanent separation of the spheres of religious activity and civil authority by comprehensively forbidding every form of public aid or support for religion. In proof, the Amendment's wording and history unite with this Court's consistent utterances whenever attention has been fixed directly upon the question. . . .

No provision of the Constitution is more closely tied to or given content by its generating history than the religious clause of the First Amendment. It is at once the refined product and the terse summation of that history. The history includes not only Madison's authorship and the proceedings before the First Congress, but also the long and intensive struggle for religious freedom in America, more especially in Virginia, of which the Amendment was the direct culmination. In the documents of the times, particularly of Madison, who was leader in the Virginia struggle before he became the Amendment's sponsor, but also in the writings of Jefferson and others and in the issues which engendered them is to be found irrefutable confirmation of the Amendment's sweeping content. . . .

Madison opposed every form and degree of official relation between religion and civil authority. For him, religion was a wholly private matter beyond the scope of civil power either to restrain or to support. Denial or abridgment of religious freedom was a violation of rights both of conscience and of natural equality. State aid was no less obnoxious or destructive to freedom and to religion itself than other forms of state interference. "Establishment" and "free exercise" were correlative and coextensive ideas, representing only different facets of the single great and fundamental freedom. The Remonstrance, following the Virginia statute's example, referred to the history of religious conflicts and the effects of all sorts of establishments, current and historical, to suppress religion's free exercise. With Jefferson, Madison believed that to tolerate any fragment of establishment would be by so much to perpetuate restraint upon that freedom. Hence, he sought to tear out the institution not partially, but root and branch, and to bar its return forever. . . .

Does New Jersey's action furnish support for religion by use of the taxing power? Certainly it does, if the test remains undiluted as Jefferson and Madison made it, that money taken by taxation from one is not to be used or given to support another's religious training or belief, or indeed one's own. Today, as then, the furnishing of "contributions of money for the propagation of opinions which he disbelieves" is the forbidden exaction, and the prohibition is absolute for whatever measure brings that consequence and whatever amount may be sought or given to that end.

The funds used here were raised by taxation. The Court does not dispute, nor could it, that their use does, in fact, give aid and encouragement to religious instruction. It only concludes that this aid is not "support" in law. But Madison and Jefferson were concerned with aid and support in fact, not as a legal conclusion "entangled in precedents." Here, parents pay money to send their children to parochial schools, and funds raised by taxation are used to reimburse them. This not only helps the children to get to school and the parents to send them. It aids them in a substantial way to get the very thing which they are sent to the particular school to secure, namely, religious training and teaching.

Believers of all faiths, and others who do not express their feeling toward ultimate issues of existence in any creedal form, pay the New Jersey tax. When the money so raised is used to pay for transportation to religious schools, the Catholic taxpayer, to the extent of his proportionate share, pays for the transportation of Lutheran, Jewish and otherwise religiously affiliated children to receive their non-Catholic religious instruction. Their parents likewise pay proportionately for the transportation of Catholic children to receive Catholic instruction. Each thus contributes to "the propagation of opinions which he disbelieves" in so far as their religions differ, as do others who accept no creed without regard to those differences. Each thus pays taxes also to support the teaching of his own religion, an exaction equally forbidden, since it denies "the comfortable liberty" of giving one's contribution to the particular agency of instruction he approves.

New Jersey's action therefore exactly fits the type of exaction and the kind of evil at which Madison and Jefferson struck. Under the test they framed, it cannot be said that the cost of transportation is no part of the cost of education or of the religious instruction given. That it is a substantial and a necessary element is shown most plainly by the continuing and increasing demand for the state to assume it. Nor is there pretense that it relates only to the secular instruction given in religious schools, or that any attempt is or could be made toward allocating proportional shares as between the secular and the religious instruction. . . .

Yet this very admixture is what was disestablished when the First Amendment forbade "an establishment of religion." Commingling the religious with the secular teaching does not divest the whole of its religious permeation and emphasis, or make them of minor part, if proportion were material. Indeed, on any other view, the constitutional prohibition always could be brought to naught by adding a modicum of the secular. . . .

It is not because religious teaching does not promote the public or the individual's welfare, but because neither is furthered when the state promotes religious education, that the Constitution forbids it to do so. Both legislatures and courts are bound by that distinction. In failure to observe it lies the fallacy of the "public function"/"social legislation" argument, a fallacy facilitated by easy transference of the argument's basing from due process unrelated to any religious aspect to the First Amendment. . . .

The reasons underlying the Amendment's policy have not vanished with time or diminished in force. Now as when it was adopted, the price of religious freedom is double. It is that the church and religion shall live both within and upon that freedom. There cannot be freedom of religion, safeguarded by the state, and intervention by the church or its agencies in the state's domain or dependency on its largesse. The great condition of religious liberty is that it be maintained free from sustenance, as also from other interferences, by the state. For when it comes to rest upon that secular foundation, it vanishes with the resting. Public money devoted to payment of religious costs, educational or other, brings the quest for more. It brings, too, the struggle of sect against sect for the larger share, or for any. Here, one by numbers alone will benefit most; there, another. That is precisely the history of societies which have had an established religion and dissident groups. It is the very thing Jefferson and Madison experienced and sought to guard against, whether in its blunt or in its more screened forms. . . .

Thus, if the present statute and its application were shown to apply equally to all religious schools of whatever faith, yet, in the light of our tradition, it could not stand. For then, the adherent of one creed still would pay for the support of another, the childless taxpayer with others more fortunate. Then too there would seem to be no bar to making appropriations for transportation and other expenses of children attending public or other secular schools, after hours in separate places and classes for their exclusively religious instruction. The person who embraces no creed also would be forced to pay for teaching what he does not believe. Again, it was the furnishing of "contributions of money for the propagation of opinions which he disbelieves" that the fathers outlawed. That consequence and effect are not removed by multiplying to all-inclusiveness the sects for which support is exacted. The Constitution requires not comprehensive identification of state with religion, but complete separation.

Justice Black's interpretation of the Establishment Clause offered an analysis that suggested little, if any, role for government in the affairs of religion. By concluding that "the wall" separating church and state must remain "high and impregnable," but holding that New Jersey's bus law benefited children and not churches, Black laid the foundation for future Establishment Clause litigation. Catholic organizations, having won the battle in *Everson*, feared that Black's near-absolutist interpretation of the Establishment Clause suggested trouble for any future effort to secure public funds beyond that which benefited children.[33] Critics of *Everson*'s holding had a much different reaction. Many religious, educational, and civic groups praised Black's rhetoric on behalf of the strict separation between church and state, but feared that the Court might use the child-benefit theory to allow other public funding efforts to fall through the cracks of Thomas Jefferson's metaphorical wall.[34] Among the justices, no one disagreed with Black's understanding of the Framers' intent behind the Establishment Clause. But the dissents of Justices Jackson and Rutledge, expressing bewilderment at Black's conclusion, firmly suggested that the Court needed to iron out the inconsistencies of the majority's holding in *Everson* by revisiting the issue as soon as possible.

After *Everson,* Catholic organizations pressed ahead in the states, where some sixteen laws similar to New Jersey's were already in place, with a more extensive campaign to secure public funds for parochial schools. Persuaded that they needed to organize their resources to match the resources of the Catholic Church, nearly two dozen Protestant agencies and church representatives convened in Washington, D.C., to establish a new organization, Protestants and Other Americans United for the Separation of Church and State (POAU). Brazenly anti-Catholic, POAU hit the ground running, organizing support and helping to draft an unsuccessful constitutional amendment to ban all government aid to parochial schools. POAU also forged legislative strategies to counter Catholic lobbying in the states, particularly in the South, where Protestants were firmly in the majority and still controlled the secular and religious content of the public schools. Finally, POAU developed the capacity to litigate, often joining lawsuits and offering *amicus* support to the ACLU and the group that soon came to dominate church-state litigation, the American Jewish Congress (AJCongress).[35]

In October 1946, Leo Pfeffer, a young AJCongress staff lawyer, believed that *Everson* offered a splendid opportunity for American Jews to enter the church-state debate. The year before, Pfeffer had compiled a report on another common program involving government and religion: released time. Under this program, public schools set aside class time during the school day to permit religious instruction from off-campus clergy. Pfeffer had discovered that released time was quite common, and broke down participation in such programs according to the religious composition of local communities. Catholics, Protestants, and Jews all participated in released-time programs, but Pfeffer found that Catholics participated in them far more than Protestants.[36] Jews, Pfeffer discovered, hardly ever participated in released time. Pfeffer ultimately concluded that released time was unconstitutional, since it opened the public schools up to religious instruction, a position with which the ACLU and most groups representing public schools and teachers agreed.[37]

But Pfeffer could not convince the AJCongress or any of the other major Jewish organizations, such as the American Jewish Committee (AJCommittee) or the Anti-Defamation League (ADL), to join the fight against the New Jersey bus law. Representatives of the AJCommittee and the ADL were concerned that organized Jewish participation would alienate the Catholic Church, and decided not to participate in *Everson.*[38] Pfeffer, who had followed with great admiration the litigation campaign of the NAACP to dismantle school segregation (see Chapter 11), believed that if African Americans had the courage to stand up and fight for their rights, Jews could certainly do the same.

In June 1947, the Court agreed to hear *McCollum* v. *Board of Education* (1948), which involved the constitutionality of on-site religious instruction in the public schools. After some careful prodding by Pfeffer, the major Jewish organizations agreed to file an *amicus* brief in *McCollum.* Numerous other civic and teachers organizations also submitted *amicus* briefs opposing released time. Justice Black offered a much clearer statement than in *Everson* about where exactly he believed the constitutional boundaries of church-state separation should be drawn.

McCollum v. *Board of Education*

333 U.S. 203 (1948)

Vashti McCollum wanted it known that it was not her antipathy toward Christianity that led her to challenge the released-time program in her son Jim's school—it was her hostility toward religion generally. She believed that religion was the opiate of the masses and a virus injected into the minds of public school children. McCollum was content, however, to keep her views to herself until her son repeatedly came home from school in tears after being forced to sit in the hall for not participating in "voluntary" religion classes. Thirty-three other states had programs similar to the one challenged in *McCollum,* enrolling anywhere between 1.2 to 3 million children. The ACLU agreed to represent Vashti McCollum.

At first, McCollum's unabashed atheism scared off many supporters of her case against released time. Leo Pfeffer, who, after *McCollum,* emerged as the key figure among advocates of strict church-state separation, inserted language into the *amicus* brief he wrote on behalf of Jewish groups disassociating them from the plaintiff's views on religion. Protestant groups, which had supported Arch Everson's historic march to the Supreme Court, did not share the same concerns about released-time programs as they did parochial school assistance. In fact, they were more concerned about the threat that parents like Vashti McCollum posed for the schools than about Catholic intrusiveness in the public education system. Many groups representing Protestant churches found themselves supporting Catholics on released time, unnerved by the prospect of "Godless" public schools.[39]

The Court's decision was 8 to 1. Justice Black delivered the opinion of the Court. Justice Jackson filed a concurring opinion. Justice Frankfurter, joined by Justices Jackson, Rutledge, and Burton, also concurred. Justice Reed dissented.

▼▲▼

MR. JUSTICE BLACK delivered the opinion of the Court.

This case relates to the power of a state to utilize its tax-supported public school system in aid of religious instruction insofar as that power may be restricted by the First and Fourteenth Amendments to the Federal Constitution. . . .

Although there are disputes between the parties as to various inferences that may or may not properly be drawn from the evidence concerning the religious program, the following facts are shown by the record without dispute. In 1940 interested members of the Jewish, Roman Catholic, and a few of the Protestant faiths formed a voluntary association called the Champaign Council on Religious Education. They obtained permission from the Board of Education to offer classes in religious instruction to public school pupils in grades four to nine inclusive. Classes were made up of pupils whose parents signed printed cards requesting that their children be permitted to attend; they were held weekly, thirty minutes for the lower grades, forty-five minutes for the higher. The council employed the religious teachers at no expense to the school authorities, but the instructors were subject to the approval and supervision of the superintendent of schools. The classes were taught in three separate religious groups by Protestant teachers, Catholic priests, and a Jewish rabbi, although for the past several years there have apparently been no classes instructed in the Jewish religion. Classes were conducted in the regular classrooms of the school building. Students who did not choose to take the religious instruction were not released from public school duties; they were required to leave their classrooms and go to some other place in the school building for pursuit of their secular studies. On the other hand, students who were released from secular study for the religious instructions were required to be present at the religious classes. Reports of their presence or absence were to be made to their secular teachers.

The foregoing facts, without reference to others that appear in the record, show the use of tax-supported property for religious instruction and the close cooperation between the school authorities and the religious council in promoting religious education. The operation of the state's compulsory education system thus assists and is integrated with the program of religious instruction carried on by separate religious sects. Pupils compelled by law to go to school for secular education are released in part from their legal duty upon the condition that they attend the religious classes. This is beyond all question a utilization of the tax-established and tax-supported public school system to aid religious groups to spread their faith. And it falls squarely under the ban of the First Amendment (made applicable to the States by the Fourteenth) as we interpreted it in *Everson* v. *Board of Education* (1947). There we said: "Neither a state nor the Federal Government can set up a church. Neither can pass laws which aid one religion, aid all religions, or prefer one religion over another. Neither can force or influence a person to go to or to remain away from church against his will or force him to profess a belief or disbelief in any religion. No person can be punished for entertaining or professing religious beliefs or disbeliefs, for church attendance or nonattendance. No tax in any amount, large or small, can be levied to support any religious activities or institutions, whatever they may be called, or whatever form they may adopt to teach or practice religion. Neither a state nor the Federal Government can, openly or secretly, participate in the affairs of any religious organizations or groups, and vice versa. In the words of Jefferson, the clause against establishment of religion by law was intended to erect "a wall of separation between Church and State." The majority in the *Everson* case, and the minority . . . agreed that the First Amendment's language, properly interpreted, had erected a wall of separation between Church and State. They disagreed as to the facts shown by the record and as to the proper application of the First Amendment's language to those facts.

Recognizing that the Illinois program is barred by the First and Fourteenth Amendments if we adhere to the views expressed both by the majority and the minority in the *Everson* case, counsel for the respondents challenge those views as dicta and urge that we reconsider and repudiate them. They argue that historically the First Amendment was intended to forbid only government preference of one religion over another, not an impartial governmental assistance of all religions. In addition they ask that we distinguish or overrule our holding in the *Everson* case that the Fourteenth Amendment made the "establishment of religion" clause of the First Amendment applicable as a prohibition against the States. After giving full consideration to the arguments presented we are unable to accept either of these contentions.

To hold that a state cannot consistently with the First and Fourteenth Amendments utilize its public school system to aid any or all religious faiths or sects in the dissemination of their doctrines and ideals does not, as counsel urge, manifest a governmental hostility to religion or religious teachings. A manifestation of such hostility would be at war with our national tradition as embodied in the First Amendment's guaranty of the free exercise of religion. For the First Amendment rests upon the premise that both religion and government can best work to achieve their lofty aims if each is left free from the other within its respective sphere. Or, as we said in the *Everson* case, the First Amendment had erected a wall between Church and State which must be kept high and impregnable.

Here not only are the state's tax-supported public school buildings used for the dissemination of religious doctrines. The State also affords sectarian groups an invaluable aid in that it helps to provide pupils for their religious classes through use of the state's compulsory public school machinery. This is not separation of Church and State.

MR. JUSTICE JACKSON, concurring.

I think it is doubtful whether the facts of this case establish jurisdiction in this Court, but in any event that we should place some bounds on the demands for interference with local schools that we are empowered or willing to entertain. I make these reservations a matter of record in view of the number of litigations likely to be started as a result of this decision.

A Federal Court may interfere with local school authorities only when they invade either a personal liberty or a property right protected by the Federal Constitution. Ordinarily this will come about in either of two ways:

First. When a person is required to submit to some religious rite or instruction or is deprived or threatened with deprivation of his freedom for resisting such unconstitutional requirement. We may then set him free or enjoin his prosecution. Typical of such cases was *West Virginia State Board of Education* v. *Barnette* (1943). There, penalties were threatened against both parent and child for refusal of the latter to perform a compulsory ritual which offended his convictions. We intervened to shield them against the penalty. But here, complainant's son may join religious classes if he chooses and if his parents so request, or he may stay out of them. The complaint is that when others join and he does not, it sets him apart as a dissenter, which is humiliating. Even admitting this to be true, it may be doubted whether the Constitution which, of course, protects the right to dissent, can be construed also to protect one from the embarrassment that always attends nonconformity, whether in religion, politics, behavior or dress. Since no legal compulsion is applied to complainant's son himself and no penalty is imposed or threatened from which we may relieve him, we can hardly base jurisdiction on this ground.

Second. Where a complaint is deprived of property by being taxed for unconstitutional purposes, such as directly or indirectly to support a religious establishment. We can protect a taxpayer against such a levy. This was the *Everson* case, as I saw it then and see it now. . . . in the *Everson* case there was a direct, substantial and measurable burden on the complainant as a taxpayer to raise funds that were used to subsidize transportation to parochial schools. Hence, we had jurisdiction to examine the constitutionality of the levy and to protect against it if a majority had agreed that the subsidy for transportation was unconstitutional. . . .

To me, the sweep and detail of [Vashti McCollum's] complaints is a danger signal which warns of the kind of local controversy we will be required to arbitrate if we do not place appropriate limitation on our decision and exact strict compliance with jurisdictional requirements. Authorities list 256 separate and substantial religious bodies to exist in the continental United States. Each of them, through the suit of some discontented but unpenalized and untaxed representative, has as good a right as this plaintiff to demand that the courts compel the schools to sift out of their teaching everything inconsistent with its doctrines. If we are to eliminate everything that is objectionable to any of these warring sects or inconsistent with any of their doctrines, we will leave public education in shreds. Nothing but educational confusion and a discrediting of the public school system can result from subjecting it to constant lawsuits. . . .

The task of separating the secular from the religious in education is one of magnitude, intricacy and delicacy. To lay down a sweeping constitutional doctrine as demanded by [McCollum] and apparently approved by the Court, applicable alike to all school boards of the nation, "to immediately adopt and enforce rules and regulations prohibiting all instruction in and teaching to religious education in all public schools," is to decree a uniform, rigid and, if we are consistent, an unchanging standard for countless school boards representing and serving highly localized groups which not only differ from each other but which themselves from time to time change attitudes. It seems to me that to do so is to allow zeal for our own ideas of what is good in public instruction to induce us to accept the role of a super board of education for every school district in the nation.

It is idle to pretend that this task is one for which we can find in the Constitution one word to help us as judges to decide where the secular ends and the sectarian begins in education. Nor can we find guidance in any other legal source. It is a matter on which we can find no law but our own prepossessions. If with no surer legal guidance we are to take up and decide every variation of this controversy, raised by persons not subject to penalty or tax but who are dissatisfied with the way schools are dealing with the problem, we are likely to have much business of the sort. And, more importantly, we are likely to make the legal "wall of separation between church and state" as winding as the famous serpentine wall designed by Mr. Jefferson for the University he founded.

McCollum received mixed reviews from the diverse range of religious and secular groups that had participated as *amicus curiae.* The major Jewish organizations hailed *McCollum* as a "milestone on the road to full application of the traditional American principle of the separation of church and state," and boasted that the Court's opinion had "followed closely" the arguments in their *amicus* brief.[40] Catholic organizations, which had feared the implications of Black's opinion in *Everson,* condemned *McCollum* as an irresponsible decision that cast aside the long-standing tradition of encouraging a place for religion in the nation's public schools. Protestant churches and groups, which had denounced *Everson* as a triumph for "the evil designs of the Catholic Church to grab ahold of the public purse," joined the chorus of Catholic criticism of *McCollum.* In the end, *Everson* and *McCollum* fundamentally reordered both modern Establishment Clause doctrine and the interest group politics that came to dominate subsequent church-state litigation. The Court's decision in *Everson* to nationalize the Establishment Clause meant that future such disputes that were once confined to state legislative corridors and local school boards had now assumed a national character. Religious minorities that had been reluctant to challenge the dominance of Christian values came to assume prominent roles in this debate. Christian America, and Protestants in particular, had received word in *Everson* and *McCollum* that its cultural preeminence in the nation's schools and civic institutions was no longer secure. Neither the Establishment Clause nor the politics that surrounded it would ever be the same.

McCollum encouraged Leo Pfeffer to think about a larger campaign to challenge religious practices in the public schools. Even before *Everson,* Pfeffer had discussed the possibility of challenging Bible reading, recitation of the Lord's Prayer, and other Christian religious practices in the public schools with other AJCongress lawyers. They agreed it was better to wait and see where the Court was going to take the Establishment Clause before they decided to mount such a controversial challenge to these popular and widespread practices. Now, with Black's *Everson dicta* on firm footing in *McCollum,* Pfeffer persuaded the AJCommittee and the ADL to cosponsor a challenge to another form of released time, this time in the New York City schools, where Catholic, Jewish, and Prostestant political power formed a combustible mix.[41] The difference between the New York City program and the Illinois program struck down in *McCollum* was the location of religious instruction. The New York program permitted students to leave school early on assigned days for religious instruction off campus.

Pfeffer took great care to select a noncontroversial plaintiff. In Tessim Zorach, he found one. An Episcopalian active in church affairs, Zorach, unlike Vashti McCollum, shunned radical politics. As part of an agreement with the other Jewish organizations, Pfeffer agreed to have the ACLU serve as Zorach's counsel of record on the court papers, but he retained control over the actual litigation. By the time the New York program reached the Supreme Court, the ACLU offered to turn the case over to Pfeffer. Bound by his earlier agreement, Pfeffer continued to operate in the shadows, coordinating *amicus* support, and writing a separate brief on behalf of the AJCongress, the AJCommittee, the ADL, and several smaller Jewish groups. Pfeffer's *amicus* brief emphasized how divided religious communities were over released time. As such, no program that divided religious groups could claim to have the best interests of religion in mind.[42]

A 6-3 Court, however, stunned Pfeffer and opponents of released time when it ruled, in *Zorach* v. *Clausen* (1952), that off-campus religious instruction posed no constitutional problems. Writing for the Court, Justice William O. Douglas, a member of the *McCollum* majority, declared:

> We would have to press the concept of separation of Church and State to . . . extremes to condemn the present law on constitutional grounds. We are a religious people whose institutions presuppose a Supreme Being. When the state encourages religious instruction or cooperates with religious authorities by adjusting the schedule of public events to sectarian needs, it follows the best of our traditions. For it then respects the religious nature of our people and accommodates the public service to their spiritual needs. To hold that it may not would be to find in the Constitution a requirement that the government show a callous indifference to religious groups. That would be preferring those who believe in no religion over those who do believe.
>
> We follow the *McCollum* case. But we cannot expand it to cover the present released-time program unless separation of Church and State means that public institutions can make no adjustments of their schedules to accommodate the religious needs of the people. We cannot read into the Bill of Rights such a philosophy of hostility to religion.[43]

Justice Robert Jackson, concurring in *McCollum,* had warned the Court against becoming a "national school board" by entering into every conflict involving religion and the public schools. Better to set firm constitutional guidelines and adhere to them than to leave educational authorities confused about the proper relationship between religion and education. Douglas's opinion in *Zorach* perplexed Jackson, who wrote:

> It takes more subtlety of mind than I possess to deny that [dismissed time] is governmental constraint in support of religion. . . . The distinction attempted between *McCollum* and this [case] is trivial, almost to the point of cynicism, magnifying its nonessential details and disparaging compulsion which was the underlying reason for invalidity. . . . The wall which the Court was professing to erect between Church and State has become even more warped and twisted than I expected. Today's judgment will be more interesting to students of psychology and of the judicial processes than to students of constitutional law.[44]

Jackson's dissent was of little consolation to Pfeffer and the organizations that had joined together to challenge New York City's released-time program. After *Zorach,* the AJCommittee and the ADL, reluctant to challenge a program so popular with Catholics and Protestants, disassociated themselves from Pfeffer and the AJCongress. They returned to their preferred emphasis on community relations to resolve church-state conflicts. The ACLU, which had formed a working partnership with the AJCongress after *McCollum,* backed away from its absolutist position on the Establishment Clause after it came under repeated fire from the Catholic Church. Stung by this criticism, the ACLU quietly lowered its profile on church-state issues after *Zorach,* dissolving its committee that monitored church-state conflicts to avoid alienating Catholics.[45]

By the late 1950s, the AJCongress had regained the confidence to pursue its litigation campaign against religious practices in the public schools. Buoyed by several important free speech victories in the Court during the same time, the ACLU decided to reenter the church-state debate. Led by Pfeffer, whose expertise in the field was by then unrivaled, the AJCongress, the ACLU and, by the early 1960s, the AJCommittee and the AJCongress, began to cooperate in challenging a far more controversial practice than released time—prayer and Bible reading in the public schools.

The School Prayer Cases

In 1952, the Court let stand a decision of the New Jersey Supreme Court upholding a state law that required public schools to offer students a verse from the Old Testament to recite before each school day began. The court ruled that "the Old Testament and the Lord's Prayer, pronounced without comment, are not sectarian, and that the short exercise provided by the statute does not constitute sectarian instruction. Such [an exercise] is but a simple recognition of the Supreme Ruler of the Universe and a deference to His majesty."[46] The ACLU sponsored the appeal, and the AJCongress, far less enthusiastic about the case, filed an *amicus* brief. Ultimately, the Court dismissed *Doremus* v. *Board of Education* (1952) on procedural grounds. For the moment, the school prayer issue was laid to rest. Leo Pfeffer believed that the ACLU's case would have been strengthened by enlisting the support of an interfaith coalition of groups to address whether a prayer could truly be "nonsectarian." But an effort to enlist the Baptist Joint Committee, the Seventh-day Adventists, and POAU failed. Even JOUAM, the plaintiff in *Everson,* filed a brief in support of the New Jersey prayer law. Pfeffer soon learned an important lesson in litigation politics that held firm until the Court's landmark decisions striking down school prayer and Bible reading in *Engel* v. *Vitale* (1962) and *Abington* v. *Schempp* (1963): Protestant groups were far more interested in eliminating public funds for parochial schools than they were in relinquishing cultural control of the public schools.[47]

In 1961, the AJCongress and the ACLU sponsored a case challenging a Maryland law that required anyone wishing to become a notary public to profess a belief in God. *Torcaso* v. *Watkins* (1961), an often overlooked but pivotal decision, realigned the Court with the firm principles guarding against government support for religion that it had articulated in *McCollum.* Justice Black, revisiting his *dicta* in *Everson,* wrote that the Court "again reaffirm[s] that neither a State nor the Federal Government can constitutionally force a person 'to profess a belief in any religion.' *Neither can constitutionally pass laws or impose requirements which aid all religions as against non-believers, and neither can aid those religions based on a belief in the existence of God as against those religions founded on different beliefs.*"[48] Black's language here is quite important. By holding that the Establishment Clause barred government support for "all religions," *Torcaso* rejected the argument of many Protestants and Catholics that as long as government support was *nonpreferential,* or available to all groups, the Establishment Clause posed no barrier to religious practices.

Meanwhile, three separate cases were moving through the lower courts that raised the far more explosive issues of prayer and Bible reading in the public schools. *Abington* v. *Schempp,* involving a Pennsylvania law that required teachers to read "at least ten verses from the Holy Bible" each day, had begun in 1957 under the cosponsorship of the Philadelphia chapters of the ACLU and the AJCongress. *Engel* v. *Vitale,* a challenge to a prayer composed by the New York Board of Regents for recitation in the public schools, was being handled by the ACLU. Finally, the AJCongress, in *Chamberlin* v. *(Miami) Dade County Board of Public Instruction,* had brought a lawsuit challenging several religious practices in the schools.[49] These practices included displaying religious symbols in classrooms, singing religious hymns in class, requiring teachers to take a religious oath as a condition of employment, and allowing teacher-led prayer and Bible reading in class. *Engel* made it to the Supreme Court first, followed by *Schempp.*

Engel v. *Vitale*

370 U.S. 421 (1962)

In 1951, the New York Board of Regents composed a one-sentence prayer for distribution to every public school in the state. It read, "Almighty God, we acknowledge our dependence upon Thee, and we beg Thy blessings upon us, our parents, our teachers and our country." Students were not required to say the prayer, but many who objected said it anyway out of fear of reprisal from their teachers or their classmates. By 1955, the New York Board of Education reported that only 10 to 20 percent of state school districts had adopted the prayer. Many schools had opted to have their students sing the fourth verse of "America," which opens, "Our father's God to thee, author of liberty, to thee we sing." Singing, too, was voluntary.

Over the objection of the national ACLU and Leo Pfeffer, the New York chapter of the ACLU agreed to represent Stephen Engel and several other parents in a lawsuit against their Long Island school district. Pfeffer had long argued that the Board of Regents prayer was so bland and devoid of sectarian biases that no court would strike it down. Instead, he believed that opponents of prayer in public school should find a case that allowed them to expose the range of religious practices taking place in public school. Pfeffer offered support to the ACLU, which gradually fell into line behind its New York office, but pursued his case in Miami, hoping that he would beat his colleagues to the Supreme Court.

In New York, the state's highest appeals court upheld the law, appearing to bear out Pfeffer's concerns that the

Regents prayer was not sufficiently offensive to pose an Establishment Clause problem.

The Court's decision was 6 to 1, with Justices White and Frankfurter not participating. Justice Black delivered the opinion of the Court. Justice Douglas filed a concurring opinion. Justice Stewart filed the Court's lone dissent.

▼▲▼

MR. JUSTICE BLACK delivered the opinion of the Court.

We think that, by using its public school system to encourage recitation of the Regents' prayer, the State of New York has adopted a practice wholly inconsistent with the Establishment Clause. There can, of course, be no doubt that New York's program of daily classroom invocation of God's blessings as prescribed in the Regents' prayer is a religious activity. It is a solemn avowal of divine faith and supplication for the blessings of the Almighty. . . .

It is a matter of history that this very practice of establishing governmentally composed prayers for religious services was one of the reasons which caused many of our early colonists to leave England and seek religious freedom in America. *The Book of Common Prayer,* which was created under governmental direction and which was approved by Acts of Parliament in 1548 and 1549, set out in minute detail the accepted form and content of prayer and other religious ceremonies to be used in the established, tax-supported Church of England. The controversies over the Book and what should be its content repeatedly threatened to disrupt the peace of that country as the accepted forms of prayer in the established church changed with the views of the particular ruler that happened to be in control at the time. Powerful groups representing some of the varying religious views of the people struggled among themselves to impress their particular views upon the Government and obtain amendments of the Book more suitable to their respective notions of how religious services should be conducted in order that the official religious establishment would advance their particular religious beliefs. Other groups, lacking the necessary political power to influence the Government on the matter, decided to leave England and its established church and seek freedom in America from England's governmentally ordained and supported religion.

It is an unfortunate fact of history that, when some of the very groups which had most strenuously opposed the established Church of England found themselves sufficiently in control of colonial governments in this country to write their own prayers into law, they passed laws making their own religion the official religion of their respective colonies. Indeed, as late as the time of the Revolutionary War, there were established churches in at least eight of the thirteen former colonies and established religions in at least four of the other five. But the successful Revolution against English political domination was shortly followed by intense opposition to the practice of establishing religion by law. This opposition crystallized rapidly into an effective political force in Virginia, where the minority religious groups such as Presbyterians, Lutherans, Quakers and Baptists had gained such strength that the adherents to the established Episcopal Church were actually a minority themselves. In 1785–1786, those opposed to the established Church, led by James Madison and Thomas Jefferson, who, though themselves not members of any of these dissenting religious groups, opposed all religious establishments by law on grounds of principle, obtained the enactment of the famous "Virginia Bill for Religious Liberty" by which all religious groups were placed on an equal footing so far as the State was concerned. Similar though less far-reaching legislation was being considered and passed in other states.

By the time of the adoption of the Constitution, our history shows that there was a widespread awareness among many Americans of the dangers of a union of Church and State. These people knew, some of them from bitter personal experience, that one of the greatest dangers to the freedom of the individual to worship in his own way lay in the Government's placing its official stamp of approval upon one particular kind of prayer or one particular form of religious services. They knew the anguish, hardship and bitter strife that could come when zealous religious groups struggled with one another to obtain the Government's stamp of approval from each King, Queen, or Protector that came to temporary power. The Constitution was intended to avert a part of this danger by leaving the government of this country in the hands of the people, rather than in the hands of any monarch. But this safeguard was not enough. Our Founders were no more willing to let the content of their prayers and their privilege of praying whenever they pleased be influenced by the ballot box than they were to let these vital matters of personal conscience depend upon the succession of monarchs. The First Amendment was added to the Constitution to stand as a guarantee that neither the power nor the prestige of the Federal Government would be used to control, support or influence the kinds of prayer the American people can say—that the people's religions must not be subjected to the pressures of government for change each time a new political administration is elected to office. Under that Amendment's prohibition against governmental establishment of religion, as reinforced by the provisions of the

Fourteenth Amendment, government in this country, be it state or federal, is without power to prescribe by law any particular form of prayer which is to be used as an official prayer in carrying on any program of governmentally sponsored religious activity.

There can be no doubt that New York's state prayer program officially establishes the religious beliefs embodied in the Regents' prayer. The respondents' argument to the contrary, which is largely based upon the contention that the Regents' prayer is "nondenominational" and the fact that the program, as modified and approved by state courts, does not require all pupils to recite the prayer, but permits those who wish to do so to remain silent or be excused from the room, ignores the essential nature of the program's constitutional defects. Neither the fact that the prayer may be denominationally neutral nor the fact that its observance on the part of the students is voluntary can serve to free it from the limitations of the Establishment Clause, as it might from the Free Exercise Clause, of the First Amendment, both of which are operative against the States by virtue of the Fourteenth Amendment. Although these two clauses may, in certain instances, overlap, they forbid two quite different kinds of governmental encroachment upon religious freedom. The Establishment Clause, unlike the Free Exercise Clause, does not depend upon any showing of direct governmental compulsion and is violated by the enactment of laws which establish an official religion whether those laws operate directly to coerce nonobserving individuals or not. This is not to say, of course, that laws officially prescribing a particular form of religious worship do not involve coercion of such individuals. When the power, prestige and financial support of government is placed behind a particular religious belief, the indirect coercive pressure upon religious minorities to conform to the prevailing officially approved religion is plain. . . .

It has been argued that to apply the Constitution in such a way as to prohibit state laws respecting an establishment of religious services in public schools is to indicate a hostility toward religion or toward prayer. Nothing, of course, could be more wrong. The history of man is inseparable from the history of religion. . . . It is neither sacrilegious nor anti-religious to say that each separate government in this country should stay out of the business of writing or sanctioning official prayers and leave that purely religious function to the people themselves and to those the people choose to look to for religious guidance.

The judgment of the Court of Appeals of New York is reversed, and the cause remanded for further proceedings not inconsistent with this opinion.

Reversed and remanded.

MR. JUSTICE DOUGLAS, concurring.

It is customary in deciding a constitutional question to treat it in its narrowest form. Yet at times the setting of the question gives it a form and content which no abstract treatment could give. The point for decision is whether the Government can constitutionally finance a religious exercise. Our system at the federal and state levels is presently honeycombed with such financing. Nevertheless, I think it is an unconstitutional undertaking whatever form it takes.

First, a word as to what this case does not involve.

Plainly, our Bill of Rights would not permit a State or the Federal Government to adopt an official prayer and penalize anyone who would not utter it. This, however, is not that case, for there is no element of compulsion or coercion in New York's regulation requiring that public schools be opened each day with the [Regents'] prayer. . . .

In short, the only one who need utter the prayer is the teacher, and no teacher is complaining of it. Students can stand mute, or even leave the classroom, if they desire. . . .

The question presented by this case is therefore an extremely narrow one. It is whether New York oversteps the bounds when it finances a religious exercise.

What New York does on the opening of its public schools is what we do when we open court. Our Crier has from the beginning announced the convening of the Court and then added "God save the United States and this Honorable Court." That utterance is a supplication, a prayer in which we, the judges, are free to join, but which we need not recite any more than the students need recite the New York prayer. . . .

In New York, the teacher who leads in prayer is on the public payroll, and the time she takes seems minuscule as compared with the salaries appropriated by state legislatures and Congress for chaplains to conduct prayers in the legislative halls. Only a bare fraction of the teacher's time is given to reciting this short 22-word prayer, about the same amount of time that our Crier spends announcing the opening of our sessions and offering a prayer for this Court. Yet, for me, the principle is the same, no matter how briefly the prayer is said, for, in each of the instances given, the person praying is a public official on the public payroll, performing a religious exercise in a governmental institution. . . .

At the same time, I cannot say that to authorize this prayer is to establish a religion in the strictly historic meaning of those words. A religion is not established in the usual sense merely by letting those who choose to do so say the prayer that the public school teacher leads. Yet once government finances a religious exercise, it inserts a divisive influence into our communities.

MR. JUSTICE STEWART, dissenting.

With all respect, I think the Court has misapplied a great constitutional principle. I cannot see how an "official religion" is established by letting those who want to say a prayer say it. On the contrary, I think that to deny the wish of these school children to join in reciting this prayer is to deny them the opportunity of sharing in the spiritual heritage of our Nation.

The Court's historical review of the quarrels over the Book of Common Prayer in England throws no light for me on the issue before us in this case. England had then and has now an established church. Equally unenlightening, I think, is the history of the early establishment and later rejection of an official church in our own States. For we deal here not with the establishment of a state church, which would, of course, be constitutionally impermissible, but with whether school children who want to begin their day by joining in prayer must be prohibited from doing so. Moreover, I think that the Court's task, in this as in all areas of constitutional adjudication, is not responsibly aided by the uncritical invocation of metaphors like the "wall of separation," a phrase nowhere to be found in the Constitution. What is relevant to the issue here is not the history of an established church in sixteenth century England or in eighteenth century America, but the history of the religious traditions of our people, reflected in countless practices of the institutions and officials of our government. . . .

The Court today says that the state and federal governments are without constitutional power to prescribe any particular form of words to be recited by any group of the American people on any subject touching religion. . . .

At the opening of each day's Session of this Court we stand, while one of our officials invokes the protection of God. Since the days of John Marshall our Crier has said, "God Save the United States and this Honorable Court." Both the Senate and the House of Representative open their daily Sessions with prayer. Each of our Presidents, from George Washington to John F. Kennedy, has upon assuming his Office asked the protection and help of God. . . .

I do not believe that this Court, or the Congress, or the President has, by the actions and practices I have mentioned, established an "official religion" in violation of the Constitution. And I do not believe the State of New York has done so in this case. What each has done has been to recognize and to follow the deeply entrenched and highly cherished spiritual traditions of our Nation—traditions which come down to us from those who almost two hundred years ago avowed their "firm Reliance on the Protection of divine Providence" when they proclaimed the freedom and independence of this brave new world.

I dissent.

Abington v. Schempp 374 U.S. 203 (1963)

At the beginning of the 1956 school year, sixteen-year-old Ellory Schempp had decided—without his parents' knowledge—to stage his own silent protest against the mandatory religious exercises at Abington (Pa.) High School. As the class read a Bible verse, Schempp sat silently and read the Koran. Schempp's homeroom teacher made him leave, but allowed him to take the Koran with him. The principal soon ordered him back into class and required him to stand during the Lord's Prayer, although he was not required to recite it. Schempp's parents contacted the Philadelphia office of the ACLU, which agreed to represent him. Ellory had graduated by the time the case made it to the Supreme Court. However, his younger brother and sister, Roger and Donna, had followed him to Abington High, where they also objected to the Bible reading practices. When their father, Edward, learned that his children's teachers had referred to his children as "oddballs" and "atheists" he was highly offended, as his family was active in the Unitarian Church.

A three-judge district court found the Pennsylvania law unconstitutional. When the Court agreed to hear *Schempp*, all the interested parties understood the outcome was foreordained. The AJCongress, the AJCommittee, the ADL, the ACLU, public education groups, and Protestant agencies came together between the announcement of the *Engel* and *Schempp* decisions to coordinate a public education effort to prepare teachers, students, and religious leaders for the changes in the rules governing religion in the public school. Indeed, after the decisions, a Baptist Joint Committee spokesperson said he "was not disturbed by the elimination of 'required prayers' from schools because he had never felt that recital of such prayers had any real religious value for children." In a similarly tolerant spirit, the National Council of Churches issued a statement that said "many Christians will welcome the decision [because] it protects the rights of minorities and guards against the development of public school religion which is neither Christianity nor Judaism but something less than neither."

The Court's decision was 8 to 1. Justice Clark delivered the opinion of the Court. Justice Douglas concurred, as did Justice Brennan. Justice Goldberg filed a concurring opinion, which Justice Harlan joined. Justice Stewart dissented.

▼▲▼

MR. JUSTICE CLARK delivered the opinion of the Court.

It is true that religion has been closely identified with our history and government. As we said in *Engel* v. *Vitale* (1962), "The history of man is inseparable from the history of religion. And . . . since the beginning of that history many people have devoutly believed that 'More things are wrought by prayer than this world dreams of.'" . . . The fact that the Founding Fathers believed devotedly that there was a God and that the unalienable rights of man were rooted in Him is clearly evidenced in their writings, from the Mayflower Compact to the Constitution itself. This background is evidenced today in our public life through the continuance in our oaths of office from the Presidency to the Alderman of the final supplication, "So help me God." Likewise each House of the Congress provides through its Chaplain an opening prayer, and the sessions of this Court are declared open by the crier in a short ceremony, the final phrase of which invokes the grace of God. Again, there are such manifestations in our military forces, where those of our citizens who are under the restrictions of military service wish to engage in voluntary worship. Indeed, only last year an official survey of the country indicated that 64% of our people have church membership. . . .

This is not to say, however, that religion has been so identified with our history and government that religious freedom is not likewise as strongly imbedded in our public and private life. Nothing but the most telling of personal experiences in religious persecution suffered by our forebears could have planted our belief in liberty of religious opinion any more deeply in our heritage. It is true that this liberty frequently was not realized by the colonists, but this is readily accountable by their close ties to the Mother Country. However, the views of Madison and Jefferson, preceded by Roger Williams, came to be incorporated not only in the Federal Constitution but likewise in those of most of our States. This freedom to worship was indispensable in a country whose people came from the four quarters of the earth and brought with them a diversity of religious opinion. Today authorities list 83 separate religious bodies, each with membership exceeding 50,000, existing among our people, as well as innumerable smaller groups. . . .

[T]his Court has rejected unequivocally the contention that the Establishment Clause forbids only governmental preference of one religion over another. Almost 20 years ago in *Everson*, the Court said that "[n]either a state nor the Federal Government can set up a church. Neither can pass laws which aid one religion, aid all religions, or prefer one religion over another." . . .

The same conclusion has been firmly maintained ever since that time, and we reaffirm it now.

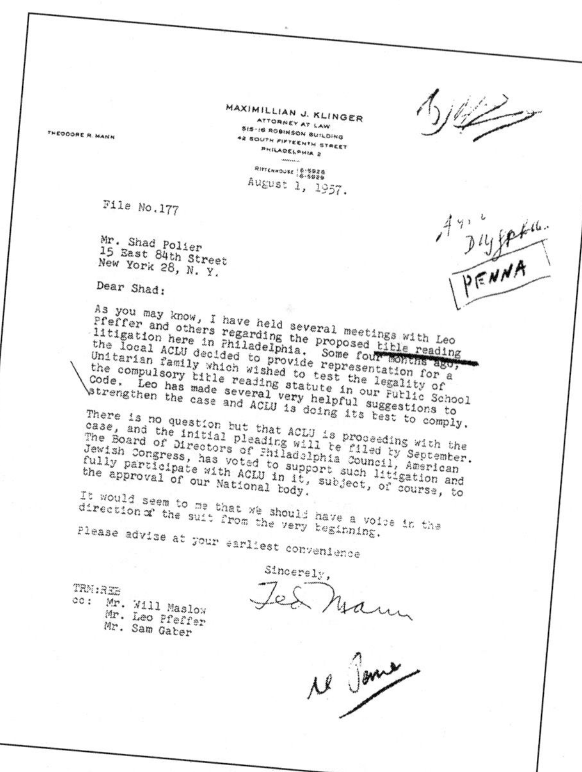

MAXIMILLIAN J. KLINGER
ATTORNEY AT LAW
515-16 ROBINSON BUILDING
42 SOUTH FIFTEENTH STREET
PHILADELPHIA 2

THEODORE R. MANN

RITTENHOUSE 6-5928
6-5929

August 1, 1957.

File No.177

Mr. Shad Polier
15 East 84th Street
New York 28, N. Y.

PENNA

Dear Shad:

As you may know, I have held several meetings with Leo Pfeffer and others regarding the proposed bible reading litigation here in Philadelphia. Some four months ago, the local ACLU decided to provide representation for a Unitarian family which wished to test the legality of the compulsory bible reading statute in our Public School Code. Leo has made several very helpful suggestions to strengthen the case and ACLU is doing its best to comply.

There is no question but that ACLU is proceeding with the case, and the initial pleading will be filed by September. The Board of Directors of Philadelphia Council, American Jewish Congress, has voted to support such litigation and fully participate with ACLU in it, subject, of course, to the approval of our National body.

It would seem to me that we should have a voice in the direction of the suit from the very beginning.

Please advise at your earliest convenience

Sincerely,

Ted Mann

TRM:REB
cc: Mr. Will Maslow
Mr. Leo Pfeffer
Mr. Sam Gater

Letter from Ted Mann to Shad Polier, both of the American Jewish Congress, outlining litigation strategy in Abington v. Schempp *(1963), the case that struck down state-sponsored Bible reading in public schools.*

While none of the parties to either of these cases has questioned these basic conclusions of the Court, both of which have been long established, recognized and consistently reaffirmed, others continue to question their history, logic and efficacy. Such contentions, in the light of the consistent interpretation in cases of this Court, seem entirely untenable and of value only as academic exercises. . . .

The wholesome "neutrality" of which this Court's cases speak thus stems from a recognition of the teachings of history that powerful sects or groups might bring about a fusion of governmental and religious functions or a concert or dependency of one upon the other to the end that official support of the State or Federal Government would be placed behind the tenets of one or of all orthodoxies. This the Establishment Clause prohibits. And a further reason for neutrality is found in the Free Exercise Clause, which recognizes the value of religious training, teaching and observance and, more particularly, the right of every person to freely choose his own course with reference thereto, free of any compulsion from the state. This the Free Exercise Clause guarantees. Thus, as we have seen, the two clauses may overlap. As we have indicated, the Establishment Clause has been directly considered by this Court eight times in the past score of years and, with only one Justice dissenting on the point, it has consistently held that the clause withdrew all legislative power respecting religious belief or the expression thereof. The test may be stated as follows: what are the purpose and the primary effect of the enactment? If either is the advancement or inhibition of religion then the enactment exceeds the scope of legislative power as circumscribed by the Constitution. That is to say that to withstand the strictures of the Establishment Clause there must be a secular legislative purpose and a primary effect that neither advances nor inhibits religion. The Free Exercise Clause, likewise considered many times here, withdraws from legislative power, state and federal, the exertion of any restraint on the free exercise of religion. Its purpose is to secure religious liberty in the individual by prohibiting any invasions thereof by civil authority. Hence it is necessary in a free exercise case for one to show the coercive effect of the enactment as it operates against him in the practice of his religion. The distinction between the two clauses is apparent—a violation of the Free Exercise Clause is predicated on coercion while the Establishment Clause violation need not be so attended.

Applying the Establishment Clause principles to the[se] cases . . . we find that the States are requiring the selection and reading at the opening of the school day of verses from the Holy Bible and the recitation of the Lord's Prayer by the students in unison. These exercises are prescribed as part of the curricular activities of students who are required by law to attend school. They are held in the school buildings under the supervision and with the participation of teachers employed in those schools. . . . The trial court . . . found that such an opening exercise is a religious ceremony and was intended by the State to be so. We agree with the trial court's finding as to the religious character of the exercises. Given that finding, the exercises and the law requiring them are in violation of the Establishment Clause.

The conclusion follows that [the law] require[s] religious exercises and such exercises are being conducted in direct violation of the rights of the appellees and petitioners. Nor are these required exercises mitigated by the fact that individual students may absent themselves upon parental request, for that fact furnishes no defense to a claim of unconstitutionality under the Establishment Clause. Further, it is no defense to urge that the religious practices here may be relatively minor encroachments on the First Amendment. The breach of neutrality that is today a trickling stream may all too soon become a raging torrent and, in the words of Madison, "it is proper to take alarm at the first experiment on our liberties."

It is insisted that unless these religious exercises are permitted a "religion of secularism" is established in the schools. We agree of course that the State may not establish a "religion of secularism" in the sense of affirmatively opposing or showing hostility to religion, thus "preferring those who believe in no religion over those who do believe." We do not agree, however, that this decision in any sense has that effect. In addition, it might well be said that one's education is not complete without a study of comparative religion or the history of religion and its relationship to the advancement of civilization. It certainly may be said that the Bible is worthy of study for its literary and historic qualities. Nothing we have said here indicates that such study of the Bible or of religion, when presented objectively as part of a secular program of education, may not be effected consistently with the First Amendment. But the exercises here do not fall into those categories. They are religious exercises, required by the States in violation of the command of the First Amendment that the Government maintain strict neutrality, neither aiding nor opposing religion.

Finally, we cannot accept that the concept of neutrality, which does not permit a State to require a religious exercise even with the consent of the majority of those affected, collides with the majority's right to free exercise of religion. While the Free Exercise Clause clearly prohibits the use of state action to deny the rights of free exercise to anyone, it has never meant that a majority could use the machinery of the State to practice its beliefs. . . .

The place of religion in our society is an exalted one, achieved through a long tradition of reliance on the home, the church and the inviolable citadel of the individual heart and mind. We have come to recognize through bitter experience that it is not within the power of government to invade that citadel, whether its purpose or effect be to aid or oppose, to advance or retard. In the relationship between man and religion, the State is firmly committed to a position of neutrality. Though the application of that rule requires interpretation of a delicate sort, the rule itself is clearly and concisely stated in the words of the First Amendment.

MR. JUSTICE STEWART, dissenting.

As a matter of history, the First Amendment was adopted solely as a limitation upon the newly created National Government. The events leading to its adoption strongly suggest that the Establishment Clause was primarily an attempt to insure that Congress not only would be powerless to establish a national church, but would also be unable to interfere with existing state establishments. Each State was left free to go its own way and pursue its own policy with respect to religion. Thus Virginia from the beginning pursued a policy of disestablishmentarianism. Massachusetts, by contrast, had an established church until well into the nineteenth century.

So matters stood until the adoption of the Fourteenth Amendment, or more accurately, until this Court's decision in *Cantwell* v. *Connecticut,* in 1940. In that case the Court said: "The First Amendment declares that Congress shall make no law respecting an establishment of religion or prohibiting the free exercise thereof. The Fourteenth Amendment has rendered the legislatures of the states as incompetent as Congress to enact such laws."

I accept without question that the liberty guaranteed by the Fourteenth Amendment against impairment by the States embraces in full the right of free exercise of religion protected by the First Amendment, and I yield to no one in my conception of the breadth of that freedom. . . . But I cannot agree with what seems to me the insensitive definition of the Establishment Clause contained in the Court's opinion, nor with the different but, I think, equally mechanistic definitions contained in the separate opinions which have been filed. . . .

Unlike other First Amendment guarantees, there is an inherent limitation upon the applicability of the Establishment Clause's ban on state support to religion. That limitation was succinctly put in *Everson* v. *Board of Education* (1947): "State power is no more to be used so as to handicap religions than it is to favor them." And in a later case, this Court recognized that the limitation was one which was itself compelled by the free exercise guarantee. "To hold that a state cannot consistently with the First and Fourteenth Amendments utilize its public school system to aid any or all religious faiths or sects in the dissemination of their doctrines and ideals does not . . . manifest a governmental hostility to religion or religious teachings. A manifestation of such hostility would be at war with our national tradition as embodied in the First Amendment's guaranty of the free exercise of religion," *McCollum* v. *Board of Education* (1948). . . .

It might . . . be argued that parents who want their children exposed to religious influences can adequately fulfill that wish off school property and outside school time. With all its surface persuasiveness, however, this argument seriously misconceives the basic constitutional justification for permitting the exercises at issue in these cases. For a compulsory state educational system so structures a child's life that if religious exercises are held to be an impermissible activity in schools, religion is placed at an artificial and state-created disadvantage. Viewed in this light, permission of such exercises for those who want them is necessary if the schools are truly to be neutral in the matter of religion. And a refusal to permit religious exercises thus is seen, not as the realization of state neutrality, but rather as the establishment of a religion of secularism, or at the least, as government support of the beliefs of those who think that religious exercises should be conducted only in private.

What seems to me to be of paramount importance, then, is recognition of the fact that the claim advanced here in favor of Bible reading is sufficiently substantial to make simple reference to the constitutional phrase "establishment of religion" as inadequate an analysis of the cases before us as the ritualistic invocation of the nonconstitutional phrase "separation of church and state." What these cases compel, rather, is an analysis of just what the "neutrality" is which is required by the interplay of the Establishment and Free Exercise Clauses of the First Amendment, as imbedded in the Fourteenth. . . .

The dangers both to government and to religion inherent in official support of instruction in the tenets of various religious sects are absent in the present cases, which involve only a reading from the Bible unaccompanied by comments which might otherwise constitute instruction. Indeed, since, from all that appears in either record, any teacher who does not wish to do so is free not to participate, it cannot even be contended that some infinitesimal part of the salaries paid by the State are made contingent upon the performance of a religious function.

In the absence of evidence that the legislature or school board intended to prohibit local schools from substituting a different set of readings where parents requested such a change, we should not assume that the provisions before us—as actually administered—may not be construed simply as authorizing religious exercises, nor that the designations may not be treated simply as indications of the promulgating body's view as to the community's preference. We are under a duty to interpret these provisions so as to render them constitutional if reasonably possible. In the *Schempp* case there is evidence which indicates that variations were in fact permitted by the very school there involved, and that further variations were not introduced only because of the absence of requests from parents. . . .

It may well be, as has been argued to us, that even the supposed benefits to be derived from noncoercive religious exercises in public schools are incommensurate with the administrative problems which they would create. The choice involved, however, is one for each local community and its school board, and not for this Court. For, as I have said, religious exercises are not constitutionally invalid if they simply reflect differences which exist in the society from which the school draws its pupils. They become constitutionally invalid only if their administration places the sanction of secular authority behind one or more particular religious or irreligious beliefs.

What our Constitution indispensably protects is the freedom of each of us, be he Jew or Agnostic, Christian or Atheist, Buddhist or Freethinker, to believe or disbelieve, to worship or not worship, to pray or keep silent, according to his own conscience, uncoerced and unrestrained by government. It is conceivable that these school boards, or even all school boards, might eventually find it impossible to administer a system of religious exercises during school hours in such a way as to meet this constitutional standard—in such a way as completely to free from any kind of official coercion those who do not affirmatively want to participate. But I think we must not assume that school boards so lack the qualities of inventiveness and good will as to make impossible the achievement of that goal.

▼▲▼

Together, *Engel* and *Abington* embroiled the Court in its greatest controversy since *Brown* v. *Board of Education*, which declared racial segregation in the public schools unconstitutional. Beyond the mainline Protestant bodies, public disapproval of *Engel* and *Schempp* was ferocious. A Gallup poll released soon after *Schempp* found that only 24 percent of Americans approved of the Court's decisions. Almost forty years later, support for the Court's school prayer decisions in public opinion has never exceeded 45 percent. In contrast, 54 percent of Americans supported *Brown* the year it was decided. Over time, support for *Brown* was so widespread that public opinion pollsters stopped asking the question.[50] Congress soon jumped on the bandwagon against *Engel* and *Schempp*. Senator Sam Ervin (D–N.C.) claimed that "the Supreme Court has declared God unconstitutional." Representative George Andrews (D–Ala.) insisted that the Court had "put Negroes in the schools and now [had] taken God out." A Florida representative suggested that Congress buy Bibles for the "personal use of each [Supreme Court] justice."[51]

By 1964, seventy-five different members of Congress had introduced over one hundred separate laws and constitutional amendments designed to overturn *Engel* and *Schempp*.[52] Only one actually emerged that garnered any significant support in the House and Senate. That was New York Representative Frank J. Becker's proposal to overturn the school prayer amendments through a constitutional amendment that read, "Nothing in this Constitution shall be deemed to prohibit the offering, reading from or listening to prayers or Biblical scriptures, if participation therein is on a voluntary basis, in any governmental or public school, institution or place." A coalition of civil liberties, education, Jewish, and Protestant groups organized by Leo Pfeffer lobbied Congress to vote down the Becker Amendment. Crucial to Pfeffer's strategy was to have prominent Christian clergy express their opposition to state-sponsored prayer, thus reassuring nervous members of Congress that a vote against the Becker Amendment was not hostile to religion.[53]

Ultimately, the Becker Amendment passed with simple majorities in the House and Senate but failed to achieve the necessary two-thirds vote to go out to the states for ratification. On numerous occasions since the uproar over *Engel* and *Schempp*, Congress has tried but failed to secure similar constitutional amendments easing the restrictions on state-sponsored religious exercises in the public schools.[54]

Two Southern Baptists, Alabamian Hugo Black and Texan Tom C. Clark, wrote the Court's opinions in *Engel* and *Schempp*, respectively. Black's short opinion left no doubt that the Court had now embraced his *dicta* from *Everson*. Chief Justice Warren's decision to assign *Schempp* to Clark was no accident, as he wanted elite opinion makers to understand that both the Court's Southerners rejected state-sponsored school prayer. But Clark's opinion gave attorneys immersed in the church-state debate a clear approach to analyzing laws and programs challenged as unconstitutional. Clark asked two questions: first, does the law have a *secular purpose*? and, second, does the law have a *secular effect* that neither advances nor inhibits religion? A law that failed just one of these tests could not stand under the Establishment Clause. The Court, in *Lemon* v. *Kurtzman* (1971), discussed later in this chapter, modified Clark's secular purpose and effect test to include a prohibition on *excessive entanglement*. Until the mid-1990s, this restriction doomed most federal and state efforts to provide public funds for parochial schools.

In 1985, the Court decided its most significant school prayer case since *Schempp*. *Wallace* v. *Jaffree* had been supported by the Reagan administration and conservative groups such as the National Legal Foundation (NLF), a creation of the politically active religious broadcaster Pat Robertson. By the early 1980s, conservatives pinned their hopes on the decreasing support for the "high wall" theory of church-state separation within the Court. In 1983, the Court ruled, in *Marsh* v. *Chambers*, that state legislatures were free to open each session with prayers led by chaplains paid with public funds because they had always done so.[55] A year later, in *Lynch* v. *Donnelly* (1984), a badly divided Court upheld the rights of states and municipalities to display a Nativity scene on public property. The majority reasoned that the "seasonal" symbols that surrounded the Nativity, such as reindeer, a plastic Santa Claus, and Christmas tree ornaments, diminished the scene's religious significance.[56] The combination of a more conservative Court and *Wallace*'s unusual procedural history, described in the accompanying SIDEBAR, along with its support from President Reagan, made this an important school prayer case.

Wallace v. *Jaffree*

472 U.S. 38 (1985)

The facts and background of this case are set out in the accompanying SIDEBAR.

The Court's decision was 6 to 3. Justice Stevens delivered the opinion of the Court. Justices O'Connor and Powell filed separate concurring opinions. Chief Justice Burger and Justices White and Rehnquist each filed separate disssents.

JUSTICE STEVENS delivered the opinion of the Court.

When the Court has been called upon to construe the breadth of the Establishment Clause, it has examined the criteria developed over a period of many years. Thus, in *Lemon* v. *Kurtzman* (1971), we wrote:

> Every analysis in this area must begin with consideration of the cumulative criteria developed by the Court over many years. Three such tests may be gleaned from our cases. First, the statute must have a secular legislative purpose; second, its principal or primary effect must be one that neither advances nor inhibits religion; finally, the statute must not foster "an excessive government entanglement with religion."

It is the first of these three criteria that is most plainly implicated by this case. . . . [N]o consideration of the second or third criteria is necessary if a statute does not have a clearly secular purpose. For even though a statute that is motivated in part by a religious purpose may satisfy the first criterion, the First Amendment requires that a statute must be invalidated if it is entirely motivated by a purpose to advance religion.

In applying the purpose test, it is appropriate to ask "whether government's actual purpose is to endorse or disapprove of religion." In this case, the answer to that question is dispositive. For the record not only provides us with an unambiguous affirmative answer, but it also reveals that the enactment of [the law] was not motivated by any clearly secular purpose—indeed, the statute had *no* secular purpose.

The sponsor of the bill that became [the law], Senator Donald Holmes, inserted into the legislative record—apparently without dissent—a statement indicating that the legislation was an "effort to return voluntary prayer" to the public schools. Later Senator Holmes confirmed this purpose before the District Court. In response to the question

SIDEBAR

WALLACE V. JAFFREE

"I'm Perceived as the Outsider"

Every day before lunch, Charlene Boyd led her kindergarten class at the Dickson Elementary School in Mobile, Alabama, in a "musical grace" that went, "God is great, God is good, Let us thank him for our food; Bow our heads, we are all fed, Give us Lord our daily bread. Amen!" On the first day of the 1981–1982 school year, five-year-old Chioke Jaffree told his teacher that he did not like having to sing the prayer and did not want to take part. Ms. Boyd told Chioke that he did not have to participate in grace. The class, however, continued to sing grace each day before they went into the cafeteria.

A couple weeks into the school year, Chioke told his father, Ishmael Jaffree, about the daily prayers before lunch. Jaffree was an attorney with a federally funded group that assisted poor clients with housing and employment matters, and was familiar with the ongoing efforts of the Alabama legislature to pass legislation authorizing prayer in the public schools. Jaffree was an agnostic, but his wife, Mozelle, was a practicing Bahai, a faith with Middle Eastern origins. The Jaffrees agreed, however, that they did not want the Mobile public schools attended by their three children to offer any sort of religious practices. Shortly after Chioke reported the daily singing of grace in his class, his eighteen-year-old sister, Makeba, told her father that her teacher recited the Lord's Prayer daily in class. The Jaffrees' eight-year-old daughter, Aakki, also said that her teacher led the class in prayer.

After Ishmael Jaffree's requests to his children's teachers to end their prayers were unsuccessful, he wrote directly to the Mobile school superintendent, Abe Lincoln Hammons, claiming that such practices were unconstitutional and should be immediately halted. Hammons refused to act on Jaffree's request. Finally, a school board lawyer responded to Jaffree that the prayers were lawful because they were voluntary and not written by the state. His children did not have to participate, but the teachers would remain free to lead their classes in prayer. Dissatisfied, Jaffree filed suit in federal district court in May 1981, claiming that Mobile's practices violated the Establishment Clause.

Alabama's political establishment stood firmly behind the right of its public schools to encourage their teachers to lead their classes in prayer. In 1978, the Alabama legislature enacted a law requiring elementary schoolteachers to establish a moment of silence for student meditation, reflection, or prayer before school started for the day. In 1981, Alabama enacted another law that gave teachers the right to provide a one-minute period of silence for meditation or "voluntary" prayer. In 1982, the legislature passed another law, this time giving "any teacher or professor . . . in any public educational institution within the state of Alabama" the right to lead "willing students" in specifically worded prayer that expressly recognized "God . . . Creator and Supreme Judge of the World." In fact, the 1981 law was enacted after Jaffree filed his legal complaint. Alabama governor Forrest "Fob" James criticized Jaffree by name during a televised address on the controversy and encouraged the legislature to take action authorizing "voluntary" prayer during the school day.

Testifying in federal district court, Jaffree expressed no qualms about his decision to challenge the religious practices that were prevalent throughout the Alabama schools. As he testified in court: "I think children on their own should be free to pray before meals, at any time they want to." Furthermore, said Jaffree, "What they are being exposed to is basically a fundamentalist, Christian philosophy. . . . I want my children not to accept everything that is told to them and be free to examine, to explore, to ponder, to think about, to be exposed to different philosophies." But Jaffree did acknowledge the social costs to his family because of his decision to challenge the prayer practices:

> My children have experienced all types of abuse from neighbors. Some of the children in our neighborhood which is mostly white [the Jaffrees were African American] have stopped playing with my children, and other children laugh at them. If [the lawsuit] is successful, then my children will be forever stamped as the children of the father who tried to take religion out of the public classrooms. How are my children going to handle this? I don't know. I have suffered emotionally myself and it has drained me. My future here in Mobile is going to be drastically altered because of this lawsuit. I'm perceived as the outsider that is disrupting Mobile's quiet tranquility.

The state called several witnesses to offer testimony about the clear and long-standing importance of prayer in the state's public schools. Charlene Boyd testified that she led her class in musical grace because, "It was one I had learned when I was in school." Children, said Boyd, should thank God for their food because "that's who I thank." Pixie Alexander, Makeba's teacher, told the court that she requested her students to pray out loud because "the power of life and death is in the tongue." The most telling statement of all, however, came from Alabama state senator Donald G. Holmes, the leading sponsor of the 1981 law. Holmes testified that law's purpose was to "return voluntary prayer to our public schools. . . . It is a beginning and a step in the right direction . . . with no other purpose in mind."

Senator Holmes's admission might have brought down a swift rebuke from other judges, but not Brevard Hand, a self-described "constitutionalist" who decorated his chambers with portraits of Confederate generals. Judge Hand, in a truly startling opinion, ruled that Alabama was free to promote school prayer because the Fourteenth Amendment did not make the Establishment Clause applicable to the states. Hand's opinion earned him the nicknamed "unlearned Hand" from one ACLU lawyer; another called him a "Hand without a head." So bizarre was his ruling that not even the Christian Legal Society and the National Association of Evangelicals, which filed *amicus* briefs supporting the Alabama prayer law, would defend Judge Hand's position on the Fourteenth Amendment. Although some of the more conservative lawyers in the Justice Department were pleased that Hand had made such a bold statement, they knew that the Supreme Court was not going to reject almost fifty years of precedent that made the First Amendment applicable to the states through the Fourteenth Amendment. After Alabama governor George Wallace decided to appeal the lower courts' rulings to the Supreme Court, the ACLU and People for the American Way, a civil liberties group founded in 1980 by Hollywood television producer Norman Lear, joined forces to support the Jaffrees.

As *Wallace* proceeded through the federal courts, a Mobile-based parents group consisting of Christian fundamentalists launched another lawsuit in Judge Hand's court asking him to strike down dozens of state-approved textbooks used in the public schools as advancing the religion of "secular humanism." Here, the Reagan administration and the conservative religious groups that were supporting Alabama's "voluntary prayer" law refused to get involved in the textbook controversy. Nonetheless, Judge Hand joined the two lawsuits together. In addition to upholding the Alabama "voluntary prayer" law, Judge Hand declared that the challenged textbooks advanced the religion of "secular humanism," making them unfit for use in the public schools. Judge Hand's decisions were reversed by the Eleventh Circuit Court of Appeals, and the judge himself was singled out for criticism for his willingness to defy the Supreme Court's long-standing doctrine making the guarantees of the Bill of Rights applicable to the states through the Fourteenth Amendment.

The Court's decision to invalidate the Alabama school prayer law in *Wallace* slowed some of the momentum that conservative Christian activists had been making in their effort to restore an official place for religion in the public schools. By the early 1990s, the Court would uphold the constitutionality of the Equal Access Act of 1984, a federal law that permitted student religious clubs to meet in public schools after-hours. But subsequent cases involving school prayer such as *Lee v. Weisman* (1992) and *Santa Fe Independent School District v. Doe* (2000) continue to demonstrate that this issue has a unique staying power and it will probably return in one form or another in the near future.

References

Irons, Peter. *The Courage of Their Convictions.* New York: Oxford University Press, 1990, pp. 357–367.

Monsma, Steven V., and J. Christopher Soper, eds. *Equal Treatment of Religion in a Pluralistic Society.* Grand Rapids, Mich.: Eerdmans Publishing Co., 1998.

whether he had any purpose for the legislation other than returning voluntary prayer to public schools, he stated: "No, I did not have no [*sic*] other purpose in mind." The State did not present evidence of *any* secular purpose. . . .

For whenever the State itself speaks on a religious subject, one of the questions that we must ask is "whether the government intends to convey a message of endorsement or disapproval of religion." The well-supported concurrent findings of the District Court and the Court of Appeals—that [the law] was intended to convey a message of state approval of prayer activities in the public schools—make it unnecessary, and indeed inappropriate, to evaluate the practical significance of the addition of the words "or voluntary prayer" to the statute. Keeping in mind, as we must, both the fundamental place held by the Establishment Clause in our constitutional scheme and the myriad, subtle ways in which Establishment Clause values can be eroded, we conclude that [the law] violates the First Amendment.

The judgment of the Court of Appeals is affirmed. . . .

JUSTICE POWELL, concurring.

My concurrence is prompted by Alabama's persistence in attempting to institute state-sponsored prayer in the public schools by enacting three successive statutes. I agree fully with JUSTICE O'CONNOR's assertion that some moment-of-silence statutes may be constitutional, a suggestion set forth in the Court's opinion as well.

I would vote to uphold the Alabama statute if it also had a clear secular purpose. Nothing in the record before us, however, identifies a clear secular purpose, and the State also has failed to identify any nonreligious reason for the statute's enactment. Under these circumstances, the Court is required by our precedents to hold that the statute fails the first prong of the *Lemon* test, and therefore violates the Establishment Clause.

Although we do not reach the other two prongs of the *Lemon* test, I note that the "effect" of a straightforward moment-of-silence statute is unlikely to "advanc[e] or inhibi[t] religion." Nor would such a statute "foster 'an excessive government entanglement with religion.'"

I join the opinion and judgment of the Court.

JUSTICE O'CONNOR, concurring in the judgment.

Twenty-five states permit or require public school teachers to have students observe a moment of silence in their classrooms. A few statutes provide that the moment of silence is for the purpose of meditation alone. The typical statute, however, calls for a moment of silence at the beginning of the schoolday during which students may meditate, pray, or reflect on the activities of the day. Federal trial courts have divided on the constitutionality of these moment of silence laws. Relying on this Court's decisions disapproving vocal prayer and Bible reading in the public schools, the courts that have struck down the moment of silence statutes generally conclude that their purpose and effect are to encourage prayer in public schools.

The *Engel* and *Abington* decisions are not dispositive on the constitutionality of moment of silence laws. In those cases, public school teachers and students led their classes in devotional exercises. . . .

A state-sponsored moment of silence in the public schools is different from state-sponsored vocal prayer or Bible reading. First, a moment of silence is not inherently religious. Silence, unlike prayer or Bible reading, need not be associated with a religious exercise. Second, a pupil who participates in a moment of silence need not compromise his or her beliefs. During a moment of silence, a student who objects to prayer is left to his or her own thoughts, and is not compelled to listen to the prayers or thoughts of others. For these simple reasons, a moment of silence statute does not stand or fall under the Establishment Clause according to how the Court regards vocal prayer or Bible reading. Scholars and at least one Member of this Court have recognized the distinction and suggested that a moment of silence in public schools would be constitutional. As a general matter, I agree. It is difficult to discern a serious threat to religious liberty from a room of silent, thoughtful schoolchildren.

By mandating a moment of silence, a State does not necessarily endorse any activity that might occur during the period. Even if a statute specifies that a student may choose to pray silently during a quiet moment, the State has not thereby encouraged prayer over other specified alternatives. Nonetheless, it is also possible that a moment of silence statute, either as drafted or as actually implemented, could effectively favor the child who prays over the child who does not. For example, the message of endorsement would seem inescapable if the teacher exhorts children to use the designated time to pray. Similarly, the face of the statute or its legislative history may clearly establish that it seeks to encourage or promote voluntary prayer over other alternatives, rather than merely provide a quiet moment that may be dedicated to prayer by those so inclined. The crucial question is whether the State has conveyed or attempted to convey the message that children should use the moment of silence for prayer. This question cannot be answered in the abstract, but instead requires courts to examine the history, language, and administration of a particular statute to determine whether it operates as an endorsement of religion. Before reviewing Alabama's moment of silence law to determine whether it endorses prayer, some general observations on the proper scope of the inquiry are in order. First, the inquiry into the purpose of the legislature in enacting a moment of silence law should be deferential and limited. In determining whether the government intends a moment of silence statute to convey a message of endorsement or disapproval of religion, a court has no license to psychoanalyze the legislators. If a legislature expresses a plausible secular purpose for a moment of silence statute in either the text or the legislative history, or if the statute disclaims an intent to encourage prayer over alternatives during a moment of silence, then courts should generally defer to that stated intent. It is particularly troublesome to denigrate an expressed secular purpose due to postenactment testimony by particular legislators or by interested persons who witnessed the drafting of the statute. Even if the text and official history of a statute express no secular purpose, the statute should be held to have an improper purpose only if it is beyond purview that endorsement of religion or a religious belief "was and is the law's reason for existence." Since there is arguably a secular pedagogical value to a moment of silence in public schools, courts should find an improper purpose behind such a statute only if the statute on its face, in its official legislative history, or in its interpretation by a responsible administrative agency suggests it has the primary purpose of endorsing prayer. . . .

The analysis above suggests that moment of silence laws in many States should pass Establishment Clause scrutiny, because they do not favor the child who chooses to pray during a moment of silence over the child who chooses to meditate or reflect. However . . . one examines its text and legislative history, however objectively one views the message attempted to be conveyed to the public, the conclusion is unavoidable that the purpose of the statute is to endorse prayer in public schools. . . .

The Court does not hold that the Establishment Clause is so hostile to religion that it precludes the States from affording schoolchildren an opportunity for voluntary silent prayer. To the contrary, the moment of silence statutes of many States should satisfy the Establishment Clause standard we have here applied. The Court holds only that Alabama has intentionally crossed the line between creating a quiet moment during which those so inclined may pray and affirmatively endorsing the particular religious practice of prayer. This line may be a fine one, but our precedents and the principles of religious liberty require that we draw it. In my view, the judgment of the Court of Appeals must be affirmed.

JUSTICE REHNQUIST, dissenting.

See Chapter 2, pp. 19–21.

Justice Stevens's opinion served as a powerful rebuke both to Judge Hand's assessment of the Establishment Clause's meaning and its applicability to the states through the Fourteenth Amendment. Note, as well, the contrast in the lessons that Stevens and Rehnquist take away from the Framers' intent in their understanding of the Establishment Clause. In a dissent that demonstrated remarkable historical range and facility, Justice Rehnquist offered a powerful critique of the Court's religion decisions. His reliance on the Framers' intent and historical sources offers an excellent example of the originalist approach to constitutional interpretation. Although Rehnquist's dissent initially caused quite a stir, it never had the impact that many observers first thought it might. Since *Wallace,* the Court has been more willing to allow religious groups access to the public schools. But the justices have never embraced Rehnquist's nonpreferential interpretation of the Establishment Clause.

In *Lee* v. *Weisman* (1992), the Bush administration, picking up where President Reagan left off, urged the Court to uphold the right of public schools to invite clergy to deliver prayer during commencement ceremonies. On first glance, nothing in *Weisman* suggested that the case raised any new or novel issues of law or fact. Indeed, the prayer challenged was not that much different from the one struck down in *Engel.* Rabbi Leslie Gutterman offered the invocation and benediction, parts of which read:

> *From the Invocation*
> God of the Free, Hope of the Brave:
>
> For the legacy of America where diversity is celebrated and the rights of minorities are protected, we thank You. May these young men and women grow up to enrich it.
>
> For the liberty of America, we thank You. May these new graduates grow up to guard it. . . .
>
> *From the Benediction*
> O God, we are grateful to You for having endowed us with the capacity for learning which we have celebrated on this joyous commencement.
>
> Happy families give thanks for seeing their children achieve an important milestone. Send Your blessings upon the teachers and administrators who helped prepare them. . . .
>
> We give thanks to You, Lord, for keeping us alive, sustaining us and allowing us to reach this special, happy occasion.

Weisman differed from *Engel* in that state educational authorities did not write the challenged prayer. Instead, the issue was whether the government may provide a platform for someone outside the school system to offer a prayer during an official school function. The Bush administration argued that no *coercion,* or government force, was involved, since graduation is generally not a mandatory school function. Besides, important free speech issues were in play, namely, the rights of private citizens to speak in public places without fear of reprisal or discrimination. Perhaps most importantly, Solicitor General Kenneth Starr asked the Court to abandon the three-part *Lemon* test, described on p. 251, in favor of the coercion argument it introduced to defend the commencement prayer.

The ACLU, which represented the Weismans, encouraged the Court to treat *Weisman* as nothing more than a simple school prayer case controlled by *Engel, Schempp,* and *Wallace.* An ecumenical coalition of over two dozen religious groups submitted an *amicus* brief urging the Court to invalidate commencement prayers, emphasizing that such a practice was good for neither religion nor community relations. School prayer opponents also encouraged the Court not to tamper with the *Lemon* test. In truth, this was a largely symbolic argument, since the Court had only selectively applied *Lemon* since the early 1980s. But it had not formally abandoned *Lemon.* Doing so in *Weisman* would send the message that the Court's approach to deciding Establishment Clause cases was now up for reconsideration.

By a 5-4 majority, the Court ruled that the challenged practice was unconstitutional and, at the same time, refused to consider the question of whether to jettison *Lemon.* Although *Weisman* certainly was a major victory for opponents of organized school prayer, many conservative groups refused to concede defeat on the issue. Shortly after *Weisman,* the American Center for Law and Justice (ACLJ), a conservative public interest law firm formed in 1990 to counter the ACLU, organized a public relations campaign emphasizing that the Court said only that public schools were prohibited from inviting clergy to direct prayer.[57] Nothing in *Weisman,* said the ACLJ, foreclosed the possibility that students could organize their own devotionals during school events as long as such participation was voluntary. In support of this effort, the ACLJ sent some ten thousand faxes to school districts across the country offering a legal analysis supportive of "student-initiated" school prayer. The ACLJ emphasized the free speech rights of students, and claimed that the Establishment Clause prohibited only direct state support for religious practices. Eight years later, that theory was put to the test in *Santa Fe Independent School District* v. *Doe* (2000).

Santa Fe Independent School District v. *Doe*

530 U.S. 290 (2000)

The Santa Fe Independent School District is located in South Texas and consists of the Santa Fe High School, two primary schools, an intermediate school, and a junior high. It enrolls four thousand students. In April 1993, a seventh-grade student was sitting in her Texas History class when her teacher distributed fliers advertising a Baptist religious revival. After learning that the student was Mormon, the teacher described the Mormon faith to her class as "cult-like" and "non-Christian." Two days later, the student's mother complained to Santa Fe School District authorities about the teacher's behavior. The teacher was formally reprimanded and ordered to apologize to the family and the class.

Nonetheless, Santa Fe continued to permit students to offer Christian prayers at graduation ceremonies and at home football games during the 1993–1994 school year. The same seventh grader attended several home football games with her family, and later asked the school district to end the prayer practice, claiming that it was unconstitutional under the Establishment Clause. After the school district refused to end the practice, the Mormon family, joined by a Catholic family, asked a federal district court to terminate student prayers at commencement exercises and football games. They were permitted to file suit as the "Does" to protect them from intimidation and harassment.

The lower court declared Santa Fe's prayer policies unconstitutional. A divided appeals court ruled that the graduation prayers could continue, but agreed that students could not use the public address system to lead prayers before football games. In September 1999, the parents of a seventeen-year-old Santa Fe student sued the school district, claiming that it was violating her free speech rights by complying with the appeals court's decision. A district court judge issued a temporary restraining order barring the school district from suspending the student's right to pray before the game. The student offered the following prayer before a Friday night football game: "God, thank you for this evening. Thank you for all the prayers that were lifted up this week for me. I pray that you'll bless each and every person here tonight."

Santa Fe subsequently appealed to the Supreme Court, claiming that the ban of student prayers violated the Free Speech Clause. The school district was represented by the ACLJ. During the early 1990s, the ACLJ had successfully argued several cases before the Supreme Court, expanding the right of religious clubs to meet in public schools (see pp. 261–262) by emphasizing the free speech rights of students. As long as government officials were not doing the speaking, the ACLJ argued that the Establishment Clause posed no barrier to student-initiated religious speech, even during official school events.

The Court's decision was 6 to 3. Justice Stevens delivered the opinion of the Court. Chief Justice Rehnquist, joined by Justices Scalia and Thomas, dissented.

JUSTICE STEVENS delivered the opinion of the Court.

In *Lee* v. *Weisman* (1992), we held that a prayer delivered by a rabbi at a middle school graduation ceremony violated that Clause. Although this case involves student prayer at a different type of school function, our analysis is properly guided by the principles that we endorsed in Lee. . . .

In this case [*Santa Fe*] first argues that this principle is inapplicable . . . because the messages are private student speech, not public speech. It reminds us that "there is a crucial difference between government speech endorsing religion, which the Establishment Clause forbids, and private speech endorsing religion, which the Free Speech and Free Exercise Clauses protect," *Board of Ed. of Westside Community Schools* v. *Mergens* (1990). We certainly agree with that distinction, but we are not persuaded that the pregame invocations should be regarded as "private speech."

These invocations are authorized by a government policy and take place on government property at government-sponsored school-related events. Of course, not every message delivered under such circumstances is the government's own. We have held, for example, that an individual's contribution to a government-created forum was not government speech, *Rosenberger* v. *Univ. of Va.* (1995). Although the District relies heavily on *Rosenberger* and similar cases involving such forums, it is clear that the pregame ceremony is not the type of forum discussed in those cases. The Santa Fe school officials simply do not "evince either 'by policy or by practice,' any intent to open the [pregame ceremony] to 'indiscriminate use,' . . . by the student body generally." Rather, the school allows only one student, the same student for the entire season, to give the invocation. The statement or invocation, moreover, is subject to particular regulations that confine the content and topic of the student's message. . . .

Granting only one student access to the stage at a time does not, of course, necessarily preclude a finding that a school has created a limited public forum. Here, however, Santa Fe's student election system ensures that only those messages deemed "appropriate" under the District's policy may be delivered. That is, the majoritarian process implemented by the District guarantees, by definition, that minority candidates will never prevail and that their views will be effectively silenced. . . .

This student election does nothing to protect minority views but rather places the students who hold such views at the mercy of the majority. Because "fundamental rights may not be submitted to vote, they depend on the outcome of no elections," *West Virginia Bd. of Ed.* v. *Barnette* (1943), the District's elections are insufficient safeguards of diverse student speech.

In *Weisman*, the school district made the related argument that its policy of endorsing only "civic or nonsectarian" prayer was acceptable because it minimized the intrusion on the audience as a whole. We rejected that claim by explaining that such a majoritarian policy "does not lessen the offense or isolation to the objectors. At best it narrows their number, at worst increases their sense of isolation and affront." Similarly, while Santa Fe's majoritarian election might ensure that most of the students are represented, it does nothing to protect the minority; indeed, it likely serves to intensify their offense.

Moreover, [Santa Fe] has failed to divorce itself from the religious content in the invocations. It has not succeeded in doing so, either by claiming that its policy is "'one of neutrality rather than endorsement'" or by characterizing the individual student as the "circuit-breaker" in the process. Contrary to [Santa Fe's] repeated assertions that it has adopted a "hands-off" approach to the pregame invocation, the realities of the situation plainly reveal that its policy involves both perceived and actual endorsement of religion. In this case, as we found in *Weisman*, the "degree of school involvement" makes it clear that the pregame prayers bear "the imprint of the State and thus put school-age children who objected in an untenable position.". . .

In addition to involving the school in the selection of the speaker, the policy, by its terms, invites and encourages religious messages. The policy itself states that the purpose of the message is "to solemnize the event." A religious message is the most obvious method of solemnizing an event. Moreover, the requirements that the message "promote good citizenship" and "establish the appropriate environment for competition" further narrow the types of message deemed appropriate, suggesting that a solemn, yet nonreligious, message, such as commentary on United States foreign policy, would be prohibited. Indeed, the only type of message that is expressly endorsed in the text is an "invocation"—a term that primarily describes an appeal for divine assistance. In fact, as used in the past at Santa Fe High School, an "invocation" has always entailed a focused religious message. Thus, the expressed purposes of the policy encourage the selection of a religious message, and that is precisely how the students understand the policy. The results of the elections described in the parties' stipulation make it clear that the students understood that the central question before them was whether prayer should be a part of the pregame ceremony. We recognize the important role that public worship plays in many communities, as well as the sincere desire to include public prayer as a part of various occasions so as to mark those occasions' significance. But such religious activity in public schools, as elsewhere, must comport with the First Amendment.

The actual or perceived endorsement of the message, moreover, is established by factors beyond just the text of the policy. Once the student speaker is selected and the message composed, the invocation is then delivered to a large audience assembled as part of a regularly scheduled, school-sponsored function conducted on school property. The message is broadcast over the school's public address system, which remains subject to the control of school officials. It is fair to assume that the pregame ceremony is clothed in the traditional indicia of school sporting events, which generally include not just the team, but also cheerleaders and band members dressed in uniforms sporting the school name and mascot. The school's name is likely written in large print across the field and on banners and flags. The crowd will certainly include many who display the school colors and insignia on their school T-shirts, jackets, or hats and who may also be waving signs displaying the school name. It is in a setting such as this that "[t]he board has chosen to permit" the elected student to rise and give the "statement or invocation."

In this context the members of the listening audience must perceive the pregame message as a public expression of the views of the majority of the student body delivered with the approval of the school administration. In cases involving state participation in a religious activity, one of the relevant questions is "whether an objective observer, acquainted with the text, legislative history, and implementation of the statute, would perceive it as a state endorsement of prayer in public schools." Regardless of the listener's support for, or objection to, the message, an objective Santa Fe High School student will unquestionably perceive the inevitable pregame prayer as stamped with her school's seal of approval. . . .

Most striking to us is the evolution of the current policy from the long-sanctioned office of "Student Chaplain" to the candidly titled "Prayer at Football Games" regulation. This history indicates that the District intended to preserve the practice of prayer before football games. The conclusion that the District viewed the October policy simply as a continuation of the previous policies is dramatically illustrated by the fact that the school did not conduct a new election, pursuant to the current policy, to replace the results of the previous election, which occurred under the former policy. Given these observations, and in light of the school's history of regular delivery of a student-led prayer at athletic events, it is reasonable to infer that the specific purpose of the policy was to preserve a popular "state-sponsored religious practice."

School sponsorship of a religious message is impermissible because it sends the ancillary message to members of the audience who are nonadherants "that they are outsiders, not full members of the political community, and an accompanying message to adherants that they are insiders, favored members of the political community." The delivery of such a message—over the school's public address system, by a speaker representing the student body, under the supervision of school faculty, and pursuant to a school policy that explicitly and implicitly encourages public prayer—is not properly characterized as "private" speech.

The District next argues that its football policy is distinguishable from the graduation prayer in *Weisman* because it does not coerce students to participate in religious observances. Its argument has two parts: first, that there is no impermissible government coercion because the pregame messages are the product of student choices; and second, that there is really no coercion at all because attendance at an extracurricular event, unlike a graduation ceremony, is voluntary. . . .

One of the purposes served by the Establishment Clause is to remove debate over this kind of issue from governmental supervision or control. We explained in *Weisman* that the "preservation and transmission of religious beliefs and worship is a responsibility and a choice committed to the private sphere." The two student elections authorized by the policy, coupled with the debates that presumably must precede each, impermissibly invade that private sphere. The election mechanism, when considered in light of the history in which the policy in question evolved, reflects a device the District put in place that determines whether religious messages will be delivered at home football games. The mechanism encourages divisiveness along religious lines in a public school setting, a result at odds with the Establishment Clause. Although it is true that the ultimate choice of student speaker is "attributable to the students," the District's decision to hold the constitutionally problematic election is clearly "a choice attributable to the State."

The District further argues that attendance at the commencement ceremonies at issue in *Weisman* "differs dramatically" from attendance at high school football games, which it contends "are of no more than passing interest to many students" and are "decidedly extracurricular," thus dissipating any coercion. Attendance at a high school football game, unlike showing up for class, is certainly not required in order to receive a diploma. Moreover, we may assume that the District is correct in arguing that the informal pressure to attend an athletic event is not as strong as a senior's desire to attend her own graduation ceremony. . . .

Even if we regard every high school student's decision to attend a home football game as purely voluntary, we are nevertheless persuaded that the delivery of a pregame prayer has the improper effect of coercing those present to participate in an act of religious worship. For "the government may no more use social pressure to enforce orthodoxy than it may use more direct means." As in *Weisman*, "[w]hat to most believers may seem nothing more than a reasonable request that the nonbeliever respect their religious practices, in a school context may appear to the nonbeliever or dissenter to be an attempt to employ the machinery of the State to enforce a religious orthodoxy." The constitutional command will not permit the District "to exact religious conformity from a student as the price" of joining her classmates at a varsity football game.

The Religion Clauses of the First Amendment prevent the government from making any law respecting the establishment of religion or prohibiting the free exercise thereof. By no means do these commands impose a prohibition on all religious activity in our public schools. Indeed, the common purpose of the Religion Clauses "is to secure religious liberty." Thus, nothing in the Constitution as interpreted by this Court prohibits any public school student from voluntarily praying at any time before, during, or after the school day. But the religious liberty protected by the Constitution is abridged when the State affirmatively sponsors the particular religious practice of prayer. . . .

The District. . . . asks us to pretend that we do not recognize what every Santa Fe High School student understands clearly—that this policy is about prayer. The District further asks us to accept what is obviously untrue: that these messages are necessary to "solemnize" a football game and that this single-student, year-long position is essential to the protection of student speech. We refuse to turn a blind eye to the context in which this policy arose, and that context quells any doubt that this policy was implemented with the purpose of endorsing school prayer. . . .

The judgment of the Court of Appeals is, accordingly, affirmed.

CHIEF JUSTICE REHNQUIST, with whom JUSTICE SCALIA and JUSTICE THOMAS join, dissenting.

The Court distorts existing precedent to conclude that the school district's student-message program is invalid on its face under the Establishment Clause. But even more disturbing than its holding is the tone of the Court's opinion; it bristles with hostility to all things religious in public life. Neither the holding nor the tone of the opinion is faithful to the meaning of the Establishment Clause, when it is recalled that George Washington himself, at the request of the very Congress which passed the Bill of Rights, proclaimed a day of "public thanksgiving and prayer, to be observed by acknowledging with grateful hearts the many and signal favors of Almighty God." . . .

The Court also relies on our decision in *Lee* v. *Weisman* (1992), to support its conclusion. In *Lee,* we concluded that the content of the speech at issue, a graduation prayer given by a rabbi, was "directed and controlled" by a school official. In other words, at issue in *Weisman* was government speech. Here, by contrast, the potential speech at issue, if the policy had been allowed to proceed, would be a message or invocation selected or created by a student. That is, if there were speech at issue here, it would be private speech. The "crucial difference between government speech endorsing religion, which the Establishment Clause forbids, and private speech endorsing religion, which the Free Speech and Free Exercise Clauses protect," applies with particular force to the question of endorsement.

Had the policy been put into practice, the students may have chosen a speaker according to wholly secular criteria—like good public speaking skills or social popularity—and the student speaker may have chosen, on her own accord, to deliver a religious message. Such an application of the policy would likely pass constitutional muster.

▼▲▼

Justice John Paul Stevens, who had written the Court's decision in *Wallace* striking down the Alabama "voluntary prayer" law, held that when a student delivers a prayer on school property, during a school-sponsored event, using the school's public address system, and in conjunction with the school district policy that encourages public prayer, it is beyond the realm of private speech. Note here that Justices Kennedy and O'Connor, who voted to strike down the commencement prayer in *Weisman,* also viewed *Santa Fe* as a school prayer case, not a case about student free speech rights. Although Chief Justice Rehnquist criticized the majority opinion as "bristl[ing]" with "hostility towards religion," the Court, in *Santa Fe,* continued to hold the line dating back to *Engel* against government sponsorship of any sort involving prayer in the public schools. It certainly does not appear that the Court is prepared to depart from this position anytime soon, despite the best efforts of conservative religious groups to persuade the justices to do so.

Beyond School Prayer: Equal Treatment for Religious Speech

After the bitter battle over the congressional school prayer amendment in 1984, many mainline Protestant groups that had joined with the ACLU, the major Jewish organizations, and public education and civil liberties groups to defeat the amendment were hurt by charges from the newly emergent Christian Right that they were anti-religious. Even the National Council of Churches, which had opposed every single measure to overturn or bypass *Engel* and *Schempp,* criticized the ACLU as "almost exclusively concerned with establishment problems and hardly at all with free exercise."[58] Sensitive to their public portrayal as hostile to religion, these normally staunch supporters of the separation principle joined forces with conservative groups, such as the Christian Legal Society and the National Association of Evangelicals, to support the Equal Access Act of 1984.

Introduced by Senator Mark Hatfield (R–Ore.), a staunch opponent of the school prayer amendment, the Equal Access Act made it unlawful for any public secondary school receiving federal financial assistance to deny equal access or fair opportunity to any students seeking to conduct a meeting on school premises on the

Students taking part in religious worship before the beginning of the school day. The Supreme Court's decisions limiting religious activities in public schools remain among its most unpopular and contoversial.
Steve Liss/TimePix

basis of religious, political, philosophical, or other speech content. The law covered noncurriculum-related student groups, and permitted them to meet on school property during noninstructional time. As reassurance to groups normally opposed to a platform for religion in schools, the law prohibited schools and their employees from influencing the form or content of prayer or other religious activity, banned any expenditure of public funds to support student groups falling under the law's definition, and required no student or school employee to attend such meetings. Leo Pfeffer, who by 1984 was no longer the centralizing force among separationist groups that he was in the 1960s and 1970s, called the diverse coalition supporting the Equal Access Act a "political miracle."[59]

In *Board of Westside Community Schools* v. *Mergens* (1990), an 8-1 Court ruled that an Omaha, Nebraska, school's decision to prohibit a Christian Bible study club from using school facilities available to other student groups violated the Equal Access Act. *Mergens* was brought by the American Center for Law and Justice. The ACLJ argued that the Equal Access Act was about free speech rights for high school students. It was not, as a small handful of the law's opponents charged, a back-door effort to promote prayer and religious worship in the public schools. Encouraged by the Court's decision, the ACLJ, in *Lamb's Chapel* v. *Center Moriches Union Free School District* (1993), decided to see whether the Court was willing to extend the principles of equal access to include the right of community-based groups to use public schools for religious purposes.

Lamb's Chapel v. *Center Moriches Union Free School District*

508 U.S. 384 (1993)

Lamb's Chapel did not involve the Equal Access Act, but the larger principle of whether state law or local school board policy could exclude religious groups from using public school facilities when they were not in use if other community groups were allowed such access. In a 1981 case, *Widmar* v. *Vincent*, the Court held that public universities could not prohibit religious clubs from using empty classrooms for meetings if other student groups were permitted use of such space. The Court ruled that an open policy for student speech furthered important educational values and encouraged "all forms of discourse." The Equal Access Act of 1984 codified the "equal access" principles established by the Court in *Widmar*. *Lamb's Chapel* was the next step in the development of equal access for religious clubs to public school facilities.

In November 1989, the Center Moriches School District in Long Island, New York, rejected an application from Lamb's Chapel pastor John Steigerwald to show a film series produced by psychologist James C. Dobson. Dobson was a founder the Family Research Council and then-president of Focus on the Family, two of the most influential and well-funded Christian groups active in contemporary legal and political debates. Dobson had produced a six-part film series called "Turn Your Heart Toward Home," which addressed family and personal problems from a Christian perspective. The school board based its decision on an understanding of the New York law regulating access to public schools for community groups. The law permitted school boards to make the final determination on "social, civic and recreational" uses of school facilities, and any other uses pertaining to the welfare of the community. Center Moriches authorized the use of school facilities for social, civic, political, and recreational purposes. It did not grant access to "any group for religious purposes."

The ACLJ, fresh from success in *Mergens,* argued that, by singling out "religious speech," the decision of Center Moriches to exclude Lamb's Chapel amounted to viewpoint-based discrimination. The year before, in *R.A.V.* v. *St. Paul* (1992) (see Chapter 4), the Court ruled that an effort by St. Paul, Minnesota, to ban certain symbols from public display was unconstitutional because the law had the effect of protecting certain viewpoints while prohibiting others. Building on *Mergens* and *R.A.V.,* ACLJ attorney Jay Sekulow emphasized the free speech issues in Lamb's Chapel, giving barely a mention to the Establishment Clause. As in *Mergens,* the ACLJ, in addition to conservative groups such as the National Association of Evangelicals and the United States Catholic Conference, had plenty of support from moderate and liberal religious and civil liberties groups, including People for the American Way (the successful cosponsor of *Wallace* v. *Jaffree),* Americans United, the ACLU, and the Baptist Joint Committee.

The Court's decision was unanimous. Justice White delivered the opinion of the Court. Justice Kennedy filed a concurring opinion. Justice Scalia, joined by Justice Thomas, also concurred.

▼▲▼

Justice White delivered the opinion of the Court.

The issue in this case is whether . . . it violates the Free Speech Clause of the First Amendment, made applicable to the States by the Fourteenth Amendment, to deny a church access to school premises to exhibit for public viewing and for assertedly religious purposes, a film series dealing with family and child-rearing issues faced by parents today.

There is no question that the District, like the private owner of property, may legally preserve the property under its control for the use to which it is dedicated. . . .

This Court suggested in *Widmar* v. *Vincent* (1981) that the interest of the State in avoiding an Establishment Clause violation "may be [a] compelling" one justifying an abridgment of free speech otherwise protected by the First Amendment; but the Court went on to hold that permitting use of university property for religious purposes under the open access policy involved there would not be incompatible with the Court's Establishment Clause cases.

We have no more trouble than did the *Widmar* Court in disposing of the claimed defense on the ground that the posited fears of an Establishment Clause violation are unfounded. The showing of this film series would not have been during school hours, would not have been sponsored by the school, and would have been open to the public, not just to church members. The District property had repeatedly been used by a wide variety of private organizations. Under these circumstances, as in *Widmar,* there would have been [no realistic danger] that the community would [think that the District was endorsing religion or any particular creed] and any benefit to religion or to the Church would have been no more than incidental. As in *Widmar,* permitting District property to be used to exhibit the film series involved in this case would not have been an establishment of religion under the three-part test articulated in *Lemon* v. *Kurtzman* (1971): the challenged governmental action has a secular purpose, does not have the principal or primary effect of advancing or inhibiting religion, and does not foster an excessive entanglement with religion. . . .

The District also submits that it justifiably denied use of its property to a "radical" church for the purpose of proselytizing, since to do so would lead to threats of public unrest and even violence. There is nothing in the record to support such a justification, which in any event would be difficult to defend as a reason to deny the presentation of a religious point of view about a subject the District otherwise opens to discussion on District property.

For the reasons stated in this opinion, the judgment of the Court of Appeals is

Reversed.

JUSTICE KENNEDY, concurring in part and concurring in the judgment.

Given the issues presented, as well as the apparent unanimity of our conclusion that this overt, viewpoint-based discrimination contradicts the Speech Clause of the First Amendment and that there has been no substantial showing of a potential Establishment Clause violation, I agree with JUSTICE SCALIA that the Court's citation of *Lemon* v. *Kurtzman* (1971) is unsettling and unnecessary. The same can be said of the Court's use of the phrase "endorsing religion," which, as I have indicated elsewhere, cannot suffice as a rule of decision consistent with our precedents and our traditions in this part of our jurisprudence. With these observations, I concur in part and concur in the judgment.

JUSTICE SCALIA, with whom JUSTICE THOMAS joins, concurring in the judgment.

I join the Court's conclusion that the District's refusal to allow use of school facilities for petitioners' film viewing, while generally opening the schools for community activities, violates petitioners' First Amendment free speech rights to the extent it compelled the District's denial. I also agree with the Court that allowing Lamb's Chapel to use school facilities poses "no realistic danger" of a violation of the Establishment Clause, but I cannot accept most of its reasoning in this regard. The Court explains that the showing of petitioners' film on school property after school hours would not cause the community to "think that the District was endorsing religion or any particular creed," and further notes that access to school property would not violate the three-part test articulated in *Lemon* v. *Kurtzman*.

As to the Court's invocation of the *Lemon* test: like some ghoul in a late-night horror movie that repeatedly sits up in its grave and shuffles abroad after being repeatedly killed and buried, *Lemon* stalks our Establishment Clause jurisprudence once again, frightening the little children and school attorneys of Center Moriches Union Free School District. Its most recent burial, only last Term, was, to be sure, not fully six feet under: Our decision in *Lee* v. *Weisman* (1992) conspicuously avoided using the supposed "test," but also declined the invitation to repudiate it. Over the years, however, no fewer than five of the currently sitting Justices have, in their own opinions, personally driven pencils through the creature's heart (the author of today's opinion repeatedly), and a sixth has joined an opinion doing so.

The secret of the *Lemon* test's survival, I think, is that it is so easy to kill. It is there to scare us (and our audience) when we wish it to do so, but we can command it to return to the tomb at will. When we wish to strike down a practice it forbids, we invoke it; see, e.g., *Aguilar* v. *Fenton* (1985); when we wish to uphold a practice it forbids, we ignore it entirely, see *Marsh* v. *Chambers* (1983). . . . Such a docile and useful monster is worth keeping around, at least in a somnolent state; one never knows when one might need him.

For my part, I agree with the long list of constitutional scholars who have criticized *Lemon* and bemoaned the strange Establishment Clause geometry of crooked lines and wavering shapes its intermittent use has produced. I will decline to apply *Lemon*—whether it validates or invalidates the government action in question—and therefore cannot join the opinion of the Court today.

I cannot join for yet another reason: the Court's statement that the proposed use of the school's facilities is constitutional because (among other things) it would not signal endorsement of religion in general. What a strange notion, that a Constitution which itself gives "religion in general" preferential treatment (I refer to the Free Exercise Clause) forbids endorsement of religion in general. The attorney general of New York not only agrees with that strange notion, he has an explanation for it: "Religious advocacy," he writes, "serves the community only in the eyes of its adherents, and yields a benefit only to those who already believe." That was not the view of those who adopted our Constitution, who believed that the public virtues inculcated by religion are a public good.

For the reasons given by the Court, I agree that the Free Speech Clause of the First Amendment forbids what respondents have done here. As for the asserted Establishment Clause justification, I would hold, simply and clearly, that giving Lamb's Chapel nondiscriminatory access to school facilities cannot violate that provision because it does not signify state or local embrace of a particular religious sect.

Justice White had little trouble concluding that Center Moriches's policy of excluding religion violated the equal access principles the Court had developed in *Widmar* and *Mergens*. Indeed, the fact that Lamb's Chapel was a private, community-based group further strengthened the equal access claim. The Court was fractured over whether any real Establishment Clause issue even existed in *Lamb's Chapel*. Justice White believed enough of an issue of government support for religion was present to apply the *Lemon* test, while Justices Kennedy, Scalia, and Thomas regarded *Lamb's Chapel* as a free speech case involving viewpoint-based discrimination. Persuading the Court to view government policies that excluded religion from public schools or public places as free speech issues and not Establishment Clause matters had been the goal of the ACLJ and other conservative Christian groups since *Mergens*. Religious worship, proselytizing, Bible reading, and the like were now, in the eyes of the Court, forms of private speech that deserved protection from discriminatory government action. Moderate and liberal groups that had supported the Equal Access Act of 1984 and *Mergens* were now beginning to wonder how far the Court was prepared to extend the concept of equal treatment for religion. In *Rosenberger* v. *Virginia* (1995), the Court again stood at the crossroads of free speech, establishment, and religious free exercise. And this time, the result was a much more divided Court, reflecting the widening disagreement among religious, educational, and civil liberties groups over when equal treatment for religious speech had crossed the threshold into the realm of impermissible government support for core religious activities.

Rosenberger v. *Virginia*

515 U.S. 819 (1995)

In 1990, Ron Rosenberger was an undergraduate at the University of Virginia, when he formed Wide Awake Productions (WAP) for the purpose of providing "a unifying focus for Christians of multicultural backgrounds." Like other student organizations, Wide Awake Productions offered several publications describing its mission, activities, and news of interest. University regulations permitted all qualifying student organizations to receive financial support from the Student Activities Fund (SAF). The SAF drew its funding from the mandatory student activity fee of $14, assessed to all full-time students each semester. WAP's main outlet was its newspaper, *Wide Awake: A Christian Perspective*, which sought to promote a "Christian perspective on both personal and community issues, especially those relevant to college students at the University of Virginia." On the paper's masthead, the editors "challenge[d] Christians to live, in word and deed, according to the faith they proclaim and to encourage students to consider what a personal relationship with Jesus Christ means."

WAP had qualified as a Contracted Independent Organization (CIO), the classification given to all groups receiving approval from the student council for university funding. University guidelines prohibited student fees from being used to pay for "religious activities," described as anything that "primarily promotes or manifests a particular belief in or about a deity or an ultimate reality." Philanthropic contributions and activities, political activities, any activity that would jeopardize the university's tax-exempt status, honoraria and speaker's fees, and social entertainment are also ineligible for student funds. The appropriations committee of the Student Council denied WAP's request for $5,862 to pay for printing costs associated with *Wide Awake*, ruling that the newspaper promoted a religious belief and thus, under CIO guidelines, was ineligible for reimbursement. Rosenberger lost an appeal before the full Student Council.

Seventy-five miles away in Washington, D.C., the Center for Individual Rights (CIR), a conservative legal group that had just won a major victory invalidating the University of Texas's affirmative action program in a federal appeals court (see Chapter 11), read about the *Wide Awake* controversy. It was willing to represent Rosenberger if he wanted to file suit against the university. CIR worked closely with the ACLJ, coordinating publicity and legal support on behalf of Ron Rosenberger's case. In contrast, the ACLU, the AJCongress, Americans United, the Baptist Joint Committee, and half a dozen other groups that had endorsed equal access and supported the right of Lamb's Chapel to use public school facilities did not interpret the University of Virginia's action as viewpoint-based discrimination. They saw *Rosenberger* as a case involving public funding for religious proselytizing, not free speech.

Rosenberger lost in federal district court and in the Fourth Circuit Court of Appeals, with the latter concluding that the entanglement prong of the *Lemon* test was "most plainly implicated by this case."

The Court's decision was 5 to 4. Justice Kennedy delivered the opinion of the Court. Justices O'Connor and Thomas filed separate concurring opinions. Justice Souter, joined by Justices Stevens, Ginsburg, and Breyer, dissented.

▼▲▼

JUSTICE KENNEDY delivered the opinion of the Court.

It is axiomatic that the government may not regulate speech based on its substantive content or the message it conveys. In the realm of private speech or expression, government regulation may not favor one speaker over another. Discrimination against speech because of its message is presumed to be unconstitutional. . . . When the government targets not subject matter but particular views taken by speakers on a subject, the violation of the First Amendment is all the more blatant. Viewpoint discrimination is thus an egregious form of content discrimination. The government must abstain from regulating speech when the specific motivating ideology or the opinion or perspective of the speaker is the rationale for the restriction.

These principles provide the framework forbidding the State from exercising viewpoint discrimination, even when the limited public forum is one of its own creation. In a case involving a school district's provision of school facilities for private uses, we declared that "[t]here is no question that the District, like the private owner of property, may legally preserve the property under its control for the use to which it is dedicated," *Lamb's Chapel* v. *Center Moriches Union Free School Dist.* (1993). . . . Thus, in determining whether the State is acting to preserve the limits of the forum it has created so that the exclusion of a class of speech is legitimate, we have observed a distinction between, on the one hand, content discrimination, which may be permissible if it preserves the purposes of that limited forum, and, on the other hand, viewpoint discrimination, which is presumed impermissible when directed against speech otherwise within the forum's limitations.

The SAF is a forum more in a metaphysical than in a spatial or geographic sense, but the same principles are applicable. The most recent and most apposite case is our decision in *Lamb's Chapel.* There, a school district had opened school facilities for use after school hours by community groups for a wide variety of social, civic, and recreational purposes. The district, however, had enacted a formal policy against opening facilities to groups for religious purposes. Invoking its policy, the district rejected a request from a group desiring to show a film series addressing various child-rearing questions from a "Christian perspective." There was no indication in the record in *Lamb's Chapel* that the request to use the school facilities was "denied for any reason other than the fact that the presentation would have been from a religious perspective." . . .

By the very terms of the SAF prohibition, the University does not exclude religion as a subject matter but selects for disfavored treatment those student journalistic efforts with religious editorial viewpoints. Religion may be a vast area of inquiry, but it also provides, as it did here, a specific premise, a perspective, a standpoint from which a variety of subjects may be discussed and considered. The prohibited perspective, not the general subject matter, resulted in the refusal to make third-party payments, for the subjects discussed were otherwise within the approved category of publications. . . .

The University tries to escape the consequences of our holding in *Lamb's Chapel* by urging that this case involves the provision of funds rather than access to facilities. The University begins with the unremarkable proposition that the State must have substantial discretion in determining how to allocate scarce resources to accomplish its educational mission. . . . [T]he University argues that content-based funding decisions are both inevitable and lawful. . . . Were the reasoning of *Lamb's Chapel* to apply to funding decisions as well as to those involving access to facilities, it is urged, its holding "would become a judicial juggernaut, constitutionalizing the ubiquitous content-based decisions that schools, colleges, and other government entities routinely make in the allocation of public funds." . . . When the government disburses public funds to private entities to convey a governmental message, it may take legitimate and appropriate steps, to ensure that its message is neither garbled nor distorted by the grantee.

It does not follow, however, and we did not suggest in *Widmar,* that viewpoint-based restrictions are proper when the University does not itself speak or subsidize transmittal of a message it favors but instead expends funds to encourage a diversity of views from private speakers. A holding that the University may not discriminate based on the viewpoint of private persons whose speech it facilitates does not restrict the University's own speech, which is controlled by different principles. The University's regulation now before us . . . has a speech-based restriction as its sole rationale and operative principle. . . .

Vital First Amendment speech principles are at stake here. The first danger to liberty lies in granting the State the power to examine publications to determine whether or not they are based on some ultimate idea and if so for the State to classify them. The second, and corollary, danger is to speech from the chilling of individual thought and expression. That danger is especially real in the University setting, where the State acts against a background and tradition of thought and experiment that is at the center of our intellectual and philosophic tradition. . . . The quality and creative power of student intellectual life to this day remains a vital measure of a school's influence and attainment. For the University, by regulation, to cast disapproval on particular viewpoints of its students risks the suppression of free speech and creative inquiry in one of the vital centers for the nation's intellectual life, its college and university campuses. . . .

Based on the principles we have discussed, we hold that the regulation invoked to deny SAF support, both in its terms and in its application to these petitioners, is a denial of their right of free speech guaranteed by the First Amendment. It remains to be considered whether the violation following from the University's action is excused by the necessity of complying with the Constitution's prohibition against state establishment of religion. We turn to that question.

A central lesson of our decisions is that a significant factor in upholding governmental programs in the face of Establishment Clause attack is their neutrality towards religion. We have decided a series of cases addressing the receipt of government benefits where religion or religious views are implicated in some degree. The first case in our modern Establishment Clause jurisprudence was *Everson v. Board of Education* (1947). There we cautioned that in enforcing the prohibition against laws respecting establishment of religion, we must "be sure that we do not inadvertently prohibit [the government] from extending its general state law benefits to all its citizens without regard to their religious belief." We have held that the guarantee of neutrality is respected, not offended, when the government, following neutral criteria and evenhanded policies, extends benefits to recipients whose ideologies and viewpoints, including religious ones, are broad and diverse. More than once have we rejected the position that the Establishment Clause even justifies, much less requires, a refusal to extend free speech rights to religious speakers who participate in broad-reaching government programs neutral in design.

The governmental program here is neutral toward religion. There is no suggestion that the University created it to advance religion or adopted some ingenious device with the purpose of aiding a religious cause. The object of the SAF is to open a forum for speech and to support various student enterprises, including the publication of newspapers, in recognition of the diversity and creativity of student life. . . . WAP did not seek a subsidy because of its Christian editorial viewpoint; it sought funding as a student journal, which it was.

Government neutrality is apparent in the State's overall scheme in a further meaningful respect. The program respects the critical difference "between government speech endorsing religion, which the Establishment Clause forbids, and private speech endorsing religion, which the Free Speech and Free Exercise Clauses protect." In this case, "the government has not willfully fostered or encouraged" any mistaken impression that the student newspapers speak for the University. The University has taken pains to disassociate itself from the private speech involved in this case. . . .

It does not violate the Establishment Clause for a public university to grant access to its facilities on a religion-neutral basis to a wide spectrum of student groups, including groups which use meeting rooms for sectarian activities, accompanied by some devotional exercises. This is so even where the upkeep, maintenance, and repair of the facilities attributed to those uses is paid from a student activities fund to which students are required to contribute. The government usually acts by spending money. Even the provision of a meeting room, as in *Mergens* and *Widmar*, involved governmental expenditure, if only in the form of electricity and heating or cooling costs. The error made by . . . the dissent lies in focusing on the money that is undoubtedly expended by the government, rather than on the nature of the benefit received by the recipient. If the expenditure of governmental funds is prohibited whenever those funds pay for a service that is, pursuant to a religion-neutral program, used by a group for sectarian purposes, then *Widmar*, *Mergens*, and *Lamb's Chapel* would have to be overruled. . . .

To obey the Establishment Clause, it was not necessary for the University to deny eligibility to student publications because of their viewpoint. The neutrality commanded of the State by the separate Clauses of the First Amendment was compromised by the University's course of action. The viewpoint discrimination inherent in the University's regulation required public officials to scan and interpret student publications to discern their underlying philosophic assumptions respecting religious theory and belief. That course of action was a denial of the right of free speech and would risk fostering a pervasive bias or hostility to religion, which could undermine the very neutrality the Establishment Clause requires. There is no Establishment Clause violation in the University's honoring its duties under the Free Speech Clause.

JUSTICE O'CONNOR, concurring.

This case lies at the intersection of the principle of government neutrality and the prohibition on state funding of religious activities. It is clear that the University has established a generally applicable program to encourage the free exchange of ideas by its students, an expressive marketplace that includes some 15 student publications with predictably divergent viewpoints. It is equally clear that petitioners' viewpoint is religious and that publication of *Wide Awake* is a religious activity, under both the University's regulation and a fair reading of our precedents. Not to finance *Wide Awake,* according to petitioners, violates the principle of neutrality by sending a message of hostility toward religion. To finance *Wide Awake,* argues the University, violates the prohibition on direct state funding of religious activities.

When two bedrock principles so conflict, understandably neither can provide the definitive answer. Reliance on categorical platitudes is unavailing. Resolution instead depends on the hard task of judging—sifting through the details and determining whether the challenged program offends the Establishment Clause. Such judgment requires courts to draw lines, sometimes quite fine, based on the particular facts of each case. . . .

The need for careful judgment and fine distinctions presents itself even in extreme cases. *Everson* v. *Board of Education* (1947) provided perhaps the strongest exposition of the no-funding principle: "No tax in any amount, large or small, can be levied to support any religious activities or institutions, whatever they may be called, or whatever form they may adopt to teach or practice religion." Yet the Court approved the use of public funds, in a general program, to reimburse parents for their children's bus fares to attend Catholic schools. Although some would cynically dismiss the Court's disposition as inconsistent with its protestations, the decision reflected the need to rely on careful judgment—not simple categories—when two principles, of equal historical and jurisprudential pedigree, come into unavoidable conflict.

So it is in this case. The nature of the dispute does not admit of categorical answers, nor should any be inferred from the Court's decision today. Instead, certain considerations specific to the program at issue lead me to conclude that by providing the same assistance to *Wide Awake* that it does to other publications, the University would not be endorsing the magazine's religious perspective.

First, the student organizations, at the University's insistence, remain strictly independent of the University. The University's agreement with the Contracted Independent Organizations (CIO)—i.e., student groups—provides: "The University is a Virginia public corporation and the CIO is not part of that corporation, but rather exists and operates independently of the University. . . ."

Second, financial assistance is distributed in a manner that ensures its use only for permissible purposes. A student organization seeking assistance must submit disbursement requests; if approved, the funds are paid directly to the third-party vendor and do not pass through the organization's coffers. . . . This feature also makes this case analogous to a school providing equal access to a generally available printing press (or other physical facilities), and unlike a block grant to religious organizations.

Third, assistance is provided to the religious publication in a context that makes improbable any perception of government endorsement of the religious message. *Wide Awake* does not exist in a vacuum. It competes with 15 other magazines and newspapers for advertising and readership. The widely divergent viewpoints of these many purveyors of opinion, all supported on an equal basis by the University, significantly diminishes the danger that the message of any one publication is perceived as endorsed by the University. . . .

The Court's decision today therefore neither trumpets the supremacy of the neutrality principle nor signals the demise of the funding prohibition in Establishment Clause jurisprudence. . . . When bedrock principles collide, they test the limits of categorical obstinacy and expose the flaws and dangers of a Grand Unified Theory that may turn out to be neither grand nor unified. The Court today does only what courts must do in many Establishment Clause cases—focus on specific features of a particular government action to ensure that it does not violate the Constitution. By withholding from *Wide Awake* assistance that the University provides generally to all other student publications, the University has discriminated on the basis of the magazine's religious viewpoint in violation of the Free Speech Clause.

JUSTICE SOUTER, with whom JUSTICE STEVENS, JUSTICE GINSBURG, and JUSTICE BREYER join, dissenting.

The Court today, for the first time, approves direct funding of core religious activities by an arm of the State. It does so, however, only after erroneous treatment of some familiar principles of law implementing the First Amendment's Establishment and Speech Clauses, and by viewing the very funds in question as beyond the reach of the Establishment Clause's funding restrictions as such. Because there is no warrant for distinguishing among public funding sources for purposes of applying the First Amendment's prohibition of religious establishment, I would hold that the University's refusal to support petitioners' religious activities is compelled by the Establishment Clause. . . .

The Court's difficulties will be all the more clear after a closer look at *Wide Awake* than the majority opinion affords. The character of the magazine is candidly disclosed on the opening page of the first issue, where the editor-in-chief announces *Wide Awake's* mission in a letter to the readership signed, "Love in Christ": it is "to challenge Christians to live, in word and deed, according to the faith they proclaim and to encourage students to consider what a personal relationship with Jesus Christ means." The masthead of every issue bears St. Paul's exhortation, that "[t]he hour has come for you to awake from your slumber, because our salvation is nearer now than when we first believed. Romans 13:11." . . .

Even featured essays on facially secular topics become platforms from which to call readers to fulfill the tenets of Christianity in their lives. Although a piece on racism has some general discussion on the subject, it proceeds beyond even the analysis and interpretation of biblical texts to conclude with the counsel to take action because that is the Christian thing to do:

> God calls us to take the risks of voluntarily stepping out of our comfort zones and to take joy in the whole richness of our inheritance in the body of Christ. We must take the love we receive from God and share it with all peoples of the world.
>
> Racism is a disease of the heart, soul, and mind, and only when it is extirpated from the individual consciousness and replaced with the love and peace of God will true personal and communal healing begin.

The same progression occurs in an article on eating disorders, which begins with descriptions of anorexia and bulimia and ends with this religious message:

> As thinking people who profess a belief in God, we must grasp firmly the truth, the reality of who we are because of Christ. Christ is the Bread of Life (John 6:35). Through Him, we are full. He alone can provide the ultimate source of spiritual fulfillment which permeates the emotional, psychological, and physical dimensions of our lives.

This writing is no merely descriptive examination of religious doctrine or even of ideal Christian practice in confronting life's social and personal problems. Nor is it merely the expression of editorial opinion that incidentally coincides with Christian ethics and reflects a Christian view of human obligation. It is straightforward exhortation to enter into a relationship with God as revealed in Jesus Christ, and to satisfy a series of moral obligations derived from the teachings of Jesus Christ. These are not the words of "student news, information, opinion, entertainment, or academic communicatio[n] . . ." but the words of "challenge [to] Christians to live, in word and deed, according to the faith they proclaim and . . . to consider what a personal relationship with Jesus Christ means." The subject is not the discourse of the scholar's study or the seminar room, but of the evangelist's mission station and the pulpit. It is nothing other than the preaching of the word, which (along with the sacraments) is what most branches of Christianity offer those called to the religious life.

Using public funds for the direct subsidization of preaching the word is categorically forbidden under the Establishment Clause, and if the Clause was meant to accomplish nothing else, it was meant to bar this use of public money. . . .

The principle against direct funding with public money is patently violated by the contested use of today's student activity fee. Like today's taxes generally, the fee is Madison's threepence. The University exercises the power of the State to compel a student to pay it, and the use of any part of it for the direct support of religious activity thus strikes at what we have repeatedly held to be the heart of the prohibition on establishment.

The Court, accordingly, has never before upheld direct state funding of the sort of proselytizing published in *Wide Awake* and, in fact, has categorically condemned state programs directly aiding religious activity. Even when the Court has upheld aid to an institution performing both secular and sectarian functions, it has always made a searching enquiry to ensure that the institution kept the secular activities separate from its sectarian ones, with any direct aid flowing only to the former and never the latter. . . .

Why does the Court not apply this clear law to these clear facts and conclude, as I do, that the funding scheme here is a clear constitutional violation? The answer must be in part that the Court fails to confront the evidence set out in the preceding section. . . . And so it is easy for the Court to lose sight of what the University students and the Court of Appeals found so obvious, and to blanch the patently and frankly evangelistic character of the magazine by unrevealing allusions to religious points of view. . . .

Although it was a taxation scheme that moved Madison to write in the first instance, the Court has never held that government resources obtained without taxation could be used for direct religious support, and our cases on direct government aid have frequently spoken in terms in no way limited to tax revenues. . . .

Nothing in the Court's opinion would lead me to end this enquiry into the application of the Establishment

Clause any differently from the way I began it. The Court is ordering an instrumentality of the State to support religious evangelism with direct funding. This is a flat violation of the Establishment Clause. . . .

The issue whether a distinction is based on viewpoint does not turn simply on whether a government regulation happens to be applied to a speaker who seeks to advance a particular viewpoint; the issue, of course, turns on whether the burden on speech is explained by reference to viewpoint. As when deciding whether a speech restriction is content-based or content-neutral, "[t]he government's purpose is the controlling consideration." So, for example, a city that enforces its excessive noise ordinance by pulling the plug on a rock band using a forbidden amplification system is not guilty of viewpoint discrimination simply because the band wishes to use that equipment to espouse antiracist views. Nor does a municipality's decision to prohibit political advertising on bus placards amount to viewpoint discrimination when in the course of applying this policy it denies space to a person who wishes to speak in favor of a particular political candidate.

Accordingly, the prohibition on viewpoint discrimination serves that important purpose of the Free Speech Clause, which is to bar the government from skewing public debate. Other things being equal, viewpoint discrimination occurs when government allows one message while prohibiting the messages of those who can reasonably be expected to respond. It is precisely this element of taking sides in a public debate that identifies viewpoint discrimination and makes it the most pernicious of all distinctions based on content. Thus, if government assists those espousing one point of view, neutrality requires it to assist those espousing opposing points of view, as well. . . .

Since I cannot see the future I cannot tell whether today's decision portends much more than making a shambles out of student activity fees in public colleges. Still, my apprehension is whetted by Chief Justice Burger's warning in *Lemon* v. *Kurtzman* (1971): "[I]n constitutional adjudication some steps, which when taken were thought to approach 'the verge,' have become the platform for yet further steps. A certain momentum develops in constitutional theory and it can be a 'downhill thrust' easily set in motion but difficult to retard or stop."

▼▲▼

On the same day it decided *Rosenberger,* the Court, 7 to 2, in *Capitol Square Review Board* v. *Pinette* (1995), ruled that the Ku Klux Klan was entitled to display an unadorned Latin cross in a downtown Columbus, Ohio, public square. Following *Lamb's Chapel, Mergens,* and *Widmar,* Justice Scalia, writing for a plurality, concluded that the cross was private speech that did not take on government endorsement by the fact that it stood alone. Justice O'Connor, joined by Justices Souter and Breyer, contended that no reasonable passersby would interpret the government's tolerance of the Klan's cross as an endorsement of religion. Unpersuaded that the cross was anything other than what most "reasonable" people assumed it was—a religious symbol—Justice Stevens dissented, concluding that "[s]ome might [perceive] the cross as a message of love, others as a message of hate, still others as a message of exclusion—a Statehouse sign calling powerfully to mind their outsider status. In any event, it was a message that the State of Ohio may not communicate to its citizens without violating the Establishment Clause."[60]

Still, all but two justices in *Pinette* agreed that the Klan's cross was private religious speech protected by the First Amendment. And just as *Pinette* brought together the intersection of free speech and the prohibition against the establishment of religion, *Rosenberger* added a third element to the mix: the use of public funds to underwrite a religious message. Two of the justices who saw *Pinette* as a free speech case, Souter and Breyer, rejected Ron Rosenberger's argument that he had a similar such right to receive public funds to underwrite *Wide Awake.* Justice Souter, who, since *Weisman,* has emerged as the Court's most ardent defender of the separation principle, saw *Rosenberger* as a case about government funding for "preaching the word," a religious activity that is "categorically forbidden by the state." The Court's decision in *Rosenberger* came down to how the justices, having had the battle lines drawn by the nearly two dozen *amici* present on behalf of the parties, saw the student council's decision to deny funds to *Wide Awake.* Was *Rosenberger* a case about equal access for student speakers or public funding for religion?

The AJCongress, the ACLU, and, to a lesser extent, separationist groups such as the AJCommittee, the ADL, and Americans United helped shape the early dynamics of church-state litigation involving religion and the public schools. As we shall see in our next section, they also played the same role in cases involving government assistance to parochial schools over a similar period of time. In like fashion, the conservative religious movement that sprang to life in the 1980s has had a formidable impact on the Court's increasing willingness to revisit some of its most important decisions in the area. *Rosenberger* might never have gotten off the ground if not for the willingness of a sympathetic group to offer its support. Prior to 1980, liberal separationist groups dominated church-state litigation; since then, conservative groups supporting a much more relaxed relationship between government and religion have taken to the courts with great success, introducing a new and powerful element into the dynamics that propel contemporary church-state litigation.[61]

Soon, the conservative religious bar turned its attention to another front—government funding of parochial schools and church-related programs. Equal treatment and nondiscrimination had been effective arguments to justify greater access for religion in public education, so why not pursue that same approach on parochial aid?

Government Funding for Parochial Schools

By the early 1960s, less than half a dozen cases had defined the boundaries of Establishment Clause law, with only one of those, *Everson* v. *Board of Education,* involving the constitutionality of public funding for parochial schools. Under Chief Justice Earl Warren (1953–1969), the Court decided the only case involving parochial aid, *Board of Education* v. *Allen* (1968), a decision that cut against the grain of its earlier decisions on school prayer.[62] In *Allen,* the Court, 6 to 3, upheld a New York law that required the state to lend secular textbooks to students in religious schools. Relying on the "child benefit theory" established in *Everson,* Justice White ruled that New York's textbook-loan program assisted children attending religious schools, and not the schools themselves. Justice White even noted that the plaintiffs, represented by the ACLU and Leo Pfeffer, had presented a "meager record" in support of their claim that textbook loans enabled religious schools to advance their beliefs at public expense. But *Everson's* author, Justice Black, saw nothing analogous in the two cases, writing that "upholding a State's power to pay bus or streetcar fares for school children cannot provide support for the validity of a state law using tax-raised funds to buy school books for a religious school."[63] Black continued in an even more ominous vein:

> [T]o authorize a State to tax its residents for such church purposes is to put the State squarely in the religious activities of certain religious groups that happen to be strong enough politically to write their own religious preferences and prejudices into the law. This links state and churches together in controlling the lives and destinies of our citizenship—a citizenship composed of people of myriad religious faiths, some of them bitterly hostile to and completely intolerant of the others.[64]

Justice White had relied upon *Schempp's* purpose and effect test to analyze the New York law. Although Black mentioned the constitutional difficulties of any financial relationship linking church and state, he offered no approach to incorporate the *Schempp* test that might prove helpful in placing limits on public funds. Earlier, in *Flast* v. *Cohen* (1968) (Volume 1, Chapter 3), the case that established the right of taxpayers to challenge public expenditures that were alleged to violate their constitutional rights, Pfeffer had argued that such a relationship created "excessive entanglement" between church and state. Ironically, *Allen* had been possible because of Pfeffer's victory in *Flast.* Having lost the initial round in the battle over public funding for religious schools, Pfeffer and the AJCongress, along with the ACLU, were determined to challenge one of the many state laws passed in the wake of *Allen.* Ultimately, they settled on two laws, one from Pennsylvania, the other from Rhode Island, each offering comprehensive public financial aid packages to parochial schools. The result was *Lemon* v. *Kurtzman* (1971), a decision that dramatically reversed the course on parochial aid chartered in *Allen. Lemon* also opened a whole new controversy over the Court's adoption of the excessive entanglement standard to augment the *Schempp* test.

Lemon v. *Kurtzman*

403 U.S. 602 (1971)

In 1965, Congress passed the Elementary and Secondary Education Act, then the most comprehensive federal aid package ever conceived to bolster the financial resources of state and local schools. The ESEA's chief purpose was to supplement lower-income school districts whose resources were inferior to those of their more affluent neighbors. But, in a departure from previous and far less ambitious federal efforts to assist education, the ESEA, for the first time, made private schools—including religious schools—eligible for government financial aid. Indeed, certain provisions of the law *required* private schools to receive money. For example, the New York law upheld in *Allen* came directly from the ESEA's mandate.

Only the major Jewish organizations and the ACLU opposed the ESEA when it was introduced in Congress. That same legislative session, Leo Pfeffer had cobbled together a coalition including education and Protestant groups to defeat the Becker Amendment, the proposal to reverse *Engel* and *Schempp*. Those same groups joined with Catholic groups and Orthodox Jewish groups to support the ESEA. Since Orthodox Jewish day schools stood to benefit from the ESEA, they joined their Christian allies to support the legislation. On this and nearly every other Establishment Clause issue, Orthodox Jews stand apart from the Reform and Conservative Jews who have always formed the core of the membership of the AJCongress, the AJCommittee, and the ADL. Protestant groups understood the dangers of the law's provisions for private schools, but believed they needed to go along or the public schools would lose federal money.

Between the ESEA's passage and the Court's decision in *Lemon,* nine states passed laws providing direct services to parochial schools, including Pennsylvania and Rhode Island, which Pfeffer considered the easiest to attack. Pennsylvania's law permitted the state superintendent of public instruction to contract for the direct purchase of so-called secular education services for use in private and parochial schools. These services included teachers' salaries, books and instructional materials, and auxiliary programs for which these schools would now be reimbursed by the state. Funding for the program was drawn from the state's horse-racing operations. The law did include a provision that prohibited parochial schools from receiving reimbursement for courses and materials that included religious content. Still, over 96 percent of nonpublic reimbursement went to religious schools, most of which were Catholic. In September 1969, after the state began reimbursing eligible schools, Pfeffer, in conjunction with the ACLU, organized a coalition of religious, educational, and civil liberties groups to challenge the statute. The organizational plaintiffs included the Pennsylvania Jewish Community Relations Council, the Protestant State Council of Churches, the NAACP, the Pennsylvania State Education Association, and the Pennsylvania office of the ACLU.

The Rhode Island Salary Supplement Act of 1969 authorized state officials to offer instructors in nonpublic schools up to 15 percent of their current annual salary in an effort to equalize compensation levels with those of their public school counterparts. Private school salaries could not exceed those paid to public school teachers, and eligible teachers in religious schools had to sign agreements that they would teach secular subjects only. Twenty-five percent of the state's elementary school students attended private schools, 95 percent of which were Catholic.

In *Robinson* v. *DiCenso* and *Earley* v. *DiCenso,* a three-judge federal district court struck down the Rhode Island law in a lawsuit brought by the American Jewish Congress, working closely with a local affiliate of the ACLU. The lower court found the parochial assistance program created "excessive entanglement" between church and state. The Court had added the excessive entanglement prong to the *Schempp* purpose and effect test during the previous term in *Walz* v. *Tax Commission* (1970), in which it ruled that tax exemptions for religious institutions did not violate the Establishment Clause. By an 8-1 margin, the Court ruled that eliminating tax exemptions would foster excessive government entanglement with religion by introducing the state into the financial affairs of churches. The Rhode Island cases were the first in which a federal court declared parochial assistance unconstitutional under what later became the *Lemon* test.

A divided three-judge federal court in Pennsylvania upheld the state's Non-Public Elementary and Secondary Education Act, finding that the law's primary purpose and effect was to aid public schools. Religious schools were only the incidental beneficiaries of public assistance. The Supreme Court granted review to all three cases and consolidated them for oral argument for the 1970–1971 term.

The Court's decision in *Lemon* was 8 to 0; in the *DiCenso* cases, the vote was 8 to 1. Chief Justice Burger delivered the opinion of the Court in all three cases. Justices Brennan and White filed concurring opinions in *Lemon*. Justice Douglas, joined by Justice Black, concurred in the *DiCenso* cases. Justice White dissented. Justice Marshall did not participate in either case.

▼▲▼

MR. CHIEF JUSTICE BURGER delivered the opinion of the Court.

These two appeals raise questions as to Pennsylvania and Rhode Island statutes providing state aid to church-related elementary and secondary schools. Both statutes are challenged as violative of the Establishment and Free Exercise Clauses of the First Amendment and the Due Process Clause of the Fourteenth Amendment. . . . We hold that both statutes are unconstitutional. . . .

In *Everson* v. *Board of Education* (1947), this Court upheld a state statute that reimbursed the parents of parochial school children for bus transportation expenses. There, MR. JUSTICE BLACK, writing for the majority, suggested that the decision carried to "the verge" of forbidden territory under the Religion Clauses. Candor compels acknowledgment, moreover, that we can only dimly perceive the lines of demarcation in this extraordinarily sensitive area of constitutional law.

The language of the Religion Clauses of the First Amendment is, at best, opaque, particularly when compared with other portions of the Amendment. Its authors did not simply prohibit the establishment of a state church or a state religion, an area history shows they regarded as very important and fraught with great dangers. Instead, they commanded that there should be "no law respecting an establishment of religion." A law may be one "respecting" the forbidden objective while falling short of its total realization. A law "respecting" the proscribed result, that is, the establishment of religion, is not always easily identifiable as one violative of the Clause. A given law might not establish a state religion, but nevertheless be one "respecting" that end in the sense of being a step that could lead to such establishment, and hence offend the First Amendment.

In the absence of precisely stated constitutional prohibitions, we must draw lines with reference to the three main evils against which the Establishment Clause was intended to afford protection: "sponsorship, financial support, and active involvement of the sovereign in religious activity," *Walz* v. *Tax Commission* (1970).

Every analysis in this area must begin with consideration of the cumulative criteria developed by the Court over many years. Three such tests may be gleaned from our cases. First, the statute must have a secular legislative purpose; second, its principal or primary effect must be one that neither advances nor inhibits religion; finally, the statute must not foster "an excessive government entanglement with religion."

Inquiry into the legislative purposes of the Pennsylvania and Rhode Island statutes affords no basis for a conclusion that the legislative intent was to advance religion. On the contrary, the statutes themselves clearly state that they are intended to enhance the quality of the secular education in all schools covered by the compulsory attendance laws. There is no reason to believe the legislatures meant anything else. A State always has a legitimate concern for maintaining minimum standards in all schools it allows to operate. . . . The legislatures of Rhode Island and Pennsylvania have concluded that secular and religious education are identifiable and separable. In the abstract, we have no quarrel with this conclusion.

The two legislatures, however, have also recognized that church-related elementary and secondary schools have a significant religious mission, and that a substantial portion of their activities is religiously oriented. They have therefore sought to create statutory restrictions designed to guarantee the separation between secular and religious educational functions, and to ensure that State financial aid supports only the former. All these provisions are precautions taken in candid recognition that these programs approached, even if they did not intrude upon, the forbidden areas under the Religion Clauses. We need not decide whether these legislative precautions restrict the principal or primary effect of the programs to the point where they do not offend the Religion Clauses, for we conclude that the cumulative impact of the entire relationship arising under the statutes in each State involves excessive entanglement between government and religion.

In *Walz*, the Court upheld state tax exemptions for real property owned by religious organizations and used for religious worship. That holding, however, tended to confine, rather than enlarge, the area of permissible state involvement with religious institutions by calling for close scrutiny of the degree of entanglement involved in the relationship. The objective is to prevent, as far as possible, the intrusion of either into the precincts of the other.

Our prior holdings do not call for total separation between church and state; total separation is not possible in an absolute sense. Some relationship between government and religious organizations is inevitable. Fire inspections, building and zoning regulations, and state requirements under compulsory school attendance laws are examples of necessary and permissible contacts. Indeed, under the statutory exemption before us in *Walz*, the State had a continuing burden to ascertain that the exempt property was, in fact, being used for religious worship. Judicial caveats against entanglement must recognize that the line of separation, far from being a "wall," is a blurred, indistinct, and variable barrier depending on all the circumstances of a particular relationship.

This is not to suggest, however, that we are to engage in a legalistic minuet in which precise rules and forms must govern. A true minuet is a matter of pure form and style, the observance of which is itself the substantive end. Here we examine the form of the relationship for the light that it casts on the substance.

In order to determine whether the government entanglement with religion is excessive, we must examine the character and purposes of the institutions that are benefited, the nature of the aid that the State provides, and the resulting relationship between the government and the religious authority. . . . Here we find that both statutes foster an impermissible degree of entanglement.

Rhode Island Program

The church schools involved in the program are located close to parish churches. This understandably permits convenient access for religious exercises, since instruction in faith and morals is part of the total educational process. The school buildings contain identifying religious symbols such as crosses on the exterior and crucifixes, and religious paintings and statues either in the classrooms or hallways. Although only approximately 30 minutes a day are devoted to direct religious instruction, there are religiously oriented extracurricular activities. Approximately two-thirds of the teachers in these schools are nuns of various religious orders. Their dedicated efforts provide an atmosphere in which religious instruction and religious vocations are natural and proper parts of life in such schools. Indeed, as the District Court found, the role of teaching nuns in enhancing the religious atmosphere has led the parochial school authorities to attempt to maintain a one-to-one ratio between nuns and lay teachers in all schools, rather than to permit some to be staffed almost entirely by lay teachers.

On the basis of these findings, the District Court concluded that the parochial schools constituted "an integral part of the religious mission of the Catholic Church." The various characteristics of the schools make them "a powerful vehicle for transmitting the Catholic faith to the next generation." This process of inculcating religious doctrine is, of course, enhanced by the impressionable age of the pupils, in primary schools particularly. In short, parochial schools involve substantial religious activity and purpose. . . .

The dangers and corresponding entanglements are enhanced by the particular form of aid that the Rhode Island Act provides. Our decisions from *Everson* to *Allen* have permitted the States to provide church-related schools with secular, neutral, or nonideological services, facilities, or materials. Bus transportation, school lunches, public health services, and secular textbooks supplied in common to all students were not thought to offend the Establishment Clause. We note that the dissenters in *Allen* seemed chiefly concerned with the pragmatic difficulties involved in ensuring the truly secular content of the textbooks provided at state expense.

We cannot . . . refuse here to recognize that teachers have a substantially different ideological character from books. In terms of potential for involving some aspect of faith or morals in secular subjects, a textbook's content is ascertainable, but a teacher's handling of a subject is not. We cannot ignore the danger that a teacher under religious control and discipline poses to the separation of the religious from the purely secular aspects of precollege education. The conflict of functions inheres in the situation.

In our view, the record shows these dangers are present to a substantial degree. The Rhode Island Roman Catholic elementary schools are under the general supervision of the Bishop of Providence and his appointed representative, the Diocesan Superintendent of Schools. In most cases, each individual parish, however, assumes the ultimate financial responsibility for the school, with the parish priest authorizing the allocation of parish funds. With only two exceptions, school principals are nuns appointed either by the Superintendent or the Mother Provincial of the order whose members staff the school. By 1969, lay teachers constituted more than a third of all teachers in the parochial elementary schools, and their number is growing. They are first interviewed by the superintendent's office and then by the school principal. The contracts are signed by the parish priest, and he retains some discretion in negotiating salary levels. Religious authority necessarily pervades the school system.

The schools are governed by the standards set forth in a "Handbook of School Regulations," which . . . states that: "Religious formation is not confined to formal courses; nor is it restricted to a single subject area." Finally, the Handbook advises teachers to stimulate interest in religious vocations and missionary work. Given the mission of the church school, these instructions are consistent and logical. . . .

We need not and do not assume that teachers in parochial schools will be guilty of bad faith or any conscious design to evade the limitations imposed by the statute and the First Amendment. We simply recognize that a dedicated religious person, teaching in a school affiliated with his or her faith and operated to inculcate its tenets, will inevitably experience great difficulty in remaining religiously neutral. Doctrines and faith are not inculcated or advanced by neutrals. With the best of intentions, such a teacher would find it hard to make a total separation between secular teaching and religious doctrine. What would appear to some to be essential to good citizenship might well for others border on or constitute instruction in religion. Further difficulties are inherent in the combination of religious discipline and the possibility of disagreement between teacher and religious authorities over the meaning of the statutory restrictions. . . .

A comprehensive, discriminating, and continuing state surveillance will inevitably be required to ensure that these restrictions are obeyed and the First Amendment otherwise respected. Unlike a book, a teacher cannot be inspected once so as to determine the extent and intent of his or her personal beliefs and subjective acceptance of the limitations imposed by the First Amendment. These prophylactic contacts will involve excessive and enduring entanglement between state and church.

There is another area of entanglement in the Rhode Island program that gives concern. The statute excludes teachers employed by nonpublic schools whose average per-pupil expenditures on secular education equal or exceed the comparable figures for public schools. In the event that the total expenditures of an otherwise eligible school exceed this norm, the program requires the government to examine the school's records in order to determine how much of the total expenditures is attributable to secular education and how much to religious activity. This kind of state inspection and evaluation of the religious content of a religious organization is fraught with the sort of entanglement that the Constitution forbids. It is a relationship pregnant with dangers of excessive government direction of church schools, and hence of churches. The Court noted "the hazards of government supporting churches" in *Walz,* and we cannot ignore here the danger that pervasive modern governmental power will ultimately intrude on religion and thus conflict with the Religion Clauses.

Pennsylvania Program

As we noted earlier, the very restrictions and surveillance necessary to ensure that teachers play a strictly nonideological role give rise to entanglements between church and state. The Pennsylvania statute, like that of Rhode Island, fosters this kind of relationship. Reimbursement is not only limited to courses offered in the public schools and materials approved by state officials, but the statute excludes "any subject matter expressing religious teaching, or the morals or forms of worship of any sect." In addition, schools seeking reimbursement must maintain accounting procedures that require the State to establish the cost of the secular, as distinguished from the religious, instruction.

The Pennsylvania statute, moreover, has the further defect of providing state financial aid directly to the church-related school. This factor distinguishes both *Everson* and *Allen,* for, in both those cases, the Court was careful to point out that state aid was provided to the student and his parents—not to the church-related school. . . .

The history of government grants of a continuing cash subsidy indicates that such programs have almost always been accompanied by varying measures of control and surveillance. The government cash grants before us now provide no basis for predicting that comprehensive measures of surveillance and controls will not follow. In particular, the government's post-audit power to inspect and evaluate a church-related school's financial records and to determine which expenditures are religious and which are secular creates an intimate and continuing relationship between church and state.

A broader base of entanglement of yet a different character is presented by the divisive political potential of these state programs. In a community where such a large number of pupils are served by church-related schools, it can be assumed that state assistance will entail considerable political activity. Partisans of parochial schools, understandably concerned with rising costs and sincerely dedicated to both the religious and secular educational missions of their schools, will inevitably champion this cause and promote political action to achieve their goals. Those who oppose state aid, whether for constitutional, religious, or fiscal reasons, will inevitably respond and employ all of the usual political campaign techniques to prevail. Candidates will be forced to declare, and voters to choose. It would be unrealistic to ignore the fact that many people confronted with issues of this kind will find their votes aligned with their faith. . . .

We have an expanding array of vexing issues, local and national, domestic and international, to debate and divide on. It conflicts with our whole history and tradition to permit questions of the Religion Clauses to assume such importance in our legislatures and in our elections that they could divert attention from the myriad issues and problems that confront every level of government. The highways of church and state relationships are not likely to be one-way streets, and the Constitution's authors sought to protect religious worship from the pervasive power of government. The history of many countries attests to the hazards of religion's intruding into the political arena or of political power intruding into the legitimate and free exercise of religious belief. . . .

The potential for political divisiveness related to religious belief and practice is aggravated in these two statutory programs by the need for continuing annual appropriations and the likelihood of larger and larger demands as costs and populations grow. The Rhode Island District Court found that the parochial school system's "monumental and deepening financial crisis" would "inescapably" require larger annual appropriations subsidizing greater percentages of the salaries of lay teachers. Although no facts have been developed in this respect in the Pennsylvania case, it appears that such pressures for expanding aid have already required the state legislature to include a portion of the state revenues from cigarette taxes in the program.

MR. JUSTICE DOUGLAS, with whom MR. JUSTICE BLACK joins, concurring.

We have announced over and over again that the use of taxpayers' money to support parochial schools violates the First Amendment, applicable to the States by virtue of the Fourteenth. . . .

Yet, in spite of this long and consistent history, there are those who have the courage to announce that a State may nonetheless finance the secular part of a sectarian school's educational program. That, however, makes a grave constitutional decision turn merely on cost accounting and bookkeeping entries. A history class, a literature class, or a science class in a parochial school is not a separate institute; it is part of the organic whole which the State subsidizes. The funds are used in these cases to pay or help pay the salaries of teachers in parochial schools; and the presence of teachers is critical to the essential purpose of the parochial school, *viz.*, to advance the religious endeavors of the particular church. It matters not that the teacher receiving taxpayers' money only teaches religion a fraction of the time. Nor does it matter that he or she teaches no religion. The school is an organism living on one budget. What the taxpayers give for salaries of those who teach only the humanities or science without any trace of proselytizing enables the school to use all of its own funds for religious training . . . And sophisticated attempts to avoid the Constitution are just as invalid as simple-minded ones.

In my view, the taxpayers' forced contribution to the parochial schools in the present cases violates the First Amendment.

On the same day the Court handed down *Lemon,* it upheld provisions of the Higher Education Facilities Act of 1963 that provided federal grants to colleges and universities, public, private, and religious, for building construction and auxiliary services against a challenge sponsored by the AJCongress and the ACLU. By a 5-4 margin, the Court, in *Tilton* v. *Richardson,* with Chief Justice Burger writing for the majority, held that the assistance was "nonideological" in nature and created no excessive entanglement between church and state. *Tilton* proved an exception, however, to the Court's direction on parochial assistance after *Lemon.* For well over the next decade, the Court invalidated several programs enacted by the states and Congress that attempted to provide financial aid to parochial schools. Between 1971 and 1985, the Court decided fourteen cases involving some form of public assistance to parochial schools; in just three of those cases did the justices uphold the challenged statute. Only *Mueller* v. *Allen* (1983) offered any real financial reimbursement to religious schools and the parents who sent their children there. In *Mueller,* the Court, 6 to 3, upheld a Minnesota law that permitted parents to deduct up to $700 in education-related expenses from their taxable income. *Mueller* was overshadowed by two cases decided two years later, *Aguilar* v. *Felton* (1985) and *Grand Rapids* v. *Ball* (1985). Together, these two cases marked the high-water mark in the Court's firm line against parochial assistance.[65] But the central argument of the majority's opinion—that such assistance was indirect and thus not directly supportive of core religious activities—later merged as a centerpiece in the Court's changing approach to parochial assistance that began in the early 1990s and continues to the current day.

After *Lemon,* Leo Pfeffer channeled most of his energy into litigation directed toward federal and state forms of parochial assistance. His organizational support structure was no longer the AJCongress, but the Committee on Public Education and Religious Liberty (PEARL), which he formed after *Flast* exclusively to monitor and litigate parochial aid issues. Pfeffer understood that the Court's decisions striking down parochial assistance were only going to encourage proponents of such programs, particularly the Roman Catholic Church, to step up their fight in the legislatures. By consolidating their resources into a single group, Pfeffer wanted to provide a centralizing force and minimize turf battles among separationist organizations over who was best qualified to litigate parochial aid cases. Among the groups belonging to PEARL were the AJCongress, the ACLU, the Baptist Joint Committee, the National Council of Churches, the AJCommittee, and the ADL. Parochial aid became the issue that defined the Establishment Clause jurisprudence of the Court under Chief Justice Burger (1969–1986), in large part because of PEARL's litigation campaign, which kept the issue moving through the courts.[66]

PEARL's last major victories on parochial aid came in *Ball* and *Aguilar*, in which the Court invalidated two programs that provided state services to parochial schools. In *Ball*, the Court, 7 to 2, struck down a Michigan "shared time" program in which classes for nonpublic school students were financed by the public school system, taught by teachers hired by the public schools, and conducted in "leased" classrooms in the nonpublic schools. *Aguilar* involved a New York remedial education program providing state-funded counseling and instructional services to parochial schools with low-income students. This case brought to the surface many of the tensions that had been building among the justices since *Lemon* over what many supporters of parochial aid believed was reasonable assistance. Students who received benefits under the New York law were precisely the ones for whom Title I of the ESEA of 1965 was written: low-income, academically at-risk, and enrolled in parochial school as a last-ditch effort to save their education. For PEARL, the decision to challenge the Title I program created by New York was a matter of principle, not hostility to the needs of low-income students.

Dissenting in *Aguilar*, Justice O'Connor joined the chorus of *Lemon*'s critics, which now included Chief Justice Burger and Justices Rehnquist and White. She argued that the "excessive entanglement" test made it impossible for the Court to grant the states any degree of freedom to develop programs under Title I that best served low-income children. Openly sympathetic to the policy goals of New York legislation, O'Connor wrote:

> For these children, the Court's decision is tragic. The Court deprives them of a program that offers a meaningful chance at success in life, and it does so on the untenable theory that public schoolteachers (most of whom are of different faiths than their students) are likely to start teaching religion merely because they have walked across the threshold of a parochial school. I reject this theory and the analysis . . . on which it is based. I cannot close my eyes to the fact that, over almost two decades, New York's public schoolteachers have helped thousands of impoverished parochial schoolchildren to overcome educational disadvantages without once attempting to inculcate religion. Their praiseworthy efforts have not eroded and do not threaten the religious liberty assured by the Establishment Clause.[67]

O'Connor's trenchant criticism of *Lemon* came on the heels of Rehnquist's dissent earlier during the same term in *Wallace* v. *Jaffree*. In that dissent Rehnquist called the Court's reliance on the "wall of separation" metaphor to describe the relationship between church and state since *Everson* "useless," "wrong," and a "constitutional theory [having] no basis in the history of the amendment it seeks to interpret." He made clear that, at some point, the Court was going to have to reconsider these issues. By the early 1990s, bolstered by three justices, Scalia, Kennedy, and Thomas, outwardly sympathetic to public funding for parochial schools, O'Connor's vision of a recalibrated Establishment Clause jurisprudence started to come into focus. Surprisingly, the Court's first major step in this direction, *Zobrest* v. *Catalina Foothills School District* (1993), would find O'Connor in the minority.

Zobrest v. *Catalina Foothills School District*

509 U.S. 1 (1993)

James Zobrest, who was born deaf, was entering the ninth grade at Salpointe Catholic High School in Tucson, Arizona, when he requested that the state provide him with a sign-language interpreter to accompany him to class. Zobrest, who had attended grades 1 through 5 at a private school for the deaf and grades 6 through 8 at a public school in the Catalina Foothills District, where he had an interpreter, claimed he was entitled to assistance under the federal Individuals with Disabilities Education Act of 1991. The school district refused his request, saying that providing an interpreter to a student attending a parochial school directly advanced a religious interest.

Zobrest divided many of the separationist groups that had come together in *Ball* and *Aguilar.* The AJCongress filed a joint brief with the Baptist Joint Committee in support of Zobrest's request, placing them on the same side of the case as the Christian Legal Society and the United States Catholic Conference, with whom they rarely agreed on the Establishment Clause. The Commission on Law and Public Affairs (COLPA), representing Orthodox Jews, also supported Zobrest. The ACLU, joined by Americans United and the Anti-Defamation League, supported the school district's decision not to award Zobrest an interpreter, a position that was endorsed by several education groups participating in the case. By the time of *Zobrest,* Leo Pfeffer had passed away, leaving separationist groups without the key figure who had shaped Establishment Clause litigation since 1945. PEARL filed a brief on behalf of Catalina Foothills, but by this time it was no longer the central force it had been during the 1970s and early 1980s.

Two lower federal courts rejected James Zobrest's request for a sign-language interpreter. Zobrest then appealed to the Supreme Court.

The Court's decision was 5 to 4. Chief Justice Rehnquist delivered the opinion of the Court. Justice O'Connor, joined by Justice Stevens, dissented. Justice Blackmun, joined by Justice Souter, also dissented.

▼▲▼

Chief Justice Rehnquist delivered the opinion of the Court.

We have never said that "religious institutions are disabled by the First Amendment from participating in publicly sponsored social welfare programs." For if the Establishment Clause did bar religious groups from receiving general government benefits, then "a church could not be protected by the police and fire departments, or have its public sidewalk kept in repair." Given that a contrary rule would lead to such absurd results, we have consistently held that government programs that neutrally provide benefits to a broad class of citizens defined without reference to religion are not readily subject to an Establishment Clause challenge just because sectarian institutions may also receive an attenuated financial benefit. Nowhere have we stated this principle more clearly than in *Mueller* v. *Allen* (1983) and *Witters* v. *Washington Dept. of Services for the Blind* (1986), two cases dealing specifically with government programs offering general educational assistance.

In *Mueller,* we rejected an Establishment Clause challenge to a Minnesota law allowing taxpayers to deduct certain educational expenses in computing their state income tax, even though the vast majority of those deductions (perhaps over 90%) went to parents whose children attended sectarian schools. Two factors, aside from States' traditionally broad taxing authority, informed our decision. We noted that the law "permits *all* parents—whether their children attend public school or private—to deduct their children's educational expenses." We also pointed out that, under Minnesota's scheme, public funds become available to sectarian schools "only as a result of numerous private choices of individual parents of school-age children," thus distinguishing *Mueller* from our other cases involving "the direct transmission of assistance from the State to the schools themselves."

Witters was premised on virtually identical reasoning. In that case, we upheld against an Establishment Clause challenge the State of Washington's extension of vocational assistance, as part of a general state program, to a blind person studying at a private Christian college to become a pastor, missionary, or youth director. Looking at the statute as a whole, we observed that any aid provided under Washington's program that ultimately flows to religious institutions does so only as a result of the genuinely independent and private choices of aid recipients. . . .

In light of these factors, we held that Washington's program—even as applied to a student who sought state assistance so that he could become a pastor—would not advance religion in a manner inconsistent with the Establishment Clause.

That same reasoning applies with equal force here. The service at issue in this case is part of a general government program that distributes benefits neutrally to any child qualifying as "handicapped" under the IDEA, without regard to the "sectarian-nonsectarian, or public-nonpublic nature" of the school the child attends. By according parents freedom to select a school of their choice, the statute ensures that a government-paid interpreter will be present in a sectarian school only as a result of the private decision of individual parents. In other words, because the IDEA creates no financial incentive for parents to choose a sectarian school, an interpreter's presence there cannot be attributed to state decisionmaking. . . .

[T]he task of a sign-language interpreter seems to us quite different from that of a teacher or guidance counselor. . . . [T]he Establishment Clause lays down no absolute bar to the placing of a public employee in a sectarian school. Such a flat rule, smacking of antiquated notions of "taint," would indeed exalt form over substance. Nothing in this record suggests that a sign-language interpreter would do more than accurately interpret whatever material is presented to the class as a whole. In fact, ethical guidelines require interpreters to "transmit everything that is said in exactly the same way it was intended." James [Zobrest's] parents have chosen of their own free will to place him in a pervasively sectarian environment. The sign-language interpreter they have requested will neither add to nor subtract from that environment, and hence the provision of such assistance is not barred by the Establishment Clause.

If a handicapped child chooses to enroll in a sectarian school, we hold that the Establishment Clause does not prevent the school district from furnishing him with a sign-language interpreter there in order to facilitate his education.

JUSTICE BLACKMUN, with whom JUSTICE SOUTER joins, and with whom JUSTICE STEVENS and JUSTICE O'CONNOR join . . . dissenting.

Until now, the Court never has authorized a public employee to participate directly in religious indoctrination. Yet that is the consequence of today's decision.

Let us be clear about exactly what is going on here. The parties have stipulated to the following facts. Petitioner requested the State to supply him with a sign-language interpreter at Salpointe High School, a private Roman Catholic school operated by the Carmelite Order of the Catholic Church. Salpointe is a "pervasively religious" institution where "[t]he two functions of secular education and advancement of religious values or beliefs are inextricably intertwined." Salpointe's overriding "objective" is to "instill a sense of Christian values." Its "distinguishing purpose" is "the inculcation in its students of the faith and morals of the Roman Catholic Church." Religion is a required subject at Salpointe, and Catholic students are "strongly encouraged" to attend daily Mass each morning. Salpointe's teachers must sign a Faculty Employment Agreement which requires them to promote the relationship among the religious, the academic, and the extracurricular. They are encouraged to do so by "assist[ing] students in experiencing how the presence of God is manifest in nature, human history, in the struggles for economic and political justice, and other secular areas of the curriculum."

The Agreement also sets forth detailed rules of conduct teachers must follow in order to advance the school's Christian mission.

At Salpointe, where the secular and the sectarian are "inextricably intertwined," governmental assistance to the educational function of the school necessarily entails governmental participation in the school's inculcation of religion. A state-employed sign-language interpreter would be required to communicate the material covered in religion class, the nominally secular subjects that are taught from a religious perspective, and the daily Masses at which Salpointe encourages attendance for Catholic students. In an environment so pervaded by discussions of the divine, the interpreter's every gesture would be infused with religious significance. . . .

The majority attempts to elude the impact of the record by offering three reasons why this sort of aid to petitioners survives Establishment Clause scrutiny. First, the majority observes that provision of a sign-language interpreter occurs as "part of a general government program that distributes benefits neutrally to any child qualifying as 'handicapped' under the IDEA, without regard to the 'sectarian-nonsectarian, or public-nonpublic' nature of the school the child attends." Second, the majority finds significant the fact that aid is provided to pupils and their parents, rather than directly to sectarian schools. . . . And, finally, the majority opines that "the task of a sign-language interpreter seems to us quite different from that of a teacher or guidance counselor."

But the majority's arguments are unavailing. As to the first two, even a general welfare program may have specific applications that are constitutionally forbidden under the Establishment Clause. For example, a general program granting remedial assistance to disadvantaged schoolchildren attending public and private, secular and sectarian schools alike would clearly offend the Establishment Clause insofar as it authorized the provision of teachers. Such a program would not be saved simply because it supplied teachers to secular, as well as sectarian, schools. Nor would the fact that teachers were furnished to pupils and their parents, rather than directly to sectarian schools, immunize such a program from Establishment Clause scrutiny. The majority's decision must turn, then, upon the distinction between a teacher and a sign-language interpreter.

Moreover, this distinction between the provision of funds and the provision of a human being is not merely one of form. It goes to the heart of the principles animating the Establishment Clause. As *Amicus* Council on Religious Freedom points out, the provision of a state-paid sign-language interpreter may pose serious problems for the church, as well as for the state. Many sectarian schools impose religiously based rules of conduct, as Salpointe has in this case. A traditional Hindu school would be likely to instruct its students and staff to dress modestly, avoid-

ing any display of their bodies. And an orthodox Jewish yeshiva might well forbid all but kosher food upon its premises. To require public employees to obey such rules would impermissibly threaten individual liberty, but to fail to do so might endanger religious autonomy. For such reasons, it long has been feared that "a union of government and religion tends to destroy government and to degrade religion." The Establishment Clause was designed to avert exactly this sort of conflict.

▼▲▼

Following the logic of *Mueller* and a 1986 decision, *Witters* v. *Washington*, which held that a sight-impaired student was eligible for vocational rehabilitation assistance from the state of Washington to attend a private Bible college, Chief Justice Rehnquist found the aid in *Zobrest* "indirect" and thus permissible under the Establishment Clause. Note how his opinion does not even mention *Lemon*, and its absence was quite telling. *Zobrest* involved just the sort of issue that led to the creation of the excessive entanglement standard. O'Connor's dissent addressed only a procedural issue; she believed the Court should not have reached the constitutional questions. The following term, however, O'Connor demonstrated again, as she had in *Weisman*, that she was not a reflexive supporter of government efforts to support religion. In one of the most unusual Establishment Clause cases the Court has decided, O'Connor emerged as a key vote in *Kiryas Joel Village School District* v. *Grumet* (1994), which continued the argument among the justices about the vitality of the *Lemon* test.

Kiryas Joel Village School District v. Grumet

512 U.S. 687 (1994)

The Village of Kiryas Joel, a community composed entirely of Satmar Hasidim Jews and located in Orange County, New York, had been part of the Monroe-Woodbury Central School District until 1989. With the support of Governor Mario Cuomo, the state legislature enacted a law that year creating a special school district to serve only the Kiryas Joel village boundaries. The special district was created to provide for children in need of special education services. Most Satmar children attended Jewish parochial schools in Kiryas Joel, but the community found the cost of providing special services for learning disabled students prohibitive. Parents were unwilling to use the public schools and receive services there because that would require them to leave the insular Satmar community, causing "panic, fear and trauma." The legislation was designed to create a public school where Satmar children would feel comfortable and allow them to receive tax-funded special education services.

The Satmar Hasidim were represented by Nathan Lewin, a former law school classmate of Justice Scalia and one of the most respected attorneys in Washington, D.C. In the late 1960s, Lewin had helped found the Commission on Law and Public Affairs (COLPA), which represents Orthodox Jews in legislative affairs and conducts litigation work. A major reason Lewin formed COLPA was to bring Orthodox Jews out from under the shadow of Leo Pfeffer and to provide a voice for Jews who rejected the strict separationist model. Since *Lemon*, the AJCongress and COLPA have appeared on the same side of an Establishment Clause case only twice, in *Witters* and *Zobrest*. None of the major Jewish organizations outside COLPA supported Kiryas Joel.

The Court's decision was 6 to 3. Justice Souter delivered the opinion of the Court. Justice Blackmun wrote a concurring opinion, as did Justices O'Connor and Kennedy. Justice Stevens filed a concurring opinion, which was joined by Justice Ginsburg. Justice Scalia, joined by Chief Justice Rehnquist and Justice Thomas, dissented.

JUSTICE SOUTER delivered the opinion of the Court.

The question is whether the Act creating the separate school district violates the Establishment Clause of the First Amendment, binding on the States through the Fourteenth Amendment. Because this unusual act is tantamount to an allocation of political power on a religious criterion and neither presupposes nor requires governmental impartiality toward religion, we hold that it violates the prohibition against establishment. . . .

"A proper respect for both the Free Exercise and the Establishment Clauses compels the State to pursue a course of 'neutrality' toward religion," favoring neither one religion over others nor religious adherents collectively over nonadherents. Chapter 748, the statute creating the Kiryas Joel Village School District, departs from this constitutional command by delegating the State's discretionary authority over public schools to a group

defined by its character as a religious community, in a legal and historical context that gives no assurance that governmental power has been or will be exercised neutrally. . . .

The Establishment Clause problem presented by Chapter 748 is . . . subtle, but it . . . teaches that a State may not delegate its civic authority to a group chosen according to a religious criterion. Authority over public schools belongs to the State, and cannot be delegated to a local school district defined by the State in order to grant political control to a religious group. What makes this litigation different . . . is the delegation here of civic power to the "qualified voters of the village of Kiryas Joel. . . . "

Although some school district franchise is common to all voters, the State's manipulation of the franchise for this district limited it to Satmars, giving the sect exclusive control of the political subdivision. In the circumstances of this case, the difference between thus vesting state power in the members of a religious group as such instead of the officers of its sectarian organization is one of form, not substance. It is true that religious people (or groups of religious people) cannot be denied the opportunity to exercise the rights of citizens simply because of their religious affiliations or commitments, for such a disability would violate the right to religious free exercise, which the First Amendment guarantees as certainly as it bars any establishment. . . . That individuals who happen to be religious may hold public office does not mean that a state may deliberately delegate discretionary power to an individual, institution, or community on the ground of religious identity. . . . Where "fusion" is an issue, the difference lies in the distinction between a government's purposeful delegation on the basis of religion and a delegation on principles neutral to religion, to individuals whose religious identities are incidental to their receipt of civic authority.

Of course, Chapter 748 delegates power not by express reference to the religious belief of the Satmar community, but to residents of the "territory of the village of Kiryas Joel." Thus the second (and arguably more important) [issue] is the identification here of the group to exercise civil authority in terms not expressly religious. But our analysis does not end with the text of the statute at issue, and the context here persuades us that Chapter 748 effectively identifies these recipients of governmental authority by reference to doctrinal adherence, even though it does not do so expressly. We find this to be the better view of the facts because of the way the boundary lines of the school district divide residents according to religious affiliation, under the terms of an unusual and special legislative act. . . .

It is undisputed that those who negotiated the village boundaries when applying the general village incorporation statute drew them so as to exclude all but Satmars, and that the New York Legislature was well aware that the village remained exclusively Satmar in 1989 when it adopted Chapter 748. The significance of this fact to the state legislature is indicated by the further fact that carving out the village school district ran counter to customary districting practices in the State. Indeed, the trend in New York is not toward dividing school districts but toward consolidating them. The thousands of small common school districts laid out in the early 19th century have been combined and recombined, first into union free school districts and then into larger central school districts, until only a tenth as many remain today. Most of these cover several towns, many of them cross county boundaries, and only one remains precisely coterminous with an incorporated village. The object of the State's practice of consolidation is the creation of districts large enough to provide a comprehensive education at affordable cost, which is thought to require at least 500 pupils for a combined junior-senior high school. The Kiryas Joel Village School District, in contrast, has only 13 local, full-time students in all (even including out-of-area and part-time students leaves the number under 200), and in offering only special education and remedial programs it makes no pretense to be a full-service district.

The origin of the district is a special act of the legislature, rather than the State's general laws governing school district reorganization. Although the legislature has established some 20 existing school districts by special act, all but one of these are districts in name only, having been designed to be run by private organizations serving institutionalized children. They have neither tax bases nor student populations of their own but serve children placed by other school districts or public agencies. The one school district petitioners point to that was formed by special act of the legislature to serve a whole community, as this one was, is a district formed for a new town, much larger and more heterogeneous than this village, being built on land that straddled two existing districts. Thus the Kiryas Joel Village School District is exceptional to the point of singularity, as the only district coming to our notice that the legislature carved from a single existing district to serve local residents. . . .

Because the district's creation ran uniquely counter to state practice, following the lines of a religious community where the customary and neutral principles would not have dictated the same result, we have good reasons to treat this district as the reflection of a religious criterion for identifying the recipients of civil authority. Not even the special needs of the children in this community can explain the legislature's unusual Act, for the State could have responded to the concerns of the Satmar parents without implicating the Establishment Clause, as we explain in some detail further on. We therefore find the legislature's Act to be substantially equivalent to defining a political subdivision and hence the qualification for its franchise by a religious test, resulting in a purposeful and forbidden "fusion of governmental and religious functions," *Larkin* v. *Grendel's Den* (1982).

The fact that this school district was created by a special and unusual Act of the legislature also gives reason for concern whether the benefit received by the Satmar community is one that the legislature will provide equally to other religious (and nonreligious) groups. . . . The fundamental source of constitutional concern here is that the legislature itself may fail to exercise governmental authority in a religiously neutral way. The anomalously case-specific nature of the legislature's exercise of state authority in creating this district for a religious community leaves the Court without any direct way to review such state action for the purpose of safeguarding a principle at the heart of the Establishment Clause, that government should not prefer one religion to another, or religion to irreligion. Because the religious community of Kiryas Joel did not receive its new governmental authority simply as one of many communities eligible for equal treatment under a general law, we have no assurance that the next similarly situated group seeking a school district of its own will receive one. . . . Nor can the historical context in this case furnish us with any reason to suppose that the Satmars are merely one in a series of communities receiving the benefit of special school district laws. Early on in the development of public education in New York, the State rejected highly localized school districts for New York City when they were promoted as a way to allow separate schooling for Roman Catholic children. And in more recent history, the special Act in this case stands alone. . . .

Here the benefit flows only to a single sect, but aiding this single, small religious group causes no less a constitutional problem than would follow from aiding a sect with more members or religion as a whole, and we are forced to conclude that the State of New York has violated the Establishment Clause. . . .

Justice Cardozo once cast the dissenter as "the gladiator making a last stand against the lions." JUSTICE SCALIA's dissent is certainly the work of a gladiator, but he thrusts at lions of his own imagining. We do not disable a religiously homogeneous group from exercising political power conferred on it without regard to religion. Unlike the states of Utah and New Mexico (which were laid out according to traditional political methodologies taking account of lines of latitude and longitude and topographical features), the reference line chosen for the Kiryas Joel Village School District was one purposely drawn to separate Satmars from non-Satmars. Nor do we impugn the motives of the New York Legislature, which no doubt intended to accommodate the Satmar community without zviolating the Establishment Clause; we simply refuse to ignore that the method it chose is one that aids a particular religious community, as such, rather than all groups similarly interested in separate schooling. . . . Indeed, under the dissent's theory, if New York were to pass a law providing school buses only for children attending Christian day schools, we would be constrained to uphold the statute against Establishment Clause attack until faced by a request from a non-Christian family for equal treatment under the patently unequal law. And to end on the point with which JUSTICE SCALIA begins, the license he takes in suggesting that the Court holds the Satmar sect to be New York's established church, is only one symptom of his inability to accept the fact that this Court has long held that the First Amendment reaches more than classic, 18th century establishments.

Our job, of course would be easier if the dissent's position had prevailed with the Framers and with this Court over the years. An Establishment Clause diminished to the dimensions acceptable to JUSTICE SCALIA could be enforced by a few simple rules, and our docket would never see cases requiring the application of a principle like neutrality toward religion as well as among religious sects. But that would be as blind to history as to precedent, and the difference between JUSTICE SCALIA and the Court accordingly turns on the Court's recognition that the Establishment Clause does comprehend such a principle and obligates courts to exercise the judgment necessary to apply it.

In this case, we are clearly constrained to conclude that the statute before us fails the test of neutrality. It delegates a power this Court has said "ranks at the very apex of the function of a State" to an electorate defined by common religious belief and practice, in a manner that fails to foreclose religious favoritism. It therefore crosses the line from permissible accommodation to impermissible establishment. The judgment of the Court of Appeals of the State of New York is accordingly

Affirmed.

JUSTICE O'CONNOR, concurring in part and concurring in the judgment.

We have time and again held that the government generally may not treat people differently based on the God or gods they worship, or don't worship. . . . This emphasis on equal treatment is, I think, an eminently sound approach. In my view, the Religion Clauses—the Free Exercise Clause, the Establishment Clause, the Religious Test Clause, Art. VI, cl. 3, and the Equal Protection Clause as applied to religion—all speak with one voice on this point: absent the most unusual circumstances, one's religion ought not affect one's legal rights or duties or benefits. As I have previously noted, "the Establishment Clause is infringed when the government makes adherence to religion relevant to a person's standing in the political community," *Wallace* v. *Jaffree* (1985).

That the government is acting to accommodate religion should generally not change this analysis. What makes accommodation permissible, even praiseworthy, is not that the government is making life easier for some particular religious group as such. Rather, it is that the government is accommodating a deeply held belief. Accommodations may thus justify treating those who share this belief differently from those who do not; but they do not justify discriminations based on sect. A state law prohibiting the consumption of alcohol may exempt sacramental wines, but it may not exempt sacramental wine use by Catholics, but not by Jews. A draft law may exempt conscientious objectors, but it may not exempt conscientious objectors whose objections are based on theistic belief (such as Quakers) as opposed to nontheistic belief (such as Buddhists) or atheistic belief. . . .

On its face, this statute benefits one group—the residents of Kiryas Joel. Because this benefit was given to this group based on its religion, it seems proper to treat it as a legislatively drawn religious classification. I realize this is a close question, because the Satmars may be the only group who currently need this particular accommodation. The legislature may well be acting without any favoritism, so that if another group came to ask for a similar district, the group might get it on the same terms as the Satmars. But the nature of the legislative process makes it impossible to be sure of this. A legislature, unlike the judiciary or many administrative decision makers, has no obligation to respond to any group's requests. A group petitioning for a law may never get a definite response, or may get a "no" based not on the merits, but on the press of other business or the lack of an influential sponsor. Such a legislative refusal to act would not normally be reviewable by a court. Under these circumstances, it seems dangerous to validate what appears to me a clear religious preference.

Our invalidation of this statute in no way means that the Satmars' needs cannot be accommodated. There is nothing improper about a legislative intention to accommodate a religious group, so long as it is implemented through generally applicable legislation. New York may, for instance, allow all villages to operate their own school districts. If it does not want to act so broadly, it may set forth neutral criteria that a village must meet to have a school district of its own; these criteria can then be applied by a state agency, and the decision would then be reviewable by the judiciary. A district created under a generally applicable scheme would be acceptable even though it coincides with a village which was consciously created by its voters as an enclave for their religious group. I do not think the Court's opinion holds the contrary.

JUSTICE KENNEDY, concurring in the judgment.

This is not a case in which the government has granted a benefit to a general class of recipients of which religious groups are just one part. It is, rather, a case in which the government seeks to alleviate a specific burden on the religious practices of a particular religious group. I agree that a religious accommodation demands careful scrutiny to ensure that it does not so burden nonadherents or discriminate against other religions as to become an establishment. I disagree, however, with the suggestion that the Kiryas Joel Village School District contravenes these basic constitutional commands. But for the forbidden manner in which the New York Legislature sought to go about it, the State's attempt to accommodate the special needs of the handicapped Satmar children would have been valid.

The Kiryas Joel Village School District thus does not suffer any of the typical infirmities that might invalidate an attempted legislative accommodation. In the ordinary case, the fact that New York has chosen to accommodate the burdens unique to one religious group would raise no constitutional problems. Without further evidence that New York has denied the same accommodation to religious groups bearing similar burdens, we could not presume from the particularity of the accommodation that the New York Legislature acted with discriminatory intent.

This particularity takes on a different cast, however, when the accommodation requires the government to draw political or electoral boundaries. "The principle that government may accommodate the free exercise of religion does not supersede the fundamental limitations imposed by the Establishment Clause," and, in my view, one such fundamental limitation is that government may not use religion as a criterion to draw political or electoral lines. Whether or not the purpose is accommodation and whether or not the government provides similar gerrymanders to people of all religious faiths, the Establishment Clause forbids the government to use religion as a line-drawing criterion. In this respect, the Establishment Clause mirrors the Equal Protection Clause. Just as the government may not segregate people on account of their race, so too it may not segregate on the basis of religion. The danger of stigma and stirred animosities is no less acute for religious line-drawing than for racial. . . . There is no serious question that the legislature configured the school district, with purpose and precision, along a religious line. This explicit religious gerrymandering violates the First Amendment Establishment Clause.

JUSTICE SCALIA, with whom THE CHIEF JUSTICE and JUSTICE THOMAS join, dissenting.

The Court today finds that the Powers That Be, up in Albany, have conspired to effect an establishment of the Satmar Hasidim. I do not know who would be more surprised at this discovery: the Founders of our Nation or Grand Rebbe Joel Teitelbaum, founder of the Satmar. The Grand Rebbe would be astounded to learn that, after escaping brutal persecution and coming to America with the modest hope of religious toleration for their ascetic form of Judaism, the Satmar had become so powerful, so closely allied with Mammon, as to have become an "establishment" of the Empire State. And the Founding Fathers would be astonished to find that the Establishment Clause—which they designed "to insure that no one powerful sect or combination of sects could use political or governmental power to punish dissenters," has been employed to prohibit characteristically and admirably American accommodation of the religious practices (or more precisely, cultural peculiarities) of a tiny minority sect. I, however, am not surprised. Once this Court has abandoned text and history as guides, nothing prevents it from calling religious toleration the establishment of religion.

Unlike most of our Establishment Clause cases involving education, these cases involve no public funding, however slight or indirect, to private religious schools. They do not involve private schools at all. The school under scrutiny is a public school specifically designed to provide a public secular education to handicapped students. The superintendent of the school, who is not Hasidic, is a 20-year veteran of the New York City public school system, with expertise in the area of bilingual, bicultural, special education. The teachers and therapists at the school all live outside the village of Kiryas Joel. While the village's private schools are profoundly religious and strictly segregated by sex, classes at the public school are co-ed and the curriculum secular. The school building has the bland appearance of a public school, unadorned by religious symbols or markings; and the school complies with the laws and regulations governing all other New York State public schools. There is no suggestion, moreover, that this public school has gone too far in making special adjustments to the religious needs of its students. In sum, these cases involve only public aid to a school that is public as can be. The only thing distinctive about the school is that all the students share the same religion. . . .

JUSTICE SOUTER's steamrolling of the difference between civil authority held by a church, and civil authority held by members of a church, is breathtaking. To accept it, one must believe that large portions of the civil authority exercised during most of our history were unconstitutional, and that much more of it than merely the Kiryas Joel School District is unconstitutional today. The history of the populating of North America is in no small measure the story of groups of people sharing a common religious and cultural heritage striking out to form their own communities. It is preposterous to suggest that the civil institutions of these communities, separate from their churches, were constitutionally suspect. And if they were, surely JUSTICE SOUTER cannot mean that the inclusion of one or two nonbelievers in the community would have been enough to eliminate the constitutional vice. If the conferral of governmental power upon a religious institution as such (rather than upon American citizens who belong to the religious institution) is not the test of *Grendel's Den* invalidity, there is no reason why giving power to a body that is overwhelmingly dominated by the members of one sect would not suffice to invoke the Establishment Clause. That might have made the entire States of Utah and New Mexico unconstitutional at the time of their admission to the Union, and would undoubtedly make many units of local government unconstitutional today. . . .

Perhaps appreciating the startling implications for our constitutional jurisprudence of collapsing the distinction between religious institutions and their members, JUSTICE SOUTER tries to limit his "unconstitutional conferral of civil authority" holding by pointing out several features supposedly unique to the present case: that the "boundary lines of the school district divide residents according to religious affiliation," that the school district was created by "a special act of the legislature," and that the formation of the school district ran counter to the legislature's trend of consolidating districts in recent years. Assuming all these points to be true (and they are not), they would certainly bear upon whether the legislature had an impermissible religious motivation in creating the district (which is JUSTICE SOUTER's next point, in the discussion of which I shall reply to these arguments). But they have nothing to do with whether conferral of power upon a group of citizens can be the conferral of power upon a religious institution. It cannot. Or if it can, our Establishment Clause jurisprudence has been transformed.

I turn, next, to JUSTICE SOUTER's second justification for finding an establishment of religion: his facile conclusion that the New York Legislature's creation of the Kiryas Joel School District was religiously motivated. But in the Land of the Free, democratically adopted laws are not so easily impeached by unelected judges. To establish the unconstitutionality of a facially neutral law on the mere basis of its asserted religiously preferential (or discriminatory) effects—or at least to establish it in conformity with our precedents—JUSTICE SOUTER "must be able to show the absence of a neutral, secular basis" for the law. . . .

There is, of course, no possible doubt of a secular basis here. The New York Legislature faced a unique problem in Kiryas Joel: a community in which all the nonhandicapped children attend private schools, and the physically and mentally disabled children who attend public school suffer the additional handicap of cultural distinctiveness. It would be troublesome enough if these peculiarly dressed, handicapped students were sent to the next town, accompanied by their similarly clad but unimpaired classmates. But all the unimpaired children of Kiryas Joel attend private school. The handicapped children suffered sufficient emotional trauma from their predicament that their parents kept them home from school. Surely the legislature could target this problem, and provide a public education for these students, in the same way it addressed, by a similar law, the unique needs of children institutionalized in a hospital. . . .

JUSTICE SOUTER's case against the statute comes down to nothing more, therefore, than his third point: the fact that all the residents of the Kiryas Joel Village School District are Satmars. But all its residents also wear unusual dress, have unusual civic customs, and have not much to do with people who are culturally different from them. The Court recognizes that "the Satmars prefer to live together 'to facilitate individual religious observance and maintain social, cultural and religious values,' but that it is not 'against their religion' to interact with others." On what basis does JUSTICE SOUTER conclude that it is the theological distinctiveness, rather than the cultural distinctiveness, that was the basis for New York State's decision? The normal assumption would be that it was the latter, since it was not theology, but dress, language, and cultural alienation that posed the educational problem for the children. JUSTICE SOUTER not only does not adopt the logical assumption, he does not even give the New York Legislature the benefit of the doubt. . . .

I have little doubt that JUSTICE SOUTER would laud this humanitarian legislation if all of the distinctiveness of the students of Kiryas Joel were attributable to the fact that their parents were nonreligious commune dwellers, or American Indians, or gypsies. The creation of a special, one-culture school district for the benefit of those children would pose no problem. The neutrality demanded by the Religion Clauses requires the same indulgence towards cultural characteristics that are accompanied by religious belief. . . .

Contrary to the Court's suggestion, I do not think that the Establishment Clause prohibits formally established "state" churches and nothing more. I have always believed, and all my opinions are consistent with the view, that the Establishment Clause prohibits the favoring of one religion over others. In this respect, it is the Court that attacks lions of straw. What I attack is the Court's imposition of novel "up front" procedural requirements on state legislatures. Making law (and making exceptions) one case at a time, whether through adjudication or through highly particularized rulemaking or legislation, violates, ex ante no principle of fairness, equal protection, or neutrality, simply because it does not announce in advance how all future cases (and all future exceptions) will be disposed of. If it did, the manner of proceeding of this Court itself would be unconstitutional. It is presumptuous for this Court to impose—out of nowhere—an unheard-of prohibition against proceeding in this manner upon the Legislature of New York State. I never heard of such a principle, nor has anyone else, nor will it ever be heard of again. Unlike what the New York Legislature has done, this is a special rule to govern only the Satmar Hasidim.

The Court's decision today is astounding. Chapter 748 involves no public aid to private schools, and does not mention religion. In order to invalidate it, the Court casts aside, on the flimsiest of evidence, the strong presumption of validity that attaches to facially neutral laws, and invalidates the present accommodation because it does not trust New York to be as accommodating toward other religions (presumably those less powerful than the Satmar Hasidim) in the future. This is unprecedented—except that it continues, and takes to new extremes, a recent tendency in the opinions of this Court to turn the Establishment Clause into a repealer of our Nation's tradition of religious toleration. I dissent.

▼▲▼

Justices O'Connor and Kennedy each concluded that New York's decision to create a special school district for Kiryas Joel was based on religion, not geography. Both justices, however, contended that New York could have accommodated the Satmar Hasidim if the state had created a district that had been neutral with regard to religion. Justice Souter, writing for the majority, rejected the idea that anything other than religion motivated the New York legislature's decision to create a school district to serve Kiryas Joel. Reasonable accommodation to provide for special educational needs was certainly within the boundaries of the Establishment Clause. But Souter also emphasized that New York could not use an unconstitutional religious preference to achieve that goal.

O'Connor and Kennedy's concurring opinions in *Kiryas Joel*, taken together with Scalia's dissent, clearly pointed to the escalating tension among the justices over whether the Court should revisit *Ball* and *Aguilar*. Five votes now existed to overturn the Court's 1985 decisions forbidding public school teachers from going into parochial schools to provide remedial instruction to economically disadvantaged children. *Rosenberger* v. *Virginia*, decided a year after *Kiryas Joel*, found O'Connor and Kennedy siding with Rehnquist, Scalia, and Thomas on the need for government to provide equal treatment for religion. Thus, it was no surprise that litigation directly challenging *Ball* and *Aguilar* was just a matter of time.

In October 1995, Rachel Agostini and several other parents of children in the New York City parochial schools joined with the New York City Board of Education to file a motion in federal court asking for relief from the Court's decision in *Aguilar*, claiming that *Witters* and *Zobrest* had created a "significant change in law." The motion, filed under Rule 60(b)(5) of the Federal Rules of Procedure, permits a court to relieve a party from a prior judgment when the party making such a request can show that it is no longer consistent with current law. The issues that had been brewing in *Zobrest*, *Kiryas Joel*, and *Rosenberger* came to a head in *Agostini* v. *Felton* (1997).

Agostini v. *Felton*

521 U.S. 203 (1997)

In response to *Aguilar*, New York City modified its Title I program to provide instruction to low-income parochial schools students inside vans parked just off the edge of school property. The city had purchased over one hundred vans to transport public school teachers to parochial schools, and these vans doubled as classrooms. Total compliance with *Aguilar* had cost the city approximately $100 million. Costs had reached the point where the city's board of education decided it either had to terminate participation in the program or had to seek relief under federal rule of procedure 60(b)(5). Rule 60 motions, as lawyers commonly call them, are rare. Two lower federal courts rejected Rachel Agostini and the school board's request, claiming that *Aguilar* was still good law.

The Court's decision to hear *Agostini* suggested that a majority of the justices was dissatisfied with *Aguilar* and *Ball*. Coming on the heels of *Zobrest* and *Rosenberger*, separationist groups that had participated in *Aguilar* and *Ball* knew the Court was going to reverse the 1985 decisions. In contrast, more than a dozen groups filed briefs encouraging the Court to overrule *Aguilar* in light of *Zobrest* and *Rosenberger*. Although *Rosenberger* dealt with a different sort of aid to religion, the majority had emphasized that religion should receive equal consideration in government funding programs intended to advance secular objectives. The Clinton administration also filed a brief asking the Court to grant the Rule 60 motion.

The Court's decision was 5 to 4. Justice O'Connor delivered the opinion of the Court. Justice Souter, joined by Justices Stevens, Ginsburg, and Breyer, dissented. Justice Ginsburg, joined by Justices Stevens, Souter, and Breyer, also dissented.

▼▲▼

JUSTICE O'CONNOR delivered the opinion of the Court.

In *Aguilar* v. *Felton* (1985), this Court held that the Establishment Clause of the First Amendment barred the city of New York from sending public school teachers into parochial schools to provide remedial education to disadvantaged children pursuant to a congressionally mandated program. . . . Twelve years later, petitioners—the parties bound by that injunction—seek relief from its operation.

Petitioners maintain that *Aguilar* cannot be squared with our intervening Establishment Clause jurisprudence, and ask that we explicitly recognize what our more recent cases already dictate: *Aguilar* is no longer good law. We agree with petitioners that *Aguilar* is not consistent with our subsequent Establishment Clause decisions, and further conclude that . . . petitioners are entitled . . . to relief from the operation of the District Court's prospective injunction. . . .

Petitioners point to three changes in the factual and legal landscape that they believe justify their claim for relief. . . . They first contend that the exorbitant costs of complying with the District Court's injunction constitute a significant factual development warranting modification of the injunction. Petitioners also argue that there have been two significant legal developments since *Aguilar* was decided: a majority of Justices have expressed their views that *Aguilar* should be reconsidered or overruled, and *Aguilar* has in any event been undermined by subsequent Establishment Clause decisions, including *Witters* v. *Washington Dept. of Servs. for Blind* (1986), *Zobrest* v. *Catalina Foothills School District* (1993), and *Rosenberger* v. *Rector and Visitors of Univ. of Va.* (1995). . . .

We agree with respondents that petitioners have failed to establish the significant change in factual conditions. . . . Both petitioners and this Court were, at the time *Aguilar* was decided, aware that additional costs would be incurred if Title I services could not be provided in parochial school classrooms. That these predictions of additional costs turned out to be accurate does not constitute a change in factual conditions warranting relief. . . .

We also agree with respondents that the statements made by five Justices in *Kiryas Joel* do not, in themselves, furnish a basis for concluding that our Establishment Clause jurisprudence has changed. . . . But the question of *Aguilar*'s propriety was not before us. The views of five Justices that the case should be reconsidered or overruled cannot be said to have effected a change in Establishment Clause law.

[Justice O'Connor then turned to the question of whether the Court's subsequent decisions involving government aid to religion "undermined" *Aguilar*.]

In order to evaluate whether Aguilar has been eroded by our subsequent Establishment Clause cases, it is necessary to understand the rationale upon which *Aguilar,* as well as its companion case, *School Dist. of Grand Rapids* v. *Ball* (1985), rested.

In *Ball,* the Court evaluated two programs implemented by the School District of Grand Rapids, Michigan. The district's Shared Time program, the one most analogous to Title I, provided remedial and "enrichment" classes at public expense, to students attending nonpublic schools. The classes were taught during regular school hours by publicly employed teachers, using materials purchased with public funds, on the premises of nonpublic schools. The Shared Time courses were in subjects designed to supplement the "core curriculum" of the nonpublic schools. Of the 41 nonpublic schools eligible for the program, 40 were "'pervasively sectarian'" in character—that is, "the purpos[e] of [those] schools [was] to advance their particular religions."

The Court conducted its analysis by applying the [purpose-effect-entanglement test] set forth in *Lemon* v. *Kurtzman* (1971). . . .

The Court acknowledged that the Shared Time program served a purely secular purpose, thereby satisfying the first part of the so-called *Lemon* test. Nevertheless, it ultimately concluded that the program had the impermissible effect of advancing religion.

The Court found that the program violated the Establishment Clause's prohibition against "government-financed or government-sponsored indoctrination into the beliefs of a particular religious faith" in at least three ways. First, . . . the Court observed that the teachers participating in the programs may become involved in intentionally or inadvertently inculcating particular religious tenets or beliefs. . . .

Accordingly, a majority found a "'substantial risk'" that teachers—even those who were not employed by the private schools—might "subtly (or overtly) conform their instruction to the [pervasively sectarian] environment in which they [taught]." The danger of "state-sponsored indoctrination" was only exacerbated by the school district's failure to monitor the courses for religious content. Notably, the Court disregarded the lack of evidence of any specific incidents of religious indoctrination as largely irrelevant, reasoning that potential witnesses to any indoctrination—the parochial school students, their parents, or parochial school officials—might be unable to detect or have little incentive to report the incidents.

The presence of public teachers on parochial school grounds had a second, related impermissible effect: it created a "graphic symbol of the 'concert or union or dependency' of church and state." The Court feared that this perception of a symbolic union between church and state would "conve[y] a message of government endorsement . . . of religion," and thereby violate a "core purpose" of the Establishment Clause.

Third, the Court found that the Shared Time program

impermissibly financed religious indoctrination by subsidizing "the primary religious mission of the institutions affected." The Court separated its prior decisions evaluating programs that aided the secular activities of religious institutions into two categories: those in which it concluded that the aid resulted in an effect that was "indirect, remote, or incidental" (and upheld the aid), and those in which it concluded that the aid resulted in "a direct and substantial advancement of the sectarian enterprise" (and invalidated the aid). [The] Grand Rapids program fell into the latter category. . . . The *Ball* Court likewise placed no weight on the fact that the program was provided to the student, rather than to the school. Nor was the impermissible effect mitigated by the fact that the program only supplemented the courses offered by the parochial schools.

The New York City Title I program challenged in *Aguilar* closely resembled the Shared Time program struck down in *Ball,* but the Court found fault with an aspect of the Title I program not present in *Ball:* the Board had "adopted a system for monitoring the religious content of publicly funded Title I classes in the religious schools." Even though this monitoring system might prevent the Title I program from being used to inculcate religion, the Court concluded . . . that the level of monitoring necessary to be "certain" that the program had an exclusively secular effect would "inevitably resul[t] in the excessive entanglement of church and state," thereby running afoul of *Lemon*'s third prong. In the majority's view, . . . the aid was provided "in a pervasively sectarian environment . . . in the form of teachers," requiring "ongoing inspection . . . to ensure the absence of a religious message." . . .

Distilled to essentials, the Court's conclusion that the Shared Time program in *Ball* had the impermissible effect of advancing religion rested on three assumptions: (i) any public employee who works on the premises of a religious school is presumed to inculcate religion in her work; (ii) the presence of public employees on private school premises creates a symbolic union between church and state; and (iii) any and all public aid that directly aids the educational function of religious schools impermissibly finances religious indoctrination, even if the aid reaches such schools as a consequence of private decisionmaking. Additionally, in *Aguilar,* there was a fourth assumption: that New York City's Title I program necessitated an excessive government entanglement with religion because public employees who teach on the premises of religious schools must be closely monitored to ensure that they do not inculcate religion.

Our more recent cases have undermined the assumptions upon which *Ball* and *Aguilar* relied. To be sure, the general principles we use to evaluate whether government aid violates the Establishment Clause have not changed since *Aguilar* was decided. For example, we continue to ask whether the government acted with the purpose of advancing or inhibiting religion, and the nature of that inquiry has remained largely unchanged. Likewise, we continue to explore whether the aid has the "effect" of advancing or inhibiting religion. What has changed since we decided *Ball* and *Aguilar* is our understanding of the criteria used to assess whether aid to religion has an impermissible effect.

As we have repeatedly recognized, government inculcation of religious beliefs has the impermissible effect of advancing religion. Our cases subsequent to *Aguilar* have, however, modified in two significant respects the approach we use to assess indoctrination. First, we have abandoned the presumption erected in . . . *Ball* that the placement of public employees on parochial school grounds inevitably results in the impermissible effect of state-sponsored indoctrination or constitutes a symbolic union between government and religion. In *Zobrest,* we examined whether the [Individuals with Disabilities Act] was constitutional as applied to a deaf student who sought to bring his state-employed sign language interpreter with him to his Roman Catholic high school. We held that this was permissible, expressly disavowing the notion that "the Establishment Clause [laid] down [an] absolute bar to the placing of a public employee in a sectarian school." "Such a flat rule, smacking of antiquated notions of 'taint,' would indeed exalt form over substance." . . . *Zobrest* also implicitly repudiated another assumption on which *Ball* and *Aguilar* turned: that the presence of a public employee on private school property creates an impermissible "symbolic link" between government and religion. . . .

[W]e have [also] departed from the rule relied on in *Ball* that all government aid that directly aids the educational function of religious schools is invalid. In *Witters,* we held that the Establishment Clause did not bar a State from issuing a vocational tuition grant to a blind person who wished to use the grant to attend a Christian college and become a pastor, missionary, or youth director. Even though the grant recipient clearly would use the money to obtain religious education, we observed that the tuition grants were "'made available generally without regard to the sectarian-nonsectarian, or public-nonpublic nature of the institution benefited.'" The grants were disbursed directly to students, who then used the money to pay for tuition at the educational institution of their choice. In our view, this transaction was no different from a State's issuing a paycheck to one of its employees, knowing that the employee would donate part or all of the check to a religious institution. In both situations, any money that ultimately went to religious institutions did so "only as a result of the genuinely independent and private choices of" individuals. The same logic applied in *Zobrest,* where we allowed the State to provide an interpreter, even though she would be a mouthpiece for religious instruction, because the IDEA's neutral eligibility criteria ensured that the interpreter's presence in a sectarian school was a "result of the private decision of individual parents" and "[could] not be attributed to *state* decision-making." . . .

Zobrest and *Witters* make clear that, under current law, the Shared Time program in *Ball* and New York City's Title I program in *Aguilar* will not, as a matter of law, be deemed to have the effect of advancing religion through indoctrination. Indeed, each of the premises upon which we relied in *Ball* to reach a contrary conclusion is no longer valid. First, there is no reason to presume that, simply because she enters a parochial school classroom, a full-time public employee such as a Title I teacher will depart from her assigned duties and instructions and embark on religious indoctrination, any more than there was a reason in *Zobrest* to think an interpreter would inculcate religion by altering her translation of classroom lectures. Certainly, no evidence has ever shown that any New York City Title I instructor teaching on parochial school premises attempted to inculcate religion in students. Thus, both our precedent and our experience require us to reject respondents' remarkable argument that we must presume Title I instructors to be "uncontrollable and sometimes very unprofessional."

As discussed above, *Zobrest* also repudiates *Ball*'s assumption that the presence of Title I teachers in parochial school classrooms will, without more, create the impression of a "symbolic union" between church and state. JUSTICE SOUTER maintains that *Zobrest* is not dispositive on this point because *Aguilar*'s implicit conclusion that New York City's Title I program created a "symbolic union" rested on more than the presence of Title I employees on parochial school grounds. To him, Title I continues to foster a "symbolic union" between the Board and sectarian schools because it mandates "the involvement of public teachers in the instruction provided within sectarian schools," and "fus[es] public and private faculties." JUSTICE SOUTER does not disavow the notion, uniformly adopted by lower courts, that Title I services may be provided to sectarian school students in off-campus locations, even though that notion necessarily presupposes that the danger of "symbolic union" evaporates once the services are provided off-campus. Taking this view, the only difference between a constitutional program and an unconstitutional one is the location of the classroom, since the degree of cooperation between Title I instructors and parochial school faculty is the same no matter where the services are provided. We do not see any perceptible (let alone dispositive) difference in the degree of symbolic union between a student receiving remedial instruction in a classroom on his sectarian school's campus and one receiving instruction in a van parked just at the school's curbside. To draw this line based solely on the location of the public employee is neither "sensible" nor "sound," and the Court in *Zobrest* rejected it.

Nor under current law can we conclude that a program placing full-time public employees on parochial campuses to provide Title I instruction would impermissibly finance religious indoctrination. In all relevant respects, the provision of instructional services under Title I is indistinguishable from the provision of sign language interpreters under the IDEA. Both programs make aid available only to eligible recipients. That aid is provided to students at whatever school they choose to attend. Although Title I instruction is provided to several students at once, whereas an interpreter provides translation to a single student, this distinction is not constitutionally significant. . . .

What is most fatal to the argument that New York City's Title I program directly subsidizes religion is that it applies with equal force when those services are provided off-campus, and *Aguilar* implied that providing the services off-campus is entirely consistent with the Establishment Clause. JUSTICE SOUTER resists the impulse to upset this implication, contending that it can be justified on the ground that Title I services are "less likely to supplant some of what would otherwise go on inside [the sectarian schools] and to subsidize what remains" when those services are offered off-campus. But JUSTICE SOUTER does not explain why a sectarian school would not have the same incentive to "make patently significant cut-backs" in its curriculum no matter where Title I services are offered, since the school would ostensibly be excused from having to provide the Title I-type services itself. Because the incentive is the same either way, we find no logical basis upon which to conclude that Title I services are an impermissible subsidy of religion when offered on-campus, but not when offered off-campus. Accordingly, contrary to our conclusion in *Aguilar,* placing full-time employees on parochial school campuses does not as a matter of law have the impermissible effect of advancing religion through indoctrination. . . .

We turn now to *Aguilar*'s conclusion that New York City's Title I program resulted in an excessive entanglement between church and state. Whether a government aid program results in such an entanglement has consistently been an aspect of our Establishment Clause analysis. We have considered entanglement both in the course of assessing whether an aid program has an impermissible effect of advancing religion and as a factor separate and apart from "effect." Regardless of how we have characterized the issue, however, the factors we use to assess whether an entanglement is "excessive" are similar to the factors we use to examine "effect." That is, to assess entanglement, we have looked to "the character and purposes of the institutions that are benefited, the nature of the aid that the State provides, and the resulting relationship between the government and religious authority." . . . [I]t is simplest to recognize why entanglement is significant and treat it—as we did in *Walz*—as an aspect of the inquiry into a statute's effect.

Not all entanglements, of course, have the effect of advancing or inhibiting religion. Interaction between church and state is inevitable, and we have always tolerated some level of involvement between the two. Entanglement must be "excessive" before it runs afoul of the Establishment Clause.

The pre-*Aguilar* Title I program does not result in an "excessive" entanglement that advances or inhibits religion. As discussed previously, the Court's finding of "excessive" entanglement in *Aguilar* rested on three grounds: (i) the program would require "pervasive monitoring by public authorities" to ensure that Title I employees did not inculcate religion; (ii) the program required "administrative cooperation" between the Board and parochial schools; and (iii) the program might increase the dangers of "political divisiveness." Under our current understanding of the Establishment Clause, the last two considerations are insufficient by themselves to create an "excessive" entanglement. They are present no matter where Title I services are offered, and no court has held that Title I services cannot be offered off-campus. Further, the assumption underlying the first consideration has been undermined. In *Aguilar,* the Court presumed that full-time public employees on parochial school grounds would be tempted to inculcate religion, despite the ethical standards they were required to uphold. Because of this risk *pervasive* monitoring would be required. But after *Zobrest.* we no longer presume that public employees will inculcate religion simply because they happen to be in a sectarian environment. Since we have abandoned the assumption that properly instructed public employees will fail to discharge their duties faithfully, we must also discard the assumption that *pervasive* monitoring of Title I teachers is required. There is no suggestion in the record before us that unannounced monthly visits of public supervisors are insufficient to prevent or to detect inculcation of religion by public employees. Moreover, we have not found excessive entanglement in cases in which States imposed far more onerous burdens on religious institutions than the monitoring system at issue here.

To summarize, New York City's Title I program does not run afoul of any of three primary criteria we currently use to evaluate whether government aid has the effect of advancing religion: it does not result in governmental indoctrination; define its recipients by reference to religion; or create an excessive entanglement. We therefore hold that a federally funded program providing supplemental, remedial instruction to disadvantaged children on a neutral basis is not invalid under the Establishment Clause when such instruction is given on the premises of sectarian schools by government employees pursuant to a program containing safeguards such as those present here. The same considerations that justify this holding require us to conclude that this carefully constrained program also cannot reasonably be viewed as an endorsement of religion. Accordingly, we must acknowledge that *Aguilar,* as well as the portion of *Ball* addressing Grand Rapids' Shared Time program, are no longer good law.

The doctrine of *stare decisis* does not preclude us from recognizing the change in our law and overruling *Aguilar* and those portions of *Ball* inconsistent with our more recent decisions. As we have often noted, "*[s]tare decisis* is not an inexorable command," but instead reflects a policy judgment that "in most matters it is more important that the applicable rule of law be settled than that it be settled right." That policy is at its weakest when we interpret the Constitution because our interpretation can be altered only by constitutional amendment or by overruling our prior decisions. Thus, we have held in several cases that *stare decisis* does not prevent us from overruling a previous decision where there has been a significant change in or subsequent development of our constitutional law. As discussed above, our Establishment Clause jurisprudence has changed significantly since we decided *Ball* and *Aguilar,* so our decision to overturn those cases rests on far more than "a present doctrinal disposition to come out differently from the Court of [1985]." We therefore overrule *Ball* and *Aguilar* to the extent those decisions are inconsistent with our current understanding of the Establishment Clause. . . .

As a final matter, we see no reason to wait for a "better vehicle" in which to evaluate the impact of subsequent cases on *Aguilar*'s continued vitality. . . . Indeed, under these circumstances, it would be particularly inequitable for us to bide our time waiting for another case to arise while the city of New York labors under a continuing injunction forcing it to spend millions of dollars on mobile instructional units and leased sites when it could instead be spending that money to give economically disadvantaged children a better chance at success in life by means of a program that is perfectly consistent with the Establishment Clause.

For these reasons, we reverse the judgment of the Court of Appeals and remand to the District Court with instructions to vacate its September 26, 1985, order.

It is so ordered.

JUSTICE SOUTER, with whom JUSTICE STEVENS and JUSTICE GINSBURG join, and with whom JUSTICE BREYER joins as to Part II, dissenting.

I believe *Aguilar* was a correct and sensible decision, and my only reservation about its opinion is that the emphasis on the excessive entanglement produced by monitoring religious instructional content obscured those facts that independently called for the application of two central tenets of Establishment Clause jurisprudence. The State is forbidden to subsidize religion directly and is just as surely forbidden to act in any way that could reasonably be viewed as religious endorsement.

As is explained elsewhere, the flat ban on subsidization antedates the Bill of Rights and has been an unwavering rule in Establishment Clause cases, qualified only by the conclusion two Terms ago that state exactions from college students are not the sort of public revenues subject to the ban, *Rosenberger* v. *Rector and Visitors of Univ. of Va.* (1995). The rule expresses the hard lesson learned over and over again in the American past and in the experiences of the countries from which we have come, that religions supported by governments are compromised just as surely as the religious freedom of dissenters is burdened when the government supports religion. . . .

The human tendency, of course, is to forget the hard lessons, and to overlook the history of governmental partnership with religion when a cause is worthy, and bureaucrats have programs. That tendency to forget is the reason for having the Establishment Clause (along with the Constitution's other structural and libertarian guarantees), in the hope of stopping the corrosion before it starts.

These principles were violated by the programs at issue in *Aguilar* and *Ball,* as a consequence of several significant features common to both Title I, as implemented in New York City before *Aguilar,* and the Grand Rapids Shared Time program: each provided classes on the premises of the religious schools, covering a wide range of subjects including some at the core of primary and secondary education, like reading and mathematics; while their services were termed "supplemental," the programs and their instructors necessarily assumed responsibility for teaching subjects that the religious schools would otherwise have been obligated to provide, the public employees carrying out the programs had broad responsibilities involving the exercise of considerable discretion, while the programs offered aid to nonpublic school students generally, participation by religious school students in each program was extensive, and, finally, aid under Title I and Shared Time flowed directly to the schools in the form of classes and programs, as distinct from indirect aid that reaches schools only as a result of independent private choice. . . .

What was true of the Title I scheme as struck down in *Aguilar* will be just as true when New York reverts to the old practices with the Court's approval after today. There is simply no line that can be drawn between the instruction paid for at taxpayers' expense and the instruction in any subject that is not identified as formally religious. While it would be an obvious sham, say, to channel cash to religious schools to be credited only against the expense of "secular" instruction, the line between "supplemental" and general education is likewise impossible to draw. If a State may constitutionally enter the schools to teach in the manner in question, it must in constitutional principle be free to assume, or assume payment for, the entire cost of instruction provided in any ostensibly secular subject in any religious school. This Court explicitly recognized this in *Ball,* and although, in *Aguilar,* the Court concentrated on entanglement it noted the similarity to *Ball*. . . .

When, moreover, [government] aid goes overwhelmingly to one religious denomination, minimal contact between state and church is the less likely to feed the resentment of other religions that would like access to public money for their own worthy projects.

In sum, if a line is to be drawn short of barring all state aid to religious schools for teaching standard subjects, the *Aguilar-Ball* line was a sensible one capable of principled adherence. It is no less sound, and no less necessary, today.

II

The Court today ignores this doctrine and claims that recent cases rejected the elemental assumptions underlying *Aguilar* and much of *Ball*. But the Court errs. Its holding that *Aguilar* and the portion of *Ball* addressing the Shared Time program are "no longer good law," rests on mistaken reading. . . .

In *Zobrest*, the Court did indeed recognize that the Establishment Clause lays down no absolute bar to placing public employees in a sectarian school, but the rejection of such a *per se* rule was hinged expressly on the nature of the employee's job, sign language interpretation (or signing) and the circumscribed role of the signer. . . .

The Court, however, ignores the careful distinction drawn in *Zobrest* and insists that a full-time public employee such as a Title I teacher is just like the signer, asserting that "there is no reason to presume that, simply because she enters a parochial school classroom, . . . [this] teacher will depart from her assigned duties and instructions and embark on religious indoctrination". . . . Whatever may be the merits of this position (and I find it short on merit), it does not enjoy the authority of *Zobrest*. The Court may disagree with *Ball*'s assertion that a publicly employed teacher working in a sectarian school is apt to reinforce the pervasive inculcation of religious beliefs, but its disagreement is fresh law. . . .

Ball did not establish that "any and all" such aid to religious schools necessarily violates the Establishment Clause. It held that the Shared Time program subsidized the religious functions of the parochial schools by taking over a significant portion of their responsibility for teaching secular subjects. The Court noted that it had "never accepted the mere possibility of subsidization . . . as sufficient to invalidate an aid program," and instead enquired whether the effect of the proffered aid was "direct and substantial" (and, so, unconstitutional) or merely "indirect and incidental" (and, so, permissible), emphasizing that the question "is one of degree." *Witters* and *Zobrest* did nothing to repudiate the principle, emphasizing rather the limited nature of the aid at issue in each case as well as the fact that religious institutions did not receive it directly from the State. In *Witters*, the Court noted that the State would issue the disputed vocational aid directly to one student who would then transmit it to the school of his choice, and that there was no record evidence that "any significant portion of the aid expended under the Washington program as a whole will end up flowing to religious education." *Zobrest* also presented an instance of a single beneficiary, and emphasized that the student (who had previously received the interpretive services in a public school) determined where the aid would be used, that the aid at issue was limited, and that the religious school was "not relieved of an expense that it otherwise would have assumed in educating its students."

It is accordingly puzzling to find the Court insisting that the aid scheme administered under Title I and considered in *Aguilar* was comparable to the programs in *Witters* and *Zobrest*. Instead of aiding isolated individuals within a school system, New York City's Title I program before *Aguilar* served about 22,000 private school students, all but 52 of whom attended religious schools. Instead of serving individual blind or deaf students, as such, Title I as administered in New York City before *Aguilar* (and as now to be revived) funded instruction in core subjects (remedial reading, reading skills, remedial mathematics, English as a second language) and provided guidance services. Instead of providing a service the school would not otherwise furnish, the Title I services necessarily relieved a religious school of "an expense that it otherwise would have assumed," and freed its funds for other, and sectarian uses.

Finally, instead of aid that comes to the religious school indirectly in the sense that its distribution results from private decision making, a public educational agency distributes Title I aid in the form of programs and services directly to the religious schools. In *Zobrest* and *Witters*, it was fair to say that individual students were themselves applicants for individual benefits on a scale that could not amount to a systemic supplement. But under Title I, a local educational agency (which in New York City is the Board of Education) may receive federal funding by proposing programs approved to serve individual students who meet the criteria of need, which it then uses to provide such programs at the religious schools, students eligible for such programs may not apply directly for Title I funds. The aid, accordingly, is not even formally aid to the individual students (and even formally individual aid must be seen as aid to a school system when so many individuals receive it that it becomes a significant feature of the system).

In sum, nothing since *Ball* and *Aguilar* and before this case has eroded the distinction between "direct and substantial" and "indirect and incidental." That principled line is being breached only here and now. . . .

III

Finally, there is the issue of precedent. *Stare decisis* is no barrier in the Court's eyes because it reads *Aguilar* and *Ball* for exaggerated propositions that *Witters* and

Zobrest are supposed to have limited to the point of abandoned doctrine. The Court's dispensation from *stare decisis* is, accordingly, no more convincing than its reading of those cases. Since *Aguilar* came down, no case has held that there need be no concern about a risk that publicly paid school teachers may further religious doctrine; no case has repudiated the distinction between direct and substantial aid and aid that is indirect and incidental; no case has held that fusing public and private faculties in one religious school does not create an impermissible union or carry an impermissible endorsement; and no case has held that direct subsidization of religious education is constitutional or that the assumption of a portion of a religious school's teaching responsibility is not direct subsidization.

The continuity of the law, indeed, is matched by the persistence of the facts. When *Aguilar* was decided, everyone knew that providing Title I services off the premises of the religious schools would come at substantial cost in efficiency, convenience, and money. Title I had begun off the premises in New York, after all, and dissatisfaction with the arrangement was what led the City to put the public school teachers into the religious schools in the first place. When *Aguilar* required the end of that arrangement, conditions reverted to those of the past and they have remained unchanged: teaching conditions are often poor, it is difficult to move children around, and it costs a lot of money. That is, the facts became once again what they were once before, as everyone including the Members of this Court knew they would be. No predictions have gone so awry as to excuse the case from the claim of precedent, let alone excuse the Court from adhering to its own prior decision in this very case.

That is not to deny that the facts just recited are regrettable; the object of Title I is worthy without doubt, and the cost of compliance is high. In the short run, there is much that is genuinely unfortunate about the administration of the scheme under *Aguilar*'s rule. But constitutional lines have to be drawn, and on one side of every one of them is an otherwise sympathetic case that provokes impatience with the Constitution and with the line. But constitutional lines are the price of constitutional government.

By overturning *Aguilar* and *Ball*, the Court, in *Agostini*, demonstrated that it was willing to chart a new direction governing the relationship between parochial schools and government educational assistance programs. Three years later, the Court, in *Mitchell* v. *Helms* (2000), ruled that parochial schools were eligible to receive technology assistance, including personal computers for classroom use, under Chapter 2 of the federal Elementary and Secondary Education Act. Also known as Title VI, the program allocates $16 million per year to private schools, almost all of which are religious. Although the justices divided 6 to 3 in favor of upholding Title VI, Justice Clarence Thomas, who wrote the majority opinion in *Helms*, could get only Chief Justice Rehnquist and Justices Kennedy and Scalia to agree with his conclusion that religious schools should be permitted to use government assistance for any aspect of their educational programs. Justice O'Connor, who wrote the majority opinion in *Agostini*, was not willing to go that far. Together, *Agostini* and *Helms* make clear that the Court is poised to reshape the legal rules limiting the eligibility of religious schools to participate in federal programs. This new environment will certainly encourage litigation on such hot-button political issues as school vouchers and federal programs making religious institutions eligible to participate in a wide array of social service and charitable functions (sometimes referred to as "charitable choice"). How a sharply divided Court rules on these questions will be closely watched by both supporters and opponents of government aid to religious institutions.

Confronting the Constitutional Order: The Free Exercise Clause

This section will examine the two major types of cases arising under the Free Exercise Clause: (1) those involving specific discrimination against religion or particular religious beliefs and (2) those involving requests for religion-based exemptions from laws that apply to the general population. Philosopher Michael Sandel has written that, for most Americans, the right to follow the dictates of conscience is not a choice but an imperative.[68] In other words, Orthodox Jews are not free to choose whether to cover their heads with a yarmulke, Seventh-day Adventists cannot substitute Sunday for the Saturday Sabbath, and Jehovah's Witnesses cannot pledge allegiance to any other authority than God. What happens when religious claims conflict with laws applicable to the general population? Is there ever a point when government may prohibit individuals or churches from following their conscience—not because it interferes with a generally applicable law, but because a majority of people find certain religious beliefs dangerous or morally repulsive?

"Whores of Babylon" and Other Heresies: The Jehovah's Witnesses, Animal Sacrifice, and Religious Free Exercise

Simply put, the foundation of free exercise doctrine in the twentieth century was built by the Jehovah's Witnesses, a small Christian denomination founded in the 1870s by Pittsburgh businessman Charles Taze Russell. Having dabbled in the Presbyterian and Congregationalist faiths, two Protestant denominations with strong roots in colonial America, Russell became convinced of Christ's imminent return and coming of Armageddon, at which point all nonbelievers would be eternally damned. By 1873, Russell had published his first tract, "The Object and Manner of the Lord's Return," in which he stated that all "living saints" would be miraculously swept away to be with their Lord when Armageddon came about. On Good Friday 1878, Russell assembled several other "living saints" and reported to the Sixth Street Bridge in downtown Pittsburgh for ascension into Heaven. Clad in white robes and standing for several hours, they waited and waited but nothing happened. The embarrassing incident was reported in local newspapers, adding to Russell's reputation as a charlatan among established religious leaders.[69]

Russell's early missteps and some unflattering attention alleging marital and financial improprieties did not leave him without adherents, who were increasingly drawn to Russell's charismatic leadership and religious prophecies. In 1884, Russell created the Watch Tower Bible and Tract Society. Although Russell's prediction that Armageddon would arrive in 1914 never came to pass, World War I did. Russell, interpreting World War I as a sign from God, revised his prophecy to claim that Armageddon's arrival would be in 1918. But in 1916, after battling a prolonged illness, Russell died before he could see the fruits of his prediction. Joseph Rutherford, a former Missouri state judge, succeeded Russell, and immediately thrust the Watch Tower society into a more prominent position through his vigorous public protests against World War I. In 1918, Rutherford and several other Watch Tower directors were briefly jailed for violating the federal Espionage Act of 1917, which prohibited a wide range of activities that interfered with the government's ability to carry on the war. Rutherford spared virtually no one in his campaign against the war, and singled out organized religion, particularly the Roman Catholic Church, for especially harsh treatment.[70]

Rutherford instituted several major changes in Watch Tower doctrine. The most significant change was his belief that beyond the "saints from birth"—original Watch Tower members and their families—there existed millions of people who could be rescued and redeemed from their evil ways through incessant proselytizing. In a 1922 address to a Watch Tower convention, Rutherford urged his followers to "herald the message far and wide. The world must know that Jehovah is God and that Jesus Christ is King of kings and

Jehovah's Witness J. B. Good, jailed in 1941 for attempting to spread his religious beliefs, looks out from his jail cell in Marianna, Arkansas.

Lord of lords. . . . You are his publicity agents. Therefore advertise, advertise, advertise the King and his kingdom." By the early 1930s, the Witnesses, as they were now more popularly known, had put together an extensive body of literature for door-to-door canvassing. They also began proselytizing on street corners, parks, and public squares.[71] These public forms of proselytizing ultimately led the Witnesses into their dramatic confrontation with government authorities over their right to follow the commands of their faith.

In contrast to litigation later undertaken by the NAACP, ACLU, and AJCongress to challenge, for example, racial discrimination and religious practices in the public schools, the Witnesses were dependent on criminal prosecution to land their day in court. Once the Witnesses decided to challenge state laws that limited their ability to proselytize, they were left with little control over litigation strategy, having to react to the charges brought against them. Still, the Witnesses were remarkably persistent in their drive to invoke the First Amendment's protection on their behalf. By the late 1930s, the ACLU began offering the Witnesses litigation support, and persuaded them to make a crucial decision that launched them toward the Supreme Court. Rather than litigate in state court, the ACLU convinced the Witnesses to take their claims into federal court, and argue that the protections of the First Amendment were applicable to the states through the Fourteenth Amendment.[72] In *Lovell* v. *Griffin* (1938) and *Schneider* v. *Irvington* (1939), the Witnesses obtained their first victories in the Supreme Court, holding that state laws banning door-to-door solicitation and distributing written materials without prior consent violated their First Amendment rights to freedom of the press. Buoyed by these groundbreaking victories, the Witnesses decided to challenge a Connecticut law prohibiting solicitation for various purposes, among them religious.

Cantwell v. *Connecticut*

310 U.S. 296 (1940)

Newton Cantwell and his wife, Esther, joined the Watch Tower Bible and Tract Society in the early 1900s, after becoming disenchanted with mainstream religious teaching. During the Great Depression, the Cantwells decided to sell their family farm and make proselytizing on behalf of the Witnesses their life's work. Esther died shortly thereafter, but Newton, along with his teenage sons, Jesse and Russell, continued the family's mission, traveling through Tennessee, Kentucky, and Virginia to spread Jehovah's word, often struggling just to eat and persevere. In 1937, the Watch Tower society selected Newton as a "special pioneer" and, with financial support, sent him to New Haven, Connecticut, to proselytize.

The Cantwells quickly ran into opposition in this overwhelmingly Catholic city. They were arrested several times by the New Haven police for breaking the city's antisolicitation laws. One April evening, the Cantwells were playing a recording of one of Joseph Rutherford's speeches that complemented his book, *Enemies*. Their activities incensed several people in the neighborhood, including a woman named Anna Rigby, who became so angry after Russell continued to preach to her that she was "mad enough to hit him if he did not go away." After Rigby complained to the police, the Cantwells were arrested for breaking the city's antisolicitation statute. All three Cantwells were convicted by a local trial court. On appeal to the Connecticut Supreme Court, Newton and Russell's convictions were thrown out; Jesse's, however, was upheld.[73]

The Witnesses' lawyer, Hayden Covington, believed that Cantwell's case was a strong one to challenge the restriction on religious activities posed by the New Haven law. Relying on the application of the Speech and Press Clauses to the states through the Due Process Clause of the Fourteenth Amendment, Covington, encouraged by the ACLU, contested Cantwell's conviction as violative of the Free Exercise Clause. Between 1938 and 1946, the Witnesses were the principal parties in twenty-three cases decided by the Supreme Court, emerging victorious in fifteen of them.[74]

The Court's decision was unanimous. Justice Roberts delivered the opinion of the Court.

MR. JUSTICE ROBERTS delivered the opinion of the Court.

The fundamental concept of liberty embodied in th[e] [Fourteenth] Amendment embraces the liberties guaranteed by the First Amendment. The First Amendment declares that Congress shall make no law respecting an establishment of religion or prohibiting the free exercise thereof. The Fourteenth Amendment has rendered the

legislatures of the states as incompetent as Congress to enact such laws. The constitutional inhibition of legislation on the subject of religion has a double aspect. On the one hand, it forestalls compulsion by law of the acceptance of any creed or the practice of any form of worship. Freedom of conscience and freedom to adhere to such religious organization or form of worship as the individual may choose cannot be restricted by law. On the other hand, it safeguards the free exercise of the chosen form of religion. Thus, the Amendment embraces two concepts—freedom to believe and freedom to act. The first is absolute, but, in the nature of things, the second cannot be. Conduct remains subject to regulation for the protection of society. The freedom to act must have appropriate definition to preserve the enforcement of that protection. In every case, the power to regulate must be so exercised as not, in attaining a permissible end, unduly to infringe the protected freedom. No one would contest the proposition that a State may not, by statute, wholly deny the right to preach or to disseminate religious views. Plainly, such a previous and absolute restraint would violate the terms of the guarantee. It is equally clear that a State may, by general and nondiscriminatory legislation, regulate the times, the places, and the manner of soliciting upon its streets, and of holding meetings thereon, and may in other respects safeguard the peace, good order, and comfort of the community without unconstitutionally invading the liberties protected by the Fourteenth Amendment. The appellants are right in their insistence that the Act in question is not such a regulation. If a certificate is procured, solicitation is permitted without restraint, but, in the absence of a certificate, solicitation is altogether prohibited.

The appellants urge that to require them to obtain a certificate as a condition of soliciting support for their views amounts to a prior restraint on the exercise of their religion within the meaning of the Constitution. The State insists that the Act, as construed by the Supreme Court of Connecticut, imposes no previous restraint upon the dissemination of religious views or teaching, but merely safeguards against the perpetration of frauds under the cloak of religion. Conceding that this is so, the question remains whether the method adopted by Connecticut to that end transgresses the liberty safeguarded by the Constitution.

The general regulation, in the public interest, of solicitation, which does not involve any religious test and does not unreasonably obstruct or delay the collection of funds, is not open to any constitutional objection, even though the collection be for a religious purpose. Such regulation would not constitute a prohibited previous restraint on the free exercise of religion or interpose an inadmissible obstacle to its exercise.

It will be noted, however, that the Act requires an application to the secretary of the public welfare council of the State; that he is empowered to determine whether the cause is a religious one, and that the issue of a certificate depends upon his affirmative action. If he finds that the cause is not that of religion, to solicit for it becomes a crime. He is not to issue a certificate as a matter of course. His decision to issue or refuse it involves appraisal of facts, the exercise of judgment, and the formation of an opinion. He is authorized to withhold his approval if he determines that the cause is not a religious one. Such a censorship of religion as the means of determining its right to survive is a denial of liberty protected by the First Amendment and included in the liberty which is within the protection of the Fourteenth. . . .

Nothing we have said is intended even remotely to imply that, under the cloak of religion, persons may, with impunity, commit frauds upon the public. Certainly penal laws are available to punish such conduct. Even the exercise of religion may be at some slight inconvenience in order that the State may protect its citizens from injury. Without doubt, a State may protect its citizens from fraudulent solicitation by requiring a stranger in the community, before permitting him publicly to solicit funds for any purpose, to establish his identity and his authority to act for the cause which he purports to represent. The State is likewise free to regulate the time and manner of solicitation generally, in the interest of public saf[ety, peace, comfort or convenience. But to condition the solicitation of aid for the perpetuation of religious views or systems upon a license, the grant of which rests in the exercise of a determination by state authority as to what is a religious cause, is to lay a forbidden burden upon the exercise of liberty protected by the Constitution. . . .

The offense known as breach of the peace embraces a great variety of conduct destroying or menacing public order and tranquility. It includes not only violent acts, but acts and words likely to produce violence in others. No one would have the hardihood to suggest that the principle of freedom of speech sanctions incitement to riot, or that religious liberty connotes the privilege to exhort others to physical attack upon those belonging to another sect. When clear and present danger of riot, disorder, interference with traffic upon the public streets, or other immediate threat to public safety, peace, or order appears, the power of the State to prevent or punish is obvious. Equally obvious is it that a State may not unduly suppress free communication of views, religious or other, under the guise of conserving desirable conditions. Here we have a situation analogous to a conviction under a statute sweeping in a great variety of conduct under a general and indefinite characterization, and leaving to the executive and judicial branches too wide a discretion in its application. . . .

In the realm of religious faith, and in that of political belief, sharp differences arise. In both fields the tenets of one man may seem the rankest error to his neighbor. To persuade others to his own point of view, the pleader, as we know, at times resorts to exaggeration, to vilification of men who have been, or are, prominent in church or state, and even to false statement. But the people of this nation have ordained, in the light of history, that, in spite of the probability of excesses and abuses, these liberties are, in the long view, essential to enlightened opinion and right conduct on the part of the citizens of a democracy.

▼▲▼

Cantwell is important for several reasons. First, the Court's decision to strike down the Connecticut law demonstrated that it was willing to extend civil liberties to groups even as distrusted as the Jehovah's Witnesses during a period when states had increasingly clamped down on any religious conduct and political dissent they found threatening. Second, *Cantwell* demonstrated the power of litigation to redress constitutional grievances and the Court's willingness to encourage minority groups to utilize litigation as an instrument of reform. Chief Justice Harlan Fiske Stone later said of the Jehovah's Witnesses cases decided during this time, "I think the Jehovah's Witnesses ought to have an endowment in view of the aid which they give in solving the legal problems of civil liberties."[75] Finally, *Cantwell* made clear that laws burdening religion had to clear the requirements of the Court's emerging *preferred freedoms* doctrine to survive judicial review. That is, a law that infringed upon a right the Court considered fundamental had to advance a government interest of the highest order, not just a rational or legitimate purpose. The New Haven law was not "neutral" and generally applicable. It applied to persons soliciting money on behalf of religious causes. Moreover, the Court held that laws burdening religion as a *class*, and not just a particular denomination or practice, would be considered presumptively unconstitutional.

Writing for the Court, Justice Roberts did hold that "belief" and "action" were subject to different levels of protection. Security for one's religious beliefs was absolute, whereas conduct compelled by the adherence to religious beliefs was not. Roberts's conclusion that "[i]n every case the power to regulate must be so exercised as not, in attaining a permissible end, unduly to infringe the protected freedom" was, however, no more than a twentieth-century application of Jefferson's position during the Virginia disestablishment debates. Recall that Jefferson had written that government was well within its power to set limits on "overt acts," even those undertaken in the name of conscience, when they conflicted with "peace and good order."

Since *Cantwell*, laws targeting religion for discriminatory treatment have been so rare that only one has reached the Supreme Court, *Church of Lukumi Babalu Aye, Inc.* v. *City of Hialeah* (1993). Political scientist Bette Evans points out that the Court has always struggled with balancing the prohibition against defining religion or determining the legitimacy of religious conduct in free exercise cases with laws resulting in harm against religion.[76] In *United States* v. *Ballard* (1944), the Court ruled that juries could not consider whether they believed the truth or falsity of claims made by religious individuals, only whether the individuals making claims believed what they said. Writing for the Court, Justice Douglas held that

> Heresy trials are foreign to our Constitution. Men may believe what they cannot prove. They may not be put to the proof of their religious doctrines or beliefs. Religious experiences which are as real as life to some may be incomprehensible to others. Yet the fact that they be beyond the ken of mortals does not mean that they can be made suspect before the law. . . . The religious view espoused by respondents might seem incredible, if not preposterous, to most people. But if those doctrines are subject to trial before a jury charged with finding their truth or falsity, then the same can be done with the religious beliefs of any sect. When the triers of fact undertake that task they enter a forbidden domain.[77]

The "preposterous" beliefs of which Douglas spoke belonged to Guy, End, and Donald Ballard, leaders of the "I Am" movement, who claimed to be the messengers of Master Saint German and to have powers to heal the incurably ill. The federal government prosecuted the Ballards for mail fraud, claiming that they did not believe their own message. The Court's conclusion in *Ballard* that it did not matter what anybody else thought as long as the Ballards claimed to believe what they said was an enormous victory for religious minorities.

Still, the Court treads near the water's edge of defining religion and assessing the legitimacy of religious practices in free exercise cases more often than it wants to acknowledge. *City of Hialeah* saw the Court relieved of the task of balancing sincere religious beliefs with harm brought about by government action because of the religion-specific nature of the contested law. Are you persuaded that the Court avoided dealing with the substance of the religious claims when it decided *City of Hialeah?* Is such detachment possible?

Church of Lukumi Babalu Aye, Inc. v. *City of Hialeah*

508 U.S. 520 (1993)

Adherents of the Santeria faith have been in the United States since the late 1950s, when Cubans fleeing Fidel Castro's revolution came to South Florida, settling principally in the Miami area, and bringing their religious practices with them. Today, about sixty thousand practitioners of Santeria live in the United States, with almost all of them living in Florida. This compares with about 100 million around the world. And while the ritual sacrifice of goats, chickens, ducks, pigeons, turtles, doves, and guinea pigs probably strikes most Americans as unusual, such practices are common in the Santeria faith. Animal sacrifice, which is accomplished by cutting the animals' neck arteries, is common at funerals, weddings, birth celebrations, and other important Santeria ceremonies.

In 1987, the Church of Lukumi Babalu Aye, which had status as a religious nonprofit corporation under Florida law, successfully petitioned the city of Hialeah for permission to build a church and related facilities. The centrality of animal sacrifice in Santeria religious ritual soon became a major public controversy, leading the city council, at the behest of animal rights groups, to adopt several ordinances banning the practice. The Hialeah laws were clearly directed at the Santeria church. They were prefaced, in fact, by a resolution "expressing 'concern' over religious practices inconsistent with public morals, peace, or safety, and declaring the city's 'commitment'" to prohibiting such practices. One ordinance defined sacrifice as unnecessarily killing an animal in a ritual that was not for food consumption, and prohibited explicitly the "possession, sacrifice, or slaughter" of an animal in "any type of ritual." Another one defined slaughter as the "killing of animals for food," and prohibited slaughter outside areas zoned for slaughterhouses. That same law included an exemption for facilities or places housing small numbers of hogs and cattle. The Santeria did not meet the requirements for exemption.

The Church of Lukumi Babalu Aye challenged the Hialeah ordinances as unconstitutional under the Free Exercise Clause. *City of Hialeah* drew a great deal of attention from religious and civil liberties groups when it reached the Supreme Court. These groups hoped the Court would use the case to revisit its controversial decision three years earlier in *Employment Division of Oregon* v. *Smith* (1990). In *Smith,* the Court, without warning or briefing, ruled that generally applicable laws burdening religion would no longer have to satisfy a compelling government interest. But *City of Hialeah* differed from *Smith* in one major way: The Florida city's law targeted the Santeria by word and deed, whereas the Oregon law in *Smith* involved general eligibility for unemployment compensation. The Court declined to revisit *Smith* in *City of Hialeah,* holding that the cases, because of the difference in the laws involved (religion-specific versus general applicability), involved different standards of review. *Smith* is discussed in detail later in this chapter.

Religious groups lined up behind the Church of Lukumi Babalu Aye, asking the Court to strike down the Hialeah ordinances as coercive and discriminatory. Americans United, AJCongress, Anti-Defamation League, the Baptist Joint Committee, the Christian Legal Society, and the National Association of Evangelicals filed a joint brief on behalf of the Santeria church, but their real motive was to ask the Court to reconsider *Smith.* The United States Catholic Conference and the National Jewish Commission on Law and Public Affairs filed separate briefs also requesting the Court to abandon *Smith.* One thing to note in free exercise cases is the completely different alignment of religious and civil liberties groups than in establishment cases. Rarely do the AJCongress and the ACLU, which helped sponsor *City of Hialeah,* appear on the same side of an Establishment Clause case as the Christian Legal

Society or the United States Catholic Conference. In fact, these three groups have supported the same party in an establishment case only three times since the late 1940s. The difference, as we noted earlier in this chapter, is that religious groups can rarely agree on when government support for prayer or public funding is good for religion. They do agree, however, that laws burdening religious practices compromise religious freedom.

The Court's decision was unanimous. Justice Kennedy delivered the opinion of the Court, which did not attract a majority. Only Justice Stevens joined in full. Chief Justice Rehnquist and Justices White, Scalia, Souter, and Thomas joined in part. Justice Scalia, joined by Chief Justice Rehnquist, filed a concurring opinion. Justice Souter filed a concurring opinion. Justice Blackmun, joined by Justice O'Connor, also concurred.

▼▲▼

JUSTICE KENNEDY delivered the opinion of the Court, except as to Part II-A-2.

The principle that government may not enact laws that suppress religious belief or practice is so well understood that few violations are recorded in our opinions. Concerned that this fundamental nonpersecution principle of the First Amendment was implicated here, however, we granted certiorari.

Our review confirms that the laws in question were enacted by officials who did not understand, failed to perceive, or chose to ignore the fact that their official actions violated the Nation's essential commitment to religious freedom. The challenged laws had an impermissible object; and in all events, the principle of general applicability was violated because the secular ends asserted in defense of the laws were pursued only with respect to conduct motivated by religious beliefs. We invalidate the challenged enactments. . . .

II

In addressing the constitutional protection for free exercise of religion, our cases establish the general proposition that a law that is neutral and of general applicability need not be justified by a compelling governmental interest even if the law has the incidental effect of burdening a particular religious practice. Neutrality and general applicability are interrelated, and, as becomes apparent in this case, failure to satisfy one requirement is a likely indication that the other has not been satisfied. A law failing to satisfy these requirements must be justified by a compelling governmental interest, and must be narrowly tailored to advance that interest. These ordinances fail to satisfy the *Smith* requirements. We begin by discussing neutrality.

A

At a minimum, the protections of the Free Exercise Clause pertain if the law at issue discriminates against some or all religious beliefs or regulates or prohibits conduct because it is undertaken for religious reasons. Indeed, it was "historical instances of religious persecution and intolerance that gave concern to those who drafted the Free Exercise Clause." These principles, though not often at issue in our Free Exercise Clause cases, have played a role in some. In *McDaniel* v. *Paty* (1978), for example, we invalidated a State law that disqualified members of the clergy from holding certain public offices, because it "impose[d] special disabilities on the basis of . . . religious status." On the same principle, . . . we [also] found that a municipal ordinance was applied in an unconstitutional manner when interpreted to prohibit preaching in a public park by a Jehovah's Witness, but to permit preaching during the course of a Catholic mass or Protestant church service. . . .

1

Although a law targeting religious beliefs as such is never permissible, if the object of a law is to infringe upon or restrict practices because of their religious motivation, the law is not neutral, and it is invalid unless it is justified by a compelling interest and is narrowly tailored to advance that interest. There are, of course, many ways of demonstrating that the object or purpose of a law is the suppression of religion or religious conduct. To determine the object of a law, we must begin with its text, for the minimum requirement of neutrality is that a law not discriminate on its face. A law lacks facial neutrality if it refers to a religious practice without a secular meaning discernable from the language or context. Petitioners contend that three of the ordinances fail this test of facial neutrality because they use the words "sacrifice" and "ritual," words with strong religious connotations. We agree that these words are consistent with the claim of facial discrimination, but the argument is not conclusive. The words "sacrifice" and "ritual" have a religious origin, but current use admits also of secular meanings. The ordinances, furthermore, define "sacrifice" in secular terms, without referring to religious practices.

We reject the contention advanced by the city, that our inquiry must end with the text of the laws at issue. Facial neutrality is not determinative. The Free Exercise Clause, like the Establishment Clause, extends beyond facial discrimination. . . . The Free Exercise Clause protects against governmental hostility which is masked, as well as overt. . . .

The record in this case compels the conclusion that suppression of the central element of the Santeria worship service was the object of the ordinances. First, though use of the words "sacrifice" and "ritual" does not compel a finding of improper targeting of the Santeria religion, the choice of these words is support for our conclusion. There are further respects in which the text of the city council's enactments discloses the improper attempt to target Santeria. . . . No one suggests, and, on this record, it cannot be maintained, that city officials had in mind a religion other than Santeria.

It becomes evident that these ordinances target Santeria sacrifice when the ordinances' operation is considered. Apart from the text, the effect of a law in its real operation is strong evidence of its object. To be sure, adverse impact will not always lead to a finding of impermissible targeting. For example, a social harm may have been a legitimate concern of government for reasons quite apart from discrimination. The subject at hand does implicate, of course, multiple concerns unrelated to religious animosity, for example, the suffering or mistreatment visited upon the sacrificed animals, and health hazards from improper disposal. But the ordinances, when considered together, disclose an object remote from these legitimate concerns. . . .

The legitimate governmental interests in protecting the public health and preventing cruelty to animals could be addressed by restrictions stopping far short of a flat prohibition of all Santeria sacrificial practice. If improper disposal, not the sacrifice itself, is the harm to be prevented, the city could have imposed a general regulation on the disposal of organic garbage. It did not do so. Indeed, counsel for the city conceded at oral argument that, under the ordinances, Santeria sacrifices would be illegal even if they occurred in licensed, inspected, and zoned slaughterhouses. Thus, these broad ordinances prohibit Santeria sacrifice even when it does not threaten the city's interest in the public health. . . . It is difficult to understand . . . how a prohibition of the sacrifices themselves, which occur in private, is enforceable if a ban on improper disposal, which occurs in public, is not. The neutrality of a law is suspect if First Amendment freedoms are curtailed to prevent isolated collateral harms not themselves prohibited by direct regulation.

Under similar analysis, narrower regulation would achieve the city's interest in preventing cruelty to animals. With regard to the city's interest in ensuring the adequate care of animals, regulation of conditions and treatment, regardless of why an animal is kept, is the logical response to the city's concern, not a prohibition on possession for the purpose of sacrifice. The same is true for the city's interest in prohibiting cruel methods of killing. . . . If the city has a real concern that other methods are less humane, however, the subject of the regulation should be the method of slaughter itself, not a religious classification that is said to bear some general relation to it. . . .

3

In sum, the neutrality inquiry leads to one conclusion: the ordinances had as their object the suppression of religion. The pattern we have recited discloses animosity to Santeria adherents and their religious practices; the ordinances, by their own terms, target this religious exercise; the texts of the ordinances were gerrymandered with care to proscribe religious killings of animals but to exclude almost all secular killings; and the ordinances suppress much more religious conduct than is necessary in order to achieve the legitimate ends asserted in their defense. These ordinances are not neutral, and the court below committed clear error in failing to reach this conclusion.

B

We turn next to a second requirement of the Free Exercise Clause, the rule that laws burdening religious practice must be of general applicability. All laws are selective to some extent, but categories of selection are of paramount concern when a law has the incidental effect of burdening religious practice. The Free Exercise Clause "protect[s] religious observers against unequal treatment," and inequality results when a legislature decides that the governmental interests it seeks to advance are worthy of being pursued only against conduct with a religious motivation.

The principle that government, in pursuit of legitimate interests, cannot in a selective manner impose burdens only on conduct motivated by religious belief is essential to the protection of the rights guaranteed by the Free Exercise Clause. The principle underlying the general applicability requirement has parallels in our First Amendment jurisprudence. In this case, we need not define with precision the standard used to evaluate whether a prohibition is of general application, for these ordinances fall well below the minimum standard necessary to protect First Amendment rights.

Respondent claims that [the Hialeah laws] advance two interests: protecting the public health and preventing cruelty to animals. The ordinances are underinclusive for those ends. They fail to prohibit nonreligious conduct that endangers these interests in a similar or greater degree than Santeria sacrifice does. The underinclusion is substantial, not inconsequential. Despite the city's proffered interest in preventing cruelty to animals, the ordinances are drafted with care to forbid few killings but those occasioned by religious sacrifice. Many types of animal deaths or kills for nonreligious reasons are either not prohibited or approved by express provision. For example, fishing—which occurs in Hialeah—is legal. Extermination of mice and rats within a home is also permitted. Florida law . . . sanctions euthanasia of "stray, neglected, abandoned, or unwanted animals," [and the] destruction of animals judicially removed from their owners "for humanitarian reasons" or when the animal "is of no commercial value." . . .

The ordinances are underinclusive as well with regard to the health risk posed by consumption of uninspected meat. Under the city's ordinances, hunters may eat their kill and fishermen may eat their catch without undergoing governmental inspection. Likewise, state law requires inspection of meat that is sold, but exempts meat from animals raised for the use of the owner and "members of his household and nonpaying guests and employees." The asserted interest in inspected meat is not pursued in contexts similar to that of religious animal sacrifice. . . .

We conclude, in sum, that each of Hialeah's ordinances pursues the city's governmental interests only against conduct motivated by religious belief. The ordinances "ha[ve] every appearance of a prohibition that society is prepared to impose upon [Santeria worshippers], but not upon itself." This precise evil is what the requirement of general applicability is designed to prevent.

III

A law burdening religious practice that is not neutral or not of general application must undergo the most rigorous of scrutiny. To satisfy the commands of the First Amendment, a law restrictive of religious practice must advance "'interests of the highest order,'" and must be narrowly tailored in pursuit of those interests. . . . A law that targets religious conduct for distinctive treatment or advances legitimate governmental interests only against conduct with a religious motivation will survive strict scrutiny only in rare cases. It follows from what we have already said that these ordinances cannot withstand this scrutiny.

JUSTICE SOUTER, concurring in part and concurring in the judgment.

This case turns on a principle about which there is no disagreement, that the Free Exercise Clause bars government action aimed at suppressing religious belief or practice. The Court holds that Hialeah's animal sacrifice laws violate that principle, and I concur in that holding without reservation.

Because prohibiting religious exercise is the object of the laws at hand, this case does not present the more difficult issue addressed in our last free exercise case, *Employment Div., Dept. of Human Resources of Oregon* v. *Smith* (1990), which announced the rule that a "neutral, generally applicable" law does not run afoul of the Free Exercise Clause even when it prohibits religious exercise in effect. The Court today refers to that rule in dicta, and, despite my general agreement with the Court's opinion, I do not join Part II . . . for I have doubts about whether the *Smith* rule merits adherence. I write separately to explain why . . . the Court should reexamine the rule *Smith* declared. . . .

That the Free Exercise Clause contains a "requirement for governmental neutrality" is hardly a novel proposition; though the term does not appear in the First Amendment, our cases have used it as shorthand to describe, at least in part, what the Clause commands. Nor is there anything unusual about the notion that the Free Exercise Clause requires general applicability, though the Court, until today, has not used exactly that term in stating a reason for invalidation.

While general applicability is, for the most part, self-explanatory, free exercise neutrality is not self-revealing. A law that is religion neutral on its face or in its purpose may lack neutrality in its effect by forbidding something that religion requires or requiring something that religion forbids. A secular law, applicable to all, that prohibits consumption of alcohol, for example, will affect members of religions that require the use of wine differently from members of other religions and nonbelievers, disproportionately burdening the practice of, say, Catholicism or Judaism. Without an exemption for sacramental wine, Prohibition may fail the test of religion neutrality. . . .

Though *Smith* used the term "neutrality" without a modifier, the rule it announced plainly assumes that free exercise neutrality is of the formal sort. Distinguishing between laws whose "object" is to prohibit religious exercise and those that prohibit religious exercise as an "incidental effect," *Smith* placed only the former within the reaches of the Free Exercise Clause; the latter, laws that satisfy formal neutrality, *Smith* would subject to no free exercise scrutiny at all, even when they prohibit religious exercise in application. The four Justices who rejected the *Smith* rule, by contrast, read the Free Exercise Clause as embracing what I have termed substantive neutrality. The enforcement of a law "neutral on its face," they said, may "nonetheless offend [the Free Exercise Clause's] requirement for government neutrality if it unduly burdens the free exercise of religion." The rule these Justices saw as flowing from free exercise neutrality, in contrast to the *Smith* rule, "requir[es] the government to justify *any* substantial burden on religiously motivated conduct by a compelling state interest and by means narrowly tailored to achieve that interest."

The proposition for which the *Smith* rule stands, then, is that formal neutrality, along with general applicability, are sufficient conditions for constitutionality under the Free Exercise Clause. That proposition is not at issue in this case, however, for Hialeah's animal sacrifice ordinances are not neutral under any definition, any more than they are generally applicable. . . .

While, as the Court observes, the Hialeah City Council has provided a rare example of a law actually aimed at suppressing religious exercise, *Smith* was typical of our free exercise cases, involving as it did a formally neutral, generally applicable law. The rule *Smith* announced, however, was decidedly untypical of the cases involving the same type of law. Because *Smith* left those prior cases standing, we are left with a free exercise jurisprudence in tension with itself, a tension that should be addressed, and that may legitimately be addressed, by reexamining the *Smith* rule in the next case that would turn upon its application. . . .

Though *Smith* sought to distinguish the free exercise cases in which the Court mandated exemptions from secular laws of general application, I am not persuaded. *Wisconsin* v. *Yoder* and *Cantwell* v. *Connecticut,* according to *Smith,* were not true free exercise cases, but "hybrid[s]" involving "the Free Exercise Clause in conjunction with other constitutional protections, such as freedom of speech and of the press, or the right of parents . . . to direct the education of their children." Neither opinion, however, leaves any doubt that "fundamental claims of religious freedom [were] at stake." And the distinction *Smith* draws strikes me as ultimately untenable. If a hybrid claim is simply one in which another constitutional right is implicated, then the hybrid exception would probably be so vast as to swallow the *Smith* rule, and, indeed, the hybrid exception would cover the situation exemplified by *Smith,* since free speech and associational rights are certainly implicated in the peyote-smoking ritual. But if a hybrid claim is one in which a litigant would actually obtain an exemption from a formally neutral, generally applicable law under another constitutional provision, then there would have been no reason for the Court in what *Smith* calls the hybrid cases to have mentioned the Free Exercise Clause at all. . . .

As for the cases on which *Smith* primarily relied as establishing the rule it embraced, *Reynolds* v. *United States* (1879) and *Minersville School Dist.* v. *Gobitis* (1940), their subsequent treatment by the Court would seem to require rejection of the *Smith* rule. *Reynolds,* which, in upholding the polygamy conviction of a Mormon, stressed the evils it saw as associated with polygamy, has been read as consistent with the principle that religious conduct may be regulated by general or targeting law only if the conduct "pose[s] some substantial threat to public safety, peace or order." And *Gobitis,* after three Justices who originally joined the opinion renounced it for disregarding the government's constitutional obligation "to accommodate itself to the religious views of minorities," was explicitly overruled in *West Virginia Board of Education* v. *Barnette* (1943) . . .

The *Smith* rule, in my view, may be reexamined consistently with principles of *stare decisis.* To begin with, the *Smith* rule was not subject to "full-dress argument" prior to its announcement. . . . [N]either party squarely addressed the proposition the Court was to embrace, that the Free Exercise Clause was irrelevant to the dispute. Sound judicial decision making requires "both a vigorous prosecution and a vigorous defense" of the issues in dispute, and a constitutional rule announced *sua sponte* [without being prompted] is entitled to less deference than one addressed on full briefing and argument.

The *Smith* rule's vitality as precedent is limited further by the seeming want of any need of it in resolving the question presented in that case. Justice O'Connor reached the same result as the majority by applying, as the parties had requested, "our established free exercise jurisprudence," and the majority never determined that the case could not be resolved on the narrower ground, going instead straight to the broader constitutional rule. But the Court's better practice, one supported by the same principles of restraint that underlie the rule of *stare decisis,* is not to "'formulate a rule of constitutional law broader than is required by the precise facts to which it is to be applied.'" While I am not suggesting that the *Smith* Court lacked the power to announce its rule, I think a rule of law unnecessary to the outcome of a case, especially one not put into play by the parties, approaches without more the sort of "dicta . . . which may be followed if sufficiently persuasive but which are not controlling."

I do not, of course, mean to imply that a broad constitutional rule announced without full briefing and argument necessarily lacks precedential weight. . . . *Smith,* however, is not such a case. By the same token, by pointing out *Smith's* recent vintage, I do not mean to suggest that novelty alone is enough to justify reconsideration. "*[S]tare decisis,*" as Justice Frankfurter wrote, "is a principle of policy, and not a mechanical formula," and the decision whether to adhere to a prior decision, particularly a constitutional decision, is a complex and difficult one that does not lend itself to resolution by application of simple, categorical rules, but that must account for a variety of often competing considerations.

One important further consideration warrants mention here, however, because it demands the reexamination I have in mind. *Smith* presents not the usual question of whether to follow a constitutional rule, but the question of which constitutional rule to follow, for *Smith* refrained from overruling prior free exercise cases that contain a free exercise rule fundamentally at odds with the rule *Smith* declared. *Smith,* indeed, announced its rule by relying squarely upon the precedent of prior cases. Since that precedent is nonetheless at odds with the *Smith* rule, as I have discussed above, the result is an intolerable tension in free exercise law which may be resolved, consistently with principles of *stare decisis,* in a case in which the tension is presented and its resolution pivotal.

While the tension on which I rely exists within the body of our extant case law, a rereading of that case law will not, of course, mark the limits of any enquiry directed to reexamining the *Smith* rule, which should be reviewed in light not only of the precedent on which it was rested, but also of the text of the Free Exercise Clause and its origins. As for text, *Smith* did not assert that the plain language of the Free Exercise Clause compelled its rule, but only that the rule was "a permissible reading" of the Clause. Suffice it to say that a respectable argument may be made that the pre-*Smith* law comes closer to fulfilling the language of the Free Exercise Clause than the rule *Smith* announced. . . . The Clause draws no distinction between laws whose object is to prohibit religious exercise and laws with that effect, on its face seemingly applying to both. . . .

The extent to which the Free Exercise Clause requires government to refrain from impeding religious exercise defines nothing less than the respective relationships in our constitutional democracy of the individual to government and to God. "Neutral, generally applicable" laws, drafted as they are from the perspective of the nonadherent, have the unavoidable potential of putting the believer to a choice between God and government. Our cases now present competing answers to the question when government, while pursuing secular ends, may compel disobedience to what one believes religion commands. The case before us is rightly decided without resolving the existing tension, which remains for another day when it may be squarely faced.

▼▲▼

The Court understood the Hialeah law as targeting religion for discriminatory treatment, and rejected the city's argument that the law was a permissible, narrowly crafted means to prevent cruelty to animals. As Justice Kennedy noted, the city did not prohibit any nonreligious killing of animals that endangered the interests of animals to a similar or greater degree than Santeria sacrifice does, such as hunting, fishing, pest extermination, or scientific experiments. Hialeah's motive was quite clear—to prohibit the practice of Santeria through a discriminatory law. The result was that the Court was not required to revisit the more controversial dimension of its free exercise jurisprudence—religious exemptions from laws that apply to the general population.

Reconciling Religious Rights with Secular Responsibilities

In the late 1800s, the Church of Jesus Christ of Latter-day Saints, more popularly known as the Mormon Church, found its practice of polygamy under attack by federal and state laws. Having migrated from Ohio to the western territories in the 1840s, the Mormons practiced polygamy in accord with the "revelation" received by their founder, Joseph Smith, who prophesied that male members of the church failing to take more than one wife would be eternally damned. The Mormons practiced polygamy privately until their leader, Brigham Young, encouraged them to make this element of their faith public after they established their State of Deseret in Utah. Around this same time, the Mormons requested admission into the United States. Congress rejected their petition, and, in 1850, established the Utah Territory instead. During and after the Civil War, Congress enacted two antipolygamy laws, the Merrill and Poland Acts, forbidding any recognition, support, or encouragement of the practice.[78]

Mormon leaders deliberately sought prosecution under the congressional laws to test their validity in the federal courts. In *Reynolds* v. *United States* (1878) and *Davis* v. *Beason* (1890), the Court rejected the Mormons' claim that the Free Exercise Clause protected their right to practice polygamy and prohibited laws denying voting rights to polygamists and anyone advocating multiple marriage.[79] In *Reynolds,* the Court first invoked the distinction between constitutional protection for religious *beliefs* and *action* motivated by such beliefs that Justice Roberts later used in *Cantwell.* Wrote Chief Justice Morrison R. Waite:

> In our opinion, the statute immediately under consideration is within the legislative power of Congress. . . . This being so, the only question which remains is, whether those who make polygamy a part of their religion are excepted from the operation of the statute. If they are, then those who do not make polygamy a part of their religious belief may be found guilty and punished, while those who do, must be acquitted and go free. This would be introducing a new element into criminal law. Laws are made for the government of actions, and while they cannot interfere with mere religious belief and opinions, they may with practices.[80]

George Reynolds, the Mormon polygamist who challenged the federal antipolygamy provisions, was imprisoned in Nebraska and Utah for several years. President Rutherford B. Hayes refused a request from the church for an executive pardon. After *Beason,* the Mormon Church eliminated polygamy from its theology and no longer required its members to practice it, a decision that highlighted just how deeply the liberty of conscience guarantee is rooted in the Protestant Christian tradition. Since *Reynolds,* no Protestant Christian denomination has ever stood before the Supreme Court to defend or account for its core religious practices against the demands of the civil and criminal law.

But *Reynolds* and *Beason* did not foreclose the federal courts to the demands of religious minorities seeking exemptions from laws applying to the general population. Almost twenty-five years after *Cantwell,* the Court, for the first time, ruled that a generally applicable state law infringing religiously motivated conduct must satisfy a "compelling" government interest, and do so through the "least restrictive" means available. *Sherbert* v. *Verner* (1963) was a major step beyond *Cantwell,* and opened the door to an entirely different conception of how far the free exercise guarantee extended to religious individuals whose practices conflicted with the secular state.

This approach reached its constitutional apex less than ten years later in *Wisconsin* v. *Yoder* (1972), when the Court confronted a conflict between one of America's oldest religious groups, the Amish, and a Wisconsin law requiring all children under the age of sixteen to attend a public or private school. Upon first glance, *Sherbert* and *Yoder* appear similar, in that a religious minority is contending that a generally applicable state law, as applied, is forcing its adherents to choose between following the dictates of their conscience or losing a secular welfare benefit. *Yoder,* however, differed in one important respect. Unlike Adell Sherbert, who was confronted with negative precedent (*Reynolds, Beason,* and the *Sunday Closing Cases*) when trying to persuade the justices to recognize a religion-based exemption to a generally applicable law, the Amish had a favorable decision on their side. In *Pierce Society of Sisters* (1925), the Court struck down an Oregon law that compelled all children between the ages of eight and sixteen to attend public school. The Court did not implicate the Free Exercise Clause in *Pierce,* relying instead on the "liberty" of parents, protected by the Due Process Clause of the Fourteenth Amendment, to direct the education of their children.

Yoder, like *West Virginia* v. *Barnette* (1943) (see Chapter 4), where the Court ruled that a state law mandating the flag salute in the public schools violated the First Amendment rights of Jehovah's Witness schoolchildren, involved what some legal scholars refer to as a *hybrid* claim. A hybrid claim involves the assertion of more than one constitutional provision on behalf of the exercise of a fundamental right. This distinction between *Sherbert* and *Yoder* emerged as a key point in the Court's decision in *Employment Division of Oregon* v. *Smith* (1990), discussed on pp. 312–318, which suggested that the Court was no longer comfortable deciding whether religion-based exceptions were appropriate under the Free Exercise Clause.

Sherbert v. *Verner*

374 U.S. 398 (1963)

Since 1934, Adell Sherbert had worked the day shift at the Spartan Mills textile plant in Spartanburg, South Carolina, with no disciplinary problems. In 1957, Sherbert joined the Seventh-day Adventist Church, which observes the Saturday Sabbath. Until June 1957, Spartan Mills had made Saturday work optional for spool tenders, such as Sherbert, and other factory workers. In a policy change, the mill announced that Saturday work was now mandatory, extending the workweek from five days to six. Sherbert refused to report for work; after six weeks, Spartan Mills fired Sherbert. Unable to find another factory job, Sherbert subsequently filed for unemployment compensation. Under South Carolina law, applicants for unemployment benefits were ineligible for assistance if they failed to accept available and suitable work without good cause. The South Carolina Employment Security Commission did not consider Sherbert's Sabbath observance "good cause" and denied her unemployment benefits.

The Seventh-day Adventist Church challenged South Carolina's decision to deny Adell Sherbert unemployment compensation benefits as unconstitutional under the Free Exercise Clause. Church lawyers contended that South Carolina's law put Sherbert in the untenable position of choosing between obedience to her religious faith and her right to public welfare assistance. The state countered that its unemployment law did not *target* Seventh-day Adventists or religion generally, as Connecticut's law in *Cantwell* did. As such, the state was only required to demonstrate that its unemployment compensation rules advanced a reasonable state interest. The "available-for-work" standard fell well within that definition.

That *Sherbert* was no ordinary free exercise case was evident when Leo Pfeffer and the AJCongress put together a coordinated *amicus* strategy to support the Seventh-day Adventist's claim. Jewish organizations, including the ADL, the AJCommittee, and numerous synagogues and community relations groups, argued that South Carolina's law placed a substantial burden on the right of Adell Sherbert to exercise freely her religious beliefs. In four cases handed down on the same day in May 1961, the Court ruled that Sunday closing laws punishing persons or businesses from doing business on that day did not violate the Establishment or Free Exercise Clauses. The AJCongress sponsored *Braunfeld* v. *Brown* and, along with the ACLU, the ADL, and the Seventh-day Adventists, filed an *amicus* brief in *Gallagher* v. *Crown Kosher Market*. Both cases involved Jewish-owned businesses that closed on Saturday for Sabbath observance but wanted to open on Sunday. The Court ruled in all four cases that Sunday closing laws promoted a reasonable state interest in leisure, recreation, and family activities from which all persons benefited. In *McGowan* v. *Maryland*, the Court noted that Maryland's Sunday closing law contained exceptions for alcohol, tobacco, bingo, movie theaters, sporting events, and other popular entertainment. Chief Justice Warren found nothing inconsistent with these exceptions and the mandate that "nonessential" businesses remain closed, even though Maryland's designated day for community relaxation fell on the Christian Sabbath.

The Court's decision was 7 to 2. Justice Brennan delivered the opinion of the Court. Justices Douglas and Stewart filed separate concurring opinions. Justice Harlan, joined by Justice White, dissented.

MR. JUSTICE BRENNAN delivered the opinion of the Court.

Plainly enough, [Sherbert's] conscientious objection to Saturday work constitutes no conduct prompted by religious principles of a kind within the reach of state legislation. If, therefore, the decision of the South Carolina Supreme Court is to withstand appellant's constitutional challenge, it must be either because her disqualification as a beneficiary represents no infringement by the State of her constitutional rights of free exercise, or because any incidental burden on the free exercise of appellant's religion may be justified by a "compelling state interest in the regulation of a subject within the State's constitutional power to regulate . . . ," *NAACP* v. *Button* (1958).

We turn first to the question whether the disqualification for benefits imposes any burden on the free exercise of appellant's religion. We think it is clear that it does. In a sense, the consequences of such a disqualification to religious principles and practices may be only an indirect result of welfare legislation within the State's general competence to enact; it is true that no criminal sanctions directly compel appellant to work a six-day week. But this is only the beginning, not the end, of our inquiry. For "[i]f the purpose or effect of a law is to impede the observance of one or all religions or is to discriminate invidiously

between religions, that law is constitutionally invalid even though the burden may be characterized as being only indirect."

Here, not only is it apparent that appellant's declared ineligibility for benefits derives solely from the practice of her religion, but the pressure upon her to forego that practice is unmistakable. The ruling forces her to choose between following the precepts of her religion and forfeiting benefits, on the one hand, and abandoning one of the precepts of her religion in order to accept work, on the other hand. Governmental imposition of such a choice puts the same kind of burden upon the free exercise of religion as would a fine imposed against appellant for her Saturday worship.

Nor may the South Carolina court's construction of the statute be saved from constitutional infirmity on the ground that unemployment compensation benefits are not appellant's "right," but merely a "privilege." It is too late in the day to doubt that the liberties of religion and expression may be infringed by the denial of or placing of conditions upon a benefit or privilege. . . .

We must next consider whether some compelling state interest enforced in the eligibility provisions of the South Carolina statute justifies the substantial infringement of appellant's First Amendment right. It is basic that no showing merely of a rational relationship to some colorable state interest would suffice; in this highly sensitive constitutional area, "[o]nly the gravest abuses, endangering paramount interests, give occasion for permissible limitation." No such abuse or danger has been advanced in the present case. The appellees suggest no more than a possibility that the filing of fraudulent claims by unscrupulous claimants feigning religious objections to Saturday work might not only dilute the unemployment compensation fund, but also hinder the scheduling by employers of necessary Saturday work. But that possibility is not apposite here, because no such objection appears to have been made before the South Carolina Supreme Court, and we are unwilling to assess the importance of an asserted state interest without the views of the state court. Nor, if the contention had been made below, would the record appear to sustain it; there is no proof whatever to warrant such fears of malingering or deceit as those which the respondents now advance. Even if consideration of such evidence is not foreclosed by the prohibition against judicial inquiry into the truth or falsity of religious beliefs—a question as to which we intimate no view, since it is not before us—it is highly doubtful whether such evidence would be sufficient to warrant a substantial infringement of religious liberties. For even if the possibility of spurious claims did threaten to dilute the fund and disrupt the scheduling of work, it would plainly be incumbent upon the appellees to demonstrate that no alternative forms of regulation would combat such abuses without infringing First Amendment rights.

In . . . *Braunfeld v. Brown* (1961), [t]he Court recognized that the Sunday closing law which that decision sustained undoubtedly served "to make the practice of [the Orthodox Jewish merchants'] . . . religious beliefs more expensive." But the statute was nevertheless saved by a countervailing factor which finds no equivalent in the instant case—a strong state interest in providing one uniform day of rest for all workers. That secular objective could be achieved, the Court found, only by declaring Sunday to be that day of rest. Requiring exemptions for Sabbatarians, while theoretically possible, appeared to present an administrative problem of such magnitude, or to afford the exempted class so great a competitive advantage, that such a requirement would have rendered the entire statutory scheme unworkable. In the present case, no such justifications underlie the determination of the state court that appellant's religion makes her ineligible to receive benefits.

In holding as we do, plainly we are not fostering the "establishment" of the Seventh-day Adventist religion in South Carolina, for the extension of unemployment benefits to Sabbatarians in common with Sunday worshippers reflects nothing more than the governmental obligation of neutrality in the face of religious differences, and does not represent that involvement of religious with secular institutions which it is the object of the Establishment Clause to forestall. Nor does the recognition of the appellant's right to unemployment benefits under the state statute serve to abridge any other person's religious liberties. Nor do we, by our decision today, declare the existence of a constitutional right to unemployment benefits on the part of all persons whose religious convictions are the cause of their unemployment. . . . Our holding today is only that South Carolina may not constitutionally apply the eligibility provisions so as to constrain a worker to abandon his religious convictions respecting the day of rest. . . .

The judgment of the South Carolina Supreme Court is reversed, and the case is remanded for further proceedings not inconsistent with this opinion.

It is so ordered.

MR. JUSTICE STEWART, concurring in the result.

Although fully agreeing with the result which the Court reaches in this case, I cannot join the Court's opinion. This case presents a double-barreled dilemma which, in all candor, I think the Court's opinion has not succeeded in papering over. The dilemma ought to be resolved.

I am convinced that no liberty is more essential to the continued vitality of the free society which our Constitution guarantees than is the religious liberty protected by the Free Exercise Clause explicit in the First Amendment and imbedded in the Fourteenth. And I regret that, on occasion . . . the Court has shown what has seemed to me a distressing insensitivity to the appropriate demands of this constitutional guarantee. By contrast, I think that the Court's approach to the Establishment Clause has, on occasion, and specifically in *Engel, Schempp,* and *Murray,* been not only insensitive but positively wooden, and that the Court has accorded to the Establishment Clause a meaning which neither the words, the history, nor the intention of the authors of that specific constitutional provision even remotely suggests.

But my views as to the correctness of the Court's decisions in these cases are beside the point here. The point is that the decisions are on the books. And the result is that there are many situations where legitimate claims under the Free Exercise Clause will run into head-on collision with the Court's insensitive and sterile construction of the Establishment Clause. The controversy now before us is clearly such a case.

Because the appellant refuses to accept available jobs which would require her to work on Saturdays, South Carolina has declined to pay unemployment compensation benefits to her. Her refusal to work on Saturdays is based on the tenets of her religious faith. The Court says that South Carolina cannot, under these circumstances, declare her to be not "available for work" within the meaning of its statute, because to do so would violate her constitutional right to the free exercise of her religion.

Yet what this Court has said about the Establishment Clause must inevitably lead to a diametrically opposite result. If the appellant's refusal to work on Saturdays were based on indolence, or on a compulsive desire to watch the Saturday television programs, no one would say that South Carolina could not hold that she was not "available for work" within the meaning of its statute. That being so, the Establishment Clause, as construed by this Court, not only permits but affirmatively requires South Carolina equally to deny the appellant's claim for unemployment compensation when her refusal to work on Saturdays is based upon her religious creed. . . .

To require South Carolina to so administer its laws as to pay public money to the appellant under the circumstances of this case is thus clearly to require the State to violate the Establishment Clause as construed by this Court. This poses no problem for me, because I think the Court's mechanistic concept of the Establishment Clause is historically unsound and constitutionally wrong. I think the process of constitutional decision in the area of the relationships between government and religion demands considerably more than the invocation of broadbrushed rhetoric of the kind I have quoted. And I think that the guarantee of religious liberty embodied in the Free Exercise Clause affirmatively requires government to create an atmosphere of hospitality and accommodation to individual belief or disbelief. In short, I think our Constitution commands the positive protection by government of religious freedom—not only for a minority, however small—not only for the majority, however large—but for each of us.

South Carolina would deny unemployment benefits to a mother unavailable for work on Saturdays because she was unable to get a babysitter. Thus, we do not have before us a situation where a State provides unemployment compensation generally, and singles out for disqualification only those persons who are unavailable for work on religious grounds. This is not, in short, a scheme which operates so as to discriminate against religion as such. But the Court nevertheless holds that the State must prefer a religious over a secular ground for being unavailable for work—that state financial support of the appellant's religion is constitutionally required to carry out "the governmental obligation of neutrality in the face of religious differences. . . . "

Yet in cases decided under the Establishment Clause, the Court has decreed otherwise. It has decreed that government must blind itself to the differing religious beliefs and traditions of the people. With all respect, I think it is the Court's duty to face up to the dilemma posed by the conflict between the Free Exercise Clause of the Constitution and the Establishment Clause as interpreted by the Court. It is a duty, I submit, which we owe to the people, the States, and the Nation, and a duty which we owe to ourselves.

JUSTICE HARLAN, whom JUSTICE WHITE joins, dissenting.

What the Court is holding is that, if the State chooses to condition unemployment compensation on the applicant's availability for work, it is constitutionally compelled to *carve out an exception*—and to provide benefits—for those whose unavailability is due to their religious convictions. Such a holding has particular significance in two respects.

First, despite the Court's protestations to the contrary, the decision necessarily overrules *Braunfeld* v. *Brown,* which held that it did not offend the "Free Exercise"

Clause of the Constitution for a State to forbid a Sabbatarian to do business on Sunday. The secular purpose of the statute before us today is even clearer than that involved in *Braunfeld.* And just as in *Braunfeld*—where exceptions to the Sunday closing laws for Sabbatarians would have been inconsistent with the purpose to achieve a uniform day of rest and would have required case-by-case inquiry into religious beliefs—so here, an exception to the rules of eligibility based on religious convictions would necessitate judicial examination of those convictions and would be at odds with the limited purpose of the statute to smooth out the economy during periods of industrial instability. Finally, the indirect financial burden of the present law is far less than that involved in *Braunfeld.* Forcing a store owner to close his business on Sunday may well have the effect of depriving him of a satisfactory livelihood if his religious convictions require him to close on Saturday as well. Here we are dealing only with temporary benefits, amounting to a fraction of regular weekly wages and running for not more than 22 weeks. Clearly, any differences between this case and *Braunfeld* cut against the present appellant.

Second, the implications of the present decision are far more troublesome than its apparently narrow dimensions would indicate at first glance. The meaning of today's holding, as already noted, is that the State must furnish unemployment benefits to one who is unavailable for work if the unavailability stems from the exercise of religious convictions. The State, in other words, must *single out* for financial assistance those whose behavior is religiously motivated, even though it denies such assistance to others whose identical behavior (in this case, inability to work on Saturdays) is not religiously motivated. It has been suggested that such singling out of religious conduct for special treatment may violate the constitutional limitations on state action. My own view, however, is that, at least under the circumstances of this case, it would be a permissible accommodation of religion for the State, if it chose to do so, to create an exception to its eligibility requirements for persons like the appellant. The constitutional obligation of "neutrality" is not so narrow a channel that the slightest deviation from an absolutely straight course leads to condemnation. . . .

For very much the same reasons, however, I cannot subscribe to the conclusion that the State is constitutionally compelled to carve out an exception to its general rule of eligibility in the present case. Those situations in which the Constitution may require special treatment on account of religion are, in my view, few and far between, and this view is amply supported by the course of constitutional litigation in this area. Such compulsion in the present case is particularly inappropriate in light of the indirect, remote, and insubstantial effect of the decision below on the exercise of appellant's religion and in light of the direct financial assistance to religion that today's decision requires.

For these reasons I respectfully dissent from the opinion and judgment of the Court.

Wisconsin v. Yoder
406 U.S. 208 (1972)

The Old Order Amish trace their origin in the United States back to the 1600s, when they first settled in Pennsylvania. Compulsory school attendance laws have existed for almost as long, although they were never really enforced until the late 1800s, when the great wave of European immigration to the United States began to challenge the dominant Protestant culture of the public schools. Public schools have always played an extremely significant role in assimilating religious and ethnic minorities into the mainstream of American life. It is for this reason, among others, that so many conflicts involving the relationship between government and religion have been fought in the public schools.

The Amish live austere lives in largely self-contained communities. They reject the elements of modern life that most Americans find indispensable, such as automobiles, electronics, modern media, and other forms of technological innovation. Amish men and women dress modestly and follow largely traditional sex roles. Along back roads in rural Pennsylvania and Wisconsin, where the Amish are largely concentrated, it is not uncommon for cars to pass horse-drawn buggies carrying Amish. But the Amish do not reject all forms of American convention, sending their children to public schools when their own communities lack their own formal schools. Amish children are permitted to attend public school only until the eighth grade, believing that high school offers too many opportunities for corruption of their way of life.

Jonas Yoder, Wallace Miller, and Adin Yutzy refused to send their children to public school in Wisconsin past the eighth grade. They were convicted and fined five dollars each for violating the state's compulsory attendance law, which they later argued in state court violated their rights under the Free Exercise Clause. Relying on *Sherbert,* the Wisconsin Supreme Court reversed.

The Court's decision was 7 to 0. Chief Justice Burger delivered the opinion of the Court. Justice White, joined by Justices Brennan and Stewart, wrote a concurring opinion. Justice Douglas wrote separately to express his views on the rights of Amish children to decide for themselves whether to attend public school or return to their communities.

▼▲▼

MR. CHIEF JUSTICE BURGER delivered the opinion of the Court.

The history of the Amish sect was given in some detail [in lower court opinions], beginning with the Swiss Anabaptists of the 16th century, who rejected institutionalized churches and sought to return to the early, simple, Christian life deemphasizing material success, rejecting the competitive spirit, and seeking to insulate themselves from the modern world. As a result of their common heritage, Old Order Amish communities today are characterized by a fundamental belief that salvation requires life in a church community separate and apart from the world and worldly influence. This concept of life aloof from the world and its values is central to their faith.

A related feature of Old Order Amish communities is their devotion to a life in harmony with nature and the soil, as exemplified by the simple life of the early Christian era that continued in America during much of our early national life. Amish beliefs require members of the community to make their living by farming or closely related activities. Broadly speaking, the Old Order Amish religion pervades and determines the entire mode of life of its adherents. Their conduct is regulated in great detail by the *Ordnung,* or rules, of the church community. Adult baptism, which occurs in late adolescence, is the time at which Amish young people voluntarily undertake heavy obligations, not unlike the Bar Mitzvah of the Jews, to abide by the rules of the church community.

Amish objection to formal education beyond the eighth grade is firmly grounded in these central religious concepts. They object to the high school, and higher education generally, because the values they teach are in marked variance with Amish values and the Amish way of life; they view secondary school education as an impermissible exposure of their children to "worldly" influence in conflict with their beliefs. The high school tends to emphasize intellectual and scientific accomplishments, self-distinction, competitiveness, worldly success, and social life with other students. Amish society emphasizes informal "learning through doing"; a life of "goodness," rather than a life of intellect; wisdom, rather than technical knowledge; community welfare, rather than competition; and separation from, rather than integration with, contemporary worldly society.

Formal high school education beyond the eighth grade is contrary to Amish beliefs not only because it places Amish children in an enviroment hostile to Amish beliefs, with increasing emphasis on competition in class work and sports and with the pressure to conform to the styles, manners, and ways of the peer group, but also because it takes them away from their community, physically and emotionally, during the crucial and formative adolescent period of life. During this period, the children must acquire Amish attitudes favoring manual work and self-reliance and the specific skills needed to perform the adult role of an Amish farmer or housewife. They must learn to enjoy physical labor. Once a child has learned basic reading, writing, and elementary mathematics, these traits, skills, and attitudes admittedly fall within the category of those best learned through example and "doing," rather than in a classroom. And, at this time in life, the Amish child must grow in his faith and his relationship to the Amish community if he is to be prepared to accept the heavy obligations imposed by adult baptism. In short, high school attendence with teachers who are not of the Amish faith—and may even be hostile to it—interposes a serious barrier to the integration of the Amish child into the Amish religious community. . . .

The Amish do not object to elementary education through the first eight grades as a general proposition, because they agree that their children must have basic skills in the "three R's" in order to read the Bible, to be good farmers and citizens, and to be able to deal with non-Amish people when necessary in the course of daily affairs. They view such a basic education as acceptable because it does not significantly expose their children to worldly values or interfere with their development in the Amish community during the crucial adolescent period. While Amish accept compulsory elementary education generally, wherever possible they have established their own elementary schools, in many respects like the small local schools of the past. In the Amish belief, higher learning tends to develop values they reject as influences that alienate man from God. . . .

There is no doubt as to the power of a State, having a high responsibility for education of its citizens, to impose reasonable regulations for the control and duration of basic education. Providing public schools ranks at the very apex of the function of a State. Yet even this paramount responsibilty was, in *Pierce,* made to yield to the right of parents to provide an equivalent education in a privately operated system. There, the Court held that Oregon's statute compelling attendence in a public school from age eight to 16 unreasonably interfered with the interest of parents in directing the rearing of their offspring, including their education in church-operated schools. As that case suggests, the values of parental direction of the religious upbringing and education of their children in their early and formative years have a high place in our society. Thus, a State's interest in universal education, however highly we rank it, is not totally free from a balancing process when it impinges on fundamental rights and interests, such as those specifically protected by the Free Exercise Clause of the First Amendment, and the traditional interest of parents with respect to the religious upbringing of their children so long as they "prepare [them] for additional obligations," *Pierce* v. *Society of Sisters* (1925).

It follows that, in order for Wisconsin to compel school attendance beyond the eighth grade against a claim that such attendance interferes with the practice of a legitimate religious belief, it must appear either that the State does not deny the free exercise of religious belief by its requirement or that there is a state interest of sufficient magnitude to override the interest claiming protection under the Free Exercise Clause. Long before there was general acknowledgment of the need for universal formal education, the Religion Clauses had specifically and firmly fixed the right to free exercise of religious beliefs, and buttressing this fundamental right was an equally firm, even if less explicit, prohibition against the establishment of any religion by government. The values underlying these two provisions relating to religion have been zealously protected, sometimes even at the expense of other interests of admittedly high social importance. . . .

The essence of all that has been said and written on the subject is that only those interests of the highest order and those not otherwise served can overbalance legitimate claims to the free exercise of religion. We can accept it as settled, therefore, however strong the State's interest in universal compulsory education, it is by no means absolute to the exclusion or subordination of all other interests.

We come then to the quality of the claims of the respondents concerning the alleged encroachment of Wisconsin's compulsory school attendance statute on their rights and the rights of their children to the free exercise of the religious beliefs they and their forebears have adhered to for almost three centuries. In evaluating those claims, we must be careful to determine whether the Amish religious faith and their mode of life are, as they claim, inseparable and interdependent. A way of life, however virtuous and admirable, may not be interposed as a barrier to reasonable state regulation of education if it is based on purely secular considerations; to have the protection of the Religion Clauses, the claims must be rooted in religious belief. Although a determination of what is a "religious" belief or practice entitled to constitutional protection may present a most delicate question, the very concept of ordered liberty precludes allowing every person to make his own standard on matters of conduct in which society as a whole has important interests. Thus, if the Amish asserted their claims because of their subjective evaluation and rejection of the contemporary secular values accepted by the majority, much as Thoreau rejected the social values of his time and isolated himself at Walden Pond, their claims would not rest on a religious basis. Thoreau's choice was philosophical and personal, rather than religious, and such belief does not rise to the demands of the Religion Clauses.

Giving no weight to such secular considerations, however, we see that the record in this case abundantly supports the claim that the traditional way of life of the Amish is not merely a matter of personal preference, but one of deep religious conviction, shared by an organized group, and intimately related to daily living. . . .

As the society around the Amish has become more populous, urban, industrialized, and complex, particularly in this century, government regulation of human affairs has correspondingly become more detailed and pervasive. The Amish mode of life has thus come into conflict increasingly with requirements of contemporary society exerting a hydraulic insistence on conformity to majoritarian standards. So long as compulsory education laws were confined to eight grades of elementary basic education imparted in a nearby schoolhouse, with a large proportion of students of the Amish faith, the Old Order Amish had little basis to fear that school attendance would expose their children to the worldly influence they reject. But modern compulsory secondary education in rural area is now largely carried on in a consolidated school, often remote from the student's home and alien to his daily home life. As the record so strongly shows, the values and programs of the modern secondary school are in sharp conflict with the fundamental mode of life mandated by the Amish religion; modern laws requiring compulsory secondary education have accordingly engendered great concern and conflict. The conclusion is inescapable that secondary schooling, by exposing Amish children to worldly influences in terms of attitudes, goals, and values contrary to beliefs, and by substantially interfering with the religious development of the Amish child and his integration into the way of life of the Amish faith community at the crucial adolescent stage of development, contravenes the basic religious tenets and practice of the Amish faith, both as to the parent and the child.

The impact of the compulsory attendance law on respondents' practice of the Amish religion is not only severe, but inescapable, for the Wisconsin law affirmatively compels them, under threat of criminal sanction, to perform acts undeniably at odds with fundamental tenets of their religious beliefs. Nor is the impact of the compulsory attendance law confined to grave interference with important Amish religious tenets from a subjective point of view. It carries with it precisely the kind of objective danger to the free exercise of religion that the First Amendment was designed to prevent. As the record shows, compulsory attendance to age 16 for Amish children carries with it a very real threat of undermining the Amish community and religious practice as they exist today; they must either abandon belief and be assimilated into society at large or be forced to migrate to some other and more tolerant region.

In sum, the unchallenged testimony of acknowledged experts in education and religious history, almost 300 years of consistent practice, and strong evidence of a sustained faith pervading and regulating respondents' entire mode of life support the claim that the enforcement of the State's requirement of compulsory formal education after the eighth grade would gravely endanger, if not destroy, the free exercise of the respondents' religious beliefs.

. . . [T]his case [cannot] be disposed of on the grounds that Wisconsin's requirement for school attendance to age 16 applies uniformly to all citizens of the state and does not, on its face, discriminate against religions or a particular religion, or that it is motivated by legitimate secular concerns. A regulation neutral on its face may, in its application, nonetheless offend the constitutional requirement for governmental neutrality if it unduly burdens the free exercise of religion. The Court must not ignore the danger that an exception from a general obligation of citizenship on religious grouds may run afoul of the Establishment Clause, but that danger cannot be allowed to prevent any exception, no matter how vital it may seem to the protection of values promoted by the right of free exercise. . . .

We turn, then, to the State's broader contention that its interest in its system of compulsory education is so compelling that even the established religious practices of the Amish must give way. Where fundamental claims of religious freedom are at stake, however, we cannot accept such a sweeping claim; despite its admitted validity in the generality of cases, we must searchingly examine the interests that the State seeks to promote by its requirement for compulsory education to age 16, and the impediment to those objectives that would flow from recognizing the claimed Amish exemption.

The State advances two primary arguments in support of its system of compulsory education. It notes, as Thomas Jefferson pointed out early in our history, that some degree of education is necessary to prepare citizens to participate effectively and intelligently in our open political system if we are to preserve freedom and independence. Further, education prepares individuals to be self-reliant and self-sufficient participants in society. We accept these propsitions.

However, the evidence adduced by the Amish in this case is persuasively to the effect that an additional one or two years of formal high school for Amish children in place of their long-established program of informal vocational education would do little to serve those interests. Respondents' experts testified at trial, without challenge, that the value of all education must be assessed in terms of its capacity to prepare the child for life. It is one thing to say that compulsory education for a year or two beyond the eighth grade may be necessary when its goal is the preparation of the child for life in modern society as the majority live, but it is quite another if the goal of education be viewed as the preparation of the child for life in the separated agrarian community that is the keystone of the Amish faith. . . .

The State . . . supports its interest in providing an additional one or two years of compulsory high school education to Amish children because of the possibility that some such children will choose to leave the Amish community, and that, if this occurs, they will be ill-equipped for life. The State argues that, if Amish children leave their church, they should not be in the position of making their way in the world without the education available in the one or two additional years the State requires. However, on this record, that argument is highly speculative. There is no specific evidence of the loss of Amish adherents by attrition, nor is there any showing that, upon leaving the Amish community, Amish children, with their practical agricultural training and habits of industry and self-reliance, would become burdens on society because of educational shortcomings. Indeed, this argument of the State appears to rest primarily on the State's mistaken assumption, already noted, that the Amish do not provide any education for their children beyond the eighth grade, but allow them to grow in "ignorance." To the contrary, not only do the Amish accept the necessity for formal schooling through the eighth grade level, but continue to provide what has been characterized by the undisputed testimony of expert educators as an "ideal" vocational education for their children in the adolescent years. . . .

Insofar as the State's claim rests on the view that a brief additional period of formal education is imperative to enable the Amish to participate effectively and intelligently in our democratic process, it must fall. The Amish alternative to formal secondary schooling education has enabled them to function effectively in their day-to-day life under self-imposed limitations on relations with the world, and to survive and prosper in contemporary society as a separate, sharply identifiable and highly self-sufficient community for more than 200 years in this country. In itself, this is strong evidence that they are capable of fulfilling social and political responsibilities of citizenship without compelled attendance beyond the eighth grade at the price of jeopardizing their free exercise of religious belief. When Thomas Jefferson emphasized the need for education as a bulwark of a free people against tyranny, there is nothing to indicate he had in mind compulsory education through any fixed age beyond a basic education. Indeed, the Amish communities singularly parallel and reflect many of the virtues of Jefferson's ideal of the "sturdy yeoman" who would form the basis of what he considered as the ideal of a democratic society. Even their idiosyncratic separateness exemplifies the diversity we profess to admire and encourage. . . .

For the reasons stated we hold, with the Supreme Court of Wisconsin, that the First and Fourteenth Amendments prevent the State from compelling respondents to cause their children to attend formal high school to age 16. Our disposition of this case, however, in no way alters our recognition of the obvious fact that courts are not school boards or legislatures, and are ill-equpped to determine the "necessity" of discrete aspects of a State's program of compulsory education. This should suggest that courts must move with great circumspection in performing the sensitive and delicate task of weighing a State's legitimate social concern when faced with religious claims for exemption from generally applicable educational requirements. It cannot be overemphasized that we are not dealing with a way of life and mode of education by a group claiming to have recently discovered some "progressive" or more enlightened process for rearing children for modern life.

JUSTICE DOUGLAS, dissenting in part.

I agree with the Court that the religious scruples of the Amish are opposed to the education of their children beyond the grade schools, yet I disagree with the Court's conclusion that the matter is within the dispensation of parents alone. The Court's analysis assumes that the only interests at stake in the case are those of the Amish parents, on the one hand, and those of the State, on the other. The difficulty with this approach is that, despite the Court's claim, the parents are seeking to vindicate not only their own free exercise claims, but also those of their high-school-age children. . . .

I think the emphasis of the Court on the "law and order" record of this Amish group of people is quite irrelevant. A religion is a religion irrespective of what the misdemeanor or felony records of its members might be. I am not at all sure how the Catholics, Episcopalians, the Baptists, Jehovah's Witnesses, the Unitarians, and my own Presbyterians would make out if subjected to such a test. It is, of course, true if a group or society was organized to perpetuate crime, and if that is its motive, we would have rather startling problems akin to those that were raised when, some years back, a particular sect was challenged here as operating on a fraudulent basis. But no such factors are present here, and the Amish, whether with a high or low criminal record, certainly qualify by all historic standards as a religion within the meaning of the First Amendment.

▼▲▼

Together, *Sherbert* and *Yoder* articulated an imposing standard that widened considerably the scope of judicial protection under the Free Exercise Clause. Neither Justice Brennan, in *Sherbert,* nor Chief Justice Burger, in *Yoder,* saw a conflict with the Establishment Clause in granting an exemption to a generally applicable law based on religious objections. Indeed, the Court's sympathies in both cases were very much with Adell Sherbert and Jonas Yoder's claims, which amounted to a last line of defense for religious minorities seeking protection from the demands of the modern welfare state. By *Yoder,* the Court seemed comfortable with the notion, advanced by the various supporting parties in that case, that an important constitutional distinction existed between laws that supported or assisted religion, and generally applicable laws that placed religious individuals in the position of having to make choices between their religion and citizenship obligations.

By holding that religion was entitled to exemptions from generally applicable laws when the government could not demonstrate a compelling government interest in enforcing the law, *Sherbert* and *Yoder* put the

Court into the business of identifying and weighing the legitimacy of religious claims against the valid purposes of state law. This stance eventually required the Court to make some difficult choices based on its perception of the importance of the religious practice in question. Moreover, the Court's willingness to engage in the weighing and balancing of competing religious and governmental interests jeopardized the notion of neutrality as a guiding principle of the Religion Clauses. If the Court was willing to grant the Amish an exemption from compulsory school attendance laws based on a religious objection, then did it seem reasonable for someone else to ask for a similar exemption based on philosophical objections to the public school curriculum? And if the courts refused to recognize such an exemption to a generally applicable law for nonreligious reasons, did that somehow favor religion in an unconstitutional way?

This tension between professed neutrality toward religion and an approach that, in the name of liberty of conscience, favored religion cut through the Court's free exercise decisions from *Yoder* until *Smith*. Despite the rhetoric of *Sherbert* and *Yoder*, the Court rarely found an asserted government interest in a free exercise case involving a generally applicable law that was not compelling. After *Yoder*, the Court ruled against an Amish carpenter who wanted an exemption from having to pay Social Security taxes; held that Hari Krishnas did not have a right to an exemption from a Minnesota law that prohibited all groups from distributing materials at state fairgrounds; revoked the tax exemption of a fundamentalist Christian college that engaged in racial discrimination; determined that an Orthodox Jewish officer in the U.S. Air Force could not wear his yarmulke because of military restrictions against headgear; refused the request of an Islamic prisoner for a special accommodation to worship; and upheld the right of the U.S. Forest Service to take a Native American ritual site on federal park land in order to harvest timber and build roads.[81] In fact, after *Yoder*, the Court rarely ventured beyond the realm of unemployment compensation when it upheld a claim against a generally applicable law.[82] In one case, the Court upheld the right of a Jehovah's Witness to cover the state motto on New Hampshire's license plate, "Live Free or Die."[83] In another, the Court struck down a Tennessee restriction that prohibited ministers from running for public office.[84]

Still, the Court's commitment to the compelling interest standard in most free exercise cases involving generally applicable claims demonstrated that it was at least willing to extend to religious minorities their day in court, even if they usually ended up losing. In *Employment Division of Oregon* v. *Smith*, however, the Court abandoned the compelling interest test in such cases, holding that government need only demonstrate a rational basis in defending a government policy that burdens religious conduct. The Court gave no indication when it accepted *Smith* for review that it was going to reconsider the *Sherbert* standard. This left the parties and their *amici* in no position to brief the Court on the potential consequences of its holding. Only the ACLU, the AJCongress, the Association on American Indian Affairs, and the Council on Religious Freedom filed *amicus* briefs in *Smith*. All these groups asked the Court to do was to decide the case according to the *Sherbert* standard. Not even the Oregon attorney general asked the Court to set aside *Sherbert* to decide *Smith*.

Employment Division of Oregon v. *Smith*

494 U.S. 872 (1990)

In October 1983, Galen Black was fired from his job as a drug and alcohol counselor for the Council on Alcohol and Drug Abuse Prevention and Treatment, a Cascadia, Oregon, treatment facility and clinic. Counselors were forbidden to use alcohol or nonprescription drugs as a condition of their employment. In September, Black had ingested a small amount of peyote, a fungus containing mescaline, a hallucinogen. About six months later, Alfred Smith was fired from his job after ingesting peyote in a show of solidarity with his fellow member of the Native American Church. Peyote use has long been a central element in the religious ritual of the Native American Church, whose presence in the United States predates the European religions that arrived with Puritan settlers in the 1600s. It is considered sacramental, and used by church members to express thanks for the past and to pray for the future.

In the 1920s, the Montana Supreme Court ruled that peyote use was not protected by the Free Exercise Clause. During the early 1960s, the California Supreme Court reached the opposite conclusion, as long as church members could demonstrate that their adherence to the peyote ritual was sincere. Since these early confrontations over peyote use, twenty-three states, including Montana and California, and the federal government have crafted legislative exemptions for peyote use by the Native American Church. Otherwise, peyote use is a criminal offense under state and federal law. The Drug Enforcement Agency categorizes peyote as a Schedule I drug, the same as heroin and LSD.

Black and Smith argued that they were entitled to unemployment compensation, since they were fired for religious reasons. The state's review board on such matters denied their claim, but the Oregon courts concluded, under *Sherbert,* that the drug counselors were entitled to receive unemployment compensation. In 1988, the United States Supreme Court, hearing an appeal by Oregon, returned the case to the Oregon Supreme Court and asked it to decide whether peyote use was prohibited by state law. The Oregon court concluded that state law made no special provision for peyote use, but it ruled nonetheless that the Free Exercise Clause of the federal Constitution protected its usage and affirmed its earlier decision. The state appealed.

The Court's decision was 6 to 3. Justice Scalia delivered the opinion of the Court. Justice O'Connor wrote an opinion concurring in the result but rejecting the majority's analysis. Justice Brennan, joined by Justice Marshall, dissented. Justice Blackmun, joined by Justices Brennan and Marshall, also dissented.

▼▲▼

JUSTICE SCALIA delivered the opinion of the Court.

The free exercise of religion means, first and foremost, the right to believe and profess whatever religious doctrine one desires. Thus, the First Amendment obviously excludes all "governmental regulation of religious beliefs as such." The government may not compel affirmation of religious belief, punish the expression of religious doctrines it believes to be false, impose special disabilities on the basis of religious views or religious status, or lend its power to one or the other side in controversies over religious authority or dogma.

But the "exercise of religion" often involves not only belief and profession but the performance of (or abstention from) physical acts: assembling with others for a worship service, participating in sacramental use of bread and wine, proselytizing, abstaining from certain foods or certain modes of transportation. It would be true, we think (though no case of ours has involved the point), that a state would be "prohibiting the free exercise [of religion]" if it sought to ban such acts or abstentions only when they are engaged in for religious reasons, or only because of the religious belief that they display. It would doubtless be unconstitutional, for example, to ban the casting of "statues that are to be used for worship purposes," or to prohibit bowing down before a golden calf.

Respondents in the present case, however, seek to carry the meaning of "prohibiting the free exercise [of religion]" one large step further. They contend that their religious motivation for using peyote places them beyond the reach of a criminal law that is not specifically directed at their religious practice, and that is concededly constitutional as applied to those who use the drug for other reasons. They assert, in other words, that "prohibiting the free exercise [of religion]" includes requiring any individual to observe a generally applicable law that requires (or forbids) the performance of an act that his religious belief forbids (or requires). As a textual matter, we do not think the words must be given that meaning. It is no more necessary to regard the collection of a general tax, for example, as "prohibiting the free exercise [of religion]" by those citizens who believe support of organized government to be sinful than it is to regard the same tax as "abridging the freedom . . . of the press" of those publishing companies that must pay the tax as a condition of staying in business. It is a permissible reading of the text, in the one case as in the other, to say that, if prohibiting the exercise of religion (or burdening the activity of printing) is not the object of the tax, but merely the incidental effect of a generally applicable and otherwise valid provision, the First Amendment has not been offended.

Our decisions reveal that the latter reading is the correct one. We have never held that an individual's religious beliefs excuse him from compliance with an otherwise valid law prohibiting conduct that the State is free to regulate. On the contrary, the record of more than a century of our free exercise jurisprudence contradicts that proposition. . . . We first had occasion to assert that principle in *Reynolds* v. *United States* (1879), where we rejected the claim that criminal laws against polygamy could not be constitutionally applied to those whose religion commanded the practice.

Subsequent decisions have consistently held that the right of free exercise does not relieve an individual of the obligation to comply with a valid and neutral law of general applicability on the ground that the law proscribes (or prescribes) conduct that his religion prescribes (or proscribes), *United States* v. *Lee* (1982). . . .

The only decisions in which we have held that the First Amendment bars application of a neutral, generally applicable law to religiously motivated action have involved not the Free Exercise Clause alone, but the Free Exercise Clause in conjunction with other constitutional protections, such as freedom of speech and of the press, or the right of parents . . . to direct the education of their children, *Wisconsin* v. *Yoder* (1972). Some of our cases prohibiting compelled expression, decided exclusively upon free speech grounds, have also involved freedom of religion. And it is easy to envision a case in which a challenge on freedom of association grounds would likewise be reinforced by Free Exercise Clause concerns.

The present case does not present such a hybrid situation, but a free exercise claim unconnected with any communicative activity or parental right. Respondents urge us to hold, quite simply, that when otherwise prohibitable conduct is accompanied by religious convictions, not only the convictions but the conduct itself must be free from governmental regulation. We have never held that, and decline to do so now. There being no contention that Oregon's drug law represents an attempt to regulate religious beliefs, the communication of religious beliefs, or the raising of one's children in those beliefs, the rule to which we have adhered ever since *Reynolds* plainly controls. . . .

Even if we were inclined to breathe into *Sherbert* some life beyond the unemployment compensation field, we would not apply it to require exemptions from a generally applicable criminal law. The *Sherbert* test, it must be recalled, was developed in a context that lent itself to individualized governmental assessment of the reasons for the relevant conduct. As a plurality of the Court noted in *Roy*, a distinctive feature of unemployment compensation programs is that their eligibility criteria invite consideration of the particular circumstances behind an applicant's unemployment. . . .

Whether or not the decisions are that limited, they at least have nothing to do with an across-the-board criminal prohibition on a particular form of conduct. Although, as noted earlier, we have sometimes used the *Sherbert* test to analyze free exercise challenges to such laws, we have never applied the test to invalidate one. We conclude today that the sounder approach, and the approach in accord with the vast majority of our precedents, is to hold the test inapplicable to such challenges. The government's ability to enforce generally applicable prohibitions of socially harmful conduct, like its ability to carry out other aspects of public policy, "cannot depend on measuring the effects of a governmental action on a religious objector's spiritual development." To make an individual's obligation to obey such a law contingent upon the law's coincidence with his religious beliefs, except where the State's interest is "compelling," *Reynolds*—permitting him, by virtue of his beliefs, "to become a law unto himself," contradicts both constitutional tradition and common sense.

The "compelling government interest" requirement seems benign, because it is familiar from other fields. But using it as the standard that must be met before the government may accord different treatment on the basis of race, or before the government may regulate the content of speech, is not remotely comparable to using it for the purpose asserted here. What it produces in those other fields—equality of treatment, and an unrestricted flow of contending speech—are constitutional norms; what it would produce here—a private right to ignore generally applicable laws—is a constitutional anomaly.

Nor is it possible to limit the impact of respondents' proposal by requiring a "compelling state interest" only when the conduct prohibited is "central" to the individual's religion. It is no more appropriate for judges to determine the "centrality" of religious beliefs before applying a "compelling interest" test in the free exercise field than it would be for them to determine the "importance" of ideas before applying the "compelling interest" test in the free speech field. What principle of law or logic can be brought to bear to contradict a believer's assertion that a particular act is "central" to his personal faith? Judging the centrality of different religious practices is akin to the unacceptable "business of evaluating the relative merits of differing religious claims," *United States* v. *Lee* (1982). . . .

If the "compelling interest" test is to be applied at all, then, it must be applied across the board, to all actions thought to be religiously commanded. Moreover, if "compelling interest" really means what it says (and watering it down here would subvert its rigor in the other fields where it is applied), many laws will not meet the test. Any society adopting such a system would be courting anarchy, but that danger increases in direct proportion to the society's diversity of religious beliefs, and its determination to coerce or suppress none of them. Precisely because "we are a cosmopolitan nation made up of people of almost every conceivable religious preference," and precisely because we value and protect that religious divergence, we cannot afford the luxury of deeming *presumptively invalid*, as applied to the religious objector, every regulation of conduct that does not protect an interest of the highest order. The rule respondents favor would open the prospect of constitutionally required religious exemptions from civic obligations of almost every conceivable kind. . . .

Values that are protected against government interference through enshrinement in the Bill of Rights are not thereby banished from the political process. Just as a society that believes in the negative protection accorded to the press by the First Amendment is likely to enact laws that affirmatively foster the dissemination of the printed word, so also a society that believes in the negative protection accorded to religious belief can be expected to be solicitous of that value in its legislation as well. It is therefore not surprising that a number of States have made an exception to their drug laws for sacramental peyote use. But to say that a nondiscriminatory religious practice exemption is permitted, or even that it is desirable, is not to say that it is constitutionally required, and that the appropriate occasions for its creation can be discerned by the courts. It may fairly be said that leaving accommodation to the political process will place at a relative disadvantage those religious practices that are not widely engaged in; but that unavoidable consequence of democratic government must be preferred to a system in which each conscience is a law unto itself or in which judges weigh the social importance of all laws against the centrality of all religious beliefs.

Because respondents' ingestion of peyote was prohibited under Oregon law, and because that prohibition is constitutional, Oregon may, consistent with the Free Exercise Clause, deny respondents unemployment compensation when their dismissal results from use of the drug. The decision of the Oregon Supreme Court is accordingly reversed.

JUSTICE O'CONNOR, with whom JUSTICE BRENNAN, JUSTICE MARSHALL, and JUSTICE BLACKMUN join as to Parts I and II, concurring in the judgment.

Although I agree with the result the Court reaches in this case, I cannot join its opinion. In my view, today's holding dramatically departs from well settled First Amendment jurisprudence, appears unnecessary to resolve the question presented, and is incompatible with our Nation's fundamental commitment to individual religious liberty.

I

[Omitted]

II

The Court today extracts from our long history of free exercise precedents the single categorical rule that "if prohibiting the exercise of religion . . . is . . . merely the incidental effect of a generally applicable and otherwise valid provision, the First Amendment has not been offended."

Indeed, the Court holds that, where the law is a generally applicable criminal prohibition, our usual free exercise jurisprudence does not even apply. To reach this sweeping result, however, the Court must not only give a strained reading of the First Amendment but must also disregard our consistent application of free exercise doctrine to cases involving generally applicable regulations that burden religious conduct. . . .

Because the First Amendment does not distinguish between religious belief and religious conduct, conduct motivated by sincere religious belief, like the belief itself, must therefore be at least presumptively protected by the Free Exercise Clause.

The Court today, however, interprets the Clause to permit the government to prohibit, without justification, conduct mandated by an individual's religious beliefs, so long as that prohibition is generally applicable. But a law that prohibits certain conduct—conduct that happens to be an act of worship for someone—manifestly does prohibit that person's free exercise of his religion. A person who is barred from engaging in religiously motivated conduct is barred from freely exercising his religion. Moreover, that person is barred from freely exercising his religion regardless of whether the law prohibits the conduct only when engaged in for religious reasons, only by members of that religion, or by all persons. It is difficult to deny that a law that prohibits religiously motivated conduct, even if the law is generally applicable, does not at least implicate First Amendment concerns.

The Court responds that generally applicable laws are "one large step" removed from laws aimed at specific religious practices. The First Amendment, however, does not distinguish between laws that are generally applicable and laws that target particular religious practices. Indeed, few States would be so naive as to enact a law directly prohibiting or burdening a religious practice as such. Our free exercise cases have all concerned generally applicable laws that had the effect of significantly burdening a religious practice. If the First Amendment is to have any vitality, it ought not be construed to cover only the extreme and hypothetical situation in which a State directly targets a religious practice. . . .

To say that a person's right to free exercise has been burdened, of course, does not mean that he has an absolute right to engage in the conduct. Under our established First Amendment jurisprudence, we have recognized that the freedom to act, unlike the freedom to believe, cannot be absolute. Instead, we have respected both the First Amendment's express textual mandate and the governmental interest in regulation of conduct by requiring the Government to justify any substantial burden on religiously motivated conduct by a compelling state interest and by means narrowly tailored to achieve that interest. . . .

The Court endeavors to escape from our decisions in *Cantwell* and *Yoder* by labeling them "hybrid" decisions, but there is no denying that both cases expressly relied on the Free Exercise Clause, and that we have consistently regarded those cases as part of the mainstream of our free exercise jurisprudence. Moreover, in each of the other cases cited by the Court to support its categorical rule, we rejected the particular constitutional claims before us only after carefully weighing the competing interests. That we rejected the free exercise claims in those cases hardly calls into question the applicability of First Amendment doctrine in the first place. Indeed, it is surely unusual to judge the vitality of a constitutional doctrine by looking to the win-loss record of the plaintiffs who happen to come before us. . . .

In my view, however, the essence of a free exercise claim is relief from a burden imposed by government on religious practices or beliefs, whether the burden is imposed directly through laws that prohibit or compel specific religious practices, or indirectly through laws that, in effect, make abandonment of one's own religion or conformity to the religious beliefs of others the price of an equal place in the civil community. . . . A State that makes criminal an individual's religiously motivated conduct burdens that individual's free exercise of religion in the severest manner possible, for it "results in the choice to the individual of either abandoning his religious principle or facing criminal prosecution." I would have thought it beyond argument that such laws implicate free exercise concerns.

Indeed, we have never distinguished between cases in which a State conditions receipt of a benefit on conduct prohibited by religious beliefs and cases in which a State affirmatively prohibits such conduct. The *Sherbert* compelling interest test applies in both kinds of cases. . . .

The Court today gives no convincing reason to depart from settled First Amendment jurisprudence. There is nothing talismanic about neutral laws of general applicability or general criminal prohibitions, for laws neutral toward religion can coerce a person to violate his religious conscience or intrude upon his religious duties just as effectively as laws aimed at religion. Although the Court suggests that the compelling interest test, as applied to generally applicable laws, would result in a "constitutional anomaly," the First Amendment unequivocally makes freedom of religion, like freedom from race discrimination and freedom of speech, a "constitutional nor[m]," not an "anomaly." Nor would application of our established free exercise doctrine to this case necessarily be incompatible with our equal protection cases. We have, in any event, recognized that the Free Exercise Clause protects values distinct from those protected by the Equal Protection Clause. As the language of the Clause itself makes clear, an individual's free exercise of religion is a preferred constitutional activity. A law that makes criminal such an activity therefore triggers constitutional concern—and heightened judicial scrutiny—even if it does not target the particular religious conduct at issue. Our free speech cases similarly recognize that neutral regulations that affect free speech values are subject to a balancing, rather than categorical, approach. The Court's parade of horribles, not only fails as a reason for discarding the compelling interest test, it instead demonstrates just the opposite: that courts have been quite capable of applying our free exercise jurisprudence to strike sensible balances between religious liberty and competing state interests.

Finally, the Court today suggests that the disfavoring of minority religions is an "unavoidable consequence" under our system of government, and that accommodation of such religions must be left to the political process. In my view, however, the First Amendment was enacted precisely to protect the rights of those whose religious practices are not shared by the majority and may be viewed with hostility. The history of our free exercise doctrine amply demonstrates the harsh impact majoritarian rule has had on unpopular or emerging religious groups such as the Jehovah's Witnesses and the Amish. . . .

III

The Court's holding today not only misreads settled First Amendment precedent; it appears to be unnecessary to this case. I would reach the same result applying our established free exercise jurisprudence. . . .

There is no dispute that Oregon's criminal prohibition of peyote places a severe burden on the ability of respondents to freely exercise their religion. Peyote is a sacrament of the Native American Church, and is regarded as vital to respondents' ability to practice their religion. . . .

Thus, the critical question in this case is whether exempting respondents from the State's general criminal prohibition "will unduly interfere with fulfillment of the governmental interest." Although the question is close, I would conclude that uniform application of Oregon's criminal prohibition is "essential to accomplish" its overriding interest in preventing the physical harm caused by the use of a Schedule I controlled substance. Oregon's criminal prohibition represents that State's judgment that the possession and use of controlled substances, even by only one person, is inherently harmful and dangerous. Because the health effects caused by the use of controlled substances exist regardless of the motivation of the user, the use of such substances, even for religious purposes, violates the very purpose of the laws that prohibit them. Moreover, in view of the societal interest in preventing trafficking in controlled substances, uniform application of the criminal prohibition at issue is essential to the effectiveness of Oregon's stated interest in preventing any possession of peyote. . . .

For these reasons, I believe that granting a selective exemption in this case would seriously impair Oregon's compelling interest in prohibiting possession of peyote by its citizens. Under such circumstances, the Free Exercise Clause does not require the State to accommodate respondents' religiously motivated conduct.

JUSTICE BLACKMUN, with whom JUSTICE BRENNAN and JUSTICE MARSHALL join, dissenting.

This Court over the years painstakingly has developed a consistent and exacting standard to test the constitutionality of a state statute that burdens the free exercise of religion. Such a statute may stand only if the law in general, and the State's refusal to allow a religious exemption in particular, are justified by a compelling interest that cannot be served by less restrictive means.

Until today, I thought this was a settled and inviolate principle of this Court's First Amendment jurisprudence. The majority, however, perfunctorily dismisses it as a "constitutional anomaly." . . . The Court discards leading free exercise cases such as *Cantwell* v. *Connecticut* (1940) and *Wisconsin* v. *Yoder* (1972) as "hybrid." The Court views traditional free exercise analysis as somehow inapplicable to criminal prohibitions (as opposed to conditions on the receipt of benefits), and to state laws of general applicability (as opposed, presumably, to laws that expressly single out religious practices). The Court cites cases in which, due to various exceptional circumstances, we found strict scrutiny inapposite, to hint that the Court has repudiated that standard altogether. In short, it effectuates a wholesale overturning of settled law concerning the Religion Clauses of our Constitution. One hopes that the Court is aware of the consequences, and that its result is not a product of overreaction to the serious problems the country's drug crisis has generated.

This distorted view of our precedents leads the majority to conclude that strict scrutiny of a state law burdening the free exercise of religion is a "luxury" that a well-ordered society cannot afford, and that the repression of minority religions is an "unavoidable consequence of democratic government." I do not believe the Founders thought their dearly bought freedom from religious persecution a "luxury," but an essential element of liberty—and they could not have thought religious intolerance "unavoidable," for they drafted the Religion Clauses precisely in order to avoid that intolerance. . . .

The State's interest in enforcing its prohibition, in order to be sufficiently compelling to outweigh a free exercise claim, cannot be merely abstract or symbolic. The State cannot plausibly assert that unbending application of a criminal prohibition is essential to fulfill any compelling interest if it does not, in fact, attempt to enforce that prohibition. In this case, the State actually has not evinced any concrete interest in enforcing its drug laws against religious users of peyote. Oregon has never sought to prosecute respondents, and does not claim that it has made significant enforcement efforts against other religious users of peyote. The State's asserted interest thus amounts only to the symbolic preservation of an unenforced prohibition. . . . Similarly, this Court's prior decisions have not allowed a government to rely on mere speculation about potential harms, but have demanded evidentiary support for a refusal to allow a religious exception.

The State proclaims an interest in protecting the health and safety of its citizens from the dangers of unlawful drugs. It offers, however, no evidence that the religious use of peyote has ever harmed anyone. The factual findings of other courts cast doubt on the State's assumption that religious use of peyote is harmful. . . . The carefully circumscribed ritual context in which respondents used peyote is far removed from the irresponsible and unrestricted recreational use of unlawful drugs. The Native American Church's internal restrictions on, and supervision of, its members' use of peyote substantially obviate the State's health and safety concerns.

Moreover, just as in *Yoder*, the values and interests of those seeking a religious exemption in this case are congruent, to a great degree, with those the State seeks to promote through its drug laws. Not only does the Church's doctrine forbid nonreligious use of peyote; it also generally advocates self-reliance, familial responsibility, and abstinence from alcohol. *See* Brief for Association on American Indian Affairs, as *amici curiae* (the Church's "ethical code" has four parts: brotherly love, care of family, self-reliance, and avoidance of alcohol (quoting from the Church membership card). . . . Far from promoting the lawless and irresponsible use of drugs, Native American Church members' spiritual code exemplifies values that Oregon's drug laws are presumably intended to foster. . . .

The State's apprehension of a flood of other religious claims is purely speculative. Almost half the States, and the Federal Government, have maintained an exemption for religious peyote use for many years, and apparently have not found themselves overwhelmed by claims to other religious exemptions. Allowing an exemption for religious peyote use would not necessarily oblige the State to grant a similar exemption to other religious groups. The unusual circumstances that make the religious use of peyote compatible with the State's interests in health and safety and in preventing drug trafficking would not apply to other religious claims. . . .

If Oregon can constitutionally prosecute them for this act of worship, they, like the Amish, may be "forced to migrate to some other and more tolerant region." This potentially devastating impact must be viewed in light of the federal policy—reached in reaction to many years of religious persecution and intolerance—of protecting the religious freedom of Native Americans. . . .

For these reasons, I conclude that Oregon's interest in enforcing its drug laws against religious use of peyote is not sufficiently compelling to outweigh respondents' right to the free exercise of their religion. Since the State could not constitutionally enforce its criminal prohibition against respondents, the interests underlying the State's drug laws cannot justify its denial of unemployment benefits.

I dissent.

▼▲▼

After *Smith,* a broad coalition of religious, education, and civil liberties groups, which ranged from liberal to moderate groups such as the AJCongress, the ACLU, and the Baptist Joint Committee to the National Parent Teacher Association to conservative groups such as the National Association of Evangelicals, Christian Legal Society, and Concerned Women for America, petitioned the Court for a rehearing to brief the issues raised by the Court's opinion. The Court denied the request.[85] Within months of *Smith,* the Court vacated several state and federal court decisions upholding the rights of churches and individuals to religious exemptions under *Sherbert.* These cases included requests from churches for exemptions from city landmark ordinances and the Amish, who wanted an exemption from a state law requiring slow-moving vehicles to display fluorescent orange triangles that would have included their horse-and-buggies.[86] Since *Smith,* no federal court has upheld a free exercise challenge to a generally applicable law under the rational basis standard.[87]

Seizing upon the internal dissension within the Court over Scalia's analysis of *Sherbert* and his interpretation of the Framers' understanding of the free exercise guarantee, the groups that came together to petition the Court for a rehearing in *Smith* formed the Coalition for the Free Exercise of Religion (CFER). Consisting of forty-five groups from all points on the religious and political spectrum, the CFER asked Congress to pass legislation to overcome *Smith.* In 1993, after three intense years of lobbying and negotiations with White House officials, Congress passed the Religious Freedom Restoration Act of 1993. During the debate over RFRA, the United States Catholic Conference expressed concern that a woman could argue she was entitled to a religious exemption from certain abortion regulations; the U.S. Department of Justice argued that the statute would hinder the ability of federal prison officials to compel religious objectors to follow disciplinary guidelines; and some members of Congress expressed concern that anyone objecting to a law could argue the law favored religion by giving religious objectors preference over secular objectors. Ultimately, the CFER was able to satisfy the Justice Department's concerns by crafting exemptions for prison officials and address congressional fears by mandating that any objection to the law had to have a "bona fide" religious basis. *Planned Parenthood* v. *Casey* (1992) (see Chapter 10), which reaffirmed *Roe* v. *Wade,* the Court's landmark 1973 decision recognizing a constitutional right to abortion, made the USCC's concerns a moot point. President Clinton signed RFRA into law in an elaborate Rose Garden ceremony.

RFRA did not reverse *Smith.* Instead, the law required federal courts hearing free exercise claims brought against generally applicable laws to use the compelling interest standard articulated in *Sherbert* and refined in *Yoder.* Moreover, RFRA did not create a substantive free exercise right. Rather, it permitted individuals whose religious liberty was burdened by a generally applicable law to have an opportunity to defend themselves in court. An early and expected challenge to RFRA's constitutionality came in *City of Boerne* v. *Flores* (1997).

City of Boerne v. *Flores, Archbishop of San Antonio*

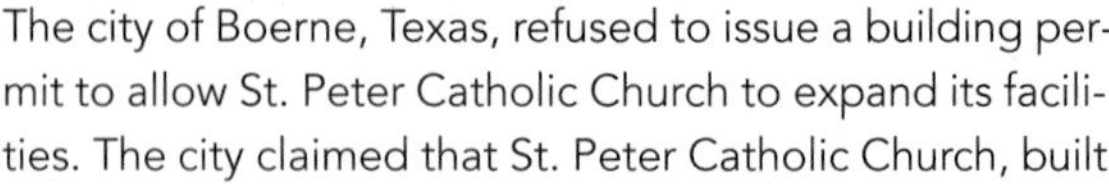

521 U.S. 507 (1997)

The city of Boerne, Texas, refused to issue a building permit to allow St. Peter Catholic Church to expand its facilities. The city claimed that St. Peter Catholic Church, built in 1923, was bound by a local law governing historic preservation in a district that included the church. The decision was challenged under RFRA. A federal district court ruled Congress exceeded the scope of its enforcement power under Section 5 of the Fourteenth Amendment when it enacted RFRA. The lower court was reversed by the Fifth Circuit Court of Appeals, one of the nation's most influential appeals courts.

The Court's decision was 6 to 3. Justice Kennedy delivered the opinion of the Court. Justice Scalia, joined by Justice Stevens, dissented. Justices O'Connor, Souter, and Breyer filed separate dissenting opinions.

JUSTICE KENNEDY delivered the opinion of the Court.

A decision by local zoning authorities to deny a church a building permit was challenged under the Religious Freedom Restoration Act of 1993 (RFRA). The case calls into question the authority of Congress to enact RFRA. We conclude the statute exceeds Congress's power. . . .

Congress enacted RFRA in direct response to the Court's decision in *Employment Div., Dept. of Human Resources of Ore.* v. *Smith* (1990). There, we considered a Free Exercise Clause claim brought by members of the Native American Church who were denied unemployment benefits when they lost their jobs because they had used peyote. Their practice was to ingest peyote for sacramental purposes, and they challenged an Oregon statute of general applicability which made use of the drug criminal. In evaluating the claim, we declined to apply the balancing test set forth in *Sherbert v. Verner* (1963), under which we would have asked whether Oregon's prohibition substantially burdened a religious practice and, if it did, whether the burden was justified by a compelling government interest. . . .

Four Members of the Court disagreed. They argued the law placed a substantial burden on the Native American Church members so that it could be upheld only if the law served a compelling state interest and was narrowly tailored to achieve that end. . . .

These points of constitutional interpretation were debated by Members of Congress in hearings and floor debates. Many criticized the Court's reasoning, and this disagreement resulted in the passage of RFRA. Congress announced:

1. [T]he framers of the Constitution, recognizing free exercise of religion as an unalienable right, secured its protection in the First Amendment to the Constitution;
2. laws 'neutral' toward religion may burden religious exercise as surely as laws intended to interfere with religious exercise;
3. governments should not substantially burden religious exercise without compelling justification;
4. in *Employment Division* v. *Smith* (1990), the Supreme Court virtually eliminated the requirement that the government justify burdens on religious exercise imposed by laws neutral toward religion; and
5. the compelling interest test as set forth in prior Federal court rulings is a workable test for striking sensible balances between religious liberty and competing prior governmental interests.

RFRA prohibits "[g]overnment" from "substantially burden[ing]" a person's exercise of religion even if the burden results from a rule of general applicability unless the government can demonstrate the burden, "(1) is in furtherance of a compelling governmental interest; and (2) is the least restrictive means of furthering that compelling governmental interest." The Act's mandate applies to any "branch, department, agency, instrumentality, and official (or other person acting under color of law) of the United States," as well as to any "State, or . . . subdivision of a State." The Act's universal coverage is confirmed in Section 2000bb-3(a), under which RFRA, "applies to all Federal and State law, and the implementation of that law, whether statutory or otherwise, and whether adopted before or after [RFRA's enactment]." In accordance with RFRA's usage of the term, we shall use "state law" to include local and municipal ordinances.

Under our Constitution, the Federal Government is one of enumerated powers. The judicial authority to determine the constitutionality of laws, in cases and controversies, is based on the premise that the "powers of the legislature are defined and limited, and that those limits may not be mistaken, or forgotten, the constitution is written," *Marbury* v. *Madison* (1803).

Congress relied on its Fourteenth Amendment enforcement power in enacting the most far reaching and substantial of RFRA's provisions, those which impose its requirements on the States. . . .

The parties disagree over whether RFRA is a proper exercise of Congress's Section 5 power "to enforce" by "appropriate legislation" the constitutional guarantee that no State shall deprive any person of "life, liberty, or property, without due process of law" nor deny any person "equal protection of the laws."

[The] respondent contends, with support from the United States as *amicus,* that RFRA is permissible enforcement legislation. Congress, it is said, is only protecting by legislation one of the liberties guaranteed by the Fourteenth Amendment's Due Process Clause, the free exercise of religion, beyond what is necessary under *Smith.* It is said the congressional decision to dispense with proof of deliberate or overt discrimination and instead concentrate on a law's effects accords with the settled understanding that Section 5 includes the power to enact legislation designed to prevent as well as remedy constitutional violations. It is further contended that Congress's Section 5 power is not limited to remedial or preventive legislation. . . .

It is also true, however, that, "[a]s broad as the congressional enforcement power is, it is not unlimited." In assessing the breadth of Section 5's enforcement power, we begin with its text. Congress has been given the power "to enforce" the "provisions of this article." We agree with respondent, of course, that Congress can enact legislation under Section 5 enforcing the constitutional right to the free exercise of religion. The "provisions of this article," to which Section 5 refers, include the Due Process Clause of the Fourteenth Amendment. . . .

Congress's power under Section 5, however, extends only to "enforc[ing]" the provisions of the Fourteenth Amendment. The Court has described this power as "remedial." The design of the Amendment and the text of Section 5 are inconsistent with the suggestion that Congress has the power to decree the substance of the Fourteenth Amendment's restrictions on the States. Legislation which alters the meaning of the Free Exercise Clause cannot be said to be enforcing the Clause. Congress does not enforce a constitutional right by changing what the right is. It has been given the power "to enforce," not the power to determine what constitutes a constitutional violation. Were it not so, what Congress would be enforcing would no longer be, in any meaningful sense, the "provisions of [the Fourteenth Amendment]."

While the line between measures that remedy or prevent unconstitutional actions and measures that make a substantive change in the governing law is not easy to discern, and Congress must have wide latitude in determining where it lies, the distinction exists and must be observed. There must be a congruence and proportionality between the injury to be prevented or remedied and the means adopted to that end. Lacking such a connection, legislation may become substantive in operation and effect. History and our case law support drawing the distinction, one apparent from the text of the Amendment. . . .

If Congress could define its own powers by altering the Fourteenth Amendment's meaning, no longer would the Constitution be "superior paramount law, unchangeable by ordinary means." It would be "on a level with ordinary legislative acts, and, like other acts, . . . alterable when the legislature shall please to alter it," *Marbury* v. *Madison*. Under this approach, it is difficult to conceive of a principle that would limit congressional power. Shifting legislative majorities could change the Constitution and effectively circumvent the difficult and detailed amendment process contained in Article V.

We now turn to consider whether RFRA can be considered enforcement legislation under Section 5 of the Fourteenth Amendment.

Respondent contends that RFRA is a proper exercise of Congress's remedial or preventive power. The Act, it is said, is a reasonable means of protecting the free exercise of religion as defined by *Smith*. It prevents and remedies laws which are enacted with the unconstitutional object of targeting religious beliefs and practices. To avoid the difficulty of proving such violations, it is said, Congress can simply invalidate any law which imposes a substantial burden on a religious practice unless it is justified by a compelling interest and is the least restrictive means of accomplishing that interest. If Congress can prohibit laws with discriminatory effects in order to prevent racial discrimination in violation of the Equal Protection Clause, then it can do the same, respondent argues, to promote religious liberty.

While preventive rules are sometimes appropriate remedial measures, there must be a congruence between the means used and the ends to be achieved. The appropriateness of remedial measures must be considered in light of the evil presented. Strong measures appropriate to address one harm may be an unwarranted response to another, lesser one.

A comparison between RFRA and the Voting Rights Act is instructive. In contrast to the record which confronted Congress and the judiciary in the voting rights cases, RFRA's legislative record lacks examples of modern instances of generally applicable laws passed because of religious bigotry. The history of persecution in this country detailed in the hearings mentions no episodes occurring in the past 40 years. . . .

Regardless of the state of the legislative record, RFRA cannot be considered remedial, preventive legislation, if those terms are to have any meaning. RFRA is so out of proportion to a supposed remedial or preventive object that it cannot be understood as responsive to, or designed to prevent, unconstitutional behavior. It appears, instead, to attempt a substantive change in constitutional protections. Preventive measures prohibiting certain types of laws may be appropriate when there is reason to believe that many of the laws affected by the congressional enactment have a significant likelihood of being unconstitutional.

RFRA is not so confined. Sweeping coverage ensures its intrusion at every level of government, displacing laws and prohibiting official actions of almost every description and regardless of subject matter. RFRA's restrictions apply to every agency and official of the Federal, State, and local Governments. RFRA applies to all federal and state law, statutory or otherwise, whether adopted before or after its enactment. RFRA has no termination date or termination mechanism. Any law is subject to challenge at any time by any individual who alleges a substantial burden on his or her free exercise of religion. . . .

Our national experience teaches that the Constitution is preserved best when each part of the government respects both the Constitution and the proper actions and determinations of the other branches. When the Court has interpreted the Constitution, it has acted within the province of the Judicial Branch, which embraces the duty to say what the law is, *Marbury* v. *Madison.* When the political branches of the Government act against the background of a judicial interpretation of the Constitution already issued, it must be understood that, in later cases and controversies, the Court will treat its precedents with the respect due them under settled principles, including *stare decisis,* and contrary expectations must be disappointed. RFRA was designed to control cases and controversies, such as the one before us; but, as the provisions of the federal statute here invoked are beyond congressional authority, it is this Court's precedent, not RFRA, which must control. . . .

It is so ordered.

JUSTICE O'CONNOR . . . dissenting.

I dissent from the Court's disposition of this case. I agree with the Court that the issue before us is whether the Religious Freedom Restoration Act (RFRA) is a proper exercise of Congress's power to enforce §5 of the Fourteenth Amendment. But as a yardstick for measuring the constitutionality of RFRA, the Court uses its holding in *Employment Div., Dept. of Human Resources of Ore.* v. *Smith* (1990), the decision that prompted Congress to enact RFRA as a means of more rigorously enforcing the Free Exercise Clause. I remain of the view that *Smith* was wrongly decided, and I would use this case to reexamine the Court's holding there. Therefore, I would direct the parties to brief the question whether *Smith* represents the correct understanding of the Free Exercise Clause and set the case for reargument. If the Court were to correct the misinterpretation of the Free Exercise Clause set forth in *Smith,* it would simultaneously put our First Amendment jurisprudence back on course and allay the legitimate concerns of a majority in Congress who believed that *Smith* improperly restricted religious liberty. We would then be in a position to review RFRA in light of a proper interpretation of the Free Exercise Clause.

Indeed, if I agreed with the Court's standard in *Smith,* I would join the opinion. As the Court's careful and thorough historical analysis shows, Congress lacks the "power to decree the substance of the Fourteenth Amendment's restrictions on the States." Rather, its power under §5 of the Fourteenth Amendment extends only to enforcing the Amendment's provisions. In short, Congress lacks the ability independently to define or expand the scope of constitutional rights by statute. Accordingly, whether Congress has exceeded its §5 powers turns on whether there is a "congruence and proportionality between the injury to be prevented or remedied and the means adopted to that end." Ante, at 10. This recognition does not, of course, in any way diminish Congress's obligation to draw its own conclusions regarding the Constitution's meaning. Congress, no less than this Court, is called upon to consider the requirements of the Constitution and to act in accordance with its dictates. But when it enacts legislation in furtherance of its delegated powers, Congress must make its judgments consistent with this Court's exposition of the Constitution and with the limits placed on its legislative authority by provisions such as the Fourteenth Amendment. . . .

I believe that we should reexamine our holding in *Smith,* and do so in this very case. In its place, I would return to a rule that requires government to justify any substantial burden on religiously motivated conduct by a compelling state interest and to impose that burden only by means narrowly tailored to achieve that interest.

JUSTICE SOUTER, dissenting.

To decide whether the Fourteenth Amendment gives Congress sufficient power to enact the Religious Freedom Restoration Act, the Court measures the legislation against the free exercise standard of *Employment Div., Dept. of Human Resources of Ore.* v. *Smith* (1990). For the reasons stated in my opinion in *Church of Lukumi Babalu Aye, Inc.* v. *Hialeah* (1993), I have serious doubts about the precedential value of the *Smith* rule and its entitlement to adherence. But without briefing and argument on the merits of that rule (which this Court has never had in any case, including *Smith* itself) . . . I am not now prepared to join Justice O'Connor in rejecting it or the majority in assuming it to be correct. In order to provide full adversarial consideration, this case should be set down for reargument permitting plenary reexamination of the issue. Since the Court declines to follow that course, our free excercise law remains marked by an "intolerable tension,"

and the constitutionality of the Act of Congress to enforce the free exercise right cannot now be soundly decided.

Justice Kennedy, in a 6-3 opinion that RFRA's supporters claimed "staked out a claim to judicial supremacy that exceed[ed] anything" any previous Court had claimed, held that Congress had far surpassed the limits of its constitutional authority when it passed legislation to curtail the impact of *Smith*.[88] Note how the *Flores* majority viewed this case as primarily about the power of Congress to encroach upon the Court's authority to decide constitutional questions, with very little attention to the substantive free exercise questions presented by RFRA's supporters. Justices O'Connor and Souter, on the other hand, continued their previous criticism of the Court's decision in *Smith*. They emphasized the need for a proper remedy to a decision they considered flawed. Although *Flores* does not raise a substantive question of religious free exercise, Kennedy's opinion does offer an important statement on the Court's willingness to permit Congress to second-guess the justices on matters of constitutional interpretation considered settled.

FOR FURTHER READING

Alley, Robert S. *The Constitution and Religion: Leading Supreme Court Cases on Church and State*. Buffalo, N.Y.: Prometheus Books, 1999.

Carter, Stephen L. *God's Name in Vain: The Wrongs and Rights of Religion in Politics*. New York: Basic Books, 2000.

Curry, Thomas J. *The First Freedoms: Church and State in America to the Passage of the First Amendment*. New York: Oxford University Press, 1986.

Davis, Derek H., and Bill Moyers, eds. *Genesis and the Millennium: An Essay on Religious Pluralism in the Twenty-First Century*. Waco, Tex.: Baylor University Press, 2000.

Evans, Bette. *Interpreting the Free Exercise of Religion*. Chapel Hill: University of North Carolina Press, 1997.

Feldman, Stephen. *Please Don't Wish Me a Merry Christmas: A Critical History of the Separation of Church and State*. New York: New York University Press, 1997.

Herberg, Will. *Protestant, Catholic, Jew: An Essay in American Religious Sociology*. Chicago: University of Chicago Press, 1960.

Ivers, Gregg. *To Build a Wall: American Jews and the Separation of Church and State*. Charlottesville: University Press of Virginia, 1995.

Long, Carolyn N. *Religious Freedom and Indian Rights: The Case of Oregon v. Smith*. Lawrence: University Press of Kansas, 2000.

Mazur, Eric Michael. *The Americanization of Religious Minorities: Confronting the Constitutional Order*. Baltimore, Md.: Johns Hopkins University Press, 1999.

Monsma, Stephen V., and J. Christopher Soper. *Equal Treatment of Religion in a Pluralistic Society*. Grand Rapids, Mich.: Eerdmans, 1998.

Peters, Shawn Francis. *Judging Jehovah's Witnesses. Religious Persecution and the Dawn of the Rights Revolution*. Lawrence: University Press of Kansas, 2000.

Pfeffer, Leo. *Church, State and Freedom*. Boston: Beacon Press, 1967.

Ravitch, Frank S. *School Prayer and Discrimination*. Boston: Northeastern University Press, 1999.

Smith, Steven D. *Foreordained Failure: The Quest for a Constitutional Principle of Religious Freedom*. New York: Oxford University Press, 1995.

Sorauf, Frank J. *The Wall of Separation: The Constitutional Politics of Church and State*. Princeton, N.J.: Princeton University Press, 1976.

Stokes, Anson Phelps. *Church and State in the United States*. New York: Harper & Bros., 1950.

Swanson, Wayne. *The Christ Child Goes to Court*. Philadelphia: Temple University Press, 1988.

Wilcox, Clyde. *God's Warriors: The Christian Right in Twentieth-Century America*. Baltimore. Md.: Johns Hopkins University Press, 1993.

Wills, Garry. *Under God*. New York: Simon & Schuster, 1990.

7 Search and Seizure

On the morning of April 16, 1992, Charles Wilson was jolted from his bed by the sound of fists pounding on the front door of his home in Rockville, Maryland, just outside Washington, D.C. He had faintly heard his nine-year-old granddaughter walk toward the door, but did not hear any other voices. Wearing only undershorts, he found a team of plainclothes officers from the United States Marshals Service and the Montgomery County Sheriff's office, accompanied by two reporters from the *Washington Post.* The officers were pointing their guns directly at him. Wilson had no idea why the police were in his home or why they were so heavily armed. After he angrily demanded an explanation, the police restrained Wilson in full view of the *Post* reporter and photographer, both of whom were recording the entire episode. By this time, Charles's wife, Geraldine, still in her nightgown, had entered the room. She was just as clueless as her husband as to why the police were in her house at such an early hour, much less why her startled husband was wearing handcuffs. After Geraldine said, "Charles," when she asked her husband what this chaos was all about, the police realized they had made a terrible mistake. Their warrant had been for Dominic Wilson, the Wilsons' son, whose last known address in local court records had been his parents' home. After offering a meek apology, the police and the *Post* reporter and photographer left.

Dominic Wilson's apprehension had been planned for quite some time as part of the United States Department of Justice's "Operation Gunsmoke," a program developed in 1992 to give the United States Marshals Service the power to enforce state arrest warrants. Operation Gunsmoke focused primarily on drug-related offenses involving violent criminals, and encouraged federal law enforcement officers to work closely with state and local authorities to apprehend suspects. Based on his prior arrest record for such felony offenses as robbery, burglary, and intent to rob, Wilson was considered likely to be heavily armed and dangerous in the event of a confrontation. And based on information drawn from Wilson's prior illegal activities, the federal marshals decided to target him as part of Operation Gunsmoke. In keeping with the Marshals Service's media ride-along policy, the *Post* team was invited to observe Operation Gunsmoke in action. In its first year, Operation Gunsmoke boasted almost 3,500 arrests in forty cities, with police seizing a total of $6.1 million in contraband. In the Washington, D.C., area, where the Wilsons lived, Operation Gunsmoke had apprehended 350 criminals and collected approximately $37,000 in illegal goods.[1]

But the Wilsons were not impressed by Operation Gunsmoke's success. On general principle, they believed that the police had no right to bring the news media into their home to observe a law enforcement operation. Moreover, the Wilsons pointed out that the Marshals Service's arrest warrant had said nothing about the *Post* reporter and photographer having the right to enter their home. The Fourth Amendment states that "The right of the people to be secure in their persons, houses, papers, and effects, against unreasonable searches and seizures, shall not be violated, and no Warrants shall issue, but upon probable cause, supported by Oath or affirmation, and particularly describing the place to be searched and the things to be seized." The arrest warrant in this case only authorized the police to "take Dominic Jerome Wilson if he/she shall be found in your bailiwick . . . to answer an indictment, or information, or criminal appeals unto the State of Maryland, of and concerning a certain charge of Robbery by him committed." The news media, in the Wilsons' view, had been guilty of trespass.

The police, on the other hand, responded that they had good reason to believe that Dominic Wilson was living with his parents. Just half an hour before the police team entered the Wilsons' home, the Montgomery County Sheriff's office had learned from Dominic's brother, who was already in police custody, that Dominic had visited his parents' home the night before. Dominic's brother also told the police that he believed Dominic had probably spent the night there. That was reason enough, the police argued, to satisfy the probable cause requirement of the Fourth Amendment. The Marshals Service argued that the Fourth Amendment's prohibition against unreasonable searches and seizures posed no barrier to third parties observing the arrest of a criminal suspect, especially when they were not government agents. Furthermore, media publicity of effective police work serves as a deterrent to crime, and also brings law enforcement operations into the public eye, thus keeping the police from engaging in abusive conduct.[2]

Ultimately, the United States Supreme Court unanimously ruled in *Wilson* v. *Layne* (1999) that the Fourth Amendment barred the news media from accompanying the police into private residences to execute an arrest warrant.[3] Homeowners are entitled to a reasonable expectation of privacy that precludes news organizations from observing and recording law enforcement operations. Since the *Post* reporter and photographer were only there to publicize Operation Gunsmoke and not aid in the actual apprehension of Dominic Wilson, the Court ruled that their presence violated the Fourth Amendment rights of Charles and Geraldine Wilson.

But suppose that the police, while standing in the Wilsons' living room, had seen an open box of hand grenades sitting on a coffee table, or what appeared to be illegal drugs carefully portioned in plastic bags. Would they have been able to seize them, even though they were not specified in the warrant, because the contraband was in plain view? Normally when police enter a home unannounced with an arrest warrant, they engage in a protective sweep—that is, officers immediately canvass the house to look for anyone who might pose a physical threat. Suppose the police, while securing the house, discovered betting slips, sexually explicit materials they believed were obscene, or a pipe with marijuana residue in the Wilsons' bedroom. Since the arrest warrant had misidentified the criminal suspect, would the police have been permitted to use the evidence they gathered on a completely unrelated search to indict and convict the Wilsons? Suppose Dominic Wilson *had* been home when the police had entered his parents' house, and found him flushing drugs down the toilet. Could they have performed a "body cavity" search to determine if Wilson had hidden other drugs in his body by ingesting them in plastic bags?

Questions such as these have preoccupied judges, prosecutors, criminal defense lawyers, and numerous groups with an interest in criminal law and procedure since the Court first began in the early 1900s to give concrete meaning to the Fourth Amendment guarantee against unreasonable searches and seizures. Although the Fourth Amendment is among the most specific of the provisions of the Bill of Rights, the Court's decisions on search and seizure have yielded numerous exceptions to the commands of the warrant requirement and have interpreted the "reasonableness" requirement for a proper search quite broadly. What has also made interpretation of the Fourth Amendment so difficult is the conflicting nature of the interests involved. Police searches and the seizure of evidence, whether physical or confessional, are inherently intrusive. And perhaps no liberty is more jealously guarded than, in Louis D. Brandeis's memorable phrase, "the right to be left alone."[4] The Framers understood quite well that when the government comes knocking on the doors of its citizens' homes with the intent to enter, search the premises, seize materials, and make arrests, the demands of an open, democratic society require some sort of basic due process before citizens may be deprived of their liberty. How the Court has resolved these competing claims surrounding the Fourth Amendment and the group dynamics that have shaped its search and seizure decisions will be the focus of this chapter.

The Framers and the Fourth Amendment: What Were They Thinking?

Many constitutional scholars consider the Fourth Amendment's prohibition on unreasonable searches and seizures the most basic freedom ensured by the Bill of Rights. Without protection from arbitrary and capricious police action, such other fundamental liberties as freedom of speech, press, assembly, and religion cannot exist. The Framers' concern for the "right of the people to be secure in their persons, houses, papers, and effects, against unreasonable searches and seizures" was drawn from the British experience of the 1600s and 1700s, when warrantless searches and later "general warrants" offered no specific basis for entering private residences or searching individuals. In 1766, the House of Commons resolved that "general" warrants, the target of much hostility among the British public, were illegal.[5]

Around the same time, American colonists were beginning to bristle at the use of "blank" warrants by British soldiers to justify raids into their homes, ships, and offices. General warrants were also used to detain individuals without specific charges. The British Crown, however, saw no need to extend the rudimentary protections it had afforded its subjects at home to the American colonists. In 1761, for example, several American merchants in Boston filed suit against the Crown for permitting British soldiers to search any house or building based on the mere suspicion that smuggled goods might be stored inside. Warrants to search the colonists' property, formally called writs of assistance, required no showing of probable cause. Lawyers for the Boston merchants later claimed that the writs of assistance were among the worst abuses of the British government and the most damaging to personal liberty. John Adams later considered the 1761 lawsuit as the most powerful experience of the colonists with unrestrained police power. "Then and there," said Adams of the Boston experience, "was the first scene of the first act of opposition to the arbitrary claims of Great Britain. Then and there the child of independence was born."[6]

The Fourth Amendment generated little controversy when James Madison, its primary author, introduced it during the First Congress. Nor was the Fourth Amendment a source of great debate among the state ratifying conventions. By the time the Fourth Amendment was introduced, all thirteen states had provisions in their own constitutions protecting the right of "the people" against "unreasonable searches and seizures." The Fourth Amendment simply reinforced at the national level the restrictions on general warrants already in place in the states. Limiting the federal government's authority to conduct searches also ensured that federal constables would not interfere with the right of the states to carry out their own law enforcement responsibilities. The Fourth Amendment, as much as any other provision of the Bill of Rights, spoke to the importance of federalism as a mechanism to secure liberty. Judges and juries serving in the state courts would be responsible for determining the reasonableness of searches, thus giving the government the closest to the people the most say in such matters.[7]

During the 1800s, the Court's encounters with the Fourth Amendment were limited to a single case, *Boyd* v. *United States* (1886), in which the justices struck down a federal law permitting government authorities to compel individuals to turn over private papers and effects as mere evidence of illegal conduct.[8] The Court ruled that the federal law operated as the equivalent of a general warrant and thus was unconstitutional under the "reasonableness" requirement of the Fourth Amendment. Since then, the Court has dealt with the Fourth Amendment as involving two central issues: The first issue involves deciding whether a search and seizure is *reasonable,* and the second is whether the police have satisfied the *probable cause* requirement. Legal scholar Akhil Reed Amar notes that the modern Court has treated the Fourth Amendment's guarantee against unreasonable searches and seizures as rooted primarily in the warrant requirement. Amar claims that the Framers did not intend for the Fourth Amendment to ban all warrantless searches. Courts can decide that searches and seizures are reasonable with or without warrants (and the modern Court has created numerous exceptions to the warrant requirement, discussed later). The warrant requirement was also a safeguard against corrupt judges tempted to issue general warrants. By requiring probable cause, the Fourth Amendment imposed a stricter requirement on police seeking judicial warrants for arrests and searches, compensating for the diminished roles of juries and the sovereign voice of the people on such matters.[9]

For the remainder of this chapter, we will examine the complex body of law that the Court has built around the competing values of the Fourth Amendment. What constitutes a reasonable search? When does the warrant requirement apply? Should evidence obtained outside the scope of a warrant be admissible in a criminal proceeding? We will look into how the Court has approached these and related questions, as well as the role that organized groups have played in shaping the debate over the Fourth Amendment.

What Is a Reasonable Search and Seizure?

The language of the Fourth Amendment appears clear enough on the question of what constitutes a reasonable search and seizure. By stating, "no Warrants shall issue, but upon probable cause, supported by Oath or affirmation," the Framers expressed their clear contempt for the British government's long-standing policy of utilizing general warrants to justify searching their colonial subjects. Accordingly, the modern Court has held that all "searches conducted outside the judicial process, without prior approval by judge or magistrate, are *per se* unreasonable under the Fourth Amendment—subject to a few specifically established and well-delineated exceptions."[10] Some scholars have suggested that the Court's interpretation of the Fourth Amendment is just a roundabout way of saying what the Framers really intended: that warrantless searches and seizures are not unconstitutional as long as they are reasonable, and that probable cause is relevant only when it becomes necessary for the police to obtain a search warrant.[11] But whether the Framers intended for the reasonableness and warrant requirements to mean separate things is essentially a moot point. The Court continues to hold that reasonableness and search warrants go together, unless there is a *compelling* reason to waive the latter. In the following section, our focus will be on the exceptions to the Fourth Amendment's warrant requirement, and how those exceptions, shaped by social and technological change, have expanded over time.

When Does the Warrant Requirement Apply? When Are Exceptions Permitted?

Whether or not the police proceed with a warrant when they engage in a search or seizure they must demonstrate, in virtually all cases, probable cause exists to intrude on a person's liberty. Determining probable cause, however, is not always easy. For example, a police detective who depends on confidential informants for information on criminal behavior may not be able to persuade a judge that her source, perhaps linked to illegal activity himself, is necessarily reliable. In some cases, a prosecutor might have offered a key witness a reduced sentence if he was willing to testify against his accomplice, thus leading defense lawyers to question the motive and accuracy of the witness's earlier statement to police. In a more controversial application, suppose the police spot someone walking through an airport who matches the "profile" of persons most frequently suspected of working as drug couriers. Do they have the right to stop and search an individual simply because he matches a general physical description of a suspected criminal "type"? In a similar context, may state troopers pull over a motorist simply because he matches a particular profile of a drug or gun courier?

Questions over what constitutes probable cause have dogged the Court since the beginning of the twentieth century, and they continue to present challenges to everyone involved in the criminal justice system. In a nutshell, though, the Court has concluded that probable cause exists when a law enforcement officer, in possession of the facts and circumstances relevant to a case, *reasonably* believes that a suspect has engaged in criminal activity. Probable cause on the part of the officer must find support from the judge or magistrate responsible for issuing a warrant.[12] If special circumstances justify an exception to the warrant requirement, juries and judges provide the safeguard to determine whether a warrantless search was reasonable.

Equally compelling questions exist concerning *when* the police or any other government official actually engage in a search or seizure. Must the police actually enter the home, office, car, boat, or other private property of an individual to engage in an actual search? If not, do the police need to satisfy the Fourth Amendment's reasonableness or warrant requirements to acquire incriminating information without physically trespassing on an individual's property? These requirements were at the heart of one of the Court's earliest Fourth Amendment decisions, *Olmstead* v. *United States* (1928). Complicating matters further, the Court was forced to assess some novel questions involving the impact of technological innovation on evidence gathering and the problems that such change potentially created for the right of individuals to a reasonable expectation of privacy.

Olmstead v. *United States*

277 U.S. 438 (1928)

One shudders to think where Roy Olmstead might rank among the titans of American industry if he had ever applied his considerable skills to a legitimate occupation. But during Prohibition, which lasted from 1919 to 1933, there was a lot of money to be made bootlegging liquor, and Olmstead was certainly getting his piece of the pie. The head honcho and, according to federal law enforcement agents, the leading conspirator in an illegal business enterprise that brought liquor into Seattle from the Canadian city of Vancouver via Puget Sound, Olmstead took in anywhere between $175,000 and $300,000 per month in gross sales. Although Olmstead was in business with eleven other partners, he had struck a tidy deal for himself that allowed him to keep 50 percent of the profits. By 1926, Olmstead employed over fifty people in various capacities and operated two boats to make the liquor runs.

Around this same time, federal agents had placed Olmstead under observation based on various bits of information they had acquired through informants. Since Olmstead's enterprise was in large part dependent on communication through telephone, federal agents placed wiretaps on several of his phone lines and those of his suspected business associates. Federal agents never entered Olmstead's home or the office or residence of anyone else. All the phones were tapped by inserting small wires into the phone lines located outside or through the main switchboard. Over time, federal agents accumulated a large body of evidence against Olmstead, who, along with several members of his gang (including his wife), was convicted of violating the Volstead Act, the federal law enforcing Prohibition.

Olmstead claimed that the government's wiretapping investigation violated his Fourth Amendment rights against unreasonable searches and seizures. Specifically, Olmstead argued that by wiretapping his phone lines the government had engaged in the equivalent of a warrantless search of his home and office, thus making the seizure of any evidence illegal. Olmstead's latter claim was based on *Weeks* v. *United States* (1914). In *Weeks*, the Court ruled that any evidence seized in violation of the Fourth Amendment could not be used against a criminal defendant. *Weeks* gave birth to the "exclusionary rule," which is discussed later in this chapter.

The nation's largest telephone company, American Telephone & Telegraph Co., along with Pacific Telephone & Telegraph Co. and the Tri-State Telephone & Telegraph Co., the nation's two largest regional telephone companies, filed a friend-of-the-court brief in *Olmstead* opposing the government's wiretapping program. The phone companies' brief argued that "criminals will not escape detection and conviction merely because evidence obtained by tapping wires of a public telephone system is inadmissible, if it should be so held; but, in any event, it is better that a few criminals escape than that the privacies of life of all the people be exposed to the agents of the government, who will act at their own discretion, the honest and the dishonest, unauthorized and unrestrained by the courts. Legislation making wiretapping a crime will not suffice if the courts nevertheless hold the evidence to be lawful."

The Court's decision was 5 to 4. Chief Justice Taft delivered the opinion of the Court. Justices Brandeis, Butler, Holmes, and Stone filed separate dissents.

Justice Brandeis's dissent represented the refinement of the more general argument he made for the right to privacy in his famous *Harvard Law Review* article. The idea that individuals had a right to a sense of personal space in which neither the government nor private citizens could intrude became the starting point in future debates over the boundaries of libel law (see Chapter 5) and the right to abortion and sexual autonomy (see Chapter 10).

▼▲▼

MR. CHIEF JUSTICE TAFT delivered the opinion of the Court.

The well known historical purpose of the Fourth Amendment, directed against general warrants and writs of assistance, was to prevent the use of governmental force

to search a man's house, his person, his papers and his effects, and to prevent their seizure against his will. This phase of the misuse of governmental power of compulsion is the emphasis of the opinion of the Court in [our previous Fourth Amendment cases]. . . .

The Amendment itself shows that the search is to be of material things—the person, the house, his papers, or his effects. The description of the warrant necessary to make the proceeding lawful is that it must specify the place to be searched and the person or *things* to be seized. . . .

The Fourth Amendment may have proper application to a sealed letter in the mail because of the constitutional provision for the Post Office Department and the relations between the Government and those who pay to secure protection of their sealed letters. . . . Congress monopolizes the carriage of letters and excludes from that business everyone else. . . . It is plainly within the words of the Amendment to say that the unlawful rifling by a government agent of a sealed letter is a search and seizure of the sender's papers or effects. The letter is a paper, an effect, and in the custody of a Government that forbids carriage except under its protection.

The United States takes no such care of telegraph or telephone messages as of mailed sealed letters. The Amendment does not forbid what was done here. There was no searching. There was no seizure. The evidence was secured by the use of the sense of hearing, and that only. There was no entry of the houses or offices of the defendants.

By the invention of the telephone fifty years ago and its application for the purpose of extending communications, one can talk with another at a far distant place. The language of the Amendment cannot be extended and expanded to include telephone wires reaching to the whole world from the defendant's house or office. The intervening wires are not part of his house or office any more than are the highways along which they are stretched. . . .

Congress may, of course, protect the secrecy of telephone messages by making them, when intercepted, inadmissible in evidence in federal criminal trials by direct legislation, and thus depart from the common law of evidence. But the courts may not adopt such a policy by attributing an enlarged and unusual meaning to the Fourth Amendment. The reasonable view is that one who installs in his house a telephone instrument with connecting wires intends to project his voice to those quite outside, and that the wires beyond his house and messages while passing over them are not within the protection of the Fourth Amendment. Here, those who intercepted the projected voices were not in the house of either party to the conversation.

Neither the cases we have cited nor any of the many federal decisions brought to our attention hold the Fourth Amendment to have been violated as against a defendant unless there has been an official search and seizure of his person, or such a seizure of his papers or his tangible material effects, or an actual physical invasion of his house "or curtilage" for the purpose of making a seizure.

We think, therefore, that the wiretapping here disclosed did not amount to a search or seizure within the meaning of the Fourth Amendment. . . .

A standard which would forbid the reception of evidence if obtained by other than nice ethical conduct by government officials would make society suffer and give criminals greater immunity than has been known heretofore. In the absence of controlling legislation by Congress, those who realize the difficulties in bringing offenders to justice may well deem it wise that the exclusion of evidence should be confined to cases where rights under the Constitution would be violated by admitting it. . . .

The judgments of the Circuit Court of Appeals are affirmed.

MR. JUSTICE BRANDEIS, dissenting.

The Government makes no attempt to defend the methods employed by its officers. Indeed, it concedes that, if wiretapping can be deemed a search and seizure within the Fourth Amendment, such wiretapping as was practiced in the case at bar was an unreasonable search and seizure, and that the evidence thus obtained was inadmissible. But it relies on the language of the Amendment, and it claims that the protection given thereby cannot properly be held to include a telephone conversation. . . .

When the Fourth and Fifth Amendments were adopted, "the form that evil had theretofore taken" had been necessarily simple. Force and violence were then the only means known to man by which a Government could directly effect self-incrimination. It could compel the individual to testify—a compulsion effected, if need be, by torture. It could secure possession of his papers and other articles incident to his private life—a seizure effected, if need be, by breaking and entry. Protection against such invasion of "the sanctities of a man's home and the privacies of life" was provided in the Fourth and Fifth Amendments by specific language. But "time works changes, brings into existence new conditions and purposes." Subtler and more far-reaching means of invading privacy have become available to the Government. Discovery and invention have made it possible for the Government, by means far more effective than stretching upon the rack, to obtain disclosure in court of what is whispered in the closet.

Moreover, "in the application of a constitution, our contemplation cannot be only of what has been but of what may be." The progress of science in furnishing the Government with means of espionage is not likely to stop with wiretapping. Ways may someday be developed by which the Government, without removing papers from secret drawers, can reproduce them in court, and by which it will be enabled to expose to a jury the most intimate occurrences of the home. Advances in the psychic and related sciences may bring means of exploring unexpressed beliefs, thoughts and emotions. . . . Can it be that the Constitution affords no protection against such invasions of individual security? . . .

The evil incident to invasion of the privacy of the telephone is far greater than that involved in tampering with the mails. Whenever a telephone line is tapped, the privacy of the persons at both ends of the line is invaded and all conversations between them upon any subject, and, although proper, confidential and privileged, may be overheard. Moreover, the tapping of one man's telephone line involves the tapping of the telephone of every other person whom he may call or who may call him. As a means of espionage, writs of assistance and general warrants are but puny instruments of tyranny and oppression when compared with wiretapping.

Time and again, this Court in giving effect to the principle underlying the Fourth Amendment, has refused to place an unduly literal construction upon it. . . .

The protection guaranteed by the [Fourth and Fifth Amendments] is much broader in scope. The makers of our Constitution undertook to secure conditions favorable to the pursuit of happiness. They recognized the significance of man's spiritual nature, of his feelings, and of his intellect. They knew that only a part of the pain, pleasure and satisfactions of life are to be found in material things. They sought to protect Americans in their beliefs, their thoughts, their emotions and their sensations. They conferred, as against the Government, the right to be let alone—the most comprehensive of rights, and the right most valued by civilized men. To protect that right, every unjustifiable intrusion by the Government upon the privacy of the individual, whatever the means employed, must be deemed a violation of the Fourth Amendment. And the use, as evidence in a criminal proceeding, of facts ascertained by such intrusion must be deemed a violation of the Fifth.

Applying to the Fourth and Fifth Amendments the established rule of construction, the defendants' objections to the evidence obtained by wiretapping must, in my opinion, be sustained. It is, of course, immaterial where the physical connection with the telephone wires leading into the defendants' premises was made. And it is also immaterial that the intrusion was in aid of law enforcement. Experience should teach us to be most on our guard to protect liberty when the Government's purposes are beneficent. Men born to freedom are naturally alert to repel invasion of their liberty by evil-minded rulers. The greatest dangers to liberty lurk in insidious encroachment by men of zeal, well meaning but without understanding. . . .

When these unlawful acts were committed, they were crimes only of the officers individually. The Government was innocent, in legal contemplation, for no federal official is authorized to commit a crime on its behalf. When the Government, having full knowledge, sought, through the Department of Justice, to avail itself of the fruits of these acts in order to accomplish its own ends, it assumed moral responsibility for the officers' crimes. And if this Court should permit the Government, by means of its officers' crimes, to effect its purpose of punishing the defendants, there would seem to be present all the elements of a ratification. If so, the Government itself would become a lawbreaker.

Will this Court, by sustaining the judgment below, sanction such conduct on the part of the Executive? The governing principle has long been settled. It is that a court will not redress a wrong when he who invokes its aid has unclean hands. The maxim of unclean hands comes from courts of equity. But the principle prevails also in courts of law. Its common application is in civil actions between private parties. Where the Government is the actor, the reasons for applying it are even more persuasive. Where the remedies invoked are those of the criminal law, the reasons are compelling. . . .

Decency, security and liberty alike demand that government officials shall be subjected to the same rules of conduct that are commands to the citizen. In a government of laws, existence of the government will be imperiled if it fails to observe the law scrupulously. Our Government is the potent, the omnipresent teacher. For good or for ill, it teaches the whole people by its example. Crime is contagious. If the Government becomes a lawbreaker, it breeds contempt for law; it invites every man to become a law unto himself; it invites anarchy. To declare that, in the administration of the criminal law, the end justifies the means—to declare that the Government may

commit crimes in order to secure the conviction of a private criminal—would bring terrible retribution. Against that pernicious doctrine this Court should resolutely set its face.

Chief Justice Taft's analysis of the federal government's wiretapping of Roy Olmstead's bootlegging operation follows a quite literal interpretation of the Fourth Amendment. Taft held that the agents had not searched Olmstead's home or office, because no physical trespass had taken place. Telephone wires were not among the "places" or "effects" entitled to Fourth Amendment protection. Conversely, Justice Brandeis's dissent offers a very different analysis of the government's newfound ability to intercept private communication over telephone wires. Taking a broader approach to the matter of personal space and privacy, Brandeis argued that individuals had a right to privacy that extended to "constitutionally protected areas" beyond their immediate proprietary interests. In other words, physical invasion of private property was not necessary to trigger the protection of the Fourth Amendment as long as the search or seizure violated an individual's right to privacy.

Olmstead was extremely unpopular with the American public. In the early 1920s, the ACLU had issued a pamphlet, *Report upon the Illegal Practices of the United States Department of Justice,* which included a section on the growing use of advanced technology in conducting warrantless surveillance on private citizens suspected of criminal wrongdoing. Although the ACLU did not submit an *amicus* brief in *Olmstead,* it helped to coordinate a successful lobbying campaign that resulted in congressional passage of the Federal Communication Act of 1934.[13] The law stated that "no person being authorized by the sender shall intercept any communication and divulge or publish the contents." Three years later, in *Nardone* v. *United States* (1939), the Court ruled that any evidence acquired through illegal wiretapping was inadmissible in court, applying the *Weeks* exclusionary rule to this still-novel method of evidence gathering.[14] But any hope on the part of civil libertarians that the Court would seize upon public dissatisfaction with *Olmstead* and overturn it disappeared in *Goldman* v. *United States* (1942). There, the Court, 5 to 3, upheld a federal electronic surveillance program that placed microphones on the exterior walls of an office to gather information inside. Relying on *Olmstead,* the Court continued to interpret a Fourth Amendment–defined search as physical trespass, not as simply the acquisition of evidence through other means.[15]

Electronic Surveillance, Domestic Security, and the Privacy Rights of Individuals

After *Goldman,* the federal government stepped up its wiretapping program to reach a wide range of suspected criminal behavior. Under Federal Bureau of Investigation (FBI) director J. Edgar Hoover, federal authorities began tapping the phones of individuals believed to harbor sympathies to America's enemies during World War II. President Roosevelt gave the FBI express authorization to use "listening devices" against "persons suspected of subversive activities against the Government of the United States, including suspected spies." Although Hoover began his unprecedented tenure as FBI director (1924–1971) opposed to wiretapping, during the late 1930s he gradually came to embrace the policy as an effective tool to keep a handle on the perceived threat posed by Communists and other "domestic radicals." By the early 1950s, just as the Cold War was reaching its peak, the FBI's vigorous electronic surveillance program to monitor America's wartime domestic and foreign enemies had taken a quantum leap forward. Hoover was a staunch ally of such prominent anti-Communists as Senator Joe McCarthy (R–Wisc.) and Senator Richard Nixon (R–Calif.), both of whom had built their early reputations in Congress as leaders of the effort to investigate suspected Communists. Having always believed that domestic subversion was America's greatest enemy, Hoover thought that an expansive program of electronic surveillance was intimately linked to the nation's national security.[16]

By the early 1960s, Hoover had turned his attention to another area of alleged domestic subversion, one that was far more personal for him than the FBI's earlier electronic surveillance of suspected Communist sympathizers. Between 1919 and 1923, Hoover had coordinated the FBI's campaign to discredit the black nationalist leader Marcus Garvey, who encouraged African Americans to demand their rights much more aggressively than other, more mainstream black voices like W. E. B.

Du Bois and, earlier, Booker T. Washington. Hoover viewed Garvey's organizing skills and radical political philosophy as a threat and ultimately succeeded in having him deported. Decades later, after Martin Luther King Jr. emerged as the civil rights movement's most prominent leader after the successful boycott of Montgomery, Alabama's bus system in 1955, Hoover ordered FBI agents to shadow his activities and those of his advisers. King's successes in leading nonviolent protests against racial discrimination throughout the South in the late 1950s and early 1960s did not receive a sympathetic audience in Hoover. Moreover, King's willingness to speak out against what he believed was the FBI's refusal to restrain the often-violent responses of Southern police to civil rights demonstrators infuriated Hoover, who took any criticism of Bureau operations personally. Having discovered through a separate domestic counterintelligence operation that one of King's closest advisers, Stanley Levison, had once been a key financial supporter of and legal counsel to the Communist Party, Hoover soon received permission from Attorney General Robert Kennedy to place wiretaps on King's home and office phones.[17]

By December 1963, Hoover succeeded in placing taps on King's motel rooms. Since King traveled most of the year leading protests, attending meetings with key supporters around the country, accepting invitations from churches to preach, and raising money, the FBI's wiretapping operation on the civil rights leader required involvement from field offices around the country. Over time, however, the FBI's concern was less with King's alleged ties to Communist agents—nothing had come from that investigation—and more with his extramarital affairs while on the road. Hoover, in particular, seized on the incriminating evidence yielded by the Bureau's wiretaps to increase pressure on King to scale back his public presence, steadily leaking bits and pieces of transcribed tapes to King detailing his sexual liaisons. In January 1965, the FBI's campaign against King reached its lowest point. FBI Assistant Director William C. Sullivan prepared a package that included an edited tape highlighting off-color remarks made by King in private as well as the sounds of people engaging in sexual activities, and an "anonymous" letter prepared by Bureau agents suggesting that King commit suicide to spare himself the public embarrassment of his "immoral" behavior. The package was sent to King's home, where his wife received it and immediately notified her husband's inner circle of advisers and confidants. The materials frightened and intimidated King, but only momentarily, as he soon resumed his normal schedule of public appearances. In fact, after 1965, King's public advocacy took on a far more confrontational and political cast than his earlier rhetoric.[18]

> KING
>
> In view of your low grade . . . I will not dignify your name with either a Mr. or a Reverend or a Dr. And, your last name calls to mind only the type of King such as King Henry the VIII. . . .
>
> King, look into your heart. You know you are a complete fraud and a great liability to all of us Negroes. White people in this country have enough frauds of their own but I am sure they don't have one at this time that is anywhere near your equal. You are no clergyman and you know it. I repeat you are a colossal fraud and an evil, vicious one at that. You could not believe in God. . . . Clearly you don't believe in any personal moral principles.
>
> King, like all frauds your end is approaching. You could have been our greatest leader. You, even at an early age have turned out to be not a leader but a dissolute, abnormal moral imbecile. We will now have to depend on our older leaders like Wilkins[,] a man of character[,] and thank God we have others like him. But you are done. Your "honorary" degrees, your Nobel Prize (what a grim farce) and other awards will not save you. King, I repeat you are done.
>
> No person can overcome facts, not even a fraud like yourself. . . . I repeat—no person can argue successfully against facts. You are finished. . . . Satan could not do more. What incredible evilness. . . . King you are done.
>
> The American public, the church organizations that have been helping—Protestant, Catholic and Jews will know you for what you are—an evil, abnormal beast. So will others who have backed you. You are done.
>
> King, there is only one thing left for you to do. You know what this is. You have just 34 days in which to do (this exact number has been selected for a specific reason, it has definite practical significant [*sic*]). You are done. There is but one way out for you. You better take it before your filthy, abnormal fraudulent self is bared to the nation.

Ultimately, the Kennedy administration and, later, President Lyndon B. Johnson refused to use the FBI's wiretapping campaign against King, working instead with him on many of the civil rights movement's major legislative goals. Nonetheless, the FBI continued to monitor King on an almost around-the-clock basis, driven more by Hoover's contempt for the civil rights leader than any important public policy objective. But King and the civil rights movement were not the only targets of the FBI during the 1960s. Student radicals, high-profile opponents of the Vietnam War, and other FBI-described "domestic subversives" all remained under the umbrella of the Bureau's electronic surveillance program. In March 1965, Attorney General Nicholas Katzenbach, unnerved by Hoover's obsession with King, ordered the FBI director to clear all requests for federal wiretaps through him. Around the same time, a Senate committee began an inquiry into the FBI's surveillance methods and the impact they had on American citizens. The committee did not like what it learned. In July 1965, President Johnson issued an executive order prohibiting federal agencies from engaging in wiretapping except in cases of national emergency. Hoover gradually ceded to the policy changes forthcoming from Congress and the executive branch, understanding full well that the FBI's credibility would suffer if it was viewed as an enemy of the people rather than as a law-abiding, law enforcement agency. Said Hoover, "I don't see what all the excitement is about. I would have no hesitance in discontinuing all techniques—technical coverage . . . microphones, trash covers, mail covers, etc. While it might handicap us I doubt they are as valuable as some believe and none warrant FBI being used to justify them."[19]

By 1967, the political tides had turned decidedly against wiretapping. Attorney General Ramsey Clark, appointed by President Johnson, took an even firmer line against electronic surveillance than any of his predecessors. That same year, the Court revisited the constitutional questions surrounding wiretapping for the first time since *Goldman*. Since 1961, when the Court ruled, in *Mapp* v. *Ohio*, that the exclusionary rule now applied to state and local criminal proceedings, the Court had revolutionized the major criminal procedure provisions of the Bill of Rights to afford criminal defendants more rights than ever before. In the process, the Court completely reworked the law of police interrogations and confessions, the assistance of counsel, and protection against unreasonable searches and seizures. The Court that decided *Katz* v. *United States* (1967) bore no relationship to the one that decided *Olmstead* and *Goldman*.

Katz v. *United States*

389 U.S. 347 (1967)

In February 1965, the FBI placed Charles Katz, a small-time Los Angeles hustler, under visual surveillance as part of a larger investigation it was conducting on college and professional sports gambling. For two weeks, federal agents watched Katz make phone calls from a row of phone booths on Sunset Boulevard, one of Los Angeles's busiest streets. They later determined that Katz was making calls to a known gambler in Massachusetts and other suspected gamblers up and down the East Coast, and placed listening devices on the exterior panels of the phone booth. FBI agents listened as Katz placed bets and exchanged gambling information on sports with individuals located in Miami and Boston. At no point in their investigation did FBI agents secure a warrant.

Katz was subsequently indicted under a federal law that prohibited anyone from using a wire communication facility to place bets or wagers on any sporting event or contest, or for transmitting information assisting in the placing of such bets or wagers. Violators were subject to a $10,000 fine or two years in prison, or both. Like Roy Olmstead, Charles Katz believed that federal agents had no right to intrude upon his telephone conversations, which he argued took place from a constitutionally protected area—a phone booth. Katz's lawyers rooted much of their argument in the Court's recent decision in *Griswold* v. *Connecticut* (1965), which invalidated an anticontraception law on right to privacy grounds. *Griswold* marked the first time the Court articulated a right to privacy in explicit terms, and the themes from Brandeis's *Olmstead* dissent are evident throughout the various opinions filed by the justices in the Connecticut case (see Chapters 2 and 10).

But the right to privacy carries many connotations. In *Griswold*, the right to privacy meant that a state could not prevent married couples from using or receiving information about contraception. Charles Katz's privacy argument is about something else entirely—the right to engage in private telephone conversations, even if the content of those conversations was criminal. Unless the government can produce a warrant or some compelling justification, Katz argued that federal officers should not be allowed to invade the personal privacy of an individual through eavesdropping.

The Court's decision was 8 to 1. Justice Stewart delivered the opinion of the Court. Justices Douglas, White, and Harlan filed concurring opinions. Justice Black dissented. Black's dissent, in particular, is a splendid example of his "literalist" approach to constitutional interpretation discussed in Chapter 2.

▼▲▼

MR. JUSTICE STEWART delivered the opinion of the Court.

We granted certiorari in order to consider the constitutional questions thus presented.

The petitioner has phrased those questions as follows:

A. Whether a public telephone booth is a constitutionally protected area so that evidence obtained by attaching an electronic listening recording device to the top of such a booth is obtained in violation of the right to privacy of the user of the booth.
B. Whether physical penetration of a constitutionally protected area is necessary before a search and seizure can be said to be violative of the Fourth Amendment to the United States Constitution.

We decline to adopt this formulation of the issues. In the first place, the correct solution of Fourth Amendment problems is not necessarily promoted by incantation of the phrase "constitutionally protected area." Secondly, the Fourth Amendment cannot be translated into a general constitutional "right to privacy." That Amendment protects individual privacy against certain kinds of governmental intrusion, but its protections go further, and often have nothing to do with privacy at all. Other provisions of the Constitution protect personal privacy from other forms of governmental invasion. But the protection of a person's *general* right to privacy—his right to be let alone by other people—is, like the protection of his property and of his very life, left largely to the law of the individual States.

Because of the misleading way the issues have been formulated, the parties have attached great significance to the characterization of the telephone booth from which the petitioner placed his calls. The petitioner has strenuously argued that the booth was a "constitutionally protected area." The Government has maintained with equal vigor that it was not. But this effort to decide whether or not a given "area," viewed in the abstract, is "constitutionally protected" deflects attention from the problem presented by this case. For the Fourth Amendment protects people, not places. What a person knowingly exposes to the public, even in his own home or office, is not a subject of Fourth Amendment protection. But what he seeks to preserve as private, even in an area accessible to the public, may be constitutionally protected.

The Government stresses the fact that the telephone booth from which the petitioner made his calls was constructed partly of glass, so that he was as visible after he entered it as he would have been if he had remained outside. But what he sought to exclude when he entered the booth was not the intruding eye—it was the uninvited ear. He did not shed his right to do so simply because he made his calls from a place where he might be seen. No less than an individual in a business office, in a friend's apartment, or in a taxicab, a person in a telephone booth may rely upon the protection of the Fourth Amendment. One who occupies it, shuts the door behind him, and pays the toll that permits him to place a call is surely entitled to assume that the words he utters into the mouthpiece will not be broadcast to the world. To read the Constitution more narrowly is to ignore the vital role that the public telephone has come to play in private communication.

The Government contends, however, that the activities of its agents in this case should not be tested by Fourth Amendment requirements, for the surveillance technique they employed involved no physical penetration of the telephone booth from which the petitioner placed his calls. It is true that the absence of such penetration was at one time thought to foreclose further Fourth Amendment inquiry, for that Amendment was thought to limit only searches and seizures of tangible property. But "[t]he premise that property interests control the right of the Government to search and seize has been discredited." Thus, although a closely divided Court supposed in *Olmstead* that surveillance without any trespass and without the seizure of any material object fell outside the ambit of the Constitution, we have since departed from the narrow view on which that decision rested. . . . Once this much is acknowledged, and once it is recognized that the Fourth Amendment protects people—and not simply "areas"—against unreasonable searches and seizures, it becomes clear that the reach of that Amendment cannot turn upon the presence or absence of a physical intrusion into any given enclosure.

We conclude that the underpinnings of *Olmstead* and *Goldman* have been so eroded by our subsequent decisions that the "trespass" doctrine there enunciated can no longer be regarded as controlling. The Government's activities in electronically listening to and recording the petitioner's words violated the privacy upon which he justifiably relied while using the telephone booth, and thus constituted a "search and seizure" within the meaning of the Fourth Amendment. The fact that the electronic device employed to achieve that end did not happen to penetrate the wall of the booth can have no constitutional significance.

The question remaining for decision, then, is whether the search and seizure conducted in this case complied with constitutional standards. In that regard, the Government's position is that its agents acted in an entirely defensible manner: they did not begin their electronic surveillance until investigation of the petitioner's activities had established a strong probability that he was using the telephone in question to transmit gambling information to persons in other States, in violation of federal law. Moreover, the surveillance was limited, both in scope and in duration, to the specific purpose of establishing the contents of the petitioner's unlawful telephonic communications. The agents confined their surveillance to the brief periods during which he used the telephone booth, and they took great care to overhear only the conversations of the petitioner himself. . . .

It is apparent that the agents in this case acted with restraint. Yet the inescapable fact is that this restraint was imposed by the agents themselves, not by a judicial officer. They were not required, before commencing the search, to present their estimate of probable cause for detached scrutiny by a neutral magistrate. They were not compelled, during the conduct of the search itself, to observe precise limits established in advance by a specific court order. Nor were they directed, after the search had been completed, to notify the authorizing magistrate in detail of all that had been seized. In the absence of such safeguards, this Court has never sustained a search upon the sole ground that officers reasonably expected to find evidence of a particular crime and voluntarily confined their activities to the least intrusive means consistent with that end. Searches conducted without warrants have been held unlawful "notwithstanding facts unquestionably showing probable cause," for the Constitution requires "that the deliberate, impartial judgment of a judicial officer . . . be interposed between the citizen and the police. . . ." "Over and again, this Court has emphasized that the mandate of the [Fourth] Amendment requires adherence to judicial processes," and that searches conducted outside the judicial process, without prior approval by judge or magistrate, are *per se* unreasonable under the Fourth Amendment—subject only to a few specifically established and well delineated exceptions.

It is difficult to imagine how any of those exceptions could ever apply to the sort of search and seizure involved in this case. Even electronic surveillance substantially contemporaneous with an individual's arrest could hardly be deemed an "incident" of that arrest. Nor could the use of electronic surveillance without prior authorization be justified on grounds of "hot pursuit." And, of course, the very nature of electronic surveillance precludes its use pursuant to the suspect's consent. . . .

These considerations do not vanish when the search in question is transferred from the setting of a home, an office, or a hotel room to that of a telephone booth. Wherever a man may be, he is entitled to know that he will remain free from unreasonable searches and seizures. The government agents here ignored "the procedure of antecedent justification . . . that is central to the Fourth Amendment," a procedure that we hold to be a constitutional precondition of the kind of electronic surveillance involved in this case. Because the surveillance here failed to meet that condition, and because it led to the petitioner's conviction, the judgment must be reversed.

It is so ordered.

MR. JUSTICE HARLAN, concurring.

I join the opinion of the Court, which I read to hold only (a) that an enclosed telephone booth is an area where, like a home, and unlike a field, a person has a constitutionally protected reasonable expectation of privacy; (b) that electronic, as well as physical, intrusion into a place that is in this sense private may constitute a violation of the Fourth Amendment, and (c) that the invasion of a constitutionally protected area by federal authorities is, as the Court has long held, presumptively unreasonable in the absence of a search warrant.

As the Court's opinion states, "the Fourth Amendment protects people, not places." The question, however, is what protection it affords to those people. Generally, as here, the answer to that question requires reference to a "place." My understanding of the rule that has emerged from prior decisions is that there is a twofold requirement, first that a person have exhibited an actual (subjective) expectation of privacy and, second, that the expectation be one that society is prepared to recognize as "reasonable." Thus, a man's home is, for most purposes, a place where he expects privacy, but objects, activities, or statements that he exposes to the "plain view" of outsiders are not "protected," because no intention to keep them to himself has been exhibited. On the other hand, conversations in the open would not be protected against being overheard, for the expectation of privacy under the circumstances would be unreasonable.

The critical fact in this case is that "[o]ne who occupies it, [a telephone booth] shuts the door behind him, and pays the toll that permits him to place a call is surely entitled to assume" that his conversation is not being intercepted. The point is not that the booth is "accessible to the public" at other times, but that it is a temporarily private place whose momentary occupants' expectations of freedom from intrusion are recognized as reasonable. . . .

Finally, I do not read the Court's opinion to declare that no interception of a conversation one-half of which occurs in a public telephone booth can be reasonable in the absence of a warrant. As elsewhere under the Fourth Amendment, warrants are the general rule, to which the legitimate needs of law enforcement may demand specific exceptions. It will be time enough to consider any such exceptions when an appropriate occasion presents itself, and I agree with the Court that this is not one.

MR. JUSTICE BLACK, dissenting.

My basic objection is two-fold: (1) I do not believe that the words of the Amendment will bear the meaning given them by today's decision, and (2) I do not believe that it is the proper role of this Court to rewrite the Amendment in order "to bring it into harmony with the times," and thus reach a result that many people believe to be desirable.

While I realize that an argument based on the meaning of words lacks the scope, and no doubt the appeal, of broad policy discussions and philosophical discourses on such nebulous subjects as privacy, for me, the language of the Amendment is the crucial place to look in construing a written document such as our Constitution. . . .

A conversation overheard by eavesdropping, whether by plain snooping or wiretapping, is not tangible and, under the normally accepted meanings of the words, can neither be searched nor seized. In addition the language of the second clause indicates that the Amendment refers not only to something tangible so it can be seized, but to something already in existence, so it can be described. Yet the Court's interpretation would have the Amendment apply to overhearing future conversations, which, by their very nature, are nonexistent until they take place. How can one "describe" a future conversation, and, if one cannot, how can a magistrate issue a warrant to eavesdrop on one in the future? It is argued that information showing what is expected to be said is sufficient to limit the boundaries of what later can be admitted into evidence; but does such general information really meet the specific language of the Amendment, which says "particularly describing"? Rather than using language in a completely artificial way, I must conclude that the Fourth Amendment simply does not apply to eavesdropping. . . .

Tapping telephone wires, of course, was an unknown possibility at the time the Fourth Amendment was adopted. But eavesdropping (and wiretapping is nothing more than eavesdropping by telephone) was. . . .

There can be no doubt that the Framers were aware of this practice, and, if they had desired to outlaw or restrict the use of evidence obtained by eavesdropping, I believe that they would have used the appropriate language to do so in the Fourth Amendment. They certainly would not have left such a task to the ingenuity of language-stretching judges. No one, it seems to me, can read the debates on the Bill of Rights without reaching the conclusion that its Framers and critics well knew the meaning of the words they used, what they would be understood to mean by others, their scope and their limitations. Under these circumstances, it strikes me as a charge against their scholarship, their common sense and their candor to give to the Fourth Amendment's language the eavesdropping meaning the Court imputes to it today. . . .

Since I see no way in which the words of the Fourth Amendment can be construed to apply to eavesdropping, that closes the matter for me. In interpreting the Bill of Rights, I willingly go as far as a liberal construction of the language takes me, but I simply cannot in good conscience give a meaning to words which they have never before been thought to have and which they certainly do not have in common ordinary usage. I will not distort the words of the Amendment in order to "keep the Constitution up to date" or "to bring it into harmony with the times." It was never meant that this Court have such power, which, in effect, would make us a continuously functioning constitutional convention.

▼▲▼

Justice Stewart's admonition that "the Fourth Amendment protects people, not places" was certainly informed by Brandeis's dissent in *Olmstead,* which argued that individuals have a *general* right of privacy that protects them from invasive government action. And the Court's conclusion that "reasonable searches" and the warrant requirement go hand-in-hand demonstrated its clear preference for judicially issued warrants to conduct searches, which, after *Katz,* set aside physical trespass as the Fourth Amendment's trigger point.

Following *Katz,* Congress enacted the Omnibus Crime Control Act of 1968, which included a provision, known as Title III, that established specific guidelines for federal and state law enforcement officers when they wanted to engage in electronic surveillance. Although Congress claimed that Title III was designed to provide legislative oversight to law enforcement wiretapping operations and thus limit electronic surveillance, the law provided so many exceptions that it actually watered down the Court's holding in *Katz*. Title III does require law enforcement agents to obtain a warrant when seeking permission to "intercept" electronic communication for a specified range of criminal offenses. But it also permits the U.S. attorney general or state prosecutors to grant exemptions to the warrant requirement based on emergency circumstances, such as threats to national security or conspiratorial activities characteristic of organized crime.

Advances in computer technology, particularly since the introduction of the Internet on a mass scale in the 1990s, have created several new, complex privacy issues for individuals who use electronic mail (e-mail), visit on-line chat rooms, or send encoded messages through specially encrypted software programs. In 2000, the FBI unveiled Carnivore, an Internet wiretapping system that enables federal agents to monitor on-line communication between computer users. FBI officials defended Carnivore as a necessary instrument to combat high-technology criminal activities, such as on-line credit card fraud, identity theft, hacking into national security databases, and trafficking in child pornography.

Carnivore is a modified version of a common network-maintenance program known as a "packet sniffer." Carnivore offers great specificity—the ability to quickly collect just the "to" and "from" information in e-mail messages, for example, and not on-line banking transactions. This gives law enforcement the equivalent of the telephone world's "pen register" and "trap and trace" data—the origin and destination of all calls related to the subject. Civil liberties groups and Internet service providers say the system raises troubling questions about what constitutes a reasonable search and seizure of electronic data. Carnivore's skeptics claim that the new technology also could scan private information about legal activities, taking in vast amounts of information from innocent people as well as the suspected criminals.[20] Certainly, the courts will take up these and other issues related to computer technology and their relationship to the Fourth Amendment's guarantee against unreasonable searches and seizures.

"Stop-and-Frisk" Searches

Broadening the rights of federal authorities to engage in electronic surveillance was not the only topic taken up by Congress in the Omnibus Crime Control Act of 1968. Congress was determined to limit and, in some

Aptos, California,
19 March, 1966.

Chief Justice
Earl Warren,
U.S. Supreme Court,
Washington, D.C.

Dear Justice:-

Greetings on your 75th anniversary!

We hope to read your obituary in the newspapers before you reach your 76th birthday anniversary.

The J.B. Lewis family.

Under Chief Justice Earl Warren (1953–1969), the Supreme Court led a revolution expanding the meaning and application of the Bill of Rights. By the early 1960s, roadside billboards reading "Impeach Earl Warren" had become common in many areas. The Chief Justice also received hate mail on a regular basis, such as this letter.

cases, reverse several key rulings of the Warren Court that expanded the rights of criminal defendants. The federal law, passed by a wide margin in the House and Senate, placed new limits on the rights of individuals convicted in state courts to seek habeas corpus relief in the federal courts and attempted to overrule three major decisions by the Court on police interrogations and confessions. Among those decisions targeted for reversal was *Miranda* v. *Arizona* (1966) (discussed in Chapter 8), the landmark ruling requiring the police to inform suspects of their right to counsel and the right to remain silent in the absence of counsel. President Lyndon Johnson signed the crime measure into law in June 1968, just two days after the Court concluded a term that was decidedly more moderate on criminal procedure issues than in recent years past.

By the late 1960s, many police departments believed that the Court's rulings on obtaining evidence, searches and seizures, interrogations, and confessions had severely handicapped their abilities to combat crime. One police technique that had come under scrutiny was the "stop-and-frisk" search, which involves stopping criminal suspects and patting them down for weapons before proceeding with questioning or a possible arrest. In light of the Court's still-evolving rules on permissible warrantless searches and seizures, the police, law enforcement associations, the ACLU, the NAACP Legal Defense Fund, and criminal defense attorneys viewed *Terry* v. *Ohio* (1968) as an important signpost for the future direction of the Fourth Amendment.

Terry v. *Ohio*

392 U.S. 1 (1968)

For Detective Martin McFadden, October 31, 1963, was just another routine afternoon on the beat spent looking for real criminals. A thirty-nine-year veteran of the Cleveland police force, McFadden had been patrolling the same area for almost thirty years in search of pickpockets and petty thieves. On that Halloween afternoon, McFadden, dressed in plainclothes, noticed suspicious behavior on the part of two men later identified as John Terry and Richard Chilton. Terry and Chilton had been taking turns walking up and down the same street to peer into a store window. By this time, McFadden noticed a third man, identified only as Katz. From his observation post three hundred feet away, McFadden counted twenty-four trips by Terry and Chilton, leading the veteran detective to conclude that the men were planning a stick-up. McFadden approached Terry and Chilton and asked them their names. After they mumbled something unintelligible, McFadden quickly turned the men so that they faced each other. McFadden patted down Terry, felt what he believed was a gun, and then ordered the men into the store they had been checking out. Once inside, McFadden removed Terry's coat and found a .38 caliber revolver in his pocket. McFadden also discovered Chilton had a gun after patting him down. McFadden arrested Terry and Chilton on concealed weapons charges. No weapon was found on Katz and he was released.

Attorneys for Terry and Chilton argued that no probable cause existed for McFadden to search their clients and wanted the guns suppressed as evidence. A trial court agreed with the defense lawyers, but rejected their contention that the officer had no right to stop and frisk someone suspected of suspicious behavior. It ruled that the guns were admissible. Richard Chilton died during the long appeals process, leaving his name off one of the most important criminal procedure decisions ever decided by the United States Supreme Court.

The Court's decision was 8 to 1. Chief Justice Warren delivered the opinion of the Court. Justice Harlan concurred. Justice Douglas dissented.

▼▲▼

MR. CHIEF JUSTICE WARREN delivered the opinion of the Court.

This case presents serious questions concerning the role of the Fourth Amendment in the confrontation on the street between the citizen and the policeman investigating suspicious circumstances. . . .

We would be less than candid if we did not acknowledge that this question thrusts to the fore difficult and troublesome issues regarding a sensitive area of police activity—issues which have never before been squarely presented to this Court. Reflective of the tensions involved are the practical and constitutional arguments pressed with great vigor on both sides of the public debate over the power of the police to "stop and frisk"—as it is sometimes euphemistically termed—suspicious persons.

On the one hand, it is frequently argued that, in dealing with the rapidly unfolding and often dangerous situations on city streets, the police are in need of an escalating set of flexible responses, graduated in relation to the amount of information they possess. For this purpose, it is urged that distinctions should be made between a "stop" and an "arrest" (or a "seizure" of a person), and between a "frisk" and a "search." Thus, it is argued, the police should be allowed to "stop" a person and detain him briefly for questioning upon suspicion that he may be connected with criminal activity. Upon suspicion that the person may be armed, the police should have the power to "frisk" him for weapons. If the "stop" and the "frisk" give rise to probable cause to believe that the suspect has committed a crime, then the police should be empowered to make a formal "arrest," and a full incident "search" of the person. This scheme is justified in part upon the notion that a "stop" and a "frisk" amount to a mere "minor inconvenience and petty indignity," which can properly be imposed upon the citizen in the interest of effective law enforcement on the basis of a police officer's suspicion.

On the other side, the argument is made that the authority of the police must be strictly circumscribed by the law of arrest and search as it has developed to date in the traditional jurisprudence of the Fourth Amendment. It is contended with some force that there is not—and cannot be—a variety of police activity which does not depend solely upon the voluntary cooperation of the citizen, and yet which stops short of an arrest based upon probable cause to make such an arrest. The heart of the Fourth Amendment, the argument runs, is a severe requirement of specific justification for any intrusion upon protected personal security, coupled with a highly developed system of judicial controls to enforce upon the agents of the State the commands of the Constitution. Acquiescence by the courts in the compulsion inherent in the field interrogation practices at issue here, it is urged, would constitute an abdication of judicial control over, and indeed an encouragement of, substantial interference with liberty and personal security by police officers whose judgment is necessarily colored by their primary involvement in "the often competitive enterprise of ferreting out crime." This, it is argued, can only serve to exacerbate police-community tensions in the crowded centers of our Nation's cities.

In this context, we approach the issues in this case mindful of the limitations of the judicial function in controlling the myriad daily situations in which policemen and citizens confront each other on the street. . . .

The exclusionary rule has its limitations, however, as a tool of judicial control. It cannot properly be invoked to exclude the products of legitimate police investigative techniques on the ground that much conduct which is closely similar involves unwarranted intrusions upon constitutional protections. Moreover, in some contexts, the rule is ineffective as a deterrent. Street encounters between citizens and police officers are incredibly rich in diversity. They range from wholly friendly exchanges of pleasantries or mutually useful information to hostile confrontations of armed men involving arrests, or injuries, or loss of life. Moreover, hostile confrontations are not all of a piece. Some of them begin in a friendly enough manner, only to take a different turn upon the injection of some unexpected element into the conversation. Encounters are initiated by the police for a wide variety of purposes, some of which are wholly unrelated to a desire to prosecute for crime. Doubtless some police "field interrogation" conduct violates the Fourth Amendment. But a stern refusal by this Court to condone such activity does not necessarily render it responsive to the exclusionary rule. Regardless of how effective the rule may be where obtaining convictions is an important objective of the police, it is powerless to deter invasions of constitutionally guaranteed rights where the police either have no interest in prosecuting or are willing to forgo successful prosecution in the interest of serving some other goal.

Proper adjudication of cases in which the exclusionary rule is invoked demands a constant awareness of these limitations. The wholesale harassment by certain elements of the police community, of which minority groups, particularly Negroes, frequently complain, will not be stopped by the exclusion of any evidence from any criminal trial. Yet a rigid and unthinking application of the exclusionary rule, in futile protest against practices which it can never be used effectively to control, may exact a high toll in human injury and frustration of efforts to prevent crime. . . .

Our first task is to establish at what point in this encounter the Fourth Amendment becomes relevant. That is, we must decide whether and when Officer McFadden "seized" Terry, and whether and when he conducted a "search." There is some suggestion in the use of such terms as "stop" and "frisk" that such police conduct is outside the purview of the Fourth Amendment because neither action rises to the level of a "search" or "seizure" within the meaning of the Constitution. We emphatically reject this notion. It is quite plain that the Fourth Amendment governs "seizures" of the person which do not eventuate in a trip to the stationhouse and prosecution for crime—"arrests" in traditional terminology. It must be recognized that, whenever a police officer accosts an individual and restrains his freedom to walk away, he has "seized" that person. And it is nothing less than sheer torture of the English language to suggest that a careful exploration of the outer surfaces of a person's clothing all over his or her body in an attempt to find weapons is not a "search." Moreover, it is simply fantastic to urge that such a procedure performed in public by a policeman while the citizen stands helpless, perhaps facing a wall with his hands raised, is a "petty indignity." It is a serious intrusion upon the sanctity of the person, which may inflict great indignity and arouse strong resentment, and it is not to be undertaken lightly.

The danger in the logic which proceeds upon distinctions between a "stop" and an "arrest," or "seizure" of the person, and between a "frisk" and a "search," is twofold. It seeks to isolate from constitutional scrutiny the initial stages of the contact between the policeman and the citizen. And, by suggesting a rigid all-or-nothing model of justification and regulation under the Amendment, it obscures the utility of limitations upon the scope, as well as the initiation, of police action as a means of constitutional regulation. This Court has held in the past that a search which is reasonable at its inception may violate the Fourth Amendment by virtue of its intolerable intensity and scope. The scope of the search must be "strictly tied to and justified by" the circumstances which rendered its initiation permissible.

The distinctions of classical "stop-and-frisk" theory thus serve to divert attention from the central inquiry under the Fourth Amendment—the reasonableness in all the circumstances of the particular governmental invasion of a citizen's personal security. "Search" and "seizure" are not talismans. We therefore reject the notions that the Fourth Amendment does not come into play at all as a limitation upon police conduct if the officers stop short of something called a "technical arrest" or a "full-blown search."

In this case, there can be no question, then, that Officer McFadden "seized" petitioner and subjected him to a "search" when he took hold of him and patted down the outer surfaces of his clothing. We must decide whether, at that point, it was reasonable for Officer McFadden to have interfered with petitioner's personal security as he did. . . .

[W]e consider first the nature and extent of the governmental interests involved. One general interest is, of course, that of effective crime prevention and detection; it is this interest which underlies the recognition that a police officer may, in appropriate circumstances and in an appropriate manner, approach a person for purposes of investigating possibly criminal behavior even though there is no probable cause to make an arrest. It was this legitimate investigative function Officer McFadden was discharging when he decided to approach petitioner and his companions. He had observed Terry, Chilton, and Katz go through a series of acts, each of them perhaps innocent in itself, but which, taken together, warranted further investigation. There is nothing unusual in two men standing together on a street corner, perhaps waiting for someone. Nor is there anything suspicious about people in such circumstances strolling up and down the street, singly or in pairs. Store windows, moreover, are made to be looked in. But the story is quite different where, as here, two men hover about a street corner for an extended period of time, at the end of which it becomes apparent that they are not waiting for anyone or anything; where these men pace alternately along an identical route, pausing to stare in the same store window roughly 24 times; where each completion of this route is followed immediately by a conference between the two men on the corner; where they are joined in one of these conferences by a third man who leaves swiftly, and where the two men finally follow the third and rejoin him a couple of blocks away. It would have been poor police work indeed for an officer of 30 years' experience in the detection of thievery from stores in this same neighborhood to have failed to investigate this behavior further. . . .

[W]e cannot blind ourselves to the need for law enforcement officers to protect themselves and other prospective victims of violence in situations where they may lack probable cause for an arrest. When an officer is justified in believing that the individual whose suspicious behavior he is investigating at close range is armed and presently dangerous to the officer or to others, it would appear to be clearly unreasonable to deny the officer the power to take necessary measures to determine whether the person is, in fact, carrying a weapon and to neutralize the threat of physical harm.

We must still consider, however, the nature and quality of the intrusion on individual rights which must be accepted if police officers are to be conceded the right to search for weapons in situations where probable cause to arrest for crime is lacking. Even a limited search of the outer clothing for weapons constitutes a severe, though brief, intrusion upon cherished personal security, and it must surely be an annoying, frightening, and perhaps humiliating experience. Petitioner contends that such an intrusion is permissible only incident to a lawful arrest, either for a crime involving the possession of weapons or for a crime the commission of which led the officer to investigate in the first place. However, this argument must be closely examined. . . .

Our evaluation of the proper balance that has to be struck in this type of case leads us to conclude that there must be a narrowly drawn authority to permit a reasonable search for weapons for the protection of the police officer, where he has reason to believe that he is dealing with an armed and dangerous individual, regardless of whether he has probable cause to arrest the individual for a crime. The officer need not be absolutely certain that the individual is armed; the issue is whether a reasonably prudent man, in the circumstances, would be warranted in the belief that his safety or that of others was in danger. . . .

We need not develop at length in this case, however, the limitations which the Fourth Amendment places upon a protective seizure and search for weapons. These limitations will have to be developed in the concrete factual circumstances of individual cases. Suffice it to note that such a search, unlike a search without a warrant incident to a lawful arrest, is not justified by any need to prevent the disappearance or destruction of evidence of crime. The sole justification of the search in the present situation is the protection of the police officer and others nearby, and it must therefore be confined in scope to an intrusion reasonably designed to discover guns, knives, clubs, or other hidden instruments for the assault of the police officer. . . .

We conclude that the revolver seized from Terry was properly admitted in evidence against him. At the time he seized petitioner and searched him for weapons, Officer McFadden had reasonable grounds to believe that petitioner was armed and dangerous, and it was necessary for the protection of himself and others to take swift measures to discover the true facts and neutralize the threat of harm if it materialized. The policeman carefully restricted his search to what was appropriate to the discovery of the particular items which he sought. Each case of this sort will, of course, have to be decided on its own facts. We merely hold today that, where a police officer observes unusual conduct which leads him reasonably to conclude in light of his experience that criminal activity may be afoot and that the persons with whom he is dealing may be armed and presently dangerous, where, in the course of investigating this behavior, he identifies himself as a policeman and makes reasonable inquiries, and where nothing in the initial stages of the encounter serves to dispel his reasonable fear for his own or others' safety, he is entitled for the protection of himself and others in the area to conduct a carefully limited search of the outer clothing of such persons in an attempt to discover weapons which might be used to assault him.

Affirmed.

MR. JUSTICE HARLAN, concurring.

While I unreservedly agree with the Court's ultimate holding in this case, I am constrained to fill in a few gaps, as I see them, in its opinion. I do this because what is said by this Court today will serve as initial guidelines for law enforcement authorities and courts throughout the land as this important new field of law develops.

A police officer's right to make an on-the-street "stop" and an accompanying "frisk" for weapons is, of course, bounded by the protections afforded by the Fourth and Fourteenth Amendments. The Court holds, and I agree, that, while the right does not depend upon possession by the officer of a valid warrant, nor upon the existence of probable cause, such activities must be reasonable under the circumstances as the officer credibly relates them in court. Since the question in this and most cases is whether evidence produced by a frisk is admissible, the problem is to determine what makes a frisk reasonable. . . .

Any person, including a policeman, is at liberty to avoid a person he considers dangerous. If and when a policeman has a right instead to disarm such a person for his own protection, he must first have a right not to avoid him, but to be in his presence. That right must be more than the liberty (again, possessed by every citizen) to address questions to other persons, for ordinarily the person addressed has an equal right to ignore his interrogator and walk away; he certainly need not submit to a frisk for the questioner's protection. I would make it perfectly clear that the right to frisk in this case depends upon the reasonableness of a forcible stop to investigate a suspected crime. . . .

The facts of this case are illustrative of a proper stop and an incident frisk. Officer McFadden had no probable cause to arrest Terry for anything, but he had observed circumstances that would reasonably lead an experienced, prudent policeman to suspect that Terry was about to engage in burglary or robbery. His justifiable suspicion afforded a proper constitutional basis for accosting Terry, restraining his liberty of movement briefly, and addressing questions to him, and Officer McFadden did so. When he did, he had no reason whatever to suppose that Terry might be armed, apart from the fact that he suspected him of planning a violent crime. McFadden asked Terry his name, to which Terry "mumbled something." Whereupon McFadden, without asking Terry to speak louder and without giving him any chance to explain his presence or his actions, forcibly frisked him.

I would affirm this conviction for what I believe to be the same reasons the Court relies on. I would, however, make explicit what I think is implicit in affirmance on the present facts. Officer McFadden's right to interrupt Terry's freedom of movement and invade his privacy arose only because circumstances warranted forcing an encounter with Terry in an effort to prevent or investigate a crime. Once that forced encounter was justified, however, the officer's right to take suitable measures for his own safety followed automatically.

MR. JUSTICE DOUGLAS, dissenting.

I agree that petitioner was "seized" within the meaning of the Fourth Amendment. I also agree that frisking petitioner and his companions for guns was a "search." But it is a mystery how that "search" and that "seizure" can be constitutional by Fourth Amendment standards unless there was "probable cause" to believe that (1) a crime had been committed or (2) a crime was in the process of being committed or (3) a crime was about to be committed.

The opinion of the Court disclaims the existence of "probable cause." If loitering were in issue and that was the offense charged, there would be "probable cause" shown. But the crime here is carrying concealed weapons; and there is no basis for concluding that the officer had "probable cause" for believing that that crime was being committed. Had a warrant been sought, a magistrate would, therefore, have been unauthorized to issue one, for he can act only if there is a showing of "probable cause." We hold today that the police have greater authority to make a "seizure" and conduct a "search" than a judge has to authorize such action. We have said precisely the opposite over and over again. . . .

The infringement on personal liberty of any "seizure" of a person can only be "reasonable" under the Fourth Amendment if we require the police to possess "probable cause" before they seize him. Only that line draws a meaningful distinction between an officer's mere inkling and the presence of facts within the officer's personal knowledge which would convince a reasonable man that the person seized has committed, is committing, or is about to commit a particular crime. . . .

To give the police greater power than a magistrate is to take a long step down the totalitarian path. Perhaps such a step is desirable to cope with modern forms of lawlessness. But if it is taken, it should be the deliberate choice of the people through a constitutional amendment. Until the Fourth Amendment, which is closely allied with the Fifth, is rewritten, the person and the effects of the individual are beyond the reach of all government agencies until there are reasonable grounds to believe (probable cause) that a criminal venture has been launched or is about to be launched.

There have been powerful hydraulic pressures throughout our history that bear heavily on the Court to water down constitutional guarantees and give the police the upper hand. That hydraulic pressure has probably never been greater than it is today.

Terry settled the issue of whether the popular stop-and-frisk practice was constitutional. The Court was absolutely clear that when a police officer had reason to believe a suspect was involved in criminal activity, the officer could stop that suspect and conduct a "pat down" search. Chief Justice Warren's opinion echoed a concern raised in the many *amicus* briefs filed on behalf of Officer McFadden. These briefs noted that, with handgun violence reaching epidemic levels, the stop-and-frisk practice was necessary to protect the police from a sudden gun-related assault. Accordingly, the Court also held that any contraband related to criminal activity seized during a "stop-and-frisk" search could later be introduced as evidence. Permitting the introduction of evidence seized during a warrantless search based on less than probable cause was an early and important limitation to the Court's decision eight years earlier in making the exclusionary rule applicable to the states.[21] *Terry* did not, however, permit the police to introduce contraband seized during a stop-and-frisk search that had no relationship to officer safety or suspected criminal wrongdoing. In *Minnesota* v. *Dickerson* (1993), the Court, by then much more sympathetic to law enforcement claims, ruled that a police officer could not seize drugs detected by police after a pat down during an otherwise valid street search for weapons.[22]

But *Terry* did have significant ramifications for warrantless searches beyond stop-and-frisk safety searches. Soon, the Court developed several more exceptions to the warrant requirement, holding that the police, acting on probable cause or, in some cases, the lesser standard of "reasonable suspicion," did not need warrants to conduct searches to protect the loss of evidence, to search a suspect after a valid arrest, to seize evidence found in "plain view," to search an automobile or individual chased in "hot pursuit," or to search open fields, trash dumps, or any other place where privacy expectations are diminished.[23]

Random Searches

Until the late 1980s the Court's rulings on the Fourth Amendment and exceptions for warrantless searches still held that probable cause was necessary to meet the constitutional requirement of reasonableness. Around this time, the Court created exceptions from the probable cause requirement, which had been necessary to authorize a warrantless search, to allow warrantless searches that do not have a basis in probable cause. Warrantless searches for which no probable cause is required include government drug-testing programs, border searches, police roadblocks to detect drunk drivers, and other such measures designed to promote broader public safety interests. In contemporary everyday life, Americans are exposed to a wide range of low-level searches that do not, for the most part, come close to implicating the Fourth Amendment. Metal detectors in airports, government buildings, and schools all involve some level of physical intrusion. Almost no one, not even the ACLU, considers them to pose a serious enough invasion of personal privacy to trigger Fourth Amendment justification. But what happens when protecting serious public safety interests, such as keeping drunk drivers off the roads and nabbing the ones out driving, result in search-and-seizure-based law enforcement programs that require persons exhibiting no suspicious behavior to surrender themselves to the police for truly invasive searches?

By the late 1980s, federal and state authorities had put drug-testing programs into place for government employees, and had begun authorizing random searches of bus, train, and airport passengers to discover drugs, guns, and other contraband. Moreover, more and more state and local police departments around the nation had begun instituting "checkpoints" to sweep drunk drivers off the roads. Here again, almost no one contested the public's interest in curtailing the flow of illegal drugs into and within the United States or containing the lethal threat posed by drunk drivers. But did the government's objectives justify the *random* nature of such searches? Two important cases decided in the early 1990s, *Michigan Department of State Police* v. *Sitz* and *Florida* v. *Bostick*, addressed these questions.

Michigan Department of State Police v. *Sitz*

496 U.S. 444 (1990)

Concerned about increasing levels of alcohol-related fatalities on Michigan's roads and highways, the Michigan state police department established a sobriety checkpoint program in early 1986. The police worked closely with local sheriffs, state prosecutors, insurance companies, and university researchers to establish guidelines for the checkpoint program. A special advisory committee to the police recommended several sites where drunken driving–related accidents were most frequent, and suggested a plan for pulling over and testing drivers. All vehicles passing through a checkpoint would be stopped and their drivers briefly examined for signs of intoxication. In cases where a checkpoint officer detected signs of intoxication, the motorist would be directed to a location out of the traffic flow.There, an officer would check the motorist's driver's license and car registration and, if necessary, conduct further sobriety tests. Should the field tests and the officer's observations suggest that the driver was intoxicated, an arrest would be made. Other drivers would be permitted to continue along their routes.

The first sobriety checkpoint went into operation in late 1986. It was conducted by Michigan state police in cooperation with the Saginaw County Sheriff's Department, whose jurisdiction includes the Detroit metropolitan area. During the seventy-five-minute duration of the checkpoint's operation, 126 drivers came through the checkpoint. The average delay for each vehicle was twenty-five seconds. Two drivers were detained for field sobriety testing, and one of the two was arrested for driving under the influence of alcohol. A third driver, who drove through without stopping, was pulled over by an officer in an observation vehicle and arrested for driving under the influence.

The day before the Michigan checkpoint was scheduled to begin, the ACLU filed suit to enjoin the police from implementing the program. The ACLU claimed that the sobriety checkpoint program violated the Fourth Amendment's ban on unreasonable searches and seizures because the Michigan police offered no probable cause to detain and search motorists. The year before, the ACLU had filed an *amicus* brief in *Treasury Employees* v. *Von Raab* (1989), in which the Court, 5 to 4, ruled that a government drug-testing program for federal border agents did not violate the Fourth Amendment. The ACLU had taken a firm line against random drug-testing programs, claiming that such programs failed to satisfy the "probable cause" requirement of the Fourth Amendment.

The American public, on the other hand, was extremely supportive of measures such as drug-testing programs and sobriety checkpoints. And no group better represented the rising sense of public outrage against drunk driving than Mothers Against Drunk Driving (MADD), founded in 1980 by a small group of California mothers, after the death of one's thirteen-year-old daughter by an intoxicated hit-and-run driver. Just two days before, that driver had been released on bail while awaiting trial on another drunk-driving crash. All told, the driver had four previous drunk-driving arrests, with two convictions, before the 1980 crash that had resulted in the young girl's death. By 2001, MADD had grown into a well-financed and politically influential group, with over 600 chapters nationwide devoted to education and lobbying on behalf of more stringent laws and punishments related to alcohol-related driving offenses. MADD filed an *amicus* brief in *Sitz*, arguing that sobriety checkpoints were effective deterrents to drunk driving, countering the ACLU's argument that the limited yield of drunk drivers that checkpoints produced did not justify the "invasive" nature of the stop and search. In addition, twenty-nine state attorneys general filed *amicus* briefs in support of sobriety checkpoints, as a Court decision declaring them unconstitutional would have a dramatic effect on their own antidrunk-driving programs.

The Court's decision was 6 to 3. Chief Justice Rehnquist delivered the opinion of the Court. Justice Blackmun filed a concurring opinion. Justice Brennan, joined by Marshall, filed a dissenting opinion. Justice Stevens, joined by Justices Brennan and Marshall, also dissented.

▼▲▼

CHIEF JUSTICE REHNQUIST delivered the opinion of the Court.

Petitioners concede, correctly in our view, that a Fourth Amendment "seizure" occurs when a vehicle is stopped at a checkpoint. The question thus becomes whether such seizures are "reasonable" under the Fourth Amendment.

It is important to recognize what our inquiry is *not* about. No allegations are before us of unreasonable treatment of any person after an actual detention at a particular checkpoint. As pursued in the lower courts, the instant action challenges only the use of sobriety checkpoints generally. We address only the initial stop of each motorist passing through a checkpoint and the associated preliminary questioning and observation by checkpoint officers. Detention of particular motorists for more extensive field sobriety testing may require satisfaction of an individualized suspicion standard.

No one can seriously dispute the magnitude of the drunken driving problem or the States' interest in eradicating it. Media reports of alcohol-related death and mutilation on the Nation's roads are legion. The anecdotal is confirmed by the statistical. "Drunk drivers cause an annual death toll of over 25,000 and in the same time span cause nearly one million personal injuries and more than five billion dollars in property damage." For decades, this Court has "repeatedly lamented the tragedy."

Conversely, the weight bearing on the other scale—the measure of the intrusion on motorists stopped briefly at sobriety checkpoints—is slight. We reached a similar conclusion as to the intrusion on motorists subjected to a brief stop at a highway checkpoint for detecting illegal aliens. We see virtually no difference between the levels of intrusion on law-abiding motorists from the brief stops necessary to the effectuation of these two types of checkpoints, which to the average motorist would seem identical save for the nature of the questions the checkpoint officers might ask. The trial court and the Court of Appeals, thus, accurately gauged the "objective" intrusion, measured by the duration of the seizure and the intensity of the investigation, as minimal.

With respect to what it perceived to be the "subjective" intrusion on motorists, however, the Court of Appeals found such intrusion substantial. The court first affirmed the trial court's finding that the guidelines governing checkpoint operation minimize the discretion of the officers on the scene. But the court also agreed with the trial court's conclusion that the checkpoints have the potential to generate fear and surprise in motorists. This was so because the record failed to demonstrate that approaching motorists would be aware of their option to make U-turns or turnoffs to avoid the checkpoints. On that basis, the court deemed the subjective intrusion from the checkpoints unreasonable.

We believe the Michigan courts misread our cases concerning the degree of "subjective intrusion" and the potential for generating fear and surprise. The "fear and surprise" to be considered are not the natural fear of one who has been drinking over the prospect of being stopped at a sobriety checkpoint but, rather, the fear and surprise engendered in law abiding motorists by the nature of the stop. . . . Here, checkpoints are selected pursuant to the guidelines, and uniformed police officers stop every approaching vehicle. . . .

In sum, the balance of the State's interest in preventing drunken driving, the extent to which this system can reasonably be said to advance that interest, and the degree of intrusion upon individual motorists who are briefly stopped, weighs in favor of the state program. We therefore hold that it is consistent with the Fourth Amendment. The judgment of the Michigan Court of Appeals is accordingly reversed, and the cause is remanded for further proceedings not inconsistent with this opinion.

It is so ordered.

JUSTICE BRENNAN, with whom JUSTICE MARSHALL joins, dissenting.

Today, the Court rejects a Fourth Amendment challenge to a sobriety checkpoint policy in which police stop all cars and inspect all drivers for signs of intoxication without any individualized suspicion that a specific driver is intoxicated. . . .

The majority opinion creates the impression that the Court generally engages in a balancing test in order to determine the constitutionality of all seizures, or at least those "dealing with police stops of motorists on public highways." This is not the case. In most cases, the police must possess probable cause for a seizure to be judged reasonable. Only when a seizure is "*substantially* less intrusive," than a typical arrest is the general rule replaced by a balancing test. I agree with the Court that the initial stop of a car at a roadblock under the Michigan State Police sobriety checkpoint policy is sufficiently less intrusive than an arrest so that the reasonableness of the seizure may be judged, not by the presence of probable cause, but by balancing "the gravity of the public concerns served by the seizure, the degree to which the seizure advances the public interest, and the severity of the interference with individual liberty." But one searches the majority opinion in vain for any acknowledgment that the reason for employing the balancing test is that the seizure is minimally intrusive.

Indeed, the opinion reads as if the minimal nature of the seizure *ends* rather than begins the inquiry into reasonableness. Once the Court establishes that the seizure is "slight," it asserts without explanation that the balance "weighs in favor of the state program." The Court ignores the fact that, in this class of minimally intrusive searches, we have generally required the Government to prove that it had reasonable suspicion for a minimally intrusive seizure to be considered reasonable. Some level of individualized suspicion is a core component of the protection the Fourth Amendment provides against arbitrary government action. By holding that no level of suspicion is necessary before the police may stop a car for the purpose of preventing drunken driving, the Court potentially subjects the general public to arbitrary or harassing conduct by the police. I would have hoped that before taking such a step, the Court would carefully explain how such a plan fits within our constitutional framework. . . .

I do not dispute the immense social cost caused by drunken drivers, nor do I slight the government's efforts to prevent such tragic losses. Indeed, I would hazard a guess that today's opinion will be received favorably by a majority of our society, who would willingly suffer the minimal intrusion of a sobriety checkpoint stop in order to prevent drunken driving. But consensus that a particular law enforcement technique serves a laudable purpose has never been the touchstone of constitutional analysis. The Fourth Amendment was designed not merely to protect against official intrusions whose social utility was less as measured by some "balancing test" than its intrusion on individual privacy; it was designed in addition to grant the individual a zone of privacy whose protections could be breached only where the "reasonable" requirements of the probable cause standard were met. Moved by whatever momentary evil has aroused their fears, officials—perhaps even supported by a majority of citizens—may be tempted to conduct searches that sacrifice the liberty of each citizen to assuage the perceived evil. But the Fourth Amendment rests on the principle that a true balance between the individual and society depends on the recognition of "the right to be let alone—the most comprehensive of rights and the right most valued by civilized men," *Olmstead* v. *United States* (1928).

In the face of the "momentary evil" of drunken driving, the Court today abdicates its role as the protector of that fundamental right. I respectfully dissent.

Florida v. *Bostick*

501 U.S. 429 (1991)

South Florida is one the major arteries for drug smugglers moving cocaine, heroin, and marijuana into the United States. Once smugglers have skirted the border patrols and customs agents, their next step is to place drugs on ground transportation to begin the distribution process throughout the rest of the country. In some cases, drug smugglers use trucks and buses to move drugs to their intended destination. Other times, individuals are given the responsibility of carrying drugs on their person or in their baggage. To combat the latter form of drug trafficking, the Broward County Sheriff's Department, acting in consultation with the United States Department of Justice, began a program known as "working the buses." This program permitted officers to board buses at undisclosed stops and request permission from passengers to search their luggage.

Terrance Bostick was a passenger on a bus bound from Miami to Atlanta. During the bus's scheduled stopover in Fort Lauderdale, two uniformed and armed Broward County officers boarded and, eyeing the passengers, asked Bostick for identification. His identification and ticket matched, and the police returned Bostick's wallet to him. The officers then asked Bostick if they could search his luggage. At this point, Bostick's account of the bus search differed from that of the police, but a Florida trial court later agreed with the police that Bostick consented to the search. (Bostick claimed that he did not object because he could not, as he was faced with armed officers on a bus.) The police found a small amount of cocaine in Bostick's luggage and later arrested him.

Bostick later claimed his detention on the bus by police amounted to an unconstitutional "seizure" of his person and the subsequent search of his luggage failed to satisfy the reasonableness requirement of the Fourth Amendment, since the police had no probable cause or even reasonable suspicion to search him. The Florida Supreme Court ultimately ruled that the police had no probable cause to seize passengers and search their luggage without clear reasons for doing so. Florida appealed to the United States Supreme Court.

Only two groups filed briefs in *Bostick*, the ACLU and the Americans for Effective Law Enforcement (AELE). The ACLU's participation in Supreme Court litigation involving the rights of the criminally accused extended all the way back to the early 1930s, when it assisted in the defense of the Scottsboro Boys in *Powell* v. *Alabama* (1932) (see Chapter 9). In *Powell*, the Court ruled that indigent defendants were entitled to a lawyer in a capital case, establishing not only an important rule of the right to counsel, but also beginning the process of the nationalization of the criminal due process guarantees of the Bill of Rights. The ACLU later became extremely influential in the Court's gradual expansion of the rights of criminal defendants in the 1960s.

The AELE, on the other hand, formed in 1966 after the Court's decision in *Miranda* v. *Arizona* (1966) (see Chapter 8), a case considered the high point in the Court's revolution in the law of criminal procedure under Chief Justice Earl Warren. Fred Inbau, a criminal law professor at Northwestern University, believed the Court had veered way off track in its rulings on behalf of criminal defendants. He also believed that the police and prosecutors had no effective voice in the courts to support their position. The AELE became that voice, filing its first *amicus* brief in *Terry* v. *Ohio* (1968).

By 2000, the AELE had filed *amicus* briefs in 155 cases. Only thirty-seven were decided unfavorably to law enforcement. Three-fourths of the cases were in the United States Supreme Court, and the remaining cases were in federal appeals or state supreme courts. Since 1968, thirty-five state attorneys general have joined AELE briefs, as have influential law enforcement groups such as the International Association of Chiefs of Police (IACP), the National Sheriffs Association (NSA), and the National District Attorneys Association (NDAA). The AELE devotes much of its *amicus* work to explaining police practices to the courts and providing social science data to support the policy positions of law enforcement. Traditionally, the ACLU and the AELE find themselves on opposite sides in criminal procedure cases.[24]

But *Bostick* was different. The ACLU and the AELE filed separate briefs arguing that the random bus searches were illegal under the Fourth Amendment. The AELE contended that Florida's "working the buses" program far exceeded existing judicial precedent, and was unnecessary in light of other, less intrusive search-and-seizure techniques available to law enforcement. Permitting random searches of bus travelers who offered no identifiable criminal tendencies was far different from authorizing drunk-driving roadblocks. The AELE argued that bus travelers offered no public safety risk, whereas the operator of a car did. Absent informant tips or other information indicating illegal behavior on the bus, the police had no right to detain passengers and search their belongings.

The Court's decision was 6 to 3. Justice O'Connor delivered the opinion of the Court. Justice Marshall, joined by Justices Blackmun and Stevens, dissented.

▼▲▼

JUSTICE O'CONNOR delivered the opinion of the Court.

We have held that the Fourth Amendment permits police officers to approach individuals at random in airport lobbies and other public places to ask them questions and to request consent to search their luggage, so long as a reasonable person would understand that he or she could refuse to cooperate. This case requires us to determine whether the same rule applies to police encounters that take place on a bus. . . .

Two facts are particularly worth noting. First, the police specifically advised Bostick that he had the right to refuse consent. Bostick appears to have disputed the point, but, as the Florida Supreme Court noted explicitly, the trial court resolved this evidentiary conflict in the State's favor. Second, at no time did the officers threaten Bostick with a gun. The Florida Supreme Court indicated that one officer carried a zipper pouch containing a pistol—the equivalent of carrying a gun in a holster—but the court did not suggest that the gun was ever removed from its pouch, pointed at Bostick, or otherwise used in a threatening manner. . . .

The sole issue presented for our review is whether a police encounter on a bus of the type described above necessarily constitutes a "seizure" within the meaning of the Fourth Amendment. The State concedes, and we accept for purposes of this decision, that the officers lacked the reasonable suspicion required to justify a seizure and that, if a seizure took place, the drugs found in Bostick's suitcase must be suppressed as tainted fruit.

Our cases make it clear that a seizure does not occur simply because a police officer approaches an individual and asks a few questions. So long as a reasonable person would feel free "to disregard the police and go about his business," the encounter is consensual, and no reasonable suspicion is required. The encounter will not trigger Fourth Amendment scrutiny unless it loses its consensual nature. The Court made precisely this point in *Terry* v. *Ohio* (1968): "Obviously, not all personal intercourse between policemen and citizens involves 'seizures' of persons. Only when the officer, by means of physical force or show of authority, has in some way restrained the liberty of a citizen may we conclude that a 'seizure' has occurred."

Since *Terry*, we have held repeatedly that mere police questioning does not constitute a seizure. . . .

There is no doubt that, if this same encounter had taken place before Bostick boarded the bus or in the lobby of the bus terminal, it would not rise to the level of a seizure. The Court has dealt with similar encounters in airports, and has found them to be "the sort of consensual encounter[s] that implicat[e] no Fourth Amendment interest." We have stated that even when officers have no basis for suspecting a particular individual, they may generally ask questions of that individual, as long as the police do not convey a message that compliance with their requests is required.

Bostick insists that this case is different because it took place in the cramped confines of a bus. A police encounter is much more intimidating in this setting, he argues, because police tower over a seated passenger and there is little room to move around. . . . Bostick maintains that a reasonable bus passenger would not have felt free to leave under the circumstances of this case because there is nowhere to go on a bus. Also, the bus was about to depart. Had Bostick disembarked, he would have risked being stranded and losing whatever baggage he had locked away in the luggage compartment.

The Florida Supreme Court found this argument persuasive, so much so that it adopted a *per se* rule prohibiting the police from randomly boarding buses as a means of drug interdiction. The state court erred, however, in focusing on whether Bostick was "free to leave," rather than on the principle that those words were intended to capture. When police attempt to question a person who is walking down the street or through an airport lobby, it makes sense to inquire whether a reasonable person would feel free to continue walking. But when the person is seated on a bus and has no desire to leave, the degree to which a reasonable person would feel that he or she could leave is not an accurate measure of the coercive effect of the encounter. . . .

The facts of this case, as described by the Florida Supreme Court, leave some doubt whether a seizure occurred. Two officers walked up to Bostick on the bus, asked him a few questions, and asked if they could search his bags. As we have explained, no seizure occurs when police ask questions of an individual, ask to examine the individual's identification, and request consent to search his or her luggage—so long as the officers do not convey a message that compliance with their requests is required. Here, the facts recited by the Florida Supreme Court indicate that the officers did not point guns at Bostick or otherwise threaten him, and that they specifically advised Bostick that he could refuse consent.

Nevertheless, we refrain from deciding whether or not a seizure occurred in this case. The trial court made no express findings of fact, and the Florida Supreme Court rested its decision on a single fact—that the encounter took place on a bus—rather than on the totality of the circumstances. We remand so that the Florida courts may evaluate the seizure question under the correct legal standard. We do reject, however, Bostick's argument that he must have been seized because no reasonable person would freely consent to a search of luggage that he or she knows contains drugs. This argument cannot prevail because the "reasonable person" test presupposes an *innocent* person. . . .

This Court, as the dissent correctly observes, is not empowered to suspend constitutional guarantees so that the Government may more effectively wage a "war on drugs." If that war is to be fought, those who fight it must respect the rights of individuals, whether or not those individuals are suspected of having committed a crime. By the same token, this Court is not empowered to forbid law enforcement practices simply because it considers them distasteful. The Fourth Amendment proscribes unreasonable searches and seizures; it does not proscribe voluntary cooperation. The cramped confines of a bus are one relevant factor that should be considered in evaluating whether a passenger's consent is voluntary. We cannot agree, however, with the Florida Supreme Court that this single factor will be dispositive in every case.

We adhere to the rule that, in order to determine whether a particular encounter constitutes a seizure, a court must consider all the circumstances surrounding the encounter to determine whether the police conduct would have communicated to a reasonable person that the person was not free to decline the officers' requests or otherwise terminate the encounter. That rule applies to encounters that take place on a city street or in an airport lobby, and it applies equally to encounters on a bus. The Florida Supreme Court erred in adopting a *per se* rule.

The judgment of the Florida Supreme Court is reversed, and the case remanded for further proceedings not inconsistent with this opinion.

It is so ordered.

JUSTICE MARSHALL, with whom JUSTICE BLACKMUN and JUSTICE STEVENS join, dissenting.

Our Nation, we are told, is engaged in a "war on drugs." No one disputes that it is the job of law enforcement officials to devise effective weapons for fighting this war. But the effectiveness of a law enforcement technique is not proof of its constitutionality. The general warrant, for example, was certainly an effective means of law enforcement. Yet it was one of the primary aims of the Fourth Amendment to protect citizens from the tyranny of being singled out for search and seizure without particularized suspicion notwithstanding the effectiveness of this method. In my view, the law enforcement technique with which we are confronted in this case—the suspicionless police sweep of buses in intrastate or interstate travel—bears all of the indicia of coercion and unjustified intrusion associated with the general warrant. Because I believe that the bus sweep at issue in this case violates the core values of the Fourth Amendment, I dissent.

At issue in this case is a "new and increasingly common tactic in the war on drugs": the suspicionless police sweep of buses in interstate or intrastate travel. Typically under this technique, a group of state or federal officers will board a bus while it is stopped at an intermediate point on its route. Often displaying badges, weapons or other indicia of authority, the officers identify themselves and announce their purpose to intercept drug traffickers. They proceed to approach individual passengers, requesting them to show identification, produce their tickets, and explain the purpose of their travels. Never do the officers advise the passengers that they are free not to speak with the officers. An "interview" of this type ordinarily culminates in a request for consent to search the passenger's luggage. . . .

To put it mildly, these sweeps "are inconvenient, intrusive, and intimidating." They occur within cramped confines, with officers typically placing themselves in between the passenger selected for an interview and the exit of the bus. Because the bus is only temporarily stationed at a point short of its destination, the passengers are in no position to leave as a means of evading the officers' questioning. Undoubtedly, such a sweep holds up the progress of the bus. Thus, this "new and increasingly common tactic," burdens the experience of traveling by bus with a degree of governmental interference to which, until now, our society has been proudly unaccustomed. . . .

The question for this Court, then, is whether the suspicionless, dragnet-style sweep of buses in intrastate and interstate travel is consistent with the Fourth Amendment. The majority suggests that this latest tactic in the drug war is perfectly compatible with the Constitution. I disagree. . . .

In my view, the Fourth Amendment clearly condemns the suspicionless, dragnet-style sweep of intrastate or interstate buses. Withdrawing this particular weapon from the government's drug war arsenal would hardly leave the police without any means of combatting the use of buses as instrumentalities of the drug trade. The police would remain free, for example, to approach passengers whom they have a reasonable, articulable basis to suspect of criminal wrongdoing. Alternatively, they could continue to confront passengers without suspicion so long as they took simple steps, like advising the passengers confronted of their right to decline to be questioned, to dispel the aura of coercion and intimidation that pervades such encounters. There is no reason to expect that such requirements would render the Nation's buses law enforcement-free zones.

The majority attempts to gloss over the violence that today's decision does to the Fourth Amendment with empty admonitions. "If th[e] [war on drugs] is to be fought," the majority intones, "those who fight it must respect the rights of individuals, whether or not those individuals are suspected of having committed a crime." The majority's actions, however, speak louder than its words.

I dissent.

Sitz and *Bostick* further widened the scope of permissible searches of individuals for which no warrant or probable cause was required. By holding that the public's interest in combating illegal drugs and potential drunk drivers justified what it acknowledged were random searches, the Court continued to move further away from the idea that reasonable searches had to have their constitutional baseline in warrants or probable cause. Several justices raised serious issues in *Sitz* and *Bostick* over the consequences of random searches. One such consequence was the disproportionate impact of random drug searches on African Americans and Latinos, a point raised by the NAACP Legal Defense Fund (NAACP LDF) in its *Bostick amicus* brief. Nonetheless, most Americans agreed with the Court that the compelling nature of drug- and alcohol-related social problems in the United States required broadening the latitude of law enforcement authorities to engage in reasonable searches, even if they lacked a basis in probable cause.

About the same time that federal and state law enforcement agencies were stepping up their efforts to curtail drug- and alcohol-related criminal conduct through random search policies, many public school authorities around the country had begun programs of their own to make their elementary and secondary schools "Drug-Free Zones." By the early 1980s, metal detectors, monitored by school officials and security guards, had become routine sights in institutions that had experienced gun violence. To complement these new security measures, many schools instituted policies that permitted administrators and teachers to search students' lockers and their personal belongings for drugs, weapons, alcohol, or any other illegal items. School officials reasoned that their position as *in locus parentis* (acting in the place of parents) made them, in essence, private parties and thus not constrained by the Fourth Amendment. Objecting students and their parents argued that searches of a student's locker required a basis in probable cause. Whether such searches were random in nature, or directed toward a particular student exhibiting suspicious behavior, school authorities were acting as the equivalent of law enforcement officers, not parents, and thus needed to conform to Fourth Amendment standards.

In *New Jersey* v. *T.L.O.* (1985), the Court agreed with a New Jersey high school student whose locker was successfully searched for drugs and drug paraphernalia that high school authorities, conducting searches of students and their property, were, like police officers, bound by the Fourth Amendment. But the Court handed school officials a much larger victory, holding that the school setting justified their right to conduct searches on the basis of *reasonable suspicion,* a less stringent standard than *probable cause.* In *T.L.O.*, the Court held that school officials need only to demonstrate they had a reason to believe that a student was engaged in illegal activity to conduct a locker search, and not probable cause, based on evidence that such activity had taken or was taking place. *T.L.O.* attracted a good deal of *amicus* activity, with the United States, the National School Boards Association, and several New Jersey education groups arguing in favor of broad discretion for public school authorities to engage in student searches. The ACLU and several groups representing the rights of children argued against such policies. The ACLU, in particular, argued that if school officials were not required to show probable cause to search students, then a similar case could be made for searches conducted entirely at random, so long as they were grounded in some larger interest related to school safety. In *Vernonia School District 47J* v. *Acton* (1995), the Court addressed a question stemming from its holding in *T.L.O.*: Did the reasonable suspicion of drug-related activity by students permit the use of random drug tests in public schools?

Vernonia School District 47J v. *Acton* 

515 U.S. 646 (1995)

In the early 1980s, the "War on Drugs" to attack drug smuggling, distribution, sales, use, and addiction reached a remote logging town in Oregon in 1989, after school authorities in the Vernonia School District decided to implement a random drug-testing policy on participants in elementary and high school athletic programs.

The facts and background of this case are set out in the accompanying SIDEBAR.

The Court's decision was 6 to 3. Justice Scalia delivered the opinion of the Court. Justice Ginsburg filed a concurring opinion. Justice O'Connor, joined by Justices Stevens and Souter, dissented.

JUSTICE SCALIA delivered the opinion of the Court.

As the text of the Fourth Amendment indicates, the ultimate measure of the constitutionality of a governmental search is "reasonableness." At least in a case such as this, where there was no clear practice, either approving or disapproving the type of search at issue at the time the constitutional provision was enacted, whether a particular search meets the reasonableness standard "is judged by balancing its intrusion on the individual's Fourth Amendment interests against its promotion of legitimate governmental interests."

Where a search is undertaken by law enforcement officials to discover evidence of criminal wrongdoing, this Court has said that reasonableness generally requires the obtaining of a judicial warrant. Warrants cannot be issued, of course, without the showing of probable cause required by the Warrant Clause. But a warrant is not required to establish the reasonableness of *all* government searches; and when a warrant is not required (and the Warrant Clause therefore not applicable), probable cause is not invariably required either. A search unsupported by probable cause can be constitutional, we have said, "when special needs, beyond the normal need for law enforcement, make the warrant and probable-cause requirement impracticable."

We have found such "special needs" to exist in the public school context. There, the warrant requirement "would unduly interfere with the maintenance of the swift and informal disciplinary procedures [that are] needed," and "strict adherence to the requirement that searches be based upon probable cause" would undercut "the substantial need of teachers and administrators for freedom to maintain order in the schools." The school search we approved in *New Jersey* v. *T.L.O.* (1985), while not based on probable cause, *was* based on individualized *suspicion* of wrongdoing. As we explicitly acknowledged, however, "'the Fourth Amendment imposes no irreducible requirement of such suspicion.'" We have upheld suspicionless searches and seizures to conduct drug testing of railroad personnel involved in train accidents, to conduct random drug testing of federal customs officers who carry arms or are involved in drug interdiction, and to maintain automobile checkpoints looking for illegal immigrants and contraband, and drunk drivers, *Michigan Dept. of State Police* v. *Sitz* (1990).

The first factor to be considered is the nature of the privacy interest upon which the search here at issue intrudes. The Fourth Amendment does not protect all subjective expectations of privacy, but only those that society recognizes as "legitimate." What expectations are legitimate varies, of course, with context, depending, for example, upon whether the individual asserting the privacy interest is at home, at work, in a car, or in a public park. In addition, the legitimacy of certain privacy expectations *vis-à-vis* the State may depend upon the individual's legal relationship with the State. . . . Central, in our view, to the present case is the fact that the subjects of the Policy are (1) children, who (2) have been committed to the temporary custody of the State as schoolmaster.

Traditionally at common law, and still today, unemancipated minors lack some of the most fundamental rights of self-determination—including even the right of liberty in its narrow sense, *i.e.*, the right to come and go at will. They are subject, even as to their physical freedom, to the control of their parents or guardians. When parents place minor children in private schools for their education, the teachers and administrators of those schools stand *in loco parentis* over the children entrusted to them. . . .

Fourth Amendment rights, no less than First and Fourteenth Amendment rights, are different in public schools than elsewhere; the "reasonableness" inquiry cannot disregard the schools' custodial and tutelary responsibility for children. For their own good and that of their classmates, public school children are routinely required to submit to various physical examinations, and to be vaccinated against various diseases. . . .

Legitimate privacy expectations are even less with regard to student athletes. School sports are not for the bashful. They require "suiting up" before each practice or event, and showering and changing afterwards. Public school locker rooms, the usual sites for these activities, are not notable for the privacy they afford. The locker rooms in Vernonia are typical: no individual dressing rooms are provided; shower heads are lined up along a wall, unseparated by any sort of partition or curtain; not even all the toilet stalls have doors. . . .

There is an additional respect in which school athletes have a reduced expectation of privacy. By choosing to "go out for the team," they voluntarily subject themselves to a degree of regulation even higher than that imposed on students generally. In Vernonia's public schools, they must submit to a pre-season physical exam, they must acquire adequate insurance coverage or sign an insurance waiver, maintain a minimum grade point average, and comply with any rules of conduct, dress, training hours and related matters as may be established for each sport by the head coach and athletic director with the principal's approval. . . .

Finally, we turn to consider the nature and immediacy of the governmental concern at issue here, and the efficacy of this means for meeting it. . . . It is a mistake, however, to think that the phrase "compelling state interest," in the Fourth Amendment context, describes a fixed, minimum quantum of governmental concern, so that one can dispose of a case by answering in isolation the question: is there a compelling state interest here? Rather, the phrase describes an interest which appears *important enough* to justify the particular search at hand, in light of other factors which show the search to be relatively intrusive upon a genuine expectation of privacy. Whether that relatively high degree of government concern is necessary in this case or not, we think it is met.

That the nature of the concern is important—indeed, perhaps compelling—can hardly be doubted. Deterring drug use by our Nation's schoolchildren is at least as important as enhancing efficient enforcement of the Nation's laws against the importation of drugs, which was the governmental concern in *National Treasury Employees v. Von Raab* (1989), or deterring drug use by engineers and trainmen, which was the governmental concern in *Skinner v. Railway Labor Executives Association* (1989). School years are the time when the physical, psychological, and addictive effects of drugs are most severe. . . .

As to the efficacy of this means for addressing the problem: it seems to us self-evident that a drug problem largely fueled by the "role model" effect of athletes' drug use, and of particular danger to athletes, is effectively addressed by making sure that athletes do not use drugs. Respondents argue that a "less intrusive means to the same end" was available, namely, "drug testing on suspicion of drug use." We have repeatedly refused to declare that only the "least intrusive" search practicable can be reasonable under the Fourth Amendment. Respondents' alternative entails substantial difficulties—if it is indeed practicable at all. It may be impracticable, for one thing, simply because the parents who are willing to accept random drug testing for athletes are not willing to accept accusatory drug testing for all students, which transforms the process into a badge of shame. Respondents' proposal brings the risk that teachers will impose testing arbitrarily upon troublesome but not drug-likely students. It generates the expense of defending lawsuits that charge such arbitrary imposition, or that simply demand greater process before accusatory drug testing is imposed. And not least of all, it adds to the ever-expanding diversionary duties of schoolteachers the new function of spotting and bringing to account drug abuse, a task for which they are ill prepared, and which is not readily compatible with their vocation. . . . In many respects, we think, testing based on "suspicion" of drug use would not be better, but worse.

Taking into account all the factors we have considered above—the decreased expectation of privacy, the relative unobtrusiveness of the search, and the severity of the need met by the search—we conclude Vernonia's Policy is reasonable, and hence constitutional.

We caution against the assumption that suspicionless drug testing will readily pass constitutional muster in other contexts. The most significant element in this case is the first we discussed: that the Policy was undertaken in furtherance of the government's responsibilities, under a public school system, as guardian and tutor of children entrusted to its care. Just as when the government conducts a search in its capacity as employer (a warrantless search of an absent employee's desk to obtain an urgently needed file, for example), the relevant question is whether that intrusion upon privacy is one that a reasonable employer might engage in, so also when the government acts as guardian and tutor the relevant question is whether the search is one that a reasonable guardian and tutor might undertake. . . .

We therefore vacate the judgment, and remand the case to the Court of Appeals for further proceedings consistent with this opinion.

It is so ordered.

JUSTICE O'CONNOR, with whom JUSTICE STEVENS and JUSTICE SOUTER join, dissenting.

The population of our Nation's public schools, grades 7 through 12, numbers around 18 million. By the reasoning

SIDEBAR

VERNONIA SCHOOL DISTRICT 47J V. ACTON

"I Never Even Got a Referral to the Principal's Office"

Located about an hour northwest of Portland, Oregon, Vernonia is a scenic rural community built around logging, one of the major industries of the Pacific Northwest. Although counting a population of less than three thousand residents, Vernonia still supports four schools, one high school and three elementary schools, enrolling approximately seven hundred students. With nearly one in four Vernonia residents enrolled in the public schools, it should come as no surprise that the community centers much of its social life on school activities. And with nearly 65 percent of high school students and 75 percent of elementary school students involved in athletics, Vernonia takes the sporting life very seriously.

And it was the decline in the performance of Vernonia's sports teams during the late 1980s that led school administrators to implement a comprehensive drug-testing program geared toward participants in the school district's athletic program. Football coaches, for example, noticed that more and more players were forgetting plays and failing to execute their assignments. One wrestler, according to another coach, suffered a serious sternum injury when he failed to react in time to an opponent's move. Teachers and administrators learned of two student clubs, the "Big Elks" and the "Drug Cartel," that were dominated by athletes who bragged about their drug use. School officials acknowledged that increased drug and alcohol use among the student body had become a problem. But they believed that by focusing on student-athletes, the most highly visible group in the schools, drug testing would draw attention to the problem and send an important message to all students that drug use would not be tolerated. Vernonia school officials had tried alternative approaches to discourage drug and alcohol use, such as drug education programs, drug-sniffing dogs on school property, and an increased police presence during the school day and at athletic events. Discouraged by their negligible impact, Randall Aultman, the acting school district superintendent and the principal of Vernonia High School, received unanimous approval in September 1989 from the parents who attended a special meeting on the community's "drug epidemic" to begin a mandatory drug-testing program on participants in the athletic program.

Under Vernonia's policy, athletes were tested at the beginning of each season and then at random until the season ended. School officials chose urinalysis as the testing method, with students providing a sample in the company of an adult. The test was able to detect the presence of marijuana, cocaine, and amphetamines. Under the school's policy, a student testing positive for drugs was required to receive counseling and submit to weekly drug tests if he or she wanted to continue to participate in the athletic program. Testing positive a second time resulted in suspension. According to Vernonia officials, the drug tests were 99.94 percent accurate.

In September 1991, James Acton, a seventh-grader at Washington Elementary School, wanted to play on the school's football team. Doing so required that James and his parents sign a consent form giving the school district permission to perform drug testing. James's parents, Judy and Wayne Acton, were furious over the drug-testing policy. "We didn't think we had to prove he wasn't taking drugs," Judy Action said. "We talked to him about it. He said, 'I'm not taking

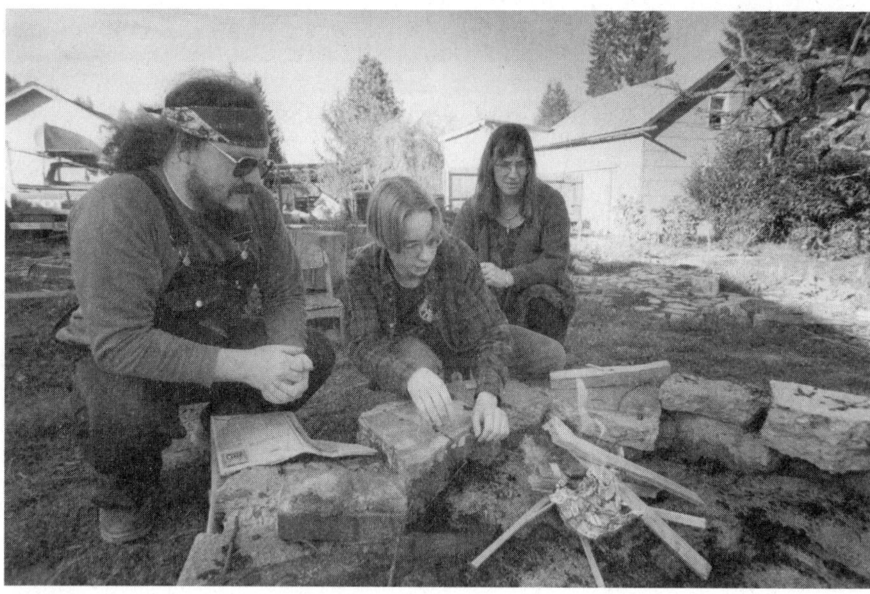

James Acton, with his parents Wayne and Judy, in their backyard at their home in Vernonia, Oregon. Marv Bondarowicz/*The Oregonian*

drugs,' and we said, 'Well, that's good enough for us.'" Commented Wayne Acton: "Suspicionless searches are illegal . . . simplistic, demagogic solutions. . . . What kind of citizens will our children be if they become accustomed to authoritarian restraints on their behavior?" The Actons refused to sign the consent form and contacted the American Civil Liberties Union about filing a lawsuit to challenge the program's constitutionality. The ACLU agreed to represent the Actons, and filed suit in federal district court, claiming that the Vernonia drug-testing policy violated the Fourth Amendment's prohibition against unreasonable searches and seizures and a similar provision under the Oregon constitution.

Vernonia school officials expected such a lawsuit and had put aside $10,000 to defend its drug-testing policy. The only thing that surprised Randall Aultman was that it had taken someone two years to challenge the program. By then, the school district had built wide-ranging support for its drug-testing program on student athletes. Not a single group submitted an *amicus* brief on behalf of the Actons. However, over a half a dozen groups, including the United States Solicitor General, the Institute for a Drug-Free Workplace, the National School Boards Association, the Washington Legal Foundation, and a joint brief representing several state and local government associations, lined up behind the school district. The community had viewed the Actons' decision to sue the school district as strange and disrespectful. According to Judy Acton, the lawsuit had "strained my relations with most people here."

Federal district court judge Malcolm Marsh of Portland ruled against the Actons, holding that the Vernonia drug-testing policy did not violate the Fourth Amendment. Said Judge Marsh, "The evidence amply demonstrated that the administration was at its wit's end and that a large segment of the student body, particularly those involved in interscholastic athletics, was in a state of rebellion." In Judge Marsh's view, the school district had demonstrated success in curbing drug use in its four schools and had made the general environment a safer one for students. The public safety far outweighed any perceived right to privacy on the part of Vernonia students.

Before the Supreme Court heard his case, James had this to say about his decision to challenge Vernonia's drug-testing policy:

> I am challenging my school district's drug testing policy because I believe in the right guaranteed to me by the Fourth Amendment of the United States Constitution. It says we have the right "to be secure in our

persons, houses, papers and effects against unreasonable searches."

This right prevents our houses from being searched against our will without a search warrant. Just as the government should not be allowed to search our house without a warrant, finding things we may wish to be private, the government should not be allowed to search our bodies either. This would say that our bodies are less private than our homes. Making kids take a drug test without any proof that they are taking drugs is just like searching a house without a warrant or proof of something wrong.

The Vernonia School District in Oregon, where I live, had no reason to think I was taking drugs. I wanted to play sports and I was one of the smartest kids in the class. I never even got a referral to the principal's office. I thought that was proof enough that I wasn't taking drugs. So I refused to take the test.

I think what I did has been made into a big deal. But I think I did the right thing and other people should also stand up for their beliefs. The government has no business searching our bodies, or our houses, without a warrant. This is part of our Constitution, which is an important part of our nation.

It may seem a little difficult to believe that a 12-year-old thought of this all by himself. But it's not too difficult to understand the right to privacy. I think everybody should be taught that they have that right.

References

ACLU, "In the Courts," www.aclu.org/court/clients.

Marquand, Robert. "Supreme Court Case Challenges Drug Test for School Athletes," *Christian Science Monitor,* March 28, 1995, p. 1.

Savage, David G. "Justices Consider Drug Tests," *Los Angeles Times,* March 29, 1995, p. A17.

of today's decision, the millions of these students who participate in interscholastic sports, an overwhelming majority of whom have given school officials no reason whatsoever to suspect they use drugs at school, are open to an intrusive bodily search.

In justifying this result, the Court dispenses with a requirement of individualized suspicion on considered policy grounds. First, it explains that precisely because *every* student athlete is being tested, there is no concern that school officials might act arbitrarily in choosing who to test. Second, a broad-based search regime, the Court reasons, dilutes the accusatory nature of the search. In making these policy arguments, of course, the Court sidesteps powerful, countervailing privacy concerns. Blanket searches, because they can involve "thousands or millions" of searches, "pos[e] a greater threat to liberty" than do suspicion-based ones, which "affec[t] one person at a time." Searches based on individualized suspicion also afford potential targets considerable control over whether they will, in fact, be searched because a person can avoid such a search by not acting in an objectively suspicious way. And given that the surest way to avoid acting suspiciously is to avoid the underlying wrongdoing, the costs of such a regime, one would think, are minimal.

But whether a blanket search is "better" than a regime based on individualized suspicion is not a debate in which we should engage. In my view, it is not open to judges or government officials to decide on policy grounds which is better and which is worse. For most of our constitutional history, mass, suspicionless searches have been generally considered *per se* unreasonable within the meaning of the Fourth Amendment. And we have allowed exceptions in recent years only where it has been clear that a suspicion-based regime would be ineffectual. Because that is not the case here, I dissent.

[N]ot all searches around the time the Fourth Amendment was adopted required individualized suspicion—although most did. A search incident to arrest was an obvious example of one that did not, but even those searches shared the essential characteristics that distinguish suspicion-based searches from abusive general searches: they only "affec[t] one person at a time," and they are generally avoidable by refraining from wrongdoing. Protection of privacy, not evenhandedness, was then and is now the touchstone of the Fourth Amendment. . . .

Thus, it remains the law that the police cannot, say, subject to drug testing every person entering or leaving a certain drug-ridden neighborhood in order to find evidence of crime. And this is true even though it is hard to think of a more compelling government interest than the need to fight the scourge of drugs on our streets and in our neighborhoods. Nor could it be otherwise, for if being evenhanded were enough to justify evaluating a search regime under an open-ended balancing test, the Warrant Clause, which presupposes that there is *some* category of searches for which individualized suspicion is non-negotiable would be a dead letter. . . .

One searches today's majority opinion in vain for recognition that history and precedent establish that individualized suspicion is "usually required" under the Fourth Amendment (regardless of whether a warrant and probable cause are also required) and that, in the area of intrusive personal searches, the only recognized exception is for situations in which a suspicion-based scheme would be likely ineffectual. Far from acknowledging anything special about individualized suspicion, the Court treats a suspicion-based regime as if it were just any run-of-the-mill, less intrusive alternative—that is, an alternative that officials may bypass if the lesser intrusion, in their reasonable estimation, is outweighed by policy concerns unrelated to practicability. . . .

In light of . . . [the] evidence of drug use by particular students [in Vernonia], there is a substantial basis for concluding that a vigorous regime of suspicion-based testing would have gone a long way toward solving Vernonia's school drug problem while preserving the Fourth Amendment rights of James Acton and others like him. And were there any doubt about such a conclusion, it is removed by indications in the record that suspicion-based testing could have been supplemented by an equally vigorous campaign to have Vernonia's parents encourage their children to submit to the District's *voluntary* drug testing program. In these circumstances, the Fourth Amendment dictates that a mass, suspicionless search regime is categorically unreasonable. . . .

It cannot be too often stated that the greatest threats to our constitutional freedoms come in times of crisis. But we must also stay mindful that not all government responses to such times are hysterical overreactions; some crises are quite real, and when they are, they serve precisely as the compelling state interest that we have said may justify a measured intrusion on constitutional rights. The only way for judges to mediate these conflicting impulses is to do what they should do anyway: stay close to the record in each case that appears before them, and make their judgments based on that alone. Having reviewed the record here, I cannot avoid the conclusion that the District's suspicionless policy of testing all student athletes sweeps too broadly, and too imprecisely, to be reasonable under the Fourth Amendment.

▼▲▼

By requiring a standard of reasonableness tied to the public interest rather than probable cause based on suspected criminal behavior, the Court has made it much easier for government authorities to engage in random searches. *Acton* and *Von Raab*, while offering government agencies and school authorities considerable leeway to mandate random drug testing of individuals who have not exhibited any drug-related behavior, have not meant that government authorities have the green light to mandate drug testing for any reason at all. In *Chandler* v. *Skinner* (1997), the Court, 8 to 1, struck down a Georgia law requiring those seeking elected public office to pass a drug test before qualifying as an official candidate. Writing for the Court, Justice Ruth Bader Ginsburg held that Georgia had offered no evidence of a drug problem among its elected state officials and thus could not justify what was admittedly a suspicionless search.

Racial Profiling

In 1967, President Lyndon Johnson appointed the National Advisory Commission on Civil Disorders, also known as the Kerner Commission, to study the growing racial unrest in the nation's major cities. The Kerner Commission found several embedded problems linked to racial discrimination in the United States, such as poverty, joblessness, broken homes, and urban violence. It also publicized one of the most common complaints of African Americans: the persistent police harassment and intimidation of young black men. More than 130 black witnesses testified in hearings held around the country during September and October 1967 that they had either witnessed an African American being stopped on foot or while driving for no obvious reason or had been the victim of what they believed was a racially motivated stop-and-frisk search. The day after the commission released its report in late February 1968, the news media began their description of its findings with its most well-known quote: "Our nation is moving toward two societies, one black and one white—separate and unequal." The report also noted that whites, by and large, would continue to think of African Americans as a predominately poor and criminal element of society as long as they were cordoned off in urban ghettos.[25]

Although America is a very different place in the early twenty-first century than it was in the late 1960s, one finding of the Kerner Commission's report that continues to haunt the relationship between African Americans and law enforcement authorities is the admitted use of racial profiling by some police departments around the country. In March 1999, for example, New Jersey governor Christine Todd Whitman fired the chief of state troopers after he defended racial profiling on the grounds that "mostly minorities" trafficked in marijuana and cocaine. In 1996, the ACLU sued the Maryland State Police after the state's own data revealed that, during the three-year period from 1994 to 1996, over 75 percent of all motorists searched during traffic stops on I-95, one of the East Coast's major interstate highways, were African American. The ACLU's lawsuit was a follow-up to a class-action lawsuit it had brought in 1993 against the Maryland state police on behalf of an African American attorney who was stopped, detained, and searched by the state police for no apparent reason. As part of the settlement, the state court required the state to maintain computer records of motorist searches to monitor for any patterns of discrimination.[26]

The Supreme Court has not confronted head-on a constitutional challenge to racial profiling practices by police departments. But in *Illinois* v. *Wardlow* (2000), the Court dealt with a closely related issue. Although *Wardlow* does not deal with racial profiling on the nation's highways and surface streets, it does address the inherent suspicion that still exists between many African Americans and the police.

Illinois v. *Wardlow*

528 U.S. 119 (2000)

On September 9, 1995, a four-car caravan of police cars drove through the Eleventh police district in downtown Chicago, an area known for heavy narcotics trafficking. Two officers, Nolan and Harvey, were in the last car in the police caravan, which was operating as a security measure in the event that any officer spotted a drug transaction. Officer Nolan noticed a forty-four-year-old African American male, Sam Wardlow, standing on a street corner holding a white bag. When Nolan made eye contact with Wardlow, Wardlow turned and started to flee. Harvey, who was driving, followed Wardlow down an alley. Nolan jumped out of the car and began chasing Wardlow, who continued to flee the uniformed officer. Nolan never announced who he was or why he was chasing after Wardlow. The officer soon cornered Wardlow and conducted a protective "stop-and-frisk" search of the sort upheld in *Terry* v. *Ohio*. After patting down the suspect, Nolan examined the bag and felt a heavy object. Inside was a.38 caliber revolver with five live rounds of ammunition. Wardlow was arrested.

During trial, Nolan said that Wardlow "looked in our direction and began fleeing." Nolan admitted that he had never seen Wardlow before and that, by standing on the street corner, Wardlow was not violating any law. The officer based his decision to chase Wardlow on the suspect's decision to flee the police. Wardlow's attorneys suggested during his trial that the only reason the police suspected their client of criminal behavior was because he was a black man standing on a street corner in a "high crime" area. The Illinois Supreme Court later ruled that the police had violated Wardlow's Fourth Amendment rights by stopping and searching him without probable cause to believe he had violated—or was about to violate—any law.

Among the groups to file *amicus* briefs with the Supreme Court after it agreed to hear Illinois's appeal was the NAACP LDF, which argued that the reason Sam Wardlow fled Officer Nolan was the inherent distrust that African Americans have for the police, a troubled relationship that extends deep into the nation's history. The NAACP LDF reported numerous statistics to the Court on the disproportionate street stops of minority residents in several major American cities, most of which never resulted in an arrest. Moreover, the NAACP LDF also cited research undertaken by the United States Department of Justice that showed African American residents in twelve major cities around the country are more than twice as likely to be dissatisfied with police practices than white residents in the same community. The NAACP LDF emphasized the racial taint that many police practices designed to deter and control street-level crime impress upon African Americans and other minorities. In contrast, the AELE and the police organizations filing *amicus* briefs in *Wardlow* argued that the right to detain and search suspects who flee the police was consistent with and a logical extension of *Terry*. For them, the right of the police to act upon "nervous, evasive behavior," not racial bias, was the issue.

The Court's decision was 5 to 4. Chief Justice Rehnquist delivered the opinion for the Court. Justice Stevens, joined by Justices Breyer, Ginsburg and Souter, dissented.

▼▲▼

CHIEF JUSTICE REHNQUIST delivered the opinion of the Court.

This case, involving a brief encounter between a citizen and a police officer on a public street, is governed by the analysis we first applied in *Terry*. In *Terry*, we held that an officer may, consistent with the Fourth Amendment, conduct a brief, investigatory stop when the officer has a reasonable, articulable suspicion that criminal activity is afoot. While "reasonable suspicion" is a less demanding standard than probable cause and requires a showing considerably less than preponderance of the evidence, the Fourth Amendment requires at least a minimal level of objective justification for making the stop. The officer must be able to articulate more than an "inchoate and unparticularized suspicion or 'hunch'" of criminal activity.

Nolan and Harvey were among eight officers in a four car caravan that was converging on an area known for heavy narcotics trafficking, and the officers anticipated encountering a large number of people in the area, including drug customers and individuals serving as lookouts. It was in this context that Officer Nolan decided to investigate Wardlow after observing him flee. An individual's presence in an area of expected criminal activity, standing alone, is not enough to support a reasonable, particularized suspicion that the person is committing a crime. But officers are not required to ignore the relevant characteristics of a location in determining whether the circumstances are sufficiently suspicious to warrant further investigation. Accordingly, we have previously noted the fact that the stop occurred in a "high crime area" among the relevant contextual considerations in a *Terry* analysis.

In this case, moreover, it was not merely respondent's presence in an area of heavy narcotics trafficking that aroused the officers' suspicion but his unprovoked flight upon noticing the police. Our cases have also recognized that nervous, evasive behavior is a pertinent factor in determining reasonable suspicion. Headlong flight—wherever it occurs—is the consummate act of evasion: it is not necessarily indicative of wrongdoing, but it is certainly suggestive of such. In reviewing the propriety of an officer's conduct, courts do not have available empirical studies dealing with inferences drawn from suspicious behavior, and we cannot reasonably demand scientific certainty from judges or law enforcement officers where none exists. Thus, the determination of reasonable suspicion must be based on commonsense judgments and inferences about human behavior. We conclude Officer Nolan was justified in suspecting that Wardlow was involved in criminal activity, and, therefore, in investigating further. . . .

Respondent and *amici* also argue that there are innocent reasons for flight from police and that, therefore, flight is not necessarily indicative of ongoing criminal activity. This fact is undoubtedly true, but does not establish a violation of the Fourth Amendment. Even in *Terry*, the conduct justifying the stop was ambiguous and susceptible of an innocent explanation. The officer observed two individuals pacing back and forth in front of a store, peering into the window and periodically conferring. All of this conduct was by itself lawful, but it also suggested that the individuals were casing the store for a planned robbery. *Terry* recognized that the officers could detain the individuals to resolve the ambiguity.

In allowing such detentions, *Terry* accepts the risk that officers may stop innocent people. Indeed, the Fourth Amendment accepts that risk in connection with more drastic police action; persons arrested and detained on probable cause to believe they have committed a crime may turn out to be innocent. The *Terry* stop is a far more minimal intrusion, simply allowing the officer to briefly investigate further. If the officer does not learn facts rising to the level of probable cause, the individual must be allowed to go on his way. But in this case the officers found respondent in possession of a handgun, and arrested him for violation of an Illinois firearms statute. No question of the propriety of the arrest itself is before us.

The judgment of the Supreme Court of Illinois is reversed, and the cause is remanded for further proceedings not inconsistent with this opinion.

It is so ordered.

JUSTICE STEVENS, with whom JUSTICE SOUTER, JUSTICE GINSBERG, and JUSTICE BREYER join, concurring in part and dissenting in part.

The State of Illinois asks this Court to announce a "bright-line rule" authorizing the temporary detention of anyone who flees at the mere sight of a police officer. Respondent counters by asking us to adopt the opposite . . . rule—that the fact that a person flees upon seeing the police can never, by itself, be sufficient to justify a temporary investigative stop of the kind authorized by *Terry v. Ohio* (1968).

The Court today wisely endorses neither *per se* rule. Instead, it rejects the proposition that "flight is . . . necessarily indicative of ongoing criminal activity," adhering to the view that "[t]he concept of reasonable suspicion . . . is not readily, or even usefully, reduced to a neat set of legal rules," but must be determined by looking to "the totality of the circumstances—the whole picture." Abiding by this framework, the Court concludes that "Officer Nolan was justified in suspecting that Wardlow was involved in criminal activity."

Although I agree with the Court's rejection of the *per se* rules proffered by the parties, unlike the Court, I am persuaded that in this case the brief testimony of the officer who seized respondent does not justify the conclusion that he had reasonable suspicion to make the stop. . . .

The question in this case concerns "the degree of suspicion that attaches to" a person's flight—or, more precisely, what "commonsense conclusions" can be drawn respecting the motives behind that flight. A pedestrian may break into a run for a variety of reasons—to catch up with a friend a block or two away, to seek shelter from an impending storm, to arrive at a bus stop before the bus leaves, to get home in time for dinner, to resume jogging after a pause for rest, to avoid contact with a bore or a bully, or simply to answer the call of nature—any of which might coincide with the arrival of an officer in the vicinity. A pedestrian might also run because he or she has just sighted one or more police officers. In the latter instance, the State properly points out "that the fleeing person may be, *inter alia,* (1) an escapee from jail; (2) wanted on a warrant, (3) in possession of contraband, (i.e., drugs, weapons, stolen goods, etc.); or (4) someone who has just committed another type of crime." In short, there are unquestionably circumstances in which a person's flight is suspicious, and undeniably instances in which a person runs for entirely innocent reasons. . . .

Even assuming we know that a person runs because he sees the police, the inference to be drawn may still vary from case to case. Flight to escape police detection, we have said, may have an entirely innocent motivation. . . .

Among some citizens, particularly minorities and those residing in high crime areas, there is also the possibility that the fleeing person is entirely innocent, but, with or without justification, believes that contact with the police can itself be dangerous, apart from any criminal activity associated with the officer's sudden presence. For such a person, unprovoked flight is neither "aberrant" nor "abnormal." Moreover, these concerns and fears are known to the police officers themselves, and are validated by law enforcement investigations into their own practices. Accordingly, the evidence supporting the reasonableness of these beliefs is too pervasive to be dismissed as random or rare, and too persuasive to be disparaged as inconclusive or insufficient. In any event, just as we do not require "scientific certainty" for our commonsense conclusion that unprovoked flight can sometimes indicate suspicious motives, neither do we require scientific certainty to conclude that unprovoked flight can occur for other, innocent reasons. . . . *

---

*See, e.g., Kotlowitz, "Hidden Casualties: Drug War's Emphasis on Law Enforcement Takes a Toll on Police," *Wall Street Journal,* Jan. 11, 1991, p. A2, col. 1 ("Black leaders complained that innocent people were picked up in the drug sweeps. . . . Some teenagers were so scared of the task force they ran even if they weren't selling drugs."). Many stops never lead to an arrest, which further exacerbates the perceptions of discrimination felt by racial minorities and people living in high-crime areas. See Goldberg, "The Color of Suspicion," *New York Times Magazine,* June 20, 1999, p. 85 (reporting that in a two-year period, New York City Police Department Street Crimes Unit made 45,000 stops, only 9,500 of which, or 20 percent, resulted in arrest); Casimir (reporting that in 1997, New York City's Street Crimes Unit conducted 27,061 stop-and-frisks, only 4,647 of which, or 17 percent, resulted in arrest). Even if these data were race neutral, they would still indicate that society as a whole is paying a significant cost in infringement on liberty by these virtually random stops.

The Chief of the Washington, D.C., Metropolitan Police Department, for example, confirmed that "sizeable percentages of Americans today—especially Americans of color—still view policing in the United States to be discriminatory, if not by policy and definition, certainly in its day-to-day application." P. Verniero, Attorney General of New Jersey, *Interim Report of the State Police Review Team Regarding Allegations of Racial Profiling* 46 (Apr. 20, 1999) (hereinafter Interim Report). And a recent survey of 650 Los Angeles Police Department officers found that 25 percent felt that "'racial bias (prejudice) on the part of officers toward minority citizens currently exists and contributes to a negative interaction between police and the community.'" Report of the Independent Comm'n on the Los Angeles Police Department 69 (1991); see also *United States Comm'n on Civil Rights, Racial and Ethnic Tensions in American Communities: Poverty, Inequality and Discrimination, The Los Angeles Report* 26 (June 1999).

New Jersey's attorney general, in a recent investigation into allegations of racial profiling on the New Jersey Turnpike, concluded that "minority motorists have been treated differently [by New Jersey State Troopers] than non-minority motorists during the course of traffic stops on the New Jersey Turnpike." "[T]he problem of disparate treatment is real—not imagined," declared the attorney general. Not surprisingly, the report concluded that this disparate treatment "engender[s] feelings of fear, resentment, hostility, and mistrust by minority citizens." See *Interim Report* 4, 7. Recently, the United States Department of Justice, citing this very evidence, announced that it would appoint an outside monitor to oversee the actions of the New Jersey state police and ensure that it enacts policy changes advocated by the Interim Report, and keeps records on racial statistics and traffic stops. See Kocieniewski, "U. S. Will Monitor New Jersey Police on Race Profiling," *New York Times,* December 23, 1999, p. 1.

The State, along with the majority of the Court, relies as well on the assumption that [Wardlow's flight] occurred in a high crime area. Even if that assumption is accurate, it is insufficient because even in a high crime neighborhood unprovoked flight does not invariably lead to reasonable suspicion. On the contrary, because many factors providing innocent motivations for unprovoked flight are concentrated in high crime areas, the character of the neighborhood arguably makes an inference of guilt less appropriate, rather than more so. Like unprovoked flight itself, presence in a high crime neighborhood is a fact too generic and susceptible to innocent explanation to satisfy the reasonable suspicion inquiry.

It is the State's burden to articulate facts sufficient to support reasonable suspicion. In my judgment, Illinois has failed to discharge that burden. I am not persuaded that the mere fact that someone standing on a sidewalk looked in the direction of a passing car before starting to run is sufficient to justify a forcible stop and frisk.

▼▲▼

Note the difference in tone between Chief Justice Rehnquist's opinion for the majority in *Wardlow,* which viewed the rights of the police in this case as a valid extension of *Terry* v. *Ohio* and made no reference to Wardlow's race, and Justice Stevens's dissent, which referred to the long-standing distrust between many police departments and minority citizens. In a separate footnote, Stevens referred to New Jersey's recent problems with racial profiling by state troopers and the fact that the United States Department of Justice would begin monitoring the New Jersey state police. Stevens's dissent in *Wardlow* is also a good example of how the justices often use such opinions to draw attention to facts and issues that they hope will be addressed in future cases or subsequent legislation arising from the case. Indeed, in some ways, the issues raised in *Terry* had not changed that much, with the safety needs of the police pitted against the nation's unfortunate history of racial discrimination by law enforcement authorities.

The Exclusionary Rule

In December 1911, United States Marshals entered the home of Fremont Weeks, who worked for an express mail company in Kansas City, Missouri. Earlier that day, Weeks had been arrested by local police officers for sending lottery tickets through the United States mail service. The marshals knew that the Kansas City police, who had received a tip identifying Weeks as a courier of illegal lottery tickets, were going to arrest him while he was working at Union Station, the city's main train terminal. Thanks to a neighbor, the marshals learned where Weeks hid the spare key to his apartment. The marshals knocked on Weeks's door, although they knew he was not home. After they entered, the marshals seized Weeks's letters, books, money, papers, notes, loan slips, stock certificates, insurance policies, candies, and clothes. The marshals ultimately found correspondence involving illegal transactions, IOUs, and lottery tickets. The search of Weeks's home and the seizure of the incriminating evidence took place without a warrant.

Weeks challenged both the warrantless search of his home and the admission of the seized evidence against him as unconstitutional under the Fourth Amendment. In essence, Weeks argued that any evidence seized during a warrantless search of an individual's home amounted to property theft and thus could not be used in a criminal proceeding. Ultimately, a unanimous Court ruled, in *Weeks* v. *United States* (1914), that evidence obtained in violation of the Fourth Amendment could not be used against a criminal defendant. The Court's justification for creating this exclusionary rule was rooted in the notion that illegally seized evidence was a form of self-incrimination, which the Fifth Amendment prohibits. Also critical in the Court's development of the exclusionary rule was the emphasis during the late nineteenth and early twentieth centuries on the centrality of property rights in constitutional theory. This combination of concerns led Justice William R. Day to conclude that

> If letters and private documents can thus be seized and held and used as evidence against a citizen accused of an offense, the protection of the Fourth Amendment declaring his right to be secure against such searches and seizures is of no value, and, so far as those thus placed are concerned, might as well be stricken from the Constitution. The efforts of the courts and their officials to bring the guilty to punishment, praiseworthy as they are, are not to be aided by the sacrifice of those great principles established by years of endeavor and suffering which have resulted in their embodiment in the fundamental law of the land.[27]

Weeks was a substantial departure from how American courts had understood the use of illegally seized evidence in a criminal prosecution. In 1822, Justice Joseph Story reached just this question when deciding a case in which the defendant made an argument for the exclusion of illegally obtained evidence against him:

> In the ordinary administration of municipal law the right of using evidence does not depend, nor, as far as I have any recollection, has ever been supposed to depend upon the lawfulness or unlawfulness of the mode, by which it is obtained. . . . In many instances, and especially in trials for crimes, evidence is often obtained from the possession of the offender by force or by contrivances, which one could not easily reconcile to a delicate sense of propriety, or support upon the foundations of municipal law. Yet I am not aware, that such evidence has upon that account ever been dismissed for incompetency.[28]

Modern skeptics of the exclusionary rule also point out that, even prior to Justice Story's opinion, the Framers never considered the Fourth Amendment to require the exclusion of illegally seized evidence. Moreover, neither British common law nor judicial decisions recognized the exclusion of evidence as a remedy for unreasonable searches and seizures. Criminals convicted with illegally seized evidence instead relied upon civil remedies, or lawsuits against the police, tried before juries, to hold the government accountable for unreasonable searches and seizures. Until *Weeks,* no federal court had ruled that the Fourth Amendment required the exclusion of evidence obtained during an unreasonable search and seizure. *Weeks,* then, was not only an innovative ruling in the law of criminal procedure, it marked a clear departure from the settled Anglo-American approach to enforcing the guarantee against unreasonable searches and seizures through civil action.[29]

By the late 1940s, criminal defense lawyers and reform-minded groups had started pushing for the application of the Fourth Amendment's guarantee against unreasonable searches and seizures, complete with exclusionary rule, to the states through the Due Process Clause of the Fourteenth Amendment. In *Wolf* v. *Colorado* (1949), the Court declined the invitation to make the exclusionary rule applicable to the states. Instead, the Court ruled that the Bill of Rights guaranteed only a "similar" right of fundamental fairness in the criminal process, including freedom from unreasonable searches and seizures, in state proceedings. In principle, the Court's opinion brought the Fourth Amendment's core guarantee against unreasonable searches and seizures to the states. Since *Wolf* did not include the exclusionary rule, however, the ruling offered no real enforcement measure to constrain state authorities.

Of greater significance in *Wolf* was that it permitted federal courts to accept evidence illegally gathered by state law enforcement authorities as long as no federal authorities had been involved. This rule was commonly referred to as the *silver platter doctrine,* since it allowed state authorities to "serve up" illegal evidence to federal courts without having to worry about its admissibility. The Court had approved this double standard in the rules of evidence in two 1927 decisions, *Byars* v. *United States* and *Gambino* v. *United States,* both of which involved enforcement of the Eighteenth Amendment (1920), which established Prohibition (later overturned by the Twenty-First Amendment in 1933).[30] In each case, the Court approved the admission of evidence into federal courts that had been illegally obtained by state law enforcement authorities. The silver platter doctrine stood until 1960, when the Court, in *Elkins* v. *United States,* ruled that permitting federal courts to consider evidence illegally obtained by state authorities undermined important principles of federalism.[31] Still, *Elkins* did not reach the question of the exclusionary rule's applicability to the states.

Unlike the expansion in civil rights and liberties that had occurred alongside the nationalization of the other areas of the Bill of Rights, the criminal procedure cases that ultimately revolutionized the Court's approach to the Fourth, Fifth, and Sixth Amendments were not the product of an interest group–sponsored litigation campaign. Rather, as political scientist Richard C. Cortner has noted, "the Court itself pushed the nationalization process by reaching out in some cases . . . or by directing in other cases that the arguments of counsel focus upon the issues of nationalization."[32] As discussed earlier in this chapter, organized interests have been frequent participants as *amici curiae* in the Court's major decisions on the Fourth Amendment, and played a crucial role in shaping the contours of debate in Fourth Amendment litigation. *Mapp* v. *Ohio* (1961), the Court's landmark decision making the exclusionary rule applicable to the states, offers a splendid example of how groups can shape the dynamics of the Court's decision-making process even when they are not a principal party in the case.

Mapp v. *Ohio*

367 U.S. 643 (1961)

When members of the Cleveland police force rang the doorbell of Dollree Mapp, better known as "Dolly," on the afternoon of May 23, 1957, they knew full well that someone with an advanced degree in street smarts was waiting inside. Once the girlfriend of Archie Moore, the world light-heavyweight boxing champion, Mapp enjoyed a reputation for being well connected in Cleveland's underworld. Indeed, the Cleveland newspapers had described her as a "confidante of numbers racketeers." Earlier that morning, the police had received an anonymous tip that a fugitive wanted in the recent bombing of boxing promoter Don King's house was hiding out in Mapp's apartment. Knowing that something was up, Mapp leaned out her window and told police they could not enter without a search warrant. By 4 P.M., the police returned with what they claimed was a warrant to search Mapp's apartment. Having consulted with her attorney, Mapp still refused to allow the police to enter. At this point, the police forced down the door leading to Mapp's apartment. When Mapp met the police in front of her apartment and demanded to see the warrant, the police waived a piece of paper in front of her. Mapp seized the paper and shoved it down her blouse. After a struggle, the police retrieved the warrant and handcuffed Dolly Mapp.[33]

A search of Mapp's apartment did not turn up the bombing suspect, but police did find several other illegal items: several sexually explicit books, photographs, and drawings. Police searched the basement of the apartment house and found a trunk containing betting and numbers slips. A separate search of the first floor apartment found the bombing suspect, Virgil Ogiltree, hiding in a closet. Mapp later admitted knowing that Ogiltree was downstairs. Mapp was arrested on misdemeanor gambling charges but later acquitted. She was indicted separately under an Ohio law banning the possession of lewd, lascivious, or obscene materials. Mapp's lawyer, A. L. Kearns, unsuccessfully contested the admission of the "obscene" materials as the product of an illegal search. During her trial, the police were unable to produce the search warrant, which was never found, that Mapp insisted was a fabrication.

After the Court agreed to hear Mapp's appeal, Kearns confined his argument to the obscenity charge that had been filed against his client, claiming that the Ohio law violated the First Amendment. Nowhere in his brief did he mention whether the evidence seized from Mapp's apartment should be held inadmissible based on the *Weeks* exclusionary rule. This omission put Kearns in hot water during oral argument, as it was clear from the start the Court was interested in the potential application of the exclusionary rule to the states. During his exchanges with the justices, Kearns could not answer even most basic questions about *Weeks, Wolf,* or any other relevant Fourth Amendment decisions. At one point, Kearns told Chief Justice Earl Warren, "I'm very sorry, I don't have all the facts in the case, only the conclusion that I reached—came to."[34]

Fortunately for Kearns, he had agreed to allot some of his oral argument time to the ACLU's lawyer, Bernard Berkman. The closing section of the ACLU's *amicus* brief had asked the Court to reconsider *Wolf* and apply the exclusionary rule to the states. During oral argument, Berkman told the Court, "We have no hesitancy about asking the Court to reconsider [*Wolf*], because we think [the exclusionary rule] is a fundamental part of due process."

The Court's decision was 6 to 3. Justice Clark delivered the opinion of the Court. Justices Black, Douglas, and Stewart filed separate concurring opinions. Justice Harlan, joined by Justices Frankfurter and Whittaker, dissented.

MR. JUSTICE CLARK delivered the opinion of the Court.

I

Seventy-five years ago, in *Boyd* v. *United States,* considering the Fourth and Fifth Amendments as running "almost into each other" on the facts before it, this Court held that the doctrines of those Amendments

> apply to all invasions on the part of the government and its employees of the sanctity of a man's home and the privacies of life. It is not the breaking of his doors, and the rummaging of his drawers, that constitutes the essence of the offence; but it is the invasion of his inde-

> feasible right of personal security, personal liberty and private property. . . . Breaking into a house and opening boxes and drawers are circumstances of aggravation; but any forcible and compulsory extortion of a man's own testimony or of his private papers to be used as evidence to convict him of crime or to forfeit his goods, is within the condemnation . . . [of those Amendments].

The Court noted that

> constitutional provisions for the security of person and property should be liberally construed. . . . It is the duty of courts to be watchful for the constitutional rights of the citizen, and against any stealthy encroachments thereon.

In this jealous regard for maintaining the integrity of individual rights, the Court gave life to Madison's prediction that

> independent tribunals of justice . . . will be naturally led to resist every encroachment upon rights expressly stipulated for in the Constitution by the declaration of rights.

Concluding, the Court specifically referred to the use of the evidence there seized as "unconstitutional."

Less than 30 years after *Boyd,* this Court, in *Weeks* v. *United States* (1914), stated that the "Fourth Amendment put the courts of the United States and Federal officials, in the exercise of their power and authority, under limitations and restraints [and] . . . forever secure[d] the people, their persons, houses, papers and effects against all unreasonable searches and seizures under the guise of law . . . , and the duty of giving to it force and effect is obligatory upon all entrusted under our Federal system with the enforcement of the laws."

Specifically dealing with the use of the evidence unconstitutionally seized, the Court concluded

> If letters and private documents can thus be seized and held and used in evidence against a citizen accused of an offense, the protection of the Fourth Amendment declaring his right to be secure against such searches and seizures is of no value, and, so far as those thus placed are concerned, might as well be stricken from the Constitution. The efforts of the courts and their officials to bring the guilty to punishment, praiseworthy as they are, are not to be aided by the sacrifice of those great principles established by years of endeavor and suffering which have resulted in their embodiment in the fundamental law of the land.

Finally, the Court in that case clearly stated that use of the seized evidence involved "a denial of the constitutional rights of the accused." Thus, in the year 1914, in the *Weeks* case, this Court "for the first time" held that, "in a federal prosecution, the Fourth Amendment barred the use of evidence secured through an illegal search and seizure." This Court has ever since required of federal law officers a strict adherence to that command which this Court has held to be a clear, specific, and constitutionally required—even if judicially implied—deterrent safeguard without insistence upon which the Fourth Amendment would have been reduced to "a form of words." . . .

There are in the cases of this Court some passing references to the *Weeks* rule as being one of evidence. But the plain and unequivocal language of *Weeks*—and its later paraphrase in *Wolf*—to the effect that the *Weeks* rule is of constitutional origin, remains entirely undisturbed. . . .

II

In 1949, 35 years after *Weeks* was announced, this Court, in *Wolf* v. *Colorado,* again for the first time, discussed the effect of the Fourth Amendment upon the States through the operation of the Due Process Clause of the Fourteenth Amendment. It said:

> [W]e have no hesitation in saying that, were a State affirmatively to sanction such police incursion into privacy, it would run counter to the guaranty of the Fourteenth Amendment.

Nevertheless, after declaring that the "security of one's privacy against arbitrary intrusion by the police" is "implicit in 'the concept of ordered liberty' and, as such, enforceable against the States through the Due Process Clause," *Palko* v. *Connecticut* (1937), and announcing that it "stoutly adhere[d]" to the *Weeks* decision, the Court decided that the *Weeks* exclusionary rule would not then be imposed upon the States as "an essential ingredient of the right." The Court's reasons for not considering essential to the right to privacy, as a curb imposed upon the States by the Due Process Clause, that which decades before had been posited as part and parcel of the Fourth Amendment's limitation upon federal encroachment of individual privacy, were bottomed on factual considerations.

While they are not basically relevant to a decision that the exclusionary rule is an essential ingredient of the Fourth Amendment as the right it embodies is vouchsafed against the States by the Due Process Clause, we will consider the current validity of the factual grounds upon which *Wolf* was based.

The Court in *Wolf* first stated that "[t]he contrariety of views of the States" on the adoption of the exclusionary rule of *Weeks* was "particularly impressive" and, in this connection, that it could not "brush aside the experience of States which deem the incidence of such conduct by the police too slight to call for a deterrent remedy . . . by overriding the [States'] relevant rules of evidence."

While, in 1949, prior to the *Wolf* case, almost two-thirds of the States were opposed to the use of the exclusionary rule, now, despite the *Wolf* case, more than half of those since passing upon it, by their own legislative or judicial decision, have wholly or partly adopted or adhered to the *Weeks* rule. . . .

It therefore plainly appears that the factual considerations supporting the failure of the *Wolf* Court to include the *Weeks* exclusionary rule when it recognized the enforceability of the right to privacy against the States in 1949, while not basically relevant to the constitutional consideration, could not, in any analysis, now be deemed controlling.

III

Today we once again examine *Wolf's* constitutional documentation of the right to privacy free from unreasonable state intrusion, and, after its dozen years on our books, are led by it to close the only courtroom door remaining open to evidence secured by official lawlessness in flagrant abuse of that basic right, reserved to all persons as a specific guarantee against that very same unlawful conduct. We hold that all evidence obtained by searches and seizures in violation of the Constitution is, by that same authority, inadmissible in a state court.

IV

Since the Fourth Amendment's right of privacy has been declared enforceable against the States through the Due Process Clause of the Fourteenth, it is enforceable against them by the same sanction of exclusion as is used against the Federal Government. Were it otherwise, then, just as without the *Weeks* rule the assurance against unreasonable federal searches and seizures would be "a form of words," valueless and undeserving of mention in a perpetual charter of inestimable human liberties, so too, without that rule, the freedom from state invasions of privacy would be so ephemeral and so neatly severed from its conceptual nexus with the freedom from all brutish means of coercing evidence as not to merit this Court's high regard as a freedom "implicit in the concept of ordered liberty." At the time that the Court held in *Wolf* that the Amendment was applicable to the States through the Due Process Clause, the cases of this Court, as we have seen, had steadfastly held that as to federal officers the Fourth Amendment included the exclusion of the evidence seized in violation of its provisions. . . . Therefore, in extending the substantive protections of due process to all constitutionally unreasonable searches—state or federal—it was logically and constitutionally necessary that the exclusion doctrine—an essential part of the right to privacy—be also insisted upon as an essential ingredient of the right newly recognized by the *Wolf* case. In short, the admission of the new constitutional right by *Wolf* could not consistently tolerate denial of its most important constitutional privilege, namely, the exclusion of the evidence which an accused had been forced to give by reason of the unlawful seizure. To hold otherwise is to grant the right but, in reality, to withhold its privilege and enjoyment. . . .

Indeed, we are aware of no restraint, similar to that rejected today, conditioning the enforcement of any other basic constitutional right. The right to privacy, no less important than any other right carefully and particularly reserved to the people, would stand in marked contrast to all other rights declared as "basic to a free society." This Court has not hesitated to enforce as strictly against the States as it does against the Federal Government the rights of free speech and of a free press, the rights to notice and to a fair, public trial, including, as it does, the right not to be convicted by use of a coerced confession, however logically relevant it be, and without regard to its reliability. And nothing could be more certain than that, when a coerced confession is involved, "the relevant rules of evidence" are overridden without regard to "the incidence of such conduct by the police," slight or frequent. Why should not the same rule apply to what is tantamount to coerced testimony by way of unconstitutional seizure of goods, papers, effects, documents, etc.? We find that, as to the Federal Government, the Fourth and Fifth Amendments and, as to the States, the freedom from unconscionable invasions of privacy and the freedom from convictions based upon coerced confessions do enjoy an "intimate relation" in their perpetuation of "principles of humanity and civil liberty [secured] . . . only after years of struggle." They express "supplementing phases of the same constitutional purpose to maintain inviolate large areas of personal privacy." The philosophy of each Amendment and of each freedom is complementary to, although not dependent upon, that of the other in its sphere of influence—the very least that together they assure in either sphere is that no man is to be convicted on unconstitutional evidence.

V

Moreover, our holding that the exclusionary rule is an essential part of both the Fourth and Fourteenth Amendments is not only the logical dictate of prior cases, but it also makes very good sense. There is no war between the Constitution and common sense. Presently, a federal prosecutor may make no use of evidence illegally seized, but a State's attorney across the street may, although he supposedly is operating under the enforceable prohibitions of the same Amendment. Thus, the State, by admitting evidence unlawfully seized, serves to encourage disobedience to the Federal Constitution which it is bound to uphold. . . .

There are those who say, as did Justice (then Judge) Cardozo, that, under our constitutional exclusionary doctrine, "[t]he criminal is to go free because the constable has blundered." In some cases, this will undoubtedly be the result. But, as was said in *Elkins*, "there is another consideration—the imperative of judicial integrity." The criminal goes free, if he must, but it is the law that sets him free. Nothing can destroy a government more quickly than its failure to observe its own laws, or worse, its disregard of the charter of its own existence. As Mr. Justice Brandeis, dissenting, said in *Olmstead* v. *United States*, "[o]ur Government is the potent, the omnipresent teacher. For good or for ill, it teaches the whole people by its example. . . . If the Government becomes a lawbreaker, it breeds contempt for law; it invites every man to become a law unto himself; it invites anarchy." . . .

The ignoble shortcut to conviction left open to the State tends to destroy the entire system of constitutional restraints on which the liberties of the people rest. Having once recognized that the right to privacy embodied in the Fourth Amendment is enforceable against the States, and that the right to be secure against rude invasions of privacy by state officers is, therefore, constitutional in origin, we can no longer permit that right to remain an empty promise. Because it is enforceable in the same manner and to like effect as other basic rights secured by the Due Process Clause, we can no longer permit it to be revocable at the whim of any police officer who, in the name of law enforcement itself, chooses to suspend its enjoyment. Our decision, founded on reason and truth, gives to the individual no more than that which the Constitution guarantees him, to the police officer no less than that to which honest law enforcement is entitled, and, to the courts, that judicial integrity so necessary in the true administration of justice.

The judgment of the Supreme Court of Ohio is reversed, and the cause remanded for further proceedings not inconsistent with this opinion.

MR. JUSTICE BLACK, concurring.

I am still not persuaded that the Fourth Amendment, standing alone, would be enough to bar the introduction into evidence against an accused of papers and effects seized from him in violation of its commands. For the Fourth Amendment does not itself contain any provision expressly precluding the use of such evidence, and I am extremely doubtful that such a provision could properly be inferred from nothing more than the basic command against unreasonable searches and seizures. Reflection on the problem, however, in the light of cases coming before the Court since *Wolf*, has led me to conclude that, when the Fourth Amendment's ban against unreasonable searches and seizures is considered together with the Fifth Amendment's ban against compelled self-incrimination, a constitutional basis emerges which not only justifies, but actually requires, the exclusionary rule.

MR. JUSTICE HARLAN, whom MR. JUSTICE FRANKFURTER and MR. JUSTICE WHITTAKER join, dissenting.

In overruling the *Wolf* case, the Court, in my opinion, has forgotten the sense of judicial restraint which, with due regard for *stare decisis*, is one element that should enter into deciding whether a past decision of this Court should be overruled. Apart from that, I also believe that the *Wolf* rule represents sounder Constitutional doctrine than the new rule which now replaces it. . . .

I think it fair to say that five members of this Court have simply "reached out" to overrule *Wolf*. With all respect, for the views of the majority, and recognizing that *stare decisis* carries different weight in Constitutional adjudication than it does in nonconstitutional decision, I can perceive no justification for regarding this case as an appropriate occasion for reexamining *Wolf*. . . .

I would not impose upon the States this federal exclusionary remedy. The reasons given by the majority for now suddenly turning its back on *Wolf* seem to me notably unconvincing.

First, it is said that "the factual grounds upon which *Wolf* was based" have since changed, in that more States now follow the *Weeks* exclusionary rule than was so at the time *Wolf* was decided. While that is true, a recent survey indicates that, at present, one-half of the States still adhere to the common law non-exclusionary rule, and one, Maryland, retains the rule as to felonies. But, in any case, surely all this is beside the point, as the majority itself indeed seems to recognize. Our concern here, as it was in *Wolf,* is not with the desirability of that rule, but only with the question whether the States are Constitutionally free to follow it or not as they may themselves determine, and the relevance of the disparity of views among the States on this point lies simply in the fact that the judgment involved is a debatable one. Moreover, the very fact on which the majority relies, instead of lending support to what is now being done, points away from the need of replacing voluntary state action with federal compulsion.

The preservation of a proper balance between state and federal responsibility in the administration of criminal justice demands patience on the part of those who might like to see things move faster among the States in this respect. Problems of criminal law enforcement vary widely from State to State. One State, in considering the totality of its legal picture, may conclude that the need for embracing the *Weeks* rule is pressing because other remedies are unavailable or inadequate to secure compliance with the substantive Constitutional principle involved. Another, though equally solicitous of Constitutional rights, may choose to pursue one purpose at a time, allowing all evidence relevant to guilt to be brought into a criminal trial, and dealing with Constitutional infractions by other means. Still another may consider the exclusionary rule too rough-and-ready a remedy, in that it reaches only unconstitutional intrusions which eventuate in criminal prosecution of the victims. Further, a State after experimenting with the *Weeks* rule for a time may, because of unsatisfactory experience with it, decide to revert to a non-exclusionary rule. And so on. . . .

I regret that I find so unwise in principle and so inexpedient in policy a decision motivated by the high purpose of increasing respect for Constitutional rights. But, in the last analysis, I think this Court can increase respect for the Constitution only if it rigidly respects the limitations which the Constitution places upon it, and respects as well the principles inherent in its own processes. In the present case, I think we exceed both, and that our voice becomes only a voice of power, not of reason.

Dollree Mapp, left, one of the most well-known figures in Cleveland's underworld during the 1950s and early 1960s, still managed to find trouble even after the Supreme Court threw out her conviction in 1961 on the grounds that police had obtained evidence against her without a proper warrant. Here, Mapp is being escorted into the headquarters of New York City's 105th precinct for questioning on racketeering charges.
AP/Wide World Photos

By bringing the exclusionary rule to the states, the Court sent a clear signal that a major revolution in American criminal procedure was on the horizon, a shift that will receive even more attention in Chapters 8 and 9. Indeed, Justice Abe Fortas, appointed to the Court in 1962, later commented that "the most radical decision in recent times was *Mapp* v. *Ohio*."[35] In addition to the consequences that the Court's opinion had for federalism, the extension of the exclusionary rule to the states touched off a major debate about the potential consequences of allowing, in Justice Tom Clark's words, "the criminal . . . to go free because the constable has blundered." Chief Justice Warren selected Clark to write *Mapp* because he knew the decision to apply the exclusionary rule to the states would be controversial, and believed the former Texas attorney general carried more credibility in the law enforcement community than any of the other justices.[36] To exclusionary rule skeptics,

Mapp heightened the possibility that more criminals would end up on the streets because of flawed searches, since the vast majority of criminal prosecutions take place at the state and local level.

Since *Mapp,* critics and supporters of the exclusionary rule have debated its constitutional legitimacy, impact on the ability of law enforcement officers to obtain evidence, and deterrent effect on criminal behavior. Since the early 1970s, the Court's decisions on the exclusionary rule have consistently favored a narrow reading of its application to evidence seized beyond the scope of the warrant. In one such case, *Stone* v. *Powell* (1976), the Court employed a cost-benefit approach to hold that the costs of excluding incriminating evidence against a criminal defendant far outweighed the potential deterrent effect it had on police misconduct. *Powell* did not deal directly with the admissibility of illegally obtained evidence in a criminal proceeding. Rather, *Powell* involved a petition for federal habeas corpus review based on a Fourth Amendment violation during a state criminal proceeding. Granting habeas corpus relief, the Court noted, would go against the principle of proportionality "essential to the concept of justice."[37]

Both these concepts—cost-benefit analysis and proportionality—were central in the Court's decision in *United States* v. *Leon* (1984). There the Court recognized a "good faith" exception to the exclusionary rule, which many law enforcement groups, such as the AELE, had argued for as far back as *Powell. Leon* attracted numerous *amicus* briefs from the exclusionary rule's supporters and opponents. Who do you think offers the more sound analysis of the exclusionary rule, Justice White, who wrote for the Court's majority, or dissenting Justices Brennan and Stevens?

United States v. *Leon*

468 U.S. 897 (1984)

In August 1981, a tip from a local confidential informant, well known on the streets as a petty, low-life drug user and criminal, to the Burbank, California, police gave this small Los Angeles suburb a major national profile. The informant told police that two persons known to him as "Armando" and "Patsy" were selling large amounts of cocaine and other narcotics in their Burbank home. The Burbank police's decision to act on the informant's tip put into motion a series of events that resulted in the "good faith" exception to the exclusionary rule established in *Weeks* and applied to the states in *Mapp*.

The police began an extensive investigation into the drug dealing operation of "Armando" and "Patsy." They later identified two cars parked outside the Burbank home identified by the informant as belonging to Armando Sanchez and Patsy Stewart, and a third automobile belonging to Ricardo Del Castillo. Sanchez and Del Castillo had previously been arrested on marijuana possession charges, while Stewart had no prior criminal record. Observation of Del Castillo's visits to Sanchez and Stewart's house led them to another drug dealer, Alberto Leon, whom Del Castillo had listed as his employer on a probation record. Police in Glendale, another Los Angeles suburb, had received information from an informant that Leon, whose police record included an arrest on drug charges, was also involved in the drug operation. Leon was also living in Burbank. Placing all four persons under extensive surveillance, the police observed numerous visits of persons known for their involvement in drug dealing shuttling between the two Burbank homes. Police later observed Sanchez and Stewart board separate flights to Miami and return to Los Angeles together. A search of their luggage turned up a small amount of marijuana, but they were released.

After the airport confrontation, a Burbank police officer with an extensive background in narcotics trafficking, Cyril Rombach, applied for a warrant to search the residences of Sanchez and Stewart, Leon, and a third party whose condominium had been the site of several comings-and-goings of related drug transactions. The subsequent search turned up large amounts of drugs in the homes and cars of Sanchez, Stewart, Del Castillo, Leon, and several others. They were arrested and indicted on several counts of cocaine possession with intent to distribute.

A federal district court suppressed the evidence, ruling that the informant's credibility did not justify probable cause to follow the defendants' trails and subsequently search their homes and cars. Officer Rombach's belief that he was acting with a proper warrant could not overcome the defective reasons for issuing it in the first place. The Reagan administration asked the Supreme Court to hear *Leon* to determine if the Fourth Amendment permitted a "good faith" exception to the exclusionary rule. U.S. Attorney General Edwin Meese had openly criticized the Court's decision in *Mapp,* and pledged that the Justice Department would make every effort to have the 1961 ruling overturned. Noting the pro-prosecution leanings of the Court's recent Fourth Amendment decisions, the Justice Department decided to place its weight behind *Leon* and come out directly for the "good faith" exception.

The Reagan administration's action was met with a powerful response. A coalition of Southern California's most prominent criminal defense lawyers affiliated with the ACLU, the National Association of Criminal Defense Lawyers, and the National Association of Trial Lawyers argued against the "good faith" exception. While the nation's district attorneys and several state attorneys general supported the Justice Department's position, the National Legal Aid and Defender Association and the NAACP LDF filed *amicus* briefs in support of Leon.

The Court's decision was 6 to 3. Justice White delivered the opinion of the Court. Justice Brennan, joined by Justice Marshall, dissented. Justice Stevens also dissented.

▼▲▼

JUSTICE WHITE delivered the opinion of the Court.

This case presents the question whether the Fourth Amendment exclusionary rule should be modified so as not to bar the use in the prosecution's case in chief of evidence obtained by officers acting in reasonable reliance on a search warrant issued by a detached and neutral magistrate but ultimately found to be unsupported by probable cause. To resolve this question, we must consider once again the tension between the sometimes competing goals of, on the one hand, deterring official misconduct and removing inducements to unreasonable invasions of privacy and, on the other, establishing procedures under which criminal defendants are "acquitted or convicted on the basis of all the evidence which exposes the truth." . . .

The Fourth Amendment contains no provision expressly precluding the use of evidence obtained in violation of its commands, and an examination of its origin and purposes makes clear that the use of fruits of a past unlawful search or seizure "work[s] no new Fourth Amendment wrong," *United States* v. *Calandra* (1974). The wrong condemned by the Amendment is "fully accomplished" by the unlawful search or seizure itself, and the exclusionary rule is neither intended nor able to "cure the invasion of the defendant's rights which he has already suffered." The rule thus operates as "a judicially created remedy designed to safeguard Fourth Amendment rights generally through its deterrent effect, rather than a personal constitutional right of the party aggrieved."

Whether the exclusionary sanction is appropriately imposed in a particular case, our decisions make clear, is "an issue separate from the question whether the Fourth Amendment rights of the party seeking to invoke the rule were violated by police conduct."

Only the former question is currently before us, and it must be resolved by weighing the costs and benefits of preventing the use in the prosecution's case in chief of inherently trustworthy tangible evidence obtained in reliance on a search warrant issued by a detached and neutral magistrate that ultimately is found to be defective.

The substantial social costs exacted by the exclusionary rule for the vindication of Fourth Amendment rights have long been a source of concern. . . . An objectionable collateral consequence of this interference with the criminal justice system's truthfinding function is that some guilty defendants may go free or receive reduced sentences as a result of favorable plea bargains. Particularly when law enforcement officers have acted in objective good faith or their transgressions have been minor, the magnitude of the benefit conferred on such guilty defendants offends basic concepts of the criminal justice system. Indiscriminate application of the exclusionary rule, therefore, may well "generat[e] disrespect for the law and administration of justice." . . .

When considering the use of evidence obtained in violation of the Fourth Amendment in the prosecution's case in chief, moreover, we have declined to adopt a *per se* or "but for" rule that would render inadmissible any evidence that came to light through a chain of causation that began with an illegal arrest. We also have held that a witness' testimony may be admitted even when his identity was discovered in an unconstitutional search. The perception underlying these decisions—that the connection between police misconduct and evidence of crime may be sufficiently attenuated to permit the use of that evidence at trial—is a product of considerations relating to the exclusionary rule and the constitutional principles it is designed to protect. . . .

The same attention to the purposes underlying the exclusionary rule also has characterized decisions not involving the scope of the rule itself. We have not required suppression of the fruits of a search incident to an arrest made in good faith reliance on a substantive criminal statute that subsequently is declared unconstitutional. Similarly, although the Court has been unwilling to conclude that new Fourth Amendment principles are always to have only prospective effect, no Fourth Amendment decision marking a "clear break with the past" has been applied retroactively. The propriety of retroactive application of a newly announced Fourth Amendment principle, moreover, has been assessed largely in terms of the contribution retroactivity might make to the deterrence of police misconduct.

As yet, we have not recognized any form of good faith exception to the Fourth Amendment exclusionary rule. But the balancing approach that has evolved during the years of experience with the rule provides strong support for the modification currently urged upon us. As we discuss below, our evaluation of the costs and benefits of suppressing reliable physical evidence seized by officers reasonably relying on a warrant issued by a detached and neutral magistrate leads to the conclusion that such evidence should be admissible in the prosecution's case in chief.

Because a search warrant "provides the detached scrutiny of a neutral magistrate, which is a more reliable safeguard against improper searches than the hurried judgment of a law enforcement officer 'engaged in the often competitive enterprise of ferreting out crime,'" we have expressed a strong preference for warrants, and declared that, "in a doubtful or marginal case, a search under a warrant may be sustainable where without one it would fall." Reasonable minds frequently may differ on the question whether a particular affidavit establishes probable cause, and we have thus concluded that the preference for warrants is most appropriately effectuated by according "great deference" to a magistrate's determination.

Deference to the magistrate, however, is not boundless. It is clear, first, that the deference accorded to a magistrate's finding of probable cause does not preclude inquiry into the knowing or reckless falsity of the affidavit on which that determination was based. Second, the courts must also insist that the magistrate purport to "perform his 'neutral and detached' function and not serve merely as a rubber stamp for the police." . . .

Third, reviewing courts will not defer to a warrant based on an affidavit that does not "provide the magistrate with a substantial basis for determining the existence of probable cause." Even if the warrant application was supported by more than a "bare bones" affidavit, a reviewing court may properly conclude that, notwithstanding the deference that magistrates deserve, the warrant was invalid because the magistrate's probable cause determination reflected an improper analysis of the totality of the circumstances, or because the form of the warrant was improper in some respect.

Only in the first of these three situations, however, has the Court set forth a rationale for suppressing evidence obtained pursuant to a search warrant; in the other areas, it has simply excluded such evidence without considering whether Fourth Amendment interests will be advanced. To the extent that proponents of exclusion rely on its behavioral effects on judges and magistrates in these areas, their reliance is misplaced. First, the exclusionary rule is designed to deter police misconduct, rather than to punish the errors of judges and magistrates. Second, there exists no evidence suggesting that judges and magistrates are inclined to ignore or subvert the Fourth Amendment, or that lawlessness among these actors requires application of the extreme sanction of exclusion.

Third, and most important, we discern no basis, and are offered none, for believing that exclusion of evidence seized pursuant to a warrant will have a significant deterrent effect on the issuing judge or magistrate. Many of the factors that indicate that the exclusionary rule cannot provide an effective "special" or "general" deterrent for individual offending law enforcement officers apply as well to judges or magistrates. And, to the extent that the rule is thought to operate as a "systemic" deterrent on a wider audience, it clearly can have no such effect on individuals empowered to issue search warrants. Judges and magistrates are not adjuncts to the law enforcement team; as neutral judicial officers, they have no stake in the outcome of particular criminal prosecutions. The threat of exclusion thus cannot be expected significantly to deter them. Imposition of the exclusionary sanction is not necessary meaningfully to inform judicial officers of their errors, and we cannot conclude that admitting evidence obtained pursuant to a warrant while at the same time declaring that the warrant was somehow defective will in any way reduce judicial officers' professional incentives to comply with the Fourth Amendment, encourage them to repeat their mistakes, or lead to the granting of all colorable warrant requests.

If exclusion of evidence obtained pursuant to a subsequently invalidated warrant is to have any deterrent effect, therefore, it must alter the behavior of individual law enforcement officers or the policies of their departments. One could argue that applying the exclusionary rule in cases where the police failed to demonstrate probable cause in the warrant application deters future inadequate presentations or "magistrate shopping," and thus promotes the ends of the Fourth Amendment. Suppressing evidence obtained pursuant to a technically defective warrant supported by probable cause also might encourage officers to scrutinize more closely the form of the warrant, and to point out suspected judicial errors. We find such arguments speculative, and conclude that suppression of evidence obtained pursuant to a warrant should be ordered only on a case-by-case basis, and only in those unusual cases in which exclusion will further the purposes of the exclusionary rule.

We have frequently questioned whether the exclusionary rule can have any deterrent effect when the offending officers acted in the objectively reasonable belief that their conduct did not violate the Fourth Amendment. . . . But even assuming that the rule effectively deters some police misconduct and provides incentives for the law enforcement profession as a whole to conduct itself in accord with the Fourth Amendment, it cannot be expected, and should not be applied, to deter objectively reasonable law enforcement activity. . . .

We conclude that the marginal or nonexistent benefits produced by suppressing evidence obtained in objectively reasonable reliance on a subsequently invalidated search warrant cannot justify the substantial costs of exclusion. We do not suggest, however, that exclusion is always inappropriate in cases where an officer has obtained a warrant and abided by its terms. . . . Nevertheless, the officer's reliance on the magistrate's probable cause determination and on the technical sufficiency of the warrant he issues must be objectively reasonable, and it is clear that, in some circumstances the officer will have no reasonable grounds for believing that the warrant was properly issued.

Suppression therefore remains an appropriate remedy if the magistrate or judge in issuing a warrant was misled by information in an affidavit that the affiant knew was false or would have known was false except for his reckless disregard of the truth. . . . Nor would an officer manifest objective good faith in relying on a warrant based on an affidavit "so lacking in indicia of probable cause as to render official belief in its existence entirely unreasonable." Finally, depending on the circumstances of the particular case, a warrant may be so facially deficient—*i.e.*, in failing to particularize the place to be searched or the things to be seized—that the executing officers cannot reasonably presume it to be valid.

In so limiting the suppression remedy, we leave untouched the probable cause standard and the various requirements for a valid warrant. Other objections to the modification of the Fourth Amendment exclusionary rule we consider to be insubstantial. The good faith exception for searches conducted pursuant to warrants is not intended to signal our unwillingness strictly to enforce the requirements of the Fourth Amendment, and we do not believe that it will have this effect. As we have already suggested, the good faith exception, turning as it does on objective reasonableness, should not be difficult to apply in practice. When officers have acted pursuant to a warrant, the prosecution should ordinarily be able to establish objective good faith without a substantial expenditure of judicial time. . . .

In the absence of an allegation that the magistrate abandoned his detached and neutral role, suppression is appropriate only if the officers were dishonest or reckless in preparing their affidavit or could not have harbored an objectively reasonable belief in the existence of probable cause. Only respondent Leon has contended that no reasonably well trained police officer could have believed that there existed probable cause to search his house; significantly, the other respondents advance no comparable argument. Officer Rombach's application for a warrant clearly was supported by much more than a "bare bones" affidavit. The affidavit related the results of an extensive investigation and, as the opinions of the divided panel of the Court of Appeals make clear, provided evidence sufficient to create disagreement among thoughtful and competent judges as to the existence of probable cause. Under these circumstances, the officers' reliance on the magistrate's determination of probable cause was objectively reasonable, and application of the extreme sanction of exclusion is inappropriate.

Accordingly, the judgment of the Court of Appeals is
Reversed.

JUSTICE BRENNAN, with whom JUSTICE MARSHALL joins, dissenting.

The Court seeks to justify [today's] result on the ground that the "costs" of adhering to the exclusionary rule in cases like those before us exceed the "benefits." But the language of deterrence and of cost/benefit analysis, if used indiscriminately, can have a narcotic effect. It creates an illusion of technical precision and ineluctability. It suggests that not only constitutional principle but also empirical data support the majority's result. When the Court's analysis is examined carefully, however, it is clear that we have not been treated to an honest assessment of the merits of the exclusionary rule, but have instead been drawn into a curious world where the "costs" of excluding illegally obtained evidence loom to exaggerated heights, and where the "benefits" of such exclusion are made to disappear with a mere wave of the hand.

The majority ignores the fundamental constitutional importance of what is at stake here. While the machinery of law enforcement, and indeed the nature of crime itself, have changed dramatically since the Fourth Amendment became part of the Nation's fundamental law in 1791, what the Framers understood then remains true today—that the task of combating crime and convicting the guilty will in every era seem of such critical and pressing concern that we may be lured by the temptations of expediency into forsaking our commitment to protecting individual liberty and privacy. It was for that very reason that the Framers of the Bill of Rights insisted that law enforcement efforts be permanently and unambiguously restricted in order to preserve personal freedoms. . . .

A proper understanding of the broad purposes sought to be served by the Fourth Amendment demonstrates that the principles embodied in the exclusionary rule rest upon a far firmer constitutional foundation than the shifting sands of the Court's deterrence rationale. But even if I were to accept the Court's chosen method of analyzing the question posed by these cases, I would still conclude that the Court's decision cannot be justified.

The Court holds that physical evidence seized by police officers reasonably relying upon a warrant issued by a detached and neutral magistrate is admissible in the prosecution's case in chief, even though a reviewing court has subsequently determined either that the warrant was defective, or that those officers failed to demonstrate when applying for the warrant that there was probable cause to conduct the search. I have no doubt that these decisions will prove in time to have been a grave mistake. But, as troubling and important as today's new doctrine may be for the administration of criminal justice in this country, the mode of analysis used to generate that doctrine also requires critical examination, for it may prove in the long run to pose the greater threat to our civil liberties.

At bottom, the Court's decision turns on the proposition that the exclusionary rule is merely a "judicially created remedy designed to safeguard Fourth Amendment rights generally through its deterrent effect, rather than a personal constitutional right." The germ of that idea is found in *Wolf* v. *Colorado* (1949), and although I had thought that such a narrow conception of the rule had been forever put to rest by our decision in *Mapp* v. *Ohio* (1961), it has been revived by the present Court and reaches full flower with today's decision. . . .

This reading of the Amendment implies that its proscriptions are directed solely at those government agents who may actually invade an individual's constitutionally protected privacy. The courts are not subject to any direct constitutional duty to exclude illegally obtained evidence, because the question of the admissibility of such evidence is not addressed by the Amendment. This view of the scope of the Amendment relegates the judiciary to the periphery. Because the only constitutionally cognizable injury has already been "fully accomplished" by the police by the time a case comes before the courts, the Constitution is not itself violated if the judge decides to admit the tainted evidence. Indeed, the most the judge can do is wring his hands and hope that perhaps, by excluding such evidence, he can deter future transgressions by the police.

Such a reading appears plausible, because, as critics of the exclusionary rule never tire of repeating, the Fourth Amendment makes no express provision for the exclusion of evidence secured in violation of its commands. A short answer to this claim, of course, is that many of the Constitution's most vital imperatives are stated in general terms, and the task of giving meaning to these precepts is therefore left to subsequent judicial decisionmaking in the context of concrete cases. . . .

A more direct answer may be supplied by recognizing that the Amendment, like other provisions of the Bill of Rights, restrains the power of the government as a whole; it does not specify only a particular agency and exempt all others. The judiciary is responsible, no less than the executive, for ensuring that constitutional rights are respected.

When that fact is kept in mind, the role of the courts and their possible involvement in the concerns of the Fourth Amendment comes into sharper focus. Because seizures are executed principally to secure evidence, and because such evidence generally has utility in our legal system only in the context of a trial supervised by a judge, it is apparent that the admission of illegally obtained evidence implicates the same constitutional concerns as the initial seizure of that evidence. Indeed, by admitting unlawfully seized evidence, the judiciary becomes a part of what is, in fact, a single governmental action prohibited by the terms of the Amendment. Once that connection between the evidence-gathering role of the police and the evidence-admitting function of the courts is acknowledged, the plausibility of the Court's interpretation becomes more suspect. Certainly nothing in the language or history of the Fourth Amendment suggests that a recognition of this evidentiary link between the police and the courts was meant to be foreclosed. It is difficult to give any meaning at all to the limitations imposed by the Amendment if they are read to proscribe only certain conduct by the police, but to allow other agents of the same government to take advantage of evidence secured by the police in violation of its requirements. The Amendment therefore must be read to condemn not only the initial unconstitutional invasion of privacy—which is done, after all, for the purpose of securing evidence—but also the subsequent use of any evidence so obtained.

The Court evades this principle by drawing an artificial line between the constitutional rights and responsibilities that are engaged by actions of the police and those that are engaged when a defendant appears before the courts. According to the Court, the substantive protections of the Fourth Amendment are wholly exhausted at the moment when police unlawfully invade an individual's privacy, and thus no substantive force remains to those protections at the time of trial when the government seeks to use evidence obtained by the police.

I submit that such a crabbed reading of the Fourth Amendment casts aside the teaching of those Justices who first formulated the exclusionary rule, and rests ultimately on an impoverished understanding of judicial responsibility in our constitutional scheme. For my part, "[t]he right of the people to be secure in their persons, houses, papers, and effects, against unreasonable searches and seizures" comprises a personal right to exclude all evidence secured by means of unreasonable searches and seizures. The right to be free from the initial invasion of privacy and the right of exclusion are coordinate components of the central embracing right to be free from unreasonable searches and seizures. . . .

[T]he Court's decisions over the past decade have made plain that the entire enterprise of attempting to assess the benefits and costs of the exclusionary rule in various contexts is a virtually impossible task for the judiciary to perform honestly or accurately. Although the Court's language in those cases suggests that some specific empirical basis may support its analyses, the reality is that the Court's opinions represent inherently unstable compounds of intuition, hunches, and occasional pieces of partial and often inconclusive data. . . . To the extent empirical data are available regarding the general costs and benefits of the exclusionary rule, such data have shown, on the one hand, as the Court acknowledges today, that the costs are not as substantial as critics have asserted in the past, and, on the other hand, that, while the exclusionary rule may well have certain deterrent effects, it is extremely difficult to determine with any degree of precision whether the incidence of unlawful conduct by police is now lower than it was prior to *Mapp*. . . .

By remaining within its redoubt of empiricism and by basing the rule solely on the deterrence rationale, the Court has robbed the rule of legitimacy. A doctrine that is explained as if it were an empirical proposition, but for which there is only limited empirical support, is both inherently unstable and an easy mark for critics. The extent of this Court's fidelity to Fourth Amendment requirements, however, should not turn on such statistical uncertainties. . . . Rather than seeking to give effect to the liberties secured by the Fourth Amendment through guesswork about deterrence, the Court should restore to its proper place the principle framed 70 years ago in *Weeks* that an individual whose privacy has been invaded in violation of the Fourth Amendment has a right grounded in that Amendment to prevent the government from subsequently making use of any evidence so obtained. . . .

What the Framers of the Bill of Rights sought to accomplish through the express requirements of the Fourth Amendment was to define precisely the conditions under which government agents could search private property so that citizens would not have to depend solely upon the discretion and restraint of those agents for the protection of their privacy. Although the self-restraint and care exhibited by the officers in this case is commendable, that alone can never be a sufficient protection for constitutional liberties. I am convinced that it is not too much to ask that an attentive magistrate take those minimum steps necessary to ensure that every warrant he issues describes with particularity the things that his independent review of the warrant application convinces him are likely to be found in the premises. And I am equally convinced that it is not too much to ask that well-trained and experienced police officers take a moment to check that the warrant they have been issued at least describes those things for which they have sought leave to search. These convictions spring not from my own view of sound criminal law enforcement policy, but are instead compelled by the language of the Fourth Amendment and the history that led to its adoption.

▼▲▼

During the same term, the Court, in *Nix v. Williams* (1984), created another exception to the exclusionary rule, the "inevitable discovery" doctrine, which holds that evidence obtained in violation of an individual's constitutional rights is admissible if the discovery of such evidence would have happened anyway.[38] *Nix* brought to a close a controversial earlier decision, *Brewer v. Williams* (1976) (see Chapter 8), in which a bitterly divided Court voted to exclude a confession from a suspect that had taken police right to the buried body of an eleven-year-old rape and murder victim. *Nix* and *Leon* elicited major protest from such groups as the ACLU, NAACP LDF, and criminal defense lawyers groups. They believed the Court had stripped criminal defendants of the only effective remedy for police misconduct. Many law enforcement groups countered with the assertion that the exclusionary rule unfairly handicapped the police in their continuing battle against an increasingly violent and technologically sophisticated criminal element. Given the different arguments you have read on behalf and against the exclusionary rule in this section, do you believe that excluding incriminating materials obtained during a legally tainted search is consistent with the Fourth Amendment's guarantee against unreasonable searches and seizures? Or do you believe the right of persons to be secure in their places, persons, houses, and effects renders the costs of the exclusionary rule too high? Should the Court abandon the exclusionary rule and instead encourage individuals who believe their Fourth Amendment rights have been violated to sue the police officers who allegedly did so for civil damages? These questions and many others will continue to draw the interest of the Court and the numerous interest groups with differing views on the meaning of the Fourth Amendment.

FOR FURTHER READING

Amar, Akhil Reed. *The Constitution and Criminal Procedure: First Principles.* New Haven, Conn.: Yale University Press, 1998.

Bradley, Craig M. *The Failure of the Criminal Procedure Revolution.* Philadelphia: University of Pennsylvania Press, 1993.

Cole, David. *No Equal Justice: Race and Class in the American Criminal Justice System.* New York: New Press, 1999.

Cortner, Richard C. *The Supreme Court and the Second Bill of Rights.* Madison: University of Wisconsin Press, 1981.

Kennedy, Randall. *Race, Crime and the Law.* New York: Pantheon, 1997.

Murphy, Walter F. *Wiretapping on Trial: A Case Study in the Judicial Process.* New York: Random House, 1965.

Pettifor, Bonnie, and Charles E. Petit. *Weeks v. United States: Illegal Search and Seizure.* Lawrence: University Press of Kansas, 2000.

Legal Representation, Confessions, and Fair Trials

Sometime on Christmas Eve 1968, ten-year-old Pamela Powers disappeared while at a basketball game with her family at a YMCA in Des Moines, Iowa. Local police soon suspected that Robert Williams, a recent escapee from a nearby mental institution who was living at the YMCA, had abducted Powers. A fourteen-year-old boy told police that Williams matched the description of the man whose car door he had held open while Williams placed a "large bundle" wrapped in a blanket on the car seat. The next day, Williams's car was found about 160 miles away near Davenport. Since Williams had a prior record of sex-related offenses involving small children, police also feared that Powers had been raped and probably killed. On December 26, two days after the police had issued an arrest warrant for him, Williams, after consulting with his attorney, surrendered to the Davenport police. Williams was a deeply religious man and Pamela's abduction had weighed heavily on his conscience. As he later admitted to the police, the small body that he claimed he had found in his room at the Des Moines YMCA and carried out to his car was probably Pamela's. Williams had been so terrified of returning to prison that he fled the state after placing her body in a ditch just off Interstate 80 in the nearby small town of Mitchellville.[1]

The Des Moines police learned where Pamela Powers was buried after Williams led the two detectives who had accompanied him from Davenport back to Des Moines to the body. Captain Leaming, the chief of detectives and a nineteen-year veteran of the Des Moines police department, and Detective Nelson, a homicide investigator with fifteen years' experience, had driven from Des Moines to Davenport to retrieve Williams for arraignment. Before Leaming and Nelson left Des Moines, Williams's attorney in Des Moines, named McKnight, told the detectives not to question his client. After turning himself in, Williams had been informed of his right to remain silent by the Davenport judge who issued the warrant for his arrest, by the Davenport police officer to whom Williams had turned himself in, and by a local Davenport attorney, named Kelley, who had represented Williams at the police station. Leaming and Nelson had also informed Williams of his right to remain silent. Williams asserted his rights several times, telling Leaming as he was being handcuffed that he would tell him "the whole story *after* I see McKnight" back in Des Moines. Leaming and Nelson permitted Williams to meet with McKnight every time he asked to do so before they started back to Des Moines.

By the time Leaming and Nelson began their trip to Des Moines, no doubt existed that the police had amply warned Williams of his right to remain silent and that anything he said could be used as evidence against him. Likewise, no doubt existed that Williams understood and asserted his right not to talk to the police about the Powers case until he was in the presence of his attorney in Des Moines. But shortly after Leaming and Nelson turned their police cruiser onto Interstate 80, Leaming, sitting in the back with Williams, began to make small talk with his prisoner, commenting on the adverse weather conditions, including freezing rain and poor visibility, that would ultimately lengthen their trip by a couple of hours. Then Leaming turned to Williams and began to talk about Pamela Powers's disappearance:

> I want to give you something to think about while we're traveling down the road. Number one, it's freezing, driving is very treacherous, visibility is poor, it's going to be dark early this evening. They are predicting several inches of snow for tonight, and I feel that you yourself are the only person that knows where this little girl's body is, that you yourself have only been there once, and if you get a snow on top of it you yourself may be unable to find it. And, since we will be going right past the area on the way into Des Moines, I feel that we could stop and locate the body, that the parents of this little girl should be entitled to a Christian burial for the little girl who was snatched away from them on Christmas Eve and murdered. And I feel we should stop and locate it on the way in rather than waiting until morning and trying to come back out after a snow storm and possibly not being able to find it at all. I don't want you to answer me. I don't want to discuss it any further. Just think about it as we're riding down the road.

Shortly after Leaming gave Williams what later became known as the "Christian burial speech," Nelson, at Williams's request, stopped the car near a gas station in Grinnell, about 50 miles east of Des Moines, where Williams said he had left Powers's shoes. A little later, Williams directed them to a rest stop near another Grinnell exit, telling Leaming he might have left the blanket near there. Search parties were already in place by the time Leaming and Nelson had arrived, as Leaming knew before they left Des Moines that pieces of Pamela's clothing had been found in Grinnell. Still, they could not find the body. Leaming, Nelson, and Williams continued their drive to Des Moines, discussing, according to Leaming, religion, intelligence, people, and friends of Williams. Then, as they got closer to Mitchellville, Williams said to Leaming, "I am going to show you where the body is," and, as an aside, asked the detective, "How did you know that it was by Mitchellville?" Leaming told Williams that it was his "job to find out such things and I just knew that it was in that area." Williams then led Leaming and Nelson to Pamela Powers's body, about two miles south of another search team that had been combing the woods and fields of rural Iowa for the young girl.

Nine years later, the United States Supreme Court, in *Brewer* v. *Williams* (1977), ruled that the Christian burial speech delivered by Captain Leaming to Robert Williams amounted to an interrogation that violated the defendant's right to remain silent in the absence of his attorney.[2] Noting that Leaming had referred to Williams as "Reverend" before he gave the Christian burial speech—an obvious reference to Williams's religious convictions—the Court concluded that the detective had deliberately set out to elicit information from the suspect. To the Court, the "conversation" between Leaming and Williams, and especially the Christian burial speech, was no different from any direct line of questioning. Leaming never denied that he was playing mind games with his suspect, but refused to concede that he had interrogated Williams. Almost ten years later, Leaming, commenting on the Court's conclusion that the Christian burial speech was a form of "psychological coercion," remarked:

> I didn't even know what those words meant, until I looked them up in the dictionary after I was accused of using it. . . .
>
> Schucks, I was just being a good old-fashioned cop, the only kind I know how to be. . . .
>
> I have never seen a prisoner physically abused, though I heard about those things in the early days. . . .
>
> That type of questioning just doesn't work. They'll just resist harder.
>
> You have to butter 'em up, sweet talk 'em, use that—what's the word?—"psychological coercion."

After the Court's decision, Williams was retried for Powers's murder without introducing his confession into evidence. Police did not attempt to introduce Williams's statements into evidence or mention that Williams had led Captain Leaming to Powers's body. Instead, the police sought—and received—permission from an Iowa trial court to introduce photos depicting the condition of the child's body after it was found and the results of post-mortem medical tests confirming that Powers had been raped. Based on the second body of evidence, Williams was convicted of raping and murdering Powers. Ultimately, the Supreme Court rebuffed an appeal by Williams, who claimed that his tainted confession made any subsequent evidence inadmissible. The Court, in *Nix* v. *Williams* (1984), ruled that, in all likelihood, the search team would have discovered Powers "within a short time" had the police not suspended the search after Williams agreed to take the police to her body.[3] In upholding Williams's conviction, the Court agreed to create an "inevitable discovery" exception to the exclusionary rule, which bans the use of illegally obtained evidence. That same term, the Court, in *United States* v. *Leon* (1984) and *Massachusetts* v. *Sheppard* (1984) (see Chapter 7), had recognized a "good faith" exception to the exclusionary rule.[4]

The "Christian burial speech" case illustrates many questions and issues involving the Fifth Amendment, which guarantees that no person "shall be compelled in any criminal case to be a witness against himself," and the Sixth Amendment, which secures the right to the "Assistance of Counsel." Did Captain Leaming's remarks constitute the equivalent of an interrogation? Did Robert Williams waive his right to counsel when he agreed to take the detectives to Pamela Powers's body? Did Williams's alleged psychological problems make him vulnerable to police manipulation, or did Leaming simply engage in good police work? Beyond these questions involving police interrogations and confessions, the Fifth and Sixth Amendments create numerous other criminal due process safeguards, including the right to a public trial by an impartial jury, the right to confront one's accusers in court, the right against double jeopardy, and the right of the accused to obtain witnesses on his or her behalf. This chapter will examine the various guarantees of the Fifth and Sixth Amendments and how they interrelate to form a crucial foundation of modern criminal due process rights.

The Right to Counsel

Over time, the Sixth Amendment guarantee to the assistance of counsel has come to mean that all persons, regardless of the nature of their alleged offense, their financial status, or their mental faculties, are *entitled* to a lawyer as soon as they become the focus of a criminal investigation. Indeed, it seems that any reasonable definition of criminal due process would include the right to legal representation when an individual is threatened with the loss of liberty. But the expansive nature of the right to counsel in the contemporary sense bears little resemblance to the Framers' original design for the Assistance of Counsel Clause. Rather, the modern meaning of the Sixth Amendment is the product of twentieth-century interest group dynamics and a Supreme Court, particularly during the 1960s, determined to reform the constitutional foundation of criminal procedure.

The Framers drew heavily on the British system of criminal procedure in establishing the due process provisions of the Bill of Rights, but added important safeguards that, by the standards of the day, made American practices much more advanced than Great Britain's. Certainly, a great deal of variation existed within the American colonies on when the criminally accused were entitled to the assistance of counsel and, separately, whether the government was required to provide lawyers to individuals who could not afford one. By 1776, however, the courts recognized the right of the criminally accused to have an attorney present during trial. Some states, such as Pennsylvania and Connecticut, legally required the appointment of a lawyer to represent an individual accused of a capital crime. In 1790, Congress enacted the Federal Crimes Act, which required the appointment of an attorney in all federal capital cases upon the defendant's request. Around the same time, Delaware and South Carolina had passed similar laws to govern state capital trials. In contrast, the British parliament did not permit the criminally accused to retain an attorney during the trial stage in felony cases until the 1830s.[5]

Even after the ratification of the Sixth Amendment in 1791, eight states, by the early 1800s, included provisions in their state constitutions pertaining to the assistance of counsel. No state constitution, however, provided the criminally accused the right to have counsel appointed in a noncapital felony case, much less one involving a less serious charge. New Jersey and Connecticut provided the criminally accused an attorney upon request in felony cases, but this right came through statutory, not constitutional, law. For almost 150 years, the Court gave little attention to what the Framers meant—or might have meant—by the right to the assistance of counsel. But as the Court, beginning in the 1920s, gradually began to make the provisions of the Bill of Rights applicable to the states through the Fourteenth Amendment, it became clear that it was only a matter of time before the justices would revisit the substance and scope of this basic due process guarantee.

The nine "Scottsboro Boys," protected by several National Guardsmen, rear, in custody after their arrest for allegedly raping two young white girls aboard a train.
©UPI Bettmann/CORBIS

Establishing the Right to Counsel

The National Association for the Advancement of Colored People (NAACP) was founded in 1909 in response to a particularly brutal spree of lynchings in Abraham Lincoln's hometown of Springfield, Illinois. In addition to its efforts to end legal discrimination in education, housing, and employment, the NAACP had always monitored the criminal justice system very carefully. In the Southern states especially, African Americans were routinely brought to trial on the flimsiest of evidence and were meted out harsh sentences for crimes to which they professed innocence. Moreover, it was not uncommon for black criminal defendants in the South to stand trial without an attorney. Later, the American Civil Liberties Union (ACLU), primarily a First Amendment rights group upon its founding in 1920, expanded its agenda to include criminal procedure reform. Like the NAACP, the ACLU was drawn to criminal justice issues primarily because of the slipshod treatment of African Americans. The NAACP and the ACLU, along with International Labor Defense, a Communist-sponsored group that operated on the fringes of the American political process, became crucial actors in *Powell* v.

Alabama (1932), a landmark decision that dramatically expanded the rights of the criminally accused in capital cases.

Powell v. *Alabama* [*The Scottsboro Boys Case*]

287 U.S. 45 (1932)

In 1931, nine young African American men between the ages of twelve and twenty were arrested in Scottsboro, Alabama, for the rape of two white girls. The alleged rape occurred aboard a freight train traveling from Chattanooga, Tennessee, en route to Memphis through rural Alabama. The girls were traveling with four or five white boys when the black youths hopped aboard the train. No one was a ticketed passenger. As was common during the Great Depression, poor people from all walks of life—families, young mothers, teenagers, old men—jumped the rails in search of adventure or, in many cases, a better life wherever the train dumped them off. On this late March afternoon, one of the white boys told his black counterpart, "Nigger bastard, this is a white man's train. . . . All you black bastards better get off." A fight ensued, and, with the exception of one, all the white boys were thrown off the train.[6]

By the time the train approached Paint Rock, Alabama, about forty miles down the tracks from where the fight had taken place, word of the confrontation had already reached the local sheriff. He had enlisted dozens of other white men, fully equipped with shotguns, baseball bats, and knives, to detain the nine black youths. The sheriff tied them together, placed them under arrest, and drove them about twenty miles down the road to Scottsboro, where they were jailed on assault and attempted murder charges. After sitting in jail for several hours, the "Scottsboro Boys," as they soon became known, were informed of an additional charge being brought against them: attempted rape. Victoria Price and Ruby Bates, the two girls aboard the train, told the sheriff that six of the nine boys had raped them.

Later that evening, an angry lynch mob carrying torches began ramming the Scottsboro jail and demanding that the sheriff "let the niggers out" or they would break the door down. The sheriff contacted the governor, who called the National Guard, which quickly descended on the jail and dispersed the lynch mob. Twelve days later, the Scottsboro Boys were divided into three separate groups and went on trial, represented by two poorly prepared lawyers. After four days, the all-white, all-male jury convicted eight of the nine Scottsboro Boys on the assault and rape charges. Clarence Norris knew exactly the fate that awaited him: "I knew if a white woman accused a black man of rape, he was as good as dead." Southern criminal law authorized the death penalty for convicted rapists, and this sentence was reserved almost exclusively for African American men convicted of raping white women.

The Court's decision was 7 to 2. Justice Sutherland delivered the opinion of the Court. Justice Butler dissented.

▼▲▼

MR. JUSTICE SUTHERLAND delivered the opinion of the Court.

It is hardly necessary to say that, the right to counsel being conceded, a defendant should be afforded a fair opportunity to secure counsel of his own choice. Not only was that not done here, but such designation of counsel as was attempted was either so indefinite or so close upon the trial as to amount to a denial of effective and substantial aid in that regard. This will be amply demonstrated by a brief review of the record. . . .

We do not overlook the case of *Hurtado* v. *California,* where this court determined that due process of law does not require an indictment by a grand jury as a prerequisite to prosecution by a state for murder. In support of that conclusion the court referred to the fact that the Fifth Amendment, in addition to containing the due process of law clause, provides in explicit terms that "No person shall be held to answer for a capital, or otherwise infamous crime, unless on a presentment or indictment of a grand jury, . . . " and said that, since no part of this important amendment could be regarded as superfluous, the obvious inference is that, in the sense of the Constitution, due process of law was not intended to include . . . the institution and procedure of a grand jury in any case, and that the same phrase, employed in the Fourteenth Amendment to restrain the action of the states, was to be interpreted as having been used in the same sense and with no greater extent, and that, if it had been the purpose of that Amendment to perpetuate the institution of the grand jury in the states, it would have embodied, as did the Fifth Amendment, an express declaration to that effect.

The Sixth Amendment, in terms, provides that, in all criminal prosecutions, the accused shall enjoy the right "to have the assistance of counsel for his defense." In the face of the reasoning of the *Hurtado* case, if it stood alone, it would be difficult to justify the conclusion that the right to counsel, being thus specifically granted by the Sixth Amendment, was also within the intendment of the due process of law clause. But the *Hurtado* case does not stand alone. [T]his court [has] held a judgment of a state court, even though authorized by statute, by which private property was taken for public use without just compensation, was in violation of the due process of law required by the Fourteenth Amendment notwithstanding that the Fifth Amendment explicitly declares that private property shall not be taken for public use without just compensation.

Likewise, this court has considered that freedom of speech and of the press are rights protected by the due process clause of the Fourteenth Amendment, although in the First Amendment, Congress is prohibited in specific terms from abridging the right, *Gitlow* v. *New York* (1925), *Stromberg* v. *California* (1931), *Near* v. *Minnesota* (1931). . . .

In the light of the facts outlined in the forepart of this opinion—the ignorance and illiteracy of the defendants, their youth, the circumstances of public hostility, the imprisonment and the close surveillance of the defendants by the military forces, the fact that their friends and families were all in other states and communication with them necessarily difficult, and, above all, that they stood in deadly peril of their lives—we think the failure of the trial court to give them reasonable time and opportunity to secure counsel was a clear denial of due process.

But passing that, and assuming their inability, even if opportunity had been given, to employ counsel, as the trial court evidently did assume, we are of opinion that, under the circumstances just stated, the necessity of counsel was so vital and imperative that the failure of the trial court to make an effective appointment of counsel was likewise a denial of due process within the meaning of the Fourteenth Amendment. Whether this would be so in other criminal prosecutions, or under other circumstances, we need not determine. All that it is necessary now to decide, as we do decide, is that, in a capital case, where the defendant is unable to employ counsel and is incapable adequately of making his own defense because of ignorance, feeble mindedness, illiteracy, or the like, it is the duty of the court, whether requested or not, to assign counsel for him as a necessary requisite of due process of law, and that duty is not discharged by an assignment at such a time or under such circumstances as to preclude the giving of effective aid in the preparation and trial of the case. To hold otherwise would be to ignore the fundamental postulate. . . . In a case such as this, whatever may be the rule in other cases, the right to have counsel appointed, when necessary, is a logical corollary from the constitutional right to be heard by counsel. . . .

The United States, by statute, and every state in the Union, by express provision of law or by the determination of its courts, make it the duty of the trial judge, where the accused is unable to employ counsel, to appoint counsel for him. In most states, the rule applies broadly to all criminal prosecutions; in others, it is limited to the more serious crimes; and in a very limited number, to capital cases. A rule adopted with such unanimous accord reflects, if it does not establish, the inherent right to have counsel appointed, at least in cases like the present, and lends convincing support to the conclusion we have reached as to the fundamental nature of that right.

The judgments must be reversed, and the causes remanded for further proceedings not inconsistent with this opinion.

Judgments reversed.

Note that Justice Sutherland's opinion relied upon the Due Process Clause of the Fourteenth Amendment, not the Assistance of Counsel Clause of the Sixth Amendment, to establish the right of criminal defendants in state capital proceedings to have an attorney appointed to represent them. Moreover, the actual holding in *Powell* was quite narrow. Although it recognized that special circumstances, such as "feeblemindedness," public opinion, age, and indigence, might warrant the right to appointed counsel in serious cases, the Court limited the right to have an attorney appointed to capital cases. Still, the Court's willingness to set federal constitutional standards in a state criminal proceeding was a stunning development, and signaled to prosecutors, criminal defense lawyers, and anyone else involved in the criminal justice system that significant changes might well be on the horizon.

Those changes, however, would not happen for quite some time. Justice Sutherland's underlying theory on the right to counsel, which emphasized what scholars have called the *fair trial rule,* proved quite durable over the next three decades. Although the Court, six years later in *Johnson* v. *Zerbst* (1938),[7] built upon *Powell* by extending the right to appointed counsel in federal criminal prosecutions, the justices drew the line on the requirements of the Sixth and Fourteenth Amendments in *Betts* v. *Brady* (1942).[8] In *Betts,* the Court, 6 to 3, ruled that a Carroll County, Maryland, man accused of robbery was not entitled to a court-appointed attorney during his trial. Carroll County, like almost every other state and local jurisdiction since *Powell,* provided counsel to defendants in rape and murder cases. It did not, however, extend such a right to the accused in other felony cases. Justice Owen Roberts, who had joined the Court's opinion in *Powell,* emphasized that no special circumstances existed that placed the defendant at a disadvantage. The defendant was knowledgeable enough to offer an alibi defense, and Roberts said this was proof that a man of "ordinary intelligence" could make his defense just fine without the assistance of counsel.

Justice Hugo Black, who had come to the Court in 1938 and had written the majority opinion in *Zerbst,* sharply dissented from Roberts's opinion. "I believe," wrote Black, "the Fourteenth Amendment made the Sixth applicable to the states." Although Black knew that such a view had "never been accepted by a majority of this Court," he used *Betts* to stake out what soon became one of his most famous and controversial positions on the Constitution: that the Fourteenth Amendment made the Bill of Rights applicable to the states. Over time, as discussed in Chapter 3, the Court, by the late 1960s, would make most of the guarantees of the Bill of Rights applicable to the states through the Fourteenth Amendment. Ironically, the Court was well on its way to making the free speech and press guarantees of the First Amendment binding upon the states, even as it refused to do so with the Sixth Amendment in *Betts.* Just over twenty years later, Black was ultimately vindicated in fact, if not in theory. In *Gideon* v. *Wainwright* (1963), the Court ruled that the criminally accused were entitled to a court-appointed lawyer in all felony cases.

Gideon v. *Wainwright*

372 U.S. 355 (1963)

Clarence Earl Gideon was a fifty-year-old drifter and career petty criminal who had never held a meaningful job for any reasonable length of time. So when Gideon was arrested on June 19, 1961, on a breaking and entering charge for burglarizing the Bay Harbor Poolroom in Panama City, Florida, he could hardly claim unfamiliarity with the criminal justice system: He had served approximately seventeen years in various federal and state prisons on four separate felony convictions. But Gideon's habitual criminality and an eighth-grade education obscured a healthy intelligence that ultimately encouraged him to assert what he believed was a basic constitutional right of any person facing the deprivation of liberty: the right to counsel. After his arrest, a local judge refused Gideon's request for representation at his trial. Like many other states, Florida did not provide indigent defendants an attorney unless they faced a murder charge. Gideon unsuccessfully attempted to defend himself, and was sentenced to five years in prison.[9]

In jail, Gideon began researching the Court's cases dealing with the right to counsel. He believed that the "special circumstances" rule established in *Betts* was far too narrow to allow poor persons to have their day in court with an attorney present. True, Gideon was an adult, literate, and understood enough legal procedure to assert his rights and subsequently challenge prior understandings of the right to counsel. After the Florida courts rejected his appeals, Gideon drafted a handwritten petition requesting a hearing in the United States Supreme Court. Wrote Gideon: "It makes no difference how old I am or what church I belong to if any. The question is I did not get a fair trial. The question is very simple, I requested the court to appoint me [an] attorney and the court refused."

The justices granted Gideon's petition, and requested the parties to address directly the question of whether *Betts* should be overruled. Gideon still needed representation, and the Court, clearly tipping its hand, appointed Abe Fortas, one of Washington's most powerful and politically well-connected lawyers, to represent him. Two years later, President Lyndon Johnson appointed Fortas, a close friend and personal adviser, to the Court, where he served until 1969. Here is how Fortas summarized the issues in *Gideon* before the Court:

> If you will look at this transcript of the record, perhaps you will share my feeling, which is a feeling of despondency. This record does not indicate that Clarence Earl Gideon is a man of inferior natural talents. This record does not indicate that Clarence Earl Gideon is a moron or a person of low intelligence. This record does not indicate that the judge of the trial court in the state of Florida, or that the prosecuting attorney in the state of Florida, was derelict in his duty. On the contrary, it indicates that they tried to help Gideon. But to me, if the

> Court please, this record indicates the basic difficulty with *Betts*. . . . And the basic difficulty with *Betts* . . . is that no man, certainly no layman, can conduct a trial in his own defense so that the trial is a fair trial.[10]

Important *amicus* briefs in support of Gideon were filed by the ACLU, which was represented by former United States solicitor general J. Lee Rankin, and twenty-two state attorneys general, who argued that states should provide indigent defendants attorneys in felony cases.

The Court's decision was unanimous. Justice Black delivered the opinion of the Court. Justices Harlan, Douglas, and Clark filed separate concurring opinions.

▼▲▼

MR. JUSTICE BLACK delivered the opinion of the Court.

Since 1942, when *Betts* v. *Brady*, was decided by a divided Court, the problem of a defendant's federal constitutional right to counsel in a state court has been a continuing source of controversy and litigation in both state and federal courts. To give this problem another review here, we granted certiorari. Since Gideon was proceeding *in forma pauperis*, we appointed counsel to represent him and requested both sides to discuss in their briefs and oral arguments the following: "Should this Court's holding in *Betts* v. *Brady* (1942) be reconsidered?"

The facts upon which Betts claimed that he had been unconstitutionally denied the right to have counsel appointed to assist him are strikingly like the facts upon which Gideon here bases his federal constitutional claim. . . . Treating due process as "a concept less rigid and more fluid than those envisaged in other specific and particular provisions of the Bill of Rights," the Court held that refusal to appoint counsel under the particular facts and circumstances in the *Betts* case was not so "offensive to the common and fundamental ideas of fairness" as to amount to a denial of due process. Since the facts and circumstances of the two cases are so nearly indistinguishable, we think the *Betts* v. *Brady* holding, if left standing, would require us to reject Gideon's claim that the Constitution guarantees him the assistance of counsel. Upon full reconsideration, we conclude that *Betts* v. *Brady* should be overruled. . . .

We think the Court in *Betts* had ample precedent for acknowledging that those guarantees of the Bill of Rights which are fundamental safeguards of liberty immune from federal abridgment are equally protected against state invasion by the Due Process Clause of the Fourteenth Amendment. This same principle was recognized, explained, and applied in *Powell* v. *Alabama* (1932). . . . In many cases other than *Powell* and *Betts*, this Court has looked to the fundamental nature of original Bill of Rights guarantees to decide whether the Fourteenth Amendment makes them obligatory on the States. Explicitly recognized to be of this "fundamental nature," and therefore made immune from state invasion by the Fourteenth, or some part of it, are the First Amendment's freedoms of speech, press, religion, assembly, association, and petition for redress of grievances. . . .

We accept *Betts* v. *Brady*'s assumption, based as it was on our prior cases, that a provision of the Bill of Rights which is "fundamental and essential to a fair trial" is made obligatory upon the States by the Fourteenth Amendment. We think the Court in *Betts* was wrong, however, in concluding that the Sixth Amendment's guarantee of counsel is not one of these fundamental rights. Ten years before *Betts* v. *Brady*, this Court, after full consideration of all the historical data examined in *Betts*, had unequivocally declared that "the right to the aid of counsel is of this fundamental character," *Powell* v. *Alabama* (1932). While the Court, at the close of its *Powell* opinion, did, by its language, as this Court frequently does, limit its holding to the particular facts and circumstances of that case, its conclusions about the fundamental nature of the right to counsel are unmistakable. . . .

In light of these and many other prior decisions of this Court, it is not surprising that the *Betts* Court, when faced with the contention that "one charged with crime, who is unable to obtain counsel, must be furnished counsel by the State," conceded that "[e]xpressions in the opinions of this court lend color to the argument. . . . " The fact is that, in deciding as it did—that "appointment of counsel is not a fundamental right, essential to a fair trial"—the Court in *Betts* v. *Brady* made an abrupt break with its own well considered precedents. In returning to these old precedents, sounder, we believe, than the new, we but restore constitutional principles established to achieve a fair system of justice. Not only these precedents, but also reason and reflection, require us to recognize that, in our adversary system of criminal justice, any person hauled into court, who is too poor to hire a lawyer, cannot be assured a fair trial unless counsel is provided for him. This seems to us to be an obvious truth. Governments, both state and federal, quite properly spend vast sums of money to establish machinery to try defendants accused of crime. Lawyers to prosecute are everywhere deemed essential to protect the public's interest in an orderly society. Similarly, there are few defendants charged with crime, few indeed, who fail to hire the best lawyers they can get to prepare and present their defenses. That government hires lawyers to prosecute and defendants who have the money hire lawyers to defend are the strongest indications of the widespread belief that lawyers in criminal courts are necessities, not luxuries. The right of one charged with crime to counsel may not be deemed fundamental and essential to fair trials in some countries, but it is in ours. From the very beginning, our state and national constitutions and laws have laid great emphasis on procedural and substantive safeguards designed to assure fair trials before impartial tribunals in which every defendant stands equal before the law. This noble ideal cannot be realized if the poor man charged with crime has to face his accusers without a lawyer to assist him. . . .

The Court in *Betts* v. *Brady* departed from the sound wisdom upon which the Court's holding in *Powell* v. *Alabama* rested. Florida, supported by two other States, has asked that *Betts* v. *Brady* be left intact. Twenty-two States, as friends of the Court, argue that *Betts* was "an anachronism when handed down," and that it should now be overruled. We agree.

The judgment is reversed, and the cause is remanded to the Supreme Court of Florida for further action not inconsistent with this opinion.

Reversed.

MR. JUSTICE HARLAN, concurring.

I agree that *Betts* v. *Brady* should be overruled, but consider it entitled to a more respectful burial than has been accorded, at least on the part of those of us who were not on the Court when that case was decided.

I cannot subscribe to the view that *Betts* v. *Brady* represented "an abrupt break with its own well considered precedents." In 1932, in *Powell* v. *Alabama*, a capital case, this Court declared that, under the particular facts there presented—the ignorance and illiteracy of the defendants, their youth, the circumstances of public hostility . . . and, above all, that they stood in deadly peril of their lives—the state court had a duty to assign counsel for the trial as a necessary requisite of due process of law. It is evident that these limiting facts were not added to the opinion as an afterthought; they were repeatedly emphasized, and were clearly regarded as important to the result.

Thus, when this Court, a decade later, decided *Betts* v. *Brady*, it did no more than to admit of the possible existence of special circumstances in noncapital, as well as capital, trials, while at the same time insisting that such circumstances be shown in order to establish a denial of due process. The right to appointed counsel had been recognized as being considerably broader in federal prosecutions, but to have imposed these requirements on the States would indeed have been "an abrupt break" with the almost immediate past. The declaration that the right to appointed counsel in state prosecutions, as established in *Powell* v. *Alabama*, was not limited to capital cases was, in truth, not a departure from, but an extension of, existing precedent. . . .

The special circumstances rule has been formally abandoned in capital cases, and the time has now come when it should be similarly abandoned in noncapital cases, at least as to offenses which, as the one involved here, carry the possibility of a substantial prison sentence. (Whether the rule should extend to all criminal cases need not now be decided.) This indeed does no more than to make explicit something that has long since been foreshadowed in our decisions.

In agreeing with the Court that the right to counsel in a case such as this should now be expressly recognized as a fundamental right embraced in the Fourteenth Amendment, I wish to make a further observation. . . . In what is done today, I do not understand the Court to depart from the principles laid down in *Palko* v. *Connecticut* (1937), or to embrace the concept that the Fourteenth Amendment "incorporates" the Sixth Amendment as such.

On these premises I join in the judgment of the Court.

Gideon, in overturning *Betts* v. *Brady*, marked, after *Mapp* v. *Ohio*, the second major shot fired in the Court's coming criminal procedure revolution. But unlike *Mapp*, Gideon's impact on the criminal justice system extended far beyond a change in the rules of procedure. By holding that indigent criminal defendants in felony cases were entitled to the assistance of counsel, the Court created an entirely new area of legal practice: the public defender's office. Prior to *Gideon*, some states provided counsel to the criminally accused by having judges appoint lawyers drawn from the membership of the local bar. Few states, however, maintained a full-time and professionally staffed public defender's office. *Gideon* required a massive overhaul in the way that states carried out the prosecution of the criminally accused. Not surprisingly, *Gideon* also encouraged several organizations that had long advocated better representation for indigent criminal defendants, such as the National Legal Aid and Defender Association, founded in 1911, and the National Association of Criminal Defense Lawyers, founded in 1958, to lobby state legislatures for

DIVISION OF CORRECTIONS

CORRESPONDENCE REGULATIONS

MAIL WILL NOT BE DELIVERED WHICH DOES NOT CONFORM WITH THESE RULES

No. 1 -- Only 2 letters each week, not to exceed 2 sheets letter-size 8 1/2 x 11" and written *on one side only*, and if ruled paper, do not write between lines. *Your complete name* must be signed at the close of your letter. *Clippings*, *stamps*, *letters* from other people, *stationery* or *cash must not be enclosed* in your letters.

No. 2 -- All *letters* must be addressed in the *complete prison name* of the inmate. *Cell number*, where applicable, and *prison number* must be placed in lower left corner of envelope, with your complete name and address in the upper left corner.

No. 3 -- *Do not send any packages without a Package Permit.* Unauthorized *packages* will be destroyed.

No. 4 -- *Letters* must be written in English only.

No. 5 -- *Books*, *magazines*, *pamphlets*, and *newspapers* of reputable character will be delivered *only if* mailed direct from the publisher.

No. 6 -- *Money* must be sent in the form of *Postal Money Orders* only, in the inmate's complete prison name and prison number.

INSTITUTION ____________ CELL NUMBER ____________

NAME ____________ NUMBER ____________

In The Supreme Court of The United States
Washington D.C.

clarence Earl Gideon
Petitioner
VS.
H.G. Cochran, Jr, as
Director, Divisions
of corrections State
of Florida

Petition for a writ
of Certiorari Directed
to The Supreme Court
State of Florida.

No. 890 Misc.
OCT. TERM 1961
U. S. Supreme Court

To: The Honorable Earl Warren, Chief
Justice of the United States

Comes now the petitioner, Clarence
Earl Gideon, a citizen of The United states
of America, in proper person, and appearing
as his own counsel. Who petitions this
Honorable Court for a Writ of Certiorari
directed to The Supreme Court of The State
of Florida. To review the order and Judge-
ment of the court below denying The
petitioner a Writ of Habeus Corpus.

Petitioner submits That The Supreme
Court of The United States has The authority
and jurisdiction to review The final Judge-
ment of The Supreme Court of The State
of Florida the highest court of The State
Under sec. 344(B) Title 28 U.S.C.A. and
Because The "Due process clause" of the

Clarence Earl Gideon's handwritten petition requesting a hearing in the United States Supreme Court on the grounds that he had been denied his constitutional right to a lawyer during his 1961 trial for breaking and entering a Panama City, Florida, pool hall.

Collection of the Supreme Court of the United States

appropriate resources. In addition, criminal defense groups wanted the Court to expand *Gideon's* scope to include misdemeanor offenses and the right to counsel on appeal.

Initially, the effort to extend the right to counsel in criminal cases beyond felony charges was successful. In *In re Gault* (1967), a case brought by the ACLU, the Court unanimously ruled that minors were entitled to the assistance of counsel in judicial proceedings in juvenile court. Five years later, the Court, in *Argersinger* v. *Hamlin* (1972), extended *Gideon* to require the assistance of counsel in all cases where the offense carried a jail term.[11] In *Argersinger*, the criminal defense bar received the support of the United States Department of Justice, which argued in its *amicus curiae* brief that the right to counsel should be broadened to include misdemeanor offenses. But the Court soon drew the line on *Gideon's* reach when it ruled, in *Ross* v. *Moffitt* (1974), that the right to counsel did not extend beyond the first appeal. Other than the National Legal Aid and Defender Association, no group supported the expansion of the right to counsel to include discretionary appeals.[12] Since *Moffitt*, the upshot on the right to counsel is this: States are free to provide counsel to indigent criminal defendants through as many layers of the appeals process as they wish, but the Sixth Amendment does not, beyond the first appeal, require them to do so.

Effective Assistance of Counsel

Powell pointed the way for the subsequent line of decisions on the right to counsel that reached its apex in *Argersinger*. But the Court not only held in *Powell* that the criminally accused in capital cases were entitled to have an attorney. It required that an attorney must be *effective*. Thus the Court, after *Powell*, ruled that the Sixth Amendment precluded courts from appointing a single lawyer to represent multiple defendants charged with the same offense. The Court also held that lawyers with insufficient experience to handle complex criminal cases had denied their clients the effective assistance of counsel, providing that their clients could show clear evidence of incompetence.[13] Beyond that, the Court has not established an expansive interpretation of the right to the effective assistance of counsel. In *Strickland* v. *Washington* (1984), the Court offered a clear rationale on what constituted the "effective" assistance of counsel.

Strickland v. *Washington*

466 U.S. 668 (1984)

The Court's decision to take this case mobilized thirty-four state attorneys general, the United States solicitor general, and several prosecution-oriented public law firms to file *amicus* briefs in support of the Washington state attorney general. The prosecution argued that the decision of a capital defendant to reject his defense lawyer's advice on matters related to his sentencing did not violate the Sixth Amendment requirement to the effective assistance of counsel. Beginning in the late 1970s, the United States Supreme Court had taken a conservative turn on criminal procedure issues, and many prosecutors and groups supportive of them had been encouraging the Court to hold the line on the rights of criminal defendants.

The Court's decision was 7 to 2. Justice O'Connor delivered the opinion of the Court. Justice Brennan concurred and dissented in part. Justice Marshall filed a dissenting opinion.

▼▲▼

JUSTICE O'CONNOR delivered the opinion of the Court.

This case requires us to consider the proper standards for judging a criminal defendant's contention that the Constitution requires a conviction or death sentence to be set aside because counsel's assistance at the trial or sentencing was ineffective. . . .

In a long line of cases that includes *Powell* v. *Alabama* (1932), *Johnson* v. *Zerbst* (1938), and *Gideon* v. *Wainwright* (1963), this Court has recognized that the Sixth Amendment right to counsel exists, and is needed, in order to protect the fundamental right to a fair trial. The Constitution guarantees a fair trial through the Due Process Clauses, but it defines the basic elements of a fair trial largely through the several provisions of the Sixth Amendment, including the Counsel Clause. . . .

Because of the vital importance of counsel's assistance, this Court has held that, with certain exceptions, a person accused of a federal or state crime has the right to have counsel appointed if retained counsel cannot be obtained. That a person who happens to be a lawyer is present at trial alongside the accused, however, is not enough to satisfy the constitutional command. The Sixth Amendment recognizes the right to the assistance of counsel because it envisions counsel's playing a role that is critical to the ability of the adversarial system to produce just results. An accused is entitled to be assisted by an attorney, whether retained or appointed, who plays the role necessary to ensure that the trial is fair.

For that reason, the Court has recognized that "the right to counsel is the right to the effective assistance of counsel." Government violates the right to effective assistance when it interferes in certain ways with the ability of counsel to make independent decisions about how to conduct the defense. Counsel, however, can also deprive a defendant of the right to effective assistance, simply by failing to render "adequate legal assistance."

The Court has not elaborated on the meaning of the constitutional requirement of effective assistance in the latter class of cases—that is, those presenting claims of "actual ineffectiveness." In giving meaning to the requirement, however, we must take its purpose—to ensure a fair trial—as the guide. The benchmark for judging any claim of ineffectiveness must be whether counsel's conduct so undermined the proper functioning of the adversarial process that the trial cannot be relied on as having produced a just result. . . .

A convicted defendant's claim that counsel's assistance was so defective as to require reversal of a conviction or death sentence has two components. First, the defendant must show that counsel's performance was deficient. This requires showing that counsel made errors so serious that counsel was not functioning as the "counsel" guaranteed the defendant by the Sixth Amendment. Second, the defendant must show that the deficient performance prejudiced the defense. This requires showing that counsel's errors were so serious as to deprive the defendant of a fair trial, a trial whose result is reliable. Unless a defendant makes both showings, it cannot be said that the conviction or death sentence resulted from a breakdown in the adversary process that renders the result unreliable. . . .

Representation of a criminal defendant entails certain basic duties. Counsel's function is to assist the defendant, and hence counsel owes the client a duty of loyalty, a duty to avoid conflicts of interest. From counsel's function as assistant to the defendant derive the overarching duty to advocate the defendant's cause and the more particular duties to consult with the defendant on important decisions and to keep the defendant informed of important developments in the course of the prosecution. Counsel also has a duty to bring to bear such skill and knowledge as will render the trial a reliable adversarial testing process. . . .

Thus, a court deciding an actual ineffectiveness claim must judge the reasonableness of counsel's challenged conduct on the facts of the particular case, viewed as of the time of counsel's conduct. A convicted defendant making a claim of ineffective assistance must identify the acts or omissions of counsel that are alleged not to have been the result of reasonable professional judgment. The court must then determine whether, in light of all the circumstances, the identified acts or omissions were outside the wide range of professionally competent assistance. In making that determination, the court should keep in mind that counsel's function, as elaborated in prevailing professional norms, is to make the adversarial testing process work in the particular case. At the same time, the court should recognize that counsel is strongly presumed to have rendered adequate assistance and made all significant decisions in the exercise of reasonable professional judgment. . . .

The reasonableness of counsel's actions may be determined or substantially influenced by the defendant's own statements or actions. Counsel's actions are usually based, quite properly, on informed strategic choices made by the defendant and on information supplied by the defendant. In particular, what investigation decisions are reasonable depends critically on such information. For example, when the facts that support a certain potential line of defense are generally known to counsel because of what the defendant has said, the need for further investigation may be considerably diminished or eliminated altogether. And when a defendant has given counsel reason to believe that pursuing certain investigations would be fruitless or even harmful, counsel's failure to pursue those investigations may not later be challenged as unreasonable. In short, inquiry into counsel's conversations with the defendant may be critical to a proper assessment of counsel's investigation decisions, just as it may be critical to a proper assessment of counsel's other litigation decisions. . . .

An error by counsel, even if professionally unreasonable, does not warrant setting aside the judgment of a criminal proceeding if the error had no effect on the judgment. The purpose of the Sixth Amendment guarantee of counsel is to ensure that a defendant has the assistance necessary to justify reliance on the outcome of the proceeding. Accordingly, any deficiencies in counsel's performance must be prejudicial to the defense in order to constitute ineffective assistance under the Constitution. . . .

[A]ctual ineffectiveness claims alleging a deficiency in attorney performance are subject to a general requirement that the defendant affirmatively prove prejudice. The government is not responsible for, and hence not able to prevent, attorney errors that will result in reversal of a conviction or sentence. Attorney errors come in an infinite variety, and are as likely to be utterly harmless in a particular case as they are to be prejudicial. They cannot be classified according to likelihood of causing prejudice.

Nor can they be defined with sufficient precision to inform defense attorneys correctly just what conduct to avoid. Representation is an art, and an act or omission that is unprofessional in one case may be sound or even brilliant in another. Even if a defendant shows that particular errors of counsel were unreasonable, therefore, the defendant must show that they actually had an adverse effect on the defense. . .

Application of the governing principles is not difficult in this case. The facts as described above make clear that the conduct of respondent's counsel at and before respondent's sentencing proceeding cannot be found unreasonable. They also make clear that, even assuming the challenged conduct of counsel was unreasonable, respondent suffered insufficient prejudice to warrant setting aside his death sentence. . . .

Failure to make the required showing of either deficient performance or sufficient prejudice defeats the ineffectiveness claim. Here there is a double failure. More generally, respondent has made no showing that the justice of his sentence was rendered unreliable by a breakdown in the adversary process caused by deficiencies in counsel's assistance. Respondent's sentencing proceeding was not fundamentally unfair.

Reversed.

The Right Against Self-Incrimination

Like the Sixth Amendment right to counsel, the Self-Incrimination Clause of the Fifth Amendment traces its origins to British common law. The right against self-incrimination emerged in England, as did virtually every other provision of criminal provision, in reaction to the Star Chamber system of justice, which relied upon secrecy and inquisitorial methods in trying and convicting criminal suspects. By the late 1600s, the American colonies, well versed in the British system, had established their own common-law right against self-incrimination. After the colonies severed their ties to England and declared independence in 1776, several of the new American states, no longer content to rely upon the common law, immediately secured the right against self-incrimination in their respective constitutions. This trend continued even after the ratification of the Constitution. And by the time the Bill of Rights was approved, ten states had provisions protecting the right against self-incrimination in their state constitutions.[14]

The Framers did not intend the right against self-incrimination to mean that the criminally accused were prohibited from confessing to charges brought against them or offering damaging information to the police or prosecutors. First and foremost, the Fifth Amendment protects the accused from *compelled* self-incrimination. The Framers knew well that freedom of speech, press, assembly, religion, the right to private property, and other fundamental liberties lived a precarious existence without effective due process guarantees to protect individuals whose views were considered dangerous by political majorities. Like the other criminal due process safeguards in the Bill of Rights, the right against self-incrimination is intimately linked to the preservation of other constitutional rights.[15]

Still, the enlightened language and evident purpose behind the Self-Incrimination Clause did not mean that it emerged fully formed in 1791, or that courts and police departments necessarily respected the right against self-incrimination after the Bill of Rights was ratified. In the nineteenth century, magistrates routinely questioned the criminally accused in pretrial proceedings and they were expected to answer. No state barred prosecutors from introducing a witness's silence during pretrial hearings into evidence before a criminal jury once the case had gone to trial. By the mid-nineteenth century, professional police departments had become more commonplace in localities across the nation. The local police assumed many of the responsibilities formerly carried out by the courts. Included in these new responsibilities was the task of obtaining evidence against the criminally accused, which included, of course, confessions.[16] Although the Self-Incrimination Clause applies in several contexts, such as formal trial testimony, congressional and administrative hearings, disputes between employees in government agencies, and government demands for personal records and materials, we will limit our discussion here to police interrogations and confessions.

Police Interrogations and Confessions

In 1897, the Court, in *Bram v. United States,* threw out a confession that it believed had been obtained improperly during police questioning. Someone had committed murder on an American passenger ship while on the high seas. When the ship arrived in Halifax, Nova Scotia, members of the crew identified a ship's mate named Bram as a possible suspect. At the request of the United States consulate, the Halifax police took Bram and another suspect into custody and detained them. The Halifax police ordered Bram to strip so that they could place him in irons. As this was taking place, a detective had the following conversation with Bram:

> When Mr. Bram came into my office, I said to him: "Bram, we are trying to unravel this horrible mystery." I said: "Our position is rather an awkward one. I have had Brown [the other suspect] in this office, and he made a statement that he saw you do the murder." He said: "He could not have seen me. Where was he?" I said: "He states he was at the wheel." "Well," he said, "he could not see me from there."

A federal trial court admitted this conversation into evidence as a confession, and Bram was convicted of murder. But the United States Supreme Court, 6 to 3, concluded that Bram's confession should never have been admitted into evidence at trial. Bram's lawyer had objected to the admission of this statement, but was overruled. The Court concluded that the trial judge had made a mistake, and ruled that Bram was entitled to a new trial.[17] *Bram* demonstrates that long before landmark cases such as *Escobedo* v. *Illinois* (1965) and *Miranda* v. *Arizona* (1966) expanded the right against self-incrimination, the Court recognized that the Fifth Amendment did not permit the criminally accused to make an unwilling contribution to their own guilt.[18]

Bram reflected the common-law emphasis on *voluntariness* as the barometer of whether confessions should be admissible against the criminally accused. For quite some time, the Court considered claims involving compelled confessions in the context of the *fair trial* or *totality of circumstances* approach to criminal due process proceedings, rather than a clear set of rules that determined a confession's admissibility. In cases such as *Brown* v. *Mississippi* (1936), *Ashcraft* v. *Tennessee* (1944), and *Spano* v. *New York* (1959), the Court ruled that confessions obtained after physical abuse, excessive detention, or psychological coercion were inconsistent with the Due Process Clause of the Fourteenth Amendment, not the Self-Incrimination Clause.[19] Parallel to the development of the right to counsel guarantee that culminated in *Gideon* v. *Wainwright* (1963), however, the Court did not make the Fifth Amendment right against self-incrimination applicable to the states through the Fourteenth Amendment until the early 1960s.

In *Malloy* v. *Hogan* (1964), the Court, for the first time, ruled that the Self-Incrimination Clause explicitly barred the states from extracting and using compelled confessions.[20] Coming on the heels of *Mapp* v. *Ohio* (1961) (see Chapter 7) and *Gideon*, *Malloy* signaled that the Court was prepared to extend further the criminal due process guarantees of the Bill of Rights to the states. In several places throughout his *Malloy* opinion, Justice Brennan mentioned that the Fourth and Fifth Amendments "almost . . . [run] into each other," thus making it impossible to apply one set of guarantees to the states without applying them in sum.[21] In *Escobedo* v. *Illinois* (1964), the Court went even further, merging the Sixth Amendment right to counsel with the Fifth Amendment right against self-incrimination to permit suspects to consult with their lawyers when

> . . . the investigation is no longer a general inquiry into an unsolved crime but has begun to focus on a particular suspect, the suspect has been taken into police custody, the police carry out a process of interrogations that lends itself to eliciting incriminating statements, the suspect has requested and been denied an opportunity to consult with his lawyer, and the police have not effectively warned him of his absolute constitutional right to remain silent, the accused has been denied "the Assistance of Counsel" in violation of the Sixth Amendment to the Constitution . . . and that no statement elicited by the police during the interrogation may be used against him at a criminal trial.[22]

By holding that illegally obtained statements could not be used against a criminal suspect, the Court also extended the *Mapp* exclusionary rule beyond the Fourth Amendment prohibition against unreasonable searches and seizures to police interrogation and confessions. The Court reasoned that if the exclusionary rule was necessary to enforce the Fourth Amendment, then it made perfect sense that the same principle should apply to illegally obtained confessions. Anticipating the criticism that would greet *Miranda* two years later, Justice Arthur Goldberg, writing for the *Escobedo* majority, noted that

> We have also learned the companion lesson of history that no system of criminal justice can, or should, survive if it

comes to depend for its continued effectiveness on the citizens' abdication through unawareness of their constitutional rights. No system worth preserving should have to fear that if an accused is permitted to consult with a lawyer, he will become aware of, and exercise, these rights. If the exercise of constitutional rights will thwart the effectiveness of a system of law enforcement, then there is something very wrong with that system.[23]

Having woven together the Fourth, Fifth, and Sixth Amendments into an elegant tapestry of rights designed to protect criminal suspects in police interrogation rooms, the Court, in *Escobedo,* nonetheless left open several important questions. If the criminally accused were entitled to consult with a lawyer once the investigative process became adversarial, did that mean that *Gideon* should now be extended to include representation when a suspect was in police custody? And if criminal suspects did not know they were entitled to an attorney while in custody, should the police—the very people trying to extract information from them—be required to tell them? Finally, should the police also have to make the criminally accused aware of their right against self-incrimination? *Miranda* v. *Arizona,* perhaps the most controversial decision of the Court's criminal procedure revolution during the 1960s, addressed all these questions, and more.

Miranda v. *Arizona*

384 U.S. 436 (1966)

The facts and background of this case are set out in the accompanying SIDEBAR.

The Court's decision was 5 to 4. Chief Justice Warren delivered the opinion of the Court. Justice White, joined by Justices Harlan and Stewart, dissented. Justice Harlan, joined by Justices White and Stewart, dissented. Justice Clark filed a separate dissenting opinion.

MR. CHIEF JUSTICE WARREN delivered the opinion of the Court.

The cases before us raise questions which go to the roots of our concepts of American criminal jurisprudence: the restraints society must observe consistent with the Federal Constitution in prosecuting individuals for crime. More specifically, we deal with the admissibility of statements obtained from an individual who is subjected to custodial police interrogation and the necessity for procedures which assure that the individual is accorded his privilege under the Fifth Amendment to the Constitution not to be compelled to incriminate himself. . . .

We start here, as we did in *Escobedo,* with the premise that our holding is not an innovation in our jurisprudence, but is an application of principles long recognized and applied in other settings. We have undertaken a thorough reexamination of the *Escobedo* decision and the principles it announced, and we reaffirm it. That case was but an explication of basic rights that are enshrined in our Constitution—that "No person . . . shall be compelled in any criminal case to be a witness against himself," and that "the accused shall . . . have the Assistance of Counsel"—rights which were put in jeopardy in that case through official overbearing. These precious rights were fixed in our Constitution only after centuries of persecution and struggle. And, in the words of Chief Justice Marshall, they were secured "for ages to come, and . . . designed to approach immortality as nearly as human institutions can approach it," *Cohen* v. *Commonwealth of Virginia* (1821). . . .

Our holding will be spelled out with some specificity in the pages which follow, but, briefly stated, it is this: the prosecution may not use statements, whether exculpatory or inculpatory, stemming from custodial interrogation of the defendant unless it demonstrates the use of procedural safeguards effective to secure the privilege against self-incrimination. By custodial interrogation, we mean questioning initiated by law enforcement officers after a person has been taken into custody or otherwise deprived of his freedom of action in any significant way. As for the procedural safeguards to be employed, unless other fully effective means are devised to inform accused persons of their right of silence and to assure a continuous opportunity to exercise it, the following measures are required. Prior to any questioning, the person must be warned that he has a right to remain silent, that any statement he does make may be used as evidence against him, and that he has a right to the presence of an attorney, either retained or appointed. The defendant may waive effectuation of these rights, provided the waiver is made voluntarily, knowingly and intelligently. If, however, he indicates in any manner and at any stage of the process that he wishes to consult with an attorney before speaking, there can be no questioning. Likewise, if the individual is alone and indicates in any manner that he does not wish to be interrogated, the police may not question him. The mere fact that he may have answered some questions or volunteered some statements on his own does not deprive him of the right to refrain from answering any further inquiries until he has consulted with an attorney and thereafter consents to be questioned.

The constitutional issue we decide in each of these cases is the admissibility of statements obtained from a defendant questioned while in custody or otherwise deprived of his freedom of action in any significant way. In each, the defendant was questioned by police officers, detectives, or a prosecuting attorney in a room in which he was cut off from the outside world. In none of these cases was the defendant given a full and effective warning of his rights at the outset of the interrogation process. In all the cases, the questioning elicited oral admissions, and in three of them, signed statements as well which were admitted at their trials. They all thus share salient features—incommunicado interrogation of individuals in a police-dominated atmosphere, resulting in self-incriminating statements without full warnings of constitutional rights.

An understanding of the nature and setting of this in-custody interrogation is essential to our decisions today. The difficulty in depicting what transpires at such interrogations stems from the fact that, in this country, they have largely taken place incommunicado. From extensive factual studies undertaken in the early 1930's, including the famous Wickersham Report to Congress by a Presidential Commission, it is clear that police violence and the "third degree" flourished at that time. In a series of cases decided by this Court long after these studies, the police resorted to physical brutality—beating, hanging, whipping—and to sustained and protracted questioning incommunicado in order to extort confessions. The Commission on Civil Rights in 1961 found much evidence to indicate that "some policemen still resort to physical force to obtain confessions." The use of physical brutality and violence is not, unfortunately, relegated to the past or to any part of the country. . . .

Unless a proper limitation upon custodial interrogation is achieved—such as these decisions will advance—there can be no assurance that practices of this nature will be eradicated in the foreseeable future. . . .

[W]e stress that the modern practice of in-custody interrogation is psychologically, rather than physically, oriented. As we have stated before, "[T]his Court has recognized that coercion can be mental as well as physical, and that the blood of the accused is not the only hallmark of an unconstitutional inquisition," *Blackburn* v. *Alabama* (1960). Interrogation still takes place in privacy. Privacy results in secrecy, and this, in turn, results in a gap in our knowledge as to what, in fact, goes on in the interrogation rooms. A valuable source of information about present police practices, however, may be found in various police manuals and texts which document procedures employed with success in the past, and which recommend various other effective tactics. These texts are used by law enforcement agencies themselves as guides. It should be noted that these texts professedly present the most enlightened and effective means presently used to obtain statements through custodial interrogation. By considering these texts and other data, it is possible to describe procedures observed and noted around the country.

The officers are told by the manuals that the "principal psychological factor contributing to a successful interrogation is *privacy*—being alone with the person under interrogation." . . .

To highlight the isolation and unfamiliar surroundings, the manuals instruct the police to display an air of confidence in the suspect's guilt and, from outward appearance, to maintain only an interest in confirming certain details. The guilt of the subject is to be posited as a fact. The interrogator should direct his comments toward the reasons why the subject committed the act, rather than court failure by asking the subject whether he did it. Like other men, perhaps the subject has had a bad family life, had an unhappy childhood, had too much to drink, had an unrequited desire for women. The officers are instructed to minimize the moral seriousness of the offense, to cast blame on the victim or on society. These tactics are designed to put the subject in a psychological state where his story is but an elaboration of what the police purport to know already—that he is guilty. Explanations to the contrary are dismissed and discouraged. . . .

The manuals suggest that the suspect be offered legal excuses for his actions in order to obtain an initial admission of guilt. Where there is a suspected revenge killing, for example, the interrogator may say:

> Joe, you probably didn't go out looking for this fellow with the purpose of shooting him. My guess is, however, that you expected something from him, and that's why you carried a gun—for your own protection. You knew him for what he was, no good. Then when you met him, he probably started using foul, abusive language and he gave some indication] that he was about to pull a gun on you, and that's when you had to act to save your own life. That's about it, isn't it, Joe? . . .

The manuals also contain instructions for police on how to handle the individual who refuses to discuss the matter entirely, or who asks for an attorney or relatives. The examiner is to concede him the right to remain silent.

> This usually has a very undermining effect. First of all, he is disappointed in his expectation of an unfavorable reaction on the part of the interrogator. Secondly, a concession of this right to remain silent impresses the subject with the apparent fairness of his interrogator. . . .

After this psychological conditioning, however, the officer is told to point out the incriminating significance of the suspect's refusal to talk:

> Joe, you have a right to remain silent. That's your privilege, and I'm the last person in the world who'll try to take it away from you. If that's the way you want to leave this, O.K. But let me ask you this. Suppose you were in my shoes, and I were in yours, and you called me in to ask me about this, and I told you, "I don't want to answer any of your questions." You'd think I had something to hide, and you'd probably be right in thinking that. That's exactly what I'll have to think about you, and so will everybody else. So let's sit here and talk this whole thing over. . . .

From these representative samples of interrogation techniques, the setting prescribed by the manuals and observed in practice becomes clear. In essence, it is this: to be alone with the subject is essential to prevent distraction and to deprive him of any outside support. The aura of confidence in his guilt undermines his will to resist. He merely confirms the preconceived story the police seek to have him describe. Patience and persistence, at times relentless questioning, are employed. To obtain a confession, the interrogator must "patiently maneuver himself or his quarry into a position from which the desired objective may be attained." When normal procedures fail to produce the needed result, the police may resort to deceptive stratagems such as giving false legal advice. It is important to keep the subject off balance, for example, by trading on his insecurity about himself or his surroundings. The police then persuade, trick, or cajole him out of exercising his constitutional rights. . . .

Even without employing brutality, the "third degree," or the specific strategems described above, the very fact of custodial interrogation exacts a heavy toll on individual liberty and trades on the weakness of individuals. . . .

It is obvious that such an interrogation environment is created for no purpose other than to subjugate the individual to the will of his examiner. This atmosphere carries its own badge of intimidation. To be sure, this is not physical intimidation, but it is equally destructive of human dignity. The current practice of incommunicado interrogation is at odds with one of our Nation's most cherished principles—that the individual may not be compelled to incriminate himself. Unless adequate protective devices are employed to dispel the compulsion inherent in custodial surroundings, no statement obtained from the defendant can truly be the product of his free choice. . . .

The question in these cases is whether the privilege is fully applicable during a period of custodial interrogation. In this Court, the privilege has consistently been accorded a liberal construction. We are satisfied that all the principles embodied in the privilege apply to informal compulsion exerted by law enforcement officers during in-custody questioning. An individual swept from familiar surroundings into police custody, surrounded by antagonistic forces, and subjected to the techniques of persuasion described above cannot be otherwise than under compulsion to speak. As a practical matter, the compulsion to speak in the isolated setting of the police station may well be greater than in courts or other official investigations, where there are often impartial observers to guard against intimidation or trickery. . . .

Today, then, there can be no doubt that the Fifth Amendment privilege is available outside of criminal court proceedings, and serves to protect persons in all settings in which their freedom of action is curtailed in any significant way from being compelled to incriminate themselves. We have concluded that, without proper safeguards, the process of in-custody interrogation of persons suspected or accused of crime contains inherently compelling pressures which work to undermine the individual's will to resist and to compel him to speak where he would not otherwise do so freely. In order to combat these pressures and to permit a full opportunity to exercise the privilege against self-incrimination, the accused must be adequately and effectively apprised of his rights, and the exercise of those rights must be fully honored.

It is impossible for us to foresee the potential alternatives for protecting the privilege which might be devised by Congress or the States in the exercise of their creative rulemaking capacities. Therefore, we cannot say that the Constitution necessarily requires adherence to any particular solution for the inherent compulsions of the interrogation process as it is presently conducted. Our decision in no way creates a constitutional straitjacket which will handicap sound efforts at reform, nor is it intended to have this effect. We encourage Congress and the States to continue their laudable search for increasingly effective ways of protecting the rights of the individual while promoting efficient enforcement of our criminal laws. However, unless we are shown other procedures which are at least as effective in apprising accused persons of their right of silence and in assuring a continuous opportunity to exercise it, the following safeguards must be observed.

At the outset, if a person in custody is to be subjected to interrogation, he must first be informed in clear and unequivocal terms that he has the right to remain silent. For those unaware of the privilege, the warning is needed simply to make them aware of it—the threshold requirement for an intelligent decision as to its exercise. More important, such a warning is an absolute prerequisite in overcoming the inherent pressures of the interrogation atmosphere. It is not just the subnormal or woefully ignorant who succumb to an interrogator's imprecations, whether implied or expressly stated, that the interrogation will continue until a confession is obtained or that silence in the face of accusation is itself damning, and will bode ill when presented to a jury. Further, the warning will show the individual that his interrogators are prepared to recognize his privilege should he choose to exercise it.

The Fifth Amendment privilege is so fundamental to our system of constitutional rule, and the expedient of giving an adequate warning as to the availability of the privilege so simple, we will not pause to inquire in individual cases whether the defendant was aware of his rights without a warning being given. Assessments of the knowledge the defendant possessed, based on information as to his age, education, intelligence, or prior contact with authorities, can never be more than speculation; a warning is a clear-cut fact. More important, whatever the background of the person interrogated, a warning at the time of the interrogation is indispensable to overcome its pressures and to insure that the individual knows he is free to exercise the privilege at that point in time.

The warning of the right to remain silent must be accompanied by the explanation that anything said can and will be used against the individual in court. This warning is needed in order to make him aware not only of the privilege, but also of the consequences of forgoing it. It is only through an awareness of these consequences that there can be any assurance of real understanding and intelligent exercise of the privilege. Moreover, this warning may serve to make the individual more acutely aware that he is faced with a phase of the adversary system—that he is not in the presence of persons acting solely in his interest.

The circumstances surrounding in-custody interrogation can operate very quickly to overbear the will of one merely made aware of his privilege by his interrogators. Therefore, the right to have counsel present at the interrogation is indispensable to the protection of the Fifth Amendment privilege under the system we delineate today. Our aim is to assure that the individual's right to choose between silence and speech remains unfettered throughout the interrogation process. A once-stated warning, delivered by those who will conduct the interrogation, cannot itself suffice to that end among those who most require knowledge of their rights. A mere warning given by the interrogators is not alone sufficient to accomplish that end. Prosecutors themselves claim that the admonishment of the right to remain silent, without more, "will benefit only the recidivist and the professional." Even preliminary advice given to the accused by his own attorney can be swiftly overcome by the secret interrogation process. Thus, the need for counsel to protect the Fifth Amendment privilege comprehends not merely a right to consult with counsel prior to questioning, but also to have counsel present during any questioning if the defendant so desires. . . .

Accordingly, we hold that an individual held for interrogation must be clearly informed that he has the right to consult with a lawyer and to have the lawyer with him during interrogation under the system for protecting the privilege we delineate today. As with the warnings of the right to remain silent and that anything stated can be used in evidence against him, this warning is an absolute prerequisite to interrogation. No amount of circumstantial evidence that the person may have been aware of this right will suffice to stand in its stead. Only through such a warning is there ascertainable assurance that the accused was aware of this right.

If an individual indicates that he wishes the assistance of counsel before any interrogation occurs, the authorities cannot rationally ignore or deny his request on the basis that the individual does not have or cannot afford a retained attorney. The financial ability of the individual has no relationship to the scope of the rights involved here. The privilege against self-incrimination secured by the Constitution applies to all individuals. . . .

In order fully to apprise a person interrogated of the extent of his rights under this system, then, it is necessary to warn him not only that he has the right to consult with an attorney, but also that, if he is indigent, a lawyer will be appointed to represent him. Without this additional warning, the admonition of the right to consult with counsel would often be understood as meaning only that he can consult with a lawyer if he has one or has the funds to obtain one. The warning of a right to counsel would be hollow if not couched in terms that would convey to the indigent—the person most often subjected to interrogation—the knowledge that he too has a right to have counsel present. As with the warnings of the right to remain silent and of the general right to counsel, only by effective and express explanation to the indigent of this right can there be assurance that he was truly in a position to exercise it.

Once warnings have been given, the subsequent procedure is clear. If the individual indicates in any manner, at any time prior to or during questioning, that he wishes to remain silent, the interrogation must cease. At this point, he has shown that he intends to exercise his Fifth Amendment privilege; any statement taken after the person invokes his privilege cannot be other than the product of compulsion, subtle or otherwise. Without the right to cut off questioning, the setting of in-custody interrogation operates on the individual to overcome free choice in producing a statement after the privilege has been once invoked. If the individual states that he wants an attorney, the interrogation must cease until an attorney is present. At that time, the individual must have an opportunity to confer with the attorney and to have him present during any subsequent questioning. If the individual cannot obtain an attorney and he indicates that he wants one before speaking to police, they must respect his decision to remain silent. . . .

The principles announced today deal with the protection which must be given to the privilege against self-incrimination when the individual is first subjected to police interrogation while in custody at the station or otherwise deprived of his freedom of action in any significant way. It is at this point that our adversary system of criminal proceedings commences, distinguishing itself at the outset from the inquisitorial system recognized in some countries. Under the system of warnings we delineate today, or under any other system which may be devised and found effective, the safeguards to be erected about the privilege must come into play at this point. . . .

To summarize, we hold that, when an individual is taken into custody or otherwise deprived of his freedom by the authorities in any significant way and is subjected to questioning, the privilege against self-incrimination is jeopardized. Procedural safeguards must be employed to protect the privilege, and unless other fully effective means are adopted to notify the person of his right of silence and to assure that the exercise of the right will be scrupulously honored, the following measures are required. He must be warned prior to any questioning that he has the right to remain silent, that anything he says can be used against him in a court of law, that he has the right to the presence of an attorney, and that, if he cannot afford an attorney one will be appointed for him prior to any questioning if he so desires. Opportunity to exercise these rights must be afforded to him throughout the interrogation. After such warnings have been given, and such opportunity afforded him, the individual may knowingly and intelligently waive these rights and agree to answer questions or make a statement. But unless and until such warnings and waiver are demonstrated by the prosecution at trial, no evidence obtained as a result of interrogation can be used against him.

A recurrent argument made in these cases is that society's need for interrogation outweighs the privilege. This argument is not unfamiliar to this Court. The whole thrust of our foregoing discussion demonstrates that the Constitution has prescribed the rights of the individual when confronted with the power of government when it provided in the Fifth Amendment that an individual cannot be compelled to be a witness against himself. That right cannot be abridged. . . .

In announcing these principles, we are not unmindful of the burdens which law enforcement officials must bear, often under trying circumstances. We also fully recognize the obligation of all citizens to aid in enforcing the criminal laws. This Court, while protecting individual rights, has always given ample latitude to law enforcement agencies in the legitimate exercise of their duties. The limits we have placed on the interrogation process should not constitute an undue interference with a proper system of law enforcement. As we have noted, our decision does not in any way preclude police from carrying out their traditional investigatory functions. Although confessions may play an important role in some convictions, the cases before us present graphic examples of the overstatement of the "need" for confessions. In each case, authorities conducted interrogations ranging up to five days in duration despite the presence, through standard investigating practices, of considerable evidence against each defendant.

Mr. Justice Clark, dissenting. . . .

It is with regret that I find it necessary to write in these cases. However, I am unable to join the majority because its opinion goes too far on too little, while my dissenting brethren do not go quite far enough. Nor can I join in the Court's criticism of the present practices of police and investigatory agencies as to custodial interrogation. The materials it refers to as "police manuals" are, as I read them, merely writings in this field by professors and some police officers. Not one is shown by the record here to be the official manual of any police department, much less in universal use in crime detection. Moreover, the examples of police brutality mentioned by the Court are rare exceptions to the thousands that appear every year in the law reports. The police agencies—all the way from municipal and state forces to the federal bureaus—are responsible for law enforcement and public safety in this country. I am proud of their efforts, which, in my view, are not fairly characterized by the Court's opinion.

MR. JUSTICE WHITE, with whom MR. JUSTICE HARLAN and MR. JUSTICE STEWART join, dissenting.

The proposition that the privilege against self-incrimination forbids in-custody interrogation without the warnings specified in the majority opinion and without a clear waiver of counsel has no significant support in the history of the privilege or in the language of the Fifth Amendment. . . .

That the Court's holding today is neither compelled nor even strongly suggested by the language of the Fifth Amendment, is at odds with American and English legal history, and involves a departure from a long line of precedent does not prove either that the Court has exceeded its powers or that the Court is wrong or unwise in its present reinterpretation of the Fifth Amendment. It does, however, underscore the obvious—that the Court has not discovered or found the law in making today's decision, nor has it derived it from some irrefutable sources; what it has done is to make new law and new public policy in much the same way that it has in the course of interpreting other great clauses of the Constitution. This is what the Court historically has done. Indeed, it is what it must do, and will continue to do until and unless there is some fundamental change in the constitutional distribution of governmental powers.

But if the Court is here and now to announce new and fundamental policy to govern certain aspects of our affairs, it is wholly legitimate to examine the mode of this or any other constitutional decision in this Court, and to inquire into the advisability of its end product in terms of the long-range interest of the country. At the very least, the Court's text and reasoning should withstand analysis, and be a fair exposition of the constitutional provision which its opinion interprets. Decisions like these cannot rest alone on syllogism, metaphysics or some ill-defined notions of natural justice, although each will perhaps play its part. In proceeding to such constructions as it now announces, the Court should also duly consider all the factors and interests bearing upon the cases, at least insofar as the relevant materials are available, and, if the necessary considerations are not treated in the record or obtainable from some other reliable source, the Court should not proceed to formulate fundamental policies based on speculation alone.

First, we may inquire what are the textual and factual bases of this new fundamental rule. To reach the result announced on the grounds it does, the Court must stay within the confines of the Fifth Amendment, which forbids self-incrimination only if compelled. Hence, the core of the Court's opinion is that, because of the "compulsion inherent in custodial surroundings, no statement obtained from [a] defendant [in custody] can truly be the product of his free choice," absent the use of adequate protective devices as described by the Court. However, the Court does not point to any sudden inrush of new knowledge requiring the rejection of 70 years' experience. Nor does it assert that its novel conclusion reflects a changing consensus among state courts, or that a succession of cases had steadily eroded the old rule and proved it unworkable. Rather than asserting new knowledge, the Court concedes that it cannot truly know what occurs during custodial questioning, because of the innate secrecy of such proceedings. It extrapolates a picture of what it conceives to be the norm from police investigatorial manuals, published in 1959 and 1962 or earlier, without any attempt to allow for adjustments in police practices that may have occurred in the wake of more recent decisions of state appellate tribunals or this Court. But even if the relentless application of the described procedures could lead to involuntary confessions, it most assuredly does not follow that each and every case will disclose this kind of interrogation or this kind of consequence. Insofar as appears from the Court's opinion, it has not examined a single transcript of any police interrogation, let alone the interrogation that took place in any one of these cases which it decides today. Judged by any of the standards for empirical investigation utilized in the social sciences, the factual basis for the Court's premise is patently inadequate. . . .

Today's result would not follow even if it were agreed that, to some extent, custodial interrogation is inherently coercive. The test has been whether the totality of circumstances deprived the defendant of a "free choice to admit, to deny, or to refuse to answer," and whether physical or psychological coercion was of such a degree that "the defendant's will was overborne at the time he confessed." The duration and nature of *incommunicado* custody, the presence or absence of advice concerning the defendant's constitutional rights, and the granting or refusal of requests to communicate with lawyers, relatives or friends have all been rightly regarded as important data bearing on the basic inquiry. But it has never been suggested, until today, that such questioning was so coercive and accused persons so lacking in hardihood that the very first response to the very first question following the commencement of custody must be conclusively presumed to be the product of an overborne will. . . .

[The Court's rationale] makes very little sense in terms of the compulsion which the Fifth Amendment proscribes. That amendment deals with compelling the accused himself. It is his free will that is involved. Confessions and incriminating admissions, as such, are not forbidden evidence; only those which are compelled are banned. I doubt that the Court observes these distinctions today. By considering any answers to any interrogation to be compelled regardless of the content and course of examination, and by escalating the requirements to prove waiver, the Court not only prevents the use of compelled confessions, but, for all practical purposes, forbids interrogation except in the presence of counsel. That is, instead of confining itself to protection of the right against compelled self-incrimination the Court has created a limited Fifth Amendment right to counsel—or, as the Court expresses it, a "need for counsel to protect the Fifth Amendment privilege. . . . " The focus then is not on the will of the accused, but on the will of counsel, and how much influence he can have on the accused. Obviously there is no warrant in the Fifth Amendment for thus installing counsel as the arbiter of the privilege.

In sum, for all the Court's expounding on the menacing atmosphere of police interrogation procedures, it has failed to supply any foundation for the conclusions it draws or the measures it adopts.

Criticism of the Court's opinion, however, cannot stop with a demonstration that the factual and textual bases for the rule it propounds are, at best, less than compelling. Equally relevant is an assessment of the rule's consequences measured against community values. The Court's duty to assess the consequences of its action is not satisfied by the utterance of the truth that a value of our system of criminal justice is "to respect the inviolability of the human personality" and to require government to produce the evidence against the accused by its own independent labors. More than the human dignity of the accused is involved; the human personality of others in the society must also be preserved. Thus, the values reflected by the privilege are not the sole desideratum; society's interest in the general security is of equal weight. . . .

The rule announced today . . . is a deliberate calculus to prevent interrogations, to reduce the incidence of confessions and pleas of guilty, and to increase the number of trials. Criminal trials, no matter how efficient the police are, are not sure bets for the prosecution, nor should they be if the evidence is not forthcoming. Under the present law, the prosecution fails to prove its case in about 30% of the criminal cases actually tried in the federal courts. But it is something else again to remove from the ordinary criminal case all those confessions which heretofore have been held to be free and voluntary acts of the accused, and to thus establish a new constitutional barrier to the ascertainment of truth by the judicial process. There is, in my view, every reason to believe that a good many criminal defendants who otherwise would have been convicted on what this Court has previously thought to be the most satisfactory kind of evidence will now, under this new version of the Fifth Amendment, either not be tried at all or will be acquitted if the State's evidence, minus the confession, is put to the test of litigation.

I have no desire whatsoever to share the responsibility for any such impact on the present criminal process.

In some unknown number of cases, the Court's rule will return a killer, a rapist or other criminal to the streets and to the environment which produced him, to repeat his crime whenever it pleases him. As a consequence, there will not be a gain, but a loss, in human dignity. The real concern is not the unfortunate consequences of this new decision on the criminal law as an abstract, disembodied series of authoritative proscriptions, but the impact on those who rely on the public authority for protection, and who, without it, can only engage in violent self-help with guns, knives and the help of their neighbors similarly inclined. There is, of course, a saving factor: the next victims are uncertain, unnamed and unrepresented in this case. . . .

Today's decision leaves open such questions as whether the accused was in custody, whether his statements were spontaneous or the product of interrogation, whether the accused has effectively waived his rights, and whether nontestimonial evidence introduced at trial is the fruit of statements made during a prohibited interrogation, all of which are certain to prove productive of uncertainty during investigation and litigation during prosecution. For all these reasons, if further restrictions on police interrogation are desirable at this time, a more flexible approach makes much more sense than the Court's constitutional straitjacket, which forecloses more discriminating treatment by legislative or rulemaking pronouncements.

▼▲▼

SIDEBAR

MIRANDA V. ARIZONA

"You Have the Right to Remain Silent"

Just a few minutes after midnight on March 3, 1963, an eighteen-year-old woman who worked as a refreshment stand clerk at a Phoenix movie theatre stepped off the bus at her usual stop and began to walk home. Even at this late hour, she often passed other people, so when a young man began purposely striding in her direction she paid him little notice. Suddenly, the man turned toward her and placed his hand on her mouth. "Don't scream," he said, "and I won't hurt you." He dragged the young woman into his car, which he had parked down the street, ordered her to lie face down in the back seat, and tied her ankles together. As her abductor drove off, the young woman pleaded for her release. About twenty minutes later, he pulled his car off into a dark stretch of desert, and then, according to the young woman, raped her. Afterward, he demanded money from her. She gave him the four dollars she had in her purse. He then ordered her to put her clothes back on and lie down in the back seat. He then drove the young woman back to the spot where he had abducted her and let her out. Before he stopped the car, he turned to her and said, "Whether you tell your mother what has happened or not is none of my business, but pray for me."

Phoenix police later arrested Ernesto Arturo Miranda, a twenty-three-year-old Mexican immigrant who drifted in and out of various jobs, for the rape and attempted murder of the young woman. Miranda had a police record and a history of sexual problems, including arrests for attempted rape, exposing himself in public, and engaging in "peeping Tom" activities. In 1960, Miranda had gone to prison for car theft. Shortly before he was released a year later, Miranda caught his hand in the electric prison gate as he waved good-bye to some visitors and lost the top third of one of his index fingers. His alleged victim mentioned no special identifying characteristics to the police.

The young woman later identified Miranda as *possibly* matching the features of her attacker, but she asked to hear his voice just to be more certain. Before that could happen, Miranda had already been led into an interrogation room, where he confessed to the rape of the young woman. The detectives later testified at Miranda's trial that Miranda, when presented with the evidence against him, simply confessed without inducement or coercion of any kind. But Miranda described the scene differently:

> Once they get you in a little room and they start badgering you with one or the other, "you'd better tell us . . . or we're going to throw the book at you" . . . that is what was told to me. They would throw the book at me. They would try to give me all the time they could. They thought there was even the possibility that there was something wrong with me. They would try to help me, get me medical care if I needed it. . . . And I haven't had any sleep since the day before. . . . I just got off work, and they have me and they are interrogating me. They mention first one crime, then another one, they are certain I am the person . . . knowing what a penitentiary is like, a person has to be frightened, scared. And not knowing if he'll be able to get back up and go home.

Before the police had settled on Miranda as their suspect, discrepancies began to emerge in the statements

Ernesto Miranda (right) after his March 1963 arrest for allegedly raping a teenage girl in Phoenix, Arizona.
© Bettmann/CORBIS

his alleged victim was giving the police. She claimed she was a virgin in her original statement, but a rape-kit test demonstrated that was not true. She claimed she had been tied up with rope and had resisted her attacker, but there were no bruises, abrasions, or rope burn marks on her body to indicate abuse or a struggle. What led the police to Miranda was the car the young woman later identified as the one that had sped past her and stopped before the man got out and followed her. When police arrived at the home belonging to Miranda's common-law wife, they peered into the car parked in the driveway. Inside, a piece of rope was strung along the back of the front seat, just as the young woman had described it.

Miranda, in accord with the Court's decision in *Gideon* v. *Wainwright,* was provided an attorney, but not until after he was in custody. No lawyer was present while he was questioned or when he confessed. Miranda's lawyer, however, did not press that argument at trial. Instead, he tried to plead that his client was temporarily insane. A jury rejected Miranda's defense and sentenced him to a term not to exceed thirty years.

Miranda's case soon came to the attention of the Phoenix affiliate of the ACLU, which enlisted the services of two of the area's most outstanding criminal and constitutional lawyers, John J. Flynn and John P. Frank, to represent Miranda on appeal. Flynn and Frank were partners in a prominent local firm that had a standing arrangement to handle two cases a year for the ACLU. After the Court's decision in *Escobedo,* most criminal attorneys understood that the next big issue for the Court was whether the Fifth and Sixth Amendments required a suspect to be *informed* of his right to have attorney present once the police had placed an individual in custody.

Flynn and Frank argued that the Court, in *Escobedo,* had stressed that criminal defendants should receive "protection" during the process of police interrogation in order for the right against self-incrimination to carry more than merely symbolic meaning. In their brief, Flynn and Frank also laid the groundwork for what became the famous "four warnings" to emerge from *Miranda*: that (1) an individual in custody must be *clearly* informed that he has the right to remain silent before police interrogation; (2) anything a suspect says can and will be used against him in court; (3) a suspect must be clearly informed that he has the right to consult with an attorney and have an attorney present during questioning; and (4) if a suspect cannot afford an attorney one will be appointed to represent him. The Court ultimately agreed with Flynn and Frank's position. In the process, the Court also joined together the privilege against self-incrimination in the Fifth Amendment with the Sixth Amendment right to counsel rule established in *Gideon* v. *Wainwright.*

Twenty-nine state attorneys general, joined by the Virgin Islands and Puerto Rico, filed a joint brief asking the Court to affirm Miranda's conviction and not to extend *Escobedo* to include the four warnings outlined in Flynn and Frank's brief. The state attorneys general also argued against a rule that would further nationalize the rights of criminal defendants. They preferred a system that gave states greater discretion in this area. The solicitor general, who represents the United States in litigation, also filed a brief opposing the position of Miranda's lawyers, as did the National District Attorneys Association. Much more effective, as discussed elsewhere in this chapter, was the brief filed by the national office of the ACLU, which emphasized, in its view, the disadvantages at which criminal defendants were placed in the process of police interrogation. The five-member majority in *Miranda* was heavily influenced by the emphasis the ACLU brief placed on deceptive and psychologically coercive police interrogation practices.

And whatever happened to Ernesto Miranda, the man whose name became synonymous with modern police practices? On January 31, 1976, Miranda, still living in Phoenix and working as a delivery man for a hardware store, was stabbed during a barroom fight over money owed in a poker game. His attackers quickly fled, but one was later caught by two officers, who read the suspect his rights in English and Spanish before taking him to police headquarters. Miranda, however, did not live to see the day. He died before his ambulance reached the hospital.

References

Baker, Liva. *Miranda: Crime, Law and Politics.* Boston: Atheneum, 1983.

Walker, Samuel. *In Defense of American Liberties: A History of the ACLU.* New York: Oxford University Press, 1990.

Not since *Engel* v. *Vitale* (1962) (see Chapter 6), which banned state-sponsored school prayer, had there been such an intense—and largely negative—public reaction to a Supreme Court decision. The political fallout from *Miranda* was tremendous. FBI Director J. Edgar Hoover immediately took steps to bring the interrogation practices of federal agents into line with the Court's decision. Congress, on the other hand, included a provision attempting to overturn *Miranda* in the 1968 Omnibus Crime Control Act, which also attempted to circumvent *Katz* v. *United States* (1967) (see Chapter 7), the Court's decision that placed limits on wiretapping. Known as Section 3501, the federal law permitted law enforcement officers to admit confessions obtained under the *voluntariness* standard, one that did not require the four warnings established by the Court's decision in *Miranda*. In reality, Congress understood it could not overturn a constitutional decision—and *Miranda* did involve the interpretation of the Fifth and Sixth Amendments—through legislation. Section 3501 was mostly an effort by Congress to sail with the negative winds of public opinion that had greeted *Miranda*. As we will discuss later in this chapter, Section 3501 went unused and stood largely neglected until it became the center of an effort by conservative groups to have the Court revisit and overturn *Miranda* in *Dickerson* v. *United States* (2000).

Civil liberties groups such as the ACLU hailed *Miranda* as a great—and long overdue—step in "cleaning up" police practices around the nation. Indeed, the ACLU's role in shaping the Court's opinion in *Miranda* cannot be overstated. In *Escobedo,* the ACLU had filed an *amicus* brief and been given oral argument time to make its argument on the right to counsel during custodial police interrogation. The ACLU brief closely paralleled Justice Goldberg's opinion for the Court. In *Miranda,* the Phoenix chapter had secured the defendant's two attorneys, John J. Flynn and John P. Frank. The ACLU national office underscored their argument by submitting an *amicus* brief, of which one legal scholar commented:

> Perhaps the most striking lesson to learn from these materials is the role an *amicus* brief can play in shaping a majority opinion, even without oral argument. Undoubtedly, the

> most effective presentation to the Court was the *amicus* brief of the American Civil Liberties Union. . . . [I]t was clear that [the ACLU brief] presented a conceptual, legal and structural formulation that is practically identical to the majority opinion. Also, it is from this brief that the Court [drew] its lengthy discussion of the contents of leading and popular police interrogation manuals. Both the ACLU brief and the Court explain that resort to the manuals is necessary because of the absence of information on what actually goes on in the privacy of police interrogation rooms. And both the Court and the ACLU brief point out that these manuals, shocking as they seem, should be understood as presenting the enlightened and fair-minded police point of view.[24]

The ACLU's pivotal role in *Miranda* represented the culmination of a decade-long effort to reform police practices. In the mid-1950s, the ACLU won a $100,000 damage award against the Chicago police after a jury concluded that an officer had unjustifiably shot and killed a potential suspect. Initially, the ACLU believed that the prospect of large damage awards would deter police misconduct, but the case proved to have little long-term impact on such behavior. In 1959, the ACLU published a report, *Secret Detention by the Chicago Police,* which examined the criminal process in over two thousand criminal cases from arrest to formal booking. Investigators found that suspects were routinely held for long periods of time without being told of the charges against them or their legal rights. What set off concern among advocates of police reform was the fact that arrest records did not exist for approximately 30 percent of the cases processed by the Chicago criminal courts. *Secret Detention* concluded by recommending several changes in police practices, most notably a law that required the police to inform suspects of their right to remain silent while in custody and another mandating the exclusion of confessions if a court determined that a suspect had been illegally detained. The ACLU report received nationwide attention, drawing positive editorial praise in several leading newspapers and requests for copies of the report from several Supreme Court justices. Foreshadowing the criminal law revolution of the 1960s, *Secret Detention*'s ultimate objective was to secure assistance for "the poor, and racial and ethnic minorities."[25]

Reaction from police departments to *Miranda,* however, was almost uniformly loud and negative. Coming on the heels of *Mapp* and *Escobedo* (*Gideon* had raised little or no protest from the police), the Court's stinging rebuke of police tactics to obtain confessions was viewed by many in the law enforcement community as a slap in the faces of the men and women who put their lives on the line every day. Moreover, many police chiefs were unsure of what to make of *Miranda*'s requirements, and were left wondering if the Court had meant to ban all confessions or just those confessions obtained in violation of the four warnings set out by Chief Justice Warren. In response, many police departments created wallet-sized cards for their officers to carry that listed the now-famous *Miranda* warnings, which often included a reminder to the officer to ask the suspect if he or she understood their rights. Impressed but angered with the ACLU's influence in *Miranda,* Northwestern University law professor Fred Inbau started Americans for Effective Law Enforcement (AELE) (see Chapter 7) to support law enforcement's view in criminal procedure cases. Inbau's textbook, *Criminal Investigations and Confessions,* had been a standard training manual in many police academies (and criticized by Chief Justice Warren in his *Miranda* opinion). He decided that the police needed a counterweight to the ACLU.[26] Other conservative public interest groups, such as the Washington Legal Foundation and Pacific Legal Foundation, were inspired by the AELE and later formed to articulate conservative positions on a wide array of constitutional issues to come before the Court, including criminal law and procedure.[27]

Even in the wake of such fierce criticism, the Court did not retreat from *Miranda.* In *Orozco* v. *Texas* (1969), the Court unanimously ruled that suspects were entitled to counsel from the point at which they came into custody, which could occur long before they entered a police station interrogation room. *Orozco* was the Court's last important self-incrimination decision under Chief Justice Earl Warren, who, as *Miranda*'s author, had been the principal target of the police and prosecutors. Warren never wavered in his belief that the Court had done the right thing in *Miranda* and in all the other controversial criminal law decisions handed down during his tenure.

Before coming to the Court in 1953, Warren had been a popular governor and, before that, state attorney general in his native California. Long before the Court began to address police misconduct, Warren earned a reputation as a scrupulously fair and ethically upright prosecutor. Perhaps the most famous example of Warren's early approach to police interrogation came during the murder investigation of his father, who was beaten to death in his home in May 1938. At that time, Warren was the district attorney of Alameda County. Several suspects were brought in for questioning, and one, after hours without food or water, was on the verge of confessing. After Warren's deputies learned that the police had detained the suspect under such conditions, they released him, a move their boss supported. Said one of the detectives supervising the investigation: "[Warren] loved his father and he wanted his murderer found, but he wouldn't break any of his rules or take advantage of his position even to convict the guilty man if he couldn't do it with solid evidence that was legally obtained."[28]

After Earl Warren's departure from the Court in 1969, the Court began to backtrack from *Miranda*. During the early 1970s, the Court ruled that the police were not required to administer warnings to individuals who volunteered to come and speak with police,[29] and held that statements made in violation of *Miranda* could be used to impeach a witness's credibility.[30] Certainly, personnel changes within the Court tipped the scales away from the rights of criminal defendants firmly in the direction of police discretion to obtain and use confessions from suspects. Before coming to the Court, Warren Burger, as a federal appeals court judge, had been a vocal critic of the Court's criminal law decisions. In fact, it was his outspoken criticism of the Court that led President Nixon, in large part, to appoint him to succeed Earl Warren as chief justice. By 1972, Nixon appointed three additional justices—Harry A. Blackmun, Lewis Powell, and William Rehnquist—to the Court, all of whom initially voted against the claims of criminal defendants quite regularly. By the late 1970s, cases in which the Court extended *Miranda* in controversial contexts, such as *Brewer* v. *Williams* (1977), discussed at the outset of this chapter, were quite rare.

Miranda critics claimed that the Court left little room for suspects to confess voluntarily once they were in police custody. Chief Justice Warren's opinion had, in fact, explicitly left room for voluntary confessions, but that provision seemed to get lost in the charged rhetoric and political gamesmanship that *Miranda* created. *Rhode Island* v. *Innis* (1980) allowed the Court to revisit several of the major questions that continued to confront police, prosecutors, criminal defense lawyers, and criminal suspects even after nearly fifteen years of post-*Miranda* cases. Is custody inherently coercive? Does all communication between police officers about a case in the presence of a suspect qualify as interrogation? Once a suspect has received his or her *Miranda* warnings, at what point do statements become admissible? *Innis* addressed all these questions and several more.

Rhode Island v. *Innis*

446 U.S. 291 (1980)

On January 16, 1975, Providence, Rhode Island, cab driver John Mulvaney was found dead in the nearby town of Coventry four days after he was dispatched to pick up a customer. Buried in a shallow grave, the veteran cab driver had been killed by a shotgun blast to the back of his head. The next day, another Providence cab driver, Gerald Aubin, phoned the local police to inform them that a man carrying a sawed-off shotgun had robbed him after he picked him up. Aubin went down to the Providence police station to give a full report. While he was waiting in a common area to speak with homicide detectives, Aubin noticed a man's picture posted on a bulletin board. That man looked remarkably like the one who had robbed him. Aubin later picked the man, Thomas Innis, out of a photo display.

Aubin had also told the police he had dropped off his assailant near Rhode Island College, located in the Mount Pleasant section of Providence. A small search team of officers combed the area looking for Innis. As one of the officers, Robert Lovell, pulled his car around a dark corner, he spotted Innis walking directly toward his car. Lovell got out, pointed his gun at Innis, and asked him to come forward with his hands up. Innis walked directly over to Lovell, who cuffed him, read him his *Miranda* rights, and, with the help of the other officers on the scene, placed him into the back of a police car.

Lovell did not talk with Innis after reading him his rights, other than to give him a cigarette, which Innis had requested. Lovell's sergeant and later his captain also read Innis his rights. The suspect said he understood them and wanted to speak with his lawyer as soon as possible. The three officers charged with taking Innis to the police station, Joseph Gleckman, Walter Williams, and Richard McKenna, were told not to question their prisoner.

As Innis sat in the back of the car, Gleckman and McKenna, sitting in the front and separated from Innis by a wire screen, began to make small talk about the potential danger that a missing—and loaded—shotgun posed for the Mount Pleasant community. Gleckman, who later testified he never spoke to Innis or directed any conversation his way, told McKenna he was familiar with the area because it was part of his beat. Every day, McKenna said, he passed a special school for disabled children and "God forbid one of them might find a weapon with shells and they might hurt themselves." Williams, who said nothing during the drive, later testified that Gleckman said, "[I]t would be too bad if the little—I believe he said girl—would pick up the gun, maybe kill herself." At this point, Innis shouted, "Stop, turn around, I'll show you where it [the gun] is." The officers' superiors were notified by radio, and met them at the location where Innis said the gun was. Innis was again apprised of his rights, but told police he "wanted to get the gun out of the way because of the kids in the area in the school."

The gun was found and matched the one used to kill Mulvaney. Innis was convicted by a state trial court, but later appealed, claiming that the conversation between Gleckman and McKenna was really a trick to get him to confess.

The Court's decision was 6 to 3. Justice Stewart delivered the opinion of the Court. Chief Justice Burger and Justice White filed separate concurring opinions. Justice Marshall, joined by Justice Brennan, dissented. Justice Stevens also filed a dissenting opinion.

▼▲▼

MR. JUSTICE STEWART delivered the opinion of the Court.

In the present case, the parties are in agreement that the respondent was fully informed of his *Miranda* rights, and that he invoked his *Miranda* right to counsel when he told [the police] that he wished to consult with a lawyer. It is also uncontested that the respondent was "in custody" while being transported to the police station.

The issue, therefore, is whether the respondent was "interrogated" by the police officers in violation of the respondent's undisputed right under *Miranda* to remain silent until he had consulted with a lawyer. In resolving this issue, we first define the term "interrogation" under *Miranda,* before turning to a consideration of the facts of this case.

The starting point for defining "interrogation" in this context is, of course, the Court's *Miranda* opinion. There the Court observed that, "[b]y custodial interrogation, we mean questioning initiated by law enforcement officers after a person has been taken into custody or otherwise deprived of his freedom of action in any significant way." This passage and other references throughout the opinion to "questioning" might suggest that the *Miranda* rules were to apply only to those police interrogation practices that involve express questioning of a defendant while in custody.

We do not, however, construe the *Miranda* opinion so narrowly. The concern of the Court in *Miranda* was that the "interrogation environment" created by the interplay of interrogation and custody would "subjugate the individual to the will of his examiner," and thereby undermine the privilege against compulsory self-incrimination. The police practices that evoked this concern included several that did not involve express questioning. For example, one of the practices discussed in *Miranda* was the use of lineups in which a coached witness would pick the defendant as the perpetrator. This was designed to establish that the defendant was, in fact, guilty as a predicate for further interrogation. A variation on this theme discussed in *Miranda* was the so-called "reverse line-up" in which a defendant would be identified by coached witnesses as the perpetrator of a fictitious crime, with the object of inducing him to confess to the actual crime of which he was suspected in order to escape the false prosecution. The Court in *Miranda* also included in its survey of interrogation practices the use of psychological ploys, such as to "posi[t]" "the guilt of the subject," to "minimize the moral seriousness of the offense," and "to cast blame on the victim or on society." It is clear that these techniques of persuasion, no less than express questioning, were thought, in a custodial setting, to amount to interrogation.

This is not to say, however, that all statements obtained by the police after a person has been taken into custody are to be considered the product of interrogation. As the Court in *Miranda* noted:

> Confessions remain a proper element in law enforcement. Any statement given freely and voluntarily without any compelling influences is, of course, admissible in evidence. *The fundamental import of the privilege while an individual is in custody is not whether he is allowed to talk to the police without the benefit of warnings and counsel, but whether he can be interrogated.* . . . Volunteered statements of any kind are not barred by the Fifth Amendment, and their admissibility is not affected by our holding today.

It is clear, therefore, that the special procedural safeguards outlined in *Miranda* are required not where a suspect is simply taken into custody, but rather where a suspect in custody is subjected to interrogation. "Interrogation," as conceptualized in the *Miranda* opinion, must reflect a measure of compulsion above and beyond that inherent in custody itself.

We conclude that the *Miranda* safeguards come into play whenever a person in custody is subjected to either express questioning or its functional equivalent. That is to say, the term "interrogation" under *Miranda* refers not only to express questioning, but also to any words or actions on the part of the police (other than those normally attendant to arrest and custody) that the police should know are reasonably likely to elicit an incriminating response from the suspect. The latter portion of this definition focuses primarily upon the perceptions of the suspect, rather than the intent of the police. This focus reflects the fact that the *Miranda* safeguards were designed to vest a suspect in custody with an added measure of protection against coercive police practices, without regard to objective proof of the underlying intent of the police. A practice that the police should know is reasonably likely to evoke an incriminating response from a suspect thus amounts to interrogation. But, since the police surely cannot be held accountable for the unforeseeable results of their words or actions, the definition of interrogation can extend only to words or actions on the part of police officers that they *should have known* were reasonably likely to elicit an incriminating response.

Turning to the facts of the present case, we conclude that the respondent was not "interrogated" within the meaning of *Miranda.* It is undisputed that the first prong of the definition of "interrogation" was not satisfied, for the conversation between Patrolmen Gleckman and McKenna included no express questioning of the respondent. Rather, that conversation was, at least in form, nothing more than a dialogue between the two officers to which no response from the respondent was invited.

Moreover, it cannot be fairly concluded that the respondent was subjected to the "functional equivalent" of questioning. It cannot be said, in short, that Patrolmen Gleckman and McKenna should have known that their conversation was reasonably likely to elicit an incriminating response from the respondent. There is nothing in the record to suggest that the officers were aware that the respondent was peculiarly susceptible to an appeal to his conscience concerning the safety of handicapped children. Nor is there anything in the record to suggest that the police knew that the respondent was unusually disoriented or upset at the time of his arrest.

The case thus boils down to whether, in the context of a brief conversation, the officers should have known that the respondent would suddenly be moved to make a self-incriminating response. Given the fact that the entire conversation appears to have consisted of no more than a few off-hand remarks, we cannot say that the officers should have known that it was reasonably likely that Innis would so respond. This is not a case where the police carried on a lengthy harangue in the presence of the suspect. Nor does the record support the respondent's contention that, under the circumstances, the officers' comments were particularly "evocative." It is our view, therefore, that the respondent was not subjected by the police to words or actions that the police should have known were reasonably likely to elicit an incriminating response from him.

The Rhode Island Supreme Court erred, in short, in equating "subtle compulsion" with interrogation. That the officers' comments struck a responsive chord is readily apparent. Thus, it may be said, as the Rhode Island Supreme Court did say, that the respondent was subjected to "subtle compulsion." But that is not the end of the inquiry. It must also be established that a suspect's incriminating response was the product of words or actions on the part of the police that they should have known were reasonably likely to elicit an incriminating response. This was not established in the present case.

For the reasons stated, the judgment of the Supreme Court of Rhode Island is vacated, and the case is remanded to that court for further proceedings not inconsistent with this opinion.

It is so ordered.

MR. JUSTICE MARSHALL, with whom MR. JUSTICE BRENNAN joins, dissenting.

I am substantially in agreement with the Court's definition of "interrogation" within the meaning of *Miranda* v. *Arizona*

(1966). In my view, the *Miranda* safeguards apply whenever police conduct is intended or likely to produce a response from a suspect in custody. . . . Thus, the Court requires an objective inquiry into the likely effect of police conduct on a typical individual, taking into account any special susceptibility of the suspect to certain kinds of pressure of which the police know or have reason to know.

I am utterly at a loss, however, to understand how this objective standard, as applied to the facts before us, can rationally lead to the conclusion that there was no interrogation. Innis was arrested at 4:30 A.M., handcuffed, searched, advised of his rights, and placed in the back seat of a patrol car. Within a short time, he had been twice more advised of his rights and driven away in a four-door sedan with three police officers. Two officers sat in the front seat, and one sat beside Innis in the back seat. Since the car traveled no more than a mile before Innis agreed to point out the location of the murder weapon, Officer Gleckman must have begun almost immediately to talk about the search for the shotgun.

The Court attempts to characterize Gleckman's statements as "no more than a few off-hand remarks" which could not reasonably have been expected to elicit a response. If the statements had been addressed to respondent, it would be impossible to draw such a conclusion. The simple message of the "talking back and forth" between Gleckman and McKenna was that they had to find the shotgun to avert a child's death.

One can scarcely imagine a stronger appeal to the conscience of a suspect—*any* suspect—than the assertion that, if the weapon is not found, an innocent person will be hurt or killed. And not just any innocent person, but an innocent child—a little girl—a helpless, handicapped little girl on her way to school. The notion that such an appeal could not be expected to have any effect unless the suspect were known to have some special interest in handicapped children verges on the ludicrous. As a matter of fact, the appeal to a suspect to confess for the sake of others, to "display some evidence of decency and honor," is a classic interrogation technique. . . .

This is not a case where police officers, speaking among themselves, are accidentally overheard by a suspect. These officers were "talking back and forth" in close quarters with the handcuffed suspect, traveling past the very place where they believed the weapon was located. They knew respondent would hear and attend to their conversation, and they are chargeable with knowledge of and responsibility for the pressures to speak which they created.

Justice Stewart, who had written the Court's opinion in *Brewer* declaring the Christian burial speech the equivalent of an interrogation, found no such coercion on the part of the officers in *Innis*. While it is possible to argue that Stewart's analysis in *Innis* draws a distinction without a difference to *Brewer*, the opinion demonstrates just how easy the Court can get around *Miranda*. The Court, a year later, unanimously ruled that the police must cease an interrogation as soon as a suspect requests an attorney—a decision that did reinforce the centrality of *Miranda*.[31] However, *Innis* was much more typical of the exceptions that the Court, since the early 1970s, had steadily created to the 1966 decision. Prominent *Miranda* critics, such as the Reagan administration and groups such as the AELE and the Washington Legal Foundation, invested a great deal of time and energy in cases they believed would be appropriate vehicles for the Court to stop creating exceptions to the decision and simply overrule it.

Below the anti-*Miranda* rhetoric, however, very little enthusiasm existed among prosecutors and police chiefs to overturn the decision. As far back as 1968, retired Supreme Court justice Tom Clark, who had dissented in *Miranda*, admitted that he had overestimated the decision's impact on the ability of police to secure convictions through confessions. Noting that "confessions were still going stronger than ever," Clark stated: "I confess error in my appraisal of *Miranda*'s effect."[32] Charles Fried, who served as solicitor general (1985–1989) during the second term of the Reagan administration, rejected various overtures from other divisions in the Department of Justice to encourage the Court to overturn *Miranda*. Fried concluded that "most experienced federal prosecutors in and out of my office were opposed to this project, and so was I."[33] Since *Miranda*, no scholarly study of police interrogation and confessions has conclusively determined that the rules that emerged from the decision have hampered law enforcement's efforts to obtain confessions.[34] On the street level, many policemen have admitted that *Miranda*'s impact on their evidence gathering and prosecutorial efforts has been, in the words of one big-city police chief, "zilch."[35]

Well into the 1990s, the Court continued the same pattern with *Miranda*. The Court reaffirmed that suspects were entitled to request an attorney at any point during questioning and the police, at that point, were required to stop their interrogation. However, the Court continued to create exceptions allowing the admission of confessions in circumstances where counsel was not present or when they were admittedly tainted by police misconduct.[36] Perhaps the most startling recent exception to *Miranda* came in *Arizona* v. *Fulminante* (1991). In *Fulminante,* five justices held that the admission of a coerced confession into evidence was a "harmless error" and thus not subject to exclusion under *Miranda.* Under the "harmless error" rule, appeals courts will not reverse lower court rulings for procedural mistakes considered minor or having no bearing on the outcome of the trial. In doing so, the Court narrowed considerably an important 1967 decision, *Chapman* v. *California,* in which the Court held that statements made by the trial judge and the prosecutor about the defendant's refusal to testify were considered so prejudicial so as not to constitute a "harmless error."[37] Note how divided the justices are over the constitutional issues in *Fulminante*, particularly the meaning of the "harmless error" rule and its application to the facts in this case. Which opinion do you consider more persuasive, Justice White's or Chief Justice Rehnquist's?

Arizona v. *Fulminante*

499 U.S. 279 (1991)

In early 1983, Oreste Fulminante began serving time in the Ray Brook Federal Correctional Institution in New York for a conviction on federal firearms possession charges. He soon became friendly with another inmate, Anthony Sarivola, who was serving a sixty-day sentence for extortion. All Fulminante knew was that Sarivola liked to brag about his high-rolling life as an organized crime figure. What Fulminante did not know was that Sarivola, a former police officer, had also become a paid informant for the FBI.

Sarivola heard a rumor that Fulminante had been involved in a child rape and murder in Arizona and tried to elicit more information from his friend about the subject. Fulminante denied knowing anything about it, saying only that he had heard that a young girl had been killed by bikers looking for drugs. Sarivola's FBI supervisors ordered him to pursue the allegation. One night, while walking around the prison track, Sarivola told Fulminante that he heard his friend was "starting to get some tough treatment and what not" from other inmates because of the rumors that he had raped and murdered a child. Sarivola told Fulminante he could protect him, but said, "You have to tell me about it, you know. I mean, in other words, for me to give you any help." Fulminante then admitted that he had driven his eleven-year-old stepdaughter, Jeneane Michelle Hunt, out to the Mesa desert on his motorcycle, sexually assaulted her, made her beg for her life, and then shot her twice in the back of her head.

Sarivola was released from prison a month after his conversation with Fulminante. In May 1984, Fulminante was released from prison. He met up with Sarivola and his wife, Donna, to whom Fulminante also described the murder of Hunt. In September 1984, after a previous arrest on firearms charges, Fulminante was indicted for the murder of Hunt. Fulminante's lawyers were unsuccessful in keeping his confession to Sarivola out of evidence. Fulminante was convicted of Hunt's murder and sentenced to death. The Arizona Supreme Court reversed the trial court, ruling that the admission of the confession was not a harmless error. It ordered Fulminante to receive a new trial. The state appealed to the Supreme Court.

The Court divided three ways on the three central questions in the case:

1. Justice White commanded five votes (Blackmun, Marshall, Scalia, and Stevens) concluding that Fulminante's confession had been coerced.
2. Justice White also commanded five votes (Blackmun, Kennedy, Marshall, and Stevens) concluding that the admission of Fulminante's confession at trial was not a harmless error beyond a reasonable doubt.
3. Chief Justice Rehnquist commanded five votes (Kennedy, O'Connor, Scalia, and Souter) on the key constitutional question of whether a coerced confession could be excused as a harmless error if other evidence supported a guilty verdict.

▼▲▼

Justice White delivered the opinion, Parts I, II, and IV of which are the opinion of the Court, and Part III of which is a dissenting opinion.

Justice Marshall, Justice Blackmun, and Justice Stevens join this opinion in its entirety; Justice Scalia joins Parts I and II; and Justice Kennedy joins Parts I and IV.

The Arizona Supreme Court ruled in this case that respondent Oreste Fulminante's confession, received in evidence at his trial for murder, had been coerced, and that its use against him was barred by the Fifth and Fourteenth Amendments to the United States Constitution. The court also held that the harmless error rule could not be used to save the conviction. We affirm the judgment of the Arizona court, although for different reasons than those upon which that court relied.

I

[Omitted]

II

We deal first with the State's contention that the court below erred in holding Fulminante's confession to have been coerced. The State argues that it is the totality of the circumstances that determines whether Fulminante's confession was coerced, but contends that, rather than apply this standard, the Arizona court applied a "but for" test, under which the court found that but for the promise given by Sarivola, Fulminante would not have confessed. In support of this argument, the State points to the Arizona court's reference to *Bram* v. *United States* (1897). Although the Court noted in *Bram* that a confession cannot be obtained by "'any direct or implied promises, however slight, nor by the exertion of any improper influence,'" it is clear this passage from *Bram,* which under current precedent does not state the standard for determining the voluntariness of a confession, was not relied on by the Arizona court in reaching its conclusion. Rather, the court cited this language as part of a longer quotation from an Arizona case which accurately described the State's burden of proof for establishing voluntariness. Indeed, the Arizona Supreme Court stated that a "determination regarding the voluntariness of a confession . . . must be viewed in a totality of the circumstances," and under that standard plainly found that Fulminante's statement to Sarivola had been coerced. . . .

Although the question is a close one, we agree with the Arizona Supreme Court's conclusion that Fulminante's confession was coerced. The Arizona Supreme Court found a credible threat of physical violence unless Fulminante confessed. Our cases have made clear that a finding of coercion need not depend upon actual violence by a government agent; a credible threat is sufficient. As we have said, "coercion can be mental as well as physical, and . . . the blood of the accused is not the only hallmark of an unconstitutional inquisition." As in *Payne* [v. *Arkansas* (1991)], where the Court found that a confession was coerced because the interrogating police officer had promised that, if the accused confessed, the officer would protect the accused from an angry mob outside the jailhouse door, so too here, the Arizona Supreme Court found that it was fear of physical violence, absent protection from his friend (and Government agent) Sarivola, which motivated Fulminante to confess. Accepting the Arizona court's finding, permissible on this record, that there was a credible threat of physical violence, we agree with its conclusion that Fulminante's will was overborne in such a way as to render his confession the product of coercion.

III

Four of us, JUSTICES MARSHALL, BLACKMUN, STEVENS and myself, would affirm the judgment of the Arizona Supreme Court on the ground that the harmless error rule is inapplicable to erroneously admitted coerced confessions. We thus disagree with the Justices who have a contrary view.

The majority today abandons what until now the Court has regarded as the "axiomatic [proposition] that a defendant in a criminal case is deprived of due process of law if his conviction is founded, in whole or in part, upon an involuntary confession, without regard for the truth or falsity of the confession, and even though there is ample evidence aside from the confession to support the conviction." The Court has repeatedly stressed that the view that the admission of a coerced confession can be harmless error because of the other evidence to support the verdict is "an impermissible doctrine," for "the admission in evidence, over objection, of the coerced confession vitiates the judgment because it violates the Due Process Clause of the Fourteenth Amendment." As [previous] . . . decisions . . . show, the rule was the same even when another confession of the defendant had been properly admitted into evidence. Today, a majority of the Court, without any justification, overrules this vast body of precedent without a word, and, in so doing, dislodges one of the fundamental tenets of our criminal justice system.

In extending to coerced confessions the harmless error rule of Chapman v. California (1967), the majority declares that because the Court has applied that analysis to numerous other "trial errors," there is no reason that it should not apply to an error of this nature as well. The four of us remain convinced, however, that we should abide by our cases that have refused to apply the harmless error rule to coerced confessions, for a coerced confession is fundamentally different from other types of erroneously admitted evidence to which the rule has been applied. Indeed, as the majority concedes, Chapman itself recognized that prior cases "have indicated that there are some constitutional rights so basic to a fair trial that their infraction can never be treated as harmless error," and it placed in that category the constitutional rule against using a defendant's coerced confession against him at his criminal trial. . . .

Chapman specifically noted three constitutional errors that could not be categorized as harmless error: using a coerced confession against a defendant in a criminal trial, depriving a defendant of counsel, and trying a defendant before a biased judge. The majority attempts to distinguish the use of a coerced confession from the other two errors listed in *Chapman* first by distorting the decision in *Payne,* and then by drawing a meaningless dichotomy between "trial errors" and "structural defects" in the trial process. . . .

As the majority concedes, there are other constitutional errors that invalidate a conviction even though there may be no reasonable doubt that the defendant is guilty and would be convicted absent the trial error. For example, a judge in a criminal trial "is prohibited from entering a judgment of conviction or directing the jury to come forward with such a verdict, regardless of how overwhelmingly the evidence may point in that direction," *United States* v. *Martin Linen Supply Co.* (1977). A defendant is entitled to counsel at trial, *Gideon* v. *Wainwright* (1963), and, as *Chapman* recognized, violating this right can never be harmless error. . . . In *Vasquez* v. *Hillery* (1986), a defendant was found guilty beyond reasonable doubt, but the conviction had been set aside because of the unlawful exclusion of members of the defendant's race from the grand jury that indicted him, despite overwhelming evidence of his guilt. The error at the grand jury stage struck at fundamental values of our society, and "undermine[d] the structural integrity of the criminal tribunal itself, and [was] not amenable to harmless error review." *Vasquez,* like *Chapman,* also noted that rule of automatic reversal when a defendant is tried before a judge with a financial interest in the outcome, despite a lack of any indication that bias influenced the decision. *Waller* v. *Georgia* (1984) recognized that violation of the guarantee of a public trial required reversal without any showing of prejudice and even though the values of a public trial may be intangible and unprovable in any particular case.

The search for truth is indeed central to our system of justice, but "certain constitutional rights are not, and should not be, subject to harmless error analysis, because those rights protect important values that are unrelated to the truthseeking function of the trial." The right of a defendant not to have his coerced confession used against him is among those rights, for using a coerced confession "abort[s] the basic trial process" and "render[s] a trial fundamentally unfair."

For the foregoing reasons, the four of us would adhere to the consistent line of authority that has recognized as a basic tenet of our criminal justice system, before and after both Miranda and Chapman, the prohibition against using a defendant's coerced confession against him at his criminal trial. *Stare decisis* is "of fundamental importance to the rule of law," *Welch* v. *Texas Highways and Public Transp.* (1987); the majority offers no convincing reason for overturning our long line of decisions requiring the exclusion of coerced confessions.

IV

Since five Justices have determined that harmless error analysis applies to coerced confessions, it becomes necessary to evaluate under that ruling the admissibility of Fulminante's confession to Sarivola. . . . Five of us are of the view that the State has not carried its burden, and accordingly affirm the judgment of the court below reversing petitioner's conviction.

A confession is like no other evidence. Indeed, "the defendant's own confession is probably the most probative and damaging evidence that can be admitted against him. . . . [T]he admissions of a defendant come from the actor himself, the most knowledgeable and unimpeachable source of information about his past conduct. Certainly, confessions have profound impact on the jury, so much so that we may justifiably doubt its ability to put them out of mind even if told to do so." While some statements by a defendant may concern isolated aspects of the crime or may be incriminating only when linked to other evidence, a full confession in which the defendant discloses the motive for and means of the crime may tempt the jury to rely upon that evidence alone in reaching its decision. In the case of a coerced confession such as that given by Fulminante to Sarivola, the risk that the confession is unreliable, coupled with the profound impact that the confession has upon the jury, requires a reviewing court to exercise extreme caution before determining that the admission of the confession at trial was harmless. . . .

Our review of the record leads us to conclude that the State has failed to meet its burden of establishing, beyond a reasonable doubt, that the admission of Fulminante's confession to Anthony Sarivola was harmless error. Three considerations compel this result.

First, the transcript discloses that both the trial court and the State recognized that a successful prosecution depended on the jury's believing the two confessions. Absent the confessions, it is unlikely that Fulminante would have been prosecuted at all, because the physical evidence from the scene and other circumstantial evidence would have been insufficient to convict. . . .

Second, the jury's assessment of the confession to Donna Sarivola could easily have depended in large part on the presence of the confession to Anthony Sarivola. Absent the admission at trial of the first confession, the jurors might have found Donna Sarivola's story unbelievable. Fulminante's confession to Donna Sarivola allegedly occurred in May, 1984, on the day he was released from Ray Brook, as she and Anthony Sarivola drove Fulminante from New York to Pennsylvania. Donna Sarivola testified that Fulminante, whom she had never before met, confessed in detail about Jeneane's brutal murder in response to her casual question concerning why he was going to visit friends in Pennsylvania instead of returning to his family in Arizona. Although she testified that she was "disgusted" by Fulminante's disclosures, she stated that she took no steps to notify authorities of what she had learned. In fact, she claimed that she barely discussed the matter with Anthony Sarivola, who was in the car and overheard Fulminante's entire conversation with Donna. Despite her disgust for Fulminante, Donna Sarivola later went on a second trip with him. Although Sarivola informed authorities that he had driven Fulminante to Pennsylvania, he did not mention Donna's presence in the car or her conversation with Fulminante. Only when questioned by authorities in June, 1985, did Anthony Sarivola belatedly recall the confession to Donna more than a year before, and only then did he ask if she would be willing to discuss the matter with authorities. . . .

Third, the admission of the first confession led to the admission of other evidence prejudicial to Fulminante. For example, the State introduced evidence that Fulminante knew of Sarivola's connections with organized crime in an attempt to explain why Fulminante would have been motivated to confess to Sarivola in seeking protection. Absent the confession, this evidence would have had no relevance, and would have been inadmissible at trial. . . .

Finally, although our concern here is with the effect of the erroneous admission of the confession on Fulminante's conviction, it is clear that the presence of the confession also influenced the sentencing phase of the trial. Under Arizona law, the trial judge is the sentencer. At the sentencing hearing, the admissibility of information regarding aggravating circumstances is governed by the rules of evidence applicable to criminal trials. In this case, "based upon admissible evidence produced at the trial," the judge found that only one aggravating circumstance existed beyond a reasonable doubt, i.e., that the murder was committed in "an especially heinous, cruel, and depraved manner." In reaching this conclusion, the judge relied heavily on evidence concerning the manner of the killing and Fulminante's motives and state of mind which could only be found in the two confessions. For example, in labeling the murder "cruel," the judge focused in part on Fulminante's alleged statements that he choked Jeneane and made her get on her knees and beg before killing her. Although the circumstantial evidence was not inconsistent with this determination, neither was it sufficient to make such a finding beyond a reasonable doubt. Indeed, the sentencing judge acknowledged that the confessions were only partly corroborated by other evidence.

In declaring that Fulminante "acted with an especially heinous and depraved state of mind," the sentencing judge relied solely on the two confessions. . . . Although the sentencing judge might have reached the same conclusions even without the confession to Anthony Sarivola, it is impossible to say so beyond a reasonable doubt. Furthermore, the judge's assessment of Donna Sarivola's credibility, and hence the reliability of the second confession, might well have been influenced by the corroborative effect of the erroneously admitted first confession. Indeed, the fact that the sentencing judge focused on the similarities between the two confessions in determining that they were reliable suggests that either of the confessions alone, even when considered with all the other evidence, would have been insufficient to permit the judge to find an aggravating circumstance beyond a reasonable doubt as a requisite prelude to imposing the death penalty.

Because a majority of the Court has determined that Fulminante's confession to Anthony Sarivola was coerced, and because a majority has determined that admitting this confession was not harmless beyond a reasonable doubt, we agree with the Arizona Supreme Court's conclusion that Fulminante is entitled to a new trial at which the confession is not admitted. Accordingly the judgment of the Arizona Supreme Court is

Affirmed.

CHIEF JUSTICE REHNQUIST, with whom JUSTICE O'CONNOR joins, JUSTICE KENNEDY and JUSTICE SOUTER join as to Parts I and II, and JUSTICE SCALIA joins as to Parts II and III.

The Court today properly concludes that the admission of an "involuntary" confession at trial is subject to harmless error analysis. Nonetheless, the independent review of the record which we are required to make shows that respondent Fulminante's confession was not, in fact, involuntary. And even if the confession were deemed to be involuntary, the evidence offered at trial, including a second, untainted confession by Fulminante, supports the conclusion that any error here was certainly harmless.

I

I am at a loss to see how the Supreme Court of Arizona reached the conclusion that it did. Fulminante offered no evidence that he believed that his life was in danger or that he, in fact, confessed to Sarivola in order to obtain the proffered protection. Indeed, he had stipulated that "[a]t no time did the defendant indicate he was in fear of other inmates, nor did he ever seek Mr. Sarivola's 'protection.'" Sarivola's testimony that he told Fulminante that "if [he] would tell the truth, he could be protected," adds little, if anything, to the substance of the parties' stipulation. The decision of the Supreme Court of Arizona rests on an assumption that is squarely contrary to this stipulation, and one that is not supported by any testimony of Fulminante.

The facts of record in the present case are quite different from those present in cases where we have found confessions to be coerced and involuntary. Since Fulminante was unaware that Sarivola was an FBI informant, there existed none of "the danger of coercion result[ing] from the interaction of custody and official interrogation." The fact that Sarivola was a government informant does not, by itself, render Fulminante's confession involuntary, since we have consistently accepted the use of informants in the discovery of evidence of a crime as a legitimate investigatory procedure consistent with the Constitution. The conversations between Sarivola and Fulminante were not lengthy, and the defendant was free at all times to leave Sarivola's company. Sarivola at no time threatened him or demanded that he confess; he simply requested that he speak the truth about the matter. Fulminante was an experienced habitue of prisons, and presumably able to fend for himself. In concluding on these facts that Fulminante's confession was involuntary, the Court today embraces a more expansive definition of that term than is warranted by any of our decided cases.

II

Since this Court's landmark decision in *Chapman* v. *California* (1967), in which we adopted the general rule that a constitutional error does not automatically require reversal of a conviction, the Court has applied harmless error analysis to a wide range of errors, and has recognized that most constitutional errors can be harmless. . . .

The admission of an involuntary confession—a classic "trial error"—is markedly different from the other two constitutional violations referred to in the *Chapman* footnote as not being subject to harmless error analysis. One of those cases, *Gideon* v. *Wainwright* (1963), involved the total deprivation of the right to counsel at trial. The other, *Tumey* v. *Ohio* (1927), involved a judge who was not impartial. These are structural defects in the constitution of the trial mechanism, which defy analysis by "harmless error" standards. The entire conduct of the trial, from beginning to end, is obviously affected by the absence of counsel for a criminal defendant, just as it is by the presence on the bench of a judge who is not impartial. Since our decision in *Chapman,* other cases have added to the category of constitutional errors which are not subject to harmless error the following: unlawful exclusion of members of the defendant's race from a grand jury, *Vasquez* v. *Hillery* (1986); the right to self-representation at trial, *McKaskle* v. *Wiggins,* and the right to public trial, *Waller* v. *Georgia* (1984). Each of these constitutional deprivations is a similar structural defect affecting the framework within which the trial proceeds, rather than simply an error in the trial process itself. "Without these basic protections, a criminal trial cannot reliably serve its function as a vehicle for determination of guilt or innocence, and no criminal punishment may be regarded as fundamentally fair."

It is evident from a comparison of the constitutional violations which we have held subject to harmless error, and those which we have held not, that involuntary statements or confessions belong in the former category. The admission of an involuntary confession is a "trial error," similar in both degree and kind to the erroneous admission of other types of evidence. The evidentiary impact of an involuntary confession, and its effect upon the composition of the record, is indistinguishable from that of a confession obtained in violation of the Sixth Amendment—of evidence seized in violation of the Fourth Amendment—or of a prosecutor's improper comment on a defendant's silence at trial in violation of the Fifth Amendment. . . .

Nor can it be said that the admission of an involuntary confession is the type of error which "transcends the criminal process." This Court has applied harmless error analysis to the violation of other constitutional rights similar in magnitude and importance, and involving the same level of police misconduct. . . . The inconsistent treatment of statements elicited in violation of the Sixth and Fourteenth Amendments, respectively, can be supported neither by evidentiary or deterrence concerns nor by a belief that there is something more "fundamental" about involuntary confessions. This is especially true in a case such as this one, where there are no allegations of physical violence on behalf of the police. The impact of a confession obtained in violation of the Sixth Amendment has the same evidentiary impact as does a confession obtained in violation of a defendant's due process rights. . . .

III

I would agree with the finding of the Supreme Court of Arizona in its initial opinion—in which it believed harmless error analysis was applicable to the admission of involuntary confessions—that the admission of Fulminante's confession was harmless. Indeed, this seems to me to be a classic case of harmless error: a second confession giving more details of the crime than the first was admitted in evidence and found to be free of any constitutional objection.

JUSTICE KENNEDY, concurring in the judgment.

For the reasons stated by THE CHIEF JUSTICE, I agree that Fulminante's confession to Anthony Sarivola was not coerced. In my view, the trial court did not err in admitting this testimony. A majority of the Court, however, finds the confession coerced, and proceeds to consider whether harmless error analysis may be used when a coerced confession has been admitted at trial. With the case in this posture, it is appropriate for me to address the harmless-error issue.

Again for the reasons stated by THE CHIEF JUSTICE, I agree that harmless-error analysis should apply in the case of a coerced confession. That said, the court conducting a harmless-error inquiry must appreciate the indelible impact a full confession may have on the trier of fact, as distinguished, for instance, from the impact of an isolated statement that incriminates the defendant only when connected with other evidence. If the jury believes that a defendant has admitted the crime, it doubtless will be tempted to rest its decision on that evidence alone, without careful consideration of the other evidence in the case. Apart, perhaps, from a videotape of the crime, one would have difficulty finding evidence more damaging to a criminal defendant's plea of innocence. For the reasons given by JUSTICE WHITE in Part IV of his opinion, I cannot with confidence find admission of Fulminante's confession to Anthony Sarivola to be harmless error.

The same majority of the Court does not agree on the three issues presented by the trial court's determination to admit Fulminante's first confession: whether the confession was inadmissible because coerced; whether harmless-error analysis is appropriate; and if so whether any error was harmless here. My own view that the confession was not coerced does not command a majority.

In the interests of providing a clear mandate to the Arizona Supreme Court in this capital case, I deem it proper to accept in the case now before us the holding of five Justices that the confession was coerced and inadmissible. I agree with a majority of the Court that admission of the confession could not be harmless error when viewed in light of all the other evidence, and so I concur in the judgment to affirm the ruling of the Arizona Supreme Court.

In 1999, the *Miranda* legacy took another interesting turn. The Fourth Circuit Court of Appeals, one of the nation's most conservative, resurrected without prompting the provision of the 1968 federal law that attempted to overrule *Miranda*, ruling that the police could use voluntary statements made by suspects even if they had not been read their rights. For thirty years, the Department of Justice had declined to enforce the statute, believing that it was unconstitutional as long as the Court directly refused to overrule *Miranda*. When the Court agreed to hear *Dickerson v. United States* (2000), all bets were off on what the justices would do: affirm *Miranda* or overturn it.

Dickerson v. United States

530 U.S. 428 (2000)

On January 24, 1997, Charles Dickerson waited impatiently in his car outside the First Virginia Bank in Old Town Alexandria, Virginia, located just across the Potomac River from Washington, D.C. Inside, his partner was holding up the bank. As alarm bells rang, Jimmy Rochester, the "inside man" on the job, raced outside and jumped in Dickerson's car, and the two robbers sped away. A few blocks later, Dickerson stopped the car. Rochester got out, put the leather bag he had used in the robbery in the trunk, and got right back in the car. The total take from the heist was $876.

An eyewitness had given police investigating the robbery the license plate of a white Oldsmobile Ciera that had been parked in front of the bank that morning. The FBI traced the car's registration to Dickerson, who lived in Takoma Park, a Maryland suburb that borders Washington, D.C. Ten FBI agents and an Alexandria police detective arrived at Dickerson's apartment on the morning of January 27 to question him. After a short conversation, Dickerson, who denied taking part in the robbery, agreed to accompany the police to an FBI field office for further questioning. As Dickerson went to his bedroom to retrieve his coat, the FBI agent following him noticed a large amount of cash sitting on his bed. When asked what he was doing with such a large amount of cash, Dickerson responded that he just returned from a successful gambling trip to Atlantic City, New Jersey.

Dickerson was not placed under arrest. After arriving at the FBI office, the agents requested and received permission for a telephone warrant to search Dickerson's apartment. The judge agreed that the agents had established probable cause by matching the license plate and discovering the cash, and granted the warrant. After FBI agents informed Dickerson they would be returning to his apartment to conduct a search, Dickerson told them he wanted to make a statement. He confessed to driving the getaway car in the Alexandria robbery, and taking part in eighteen previous bank robberies in Virginia, Maryland, and Georgia. Police then placed Dickerson under arrest and read him his *Miranda* rights.

A federal trial judge threw out Dickerson's confession, ruling that the FBI's failure to read the suspect his *Miranda* rights prior to his confession made any subsequent statements inadmissible. A divided panel of the Fourth Circuit Court of Appeals then reversed, claiming that under Section 3501 of the Omnibus Crime Control Act of 1968 the admissibility of a confession was based solely on whether it was voluntary. The Department of Justice had not argued to apply Section 3501, believing that the *Miranda* decision had made it unconstitutional. The Fourth Circuit opinion was very critical of the Justice Department's position, claiming it was motivated by "politics over law." In truth, seven presidential administrations had come and gone since *Miranda* was decided, and not one, including the conservative Reagan administration, had ever invoked Section 3501 to challenge the 1966 decision. Only the Washington Legal Foundation, in its *amicus* brief, urged the appeals court to bypass *Miranda* by relying on Section 3501.

After the Supreme Court agreed to hear Dickerson's appeal, Attorney General Janet Reno stated that the Justice Department would not defend the Fourth Circuit's decision. The Court appointed Paul Cassell, a law professor and outspoken critic of *Miranda*, to represent the United States against Dickerson's appeal. Cassell, who had served as a law clerk for Justice Scalia before Scalia was appointed to the Court in 1986, had helped to write the Washington Legal Foundation's brief submitted to the Fourth Circuit. Several law enforcement groups lined up behind Cassell's brief, urging the Court to uphold the Fourth Circuit's application of Section 3501. Not a single group, however, supported Cassell's position to overturn *Miranda* outright.

The Court's decision was 7 to 2. Chief Justice Rehnquist delivered the opinion of the Court. Justice Scalia, joined by Justice Thomas, dissented.

▼▲▼

CHIEF JUSTICE REHNQUIST delivered the opinion of the Court.

In *Miranda* v. *Arizona* (1966), we held that certain warnings must be given before a suspect's statement made during custodial interrogation could be admitted in evidence. In the wake of that decision, Congress enacted 18 U.S.C. § 3501, which in essence laid down a rule that the admissibility of such statements should turn only on whether or not they were voluntarily made. We hold that *Miranda*, being a constitutional decision of this Court, may not be in effect overruled by an Act of Congress, and we decline to overrule *Miranda* ourselves. We therefore hold that *Miranda* and its progeny in this Court govern the admissibility of statements made during custodial interrogation in both state and federal courts. . . .

Given § 3501's express designation of voluntariness as the touchstone of admissibility, its omission of any warning requirement, and the instruction for trial courts to consider a nonexclusive list of factors relevant to the circumstances of a confession, we agree with the Court of Appeals that Congress intended by its enactment to overrule *Miranda*. Because of the obvious conflict between our decision in *Miranda* and § 3501, we must address whether Congress has constitutional authority to thus supersede *Miranda*. If Congress has such authority, § 3501's totality-of-the-circumstances approach must prevail over *Miranda*'s requirement of warnings; if not, that section must yield to *Miranda*'s more specific requirements.

The law in this area is clear. This Court has supervisory authority over the federal courts, and we may use that authority to prescribe rules of evidence and procedure that are binding in those tribunals. However, the power to judicially create and enforce nonconstitutional "rules of procedure and evidence for the federal courts exists only in the absence of a relevant Act of Congress." Congress retains the ultimate authority to modify or set aside any judicially created rules of evidence and procedure that are not required by the Constitution.

But Congress may not legislatively supersede our decisions interpreting and applying the Constitution. This case therefore turns on whether the *Miranda* Court announced a constitutional rule or merely exercised its supervisory authority to regulate evidence in the absence of congressional direction. Recognizing this point, the Court of Appeals surveyed *Miranda* and its progeny to determine the constitutional status of the *Miranda* decision. Relying on the fact that we have created several exceptions to *Miranda*'s warnings requirement and that we have repeatedly referred to the *Miranda* warnings as "prophylactic," *New York* v. *Quarles* (1984), and "not themselves rights protected by the Constitution," *Michigan* v. *Tucker* (1974), the Court of Appeals concluded that the protections announced in Miranda are not constitutionally required. . . .

The *Miranda* opinion itself begins by stating that the Court granted certiorari "to explore some facets of the problems . . . of applying the privilege against self-incrimination to in-custody interrogation, and to give concrete constitutional guidelines for law enforcement agencies and courts to follow." In fact, the majority opinion is replete with statements indicating that the majority thought it was announcing a constitutional rule. Indeed, the Court's ultimate conclusion was that the unwarned confessions obtained in the four cases before the Court in *Miranda* "were obtained from the defendant under circumstances that did not meet constitutional standards for protection of the privilege." . . .

Additional support for our conclusion that *Miranda* is constitutionally based is found in the *Miranda* Court's invitation for legislative action to protect the constitutional right against coerced self-incrimination. After discussing the "compelling pressures" inherent in custodial police interrogation, the *Miranda* Court concluded that, "[i]n order to combat these pressures and to permit a full opportunity to exercise the privilege against self-incrimination, the accused must be adequately and effectively apprised of his rights and the exercise of those rights must be fully honored." However, the Court emphasized that it could not foresee "the potential alternatives for protecting the privilege which might be devised by Congress or the States," and it accordingly opined that the Constitution would not preclude legislative solutions that differed from the prescribed *Miranda* warnings but which were "at least as effective in apprising accused persons of their right of silence and in assuring a continuous opportunity to exercise it." . . .

[A]fter our *Miranda* decision, [we have] made exceptions from its rule in cases such as *New York* v. *Quarles* (1984) and *Harris* v. *New York* (1971). But we have also broadened the application of the *Miranda* doctrine. . . . These decisions illustrate the principle—not that *Miranda* is not a constitutional rule—but that no constitutional rule is immutable. No court laying down a general rule can possibly foresee the various circumstances in which counsel will seek to apply it, and the sort of modifications represented by these cases are as much a normal part of constitutional law as the original decision. . . .

We agree with the amicus' [Paul Cassell] contention that there are more remedies available for abusive police conduct than there were at the time *Miranda* was decided to hold that a suspect may bring a federal cause of action under the Due Process Clause for police misconduct during custodial interrogation. But we do not agree that these additional measures supplement § 3501's protections sufficiently to meet the constitutional minimum. *Miranda* requires procedures that will warn a suspect in custody of his right to remain silent and which will assure the suspect that the exercise of that right will be honored. As discussed above, § 3501 explicitly eschews a requirement of pre-interrogation warnings in favor of an approach that looks to the administration of such warnings as only one factor in determining the voluntariness of a suspect's confession. The additional remedies cited by amicus do not, in our view, render them, together with § 3501, an adequate substitute for the warnings required by *Miranda*.

Whether or not we would agree with *Miranda*'s reasoning and its resulting rule, were we addressing the issue in the first instance, the principles of *stare decisis* weigh heavily against overruling it now. While "*stare decisis* is not an inexorable command," *Payne* v. *Tennessee* (1991), particularly when we are interpreting the Constitution, "even in constitutional cases, the doctrine carries such persuasive force that we have always required a departure from precedent to be supported by some 'special justification,'" *United States* v. *International Business Machines Corp.* (1996).

We do not think there is such justification for overruling *Miranda*. *Miranda* has become embedded in routine police practice to the point where the warnings have become part of our national culture. While we have overruled our precedents when subsequent cases have undermined their doctrinal underpinnings, we do not believe that this has happened to the *Miranda* decision. If anything, our subsequent cases have reduced the impact of the *Miranda* rule on legitimate law enforcement while reaffirming the decision's core ruling that unwarned statements may not be used as evidence in the prosecution's case in chief.

The disadvantage of the *Miranda* rule is that statements which may be by no means involuntary, made by a defendant who is aware of his "rights," may nonetheless be excluded and a guilty defendant go free as a result. But experience suggests that the totality-of-the-circumstances test which § 3501 seeks to revive is more difficult than Miranda for law enforcement officers to conform to, and for courts to apply in a consistent manner. . . .

In sum, we conclude that *Miranda* announced a constitutional rule that Congress may not supersede legislatively. Following the rule of *stare decisis*, we decline to overrule *Miranda* ourselves. The judgment of the Court of Appeals is therefore

Reversed.

JUSTICE SCALIA, with whom JUSTICE THOMAS joins, dissenting.

Those to whom judicial decisions are an unconnected series of judgments that produce either favored or disfavored results will doubtless greet today's decision as a paragon of moderation, since it declines to overrule *Miranda* v. *Arizona* (1966). Those who understand the judicial process will appreciate that today's decision is not a reaffirmation of *Miranda,* but a radical revision of the most significant element of *Miranda* (as of all cases): the rationale that gives it a permanent place in our jurisprudence. . . .

It takes only a small step to bring today's opinion out of the realm of power-judging and into the mainstream of legal reasoning: The Court need only go beyond its carefully couched iterations that "*Miranda* is a constitutional decision," that "*Miranda* is constitutionally based," that *Miranda* has "constitutional underpinnings," and come out and say quite clearly: "We reaffirm today that custodial interrogation that is not preceded by Miranda warnings or their equivalent violates the Constitution of the United States." It cannot say that, because a majority of the Court does not believe it. The Court therefore acts in plain violation of the Constitution when it denies effect to this Act of Congress. . . .

[T]he Court asserts that *Miranda* must be a "constitutional decision" announcing a "constitutional rule," and thus immune to congressional modification, because we have since its inception applied it to the States. If this argument is meant as an invocation of *stare decisis,* it fails because, though it is true that our cases applying *Miranda* against the States must be reconsidered if *Miranda* is not required by the Constitution, it is likewise true that our cases (discussed above) based on the principle that *Miranda* is not required by the Constitution will have to be reconsidered if it is. So the *stare decisis* argument is a wash. If, on the other hand, the argument is meant as an appeal to logic rather than *stare decisis,* it is a classic example of begging the question: Congress's attempt to set aside *Miranda,* since it represents an assertion that violation of *Miranda* is not a violation of the Constitution, also represents an assertion that the Court has no power to impose *Miranda* on the States. To answer this assertion—not by showing why violation of *Miranda* is a violation of the Constitution—but by asserting that *Miranda* does apply against the States, is to assume precisely the point at issue. In my view, our continued application of the *Miranda* code to the States despite our consistent statements that running afoul of its dictates does not necessarily—or even usually—result in an actual constitutional violation, represents not the source of *Miranda*'s salvation but rather evidence of its ultimate illegitimacy. As Justice Stevens has elsewhere explained, "[t]his Court's power to require state courts to exclude probative self-incriminatory statements rests entirely on the premise that the use of such evidence violates the Federal Constitution. . . . If the Court does not accept that premise, it must regard the holding in the *Miranda* case itself, as well as all of the federal jurisprudence that has evolved from that decision, as nothing more than an illegitimate exercise of raw judicial power." Quite so. . . .

[W]hile I agree with the Court that § 3501 cannot be upheld without also concluding that *Miranda* represents an illegitimate exercise of our authority to review state-court judgments, I do not share the Court's hesitation in reaching that conclusion. For while the Court is also correct that the doctrine of *stare decisis* demands some "special justification" for a departure from longstanding precedent—even precedent of the constitutional variety —that criterion is more than met here. To repeat Justice Stevens' cogent observation, it is "[o]bviou[s]" that "the Court's power to reverse *Miranda*'s conviction rested entirely on the determination that a violation of the Federal Constitution had occurred." Despite the Court's Orwellian assertion to the contrary, it is undeniable that later cases have "undermined [*Miranda*'s] doctrinal underpinnings," denying constitutional violation and thus stripping the holding of its only constitutionally legitimate support. *Miranda*'s critics and supporters alike have long made this point. . . .

[Nor] am I persuaded by the argument for retaining *Miranda* that touts its supposed workability as compared with the totality-of-the-circumstances test it purported to replace. *Miranda*'s proponents cite ad nauseam the fact that the Court was called upon to make difficult and subtle distinctions in applying the "voluntariness" test in some 30-odd due process "coerced confessions" cases in the 30 years between *Brown* v. *Mississippi* (1936) and *Miranda.* It is not immediately apparent, however, that the judicial burden has been eased by the "bright-line" rules adopted in *Miranda.* In fact, in the 34 years since *Miranda* was decided, this Court has been called upon to decide nearly 60 cases involving a host of *Miranda* issues, most of them predicted with remarkable prescience by Justice White in his *Miranda* dissent. . . .

Finally, I am not convinced by petitioner's argument that *Miranda* should be preserved because the decision occupies a special place in the "public's consciousness." As far as I am aware, the public is not under the illusion that we are infallible. I see little harm in admitting that we made a mistake in taking away from the people the ability to decide for themselves what protections (beyond those required by the Constitution) are reasonably affordable in the criminal investigatory process. And I see much to be gained by reaffirming for the people the wonderful reality that they govern themselves—which means that "[t]he powers not delegated to the United States by the Constitution" that the people adopted, "nor prohibited . . . . to the States" by that Constitution, "are reserved to the States respectively, or to the people."

In imposing its Court-made code upon the States, [*Miranda*] at least asserted that it was demanded by the Constitution. Today's decision does not pretend that it is—and yet still asserts the right to impose it against the will of the people's representatives in Congress. Far from believing that *stare decisis* compels this result, I believe we cannot allow to remain on the books even a celebrated decision—especially a celebrated decision—that has come to stand for the proposition that the Supreme Court has power to impose extraconstitutional constraints upon Congress and the States. This is not the system that was established by the Framers, or that would be established by any sane supporter of government by the people.

I dissent from today's decision, and, until § 3501 is repealed, will continue to apply it in all cases where there has been a sustainable finding that the defendant's confession was voluntary.

For Chief Justice Rehnquist to assign *Dickerson* to himself was a decision of no small symbolic importance. Since coming to the Court in 1972, Rehnquist had been a persistent and vocal critic of *Miranda,* claiming that its roots in the Constitution were suspect. And while Rehnquist wrote in *Dickerson* that, in all likelihood, he would not have joined the original five-member majority in *Miranda,* he also acknowledged that the 1966 decision had become an "embedded constitutional rule" that, by and large, posed no problems for the police. Although no constitutional rule, as Rehnquist pointed out, is immutable, the probability that the Court, after *Dickerson,* will overturn *Miranda* seems to have finally passed. *Dickerson* is also consistent with the Court's desire to protect what it believes is its supreme authority to interpret the Constitution. Note how Chief Justice Rehnquist makes clear that Congress has no power to circumvent a constitutional decision by the Court. Like it or not, said the justices, *Miranda* is a constitutional rule subject only to reversal by the Court itself or by constitutional amendment. In this sense, *Dickerson* compares favorably with *City of Boerne* v. *Flores* (1997) (see Volume 1, Chapter 3; Volume 2, Chapter 6), in which the Court invalidated a federal law intended to modify a previous constitutional ruling.[38]

Fairness in the Courtroom

Our discussions of the right to counsel and the right against self-incrimination are intimately linked to the broader guarantee of fairness during trial. So embedded is the right of the criminally accused to a trial by jury in the Anglo-American legal tradition that this right appears in both Article III of the original Constitution and in the Fifth (grand juries) and Sixth (trial juries) Amendments of the Bill of Rights. Indeed, the importance of the jury system to the Framers is hard to overlook. Between 1776 and 1787, the right to a jury trial in criminal cases was the *only* right secured in every single state constitution. Of the six state conventions that convened in 1788 to consider adopting a bill of rights, five offered two or more proposals for jury trials in criminal proceedings. In the Colonial era and into the early Republic, early victories for civil liberties claims were often won when juries, not judges, ruled against the government.[39] One such example involved the famous 1735 trial of John Peter Zenger, a newspaper publisher, who was acquitted of libel against the colonial New York government when a jury accepted truth as a

JURIES AND JURY SELECTION IN CRIMINAL TRIALS

Grand Jury	A jury that examines accusations against persons charged with crime and, if the evidence warrants, makes formal charges on which the accused persons are later tried.
Petit Jury	A jury that is selected to try and to decide the facts at issue in a trial.
Voir Dire	The process of questioning prospective jurors to determine which are qualified and suited for service on a jury.
Peremptory Strike	The procedure that allows lawyers to strike prospective jurors for any reason, so long as such strikes are not motivated by racial or gender discrimination. See *Batson* v. *Kentucky* (1986) (pp. 412–418) and *J.E.B.* v. *Alabama ex. rel. T.B.* (1994) (pp. 418–422). Lawyers have a limited number of peremptory strikes.
Strike for Cause	The procedure that allows lawyers to remove prospective jurors whom they believe have demonstrated that they cannot hear the evidence and decide the case impartially. Lawyers generally have unlimited power to strike for cause.

defense, something that few judges of that era were willing to do. The *Zenger* verdict had broad ramifications for the later establishment of the First Amendment guarantee of freedom of the press.[40]

This section focuses on one aspect on fairness in jury trials: jury composition and the right to trial by one's peers. Certainly, the Sixth Amendment guarantee to a speedy and public trial highlights the Framers' concern over the worst excesses of the delays, secrecy, and inquisitorial methods of the British criminal justice system. By bringing criminal trials into the open and emphasizing the role of juries, the Framers offered an innovative contribution to the constitutional idea of democratic self-government. Juries would be drawn from the community, which would be based on reasonable geographic boundaries. Thus, in another departure from the British common-law tradition, individuals would receive a trial by a jury of their peers. In theory, then, the Constitution included an equal protection component in the fair trial guarantees of the Sixth Amendment.

In reality, however, juries have only recently become more representative of the local communities they serve. Women were excluded by law from jury service well into the twentieth century, a rule that had its place in the "separate spheres" understanding of the roles of men and women in society. As recently as 1961, the Supreme Court, in *Hoyt* v. *Florida*, ruled that a Florida law giving women an automatic exemption from jury service did not violate the Fourteenth Amendment. Chief Justice Earl Warren, who had written many of the Court's landmark decisions outlawing racial segregation, concluded that states had a reasonable interest in making sure that a woman was not drawn into civic or community service unless it was "consistent with her own 'special responsibilities'."[41] *Hoyt* remained good law until 1975, until the Court overruled it in *Taylor* v. *Louisiana* (1975), holding that deliberate efforts by the states to exclude women from jury service violated the Sixth and Fourteenth Amendments.[42]

Before the Civil War, rare was the case that African Americans were permitted to participate as jurors in criminal trials. After the Civil War, the Court, in *Strauder* v. *West Virginia* (1879), demonstrated that it was willing to extend the Equal Protection Clause of the Fourteenth Amendment to jury trials. In *Strauder*, a black criminal defendant, who had been accused of a capital crime, argued that he could not receive a fair trial in West Virginia because state law excluded blacks from serving on grand and trial juries. But *Strauder* only hinted at the layers of prejudice that existed against

African Americans in the criminal justice system. After the collapse of Reconstruction in 1877 and the subsequent rise of the "separate but equal" interpretation of the Fourteenth Amendment, the Court simply ignored the racial discrimination rampant in everyday American life. This meant the systematic exclusion of blacks from jury pools and service, as long as the state was using means other than direct prohibition of the kind struck down in *Strauder.* Such discrimination was concentrated in the South, and took the form of such qualifications as voter registration, property ownership, and literacy tests to become eligible for jury service. Fearful of violence and retribution from local police and terrorist organizations such as the Ku Klux Klan, many blacks simply did not question their exclusion from the jury rolls, even if that meant watching black criminal defendants get convicted on flimsy evidence by indifferent judges and racist juries.

Powell v. *Alabama,* however, demonstrated to African Americans that the Court was willing to come down hard on states that engaged in racially motivated denials of basic due process guarantees. In *Hale* v. *Kentucky* (1938), the Court agreed with a black capital defendant that McCracken County, Kentucky, had arbitrarily excluded African Americans from its list of eligible jurors and thus violated that defendant's Fourteenth Amendment rights. At that time, the NAACP was still in the early stages of its litigation campaign to dismantle legal segregation in the United States (see Chapter 11, where the NAACP's legal efforts are discussed extensively). The organization obtained records showing that despite a black population of 8,000 in a county of 48,000, not one African American from 1906 to 1936 had served on a McCracken County jury. Undaunted, the Southern white supremacist political structure continued to exclude African Americans from jury service, except now it used the most powerful legal weapon in its arsenal, one that was fully exempted from constitutional challenge: *the peremptory challenge.*

Lawyers assembling their juries for trial may strike potential jurors either for *cause* (i.e., the juror believes the defendant is probably guilty, is related to the prosecutor, had a bad run-in with a police officer, has a sister who is a police officer, indicates prejudicial attitudes, and so on) or by a peremptory challenge, which permits the dismissal of a juror for no reason. The purpose of peremptory challenges during the early years of the American jury system is not altogether clear, but many scholars believe it served as a polite way of excusing jurors with an intimate knowledge of the case, of the parties, or both.[43] Peremptory challenges have long been valued by trial lawyers, as they believe it gives them an important tool to allow them to use their "sixth sense" about jurors. Over time, peremptory challenges in the hands of racist prosecutors and judges, who, in some cases, handle *voir dire* themselves, became a way to remove African Americans from the available jury pool.

Suppose, in the Jim Crow South, that thirty people were called in for jury selection, and that six of them were black. Prosecutors could then use their peremptory challenges to remove the six African American members of the jury pool without having to worry about offending the Constitution. And so they did, even after the NAACP attempted to halt such practices in *Swain* v. *Alabama* (1965). But the Court, in *Swain,* rejected the NAACP's argument that peremptory challenges, even if used to eliminate blacks from juries, were barred by the Sixth and Fourteenth Amendments. However, the Court offered no real defense of peremptory challenges other than to appeal to their long-standing use as part of the trial process. Writing for a unanimous Court, Justice White ruled that the NAACP had offered no compelling evidence that such systematic discrimination existed against blacks.

In *Batson* v. *Kentucky* (1986), the Court revisited the issue of racially motivated peremptory challenges in criminal trials. The NAACP did not sponsor *Batson,* but it did assemble a powerful coalition of civil rights organizations to file a joint *amicus* brief. In fact, Justice Powell's majority opinion, citing the NAACP's joint *amicus* brief, referred to the importance of the equal protection issues in *Batson* right at the outset.[44]

Batson v. *Kentucky*

476 U.S. 79 (1986)

In January 1982, James Batson, a young African American man, was indicted in Jefferson County, Kentucky, on second-degree burglary charges and for receiving stolen goods. Batson was not a first-time offender. As such, he was eligible to receive a heavier sentence if convicted.

Batson pled innocent and the parties proceeded to trial. When the jurors were brought into the courtroom for *voir dire,* Batson's lawyer noticed that, of the forty persons called to serve, only four were black. The Kentucky prosecutor trying Batson's case used his peremptory challenges to eliminate the African American jurors from the pool. Batson was then left in an unfavorable position for a black criminal defendant in a small Southern town, even in the 1980s: He now faced an all-white jury.

Batson was convicted on both counts and sentenced to twenty years in prison. His lawyers appealed, claiming that the prosecutor had engaged in a racially discriminatory pattern of behavior by striking all the eligible blacks from the jury pool. Claiming that *Swain* was too limited in scope to guarantee equal treatment in jury selection, Batson's lawyers argued that the Court should extend the equal protection guarantee established there by holding that the exclusion of African Americans from juries was the logical extension of forbidding their exclusion from the jury pool. Kentucky countered that creating a constitutional barrier to the unrestricted use of peremptory barriers in jury selection amounted to a reckless intrusion into a lawyer's right to secure the most favorable conditions for a client's trial.

Batson received strong support from civil rights and criminal defense groups. The NAACP LDF, the American Jewish Committee, and the American Jewish Congress filed a joint brief arguing that peremptory challenges should be subject to strict scrutiny under the Equal Protection Clause when a defendant could establish a pattern of discrimination. Discrimination against blacks in the criminal justice system at all levels has been well documented. The involvement of Jewish organizations is interesting, as it recalled the "last name" discrimination used to identify Jewish jurors and exclude them in criminal cases involving Jewish defendants. Moreover, to many Southern prosecutors in the pre–civil rights era South, Jews were viewed as more sympathetic to black defendants in criminal proceedings and routinely stricken from juries.[45] The National Legal Aid and Defender Association, whose clients include a disproportionate number of African American defendants, also filed a brief urging the Court to bring peremptory challenges under the scope of the Equal Protection Clause. The Department of Justice, which, since the election of President Ronald Reagan in 1980, had urged the Court to revisit such cases as *Mapp* v. *Ohio* (see Chapter 7) and *Miranda* v. *Arizona,* supported Kentucky.

The Court's decision was 7 to 2. Justice Powell delivered the opinion of the Court. Justices Marshall, O'Connor, Stevens, and White filed separate concurring opinions. Chief Justice Burger, joined by Justice Rehnquist, filed a dissenting opinion. Justice Rehnquist, joined by the Chief Justice, also dissented.

▼▲▼

JUSTICE POWELL delivered the opinion of the Court.

This case requires us to reexamine that portion of *Swain* v. *Alabama* (1965) concerning the evidentiary burden placed on a criminal defendant who claims that he has been denied equal protection through the State's use of peremptory challenges to exclude members of his race from the petit jury. . . .

In *Swain,* this Court recognized that a "State's purposeful or deliberate denial to Negroes on account of race of participation as jurors in the administration of justice violates the Equal Protection Clause." This principle has been "consistently and repeatedly" reaffirmed in numerous decisions of this Court both preceding and following *Swain.* We reaffirm the principle today.

More than a century ago, the Court decided that the State denies a black defendant equal protection of the laws when it puts him on trial before a jury from which members of his race have been purposefully excluded, *Strauder* v. *West Virginia* (1880). That decision laid the foundation for the Court's unceasing efforts to eradicate racial discrimination in the procedures used to select the venire from which individual jurors are drawn. In *Strauder,* the Court explained that the central concern of the recently ratified Fourteenth Amendment was to put an end to governmental discrimination on account of race. Exclusion of black citizens from service as jurors constitutes a primary example of the evil the Fourteenth Amendment was designed to cure.

In holding that racial discrimination in jury selection offends the Equal Protection Clause, the Court in *Strauder* recognized, however, that a defendant has no right to a "petit jury composed in whole or in part of persons of his own race." . . . But the defendant does have the right to be tried by a jury whose members are selected pursuant to nondiscriminatory criteria. The Equal Protection Clause guarantees the defendant that the State will not exclude members of his race from the jury venire on account of race, *Strauder,* or on the false assumption that members of his race as a group are not qualified to serve as jurors.

Purposeful racial discrimination in selection of the [jury] violates a defendant's right to equal protection because it denies him the protection that a trial by jury is intended to secure. "The very idea of a jury is a body . . . composed of the peers or equals of the person whose rights it is selected or summoned to determine; that is, of his neighbors, fellows, associates, persons having the same legal status in society as that which he holds." The petit jury has occupied a central position in our system of justice by safeguarding a person accused of crime against the arbitrary exercise of power by prosecutor or judge. . . .

The harm from discriminatory jury selection extends beyond that inflicted on the defendant and the excluded juror to touch the entire community. Selection procedures that purposefully exclude black persons from juries undermine public confidence in the fairness of our system of justice. Discrimination within the judicial system is most pernicious because it is "a stimulant to that race prejudice which is an impediment to securing to [black citizens] that equal justice which the law aims to secure to all others."

In *Strauder*, the Court invalidated a state statute that provided that only white men could serve as jurors. We can be confident that no State now has such a law. The Constitution requires, however, that we look beyond the face of the statute defining juror qualifications and also consider challenged selection practices to afford "protection against action of the State through its administrative officers in effecting the prohibited discrimination." Thus, the Court has found a denial of equal protection where the procedures implementing a neutral statute operated to exclude persons from the venire on racial grounds, and has made clear that the Constitution prohibits all forms of purposeful racial discrimination in selection of jurors. While decisions of this Court have been concerned largely with discrimination during selection of the venire, the principles announced there also forbid discrimination on account of race in selection of the petit jury. . . .

Accordingly, the component of the jury selection process at issue here, the State's privilege to strike individual jurors through peremptory challenges, is subject to the commands of the Equal Protection Clause. Although a prosecutor ordinarily is entitled to exercise permitted peremptory challenges "for any reason at all, as long as that reason is related to his view concerning the outcome" of the case to be tried, the Equal Protection Clause forbids the prosecutor to challenge potential jurors solely on account of their race or on the assumption that black jurors as a group will be unable impartially to consider the State's case against a black defendant.

The principles announced in *Strauder* never have been questioned in any subsequent decision of this Court. Rather, the Court has been called upon repeatedly to review the application of those principles to particular facts. A recurring question in these cases, as in any case alleging a violation of the Equal Protection Clause, was whether the defendant had met his burden of proving purposeful discrimination on the part of the State. That question also was at the heart of the portion of *Swain* v. *Alabama* we reexamine today.

Swain required the Court to decide, among other issues, whether a black defendant was denied equal protection by the State's exercise of peremptory challenges to exclude members of his race from the petit jury. The record in *Swain* showed that the prosecutor had used the State's peremptory challenges to strike the six black persons included on the petit jury venire. While rejecting the defendant's claim for failure to prove purposeful discrimination, the Court nonetheless indicated that the Equal Protection Clause placed some limits on the State's exercise of peremptory challenges.

The Court sought to accommodate the prosecutor's historical privilege of peremptory challenge free of judicial control, and the constitutional prohibition on exclusion of persons from jury service on account of race. While the Constitution does not confer a right to peremptory challenges, those challenges traditionally have been viewed as one means of assuring the selection of a qualified and unbiased jury. To preserve the peremptory nature of the prosecutor's challenge, the Court in Swain declined to scrutinize his actions in a particular case by relying on a presumption that he properly exercised the State's challenges.

The Court went on to observe, however, that a State may not exercise its challenges in contravention of the Equal Protection Clause. It was impermissible for a prosecutor to use his challenges to exclude blacks from the jury "for reasons wholly unrelated to the outcome of the particular case on trial" or to deny to blacks "the same right and opportunity to participate in the administration of justice enjoyed by the white population." Accordingly, a black defendant could make out a *prima facie* case of purposeful discrimination on proof that the peremptory challenge system was "being perverted" in that manner. For example, an inference of purposeful discrimination would be raised on evidence that a prosecutor, "in case after case, whatever the circumstances, whatever the crime and whoever the defendant or the victim may be, is responsible for the removal of Negroes who have been selected as qualified jurors by the jury commissioners and who have survived challenges for cause, with the result that no Negroes ever serve on petit juries." Evidence offered by the defendant in *Swain* did not meet that standard. While the defendant showed that prosecutors in the jurisdiction had exercised their strikes to exclude blacks from the jury, he offered no proof of the circumstances under which prosecutors were responsible for striking black jurors beyond the facts of his own case. . . .

[S]ince the decision in *Swain*, this Court has recognized that a defendant may make a *prima facie* showing of purposeful racial discrimination in selection of the venire by relying solely on the facts concerning its selection in his case. These decisions are in accordance with the proposition . . . that "a consistent pattern of official racial discrimination" is not "a necessary predicate to a violation of the Equal Protection Clause. A single invidiously discriminatory governmental act" is not "immunized by the absence of such discrimination in the making of other comparable decisions." For evidentiary requirements to dictate that "several must suffer discrimination" before one could object, would be inconsistent with the promise of equal protection to all. . . .

The State contends that our holding will eviscerate the fair trial values served by the peremptory challenge. Conceding that the Constitution does not guarantee a right to peremptory challenges and that *Swain* did state that their use ultimately is subject to the strictures of equal protection, the State argues that the privilege of unfettered exercise of the challenge is of vital importance to the criminal justice system.

While we recognize, of course, that the peremptory challenge occupies an important position in our trial procedures, we do not agree that our decision today will undermine the contribution the challenge generally makes to the administration of justice. The reality of practice, amply reflected in many state- and federal-court opinions, shows that the challenge may be, and unfortunately at times has been, used to discriminate against black jurors. By requiring trial courts to be sensitive to the racially discriminatory use of peremptory challenges, our decision enforces the mandate of equal protection and furthers the ends of justice. In view of the heterogeneous population of our Nation, public respect for our criminal justice system and the rule of law will be strengthened if we ensure that no citizen is disqualified from jury service because of his race.

Justice Marshall, concurring.

I join Justice Powell's eloquent opinion for the Court, which takes a historic step toward eliminating the shameful practice of racial discrimination in the selection of juries. The Court's opinion cogently explains the pernicious nature of the racially discriminatory use of peremptory challenges, and the repugnancy of such discrimination to the Equal Protection Clause. The Court's opinion also ably demonstrates the inadequacy of any burden of proof for racially discriminatory use of peremptories that requires that "justice . . . sit supinely by" and be flouted in case after case before a remedy is available. I nonetheless write separately to express my views. The decision today will not end the racial discrimination that peremptories inject into the jury-selection process. That goal can be accomplished only by eliminating peremptory challenges entirely. . . .

Misuse of the peremptory challenge to exclude black jurors has become both common and flagrant. Black defendants rarely have been able to compile statistics showing the extent of that practice, but the few cases setting out such figures are instructive. Prosecutors have explained to courts that they routinely strike black jurors. An instruction book used by the prosecutor's office in Dallas County, Texas, explicitly advised prosecutors that they conduct jury selection so as to eliminate "'any member of a minority group.'" In 100 felony trials in Dallas County in 1983–1984, prosecutors peremptorily struck 405 out of 467 eligible black jurors; the chance of a qualified black sitting on a jury was 1 in 10, compared to 1 in 2 for a white. . . .

The inherent potential of peremptory challenges to distort the jury process by permitting the exclusion of jurors on racial grounds should ideally lead the Court to ban them entirely from the criminal justice system. Justice Goldberg, dissenting in *Swain*, emphasized that "[w]ere it necessary to make an absolute choice between the right of a defendant to have a jury chosen in conformity with the requirements of the Fourteenth Amendment and the right to challenge peremptorily, the Constitution compels a choice of the former." I believe that this case presents just such a choice, and I would resolve that choice by eliminating peremptory challenges entirely in criminal cases.

Justice Rehnquist, with whom The Chief Justice joins, dissenting.

I cannot subscribe to the Court's unprecedented use of the Equal Protection Clause to restrict the historic scope of the peremptory challenge, which has been described as "a necessary part of trial by jury." In my view, there is simply nothing "unequal" about the State's using its peremptory challenges to strike blacks from the jury in cases involving black defendants, so long as such challenges are also used to exclude whites in cases involving white defendants, Hispanics in cases involving Hispanic defendants, Asians in cases involving Asian defendants, and so on. This

RACE IN THE COURTROOM

Thurgood Marshall Meets the Jim Crow Jury System

Thurgood Marshall is perhaps best known as a key architect of and chief courtroom lawyer for the NAACP's campaign to defeat legal segregation. While much attention has been given to Marshall's work in the school segregation and voting rights cases, he also continued to press the NAACP's long-standing concern with racial inequities in the criminal justice system. Below is an excerpt taken from Juan Williams's biography of Thurgood Marshall, *Thurgood Marshall: American Revolutionary.* It describes one of Marshall's initial efforts to break the back of the discriminatory jury system in Texas, a system that was common throughout the South (and in many other parts of the nation) when Marshall visited there in 1938.

The story began on September 26, 1938, when George Porter was summoned for jury service with a randomly selected group of Dallas citizens that included several other blacks. As was the segregationist tradition in Dallas, the judge immediately dismissed all black jurors. But Porter knew this dance. He had been summoned to jury duty twice before. Both times white jurors and court officials had threatened to beat him, even lynch him if he persisted in trying to serve. And both times the balding, dark-skinned Porter had left without resistance.

In September 1938, however, Porter made his stand. A deputy sheriff ordered all the blacks in the jury pool to stay behind while the white jurors went to lunch. The deputy sheriff took them into a darkened room, and as the black jurors grew fearful, the deputy told them to go home. Most people quickly headed for the door, but Porter demanded to see the judge, Paine Bush. The deputy stared down at him, not budging until Judge Bush walked into the courtroom. The judge told Porter he could protest the dismissal, but it was too late for him to serve on this jury.

Porter had anticipated the judge's words. He told the surprised judge that he had already filed a protest in advance of being dismissed. The judge was trapped. If he dismissed Porter now it would create a controversy and possibly tar the judge's name. Bush walked away in disgust. He told Porter that he could stay, but at his own risk.

Porter went to lunch, but when he returned a young white man ran into the jury room and threatened to beat him up. Porter ignored the threat, but soon another white man came in. This time there was no warning. The man grabbed the unsuspecting Porter by the collar, dragging him through the halls of the courthouse. When he got him to the front door, with Porter still struggling to regain his balance, he threw the junior-college president out the door and down the front steps.

Looking at the holes in his good suit and wiping his handkerchief over the cuts and bruises on his body, Porter marched back up the steps. At the top, a line of white men stood in front of the door and circled him. Staring past their scowling faces, Porter pushed through and ran back into the courthouse. The white men stopped their pursuit when he ran into Judge Bush's courtroom.

Porter's bravery was not rewarded. The judge filled the grand jury, then dismissed Porter along with sixteen whites.

Just as Marshall was preparing to leave for Dallas, he heard from NAACP officials there that the chief of police was making special plans for his visit. The chief had called his top officers in and told them that a black NAACP lawyer from New York was coming to stir up trouble. And he told them they were not to allow any acts of intimidation against the lawyer. "Don't lay a hand on him," the chief ordered. "Don't touch Thurgood Marshall. Because I personally will take him and kick the shit out of him. Personally."

Marshall was genuinely worried: "I sort of considered the idea of having a bad cold or something and not going down there," he said. "But I couldn't get a cold."

To ease his mind Marshall decided to find out about the police chief and the rumored threat. He heard that Texas goveror James Allred was a fair man and placed a call. Allred said he had heard the rumor too. "Aw no," the governor told Marshall. "I give you my word, if you come down here, you'll not be injured."

"And sure enough," Marshall said, "when I got down there, a Texas Ranger was there." But the ranger assigned to protect him did not seem initially to Marshall's liking. "As he talked he kept saying 'boy.' I said, 'This ain't the man I need.' So I called the governor, and he said, "He's the best trained I've got. And if I straighten him out, will that be okay?' And I said sure. So I put him on the phone. And, oh, you should have seen his face!"

Luckily for Marshall, the Texas Ranger proved to be the right man for the job. Near the end of his first week in town, after talking with judges, Marshall was leaving the courthouse late one afternoon and walking over to his car, where the ranger was waiting for him. Suddenly Marshall saw the chief of police charging out of the nearby police headquarters, with his gun drawn. Stiff and wide-eyed, Marshall could not move. Running toward him, the chief shouted: "Hi, you black son of a bitch, I've got you now." Those words broke Marshall's trance, and he began to run to the car. The ranger, who had been sitting on the hood of the car, calmly pulled his gun and faced the chief. "Fella, just stay right where you are," he said.

Sweating and huffing, Marshall got in the car and slammed the door as the chief stood there gritting his teeth. The ranger, still holding the gun out, got in the driver's seat, started the car, and drove away.

Despite the investigation Marshall was not able to prosecute anyone in the case. But his trip to Texas put court officials throughout the South on alert. The NAACP, through Marshall's presence, had announced that it had the legal know-how, the political power, and the people to put up a fight for the rights of blacks. By putting pressure on the governor and drawing press attention to rude handling of black jurors in Texas, Marshall got Judge Bush to reverse his position. A few weeks after the trip, Bush allowed a black juror, W. L. Dickson, to remain on a jury. Governor Allred then assigned rangers to protect black jurors in the courthouse. And blacks gradually began to do regular service on juries throughout Texas.

case-specific use of peremptory challenges by the State does not single out blacks, or members of any other race for that matter, for discriminatory treatment. Such use of peremptories is at best based upon seat-of-the-pants instincts, which are undoubtedly crudely stereotypical and may in many cases be hopelessly mistaken. But as long as they are applied across-the-board to jurors of all races and nationalities, I do not see—and the Court most certainly has not explained—how their use violates the Equal Protection Clause.

Nor does such use of peremptory challenges by the State infringe upon any other constitutional interests. The Court does not suggest that exclusion of blacks from the jury through the State's use of peremptory challenges results in a violation of either the fair-cross-section or impartiality component of the Sixth Amendment. And because the case-specific use of peremptory challenges by the State does not deny blacks the right to serve as jurors in cases involving nonblack defendants, it harms neither the excluded jurors nor the remainder of the community.

The use of group affiliations, such as age, race, or occupation, as a "proxy" for potential juror partiality, based on the assumption or belief that members of one group are more likely to favor defendants who belong to the same group, has long been accepted as a legitimate basis for the State's exercise of peremptory challenges. Indeed, given the need for reasonable limitations on the time devoted to voir dire, the use of such "proxies" by both the State and the defendant may be extremely useful in eliminating from the jury persons who might be biased in one way or another. The Court today holds that the State may not use its peremptory challenges to strike black prospective jurors on this basis without violating the Constitution. But I do not believe there is anything in the Equal Protection Clause, or any other constitutional provision, that justifies such a departure from the substantive holding contained in . . . *Swain*. Petitioner in the instant case failed to make a sufficient showing to overcome the presumption announced in *Swain* that the State's use of peremptory challenges was related to the context of the case. I would therefore affirm the judgment of the court below.

▼▲▼

By overruling *Swain*, the Court, in *Batson*, opened the door for future challenges to the racially motivated use of peremptory challenges. Indeed, by the early 1990s, the Court had extended *Batson* to ban defense lawyers, not just prosecutors, from using peremptory strikes to exclude jurors on the basis of race.[46] With racially discriminatory claims involving peremptory strikes in jury selection now firmly housed under the Equal Protection Clause of the Fourteenth Amendment, it was only a matter of time before someone stepped up to argue that sex-based peremptory challenges were unconstitutional as well. In *J.E.B. v. Alabama ex. rel. T.B.* (1994), the Court revisited *Taylor*, and fused it with an update of the equal protection guarantee outlined in *Batson*.

J.E.B. v. *Alabama ex rel. T.B.*

511 U.S. 127 (1994)

In October 1989, Teresia Bible, with the support of the Alabama attorney general's office, filed suit against James Edward Bowman, Sr. Bible was seeking child support on behalf of Phillip Rhett Bowman Bible, a six-month-old infant whom she claimed was Bowman's biological son. Adamantly denying Bible's charge, Bowman demanded to take a blood test in order to establish paternity. Whether Bowman thought that such a bold move would force Bible to reconsider her claim was not clear, but his decision backfired: The test results showed a 99.9 percent probability that Bowman was the father of Bible's child. Undaunted, Bowman filed suit against Bible, claiming that, test results to the contrary, a man named Ricky Stone was the father. Bowman had only dug himself a deeper hole: A blood test on Stone revealed absolutely no possibility that Stone could have fathered Bible's child. A state trial court ruled that Bowman was the father and ordered him to pay child support. Nonetheless, Bowman pressed his lawsuit against Bible and appealed the verdict.

In December 1991, a panel of thirty-six jurors was assembled in the Jackson County, Alabama, courtroom to begin Bowman's suit challenging the paternity claim. Twenty-four of the jurors were women. The judge dismissed three of the jurors for cause, leaving twenty-two women and ten men. The state used nine of its ten peremptory strikes to eliminate all but one of the men from the jury panel. Bowman's attorney used his peremptory strikes to remove nine women and one man. Continuing his bad fortune, Bowman was left to start his trial with an all-female jury.

Bowman's attorney argued that the state's use of its peremptory strikes was a deliberate effort to keep men off the jury, and thus violated the Equal Protection Clause. Citing *Batson*, Bowman's attorney claimed that sex-based discrimination in jury selection was no more permissible than race-based discrimination. The trial judge rejected that argument, and permitted the trial to go forward. The jury found that Bowman was the father of Bible's child, and ordered him to pay child support. Bowman's subsequent appeals through the Alabama courts failed.

Whereas James Batson had to contend with the United States Justice Department arguing against his claim that race-based peremptory strikes violated his constitutional rights, James Bowman received the support of the Justice Department. Under President Bill Clinton (1993–2001), the Justice Department reversed many of the Bush and Reagan administration's positions on civil rights claims. In addition, a coalition of seventeen women's rights and civil liberties groups, including the NOW LDF, the ACLU, People for the American Way, and the National Women's Law Center, filed a brief in support of Bowman's claim.

The Court's decision was 6 to 3. Justice Blackmun delivered the opinion of the Court. Justices O'Connor and Kennedy filed separate concurring opinions. Chief Justice Rehnquist dissented. Justice Scalia, joined by Justices Thomas and Rehnquist, also dissented.

▼▲▼

JUSTICE BLACKMUN delivered the opinion of the Court.

In *Batson* v. *Kentucky* (1986), this Court held that the Equal Protection Clause of the Fourteenth Amendment governs the exercise of peremptory challenges by a prosecutor in a criminal trial. The Court explained that, although a defendant has "no right to a 'petit jury composed in whole or in part of persons of his own race,'" *Strauder* v. *West Virginia* (1880), the "defendant does have the right to be tried by a jury whose members are selected pursuant to nondiscriminatory criteria." Since *Batson,* we have reaffirmed repeatedly our commitment to jury selection procedures that are fair and nondiscriminatory. We have recognized that, whether the trial is criminal or civil, potential jurors, as well as litigants, have an equal protection right to jury selection procedures that are free from state-sponsored group stereotypes rooted in, and reflective of, historical prejudice.

Today we are faced with the question whether the Equal Protection Clause forbids intentional discrimination on the basis of gender, just as it prohibits discrimination on the basis of race. We hold that gender, like race, is an unconstitutional proxy for juror competence and impartiality. . . .

Discrimination on the basis of gender in the exercise of peremptory challenges is a relatively recent phenomenon. Gender-based peremptory strikes were hardly practicable for most of our country's existence, since, until the 19th century, women were completely excluded from jury service. So well-entrenched was this exclusion of women that, in 1880, this Court, while finding that the exclusion of African-American men from juries violated the Fourteenth Amendment, expressed no doubt that a State "may confine the selection [of jurors] to males.". . . .

This Court, in *Ballard* v. *United States* (1946), first questioned the fundamental fairness of denying women the right to serve on juries. Relying on its supervisory powers over the federal courts, it held that women may not be excluded from the venire in federal trials in States where women were eligible for jury service under local law. . . .

Fifteen years later, however, the Court still was unwilling to translate its appreciation for the value of women's contribution to civic life into an enforceable right to equal treatment under state laws governing jury service. In *Hoyt* v. *Florida* [1961], the Court found it reasonable, "despite the enlightened emancipation of women," to exempt women from mandatory jury service by statute, allowing women to serve on juries only if they volunteered to serve. The Court justified the differential exemption policy on the ground that women, unlike men, occupied a unique position "as the center of home and family life."

In 1975, the Court finally repudiated the reasoning of *Hoyt* and struck down, under the Sixth Amendment, an affirmative registration statute nearly identical to the one at issue in *Hoyt, Taylor* v. *Louisiana* (1975). We explained: "Restricting jury service to only special groups or excluding identifiable segments playing major roles in the community cannot be squared with the constitutional concept of jury trial." The diverse and representative character of the jury must be maintained "'partly as assurance of a diffused impartiality and partly because sharing in the administration of justice is a phase of civic responsibility.'" . . .

Despite the heightened scrutiny afforded distinctions based on gender, respondent argues that gender discrimination in the selection of the petit jury should be permitted, though discrimination on the basis of race is not. Respondent suggests that "gender discrimination in this country. . . . has never reached the level of discrimination" against African-Americans, and therefore gender discrimination, unlike racial discrimination, is tolerable in the courtroom.

While the prejudicial attitudes toward women in this country have not been identical to those held toward racial minorities, the similarities between the experiences of racial minorities and women, in some contexts, "overpower those differences." . . .

Certainly, with respect to jury service, African-Americans and women share a history of total exclusion, a history which came to an end for women many years after the embarrassing chapter in our history came to an end for African-Americans. We need not determine, however, whether women or racial minorities have suffered more at the hands of discriminatory state actors during the decades of our Nation's history. It is necessary only to acknowledge that "our Nation has had a long and unfortunate history of sex discrimination," a history which warrants the heightened scrutiny we afford all gender-based classifications today. Under our equal protection jurisprudence, gender-based classifications require "an exceedingly persuasive justification" in order to survive constitutional scrutiny. Thus, the only question is whether discrimination on the basis of gender in jury selection substantially furthers the State's legitimate interest in achieving a fair and impartial trial. In making this assessment, we do not weigh the value of peremptory challenges as an institution against our asserted commitment to eradicate invidious discrimination from the courtroom. Instead, we consider whether peremptory challenges based on gender stereotypes provide substantial aid to a litigant's effort to secure a fair and impartial jury. . . .

Discrimination in jury selection, whether based on race or on gender, causes harm to the litigants, the community, and the individual jurors who are wrongfully excluded from participation in the judicial process. The litigants are harmed by the risk that the prejudice which motivated the discriminatory selection of the jury will infect the entire proceedings. The community is harmed by the State's participation in the perpetuation of invidious group stereotypes and the inevitable loss of confidence in our judicial system that state-sanctioned discrimination in the courtroom engenders.

When state actors exercise peremptory challenges in reliance on gender stereotypes, they ratify and reinforce prejudicial views of the relative abilities of men and women. Because these stereotypes have wreaked injustice in so many other spheres of our country's public life, active discrimination by litigants on the basis of gender during jury selection "invites cynicism respecting the jury's neutrality and its obligation to adhere to the law." The potential for cynicism is particularly acute in cases where gender-related issues are prominent, such as cases involving rape, sexual harassment, or paternity. Discriminatory use of peremptory challenges may create the impression that the judicial system has acquiesced in suppressing full participation by one gender or that the "deck has been stacked" in favor of one side. . . .

Our conclusion that litigants may not strike potential jurors solely on the basis of gender does not imply the elimination of all peremptory challenges. Neither does it conflict with a State's legitimate interest in using such challenges in its effort to secure a fair and impartial jury. Parties still may remove jurors whom they feel might be less acceptable than others on the panel; gender simply may not serve as a proxy for bias. Parties may also exercise their peremptory challenges to remove from the venire any group or class of individuals normally subject to "rational basis" review. Even strikes based on characteristics that are disproportionately associated with one gender could be appropriate, absent a showing of pretext. . . .

Failing to provide jurors the same protection against gender discrimination as race discrimination could frustrate the purpose of *Batson* itself. Because gender and race are overlapping categories, gender can be used as a pretext for racial discrimination. Allowing parties to remove racial minorities from the jury not because of their race, but because of their gender, contravenes well-established equal protection principles and could insulate effectively racial discrimination from judicial scrutiny.

Equal opportunity to participate in the fair administration of justice is fundamental to our democratic system. It not only furthers the goals of the jury system. It reaffirms the promise of equality under the law—that all citizens, regardless of race, ethnicity, or gender, have the chance to take part directly in our democracy. When persons are excluded from participation in our democratic processes solely because of race or gender, this promise of equality dims, and the integrity of our judicial system is jeopardized.

In view of these concerns, the Equal Protection Clause prohibits discrimination in jury selection on the basis of gender, or on the assumption that an individual will be biased in a particular case for no reason other than the fact that the person happens to be a woman or happens to be a man. As with race, the "core guarantee of equal protection, ensuring citizens that their State will not discriminate . . . , would be meaningless were we to approve the exclusion of jurors on the basis of such assumptions, which arise solely from the jurors' [gender]," *Batson* v. *Kentucky* (1986).

The judgment of the Court of Civil Appeals of Alabama is reversed and the case is remanded to that court for further proceedings not inconsistent with this opinion.

It is so ordered.

JUSTICE KENNEDY, concurring in the judgment.

There is no doubt under our precedent . . . that the Equal Protection Clause prohibits sex discrimination in the selection of jurors. The only question is whether the Clause also prohibits peremptory challenges based on sex. The Court is correct to hold that it does. The Equal Protection Clause and our constitutional tradition are based on the theory that an individual possesses rights that are protected against lawless action by the government. The neutral phrasing of the Equal Protection Clause, extending its guarantee to "any person," reveals its concern with rights of individuals, not groups (though group disabilities are sometimes the mechanism by which the State violates the individual right in question). "At the heart of the Constitution's guarantee of equal protection lies the simple command that the Government must treat citizens as individuals, not as simply components of a racial [or] sexual . . . class," *Metro Broadcasting, Inc.* v. *FCC* (1990). For purposes of the Equal Protection Clause, an individual denied jury service because of a peremptory challenge exercised against her on account of her sex is no less injured than the individual denied jury service because of a law banning members of her sex from serving as jurors. The injury is to personal dignity and to the individual's right to participate in the political process. The neutrality of the Fourteenth Amendment's guarantee is confirmed by the fact that the Court has no difficulty in finding a constitutional wrong in this case, which involves males excluded from jury service because of their gender.

The importance of individual rights to our analysis prompts a further observation concerning what I conceive to be the intended effect of today's decision. We do not prohibit racial and gender bias in jury selection only to encourage it in jury deliberations. Once seated, a juror should not give free rein to some racial or gender bias of his or her own. The jury system is a kind of compact by which power is transferred from the judge to jury, the jury in turn deciding the case in accord with the instructions defining the relevant issues for consideration. The wise limitations on the authority of courts to inquire into the reasons underlying a jury's verdict does not mean that a jury ought to disregard the court's instructions. A juror who allows racial or gender bias to influence assessment of the case breaches the compact and renounces his or her oath. . . .

In this regard, it is important to recognize that a juror sits not as a representative of a racial or sexual group, but as an individual citizen. Nothing would be more pernicious to the jury system than for society to presume that persons of different backgrounds go to the jury room to voice prejudice. The jury pool must be representative of the community, but that is a structural mechanism for preventing bias, not enfranchising it. . . . Thus, the Constitution guarantees a right only to an impartial jury, not to a jury composed of members of a particular race or gender.

For these reasons, I concur in the judgment of the Court holding that peremptory strikes based on gender violate the Equal Protection Clause.

JUSTICE SCALIA, with whom THE CHIEF JUSTICE and JUSTICE THOMAS join, dissenting.

Today's opinion is an inspiring demonstration of how thoroughly up-to-date and right-thinking we Justices are in matters pertaining to the sexes (or as the Court would have it, the genders), and how sternly we disapprove the male chauvinist attitudes of our predecessors. The price to be paid for this display—a modest price, surely—is that most of the opinion is quite irrelevant to the case at hand. The hasty reader will be surprised to learn, for example, that this lawsuit involves a complaint about the use of peremptory challenges to exclude men from a petit jury. To be sure, petitioner, a man, used all but one of his peremptory strikes to remove women from the jury (he used his last challenge to strike the sole remaining male from the pool), but the validity of his strikes is not before us. Nonetheless, the Court treats itself to an extended discussion of the historic exclusion of women not only from jury service, but also from service [in the legal profession] (which is rather like jury service, in that it involves going to the courthouse a lot). . . .

The Court also spends time establishing that the use of sex as a proxy for particular views or sympathies is unwise, and perhaps irrational. The opinion stresses the lack of statistical evidence to support the widely held belief that at least in certain types of cases, a juror's sex has some statistically significant predictive value as to how the juror will behave. This assertion seems to place the Court in opposition to its earlier Sixth Amendment "fair cross-section" cases. But times and trends do change, and unisex is unquestionably in fashion. Personally, I am less inclined to demand statistics, and more inclined to credit the perceptions of experienced litigators who have had money on the line. But it does not matter. The Court's fervent defense of the proposition il n'y a pas de difference entre les hommes et les femmes (it stereotypes the opposite view as hateful "stereotyping") turns out to be, like its recounting of the history of sex discrimination against women, utterly irrelevant. Even if sex was a remarkably good predictor in certain cases, the Court would find its use in peremptories unconstitutional. . . .

The core of the Court's reasoning is that peremptory challenges on the basis of any group characteristic subject to heightened scrutiny are inconsistent with the guarantee of the Equal Protection Clause. That conclusion can be reached only by focusing unrealistically upon individual exercises of the peremptory challenge, and ignoring the totality of the practice. Since all groups are subject to the peremptory challenge (and will be made the object of it, depending upon the nature of the particular case) it is hard to see how any group is denied equal protection. That explains why peremptory challenges coexisted with the Equal Protection Clause for 120 years. This case is a perfect example of how the system as a whole is evenhanded. While the only claim before the Court is petitioner's complaint that the prosecutor struck male jurors, for every man struck by the government, petitioner's own lawyer struck a woman. To say that men were singled out for discriminatory treatment in this process is preposterous. The situation would be different if both sides systematically struck individuals of one group, so that the strikes evinced group-based animus and served as a proxy for segregated venire lists. The pattern here, however, displays not a systemic sex-based animus, but each side's desire to get a jury favorably disposed to its case. That is why the Court's characterization of respondent's argument as "reminiscent of the arguments advanced to justify the total exclusion of women from juries" is patently false. Women were categorically excluded from juries because of doubt that they were competent; women are stricken from juries by peremptory challenge because of doubt that they are well disposed to the striking party's case. There is discrimination and dishonor in the former, and not in the latter—which explains the 106-year interlude between our holding that exclusion from juries on the basis of race was unconstitutional, *Strauder* v. *West Virginia* (1880), and our holding that peremptory challenges on the basis of race were unconstitutional, *Batson* v. *Kentucky*. . . .

The irrationality of today's strike-by-strike approach to equal protection is evident from the consequences of extending it to its logical conclusion. If a fair and impartial trial is a prosecutor's only legitimate goal; if adversarial trial stratagems must be tested against that goal in abstraction from their role within the system as a whole; and if, so tested, sex-based stratagems do not survive heightened scrutiny—then the prosecutor presumably violates the Constitution when he selects a male or female police officer to testify because he believes one or the other sex might be more convincing in the context of the particular case, or because he believes one or the other might be more appealing to a predominantly male or female jury. A decision to stress one line of argument or present certain witnesses before a mostly female jury—for example, to stress that the defendant victimized women—becomes, under the Court's reasoning, intentional discrimination by a state actor on the basis of gender.

In order, it seems to me, not to eliminate any real denial of equal protection, but simply to pay conspicuous obeisance to the equality of the sexes, the Court imperils a practice that has been considered an essential part of fair jury trial since the dawn of the common law. The Constitution of the United States neither requires nor permits this vandalizing of our people's traditions.

For these reasons, I dissent.

Confronting Witnesses

The Sixth Amendment also guarantees the criminally accused the right to confront witnesses testifying against them in an open courtroom. The meaning of the Confrontation Clause is pretty clear: Defendants have the right to attend their own trials, get a look at the witnesses called to testify against them, and cross-examine them. Generally, the Court has remained true to the language of the Confrontation Clause, holding that, except in cases involving defendant misconduct, no compelling reason exists to excuse a defendant during witness testimony.[47] In *Maryland v. Craig* (1990), our final case in this chapter, the Court created an important exception to the Confrontation Clause, one that provoked a heated exchange between Justice O'Connor, writing for the majority, and Justice Scalia, writing in dissent.

Maryland v. *Craig*

497 U.S. 836 (1990)

In October 1986, a Howard County, Maryland, grand jury indicted Sandra Ann Craig, who owned and operated a preschool and kindergarten, on several counts of child abuse, including sexual assault and battery. Craig's alleged victim on all counts was a six-year-old girl who had attended Craig's school from August 1984 to June 1986. Before the case went to trial in March 1987, Maryland prosecutors requested that they be permitted to offer the girl's testimony via one-way closed-circuit television. A Maryland law authorized such a procedure if the presiding judge determined that the alleged child abuse victim's testifying in open court would "result in the child suffering serious emotional distress such that the child cannot reasonably communicate." If the judge grants the request, then the witness is examined by prosecuting and defense lawyers in a room separate from the defendant, the jury, and the judge. At no point does the witness ever see or communicate with the defendant.

The Maryland trial judge ruled that "the expert testimony in each case suggested" that the young girl bringing abuse charges against Craig would be unable to communicate effectively in her presence. The judge permitted the trial to proceed under the special circumstances rule. Craig's lawyers objected on Sixth Amendment grounds, claiming that Maryland law denied their client the right to confront her accuser. The Maryland Court of Appeals reversed the trial judge's ruling, setting the stage for the state's appeal to the United States Supreme Court.

Thirty-eight states plus Puerto Rico and the Virgin Islands filed a joint *amicus* brief defending Maryland's testimonial exception in child abuse cases. All these states had such laws themselves, many of which had been enacted in the early 1980s after some alleged child abuse cases involving day care centers had received national attention. The American Psychological Association filed a brief in support of Maryland's law, claiming that forcing children to confront their abusers could have traumatic and irreversible effects on their mental health. The National Association of Criminal Defense Lawyers filed a brief in support of Craig's argument.

The Court's decision was 5 to 4. Justice O'Connor delivered the opinion of the Court. Justice Scalia, joined by Justices Brennan, Marshall, and Stevens, dissented.

▼▲▼

JUSTICE O'CONNOR delivered the opinion of the Court.

This case requires us to decide whether the Confrontation Clause of the Sixth Amendment categorically prohibits a child witness in a child abuse case from testifying against a defendant at trial, outside the defendant's physical presence, by one-way closed-circuit television. . . .

The Confrontation Clause of the Sixth Amendment, made applicable to the States through the Fourteenth Amendment, provides: "In all criminal prosecutions, the accused shall enjoy the right . . . to be confronted with the witnesses against him."

We observed in *Coy* v. *Iowa* that "the Confrontation Clause guarantees the defendant a face-to-face meeting with witnesses appearing before the trier of fact." This interpretation derives not only from the literal text of the Clause, but also from our understanding of its historical roots.

We have never held, however, that the Confrontation Clause guarantees criminal defendants the absolute right to a face-to-face meeting with witnesses against them at trial. . . .

The central concern of the Confrontation Clause is to ensure the reliability of the evidence against a criminal defendant by subjecting it to rigorous testing in the context of an adversary proceeding before the trier of fact. The word "confront," after all, also means a clashing of forces or ideas, thus carrying with it the notion of adversariness. . . .

[T]he right guaranteed by the Confrontation Clause includes not only a "personal examination," but also "(1) insures that the witness will give his statements under oath—thus impressing him with the seriousness of the matter and guarding against the lie by the possibility of a penalty for perjury; (2) forces the witness to submit to cross-examination, the "greatest legal engine ever invented for the discovery of truth;" [and] (3) permits the jury that is to decide the defendant's fate to observe the demeanor of the witness in making his statement, thus aiding the jury in assessing his credibility." . . .

The combined effect of these elements of confrontation—physical presence, oath, cross-examination, and observation of demeanor by the trier of fact—serves the purposes of the Confrontation Clause by ensuring that evidence admitted against an accused is reliable and subject to the rigorous adversarial testing that is the norm of Anglo-American criminal proceedings. . . .

[W]e have never insisted on an actual face-to-face encounter at trial in every instance in which testimony is admitted against a defendant. Instead, we have repeatedly held that the Clause permits, where necessary, the admission of certain hearsay statements against a defendant despite the defendant's inability to confront the [witness] at trial. . . .

Given our hearsay cases, the word "confront," as used in the Confrontation Clause, cannot simply mean face-to-face confrontation, for the Clause would then, contrary to our cases, prohibit the admission of any accusatory hearsay statement made by an absent declarant—a declarant who is undoubtedly as much a "witness against" a defendant as one who actually testifies at trial.

In sum, our precedents establish that "the Confrontation Clause reflects a preference for face-to-face confrontation at trial," a preference that "must occasionally give way to considerations of public policy and the necessities of the case." "[W]e have attempted to harmonize the goal of the Clause—placing limits on the kind of evidence that may be received against a defendant—with a societal interest in accurate factfinding, which may require consideration of out-of-court statements. We have accordingly interpreted the Confrontation Clause in a manner sensitive to its purposes and sensitive to the necessities of trial and the adversary process. Thus, though we reaffirm the importance of face-to-face confrontation with witnesses appearing at trial, we cannot say that such confrontation is an indispensable element of the Sixth Amendment's guarantee of the right to confront one's accusers. . . .

That the face-to-face confrontation requirement is not absolute does not, of course, mean that it may easily be dispensed with. . . . [O]ur precedents confirm that a defendant's right to confront accusatory witnesses may be satisfied absent a physical, face-to-face confrontation at trial only where denial of such confrontation is necessary to further an important public policy and only where the reliability of the testimony is otherwise assured.

Maryland's statutory procedure, when invoked, prevents a child witness from seeing the defendant as he or she testifies against the defendant at trial. We find it significant, however, that Maryland's procedure preserves all of the other elements of the confrontation right: the child witness must be competent to testify and must testify under oath; the defendant retains full opportunity for contemporaneous cross-examination; and the judge, jury, and defendant are able to view (albeit by video monitor) the demeanor (and body) of the witness as he or she testifies. Although we are mindful of the many subtle effects face-to-face confrontation may have on an adversary criminal proceeding, the presence of these other elements of confrontation—oath, cross-examination, and observation of the witness' demeanor—adequately ensures that the testimony is both reliable and subject to rigorous adversarial testing in a manner functionally equivalent to that accorded live, in-person testimony. These safeguards of reliability and adversariness render the use of such a procedure a far cry from the undisputed prohibition of the Confrontation Clause: trial by ex parte affidavit or inquisition. Rather, we think these elements of effective confrontation not only permit a defendant to "confound and undo the false accuser, or reveal the child coached by a malevolent adult," but may well aid a defendant in eliciting favorable testimony from the child witness. Indeed, to the extent the child witness' testimony may be said to be technically given out-of-court (though we do not so hold), these assurances of reliability and adversariness are far greater than those required for admission of hearsay testimony under the Confrontation Clause. We are therefore confident that use of the one-way closed-circuit television procedure, where necessary to further an important state interest, does not impinge upon the truth-seeking or symbolic purposes of the Confrontation Clause.

The critical inquiry in this case, therefore, is whether use of the procedure is necessary to further an important state interest. The State contends that it has a substantial interest in protecting children who are allegedly victims of child abuse from the trauma of testifying against the alleged perpetrator, and that its statutory procedure for receiving testimony from such witnesses is necessary to further that interest. . . .

We . . . conclude today that a State's interest in the physical and psychological wellbeing of child abuse victims may be sufficiently important to outweigh, at least in some cases, a defendant's right to face his or her accusers in court. That a significant majority of States has enacted statutes to protect child witnesses from the trauma of giving testimony in child abuse cases attests to the widespread belief in the importance of such a public policy. Thirty-seven States, for example, permit the use of videotaped testimony of sexually abused children; 24 States have authorized the use of one-way closed-circuit television testimony in child abuse cases; and 8 States authorize the use of a two-way system in which the child-witness is permitted to see the courtroom and the defendant on a video monitor and in which the jury and judge is permitted to view the child during the testimony. . . .

Given the State's traditional and "'transcendent interest in protecting the welfare of children,'" and buttressed by the growing body of academic literature documenting the psychological trauma suffered by child abuse victims who must testify in court, we will not second-guess the considered judgment of the Maryland Legislature regarding the importance of its interest in protecting child abuse victims from the emotional trauma of testifying. Accordingly, we hold that, if the State makes an adequate showing of necessity, the state interest in protecting child witnesses from the trauma of testifying in a child abuse case is sufficiently important to justify the use of a special procedure that permits a child witness in such cases to testify at trial against a defendant in the absence of face-to-face confrontation with the defendant. . . .

To be sure, face-to-face confrontation may be said to cause trauma for the very purpose of eliciting truth, but we think that the use of Maryland's special procedure, where necessary to further the important state interest in preventing trauma to child witnesses in child abuse cases, adequately ensures the accuracy of the testimony and preserves the adversary nature of the trial. Indeed, where face-to-face confrontation causes significant emotional distress in a child witness, there is evidence that such confrontation would in fact disserve the Confrontation Clause's truth-seeking goal. . . .

In sum, we conclude that, where necessary to protect a child witness from trauma that would be caused by testifying in the physical presence of the defendant, at least where such trauma would impair the child's ability to communicate, the Confrontation Clause does not prohibit use of a procedure that, despite the absence of face-to-face confrontation, ensures the reliability of the evidence by subjecting it to rigorous adversarial testing and thereby preserves the essence of effective confrontation. Because there is no dispute that the child witnesses in this case testified under oath, were subject to full cross-examination, and were able to be observed by the judge, jury, and defendant as they testified, we conclude that, to the extent that a proper finding of necessity has been made, the admission of such testimony would be consonant with the Confrontation Clause.

JUSTICE SCALIA, with whom JUSTICE BRENNAN, JUSTICE MARSHALL, and JUSTICE STEVENS join, dissenting.

Seldom has this Court failed so conspicuously to sustain a categorical guarantee of the Constitution against the tide of prevailing current opinion. The Sixth Amendment provides, with unmistakable clarity, that "[i]n all criminal prosecutions, the accused shall enjoy the right . . . to be confronted with the witnesses against him." The purpose of enshrining this protection in the Constitution was to assure that none of the many policy interests from time to time pursued by statutory law could overcome a defendant's right to face his or her accusers in court. . . .

Because of this subordination of explicit constitutional text to currently favored public policy, the following scene can be played out in an American courtroom for the first time in two centuries: A father whose young daughter has been given over to the exclusive custody of his estranged wife, or a mother whose young son has been taken into custody by the State's child welfare department, is sentenced to prison for sexual abuse on the basis of testimony by a child the parent has not seen or spoken to for many months, and the guilty verdict is rendered without giving the parent so much as the opportunity to sit in the presence of the child, and to ask, personally or through counsel, "it is really not true, is it, that I—your father (or mother) whom you see before you—did these terrible things?" Perhaps that is a procedure today's society desires; perhaps (though I doubt it) it is even a fair procedure; but it is assuredly not a procedure permitted by the Constitution.

Because the text of the Sixth Amendment is clear, and because the Constitution is meant to protect against, rather than conform to, current "widespread belief," I respectfully dissent. . . .

The Court today has applied "interest-balancing" analysis where the text of the Constitution simply does not permit it. We are not free to conduct a cost-benefit analysis of clear and explicit constitutional guarantees, and then to adjust their meaning to comport with our findings. The Court has convincingly proved that the Maryland procedure serves a valid interest, and gives the defendant virtually everything the Confrontation Clause guarantees (everything, that is, except confrontation). I am persuaded, therefore, that the Maryland procedure is virtually constitutional. Since it is not, however, actually constitutional, I would affirm the judgment of the Maryland Court of Appeals reversing the judgment of conviction.

FOR FURTHER READING

Abramson, Jeffrey. *We, the Jury: The Jury System and the Ideal of Democracy.* New York: Basic Books, 1994.

Amar, Akhil Reed. *The Constitution and Criminal Procedure: First Principles.* New Haven, Conn.: Yale University Press, 1998.

Baker, Liva. *Miranda: Crime, Law and Politics.* New York: Atheneum, 1983.

Bodenhamer, David J. *Fair Trial: Rights of the Accused in American History.* New York: Oxford University Press, 1992.

Carter, Dan. *A Tragedy of the American South.* Baton Rouge: Louisiana State University Press, 1979.

Cole, David. *No Equal Justice: Race and Class in the American Criminal Justice System.* New York: New Press, 1999.

Cortner, Richard C. *A Mob Intent on Death.* Middletown, Conn.: Wesleyan University Press, 1988.

Curriden, Mark, and Leroy Phillips, Jr. *Contempt of Court: The Turn-of-the Century Lynching That Launched a Hundred Years of Federalism.* New York: Faber and Faber, 1999.

Goodman, James. *Stories of Scottsboro.* New York: Pantheon, 1994.

Graham, Fred P. *The Self-Inflicted Wound.* New York: Macmillan, 1970.

Kalven, Harry, and Hans Zeizel. *The American Jury.* Chicago: University of Chicago Press, 1966.

Kamisar, Yale. *Police Interrogation and Confessions.* Ann Arbor: University of Michigan Press, 1980.

Levy, Leonard. *Origins of the Fifth Amendment.* New York: Oxford University Press, 1968.

Lewis, Anthony. *Gideon's Trumpet.* New York: Vintage Books, 1979.

Medalie, Richard J. *From Escobedo to Miranda: The Anatomy of a Supreme Court Decision.* Washington, D.C.: Lerner Law Book Co., 1966.

9 Cruel and Unusual Punishment

Andrew Thomas, a pharmacist in the small Louisiana bayou town of St. Martinsville, was murdered in November 1944. Apparently the motive was robbery; when the police found Thomas, his wallet and watch, as well as four dollars, were missing. For nine months, the St. Martinsville police were unable to locate a suspect. Then, one night in August 1945, while pursuing a narcotics suspect into Port Arthur, Texas (located just over the Louisiana state line), a St. Martinsville police officer identified a familiar figure hanging around the local train station: sixteen-year-old Willie Francis, who had worked on and off for Thomas as a delivery boy. Francis was taken into custody. Very shortly thereafter, Francis turned over Thomas's wallet, which he had been keeping in his pocket, to the police. Although Francis later named several other accomplices in the pharmacist's murder, he ultimately confessed to pulling the trigger himself. In barely legible and semiliterate scrawl, Francis produced a statement describing what had happened. After taking the police to the spot where he had thrown the holster of the murder weapon, Francis was formally arrested.[1]

Francis was an indigent in the classic sense—he was one of fifteen children whose farm-laborer father earned just $9 a week. Since *Powell* v. *Alabama* (the Scottsboro Boys case) thirteen years before (see Chapter 8), the Court required state courts to provide representation to defendants in capital cases. Two local attorneys were appointed to represent Francis one month after he was arrested and less than a week before he began his trial. From start to finish, Francis was tried, convicted, and sentenced to death in only eight days. At no point during his trial did Francis's attorneys call witnesses or offer any evidence on their client's behalf, despite Francis's decision to recant his confession and plead not guilty. On September 13, an all-white, all-male jury found Francis, an African American, guilty of first-degree murder. The next day, the trial judge sentenced Francis to death.

Francis lingered in prison for eight months before the state made arrangements to carry out his execution. Louisiana did not have a prison that served as a "death row" for inmates scheduled for execution. Instead, capital offenders were transported into the jurisdiction where they had committed their offense. The state then brought its one electric chair into the local jail, where the execution would then take place. On May 3, 1946, Francis made the fifteen-minute trip from New Iberia, where he had been held, to St. Martinsville, where he was scheduled for execution that evening in front of witnesses who knew him and the murdered pharmacist. After Francis arrived in St. Martinsville, he was quickly prepared for the electric chair. A fellow inmate shaved the hair of his head and body, and another inmate helped prison authorities prepare the electric chair. Jailers strapped Francis into the chair, attached electrodes to his body, and placed a mask over his face. As the witnesses steeled themselves for the execution, several other people hung around outside the prison, including Francis's father, who had arrived bearing a coffin for his son.

As a prison guard tightened the hood around Francis's face, Willie said, "It hurts me the way you're doing it." The guard, after sealing the mask around Francis's

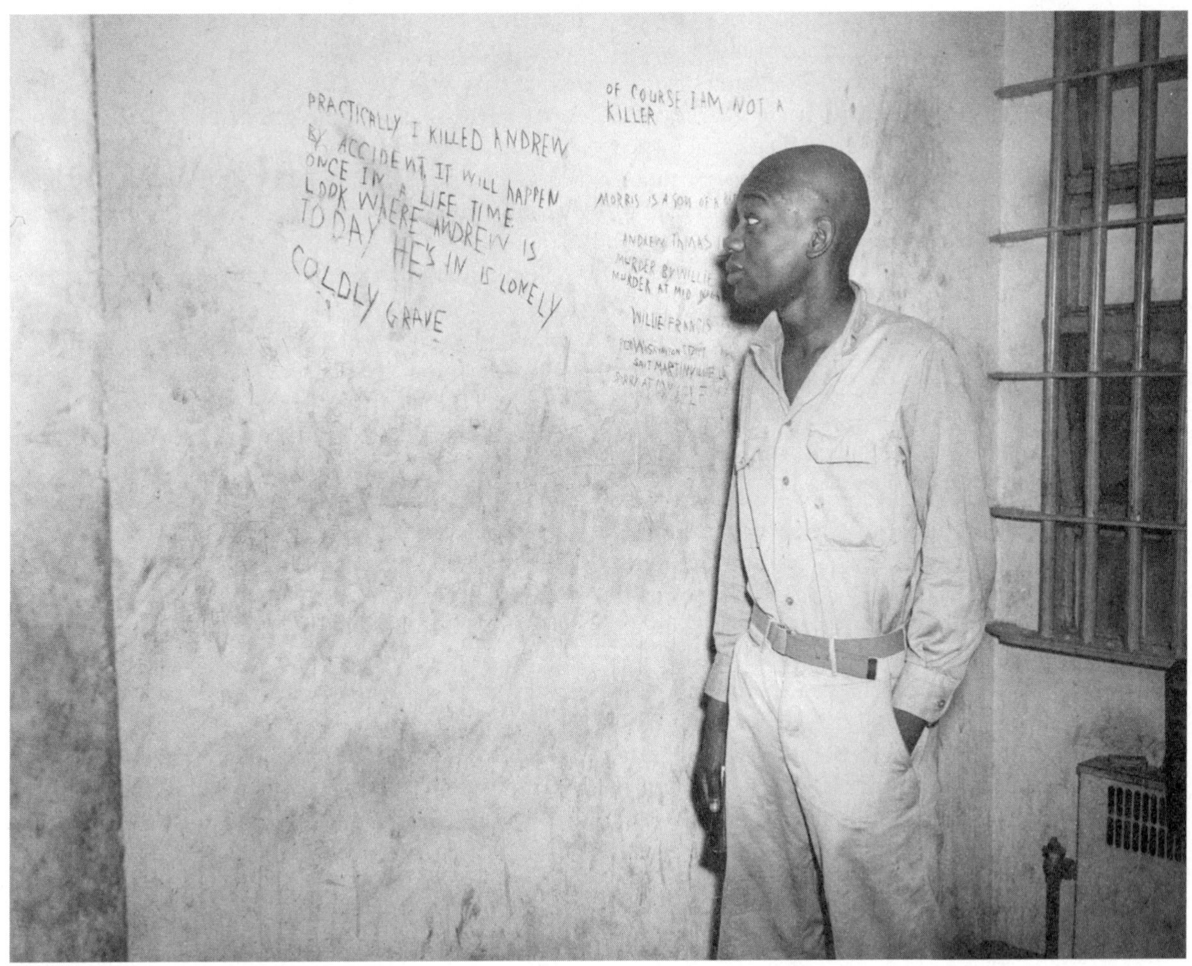

A barely literate Willie Francis looking at his own writing on the wall of his Louisiana jail cell. Francis's lawyers claimed that the state's initial failed effort to electrocute him prevented a second such attempt. The Supreme Court, in Francis v. Resweber *(1947), disagreed, and Francis was subsequently executed.*
AP/Wide World Photos

lips, told the doomed inmate, "It'll hurt more after a while, Willie."

The generator began to hum, and a few moments later the guard flipped the switch. Hundreds of volts of electric current entered Francis's body, which began to tremble and shake, bringing the rickety wooden chair off the floor. The guard flipped the switch again, sending another charge into Francis's body and smoke into the air, except this time the condemned man yelled, "TAKE IT OFF—LET ME BREATHE!" The St. Martinsville sheriff supervising the execution ordered the guard to stop. Francis was released and taken back to a holding cell. The Louisiana governor, Jimmie Davis, and prison officials and local police responsible for carrying out Francis's death sentence agreed not to attempt another electrocution. Francis was returned to New Iberia, and his execution was rescheduled for May 10.

Willie Francis's botched execution created quite a commotion outside the prison, which was located next to the courthouse in the St. Martinsville town square.

No one standing there was prepared to see Francis, surrounded by sheriff's deputies, walk out of his own execution. One observer was Bertrand De Blanc, a young attorney and childhood friend of the murder victim, who decided that no civilized system of criminal justice could send a condemned man to his own execution twice. After meeting with Francis, De Blanc decided to represent him. He explained why:

> The question of guilt or innocence was beside the point. . . . The question was whether the man goes to the chair twice for the same offense. . . . The whole thing about capital punishment in my opinion is the anticipation. For two weeks, three weeks, a month, you know you're going to die the moment they pull the switch. . . . You die. You blow that, you blow the whole thing.

De Blanc quickly went to work to save Francis's life. The local district attorney had no qualms about sending Francis to the electric chair again, telling the state board of pardons that executing Francis would spare him an almost certain lynching. The board ultimately refused to grant Francis a pardon, but De Blanc, working with attorneys in Washington, persuaded the United States Supreme Court to hear Francis's case. The question Francis's lawyers put before the Court was straightforward: Did the Cruel and Unusual Punishment Clause of the Eighth Amendment and the Double Jeopardy Clause of the Fifth Amendment prohibit Louisiana from sending Willie Francis to the electric chair for a second time? By now, the second part of their argument should have a familiar ring: Did the Due Process Clause of the Fourteenth Amendment make these guarantees of the Bill of Rights applicable to the states?

Dividing 5 to 4, the Court, in *Francis* v. *Resweber* (1947), ruled that Louisiana had not violated the Fifth and Eighth Amendments by failing to execute Willie Francis the first time.[2] Four justices in the majority acknowledged that federal guarantees against double jeopardy and cruel and unusual punishment would protect an individual in the event that a state violated the Due Process Clause of the Fourteenth Amendment. Such a violation, however, was not present here. Casting the fifth vote, Justice Felix Frankfurter rejected the notion that the Fourteenth Amendment made the specific guarantees of the Bill of Rights applicable to the states, writing that it placed "no specific restraints upon the States in the formulation or the administration of their criminal law."[3] Returning to the more general guarantee established in *Palko* v. *Connecticut* (1937) (see Chapter 3), Frankfurter believed that the Fourteenth Amendment shielded the states from a uniform standard of fairness in criminal proceedings, unless the action "offend[ed] a principle of justice so rooted in the traditions and conscience of our people as to be ranked as fundamental."[4]

Frankfurter's icy position on the Fourteenth Amendment concealed from the general public his lifelong opposition to the death penalty. While still a Harvard law professor in the 1920s, Frankfurter worked with the ACLU and the NAACP in several capital cases where he believed a miscarriage of justice, usually involving race or ethnic origin discrimination, had taken place. After coming to the Court in the late 1930s, he often wrote friends in state legislatures around the country encouraging them to drop the death penalty. Willie Francis's case was no exception. No sooner had the ink dried on Frankfurter's opinion than this stickler for judicial process began a series of letters and phone calls to friends in Louisiana encouraging the state to commute Francis's sentence. But Frankfurter's efforts, along with those of Francis's attorneys, could not derail Louisiana's determination to carry out the execution. On May 10, 1947, Willie Francis was taken to the St. Martinsville prison, a generator was parked next to the courthouse, and the execution went off without a hitch. This time, the coffin that Francis's father brought with him was used.

The Willie Francis case raises several questions that still form the heart of the debate over the death penalty in contemporary American society. Is the death penalty itself a form of cruel and unusual punishment? Does the Constitution require only that death penalties meet certain due process guidelines? Does racial discrimination influence how criminal defendants are tried and sentenced in capital cases? How much discretion should juries have in handing down capital sentences? Should juveniles be eligible for the death penalty? This chapter addresses these questions and related matters involving the administration of capital punishment in the United States. In this chapter, you will also note how organized interests, particularly the NAACP Legal Defense Fund (LDF), have been particularly active in the capital punishment cases that have come before the Supreme Court.

Finally, this chapter also briefly addresses the application of the Cruel and Unusual Punishment Clause in cases involving noncapital offenses, and how the Court has dealt with the proportionality of sentencing in this particular context. Although the death penalty and capital sentencing command the lion's share of attention when the Cruel and Unusual Punishment Clause is mentioned, the Court has also dealt with some important questions dealing with proportionality in sentencing and the nature of criminal behavior itself.

Launching the Capital Punishment Debate

Generally, scholars who believe that the Constitution does not prohibit the death penalty point to two sources for support. First, they note the uniform acceptance of capital punishment by the states when the Eighth Amendment ban on cruel and unusual punishment was adopted. Second, they interpret the language of the Fifth Amendment—that no person shall be "deprived of life, liberty, or property, without due process of law"—to mean that life, just like liberty and property, can be taken as long as an individual had been afforded the due process of law. Indeed, the Eighth Amendment was viewed less as a substantive guarantee against specific punishments and more as a restraint on congressional interference with the still-emerging systems of criminal justice in the states. And since no state prohibited capital punishment, the fundamental debate during the Founding period centered on the extent of due process guarantees for capital defendants and what crimes merited the death penalty. In the late 1700s, many states authorized the death penalty for crimes such as robbery and rape, and for civil offenses such as forgery and adultery. By the early 1800s, most states had eliminated the death penalty for civil offenses, and many had modified their criminal laws to abolish death for noncapital offenses. Some states had even begun to create different "degrees" of murder, with only premeditated killing, or what is now called first-degree murder, punishable by death.[5]

But reform of the criminal law only went so far. Although many states continued to reduce their number of death-eligible offenses and, by the 1840s, Michigan and Wisconsin had completely abolished capital punishment,[6] the Southern states remained an exception to this trend. Rape and robbery were still death-eligible offenses in the South, and many of the "cruder" forms of execution—such as death by hanging and firing squad—were still practiced throughout the region. Controlling slaves and underscoring the racial boundaries that existed between free Southern blacks and whites accounted for much of the South's criminal code. Indeed, so entrenched was the element of racial control in the criminal laws of the Southern states that they survived the Civil War and Reconstruction well intact.[7] Because Southern judges and juries sent African American capital offenders to their death much more often than whites, especially if the victim was white, during the 1960s and 1970s the NAACP LDF made the region the target of its nearly successful litigation campaign to abolish the death penalty.[8]

Until the early 1960s, the Court had never questioned the constitutionality of capital punishment, adhering to the standard interpretation that the Eighth and Fourteenth Amendments ensured only that capital defendants receive fair treatment from their accusers. Recall, for example, how the Court viewed *Powell* v. *Alabama*. The issue was not whether Alabama could seek the death penalty against the nine African American young men for allegedly raping a white girl aboard a train, but whether, given the seriousness of the offense and potential punishment, the Sixth and Fourteenth Amendments required the state to provide counsel to the defendants. Then, in *Trop* v. *Dulles* (1958), Chief Justice Earl Warren wrote that the Eighth Amendment was neither "precise" nor "static," instead drawing "its meaning from the evolving standards of decency that mark the progress of a maturing society."[9] Granted, Warren's statement was rather abstract, and *Trop* was concerned with whether the United States could strip the citizenship of an Army deserter, not with capital punishment. But to opponents of the death penalty, *Trop* suggested that the Court might well be inclined to address whether societal standards had evolved to the point where capital punishment was no longer acceptable. After all, the Warren Court was no stranger to controversy, having declared, in *Brown* v. *Board of Education* (1954), racial segregation in the nation's public schools unconstitutional. If the Court could rewrite the Equal Protection Clause to conform to "evolving societal standards" in *Brown,* was there a possibility that it might do the same for capital punishment?

An affirmative answer came five years later in *Rudolph* v. *Alabama* (1963) and *Snider* v. *Cunningham* (1963), when Justice Arthur Goldberg publicly dissented from the Court's decision to deny review in two cases involving appeals by black men convicted of raping white women. *Rudolph* did not involve a challenge to the death penalty; instead, the defendant argued that his confession had been coerced, producing the evidence that ultimately led to his conviction. Goldberg, joined by Justices William Brennan and William Douglas, believed that *Rudolph* and *Snider* offered the Court an appropriate opportunity to consider head-on the constitutionality of the death penalty. Three questions, wrote Goldberg, were "relevant and worthy of argument and consideration by the Court":

1. In light of the trend in this country and throughout the world against punishing rape by death, does the imposition of the death penalty by those states which retain it for rape violate "evolving standards of decency that mark the progress of [our] maturing society," or standards of decency more or less universally accepted?
2. Is the taking of human life to protect a value other than human life consistent with the constitutional proscription against "punishments which by their excessive . . . severity are greatly disproportioned to the offenses charged"?
3. Can the permissible aims of punishment (e.g., deterrence, isolation, rehabilitation) be achieved as effectively by punishing rape less severely than by death—e.g., by life imprisonment? If so, does the imposition of the death penalty for rape constitute "unnecessary cruelty"?[10]

Goldberg did not mention racial discrimination in meting out the death penalty for rape, a problem endemic in the South and one that the NAACP LDF and the ACLU had wanted to challenge for some time. But in 1963, even the most ardent opponents of the death penalty understood that the Court was not about to invalidate a capital punishment law by entering the minefield of interracial rape. Indeed, the Court was already a lightning rod for criticism for its civil rights decisions and, since 1961, its willingness to expand the due process rights of criminal defendants (see Chapters 7 and 8). Nonetheless, Goldberg's dissent held out the possibility that, if proven, a constitutional claim could be brought against Southern states that reserved the death penalty for African American men accused of raping white women. Accordingly, Jack Greenberg, who had succeeded Thurgood Marshall as the legal director of the NAACP LDF, announced that the civil rights group would now begin a campaign to abolish capital punishment for rape, charging that such sentences violated the Eighth Amendment's ban against cruel and unusual punishment and the Equal Protection and Due Process Clauses of the Fourteenth Amendment.[11]

The NAACP LDF Campaign Begins

Greenberg did not need much persuading to marshal the NAACP LDF's litigation muscle behind an attack on the death penalty. Having joined the organization in 1948, Greenberg had participated in numerous criminal cases involving coerced confessions, the right to counsel, racially exclusive juries, and interracial rape, most of which shared a common trait—they resulted in the death of a black man for committing a crime against a white person. Like many young civil rights lawyers, Greenberg was familiar with *Powell* from journalistic accounts and the stories told by older lawyers in the civil rights community who were there. After joining the NAACP LDF, Greenberg soon discovered that "Little Scottsboros" permeated the American criminal justice system, particularly in the South. By the early 1960s, but before Goldberg's dissent in *Rudolph,* Greenberg believed the legal climate had developed enough to consider an attack on capital punishment for rape. In 1961, the NAACP LDF agreed to defend an African American man who had been convicted of rape for entering the home of an elderly white woman and exposing his genitals to her. Although the man never touched or threatened the woman, an Alabama jury nonetheless found him guilty of rape and sentenced him to death. Ultimately, the Supreme Court, in *Hamilton* v. *Alabama* (1961), reversed the defendant's conviction on assistance of counsel grounds. A second trial resulted in a lesser charge, one not involving the death penalty.[12]

After *Rudolph,* the NAACP LDF, in conjunction with the ACLU and several other student civil rights organizations, sent researchers into the Deep South to investigate judicial records in rape cases. Not surprisingly, the researchers found that 90 percent of convicted rapists put to death since 1930 had been African Americans,

SIDEBAR

WANTED: WITNESS TO THE EXECUTION

by Geraldine Sealey

Help wanted: Law enforcement official, criminologist, student or curious citizen for one-time, volunteer opportunity. Evenings and late nights necessary. Faint-hearted need not apply.

Prison officials have yet to resort to traditional classified ads, but many have found themselves struggling recently to recruit civilian witnesses to executions.

Of the 38 states that have the death penalty, more than a dozen require the presence of civilians at executions—on average, these states require a half-dozen witnesses with no connection to the crime victim or perpetrator and who are not members of the media.

For years after the Supreme Court reinstated the death penalty in 1976, finding witnesses was no problem. But as the pace of executions has picked up—there were 98 executions in 1999, compared to 11 during the first eight years after reinstatement—states have found themselves scrambling for witnesses.

In Missouri, legislators solved the problem by lowering the required number of citizen witnesses from 12 to eight. But other states have maintained their limits while stepping up publicity efforts.

Stocking the Witness Pool

When Arizona prison officials learned in late 1998 that 11 inmates could face execution the following year, they hunted for witnesses. State law requires that 12 citizen witnesses attend each execution.

Although officials keep a running list of citizens interested in attending executions, the nearly dozen executions scheduled for 1999 would have exhausted Arizona's pool of volunteers. "Our list was becoming depleted very rapidly," says Camilla Strongin, a prison department spokeswoman.

Prison officials began spreading word of their witness shortage to members of the law enforcement community and the media. They also posted a message on the corrections department Web site.

The open letter on the Web site asks "reputable citizens" who are at least 18 years old to submit a letter to the corrections director including a general statement of why the applicant would want to attend an execution.

So far, Strongin says, the publicity push has worked. The state currently has almost 100 citizens in its pool of potential witnesses. Although executions have slowed in the state this year—only two carried out so far in 2000, compared to seven in 1999—the witness pool is stocked if the pace quickens.

Press Release Successful

Pennsylvania has achieved similar success with its witness recruitment efforts. Five years ago, the state was poised to execute its first inmate since the death penalty was reinstated. State law requires the presence of six civilian witnesses at executions. So, prison officials issued a press release titled "Corrections Seeks Execution Witnesses."

The problem was solved. Now, Pennsylvania has hundreds of citizens in its pool of potential witnesses, says Jeffrey Rackovan, assistant to the superintendent at the state's death house.

Since executions are not common in the state—only three inmates have been put to death since the

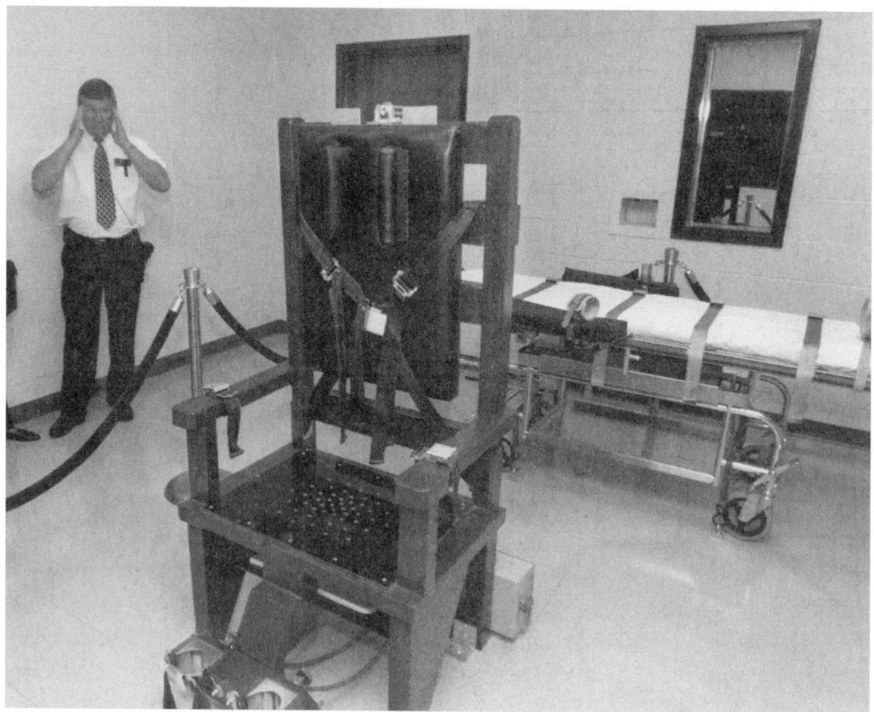

Ricky Bell, the warden at Riverbend Maximum Security Institution in Nashville, Tennessee, gives a tour of the prison's execution chamber. Of the thirty-eight states that have the death penalty, more than a dozen require the presence of civilians at executions.
AP/Wide World Photos

early 1970s—officials are not likely to run out of volunteers.

Few Questions Asked

Most states that invite civilian witnesses into the death chamber are not picky about the motivations or qualifications of the volunteers.

Although most states ask citizens to explain why they want to see an execution, few volunteers are ever turned away. In Florida, for example, officials perform background checks on potential witnesses, but applicants' motivations are not heavily scrutinized.

Most applicants for the state's 12 witness slots are law enforcement officials or students of criminal justice, says prison spokeswoman Debbie Buchanan. So far, with 150 to 200 volunteers on its waiting list, Florida has had no problem attracting civilian witnesses.

In Pennsylvania, the prison superintendent reviews witness requests. Applicants are asked to explain why they want to witness the execution, but most would not be turned away unless they expressed some "radical" viewpoint, Rackovan says.

Most witness applicants in Arizona have some connection to law enforcement or education, Strongin says. But others have been activists in the death penalty or even just interested citizens.

Regardless of their motivations, Strongin says inviting citizens into the death chamber is critical to the execution of justice. "We feel strongly about it," she says. "The voters in Arizona support capital punishment and should be able to see it carried out if they so choose."

Source: From Geraldine Sealey, "Wanted: Witness to the Execution." Reprinted courtesy of ABCNEWS.com.

lending firm support to what many civil rights lawyers had known already through their own experience. By the mid-1960s, the NAACP LDF was handling almost twenty cases involving capital punishment for rape. By 1970, that number increased to thirty-five, as the group, to build support for opposition to the death penalty more generally, had begun representing white capital defendants in murder cases. Going back to the early twentieth century, when such records first started being kept with any regularity, only one white man had ever been executed for murdering a black man in the United States. Still, as NAACP LDF strategy evolved on capital punishment in the late 1960s and early 1970s, its lawyers emphasized three major points: the race of the victim; the arbitrary, random, and undisciplined nature of the death penalty's application; and the lack of separate trial and sentencing phases in capital cases.[13]

In 1968, the Court handed death penalty opponents a major victory, declaring unconstitutional an Illinois law that permitted prosecutors to exclude individuals with "conscientious scruples against capital punishment" from juries hearing capital cases. The NAACP LDF filed an influential *amicus* brief supporting the arguments of William Witherspoon's lawyers, who claimed the Illinois law did not allow capital defendants a jury trial before a cross section of the community. Originally, the Court voted not to hear *Witherspoon.* Justice Potter Stewart, who often favored the prosecution in criminal cases, wrote a memo to his colleagues noting that "half the country [at that time] opposed capital punishment." This raised the question of whether a capital defendant could receive a proper jury trial, causing the justices to change their minds and agree to hear *Witherspoon.*[14] Stewart ultimately wrote the Court's opinion, stating that, "Whatever else might be said of capital punishment it is at least clear that its imposition by a hanging jury cannot be squared with the Constitution."[15]

In 1971, the Court decided to confront directly the constitutionality of the death penalty. By this time, about 120 capital cases were on their way to the Court, affecting approximately 640 death row inmates, half of whom were represented by the NAACP LDF. On the one hand, the Court continued to reject quite firmly the idea that the Eighth Amendment prohibited capital punishment. Justice Black's literalist approach to the Constitution summed up this position: "It is inconceivable to me that the Framers intended to end capital punishment by the [Eighth] Amendment. Although some people have urged that the Court should amend the Constitution by interpretation to keep it abreast of modern ideas, I have never believed that lifetime judges in our system have any such legislative power."[16] Yet, the Court did not hesitate to set aside convictions in capital cases where due process had been denied or racial discrimination was clearly present. On June 28, 1971, the Court agreed to hear four capital cases—two involving rape and two involving murder—that brought together all the issues the NAACP LDF had been litigating in the courts since the mid-1960s. A year and a day later, the Court handed down decisions in three of the four cases, which were decided together as *Furman* v. *Georgia* (1972).

Furman v. *Georgia*

408 U.S. 238 (1972)

Leading the NAACP LDF's campaign to abolish the death penalty was Anthony Amsterdam, a University of Pennsylvania law professor. Amsterdam had coordinated the litigation strategy and crafted the legal arguments in the nine-year period between 1963, when Justice Goldberg dissented in *Rudolph,* and 1972, when the Court decided to hear *Furman, Jackson* v. *Georgia,* and *Branch* v. *Texas. Furman* and *Jackson* were murder cases; *Branch* tested Texas's law imposing capital punishment for rape. For the first time, the Court ordered the parties in *Furman* to limit their briefs to the following question: "Does the imposition and carrying out of the death penalty in this case constitute cruel and unusual punishment in violation of the Eighth and Fourteenth Amendments?"

Amsterdam emphasized two major points in the NAACP LDF's briefs. First, he argued that the death penalty violated "basic standards of human decency," as measured by "evolving societal standards." Clearly making a reference to Chief Justice Warren's opinion in *Trop* v. *Dulles,* Amsterdam emphasized the "freakish" nature of the death penalty's imposition, its arbitrariness, and its racially discriminatory context. He claimed that these factors made capital punishment a cruel and unusual punishment, and thus one prohibited by the Eighth Amendment. Second, Amsterdam argued that the Court had the obligation to protect minority rights, and capital punishment laws affected a distinct and unpopular minority.

Amsterdam assembled numerous sympathetic parties to submit *amicus* briefs in *Furman*. The ACLU, which had worked closely with the NAACP LDF in several capital punishment cases during the 1960s and early 1970s, filed a brief emphasizing the death penalty's lack of deterrent value. Religious organizations such as the Synagogue Council of America, American Jewish Congress, and National Council of Churches filed briefs stating the opposition of most religious denominations in the United States to capital punishment.

The Court's vote was 5 to 4, but the justices offered no majority opinion. After issuing a short *per curiam* order declaring the Georgia and Texas laws unconstitutional, each justice wrote a separate opinion explaining his vote. The opinions comprised 243 pages and 50,000 words, the longest in the Court's history.

▼▲▼

PER CURIAM.

The Court holds that the imposition and carrying out of the death penalty in these cases constitute cruel and unusual punishment in violation of the Eighth and Fourteenth Amendments. The judgment in each case is therefore reversed insofar as it leaves undisturbed the death sentence imposed, and the cases are remanded for further proceedings.

So ordered. . . .

JUSTICE DOUGLAS, concurring.

The generality of a law inflicting capital punishment is one thing. What may be said of the validity of a law on the books and what may be done with the law in its application do, or may, lead to quite different conclusions.

It would seem to be incontestable that the death penalty inflicted on one defendant is "unusual" if it discriminates against him by reason of his race, religion, wealth, social position, or class, or if it is imposed under a procedure that gives room for the play of such prejudices. . . .

Those who wrote the Eighth Amendment knew what price their forebears had paid for a system based, not on equal justice, but on discrimination. In those days the target was not the blacks or the poor, but the dissenters, those who opposed absolutism in government, who struggled for a parliamentary regime, and who opposed governments' recurring efforts to foist a particular religion on the people. But the tool of capital punishment was used with vengeance against the opposition and those unpopular with the regime. One cannot read this history without realizing that the desire for equality was reflected in the ban against "cruel and unusual punishments" contained in the Eighth Amendment. . . .

In a Nation committed to equal protection of the laws there is no permissible "caste" aspect of law enforcement. Yet we know that the discretion of judges and juries in imposing the death penalty enables the penalty to be selectively applied, feeding prejudices against the accused if he is poor and despised, and lacking political clout, or if he is a member of a suspect or unpopular minority, and saving those who by social position may be in a more protected position. In ancient Hindu law a Brahman was exempt from capital punishment, and under that law, "[g]enerally, in the law books, punishment increased in severity as social status diminished." We have, I fear, taken in practice the same position, partially as a result of making the death penalty discretionary and partially as a result of the ability of the rich to purchase the services of the most respected and most resourceful legal talent in the Nation.

The high service rendered by the "cruel and unusual" punishment clause of the Eighth Amendment is to require legislatures to write penal laws that are evenhanded, nonselective, and nonarbitrary, and to require judges to see to it that general laws are not applied sparsely, selectively, and spottily to unpopular groups. . . .

Any law which is nondiscriminatory on its face may be applied in such a way as to violate the Equal Protection Clause of the Fourteenth Amendment. Such conceivably might be the fate of a mandatory death penalty, where equal or lesser sentences were imposed on the elite, a harsher one on the minorities or members of the lower castes. Whether a mandatory death penalty would otherwise be constitutional is a question I do not reach.

JUSTICE BRENNAN, concurring.

Justice Brennan's concurring opinion is excerpted in Chapter 2, pp. 29–31.

JUSTICE STEWART, concurring.

The penalty of death differs from all other forms of criminal punishment, not in degree but in kind. It is unique in its total irrevocability. It is unique in its rejection of rehabilitation of the convict as a basic purpose of criminal justice. And it is unique, finally, in its absolute renunciation of all that is embodied in our concept of humanity.

For these and other reasons, at least two of my Brothers have concluded that the infliction of the death penalty is constitutionally impermissible in all circumstances under the Eighth and Fourteenth Amendments. Their case is a strong one. But I find it unnecessary to reach the ultimate question they would decide. . . .

Legislatures—state and federal—have sometimes specified that the penalty of death shall be the mandatory punishment for every person convicted of engaging in certain designated criminal conduct. . . .

I cannot agree that retribution is a constitutionally impermissible ingredient in the imposition of punishment. The instinct for retribution is part of the nature of man, and channeling that instinct in the administration of criminal justice serves an important purpose in promoting the stability of a society governed by law. When people begin to believe that organized society is unwilling or unable to impose upon criminal offenders the punishment they "deserve," then there are sown the seeds of anarchy—of self-help, vigilante justice, and lynch law.

The constitutionality of capital punishment in the abstract is not, however, before us in these cases. For the Georgia and Texas Legislatures have not provided that the death penalty shall be imposed upon all those who are found guilty of forcible rape. And the Georgia Legislature has not ordained that death shall be the automatic punishment for murder. In a word, neither State has made a legislative determination that forcible rape and murder can be deterred only by imposing the penalty of death upon all who perpetrate those offenses. . . .

Instead, the death sentences now before us are the product of a legal system that brings them, I believe, within the very core of the Eighth Amendment's guarantee against cruel and unusual punishments, a guarantee applicable against the States through the Fourteenth Amendment. In the first place, it is clear that these sentences are "cruel" in the sense that they excessively go beyond, not in degree but in kind, the punishments that the state legislatures have determined to be necessary. In the second place, it is equally clear that these sentences are "unusual" in the sense that the penalty of death is infrequently imposed for murder, and that its imposition for rape is extraordinarily rare. But I do not rest my conclusion upon these two propositions alone.

These death sentences are cruel and unusual in the same way that being struck by lightning is cruel and unusual. . . . [T]he petitioners are among a capriciously selected random handful upon whom the sentence of death has in fact been imposed. My concurring Brothers have demonstrated that, if any basis can be discerned for the selection of these few to be sentenced to die, it is the constitutionally impermissible basis of race. But racial discrimination has not been proved, and I put it to one side. I simply conclude that the Eighth and Fourteenth Amendments cannot tolerate the infliction of a sentence of death under legal systems that permit this unique penalty to be so wantonly and so freakishly imposed.

For these reasons I concur in the judgments of the Court.

Mr. Justice White, concurring.

In joining the Court's judgments, therefore, I do not at all intimate that the death penalty is unconstitutional per se or that there is no system of capital punishment that would comport with the Eighth Amendment. That question, ably argued by several of my Brethren, is not presented by these cases and need not be decided. . . .

I cannot avoid the conclusion that as the statutes before us are now administered, the penalty is so infrequently imposed that the threat of execution is too attenuated to be of substantial service to criminal justice. . . .

I add only that past and present legislative judgment with respect to the death penalty loses much of its force when viewed in light of the recurring practice of delegating sentencing authority to the jury and the fact that a jury, in its own discretion and without violating its trust or any statutory policy, may refuse to impose the death penalty no matter what the circumstances of the crime. Legislative "policy" is thus necessarily defined not by what is legislatively authorized but by what juries and judges do in exercising the discretion so regularly conferred upon them. In my judgment what was done in these cases violated the Eighth Amendment.

I concur in the judgments of the Court.

Mr. Justice Marshall, concurring.

Candor compels me to confess that I am not oblivious to the fact that this is truly a matter of life and death. Not only does it involve the lives of these three petitioners, but those of the almost 600 other condemned men and women in this country currently awaiting execution. While this fact cannot affect our ultimate decision, it necessitates that the decision be free from any possibility of error. . . .

In order to assess whether or not death is an excessive or unnecessary penalty, it is necessary to consider the reasons why a legislature might select it as punishment for one or more offenses, and examine whether less severe penalties would satisfy the legitimate legislative wants as well as capital punishment. If they would, then the death penalty is unnecessary cruelty, and, therefore, unconstitutional.

There are six purposes conceivably served by capital punishment: retribution, deterrence, prevention of repetitive criminal acts, encouragement of guilty pleas and confessions, eugenics, and economy. . . .

[Justice Marshall then gave extensive review to each purpose and concluded that capital punishment did not accomplish any one of them.]

[E]ven if capital punishment is not excessive, it nonetheless violates the Eighth Amendment because it is morally unacceptable to the people of the United States at this time in their history.

In judging whether or not a given penalty is morally acceptable, most courts have said that the punishment is valid unless "it shocks the conscience and sense of justice of the people." Judge Frank once noted the problems inherent in the use of such a measuring stick: "[The court,] before it reduces a sentence as 'cruel and unusual,' must have reasonably good assurances that the sentence offends the 'common conscience.' And, in any context, such a standard—the community's attitude—is usually an unknowable. It resembles a slithery shadow, since one can seldom learn, at all accurately, what the community, or a majority, actually feels. Even a carefully-taken 'public opinion poll' would be inconclusive in a case like this."

While a public opinion poll obviously is of some assistance in indicating public acceptance or rejection of a specific penalty, its utility cannot be very great. This is because whether or not a punishment is cruel and unusual depends, not on whether its mere mention "shocks the conscience and sense of justice of the people," but on whether people who were fully informed as to the purposes of the penalty and its liabilities would find the penalty shocking, unjust, and unacceptable.

In other words, the question with which we must deal is not whether a substantial proportion of American citizens would today, if polled, opine that capital punishment is barbarously cruel, but whether they would find it to be so in the light of all information presently available.

This is not to suggest that with respect to this test of unconstitutionality people are required to act rationally; they are not. With respect to this judgment, a violation of the Eighth Amendment is totally dependent on the predictable subjective, emotional reactions of informed citizens.

It has often been noted that American citizens know almost nothing about capital punishment. Some of the conclusions arrived at in the preceding section and the supporting evidence would be critical to an informed judgment on the morality of the death penalty: e.g., that the death penalty is no more effective a deterrent than life imprisonment, that convicted murderers are rarely executed, but are usually sentenced to a term in prison; that convicted murderers usually are model prisoners, and that they almost always become law-abiding citizens upon their release from prison; that the costs of executing a capital offender exceed the costs of imprisoning him for life; that while in prison, a convict under sentence of death performs none of the useful functions that life prisoners perform; that no attempt is made in the sentencing process to ferret out likely recidivists for execution; and that the death penalty may actually stimulate criminal activity.

This information would almost surely convince the average citizen that the death penalty was unwise, but a problem arises as to whether it would convince him that the penalty was morally reprehensible. This problem arises from the fact that the public's desire for retribution, even though this is a goal that the legislature cannot constitutionally pursue as its sole justification for capital punishment, might influence the citizenry's view of the morality of capital punishment. The solution to the problem lies in the fact that no one has ever seriously advanced retribution as a legitimate goal of our society. Defenses of capital punishment are always mounted on deterrent or other similar theories. This should not be surprising. It is the people of this country who have urged in the past that prisons rehabilitate as well as isolate offenders, and it is the people who have injected a sense of purpose into our penology. I cannot believe that at this stage in our history, the American people would ever knowingly support purposeless vengeance. Thus, I believe that the great mass of citizens would conclude on the basis of the material already considered that the death penalty is immoral and therefore unconstitutional.

But, if this information needs supplementing, I believe that the following facts would serve to convince even the most hesitant of citizens to condemn death as a sanction: capital punishment is imposed discriminatorily against certain identifiable classes of people; there is evidence that innocent people have been executed before their innocence can be proved; and the death penalty wreaks havoc with our entire criminal justice system. . . .

Assuming knowledge of all the facts presently available regarding capital punishment, the average citizen would, in my opinion, find it shocking to his conscience and sense of justice. For this reason alone capital punishment cannot stand. . . .

MR. CHIEF JUSTICE BURGER, with whom MR. JUSTICE BLACKMUN, MR. JUSTICE POWELL, and MR. JUSTICE REHNQUIST join, dissenting.

If we were possessed of legislative power, I would either join with MR. JUSTICE BRENNAN and MR. JUSTICE MARSHALL or, at the very least, restrict the use of capital punishment to a small category of the most heinous crimes. Our constitutional inquiry, however, must be divorced from personal feelings as to the morality and efficacy of the death penalty, and be confined to the meaning and applicability of the uncertain language of the Eighth Amendment. There is no novelty in being called upon to interpret a constitutional provision that is less than self-defining, but, of all our fundamental guarantees, the ban on "cruel and unusual punishments" is one of the most difficult to translate into judicially manageable terms. The widely divergent views of the Amendment expressed in today's opinions reveal the haze that surrounds this constitutional command. Yet it is essential to our role as a court that we not seize upon the enigmatic character of the guarantee as an invitation to enact our personal predilections into law. . . .

Today the Court has not ruled that capital punishment is per se violative of the Eighth Amendment; nor has it ruled that the punishment is barred for any particular class or classes of crimes. The substantially similar concurring opinions of MR. JUSTICE STEWART and MR. JUSTICE WHITE, which are necessary to support the judgment setting aside petitioners' sentences, stop short of reaching the ultimate question. The actual scope of the Court's ruling, which I take to be embodied in these concurring opinions, is not entirely clear. This much, however, seems apparent: if the legislatures are to continue to authorize capital punishment for some crimes, juries and judges can no longer be permitted to make the sentencing determination in the same manner they have in the past. This approach—not urged in oral arguments or briefs—misconceives the nature of the constitutional command against "cruel and unusual punishments," disregards controlling case law, and demands a rigidity in capital cases which, if possible of achievement, cannot be regarded as a welcome change. Indeed the contrary seems to be the case.

As I have earlier stated, the Eighth Amendment forbids the imposition of punishments that are so cruel and inhumane as to violate society's standards of civilized conduct. The Amendment does not prohibit all punishments the States are unable to prove necessary to deter or control crime. The Amendment is not concerned with the process by which a State determines that a particular punishment is to be imposed in a particular case. And the Amendment most assuredly does not speak to the power of legislatures to confer sentencing discretion on juries, rather than to fix all sentences by statute. . . .

While I would not undertake to make a definitive statement as to the parameters of the Court's ruling, it is clear that if state legislatures and the Congress wish to maintain the availability of capital punishment, significant statutory changes will have to be made. Since the two pivotal concurring opinions turn on the assumption that the punishment of death is now meted out in a random and unpredictable manner, legislative bodies may seek to bring their laws into compliance with the Court's ruling by providing standards for juries and judges to follow in determining the sentence in capital cases or by more narrowly defining the crimes for which the penalty is to be imposed. If such standards can be devised or the crimes more meticulously defined, the result cannot be detrimental. . . . But even assuming that suitable guidelines can be established, there is no assurance that sentencing patterns will change so long as juries are possessed of the power to determine the sentence or to bring in a verdict of guilt on a charge carrying a lesser sentence; juries have not been inhibited in the exercise of these powers in the past. Thus, unless the Court in *McGautha* misjudged the experience of history, there is little reason to believe that sentencing standards in any form will substantially alter the discretionary character of the prevailing system of sentencing in capital cases. That system may fall short of perfection, but it is yet to be shown that a different system would produce more satisfactory results.

Real change could clearly be brought about if legislatures provided mandatory death sentences in such a way as to deny juries the opportunity to bring in a verdict on a lesser charge; under such a system, the death sentence could only be avoided by a verdict of acquittal. If this is the only alternative that the legislatures can safely pursue under today's ruling, I would have preferred that the Court opt for total abolition. . . .

Since there is no majority of the Court on the ultimate issue presented in these cases, the future of capital punishment in this country has been left in an uncertain limbo. Rather than providing a final and unambiguous answer on the basic constitutional question, the collective impact of the majority's ruling is to demand an undetermined measure of change from the various state legislatures and the Congress. While I cannot endorse the process of decision-making that has yielded today's result and the restraints that that result imposes on legislative action, I am not altogether displeased that legislative bodies have been given the opportunity, and indeed unavoidable responsibility, to make a thorough re-evaluation of the entire subject of capital punishment. If today's opinions demonstrate nothing else, they starkly show that this is an area where legislatures can act far more effectively than courts.

The legislatures are free to eliminate capital punishment for specific crimes or to carve out limited exceptions to a general abolition of the penalty, without adherence to the conceptual strictures of the Eighth Amendment. The legislatures can and should make an assessment of the deterrent influence of capital punishment, both generally and as affecting the commission of specific types of crimes. If legislatures come to doubt the efficacy of capital punishment, they can abolish it, either completely or on a selective basis. If new evidence persuades them that they have acted unwisely, they can reverse their field and reinstate the penalty to the extent it is thought warranted. An Eighth Amendment ruling by judges cannot be made with such flexibility or discriminating precision.

The highest judicial duty is to recognize the limits on judicial power and to permit the democratic processes to deal with matters falling outside of those limits. The "hydraulic pressure[s]" that [Justice] Holmes spoke of as being generated by cases of great import have propelled the Court to go beyond the limits of judicial power, while fortunately leaving some room for legislative judgment.

MR. JUSTICE BLACKMUN, dissenting.

I . . . add only the following, somewhat personal, comments.

. . . Cases such as these provide for me an excruciating agony of the spirit. I yield to no one in the depth of my distaste, antipathy, and, indeed, abhorrence, for the death penalty, with all its aspects of physical distress and fear and of moral judgment exercised by finite minds. That distaste is buttressed by a belief that capital punishment serves no useful purpose that can be demonstrated. For me, it violates childhood's training and life's experiences, and is not compatible with the philosophical convictions I have been able to develop. It is antagonistic to any sense of "reverence for life." Were I a legislator, I would vote against the death penalty for the policy reasons argued by counsel for the respective petitioners and expressed and adopted in the several opinions filed by the Justices who vote to reverse these judgments. . . .

I do not sit on these cases, however, as a legislator, responsive, at least in part, to the will of constituents. Our task here, as must so frequently be emphasized and re-emphasized, is to pass upon the constitutionality of legislation that has been enacted and that is challenged. This is the sole task for judges. We should not allow our personal preferences as to the wisdom of legislative and congressional action, or our distaste for such action, to guide our judicial decision in cases such as these. The temptations to cross that policy line are very great. In fact, as today's decision reveals, they are almost irresistible. . . .

It is not without interest, also, to note that, although the several concurring opinions acknowledge the heinous and atrocious character of the offenses committed by the petitioners, none of those opinions makes reference to the misery the petitioners' crimes occasioned to the victims, to the families of the victims, and to the communities where the offenses took place. The arguments for the respective petitioners, particularly the oral arguments, were similarly and curiously devoid of reference to the victims. There is risk, of course, in a comment such as this, for it opens one to the charge of emphasizing the retributive. Nevertheless, these cases are here because offenses to innocent victims were perpetrated. This fact, and the terror that occasioned it, and the fear that stalks the streets of many of our cities today perhaps deserve not to be entirely overlooked. Let us hope that, with the Court's decision, the terror imposed will be forgotten by those upon whom it was visited, and that our society will reap the hoped-for benefits of magnanimity.

Although personally I may rejoice at the Court's result, I find it difficult to accept or to justify as a matter of history, of law, or of constitutional pronouncement. I fear the Court has overstepped. It has sought and has achieved an end.

JUSTICE POWELL, with whom THE CHIEF JUSTICE, MR. JUSTICE BLACKMUN, and MR. JUSTICE REHNQUIST join, dissenting.

The Court rejects as not decisive the clearest evidence that the Framers of the Constitution and the authors of the Fourteenth Amendment believed that those documents posed no barrier to the death penalty. The Court also brushes aside an unbroken line of precedent reaffirming the heretofore virtually unquestioned constitutionality of capital punishment. Because of the pervasiveness of the constitutional ruling sought by petitioners, and accepted in varying degrees by five members of the Court, today's departure from established precedent invalidates a staggering number of state and federal laws. The capital punishment laws of no less than 39 States and the District of Columbia are nullified. . . . The Court's judgment not only wipes out laws presently in existence, but denies to Congress and to the legislatures of the 50 States the power to adopt new policies contrary to the policy selected by the Court. Indeed, it is the view of two of my Brothers that the people of each State must be denied the prerogative to amend their constitutions to provide for capital punishment even selectively for the most heinous crime.

In terms of the constitutional role of this Court, the impact of the majority's ruling is all the greater because the decision encroaches upon an area squarely within the historic prerogative of the legislative branch—both state and federal—to protect the citizenry through the designation of penalties for prohibitable conduct. It is the very sort of judgment that the legislative branch is competent to make and for which the judiciary is ill-equipped. Throughout our history, Justices of this Court have emphasized the gravity of decisions invalidating legislative judgments, admonishing the nine men who sit on this bench of the duty of self-restraint, especially when called upon to apply the expansive due process and cruel and unusual punishment rubrics. I can recall no case in which, in the name of deciding constitutional questions, this Court has subordinated national and local democratic processes to such an extent.

MR. JUSTICE REHNQUIST, with whom THE CHIEF JUSTICE, MR. JUSTICE BLACKMUN, and MR. JUSTICE POWELL join, dissenting.

Whatever its precise rationale, today's holding necessarily brings into sharp relief the fundamental question of the role of judicial review in a democratic society. How can government by the elected representatives of the people co-exist with the power of the federal judiciary, whose members are constitutionally insulated from responsiveness to the popular will, to declare invalid laws duly enacted by the popular branches of government?

The answer, of course, is found in Hamilton's *Federalist Paper* No. 78 and in Chief Justice Marshall's classic opinion in *Marbury* v. *Madison* (1803). An oft-told story since then, it bears summarization once more. Sovereignty resides ultimately in the people as a whole and, by adopting through their States a written Constitution for the Nation and subsequently adding amendments to that instrument, they have both granted certain powers to the National Government, and denied other powers to the National and the State Governments. Courts are exercising no more than the judicial function conferred upon them by Art. III of the Constitution when they assess, in a case before them, whether or not a particular legislative enactment is within the authority granted by the Constitution to the enacting body, and whether it runs afoul of some limitation placed by the Constitution on the authority of that body. For the theory is that the people themselves have spoken in the Constitution, and therefore its commands are superior to the commands of the legislature, which is merely an agent of the people.

The Founding Fathers thus wisely sought to have the best of both worlds, the undeniable benefits of both democratic self-government and individual rights protected against possible excesses of that form of government. . . .

Rigorous attention to the limits of this Court's authority is likewise enjoined because of the natural desire that beguiles judges along with other human beings into imposing their own views of goodness, truth, and justice upon others. Judges differ only in that they have the power, if not the authority, to enforce their desires. This is doubtless why nearly two centuries of judicial precedent from this Court counsel the sparing use of that power. The most expansive reading of the leading constitutional cases does not remotely suggest that this Court has been granted a roving commission, either by the Founding Fathers or by the framers of the Fourteenth Amendment, to strike down laws that are based upon notions of policy or morality suddenly found unacceptable by a majority of this Court. . . .

A separate reason for deference to the legislative judgment is the consequence of human error on the part of the judiciary with respect to the constitutional issue before it. Human error there is bound to be, judges being men and women, and men and women being what they are. But an error in mistakenly sustaining the constitutionality of a particular enactment, while wrongfully depriving the individual of a right secured to him by the Constitution, nonetheless does so by simply letting stand a duly enacted law of a democratically chosen legislative body. The error resulting from a mistaken upholding of an individual's constitutional claim against the validity of a legislative enactment is a good deal more serious. For the result in such a case is not to leave standing a law duly enacted by a representative assembly, but to impose upon the Nation the judicial fiat of a majority of a court of judges whose connection with the popular will is remote at best.

The Court's nine separate opinions revealed the wide range of views among the justices. Only two justices, Brennan and Marshall, agreed with the NAACP LDF's position that the death penalty, in light of evolving societal standards, was inherently cruel and unusual. Amsterdam, however, had emphasized the procedural deficiencies that plagued the administration of the death penalty in the United States. Justices Douglas, Stewart, and White all emphasized different issues in their opinions striking down the Georgia and Texas laws, but a common theme ran through them all: The death penalty, as *imposed*, was arbitrary, carried racially discriminatory overtones, and lacked clear judicial guidelines in the sentencing stages. All five justices agreed that a death row inmate's chances of getting executed were completely random, and thus served no deterrent value. Note how Stewart borrowed Amsterdam's earlier description of the death penalty to describe his own position on the death penalty's current application. Executions, wrote Stewart, were "freakish," "wanton," and akin to being "struck by lightning."

The Response to *Furman*

Furman stunned the NAACP LDF and the other groups that had campaigned against the death penalty in the courts and the legislatures for the previous decade. Just the year before, the Court had upheld the "standardless" sentencing guidelines it subsequently invalidated in *Furman*.[17] NAACP LDF legal director Jack Greenberg had no explanation for the Court's sudden about-face on the issue, other than to suggest that Amsterdam's arguments and advocacy packed a powerful punch. Moreover, the California Supreme Court's recent decision to declare the state's capital punishment laws unconstitutional showed the Court that declaring the death penalty unconstitutional was not unthinkable.[18]

In the short term, why the Court found the death penalty unconstitutional was less important than *Furman*'s immediate impact on the nation's capital punishment laws. Although no state had carried out an execution since 1967, all 629 persons on death row when *Furman* was decided had their sentences vacated, but not their convictions. Their punishment became life imprisonment.[19] With the death penalty laws of thirty-nine states and the District of Columbia now invalidated, many participants in the death penalty debate believed that *Furman* spelled the end of capital punishment in the United States. Even though public opinion had again become very supportive of capital punishment, many state legislators believed the Court's stringent new due process standards had erected a formidable barrier to the creation of capital punishment laws that could satisfy the concerns of Douglas, Stewart, and White. In the end, did capital punishment laws, which most states knew suffered from the administrative defects pointed out by the Court, merit rebuilding from the ground up?

A careful parsing of Chief Justice Burger's dissent in *Furman* helps explain why thirty-five states introduced new death penalty laws between 1972 and 1976. "It is clear that if state legislatures . . . wish to maintain the availability of capital punishment, significant statutory changes will have to be made. . . . [L]egislative bodies may seek to bring their laws into compliance with the Court's ruling by providing standards for judges and juries to follow . . . or by more narrowly defining crimes for which the penalty is imposed." After four years of legislative fine-tuning to bring their laws into what they believed was compliance with *Furman* (remember, only Brennan and Marshall had declared the death penalty unconstitutional per se), the states now had over six hundred inmates back on death row. In January 1976, the Court agreed to hear five capital cases involving clear challenges to procedural defects cited by Stewart and White in *Furman*. The NAACP LDF, which represented about one in four death row inmates in the United States, soon found itself back before the Court. Six months later, the Court handed down decisions in all five cases. By a 5 to 4 margin, the Court ruled that two laws mandating death sentences for certain crimes violated the Eighth Amendment.[20] These were both NAACP LDF cases. But in three other cases, the Court upheld new sentencing laws from Florida, Georgia, and Texas that separated the trial and sentencing phases of capital trials, and permitted juries to consider "aggravating" and "mitigating" circumstances in their decision to impose life or death. *Gregg* v. *Georgia* (1976) featured a contentious oral argument between NAACP LDF attorney Anthony Amsterdam and the justices.

Gregg v. *Georgia*

428 U.S. 153 (1976)

Troy Gregg had been sentenced to death under Georgia's new "bifurcated" trial system, which divided the trial and sentencing phases of death-eligible crimes into two parts. The law required juries to weigh the "aggravating" circumstances involved in a capital offense—such as the brutality of the crime, whether it included a sexual offense, the killing of a police officer—against the "mitigating" circumstances"—such as the defendant's age, mental health, family background, previous criminal record, and prospects for rehabilitation. A jury convicted Gregg of murdering the driver who picked him up while he and a companion were hitchhiking in northern Florida. Gregg then received the death sentence. A public defender had been assigned to Gregg, but the NAACP LDF effectively handled the case. Anthony Amsterdam was responsible for *Jurek* v. *Texas*, one of the companion cases brought with *Gregg*, but his argument canvassed over all three statutes. And it became clear during oral argument that the justices saved their most serious questions about the new laws for Amsterdam.

Amsterdam argued that many of the new laws simply carried forward the same procedural defects as the old ones. They were arbitrary, random, and discriminatory. Even with the new "bifurcated" trial systems, these laws still gave juries too much discretion in determining life or death. Invoking *Witherspoon* v. *Illinois*, Amsterdam also pointed out that prosecutors in the Texas case had been allowed to exclude jurors who opposed the death penalty, thus raising a Sixth Amendment argument as well. But the core of Amsterdam's argument came down to the finality of death itself as a punishment. Consider this exchange with Justice Potter Stewart:

> Stewart: Doesn't your argument prove too much? In other words, in our system of adversary criminal justice, we have prosecutorial discretion; we have jury discretion, including jury nullification, as it's known; we have the practice of submitting to the jury the option of returning verdicts of lesser included offenses; we have appellate review; and we have the possibility of executive clemency. And that's true throughout our adversary system of justice. And if a person is sentenced to anything as the end product of that system, under your argument, his sentence, be it life imprisonment or five years imprisonment, is a cruel and unusual punishment because it's the product of this system. That's your argument, isn't it?
>
> Amsterdam: No.
>
> Stewart: And why not?
>
> Amsterdam: It is not. Our argument is essentially that death is different. If you don't accept the view that for constitutional purposes death is different, we lose this case, let me make that very clear. There is nothing that we argue in this case that will touch imprisonment, life imprisonment, any of those things. . . .
>
> Why do we say death is different? Our legal system as a whole has always treated death differently. We allow more peremptory challenges; we allow automatic appeals; we have different rules of harmless error; we have indictment requirements; unanimous verdict requirements in some jurisdictions, because death is different.
>
> Death is factually different. Death is final. Death [cannot be remedied]. . . . Death is different because even if exactly the same discretionary procedures are used to decide issues of five years versus ten years, or life versus death, the result will be more arbitrary on the life or death choice.[21]

Many accounts of Amsterdam's argument in the 1976 death penalty cases suggest that his emphasis on the "death is different" strategy did not impress the justices. Chief Justice Burger, who dissented in *Furman*, turned Amsterdam's argument against him, concluding that "death was different" for victims too. Moreover, the fact that thirty-five states had responded so quickly to *Furman* suggested that, to a majority of the justices, the "evolving societal standards" argument undercut Amsterdam's view that the death penalty was unconstitutional. Between public opinion, which, by 1976, firmly supported the death penalty, and post-*Furman* legislative enactments by the states, it seemed that capital punishment was firmly in line with contemporary societal standards.

Seven justices voted to uphold the Georgia, Texas, and Florida laws, but formed no majority opinion. Justices Stevens, Stewart, and Powell wrote one opinion upholding the laws; Justices Rehnquist and White and Chief Justice Burger wrote a separate opinion; Justice Blackmun wrote a separate concurring opinion. Justices Brennan and Marshall wrote separate dissenting opinions.

▼▲▼

Judgment of the Court, and opinion of MR. JUSTICE STEWART, MR. JUSTICE POWELL, and MR. JUSTICE STEVENS, announced by MR. JUSTICE STEWART.

. . . [U]ntil *Furman* v. *Georgia* (1972), the Court never confronted squarely the fundamental claim that the punishment of death always, regardless of the enormity of the offense or the procedure followed in imposing the sentence, is cruel and unusual punishment in violation of the Constitution. Although this issue was presented and addressed in *Furman*, it was not resolved by the Court. Four Justices would have held that capital punishment is not unconstitutional per se; two Justices would have reached the opposite conclusion; and three Justices, while agreeing that the statutes then before the Court were invalid as applied, left open the question whether such

punishment may ever be imposed. We now hold that the punishment of death does not invariably violate the Constitution. . . .

In the earliest cases raising Eighth Amendment claims, the Court focused on particular methods of execution to determine whether they were too cruel to pass constitutional muster. The constitutionality of the sentence of death itself was not at issue, and the criterion used to evaluate the mode of execution was its similarity to "torture" and other "barbarous" methods.

But the Court has not confined the prohibition embodied in the Eighth Amendment to "barbarous" methods that were generally outlawed in the 18th century. Instead, the Amendment has been interpreted in a flexible and dynamic manner. The Court early recognized that "a principle to be vital must be capable of wider application than the mischief which gave it birth." Thus, the Clause forbidding "cruel and unusual" punishments "is not fastened to the obsolete, but may acquire meaning as public opinion becomes enlightened by a humane justice." . . .

[T]the Eighth Amendment has not been regarded as a static concept. As Mr. Chief Justice Warren said, in an oft-quoted phrase, "[t]he Amendment must draw its meaning from the evolving standards of decency that mark the progress of a maturing society," *Trop* v. *Dulles* (1958). Thus, an assessment of contemporary values concerning the infliction of a challenged sanction is relevant to the application of the Eighth Amendment. As we develop below more fully, this assessment does not call for a subjective judgment. It requires, rather, that we look to objective indicia that reflect the public attitude toward a given sanction.

But our cases also make clear that public perceptions of standards of decency with respect to criminal sanctions are not conclusive. A penalty also must accord with "the dignity of man," which is the "basic concept underlying the Eighth Amendment." This means, at least, that the punishment not be "excessive." When a form of punishment in the abstract (in this case, whether capital punishment may ever be imposed as a sanction for murder), rather than in the particular (the propriety of death as a penalty to be applied to a specific defendant for a specific crime), is under consideration, the inquiry into "excessiveness" has two aspects. First, the punishment must not involve the unnecessary and wanton infliction of pain. Second, the punishment must not be grossly out of proportion to the severity of the crime.

Of course, the requirements of the Eighth Amendment must be applied with an awareness of the limited role to be played by the courts. This does not mean that judges have no role to play, for the Eighth Amendment is a restraint upon the exercise of legislative power.

Judicial review, by definition, often involves a conflict between judicial and legislative judgment as to what the Constitution means or requires. In this respect, Eighth Amendment cases come to us in no different posture. It seems conceded by all that the Amendment imposes some obligations on the judiciary to judge the constitutionality of punishment, and that there are punishments that the Amendment would bar whether legislatively approved or not. But, while we have an obligation to insure that constitutional bounds are not overreached, we may not act as judges as we might as legislators. . . .

Therefore, in assessing a punishment selected by a democratically elected legislature against the constitutional measure, we presume its validity. We may not require the legislature to select the least severe penalty possible so long as the penalty selected is not cruelly inhumane or disproportionate to the crime involved. And a heavy burden rests on those who would attack the judgment of the representatives of the people. . . .

We now consider specifically whether the sentence of death for the crime of murder is a per se violation of the Eighth and Fourteenth Amendments to the Constitution. We note first that history and precedent strongly support a negative answer to this question.

The imposition of the death penalty for the crime of murder has a long history of acceptance both in the United States and in England. . . . And the penalty continued to be used into the 20th century by most American States, although the breadth of the common law rule was diminished, initially by narrowing the class of murders to be punished by death and subsequently by widespread adoption of laws expressly granting juries the discretion to recommend mercy.

It is apparent from the text of the Constitution itself that the existence of capital punishment was accepted by the Framers. At the time the Eighth Amendment was ratified, capital punishment was a common sanction in every State. Indeed, the First Congress of the United States enacted legislation providing death as the penalty for specified crimes. The Fifth Amendment, adopted at the same time as the Eighth, contemplated the continued existence of the capital sanction by imposing certain limits on the prosecution of capital cases. . . .

For nearly two centuries, this Court, repeatedly and often expressly, has recognized that capital punishment is not invalid *per se*. . . .

Four years ago, the petitioners in *Furman* and its companion cases predicated their argument primarily upon the asserted proposition that standards of decency had evolved to the point where capital punishment no longer could be tolerated. The petitioners in those cases said, in effect, that the evolutionary process had come to an end, and that standards of decency required that the Eighth Amendment be construed finally as prohibiting capital punishment for any crime, regardless of its depravity and impact on society. This view was accepted by two Justices. Three other Justices were unwilling to go so far; focusing on the procedures by which convicted defendants were selected for the death penalty, rather than on the actual punishment inflicted, they joined in the conclusion that the statutes before the Court were constitutionally invalid.

The petitioners in the capital cases before the Court today renew the "standards of decency" argument, but developments during the four years since *Furman* have undercut substantially the assumptions upon which their argument rested. Despite the continuing debate, dating back to the 19th century, over the morality and utility of capital punishment, it is now evident that a large proportion of American society continues to regard it as an appropriate and necessary criminal sanction.

The most marked indication of society's endorsement of the death penalty for murder is the legislative response to *Furman.* The legislatures of at least 35 States have enacted new statutes that provide for the death penalty for at least some crimes that result in the death of another person. And the Congress of the United States, in 1974, enacted a statute providing the death penalty for aircraft piracy that results in death. These recently adopted statutes have attempted to address the concerns expressed by the Court in *Furman* primarily (i) by specifying the factors to be weighed and the procedures to be followed in deciding when to impose a capital sentence, or (ii) by making the death penalty mandatory for specified crimes. But all of the post-*Furman* statutes make clear that capital punishment itself has not been rejected by the elected representatives of the people. . . .

The jury also is a significant and reliable objective index of contemporary values, because it is so directly involved. The Court has said that one of the most important functions any jury can perform in making . . . a selection [between life imprisonment and death for a defendant convicted in a capital case] is to maintain a link between contemporary community values and the penal system. It may be true that evolving standards have influenced juries in recent decades to be more discriminating in imposing the sentence of death. But the relative infrequency of jury verdicts imposing the death sentence does not indicate rejection of capital punishment per se. Rather, the reluctance of juries in many cases to impose the sentence may well reflect the humane feeling that this most irrevocable of sanctions should be reserved for a small number of extreme cases. Indeed, the actions of juries in many States since *Furman* are fully compatible with the legislative judgments, reflected in the new statutes, as to the continued utility and necessity of capital punishment in appropriate cases. . . .

As we have seen, however, the Eighth Amendment demands more than that a challenged punishment be acceptable to contemporary society. The Court also must ask whether it comports with the basic concept of human dignity at the core of the Amendment. Although we cannot "invalidate a category of penalties because we deem less severe penalties adequate to serve the ends of penology," the sanction imposed cannot be so totally without penological justification that it results in the gratuitous infliction of suffering.

The death penalty is said to serve two principal social purposes: retribution and deterrence of capital crimes by prospective offenders.

In part, capital punishment is an expression of society's moral outrage at particularly offensive conduct. This function may be unappealing to many, but it is essential in an ordered society that asks its citizens to rely on legal processes, rather than self-help, to vindicate their wrongs. The instinct for retribution is part of the nature of man, and channeling that instinct in the administration of criminal justice serves an important purpose in promoting the stability of a society governed by law. When people begin to believe that organized society is unwilling or unable to impose upon criminal offenders the punishment they "deserve," then there are sown the seeds of anarchy—of self-help, vigilante justice, and lynch law. . . . Indeed, the decision that capital punishment may be the appropriate sanction in extreme cases is an expression of the community's belief that certain crimes are themselves so grievous an affront to humanity that the only adequate response may be the penalty of death.

Statistical attempts to evaluate the worth of the death penalty as a deterrent to crimes by potential offenders have occasioned a great deal of debate. The results simply have been inconclusive. As one opponent of capital punishment has said:

> [A]fter all possible inquiry, including the probing of all possible methods of inquiry, we do not know, and, for systematic and easily visible reasons, cannot know, what the truth about this "deterrent" effect may be. . . . The inescapable flaw is . . . that social conditions in any state

> are not constant through time, and that social conditions are not the same in any two states. If an effect were observed (and the observed effects, one way or another, are not large), then one could not at all tell whether any of this effect is attributable to the presence or absence of capital punishment. A "scientific"—that is to say, a soundly based—conclusion is simply impossible, and no methodological path out of this tangle suggests itself. C. Black, *Capital Punishment: The Inevitability of Caprice and Mistake* (1974). . . .

In sum, we cannot say that the judgment of the Georgia Legislature that capital punishment may be necessary in some cases is clearly wrong. Considerations of federalism, as well as respect for the ability of a legislature to evaluate, in terms of its particular State, the moral consensus concerning the death penalty and its social utility as a sanction, require us to conclude, in the absence of more convincing evidence, that the infliction of death as a punishment for murder is not without justification, and thus is not unconstitutionally severe.

Finally, we must consider whether the punishment of death is disproportionate in relation to the crime for which it is imposed. There is no question that death, as a punishment, is unique in its severity and irrevocability. When a defendant's life is at stake, the Court has been particularly sensitive to insure that every safeguard is observed. But we are concerned here only with the imposition of capital punishment for the crime of murder, and, when a life has been taken deliberately by the offender, we cannot say that the punishment is invariably disproportionate to the crime. It is an extreme sanction, suitable to the most extreme of crimes.

We hold that the death penalty is not a form of punishment that may never be imposed, regardless of the circumstances of the offense, regardless of the character of the offender, and regardless of the procedure followed in reaching the decision to impose it.

We now consider whether Georgia may impose the death penalty on the petitioner in this case.

Furman mandates that, where discretion is afforded a sentencing body on a matter so grave as the determination of whether a human life should be taken or spared, that discretion must be suitably directed and limited so as to minimize the risk of wholly arbitrary and capricious action. . . .

Jury sentencing has been considered desirable in capital cases in order to maintain a link between contemporary community values and the penal system—a link without which the determination of punishment could hardly reflect "the evolving standards of decency that mark the progress of a maturing society."

But it creates special problems. Much of the information that is relevant to the sentencing decision may have no relevance to the question of guilt, or may even be extremely prejudicial to a fair determination of that question. This problem, however, is scarcely insurmountable. Those who have studied the question suggest that a bifurcated procedure—one in which the question of sentence is not considered until the determination of guilt has been made—is the best answer. . . . When a human life is at stake, and when the jury must have information prejudicial to the question of guilt but relevant to the question of penalty in order to impose a rational sentence, a bifurcated system is more likely to ensure elimination of the constitutional deficiencies identified in *Furman*.

The idea that a jury should be given guidance in its decision making is also hardly a novel proposition. Juries are invariably given careful instructions on the law and how to apply it before they are authorized to decide the merits of a lawsuit. It would be virtually unthinkable to follow any other course in a legal system that has traditionally operated by following prior precedents and fixed rules of law. When erroneous instructions are given, retrial is often required. It is quite simply a hallmark of our legal system that juries be carefully and adequately guided in their deliberations.

While some have suggested that standards to guide a capital jury's sentencing deliberations are impossible to formulate, the fact is that such standards have been developed. . . . While such standards are, by necessity, somewhat general, they do provide guidance to the sentencing authority, and thereby reduce the likelihood that it will impose a sentence that fairly can be called capricious or arbitrary. Where the sentencing authority is required to specify the factors it relied upon in reaching its decision, the further safeguard of meaningful appellate review is available to ensure that death sentences are not imposed capriciously or in a freakish manner.

In summary, the concerns expressed in *Furman* that the penalty of death not be imposed in an arbitrary or capricious manner can be met by a carefully drafted statute that ensures that the sentencing authority is given adequate information and guidance. As a general proposition, these concerns are best met by a system that provides for a bifurcated proceeding at which the sentencing authority is apprised of the information relevant to the imposition of sentence and provided with standards to guide its use of the information. . . .

As an important additional safeguard against arbitrariness and caprice, the Georgia statutory scheme provides for automatic appeal of all death sentences to the State's Supreme Court. That court is required by statute to review each sentence of death and determine whether it was imposed under the influence of passion or prejudice, whether the evidence supports the jury's finding of a statutory aggravating circumstance, and whether the sentence is disproportionate compared to those sentences imposed in similar cases.

In short, Georgia's new sentencing procedures require, as a prerequisite to the imposition of the death penalty, specific jury findings as to the circumstances of the crime or the character of the defendant. Moreover, to guard further against a situation comparable to that presented in *Furman*, the Supreme Court of Georgia compares each death sentence with the sentences imposed on similarly situated defendants to ensure that the sentence of death in a particular case is not disproportionate. On their face, these procedures seem to satisfy the concerns of *Furman*. No longer should there be "no meaningful basis for distinguishing the few cases in which [the death penalty] is imposed from the many cases in which it is not." . . .

The basic concern of *Furman* centered on those defendants who were being condemned to death capriciously and arbitrarily. Under the procedures before the Court in that case, sentencing authorities were not directed to give attention to the nature or circumstances of the crime committed or to the character or record of the defendant. Left unguided, juries imposed the death sentence in a way that could only be called freakish. The new Georgia sentencing procedures, by contrast, focus the jury's attention on the particularized nature of the crime and the particularized characteristics of the individual defendant. While the jury is permitted to consider any aggravating or mitigating circumstances, it must find and identify at least one statutory aggravating factor before it may impose a penalty of death. In this way, the jury's discretion is channeled. No longer can a jury wantonly and freakishly impose the death sentence; it is always circumscribed by the legislative guidelines. In addition, the review function of the Supreme Court of Georgia affords additional assurance that the concerns that prompted our decision in *Furman* are not present to any significant degree in the Georgia procedure applied here.

For the reasons expressed in this opinion, we hold that the statutory system under which Gregg was sentenced to death does not violate the Constitution. Accordingly, the judgment of the Georgia Supreme Court is affirmed.

MR. JUSTICE WHITE, with whom THE CHIEF JUSTICE and MR. JUSTICE REHNQUIST join, concurring in the judgment.

In *Furman* v. *Georgia* (1972), this Court held the death penalty, as then administered in Georgia, to be unconstitutional. That same year, the Georgia Legislature enacted a new statutory scheme under which the death penalty may be imposed for several offenses, including murder. The issue in this case is whether the death penalty imposed for murder on petitioner Gregg under the new Georgia statutory scheme may constitutionally be carried out. I agree that it may.

The threshold question in this case is whether the death penalty may be carried out for murder under the Georgia legislative scheme consistent with the decision in *Furman* v. *Georgia*. In *Furman*, this Court held that, as a result of giving the sentencer unguided discretion to impose or not to impose the death penalty for murder, the penalty was being imposed discriminatorily, wantonly and freakishly, and so infrequently, that any given death sentence was cruel and unusual. Petitioner argues that, as in *Furman*, the jury is still the sentencer; that the statutory criteria to be considered by the jury on the issue of sentence under Georgia's new statutory scheme are vague, and do not purport to be all-inclusive; and that, in any event, there are no circumstances under which the jury is required to impose the death penalty. Consequently, the petitioner argues that the death penalty will inexorably be imposed in as discriminatory, standardless, and rare a manner as it was imposed under the scheme declared invalid in *Furman*.

The argument is considerably overstated. The Georgia Legislature has made an effort to identify those aggravating factors which it considers necessary and relevant to the question whether a defendant convicted of capital murder should be sentenced to death. The jury which imposes sentence is instructed on all statutory aggravating factors which are supported by the evidence, and is told that it may impose the death penalty unless it unanimously finds at least one of those factors to have been established beyond a reasonable doubt. The Georgia Legislature has plainly made an effort to guide the jury in the exercise of its discretion, while, at the same time, permitting the jury to dispense mercy on the basis of factors too intangible to write into a statute, and I cannot accept the naked assertion that the effort is bound to fail. As the types of murders for which the death penalty may be imposed become more narrowly defined and are limited to those which are particularly serious or for which the death penalty is peculiarly appropriate, as they are in

Georgia by reason of the aggravating circumstance requirement, it becomes reasonable to expect that juries—even given discretion not to impose the death penalty—will impose the death penalty in a substantial portion of the cases so defined. If they do, it can no longer be said that the penalty is being imposed wantonly and freakishly, or so infrequently that it loses its usefulness as a sentencing device. There is, therefore, reason to expect that Georgia's current system would escape the infirmities which invalidated its previous system under *Furman*. However, the Georgia Legislature was not satisfied with a system which might, but also might not, turn out in practice to result in death sentences being imposed with reasonable consistency for certain serious murders. Instead, it gave the Georgia Supreme Court the power and the obligation to perform precisely the task which three Justices of this Court, whose opinions were necessary to the result, performed in *Furman:* namely, the task of deciding whether, in fact, the death penalty was being administered for any given class of crime in a discriminatory, standardless, or rare fashion. . . .

Petitioner's argument that there is an unconstitutional amount of discretion in the system which separates those suspects who receive the death penalty from those who receive life imprisonment, a lesser penalty, or are acquitted or never charged, seems to be, in final analysis, an indictment of our entire system of justice. Petitioner has argued, in effect, that no matter how effective the death penalty may be as a punishment, government, created and run as it must be by humans, is inevitably incompetent to administer it. This cannot be accepted as a proposition of constitutional law. Imposition of the death penalty is surely an awesome responsibility for any system of justice and those who participate in it. Mistakes will be made, and discriminations will occur which will be difficult to explain. However, one of society's most basic tasks is that of protecting the lives of its citizens, and one of the most basic ways in which it achieves the task is through criminal laws against murder. I decline to interfere with the manner in which Georgia has chosen to enforce such laws on what is simply an assertion of lack of faith in the ability of the system of justice to operate in a fundamentally fair manner.

MR. JUSTICE BRENNAN, dissenting.

This Court inescapably has the duty, as the ultimate arbiter of the meaning of our Constitution, to say whether, when individuals condemned to death stand before our Bar, "moral concepts" require us to hold that the law has progressed to the point where we should declare that the punishment of death, like punishments on the rack, the screw, and the wheel, is no longer morally tolerable in our civilized society. My opinion in *Furman* v. *Georgia* concluded that our civilization and the law had progressed to this point, and that, therefore, the punishment of death, for whatever crime and under all circumstances, is "cruel and unusual" in violation of the Eighth and Fourteenth Amendments of the Constitution. I shall not again canvass the reasons that led to that conclusion. I emphasize only that foremost among the "moral concepts" recognized in our cases and inherent in the Clause is the primary moral principle that the State, even as it punishes, must treat its citizens in a manner consistent with their intrinsic worth as human beings—a punishment must not be so severe as to be degrading to human dignity. A judicial determination whether the punishment of death comports with human dignity is therefore not only permitted, but compelled, by the Clause.

I do not understand that the Court disagrees that, "[i]n comparison to all other punishments today . . . , the deliberate extinguishment of human life by the State is uniquely degrading to human dignity." For three of my Brethren hold today that mandatory infliction of the death penalty constitutes the penalty cruel and unusual punishment. I perceive no principled basis for this limitation. Death, for whatever crime and under all circumstances, is truly an awesome punishment. The calculated killing of a human being by the State involves, by its very nature, a denial of the executed person's humanity. . . . An executed person has indeed "lost the right to have rights." Death is not only an unusually severe punishment, unusual in its pain, in its finality, and in its enormity, but it serves no penal purpose more effectively than a less severe punishment; therefore the principle inherent in the Clause that prohibits pointless infliction of excessive punishment when less severe punishment can adequately achieve the same purposes invalidates the punishment.

The fatal constitutional infirmity in the punishment of death is that it treats members of the human race as nonhumans, as objects to be toyed with and discarded. [It is] thus inconsistent with the fundamental premise of the Clause that even the vilest criminal remains a human being possessed of common human dignity.

As such, it is a penalty that "subjects the individual to a fate forbidden by the principle of civilized treatment guaranteed by the [Clause]." I therefore would hold, on that ground alone, that death is today a cruel and unusual punishment prohibited by the Clause. Justice of this kind is obviously no less shocking than the crime itself, and the new "official" murder, far from offering redress for the offense committed against society, adds instead a second defilement to the first.

MR. JUSTICE MARSHALL, dissenting.

I have no intention of retracing the "long and tedious journey" that led to my conclusion in *Furman.* My sole purposes here are to consider the suggestion that my conclusion in *Furman* has been undercut by developments since then, and briefly to evaluate the basis for my Brethren's holding that the extinction of life is a permissible form of punishment under the Cruel and Unusual Punishments Clause.

In *Furman,* I concluded that the death penalty is constitutionally invalid for two reasons. First, the death penalty is excessive. And second, the American people, fully informed as to the purposes of the death penalty and its liabilities, would, in my view, reject it as morally unacceptable.

Since the decision in *Furman,* the legislatures of 35 States have enacted new statutes authorizing the imposition of the death sentence for certain crimes, and Congress has enacted a law providing the death penalty for air piracy resulting in death. I would be less than candid if I did not acknowledge that these developments have a significant bearing on a realistic assessment of the moral acceptability of the death penalty to the American people. But if the constitutionality of the death penalty turns, as I have urged, on the opinion of an informed citizenry, then even the enactment of new death statutes cannot be viewed as conclusive. In *Furman,* I observed that the American people are largely unaware of the information critical to a judgment on the morality of the death penalty, and concluded that, if they were better informed, they would consider it shocking, unjust, and unacceptable. A recent study, conducted after the enactment of the post-*Furman* statutes, has confirmed that the American people know little about the death penalty, and that the opinions of an informed public would differ significantly from those of a public unaware of the consequences and effects of the death penalty.

Even assuming, however, that the post-*Furman* enactment of statutes authorizing the death penalty renders the prediction of the views of an informed citizenry an uncertain basis for a constitutional decision, the enactment of those statutes has no bearing whatsoever on the conclusion that the death penalty is unconstitutional because it is excessive. An excessive penalty is invalid under the Cruel and Unusual Punishments Clause "even though popular sentiment may favor" it. The inquiry here, then, is simply whether the death penalty is necessary to accomplish the legitimate legislative purposes in punishment, or whether a less severe penalty—life imprisonment—would do as well. . . .

The concept of retribution is a multifaceted one, and any discussion of its role in the criminal law must be undertaken with caution. On one level, it can be said that the notion of retribution or reprobation is the basis of our insistence that only those who have broken the law be punished, and, in this sense, the notion is quite obviously central to a just system of criminal sanctions. But our recognition that retribution plays a crucial role in determining who may be punished by no means requires approval of retribution as a general justification for punishment. It is the question whether retribution can provide a moral justification for punishment—in particular, capital punishment—that we must consider. . . . .

[I]t may be suggested that the expression of moral outrage through the imposition of the death penalty serves to reinforce basic moral values—that it marks some crimes as particularly offensive, and therefore to be avoided. The argument is akin to a deterrence argument, but differs in that it contemplates the individual's shrinking from antisocial conduct not because he fears punishment, but because he has been told in the strongest possible way that the conduct is wrong. This contention, like the previous one, provides no support for the death penalty. It is inconceivable that any individual concerned about conforming his conduct to what society says is "right" would fail to realize that murder is "wrong" if the penalty were simply life imprisonment.

The foregoing contentions—that society's expression of moral outrage through the imposition of the death penalty preempts the citizenry from taking the law into its own hands and reinforces moral values—are not retributive in the purest sense. They are essentially utilitarian, in that they portray the death penalty as valuable because of its beneficial results. These justifications for the death penalty are inadequate because the penalty is, quite clearly I think, not necessary to the accomplishment of those results.

The death penalty, unnecessary to promote the goal of deterrence or to further any legitimate notion of retribution, is an excessive penalty forbidden by the Eighth and Fourteenth Amendments. I respectfully dissent from the Court's judgment upholding the sentences of death imposed upon the petitioners in these cases.

Gregg made clear what anti–death penalty advocates were reluctant to admit after *Furman:* No majority existed within the Court that believed the death penalty per se was unconstitutional. Only Brennan and Marshall had subscribed to that view. In the eyes of Stewart and White—Douglas had retired by the time of *Gregg*—the Texas, Georgia, and Florida laws had eliminated the procedural deficiencies that concerned them in *Furman*. The "death is different" argument offered by Amsterdam did not persuade the justices. If anything, the Court, with the exception of Brennan and Marshall, believed that the "death is different" argument actually supported the death penalty. For the first time, the Court said that retribution was a perfectly reasonable justification to impose capital punishment when the "aggravating" circumstances of a crime warranted it. Trying to understand what combination of forces—the argument advanced by the NAACP LDF, public opinion, political pressure, or the hardened legal views of the individual justices—led the Court to reinstitute capital punishment after a four-year moratorium is difficult to say.[22] This much, however, is true. *Gregg* repopulated death row as fast as *Furman* had cleared it. By 1980, approximately 1,000 inmates were on death row; by 1985, that figure stood at approximately 1,450. By 2000, that number more than doubled to approximately 3,600.[23] To demonstrate that the doors to execution were now open, Utah carried out the nation's first death sentence since 1967 when a firing squad executed Gary Gilmore in January 1977.

Regulating the Death Penalty: Capital Punishment After *Gregg*

Gregg's restoration of the death penalty did not mean, however, that the Court was prepared to abandon its supervision of how capital punishment was administered nationwide. One year later, the NAACP LDF won a small consolation of sorts when the Court, in *Coker* v. *Georgia* (1977), held that the death penalty for rape violated the Eighth Amendment, the very issue that gave birth to the group's capital punishment litigation campaign in the early 1960s.[24] In *Lockett* v. *Ohio* (1978), the Court held that states could not limit the number of mitigating factors capital defendants could introduce during the sentencing phase of their trials, reinforcing *Furman's* insistence on individualized sentencing in death penalty cases.[25] And, even into the mid-1980s, when the Court began to heed a more conservative line in criminal cases, slim majorities nonetheless held that states could not execute a capital defendant who went insane on death row or accomplices in capital murder cases who did not engage in violent acts.[26]

After *Gregg*, the NAACP LDF still represented more capital defendants than any other law firm in the country. Constant involvement in death penalty cases since the late 1960s had left one unshakable impression in

FIGURE 9.1 Number of Executions Since 1976

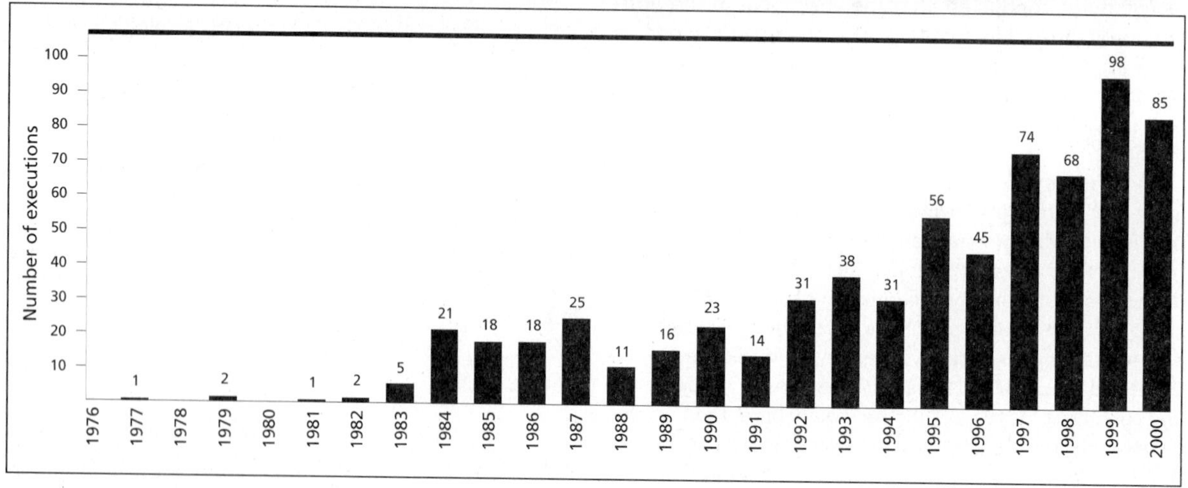

Reprinted by permission of the Death Penalty Information Center.

the minds of NAACP LDF lawyers: Race had everything to do with how capital defendants were tried and sentenced. Blacks who killed whites were much more likely to receive the death sentence than were whites who killed whites. Blacks who killed blacks rarely were sentenced to death. By the time *Gregg* was decided, the NAACP LDF, the ACLU, and other groups opposed to the death penalty had uncovered a telling statistic: No white person convicted of killing an African American had *ever* been executed since such statistics began being kept in the early 1930s. Hoping that pervasive evidence of racial discrimination would persuade the Court to revisit similar concerns raised in *Furman*, the NAACP LDF hired David Baldus, a leading authority on racial discrimination in the criminal justice system, to engage in a systematic study of the role of race in capital sentencing. Baldus, along with several colleagues, developed a complex statistical analysis demonstrating that criminal defendants charged with killing white victims were 4.3 times as likely to receive the death sentence as those charged with killing African Americans. The NAACP LDF had Baldus testify in a death penalty case, *McCleskey* v. *Kemp*, it was currently handling in Georgia involving a black man convicted of killing a white police officer. Even with the Baldus study, the NAACP LDF lost in the lower courts, opening the door for one last major challenge to the death penalty in the Supreme Court.

McCleskey v. *Kemp*

481 U.S. 279 (1987)

In October 1978, Warren McCleskey was convicted of robbing a furniture store and killing a City of Atlanta police officer who had responded to a silent alarm triggered by one of the store's employees. The jury consisted of eleven whites and one black man, a retired county worker. McCleskey would contest his conviction on several grounds over the years, including that he had been coerced into confessing by a jailhouse informant. That charge resulted in separate litigation that culminated in another Supreme Court decision, *McCleskey* v. *Zant* (1991). McCleskey was no more successful the second time. The justices used *Zant* to limit the number of habeas corpus petitions that death row inmates could file in federal court.

McCleskey's second trip to the Court may never have been necessary had the Baldus study persuaded the justices that racial discrimination was so pervasive in the nation's system of capital punishment that it violated the Eighth and Fourteenth Amendments. NAACP LDF lawyers knew that the Baldus study offered their best hope in years

FIGURE 9.2 Public Support for the Death Penalty

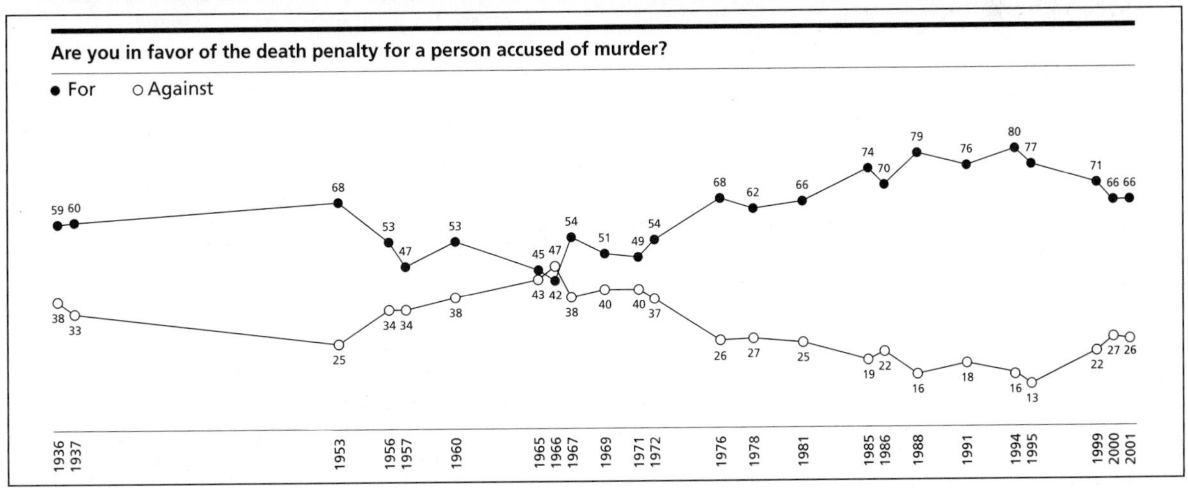

Source: www.gallup.com/poll

of calling into question the death penalty as administered. And the Georgia statute offered a particularly inviting target for a racial discrimination argument. Between 1930 and 1972, Georgia had executed sixty-nine persons for rape; sixty-six were black. After *Furman*, Georgia was the only state to impose capital punishment for rape. Like every other state with capital punishment, Georgia had never executed a white man for killing a black man. As NAACP LDF lawyer Jack Boger said during oral argument, the Baldus study was "not some kind of statistical aberration. We have a century-old pattern in the state of Georgia."

Prosecutors and their *amici*, including the Washington Legal Foundation, a group active in other areas of criminal law (see Chapters 7 and 8), argued that the Baldus study offered no *proof of purposeful discrimination* in capital sentencing. Evidence of racial disparities did not translate into willful discrimination. Another point raised against the Baldus study was the potential it held to disrupt the nation's criminal justice system. If the Court invalidated McCleskey's sentence on racial grounds, every state capital sentencing process would be called into question, running the risk of another judicially imposed moratorium on the death penalty, as in *Furman*. Might these arguments have influenced the justices?

The Court's vote was 5 to 4. Justice Powell delivered the opinion of the Court. Justice Blackmun, joined by Justices Brennan, Marshall, and Stevens, dissented. Justice Brennan dissented, and was joined by Justices Blackmun, Marshall, and Stevens. Justice Stevens, joined by Justice Blackmun, also dissented.

▼▲▼

JUSTICE POWELL delivered the opinion of the Court.

This case presents the question whether a complex statistical study that indicates a risk that racial considerations enter into capital sentencing determinations proves that petitioner McCleskey's capital sentence is unconstitutional under the Eighth or Fourteenth Amendment. . . .

Our analysis begins with the basic principle that a defendant who alleges an equal protection violation has the burden of proving "the existence of purposeful discrimination." A corollary to this principle is that a criminal defendant must prove that the purposeful discrimination "had a discriminatory effect" on him. Thus, to prevail under the Equal Protection Clause, McCleskey must prove that the decision makers in his case acted with discriminatory purpose. He offers no evidence specific to his own case that would support an inference that racial considerations played a part in his sentence. Instead, he relies solely on the Baldus study. McCleskey argues that the Baldus study compels an inference that his sentence rests on purposeful discrimination. McCleskey's claim that these statistics are sufficient proof of discrimination, without regard to the facts of a particular case, would extend to all capital cases in Georgia, at least where the victim was white and the defendant is black.

The Court has accepted statistics as proof of intent to discriminate in certain limited contexts. First, this Court has accepted statistical disparities as proof of an equal protection violation in the selection of the jury venire in a particular district. Although statistical proof normally must present a "stark" pattern to be accepted as the sole proof of discriminatory intent under the Constitution, . . . [b]ecause of the nature of the jury-selection task, . . . we have permitted a finding of constitutional violation even when the statistical pattern does not approach [such] extremes. Second, this Court has accepted statistics in the form of multiple-regression analysis to prove statutory violations under Title VII of the Civil Rights Act of 1964.

But the nature of the capital sentencing decision, and the relationship of the statistics to that decision, are fundamentally different from the corresponding elements in the venire selection or Title VII cases. Most importantly, each particular decision to impose the death penalty is made by a petit jury selected from a properly constituted venire. Each jury is unique in its composition, and the Constitution requires that its decision rest on consideration of innumerable factors that vary according to the characteristics of the individual defendant and the facts of the particular capital offense. Thus, the application of an inference drawn from the general statistics to a specific decision in a trial and sentencing simply is not comparable to the application of an inference drawn from general statistics to a specific venire-selection or Title VII case. In those cases, the statistics relate to fewer entities, and fewer variables are relevant to the challenged decisions.

Another important difference between the cases in which we have accepted statistics as proof of discriminatory intent and this case is that, in the venire-selection and Title VII contexts, the decision maker has an opportunity to explain the statistical disparity. Here, the State has no practical opportunity to rebut the Baldus study. . . . Moreover, absent far stronger proof, it is unnecessary to seek such a rebuttal, because a legitimate and unchallenged explanation for the decision is apparent from the record: McCleskey committed an act for which the United States Constitution and Georgia laws permit imposition of the death penalty.

Finally, McCleskey's statistical proffer must be viewed in the context of his challenge. McCleskey challenges decisions at the heart of the State's criminal justice system. . . . [O]ne of society's most basic tasks is that of protecting the lives of its citizens, and one of the most basic ways in which it achieves the task is through criminal laws against murder. Implementation of these laws necessarily requires discretionary judgments. Because discretion is essential to the criminal justice process, we would demand exceptionally clear proof before we would infer that the discretion has been abused. The unique nature of the decisions at issue in this case also counsels against adopting such an inference from the disparities indicated by the Baldus study. Accordingly, we hold that the Baldus study is clearly insufficient to support an inference that any of the decision makers in McCleskey's case acted with discriminatory purpose.

McCleskey also suggests that the Baldus study proves that the State as a whole has acted with a discriminatory purpose. . . . For this claim to prevail, McCleskey would have to prove that the Georgia Legislature enacted or maintained the death penalty statute because of an anticipated racially discriminatory effect. In *Gregg* v. *Georgia*, this Court found that the Georgia capital sentencing system could operate in a fair and neutral manner. There was no evidence then, and there is none now, that the Georgia Legislature enacted the capital punishment statute to further a racially discriminatory purpose. Nor has McCleskey demonstrated that the legislature maintains the capital punishment statute because of the racially disproportionate impact suggested by the Baldus study. As legislatures necessarily have wide discretion in the choice of criminal laws and penalties, and as there were legitimate reasons for the Georgia Legislature to adopt and maintain capital punishment, we will not infer a discriminatory purpose on the part of the State of Georgia. Accordingly, we reject McCleskey's equal protection claims.

McCleskey also argues that the Baldus study demonstrates that the Georgia capital sentencing system violates the Eighth Amendment.

Two principal decisions guide our resolution of McCleskey's Eighth Amendment claim. In *Furman*, the Court concluded that the death penalty was so irrationally imposed that any particular death sentence could be presumed excessive. . . .

In *Gregg*, the Court specifically addressed the question left open in *Furman*—whether the punishment of death for murder is "under all circumstances, 'cruel and unusual' in violation of the Eighth and Fourteenth Amendments of the Constitution." . . .

The second question before the Court in *Gregg* was the constitutionality of the particular procedures embodied in the Georgia capital punishment statute. We explained the fundamental principle of *Furman*, that, "where discretion is afforded a sentencing body on a matter so grave as the determination of whether a human life should be taken or spared, that discretion must be suitably directed and limited so as to minimize the risk of wholly arbitrary and capricious action." Numerous features of the then-new Georgia statute met the concerns articulated in *Furman*. The Georgia system bifurcates guilt and sentencing proceedings, so that the jury can receive all relevant information for sentencing without the risk that evidence irrelevant to the defendant's guilt will influence the jury's consideration of that issue. The statute narrows the class of murders subject to the death penalty to cases in which the jury finds at least one statutory aggravating circumstance beyond a reasonable doubt. Conversely, it allows the defendant to introduce any relevant mitigating evidence that might influence the jury not to impose a death sentence. The procedures also require a particularized inquiry into "'the circumstances of the offense, together with the character and propensities of the offender.'" . . .

Moreover, the Georgia system adds "an important additional safeguard against arbitrariness and caprice" in a provision for automatic appeal of a death sentence to the State Supreme Court. The statute requires the court to review each sentence to determine whether it was imposed under the influence of passion or prejudice, whether the evidence supports the jury's finding of a statutory aggravating circumstance, and whether the sentence is disproportionate to sentences imposed in generally similar murder cases. To aid the court's review, the trial judge answers a questionnaire about the trial, including detailed questions as to "the quality of the defendant's representation [and] whether race played a role in the trial." . . .

In sum, our decisions since *Furman* have identified a constitutionally permissible range of discretion in imposing the death penalty. First, there is a required threshold below which the death penalty cannot be imposed. In this context, the State must establish rational criteria that narrow the decision maker's judgment as to whether the circumstances of a particular defendant's case meet the threshold. Moreover, a societal consensus that the death penalty is disproportionate to a particular offense prevents a State from imposing the death penalty for that offense. Second, States cannot limit the sentencer's consideration of any relevant circumstance that could cause it to decline to impose the penalty. In this respect, the State cannot channel the sentencer's discretion, but must allow it to consider any relevant information offered by the defendant.

In light of our precedents under the Eighth Amendment, McCleskey cannot argue successfully that his sentence is "disproportionate to the crime in the traditional sense." He does not deny that he committed a murder in the course of a planned robbery, a crime for which this Court has determined that the death penalty constitutionally may be imposed. His disproportionality claim "is of a different sort." McCleskey argues that the sentence in his case is disproportionate to the sentences in other murder cases.

. . . [H]e cannot base a constitutional claim on an argument that his case differs from other cases in which defendants did receive the death penalty. On automatic appeal, the Georgia Supreme Court found that McCleskey's death sentence was not disproportionate to other death sentences imposed in the State. . . .

[A]bsent a showing that the Georgia capital punishment system operates in an arbitrary and capricious manner, McCleskey cannot prove a constitutional violation by demonstrating that other defendants who may be similarly situated did not receive the death penalty. . . .

Because McCleskey's sentence was imposed under Georgia sentencing procedures that focus discretion "on the particularized nature of the crime and the particularized characteristics of the individual defendant," we lawfully may presume that McCleskey's death sentence was not "wantonly and freakishly" imposed, and thus that the sentence is not disproportionate within any recognized meaning under the Eighth Amendment. . . .

To evaluate McCleskey's challenge, we must examine exactly what the Baldus study may show. Even Professor Baldus does not contend that his statistics prove that race enters into any capital sentencing decisions, or that race was a factor in McCleskey's particular case. Statistics, at most, may show only a likelihood that a particular factor entered into some decisions. There is, of course, some risk of racial prejudice influencing a jury's decision in a criminal case. There are similar risks that other kinds of prejudice will influence other criminal trials. The question "is at what point that risk becomes constitutionally unacceptable." McCleskey asks us to accept the likelihood allegedly shown by the Baldus study as the constitutional measure of an unacceptable risk of racial prejudice influencing capital sentencing decisions. This we decline to do. . . .

McCleskey's argument that the Constitution condemns the discretion allowed decision makers in the Georgia capital sentencing system is antithetical to the fundamental role of discretion in our criminal justice system. Discretion in the criminal justice system offers substantial benefits to the criminal defendant. Not only can a jury decline to impose the death sentence, it can decline to convict or choose to convict of a lesser offense. Whereas decisions against a defendant's interest may be reversed by the trial judge or on appeal, these discretionary exercises of leniency are final and unreviewable. Similarly, the capacity of prosecutorial discretion to provide individualized justice is "only entrenched in American law." As we have noted, a prosecutor can decline to charge, offer a plea bargain, or decline to seek a death sentence in any particular case. Of course, "the power to be lenient [also] is the power to discriminate," but a capital punishment system that did not allow for discretionary acts of leniency "would be totally alien to our notions of criminal justice," *Gregg* v. *Georgia* (1976).

At most, the Baldus study indicates a discrepancy that appears to correlate with race. Apparent disparities in sentencing are an inevitable part of our criminal justice system. . . . As this Court has recognized, any mode for determining guilt or punishment "has its weaknesses and the potential for misuse." Specifically, "there can be 'no perfect procedure for deciding in which cases governmental authority should be used to impose death.'" Despite these imperfections, our consistent rule has been that constitutional guarantees are met when "the mode [for determining guilt or punishment] itself has been surrounded with safeguards to make it as fair as possible." Where the discretion that is fundamental to our criminal process is involved, we decline to assume that what is unexplained is invidious. In light of the safeguards designed to minimize racial bias in the process, the fundamental value of jury trial in our criminal justice system, and the benefits that discretion provides to criminal defendants, we hold that the Baldus study does not demonstrate a constitutionally significant risk of racial bias affecting the Georgia capital sentencing process.

Two additional concerns inform our decision in this case. First, McCleskey's claim, taken to its logical conclusion, throws into serious question the principles that underlie our entire criminal justice system. The Eighth Amendment is not limited in application to capital punishment, but applies to all penalties. Thus, if we accepted McCleskey's claim that racial bias has impermissibly tainted the capital sentencing decision, we could soon be faced with similar claims as to other types of penalty. Moreover, the claim that his sentence rests on the irrelevant factor of race easily could be extended to apply to claims based on unexplained discrepancies that correlate to membership in other minority groups, and even to gender. . . . If arbitrary and capricious punishment is the touchstone under the Eighth Amendment, such a claim could—at least in theory—be based upon any arbitrary variable, such as the defendant's facial characteristics, or the physical attractiveness of the defendant or the victim, that some statistical study indicates may be influential in jury decision making. As these examples illustrate, there is no limiting principle to the type of challenge brought by McCleskey. The Constitution does not require that a State eliminate any demonstrable disparity that correlates with a potentially irrelevant factor in order to operate a criminal justice system that includes capital punishment. . . .

Second, McCleskey's arguments are best presented to the legislative bodies. It is not the responsibility—or indeed even the right—of this Court to determine the appropriate punishment for particular crimes. Legislatures . . . are better qualified to weigh and evaluate the results of statistical studies in terms of their own local conditions and with a flexibility of approach that is not available to the courts. Capital punishment is now the law in more than two-thirds of our States. It is the ultimate duty of courts to determine on a case-by-case basis whether these laws are applied consistently with the Constitution. Despite McCleskey's wide-ranging arguments that basically challenge the validity of capital punishment in our multiracial society, the only question before us is whether, in his case, the law of Georgia was properly applied. We agree with the District Court and the Court of Appeals for the Eleventh Circuit that this was carefully and correctly done in this case.

Accordingly, we affirm the judgment of the Court of Appeals for the Eleventh Circuit.

It is so ordered.

JUSTICE BRENNAN, with whom JUSTICE MARSHALL joins, and with whom JUSTICE BLACKMUN and JUSTICE STEVENS join in all but Part I, dissenting.

I

Adhering to my view that the death penalty is in all circumstances cruel and unusual punishment forbidden by the Eighth and Fourteenth Amendments, I would vacate the decision below insofar as it left undisturbed the death sentence imposed in this case. . . .

Even if I did not hold this position, however, I would reverse the Court of Appeals, for petitioner McCleskey has clearly demonstrated that his death sentence was imposed in violation of the Eighth and Fourteenth Amendments. . . . McCleskey . . . demonstrate[s] precisely the type of risk of irrationality in sentencing that we have consistently condemned in our Eighth Amendment jurisprudence.

II

At some point in this case, Warren McCleskey doubtless asked his lawyer whether a jury was likely to sentence him to die. A candid reply to this question would have been disturbing. First, counsel would have to tell McCleskey that few of the details of the crime or of McCleskey's past criminal conduct were more important than the fact that his victim was white. Furthermore, counsel would feel bound to tell McCleskey that defendants charged with killing white victims in Georgia are 4.3 times as likely to be sentenced to death as defendants charged with killing blacks. In addition, frankness would compel the disclosure that it was more likely than not that the race of McCleskey's victim would determine whether he received a death sentence: 6 of every 11 defendants convicted of killing a white person would not have received the death penalty if their victims had been black, while, among defendants with aggravating and mitigating factors comparable to McCleskey's, 20 of every 34 would not have been sentenced to die if their victims had been black. Finally, the assessment would not be complete without the information that cases involving black defendants and white victims are more likely to result in a death sentence than cases featuring any other racial combination of defendant and victim. The story could be told in a variety of ways, but McCleskey could not fail to grasp its essential narrative line: there was a significant chance that race would play a prominent role in determining if he lived or died.

The Court today holds that Warren McCleskey's sentence was constitutionally imposed. It finds no fault in a system in which lawyers must tell their clients that race casts a large shadow on the capital sentencing process. The Court arrives at this conclusion by stating that the Baldus study cannot "prove that race enters into any capital sentencing decisions or that race was a factor in McCleskey's particular case." Since, according to Professor Baldus, we cannot say "to a moral certainty" that race influenced a decision, we can identify only "a likelihood that a particular factor entered into some decisions," and "a discrepancy that appears to correlate with race." This "likelihood" and "discrepancy," holds the Court, is insufficient to establish a constitutional violation. The Court reaches this conclusion by placing four factors on the scales opposite McCleskey's evidence: the desire to encourage sentencing discretion, the existence of "statutory safeguards" in the Georgia scheme, the fear of encouraging widespread challenges to other sentencing decisions, and the limits of the judicial role. The Court's evaluation of the significance of petitioner's evidence is fundamentally at odds with our consistent concern for rationality in capital sentencing, and the considerations that the majority invokes to discount that evidence cannot justify ignoring its force.

III

The statistical evidence in this case thus relentlessly documents the risk that McCleskey's sentence was influenced by racial considerations. This evidence shows that there is a better than even chance in Georgia that race will influence the decision to impose the death penalty: a majority of defendants in white-victim crimes would not have been sentenced to die if their victims had been black. In determining whether this risk is acceptable, our judgment must be shaped by the awareness that "[t]he risk of racial prejudice infecting a capital sentencing proceeding is especially serious in light of the complete finality of the death sentence,"and that "[i]t is of vital importance to the defendant and to the community that any decision to impose the death sentence be, and appear to be, based on reason rather than caprice or emotion." In determining the guilt of a defendant, a State must prove its case beyond a reasonable doubt. That is, we refuse to convict if the chance of error is simply less likely than not. Surely, we should not be willing to take a person's life if the chance that his death sentence was irrationally imposed is more likely than not. In light of the gravity of the interest at stake, petitioner's statistics, on their face, are a powerful demonstration of the type of risk that our Eighth Amendment jurisprudence has consistently condemned. . . .

Evaluation of McCleskey's evidence cannot rest solely on the numbers themselves. We must also ask whether the conclusion suggested by those numbers is consonant with our understanding of history and human experience. Georgia's legacy of a race-conscious criminal justice system, as well as this Court's own recognition of the persistent danger that racial attitudes may affect criminal proceedings, indicates that McCleskey's claim is not a fanciful product of mere statistical artifice.

For many years, Georgia operated openly and formally precisely the type of dual system the evidence shows is still effectively in place. The criminal law expressly differentiated between crimes committed by and against blacks and whites, distinctions whose lineage traced back to the time of slavery. During the colonial period, black slaves who killed whites in Georgia, regardless of whether in self-defense or in defense of another, were automatically executed. . . .

By the time of the Civil War, a dual system of crime and punishment was well established in Georgia. The state criminal code contained separate sections for "Slaves and Free Persons of Color." The code provided, for instance, for an automatic death sentence for murder committed by blacks, but declared that anyone else convicted of murder might receive life imprisonment if the conviction were founded solely on circumstantial testimony or simply if the jury so recommended. The code established that the rape of a free white female by a black "shall be" punishable by death. However, rape by anyone else of a free white female was punishable by a prison term not less than 2 nor more than 20 years. The rape of blacks was punishable "by fine and imprisonment, at the discretion of the court." . . .

[Here, Justice Brennan reviewed the history of laws formally punishing blacks for crimes against whites. Identical crimes committed by whites against whites were always punished less severely.]

History and its continuing legacy thus buttress the probative force of McCleskey's statistics. Formal dual criminal laws may no longer be in effect, and intentional discrimination may no longer be prominent. Nonetheless, . . . the Georgia system gives such attitudes considerable room to operate. The conclusions drawn from McCleskey's statistical evidence are therefore consistent with the lessons of social experience. . . .

It is tempting to pretend that minorities on death row share a fate in no way connected to our own, that our treatment of them sounds no echoes beyond the chambers in which they die. Such an illusion is ultimately corrosive, for the reverberations of injustice are not so easily confined. "The destinies of the two races in this country are indissolubly linked together" (Harlan, J., dissenting), and the way in which we choose those who will die reveals the depth of moral commitment among the living.

The Court's decision today will not change what attorneys in Georgia tell other Warren McCleskeys about their chances of execution. Nothing will soften the harsh message they must convey, nor alter the prospect that race undoubtedly will continue to be a topic of discussion. McCleskey's evidence will not have obtained judicial acceptance, but that will not affect what is said on death row. However many criticisms of today's decision may be rendered, these painful conversations will serve as the most eloquent dissents of all.

JUSTICE BLACKMUN, with whom JUSTICE MARSHALL and JUSTICE STEVENS join, and with whom JUSTICE BRENNAN joins . . .

The Court today seems to give a new meaning to our recognition that death is different. Rather than requiring "a correspondingly greater degree of scrutiny of the capital sentencing determination," the Court relies on the very fact that this is a case involving capital punishment to apply a lesser standard of scrutiny under the Equal Protection Clause. The Court concludes that "legitimate" explanations outweigh McCleskey's claim that his death sentence reflected a constitutionally impermissible risk of racial discrimination. The Court explains that McCleskey's evidence is too weak to require rebuttal because a legitimate and unchallenged explanation for the decision is apparent from the record: McCleskey committed an act for which the United States Constitution and Georgia laws permit imposition of the death penalty. The Court states that it will not infer a discriminatory purpose on the part of the state legislature, because "there were legitimate reasons for the Georgia Legislature to adopt and maintain capital punishment."

The Court's assertion that the fact of McCleskey's conviction undermines his constitutional claim is inconsistent with a long and unbroken line of this Court's case law. The Court on numerous occasions during the past century has recognized that an otherwise legitimate basis for a conviction does not outweigh an equal protection violation. In cases where racial discrimination in the administration of the criminal justice system is established, it has held that setting aside the conviction is the appropriate remedy. . . .

There can be no dispute that McCleskey has made the requisite showing. . . . The Baldus study demonstrates that black persons are a distinct group that are singled out for different treatment in the Georgia capital sentencing system. The Court acknowledges, as it must, that the raw statistics included in the Baldus study and presented by petitioner indicate that it is much less likely that a death sentence will result from a murder of a black person than from a murder of a white person. White-victim cases are nearly 11 times more likely to yield a death sentence than are black-victim cases. The raw figures also indicate that, even within the group of defendants who are convicted of killing white persons and are thereby more likely to receive a death sentence, black defendants are more likely than white defendants to be sentenced to death. . . .

I do not believe acceptance of McCleskey's claim would eliminate capital punishment in Georgia. I [believe] that narrowing the class of death-eligible defendants is not too high a price to pay for a death penalty system that does not discriminate on the basis of race. Moreover, the establishment of guidelines for Assistant District Attorneys as to the appropriate basis for exercising their discretion at the various steps in the prosecution of a case would provide at least a measure of consistency. The Court's emphasis on the procedural safeguards in the system ignores the fact that there are none whatsoever during the crucial process leading up to trial. . . . I find the risk that racial prejudice may have infected petitioner's capital sentencing unacceptable in light of the ease with which that risk could have been minimized. I dissent.

In rejecting the Baldus study, the Court effectively erected a stone wall against further challenges against the death penalty on grounds that capital punishment was imposed in a racially discriminatory manner. Although the Court confined the issue in *McCleskey* to whether the defendant had demonstrated intentional racial discrimination in his particular case, none of the parties involved had any illusions about what this meant for the future. The Baldus study was the most comprehensive social science effort to date attempting to demonstrate the role that race played in capital sentencing. Note that Justice Powell did not contest the validity of Baldus's study or the presence of racial disparities in Georgia's capital sentencing scheme; he simply found that it did not demonstrate a causal relationship between race and the imposition of the death penalty. The NAACP LDF introduced additional data demonstrating racial disparities in capital punishment: From 1930, when such statistics started being kept, through 1987, no white offender had ever been executed for murdering a black man. By 1993 that changed, when the first ever such execution was carried out. Since *Gregg*, 175 persons have been executed for interracial murders through July 2001; 164 of those executions involved an African American defendant and a white victim.[27]

Although the Court upheld Warren McCleskey's death sentence and, by extension, how the death penalty was imposed and carried out in virtually every state that had capital punishment, several of the justices were clearly troubled by what they saw in the Baldus study. Justice Antonin Scalia, an ardent supporter of capital punishment then and now, wrote to his colleagues before *McCleskey* was decided that "[T]he unconscious operation of irrational sympathies and antipathies, including racial, upon jury decisions and (hence) prosecutorial decisions is real, acknowledged in the decisions of this court, and ineradicable."[28] Powell, who retired in 1987, later expressed serious regret over voting with the majority and writing the opinion in *McCleskey*. In the early 1990s, as Powell was discussing his Court career with his biographer, he was asked whether he would change his vote in any case.

Powell: "Yes, *McCleskey* v. *Kemp*."
"Do you mean you would now accept the argument from statistics?"
Powell: "No, I would vote that way in any capital case."
"In *any* capital case?"
Powell: "Yes."
"Even in *Furman* v. *Georgia*?"
Powell: "Yes, I have come to think that capital punishment should be abolished."[29]

The Court has not entertained a frontal challenge to the death penalty since *McCleskey* and appears to have no interest in doing so. Since the late 1980s, the Court has expanded the range of persons eligible for the death penalty, including juveniles and the mentally retarded. The justices have also revisited and, in some cases, overturned decisions involving the discretion of prosecutors to select "death qualified" juries and introduce "victim impact" statements to juries during the sentencing phase of a capital trial. But the introduction of new evidence-gathering techniques, particularly the use of DNA testing by defense attorneys to establish the innocence of their clients on death row, has raised new questions about due process and the imposition of the death penalty. DNA testing and the repercussions it has had for the death penalty debate in the United States is discussed in the accompanying SIDEBAR, "Executing the Innocent?"

Death Penalty for Juveniles

Of the thirty-eight states that had death penalty laws on their books as of June 2001, thirty have carried out executions since 1976. Of these thirty states, twenty-three permit the execution of juveniles—individuals under eighteen years old—for capital crimes committed under the age of eighteen. Since the reinstatement of the death penalty in *Gregg*, no state has executed an individual while still a juvenile. Through June 2001, the youngest person executed in the United States has been a twenty-three-year-old for a crime committed as a seventeen-year-old. But the issue of whether juveniles should be death-eligible for capital crimes is a controversial topic. That only seven states have executed individuals for crimes committed as minors suggests that not all death penalty supporters necessarily believe juveniles should be eligible for capital punishment.[30]

The Court first confronted the issue of whether juveniles should be death-eligible for capital crimes in *Eddings* v. *Oklahoma* (1982).[31] By a 5 to 4 majority, the Court vacated the death sentence of sixteen-year-old Monty Lee Eddings, who had been sentenced to death for killing an Oklahoma state trooper with a point-blank shotgun blast to the face. The Court concluded that the trial judge's failure to allow the jury to consider every mitigating circumstance introduced by his lawyers during the sentencing phase violated Eddings's rights under the Eighth and Fourteenth Amendments. But the justices did not reach the question of whether the Cruel and Unusual Punishment Clause barred the consideration of juveniles for the death penalty. Three years later, in *Thompson* v. *Oklahoma* (1985), the same 5 to 4 majority concluded that fifteen-year-olds could not be considered death-eligible in the absence of a national consensus on the appropriate minimum age for capital punishment. Four justices, Blackmun, Brennan, Marshall, and Stevens, believed that the Eighth Amendment barred the consideration of fifteen-year-olds for capital punishment. Casting the fifth vote, Justice O'Connor did not reach this issue, instead concluding that the flaw in *Thompson* rested with the lack of legislative consensus on the minimum age for death-eligibility in capital cases.[32] In *Stanford* v. *Kentucky* (1989) and *Wilkins* v. *Missouri* (1989), the Court offered a more definitive opinion about death-eligibility for juveniles in capital cases.

Stanford v. *Kentucky*
Wilkins v. *Missouri*

492 U.S. 361 (1989)

On January 7, 1981, Kevin Stanford and an accomplice robbed a gas station in rural Jefferson County, Kentucky, of three hundred cartons of cigarettes, two gallons of gas, and some petty cash. During and after the robbery, they took turns beating and raping their victim, a twenty-year-old woman who worked at the gas station as an attendant. Stanford and his accomplice then drove their victim to a secluded area behind the gas station, where Stanford put his shotgun to her face and sent a blast through the back of her head. He then turned her around and shot her again through the head. After Stanford was placed in custody, a

EXECUTING THE INNOCENT?

"I Thought My Life's Over, Literally Over"

In 1998, both Greg Wilhout and Ron Williamson were convicted of brutal murders, sentenced to death, and sent to wait their turn on death row at the Oklahoma state prison. Wilhout, a big, strong ironworker, had been convicted of beating and killing his wife in the presence of the couple's two young daughters. Williamson, a former star high school baseball player on his way to the major leagues until he was derailed by an injury, had been found guilty of raping and strangling a young waitress in Ada, Oklahoma. Williamson was considered a loner since his arrival in town, and police quickly made him their chief suspect. (Williamson also had a criminal record and a history of mental illness.) Their investigation turned up stray hairs that they claimed were Williamson's. These hairs, examined under a microscope alongside sample hairs taken from Williamson, formed the prosecution's core case against the defendant. In Wilhout's case, prosecutors focused on his recent separation from his wife, a bite mark identified as Wilhout's that was found on his wife's dead body, and his inability to produce an alibi for the night of her murder. Both men insisted on their innocence and set about trying to free themselves.

For his trial, Wilhout received a court-appointed lawyer to defend him, but one who had earned a reputation as the "town drunk." Said his second lawyer, Mark Barrett, a public defender who represented Wilhout on appeal, "His lawyer was . . . enough of a town drunk that he had wet himself in some courtrooms, [and] thrown up in some courtrooms." After eight years on death row, Wilhout won a new trial when Barrett introduced reports from eleven forensic specialists concluding that the bite mark on the murder victim was not his client's. During Wilhout's first trial, the police had relied on the testimony of two dentists to identify the bite marks. Wilhout was granted a new trial, and the prosecution again contended that the defendant had killed his wife. This time, however, the state, unable to introduce the dentists' conclusions, had no physical evidence to link the defendant to the victim. Halfway through the trial, the judge called a halt to the proceedings and set Wilhout free.

Barrett also took up Williamson's appeal, convinced that his first lawyer had made no real effort to challenge the prosecution's case. Police had relied upon microscopic similarities between his hair and the hair found on his alleged victim's body. Plans for Williamson's execution had progressed to the point where his sister had received a letter from prison authorities instructing her on the correct procedure to claim his body. Barrett fought for over ten years to have the hairs used to convict Williamson examined through DNA testing, a procedure that was not widely available in 1988. Finally, in 1999, Barrett, working with Barry Scheck, a defense attorney who had pioneered the use of DNA evidence to defend his clients, introduced DNA reports showing that the hairs used to convict Williamson were not his after all. Williamson, with his old prison buddy Greg Wilhout looking on in the courtroom, was freed.

Wilhout's and Williamson's ordeals illuminate in

very human terms a problem that many capital punishment opponents claim afflicts the current administration of the death penalty in the United States. Bad defense lawyers, slippery prosecutions, and recent decisions from the United States Supreme Court limiting the number of appeals by death row inmates, they claim, have resulted in a system of capital punishment that sends innocent persons to the execution chamber. From 1973 to 2000, eighty-five death row inmates have been exonerated or freed across the nation. In Florida, which has executed forty-nine persons since 1976, eighteen death row inmates have been set free. Texas, which has carried out 231 executions during this period—almost 150 more than any other state—has released seven death row inmates. And Oklahoma, which has executed thirty persons, has set free seven individuals slated for execution, including Greg Wilhout and Ron Williamson.

Ron Williamson (right), shown here with lawyer Dennis Fritz, and Greg Wilhout were nearly executed for crimes they did not commit.
AP/Wide World Photos

But perhaps the most compelling evidence that serious problems exist in how death sentences are imposed and carried out in the United States arose in January 2000, when Illinois Governor George Ryan imposed a moratorium on all executions until the state's system of capital punishment had undergone a thorough review. Ryan's announcement came after journalism students at Northwestern University had uncovered evidence exonerating death row inmate Anthony Porter, who had once come within two days of execution by lethal injection. The *Chicago Tribune* had also just completed a series of articles on capital punishment in Illinois that uncovered some damning pieces of information. Thirty-three death row inmates had been represented by attorneys who were subsequently disbarred or suspended. Appeals courts had either reversed or vacated lower court rulings in over half of the state's capital cases. What troubled Governor Ryan most was when he learned that more death row inmates (thirteen) had been freed than executed (twelve) since Illinois had reinstated capital punishment after *Gregg* in 1977. Governors in several other states followed Ryan's lead and ordered a halt on executions until they could investigate irregularities in their capital punishment systems.

Several factors account for the renewed attention focused on the flaws in the administration of capital punishment in the United States. Racial disparities continue to exist in capital sentencing and executions. Many capital defendants are now armed with better statistical evidence demonstrating racial bias in the prosecution and sentencing of minority capital defendants, particularly when white victims are involved. Other sophisticated statistical analyses have been made showing that between 1973 and 1995 state or federal appeals courts threw out convictions or death sentences in 68 percent of the cases because of faulty legal representation or unreliable evidence. Moreover, DNA testing has become more prominent in capital cases, offering defendants the chance to demonstrate their innocence with scientific precision.

Many supporters of capital punishment have dismissed these recent studies and developments as ideologically driven efforts to abolish capital punishment. Although support for the death penalty has dropped to its lowest levels since the early 1980s (see Figure 9.2 on page 449), nearly two thirds of Americans—64 percent—support the death penalty. And many death penalty supporters argue that there is nothing wrong with increasing the use of DNA evidence in

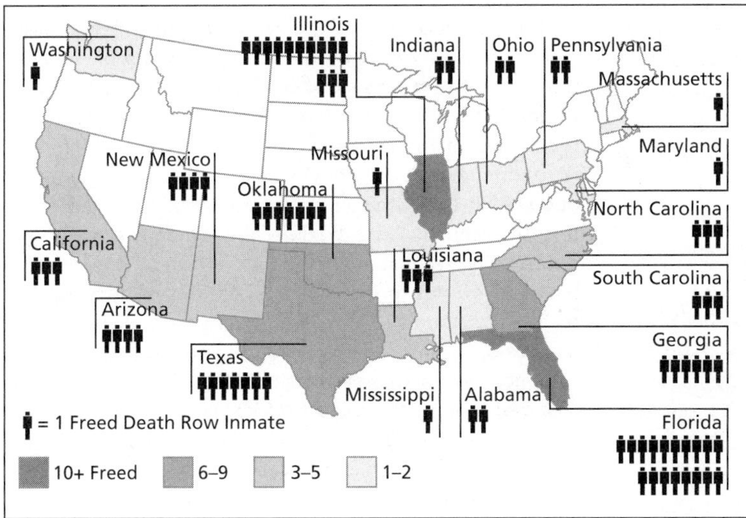

Since 1973, eighty-five death-row prisoners have been exonerated and freed across the nation. The prisoners spent an average of 7.5 years on death row prior to being released. New DNA evidence played a substantial factor in establishing the innocence of eight freed prisoners.
Source: Death Penalty Information Center (www.ABCNEWS.com/)

capital cases, since such evidence stands to confirm the guilty and to free those inmates who are innocent. But with more and more elected officials calling into question the fairness of capital punishment in the United States, the death penalty debate, one of the most emotional and gut-wrenching in American politics, is not going to disappear anytime soon.

References

"Through Thick and Thin," www.abcnews.com/onair/2020/2020_0018_deathrow_feature.html
Geraldine Sealey, "Moratorium on Execution in Illinois," www.abcnews.com, January 31, 2000.
Data and graphs: Death Penalty Information Center, Washington, D.C. (www.deathpenaltyinfo.org).

corrections officer testified during Stanford's trial that the defendant told him, "I had to shoot her, [since] she lived next door to me and she would recognize me. . . . I guess we could have tied her up . . . and tell her if she tells, we would kill her." According to the officer, Stanford started laughing after he told the story.

On July 25, 1985, Heath Wilkins and Patrick Stevens robbed a convenience store in Avondale, Missouri, owned and operated by Nancy Allen, a twenty-six-year-old mother of two young children, and her husband, David. After entering the store, Stevens grabbed Nancy Allen, who was working behind the counter, and held her while Wilkins stabbed her, causing her to fall to the floor. Stevens attempted to open the cash register, but could not make it work. Allen tried to tell him what to do, leading Wilkins to stab her three more times in the chest. As Allen coughed and gagged, Wilkins stabbed her again in the chest, opening her carotid artery and causing blood to spurt everywhere. Wilkins and Stevens stole some liquor, cigarettes, rolling papers, and approximately $450 in cash and checks. They hustled out of the store, and left Allen to die on the floor.

Stanford was seventeen years and four months old when he committed the rape and murder of his twenty-year-old victim. Wilkins was sixteen years and six months old when he stabbed Nancy Allen to death. Stanford and Wilkins were tried as adults and received the death penalty.

Both defendants based their argument on the Court's holdings in *Eddings* and *Thompson,* claiming that no national consensus existed on the minimum age at which capital offenders became death-eligible. Moreover, Stanford and Wilkins argued that juveniles are less aware of their actions and thus less culpable for the crimes they commit, even ones as heinous as those for which they were convicted. Stanford and Wilkins drew several supporting *amici* ranging from the American Bar Association, which by then was on record as opposing the death penalty, to religious groups to psychiatric and children's rights organizations. Kentucky and Missouri were supported by a joint *amicus* brief from fifteen state attorneys general arguing on behalf of death-eligibility for juveniles convicted of capital crimes.

The Court's decision was 5 to 4 to uphold the Kentucky and Missouri laws. Justice Scalia wrote the Court's opinion, which was not joined in full by a majority of the justices. Justice O'Connor wrote a concurring opinion. Justice Brennan, joined by Justices Blackmun, Marshall, and Stevens, dissented.

JUSTICE SCALIA announced the judgment of the Court and delivered the opinion of the Court.

These two consolidated cases require us to decide whether the imposition of capital punishment on an individual for a crime committed at 16 or 17 years of age constitutes cruel and unusual punishment under the Eighth Amendment. . . .

The thrust of both Wilkins' and Stanford's arguments is that imposition of the death penalty on those who were juveniles when they committed their crimes falls within the Eighth Amendment's prohibition against "cruel and unusual punishments." Wilkins would have us define juveniles as individuals 16 years of age and under; Stanford would draw the line at 17. . . .

Neither petitioner asserts that his sentence constitutes one of "those modes or acts of punishment that had been considered cruel and unusual at the time that the Bill of Rights was adopted." Nor could they support such a contention. At that time, the common law set the rebuttable presumption of incapacity to commit any felony at the age of 14, and theoretically permitted capital punishment to be imposed on anyone over the age of 7. In accordance with the standards of this common law tradition, at least 281 offenders under the age of 18 have been executed in this country, and at least 126 under the age of 17.

Thus, petitioners are left to argue that their punishment is contrary to the "evolving standards of decency that mark the progress of a maturing society," *Trop* v. *Dulles* (1958). They are correct in asserting that this Court has "not confined the prohibition embodied in the Eighth Amendment to 'barbarous' methods that were generally outlawed in the 18th century," but instead has interpreted the Amendment "in a flexible and dynamic manner." In determining what standards have "evolved," however, we have looked not to our own conceptions of decency, but to those of modern American society as a whole. As we have said, "Eighth Amendment judgments should not be, or appear to be, merely the subjective views of individual Justices; judgment should be informed by objective factors to the maximum possible extent," *Coker* v. *Georgia* (1977). This approach is dictated both by the language of the Amendment—which proscribes only those punishments that are both "cruel and unusual"—and by the "deference we owe to the decisions of the state legislatures under our federal system," *Gregg* v. *Georgia* (1976).

"[F]irst" among the "'objective indicia that reflect the public attitude toward a given sanction'" are statutes passed by society's elected representatives. Of the 37 States whose laws permit capital punishment, 15 decline to impose it upon 16-year-old offenders and 12 decline to impose it on 17-year-old offenders. This does not establish the degree of national consensus this Court has previously thought sufficient to label a particular punishment cruel and unusual. In invalidating the death penalty for rape of an adult woman, we stressed that Georgia was the sole jurisdiction that authorized such a punishment. In striking down capital punishment for participation in a robbery in which an accomplice takes a life, we emphasized that only eight jurisdictions authorized similar punishment. In finding that the Eighth Amendment precludes execution of the insane, and thus requires an adequate hearing on the issue of sanity, we relied upon (in addition to the common law rule) the fact that "no State in the Union" permitted such punishment. And in striking down a life sentence without parole under a recidivist statute, we stressed that "[i]t appears that [petitioner] was treated more severely than he would have been in any other State." . . .

Wilkins and Stanford argue, however, that even if the laws themselves do not establish a settled consensus, the application of the laws does. That contemporary society views capital punishment of 16- and 17-year-old offenders as inappropriate is demonstrated, they say, by the reluctance of juries to impose, and prosecutors to seek, such sentences. Petitioners are quite correct that a far smaller number of offenders under 18 than over 18 have been sentenced to death in this country. From 1982 through 1988, for example, out of 2,106 total death sentences, only 15 were imposed on individuals who were 16 or under when they committed their crimes, and only 30 on individuals who were 17 at the time of the crime. And it appears that actual executions for crimes committed under age 18 accounted for only about two percent of the total number of executions that occurred between 1642 [492 U.S. 374] and 1986. As Wilkins points out, the last execution of a person who committed a crime under 17 years of age occurred in 1959. These statistics, however, carry little significance. Given the undisputed fact that a far smaller percentage of capital crimes are committed by persons under 18 than over 18, the discrepancy in treatment is much less than might seem. Granted, however, that a substantial discrepancy exists, that does not establish the requisite proposition that the death sentence for offenders under 18 is categorically unacceptable to prosecutors and juries. To the contrary, it is not only possible, but overwhelmingly probable, that the very considerations which induce petitioners and their supporters to believe that death should never be imposed on offenders under 18 cause prosecutors and juries to believe that it should rarely be imposed.

This last point suggests why there is also no relevance to the laws cited by petitioners and their amici which set 18 or more as the legal age for engaging in various activities, ranging from driving to drinking alcoholic beverages to voting. It is, to begin with, absurd to think that one must be mature enough to drive carefully, to drink responsibly, or to vote intelligently, in order to be mature enough to understand that murdering another human being is profoundly wrong, and to conform one's conduct to that most minimal of all civilized standards. But even if the requisite degrees of maturity were comparable, the age statutes in question would still not be relevant. They do not represent a social judgment that all persons under the designated ages are not responsible enough to drive, to drink, or to vote, but at most a judgment that the vast majority are not. These laws set the appropriate ages for the operation of a system that makes its determinations in gross, and that does not conduct individualized maturity tests for each driver, drinker, or voter. The criminal justice system, however, does provide individualized testing. In the realm of capital punishment in particular, "individualized consideration [is] a constitutional requirement," and one of the individualized mitigating factors that sentencers must be permitted to consider is the defendant's age. Twenty-nine States, including both Kentucky and Missouri, have codified this constitutional requirement in laws specifically designating the defendant's age as a mitigating factor in capital cases. Moreover, the determinations required by juvenile transfer statutes to certify a juvenile for trial as an adult ensure individualized consideration of the maturity and moral responsibility of 16- and 17-year-old offenders before they are even held to stand trial as adults. The application of this particularized system to the petitioners can be declared constitutionally inadequate only if there is a consensus, not that 17 or 18 is the age at which most persons, or even almost all persons, achieve sufficient maturity to be held fully responsible for murder; but that 17 or 18 is the age before which no one can reasonably be held fully responsible. What displays society's views on this latter point are not the ages set forth in the generalized system of driving, drinking, and voting laws cited by petitioners and their amici, but the ages at which the States permit their particularized capital punishment systems to be applied.

Having failed to establish a consensus against capital punishment for 16- and 17-year-old offenders through state and federal statutes and the behavior of prosecutors and juries, petitioners seek to demonstrate it through other indicia, including public opinion polls, the views of interest groups, and the positions adopted by various professional associations. We decline the invitation to rest constitutional law upon such uncertain foundations. A revised national consensus so broad, so clear, and so enduring as to justify a permanent prohibition upon all units of democratic government must appear in the operative acts (laws and the application of laws) that the people have approved. . . .

We discern neither a historical nor a modern societal consensus forbidding the imposition of capital punishment on any person who murders at 16 or 17 years of age. Accordingly, we conclude that such punishment does not offend the Eighth Amendment's prohibition against cruel and unusual punishment. . . .

Affirmed.

JUSTICE O'CONNOR, concurring in part and concurring in the judgment.

Last Term, in *Thompson* v. *Oklahoma* (1988), I expressed the view that a criminal defendant who would have been tried as a juvenile under state law, but for the granting of a petition waiving juvenile court jurisdiction, may only be executed for a capital offense if the State's capital punishment statute specifies a minimum age at which the commission of a capital crime can lead to an offender's execution and the defendant had reached that minimum age at the time the crime was committed. As a threshold matter, I indicated that such specificity is not necessary to avoid constitutional problems if it is clear that no national consensus forbids the imposition of capital punishment for crimes committed at such an age. Applying this two-part standard in *Thompson,* I concluded that Oklahoma's imposition of a death sentence on an individual who was 15 years old at the time he committed a capital offense should be set aside. Applying the same standard today, I conclude that the death sentences for capital murder imposed by Missouri and Kentucky on petitioners Wilkins and Stanford respectively should not be set aside, because it is sufficiently clear that no national consensus forbids the imposition of capital punishment on 16- or 17-year-old capital murderers. . . .

I am unable, however, to join the remainder of the plurality's opinion . . . [that] "emphatically reject[s]," the suggestion that, beyond an assessment of the specific enactments of American legislatures, there remains a constitutional obligation imposed upon this Court to judge whether the "'nexus between the punishment imposed and the defendant's blameworthiness'" is proportional. . . . [T]he plurality's opinion specifically rejects as irrelevant to Eighth Amendment considerations state statutes that distinguish juveniles from adults for a variety of other purposes. In my view, this Court does have a constitutional obligation to conduct proportionality analysis. In *Thompson,* I specifically identified age-based statutory classifications as "relevant to Eighth Amendment proportionality analysis." Thus, although I do not believe that these particular cases can be resolved through proportionality analysis, I reject the suggestion that the use of such analysis is improper as a matter of Eighth Amendment jurisprudence.

JUSTICE BRENNAN, with whom JUSTICE MARSHALL, JUSTICE BLACKMUN, and JUSTICE STEVENS join, dissenting.

I believe that to take the life of a person as punishment for a crime committed when below the age of 18 is cruel and unusual, and hence is prohibited by the Eighth Amendment. . . .

Our judgment about the constitutionality of a punishment under the Eighth Amendment is informed, though not determined, by an examination of contemporary attitudes toward the punishment, as evidenced in the actions of legislatures and of juries. The views of organizations with expertise in relevant fields and the choices of governments elsewhere in the world also merit our attention as indicators whether a punishment is acceptable in a civilized society. . . .

The Court's discussion of state laws concerning capital sentencing gives a distorted view of the evidence of contemporary standards that these legislative determinations provide. Currently, 12 of the States whose statutes permit capital punishment specifically mandate that offenders under age 18 not be sentenced to death. When one adds to these 12 States the 15 (including the District of Columbia) in which capital punishment is not authorized at all, it appears that the governments in fully 27 of the States have concluded that no one under 18 should face the death penalty. A further three States explicitly refuse to authorize sentences of death for those who committed their offense when under 17, making a total of 30 States that would not tolerate the execution of petitioner Wilkins. Congress' most recent enactment of a death penalty statute also excludes those under 18.

In 19 States that have a death penalty, no minimum age for capital sentences is set in the death penalty statute. The notion that these States have consciously authorized the execution of juveniles derives from the congruence in those jurisdictions of laws permitting state courts to hand down death sentences, on the one hand, and, on the other, statutes permitting the transfer of offenders under 18 from the juvenile to state court systems for trial in certain circumstances. I would not assume, however, in considering how the States stand on the moral issue that underlies the constitutional question with which we are presented, that a legislature that has never specifically considered the issue has made a conscious moral choice to permit the execution of juveniles. On a matter of such moment that most States have expressed an explicit and contrary judgment, the decisions of legislatures that are only implicit, and that lack the "earmarks of careful consideration that we have required for other kinds of decisions leading to the death penalty," must count for little. I do not suggest, of course, that laws of these States cut against the constitutionality of the juvenile death penalty—only that accuracy demands that the baseline for our deliberations should be that 27 States refuse to authorize a sentence of death in the circumstances of petitioner Stanford's case, and 30 would not permit Wilkins' execution; that 19 States have not squarely faced the question; and that only the few remaining jurisdictions have explicitly set an age below 18 at which a person may be sentenced to death. . . .

There may be exceptional individuals who mature more quickly than their peers, and who might be considered fully responsible for their actions prior to the age of 18, despite their lack of the experience upon which judgment depends. In my view, however, it is not sufficient to accommodate the facts about juveniles that an individual youth's culpability may be taken into account in the decision to transfer him or her from the juvenile to the adult court system for trial, or that a capital sentencing jury is instructed to consider youth and other mitigating factors. I believe that the Eighth Amendment requires that a person who lacks that full degree of responsibility for his or her actions associated with adulthood not be sentenced to death. Hence it is constitutionally inadequate that a juvenile offender's level of responsibility be taken into account only along with a host of other factors that the court or jury may decide outweigh that want of responsibility.

Immaturity that constitutionally should operate as a bar to a disproportionate death sentence does not guarantee that a minor will not be transferred for trial to the adult court system. Rather, the most important considerations in the decision to transfer a juvenile offender are the seriousness of the offense, the extent of prior delinquency, and the response to prior treatment within the juvenile justice system. Psychological, intellectual, and other personal characteristics of juvenile offenders receive little attention at the transfer stage, and cannot account for differences between those transferred and those who remain in the juvenile court system. Nor is an adolescent's lack of full culpability isolated at the sentencing stage as a factor that determinatively bars a death sentence. A jury is free to weigh a juvenile offender's youth and lack of full responsibility against the heinousness of the crime and other aggravating factors—and, finding the aggravating factors weightier, to sentence even the most immature of 16- or 17-year-olds to be killed. By no stretch of the imagination, then, are the transfer and sentencing decisions designed to isolate those juvenile offenders who are exceptionally mature and responsible, and who thus stand out from their peers as a class. . . .

There are strong indications that the execution of juvenile offenders violates contemporary standards of decency: a majority of States decline to permit juveniles to be sentenced to death; imposition of the sentence upon minors is very unusual even in those States that permit it; and respected organizations with expertise in relevant areas regard the execution of juveniles as unacceptable, as does international opinion. These indicators serve to confirm, in my view, my conclusion that the Eighth Amendment prohibits the execution of persons for offenses they committed while below the age of 18, because the death penalty is disproportionate when applied to such young offenders and fails measurably to serve the goals of capital punishment. I dissent.

Only one state, Oklahoma, has executed an individual for a capital crime committed while sixteen years old. The other sixteen individuals executed since *Gregg* for capital crimes committed as juveniles were all seventeen years old when they committed their offenses. Since *Stanford*, fourteen juvenile capital offenders have been executed, compared to three between 1976 and 1989.[33] *Stanford* effectively settled the constitutional debate over the death penalty for juveniles. No serious challenge has since been mounted to the minimum age requirement for death-eligibility in capital cases.

Victim Impact Statements

Throwing further confusion into the procedural dimension of capital punishment law, the Court, soon after rejecting the NAACP LDF's argument in *McCleskey* that race played a critical role in the imposition of the death penalty, ruled that prosecutors could not introduce statements or call witnesses during the sentencing phase of a capital trial attesting to the impact of the crime on loved ones and family. Bare majorities in *Booth* v. *Maryland* (1987) and *South Carolina* v. *Gathers* (1989) held that prosecutors could not introduce *victim impact* evidence during the sentencing phase of capital trials because such evidence was unnecessary to understand the significance of the crime.[34] Defense lawyers argued that victim impact statements were emotional appeals designed to inflame the jury. Proponents of such evidence argued that since defendants could introduce as many mitigating circumstances as they wanted, it was only reasonable that prosecutors should be permitted to do the same. By the late 1980s, a growing movement of victims' rights and assistance organizations, distraught by what they believed was too much emphasis on the rights of violent offenders, had exerted a firm influence in state legislatures and Congress. Despite *Booth* and *Gathers*, lawmakers continued to amend their capital punishment laws to permit victim impact statements and prosecutors continued to use them in capital cases. In *Payne* v. *Tennessee* (1991), the Court revisited the constitutionality of victim impact statements. Rarely does the Court explicitly reconsider recently decided cases, but in *Payne* the justices did just that, a decision that disturbed anti–death penalty groups, which believed that such evidence was inherently prejudicial, and encouraged pro–capital punishment forces, which believed that juries had a right to consider the impact of capital offenses on a victim's family.

Payne v. *Tennessee*

501 U.S. 808 (1991)

On June 27, 1987, Pervis Tyrone Payne went to visit his girlfriend in the small Tennessee town of Millington, expecting that she would have returned home from visiting her mother in Arkansas. Payne made several trips, but never found anyone home. Between trips to his girlfriend's apartment, Payne drove around drinking beer and injecting cocaine. After several failed attempts at finding his girlfriend home, Payne entered the apartment of Charisse Christopher, who lived across the hall with her two small children. Intoxicated on alcohol and drugs, Payne made several sexual advances toward Christopher, who resisted. Payne then became violent, after which Christopher began screaming, "Get out, get out!" A neighbor heard what she later told police was a bloodcurdling scream from Christopher's apartment and called the police. The police arrived to find her and her two-year-old daughter dead of multiple stab wounds. Christopher's son, Nicholas, had also been stabbed several times, but somehow managed to survive.

Payne professed innocence throughout his trial, but a jury found the overwhelming physical evidence introduced against him—fingerprints, blood matches on his body and clothing, eyewitness identification—much more compelling. During the sentencing phase, Payne called his relatives, minister, and girlfriend to the stand to testify to his character and background. The prosecutor, asking for the death penalty, then put Christopher's mother on the stand:

> He [Christopher's son] cries for his mom. He doesn't seem to understand why she doesn't come home. And he cries for his sister Lacie. He comes to me many times during the week and asks me, Grandmama, do you miss my Lacie? And I tell him yes. He says, I'm worried about my Lacie.

The prosecutor introduced the following statement:

> But we do know that Nicholas was alive. And Nicholas was in the same room. Nicholas was still conscious. His eyes were open. He responded to the paramedics. He was able to follow their directions. He was able to hold his intestines in as he was carried to the ambulance. So he knew what happened to his mother and baby sister.
>
> There is nothing you can do to ease the pain of any of the families involved in this case. . . . There is obviously nothing you can do for Charisse and Lacie Jo. But there is something that you can do for Nicholas. Somewhere down the road Nicholas is going to grow up, hopefully. He's going to want to know what happened. And he is going to know what happened to his baby sister and his mother. He is going to want to know what type of justice was done. He is going to want to know what happened. With your verdict, you will provide the answer.

Payne's lawyers contended that the prosecutor's victim impact statements all but ensured their client's fate, later arguing in the courts that such evidence was banned by *Booth* and *Gathers*.

The Court's decision was 6 to 3. Chief Justice Rehnquist delivered the opinion of the Court. Justice O'Connor, joined by Justices White and Kennedy, wrote a concurring opinion. Justice Marshall, joined by Justice Blackmun, dissented. Justice Stevens, joined by Justice Blackmun, also dissented.

CHIEF JUSTICE REHNQUIST delivered the opinion of the Court.

In this case, we reconsider our holdings in *Booth* v. *Maryland* (1987) and *South Carolina* v. *Gathers* (1989) that the Eighth Amendment bars the admission of victim impact evidence during the penalty phase of a capital trial. . . .

Booth and Gathers were based on two premises: that evidence relating to a particular victim or to the harm that a capital defendant causes a victim's family do not in general reflect on the defendant's "blameworthiness," and that only evidence relating to "blameworthiness" is relevant to the capital sentencing decision. However, the assessment of harm caused by the defendant as a result of the crime charged has understandably been an important concern of the criminal law, both in determining the elements of the offense and in determining the appropriate punishment. Thus, two equally blameworthy criminal defendants may be guilty of different offenses solely because their acts cause differing amounts of harm. If a bank robber aims his gun at a guard, pulls the trigger, and kills his target, he may be put to death. If the gun unexpectedly misfires, he may not. His moral guilt in both cases is identical, but his responsibility in the former is greater.

We have held that a State cannot preclude the sentencer from considering "any relevant mitigating evidence" that the defendant proffers in support of a sentence less than death. Thus, we have, as the Court observed in *Booth*, required that the capital defendant be treated as a "'uniquely individual human bein[g].'" But it was never held or even suggested in any of our cases preceding *Booth* that the defendant, entitled as he was to individualized consideration, was to receive that consideration wholly apart from the crime which he had committed. . . .

The *Booth* Court reasoned that victim impact evidence must be excluded because it would be difficult, if not impossible, for the defendant to rebut such evidence without shifting the focus of the sentencing hearing away from the defendant, thus creating a "'mini-trial' on the victim's character." In many cases, the evidence relating to the victim is already before the jury, at least in part because of its relevance at the guilt phase of the trial. But even as to additional evidence admitted at the sentencing phase, the mere fact that, for tactical reasons, it might not be prudent for the defense to rebut victim impact evidence makes the case no different than others in which a party is faced with this sort of a dilemma. As we explained in rejecting the contention that expert testimony on future dangerousness should be excluded from capital trials, "the rules of evidence generally extant at the federal and state levels anticipate that relevant, unprivileged evidence should be admitted and its weight left to the factfinder, who would have the benefit of cross-examination and contrary evidence by the opposing party," *Barefoot* v. *Estelle* (1983).

Payne echoes the concern voiced in Booth's case that the admission of victim impact evidence permits a jury to find that defendants whose victims were assets to their community are more deserving of punishment than those whose victims are perceived to be less worthy. As a general matter, however, victim impact evidence is not offered to encourage comparative judgments of this kind—for instance, that the killer of a hardworking, devoted parent deserves the death penalty, but that the murderer of a reprobate does not. It is designed to show, instead, each victim's "uniqueness as an individual human being," whatever the jury might think the loss to the community resulting from his death might be. The facts of *Gathers* are an excellent illustration of this: the evidence showed that the victim was an out-of-work, mentally handicapped individual, perhaps not, in the eyes of most, a significant contributor to society, but nonetheless a murdered human being.

Under our constitutional system, the primary responsibility for defining crimes against state law, fixing punishments for the commission of these crimes, and establishing procedures for criminal trials rests with the States. The state laws respecting crimes, punishments, and criminal procedure are, of course, subject to the overriding provisions of the United States Constitution. Where the State imposes the death penalty for a particular crime, we have held that the Eighth Amendment imposes special limitations upon that process. . . .

Within the constitutional limitations defined by our cases, the States enjoy their traditional latitude to prescribe the method by which those who commit murder shall be punished. The States remain free, in capital cases, as well as others, to devise new procedures and new remedies to meet felt needs. Victim impact evidence is simply another form or method of informing the sentencing authority about the specific harm caused by the crime in question, evidence of a general type long considered by sentencing authorities. We think the *Booth* Court was wrong in stating that this kind of evidence leads to the arbitrary imposition of the death penalty. In the majority of cases, and in this case, victim impact evidence serves entirely legitimate purposes. In the event that evidence is introduced that is so unduly prejudicial that it renders the trial fundamentally unfair, the Due Process Clause of the Fourteenth Amendment provides a mechanism for relief. Courts have always taken into consideration the harm done by the defendant in imposing sentence, and the evidence adduced in this case was illustrative of the harm caused by Payne's double murder.

We are now of the view that a State may properly conclude that, for the jury to assess meaningfully the defendant's moral culpability and blameworthiness, it should have before it at the sentencing phase evidence of the specific harm caused by the defendant. . . . By turning the victim into a "faceless stranger at the penalty phase of a capital trial," *Booth* deprives the State of the full moral force of its evidence, and may prevent the jury from having before it all the information necessary to determine the proper punishment for a first-degree murder. . . .

Payne and his *amicus* argue that, despite these numerous infirmities in the rule created by *Booth* and *Gathers*, we should adhere to the doctrine of *stare decisis* and stop short of overruling those cases. *Stare decisis* is the preferred course, because it promotes the evenhanded, predictable, and consistent development of legal principles, fosters reliance on judicial decisions, and contributes to the actual and perceived integrity of the judicial process. Adhering to precedent "is usually the wise policy, because, in most matters, it is more important that the applicable rule of law be settled than it be settled right." Nevertheless, when governing decisions are unworkable or are badly reasoned, "this Court has never felt constrained to follow precedent." *Stare decisis* is not an inexorable command; rather, it "is a principle of policy and not a mechanical formula of adherence to the latest decision."

This is particularly true in constitutional cases, because in such cases "correction through legislative action is practically impossible." Considerations in favor of *stare decisis* are at their acme in cases involving property and contract rights, where reliance interests are involved; the opposite is true in cases, such as the present one, involving procedural and evidentiary rules.

Booth and *Gathers* were decided by the narrowest of margins, over spirited dissents challenging the basic underpinnings of those decisions. They have been questioned by Members of the Court in later decisions and have defied consistent application by the lower courts. Reconsidering these decisions now, we conclude, for the reasons heretofore stated, that they were wrongly decided and should be, and now are, overruled.

JUSTICE O'CONNOR, with whom JUSTICE WHITE and JUSTICE KENNEDY join, concurring.

In my view, a State may legitimately determine that victim impact evidence is relevant to a capital sentencing proceeding. A State may decide that the jury, before determining whether a convicted murderer should receive the death penalty, should know the full extent of the harm caused by the crime, including its impact on the victim's family and community. A State may decide also that the jury should see "a quick glimpse of the life petitioner chose to extinguish," to remind the jury that the person whose life was taken was a unique human being. . . .

We do not hold today that victim impact evidence must be admitted, or even that it should be admitted. We hold merely that, if a State decides to permit consideration of this evidence, "the Eighth Amendment erects no per se bar." If, in a particular case, a witness' testimony or a prosecutor's remark so infects the sentencing proceeding as to render it fundamentally unfair, the defendant may seek appropriate relief under the Due Process Clause of the Fourteenth Amendment.

JUSTICE MARSHALL, with whom JUSTICE BLACKMUN joins, dissenting.

Power, not reason, is the new currency of this Court's decision making. Four Terms ago, a five-Justice majority of this Court held that "victim impact" evidence of the type at issue in this case could not constitutionally be introduced during the penalty phase of a capital trial, *Booth* v. *Maryland* (1987). By another 5-4 vote, a majority of this Court rebuffed an attack upon this ruling just two Terms ago, *South Carolina* v. *Gathers* (1989). Nevertheless, having expressly invited respondent to renew the attack, today's majority overrules *Booth* and *Gathers* and credits the dissenting views expressed in those cases. Neither the law nor the facts supporting *Booth* and *Gathers* underwent any change in the last four years. Only the personnel of this Court did.

In dispatching *Booth* and *Gathers* to their graves, today's majority ominously suggests that an even more extensive upheaval of this Court's precedents may be in store. Renouncing this Court's historical commitment to a conception of "the judiciary as a source of impersonal and reasoned judgments," the majority declares itself free to discard any principle of constitutional liberty which was recognized or reaffirmed over the dissenting votes of four Justices and with which five or more Justices now disagree. The implications of this radical new exception to the doctrine of *stare decisis* are staggering. The majority today sends a clear signal that scores of established constitutional liberties are now ripe for reconsideration, thereby inviting the very type of open defiance of our precedents that the majority rewards in this case. Because I believe that this Court owes more to its constitutional precedents in general and to *Booth* and *Gathers* in particular. I dissent. . . .

The overruling of one of this Court's precedents ought to be a matter of great moment and consequence. . . . Consequently, this Court has never departed from precedent without "special justification." Such justifications include the advent of "subsequent changes or development in the law" that undermine a decision's rationale, the need "to bring [a decision] into agreement with experience and with facts newly ascertained," and a showing that a particular precedent has become a "detriment to coherence and consistency in the law."

The majority cannot seriously claim that any of these traditional bases for overruling a precedent applies to *Booth* or *Gathers*. The majority does not suggest that the legal rationale of these decisions has been undercut by changes or developments in doctrine during the last two years. Nor does the majority claim that experience over that period of time has discredited the principle that "any decision to impose the death sentence be, and appear to be, based on reason rather than caprice or emotion," the larger postulate of political morality on which *Booth* and *Gathers* rest. . . .

Th[e] truncation of the Court's duty to stand by its own precedents is astonishing. By limiting full protection of the doctrine of *stare decisis* to "cases involving property and contract rights," the majority sends a clear signal that essentially all decisions implementing the personal liberties protected by the Bill of Rights and the Fourteenth Amendment are open to reexamination. Taking into account the majority's additional criterion for overruling—that a case either was decided or reaffirmed by a 5-4 margin "over spirited dissen[t]"—the continued vitality of literally scores of decisions must be understood to depend on nothing more than the proclivities of the individuals who now comprise a majority of this Court. . . .

In my view, this impoverished conception of *stare decisis* cannot possibly be reconciled with the values that inform the proper judicial function. Contrary to what the majority suggests, *stare decisis* is important not merely because individuals rely on precedent to structure their commercial activity, but because fidelity to precedent is part and parcel of a conception of "the judiciary as a source of impersonal and reasoned judgments." Indeed, this function of *stare decisis* is in many respects even more critical in adjudication involving constitutional liberties than in adjudication involving commercial entitlements. Because enforcement of the Bill of Rights and the Fourteenth Amendment frequently requires this Court to rein in the forces of democratic politics, this Court can legitimately lay claim to compliance with its directives only if the public understands the Court to be implementing "principles . . . founded in the law, rather than in the proclivities of individuals." . . .

Carried to its logical conclusion, the majority's debilitated conception of *stare decisis* would destroy the Court's very capacity to resolve authoritatively the abiding conflicts between those with power and those without. If this Court shows so little respect for its own precedents, it can hardly expect them to be treated more respectfully by the state actors whom these decisions are supposed to bind. By signaling its willingness to give fresh consideration to any constitutional liberty recognized by a 5-4 vote "over spirited dissen[t]," the majority invites state actors to renew the very policies deemed unconstitutional in the hope that this Court may now reverse course, even if it has only recently reaffirmed the constitutional liberty in question.

Today's decision charts an unmistakable course. If the majority's radical reconstruction of the rules for overturning this Court's decisions is to be taken at face value—and the majority offers us no reason why it should not—then the overruling of *Booth* and *Gathers* is but a preview of an even broader and more far-reaching assault upon this Court's precedents. Cast aside today are those condemned to face society's ultimate penalty. Tomorrow's victims may be minorities, women, or the indigent. Inevitably, this campaign to resurrect yesterday's "spirited dissents" will squander the authority and the legitimacy of this Court as a protector of the powerless.

The Contemporary Court and the Death Penalty

Since *Payne*, the Court has continued to decide cases involving the death penalty in favor of supporters of capital punishment. In two cases decided during the same term as *Payne*—*McCleskey* v. *Zant* (1991) and *Coleman* v. *Thompson* (1991) (see Chapter 3)—the Court narrowed considerably the right of death row inmates to file habeas corpus petitions in federal court once a state court has entered a final judgment. In *Zant*, Warren McCleskey, who had failed four years before, in *McCleskey* v. *Kemp*, to persuade the Court that Georgia's death penalty law was carried out in a racially prejudicial manner, lost a separate appeal arguing that he should have the right to seek federal review of a state court judgment upholding the admission of an alleged "coerced" confession.[35] In *Coleman*, the Court rejected the appeal of a death row inmate who sought a review in federal court of his claim that his right to the effective assistance of counsel had been violated.[36] *Zant* and *Coleman* were decided by the same 6-3 majority that had decided *Payne*. In both cases, the Court, taking two different approaches, emphasized the finality of state court judgments involving habeas corpus petitions. Writing for the *Zant* majority, Justice Anthony Kennedy held that state prosecutors could contest any writ of habeas corpus filed after the first one as "abusive" except when an inmate could (1) demonstrate a clear reason for failing to raise the issue earlier and (2) demonstrate that an error from his trial, conviction, or sentencing amounted to "actual prejudice." In *Coleman*, Justice Sandra Day O'Connor held that tightening the rules on habeas petitions was consistent with respect for the position of state courts in the American federal structure.

No current justice on the Court, as of August 2001, has written that the death penalty is unconstitutional per se. Not since 1994, when Justice Harry Blackmun, dissenting from the Court's decision not to hear *Callins* v. *Collins*, wrote that "[f]rom this day forward, I shall no longer tinker with the machinery of death," has a sitting justice concluded that the death penalty cannot, under any circumstance, be administered in a constitutionally fair manner. Recall that Blackmun had joined the dissenters in *Furman* and the majority in *Gregg* upholding the administration of the death penalty. In both cases,

Blackmun wrote of his personal opposition to the death penalty, going so far as to say in *Furman*, "I yield to no one in the depth of my distaste, antipathy, and, indeed, abhorrence, for the death penalty . . . that distaste is buttressed by a belief that capital punishment serves no useful purpose that can be demonstrated." Still, he believed that the Constitution did not prevent the imposition of the death penalty, if administered in accord with due process. Blackmun's change of heart—that the death penalty could never be administered fairly—came during his final term on the Court. By that point he was a minority of one. More consistent with the current majority's approach to the death penalty is Justice Scalia's response to Blackmun's dissent in *Collins*. Wrote Scalia:

> Convictions in opposition to the death penalty are often passionate and deeply held. That would be no excuse for reading them into a Constitution that does not contain them, even if they represented the convictions of a majority of Americans. Much less is there any excuse for using that course to thrust a minority's views upon the people. . . . If the people conclude that . . . brutal deaths may be deterred by capital punishment; indeed, if they merely conclude that justice requires such brutal deaths to be avenged by capital punishment; the creation of false, untextual and unhistorical contradictions within "the Court's Eighth Amendment jurisprudence" should not prevent them.[37]

Since *Collins*, two presidents, Bill Clinton, a Democrat, and George W. Bush, a Republican, have been elected (Clinton, 1996; Bush, 2000) who support the death penalty in capital cases. Neither of President Clinton's two appointments to the Court, Stephen Breyer and Ruth Bader Ginsburg, has thus far given any indication that they believe the death penalty can never be constitutionally applied. While governor of Texas from 1994 to 2000, Bush presided over more executions than any other governor during this same time.[38] Having restated his support for the death penalty during his successful presidential campaign, it is highly unlikely that President Bush will appoint justices who are on record as opposing capital punishment. Although the possibility exists that a sitting justice could change his or her mind on the death penalty, as Justice Blackmun did, it would stretch the boundaries of credibility to suggest that the majority of the current justices will change their minds anytime soon. On this point, *Felker v. Turpin* (1996) is particularly instructive: A unanimous Court upheld the provisions of the federal Antiterrorism and Effective Death Penalty Act of 1996 preventing state prisoners from filing a second (or successive) habeas corpus petition if such a claim failed to present a new issue.

Beyond the Death Penalty: Cruel and Unusual Punishment in Noncapital Cases

Although most discussion of what constitutes cruel and unusual punishment is synonymous with the death penalty, the Court has ruled that this provision of the Eighth Amendment applies to punishments that involve noncapital criminal offenses. In fact, the Court's first decision that explicitly incorporated the guarantee against cruel and unusual punishment into the Fourteenth Amendment, thus making it applicable to the states, came in *Robinson v. California* (1962), a case that had nothing to do with capital punishment. Recall that in *Francis v. Resweber* (1947) (the death penalty case involving the malfunctioning electric chair in Louisiana that opened this chapter), the Court refused to hold that the Cruel and Unusual Punishment Clause applied to the states. *Robinson*, as you will note, involved a very different issue: May a state criminally punish an individual on the basis of social status or condition and not conduct?

Robinson v. California
370 U.S. 660 (1962)

A Los Angeles police officer arrested Lawrence Robinson for violating a California law that made it illegal to "be addicted to the use of narcotics." The arresting officer claimed that on several occasions while on patrol he had observed Robinson under the influence of drugs. The officer later claimed that he had noticed "scar tissue and discoloration on the inside" of Robinson's right arm, and also "what appeared to be numerous needle marks and a scab which was approximately three inches below the crook of the elbow" in the same place. According to the officer, Robinson had also admitted under questioning to the occasional use of narcotics. During his trial, Robinson later denied using drugs or being addicted to them, claiming that the marks on his arm were due to an allergic condition he contracted during military service.

Robinson was convicted and lost a subsequent appeal in the Los Angeles County Superior Court. The United States Supreme Court agreed to hear the case, and focused solely on whether the California law violated the Eighth Amendment's ban on cruel and unusual punishment.

The Court's decision was 6 to 2. Justice Stewart delivered the opinion of the Court. Justices Douglas and Harlan wrote separate concurring opinions. Justices Clark and White wrote separate dissenting opinions. Justice Frankfurter did not participate.

▼▲▼

MR. JUSTICE STEWART delivered the opinion of the Court.

This statute . . . is not one which punishes a person for the use of narcotics, for their purchase, sale or possession, or for antisocial or disorderly behavior resulting from their administration. It is not a law which even purports to provide or require medical treatment. Rather, we deal with a statute which makes the "status" of narcotic addiction a criminal offense, for which the offender may be prosecuted "at any time before he reforms." California has said that a person can be continuously guilty of this offense, whether or not he has ever used or possessed any narcotics within the State, and whether or not he has been guilty of any antisocial behavior there.

It is unlikely that any State at this moment in history would attempt to make it a criminal offense for a person to be mentally ill, or a leper, or to be afflicted with a venereal disease. A State might determine that the general health and welfare require that the victims of these and other human afflictions be dealt with by compulsory treatment, involving quarantine, confinement, or sequestration. But, in the light of contemporary human knowledge, a law which made a criminal offense of such a disease would doubtless be universally thought to be an infliction of cruel and unusual punishment in violation of the Eight and Fourteenth Amendments.

We cannot but consider the statute before us as of the same category. In this Court counsel for the State recognized that narcotic addiction is an illness. Indeed, it is apparently an illness which may be contracted innocently or involuntarily. We hold that a state law which imprisons a person thus afflicted as a criminal, even though he has never touched any narcotic drug within the State or been guilty of any irregular behavior there, inflicts a cruel and unusual punishment in violation of the Fourteenth Amendment. To be sure, imprisonment for ninety days is not, in the abstract, a punishment which is either cruel or unusual. But the question cannot be considered in the abstract. Even one day in prison would be a cruel and unusual punishment for the "crime" of having a common cold.

We are not unmindful that the vicious evils of the narcotics traffic have occasioned the grave concern of government. There are, as we have said, countless fronts on which those evils may be legitimately attacked. We deal in this case only with an individual provision of a particularized local law as it has so far been interpreted by the California courts.

Reversed.

MR. JUSTICE DOUGLAS, concurring.

The impact that an addict has on a community causes alarm and often leads to punitive measures. Those measures are justified when they relate to acts of transgression. But I do not see how under our system being an addict can be punished as a crime. If addicts can be punished for their addiction, then the insane can also be punished for their insanity. Each has a disease and each must be treated as a sick person . . .

We should show . . . discernment respecting drug addiction. The addict is a sick person. He may, of course, be confined for treatment or for the protection of society. Cruel and unusual punishment results not from confinement, but from convicting the addict of a crime. The purpose of 11721 is not to cure, but to penalize. Were the purpose to cure, there would be no need for a mandatory jail term of not less than 90 days. Contrary to my Brother CLARK, I think the means must stand constitutional scrutiny, as well as the end to be achieved. A prosecution for addiction, with its resulting stigma and irreparable damage to the good name of the accused, cannot be justified as a means of protecting society, where a civil commitment would do as well. Indeed, in 5350 of the Welfare and Institutions Code, California has expressly provided for civil proceedings for the commitment of habitual addicts. Section 11721 is, in reality, a direct attempt to punish those the State cannot commit civilly. This prosecution has no relationship to the curing of an illness. Indeed, it cannot, for the prosecution is aimed at penalizing an illness, rather than at providing medical care for it. We would forget the teachings of the Eighth Amendment if we allowed sickness to be made a crime and permitted sick people to be punished for being sick. This age of enlightenment cannot tolerate such barbarous action.

MR. JUSTICE CLARK, dissenting.

Apart from prohibiting specific acts such as the purchase, possession and sale of narcotics, California has taken certain legislative steps in regard to the status of being a narcotic addict—a condition commonly recognized as a threat to the State and to the individual. The Code deals with this problem in realistic stages. . . .

There was no suggestion that the term "narcotic addict" as here used included a person who acted without volition or who had lost the power of self-control. Although the section is penal in appearance—perhaps a carry-over from a less sophisticated approach—its present provisions are quite similar to those for civil commitment and treatment of addicts who have lost the power of self-control, and its present purpose is reflected in a statement which closely follows 11721: "The rehabilitation of narcotic addicts and the prevention of continued addiction to narcotics is a matter of statewide concern."

Where narcotic addiction has progressed beyond the incipient, volitional stage, California provides for commitment of three months to two years in a state hospital. . . .

The majority strikes down the conviction primarily on the grounds that petitioner was denied due process by the imposition of criminal penalties for nothing more than being in a status. This viewpoint is premised upon the theme that 11721 is a "criminal" provision authorizing a punishment, for the majority admits that "a State might establish a program of compulsory treatment for those addicted to narcotics" which "might require periods of involuntary confinement." I submit that California has done exactly that. The majority's error is in instructing the California Legislature that hospitalization is the only treatment for narcotics addiction—that anything less is a punishment denying due process. California has found otherwise after a study which I suggest was more extensive than that conducted by the Court. Even in California's program for hospital commitment of nonvolitional narcotic addicts—which the majority approves—it is recognized that some addicts will not respond to or do not need hospital treatment. As to these persons its provisions are identical to those of 11721—confinement for a period of not less than 90 days. Section 11721 provides this confinement as treatment for the volitional addicts to whom its provisions apply, in addition to parole with frequent tests to detect and prevent further use of drugs. The fact that 11721 might be labeled "criminal" seems irrelevant, not only to the majority's own "treatment" test but to the "concept of ordered liberty" to which the States must attain under the Fourteenth Amendment. The test is the overall purpose and effect of a State's act, and I submit that California's program relative to narcotic addicts—including both the "criminal" and "civil" provisions—is inherently one of treatment and lies well within the power of a State . . .

It is no answer to suggest that we are dealing with an involuntary status and thus penal sanctions will be ineffective and unfair. The section at issue applies only to persons who use narcotics often or even daily but not to the point of losing self-control. When dealing with involuntary addicts California moves only through 5355 of its Welfare Institutions Code which clearly is not penal. Even if it could be argued that 11721 may not be limited to volitional addicts, the petitioner in the instant case undeniably retained the power of self-control and thus to him the statute would be constitutional. Moreover, "status" offenses have long been known and recognized in the criminal law. A ready example is drunkenness, which plainly is as involuntary after addiction to alcohol as is the taking of drugs.

Nor is the conjecture relevant that petitioner may have acquired his habit under lawful circumstances. There was no suggestion by him to this effect at trial, and surely the State need not rebut all possible lawful sources of addiction as part of its prima facie case.

The argument that the statute constitutes a cruel and unusual punishment is governed by the discussion above. Properly construed, the statute provides a treatment rather than a punishment. But even if interpreted as penal, the sanction of incarceration for 3 to 12 months is not unreasonable when applied to a person who has voluntarily placed himself in a condition posing a serious threat to the State. Under either theory, its provisions for 3 to 12 months' confinement can hardly be deemed unreasonable. . . .

Robinson was potentially a far-reaching case. By holding that narcotics addiction was an illness and not a crime, the Court opened the possibility that criminal penalties for other diseases having negative social consequences—alcoholism, for example—were cruel and unusual forms of punishment. Just that issue arose in *Powell* v. *Texas* (1968), where the Court considered whether a Texas law that punished public drunkenness violated the Eighth Amendment.[39] Writing for a 5-4 majority, Justice Thurgood Marshall rejected the argument of Leroy Powell, who claimed that he was powerless to control his drinking because he suffered from "the disease of chronic alcoholism." Marshall distinguished *Robinson* from *Powell*, noting that

> On its face the present case does not fall within that holding, since appellant was convicted, not for being a chronic alcoholic, but for being in public while drunk on a particular occasion. The State of Texas has not sought to punish a mere status, as California did in *Robinson*; nor has it attempted to regulate appellant's behavior in the privacy of his own home. Rather, it has imposed upon appellant a criminal sanction for public behavior which may create substantial health and safety hazards, both for appellant and for members of the general public. . . .
>
> Ultimately . . . the most troubling aspects of this case, were *Robinson* to be extended to meet it, would be the scope and content of what could only be a constitutional doctrine of criminal responsibility. . . .

Was Justice Marshall suggesting that, had the Court found the Texas law unconstitutional, states would have been powerless to mandate criminal punishment for sexual offenders, gamblers, and habitual shoplifters because their behavior is considered by segments of the medical community to have roots in mental illness? Clearly, Marshall was uncomfortable with the idea of the courts becoming responsible for defining what was and what was not criminal behavior. *Powell* drew a constitutional line where it believed *Robinson* had ended, and that was on the question of whether an individual could be punished on the basis of status or a condition. States cannot punish alcoholics or drug addicts for their condition, but they can make them criminally responsible for any behavior that stems from their condition.

More indicative of the Court's recent decisions involving the Cruel and Unusual Punishment Clause's application to noncapital offenses is *Harmelin* v. *Michigan* (1991), which involved an Eighth Amendment "proportionality" challenge to a Michigan drug possession law that was then the nation's most severe. In two cases decided before *Harmelin, Rummel* v. *Estelle* (1980) and *Solem* v. *Helm* (1983), the Court had issued somewhat conflicting opinions on the centrality of "proportionality" as a major theme of the Cruel and Unusual Punishment Clause.[40] In *Rummel*, a 5-4 Court upheld a Texas law that sentenced three-time felony offenders to life imprisonment, regardless of the severity of their offenses. In *Solem*, however, the Court, again divided 5 to 4, struck down as unconstitutional a sentence that sent Jerry Helm to prison for life for writing a bad check in the amount of $100. Although Helm had six nonviolent offenses on his criminal record, the Court nonetheless concluded that the life sentence in that case was disproportionate to the offense.

Harmelin revived the debate over whether the Cruel and Unusual Punishment Clause includes a proportionality requirement. Note that Justice Scalia's opinion for the Court upholding a sentence of life imprisonment without parole for cocaine possession did not garner a majority for his conclusion that the Cruel and Unusual Punishment Clause did not require any consideration of proportionality between crime and punishment in noncapital cases. Only Chief Justice Rehnquist agreed with Scalia on this point. Justice White, normally a reliable vote to uphold crime control measures, vigorously dissented in *Harmelin*. Who do you believe makes the better point about proportionality as a constitutional requirement, Scalia or White? Do you believe that states should be free to impose such sentences as mandatory life imprisonment without parole if the criminal offense is not violent or sufficiently threatening to public safety? What should be the proper boundaries in such cases?

Harmelin v. *Michigan*

501 U.S. 957 (1991)

Harmelin was convicted of violating a Michigan drug law that mandated life imprisonment without parole for possessing over 650 grams of cocaine. He claimed his sentence was unconstitutional for two reasons. First, Harmelin claimed that life imprisonment without parole was significantly disproportionate to the crime he had committed. Second, he claimed that the sentencing judge was required to impose the penalty without being able to consider the particular circumstances of the crime and Harmelin's background. The Michigan courts rejected his contention that the sentence was cruel and unusual punishment in violation of the Eighth Amendment.

Justice Scalia delivered the judgment of the Court. Four Justices joined Section IV of Scalia's opinion and agreed that the Michigan law did not violate the Eighth Amendment. Only Chief Justice Rehnquist joined Parts I, II, and III of Scalia's opinion. Justice White, joined by Justices Blackmun and Stevens, filed a dissenting opinion.

Justice Marshall filed a dissenting opinion. Justice Stevens, joined by Justice Blackmun, also dissented.

▼▲▼

JUSTICE SCALIA announced the judgment of the Court and delivered the opinion of the Court with respect to Part IV, and an opinion with respect to Parts I, II, and III, in which THE CHIEF JUSTICE joins.

Petitioner claims that his sentence is unconstitutionally "cruel and unusual" for two reasons: first, because it is "significantly disproportionate" to the crime he committed; second, because the sentencing judge was statutorily required to impose it, without taking into account the particularized circumstances of the crime and of the criminal. . . .

I

The Eighth Amendment, which applies against the States by virtue of the Fourteenth Amendment, *Robinson* v. *California* (1962), provides: "Excessive bail shall not be required, nor excessive fines imposed, nor cruel and unusual punishments inflicted." In *Rummel* v. *Estelle* (1980), we held that it did not constitute "cruel and unusual punishment" to impose a life sentence, under a recidivist statute, upon a defendant who had been convicted, successively, of fraudulent use of a credit card to obtain $80 worth of goods or services, passing a forged check in the amount of $28.36, and obtaining $120.75 by false pretenses. We said that "one could argue without fear of contradiction by any decision of this Court that for crimes concededly classified and classifiable as felonies, that is, as punishable by significant terms of imprisonment in a state penitentiary, the length of the sentence actually imposed is purely a matter of legislative prerogative." We specifically rejected the proposition . . . that unconstitutional disproportionality could be established by weighing three factors: (1) gravity of the offense compared to severity of the penalty, (2) penalties imposed within the same jurisdiction for similar crimes, and (3) penalties imposed in other jurisdictions for the same offense. A footnote in the opinion, however, said: "This is not to say that a proportionality principle would not come into play in the extreme example mentioned by the dissent, . . . if a legislature made overtime parking a felony punishable by life imprisonment." . . .

Solem v. *Helm* (1983) set aside under the Eighth Amendment, because it was disproportionate, a sentence of life imprisonment without possibility of parole, imposed under a South Dakota recidivist statute for successive offenses that included three convictions of third-degree burglary, one of obtaining money by false pretenses, one of grand larceny, one of third-offense driving while intoxicated, and one of writing a "no account" check with intent to defraud. In the *Solem* account, *Weems* no longer involved punishment of a "unique nature," but was the "leading case," exemplifying the "general principle of proportionality," which was "deeply rooted and frequently repeated in common-law jurisprudence," had been embodied in the English Bill of Rights "in language that was later adopted in the Eighth Amendment," and had been "recognized explicitly in this Court for almost a century." . . .

It should be apparent from the above discussion that our 5-to-4 decision eight years ago in *Solem* was scarcely the expression of clear and well-accepted constitutional law. We have long recognized, of course, that the doctrine of *stare decisis* is less rigid in its application to constitutional precedents, see *Payne* v. *Tennessee* (1991) . . . and we think that to be especially true of a constitutional precedent that is both recent and in apparent tension with other decisions. Accordingly, we have addressed anew, and in greater detail, the question whether the Eighth Amendment contains a proportionality guarantee—with particular attention to the background of the Eighth Amendment (which *Solem* discussed in only two pages), and to the understanding of the Eighth Amendment before the end of the 19th century. We conclude from this examination that *Solem* was simply wrong; the Eighth Amendment contains no proportionality guarantee. . . .

II

. . . *Solem* found relevant [three factors] to the proportionality determination: (1) the inherent gravity of the offense, (2) the sentences imposed for similarly grave offenses in the same jurisdiction, and (3) sentences imposed for the same crime in other jurisdictions. As to the first factor: of course some offenses, involving violent harm to human beings, will always and everywhere be regarded as serious, but that is only half the equation. The issue is what else should be regarded to be as serious as these offenses, or even to be more serious than some of them. On that point, judging by the statutes that Americans have enacted, there is enormous variation—even within a given age, not to mention across the many generations ruled by the Bill of Rights. . . .

III

The first holding of this Court unqualifiedly applying a requirement of proportionality to criminal penalties was issued 185 years after the Eighth Amendment was adopted. In *Coker* v. *Georgia,* the Court held that, because of the disproportionality, it was a violation of the

Cruel and Unusual Punishments Clause to impose capital punishment for rape of an adult woman. Five years later, in *Enmund* v. *Florida* (1982), we held that it violates the Eighth Amendment, because of disproportionality, to impose the death penalty upon a participant in a felony that results in murder, without any inquiry into the participant's intent to kill. *Rummel* treated this line of authority as an aspect of our death penalty jurisprudence, rather than a generalizable aspect of Eighth Amendment law. We think that is an accurate explanation, and we reassert it. Proportionality review is one of several respects in which we have held that "death is different," and have imposed protections that the Constitution nowhere else provides. We would leave it there, but will not extend it further.

IV

Petitioner claims that his sentence violates the Eighth Amendment for a reason in addition to its alleged disproportionality. He argues that it is "cruel and unusual" to impose a mandatory sentence of such severity, without any consideration of so-called mitigating factors such as, in his case, the fact that he had no prior felony convictions. He apparently contends that the Eighth Amendment requires Michigan to create a sentencing scheme whereby life in prison without possibility of parole is simply the most severe of a range of available penalties that the sentencer may impose after hearing evidence in mitigation and aggravation.

As our earlier discussion should make clear, this claim has no support in the text and history of the Eighth Amendment. Severe, mandatory penalties may be cruel, but they are not unusual in the constitutional sense, having been employed in various forms throughout our Nation's history. As noted earlier, mandatory death sentences abounded in our first Penal Code. They were also common in the several States—both at the time of the founding and throughout the 19th century. There can be no serious contention, then, that a sentence which is not otherwise cruel and unusual becomes so simply because it is "mandatory." . . .

It is true that petitioner's sentence is unique in that it is the second most severe known to the law; but life imprisonment with possibility of parole is also unique in that it is the third most severe. And if petitioner's sentence forecloses some "flexible techniques" for later reducing his sentence, it does not foreclose all of them, since there remain the possibilities of retroactive legislative reduction and executive clemency. In some cases, moreover, there will be negligible difference between life without parole and other sentences of imprisonment—for example, a life sentence with eligibility for parole after 20 years, or even a lengthy term sentence without eligibility for parole, given to a 65-year-old man. But even where the difference is the greatest, it cannot be compared with death. We have drawn the line of required individualized sentencing at capital cases, and see no basis for extending it further.

The judgment of the Michigan Court of Appeals is
Affirmed.

JUSTICE WHITE, with whom JUSTICE BLACKMUN and JUSTICE STEVENS join, dissenting.

The language of the [Eighth] Amendment does not refer to proportionality in so many words, but it does forbid "excessive" fines, a restraint that suggests that a determination of excessiveness should be based at least in part on whether the fine imposed is disproportionate to the crime committed. Nor would it be unreasonable to conclude that it would be both cruel and unusual to punish overtime parking by life imprisonment, or more generally, to impose any punishment that is grossly disproportionate to the offense for which the defendant has been convicted. . . .

Not only is it undeniable that our cases have construed the Eighth Amendment to embody a proportionality component, but it is also evident that none of the Court's cases suggest that such a construction is impermissible. Indeed, *Rummel* v. *Estelle* (1980), the holding of which JUSTICE SCALIA does not question, itself recognized that the Eighth Amendment contains a proportionality requirement, for it did not question *Coker* and indicated that the proportionality principle would come into play in some extreme, nonfelony cases. . . .

What is more, the Court's jurisprudence concerning the scope of the prohibition against cruel and unusual punishments has long understood the limitations of a purely historical analysis, *Trop* v. *Dulles* (1958). Thus, "this Court has 'not confined the prohibition embodied in the Eighth Amendment to "barbarous" methods that were generally outlawed in the 18th century,' but instead has interpreted the Amendment 'in a flexible and dynamic manner,'" *Stanford* v. *Kentucky* (1989), quoting *Gregg* v. *Georgia* (1976). . . .

The Court therefore has recognized that a punishment may violate the Eighth Amendment if it is contrary to the "evolving standards of decency that mark the progress of a maturing society." In evaluating a punishment under this test, "we have looked not to our own conceptions of decency, but to those of modern American society as a whole" in determining what standards have "evolved," and thus have focused not on "the subjective views of individual Justices," but on "objective factors to the maximum possible extent." It is this type of objective factor which forms the basis for the tripartite proportionality analysis set forth in *Solem*. . . .

Petitioner, a first-time offender, was convicted of possession of 672 grams of cocaine. The statute under which he was convicted . . . provides that a person who knowingly or intentionally possesses any of various narcotics, including cocaine, "[w]hich is in an amount of 650 grams or more of any mixture containing that controlled substance is guilty of a felony and shall be imprisoned for life." No particular degree of drug purity is required for a conviction. Other statutes make clear that an individual convicted of possessing this quantity of drugs is not eligible for parole. A related statute . . . which was enacted at the same time as the statute under which petitioner was convicted, mandates the same penalty of life imprisonment without possibility of parole for someone who "manufacture[s], deliver[s], or possess[es] with intent to manufacture or deliver" 650 grams or more of a narcotic mixture. There is no room for judicial discretion in the imposition of the life sentence upon conviction. The asserted purpose of the legislative enactment of these statutes was to "'stem drug traffic'" and reach "'drug dealers.'" . . .

Drugs are without doubt a serious societal problem. To justify such a harsh mandatory penalty as that imposed here, however, the offense should be one which will always warrant that punishment. Mere possession of drugs—even in such a large quantity—is not so serious an offense that it will always warrant, much less mandate, life imprisonment without possibility of parole. Unlike crimes directed against the persons and property of others, possession of drugs affects the criminal who uses the drugs most directly. The ripple effect on society caused by possession of drugs, through related crimes, lost productivity, health problems, and the like is often not the direct consequence of possession, but of the resulting addiction, something which this Court held in *Robinson* v. *California* [1962] cannot be made a crime. . . .

[T]here is no death penalty in Michigan; consequently, life without parole, the punishment mandated here, is the harshest penalty available. It is reserved for three crimes: first-degree murder, manufacture, distribution, or possession with intent to manufacture or distribute 650 grams or more of narcotics; and possession of 650 grams or more of narcotics. Crimes directed against the persons and property of others—such as second-degree murder, and armed robbery—do not carry such a harsh mandatory sentence, although they do provide for the possibility of a life sentence in the exercise of judicial discretion. It is clear that petitioner "has been treated in the same manner as, or more severely than, criminals who have committed far more serious crimes."

The third factor set forth in *Solem* examines "the sentences imposed for commission of the same crime in other jurisdictions." . . . No other jurisdiction imposes a punishment nearly as severe as Michigan's for possession of the amount of drugs at issue here. Of the remaining 49 States, only Alabama provides for a mandatory sentence of life imprisonment without possibility of parole for a first-time drug offender, and then only when a defendant possesses 10 kilograms or more of cocaine. Possession of the amount of cocaine at issue here would subject an Alabama defendant to a mandatory minimum sentence of only five years in prison. Even under the Federal Sentencing Guidelines, with all relevant enhancements, petitioner's sentence would barely exceed 10 years. Thus, "[i]t appears that [petitioner] was treated more severely than he would have been in any other State." Indeed, the fact that no other jurisdiction provides such a severe, mandatory penalty for possession of this quantity of drugs is enough to establish "the degree of national consensus this Court has previously thought sufficient to label a particular punishment cruel and unusual."

Application of *Solem*'s proportionality analysis leaves no doubt that the Michigan statute at issue fails constitutional muster. The statutorily mandated penalty of life without possibility of parole for possession of narcotics is unconstitutionally disproportionate in that it violates the Eighth Amendment's prohibition against cruel and unusual punishment. Consequently, I would reverse the decision of the Michigan Court of Appeals.

JUSTICE STEVENS, with whom JUSTICE BLACKMUN joins, dissenting.

The severity of the sentence that Michigan has mandated for the crime of possession of more than 650 grams of cocaine, whether diluted or undiluted, does not place the sentence in the same category as capital punishment. I remain convinced that Justice Stewart correctly characterized the penalty of death as "unique" because of "its absolute renunciation of all that is embodied in our concept of humanity," *Furman* v. *Georgia* [1972] (Stewart, J., concurring). Nevertheless, a mandatory sentence of life imprisonment without the possibility of parole does share one important characteristic of a death sentence: The offender will never regain his freedom. Because such a sentence does not even purport to serve a rehabilitative function, the sentence must rest on a rational determination that the punished "criminal conduct is so atrocious that society's interest in deterrence and retribution wholly outweighs any considerations of reform or rehabilitation of the perpetrator." Serious as this defendant's crime was, I believe it is irrational to conclude that every similar offender is wholly incorrigible.

The death sentences that were at issue and invalidated

in *Furman* were "cruel and unusual in the same way that being struck by lightning is cruel and unusual." In my opinion the imposition of a life sentence without possibility of parole on this petitioner is equally capricious. As JUSTICE WHITE has pointed out, under the Federal Sentencing Guidelines, with all relevant enhancements, petitioner's sentence would barely exceed 10 years. In most States, the period of incarceration for a first offender like petitioner would be substantially shorter. No jurisdiction except Michigan has concluded that the offense belongs in a category where reform and rehabilitation are considered totally unattainable. Accordingly, the notion that this sentence satisfies any meaningful requirement of proportionality is itself both cruel and unusual.

I respectfully dissent.

Although the Court did not say it, *Harmelin* suggests that the Cruel and Unusual Punishment Clause has very little application outside the death penalty. Certainly, *Harmelin* ensures that the "three strikes and you're out laws" mandating life sentences for repeat offenders that were passed by Congress and numerous state legislatures in the 1980s and 1990s are in no constitutional jeopardy. In *Hudson* v. *McMillian* (1992), the Court did hold that a prison inmate who had been severely beaten by two corrections officers was entitled to protection from such behavior under the Eighth Amendment.[41] But *Hudson* is an exception in the Court's more recent approach to noncapital punishment that has emphasized deference to sentencing authorities. Scalia's opinion in *Harmelin* rejecting a proportionality component in the Cruel and Unusual Punishment Clause did not carry the day, but it is fair to say that the Court is not prepared to second-guess the crime control measures enacted by Congress and the states, no matter how strong the argument is that a particular punishment does not fit the crime.

FOR FURTHER READING

Baldus, David, George Woodruff, and Charles Pulaski. *Equal Justice and the Death Penalty.* Boston: Northeastern University Press, 1990.

Bedau, Hugo Adam, ed. *The Death Penalty in America: Current Controversies.* New York: Oxford University Press, 1998.

Burns, Walter. *For Capital Punishment.* New York: Basic Books, 1979.

Cabana, Donald A. *Death at Midnight: The Confession of an Executioner.* Boston: Northeastern University Press, 1996.

Epstein, Lee, and Joseph F. Kobylka. *The Supreme Court and Legal Change: Abortion and the Death Penalty.* Chapel Hill: University of North Carolina Press, 1992.

Johnson, Robert. *Death Work: A Study in Modern Execution Process.* New York: Wadsworth, 1997.

Mello, Michael A. *Dead Wrong.* Madison: University of Wisconsin Press, 1998.

Meltsner, Michael. *Cruel and Unusual Punishment: The Supreme Court and Capital Punishment.* New York: Random House, 1973.

Prejean, Helen. *Dead Man Walking: An Eyewitness Account of the Death Penalty in the United States.* New York: Vintage Books, 1996.

Prettyman, E. Barrett. *Death and the Supreme Court.* New York: Harcourt, Brace & World, 1961.

Sarat, Austin, ed. *The Killing State: Capital Punishment in Law, Politics, and Culture.* New York: Oxford University Press, 1998.

———. *When the State Kills: Capital Punishment and the American Condition.* Princeton, N.J.: Princeton University Press, 2001.

10 The Right to Privacy

By her eighteenth birthday, Carrie Buck had experienced more personal difficulties than most people do in an entire lifetime. She had been born to a mother who had been in and out of mental institutions and described by the mental health authorities of the state of Virginia as "feeble-minded, worthless, maritally unworthy, shiftless and ignorant." Carrie had spent time in several foster homes, where she did not always receive the most attentive and loving care. In 1924, after struggling to perform even menial jobs, Carrie joined her mother at the Virginia State Colony for Epileptics and Feeble-Minded after the state determined that she, too, was "feeble-minded" and a burden to society. Carrie had given birth to a baby girl shortly after she turned seventeen, one that state mental authorities described as an "illegitimate feeble-minded child." Fate promised to deal an even more uncomfortable hand to Carrie: In March 1924, Virginia had passed a law that permitted state mental health authorities to sterilize "mental defectives" if those authorities concluded that such persons would become an menace to society if released from care and allowed to procreate. Later that year, Carrie unsuccessfully contended the state's decision to sterilize her before a state health board and in the Virginia courts.

On appeal, Carrie was represented by Irving Whitehead, a former director of the state mental health colony. As it turned out, Whitehead was close friends with Aubrey Strode, the Virginia state senator who had written the sterilization law. After obliging Carrie's request to appeal the decision to the United States Supreme Court, Whitehead put together a half-hearted, eight-page brief on her behalf. In contrast, Strode offered a forty-five-page brief in defense of the law, complete with citations to scientific authorities. The state's position was consistent with the emergent eugenics movement of the Progressive era. Eugenics was rooted in the belief that it was possible to create a better society by eliminating the transmission of bad genes from generation to generation. One way to do that within humanitarian boundaries, argued its proponents, was to sterilize society's "mental defectives" in a compassionate, properly supervised manner.

Strode's arguments found a receptive audience on the Court. Writing for an 8-1 majority, Justice Oliver Wendell Holmes, commenting on Carrie Buck's unfortunate background, wrote, "It is better for all the world if instead of waiting to execute degenerate offspring for crime, or to let them starve for their imbecility, society can prevent those who are manifestly unfit from continuing their kind. The principle that sustains compulsory vaccination is broad enough to cover cutting the Fallopian tubes. Three generations of imbeciles are enough."[1] By modern standards, this is an astonishing statement, especially coming from Holmes, widely considered one the greatest figures in American law. But it quite accurately reflected Holmes's own sentiments on the human condition and, as strange as it might seem now, elite opinion more generally. For Holmes, however, the issue in *Buck* v. *Bell* (1927) was not his own distaste for the less fortunate, but rather the idea that Carrie Buck had some abstract right to bodily integrity anchored in the Constitution that protected her against a law such as Virginia's.

Holmes rejected Carrie's claim that the Due Process Clause of the Fourteenth Amendment afforded her such a right, just he had argued in *Lochner* v. *New York* (1905) (Volume 1, Chapter 9) that the same constitutional provision did not include a fundamental right to "liberty of contract" protecting business owners from government regulation intended to promote the public welfare.[2] In *Lochner,* the Court struck down the New York Bakeshop Law of 1897, which limited the maximum number of hours that bakers could work per day and per week. The Court ruled that the law offered "no reasonable ground for interfering with the liberty of person or the right of free contract" between employer and employee. Economic markets, as the Court understood them in *Lochner,* simply existed in some kind of natural state, and were not the product of political choices protected by law. Dissenting, Holmes wrote that "[t]his case is decided upon an economic theory which a large part of the country does not entertain. If it were a question whether I agreed with that theory, I should desire to study it further and long before making up my mind. But I do not conceive that to be my duty, because I strongly believe that my agreement or disagreement has nothing to do with right of the majority to embody their opinions in law." Holmes then turned his attention to the idea that the Constitution authorized judges to create rights, such as "liberty of contract," not specifically enumerated or understood as part of the nation's tradition:

> [A] Constitution . . . is made for people of fundamentally differing views, and the accident of our finding certain opinions natural and familiar, or novel, and even shocking, ought not to conclude our judgment upon the question whether statutes embodying them conflict with the Constitution of the United States.
>
> General propositions do not decide concrete cases. The decision will depend on a judgment of intuition more subtle than any articulate major premise. But I think that the proposition just stated, if it is accepted, will carry us far toward the end. Every opinion tends to become a law. I think that the word 'liberty,' in the Fourteenth Amendment, is perverted when it is held to prevent the natural outcome of a dominant opinion, unless it can be said that a rational and fair man necessarily would admit that the statute proposed would infringe fundamental principles as they have been understood by the traditions of our people and our law.[3]

Holmes rejected the notion that the Due Process Clause protected a substantive right to "liberty of contract," and he viewed with equal disdain the idea that it protected other rights without a recognized place in the American constitutional tradition. Even though Holmes was a social Darwinist who detested "do-gooders" and their desire to tinker with the "natural order of things," he remained convinced that "the people" had the right to experiment with solutions to social and economic problems as they saw fit. Or, as he once told Harlan Fiske Stone, an unwavering ally of Holmes during the seven years they served on the Court together: "When the people . . . want to do something that I can't find anything in the Constitution expressly forbidding them to do, I say, whether I like it or not, 'Goddamit, let 'em do it.'"[4]

Just as Holmes believed that the New York legislature had acted reasonably in limiting the number of hours bakers could work, he also concluded that nothing in the Constitution prohibited Virginia from carrying out its program of eugenic sterilization. Noting that the law included "very careful provisions by which the act protects the patients from possible abuse," Holmes concluded that Virginia had met the only requirement at issue in Carrie Buck's challenge. And that requirement was whether the state had complied with the procedural guarantees of the Due Process Clause. Holmes's opinion in *Buck* is his most heavily criticized, as much for its steely-eyed cold-heartedness as for its logical reasoning, but it was entirely consistent with his stance on *substantive* due process claims. Give judges the opportunity to roam the Constitution at will, reasoned Holmes, and they will interpret it to suit their own personal prejudices, subverting democracy in the process by preventing the right of dominant opinion to become law.

After *Buck,* numerous states followed Virginia's lead, enacting laws that permitted them to sterilize mental patients afflicted with "insanity" or "imbecility," or who possessed any "defective" trait that might place future generations at risk. In Virginia alone, over 8,300 people were sterilized between 1924 and 1972, when the state discontinued the practice. Many of those sterilized were never informed of the procedure. Fifty years after *Buck,* investigative reporting and scholarly research into Carrie Buck's case revealed some alarming information about the circumstances of her confinement and sterilization.

Carrie, in turns out, had been raped by a prominent—and married—Virginia doctor for whom she once worked as a housekeeper. Well-connected to the authorities who ran the state's mental health colony, Carrie's assailant arranged to have her sent away to have her baby where no one would ever discover the true circumstances of her pregnancy. As far as the public record was concerned, Carrie was a mentally retarded woman who was incapable of understanding her own sexuality, scoring as a nine-year-old on the Binet-Simon I.Q. test. That part of the story was also fabricated. Carrie was not a "mental defective" or "imbecile," as Justice Holmes described her. Like her mother, Emma, Carrie was a woman of slightly below-average intelligence from a lower-class background. Carrie's daughter, Vivian, was a healthy baby girl of normal intelligence who had the misfortune of being born to a socially upright married man with enough political influence to seek an effective and scientifically well-respected cover for his actions.

Dr. Alberty S. Priddy, the physician who led the crusade on behalf of the Virginia sterilization law, was later honored by Adolf Hitler's Nazi Germany, which enacted its "Race Hygiene" law based in large part on his work and with his assistance. None of this, of course, was known to Holmes or the seven other justices who joined him in *Buck*. By the time of *Buck*, Holmes had, for twenty years, watched the Court distort the Due Process Clause on behalf of a "liberty of contract" right that prevented legislatures from responding to the social and economic ills of the day. Holmes was willing to accept the record in Carrie Buck's case, as he had been willing to accept the record of the New York legislature in *Lochner*. By all accounts, the record in *Buck* seemed reasonable and well-informed.[5]

Justice Holmes's dissent in *Lochner* is considered by many legal scholars his most important contribution to American constitutional development during his service on the Court. As legal scholar Richard Posner has commented, Holmes, in *Lochner*, "created the modern theory of federalism, the theory of judicial self-restraint . . . and the idea of the 'living Constitution'—the idea that the Constitution should be construed flexibly, liberally, rather than strictly, narrowly."[6] But Holmes's commitment to judicial deference in cases involving economic rights also had consequences in cases raising delicate and intimate matters of personal privacy such as *Buck* v. *Bell*. Had Holmes demonstrated the same skepticism toward the Virginia legislature's invasive eugenics law as he did toward political majorities that sought to limit free speech rights (see Capter 4), the law of personal privacy might have taken an entirely different course. Having folded Carrie Buck's claim to a right of "bodily integrity" into what he viewed as the illegitimate doctrine of economic substantive due process, Holmes successfully set aside any meaningful discussion of whether the Constitution protected a fundamental right to personal privacy.

The *Lochner* era lasted until the Constitutional Revolution of 1937, which rejected the conception of *laissez faire* that had dominated the Court's approach to cases involving economic and ownership rights. But the notion that *Lochner* represented a distortion of the Due Process Clause that went completely uncorrected until the late 1930s is a bit of a misconception. After *Lochner*, the Court also held that the Due Process Clause protected the right of public schools to offer foreign language instruction and, separately, the right of parents to send their children to private schools. In *Meyer* v. *Nebraska* (1923), the Court invalidated a Nebraska law, enacted in 1919 as an emergency measure to guard against subversion by America's World War I enemies, that prohibited its public schools from offering instruction in any foreign language to students below the eighth grade. Justice James McReynolds concluded that the Due Process Clause protected the right "generally to enjoy those privileges long recognized at common law as essential to the orderly pursuit of happiness by free men," even though he could point to no specific textual provision securing such privileges. The Court noted that "the American people have always regarded education and acquisition of knowledge as matters of supreme importance which should be diligently promoted."[7]

Two years later, the Court ruled in *Pierce* v. *Society of Sisters* (1925) that the Due Process Clause permitted parents to establish and send their children to private parochial schools. In overturning a 1922 Oregon law that required all children between the ages of eight and sixteen to attend public schools, the Court, with Justice McReynolds again writing for the majority, concluded that "the fundamental theory of liberty . . . excludes any general power of the State to standardize its children by forcing them to accept instruction from public teachers only." Such a law, concluded the Court, "unreasonably interferes with the liberty of parents and guardians to direct the upbringing and education of children under their control."[8] Again, the Court relied upon an abstract conception of the "liberty" provision of the Due Process Clause, in a sense arguing that it protected rights so fundamental to human existence that no constitutional specification was required.

Justice Holmes dissented in *Meyer,* arguing that the state had a perfectly reasonable interest in promoting English as the nation's common language, but joined the Court's unanimous opinion in *Pierce* upholding the *fundamental* but unspecified right of parents to direct the education of their children. What was it that led Holmes, the Court's most articulate voice against substantive due process, to conclude that state legislatures had the right to prohibit public schools from teaching foreign languages, but no such power to compel parents to send their children to public schools? Perhaps the answer lies in Holmes's dissent in *Lochner:* "General propositions do not decide concrete cases. The decision will depend on a judgment of intuition more subtle than any articulate major premise." In other words, judicial detachment from the substance of legislation is not always possible or, as Louis Brandeis, the Court's first major exponent of sociological jurisprudence, argued, even desirable.

Sometimes judges must eschew abstract theories of constitutional interpretation for a more pragmatic approach. This was evident in the legal realism of Holmes and Brandeis, discussed in Chapter 2, and a central point of Holmes's *Lochner* dissent: Courts should not strike down legislation "unless it can be said that a rational and fair man necessarily would admit that the statute proposed would infringe fundamental principles as they have been understood by the traditions of our people and our law." But no precise formula exists to tell judges the difference between legislation that is reasonable and that which is arbitrary and inconsistent with "the traditions of our people and our law." Giving meaning to the "liberties" protected by the Due Process Clause is a much more subjective enterprise than even Holmes was willing to admit.

Buck, much more so than *Meyer* and *Pierce,* raised the sort of issue that dominates contemporary discussion of the right to privacy, a liberty the Court has since concluded is protected by the Due Process Clause of the Fourteenth Amendment. The Court did not treat the right of parents to control the education of their children—the common theme running through *Meyer* and *Pierce*—as one anchored in a right to privacy, but as one closely tied to other fundamental rights protected by the Constitution. *Pierce,* for example, also raised issues that went directly to the guarantees protected by the Free Exercise Clause of the First Amendment—specifically, the right of churches to establish their own parochial schools. The Oregon law struck down in *Pierce* was the product of a successful campaign led by the Ku Klux Klan and various fraternal and civic groups that shared the Klan's anti-Catholic bias. Although only one of the two schools that brought suit against the Oregon law was religious, the Court weighed the implications for religious freedom quite heavily. In fact, many scholars today consider *Pierce* the Court's first major interpretation of the scope of religious freedom protected by the Free Exercise Clause.[9]

By raising eugenic sterilization as a violation of her right to "bodily integrity," Carrie Buck offered a distinctly personal claim to a right of privacy that differed from the liberties the Court said were protected by the Due Process Clause in *Meyer* and *Pierce.* As such, Carrie Buck's case foreshadowed such future conflicts over the right to purchase and use birth control, the right to abortion, the right to sexual privacy, and the right to die, the issues with which the right to personal privacy is now most closely associated. The Court has never overruled *Buck,* but, as we shall see, it has recognized a right to privacy originating in the Due Process Clause of the Fourteenth Amendment broad enough to encompass many of the rights described above. In doing so, the Court has engaged in a vigorous internal debate about the constitutional origins of the right to privacy. The Court's privacy decisions have also spurred an intense public debate that continues to have a major presence in the nation's courtrooms and legislatures, particularly since *Roe* v. *Wade* (1973), the decision that established a constitutional right to abortion.

This chapter will examine the struggle to establish a right to personal privacy, the Court's major decisions in such areas as abortion, marital relations, and sexual autonomy, and, most recently and no less controversial, the right to refuse unwanted medical treatment and the right to physician-assisted suicide. We will also give considerable attention to the forces that have shaped the dynamics of this litigation and the broader social and political consequences of the Court's right to privacy decisions.

Establishing a Right of Personal Privacy

Until the late nineteenth century, any discussion of a constitutional right to privacy centered on property and places, not people. In 1888, Thomas M. Cooley, the legal theorist whose book *Constitutional Limitations* (1868) emerged as the single most influential argument on behalf of the laissez-faire conception of the Due Process Clause, coined the phrase that later became synonymous with the notion that privacy was a personal right: "The right to one's person may be said to be a right of complete immunity—to be let alone."[10] Two years later, Louis Brandeis, then a successful Boston trial lawyer, and his law partner, Samuel Warren, published a highly influential article that took Cooley's key point and developed it an additional major step. Noting that "political, social, and economic changes entail the recognition of new rights," Brandeis and Warren argued that "the private life, habits, acts, and relations of an individual" deserved legal protection. What motivated Brandeis and Warren to write their article was not a desire to protect the right to abortion or some other "private . . . relations of an individual," but to establish a legal argument to allow individuals to sue for invasive reporting and commentary by the news media. Unauthorized invasion of one's "general right to privacy for thoughts, emotions, and sensations," Brandeis and Warren argued, violated a fundamental right of personal liberty. Most critically for the development of modern privacy doctrine, this violation amounted to a form of personal injury and thus a legal wrong.[11]

By the time Brandeis joined the Court in 1916, the idea that privacy extended beyond property and places to individuals had gained considerable acceptance within the legal profession. Several state courts had endorsed the Brandeis/Warren concept in decisions favoring plaintiffs who brought invasion of privacy lawsuits against companies that had used plaintiffs' likenesses or published information about them without their permission. The Georgia Supreme Court, for example, concluded that "[e]ach person has a liberty of privacy derived from natural law."[12] This trend continued throughout the 1920s, with Brandeis offering the most succinct explanation of his position on personal privacy in *Olmstead* v. *United States* (1928) (see Chapter 7). Dissenting from the Court's ruling upholding warrantless electronic surveillance by federal law enforcement agents, Brandeis wrote that "the makers of our Constitution . . . conferred, as against the Government, the right to be let alone—the most comprehensive of rights and the right most valued by civilized men."[13] Although Brandeis was writing firmly within the context of the Fourth Amendment's prohibition against unreasonable searches and seizures, his *Olmstead* dissent is considered by many his most complete statement on privacy as an inherently personal right that deserved constitutional protection.

Fourteen years later, the Court revisited the issue of state-mandated sterlization, this time for individuals convicted of two or more crimes of "moral terpitude." Unlike in *Buck,* the Court in *Skinner* v. *Oklahoma* (1942) concluded that sterilization served no legitimate societal purpose. And while the Court did not reach the question of whether compulsory sterilization violated the privacy rights of individuals, Justice William O. Douglas did make explicit reference to marriage and procreation as two of civilization's most "fundamental" rights. Note, however, where Douglas centered the constitutional protection for these rights, and the response it drew from Chief Justice Harlan Fiske Stone and Justice Robert Jackson.

Skinner v. *Oklahoma*

316 U.S. 535 (1942)

Arthur Skinner never met Louis Brandeis and, as a professional thief, probably did not know anyone who had. But the Court's decision to declare Oklahoma's Habitual Criminal Sterilization Act of 1935 unconstitutional, and thus spare Skinner the fate that had befallen Carrie Buck, represented the first forceful application of Brandeis's contention that the Constitution afforded a right to a privacy of the most personal and intimate sort. After three convictions in eight years for theft and armed robbery, including one for stealing chickens, Skinner was facing proceedings by Oklahoma's attorney general to have him sterilized. By the narrowest of margins, the Oklahoma Supreme Court upheld a lower court ruling ordering Skinner to undergo a vasectomy.

In 1942, America was still largely ignorant of Nazi Germany's campaign to exterminate European Jews, homosexuals, Jehovah's Witnesses, gypsies, and others who did not fit into the Nazis' conception of the "master race." But the Court was not, as Douglas's careful but unstated reference to Hitler made clear. In 1946, after World War II, Justice Jackson took leave from the Court to serve as the chief counsel for the United States at the Nuremberg Trials, where he learned first-hand of the evils of the Holocaust, including the eugenic experiments of Nazi doctors.

The Court's opinion was unanimous. Justice Douglas delivered the opinion of the Court. Chief Justice Stone and Justice Jackson filed separate concurring opinions.

▼▲▼

MR. JUSTICE DOUGLAS delivered the opinion of the Court.

This case touches a sensitive and important area of human rights. Oklahoma deprives certain individuals of a right which is basic to the perpetuation of a race—the right to have offspring. . . .

Several objections to the constitutionality of the Act have been pressed upon us. It is urged that the Act cannot be sustained as an exercise of the police power, in view of the state of scientific authorities respecting inheritability of criminal traits. It is argued that due process is lacking because, under this Act, unlike the Act upheld in *Buck* v. *Bell* (1927), the defendant is given no opportunity to be heard on the issue as to whether he is the probable potential parent of socially undesirable offspring. It is also suggested that the Act is penal in character, and that the sterilization provided for is cruel and unusual punishment and violative of the Fourteenth Amendment. We pass those points without intimating an opinion on them, for there is a feature of the Act which clearly condemns it. That is its failure to meet the requirements of the equal protection clause of the Fourteenth Amendment.

We do not stop to point out all of the inequalities in this Act. A few examples will suffice. In Oklahoma, grand larceny is a felony. Larceny is grand larceny when the property taken exceeds $20 in value. Embezzlement is punishable "in the manner prescribed for feloniously stealing property of the value of that embezzled. Hence, he who embezzles property worth more than $20 is guilty of a felony. A clerk who appropriates over $20 from his employer's till and a stranger who steals the same amount are thus both guilty of felonies. If the latter repeats his act and is convicted three times, he may be sterilized. But the clerk is not subject to the pains and penalties of the Act no matter how large his embezzlements nor how frequent his convictions. A person who enters a chicken coop and steals chickens commits a felony, and he may be sterilized if he is thrice convicted. If, however, he is a bailee of the property and fraudulently appropriates it, he is an embezzler. Hence, no matter how habitual his proclivities for embezzlement are, and no matter how often his conviction, he may not be sterilized. Thus, the nature of the two crimes is intrinsically the same, and they are punishable in the same manner. . . . There may be larceny by fraud, rather than embezzlement, even where the owner of the personal property delivers it to the defendant, if the latter has, at that time, "a fraudulent intention to make use of the possession as a means of converting such property to his own use, and does so convert it." If the fraudulent intent occurs later, and the defendant converts the property, he is guilty of embezzlement. Whether a particular act is larceny by fraud or embezzlement thus turns not on the intrinsic quality of the act, but on when the felonious intent arose—a question for the jury under appropriate instructions.

It was stated in *Buck* that the claim that state legislation violates the equal protection clause of the Fourteenth Amendment is "the usual last resort of constitutional arguments." Under our constitutional system, the States, in determining the reach and scope of particular legislation, need not provide "abstract symmetry." They may mark and set apart the classes and types of problems according to the needs and as dictated or suggested by experience. . . .

[T]he instant legislation runs afoul of the equal protection clause, though we give Oklahoma that large deference which the rule of the foregoing cases requires. We are dealing here with legislation which involves one of the basic civil rights of man. Marriage and procreation are fundamental to the very existence and survival of the race. The power to sterilize, if exercised, may have subtle, far-reaching and devastating effects. In evil or reckless hands, it can cause races or types which are inimical to the dominant group to wither and disappear. There is no redemption for the individual whom the law touches. Any experiment which the State conducts is to his irreparable injury. He is forever deprived of a basic liberty. We mention these matters not to reexamine the scope of the police power of the States. We advert to them merely in emphasis of our view that strict scrutiny of the classification which a State makes in a sterilization law is essential, lest unwittingly, or otherwise, invidious discriminations are made against groups or types of individuals in violation of the constitutional guaranty of just and equal laws. The guaranty of "equal protection of the laws is a pledge of the protection of equal laws." When the law lays an unequal hand on those who have committed intrinsically the same quality of offense and sterilizes one and not the other, it has made as invidious a discrimination as if it had selected a particular race or nationality for oppressive treatment. Sterilization of those who have thrice committed grand larceny, with immunity for those who are embezzlers, is a clear, pointed, unmistakable discrimination. Oklahoma makes no attempt to say that he who commits larceny by trespass or trick or fraud has biologically inheritable traits which he who commits embezzlement lacks. Oklahoma's line between larceny by fraud and embezzlement is determined, as we have noted, "with reference to the time when the fraudulent intent to convert the property to the taker's own use" arises. We have not the slightest basis for inferring that that line has any significance in eugenics, nor that the inheritability of criminal traits follows the neat legal distinctions which the law has marked between those two offenses. In terms of fines and imprisonment, the crimes of larceny and embezzlement rate the same under the Oklahoma code. Only when it comes to sterilization are the pains and penalties of the law different. The equal protection clause would indeed be a formula of empty words if such conspicuously artificial lines could be drawn. In *Buck*, the Virginia statute was upheld though it applied only to feeble-minded persons in institutions of the State. But it was pointed out that, "so far as the operations enable those who otherwise must be kept confined to be returned to the world, and thus open the asylum to others, the equality aimed at will be more nearly reached." Here there is no such saving feature. Embezzlers are forever free. Those who steal or take in other ways are not. . . .

Reversed.

MR. CHIEF JUSTICE STONE, concurring.

I concur in the result, but I am not persuaded that we are aided in reaching it by recourse to the equal protection clause.

If Oklahoma may resort generally to the sterilization of criminals on the assumption that their propensities are transmissible to future generations by inheritance, I seriously doubt that the equal protection clause requires it to apply the measure to all criminals in the first instance, or to none.

Moreover, if we must presume that the legislature knows—what science has been unable to ascertain—that the criminal tendencies of any class of habitual offenders are transmissible regardless of the varying mental characteristics of its individuals, I should suppose that we must likewise presume that the legislature, in its wisdom, knows that the criminal tendencies of some classes of offenders are more likely to be transmitted than those of others. And so I think the real question we have to consider is not one of equal protection, but whether the wholesale condemnation of a class to such an invasion of personal liberty, without opportunity to any individual to show that his is not the type of case which would justify resort to it, satisfies the demands of due process.

JUSTICE JACKSON, concurring.

I also think the present plan to sterilize the individual in pursuit of a eugenic plan to eliminate from the race characteristics that are only vaguely identified and which, in our present state of knowledge, are uncertain as to transmissibility presents other constitutional questions of gravity. This Court has sustained such an experiment with respect to an imbecile, a person with definite and observable characteristics, where the condition had persisted through three generations and afforded grounds for the belief that it was transmissible, and would continue to manifest itself in generations to come.

There are limits to the extent to which a legislatively represented majority may conduct biological experiments at the expense of the dignity and personality and natural powers of a minority—even those who have been guilty of what the majority define as crimes. But this Act falls down before reaching this problem, which I mention only to avoid the implication that such a question may not exist because not discussed. On it, I would also reserve judgment.

By exempting "white collar" crimes such as fraud and embezzlement from the class of crimes that made convicted felons eligible for sterilization, the Court held that the Oklahoma law violated the Equal Protection Clause. Perhaps the specter of reviving *Lochner*-era substantive due process so shortly after the Constitutional Revolution of 1937 discouraged Douglas from considering criminal sterilization as a violation of personal liberties protected by the Due Process Clause. Nonetheless, the Court's unanimous decision that marriage and procreation were substantive liberties protected by the

Constitution was something the Court had not recognized up until *Skinner.* But the Court left open a question that would soon come to dominate the debate over a constitutional right to personal privacy: Did the Constitution also include a right not to have children? And if so, where was such a right found in the Constitution?

"An Uncommonly Silly Law": Contraception, the Constitution, and *Griswold*

In 1821, Connecticut became the first state to outlaw the distribution of birth control information and contraceptives. By the late nineteenth century, twenty-two states had followed suit, taking their lead from the congressional passage of the federal "Comstock Act" of 1873, named for its sponsor, Anthony Comstock, a New York–based, self-proclaimed crusader against "smut and obscenity." The Comstock Act banned the transmission over state lines or through the United States mail of any material deemed pornographic and obscene, including "any drug, medicine, article or thing designed, adapted, or intended for preventing contraception," as well any "abortion device." Deterred by the fact that distribution of birth control information meant near-certain arrest under federal law or perhaps one of the states' "little Comstock laws," public discussion of contraception and family planning went underground. It would resurface in the early 1900s, after women active in various Progressive-era reform groups insisted on bringing the issue into the public light.[14]

Margaret Sanger, a former nurse turned social activist, emerged as the first major national leader of the movement to legalize birth control and promote family planning awareness. In 1914, Sanger began publishing her own monthly magazine, *The Woman Rebel,* to advocate the right of women to control their reproductive choices. That same year, federal authorities charged her with violating the Comstock Act, which was just what Sanger wanted. She believed that an arrest would allow her to challenge the anticontraception law's enforcement. Rather than stand trial, Sanger left the United States for Europe, where the discussion and use of birth control was permitted. During Sanger's absence, her husband was arrested for publishing a pamphlet Sanger had written after her arrest. Bill Sanger was convicted of violating the Comstock Act and sentenced to thirty days in jail, an event that drew national attention and helped mobilize hundreds of people into the birth control movement. Around this time, several well-to-do women in New York and Connecticut formed the first national birth control advocacy group, the National Birth Control League (NBCL). Soon after, Sanger formed her own group, the American Birth Control League (ABCL), which was considered by physicians the more mainstream of the two organizations, focusing only on birth control and not, like the NBCL, on other women's issues such as voting rights and various social welfare causes.[15]

In 1936, the Second Circuit Court of Appeals in New York ruled, in *United States* v. *One Package,* that the Comstock Act could not be applied if the result was to obstruct legitimate public health goals. Attorney General Homer Cummings announced that the Department of Justice would not appeal *One Package,* thus bringing to an end any federal prohibition on the dissemination of birth control information and contraceptive devices. Margaret Sanger, who had been instrumental in putting together the organization that brought the lawsuit against the Comstock Act, called *One Package* "an emancipation proclamation to the motherhood of America." Shortly thereafter, Sanger and other birth control proponents received even more good news: The American Medical Association (AMA), an early nineteenth-century advocate of anticontraception laws, announced that it now supported "the dissemination and teaching of the best methods of birth control." And although public opinion had firmly moved behind the idea of legal contraception—by the late 1930s several polls taken of American women showed that roughly three-quarters of those polled supported the birth control movement—many activists were concerned that the term "birth control" was too controversial. In 1942, the ABCL and NBCL combined to form the Planned Parenthood Federation of America, which soon became synonymous with family planning education and, later, the movement in support of contraception and abortion rights.[16]

Planned Parenthood, working closely with state and local activists, continued to press for the legislative repeal of restrictive state birth control laws. By the late 1950s, only Massachusetts and Connecticut continued to enforce their anticontraception laws, a reflection of the political strength of the Roman Catholic Church in those states. In 1942, Massachusetts voters overwhelming rejected a proposed statewide referendum that would have permitted doctors to prescribe birth control to married women, a result heavily influenced by the Church's advertising campaign that featured the slogan: "Birth Control Is Against God's Law—Vote NO." On several occasions the Connecticut chapter of Planned Parenthood mounted legal challenges against the state's birth control laws, two of which reached the Supreme Court.[17] In *Tileston* v. *Ullman* (1943), a unanimous Court dismissed Planned Parenthood's claim that Connecticut's birth control law, which had been revised in 1879 to prohibit the actual *use* of any contraceptive device, violated the Due Process Clause of the Fourteenth Amendment. The law posed no threat to the physicians who challenged it; rather, it was their patients who experienced any deprivation of life or liberty stemming from the law's enforcement. Any challenge to the state's law would have to come from persons *affected* by the law.[18]

In *Poe* v. *Ullman* (1961), Planned Parenthood fell a single vote shy of persuading the Court to overturn Connecticut's birth control law. Writing for the five-member majority, Justice Felix Frankfurter concluded there was "no realistic fear of prosecution" of anyone who violated the law's prohibition on contraceptive use. There was no point, Frankfurter reasoned, in making the Court an "umpire to debates concerning harmless, empty shadows." Concurring, Justice William Brennan agreed with Frankfurter that Planned Parenthood had failed to present a "real and substantial controversy." But he made the subtle observation that future litigation might concern itself with the law's impact on the right of birth control clinics to open and operate. Should physicians find themselves prosecuted for practicing family planning, the Court could then "decide the constitutional questions urged upon us."[19]

In dissent, Justice John Harlan offered a very different view of the constitutional problems posed by the Connecticut law. Concluding that Planned Parenthood had "presented a very pressing claim for constitutional protection" against the "utter novelty" of Connecticut's "obnoxiously intrusive" law, Harlan wrote that the Due Process Clause protected the private realm of family life: "It is difficult to imagine what is more private or more intimate than a husband and wife's marital relations." Turning to the conception of personal privacy raised by Brandeis, Harlan concluded that the protection afforded by the Due Process Clause's protection against "arbitrary impositions and purposeless restraints" included the right to privacy in the home. That right went beyond the Fourth Amendment's guarantee against unreasonable searches and seizures to include "unreasonable intrusion of whatever character." Such a right of privacy, Harlan acknowledged, was

> [n]ot an absolute. Thus, I would not suggest that adultery, homosexuality, fornication and incest are immune from criminal enquiry, however privately practiced. [But] the intimacy of husband and wife is necessarily an essential and accepted feature of the institution of marriage, an institution which the State not only must allow, but which always and in every age it has fostered and protected. It is one thing when the State exerts its power either to forbid extramarital sexuality altogether, or to say who may marry, but it is quite another when, having acknowledged a marriage and the intimacies inherent in it, it undertakes to regulate by means of the criminal law the details of that intimacy.[20]

Planned Parenthood and its lawyers were not terribly surprised that the Court refused to rule on the constitutionality of the Connecticut law. But *Poe* encouraged them on two levels. First, Brennan's concurring opinion offered an alternative litigation strategy easily available to Planned Parenthood—one that demonstrated how the law interfered with an individual's right to open a family planning clinic and dispense contraception in accord with sound medical advice. Second, Harlan's dissent suggesting that extending the right to privacy beyond property and places to persons, coming as it did from one of the Court's more conservative justices, might persuade a majority to adopt a personal right of privacy that reached marital intimacy. Four years later, in *Griswold* v. *Connecticut* (1965), the Court again considered the constitutionality of the Connecticut birth control law, this time with dramatically different results.

Griswold v. *Connecticut*

381 U.S. 489 (1965)

P. T. Barnum is best remembered for giving America the traveling three-ring circus and other forms of peerless spectacle that forever cemented his legacy as one of the all-time great promoters of public entertainment. And while there is no proof that Barnum ever uttered the phrase, "there's a sucker born every minute," another of his legacies stands beyond any doubt. Barnum, a Bridgeport, Connecticut, native, also served in the Connecticut legislature. In 1879, Barnum, a vocal supporter of Anthony Comstock's "public morals" campaign, introduced legislation prohibiting the "use of any drug, medicine, article, or instrument" for the purpose of preventing contraception, which passed with strong majorities. This law stood undisturbed for over eighty years.

In November 1961, Planned Parenthood opened a family planning clinic in New Haven, a heavily Catholic city that was also the home to the Yale University Medical School. The organization did so knowing that such an audacious move might lead to arrests. And within a week, the New Haven police arrested Estelle Griswold, the Connecticut chapter's executive director who ran the clinic, for providing contraceptives to a married couple. Griswold was happy to see the police, as she welcomed the chance to begin the chain of events that would challenge the constitutionality of the 1879 law. Just to make sure she left no stone unturned, Griswold offered the police copies of Planned Parenthood's literature, which described how physicians fit women with diaphragms, and outlined the advantages of different forms of contraception.

Griswold's arrest satisfied Justice Brennan's qualification in *Poe*, so there was little doubt in the minds of her lawyers that the Court would decide her case on the merits. But Thomas Emerson, who represented Griswold, decided not to follow Harlan's emphasis on marital privacy as a right protected by the Due Process Clause, but the argument laid out by Justice William Douglas, who also dissented in *Poe*. Douglas believed that the right to privacy emanated from the "totality of the constitutional scheme under which we live," a position that foreshadowed his majority opinion in *Griswold*. Emerson and Douglas were close personal friends and shared a passion for liberal political causes. They were, however, quite different in temperament, with Emerson's reserved, detached nature a distinct counterpoint to Douglas's bold, extroverted personality.

Emerson argued that Connecticut's law violated the Due Process Clause of the Fourteenth Amendment and the composite of privacy rights protected by the Third, Fourth, Fifth, and Ninth Amendments. In sum, he asserted that the Connecticut law unconstitutionally intruded upon the sanctity of the home and the sexual intimacies of the marital relationship.

The Court's decision was 7 to 2. Justice Douglas delivered the opinion of the Court. Justices Harlan and White filed separate concurring opinions. Justice Goldberg, joined by Chief Justice Warren and Justice Brennan, also wrote a concurring opinion. Justice Black, joined by Justice Stewart, dissented. Justice Stewart wrote a separate dissent, which Justice Black joined.

For discussion of *Griswold* as a controversy in constitutional interpretation, see Chapter 2. Justice Goldberg's and Justice Brennan's opinions can be found there.

▼▲▼

MR. JUSTICE DOUGLAS delivered the opinion of the Court.

. . . [W]e are met with a wide range of questions that implicate the Due Process Clause of the Fourteenth Amendment. Overtones of some arguments suggest that *Lochner* v. *New York* should be our guide. But we decline that invitation, as we did in *West Coast Hotel* v. *Parrish* (1937) [and several subsequent cases raising substantive due process claims]. We do not sit as a super-legislature to determine the wisdom, need, and propriety of laws that touch economic problems, business affairs, or social conditions. This law, however, operates directly on an intimate relation of husband and wife and their physician's role in one aspect of that relation.

The association of people is not mentioned in the Constitution nor in the Bill of Rights. The right to educate a child in a school of the parents' choice—whether public or private or parochial—is also not mentioned. Nor is the right to study any particular subject or any foreign language. Yet the First Amendment has been construed to include certain of those rights.

. . . [T]he State may not, consistently with the spirit of the First Amendment, contract the spectrum of available knowledge. The right of freedom of speech and press includes not only the right to utter or to print, but the right to distribute, the right to receive, the right to read and freedom of inquiry, freedom of thought, and freedom to teach—indeed, the freedom of the entire university community. Without those peripheral rights, the specific rights would be less secure. And so we reaffirm the principle of the *Pierce* and the *Meyer* cases. . . .

[T]he First Amendment has a penumbra where privacy is protected from governmental intrusion. In like context, we have protected forms of "association" that are not political in the customary sense, but pertain to the social, legal, and economic benefit of the members.

. . . [Previous] cases suggest that specific guarantees in the Bill of Rights have penumbras, formed by emanations from those guarantees that help give them life and substance. Various guarantees create zones of privacy. The right of association contained in the penumbra of the First Amendment is one, as we have seen. The Third Amendment, in its prohibition against the quartering of soldiers "in any house" in time of peace without the consent of the owner, is another facet of that privacy. The Fourth Amendment explicitly affirms the "right of the people to be secure in their persons, houses, papers, and effects, against unreasonable searches and seizures." The Fifth Amendment, in its Self-Incrimination Clause, enables the citizen to create a zone of privacy which government may not force him to surrender to his detriment. The Ninth Amendment provides: "The enumeration in the Constitution, of certain rights, shall not be construed to deny or disparage others retained by the people." . . .

We have had many controversies over these penumbral rights of "privacy and repose," *Skinner* v. *Oklahoma* (1942). These cases bear witness that the right of privacy which presses for recognition here is a legitimate one.

The present case, then, concerns a relationship lying within the zone of privacy created by several fundamental constitutional guarantees. And it concerns a law which, in forbidding the use of contraceptives, rather than regulating their manufacture or sale, seeks to achieve its goals by means having a maximum destructive impact upon that relationship. Such a law cannot stand in light of the familiar principle, so often applied by this Court, that a "governmental purpose to control or prevent activities constitutionally subject to state regulation may not be achieved by means which sweep unnecessarily broadly and thereby invade the area of protected freedoms." Would we allow the police to search the sacred precincts of marital bedrooms for telltale signs of the use of contraceptives? The very idea is repulsive to the notions of privacy surrounding the marriage relationship.

We deal with a right of privacy older than the Bill of Rights—older than our political parties, older than our school system. Marriage is a coming together for better or for worse, hopefully enduring, and intimate to the degree of being sacred. It is an association that promotes a way of life, not causes; a harmony in living, not political faiths; a bilateral loyalty, not commercial or social projects. Yet it is an association for as noble a purpose as any involved in our prior decisions.

Reversed.

MR. JUSTICE GOLDBERG, with whom THE CHIEF JUSTICE and MR. JUSTICE BRENNAN join, concurring.

(For Justice Goldberg's concurring opinion, see Chapter 2, pp. 33–34.)

MR. JUSTICE HARLAN, concurring in the judgment.

I fully agree with the judgment of reversal, but find myself unable to join the Court's opinion. The reason is that it seems to me to evince an approach to this case very much like that taken by my Brothers BLACK and STEWART in dissent, namely: the Due Process Clause of the Fourteenth Amendment does not touch this Connecticut statute unless the enactment is found to violate some right assured by the letter or penumbra of the Bill of Rights.

In other words, what I find implicit in the Court's opinion is that the "incorporation" doctrine may be used to restrict the reach of Fourteenth Amendment Due Process. For me, this is just as unacceptable constitutional doctrine as is the use of the "incorporation" approach to impose upon the States all the requirements of the Bill of Rights as found in the provisions of the first eight amendments and in the decisions of this Court interpreting them. . . .

In my view, the proper constitutional inquiry in this case is whether this Connecticut statute infringes the Due Process Clause of the Fourteenth Amendment because the enactment violates basic values "implicit in the concept of ordered liberty," *Palko* v. *Connecticut* (1937). For reasons stated at length in my dissenting opinion in *Poe* v. *Ullman,* I believe that it does. While the relevant inquiry may be aided by resort to one or more of the provisions of the Bill of Rights, it is not dependent on them or any of their radiations. The Due Process Clause of the Fourteenth Amendment stands, in my opinion, on its own bottom.

A further observation seems in order respecting the justification of my Brothers BLACK and STEWART for their "incorporation" approach to this case. Their approach does not rest on historical reasons, which are, of course, wholly lacking, . . . but on the thesis that, by limiting the content of the Due Process Clause of the Fourteenth Amendment to the protection of rights which can be found elsewhere in the Constitution, in this instance, in the Bill of Rights, judges will thus be confined to "interpretation" of specific constitutional provisions, and will thereby be restrained from introducing their own notions of constitutional right and wrong into the "vague contours of the Due Process Clause." While I could not more heartily agree that judicial "self-restraint" is an indispensable ingredient of sound constitutional adjudication, I do submit that the formula suggested for achieving it is more hollow than real. "Specific" provisions of the Constitution, no less than "due process," lend themselves as readily to "personal" interpretations by judges whose constitutional outlook is simply to keep the Constitution in supposed "tune with the times." . . .

Judicial self-restraint will not, I suggest, be brought about in the "due process" area by the historically unfounded incorporation formula long advanced by my Brother BLACK, and now in part espoused by my Brother STEWART. It will be achieved in this area, as in other constitutional areas, only by continual insistence upon respect for the teachings of history, solid recognition of the basic values that underlie our society, and wise appreciation of the great roles that the doctrines of federalism and separation of powers have played in establishing and preserving American freedoms. Adherence to these principles will not, of course, obviate all constitutional differences of opinion among judges, nor should it. Their continued recognition will, however, go farther toward keeping most judges from roaming at large in the constitutional field than will the interpolation into the Constitution of an artificial and largely illusory restriction on the content of the Due Process Clause.

MR. JUSTICE BLACK, with whom MR. JUSTICE STEWART joins, dissenting.

(For Justice Black's dissenting opinion, see Chapter 2, pp. 34–35)

MR. JUSTICE STEWART, with whom MR. JUSTICE BLACK joins, dissenting.

Since 1879, Connecticut has had on its books a law which forbids the use of contraceptives by anyone. I think this is an uncommonly silly law. As a practical matter, the law is obviously unenforceable, except in the oblique context of the present case. As a philosophical matter, I believe the use of contraceptives in the relationship of marriage should be left to personal and private choice, based upon each individual's moral, ethical, and religious beliefs. As a matter of social policy, I think professional counsel about methods of birth control should be available to all, so that each individual's choice can be meaningfully made. But we are not asked in this case to say whether we think this law is unwise, or even asinine. We are asked to hold that it violates the United States Constitution. And that I cannot do.

In the course of its opinion, the Court refers to no less than six Amendments to the Constitution: the First, the Third, the Fourth, the Fifth, the Ninth, and the Fourteenth. But the Court does not say which of these Amendments, if any, it thinks is infringed by this Connecticut law.

We are told that the Due Process Clause of the Fourteenth Amendment is not, as such, the "guide" in this case. With that much, I agree. There is no claim that this law, duly enacted by the Connecticut Legislature, is unconstitutionally vague. There is no claim that the appellants were denied any of the elements of procedural due process at their trial, so as to make their convictions constitutionally invalid. And, as the Court says, the day has long passed since the Due Process Clause was regarded as a proper instrument for determining "the wisdom, need, and propriety" of state laws. . . .

What provision of the Constitution, then, does make this state law invalid? The Court says it is the right of privacy "created by several fundamental constitutional guarantees." With all deference, I can find no such general right of privacy in the Bill of Rights, in any other part of the Constitution, or in any case ever before decided by this Court.

▼▲▼

Note that Douglas did not mention *Skinner* in his opinion, or anchor the Court's newly minted privacy right in the Due Process Clause of the Fourteenth Amendment. Mostly likely, Douglas purposely avoided relying solely on the Due Process Clause to avoid dredging up the ghosts of *Lochner*-era substantive due process. "We do not sit as a super-legislature," wrote Chief Justice Charles Evans Hughes in *West Coast Hotel* v. *Parrish* (1937), the case that brought down the curtain on *Lochner,* "to determine the wisdom, need, and propriety of laws that touch economic problems, business affairs, or social conditions."[21] Douglas and Black were the only justices who were actually connected to the Constitutional Revolution of 1937, having been appointed to the Court in the late 1930s in no small part because of their support for the New Deal.[22] Black, however, could not join the Court's opinion, having written as recently as two years earlier that substantive due process was a "discredited" doctrine, regardless of how it was applied.[23]

Justice Harlan found Douglas's constitutional arithmetic unnecessary. For him, marital privacy was so fundamental to the concept of liberty that no other explanation was required beyond that which he laid out in his *Poe* dissent. Justice Goldberg was also quite critical of Douglas's approach. Relying on the Ninth Amendment, Goldberg argued that marital privacy was certainly among the rights "retained by the people" under the Constitution. Dissenting, Justice Stewart conceded that Connecticut's was an "uncommonly silly law," but that nothing in the Constitution prohibited the enactment of laws that were "unwise, even asinine," barring a specific prohibition to the contrary.

Not a single justice defended Connecticut's law as public policy. The Court's differences in *Griswold* were over constitutional interpretation: how and where to center rights in the Constitution and whether the power to do so should rest with the courts or the legislatures. In establishing the constitutional right to personal privacy, however, the Court opened up many more questions about the scope of this new guarantee. Did the Court's emphasis in *Griswold* on the private nature of the marital relationship mean that states were within their rights to forbid unmarried persons from receiving birth control information and using contraceptives? What power remained with the state to regulate the freedom to marry? Did the right to prevent unwanted pregnancies through the use of contraceptives encompass a right broad enough to include the right to abortion?

The Court addressed the first two questions rather quickly. In *Loving* v. *Virginia* (1967), a unanimous Court invalidated one of the last remaining relics of the Black Codes on the Southern law books, the ban on interracial marriage. Turning to *Skinner*, Chief Justice Warren noted that "marriage is one of the 'basic civil rights of man.'" Warren concluded that the Virginia law violated the Due Process and Equal Protection Clauses of the Fourteenth Amendment. Note that Warren did not mention *Griswold*, following the *Meyer-Pierce-Skinner* line of reasoning instead. But given the emphasis on marital privacy in *Griswold*, there was little doubt about how the Court would decide *Loving*.

Loving v. *Virginia*

388 U.S. 1 (1967)

Virginia enacted its first law banning interracial marriage in 1691, setting an example that most other states, North and South, followed until well after World War II. By the time Richard and Mildred Loving were arrested in July 1958 for violating a modified antimiscegenation law, sixteen Southern and border states continued to enforce similar such laws. The state judge who presided over the Lovings' case told them, "Almighty God created the races white, black, yellow and red, and he placed them on separate continents. And but for the interference with his arrangement there would be no cause for such marriages. The fact that he separated the races shows that he did not intend for the races to mix." He agreed, however, to suspend their one-year sentence if they would leave the state.

The Lovings moved to Washington, D.C. There, they wrote a letter describing their ordeal to United States Attorney General Robert F. Kennedy, who forwarded it to the American Civil Liberties Union. Two Virginia lawyers, Bernard Cohen and Philip Hirschkopf, agreed to represent the Lovings. Before the Supreme Court, Hirschkopf emphasized the racist origins of the Virginia law, which had been rewritten in 1924 as "A Bill to Preserve the Integrity of the White Race." Questioned by the justices about the law's application to other ethnic groups in Virginia, Hirschkopf noted:

> In Virginia it's only a crime for white and Negro to intermary, and the law is couched in such terms that they say white may only marry white . . . but it goes on from there to make it a crime only for whites and Negroes to intermarry. There's no crime for a Malaysian to marry a Negro, and it's a valid marriage in Virginia. But it would be a void marriage for a Malaysian or any other race, aside from Negro, to marry a white person. A void marriage, but there would be no criminal penalty against anyone but the white person. They were not concerned with racial integrity, but racial supremacy of the white race.

Virginia's attorney general tried to argue that the state's authority to ban interracial marriages "stands on the same footing as the prohibition of polygamous marriage, or incestuous marriage, or the prescription of minimum ages at which people can marry."[24] Justice Harlan had written in his *Poe* dissent that not all aspects of marital freedom and privacy were free from state regulation. Clearly, though, a law forbidding interracial marriage did fall within this grouping, as Justice Harlan joined the Court's majority opinion without comment.

The Court's decision was unanimous. Chief Justice Warren delivered the opinion of the Court.

MR. CHIEF JUSTICE WARREN delivered the opinion of the Court.

This case presents a constitutional question never addressed by this Court: whether a statutory scheme adopted by the State of Virginia to prevent marriages be-

tween persons solely on the basis of racial classifications violates the Equal Protection and Due Process Clauses of the Fourteenth Amendment. For reasons which seem to us to reflect the central meaning of those constitutional commands, we conclude that these statutes cannot stand consistently with the Fourteenth Amendment. . . .

[Virginia] does not contend in its argument before this Court that its powers to regulate marriage are unlimited notwithstanding the commands of the Fourteenth Amendment. Nor could it do so in light of *Meyer* v. *Nebraska* (1923) and *Skinner* v. *Oklahoma* (1942). Instead, the State argues that the meaning of the Equal Protection Clause, as illuminated by the statements of the Framers, is only that state penal laws containing an interracial element as part of the definition of the offense must apply equally to whites and Negroes in the sense that members of each race are punished to the same degree. Thus, the State contends that, because its miscegenation statutes punish equally both the white and the Negro participants in an interracial marriage, these statutes, despite their reliance on racial classifications, do not constitute an invidious discrimination based upon race. The second argument advanced by the State assumes the validity of its equal application theory. The argument is that, if the Equal Protection Clause does not outlaw miscegenation statutes because of their reliance on racial classifications, the question of constitutionality would thus become whether there was any rational basis for a State to treat interracial marriages differently from other marriages. On this question, the State argues, the scientific evidence is substantially in doubt and, consequently, this Court should defer to the wisdom of the state legislature in adopting its policy of discouraging interracial marriages.

Because we reject the notion that the mere "equal application" of a statute containing racial classifications is enough to remove the classifications from the Fourteenth Amendment's proscription of all invidious racial discriminations, we do not accept the State's contention that these statutes should be upheld if there is any possible basis for concluding that they serve a rational purpose. The mere fact of equal application does not mean that our analysis of these statutes should follow the approach we have taken in cases involving no racial discrimination. . . .

In . . . cases . . . involving distinctions not drawn according to race, the Court has merely asked whether there is any rational foundation for the discriminations, and has deferred to the wisdom of the state legislatures. In the case [before us], however, we deal with statutes containing racial classifications, and the fact of equal application does not immunize the statute from the very heavy burden of justification which the Fourteenth Amendment has traditionally required of state statutes drawn according to race.

The State argues that statements in the Thirty-ninth Congress about the time of the passage of the Fourteenth Amendment indicate that the Framers did not intend the Amendment to make unconstitutional state miscegenation laws. Many of the statements alluded to by the State concern the debates over the Freedmen's Bureau Bill, which President Johnson vetoed, and the Civil Rights Act of 1866, enacted over his veto. While these statements have some relevance to the intention of Congress in submitting the Fourteenth Amendment, it must be understood that they pertained to the passage of specific statutes, and not to the broader, organic purpose of a constitutional amendment. As for the various statements directly concerning the Fourteenth Amendment, we have said in connection with a related problem that, although these historical sources "cast some light" they are not sufficient to resolve the problem. . . . We have rejected the proposition that the debates in the Thirty-ninth Congress or in the state legislatures which ratified the Fourteenth Amendment supported the theory advanced by the State, that the requirement of equal protection of the laws is satisfied by penal laws defining offenses based on racial classifications so long as white and Negro participants in the offense were similarly punished. . . .

There can be no question but that Virginia's miscegenation statutes rest solely upon distinctions drawn according to race. The statutes proscribe generally accepted conduct if engaged in by members of different races. Over the years, this Court has consistently repudiated "[d]istinctions between citizens solely because of their ancestry" as being "odious to a free people whose institutions are founded upon the doctrine of equality," *Hirabayashi* v. *United States* (1943). At the very least, the Equal Protection Clause demands that racial classifications, especially suspect in criminal statutes, be subjected to the "most rigid scrutiny," and, if they are ever to be upheld, they must be shown to be necessary to the accomplishment of some permissible state objective, independent of the racial discrimination which it was the object of the Fourteenth Amendment to eliminate. . . .

There is patently no legitimate overriding purpose independent of invidious racial discrimination which justifies this classification. The fact that Virginia prohibits only interracial marriages involving white persons demonstrates that the racial classifications must stand on their own justification, as measures designed to maintain White Supremacy. We have consistently denied the constitutionality of measures which restrict the rights of citizens on account of race. There can be no doubt that restricting the freedom to marry solely because of racial classifications violates the central meaning of the Equal Protection Clause.

These statutes also deprive the Lovings of liberty without due process of law in violation of the Due Process Clause of the Fourteenth Amendment. The freedom to marry has long been recognized as one of the vital personal rights essential to the orderly pursuit of happiness by free men.

Marriage is one of the "basic civil rights of man," fundamental to our very existence and survival. To deny this fundamental freedom on so unsupportable a basis as the racial classifications embodied in these statutes, classifications so directly subversive of the principle of equality at the heart of the Fourteenth Amendment, is surely to deprive all the State's citizens of liberty without due process of law. The Fourteenth Amendment requires that the freedom of choice to marry not be restricted by invidious racial discriminations. Under our Constitution, the freedom to marry, or not marry, a person of another race resides with the individual, and cannot be infringed by the State.

These convictions must be reversed.

It is so ordered.

▼▲▼

Any question of whether the Court viewed *Griswold* as fundamentally about marital privacy was answered seven years later in *Eisenstadt* v. *Baird* (1972). There, the Court ruled that a Massachusetts law prohibiting the use of contraceptives by unmarried persons violated the Due Process Clause. Like *Griswold, Eisenstadt* involved a deliberate effort to test the constitutionality of an anticontraception law. This time, however, the challenge was not the work of Planned Parenthood, but of an individual. Rebellious and young, former medical student Bill Baird had left his job with a pharmaceutical company to travel the country speaking out on the need to legalize birth control and abortion. Baird's case attracted considerable *amicus* support, including a notable brief by the ACLU, which stressed that *Griswold's* real significance had been to create a right of individual sexual privacy, a right not just attached to the marital relationship.

Writing for a 6-1 Court, Justice Brennan noted it was "true that in *Griswold* the right of privacy in question inhered in the marital relationship. Yet the marital couple is not an independent entity with a mind and heart of its own, but an association of two individuals each with a separate intellectual and emotional makeup. If the right of privacy means anything, it is the right of the *individual,* married or single, to be free from unwarranted intrusion into matters so fundamentally affecting a person as the decision whether to bear or beget a child."[25] Commentators seized upon that last sentence in *Eisenstadt* as proof positive that *Griswold* was based on the idea of sexual liberty rather than personal privacy and suggested that "the family rationale of 1965 was simply a fabrication." Several of Brennan's clerks who worked with him on *Eisenstadt* firmly believed that sentence was meant to open the door to a full consideration of the issue that *Griswold* had left ajar, and that was whether the right to privacy included the right of women to terminate their pregnancies.[26]

Abortion

The Court decided *Eisenstadt* in March 1972; by this time, the Court had already heard oral arguments in three abortion cases: *United States* v. *Vuitich* (1971), *Roe* v. *Wade* (1973), and *Doe* v. *Bolton* (1973). In *Vuitich,* the Court refused to consider the constitutionality of a Washington, D.C., law that prohibited abortions except in cases involving the mother's life and health. A lower federal court had declared the law unconstitutional on the grounds that it was vague and unenforceable, and suggested further that the law might well interfere with the right of women to "remove an unwanted child." The Court did not reach those issues; instead, it ruled that the law was not vague, and ordered the doctor convicted under it to stand trial so that a jury could decide if he had, in fact, violated its "life and health" provisions. But the Court's decision to hear the case indicated, in retrospect, what had been obvious after *Griswold:* Sooner or later, the Court was going to have deal with the small but growing abortion rights movement.

By the time the Court heard *Vuitich,* federal and state courts across the country had invalidated over half a dozen state criminal abortion laws, but offered no coherent constitutional reasoning other than such laws violated the reproductive freedom of women. These laws had been challenged by the ACLU, the National Association for the Repeal of Abortion Laws (NARAL, which, in 1973, changed its name to the National Abortion Rights Action League), Planned Parenthood, the National Organization for Women (NOW), and a loose confederation of physician-activists, law professors, public interest lawyers, and attorneys in private practice who favored a constitutional right to abortion. Litigation as an instrument to reform the nation's criminal abortion law had emerged alongside the abortion rights movement's state-by-state effort to persuade legislatures to reform or repeal their existing abortion codes. Allied with them in this effort were the American Bar Association (ABA), the American Medical Association (AMA), the American Public Health Association (APHA), and the American Law Institute (ALI), which gave abortion rights advocates the support of the legal and medical establishments.[27] The late 1960s was not the first time that a call for abortion rights had produced political sparks in the nation's legislatures and courtrooms. Our SIDEBAR on the history of abortion in the United States offers a more detailed background on abortion as a source of ethical, political, and legal disagreement in American politics, and how various social forces came to shape its development as public policy.

Six weeks after *Eisenstadt,* Justice Harry Blackmun circulated the first draft of his opinion in *Roe,* which offered a very tentative conclusion that an 1854 Texas law banning abortion except when the mother's life was at stake was unconstitutional. In *Roe,* a three-judge federal court, ignoring Justice Douglas's opinion in *Griswold,* ruled that Texas's law violated the right to privacy inherent in the Ninth Amendment, the position taken by Justice Goldberg. The lower court, however, refused to enjoin Texas from enforcing the law, giving both sides grounds for an appeal. Shortly thereafter, Blackmun distributed a draft of his *Doe* opinion, a case argued the same day as *Roe,* holding there that a Georgia law, directly modeled on the reforms suggested by the ALI, was unconstitutional. In contrast to the Texas law, the Georgia law permitted exceptions in three cases: (1) when the health, not just the life, of the mother was severely threatened; (2) when there was a substantial chance that the fetus would be born with severe birth defects; or (3) when the pregnancy was the result of rape or incest. The law also offered a complex licensing and reporting scheme, which included requiring doctors to certify with signatures from two other physicians that the abortion was being performed for one the reasons set out in the law. Any report of rape had to be certified as well.

Blackmun's *Roe* draft received a less than enthusiastic reception from the other justices, six of whom would eventually join him in striking down the Texas and Georgia laws. The justices most firmly favoring a right to abortion—Brennan, Marshall, Douglas, and Stewart—did not believe Blackmun, who had emphasized the vagueness of the Texas law, had sufficiently addressed the constitutional question. They encouraged him to extend the right to privacy established in *Griswold* and *Eisenstadt* to include a woman's right to continue her pregnancy. His *Doe* opinion fared better, receiving only minor suggestions from the four other justices who were already committed to *Roe.* After circulating several drafts of his *Roe* and *Doe* opinions, it appeared that Blackmun would have an opinion ready by June 1972, the end of the term. Chief Justice Warren Burger, however, persuaded four members of the Court, Blackmun, Byron White, Lewis Powell, and William Rehnquist (the latter two had not been confirmed until after the oral arguments in *Roe* and *Doe* in December 1971), to hold the case over for reargument the following term. Burger's behind-the-scenes move to delay the Court's decisions in *Roe* and *Doe* infuriated Brennan, Douglas, Marshall, and Stewart, who believed that Burger was attempting to manipulate Blackmun, whom he had known since their childhood together in St. Paul, Minnesota. Douglas, in particular, suspected that Burger wanted another opportunity to change Blackmun's mind. Hearing the cases again, this time with Powell and Rehnquist able to participate in oral argument, would give Burger that chance.[28]

Eight days after the Court's decision, the *Washington Post* carried a front-page story headlined, "Move by Burger May Shift Court's Stand on Abortion." The story, which carried no reporter's by-line, stated that a majority of the seven justices who heard the abortion cases favored a constitutional right to abortion, with only White and Burger dissenting. A day later, the *New York Times* carried a similar story, claiming that "sources close to the Court" had confirmed what the *Washington Post* had reported. When Douglas, who was the most strenuous objector to Burger's tactics, learned of the news reports while vacationing in Washington State, he wrote

ABORTION IN AMERICA

In 1812, the Massachusetts Supreme Court ruled that "miscarrying" a child early in a woman's pregnancy was not a criminal offense. Following British common law and American attitudes toward the practice, the court ruled that prior to a woman's ability to feel the fetus move in her womb, the decision to continue or abort her pregnancy remained with her. "Quickening," as this rule was better known, generally did not occur until the fourth or fifth month—the second trimester in a woman's pregnancy. Although debate over whether the fetus was a person and thus deserving of legal protection from abortion had been debated for thousands of years, American courts relied on the quickening doctrine to determine the legal status of the fetus.

While no statistics or records exist that offer a complete picture of the frequency of abortion during the late eighteenth and early nineteenth centuries, the practice was not uncommon. Generally, poor women who feared the financial consequences of an unwanted pregnancy, women who had been raped or lived with abusive husbands, and well-to-do women who could not bear the social stigma of an illegitimate child most often sought abortion services. Abortion was not then, as it is now, an invasive medical procedure. Women who wanted abortions either attempted to induce a miscarriage on their own, or sought the assistance of midwives and specialists, who usually administered a combination of drugs and herbs to end the pregnancy.

In 1821, in response to a public morals movement that also resulted in the nation's first law banning contraception, Connecticut made abortion illegal after the fetus had quickened. Women were not the target of the statute; abortion providers were, and a woman or the fetus had to die or suffer severe damage to warrant criminal charges. New York followed suit in 1829 with a similar law. By 1840, thirteen more states had enacted laws that punished abortions on quickened fetuses, with harsher penalties meted out to those who performed abortions after this stage. The forces behind the first major wave of restrictive abortion legislation were state and local medical societies, not temperance organizations or religious activists. Trained physicians believed that abortion was too often left in the hands of amateurs, and that by restricting who could perform abortions, the health and welfare of pregnant women were better protected. Many of these same physicians were willing to perform abortions on women carrying "unquickened" fetuses, thus exposing one of the major reasons the medical industry decided to regulate the practice: It limited competition for patients and allowed doctors to professionalize the practice.

In 1859, the American Medical Association (AMA) became the first group in the United States to issue a major statement on the abortion issue. In doing so, the AMA shifted the debate away from the public health aspects of the practice to the moral dimension of abortion. Calling for legislation to prohibit the "unwarrantable destruction of human life," the AMA recommended banning abortion in all circumstances, except when the mother's life, though not necessarily her health, was at stake. To bolster its vigorous legislative campaign in the states, the AMA tried hard to enlist the support of organized religion, but had little success. Many church leaders were reluctant to enter the abortion debate, much less the political arena, as many religious denominations had not developed an official position on the issue. The AMA had tried especially to enlist Protestant denominations, making public a report showing that most abortions were performed on Protestant women. Nonetheless, several Protestant churches believed a woman's right to determine her own future to be as morally compelling as the far from clear-cut issues involved in the termination of a gestating fetus. As a result, many churches decided to let individual members decide the matter for themselves. Other Protestant churches endorsed the AMA's antiabortion campaign and openly encouraged their congregations to support it.

A major turning point in the campaign to criminalize abortion came after the Civil War. The Roman Catholic Church issued a statement in support of the AMA's campaign, calling abortion a "sin so directly opposite to the first laws of nature, and to the designs of God, our Creator, that it cannot fail to draw down a curse upon the land where it is generally practiced." In 1869, Pope Pius IX issued a declaration making excommunication a punishment for abortion, a position the Vatican refined in the early twentieth century to include even abortions necessary to save the life of the mother. Although the relationship between organized religion and the AMA never flourished, the support of the Catholic Church and splinter spokespersons from American Protestant denominations gave the antiabortion physicians a moral foundation to their campaign. By the late 1880s, every state had enacted a criminal abortion law; these laws would remain relatively unchanged until the late 1960s. In the end, however, the criminalization of abortion in the United States during the nineteenth century owed little to the influence or activities of organized religion.

After *Roe,* the movement to restrict abortion was decidedly different from its nineteenth-century predecessor. The Roman Catholic Church, gradually supported by conservative Protestant and Orthodox Jewish denominational representatives, emerged as the primary organizational force on behalf of what was now a *pro-life* movement. No longer was the emphasis on medical ethics and professional control. The movement to ban abortion had deep roots in theological and moral opposition to the practice. In contrast to the late-nineteenth-century effort to restrict abortion, pro-life forces relied on modern campaign and advertising techniques, and borrowed a page from the civil rights movement by emphasizing grassroots organizing and public protests. By the early 1960s, the AMA had changed its position on abortion to favor the right of women to terminate their pregnancies, leaving a void that was filled by religious and other pro-life public interest organizations incensed by the Court's decision to legalize abortion in *Roe.*

References

Craig, Barbara Hinkson, and David M. O'Brien. *Abortion and American Politics.* Chatham, N.J.: Chatham House, 1993.

Mohr, James C. *Abortion in America: The Origins and Evolution of National Policy.* New York: Oxford University Press, 1978.

Noonan, John T. Jr. *A Private Choice: Abortion in America During the Seventies.* New York: Free Press, 1979.

the Chief Justice a letter denying that he had leaked anything to the press. Wrote Douglas:

> I am upset and appalled. I have never breathed a word concerning these cases, or my memo, to anyone outside the Court. I have no idea where the writer got the story.
>
> We have our differences; but so far as I am concerned they are wholly internal; and if revealed, they are mirrored in opinions filed, never in "leaks" to the press.
>
> I am taking the liberty of sending a copy of this letter to you to the other Brethren.

Neither Douglas nor some disgruntled clerk leaked the story, but Potter Stewart, who enjoyed a long friendship with a veteran reporter at the *Washington Post,* did. More so than even Douglas, Stewart resented Burger's tactics, which he believed were self-serving and utterly unrelated to the merits of the case.[29]

In August 1972, a Gallup poll revealed that 64 percent of Americans believed that "the decision to have an abortion should be made solely by a woman and her physician," an increase of 7 percent from a previous poll released in January. Two particularly notable results of this poll were that 56 percent of Roman Catholic respondents agreed with this statement, and that only 7 percent of all persons polled opposed abortion under any circumstance. Moreover, by 1971, four states—

Alaska, Hawaii, New York, and Washington—and Washington, D.C., had modified their abortion laws to the point where they would become the only ones in the country unaffected by *Roe*. Still, that left forty-six other states, including those that had adopted the ALI reforms, with abortion laws that would not survive the Court's dramatic decision in January 1973.

Roe v. *Wade*

410 U.S. 173 (1973)

In January 1970, Norma McCorvey returned home to Texas after working for a traveling carnival. She then met Linda Coffee and Sarah Weddington, two young lawyers active in the abortion rights movement, in a Dallas pizza parlor. Pregnant with her third child, McCorvey hoped that Coffee and Weddington could assist her in obtaining an abortion. The lawyers, however, were there to persuade McCorvey to become a plaintiff in a test case challenging Texas's restrictive abortion law. A friend of Coffee and Weddington had arranged for the legal adoption of McCorvey's still-unborn child and agreed to pay all the childbirth expenses. The two lawyers assured McCorvey that they would protect her anonymity by listing her only as "Jane Roe" on the legal papers.

Coffee and Weddington, working closely with some law school friends from the University of Texas, began work on *Roe* in February. By May, they obtained a hearing before a three-judge panel of federal judges. Coffee had clerked for one of the judges, Sarah Hughes, in her first year out of law school. All three judges had been appointed by Democratic presidents, and were considered liberal by civil rights lawyers. In fact, before Coffee and Weddington appeared before them, Hughes and one other judge had already decided to declare the Texas law unconstitutional. They were using the hearing to help shape the record for what everyone involved knew would be an eventual appeal. Their victory in June 1970 attracted the attention of abortion reformers across the country, a development that intensified further when, on the last day of July, a federal panel of judges in Atlanta declared Georgia's ALI-model abortion law unconstitutional. *Doe* v. *Bolton* had been brought by the Georgia chapter of the ACLU, and marked the first time that a liberalized abortion law had been declared unconstitutional.

Roe and *Doe* attracted numerous *amicus* briefs, most of which encouraged the Court to strike down the Texas and Georgia laws. Emphasis in the *amicus* coordination on behalf of the abortion rights position was less on the constitutional argument and more on demonstrating the level of support that existed within the medical and legal communities for legal abortion. One such brief included the American College of Obstetricians and Gynecologists, the American Medical Women's Association, the American Psychiatric Association, and 178 individual signatories, two dozen of which were based in Minnesota and included physicians affiliated with the Mayo Clinic. Justice Blackmun had served as an in-house counsel for the Mayo Clinic before ascending to the federal bench. Several other *amicus* briefs emphasized a recent law review article written by former Supreme Court justice Tom Clark, who had been part of the *Griswold* majority. He wrote: the "right of a woman to choose whether or not to bear a child is an aspect of her right to privacy and liberty." Groups that later became active and influential forces in the pro-life movement that emerged after *Roe*, such as the National Right to Life Committee, filed briefs in support of the Texas and Georgia laws.

During the first round of oral arguments, Weddington, who argued the case, had come across as self-conscious and nervous, and had given the justices no concrete argument in favor of the constitutional basis for the right to abortion. Texas assistant attorney general Jay Floyd began his presentation with no such lack of confidence. "It's an old joke," Floyd told the Court, "but when a man argues against two beautiful ladies like this, they are going to have the last word." No one laughed, and Floyd was replaced by Robert Flowers to defend Texas's law when *Roe* was reargued the following term. Weddington, on the other hand, was much more composed. In the face of repeated interruptions and questions, she stuck to her argument that the Fourteenth Amendment secured a right of privacy broad enough to include an elective abortion early in a woman's pregnancy.

The Court's decision was 7 to 2. Justice Blackmun delivered the opinion of the Court. Chief Justice Burger concurred, and Justices Douglas and Stewart filed separate concurring opinions. Justices Rehnquist and White filed separate dissents.

▼▲▼

MR. JUSTICE BLACKMUN delivered the opinion of the Court.

We forthwith acknowledge our awareness of the sensitive and emotional nature of the abortion controversy, of the vigorous opposing views, even among physicians, and of the deep and seemingly absolute convictions that the subject inspires. One's philosophy, one's experiences, one's exposure to the raw edges of human existence, one's religious training, one's attitudes toward life and family and their values, and the moral standards one establishes and seeks to observe, are all likely to influence and to color one's thinking and conclusions about abortion.

In addition, population growth, pollution, poverty, and racial overtones tend to complicate and not to simplify the problem.

Our task, of course, is to resolve the issue by constitutional measurement, free of emotion and of predilection. We seek earnestly to do this, and, because we do, we have inquired into, and in this opinion place some emphasis upon, medical and medical-legal history and what that history reveals about man's attitudes toward the abortion procedure over the centuries. We bear in mind, too, Mr. Justice Holmes's admonition in his now-vindicated dissent in *Lochner* v. *New York* (1905): "[The Constitution] is made for people of fundamentally differing views, and the accident of our finding certain opinions natural and familiar or novel and even shocking ought not to conclude our judgment upon the question whether statutes embodying them conflict with the Constitution of the United States." . . .

The principal thrust of appellant's attack on the Texas statutes is that they improperly invade a right, said to be possessed by the pregnant woman, to choose to terminate her pregnancy. Appellant would discover this right in the concept of personal "liberty" embodied in the Fourteenth Amendment's Due Process Clause; or in personal, marital, familial, and sexual privacy said to be protected by the Bill of Rights or its penumbras, or among those rights reserved to the people by the Ninth Amendment. Before addressing this claim, we feel it desirable briefly to survey, in several aspects, the history of abortion, for such insight as that history may afford us, and then to examine the state purposes and interests behind the criminal abortion laws. . . .

It perhaps is not generally appreciated that the restrictive criminal abortion laws in effect in a majority of States today are of relatively recent vintage. Those laws, generally proscribing abortion or its attempt at any time during pregnancy except when necessary to preserve the pregnant woman's life, are not of ancient or even of common law origin. Instead, they derive from statutory changes effected, for the most part, in the latter half of the 19th century. . . .

Three reasons have been advanced to explain historically the enactment of criminal abortion laws in the 19th century and to justify their continued existence.

It has been argued occasionally that these laws were the product of a Victorian social concern to discourage illicit sexual conduct. Texas, however, does not advance this justification in the present case, and it appears that no court or commentator has taken the argument seriously. The appellants and *amici* contend, moreover, that this is not a proper state purpose at all and suggest that, if it were, the Texas statutes are overbroad in protecting it, since the law fails to distinguish between married and unwed mothers.

A second reason is concerned with abortion as a medical procedure. When most criminal abortion laws were first enacted, the procedure was a hazardous one for the woman. This was particularly true prior to the development of antisepsis. Antiseptic techniques, of course, were based on discoveries by Lister, Pasteur, and others first announced in 1867, but were not generally accepted and employed until about the turn of the century. Abortion mortality was high. Even after 1900, and perhaps until as late as the development of antibiotics in the 1940s, standard modern techniques such as dilation and curettage were not nearly so safe as they are today. Thus, it has been argued that a State's real concern in enacting a criminal abortion law was to protect the pregnant woman, that is, to restrain her from submitting to a procedure that placed her life in serious jeopardy.

Modern medical techniques have altered this situation. Appellants and various *amici* refer to medical data indicating that abortion in early pregnancy, that is, prior to the end of the first trimester, although not without its risk, is now relatively safe. Mortality rates for women undergoing early abortions, where the procedure is legal, appear to be as low as or lower than the rates for normal childbirth. Consequently, any interest of the State in protecting the woman from an inherently hazardous procedure, except when it would be equally dangerous for her to forgo it, has largely disappeared. Of course, important state interests in the areas of health and medical standards do remain. The State has a legitimate interest in seeing to it that abortion, like any other medical procedure, is performed under circumstances that insure maximum safety for the patient. . . .

The third reason is the State's interest—some phrase it in terms of duty—in protecting prenatal life. Some of the argument for this justification rests on the theory that a new human life is present from the moment of conception. The State's interest and general obligation to protect life then extends, it is argued, to prenatal life. Only when the life of the pregnant mother herself is at stake, balanced against the life she carries within her, should the interest of the embryo or fetus not prevail. Logically, of course, a legitimate state interest in this area need not stand or fall on acceptance of the belief that life begins at conception or at some other point prior to live birth. In assessing the State's interest, recognition may be given to the less rigid claim that as long as at least potential life is involved, the State may assert interests beyond the protection of the pregnant woman alone. . . .

It is with these interests, and the eight to be attached to them, that this case is concerned.

The Constitution does not explicitly mention any right of privacy. . . . [but] the Court has recognized that a right of personal privacy, or a guarantee of certain areas or zones of privacy, does exist under the Constitution. In varying contexts, the Court or individual Justices have, indeed, found at least the roots of that right in the First Amendment, in the Fourth and Fifth Amendments, in the penumbras of the Bill of Rights, in the Ninth Amendment, or in the concept of liberty guaranteed by the first section of the Fourteenth Amendment. These decisions make it clear that only personal rights that can be deemed "fundamental" or "implicit in the concept of ordered liberty," *Palko* v. *Connecticut* (1937), are included in this guarantee of personal privacy. They also make it clear that the right has some extension to activities relating to marriage, procreation, contraception, family relationships, and childrearing and education.

This right of privacy, whether it be founded in the Fourteenth Amendment's concept of personal liberty and restrictions upon state action, as we feel it is, or, as the District Court determined, in the Ninth Amendment's reservation of rights to the people, is broad enough to encompass a woman's decision whether or not to terminate her pregnancy. The detriment that the State would impose upon the pregnant woman by denying this choice altogether is apparent. Specific and direct harm medically diagnosable even in early pregnancy may be involved. Maternity, or additional offspring, may force upon the woman a distressful life and future. Psychological harm may be imminent. Mental and physical health may be taxed by child care. There is also the distress, for all concerned, associated with the unwanted child, and there is the problem of bringing a child into a family already unable, psychologically and otherwise, to care for it. In other cases, as in this one, the additional difficulties and continuing stigma of unwed motherhood may be involved. All these are factors the woman and her responsible physician necessarily will consider in consultation.

On the basis of elements such as these, appellant and some *amici* argue that the woman's right is absolute and that she is entitled to terminate her pregnancy at whatever time, in whatever way, and for whatever reason she alone chooses. With this we do not agree. Appellant's arguments that Texas either has no valid interest at all in regulating the abortion decision, or no interest strong enough to support any limitation upon the woman's sole determination, are unpersuasive. The Court's decisions recognizing a right of privacy also acknowledge that some state regulation in areas protected by that right is appropriate. As noted above, a State may properly assert important interests in safeguarding health, in maintaining medical standards, and in protecting potential life. At some point in pregnancy, these respective interests become sufficiently compelling to sustain regulation of the factors that govern the abortion decision. The privacy right involved, therefore, cannot be said to be absolute. In fact, it is not clear to us that the claim asserted by some *amici* that one has an unlimited right to do with one's body as one pleases bears a close relationship to the right of privacy previously articulated in the Court's decisions. The Court has refused to recognize an unlimited right of this kind in the past.

We, therefore, conclude that the right of personal privacy includes the abortion decision, but that this right is not unqualified, and must be considered against important state interests in regulation. . . .

Where certain "fundamental rights" are involved, the Court has held that regulation limiting these rights may be justified only by a "compelling state interest," and that legislative enactments must be narrowly drawn to express only the legitimate state interests at stake.

In the recent abortion cases [decided in the lower federal courts], courts have recognized these principles. Those striking down state laws have generally scrutinized the State's interests in protecting health and potential life, and have concluded that neither interest justified broad limitations on the reasons for which a physician and his pregnant patient might decide that she should have an abortion in the early stages of pregnancy. Courts sustaining state laws have held that the State's determinations to protect health or prenatal life are dominant and constitutionally justifiable. . . .

The appellee and certain *amici* argue that the fetus is a "person" within the language and meaning of the

Fourteenth Amendment. In support of this, they outline at length and in detail the well known facts of fetal development. . . .

[The Court summarized all the places where the word "person" appears in the Constitution, and concluded that] . . . the use of the word is such that it has application only post-natally. None indicates, with any assurance, that it has any possible pre-natal application.

All this, together with our observation, that, throughout the major portion of the 19th century, prevailing legal abortion practices were far freer than they are today, persuades us that the word "person," as used in the Fourteenth Amendment, does not include the unborn. . . .

The pregnant woman cannot be isolated in her privacy. She carries an embryo and, later, a fetus, if one accepts the medical definitions of the developing young in the human uterus. The situation therefore is inherently different from marital intimacy, or bedroom possession of obscene material, or marriage, or procreation, or education, with which *Eisenstadt* and *Griswold, Stanley, Loving, Skinner,* and *Pierce* and *Meyer* were respectively concerned. As we have intimated above, it is reasonable and appropriate for a State to decide that, at some point in time another interest, that of health of the mother or that of potential human life, becomes significantly involved. The woman's privacy is no longer sole and any right of privacy she possesses must be measured accordingly.

Texas urges that, apart from the Fourteenth Amendment, life begins at conception and is present throughout pregnancy, and that, therefore, the State has a compelling interest in protecting that life from and after conception. We need not resolve the difficult question of when life begins. When those trained in the respective disciplines of medicine, philosophy, and theology are unable to arrive at any consensus, the judiciary, at this point in the development of man's knowledge, is not in a position to speculate as to the answer. . . .

In areas other than criminal abortion, the law has been reluctant to endorse any theory that life, as we recognize it, begins before live birth, or to accord legal rights to the unborn except in narrowly defined situations and except when the rights are contingent upon live birth. . . .

In view of all this, we do not agree that, by adopting one theory of life, Texas may override the rights of the pregnant woman that are at stake. We repeat, however, that the State does have an important and legitimate interest in preserving and protecting the health of the pregnant woman, whether she be a resident of the State or a nonresident who seeks medical consultation and treatment there, and that it has still *another* important and legitimate interest in protecting the potentiality of human life. These interests are separate and distinct. Each grows in substantiality as the woman approaches term and, at a point during pregnancy, each becomes "compelling."

With respect to the State's important and legitimate interest in the health of the mother, the "compelling" point, in the light of present medical knowledge, is at approximately the end of the first trimester. This is so because of the now-established medical fact, referred to above at that, until the end of the first trimester mortality in abortion may be less than mortality in normal childbirth. It follows that, from and after this point, a State may regulate the abortion procedure to the extent that the regulation reasonably relates to the preservation and protection of maternal health. Examples of permissible state regulation in this area are requirements as to the qualifications of the person who is to perform the abortion; as to the licensure of that person; as to the facility in which the procedure is to be performed, that is, whether it must be a hospital or may be a clinic or some other place of less-than-hospital status; as to the licensing of the facility; and the like.

This means, on the other hand, that, for the period of pregnancy prior to this "compelling" point, the attending physician, in consultation with his patient, is free to determine, without regulation by the State, that, in his medical judgment, the patient's pregnancy should be terminated. If that decision is reached, the judgment may be effectuated by an abortion free of interference by the State.

With respect to the State's important and legitimate interest in potential life, the "compelling" point is at viability. This is so because the fetus then presumably has the capability of meaningful life outside the mother's womb. State regulation protective of fetal life after viability thus has both logical and biological justifications. If the State is interested in protecting fetal life after viability, it may go so far as to proscribe abortion during that period, except when it is necessary to preserve the life or health of the mother.

Measured against these standards, [the Texas law], in restricting legal abortions to those "procured or attempted by medical advice for the purpose of saving the life of the mother," sweeps too broadly. The statute makes no distinction between abortions performed early in pregnancy and those performed later, and it limits to a single reason, "saving" the mother's life, the legal justification for the procedure. The statute, therefore, cannot survive the constitutional attack made upon it here. . . .

To summarize and to repeat:

1. A state criminal abortion statute of the current Texas type, that excepts from criminality only a lifesaving procedure on behalf of the mother, without regard to pregnancy stage and without recognition of the other interests involved, is violative of the Due Process Clause of the Fourteenth Amendment.
   a. For the stage prior to approximately the end of the first trimester, the abortion decision and its effectuation must be left to the medical judgment of the pregnant woman's attending physician.
   b. For the stage subsequent to approximately the end of the first trimester, the State, in promoting its interest in the health of the mother, may, if it chooses, regulate the abortion procedure in ways that are reasonably related to maternal health.
   c. For the stage subsequent to viability, the State in promoting its interest in the potentiality of human life may, if it chooses, regulate, and even proscribe, abortion except where it is necessary, in appropriate medical judgment, for the preservation of the life or health of the mother. . . .

This holding, we feel, is consistent with the relative weights of the respective interests involved, with the lessons and examples of medical and legal history, with the lenity of the common law, and with the demands of the profound problems of the present day. The decision leaves the State free to place increasing restrictions on abortion as the period of pregnancy lengthens, so long as those restrictions are tailored to the recognized state interests. The decision vindicates the right of the physician to administer medical treatment according to his professional judgment up to the points where important state interests provide compelling justifications for intervention. Up to those points, the abortion decision in all its aspects is inherently, and primarily, a medical decision, and basic responsibility for it must rest with the physician. If an individual practitioner abuses the privilege of exercising proper medical judgment, the usual remedies, judicial and intra-professional, are available.

MR. JUSTICE STEWART, concurring.

In 1963, this Court, in *Ferguson* v. *Skrupa* (1963), purported to sound the death knell for the doctrine of substantive due process, a doctrine under which many state laws had in the past been held to violate the Fourteenth Amendment. As Mr. Justice Black's opinion for the Court in *Skrupa* put it: "We have returned to the original constitutional proposition that courts do not substitute their social and economic beliefs for the judgment of legislative bodies, who are elected to pass laws."

Barely two years later, in *Griswold* v. *Connecticut*, the Court held a Connecticut birth control law unconstitutional. In view of what had been so recently said in *Skrupa*, the Court's opinion in *Griswold* understandably did its best to avoid reliance on the Due Process Clause of the Fourteenth Amendment as the ground for decision. Yet the Connecticut law did not violate any provision of the Bill of Rights, nor any other specific provision of the Constitution. So it was clear to me then, and it is equally clear to me now, that the *Griswold* decision can be rationally understood only as a holding that the Connecticut statute substantively invaded the "liberty" that is protected by the Due Process Clause of the Fourteenth Amendment. As so understood, *Griswold* stands as one in a long line of pre-*Skrupa* cases decided under the doctrine of substantive due process, and I now accept it as such. . . .

Several decisions of this Court make clear that freedom of personal choice in matters of marriage and family life is one of the liberties protected by the Due Process Clause of the Fourteenth Amendment. As recently as last Term, *Eisenstadt* v. *Baird*, we recognized "the right of the *individual*, married or single, to be free from unwarranted governmental intrusion into matters so fundamentally affecting a person as the decision whether to bear or beget a child." That right necessarily includes the right of a woman to decide whether or not to terminate her pregnancy. . . .

The asserted state interests are protection of the health and safety of the pregnant woman, and protection of the potential future human life within her. These are legitimate objectives, amply sufficient to permit a State to regulate abortions as it does other surgical procedures, and perhaps sufficient to permit a State to regulate abortions more stringently, or even to prohibit them in the late stages of pregnancy. But such legislation is not before us, and I think the Court today has thoroughly demonstrated that these state interests cannot constitutionally support the broad abridgment of personal liberty worked by the existing Texas law. Accordingly, I join the Court's opinion holding that that law is invalid under the Due Process Clause of the Fourteenth Amendment.

MR. JUSTICE REHNQUIST, dissenting.

The Court's opinion brings to the decision of this troubling question both extensive historical fact and a wealth of legal scholarship. While the opinion thus commands my respect, I find myself nonetheless in fundamental disagreement with those parts of it that invalidate the Texas statute in question, and therefore dissent. . . .

If the Court means by the term "privacy" no more than that the claim of a person to be free from unwanted state regulation of consensual transactions may be a form of "liberty" protected by the Fourteenth Amendment, there is no doubt that similar claims have been upheld in our earlier decisions on the basis of that liberty. I agree with . . . Justice Stewart in his concurring opinion that the "liberty," against deprivation of which without due process the Fourteenth Amendment protects, embraces more than the rights found in the Bill of Rights. But that liberty is not guaranteed absolutely against deprivation, only against deprivation without due process of law. The test traditionally applied in the area of social and economic legislation is whether or not a law such as that challenged has a rational relation to a valid state objective. The Due Process Clause of the Fourteenth Amendment undoubtedly does place a limit, albeit a broad one, on legislative power to enact laws such as this. If the Texas statute were to prohibit an abortion even where the mother's life is in jeopardy, I have little doubt that such a statute would lack a rational relation to a valid state objective. . . . But the Court's sweeping invalidation of any restrictions on abortion during the first trimester is impossible to justify under that standard, and the conscious weighing of competing factors that the Court's opinion apparently substitutes for the established test is far more appropriate to a legislative judgment than to a judicial one. . . .

While the Court's opinion quotes from the dissent of Justice Holmes in *Lochner,* . . . the result it reaches is more closely attuned to the majority opinion of Justice Peckham in that case. As in *Lochner* and similar cases applying substantive due process standards to economic and social welfare legislation, the adoption of the compelling state interest standard will inevitably require this Court to examine the legislative policies and pass on the wisdom of these policies in the very process of deciding whether a particular state interest put forward may or may not be "compelling." The decision here to break pregnancy into three distinct terms and to outline the permissible restrictions the State may impose in each one, for example, partakes more of judicial legislation than it does of a determination of the intent of the drafters of the Fourteenth Amendment.

The fact that a majority of the States reflecting, after all, the majority sentiment in those States, have had restrictions on abortions for at least a century is a strong indication, it seems to me, that the asserted right to an abortion is not "so rooted in the traditions and conscience of our people as to be ranked as fundamental." Even today, when society's views on abortion are changing, the very existence of the debate is evidence that the "right" to an abortion is not so universally accepted as the appellant would have us believe. . . .

There apparently was no question concerning the validity of this provision or of any of the other state statutes when the Fourteenth Amendment was adopted. The only conclusion possible from this history is that the drafters did not intend to have the Fourteenth Amendment withdraw from the States the power to legislate with respect to this matter.

Justice Blackmun's opinion attracted more commentary, both supportive and critical, than any Supreme Court decision since *Brown* v. *Board of Education* (1954), which declared racial segregation in elementary and secondary public schools unconstitutional. The nation's major newspapers, including the *New York Times,* the *Washington Post,* the *Los Angeles Times,* the *Raleigh News and Observer,* the *Atlanta Constitution,* the *Wall Street Journal,* and the *Houston Chronicle,* overwhelmingly endorsed the Court's decision in the abortion cases. Editorial writers described Blackmun's opinion in such terms as "sound," "sensible," "humane," "compassionate and intelligent," and consistent with America's commitment to personal freedom. But *Christianity Today,* an influential monthly, asserted that "the majority of the Supreme Court has explicitly rejected Christian moral teaching." The *New Republic,* a liberal weekly, endorsed Rehnquist's dissent, and concluded that abortion was an issue best left to the legislative process. Law reviews and legal journals soon found their pages filled with scholarly—and often bitterly divided—commentary on *Roe* and the Court's proper role in the abortion debate.[30] One such critic of *Roe* was none other than Ruth Bader Ginsburg, then a prominent women's rights lawyer who, in 1993, was appointed to the Court by President Bill Clinton to succeed Harry Blackmun. Although staunchly pro-choice, Ginsburg, prior to her appointment, had written that *Roe* "prolonged divisiveness and deferred stable settlement of the [abortion] issue" by preempting legislative reform. On another occasion, Ginsburg criticized Roe as "heavy-handed" and claimed that it "ventured too far in the change it ordered."[31]

Two developments have generally been attributed to *Roe.* The first is that it brought the debate over abortion rights out of the courtrooms and into the public eye. The second is that *Roe* encouraged the rise of the pro-life movement to take quick and decisive action to limit the breadth of the Court's decision. While it is true that *Roe's* comprehensive holding did galvanize pro- *and* anti-abortion rights forces in the early 1970s, the battle over a woman's right to abortion dated back to the early nineteenth century. *Griswold, Eisenstadt,* and, ultimately, *Roe* were the culmination of efforts that began when bold feminists such as Margaret Sanger and reserved physicians such as Wilder Tileston, who shared a deep commitment to birth control reform, decided to challenge in the legislatures and the courts P. T. Barnum's 1879 Connecticut anticontraception law. By the time it was decided, *Roe* was not, in Justice Blackmun's own words, "such a revolutionary opinion at the time."[32] The movement had been building in that direction for nearly a century.

Moreover, Ginsburg's argument that *Roe* allowed the courts to seize control of the abortion issue before the reform process had played out in state legislatures is not borne out by the evidence gleaned from public opinion and legislative activity in the early 1970s. Seventeen of the eighteen states that reformed their abortion laws in line with the ALI model statute did so between 1966 and 1970; after 1970, just one state modified its law before *Roe* was decided.[33] Moreover, public opinion, which had been highly supportive of *Roe's* core holding around the time it was argued, had begun to turn in the other direction by the time *Roe* was decided. Pro-life groups had begun an intense lobbying effort to defeat several state referenda drives on behalf of legal abortion *before Roe* and to publicize their cause after several federal courts had invalidated restrictive abortion statutes between 1969 and 1972. Soon after *Roe,* Gallup released a poll showing that 46 percent of Americans supported the Court's decision and 45 percent did not. Thus, as legal scholar Neal Devins points out, "In plain terms, there is little reason to think that the pre-*Roe* liberalization movement would have avalanched into sweeping abortion reform throughout the nation."[34]

Abortion Politics and Litigation After *Roe*

While the social, political, and legal dynamics of the abortion debate were much more complex prior to *Roe* than many commentators have suggested, what is clear is that Justice Blackmun's sweeping opinion left open the question of whether states still retained any authority under the Constitution to regulate abortion. This gave pro-life advocates broad room to launch a massive counteroffensive in Congress and the state legislatures. Within a year after *Roe,* over 2,600 laws attempting to restrict abortion were introduced in the states; by 1976, some 50 different provisions were introduced in Congress to limit or prohibit abortion. These ranged from laws removing the jurisdiction of the federal courts to hear abortion cases to constitutional amendments defining the fetus as a person and thus protected by the Fifth and Fourteenth Amendments. By 1978, thirty-three states had enacted laws placing restrictions on abortions. The technique most favored by the pro-life groups involved "burden-creation" laws—that is, laws that made it more difficult to obtain an abortion by forbidding certain abortion procedures, requiring that all abortions be performed in hospitals, increasing their costs by mandating the presence of additional physicians to assist with the procedure, requiring women to receive "counseling," or wait anywhere from one to seventy-two hours prior to receiving an abortion. Few, if any, of these provisions, were upheld by the federal courts or enforced by the states.[35]

Persuaded that *Roe* had, once and for all, settled the constitutional question, abortion-rights groups conceded the legislative battleground to pro-life forces, preferring to invest their time and resources in litigation. In fact, abortion-rights groups, by the late 1970s, had reached a consensus not to contest even the most severe restrictions on abortion passed by state legislatures, confident they could go into court and have them enjoined or declared unconstitutional.[36] And until 1980 this was a highly successful strategy, as the Court struck down, in *Planned Parenthood* v. *Danforth* (1976) and *Belotti* v. *Baird* (1979), state laws that required women to obtain consent from their spouses or, if they were minors, from their parents. In *Danforth,* the Court also declared unconstitutional a regulation that prohibited certain abortion procedures in the first trimester and subjected doctors to criminal sanctions if they did not exercise "due care and skill" to preserve the life of the fetus.

But in *Harris* v. *McRae* (1980), the Court handed abortion-rights advocates their first major defeat since their victory in *Roe,* holding that a 1976 amendment to the federal Medicaid program banning the use of public funds for abortions, except in cases where the woman's life is at stake or she was a victim of rape or incest, was not unconstitutional. Named for its chief sponsor, Representative Henry J. Hyde (R-Ill.), the amendment generated heated debate in Congress between pro-life and abortion-rights forces, with the latter claiming that funding restrictions were discriminatory because they, in effect, left poor women with no choice whether to continue their pregnancies. The original version of the Hyde Amendment prohibited federal funding of all abortions, with the maternal health and rape and incest exceptions coming only after abortion-rights forces in the Senate succeeded in obtaining a compromise. A federal district court declared the Hyde Amendment unconstitutional, ruling that it violated the Due Process Clause of the Fifth Amendment and, by effectively denying poor women abortions, the equal protection component of the same provision as well. In addition, the lower court also ruled that the Hyde Amendment violated the Free Exercise Clause of the First Amendment, a conclusion that reflected the increasingly prominent role that religious organizations were playing in driving the debate over abortion rights. While the Court rejected that argument, along with all the others mounted against the Hyde Amendment, *McRae* did much to expose the deep division within organized American religion over the ethics and propriety in the choices involved in abortion.

Harris v. McRae

448 U.S. 297 (1980)

In 1975, prior the enactment of the Hyde Amendment, the Department of Health, Education and Welfare—now the Department of Health and Human Services—funded approximately 275,000 of the estimated 1 million abortions performed in the United States. During debate over his proposal to eliminate federal funding of abortion, Representative Hyde described the trauma inflicted upon an "unborn child . . . as a member of the innocently inconvenient . . . [who] deserve[d] better than to be flushed down a toilet or burned in an incinerator." Although Hyde's rhetoric was certainly provocative, his fundamental objective of prohibiting the federal government from funding abortion had widespread support within Congress and from President Jimmy Carter's administration, even though two years before Congress had rejected similar proposals.

The most influential of the pro-life organizations seeking to shape the abortion debate, the National Right to Life Committee (NRLC), was formed after *Roe*, but the real force behind this movement was the United States Catholic Conference (USCC) and the National Conference of Catholic Bishops (NCCB). The USCC and the NCCB, representing the Roman Catholic Church in the United States, developed a comprehensive program that called upon "all Church sponsored or identifiable Catholic national, regional, diocesan and parochial organizations and agencies . . . to persuade . . . the democratic process" to enact restrictive abortion laws in the states and press for a federal constitutional amendment to overturn *Roe*. The NRLC was, in essence, the lay representative of the Catholic Church. Other pro-life denominations soon entered the legislative and judicial battle over abortion, including the National Association of Evangelicals and the Christian Life Commission of the Southern Baptist Convention.

In *McRae*, several religious organizations supported the plaintiffs contesting the constitutionality of the Hyde Amendment. The most theologically diverse of the these groups was the Religious Coalition for Abortion Rights (RCAR), which included the American Jewish Congress, United Methodist Church, the Baptist Joint Committee on Public Affairs, Union of American Hebrew Congregations, American Baptist Churches, and Catholics for a Free Choice. RCAR argued that the Hyde Amendment not only put poor women in the position of having to give birth, but also forced them to violate their religious beliefs if they did not believe that abortion was morally or theologically repugnant. The district court, in striking down the Hyde Amendment, ruled that a "woman's conscientious decision . . . to terminate her pregnancy because that is necessary to her health [is] surely part of the liberty protected by the Fifth Amendment, doubly protected when the liberty is exercised in conformity with religious belief and teaching protected by the First Amendment."

The Court's decision was 5 to 4. Justice Stewart delivered the opinion of the Court. Justice Brennan, joined by Justices Blackmun and Marshall, dissented. Justices Blackmun, Marshall, and Stevens each filed separate dissents.

▼▲▼

MR. JUSTICE STEWART delivered the opinion of the Court.

The constitutional question . . . is whether the Hyde Amendment, by denying public funding for certain medically

necessary abortions, contravenes the liberty or equal protection guarantees of the Due Process Clause of the Fifth Amendment, or either of the Religion Clauses of the First Amendment. . . .

It is well settled that, quite apart from the guarantee of equal protection, if a law "impinges upon a fundamental right explicitly or implicitly secured by the Constitution, [it] is presumptively unconstitutional." Accordingly, before turning to the equal protection issue in this case, we examine whether the Hyde Amendment violates any substantive rights secured by the Constitution.

We address first the appellees' argument that the Hyde Amendment, by restricting the availability of certain medically necessary abortions under Medicaid, impinges on the "liberty" protected by the Due Process Clause as recognized in *Roe* v. *Wade* and its progeny.

In [*Roe*], this Court held unconstitutional a Texas statute making it a crime to procure or attempt an abortion except on medical advice for the purpose of saving the mother's life. The constitutional underpinning of [*Roe*] was a recognition that the "liberty" protected by the Due Process Clause of the Fourteenth Amendment includes not only the freedoms explicitly mentioned in the Bill of Rights, but also a freedom of personal choice in certain matters of marriage and family life. This implicit constitutional liberty, the Court in [*Roe*] held, includes the freedom of a woman to decide whether to terminate a pregnancy.

But the Court in [*Roe*] also recognized that a State has legitimate interests during a pregnancy in both ensuring the health of the mother and protecting potential human life. These state interests, which were found to be "separate and distinct" and to "gro[w] in substantiality as the woman approaches term," pose a conflict with a woman's untrammeled freedom of choice. In resolving this conflict, the Court held that, before the end of the first trimester of pregnancy, neither state interest is sufficiently substantial to justify any intrusion on the woman's freedom of choice. In the second trimester, the state interest in maternal health was found to be sufficiently substantial to justify regulation reasonably related to that concern. And at viability, usually in the third trimester, the state interest in protecting the potential life of the fetus was found to justify a criminal prohibition against abortions, except where necessary for the preservation of the life or health of the mother. Thus, inasmuch as the Texas criminal statute allowed abortions only where necessary to save the life of the mother and without regard to the stage of the pregnancy, the Court held in [*Roe*] that the statute violated the Due Process Clause of the Fourteenth Amendment.

In *Maher* v. *Roe* (1977), the Court was presented with the question whether the scope of personal constitutional freedom recognized in *Roe* v. *Wade* included an entitlement to Medicaid payments for abortions that are not medically necessary. At issue in *Maher* was a Connecticut welfare regulation under which Medicaid recipients received payments for medical services incident to childbirth, but not for medical services incident to nontherapeutic abortions. The District Court held that the regulation violated the Equal Protection Clause of the Fourteenth Amendment because the unequal subsidization of childbirth and abortion impinged on the "fundamental right to abortion" recognized in [*Roe*] and its progeny. . . .

[T]he constitutional freedom recognized in [*Roe*] and its progeny, the *Maher* Court explained, did not prevent Connecticut from making "a value judgment favoring childbirth over abortion, and . . . implement[ing] that judgment by the allocation of public funds." . . .

Thus, even though the Connecticut regulation favored childbirth over abortion by means of subsidization of one and not the other, the Court in *Maher* concluded that the regulation did not impinge on the constitutional freedom recognized in [*Roe*] because it imposed no governmental restriction on access to abortions.

The Hyde Amendment . . . places no governmental obstacle in the path of a woman who chooses to terminate her pregnancy, but rather, by means of unequal subsidization of abortion and other medical services, encourages alternative activity deemed in the public interest. . . . [A]ppellees argue that, because the Hyde Amendment affects a significant interest not present or asserted in *Maher*—the interest of a woman in protecting her health during pregnancy—and because that interest lies at the core of the personal constitutional freedom recognized in *Roe*, the present case is constitutionally different from *Maher*. It is the appellees' view that, to the extent that the Hyde Amendment withholds funding for certain medically necessary abortions, it clearly impinges on the constitutional principle recognized in *Roe*. . . .

[R]egardless of whether the freedom of a woman to choose to terminate her pregnancy for health reasons lies at the core or the periphery of the due process liberty recognized in *Roe*, it simply does not follow that a woman's freedom of choice carries with it a constitutional entitlement to the financial resources to avail herself of the full range of protected choices. . . . The financial constraints that restrict an indigent woman's ability to enjoy the full range of constitutionally protected freedom of choice are the product not of governmental restrictions on access to abortions, but rather of her indigency. Although Congress has opted to subsidize medically necessary services generally, but not certain medically necessary abortions, the fact remains that the Hyde Amendment leaves an indigent woman with at least the same range of choice in deciding whether to obtain a medically necessary abortion as she would have had if Congress had chosen to subsidize no health care costs at all. We are thus not persuaded that the Hyde Amendment impinges on the constitutionally protected freedom of choice recognized in *Wade*.

Although the liberty protected by the Due Process Clause affords protection against unwarranted government interference with freedom of choice in the context of certain personal decisions, it does not confer an entitlement to such funds as may be necessary to realize all the advantages of that freedom. To hold otherwise would mark a drastic change in our understanding of the Constitution. It cannot be that, because government may not prohibit the use of contraceptives, or prevent parents from sending their child to a private school, government therefore has an affirmative constitutional obligation to ensure that all persons have the financial resources to obtain contraceptives or send their children to private schools. To translate the limitation on governmental power implicit in the Due Process Clause into an affirmative funding obligation would require Congress to subsidize the medically necessary abortion of an indigent woman even if Congress had not enacted a Medicaid program to subsidize other medically necessary services. Nothing in the Due Process Clause supports such an extraordinary result. Whether freedom of choice that is constitutionally protected warrants federal subsidization is a question for Congress to answer, not a matter of constitutional entitlement. Accordingly, we conclude that the Hyde Amendment does not impinge on the due process liberty recognized in *Roe* v. *Wade*.

The appellees also argue that the Hyde Amendment contravenes rights secured by the Religion Clauses of the First Amendment. It is the appellees' view that the Hyde Amendment violates the Establishment Clause because it incorporates into law the doctrines of the Roman Catholic Church concerning the sinfulness of abortion and the time at which life commences. Moreover, insofar as a woman's decision to seek a medically necessary abortion may be a product of her religious beliefs under certain Protestant and Jewish tenets, the appellees assert that the funding limitations of the Hyde Amendment impinge on the freedom of religion guaranteed by the Free Exercise Clause.

It is well settled that "a legislative enactment does not contravene the Establishment Clause if it has a secular legislative purpose, if its principal or primary effect neither advances nor inhibits religion, and if it does not foster an excessive governmental entanglement with religion." Applying this standard, the District Court properly concluded that the Hyde Amendment does not run afoul of the Establishment Clause. Although neither a State nor the Federal Government can constitutionally "pass laws which aid one religion, aid all religions, or prefer one religion over another," it does not follow that a statute violates the Establishment Clause because it "happens to coincide or harmonize with the tenets of some or all religions." That the Judaeo-Christian religions oppose stealing does not mean that a State or the Federal Government may not, consistent with the Establishment Clause, enact laws prohibiting larceny. The Hyde Amendment, as the District Court noted, is as much a reflection of "traditionalist" values towards abortion as it is an embodiment of the views of any particular religion. In sum, we are convinced that the fact that the funding restrictions in the Hyde Amendment may coincide with the religious tenets of the Roman Catholic Church does not, without more, contravene the Establishment Clause. . . .

It remains to be determined whether the Hyde Amendment violates the equal protection component of the Fifth Amendment. This challenge is premised on the fact that, although federal reimbursement is available under Medicaid for medically necessary services generally, the Hyde Amendment does not permit federal reimbursement of all medically necessary abortions. The District Court held, and the appellees argue here, that this selective subsidization violates the constitutional guarantee of equal protection.

The guarantee of equal protection under the Fifth Amendment is not a source of substantive rights or liberties, but rather a right to be free from invidious discrimination in statutory classifications and other governmental activity. It is well settled that where a statutory classification does not itself impinge on a right or liberty protected by the Constitution, the validity of classification must be sustained unless "the classification rests on grounds wholly irrelevant to the achievement of [any legitimate governmental] objective." This presumption of constitutional validity, however, disappears if a statutory classification is predicated on criteria that are, in a constitutional sense, "suspect," the principal example of which is a classification based on race. . . .

It follows that the Hyde Amendment, by encouraging childbirth except in the most urgent circumstances, is rationally related to the legitimate governmental objective of protecting potential life. By subsidizing the medical expenses of indigent women who carry their pregnancies to term while not subsidizing the comparable expenses of women who undergo abortions (except those whose lives are threatened), Congress has established incentives that make childbirth a more attractive alternative than abortion for persons eligible for Medicaid. These incentives bear a direct relationship to the legitimate congressional interest in protecting potential life. Nor is it irrational that Congress has authorized federal reimbursement for medically necessary services generally, but not for certain medically necessary abortions. Abortion is inherently different from other medical procedures, because no other procedure involves the purposeful termination of a potential life. . . .

We . . . hold that the funding restrictions of the Hyde Amendment violate neither the Fifth Amendment nor the Establishment Clause of the First Amendment. It is also our view that the appellees lack standing to raise a challenge to the Hyde Amendment under the Free Exercise Clause of the First Amendment. Accordingly, the judgment of the District Court is reversed, and the case is remanded to that court for further proceedings consistent with this opinion.

It is so ordered.

MR. JUSTICE BRENNAN, with whom MR. JUSTICE MARSHALL and MR. JUSTICE BLACKMUN join, dissenting.

Roe v. *Wade* held that the constitutional right to personal privacy encompasses a woman's decision whether or not to terminate her pregnancy. *Roe* and its progeny established that the pregnant woman has a right to be free from state interference with her choice to have an abortion—a right which, at least prior to the end of the first trimester, absolutely prohibits any governmental regulation of that highly personal decision. The proposition for which these cases stand thus is not that the State is under an affirmative obligation to ensure access to abortions for all who may desire them; it is that the State must refrain from wielding its enormous power and influence in a manner that might burden the pregnant woman's freedom to choose whether to have an abortion. The Hyde Amendment's denial of public funds for medically necessary abortions plainly intrudes upon this constitutionally protected decision, for both by design and in effect, it serves to coerce indigent pregnant women to bear children that they would otherwise elect not to have. . . .

Moreover, it is clear that the Hyde Amendment not only was designed to inhibit, but does in fact inhibit, the woman's freedom to choose abortion over childbirth. . . .

By thus injecting coercive financial incentives favoring childbirth into a decision that is constitutionally guaranteed to be free from governmental intrusion, the Hyde Amendment deprives the indigent woman of her freedom to choose abortion over maternity, thereby impinging on the due process liberty right recognized in *Roe* v. *Wade*. . . .

A poor woman in the early stages of pregnancy confronts two alternatives: she may elect either to carry the fetus to term or to have an abortion. In the abstract, of course, this choice is hers alone, and the Court rightly observes that the Hyde Amendment "places no governmental obstacle in the path of a woman who chooses to terminate her pregnancy." But the reality of the situation is that the Hyde Amendment has effectively removed this choice from the indigent woman's hands. By funding all of the expenses associated with childbirth and none of the expenses incurred in terminating pregnancy, the Government literally makes an offer that the indigent woman cannot afford to refuse. It matters not that, in this instance, the Government has used the carrot, rather than the stick. What is critical is the realization that, as a practical matter, many poverty-stricken women will choose to carry their pregnancy to term simply because the Government provides funds for the associated medical services, even though these same women would have chosen to have an abortion if the Government had also paid for that option, or indeed if the Government had stayed out of the picture altogether and had defrayed the costs of neither procedure. . . .

MR. JUSTICE STEVENS, dissenting.

These cases involve a special exclusion of women who, by definition, are confronted with a choice between two serious harms: serious health damage to themselves on the one hand and abortion on the other. The competing interests are the interest in maternal health and the interest in protecting potential human life. It is now part of our law that the pregnant woman's decision as to which of these conflicting interests shall prevail is entitled to constitutional protection. . . .

If a woman has a constitutional right to place a higher value on avoiding either serious harm to her own health or perhaps an abnormal childbirth than on protecting potential life, the exercise of that right cannot provide the basis for the denial of a benefit to which she would otherwise be entitled. The Court's sterile equal protection analysis evades this critical, though simple, point. The Court focuses exclusively on the "legitimate interest in protecting the potential life of the fetus." It concludes that, since the Hyde Amendments further that interest, the exclusion they create is rational, and therefore constitutional. But it is misleading to speak of the Government's legitimate interest in the fetus without reference to the context in which that interest was held to be legitimate. For *Roe* v. *Wade* squarely held that the States may not protect that interest when a conflict with the interest in a pregnant woman's health exists. It is thus perfectly clear that neither the Federal Government nor the States may exclude a woman from medical benefits to which she would otherwise be entitled solely to further an interest in potential life when a physician, "in appropriate medical judgment," certifies that an abortion is necessary "for the preservation of the life or health of the mother." . . .

It cannot be denied that the harm inflicted upon women in the excluded class is grievous. As the Court's comparison of the differing forms of the Hyde Amendment that have been enacted since 1976 demonstrates, the Court expressly approves the exclusion of benefits in "instances where severe and long-lasting physical health damage to the mother" is the predictable consequence of carrying the pregnancy to term. Indeed, as the Solicitor General acknowledged with commendable candor, the logic of the Court's position would justify a holding that it would be constitutional to deny funding to a medically and financially needy person even if abortion were the only lifesaving medical procedure available. Because a denial of benefits for medically necessary abortions inevitably causes serious harm to the excluded women, it is tantamount to severe punishment. In my judgment, that denial cannot be justified unless government may, in effect, punish women who want abortions. But as the Court unequivocally held in *Roe* v. *Wade*, this the government may not do.

After *McRae*, religious organizations supporting and opposing abortion rights continued to participate in abortion litigation, giving the debate over the constitutional right to abortion a theological dimension to complement the traditional arguments over the scope of personal privacy rights. In the 1980s, the infusion of religious groups into the abortion debate coincided with a much more dynamic and contentious litigation environment, fueled in part by the determination of the Reagan administration to overturn *Roe*. On several occasions between 1983 and 1989, the Department of Justice asked the Court to overturn *Roe*, coming within an eyelash in two separate cases, *Planned Parenthood* v. *Thornburgh* (1986) and *Webster* v. *Reproductive Health Services* (1989), both of which were decided by 5-4 votes.[37] Each successive abortion case during the 1980s drew increasing levels of interest group participation, as anti-*Roe* justices on the Court sent signals that they would use the first opportunity to revisit and possibly overturn the landmark abortion case. By *Webster*, anti-*Roe* justices appeared to command a majority of the Court, prompting the largest submission of *amicus* briefs ever—seventy-eight briefs representing over five thousand organizations and individuals. Abortion-rights advocates, in particular, undertook a massive drive to generate *amicus* support in *Webster*, soliciting briefs from civil rights groups, social historians, family planning specialists, religious organizations, and public health groups to demonstrate that firm support for *Roe* existed beyond the perception created by pro-life forces. One such brief prepared by NARAL and the NOW Legal Defense Fund took the unusual approach of using interviews with over one thousand women who had obtained abortions, some legal and some not, to underscore, in personal terms, the importance of their right to terminate their pregnancies.[38]

Despite the anticipation that had built up around *Webster*, the Court declined to use a challenge brought by Planned Parenthood against a Missouri law prohibiting the use of public hospitals, public employees, and public funds to perform all but medically necessary abortions to overturn *Roe*. The law also permitted doctors to determine whether the fetus was viable prior to the end of the twenty-fourth week, a direct challenge to *Roe*'s trimester system. And, in a nod to the lawyers for the Missouri Catholic Conference who had helped draft the bill, the law contained a preamble declaring that the "life of each human being begins at conception."[39] This last provision encouraged over four dozen religious organizations and congregational representatives to submit arguments in support of or opposition to this statement. Solicitor General Charles Fried, arguing on behalf of the Bush administration, which had picked up the case from President Reagan's justice department, urged the Court to abandon *Roe*. Fried told the Justices that such a decision was possible without "unravel[ing] the fabric of unenumerated and privacy rights which this Court has woven in cases like *Griswold*."[40] Several state attorneys general endorsed Fried's argument, but a half dozen more did not. In a separate brief filed along with over six hundred state legislators, these attorney generals supportive of *Roe* argued that the responsibility for defining "the constitutional boundaries within which to legislate" on abortion and privacy matters belonged to the courts.[41]

Of the five justices that formed the majority in *Webster,* only Justice Scalia, participating in his first abortion case, called for the Court to overturn *Roe.* Scalia was most upset with Justice O'Connor. In her concurring opinion, O'Connor wrote that a "fundamental rule of judicial restraint" required the Court to wait until "the constitutional validity of a State's abortion statute actually turns on the constitutional validity of *Roe*" to reexamine the 1973 decision. Even though O'Connor had voted to uphold every single restriction on abortion challenged in the Court since coming to the bench in 1981, Scalia severely criticized her analysis, deriding it as one that "cannot be taken seriously." For Scalia, the Court's obligation was quite clear:

> The real question, then, is whether there are valid reasons to go beyond the most stingy possible holding today. It seems to me there are not only valid but compelling ones. Ordinarily, speaking no more broadly than is absolutely required avoids throwing settled law into confusion; doing so today preserves a chaos that is evident to anyone who can read and count. Alone sufficient to justify a broad holding is the fact that our retaining control, through *Roe,* of what I believe to be, and many of our citizens recognize to be, a political issue continuously distorts the public perception of the role of this Court. We can now look forward to at least another Term with carts full of mail from the public, and streets full of demonstrators, urging us—their unelected and life tenured judges who have been awarded those extraordinary, undemocratic characteristics precisely in order that we might follow the law despite the popular will—to follow the popular will. Indeed, I expect we can look forward to even more of that than before, given our indecisive decision today.[42]

Justice Scalia was right about one thing—*Webster* did encourage pro-life and pro-choice advocates to take their cause to the public with even greater vigor, offering the most visible evidence to date of just how deeply divided the nation was over abortion. Two weeks before *Webster,* a coalition of pro-choice organizations, assembling some 300,000 marchers, had put together the largest demonstration on behalf of abortion rights since *Roe.* Shortly after *Webster,* the Christian Action Council led a campaign of approximately two dozen pro-life groups to encourage their members to boycott companies that supported family planning organizations, including such corporate giants as American Express and AT&T. Ultimately, AT&T and ten other major companies ended their support of Planned Parenthood and other family planning groups. Gallup polls indicated that a majority of people believed that the Court should not abandon *Roe,* but did agree that states should have wide latitude to regulate abortion as set out in the Missouri statute.[43]

The Court heard two more abortion cases the following term, *Ohio* v. *Akron Center for Reproductive Health* (1990) and *Hodgson* v. *Minnesota* (1990).[44] In *Akron Center,* the Court, with the usually pro-choice Justice Stevens in the majority, upheld an Ohio law that required minors to provide notice to one parent before having an abortion, with a "judicial bypass" available for minors who were the victims of incest or parental abuse or who could otherwise demonstrate that notification was not in their best interest. A "judicial bypass" permits the party seeking an abortion to make her request directly before a judge rather than comply with the consent provisions. But in *Hodgson,* Justice O'Connor, using her "unduly burdensome" analysis, provided the fifth vote to give the *Roe* supporters a majority to strike down a Minnesota law that required a minor to provide *both* parents notice that she was having an abortion. In the same case, O'Connor joined the *Webster* majority to uphold a separate provision authorizing a judicial bypass for minors. Still, O'Connor's decision to join the Court's pro-choice wing marked the first time since coming to the bench nine years before that she had voted to strike down *any* abortion regulation. *Roe* supporters were relieved that one of the landmark decision's fiercest critics was more disturbed by its reasoning than by its fundamental holding. Thus it became clear that if the Court was going to overturn *Roe,* O'Connor was not going to be among the majority voting to do so.

By 1992, of the seven-person majority that had established a constitutional right to abortion in *Roe,* only Justice Blackmun remained. After *Hodgson* and *Akron Center,* two more members of the original *Roe* majority, Brennan and Marshall, had retired. President George Bush, who, while serving in the House of Representatives, had sponsored the federal law that overturned the Comstock Act of 1873 banning any "trafficking" in contraception, had changed his position after serving as Ronald Reagan's vice president from 1981 to 1989. In 1970, Congressman Bush wrote to one constituent that the decision to give birth to a child "should always remain a matter of individual choice." During the 1992 presidential campaign, President Bush affirmed his support for "adoption, not abortion." Speaking before the National Association of Evangelicals, Bush said that he would veto any effort by Congress to protect the rights established in *Roe* through federal legislation. President Bush's commitment to the pro-life position led many people to believe that the two men he appointed to replace Brennan and Marshall, David Souter and Clarence Thomas, shared those views and would vote to overturn *Roe.*[45]

In March 1992, the Court announced that it would hear a challenge in April to a Pennsylvania law, modified in the wake of *Webster,* that placed several restrictions on abortion in the pre-viability stage of a woman's pregnancy. Continuing where it left off in *Webster,* the Department of Justice asked the Court if it could join Pennsylvania in arguing to overturn *Roe,* a request the justices granted. Abortion-rights supporters adopted a somewhat different legal strategy in *Casey* than in previous cases challenging *Roe's* vitality. Rather than submit the usual dozens of briefs offering, more or less, similar arguments on behalf of broad abortion rights, 178 organizations signed on to a single *amicus* brief, coauthored by Sarah Weddington, that encouraged the Court either to reaffirm or reject *Roe.* The abortion-rights groups did not want another decision like *Webster,* which left everyone uncertain on the status of abortion law. If the Court was going to overturn a woman's constitutional right to abortion, pro-choice advocates wanted that decision on record in time to make it a campaign issue in the 1992 presidential election. Pro-life groups mounted an aggressive *amicus* effort as well, also encouraging the Court to resolve the status of *Roe* once and for all. By most accounts, pro-choice advocates expected the Court to decide against them. Even with O'Connor committed to some constitutional basis for abortion rights, Kennedy had demonstrated hostility to *Roe* in *Webster,* and Clarence Thomas's impeccable conservative credentials led most students of the Court to conclude that a five-person majority was prepared to overturn *Roe.*

Planned Parenthood v. *Casey*

505 U.S. 833 (1992)

In November 1989, five months after *Webster,* Pennsylvania governor Robert P. Casey signed an amended version of the state's Abortion Control Act, sections of which had been invalidated three years before in *Planned Parenthood* v. *Thornburgh.* Among other things, the law required women to wait twenty-four hours before receiving an abortion; sign a form indicating they had received information about alternatives to abortion, including adoption; provide a statement, if married, indicating that their husbands had been notified of their decision to have an abortion; and, if minors, provide documentation that one parent had given their consent for an abortion. A federal district court blocked the law from going into effect, but an appeals court reversed, upholding all but the spousal notification provision. Around this same time, Idaho's governor had vetoed a model anti-abortion law ghostwritten by pro-life groups; and Connecticut, one of the last states to maintain a legal ban on contraception, enacted a statute that codified *Roe's* holding into state law.

By the time *Casey* reached the Court, fewer and fewer doctors were willing to perform abortions. They were fearful of the violence that had recently plagued clinics and abortion providers. Many more doctors stopped performing them because they felt stigmatized by their colleagues. By the early 1990s, approximately 85 percent of all abortions were being performed in specialized clinics, not hospitals. Less than 15 percent of all medical students in obstetrics and gynecology programs were receiving training in abortion techniques. Public opinion continued to support a woman's right to choose abortion, but, as was the case after *Webster,* also endorsed the idea of regulation. America's view on abortion appeared to be one of trust, but verify.

When Kathryn Kolbert, an ACLU lawyer who had headed the group's Reproductive Rights Project during the 1980s, took the lectern on the morning of April 22, 1992, she told the justices to confront *Roe* head-on:

Whether our Constitution endows government with the power to force a woman to continue or to end a pregnancy against her will is the central question in this case.

Since this Court's decision in *Roe* v. *Wade*, a generation of American women have come of age secure in the knowledge that the Constitution provides the highest level of protection for their childbearing decisions.

This landmark decision, which necessarily and logically flows from a century of this Court's jurisprudence, not only protects rights of bodily integrity and autonomy, but has enabled millions of women to participate fully and equally in society.

Pennsylvania's attorney general, Ernest D. Preate Jr., and United States Solicitor General Kenneth Starr urged the Court to overturn *Roe*. For the United States, *Casey* marked the sixth time in nine years that it had asked the Court to abandon *Roe*, a tactic that appeared to test the patience of the pro-*Roe* justices, including O'Connor.

Nine weeks later, on June 29, the last day of the Court's term, a crowded courtroom assembled to hear the justices determine *Roe*'s fate. When Chief Justice Rehnquist announced that Justices O'Connor, Kennedy, and Souter would deliver a jointly signed opinion in *Casey*, sections of which were joined by Justices Blackmun and Stevens, seasoned Court-watchers were baffled. What could this mean? O'Connor's position on abortion by now was clear, but Kennedy had demonstrated no sympathy for abortion rights since joining the Court in 1987. What was Blackmun, *Roe*'s author, doing joining, in part, an opinion in which Kennedy was a coauthor? Only once before had the Court handed down a decision in which more than one justice signed the majority opinion, and that had come thirty-four years before in *Cooper* v. *Aaron* (1958), which reaffirmed the Court's landmark school desegregation decision of *Brown* v. *Board of Education* (1954) (see Chapter 11).

The Court's decision was 5 to 4 to reaffirm the core holding of *Roe*—that women, prior to the viability of the fetus, retained the right to decide whether to continue their pregnancy—and 5 to 4 to uphold all but the spousal notice provision of the Pennsylvania law. Justices Kennedy, O'Connor, and Souter announced the judgment of the Court and delivered the opinion. Justice Blackmun filed an opinion concurring in part and dissenting in part, as did Justice Stevens. Chief Justice Rehnquist, joined by Justices White, Scalia, and Thomas, filed an opinion concurring in part and dissenting in part. Justice Scalia, joined by Chief Justice Rehnquist and Justices White and Thomas, filed an opinion concurring in part and dissenting in part.

JUSTICE O'CONNOR, JUSTICE KENNEDY, and JUSTICE SOUTER announced the judgment of the Court and delivered the opinion of the Court with respect to Parts I, II, III, V-A, V-C, and VI, an opinion with respect to Part V-E, in which JUSTICE STEVENS joins, and an opinion with respect to Parts IV, V-B, and V-D.

I

Liberty finds no refuge in a jurisprudence of doubt. Yet, 19 years after our holding that the Constitution protects a woman's right to terminate her pregnancy in its early stages, *Roe* v. *Wade* (1973), that definition of liberty is still questioned. Joining the respondents as *amicus curiae*, the United States, as it has done in five other cases in the last decade, again asks us to overrule *Roe*. . . .

After considering the fundamental constitutional questions resolved by *Roe*, principles of institutional integrity, and the rule of *stare decisis*, we are led to conclude this: the essential holding of *Roe* v. *Wade* should be retained and once again reaffirmed.

It must be stated at the outset and with clarity that *Roe*'s essential holding, the holding we reaffirm, has three parts. First is a recognition of the right of the woman to choose to have an abortion before viability and to obtain it without undue interference from the State. Before viability, the State's interests are not strong enough to support a prohibition of abortion or the imposition of a substantial obstacle to the woman's effective right to elect the procedure. Second is a confirmation of the State's power to restrict abortions after fetal viability if the law contains exceptions for pregnancies which endanger a woman's life or health. And third is the principle that the State has legitimate interests from the outset of the pregnancy in protecting the health of the woman and the life of the fetus that may become a child. These principles do not contradict one another; and we adhere to each.

II

The inescapable fact is that adjudication of substantive due process claims may call upon the Court in interpreting the Constitution to exercise that same capacity which, by tradition, courts always have exercised: reasoned judgment. Its boundaries are not susceptible of expression as a simple rule. That does not mean we are free to invalidate state policy choices with which we disagree; yet neither does it permit us to shrink from the duties of our office. . . .

Men and women of good conscience can disagree, and we suppose some always shall disagree, about the profound moral and spiritual implications of terminating a pregnancy, even in its earliest stage. Some of us as individuals find abortion offensive to our most basic principles of morality, but that cannot control our decision. Our obligation is to define the liberty of all, not to mandate our own moral code. The underlying constitutional issue is whether the State can resolve these philosophic questions in such a definitive way that a woman lacks all choice in the matter, except perhaps in those rare circumstances in which the pregnancy is itself a danger to her own life or health, or is the result of rape or incest.

It is conventional constitutional doctrine that, where reasonable people disagree, the government can adopt one position or the other. That theorem, however, assumes a state of affairs in which the choice does not intrude upon a protected liberty. Thus, while some people might disagree about whether or not the flag should be saluted, or disagree about the proposition that it may not be defiled, we have ruled that a State may not compel or enforce one view or the other. . . .

At the heart of liberty is the right to define one's own concept of existence, of meaning, of the universe, and of the mystery of human life. Beliefs about these matters could not define the attributes of personhood were they formed under compulsion of the State. . . .

These considerations begin our analysis of the woman's interest in terminating her pregnancy, but cannot end it, for this reason: though the abortion decision may originate within the zone of conscience and belief, it is more than a philosophic exercise. Abortion is a unique act. It is an act fraught with consequences for others: for the woman who must live with the implications of her decision; for the persons who perform and assist in the procedure; for the spouse, family, and society which must confront the knowledge that these procedures exist, procedures some deem nothing short of an act of violence against innocent human life; and, depending on one's beliefs, for the life or potential life that is aborted. Though abortion is conduct, it does not follow that the State is entitled to proscribe it in all instances. That is because the liberty of the woman is at stake in a sense unique to the human condition, and so, unique to the law. The mother who carries a child to full term is subject to anxieties, to physical constraints, to pain that only she must bear. That these sacrifices have from the beginning of the human race been endured by woman with a pride that ennobles her in the eyes of others and gives to the infant a bond of love cannot alone be grounds for the State to insist she make the sacrifice. Her suffering is too intimate and personal for the State to insist, without more, upon its own vision of the woman's role, however dominant that vision has been in the course of our history and our culture. The destiny of the woman must be shaped to a large extent on her own conception of her spiritual imperatives and her place in society.

It should be recognized, moreover, that in some critical respects, the abortion decision is of the same character as the decision to use contraception, to which *Griswold* v. *Connecticut*, *Eisenstadt* v. *Baird*, and *Carey* v. *Population Services International* afford constitutional protection. We have no doubt as to the correctness of those decisions. They support the reasoning in *Roe* relating to the woman's liberty, because they involve personal decisions concerning not only the meaning of procreation but also human responsibility and respect for it. As with abortion, reasonable people will have differences of opinion about these matters. One view is based on such reverence for the wonder of creation that any pregnancy ought to be welcomed and carried to full term, no matter how difficult it will be to provide for the child and ensure its wellbeing. Another is that the inability to provide for the nurture and care of the infant is a cruelty to the child and an anguish to the parent. These are intimate views with infinite variations, and their deep, personal character underlay our decisions in *Griswold* [and] *Eisenstadt*. The same concerns are present when the woman confronts the reality that, perhaps despite her attempts to avoid it, she has become pregnant.

It was this dimension of personal liberty that *Roe* sought to protect, and its holding invoked the reasoning and the tradition of the precedents we have discussed, granting protection to substantive liberties of the person. *Roe* was, of course, an extension of those cases and, as the decision itself indicated, the separate States could act in some degree to further their own legitimate interests in protecting prenatal life. The extent to which the legislatures of the States might act to outweigh the interests of the woman in choosing to terminate her pregnancy was a subject of debate both in *Roe* itself and in decisions following it.

While we appreciate the weight of the arguments made on behalf of the State in the case before us, arguments which in their ultimate formulation conclude that *Roe* should be overruled, the reservations any of us may have in reaffirming the central holding of *Roe* are outweighed by the explication of individual liberty we have given, combined with the force of *stare decisis.* We turn now to that doctrine.

III

A

Although *Roe* has engendered opposition, it has in no sense proven "unworkable," representing as it does a simple limitation beyond which a state law is unenforceable. While *Roe* has, of course, required judicial assessment of state laws affecting the exercise of the choice guaranteed against government infringement, and although the need for such review will remain as a consequence of today's decision, the required determinations fall within judicial competence. . . .

No evolution of legal principle has left *Roe*'s doctrinal footings weaker than they were in 1973. No development of constitutional law since the case was decided has implicitly or explicitly left *Roe* behind as a mere survivor of obsolete constitutional thinking. . . .

Roe, however, may be seen not only as an exemplar of *Griswold* liberty but as a rule (whether or not mistaken) of personal autonomy and bodily integrity, with doctrinal affinity to cases recognizing limits on governmental power to mandate medical treatment or to bar its rejection. If so, our cases since *Roe* accord with *Roe*'s view that a State's interest in the protection of life falls short of justifying any plenary override of individual liberty claims. . . .

We have seen how time has overtaken some of *Roe*'s factual assumptions: advances in maternal health care allow for abortions safe to the mother later in pregnancy than was true in 1973, and advances in neonatal care have advanced viability to a point somewhat earlier. But these facts go only to the scheme of time limits on the realization of competing interests, and the divergences from the factual premises of 1973 have no bearing on the validity of *Roe*'s central holding, that viability marks the earliest point at which the State's interest in fetal life is constitutionally adequate to justify a legislative ban on nontherapeutic abortions. The soundness or unsoundness of that constitutional judgment in no sense turns on whether viability occurs at approximately 28 weeks, as was usual at the time of *Roe,* at 23 to 24 weeks, as it sometimes does today, or at some moment even slightly earlier in pregnancy, as it may if fetal respiratory capacity can somehow be enhanced in the future. Whenever it may occur, the attainment of viability may continue to serve as the critical fact, just as it has done since *Roe* was decided; which is to say that no change in *Roe*'s factual underpinning has left its central holding obsolete, and none supports an argument for overruling it.

C

The sum of the precedential inquiry to this point shows *Roe*'s underpinnings unweakened in any way affecting its central holding. While it has engendered disapproval, it has not been unworkable. An entire generation has come of age free to assume *Roe*'s concept of liberty in defining the capacity of women to act in society, and to make reproductive decisions; no erosion of principle going to liberty or personal autonomy has left *Roe*'s central holding a doctrinal remnant; *Roe* portends no developments at odds with other precedent for the analysis of personal liberty; and no changes of fact have rendered viability more or less appropriate as the point at which the balance of interests tips. Within the bounds of normal *stare decisis* analysis, then, and subject to the considerations on which it customarily turns, the stronger argument is for affirming *Roe*'s central holding, with whatever degree of personal reluctance any of us may have, not for overruling it. . . .

Because neither the factual underpinnings of *Roe*'s central holding nor our understanding of it has changed (and because no other indication of weakened precedent has been shown), the Court could not pretend to be reexamining the prior law with any justification beyond a present doctrinal disposition to come out differently from the Court of 1973. To overrule prior law for no other reason than that would run counter to the view, repeated in our cases, that a decision to overrule should rest on some special reason over and above the belief that a prior case was wrongly decided. . . .

Our analysis would not be complete, however, without explaining why overruling *Roe*'s central holding would not only reach an unjustifiable result under principles of *stare decisis,* but would seriously weaken the Court's capacity to exercise the judicial power and to function as the Supreme Court of a Nation dedicated to the rule of law. To understand why this would be so, it is necessary to understand the source of this Court's authority, the conditions necessary for its preservation, and its relationship to the country's understanding of itself as a constitutional Republic.

The root of American governmental power is revealed most clearly in the instance of the power conferred by the Constitution upon the Judiciary of the United States, and specifically upon this Court. As Americans of each succeeding generation are rightly told, the Court cannot buy support for its decisions by spending money, and, except to a minor degree, it cannot independently coerce obedience to its decrees. The Court's power lies, rather, in its legitimacy, a product of substance and perception that shows itself in the people's acceptance of the Judiciary as fit to determine what the Nation's law means, and to declare what it demands.

The underlying substance of this legitimacy is of course the warrant for the Court's decisions in the Constitution and the lesser sources of legal principle on which the Court draws. That substance is expressed in the Court's opinions, and our contemporary understanding is such that a decision without principled justification would be no judicial act at all. But even when justification is furnished by apposite legal principle, something more is required. Because not every conscientious claim of principled justification will be accepted as such, the justification claimed must be beyond dispute. The Court must take care to speak and act in ways that allow people to accept its decisions on the terms the Court claims for them, as grounded truly in principle, not as compromises with social and political pressures having, as such, no bearing on the principled choices that the Court is obliged to make. Thus, the Court's legitimacy depends on making legally principled decisions under circumstances in which their principled character is sufficiently plausible to be accepted by the Nation.

The need for principled action to be perceived as such is implicated to some degree whenever this, or any other appellate court, overrules a prior case. This is not to say, of course, that this Court cannot give a perfectly satisfactory explanation in most cases. People understand that some of the Constitution's language is hard to fathom, and that the Court's Justices are sometimes able to perceive significant facts or to understand principles of law that eluded their predecessors and that justify departures from existing decisions. However upsetting it may be to those most directly affected when one judicially derived rule replaces another, the country can accept some correction of error without necessarily questioning the legitimacy of the Court.

In two circumstances, however, the Court would almost certainly fail to receive the benefit of the doubt in overruling prior cases. There is, first, a point beyond which frequent overruling would overtax the country's belief in the Court's good faith. Despite the variety of reasons that may inform and justify a decision to overrule, we cannot forget that such a decision is usually perceived (and perceived correctly) as, at the least, a statement that a prior decision was wrong. There is a limit to the amount of error that can plausibly be imputed to prior courts. If that limit should be exceeded, disturbance of prior rulings would be taken as evidence that justifiable reexamination of principle had given way to drives for particular results in the short term. The legitimacy of the Court would fade with the frequency of its vacillation.

That first circumstance can be described as hypothetical; the second is to the point here and now. Where, in the performance of its judicial duties, the Court decides a case in such a way as to resolve the sort of intensely divisive controversy reflected in *Roe* and those rare, comparable cases, its decision has a dimension that the resolution of the normal case does not carry. It is the dimension present whenever the Court's interpretation of the Constitution calls the contending sides of a national controversy to end their national division by accepting a common mandate rooted in the Constitution.

The Court is not asked to do this very often, having thus addressed the Nation only twice in our lifetime, in the decisions of *Brown* and *Roe*. But when the Court does act in this way, its decision requires an equally rare precedential force to counter the inevitable efforts to overturn it and to thwart its implementation. Some of those efforts may be mere unprincipled emotional reactions; others may proceed from principles worthy of profound respect. But whatever the premises of opposition may be, only the most convincing justification under accepted standards of precedent could suffice to demonstrate that a later decision overruling the first was anything but a surrender to political pressure and an unjustified repudiation of the principle on which the Court staked its authority in the first instance. So to overrule under fire in the absence of the most compelling reason to reexamine a watershed decision would subvert the Court's legitimacy beyond any serious question.

The country's loss of confidence in the judiciary would be underscored by an equally certain and equally reasonable condemnation for another failing in overruling unnecessarily and under pressure. Some cost will be paid by anyone who approves or implements a constitutional decision where it is unpopular, or who refuses to work to undermine the decision or to force its reversal. The price may be criticism or ostracism, or it may be violence. An extra price will be paid by those who themselves disapprove of the decision's results when viewed outside of constitutional terms, but who nevertheless struggle to accept it, because they respect the rule of law. To all those who will be so tested by following, the Court implicitly undertakes to remain steadfast, lest in the end a price be paid for nothing. The promise of constancy, once given, binds its maker for as long as the power to stand by the decision survives and the understanding of the issue has not changed so fundamentally as to render the commitment obsolete. From the obligation of this promise, this Court cannot and should not assume any exemption when duty requires it to decide a case in conformance with the Constitution. A willing breach of it would be nothing less than a breach of faith, and no Court that broke its faith with the people could sensibly expect credit for principle in the decision by which it did that. . . .

The Court's duty in the present case is clear. In 1973, it confronted the already-divisive issue of governmental power to limit personal choice to undergo abortion, for which it provided a new resolution based on the due process guaranteed by the Fourteenth Amendment. Whether or not a new social consensus is developing on that issue, its divisiveness is no less today than in 1973, and pressure to overrule the decision, like pressure to retain it, has grown only more intense. A decision to overrule *Roe*'s essential holding under the existing circumstances would address error, if error there was, at the cost of both profound and unnecessary damage to the Court's legitimacy, and to the Nation's commitment to the rule of law. It is therefore imperative to adhere to the essence of *Roe*'s original decision, and we do so today.

IV

From what we have said so far, it follows that it is a constitutional liberty of the woman to have some freedom to terminate her pregnancy. We conclude that the basic decision in *Roe* was based on a constitutional analysis which we cannot now repudiate. . . .

That brings us, of course, to the point where much criticism has been directed at *Roe*, a criticism that always inheres when the Court draws a specific rule from what in the Constitution is but a general standard. We conclude, however, that the urgent claims of the woman to retain the ultimate control over her destiny and her body, claims implicit in the meaning of liberty, require us to perform that function. Liberty must not be extinguished for want of a line that is clear. And it falls to us to give some real substance to the woman's liberty to determine whether to carry her pregnancy to full term.

We conclude the line should be drawn at viability, so that, before that time, the woman has a right to choose to terminate her pregnancy. We adhere to this principle for two reasons. First, as we have said, is the doctrine of *stare decisis*. Any judicial act of line-drawing may seem somewhat arbitrary, but *Roe* was a reasoned statement, elaborated with great care. . . .

The second reason is that the concept of viability, as we noted in *Roe*, is the time at which there is a realistic possibility of maintaining and nourishing a life outside the womb, so that the independent existence of the second life can, in reason and all fairness, be the object of state protection that now overrides the rights of the woman. Consistent with other constitutional norms, legislatures may draw lines which appear arbitrary without the necessity of offering a justification. But courts may not. We must justify the lines we draw. And there is no line other than viability which is more workable. To be sure, as we have said, there may be some medical developments that affect the precise point of viability, but this is an imprecision within tolerable limits, given that the medical community and all those who must apply its discoveries will continue to explore the matter. The viability line also has, as a practical matter, an element of fairness. In some broad sense, it might be said that a woman who fails to act before viability has consented to the State's intervention on behalf of the developing child.

The woman's right to terminate her pregnancy before viability is the most central principle of *Roe* v. *Wade*. It is a rule of law and a component of liberty we cannot renounce.

On the other side of the equation is the interest of the State in the protection of potential life. The *Roe* Court recognized the State's "important and legitimate interest in protecting the potentiality of human life." The weight to be given this state interest, not the strength of the woman's interest, was the difficult question faced in *Roe*. We do not need to say whether each of us, had we been Members of the Court when the valuation of the State interest came before it as an original matter, would have concluded, as the *Roe* Court did, that its weight is insufficient to justify a ban on abortions prior to viability even when it is subject to certain exceptions. The matter is not before us in the first instance, and, coming as it does after nearly 20 years of litigation in *Roe*'s wake we are satisfied that the immediate question is not the soundness of *Roe*'s resolution of the issue, but the precedential force that must be accorded to its holding. And we have concluded that the essential holding of *Roe* should be reaffirmed.

Yet it must be remembered that *Roe* v. *Wade* speaks with clarity in establishing not only the woman's liberty but also the State's "important and legitimate interest in potential life." That portion of the decision in *Roe* has been given too little acknowledgement and implementation by the Court in its subsequent cases. Those cases decided that any regulation touching upon the abortion decision must survive strict scrutiny, to be sustained only if drawn in narrow terms to further a compelling state interest. Not all of the cases decided under that formulation can be reconciled with the holding in *Roe* itself that the State has legitimate interests in the health of the woman and in protecting the potential life within her. In resolving this tension, we choose to rely upon *Roe*, as against the later cases.

Roe established a trimester framework to govern abortion regulations. Under this elaborate but rigid construct, almost no regulation at all is permitted during the first trimester of pregnancy; regulations designed to protect the woman's health, but not to further the State's interest in potential life, are permitted during the second trimester; and, during the third trimester, when the fetus is viable, prohibitions are permitted provided the life or health of the mother is not at stake. Most of our cases since *Roe* have involved the application of rules derived from the trimester framework.

The trimester framework no doubt was erected to ensure that the woman's right to choose not become so subordinate to the State's interest in promoting fetal life that her choice exists in theory, but not in fact. We do not agree, however, that the trimester approach is necessary to accomplish this objective. A framework of this rigidity was unnecessary, and, in its later interpretation, sometimes contradicted the State's permissible exercise of its powers. . . .

We reject the trimester framework, which we do not consider to be part of the essential holding of *Roe*. Measures aimed at ensuring that a woman's choice contemplates the consequences for the fetus do not necessarily interfere with the right recognized in *Roe*, although those measures have been found to be inconsistent with the rigid trimester framework announced in that case. A logical reading of the central holding in *Roe* itself, and a necessary reconciliation of the liberty of the woman and the interest of the State in promoting prenatal life, require, in our view, that we abandon the trimester framework as a rigid prohibition on all pre-viability regulation aimed at the protection of fetal life. The trimester framework suffers from these basic flaws: in its formulation, it misconceives the nature of the pregnant woman's interest; and in practice, it undervalues the State's interest in potential life, as recognized in *Roe*. . . .

Some guiding principles should emerge. What is at stake is the woman's right to make the ultimate decision, not a right to be insulated from all others in doing so. Regulations which do no more than create a structural mechanism by which the State, or the parent or guardian of a minor, may express profound respect for the life of the unborn are permitted, if they are not a substantial obstacle to the woman's exercise of the right to choose. Unless it has that effect on her right of choice, a state measure designed to persuade her to choose childbirth over abortion will be upheld if reasonably related to that goal. Regulations designed to foster the health of a woman seeking an abortion are valid if they do not constitute an undue burden. . . .

Even when jurists reason from shared premises, some disagreement is inevitable. That is to be expected in the application of any legal standard which must accommodate life's complexity. We do not expect it to be otherwise with respect to the undue burden standard. We give this summary:

a. To protect the central right recognized by *Roe* v. *Wade* while at the same time accommodating the State's profound interest in potential life, we will employ the undue burden analysis as explained in this opinion. An undue burden exists, and therefore a provision of law is invalid, if its purpose or effect is to place a substantial obstacle in the path of a woman seeking an abortion before the fetus attains viability.

b. We reject the rigid trimester framework of *Roe* v. *Wade*. To promote the State's profound interest in potential life, throughout pregnancy, the State may take measures to ensure that the woman's choice is informed, and measures designed to advance this interest will not be invalidated as long as their purpose is to persuade the woman to choose childbirth over abortion. These measures must not be an undue burden on the right.

c. As with any medical procedure, the State may enact regulations to further the health or safety of a woman seeking an abortion. Unnecessary health regulations that have the purpose or effect of presenting a substantial obstacle to a woman seeking an abortion impose an undue burden on the right.

d. Our adoption of the undue burden analysis does not disturb the central holding of *Roe* v. *Wade*, and we reaffirm that holding. Regardless of whether exceptions are made for particular circumstances, a State may not prohibit any woman from making the ultimate decision to terminate her pregnancy before viability.

e. We also reaffirm *Roe*'s holding that, "subsequent to viability, the State, in promoting its interest in the potentiality of human life, may, if it chooses, regulate, and even proscribe, abortion except where it is necessary, in appropriate medical judgment, for the preservation of the life or health of the mother."

These principles control our assessment of the Pennsylvania statute, and we now turn to the issue of the validity of its challenged provisions.

V

[Informed Consent]

We . . . consider [now] the informed consent requirement. . . .

Our prior decisions establish that, as with any medical procedure, the State may require a woman to give her written informed consent to an abortion. In this respect, the statute is unexceptional. Petitioners challenge the statute's definition of informed consent because it includes the provision of specific information by the doctor and the mandatory 24-hour waiting period. The conclusions reached by a majority of the Justices in the separate opinions filed today and the undue burden standard adopted in this opinion require us to overrule in part some of the Court's past decisions, decisions driven by the trimester framework's prohibition of all pre-viability regulations designed to further the State's interest in fetal life. . . .

It cannot be questioned that psychological wellbeing is a facet of health. Nor can it be doubted that most women considering an abortion would deem the impact on the fetus relevant, if not dispositive, to the decision. In attempting to ensure that a woman apprehend the full consequences of her decision, the State furthers the legitimate purpose of reducing the risk that a woman may elect an abortion, only to discover later, with devastating psychological consequences, that her decision was not fully informed. If the information the State requires to be made available to the woman is truthful and not misleading, the requirement may be permissible. . . .

We are left with the argument that the various aspects of the informed consent requirement are unconstitutional because they place barriers in the way of abortion on demand. Even the broadest reading of *Roe,* however, has not suggested that there is a constitutional right to abortion on demand. Rather, the right protected by *Roe* is a right to decide to terminate a pregnancy free of undue interference by the State. Because the informed consent requirement facilitates the wise exercise of that right, it cannot be classified as an interference with the right *Roe* protects. The informed consent requirement is not an undue burden on that right. . . .

C
[Spousal Notification]

. . . Pennsylvania's abortion law provides, except in cases of medical emergency, that no physician shall perform an abortion on a married woman without receiving a signed statement from the woman that she has notified her spouse that she is about to undergo an abortion. The woman has the option of providing an alternative signed statement certifying that her husband is not the man who impregnated her; that her husband could not be located; that the pregnancy is the result of spousal sexual assault which she has reported; or that the woman believes that notifying her husband will cause him or someone else to inflict bodily injury upon her. A physician who performs an abortion on a married woman without receiving the appropriate signed statement will have his or her license revoked, and is liable to the husband for damages. . . .

[Here, the Court summarized the findings of fact by the lower court on domestic violence against women, and the problems that spousal consent might pose for women who are carrying unwanted babies.]

These findings are supported by studies of domestic violence. The American Medical Association (AMA) has published a summary of the recent research in this field, which indicates that, in an average 12-month period in this country, approximately two million women are the victims of severe assaults by their male partners. In a 1985 survey, women reported that nearly one of every eight husbands had assaulted their wives during the past year. The AMA views these figures as "marked underestimates," because the nature of these incidents discourages women from reporting them, and because surveys typically exclude the very poor, those who do not speak English well, and women who are homeless or in institutions or hospitals when the survey is conducted. . . . [O]n an average day in the United States, nearly 11,000 women are severely assaulted by their male partners. Many of these incidents involve sexual assault. In families where wife-beating takes place, moreover, child abuse is often present as well. . . .

The limited research that has been conducted with respect to notifying one's husband about an abortion, although involving samples too small to be representative, also supports the District Court's findings of fact. The vast majority of women notify their male partners of their decision to obtain an abortion. In many cases in which married women do not notify their husbands, the pregnancy is the result of an extramarital affair. Where the husband is the father, the primary reason women do not notify their husbands is that the husband and wife are experiencing marital difficulties, often accompanied by incidents of violence. . . .

In well functioning marriages, spouses discuss important intimate decisions such as whether to bear a child. But there are millions of women in this country who are the victims of regular physical and psychological abuse at the hands of their husbands. Should these women become pregnant, they may have very good reasons for not wishing to inform their husbands of their decision to obtain an abortion. Many may have justifiable fears of physical abuse, but may be no less fearful of the consequences of reporting prior abuse to the Commonwealth of Pennsylvania. Many may have a reasonable fear that notifying their husbands will provoke further instances of child abuse; these women are not exempt from [the law's] notification requirement.

The spousal notification requirement is thus likely to prevent a significant number of women from obtaining an abortion. It does not merely make abortions a little more difficult or expensive to obtain; for many women, it will impose a substantial obstacle. We must not blind ourselves to the fact that the significant number of women who fear for their safety and the safety of their children are likely to be deterred from procuring an abortion as surely as if the Commonwealth had outlawed abortion in all cases. . . .

The husband's interest in the life of the child his wife is carrying does not permit the State to empower him with this troubling degree of authority over his wife. The contrary view leads to consequences reminiscent of the common law. A husband has no enforceable right to require a wife to advise him before she exercises her personal choices. If a husband's interest in the potential life of the child outweighs a wife's liberty, the State could require a married woman to notify her husband before she uses a post-fertilization contraceptive. Perhaps next in line would be a statute requiring pregnant married women to notify their husbands before engaging in conduct causing risks to the fetus. After all, if the husband's interest in the fetus' safety is a sufficient predicate for state regulation, the State could reasonably conclude that pregnant wives should notify their husbands before drinking alcohol or smoking. Perhaps married women should notify their husbands before using contraceptives or before undergoing any type of surgery that may have complications affecting the husband's interest in his wife's reproductive organs. And if a husband's interest justifies notice in any of these cases, one might reasonably argue that it justifies exactly what the *Danforth* Court held it did not justify—a requirement of the husband's consent as well. A State may not give to a man the kind of dominion over his wife that parents exercise over their children. . . .

D

[Parental Consent]

We next consider the parental consent provision. Except in a medical emergency, an unemancipated young woman under 18 may not obtain an abortion unless she and one of her parents (or guardian) provides informed consent as defined above. If neither a parent nor a guardian provides consent, a court may authorize the performance of an abortion upon a determination that the young woman is mature and capable of giving informed consent and has, in fact, given her informed consent, or that an abortion would be in her best interests.

We have been over most of this ground before. Our cases establish, and we reaffirm today, that a State may require a minor seeking an abortion to obtain the consent of a parent or guardian, provided that there is an adequate judicial bypass procedure. Under these precedents, in our view, the one-parent consent requirement and judicial bypass procedure are constitutional. . . .

E

[Omitted]

VI

Our Constitution is a covenant running from the first generation of Americans to us, and then to future generations. It is a coherent succession. Each generation must learn anew that the Constitution's written terms embody ideas and aspirations that must survive more ages than one. We accept our responsibility not to retreat from interpreting the full meaning of the covenant in light of all of our precedents. We invoke it once again to define the freedom guaranteed by the Constitution's own promise, the promise of liberty. . . .

It is so ordered.

Justice Stevens, concurring in part and dissenting with respect to Parts IV, V-B, and V-D.

The portions of the Court's opinion that I have joined are more important than those with which I disagree. . . .

The Court is unquestionably correct in concluding that the doctrine of *stare decisis* has controlling significance in a case of this kind, notwithstanding an individual justice's concerns about the merits. The central holding of *Roe* v. *Wade* (1973) has been a "part of our law" for almost two decades. It was a natural sequel to the protection of individual liberty established in *Griswold* v. *Connecticut* (1965). The societal costs of overruling *Roe* at this late date would be enormous. *Roe* is an integral part of a correct understanding of both the concept of liberty and the basic equality of men and women. . . .

Justice Blackmun, concurring in part, concurring in the judgment in part, and dissenting in part.

I join parts I, II, III, V-A, V-C, and VI of the joint opinion of Justices O'Connor, Kennedy, and Souter.

Three years ago, in *Webster* v. *Reproductive Health Services* (1989), four Members of this Court appeared poised to "cas[t] into darkness the hopes and visions of every woman in this country" who had come to believe that the Constitution guaranteed her the right to reproductive choice. All that remained between the promise of *Roe* and the darkness of the plurality was a single, flickering flame. Decisions since *Webster* gave little reason to hope that this flame would cast much light But now, just when so many expected the darkness to fall, the flame has grown bright.

I do not underestimate the significance of today's joint opinion. Yet I remain steadfast in my belief that the right to reproductive choice is entitled to the full protection afforded by this Court before *Webster.* And I fear for the darkness as four Justices anxiously await the single vote necessary to extinguish the light.

I

Make no mistake, the joint opinion of JUSTICES O'CONNOR, KENNEDY, and SOUTER is an act of personal courage and constitutional principle. In contrast to previous decisions in which JUSTICES O'CONNOR and KENNEDY postponed reconsideration of *Roe,* the authors of the joint opinion today join JUSTICE STEVENS and me in concluding that "the essential holding of *Roe* should be retained and once again reaffirmed." In brief, five Members of this Court today recognize that "the Constitution protects a woman's right to terminate her pregnancy in its early stages."

A fervent view of individual liberty and the force of *stare decisis* have led the Court to this conclusion. Today a majority reaffirms that the Due Process Clause of the Fourteenth Amendment establishes "a realm of personal liberty which the government may not enter"—a realm whose outer limits cannot be determined by interpretations of the Constitution that focus only on the specific practices of States at the time the Fourteenth Amendment was adopted. . . .

What has happened today should serve as a model for future Justices and a warning to all who have tried to turn this Court into yet another political branch. . . .

II

[Omitted]

III

At long last, THE CHIEF JUSTICE and those who have joined him admit it. Gone are the contentions that the issue need not be (or has not been) considered. There, on the first page, for all to see, is what was expected: "We believe that *Roe* was wrongly decided, and that it can and should be overruled consistently with our traditional approach to *stare decisis* in constitutional cases." If there is much reason to applaud the advances made by the joint opinion today, there is far more to fear from THE CHIEF JUSTICE's opinion.

THE CHIEF JUSTICE's criticism of *Roe* follows from his stunted conception of individual liberty. While recognizing that the Due Process Clause protects more than simple physical liberty, he then goes on to construe this Court's personal liberty cases as establishing only a laundry list of particular rights, rather than a principled account of how these particular rights are grounded in a more general right of privacy. This constricted view is reinforced by THE CHIEF JUSTICE's exclusive reliance on tradition as a source of fundamental rights. He argues that the record in favor of a right to abortion is no stronger than the . . . fundamental right to visitation privileges by an adulterous father, or in *Bowers* v. *Hardwick* (1986), where the Court found no fundamental right to engage in homosexual sodomy. . . . In THE CHIEF JUSTICE's world, a woman considering whether to terminate a pregnancy is entitled to no more protection than adulterers, murderers, and so-called "sexual deviates." Given THE CHIEF JUSTICE's exclusive reliance on tradition, people using contraceptives seem the next likely candidate for his list of outcasts. . . .

But, we are reassured [by the CHIEF JUSTICE and JUSTICE SCALIA], there is always the protection of the democratic process. While there is much to be praised about our democracy, our country, since its founding, has recognized that there are certain fundamental liberties that are not to be left to the whims of an election. A woman's right to reproductive choice is one of those fundamental liberties. Accordingly, that liberty need not seek refuge at the ballot box.

IV

In one sense, the Court's approach is worlds apart from that of THE CHIEF JUSTICE and JUSTICE SCALIA. And yet, in another sense, the distance between the two approaches is short—the distance is but a single vote.

I am 83 years old. I cannot remain on this Court forever, and when I do step down, the confirmation process for my successor well may focus on the issue before us today. That, I regret, may be exactly where the choice between the two worlds will be made.

CHIEF JUSTICE REHNQUIST, with whom JUSTICE WHITE, JUSTICE SCALIA, and JUSTICE THOMAS join, concurring in the judgment in part and dissenting in part.

The joint opinion, following its newly minted variation on *stare decisis,* retains the outer shell of *Roe* v. *Wade,* but beats a wholesale retreat from the substance of that case. We believe that *Roe* was wrongly decided, and that it can and should be overruled consistently with our traditional approach to *stare decisis* in constitutional cases. We would adopt the approach of the plurality in *Webster* v. *Reproductive Health Services* (1989), and uphold the challenged provisions of the Pennsylvania statute in their entirety. . . .

I

We believe that the sort of constitutionally imposed abortion code of the type illustrated by our decisions following *Roe* is inconsistent "with the notion of a Constitution cast in general terms, as ours is, and usually speaking in general principles, as ours does." The Court in *Roe* reached too far when it analogized the right to abort a fetus to the rights involved in *Griswold,* and thereby deemed the right to abortion fundamental.

II

The joint opinion of JUSTICES O'CONNOR, KENNEDY, and SOUTER cannot bring itself to say that *Roe* was correct as an original matter, but the authors are of the view that "the immediate question is not the soundness of *Roe's* resolution of the issue, but the precedential force that must be accorded to its holding." Instead of claiming that *Roe* was correct as a matter of original constitutional interpretation, the opinion therefore contains an elaborate discussion of *stare decisis.* This discussion of the principle of *stare decisis* appears to be almost entirely dicta, because the joint opinion does not apply that principle in dealing with *Roe. Roe* decided that a woman had a fundamental right to an abortion. The joint opinion rejects that view. *Roe* decided that abortion regulations were to be subjected to "strict scrutiny," and could be justified only in the light of "compelling state interests." The joint opinion rejects that view. *Roe* analyzed abortion regulation under a rigid trimester framework, a framework which has guided this Court's decision making for 19 years. The joint opinion rejects that framework. . . .

In our view, authentic principles of *stare decisis* do not require that any portion of the reasoning in *Roe* be kept intact. "*Stare decisis* is not . . . a universal, inexorable command," especially in cases involving the interpretation of the Federal Constitution. Erroneous decisions in such constitutional cases are uniquely durable, because correction through legislative action, save for constitutional amendment, is impossible. It is therefore our duty to reconsider constitutional interpretations that "depar[t] from a proper understanding" of the Constitution. Our constitutional watch does not cease merely because we have spoken before on an issue; when it becomes clear that a prior constitutional interpretation is unsound, we are obliged to reexamine the question. . . .

In the end, having failed to put forth any evidence to prove any true reliance, the joint opinion's argument is based solely on generalized assertions about the national psyche, on a belief that the people of this country have grown accustomed to the *Roe* decision over the last 19 years and have "ordered their thinking and living around" it. As an initial matter, one might inquire how the joint opinion can view the "central holding" of *Roe* as so deeply rooted in our constitutional culture when it so casually uproots and disposes of that same decision's trimester framework. Furthermore, at various points in the past, the same could have been said about this Court's erroneous decisions that the Constitution allowed "separate but equal" treatment of minorities, or that "liberty" under the Due Process Clause protected "freedom of contract." The "separate but equal" doctrine lasted 58 years after *Plessy,* and *Lochner's* protection of contractual freedom lasted 32 years. However, the simple fact that a generation or more had grown used to these major decisions did not prevent the Court from correcting its errors in those cases, nor should it prevent us from correctly interpreting the Constitution here. . . .

There is also a suggestion in the joint opinion that the propriety of overruling a "divisive" decision depends in part on whether "most people" would now agree that it should be overruled. Either the demise of opposition or its progression to substantial popular agreement apparently is required to allow the Court to reconsider a divisive decision. How such agreement would be ascertained, short of a public opinion poll, the joint opinion does not say. But surely even the suggestion is totally at war with the idea of "legitimacy" in whose name it is invoked. The Judicial Branch derives its legitimacy not from following public opinion, but from deciding by its best lights whether legislative enactments of the popular branches of Government comport with the Constitution. The doctrine of *stare decisis* is an adjunct of this duty, and should be no more subject to the vagaries of public opinion than is the basic judicial task. . . .

The end result of the joint opinion's paeans of praise for legitimacy is the enunciation of a brand new standard for evaluating state regulation of a woman's right to abortion—the "undue burden" standard. As indicated above, *Roe* v. *Wade* adopted a "fundamental right" standard under which state regulations could survive only if they met the requirement of "strict scrutiny." While we disagree with that standard, it at least had a recognized basis in constitutional law at the time *Roe* was decided. The same cannot be said for the "undue burden" standard, which is created largely out of whole cloth by the authors of the joint opinion. It is a standard which even today does not command the support of a majority of this Court. And it will not, we believe, result in the sort of "simple limitation," easily applied, which the joint opinion anticipates. In sum, it is a standard which is not built to last.

III

[Omitted]

IV

For the reasons stated, we therefore would hold that each of the challenged provisions of the Pennsylvania statute is consistent with the Constitution. It bears emphasis that our conclusion in this regard does not carry with it any necessary approval of these regulations. Our task is, as always, to decide only whether the challenged provisions of a law comport with the United States Constitution. If, as we believe, these do, their wisdom as a matter of public policy is for the people of Pennsylvania to decide.

JUSTICE SCALIA, with whom THE CHIEF JUSTICE, JUSTICE WHITE, and JUSTICE THOMAS join, concurring in the judgment in part and dissenting in part.

My views on this matter are unchanged. . . . The States may, if they wish, permit abortion on demand, but the Constitution does not *require* them to do so. The permissibility of abortion, and the limitations upon it, are to be resolved like most important questions in our democracy: by citizens trying to persuade one another and then voting. As the Court acknowledges, "where reasonable people disagree, the government can adopt one position or the other." The Court is correct in adding the qualification that this "assumes a state of affairs in which the choice does not intrude upon a protected liberty," but the crucial part of that qualification is the penultimate word. A State's choice between two positions on which reasonable people can disagree is constitutional even when (as is often the case) it intrudes upon a "liberty" in the absolute sense. Laws against bigamy, for example—which entire societies of reasonable people disagree with—intrude upon men and women's liberty to marry and live with one another. But bigamy happens not to be a liberty specially "protected" by the Constitution.

That is, quite simply, the issue in this case: not whether the power of a woman to abort her unborn child is a "liberty" in the absolute sense; or even whether it is a liberty of great importance to many women. Of course it is both. The issue is whether it is a liberty protected by the Constitution of the United States. I am sure it is not. I reach that conclusion not because of anything so exalted as my views concerning the "concept of existence, of meaning, of the universe, and of the mystery of human life." *Ibid.* Rather, I reach it for the same reason I reach the conclusion that bigamy is not constitutionally protected—because of two simple facts: (1) the Constitution says absolutely nothing about it, and (2) the longstanding traditions of American society have permitted it to be legally proscribed. . . .

[Here, Justice Scalia responded to the joint opinion's various arguments, which he called "beyond human nature to leave unanswered."]

Liberty finds no refuge in a jurisprudence of doubt.

One might have feared to encounter this august and sonorous phrase in an opinion defending the real *Roe* v. *Wade,* rather than the revised version fabricated today by the authors of the joint opinion. The shortcomings of *Roe* did not include lack of clarity: virtually all regulation of abortion before the third trimester was invalid. But to come across this phrase in the joint opinion—which calls upon federal district judges to apply an "undue burden" standard as doubtful in application as it is unprincipled in origin—is really more than one should have to bear.

The joint opinion frankly concedes that the amorphous concept of "undue burden" has been inconsistently applied by the Members of this Court in the few brief years since that "test" was first explicitly propounded by JUSTICE O'CONNOR in [a previous case]. Because the three Justices now wish to "set forth a standard of general application," the joint opinion announces that "it is important to clarify what is meant by an undue burden." I certainly agree with that, but I do not agree that the joint opinion succeeds in the announced endeavor. To the contrary, its efforts at clarification make clear only that the standard is inherently manipulable, and will prove hopelessly unworkable in practice.

The joint opinion explains that a state regulation imposes an "undue burden" if it "has the purpose or effect of placing a substantial obstacle in the path of a woman seeking an abortion of a nonviable fetus." An obstacle is "substantial," we are told, if it is "calculated[,] [not] to inform the woman's free choice, [but to] hinder it." This latter statement cannot possibly mean what it says. *Any* regulation of abortion that is intended to advance what the joint opinion concedes is the State's "substantial" interest in protecting unborn life will be "calculated [to] hinder" a decision to have an abortion. It thus seems more accurate to say that the joint opinion would uphold abortion regulations only if they do not *unduly* hinder the woman's decision. That, of course, brings us right back to square one: defining an "undue burden" as an "undue hindrance" (or a "substantial obstacle") hardly "clarifies" the test. Consciously or not, the joint opinion's verbal shell game will conceal raw judicial policy choices concerning what is "appropriate" abortion legislation. . . .

To the extent I can discern any meaningful content in the "undue burden" standard as applied in the joint opinion, it appears to be that a State may not regulate abortion in such a way as to reduce significantly its incidence. The joint opinion repeatedly emphasizes that an important factor in the "undue burden" analysis is whether the regulation "prevent[s] a significant number of women from obtaining an abortion," whether a "significant number of women . . . are likely to be deterred from procuring an abortion," and whether the regulation often "deters" women from seeking abortions. We are not told, however, what forms of "deterrence" are impermissible or what degree of success in deterrence is too much to be tolerated. If, for example, a State required a woman to read a pamphlet describing, with illustrations, the facts of fetal development before she could obtain an abortion, the effect of such legislation might be to "deter" a "significant number of women" from procuring abortions, thereby seemingly allowing a district judge to invalidate it as an undue burden. Thus, despite flowery rhetoric about the State's "substantial" and "profound" interest in "potential human life," and criticism of *Roe* for undervaluing that interest, the joint opinion permits the State to pursue that interest only so long as it is not too successful. As Justice Blackmun recognizes (with evident hope), the "undue burden" standard may ultimately require the invalidation of each provision upheld today if it can be shown, on a better record, that the State is too effectively "express[ing] a preference for childbirth over abortion." Reason finds no refuge in this jurisprudence of confusion.

> While we appreciate the weight of the arguments . . . that *Roe* should be overruled, the reservations any of us may have in reaffirming the central holding of *Roe* are outweighed by the explication of individual liberty we have given combined with the force of *stare decisis.*

The Court's reliance upon *stare decisis* can best be described as contrived. It insists upon the necessity of adhering not to all of *Roe,* but only to what it calls the "central holding." It seems to me that *stare decisis* ought to be applied even to the doctrine of *stare decisis,* and I confess never to have heard of this new, keep-what-you-want-and-throw-away-the-rest version. I wonder whether, as applied to *Marbury* v. *Madison* (1803), for example, the new version of *stare decisis* would be satisfied if we allowed courts to review the constitutionality of only those statutes that (like the one in *Marbury*) pertain to the jurisdiction of the courts. . . .

> Where, in the performance of its judicial duties, the Court decides a case in such a way as to resolve the sort of intensely divisive controversy reflected in *Roe* . . . its decision has a dimension that the resolution of the normal case does not carry. It is the dimension present whenever the Court's interpretation of the Constitution calls the contending sides of a national controversy to end their national division by accepting a common mandate rooted in the Constitution.

The Court's description of the place of *Roe* in the social history of the United States is unrecognizable. Not only did *Roe* not, as the Court suggests, *resolve* the deeply divisive issue of abortion; it did more than anything else to nourish it, by elevating it to the national level, where it is infinitely more difficult to resolve. National politics were not plagued by abortion protests, national abortion lobbying, or abortion marches on Congress, before *Roe* v. *Wade* was decided. Profound disagreement existed among our citizens over the issue—as it does over other issues, such as the death penalty—but that disagreement was being worked out at the state level. As with many other issues, the division of sentiment within each State was not as closely balanced as it was among the population of the Nation as a whole, meaning not only that more people would be satisfied with the results of state-by-state resolution, but also that those results would be more stable. Pre-*Roe,* moreover, political compromise was possible.

Roe's mandate for abortion on demand destroyed the compromises of the past, rendered compromise impossible for the future, and required the entire issue to be resolved uniformly, at the national level. At the same time, *Roe* created a vast new class of abortion consumers and abortion proponents by eliminating the moral opprobrium that had attached to the act. ("If the Constitution *guarantees* abortion, how can it be bad?"—not an accurate line of thought, but a natural one.) Many favor all of those developments, and it is not for me to say that they are wrong. But to portray *Roe* as the statesmanlike "settlement" of a divisive issue, a jurisprudential Peace of Westphalia that is worth preserving, is nothing less than Orwellian. *Roe* fanned into life an issue that has inflamed our national politics in general, and has obscured with its smoke the selection of Justices to this Court, in particular, ever since. . . .

> [T]o overrule under fire . . . would subvert the Court's legitimacy. . . .
>
> To all those who will be . . . tested by following, the Court implicitly undertakes to remain steadfast. . . . The promise of constancy, once given, binds its maker for as long as the power to stand by the decision survives and . . . the commitment [is not] obsolete. . . .
>
> [The American people's] belief in themselves as . . . a people [who aspire to live according to the rule of law] is not readily separable from their understanding of the Court invested with the authority to decide their constitutional cases and speak before all others for their constitutional ideals. If the Court's legitimacy should be undermined, then so would the country be in its very ability to see itself through its constitutional ideals.

The Imperial Judiciary lives. It is instructive to compare this Nietzschean vision of us unelected, life-tenured judges—leading a Volk who will be "tested by following," and whose very "belief in themselves" is mystically bound up in their "understanding" of a Court that "speak[s] before all others for their constitutional ideals"—with the somewhat more modest role envisioned for these lawyers by the Founders. . . .

I cannot agree with, indeed I am appalled by, the Court's suggestion that the decision whether to stand by an erroneous constitutional decision must be strongly influenced—*against* overruling, no less—by the substantial and continuing public opposition the decision has generated. The Court's judgment that any other course would "subvert the Court's legitimacy" must be another consequence of reading the error-filled history book that described the deeply divided country brought together by *Roe*. In my history book, the Court was covered with dishonor and deprived of legitimacy by *Dred Scott* v. *Sandford* (1857), an erroneous (and widely opposed) opinion that it did not abandon, rather than by *West Coast Hotel Co.* v. *Parrish* (1937), which produced the famous "switch in time" from the Court's erroneous (and widely opposed) constitutional opposition to the social measures of the New Deal. Both *Dred Scott* and one line of the cases resisting the New Deal rested upon the concept of "substantive due process" that the Court praises and employs today. . . .

In truth, I am as distressed as the Court is . . . about the "political pressure" directed to the Court: the marches, the mail, the protests aimed at inducing us to change our opinions. How upsetting it is, that so many of our citizens (good people, not lawless ones, on both sides of this abortion issue, and on various sides of other issues as well) think that we Justices should properly take into account their views, as though we were engaged not in ascertaining an objective law, but in determining some kind of social consensus. The Court would profit, I think, from giving less attention to the *fact* of this distressing phenomenon, and more attention to the *cause* of it. That cause permeates today's opinion: a new mode of constitutional adjudication that relies not upon text and traditional practice to determine the law, but upon what the Court calls "reasoned judgment," which turns out to be nothing but philosophical predilection and moral intuition. . . .

What makes all this relevant to the bothersome application of "political pressure" against the Court are the twin facts that the American people love democracy and the American people are not fools. As long as this Court thought (and the people thought) that we Justices were doing essentially lawyers' work up here—reading text and discerning our society's traditional understanding of that text—the public pretty much left us alone. Texts and traditions are facts to study, not convictions to demonstrate about. But if in reality, our process of constitutional adjudication consists primarily of making *value judgments;* if we can ignore a long and clear tradition clarifying an ambiguous text, as we did, for example, five days ago in declaring unconstitutional invocations and benedictions at public high school graduation ceremonies, *Lee* v. *Weisman* (1992); if, as I say, our pronouncement of constitutional law rests primarily on value judgments, then a free and intelligent people's attitude towards us can be expected to be (*ought* to be) quite different. The people know that their value judgments are quite as good as those taught in any law school—maybe better. If, indeed, the "liberties" protected by the Constitution are, as the Court says, undefined and unbounded, then the people *should* demonstrate, to protest that we do not implement *their* values instead of *ours*. Not only that, but the confirmation hearings for new Justices *should* deteriorate into question-and-answer sessions in which Senators go through a list of their constituents' most favored and most disfavored alleged constitutional rights, and seek the nominee's commitment to support or oppose them. Value judgments, after all, should be voted on, not dictated; and if our Constitution has somehow accidently committed them to the Supreme Court, at least we can have a sort of plebiscite each time a new nominee to that body is put forward. JUSTICE BLACKMUN not only regards this prospect with equanimity, he solicits it. . . .

We should get out of this area, where we have no right to be, and where we do neither ourselves nor the country any good by remaining.

TABLE 10.1 Current Status of State Abortion Laws

Planned Parenthood v. *Casey* (1992), while retaining the fundamental core holding of *Roe,* allowed states greater leeway to regulate abortion. Below is the current status, as of February 2000, of abortion law throughout the United States. Note that these reflect the regulations that were upheld in the *Casey* decision. Also note that *Stenberg* v. *Carhart* (2000) placed the constitutionality of every state "partial-birth" abortion law in jeopardy.

	Parental Consent or Notification Required for Minor to Obtain Abortion	Mandatory State-Directed Counseling	Mandatory Waiting Period Following Counseling	"Partial Birth" Abortion Banned
Alabama	Consent	—	—	Yes†
Alaska	Consent*	Yes	—	Yes*
Arizona	Consent*	—	—	Yes*
Arkansas	Notification	—	—	Yes*
California	Consent*	Yes	—	—
Colorado	Notification*	—	—	—
Connecticut	—	Yes	—	—
Delaware	Notification	Yes*	24 hours*	—
District of Columbia				
Florida	Notification*	Yes*	—	Yes*
Georgia	Notification	—	—	Yes†
Hawaii	—	—	—	—
Idaho	Consent	Yes	24 hours	Yes*
Illinois	Notification*	—	—	Yes‡
Indiana	Consent	Yes	18 hours	Yes
Iowa	Notification	—	—	Yes*
Kansas	Notification	Yes	24 hours	Yes[1]
Kentucky	Consent	Yes*	24 hours*	Yes*
Louisiana	Consent	Yes	24 hours	Yes*
Maine	—	Yes	—	—
Maryland	Notification	—	—	—
Massachusetts	Consent	Yes*	24 hours*	—
Michigan	Consent	Yes	24 hours	Yes*
Minnesota	Notification	Yes	—	—
Mississippi	Consent	Yes	24 hours	Yes
Missouri	Consent	Yes*	—	Yes
Montana	Notification*	Yes*	24 hours*	Yes*[2]
Nebraska	Notification	Yes	24 hours	Yes*
Nevada	Notification*	Yes	—	—
New Hampshire	—	—	—	—
New Jersey	Notification*	—	—	Yes*
New Mexico	Consent*	—	—	—
New York	—	—	—	—
North Carolina	Consent	—	—	—

(continues)

TABLE 10.1 Current Status of State Abortion Laws (*continued*)

	Parental Consent or Notification Required for Minor to Obtain Abortion	Mandatory State-Directed Counseling	Mandatory Waiting Period Following Counseling	"Partial Birth" Abortion Banned
North Dakota	Consent	Yes	24 hours	Yes
Ohio	Notification	Yes	24 hours	Yes[3]
Oklahoma	—	—	—	Yes
Oregon	—	—	—	—
Pennsylvania	Consent	Yes	24 hours	—
Rhode Island	Consent	Yes	—	Yes[*]
South Carolina	Consent[4]	Yes	1 hour	Yes
South Dakota	Notification	Yes	24 hours	Yes
Tennessee	Consent	Yes[*]	48–72 hours[*]	Yes
Texas	Notification	—	—	—
Utah	Notification	Yes	24 hours	Yes[5]
Vermont	—	—	—	—
Virginia	Notification[6]	Yes	—	Yes[7]
Washington	—	—	—	—
West Virginia	Notification	—	—	Yes
Wisconsin	Consent	Yes	24 hours	Yes‡
Wyoming	Consent	—	—	—

[1]Includes a narrow health exception for the mother, and prohibits "partial-birth" abortion after viability.
[2]A new law is temporarily enjoined pending trial; prior law permanently enjoined.
[3]As defined by legislature, prohibits "dilation and extraction" abortions.
[4]Grandparent may consent.
[5]Prohibits the following: "partial-birth," "dilation and extraction," and saline abortion after viability as defined by the state legislature. Also includes health exception.
[6]Notification requirement may be waived by a physician, if the minor claims she is the victim of abuse or neglect.
[7]Law was permanently blocked by federal court; pending resolution of an appeal, it will be enforced.
[*]Requirement is enjoined.
†Limited enforcement.
‡Pending resolution of a legal challenge, enforcement is delayed.
Source: Planned Parenthood Federation of America Litigation and Law Division & The Alan Guttmacher Institute Special Report: The Status of Major Abortion-Related Laws & Policies in the States, February 2000.

After *Casey,* pro-life activity in the states took a different direction. Many states already had restrictions in place similar to those approved in *Casey.* With the Court now unquestionably firm in its support for *Roe,* pro-life groups saw no need to push for laws completely outlawing abortion. Instead, pro-life groups concentrated their efforts on restricting abortion availability in the states by attempting to outlaw a rare late-term procedure sometimes called a "partial-birth abortion." Abortion-rights supporters object to the phrase "partial-birth abortion" because it is not, in their view, a recognizable medical term. Pro-life activists claim that the term accurately describes the abortion procedure after the fetus has become viable. By the late 1990s, thirty-one states had banned medical procedures used to perform late-term abortions. Although *Casey* had held that states were free to ban abortion for any reason except to preserve the life or health of the mother subsequent to the viability of the fetus, no state could ban a procedure also used in previability pregnancies. In *Stenberg* v. *Carhart* (2000), the Court entered the abortion controversy for the first time since *Casey* to address whether a state law banning a specific procedure used in late-term abortions was unconstitutional because the same procedure could be used to perform a previability abortion.

Stenberg v. *Carhart*

530 U.S. 914 (2000)

On June 9, 1997, a Nebraska law went into effect prohibiting what it described as "partial-birth abortions." The law defined a partial-birth abortion as "an abortion procedure in which the person performing the abortion partially delivers vaginally a living unborn child before killing the unborn child and completing the delivery." The phrase, "killing the unborn child before completing the delivery," referred to a particular abortion technique known as dilation and extraction (D&X), in which the fetus is pulled into the vagina, where the skull is emptied by the doctor. The D&X procedure is extremely rare. The much more common second-semester abortion technique is the dilation and evacuation (D&E) procedure, in which the fetus is pulled into the vagina and dismembered. During the early 1970s, the most common second-trimester abortion method involved injecting saline into a woman's uterus to induce labor. Today, the D&E procedure accounts for 95 percent of all second-trimester abortions. Only when the gestated fetus has grown too large is the D&X procedure used. Less than 10 percent of all abortions in the United States are performed after the first trimester, or the twelfth week of pregnancy.

Dr. LeRoy Carhart, a physican who had performed abortions in his Bellvue, Nebraska, clinic since the early 1970s, filed a lawsuit in federal district court as soon as the law went into effect. Carhart claimed that the law imposed an "undue burden" on him and his female patients because, by targeting the D&X technique, the law effectively banned the D&E procedure, used in second-trimester previability abortions. The district court agreed with Carhart that the law was unconstitutional, and the Eighth Circuit Court of Appeals affirmed. Writing for the unanimous three-judge panel, Judge Richard Arnold noted that "the difficulty is that the statute covers a great deal more [than the D&X procedure]. It would also prohibit, in many circumstances, the most common method of second-trimester abortion, called a dilation and evacuation (D&E)."

The Center for Reproductive Law and Policy, a pro-choice group, represented Dr. Carhart. After Nebraska appealed the case to the Supreme Court, several more pro-choice groups filed *amicus* briefs asking the justices to affirm the Eighth Circuit's decision. The American College of Obstretricians and Gynecologists, which is the largest professional association representing physicians that perform abortions, filed an *amicus* brief urging the Court to strike down the Nebraska law. The ACLU, the Religious Coalition for Reproductive Choice (formerly the Religious Coalition for Abortion Rights), and NARAL all filed briefs urging the Court to declare the law unconstitutional.

Numerous pro-life organizations lined up behind Nebraska. The National Right to Life Committee, which had been instrumental in drafting many of the "partial-birth abortion" laws enacted by the states after *Casey,* asked the Court to uphold the law. The American Center for Law and Justice (a conservative public interest law firm with strong ties to the Christian Coaltion), the United States Catholic Conference, Agudath Israel (an Orthodox Jewish group), Feminists for Life, and four state attorneys general also filed briefs in support of the Nebraska law.

The Court's decision was 5 to 4. Justice Breyer delivered the opinion of the Court. Justice Stevens, joined by Justice Ginsburg, filed a concurring opinion. Justice O'Connor filed a concurring opinion. Justice Ginsburg, joined by Justice Stevens, also filed a concurring opinion. Justices Scalia and Kennedy filed separate dissenting opinions. Justice Thomas, joined by Chief Justice Rehnquist and Justice Scalia, also dissented.

Justice Breyer delivered the opinion of the Court.

We again consider the right to an abortion. We understand the controversial nature of the problem. Millions of Americans believe that life begins at conception and consequently that an abortion is akin to causing the death of an innocent child; they recoil at the thought of a law that would permit it. Other millions fear that a law that forbids abortion would condemn many American women to lives that lack dignity, depriving them of equal liberty and leading those with least resources to undergo illegal abortions with the attendant risks of death and suffering. Taking account of these virtually irreconcilable points of view,

aware that constitutional law must govern a society whose different members sincerely hold directly opposing views, and considering the matter in light of the Constitution's guarantees of fundamental individual liberty, this Court, in the course of a generation, has determined and then redetermined that the Constitution offers basic protection to the woman's right to choose, *Roe* v. *Wade* (1973); *Planned Parenthood of Southeastern Pa.* v. *Casey* (1992). We shall not revisit those legal principles. Rather, we apply them to the circumstances of this case.

Three established principles determine the issue before us. We shall set them forth in the language of the joint opinion in *Casey.* First, before "viability . . . the woman has a right to choose to terminate her pregnancy."

Second, "a law designed to further the State's interest in fetal life which imposes an undue burden on the woman's decision before fetal viability" is unconstitutional. An "undue burden is . . . shorthand for the conclusion that a state regulation has the purpose or effect of placing a substantial obstacle in the path of a woman seeking an abortion of a nonviable fetus."

Third, "'subsequent to viability, the State in promoting its interest in the potentiality of human life may, if it chooses, regulate, and even proscribe, abortion except where it is necessary, in appropriate medical judgment, for the preservation of the life or health of the mother.'"

We apply these principles to a Nebraska law banning "partial birth abortion[,]" . . . [and] hold that [it] violates the Constitution. . . .

The question before us is whether Nebraska's statute, making criminal the performance of a "partial birth abortion," violates the Federal Constitution, as interpreted in *Casey* and *Roe.* We conclude that it does for at least two independent reasons. First, the law lacks any exception "for the preservation of the . . . health of the mother." Second, it "imposes an undue burden on a woman's ability" to choose a D&E abortion, thereby unduly burdening the right to choose abortion itself. We shall discuss each of these reasons in turn. . . .

The quoted standard also depends on the state regulations "promoting [the State's] interest in the potentiality of human life." The Nebraska law, of course, does not directly further an interest "in the potentiality of human life" by saving the fetus in question from destruction, as it regulates only a method of performing abortion. Nebraska describes its interests differently. It says the law "'show[s] concern for the life of the unborn,'" "prevent[s] cruelty to partially born children," and "preserve[s] the integrity of the medical profession." But we cannot see how the interest-related differences could make any difference to the question at hand, namely, the application of the "health" requirement.

Consequently, the governing standard requires an exception "where it is necessary, in appropriate medical judgment for the preservation of the life or health of the mother," for this Court has made clear that a State may promote but not endanger a woman's health when it regulates the methods of abortion. . . . Our cases have repeatedly invalidated statutes that in the process of regulating the methods of abortion, imposed significant health risks. They make clear that a risk to a women's health is the same whether it happens to arise from regulating a particular method of abortion, or from barring abortion entirely. Our holding does not go beyond those cases, as ratified in *Casey.* . . .

Nebraska responds that the law does not require a health exception unless there is a need for such an exception. And here there is no such need, it says. It argues that "safe alternatives remain available" and "a ban on partial-birth abortion/D&X would create no risk to the health of women." The problem for Nebraska is that the parties strongly contested this factual question in the trial court below; and the findings and evidence support Dr. Carhart. The State fails to demonstrate that banning D&X without a health exception may not create significant health risks for women, because the record shows that significant medical authority supports the proposition that in some circumstances, D&X would be the safest procedure.

We shall reiterate in summary form the relevant findings and evidence. On the basis of medical testimony the District Court concluded that "Carhart's D&X procedure is . . . safer tha[n] the D&E and other abortion procedures used during the relevant gestational period in the 10 to 20 cases a year that present to Dr. Carhart." It found that the D&X procedure permits the fetus to pass through the cervix with a minimum of instrumentation. It thereby "reduces operating time, blood loss and risk of infection; reduces complications from bony fragments; reduces instrument-inflicted damage to the uterus and cervix; prevents the most common causes of maternal mortality (DIC and amniotic fluid embolus); and eliminates the possibility of 'horrible complications' arising from retained fetal parts." . . .

Nebraska, along with supporting *amici,* replies that these findings are irrelevant, wrong, or applicable only in a tiny number of instances. It says (1) that the D&X procedure is "little-used," (2) by only "a handful of doctors." It argues (3) that D&E and labor induction are at all times "safe alternative procedures." Id., at 36. It refers to the testimony of petitioners' medical expert, who testified (4) that the ban would not increase a woman's risk of several rare abortion complications (disseminated intravascular coagulopathy and amniotic fluid embolus).

The Association of American Physicians and Surgeons et al., *amici* supporting Nebraska, argue (5) that elements of the D&X procedure may create special risks, including cervical incompetence caused by overdilation, injury caused by conversion of the fetal presentation, and dangers arising from the "blind" use of instrumentation to pierce the fetal skull while lodged in the birth canal.

Nebraska further emphasizes (6) that there are no medical studies "establishing the safety of the partial-birth abortion/D&X procedure," and "no medical studies comparing the safety of partial-birth abortion/D&X to other abortion procedures," (7) an American Medical Association policy statement that "'there does not appear to be any identified situation in which intact D&X is the only appropriate procedure to induce abortion." And it points out (8) that the American College of Obstetricians and Gynecologists qualified its statement that D&X "may be the best or most appropriate procedure," by adding that the panel "could identify no circumstances under which [the D&X] procedure . . . would be the only option to save the life or preserve the health of the woman."

We find these eight arguments insufficient to demonstrate that Nebraska's law needs no health exception. For one thing, certain of the arguments are beside the point. The D&X procedure's relative rarity (argument [1]) is not highly relevant. The D&X is an infrequently used abortion procedure; but the health exception question is whether protecting women's health requires an exception for those infrequent occasions. A rarely used treatment might be necessary to treat a rarely occurring disease that could strike anyone—the State cannot prohibit a person from obtaining treatment simply by pointing out that most people do not need it. Nor can we know whether the fact that only a "handful" of doctors use the procedure (argument [2]) reflects the comparative rarity of late second term abortions, the procedure's recent development, the controversy surrounding it, or, as Nebraska suggests, the procedure's lack of utility.

For another thing, the record responds to Nebraska's (and *amici*'s) medically based arguments. In respect to argument (3), for example, the District Court agreed that alternatives, such as D&E and induced labor, are "safe" but found that the D&X method was significantly safer in certain circumstances. In respect to argument (4), the District Court simply relied on different expert testimony—testimony stating that "'[a]nother advantage of the Intact D&E is that it eliminates the risk of embolism of cerebral tissue into the woman's blood stream.'"

In response to *amici's* argument (5), the American College of Obstetricians and Gynecologists, in its own *amici* brief, denies that D&X generally poses risks greater than the alternatives. It says that the suggested alternative procedures involve similar or greater risks of cervical and uterine injury, for "D&E procedures, involve similar amounts of dilation" and "of course childbirth involves even greater cervical dilation." The College points out that Dr. Carhart does not reposition the fetus, thereby avoiding any risks stemming from conversion to breech presentation, and that, as compared with D&X, D&E involves the same, if not greater, "blind" use of sharp instruments in the uterine cavity.

We do not quarrel with Nebraska's argument (6), for Nebraska is right. There are no general medical studies documenting comparative safety. Neither do we deny the import of the American Medical Association's statement (argument [7])—even though the State does omit the remainder of that statement: "The AMA recommends that the procedure not be used unless alternative procedures pose materially greater risk to the woman."

We cannot, however, read the American College of Obstetricians and Gynecologists panel's qualification (that it could not "identify" a circumstance where D&X was the "only" life- or health-preserving option) as if, according to Nebraska's argument (8), it denied the potential health-related need for D&X. That is because the College writes the following in its *amici* brief: "Depending on the physician's skill and experience, the D&X procedure can be the most appropriate abortion procedure for some women in some circumstances. D&X presents a variety of potential safety advantages over other abortion procedures used during the same gestational period." . . .

The upshot is a District Court finding that D&X significantly obviates health risks in certain circumstances, a highly plausible record-based explanation of why that might be so, a division of opinion among some medical experts over whether D&X is generally safer, and an absence of controlled medical studies that would help answer these medical questions. Given these medically related evidentiary circumstances, we believe the law requires a health exception.

The word "necessary" in *Casey*'s phrase "necessary, in appropriate medical judgment, for the preservation of the life or health of the mother," cannot refer to an absolute necessity or to absolute proof. Medical treatments and procedures are often considered appropriate in light of estimated comparative health risks (and health benefits) in particular cases. Neither can that phrase require unanimity of medical opinion. Doctors often differ in their estimation of comparative health risks and appropriate treatment. And *Casey*'s words "appropriate medical judgment" must embody the judicial need to tolerate responsible differences of medical opinion—differences of a sort that the American Medical Association and American College of Obstetricians and Gynecologists' statements together indicate are present here.

For another thing, the division of medical opinion about the matter at most means uncertainty, a factor that signals the presence of risk, not its absence. That division here involves highly qualified knowledgeable experts on both sides of the issue. Where a significant body of medical opinion believes a procedure may bring with it greater safety for some patients and explains the medical reasons supporting that view, we cannot say that the presence of a different view by itself proves the contrary. Rather, the uncertainty means a significant likelihood that those who believe that D&X is a safer abortion method in certain circumstances may turn out to be right. If so, then the absence of a health exception will place women at an unnecessary risk of tragic health consequences. If they are wrong, the exception will simply turn out to have been unnecessary.

In sum, Nebraska has not convinced us that a health exception is "never necessary to preserve the health of women." Rather, a statute that altogether forbids D&X creates a significant health risk. The statute consequently must contain a health exception. This is not to say, as Justice Thomas and Justice Kennedy claim, that a State is prohibited from proscribing an abortion procedure whenever a particular physician deems the procedure preferable. By no means must a State grant physicians "unfettered discretion" in their selection of abortion methods. But where substantial medical authority supports the proposition that banning a particular abortion procedure could endanger women's health, *Casey* requires the statute to include a health exception when the procedure is "necessary, in appropriate medical judgment, for the preservation of the life or health of the mother." . . . Requiring such an exception in this case is no departure from *Casey,* but simply a straightforward application of its holding.

The Eighth Circuit found the Nebraska statute unconstitutional because, in *Casey*'s words, it has the "effect of placing a substantial obstacle in the path of a woman seeking an abortion of a nonviable fetus." It thereby places an "undue burden" upon a woman's right to terminate her pregnancy before viability. Nebraska does not deny that the statute imposes an "undue burden" if it applies to the more commonly used D&E procedure as well as to D&X And we agree with the Eighth Circuit that it does so apply. . . .

In sum, using this law some present prosecutors and future Attorneys General may choose to pursue physicians who use D&E procedures, the most commonly used method for performing previability second trimester abortions. All those who perform abortion procedures using that method must fear prosecution, conviction, and imprisonment. The result is an undue burden upon a woman's right to make an abortion decision. We must consequently find the statute unconstitutional.

The judgment of the Court of Appeals is affirmed.

Justice Stevens, with whom Justice Ginsburg joins, concurring.

Although much ink is spilled today describing the gruesome nature of late-term abortion procedures, that rhetoric does not provide me a reason to believe that the procedure Nebraska here claims it seeks to ban is more brutal, more gruesome, or less respectful of "potential life" than the equally gruesome procedure Nebraska claims it still allows. Justice Ginsburg [has] . . . correctly diagnosed the underlying reason for the enactment of this legislation—a reason that also explains much of the Court's rhetoric directed at an objective that extends well beyond the narrow issue that this case presents. The rhetoric is almost, but not quite, loud enough to obscure the quiet fact that during the past 27 years, the central holding of *Roe* v. *Wade* (1973) has been endorsed by all but 4 of the 17 Justices who have addressed the issue. That holding—that the word "liberty" in the Fourteenth Amendment includes a woman's right to make this difficult and extremely personal decision—makes it impossible for me to understand how a State has any legitimate interest in requiring a doctor to follow any procedure other than the one that he or she reasonably believes will best protect the woman in her exercise of this constitutional liberty. But one need not even approach this view today to conclude that Nebraska's law must fall. For the notion that either of these two equally gruesome procedures performed at this late stage of gestation is more akin to infanticide than the other, or that the State furthers any legitimate interest by banning one but not the other, is simply irrational.

Justice O'Connor, concurring.

I agree that Nebraska's statute cannot be reconciled with our decision in *Planned Parenthood of Southeastern Pa.* v. *Casey* (1992), and is therefore unconstitutional. I write separately to emphasize the following points.

First, the Nebraska statute is inconsistent with *Casey* because it lacks an exception for those instances when the banned procedure is necessary to preserve the health of the mother. Importantly, Nebraska's own statutory scheme underscores this constitutional infirmity. As we held in *Casey,* prior to viability "the woman has a right to choose to terminate her pregnancy." After the fetus has become viable, States may substantially regulate and even proscribe abortion, but any such regulation or proscription must contain an exception for instances "where it is necessary, in appropriate medical judgment, for the preservation of the life or health of the mother." Nebraska has recognized this constitutional limitation in its separate statute generally proscribing postviability abortions. That statute provides that "[n]o abortion shall be performed after the time at which, in the sound medical judgment of the attending physician, the unborn child clearly appears to have reached viability, except when necessary to preserve the life or health of the mother." Because even a postviability proscription of abortion would be invalid absent a health exception, Nebraska's ban on previability partial-birth abortions, under the circumstances presented here, must include a health exception as well, since the State's interest in regulating abortions before viability is "considerably weaker" than after viability. The statute at issue here, however, only excepts those procedures "necessary to save the life of the mother whose life is endangered by a physical disorder, physical illness, or physical injury." This lack of a health exception necessarily renders the statute unconstitutional.

. . . [T]he need for a health exception does not arise from "the individual views of Dr. Carhart and his supporters." Rather, as the majority explains, where, as here, "a significant body of medical opinion believes a procedure may bring with it greater safety for some patients and explains the medical reasons supporting that view," then Nebraska cannot say that the procedure will not, in some circumstances, be "necessary to preserve the life or health of the mother." Accordingly, our precedent requires that the statute include a health exception.

Second, Nebraska's statute is unconstitutional on the alternative and independent ground that it imposes an undue burden on a woman's right to choose to terminate her pregnancy before viability. Nebraska's ban covers not just the dilation and extraction (D&X) procedure, but also the dilation and evacuation (D&E) procedure, "the most commonly used method for performing previability second trimester abortions." The statute defines the banned procedure as "deliberately and intentionally delivering into the vagina a living unborn child, or a substantial portion thereof, for the purpose of performing a procedure that the person performing such procedure knows will kill the unborn child and does kill the unborn child." As the Court explains, the medical evidence establishes that the D&E procedure is included in this definition. Thus, it is not possible to interpret the statute's language as applying only to the D&X procedure. . . . We have stated on several occasions that we ordinarily defer to the construction of a state statute given it by the lower federal courts unless such a construction amounts to plain error. Such deference is not unique to the abortion context, but applies generally to state statutes addressing all areas of the law. Given this construction, the statute is impermissible. Indeed, Nebraska conceded at oral argument that "the State could not prohibit the D&E procedure." By proscribing the most commonly used method for previability second trimester abortions, the statute creates a "substantial obstacle to a woman seeking an abortion," and therefore imposes an undue burden on a woman's right to terminate her pregnancy prior to viability. . . .

If Nebraska's statute limited its application to the D&X procedure and included an exception for the life and health of the mother, the question presented would be quite different than the one we face today. As we held in *Casey,* an abortion regulation constitutes an undue burden if it "has the purpose or effect of placing a substantial obstacle in the path of a woman seeking an abortion of a nonviable fetus." If there were adequate alternative methods for a woman safely to obtain an abortion before viability, it is unlikely that prohibiting the D&X procedure alone would "amount in practical terms to a substantial obstacle to a woman seeking an abortion." Thus, a ban on partial-birth abortion that only proscribed the D&X method of abortion and that included an exception to preserve the life and health of the mother would be constitutional in my view.

Nebraska's statute, however, does not meet these criteria. It contains no exception for when the procedure, in appropriate medical judgment, is necessary to preserve the health of the mother; and it proscribes not only the D&X procedure but also the D&E procedure, the most commonly used method for previability second trimester abortions, thus making it an undue burden on a woman's right to terminate her pregnancy. For these reasons, I agree with the Court that Nebraska's law is unconstitutional.

JUSTICE GINSBURG, with whom JUSTICE STEVENS joins, concurring.

I write separately only to stress that amidst all the emotional uproar caused by an abortion case, we should not lose sight of the character of Nebraska's "partial birth abortion" law. As the Court observes, this law does not save any fetus from destruction, for it targets only "a method of performing abortion." Nor does the statute seek to protect the lives or health of pregnant women. Moreover, . . . the most common method of performing previability second trimester abortions is no less distressing or susceptible to gruesome description. . . .

A state regulation that "has the purpose or effect of placing a substantial obstacle in the path of a woman seeking an abortion of a nonviable fetus" violates the Constitution, *Casey*. Such an obstacle exists if the State stops a woman from choosing the procedure her doctor "reasonably believes will best protect the woman in [the] exercise of [her] constitutional liberty." . . .

JUSTICE SCALIA, dissenting.

I am optimistic enough to believe that, one day, *Stenberg* v. *Carhart* will be assigned its rightful place in the history of this Court's jurisprudence beside *Korematsu and Dred Scott*. The method of killing a human child—one cannot even accurately say an entirely unborn human child—proscribed by this statute is so horrible that the most clinical description of it evokes a shudder of revulsion. And the Court must know (as most state legislatures banning this procedure have concluded) that demanding a "health exception"—which requires the abortionist to assure himself that, in his expert medical judgment, this method is, in the case at hand, marginally safer than others (how can one prove the contrary beyond a reasonable doubt?)—is to give live-birth abortion free rein. The notion that the Constitution of the United States, designed, among other things, "to establish Justice, insure domestic Tranquility, . . . and secure the Blessings of Liberty to ourselves and our Posterity," prohibits the States from simply banning this visibly brutal means of eliminating our half-born posterity is quite simply absurd. . . .

. . . I [believe] that today's decision is an "unprecedented expansio[n]" of our prior cases," is not mandated" by *Casey*'s "undue burden" test, and can even be called (though this pushes me to the limit of my belief) "obviously irreconcilable with *Casey*'s explication of what its undue-burden standard requires." But I never put much stock in *Casey*'s explication of the inexplicable. In the last analysis, my judgment that *Casey* does not support today's tragic result can be traced to the fact that what I consider to be an "undue burden" is different from what the majority considers to be an "undue burden"—a conclusion that cannot be demonstrated true or false by factual inquiry or legal reasoning. It is a value judgment, dependent upon how much one respects (or believes society ought to respect) the life of a partially delivered fetus, and how much one respects (or believes society ought to respect) the freedom of the woman who gave it life to kill it. Evidently, the five Justices in today's majority value the former less, or the latter more, (or both), than the four of us in dissent. Case closed. There is no cause for anyone who believes in *Casey* to feel betrayed by this outcome. It has been arrived at by precisely the process *Casey* promised—a democratic vote by nine lawyers, not on the question whether the text of the Constitution has anything to say about this subject (it obviously does not); nor even on the question (also appropriate for lawyers) whether the legal traditions of the American people would have sustained such a limitation upon abortion (they obviously would); but upon the pure policy question whether this limitation upon abortion is "undue"—i.e., goes too far.

In my dissent in *Casey*, I wrote that the "undue burden" test made law by the joint opinion created a standard that was "as doubtful in application as it is unprincipled in origin," "hopelessly unworkable in practice." Today's decision is the proof. As long as we are debating this issue of necessity for a health-of-the-mother exception on the basis of *Casey*, it is really quite impossible for us dissenters to contend that the majority is wrong on the law—any more than it could be said that one is wrong in law to support or oppose the death penalty, or to support or oppose mandatory minimum sentences. The most that we can honestly say is that we disagree with the majority on their policy-judgment-couched-as-law. And those who believe that a 5-to-4 vote on a policy matter by unelected lawyers should not overcome the judgment of 30 state legislatures have a problem, not with the application of *Casey*, but with its existence. *Casey* must be overruled.

While I am in an I-told-you-so mood, I must recall my bemusement, in *Casey*, at the joint opinion's expressed belief that *Roe* v. *Wade* had "call[ed] the contending sides of a national controversy to end their national division by accepting a common mandate rooted in the Constitution," and that the decision in *Casey* would ratify that happy truce. It seemed to me, quite to the contrary, that "*Roe* fanned into life an issue that has inflamed our national politics in general, and has obscured with its smoke the selection of Justices to this Court in particular, ever since"; and that, "by keeping us in the abortion-umpiring business, it is the perpetuation of that disruption, rather than of any Pax Roeana, that the Court's new majority decrees." Today's decision, that the Constitution of the United States prevents the prohibition of a horrible mode of abortion, will be greeted by a firestorm of criticism—as well it should. I cannot understand why those who acknowledge that, in the opening words of JUSTICE O'CONNOR'S concurrence, "[t]he issue of abortion is one of the most contentious and controversial in contemporary American society," persist in the belief that this Court, armed with neither constitutional text nor accepted tradition, can resolve that contention and controversy rather than be consumed by it. If only for the sake of its own preservation, the Court should return this matter to the people—where the Constitution, by its silence on the subject, left it—and let them decide, State by State, whether this practice should be allowed. *Casey* must be overruled.

JUSTICE KENNEDY, with whom THE CHIEF JUSTICE joins, dissenting.

For close to two decades after *Roe* v. *Wade* (1973), the Court gave but slight weight to the interests of the separate States when their legislatures sought to address persisting concerns raised by the existence of a woman's right to elect an abortion in defined circumstances. When the Court reaffirmed the essential holding of *Roe*, a central premise was that the States retain a critical and legitimate role in legislating on the subject of abortion, as limited by the woman's right the Court restated and again guaranteed, *Planned Parenthood of Southeastern Pa.* v. *Casey* (1992). The political processes of the State are not to be foreclosed from enacting laws to promote the life of the unborn and to ensure respect for all human life and its potential. The State's constitutional authority is a vital means for citizens to address these grave and serious issues, as they must if we are to progress in knowledge and understanding and in the attainment of some degree of consensus.

The Court's decision today, in my submission, repudiates this understanding by invalidating a statute advancing critical state interests, even though the law denies no woman the right to choose an abortion and places no undue burden upon the right. The legislation is well within the State's competence to enact. Having concluded Nebraska's law survives the scrutiny dictated by a proper understanding of *Casey*, I dissent from the judgment invalidating it.

Note how differently the majority and concurring opinions in *Carhart* view the state's interest banning the D&X procedure from the dissents. Is Justice Breyer's opinion concluding that the Nebraska law poses an "undue burden" on the right of women to obtain an abortion more persuasive than Justice Scalia's dissent concluding that the Court has authorized "infanticide" by striking down the D&X ban? Also worth noting in *Carhart* is Justice Stevens's observation than only four of the seventeen justices who have served on the Court from *Roe* through *Carhart* have rejected the "core" holding of *Roe*—that women have the "right to make this difficult and extremely personal decision [to have an abortion]." But Justice Kennedy, who voted to retain *Roe* in *Casey*, rejected the notion that bans on "partial-birth" abortion are controlled by the logic of the Court's previous abortion decisions. In the area of abortion rights, the sharp differences among the justices mirror the interest group politics at play in society. It seems fair to say that regardless of the Court's efforts to "settle" the issue, the battle over the limits of legal abortion will continue to hold a prominent place in the legislative and judicial arenas.

Personal Privacy and Sexual Autonomy

In *Skinner*, the Court put into plain language what most people have always assumed: that individuals have the right to procreate, and that right may not be limited or denied except under the most compelling of circumstances. After the Court's decisions in *Griswold, Eisenstadt,* and *Roe* that established a right not to have children, many legal commentators assumed that this umbrella of personal privacy extended to consensual sexual relations of any kind between adults. By holding that men and (especially) women have a right, to paraphrase Justice Brennan in *Eisenstadt*, to decide whether to bear or beget a child, the Court acknowledged that not all sexual activity is designed to produce children.

One issue that the Court had not confronted involving privacy and sexual behavior was the constitutionality of laws prohibiting homosexual sexual conduct. In *Poe* v. *Ullman*, Justice Harlan, in laying out the argument on behalf of a Fourteenth Amendment right of privacy for married couples that included the right to use birth control, suggested "adultery, homosexuality and the like" were still within the purview of state regulatory power. Unlike marriage, however, extramarital sex and homosexuality had been actively discouraged and punished, not "fostered and protected," by state laws. The opportunity to decide the acceptable boundaries of state power to regulate intimate and private sexual matters between same sex partners came in *Bowers* v. *Hardwick* (1986).

Bowers v. *Hardwick*

478 U.S. 1986 (1986)

The facts and background of this case are set out in the accompanying SIDEBAR.

The Court's decision was 5 to 4. Justice White delivered the opinion of the Court. Chief Justice Burger and Justice Powell filed separate concurring opinions. Justice Blackmun, joined by Justices Brennan, Marshall, and Stevens, dissented. Justice Stevens dissented, and was joined by Justices Brennan and Marshall.

JUSTICE WHITE delivered the opinion of the Court.

This case does not require a judgment on whether laws against sodomy between consenting adults in general, or between homosexuals in particular, are wise or desirable. It raises no question about the right or propriety of state legislative decisions to repeal their laws that criminalize homosexual sodomy, or of state court decisions invalidating those laws on state constitutional grounds. The issue presented is whether the Federal Constitution confers a fundamental right upon homosexuals to engage in sodomy, and hence invalidates the laws of the many States that still make such conduct illegal, and have done so for a very long time. The case also calls for some judgment about the limits of the Court's role in carrying out its constitutional mandate. . . .

We first register our disagreement with the . . . respondent that the Court's prior cases have construed the Constitution to confer a right of privacy that extends to homosexual sodomy and, for all intents and purposes, have decided this case. [Here, the Court cited its cases on privacy and personal autonomy, including the right to procreation, the right of married and unmarried persons to receive and use contraception, and the right to abortion.] The latter . . . cases were interpreted as construing the Due Process Clause of the Fourteenth Amendment to confer a fundamental individual right to decide whether or not to beget or bear a child.

Accepting the decisions in these cases and the above description of them, we think it evident that none of the rights announced in those cases bears any resemblance to the claimed constitutional right of homosexuals to engage in acts of sodomy that is asserted in this case. No connection between family, marriage, or procreation, on the one hand, and homosexual activity, on the other, has been demonstrated, either by the Court of Appeals or by respondent. Moreover, any claim that these cases nevertheless stand for the proposition that any kind of private sexual conduct between consenting adults is constitutionally insulated from state proscription is unsupportable. Indeed, the Court's opinion in *Carey* twice asserted that the privacy right, which the *Griswold* line of cases found to be one of the protections provided by the Due Process Clause, did not reach so far.

Precedent aside, however, respondent would have us announce . . . a fundamental right to engage in homosexual sodomy. This we are quite unwilling to do. It is true that, despite the language of the Due Process Clauses of the Fifth and Fourteenth Amendments, which appears to focus only on the processes by which life, liberty, or property is taken, the cases are legion in which those Clauses have been interpreted to have substantive content, subsuming rights that to a great extent are immune from federal or state regulation or proscription. Among such cases are those recognizing rights that have little or no textual support in the constitutional language. . . .

Striving to assure itself and the public that announcing rights not readily identifiable in the Constitution's text involves much more than the imposition of the Justices' own choice of values on the States and the Federal Government, the Court has sought to identify the nature of the rights qualifying for heightened judicial protection. In *Palko* v. *Connecticut* (1937), it was said that this category includes those fundamental liberties that are "implicit in the concept of ordered liberty," such that "neither liberty nor justice would exist if [they] were sacrificed." A different description of fundamental liberties [later] appeared . . . where they are characterized as those liberties that are "deeply rooted in this Nation's history and tradition."

It is obvious to us that neither of these formulations would extend a fundamental right to homosexuals to engage in acts of consensual sodomy. Proscriptions against that conduct have ancient roots. Sodomy was a criminal offense at common law, and was forbidden by the laws of the original 13 States when they ratified the Bill of Rights. In 1868, when the Fourteenth Amendment was ratified, all but 5 of the 37 States in the Union had criminal sodomy laws. In fact, until 1961, all 50 States outlawed sodomy, and today, 24 States and the District of Columbia continue to provide criminal penalties for sodomy performed in private and between consenting adults. Against this background, to claim that a right to engage in such conduct is "deeply rooted in this Nation's history and tradition" or "implicit in the concept of ordered liberty" is, at best, facetious.

Nor are we inclined to take a more expansive view of our authority to discover new fundamental rights imbedded in the Due Process Clause. The Court is most vulnerable and comes nearest to illegitimacy when it deals with judge-made constitutional law having little or no cognizable roots in the language or design of the Constitution. That this is so was painfully demonstrated by the face-off between the Executive and the Court in the 1930's, which resulted in the repudiation of much of the substantive gloss that the Court had placed on the Due Process Clauses of the Fifth and Fourteenth Amendments. There should be, therefore, great resistance to expand the substantive reach of those Clauses, particularly if it requires redefining the category of rights deemed to be fundamental. Otherwise, the Judiciary necessarily takes to itself further authority to govern the country without express constitutional authority. The claimed right pressed on us today falls far short of overcoming this resistance.

Respondent, however, asserts that the result should be different where the homosexual conduct occurs in the privacy of the home. He relies on *Stanley* v. *Georgia* (1969), where the Court held that the First Amendment prevents conviction for possessing and reading obscene material in the privacy of one's home: "If the First Amendment means anything, it means that a State has no business telling a man, sitting alone in his house, what books he may read or what films he may watch."

Stanley did protect conduct that would not have been protected outside the home, and it partially prevented the enforcement of state obscenity laws; but the decision was firmly grounded in the First Amendment. The right pressed upon us here has no similar support in the text of the Constitution, and it does not qualify for recognition under the prevailing principles for construing the Fourteenth Amendment. Its limits are also difficult to discern. Plainly enough, otherwise illegal conduct is not always immunized whenever it occurs in the home. Victimless crimes, such as the possession and use of illegal drugs, do not escape the law where they are committed at home. *Stanley* itself recognized that its holding offered no protection for the possession in the home of drugs, firearms, or stolen goods. And if respondent's submission is limited to the voluntary sexual conduct between consenting adults, it would be difficult, except by fiat, to limit the claimed right to homosexual conduct while leaving exposed to prosecution adultery, incest, and other sexual crimes even though they are committed in the home. We are unwilling to start down that road.

Even if the conduct at issue here is not a fundamental right, respondent asserts that there must be a rational basis for the law, and that there is none in this case other than the presumed belief of a majority of the electorate in Georgia that homosexual sodomy is immoral and unacceptable. This is said to be an inadequate rationale to support the law. The law, however, is constantly based on notions of morality, and if all laws representing essentially moral choices are to be invalidated under the Due Process Clause, the courts will be very busy indeed. Even respondent makes no such claim, but insists that majority sentiments about the morality of homosexuality should be declared inadequate. We do not agree, and are unpersuaded that the sodomy laws of some 25 States should be invalidated on this basis. . . .

Reversed.

Justice Powell, concurring.

I join the opinion of the Court. I agree with the Court that there is no fundamental right—i.e., no substantive right under the Due Process Clause—such as that claimed by respondent Hardwick, and found to exist by the Court of Appeals. This is not to suggest, however, that respondent may not be protected by the Eighth Amendment of the Constitution. The Georgia statute at issue in this case authorizes a court to imprison a person for up to 20 years for a single private, consensual act of sodomy. In my view, a prison sentence for such conduct—certainly a sentence of long duration—would create a serious Eighth Amendment issue. Under the Georgia statute, a single act of sodomy, even in the private setting of a home, is a felony comparable in terms of the possible sentence imposed to serious felonies such as aggravated battery.

In this case, however, respondent has not been tried, much less convicted and sentenced. Moreover, respondent has not raised the Eighth Amendment issue below. For these reasons this constitutional argument is not before us.

Justice Blackmun, with whom Justice Brennan, Justice Marshall, and Justice Stevens join, dissenting.

This case is no more about "a fundamental right to engage in homosexual sodomy," as the Court purports to declare, than *Stanley* v. *Georgia* (1969) was about a fundamental

SIDEBAR

BOWERS V. HARDWICK

"A Knock at the Door"

> "While I nodded, nearly napping, suddenly there came a tapping, as of someone gently rapping, rapping at my chamber door."
>
> —Edgar Allan Poe, "The Raven"

By the time Michael Hardwick walked out of the Atlanta bar where he worked and into another scorching July afternoon, he was so tired from setting up the dance floor's elaborate lighting system that he forgot about the cold beer he was carrying in his hand. He took a final sip, poured the rest out, and threw the bottle into a trash can located in the bar's parking lot. No sooner had Hardwick taken his next step than he saw a police car make a U-turn and begin to head in his direction. The car pulled up to Hardwick and stopped. K. R. Torick, an Atlanta beat cop who often patrolled the predominantly gay neighborhood in which Hardwick lived, stepped out and asked the twenty-eight-year-old bartender to put his hands against the car. Torick frisked Hardwick and asked him for identification. After Hardwick produced his driver's license, Torick asked him where he had tossed the beer bottle. Hardwick pointed to the trash can outside the bar. Torick refused to believe him, and proceeded to write him a ticket for drinking in public.

On the top left-hand corner of the ticket, Torick had written "Wed Thurs," but further down had filled in July 13, a Tuesday, as the day to appear in court. Confused, Hardwick failed to appear on the morning of the appointed date. At two-thirty that afternoon, Torick showed up at Hardwick's apartment. He entered without permission and questioned a couple of guests sitting in the living room. After he checked their identification, Torick left. On his way out, he said, "Tell him [Hardwick] I'll be back." When Hardwick arrived home that afternoon, his friends told him what had happened. Concerned, Hardwick called the courthouse and asked when he could come down and pay the fine. The clerk told Hardwick that he could come in the following morning. He did.

On the first Monday in August, Officer Torick, holding an arrest warrant, again drove to Hardwick's apartment, unaware that Hardwick had paid the fine. Torick entered Hardwick's apartment, the front door left open by a friend who lay passed out on the couch. Walking down the hall, Torick, without knocking, opened Hardwick's bedroom door. He found Hardwick engaged in oral sex with another man. Torick told both men to get up, get dressed, and come down to the police station with him. On the way out, he noticed a small bowl of marijuana and confiscated it. Torick told Hardwick and his friend that they were under arrest for sodomy and marijuana possession. At no point were either of the accused men advised of their *Miranda* rights. Hardwick told Torick that he had paid his fine, and if he would take him by the bar where he worked he would show the receipt to him. Torick declined, saying he "did not run a goddamned taxi service." He also declined to phone the courthouse clerk to verify Hardwick's account.

Lewis Slaton, the Fulton County district attorney, declined to prosecute Hardwick, saying that the city had already spent too much money on the case. A tough veteran prosecutor with keen political instincts, Slaton knew enough not to push the buttons of Atlanta's sizable gay community by going forward with a prosecution. For years, Slaton believed that sodomy should be a misdemeanor, not a felony, and prosecuted only if police spotted individuals in public places. Consensual sodomy in the home, Slaton believed, was not something his office had any time or interest in prosecuting. Torick's conduct had offended his personal and professional sensibilities, and he believed he was doing the police a favor by not giving Hardwick's potential lawyers a public stage to describe the officer's warrantless search and what he believed was persistent harassment of Hardwick.

Slaton's decision not to prosecute Hardwick did not mean, however, that the beleaguered bartender was without recourse to challenge his arrest on other grounds. An ACLU attorney had contacted Hardwick shortly after his arrest to see if he would be willing to challenge the Georgia sodomy law as a violation of his privacy rights. Hardwick's decision carried far different risks than did challenging a civil law; if the state did decide to prosecute—the law carried a four-year statute of limitations—he could go to jail for twenty years. Ultimately, Hardwick received an outpouring of support from Atlanta's gay community. This led him to serve as the plaintiff in a case that the ACLU clearly hoped would go to the United States Supreme Court.

Georgia's sodomy law had been enacted in 1816, but the common law prohibition against "unnatural" sexual acts, as oral and anal sex were considered, reached back for centuries. In the United States, not even the Bill of Rights served as a bar to sodomy laws. Antisodomy laws were usually among the first criminal laws enacted by new states upon their admission into the union. These laws stood until the early 1960s, when the American Law Institute (ALI), the same group that encouraged states to liberalize their abortion laws later in the decade, offered a model law to states encouraging them to decriminalize consensual sexual conduct between adults. By 1986, when the Court decided *Bowers,* twenty-seven states had either repealed their sodomy laws or had them declared unconstitutional by state courts.

Michael Bowers, Georgia's popular attorney general, argued that his state's restrictive sodomy law reflected a moral consensus over the "delinquency" of this form of sexual conduct. Homosexual sodomy, Bowers claimed in the state's brief, led to "deviate practices such as sadomasochism, group orgies, or transvestism, to name only a few." Citing the recent concern over AIDS, which, in the mid-1980s, had entered the nation's public health consciousness for the first time, Bowers argued that the law was necessary to combat the spread of this mysterious disease. What the attorney general failed to note was that Georgia's law had been enacted one hundred and fifty years before anyone even knew what AIDS was or how it was transmitted.

As Bowers emphasized the need to control homosexual sexual conduct through the state's restrictive sodomy laws, he neglected one important aspect in his presentation to the Court: Georgia's law prohibited oral and anal sex between all consenting adults, whether gay or straight. Bowers and his deputy, Michael E. Hobbs, had framed the issue as "whether the Federal Constitution confers a fundamental right

WED THURS
COURT CODE
CITY OF ATLANTA MUNICIPAL COURT
G1150236
165 Decatur Street, S.E.

ARREST NUMBER
DOCKET NUMBER

TO MICHAEL DAVID HARDWICK
ADDRESS 811 PONCE DE LEON PL. N.E.
RACE W SEX M DOB 2-23-54 (MO. DAY YR)
SS 262211099

YOU ARE HEREBY COMMANDED, to be and appear at the MUNICIPAL COURT, GENERAL DIVISION, of the City of Atlanta, to be held in the Municipal Court Room, 165 Decatur Street, S.E., at:
9A M. on the 13th Day of JULY
19 82, to answer to the charge and NCIC Code DRINKING IN PUBLIC ( ) MISD ( ) FEL
Place of arrest 1310 MONROE DR. N.E. 1030 a.m./p.m.
Place of offense SAME a.m./p.m.
In the City of Atlanta on the 5th day of JULY 19 82, this 5th day of JULY 19 82
Officer K.R. TORICK S.S. No. 381689165
Officer ______ S.S. No. ______
COPY REC'D - Transporting Officer
Complaint No. 2215
( ) Arrested (X) Copy Assignment

A citation given to Michael Hardwick for drinking in public in July 1982. Confusion over whether Hardwick had paid his fine led to the sequence of events that resulted in his arrest for violating Georgia's sodomy law.

upon homosexuals to engage in sodomy." A five-member Court majority accepted Georgia's characterization of the case, and treated it as one involving the right to control sexual conduct considered deviant. The minority, on the other hand, agreed with Hardwick's lawyers that the case was about the right of sexual privacy between consenting adults.

Michael Hardwick did not prevail on that last day of June in 1986, but he did in the long run. Since 1986, seven more states have either repealed their sodomy laws or had them declared unconstitutional by state courts. In contrast to *Roe,* which spurred a move toward restrictive abortion statutes, *Hardwick* encouraged states to liberalize their sodomy statutes. Of the sixteen states that still have sodomy laws on the books, only four confine the sexual prohibition to same-sex partners. In 1998, the Georgia Supreme Court wrote the final chapter in the saga of Michael Bowers and Michael Hardwick, ruling that the state's sodomy law violated the right of privacy under the state constitution.

Michael Hardwick left Atlanta for Miami, where he was born and raised, after the Court's decision bearing his name. In 1996, Michael Bowers, by then serving his fourth elected term as the state's leading law enforcement officer, announced he was running for governor. Early on in his campaign, Bowers confirmed rumors that he had, since serving as Georgia's attorney general, engaged in an adulterous affair. That same year, Bowers had successfully defended his decision to withdraw an employment offer to a woman after he found out she was a lesbian. Bowers claimed that Robin Shahar, who had "married" her female partner in a private ceremony in 1991, could not enforce laws that she was violating. Shahar ended her appeal in 1996 after the Eleventh Circuit Court of Appeals found in favor of the state's position. After the revelations about Bowers's conduct she petitioned the appeals court for a rehearing, claiming that the attorney general had violated the state's adultery and fornication laws over the course his eleven-year affair. The Eleventh Circuit denied Shahar a rehearing. Michael Bowers, on the other hand, withdrew from the governor's race, almost ten years to the day the Supreme Court decided to follow his recommendation and make Michael Hardwick an example in contemporary sexual ethics.

References

Irons, Peter. *A People's History of the Supreme Court.* New York: Viking, 1999, pp. 457–63.

Joseph, Joel D. *Black Mondays: Worst Decisions of the Supreme Court.* Washington, D.C.: National Press Books, 1990, pp. 65–74.

right to watch obscene movies, or *Katz* v. *United States* (1967) was about a fundamental right to place interstate bets from a telephone booth. Rather, this case is about "the most comprehensive of rights and the right most valued by civilized men," namely, "the right to be let alone," *Olmstead* v. *United States* (1928) (Brandeis, J., dissenting). . . .

First, the Court's almost obsessive focus on homosexual activity is particularly hard to justify in light of the broad language Georgia has used. Unlike the Court, the Georgia Legislature has not proceeded on the assumption that homosexuals are so different from other citizens that their lives may be controlled in a way that would not be tolerated if it limited the choices of those other citizens. Rather, Georgia has provided that

> [a] person commits the offense of sodomy when he performs or submits to any sexual act involving the sex organs of one person and the mouth or anus of another.

The sex or status of the persons who engage in the act is irrelevant as a matter of state law. In fact, to the extent I can discern a legislative purpose for [the Georgia law] that purpose seems to have been to broaden the coverage of the law to reach heterosexual as well as homosexual activity. I therefore see no basis for the Court's decision to treat this . . . solely on the grounds that it prohibits homosexual activity. Michael Hardwick's standing may rest in significant part on Georgia's apparent willingness to enforce against homosexuals a law it seems not to have any desire to enforce against heterosexuals. But his claim that [the law] involves an unconstitutional intrusion into his privacy and his right of intimate association does not depend in any way on his sexual orientation.

Second, I disagree with the Court's refusal to consider whether [the law] runs afoul of the Eighth or Ninth Amendments or the Equal Protection Clause of the Fourteenth Amendment. Respondent's complaint expressly invoked the Ninth Amendment, which identifies that Amendment as one of the specific constitutional provisions giving "life and substance" to our understanding of privacy. . . .

In construing the right to privacy, the Court has proceeded along two somewhat distinct, albeit complementary, lines. First, it has recognized a privacy interest with reference to certain decisions that are properly for the individual to make. Second, it has recognized a privacy interest with reference to certain places without regard for the particular activities in which the individuals who occupy them are engaged. The case before us implicates both the decisional and the spatial aspects of the right to privacy.

The Court concludes today that none of our prior cases dealing with various decisions that individuals are entitled to make free of governmental interference "bears any resemblance to the claimed constitutional right of homosexuals to engage in acts of sodomy that is asserted in this case." While it is true that these cases may be characterized by their connection to protection of the family, the Court's conclusion that they extend no further than this boundary ignores the warning in *Moore* v. *East Cleveland* (1977), against "clos[ing] our eyes to the basic reasons why certain rights associated with the family have been accorded shelter under the Fourteenth Amendment's Due Process Clause." We protect those rights not because they contribute, in some direct and material way, to the general public welfare, but because they form so central a part of an individual's life. "[T]he concept of privacy embodies the 'moral fact that a person belongs to himself, and not others nor to society as a whole.'" . . . And so we protect the decision whether to marry precisely because marriage "is an association that promotes a way of life, not causes; a harmony in living, not political faiths; a bilateral loyalty, not commercial or social projects." We protect the decision whether to have a child because parenthood alters so dramatically an individual's self-definition, not because of demographic considerations or the Bible's command to be fruitful and multiply. And we protect the family because it contributes so powerfully to the happiness of individuals, not because of a preference for stereotypical households. . . .

Only the most willful blindness could obscure the fact that sexual intimacy is "a sensitive, key relationship of human existence, central to family life, community welfare, and the development of human personality." The fact that individuals define themselves in a significant way through their intimate sexual relationships with others suggests, in a Nation as diverse as ours, that there may be many "right" ways of conducting those relationships, and that much of the richness of a relationship will come from the freedom an individual has to choose the form and nature of these intensely personal bonds.

In a variety of circumstances, we have recognized that a necessary corollary of giving individuals freedom to choose how to conduct their lives is acceptance of the fact that different individuals will make different choices. For example, in holding that the clearly important state interest in public education should give way to a competing claim by the Amish to the effect that extended formal schooling threatened their way of life, the Court declared: "There can be no assumption that today's majority is 'right' and the Amish and others like them are 'wrong'. A way of life that is odd or even erratic, but interferes with no rights or interests of others, is not to be condemned because it is different," *Wisconsin* v. *Yoder* (1972). The Court claims that its decision today merely refuses to recognize a fundamental right to engage in homosexual sodomy; what the Court really has refused to recognize is the fundamental interest all individuals have in controlling the nature of their intimate associations with others. . . .

This case involves no real interference with the rights of others, for the mere knowledge that other individuals do not adhere to one's value system cannot be a legally cognizable interest, let alone an interest that can justify invading the houses, hearts, and minds of citizens who choose to live their lives differently.

In his concurring opinion, a reluctant Lewis Powell agreed with the majority that the Fourteenth Amendment offered no "substantive right" to support Michael Hardwick's claim. However, he did suggest that the substantial penalties for conviction under the Georgia sodomy law—twenty years—might raise an Eighth Amendment issue of cruel and unusual punishment. Since that issue was not before the Court, Powell declined to elaborate further. Three years after his retirement, Powell told the *New York Times*, "I think I probably made a mistake."[46] The Court has yet to revisit this issue.

TABLE 10.2 Current Status of State Sodomy Laws

	States That Prohibit Sodomy Between Homosexual Partners Only	States That Prohibit Sodomy Between Homosexual and Heterosexual Partners	States That Have No Sodomy Laws
Alabama		•	
Alaska			•
Arizona		•	
Arkansas	•		
California			•
Colorado			•
Connecticut			•
Delaware			•
District of Columbia			•
Florida		•	
Georgia			•
Hawaii			•
Idaho		•	
Illinois			•
Indiana			•
Iowa			•
Kansas	•		
Kentucky			•
Louisiana		•	
Maine			•
Maryland			•
Massachusetts		•	
Michigan			•
Minnesota			•
Mississippi		•	
Missouri			•
Montana			•
Nebraska			•
Nevada			•
New Hampshire			•
New Jersey			•
New Mexico			•
New York			•
North Carolina		•	
North Dakota			•
Ohio			•
Oklahoma	•		
Oregon			•
Pennsylvania			•
Rhode Island			•
South Carolina		•	
South Dakota			•
Tennessee			•
Texas	•		
Utah		•	
Vermont			•
Virginia		•	
Washington			•
West Virginia			•
Wisconsin			•
Wyoming			•

The Right to Die

If the Due Process Clause protects the right to procreate, the right to use contraception, the right of women to terminate their pregnancies, and, *Bowers* aside, the right to a substantial degree of sexual autonomy, does it follow that the "right to die" is also among the personal rights of privacy protected by the Fourteenth Amendment? In 1976, the New Jersey Supreme Court decided *The Matter of Karen Ann Quinlan,* a case involving a young woman who remained alive only because of life-support equipment. Quinlan's parents petitioned to have their daughter removed from the respirator that kept her alive. Their battle with medical and legal authorities attracted national attention, and elevated the question of whether individuals should have a right to control the end of their lives from a moral dilemma into a constitutional issue. The New Jersey court concluded that Karen Ann Quinlan had a right to "die with dignity," and that such a right was consistent with Louis Brandeis's understanding of privacy as "the right to be let alone."[47]

After *Quinlan,* federal and state courts began hearing more right to die claims, but most were reluctant to extend that right without informed consent on the part of individuals attached to life-support equipment. In 1990, in *Cruzan* v. *Director, Missouri Department of Health,* the Supreme Court heard its first such case, and affirmed the position taken by the lower federal courts. Writing for a 5-4 Court, Chief Justice Rehnquist refused to extend a substantive due process right to a family's request to remove a feeding tube from their daughter, who, like Karen Ann Quinlan, lay in a "permanent vegetative state" as the result of a car accident. Relying on the doctrine of informed consent, Rehnquist held that the right of privacy did not include the right of "substituted judgment," or the right of one person to make decisions for another in the absence of clear intent. However, the majority, with the exception of Scalia, agreed with the dissenters that the right to informed consent also included a right to *refuse* medical treatment. The Court strongly implied that a living will offered the kind of "clear and convincing" evidence necessary to permit the withdrawal of medical treatment in the event that an individual was no longer competent to make such a decision.[48]

In *Washington* v. *Glucksberg* (1997), the Court faced the right to die issue from a different angle: Did the doctrine of informed consent include the right of competent persons to end their lives with the assistance of a physician? Note the differences in the Court's approach to death, dying, and the liberty interest that attach to these decisions based on the circumstances of the individuals involved.

Washington v. *Glucksberg*

521 U.S. 702 (1997)

Cruzan gave the "right to die" issue a major public profile. Certainly, the idea that families faced difficult decisions over whether to continue life support for their loved ones in medically unalterable states was not new. A grasp of the legal issues involved in making such a decision, however, was foreign for many people. *Cruzan* clarified the difference between "substituted judgment"—that is, making a decision in lieu of formal consent—and the right of a designated family member or friend to authorize an attending physician to remove life-supporting medical treatment. "Living wills"—legal documents in which, for example, a husband grants permission to his wife or children to withdraw a feeding tube or terminate the use of a respirator—became much more popular after *Cruzan.*

By the early 1990s, another issue emerged alongside the right to withdraw life support: physician-assisted suicide. Jack Kevorkian, a Michigan physician, began making news after he disclosed to reporters that he had "assisted" several terminally ill patients with suicide. His methods were crude, usually involving a lethal drug prescription administered intravenously. Kevorkian's news appeal, however, rested with his unapologetic attitude toward assisted suicide. Kevorkian believed his was a humanitarian mission. He was simply putting people out of their misery—cancer patients, Alzheimer's sufferers, and victims of other terminal diseases—not murdering them. Kevorkian's fame reached its zenith in 1999 after CBS television broadcast a Kevorkian-assisted suicide of a patient with Lou Gehrig's disease. Kevorkian was convicted of murder in Michigan. This marked the first successful prosecution of Kevorkian since he had begun his national crusade.

Kevorkian's dramatics obscured a larger debate taking place in many legislatures around the nation over the scope of the right to die. In Washington State, the legislature passed a "natural death law" permitting physicians, with consent, to withdraw life-supporting sustenance and medical treatment, but specifically barred physicians from prescribing drugs or taking any other action to hasten death. Harold Glucksberg and several physicians challenged the law as a violation of the Due Process Clause of the Fourteenth Amendment.

▼▲▼

CHIEF JUSTICE REHNQUIST delivered the opinion of the Court.

The question presented in this case is whether Washington's prohibition against "caus[ing]" or "aid[ing]" a suicide offends the Fourteenth Amendment to the United States Constitution. We hold that it does not. . . .

We begin, as we do in all due process cases, by examining our Nation's history, legal traditions, and practices. In almost every State—indeed, in almost every western democracy—it is a crime to assist a suicide. The States' assisted suicide bans are not innovations. Rather, they are longstanding expressions of the States' commitment to the protection and preservation of all human life. Indeed, opposition to and condemnation of suicide—and, therefore, of assisting suicide—are consistent and enduring themes of our philosophical, legal, and cultural heritages.

Though deeply rooted, the States' assisted suicide bans have in recent years been reexamined and, generally, reaffirmed. Because of advances in medicine and technology, Americans today are increasingly likely to die in institutions, from chronic illnesses. Public concern and democratic action are therefore sharply focused on how best to protect dignity and independence at the end of life, with the result that there have been many significant changes in state laws and in the attitudes these laws reflect. Many States, for example, now permit "living wills," surrogate health care decision making, and the withdrawal or refusal of life-sustaining medical treatment. At the same time, however, voters and legislators continue for the most part to reaffirm their States' prohibitions on assisting suicide.

The Washington statute at issue in this case was enacted in 1975 as part of a revision of that State's criminal code. Four years later, Washington passed its Natural Death Act, which specifically stated that the "withholding or withdrawal of life-sustaining treatment . . . shall not, for any purpose, constitute a suicide" and that "[n]othing in this chapter shall be construed to condone, authorize, or approve mercy killing. . . . " In 1991, Washington voters rejected a ballot initiative which, had it passed, would have permitted a form of physician-assisted suicide. Washington then added a provision to the Natural Death Act expressly excluding physician-assisted suicide.

California voters rejected an assisted suicide initiative similar to Washington's in 1993. On the other hand, in 1994, voters in Oregon enacted, also through ballot initiative, that State's "Death With Dignity Act," which legalized physician-assisted suicide for competent, terminally ill adults. Since the Oregon vote, many proposals to legalize assisted suicide have been and continue to be introduced in the States' legislatures, but none has been enacted. And, just last year, Iowa and Rhode Island joined the overwhelming majority of States explicitly prohibiting assisted suicide. Also, on April 30, 1997, President Clinton signed the Federal Assisted Suicide Funding Restriction Act of 1997, which prohibits the use of federal funds in support of physician-assisted suicide.

Thus, the States are currently engaged in serious, thoughtful examinations of physician-assisted suicide and other similar issues. For example, New York State's Task Force on Life and the Law—an ongoing, blue-ribbon commission composed of doctors, ethicists, lawyers, religious leaders, and interested laymen—was convened in 1984 and commissioned with "a broad mandate to recommend public policy on issues raised by medical advances." Over the past decade, the Task Force has recommended laws relating to end of life decisions, surrogate pregnancy, and organ donation. After studying physician-assisted suicide, however, the Task Force unanimously concluded that "[l]egalizing assisted suicide and euthanasia would pose profound risks to many individuals who are ill and vulnerable. . . . [T]he potential dangers of this dramatic change in public policy would outweigh any benefit that might be achieved."

Attitudes toward suicide itself have changed since [the 13th century], but our laws have consistently condemned, and continue to prohibit, assisting suicide. Despite changes in medical technology and notwithstanding an increased emphasis on the importance of end of life decision making, we have not retreated from this prohibition. Against this backdrop of history, tradition, and practice, we now turn to respondents' constitutional claim.

The Due Process Clause guarantees more than fair process, and the "liberty" it protects includes more than the absence of physical restraint. The Clause also provides heightened protection against government interference with certain fundamental rights and liberty interests. In a

Dr. Jack Kevorkian, right, with pelvic disease sufferer Marjorie Wantz, making his case for physician-assisted suicide. Kevorkian assisted Wantz with her suicide in October 1991.
Dennis Cox/TimePix

long line of cases, we have held that, in addition to the specific freedoms protected by the Bill of Rights, the "liberty" specially protected by the Due Process Clause includes the rights to marry, *Loving* v. *Virginia* (1967); to have children, *Skinner* v. *Oklahoma* (1942); to direct the education and upbringing of one's children, *Meyer* v. *Nebraska* (1923); *Pierce* v. *Society of Sisters* (1925); to marital privacy, *Griswold* v. *Connecticut* (1965); to use contraception, *Eisenstadt* v. *Baird* (1972); . . . and to abortion, *Planned Parenthood* v. *Casey (1992).* We have also assumed, and strongly suggested, that the Due Process Clause protects the traditional right to refuse unwanted lifesaving medical treatment. . . .

Our established method of substantive due process analysis has two primary features: First, we have regularly observed that the Due Process Clause specially protects those fundamental rights and liberties which are, objectively, "deeply rooted in this Nation's history and tradition," and "implicit in the concept of ordered liberty," such that "neither liberty nor justice would exist if they were sacrificed." Second, we have required in substantive due process cases a "careful description" of the asserted fundamental liberty interest. Our Nation's history, legal traditions, and practices thus provide the crucial "guideposts for responsible decisionmaking," that direct and restrain our exposition of the Due Process Clause. . . .

In our view, . . . the development of this Court's substantive due process jurisprudence, described briefly above, has been a process whereby the outlines of the "liberty" specially protected by the Fourteenth Amendment—never fully clarified, to be sure, and perhaps not capable of being fully clarified—have at least been carefully refined by concrete examples involving fundamental rights found to be deeply rooted in our legal tradition. This approach tends to rein in the subjective elements that are necessarily present in due process judicial review. In addition, by establishing a threshold requirement—that a challenged state action implicate a fundamental right—before requiring more than a reasonable relation to a legitimate state interest to justify the action, it avoids the need for complex balancing of competing interests in every case. . . .

According to respondents, our liberty jurisprudence, and the broad, individualistic principles it reflects, protects the "liberty of competent, terminally ill adults to make end of life decisions free of undue government interference." The question presented in this case, however, is whether the protections of the Due Process Clause include a right to commit suicide with another's assistance. With this "careful description" of respondents' claim in mind, we turn to *Casey* and *Cruzan*. . . .

Respondents contend that, in *Cruzan,* we "acknowledged that competent, dying persons have the right to direct the removal of life-sustaining medical treatment, and thus hasten death," and that "the constitutional principle behind recognizing the patient's liberty to direct the withdrawal of artificial life support applies at least as strongly to the choice to hasten impending death by consuming lethal medication." . . .

The right assumed in *Cruzan,* however, was not simply deduced from abstract concepts of personal autonomy. Given the common law rule that forced medication was a battery, and the long legal tradition protecting the decision to refuse unwanted medical treatment, our assumption was entirely consistent with this Nation's history and constitutional traditions. The decision to commit suicide with the assistance of another may be just as personal and profound as the decision to refuse unwanted medical treatment, but it has never enjoyed similar legal protection. Indeed, the two acts are widely and reasonably regarded as quite distinct. In *Cruzan* itself, we recognized that most States outlawed assisted suicide—and even more do today—and we certainly gave no intimation that the right to refuse unwanted medical treatment could be somehow transmuted into a right to assistance in committing suicide. . . .

[The] respondents emphasize the statement in *Casey* that: "At the heart of liberty is the right to define one's own concept of existence, of meaning, of the universe, and of the mystery of human life. Beliefs about these matters could not define the attributes of personhood were they formed under compulsion of the State." By choosing this language, the Court's opinion in *Casey* described, in a general way and in light of our prior cases, those personal activities and decisions that this Court has identified as so deeply rooted in our history and traditions, or so fundamental to our concept of constitutionally ordered liberty, that they are protected by the Fourteenth Amendment. The opinion moved from the recognition that liberty necessarily includes freedom of conscience and belief about ultimate considerations to the observation that "though the abortion decision may originate within the zone of conscience and belief, it is *more than a philosophic exercise.*" That many of the rights and liberties protected by the Due Process Clause sound in personal autonomy does not warrant the sweeping conclusion that any and all important, intimate, and personal decisions are so protected, and *Casey* did not suggest otherwise.

The history of the law's treatment of assisted suicide in this country has been and continues to be one of the rejection of nearly all efforts to permit it. That being the case, our decisions lead us to conclude that the asserted "right" to assistance in committing suicide is not a fundamental liberty interest protected by the Due Process Clause. . . .

[Here, the Court turned to whether the Washington law bore a "rational relationship" to a "legitimate" public policy objective.]

First, Washington has an "unqualified interest in the preservation of human life." The State's prohibition on assisted suicide, like all homicide laws, both reflects and advances its commitment to this interest. This interest is symbolic and aspirational, as well as practical: "While suicide is no longer prohibited or penalized, the ban against assisted suicide and euthanasia shores up the notion of limits in human relationships. It reflects the gravity with which we view the decision to take one's own life or the life of another, and our reluctance to encourage or promote these decisions." . . .

The State also has an interest in protecting the integrity and ethics of the medical profession. . . . [T]he American Medical Association, like many other medical and physicians' groups, has concluded that "[p]hysician-assisted suicide is fundamentally incompatible with the physician's role as healer And physician-assisted suicide could, it is argued, undermine the trust that is essential to the doctor-patient relationship by blurring the time-honored line between healing and harming.

Next, the State has an interest in protecting vulnerable groups—including the poor, the elderly, and disabled persons—from abuse, neglect, and mistakes. . . .

The State's interest here goes beyond protecting the vulnerable from coercion; it extends to protecting disabled and terminally ill people from prejudice, negative and inaccurate stereotypes, and "societal indifference." The State's assisted suicide ban reflects and reinforces its policy that the lives of terminally ill, disabled, and elderly people must be no less valued than the lives of the young and healthy, and that a seriously disabled person's suicidal impulses should be interpreted and treated the same way as anyone else's.

Finally, the State may fear that permitting assisted suicide will start it down the path to voluntary and perhaps even involuntary euthanasia. . . . [I]t turns out that what is couched as a limited right to "physician-assisted suicide" is likely, in effect, a much broader license, which could prove extremely difficult to police and contain. Washington's ban on assisting suicide prevents such erosion.

This concern is further supported by evidence about the practice of euthanasia in the Netherlands. The Dutch government's own study revealed that in 1990, there were 2,300 cases of voluntary euthanasia (defined as "the deliberate termination of another's life at his request"), 400 cases of assisted suicide, and more than 1,000 cases of euthanasia without an explicit request. In addition to these latter 1,000 cases, the study found an additional 4,941 cases where physicians administered lethal morphine overdoses without the patients' explicit consent. This study suggests that, despite the existence of various reporting procedures, euthanasia in the Netherlands has not been limited to competent, terminally ill adults who are enduring physical suffering, and that regulation of the practice may not have prevented abuses in cases involving vulnerable persons, including severely disabled neonates and elderly persons suffering from dementia. Washington, like most other States, reasonably ensures against this risk [of abusing vulnerable persons] by banning, rather than regulating, assisting suicide. . . .

Throughout the Nation, Americans are engaged in an earnest and profound debate about the morality, legality, and practicality of physician-assisted suicide. Our holding permits this debate to continue, as it should in a democratic society. The decision of the en banc Court of Appeals is reversed, and the case is remanded for further proceedings consistent with this opinion.

It is so ordered.

JUSTICE O'CONNOR, concurring.

Death will be different for each of us. For many, the last days will be spent in physical pain and perhaps the despair that accompanies physical deterioration and a loss of control of basic bodily and mental functions. Some will seek medication to alleviate that pain and other symptoms.

The Court frames the issue in this case as whether the Due Process Clause of the Constitution protects a "right to commit suicide which itself includes a right to assistance in doing so," and concludes that our Nation's history, legal traditions, and practices do not support the existence of such a right. I join the Court's opinions because I agree that there is no generalized right to "commit suicide." But respondents urge us to address the narrower question whether a mentally competent person who is experiencing great suffering has a constitutionally cognizable interest in controlling the circumstances of his or her imminent death. I see no need to reach that question in the context of the facial challenges to the New York and Washington laws at issue here. The parties and *amici* agree that, in these States, a patient who is suffering from a terminal illness and who is experiencing great pain has no legal barriers to obtaining medication, from qualified physicians, to alleviate that suffering, even to the point of causing unconsciousness and hastening death. In this light, even assuming that we would recognize such an interest, I agree that the State's interests in protecting those who are not truly competent or facing imminent death, or those whose decisions to hasten death would not truly be voluntary, are sufficiently weighty to justify a prohibition against physician-assisted suicide.

Every one of us at some point may be affected by our own or a family member's terminal illness. There is no reason to think the democratic process will not strike the proper balance between the interests of terminally ill, mentally competent individuals who would seek to end their suffering and the State's interests in protecting those who might seek to end life mistakenly or under pressure. As the Court recognizes, States are presently undertaking extensive and serious evaluation of physician-assisted suicide and other related issues. . . .

In sum, there is no need to address the question whether suffering patients have a constitutionally cognizable interest in obtaining relief from the suffering that they may experience in the last days of their lives. There is no dispute that dying patients in Washington and New York can obtain palliative care, even when doing so would hasten their deaths. The difficulty in defining terminal illness and the risk that a dying patient's request for assistance in ending his or her life might not be truly voluntary justifies the prohibitions on assisted suicide we uphold here.

JUSTICE STEVENS, concurring in the judgment.

I write separately to make it clear that there is also room for further debate about the limits that the Constitution places on the power of the States to punish the practice. . . .

History and tradition provide ample support for refusing to recognize an open-ended constitutional right to commit suicide. Much more than the State's paternalistic interest in protecting the individual from the irrevocable consequences of an ill-advised decision motivated by temporary concerns is at stake. There is truth in John Donne's observation that "No man is an island." The State has an interest in preserving and fostering the benefits that every human being may provide to the community—a community that thrives on the exchange of ideas, expressions of affection, shared memories and humorous incidents as well as on the material contributions that its members create and support. The value to others of a person's life is far too precious to allow the individual to claim a constitutional entitlement to complete autonomy in making a decision to end that life. Thus, I fully agree with the Court that the "liberty" protected by the Due Process Clause does not include a categorical "right to commit suicide which itself includes a right to assistance in doing so."

But just as our conclusion that capital punishment is not always unconstitutional did not preclude later decisions holding that it is sometimes impermissibly cruel, so is it equally clear that a decision upholding a general statutory prohibition of assisted suicide does not mean that every possible application of the statute would be valid. A State, like Washington, that has authorized the death penalty and thereby has concluded that the sanctity of human life does not require that it always be preserved, must acknowledge that there are situations in which an interest in hastening death is legitimate. Indeed, not only is that interest sometimes legitimate, I am also convinced that there are times when it is entitled to constitutional protection. . . .

Cruzan was not [a] normal case. Given the irreversible nature of her illness and the progressive character of her suffering, Nancy Cruzan's interest in refusing medical care was incidental to her more basic interest in controlling the manner and timing of her death. In finding that her best interests would be served by cutting off the nourishment that kept her alive, the trial court did more than simply vindicate Cruzan's interest in refusing medical treatment; the court, in essence, authorized affirmative conduct that would hasten her death. When this Court reviewed the case and upheld Missouri's requirement that there be clear and convincing evidence establishing Nancy Cruzan's intent to have life-sustaining nourishment withdrawn, it made two important assumptions: (1) that there was a "liberty interest" in refusing unwanted treatment protected by the Due Process Clause; and (2) that this liberty interest did not "end the inquiry" because it might be outweighed by relevant state interests. I agree with both of those assumptions, but I insist that the source of Nancy Cruzan's right to refuse treatment was not just a common law rule. Rather, this right is an aspect of a far broader and more basic concept of freedom that is even older than the common law. This freedom embraces not merely a person's right to refuse a particular kind of unwanted treatment, but also her interest in dignity, and in determining the character of the memories that will survive long after her death. In recognizing that the State's interests did not outweigh Nancy Cruzan's liberty interest in refusing medical treatment, *Cruzan* rested not simply on the common law right to refuse medical treatment, but—at least implicitly—on the even more fundamental right to make this "deeply personal decision."

While I agree with the Court that *Cruzan* does not decide the issue presented by these cases, *Cruzan* did give recognition, not just to vague, unbridled notions of autonomy, but to the more specific interest in making decisions about how to confront an imminent death. Although there is no absolute right to physician-assisted suicide, *Cruzan* makes it clear that some individuals who no longer have the option of deciding whether to live or to die because they are already on the threshold of death have a constitutionally protected interest that may outweigh the State's interest in preserving life at all costs. The liberty interest at stake in a case like this differs from, and is stronger than, both the common law right to refuse medical treatment and the unbridled interest in deciding whether to live or die. It is an interest in deciding how, rather than whether, a critical threshold shall be crossed. . . .

There remains room for vigorous debate about the outcome of particular cases that are not necessarily resolved by the opinions announced today. How such cases may be decided will depend on their specific facts. In my judgment, however, it is clear that the so-called "unqualified interest in the preservation of human life," is not itself sufficient to outweigh the interest in liberty that may justify the only possible means of preserving a dying patient's dignity and alleviating her intolerable suffering.

JUSTICE SOUTER, concurring in the judgment.

One must bear in mind that the nature of the right claimed, if recognized as one constitutionally required, would differ in no essential way from other constitutional rights guaranteed by enumeration or derived from some more definite textual source than "due process." An unenumerated right should not therefore be recognized, with the effect of displacing the legislative ordering of things, without the assurance that its recognition would prove as durable as the recognition of those other rights differently derived. To recognize a right of lesser promise would simply create a constitutional regime too uncertain to bring with it the expectation of finality that is one of this Court's central obligations in making constitutional decisions.

Legislatures, however, are not so constrained. The experimentation that should be out of the question in constitutional adjudication displacing legislative judgments is entirely proper, as well as highly desirable, when the legislative power addresses an emerging issue like assisted suicide. The Court should accordingly stay its hand to allow reasonable legislative consideration. While I do not decide for all time that respondents' claim should not be recognized, I acknowledge the legislative institutional competence as the better one to deal with that claim at this time.

JUSTICE BREYER, concurring in the judgment.

I believe that JUSTICE O'CONNOR's views, which I share, have greater legal significance than the Court's opinion suggests. . . . I shall briefly explain how I differ from the Court.

I agree with the Court . . . that the articulated state interests justify the distinction drawn between physician-assisted suicide and withdrawal of life-support. I also agree with the Court that the critical question in both of the cases before us is whether "the 'liberty' specially protected by the Due Process Clause includes a right" of the sort that the respondents assert. I do not agree, however, with the Court's formulation of that claimed "liberty" interest. The Court describes it as a "right to commit suicide with another's assistance." But I would not reject the respondents' claim without considering a different formulation, for which our legal tradition may provide greater support. That formulation would use words roughly like a "right to die with dignity." But irrespective of the exact words used at its core would lie personal control over the manner of death, professional medical assistance, and the avoidance of unnecessary and severe physical suffering combined. . . .

[In *Poe* v. *Ullman* (1961)], Justice Harlan, [dissenting], concluded that marital privacy was such a "special interest." He found in the Constitution a right of "privacy of the home"—with the home, the bedroom, and "intimate details of the marital relation" at its heart—by examining the protection that the law had earlier provided for related, but not identical, interests described by such words as "privacy," "home," and "family." The respondents here essentially ask us to do the same. They argue that one can find a "right to die with dignity" by examining the protection the law has provided for related, but not identical, interests relating to personal dignity, medical treatment, and freedom from state-inflicted pain.

I do not believe, however, that this Court need or now should decide whether or a not such a right is "fundamental." That is because, in my view, the avoidance of severe physical pain (connected with death) would have to comprise an essential part of any successful claim and because, as JUSTICE O'CONNOR points out, the laws before us do not *force* a dying person to undergo that kind of pain. Rather, the laws of New York and of Washington do not prohibit doctors from providing patients with drugs sufficient to control pain despite the risk that those drugs themselves will kill. And under these circumstances the law . . . [of] Washington would overcome any remaining significant interests and would be justified, regardless. . . .

Were the legal circumstances different—for example, were state law to prevent the provision of palliative care, including the administration of drugs as needed to avoid pain at the end of life—then the law's impact upon serious and otherwise unavoidable physical pain (accompanying death) would be more directly at issue. And, as JUSTICE O'CONNOR suggests, the Court might have to revisit its conclusions in these cases.

▼▲▼

Glucksberg provides firm notice that, at least for now, the Court is not prepared to extend substantive claims to liberty under the Due Process Clause to include a right to physician-assisted suicide. Chief Justice Rehnquist's opinion offers an insightful comparison of the Court's approach to substantive due process analysis in the post-*Lochner* era. His opinion never questions the legitimacy of substantive claims to liberty, noting the Due Process Clause "guarantees more than fair process, and . . . protect[ion] against physical restraint. [I]t also provides heightened protection against government interference with certain fundamental rights and liberty interests."[49]

The Court also emphasized the role of tradition in deciding whether the right to physician-assisted suicide deserved any protection under the Due Process Clause. Here, as opposed to *Roe* and *Casey*, the Court concluded that it could not recognize a right to die because it was not rooted in societal tradition. But neither the right to abortion, the right to interracial marriage, nor the right of unmarried persons to purchase and use contraception held a place in societal tradition when the Court decided each such right was protected by the Due Process Clause. In fact, the Court's line of substantive due process decisions involving privacy and autonomy is more notable for going *against* the consensus of law and social values prevalent at the time than giving constitutional recognition to rights understood as a matter of tradition.[50]

How then do we explain the apparent contradiction between the Court's conception of substantive due process before and after the Constitutional Revolution of 1937? If one sees no difference between an asserted right to liberty of contract and the right to receive contraceptives, then explaining the Court's rejection of *Lochner* and embrace of *Roe* is difficult. But, as supporters of the Court's modern privacy doctrine suggest, if wholly different state interests exist in promoting workplace safety than in limiting reproductive freedom, then the differences between the two cases are more readily understood. Rejection of the economic, social, and political status quo was the fundamental legacy of the Court's 1937 ratification of the New Deal.

The continuing debate over the Court's role in defining and protecting liberties outside the specific protections of the Bill of Rights offers a clear illustration of how intertwined its conception of the proper relationship between political power and individual rights is with the thread of social and political change. The Court's decisions in *Lochner, Roe, Casey,* and *Glucksberg* are proof positive that the justices, to paraphrase Justice Benjamin Cardozo, are not immune from the great tides and currents that constantly reshape the values of American society and its political institutions.

FOR FURTHER READING

Chauncey, George. *Gay New York: Gender, Urban Culture, and the Making of the Gay Male World, 1890–1940.* New York: Basic Books, 1994.

Dworkin, Ronald. *Life's Dominion: An Argument About Abortion, Euthanasia and Individual Freedom.* New York: Alfred A. Knopf, 1993.

Garrow, David. *Liberty and Sexuality: The Right to Privacy and the Making of Roe v. Wade.* New York: Macmillan, 1994.

Glick, Henry. *The Right to Die.* New York: Columbia University Press, 1992.

Graber, Mark A. *Rethinking Abortion.* Princeton, N.J.: Princeton University Press, 1996.

Lee, Ellie. *Abortion Law and Politics Today.* New York: St. Martin's Press, 1998.

Noonan, John T., Jr. *A Private Choice: Abortion in America in the Seventies.* New York: Free Press, 1979.

Sullivan, Andrew. *Virtually Normal: An Argument About Homosexuality.* New York: Vintage Books, 1996.

Tribe, Laurence I. *Abortion: The Clash of Absolutes.* New York: W. W. Norton, 1990.

Urofsky, Melvin I. *Letting Go: Death, Dying and the Law.* New York: Scribner's, 1993.

———. *Lethal Judgments: Assisted Suicide & American Law.* Lawrence: University Press of Kansas, 2000.

Weddington, Sarah. *A Question of Choice.* New York: Grosset/Putnam, 1992.

11 Equal Protection

In July 1955, Mamie Bradley put her fourteen-year-old son, Emmett Till, on the Illinois Central train bound for Mississippi, where he was to spend the rest of the summer with his cousin, Curtis Jones. Bradley and her son lived in a working-class African American neighborhood on the south side of Chicago and were well-versed in the city's informal racial boundaries. But the racial segregation that Till would encounter once he got to Mississippi was far greater than he could ever have imagined, living as he did in a city where blacks could vote, hold decent jobs in factories, staff government agencies, and enjoy at least some of the fruits of Chicago's well-known patronage politics. His mother knew what Mississippi held in store for a young black man unfamiliar with its rigid code of racial apartheid. Her own family had left the Mississippi Delta for Chicago when she was two years old for a chance at personal and economic freedom. As she put him on the train, Bradley told her son: "If you have to get on your knees and bow when a white person goes past, do it willingly."

Till made a quick impression on Jones, who both admired and feared his cousin's extroverted nature. Till had a penchant for showing off and pulling pranks, anything to get a little attention and a laugh. One August evening, Jones borrowed his grandfather's 1941 Ford so he and Till could meet up with some friends at Bryant's Grocery and Meat Market, the country store and hangout closest to Jones's home. Following custom, Jones pulled to the rear of the building and parked his car. He spotted an old black man sitting by himself at an outside table, apparently awaiting a checkers opponent. Jones sat down to play checkers, while Till walked over to some other kids and struck up a conversation. Jones overheard Till bragging to the locals that he dated a white girl back in Chicago. He shook his head, not knowing if Till was telling the truth or making up a story. One of the kids said to Till, "There's a [white] girl in that store there. I bet you won't go in there and talk to her." Till took the dare. As he left the store, he turned to a white woman named Carolyn Bryant and said, "Bye, baby."

Three days later, Roy Bryant, Carolyn's husband, and his brother-in-law, J. W. Milam, drove out to the home of Mose Wright, Jones's grandfather, whose unpainted cabin was located adjacent to one of the county's largest cotton fields. Arriving shortly after midnight, Bryant and Milam demanded that Wright produce "the boy who done the talkin'." Wright told Bryant and Milam that Till was a teenager from "up nawth," who didn't know how "colored folks" were supposed to act around whites down South. Just give him a good whipping and leave it at that. Bryant and Milam responded that if Wright wanted to live to be sixty-five, he should get out of the way and not cause any trouble. They bound and gagged Till, shoved him into their car, and drove away.

Wright never told the police what happened. But the next morning, Curtis Jones phoned the local sheriff and reported Till's abduction. Bryant and Milam were charged with kidnapping. When the police pulled Till's nearly unrecognizable body out of a river three days after Jones's call, the charge was upgraded to murder. The savagery of Till's murder—he was found with an eye gouged out, his forehead crushed, and head nearly severed from the rest of his body after the cotton gin tied around his neck got caught on a river root—stunned even Mississippi's white supremacist political establishment, so much so that no local white lawyer would represent Bryant and Milam at trial.

Mamie Bradley wanted her son's body sent back to Chicago so she could identify it. Part of her wanted to believe the police had made a mistake and that Emmett was still alive and in hiding from local lynch mobs. The other part of her was braced for the worst. If that mangled body was indeed Emmett, Bradley wanted the entire world to see that racist violence in Mississippi did not exempt innocent children. She confirmed her son's identity for the police. An open-casket funeral was held so that the entire world could view what Bryant and Milam had done to her son.

Two weeks later, Bryant and Milam were tried in a Sumner, Mississippi, courtroom before a jury of twelve white men. Even though the state had secured evidence placing Bryant and Milam with Till on the night he died, it needed an eyewitness to confirm that fact. In the Jim Crow South, and especially in Mississippi, blacks simply did not testify against whites in criminal proceedings. But this murder was so brutal that it led Mose Wright, the man who watched Bryant and Milam carry Till out of his home, to take the stand for the prosecution. Wright received several clandestine warnings to keep his mouth shut or take his family and leave town. He stayed put. At trial, Wright stood up in the witness box and, in front of a white judge, a white jury, and armed white guards, pointed at Milam and said, "Thar' he." He also identified Bryant. It was the first time that anybody covering the trial could remember a black witness standing up in a Mississippi courtroom and

Roy Bryant's Store and Meat Market in Sumner, Mississippi, where Emmett Till, a fourteen-year-old African American boy from Chicago, violated the most deeply held custom of the segregated South by making a flirtatious remark to a white woman.
Ed Clark/TimePix

pointing to a white man as the murderer of an African American.

The defendants never testified. The attorneys assigned to represent Bryant and Tilam offered no other defense than a half-dozen character witnesses. In his closing argument, John C. Whitten, the defendants' attorney, left the jury with the following thought: "Your fathers will turn over in their graves if [you find Milam and Bryant guilty] and I'm sure that every last Anglo-Saxon one of you has the courage to free these men in the face of that pressure."

Just over an hour later, the jury returned a verdict of not guilty. The jury foreman later told the assembled news media that "the state failed to prove the identity of the body."

African American newspapers around the nation reacted with shock, and encouraged blacks to demand justice through protest. Newspapers such as the *New York Times* and the *Washington Post* expressed their indignation over the verdict, and called for decisive federal action to address America's "race issue." One writer compared Till to Anne Frank, the young Jewish girl whose diaries described the fears of Jews living in Nazi Germany and the atrocities of the Holocaust.

Mose Wright left Mississippi, never to return, after he testified against the men who lynched and murdered Emmett Till. He drove his '41 Ford to the train station, got on the Illinois Central, and headed for Chicago. Two months after the jury's verdict, Milam and Bryant sold their story to a white journalist from Alabama. They admitted killing Till, but insisted they never meant to hurt him. Because a fourteen-year-old black child refused to repent or beg for his life, Milam and Bryant felt they had no choice but to kill him. "What else could we do," said Milam. "He was hopeless . . . I never hurt a nigger in my life. I like niggers in their place . . . but I just decided it was time a few people got put on notice." Mamie Bradley traveled the country, encouraging African Americans to stand up for their rights. "Two months ago I had a nice apartment in Chicago. I had a good job. I had a son. When something happened to the Negroes in the South I said, 'That's their business, not mine.' Now I know how wrong I was."

The *Montgomery Advertiser,* a white-owned newspaper in Montgomery, Alabama, that, by Southern standards, was considered liberal on race issues—it had long crusaded against lynching, the Ku Klux Klan, and other forms of racial violence—gave the Till story prominent display. And African Americans took heed. Three months after the Till trial, on December 1, 1955, Rosa Parks, a black seamstress, refused to give up her seat to a white person on a Montgomery city bus. Parks, like Mose Wright, was an ordinary person who simply decided that enough was enough. Under the leadership of an Atlanta-born twenty-six-year-old Baptist preacher, Martin Luther King Jr., Montgomery's African Americans launched a boycott of the public transportation system that brought the city's white economic and political establishments to their knees. The civil rights movement was born, and America would never be the same.[1]

Emmett Till's lynching exposed in the starkest terms a cold, hard fact of American social and political life: that racial and ethnic minorities, especially African Americans, lived under a different Constitution than white Americans. If violence that resulted in death represented racial bigotry in its most extreme manifestation, then such indignities as inadequate schools, an elaborate system of rigorously enforced racial segregation, political disenfranchisement, and housing and job discrimination represented America's culturally entrenched and legally protected order of racial supremacy in its everyday form. Even though the Supreme Court had opened the door to a new era in equal protection law the year before in *Brown* v. *Board of Education* (1954), its landmark decision holding segregated public schools unconstitutional, it took well over a decade before African Americans saw any real change in their social and political status. Litigation is certainly a powerful tool of reform, but law, by itself, cannot sweep away deeply held prejudice without the support of public opinion and political bodies willing to turn abstract constitutional guarantees into reality.[2] Our discussion of the evolution of the Constitution's guarantee of equal protection under the law will illustrate the complex interplay between law, on the one hand, and social and political attitudes, on the other.

The journey of African Americans from slavery to their place in contemporary society as equals in the American constitutional order has been long and arduous. It should come as no surprise that cases involving racial discrimination have dominated the Court's decisions to define the substance and scope of the Fourteenth

Amendment. But legally enforced discrimination and social prejudice are not the sole province of America's persistent struggle with racial equality. This chapter will examine the evolution of the equal protection guarantee beyond the borders of racial prejudice to include the rights of women, ethnic and religious minorities, and gays and lesbians, all of whom have felt the sting of discrimination. Our focus will be not only on the Court and the law, but also on the social and political forces that were critical in bringing about constitutional change.

The Development of the Equal Protection Guarantee

Equality is considered one of the most fundamental principles in the American constitutional order—so basic to our social and political culture that it is often surprising for people to learn that the original Constitution contained no explicit mention of a guarantee to the equal protection of the law. Indeed, one of the most majestic and often quoted phrases of the Constitution, that "No State shall . . . deny to any person . . . the equal protection of the laws," did not become the law of the land until ratification of the Fourteenth Amendment in 1868, after the Civil War. As a condition of their readmission into the Union, the former Confederate states were required to ratify the Fourteenth Amendment, just as they had been required to approve the Thirteenth Amendment in 1865, which abolished slavery and involuntary servitude. In 1870, the states ratified the Fifteenth Amendment, which established the right to vote regardless of color.

The Civil War Amendments, as the Thirteenth, Fourteenth, and Fifteenth Amendments are often called, established formal constitutional equality for African Americans, regardless of their status before the Civil War. They did not, as we will discuss later in this chapter, eliminate the deeply held prejudice that existed against African Americans in both the defeated South as well as in the victorious North. The nation's different regions would respond differently to the formal emancipation of African slaves and the new sense of constitutional purpose that existed among free blacks. They would find clever ways to enforce the long-standing notion of white supremacy so deeply embedded in American law and culture. In doing so, the states would receive several critical assists from the Supreme Court.

The distance between the parchment promises of the Civil War Amendments and how they were interpreted by the Court and applied by Congress, state legislatures, and the common institutions of American life—businesses, schools, hospitals, restaurants and hotels, and housing authorities—remained deep and wide well into the twentieth century. By this time, of course, slavery no longer existed. But racial discrimination was the norm nationwide. In the South, a meticulously planned system of racial segregation replaced the pre–Civil War system of slavery. Historians have been unable to trace the precise origin of the phrase "Jim Crow," the adjective used to describe the South's segregation laws and practices. Its enforcement was rigid and steeped in the most minute detail—in South Carolina, for example, black and white cotton-mill workers were forbidden by law to look out of the same window. Jim Crow was also often brutal, leading some African Americans who experienced life in the pre– and post–Civil War South to describe it as even worse than slavery itself.[3]

By the time the Court began to reconsider the law of equal protection in the late 1940s and early 1950s, a consensus had emerged among the various parties involved in the different facets of the struggle for African American equality. No discussion of how to interpret the guarantees of the Fourteenth Amendment could proceed without revisiting the status of blacks before the Civil War, the shattered promise of Reconstruction, and the social and political forces that created the legal infrastructure behind the system of Jim Crow.

Slavery and Its Consequences

The first African slaves arrived in the port city of Jamestown, Virginia, in 1619. By the time of the Revolutionary War in 1776, slavery was so well established in the Southern colonies that African slaves made up approximately 40 percent of the population. Later, during the Constitutional Convention of 1787, delegates from the Northern and Southern states clashed heatedly over whether to count slaves as persons for the purposes of congressional representation. Southern delegates wanted to count slaves as people, even though they were considered the equivalent of domestic animals and treated as such. Northern delegates argued that slaves should not be counted equally with free men, since they were without rights. The political stakes of this disagreement were quite high: If the Southern states were able to include slaves in their census counts, they would gain additional seats in the House of Representatives. Northern states rejected the South's proposal not on humanitarian grounds, but because it would have weakened their own position in the House. The delegates finally agreed on the Three-Fifths Compromise, found in Article I, Section 2: taxes and representatives in the House would be apportioned based on the number of "free Persons" and "three-fifths of all other Persons . . . excluding Indians not taxed" living in the states.[4]

Seeing slavery as a sectional conflict about political power and not a moral conflict reflected the tenor of the times. From the Jamestown settlement until the 1790s, no serious abolition movement existed in any of the states. Slavery thrived in all thirteen colonies, and none formally abolished the institution until after the Revolutionary War. While the life of a house servant in New England was different from that of a cotton-picking field hand on a Southern plantation, and the degree of humanity in the relationship between slaves and their masters varied widely, the essential norms of the institution were the same from North to South. African slaves were indentured to their masters for life, as were any of their children. Husbands and wives, mothers and children, and brothers and sisters could be sold and dispersed on the whim of their owner, and frequently they were.[5]

By the late 1780s and early 1790s, the first serious anti-slavery sentiments appeared in state and national politics. The New England states and Pennsylvania had abolished slavery by this time. In 1777, Vermont became the first state to enter the Union that expressly prohibited slavery. Maryland, Delaware, and even Virginia permitted owners to release their slaves without legal reprisal for either master or slave. Abolition societies formed in every state north of Virginia, with prominent national figures such as John Jay and Benjamin Franklin in leading roles in their respective states of New York and Pennsylvania. By 1804, New Jersey and New York had abolished slavery, leaving only those states from Virginia southward with legal codes protecting the institution. By then, the sectional divisiveness over slavery that emerged with force during the Constitutional Convention in 1787 was firmly entrenched.[6]

Even so, the Northern states were reluctant to use their majority advantage in Congress to force the slavery issue. For one, not even such statesmen as Jay, Franklin, and John Adams were prepared to compromise the fragility of the Union over the issue. Adams, as the most outspoken opponent of slavery, often incurred the wrath of the other giants of the Founding generation, such as James Madison, George Washington, and Thomas Jefferson. Moreover, key Framers such as Madison and Jefferson, each of whom held slaves, genuinely believed that history would free the slaves. In other words, the moral and political sensibilities of future generations would have no room for the notion that the Constitution protected, in Madison's words, "the idea that there could be property in men." Political scientist William Lee Miller has commented that "[I]n its silent way, [Madison's comment] was . . . a touching appeal to future generations to do what the Framers themselves were not able to do. They would not speak the word, not in this document."[7]

Slavery is nowhere mentioned by name in the original Constitution, although its presence radiates throughout the document. In addition to the Three-Fifths Compromise, there were two other clear references to slavery in the Constitution. Article I, Section 9, contained the Slave-Trade Clause, which discouraged the importation of "such Persons" (referring to the Three-Fifths Compromise) after the year 1808 by authorizing Congress to impose taxes on all slave labor brought to the United States. Article IV, Section 2, included the Fugitive-Slave Clause. This provision read that "No Person *legally* held to Service or Labour in one State, under the Laws thereof, escaping into another, shall . . . be discharged from such Service or Labour, but shall be delivered up on Claim of the Party to whom such Service or Labour may be due." The original version of the Fugitive-Slave Clause read, "No Person *legally* held to Service," and did not include the phrase "the Laws thereof" when referring to the States. Here, one sees the more ambivalent side of the Framers toward slavery: the refusal to mention the institution by name to discourage the notion that it was legally protected by the Constitution, the hope that punitive taxing measures would discourage its permanence, and, by leaving states responsible for the recovery and punishment of slaves, the strong suggestion that slavery was a state and local, and not a national, matter.[8]

Despite the careful and circumspect manner in which the Framers treated slavery, there is no escaping the basic truth that America's great and tragic original sin, the enslavement of Africans, was fully protected by the Constitution. The Framers wanted to have it both ways, but the demands of nation-building and the precarious nature of the alliance between the North and South left them with little choice but to acknowledge and preserve the institution by law. Historian Don Fehrenbacher offers a succinct description of the Framers' legacy: "It is as though the Framers were half-consciously trying to frame two constitutions, one for their own time, and the other for the ages, with slavery viewed bifocally—that is, plainly visible at their feet, but disappearing when they lifted their eyes."[9]

Free of constitutional constraints, states developed and enforced their own slave codes, which remained in place until the end of the Civil War. For the purpose of civil law, slaves were considered property. Disputes over slave ownership and obligations were matters of civil, not criminal, law. But if a slave committed a criminal offense, such as arson, poisoning, or assault against a white person, he was considered responsible and punishable under criminal law. Punishment for capital offenses proved especially tricky under the slave codes. If a slave was put to death or imprisoned for a long period, it meant the loss of valuable property for the owner. Thus, whipping, not death or incarceration, became the standard punishment for disobedient slaves.[10]

A cornerstone of the slave codes was the prohibition of any form of "proper" education for slaves. It was against the law in all the slave-holding states to teach slaves to read and write, as it was to expose them to abolitionist materials. Free blacks permitted access to public education in the South were not offered the same curriculum as white children. Instead, they were channeled into agricultural and trade schools so that they could better serve the region's farm-based economy. Even after the Civil War, this continued to be the pattern of education for whites and blacks in the South until well into the twentieth century.[11]

From 1790 until around 1830, the free and slave states accommodated each other on matters governing the maintenance of slavery. Northern states cooperated with Southern states on the return of fugitive slaves; Southern states, in turn, recognized that the indefinite or permanent residence of a former slave in a free state resulted in emancipation. As the 1830s progressed, however, it became increasingly evident that the Constitution's muted tones on slavery could not prevent it from becoming a national issue. The infamous slave rebellion led by Nat Turner in 1831 caused the Southern states to tighten their control over the institution. By 1837, abolition societies in the South no longer existed, and Northerners visiting the region on business were often followed and harassed to ensure that they were not abolitionists in disguise. Moreover, several state courts in the North had ruled that slavery was inconsistent with natural law, and as such inconsistent with any reasonable notion of personal liberty.

Many Northern states that had once cooperated with the slave states on fugitive and sojourning slaves now began to treat slaves on their soil as emancipated, refusing to return them to their owners.[12] Congress, more so than ever before, was drawn into this rapidly unfolding chain of events. In 1836, several Southern senators successfully introduced a "gag rule" in Congress barring the introduction of any anti-slavery petitions on the floor of the House of Representatives. After a nine-year fight, anti-slavery members, led by former president and then Massachusetts representative John Quincy Adams, fought to repeal the gag rule, often in the face of death threats and accusations of treason.

Perhaps more so than any humanitarian impulse, it was the sectional hardening of the nation's political arteries over the status of slavery in the territories that ultimately led the Union to dissolve. The Compromise of 1850 was Congress's last-ditch effort to accommodate the South's demands for "popular sovereignty" in the territories while remaining true to the Missouri Compromise of 1820. The Compromise of 1850 ultimately left the South in a stronger position to argue that the national government had abandoned its "neutral" position toward the positive recognition of slavery. In 1820, after several efforts to introduce legislation to give the national government power to abolish slavery in territories applying for admission to the Union failed, Congress passed legislation that permitted Missouri to enter the Union as a slave state. This was balanced by the admission of Maine as a free state. The legislation's key feature, however, was a congressional ban on slavery in all territories above the 36.30′ line, which ran across Missouri's southern border. In 1850, Congress agreed to admit California as a free state, but permitted the territories of New Mexico and Utah to decide the slavery question as a matter of popular sovereignty. The Northern states' willingness to compromise on national control of territorial slavery was primarily out of fear that the Southern states would make good on their threat to secede from the Union. It also had the effect of permitting slavery in national territories where it had been previously excluded by law.[13]

In 1854, Congress provoked another political upheaval when it passed the Kansas-Nebraska Act, a direct challenge to the 1820 and 1850 compromises. The legislation was spearheaded by Representative Stephen A. Douglas, a Democrat from Illinois, who later ran against and defeated Abraham Lincoln in 1858 for a Senate seat. Douglas argued that the territories west of Missouri should be permitted to retain or permit slavery, just as New Mexico and Utah had. This time, however, territorial slavery was not simply a matter of popular sovereignty, but a matter of right under the Constitution. Douglas believed that Congress had no power to impose restrictions on slavery in the territories. As such, the Missouri Compromise of 1820 was "inoperable and void." In a sense, the Democrats argued that the Constitution took a position on slavery by *not* taking a position on slavery.

The political consequences of the Kansas-Nebraska Act were fast and furious. A civil war broke out in Kansas between pro- and anti-slavery territorial governments, forcing Congress to decide whether to admit it as a free state. The House approved Kansas's admission as a free state, but the Senate rejected it. Politically, the Democrats further strengthened their standing as a national pro-slavery party, while the continuing disputes in the territories elevated the Republican party, once a sectional anti-slavery party, to national party status. These disputes favored the fortunes of the Democrats, who knew the uncertain legal status of the 1820 and 1850 compromises created by the Kansas-Nebraska legislation all but invited the Supreme Court to decide the constitutional question of congressional power to restrict slavery in the territories.[14] The result was *Dred Scott* v. *Sandford* (1857), a case that brought to the fore the political and humanitarian consequences of slavery's failure to disappear into the dustbin of history.

Dred Scott v. *Sandford*

60 U.S. 393 (1857)

Dred Scott is often discussed as representative of the Court's pre–Civil War attitude toward the rights of African Americans or in the context of what happens when the Court exceeds the scope of its own authority. It is easy to forget, then, that Dred Scott was actually a real person. In 1833, Dred Scott was sold to Dr. John Emerson, an army doctor, by the family of Peter Blow, who had brought Scott and five other slaves to Missouri from Alabama in 1830. Historical records are somewhat vague about the origin of Dred Scott's name. Some evidence exists suggesting that Emerson bestowed the name, Dred Scott, on the male slave he purchased from the Blows. Up until then, he had simply been known as "Sam."

Accompanying Emerson on his travels to Illinois and the Wisconsin territory at various times during the 1830s and 1840s, Scott decided to petition the courts for his freedom. The Blow family helped support Scott's lawsuit, providing him money and other assistance during the ten years he and his two daughters, Eliza and Lizzie, pursued their claim. After the Court ruled that Scott was indeed a slave, the Blows purchased him and then set him free. In 1858, Scott died of tuberculosis in St. Louis, where he worked as a hotel porter.[15]

Additional facts and background of this case are set out in the accompanying SIDEBAR.

The Court's opinion was 7 to 2. Chief Justice Taney delivered the opinion of the Court. Justices Wayne, Nelson, Grier, Campbell, and Catron each filed concurring opinions. Justices Curtis and McClean wrote separate dissents.

CHIEF JUSTICE TANEY delivered the opinion of the Court.

The question is simply this: Can a negro, whose ancestors were imported into this country, and sold as slaves, become a member of the political community formed and brought into existence by the Constitution of the United States, and as such become entitled to all the rights, and privileges, and immunities, guarantied by that instrument to the citizen? One of which rights is the privilege of suing in a court of the United States in the cases specified in the Constitution. . . .

The words "people of the United States" and "citizens" are synonymous terms, and mean the same thing. They both describe the political body who, according to our republican institutions, form the sovereignty, and who hold the power and conduct the Government through their representatives. They are what we familiarly call the "sovereign people," and every citizen is one of this people, and a constituent member of this sovereignty. The question before us is, whether the class of persons described in the plea in abatement compose a portion of this people, and are constituent members of this sovereignty? We think they are not, and that they are not included, and were not intended to be included, under the word "citizens" in the Constitution, and can therefore claim none of the rights and privileges which that instrument provides for and secures to citizens of the United States. On the contrary, they were at that time considered as a subordinate and inferior class of beings, who had been subjugated by the dominant race, and, whether emancipated or not, yet remained subject to their authority, and had no rights or privileges but such as those who held the power and the Government might choose to grant them.

It is not the province of the court to decide upon the justice or injustice, the policy or impolicy, of these laws. The decision of that question belonged to the political or law-making power; to those who formed the sovereignty and framed the Constitution. The duty of the court is to interpret the instrument they have framed, with the best lights we can obtain on the subject, and to administer it as we find it, according to its true intent and meaning when it was adopted.

In discussing this question, we must not confound the rights of citizenship which a State may confer within its own limits, and the rights of citizenship as a member of the Union. It does not by any means follow, because he has all the rights and privileges of a citizen of a State, that he must be a citizen of the United States. He may have all of the rights and privileges of the citizen of a State, and yet not be entitled to the rights and privileges of a citizen in any other State. For, previous to the adoption of the Constitution of the United States, every State had the undoubted right to confer on whomsoever it pleased the character of citizen, and to endow him with all its rights. But this character of course was confined to the boundaries of the State, and gave him no rights or privileges in other States beyond those secured to him by the laws of nations and the comity of States. Nor have the several States surrendered the power of conferring these rights and privileges by adopting the Constitution of the United States. Each State may still confer them upon an alien, or any one it thinks proper, or upon any class or description of persons; yet he would not be a citizen in the sense in which that word is used in the Constitution of the United States, nor entitled to sue as such in one of its courts, nor to the privileges and immunities of a citizen in the other States. The rights which he would acquire would be restricted to the State which gave them. The Constitution has conferred on Congress the right to establish an uniform rule of naturalization, and this right is evidently exclusive, and has always been held by this court to be so. Consequently, no State, since the adoption of the Constitution, can by naturalizing an alien invest him with the rights and privileges secured to a citizen of a State under the Federal Government, although, so far as the State alone was concerned, he would undoubtedly be entitled to the rights of a citizen, and clothed with all the rights and immunities which the Constitution and laws of the State attached to that character.

It is very clear, therefore, that no State can, by any act or law of its own, passed since the adoption of the Constitution, introduce a new member into the political community created by the Constitution of the United States. It cannot make him a member of this community by making him a member of its own. And for the same reason it cannot introduce any person, or description of persons, who were not intended to be embraced in this new political family, which the Constitution brought into existence, but were intended to be excluded from it.

The question then arises, whether the provisions of the Constitution, in relation to the personal rights and privileges to which the citizen of a State should be entitled, embraced the negro African race, at that time in this country, or who might afterwards be imported, who had then or should afterwards be made free in any State; and to put it in the power of a single State to make him a citizen of the United States, and endue him with the full rights of citizenship in every other State without their consent? Does the Constitution of the United States act upon him whenever he shall be made free under the laws of a State, and raised there to the rank of a citizen, and immediately clothe him with all the privileges of a citizen in every other State, and in its own courts?

The court thinks the affirmative of these propositions cannot be maintained. And if it cannot, the plaintiff in error could not be a citizen of the State of Missouri, within the meaning of the Constitution of the United States, and, consequently, was not entitled to sue in its courts. . . .

In the opinion of the court, the legislation and histories of the times, and the language used in the Declaration of

S I D E B A R

DRED SCOTT V. SANDFORD

"No Rights the White Man Are Bound to Respect"

Dred Scott, as a slave in the company of his master, Dr. John Emerson, had traveled into territory north of the 36.30′ line established by the Missouri Compromise. In 1856, when *Dred Scott* was argued before the Supreme Court, five of the nine justices on the Court were Southerners with strong political ties to slave-holding interests. Chief Justice Roger Taney, appointed by Andrew Jackson in 1835 to succeed John Marshall, was the most prominent among them. Since the outcome of Scott's claim on the citizenship question was considered a foregone conclusion, the crucial question was really whether the Court was prepared to issue a definitive opinion on what the Constitution said about slavery. During the presidential election of 1856, the candidates, including the ultimate victor, Democrat James Buchanan, whose party remained divided on whether slavery was a matter of popular sovereignty or a constitutional right, avoided the slavery question. This further increased expectations that the Court would resolve the issue. Few people connected to the *Dred Scott* case believed the Court would actually decide that Dred Scott was a free man and a citizen of the United States.[16]

The Court, after hearing its second set of arguments on the case in December 1856, issued its ruling in March 1857. During this time, the voting alignments and various issues in the case shifted several times, for the simple reason that no one issue or resolution carried the same majority. Seven justices agreed that Dred Scott should remain a slave, but disagreed over whether to extend the scope of the ruling to hold the Missouri Compromise unconstitutional. The 1820 law had not been an issue in any of the lower court proceedings, and the Court had not even asked the parties for a briefing on it. Lawyers for John Emerson's estate—he had died while the case was in litigation—decided that the time was ripe for the Court to decide the slavery question. Putting the constitutionality of the Missouri Compromise before the Justices was one way to ensure a broader ruling than merely the citizenship status of Dred Scott. After an intense internal debate, Chief Justice Taney decided to throw the initial, more cautious opinion of Justice Nelson, which held simply that Dred Scott was a slave under Missouri law and had no standing to sue, to the wind and declare the anti-slavery provision of the Missouri Compromise unconstitutional.

In an exchange inconceivable today, President Buchanan had written Justice John Catron, an old friend, urging him to have the Court decide the case quickly so he could speak definitively on the slavery question before his inaugural address. Catron replied that the Court would dispose of the case before his inauguration, but without a ruling on the Missouri Compromise. Buchanan, under pressure from his party's Southern wing in Congress, wanted the Court to strike down the anti-slavery provision so he could claim judicial approval for his political agenda. Taney, now working in concert with Buchanan and Catron, argued to his pro-slavery colleagues that the Court's opinion would be stronger if one of their Northern brethren could be persuaded to join. Buchanan wrote Justice Robert Grier, a fellow Pennsylvanian, to explain his position. Replied Grier: "I am anxious that it should not appear that the line of latitude should mark the line of division in the court." He agreed to defer to Chief Justice Taney on the Missouri Compromise. Grier did insist, however, that the Court not issue its opinion in *Dred Scott* until after Buchanan's inauguration. Buchanan referred to *Dred Scott,* although not by name, during his address, noting that, as president, he was obliged to follow the Court's ruling on territorial slavery. Few in Washington doubted, however, that Buchanan had the inside track on the case's outcome.

Two days after President Buchanan's inauguration, Chief Justice Taney read his fifty-five-page, finely printed opinion before a hushed, crowded chamber. He addressed four major questions: (1) Had Scott's status on free soil made him a citizen and thus allowed him to sue to contest his status in federal court? (2) Could Scott, or any "Negro of the African race," be a citizen of the United States? (3) Was the Missouri Compromise of 1820 unconstitutional? (4) Did the laws of Missouri compel Scott's return to slave status even after his residence north the 36.30′ line? Scholars disagree over the force of Taney's opinion. Some claim that because none of the seven justices who agreed that Scott must remain a slave objected to any of his other conclusions, Taney's opinion had their implied consent. Others argued that because only two justices stated their explicit agreement with Taney's conclusion on the status of all blacks under the Constitution, Justice Nelson's much narrower concurrence, which dealt only with Scott's status as a free man, represented the Court's opinion.

In 1857, however, all that mattered was Taney's opinion. On all four questions, he was quite clear. Scott's presence on free soil did not make him a citizen of the United States. He had not become a free man during his residence with Dr. Emerson in Illinois and thus was bound, upon his return to Missouri, by the laws of that state. The anti-slavery restrictions in the 1820 compromise were unconstitutional. Finally, in the most inflammatory section of his opinion, Chief Justice Taney ruled that no black, whether free or enslaved, could be considered a citizen under the Constitution. As President Jackson's attorney general, Taney had prepared an opinion on a slavery-related legal matter in which he referred to the African race as a "degraded class." Now, as Chief Justice, Taney found that he could use *Dred Scott* to leave a permanent imprint of his racist views toward blacks in American constitutional law.

The consequences of *Dred Scott,* legally and politically, were enormous. Taney's opinion, in effect, said that slavery was national and freedom local.[17] His holding that blacks, regardless of their status, were not citizens under the Constitution flew in the face of the history of free blacks in the United States before 1789. Free blacks were permitted to enter into contracts, marry, bequeath property, and seek redress in the courts during the Founding era, just as they were in 1857. This is not to say that blacks in the North as well as in the South were considered the equals of whites—they most decidedly were not. But Taney's desire to consecrate the constitutional status of slavery by combining the status of all persons of African descent in the United States revealed the transparency of his racist views, and above all, his desire to uphold the South's sectional interests in national politics.

Politically, *Dred Scott* left the Democrats firmly cast as a pro-slavery party. Taney's opinion effectively nullified the popular sovereignty position of the Stephen Douglas–led wing of the Democratic Party. In holding that blacks were property and not people, Taney affirmed that the right to own slaves was inherent in the property rights of man, and thus trumped any decision of a territorial legislature. *Dred Scott* would loom large over Douglas in his historic 1858 campaign against Abraham Lincoln for the vacant Senate seat in Illinois. Douglas continued to press popular sovereignty as the instrument to maintain national unity, but that argument no longer appealed to the Southerners in his party, who believed Taney had settled the slavery issue, and that it was now a matter of positive right. Lincoln, on the other hand, rejected slavery on moral and political grounds. It was morally wrong because it contradicted the fundamental principle of equality, expressed in the Declaration of Independence and the Constitution. The nation could no longer exist half-slave and half-free, said Lincoln. His belief that slavery was inconsistent with the principles of republican government made it clear that the institution had to dissolve under the weight of its own immorality.

Douglas defeated Lincoln in 1858. Lincoln, of

course, won the 1860 presidential election, largely because he was able to capitalize on intractable division within the Democratic Party over the extension and justification for slavery. In March 1861, in a moment of great historical irony, Lincoln was sworn in as president by Chief Justice Taney. With the Chief Justice sitting uncomfortably behind him, Lincoln left no doubt that he was prepared to confront the slavery question head on. His criticism of *Dred Scott* was visible to anyone who listened or later read Lincoln's speech:

> [I]f the policy of the government, upon vital questions affecting the whole people, is to be irrevocably fixed by decisions of the Supreme Court, the instant they are made, in ordinary litigation between parties in personal actions, the people will have ceased to be their own rulers, having to that extent practically resigned their government into the hands of that eminent tribune.

Five weeks after Lincoln was sworn in as the nation's sixteenth president, Confederate forces fired on Fort Sumter, a federal post located just outside of Charleston, South Carolina. After two days, its defenders surrendered; that same day, April 14, 1861, President Lincoln called a special session of Congress to inform it that he was calling out the state militias to "cause the laws to be duly executed." The Civil War had begun. Its first shots, however, had been fired by the Supreme Court in *Dred Scott*.

References

Fehrenbacher, Don E. *Slavery, Law & Politics: The Dred Scott Case in Historical Perspective*. New York: Oxford University Press, 1981.

Irons, Peter. *A People's History of the Supreme Court*. New York: Viking Press, 1999, pp. 164–170.

Independence, show, that neither the class of persons who had been imported as slaves, nor their descendants, whether they had become free or not, were then acknowledged as a part of the people, nor intended to be included in the general words used in that memorable instrument.

It is difficult at this day to realize the state of public opinion in relation to that unfortunate race, which prevailed in the civilized and enlightened portions of the world at the time of the Declaration of Independence, and when the Constitution of the United States was framed and adopted. But the public history of every European nation displays it in a manner too plain to be mistaken.

They had for more than a century before been regarded as beings of an inferior order, and altogether unfit to associate with the white race, either in social or political relations; and so far inferior, that they had no rights which the white man was bound to respect; and that the negro might justly and lawfully be reduced to slavery for his benefit. He was bought and sold, and treated as an ordinary article of merchandise and traffic, whenever a profit could be made by it. This opinion was at that time fixed and universal in the civilized portion of the white race. It was regarded as an axiom in morals as well as in politics, which no one thought of disputing, or supposed to be open to dispute; and men in every grade and position in society daily and habitually acted upon it in their private pursuits, as well as in matters of public concern, without doubting for a moment the correctness of this opinion.

And in no nation was this opinion more firmly fixed or more uniformly acted upon than by the English Government and English people. They not only seized them on the coast of Africa, and sold them or held them in slavery for their own use; but they took them as ordinary articles of merchandise to every country where they could make a profit on them, and were far more extensively engaged in this commerce than any other nation in the world.

The opinion thus entertained and acted upon in England was naturally impressed upon the colonies they founded on this side of the Atlantic. And, accordingly, a negro of the African race was regarded by them as an article of property, and held, and bought and sold as such, in every one of the thirteen colonies which united in the Declaration of Independence, and afterwards formed the Constitution of the United States. The slaves were more or less numerous in the different colonies, as slave labor was found more or less profitable. But no one seems to have doubted the correctness of the prevailing opinion of the time. . . .

The language of the Declaration of Independence is . . . conclusive:

It begins by declaring that, "when in the course of human events it becomes necessary for one people to dissolve the political bands which have connected them with another, and to assume among the powers of the earth the separate and equal station to which the laws of nature and nature's God entitle them, a decent respect for the opinions of mankind requires that they should declare the causes which impel them to the separation."

It then proceeds to say: "We hold these truths to be self-evident: that all men are created equal; that they are endowed by their Creator with certain unalienable rights; that among them is life, liberty, and the pursuit of happiness; that to secure these rights, Governments are instituted, deriving their just powers from the consent of the governed."

The general words above quoted would seem to embrace the whole human family, and if they were used in a similar instrument at this day would be so understood. But it is too clear for dispute, that the enslaved African race were not intended to be included, and formed no part of the people who framed and adopted this declaration; for if the language, as understood in that day, would embrace them, the conduct of the distinguished men who framed the Declaration of Independence would have been utterly and flagrantly inconsistent with the principles they asserted; and instead of the sympathy of mankind, to which they so confidently appealed, they would have deserved and received universal rebuke and reprobation.

Yet the men who framed this declaration were great men—high in literary acquirements—high in their sense of honor, and incapable of asserting principles inconsistent with those on which they were acting. They perfectly understood the meaning of the language they used, and how it would be understood by others; and they knew that it would not in any part of the civilized world be supposed to embrace the negro race, which, by common consent, had been excluded from civilized Governments and the family of nations, and doomed to slavery. They spoke and acted according to the then established doctrines and principles, and in the ordinary language of the day, and no one misunderstood them. The unhappy black race were separated from the white by indelible marks, and laws long before established, and were never thought of or spoken of except as property, and when the claims of the owner or the profit of the trader were supposed to need protection. . . .

[T]here are two clauses in the Constitution which point directly and specifically to the negro race as a separate class of persons, and show clearly that they were not regarded as a portion of the people or citizens of the Government then formed.

One of these clauses reserves to each of the thirteen States the right to import slaves until the year 1808, if it thinks proper. And the importation which it thus sanctions was unquestionably of persons of the race of which we are speaking, as the traffic in slaves in the United States had always been confined to them. And by the other provision the States pledge themselves to each other to maintain the right of property of the master, by delivering up to him any slave who may have escaped from his service, and be found within their respective territories. By the first above-mentioned clause, therefore, the right to purchase and hold this property is directly sanctioned and authorized for twenty years by the people who framed the Constitution. And by the second, they pledge themselves to maintain and uphold the right of the master in the manner specified, as long as the Government they then formed should endure. And these two provisions show, conclusively, that neither the description of persons therein referred to, nor their descendants, were embraced in any of the other provisions of the Constitution; for certainly these two clauses were not intended to confer on them or their posterity the blessings of liberty, or any of the personal rights so carefully provided for the citizen.

No one of that race had ever migrated to the United States voluntarily; all of them had been brought here as articles of merchandise. The number that had been emancipated at that time were but few in comparison with those held in slavery; and they were identified in the public mind with the race to which they belonged, and regarded as a part of the slave population rather than the free. It is obvious that they were not even in the minds of the framers of the Constitution when they were conferring special rights and privileges upon the citizens of a State in every other part of the Union.

Indeed, when we look to the condition of this race in the several States at the time, it is impossible to believe that these rights and privileges were intended to be extended to them. . . .

[U]pon a full and careful consideration of the subject, the court is of the opinion that, upon the facts stated in the plea in abatement, Dred Scott was not a citizen of Missouri within the meaning of the Constitution of the United States, and not entitled as such to sue in its courts; and, consequently, that the Circuit Court had no jurisdiction of the case, and that the judgment on the plea in abatement is erroneous.

The Collapse of Reconstruction and the Rise of "Separate But Equal"

Dred Scott was overturned by the Civil War Amendments, but its stain permeated the development of the equal protection guarantee until well into the twentieth century. The Thirteenth Amendment addressed the institution of slavery by abolishing it and other forms of "servitude." The Fourteenth Amendment addressed the question left open by the near-overnight rise in the population of free blacks, which increased from 500,000 to nearly 5 million after the Civil War. Its very first sentence, "All persons born or naturalized in the United States, and subsequent to the jurisdiction thereof, are citizens of the United States and of the State wherein they reside," rejected Taney's declaration that blacks were not and never had been citizens of the United States. Moreover, two major civil rights acts enacted by Congress in 1866 and 1875 repudiated further Taney's claim that blacks had "no rights the white man was bound to respect." In 1869, Congress approved the Fifteenth Amendment, extending the right to vote "regardless of color or previous condition of servitude," which the states ratified the following year. The Fifteenth Amendment, even more so than the Fourteenth, was considered by its advocates and its opponents the "most revolutionary measure" in the name of black equality ever to receive congressional sanction.[18]

The constitutional, social, and political reorganization of the old Union in the period after the Civil War is known as Reconstruction. Centered on the sudden freedom of over 4 million slaves, Reconstruction was

MAJOR RECONSTRUCTION-ERA CIVIL RIGHTS LEGISLATION

The Civil Rights Act of 1866	This law established, for the first time, citizenship to "all persons born in the United States . . . of every race and color, without regard to any previous condition of slavery or involuntary servitude." The law also declared that all citizens were to have the same rights to make contracts and have them enforced by the courts, own property, and enjoy the "full and equal" benefits of all laws previously limited to "white citizens." Congress enacted this law under Section 2 of the Thirteenth Amendment, claiming that it was necessary to eradicate any "badge" or condition of slavery.
The Civil Rights Act of 1870	Congress enacted this law under Section 2 of the Fifteenth Amendment. This statute prohibited the denial of the right to vote based on "race, color, or previous servitude."
The Civil Rights Act of 1871	Congress enacted this law under Section 5 of the Fourteenth Amendment. This law was the third major Reconstruction "enforcement" act designed to establish Northern governing authority over the former Confederate states. Also known as the Ku Klux Klan Act, the 1871 law made it a federal crime for any person to form an "unlawful combination" to deprive any other person of their constitutional rights. Such action was considered a "rebellion against the government of the United States." This law proved very difficult to enforce and ultimately did little to curb Southern violence against African Americans.
The Civil Rights Act of 1875	Congress attempted to use its Section 5 power under the Fourteenth Amendment to ban racial discrimination in public accommodations. A draft version of the 1875 law also banned racially segregated public schools. This provision did not survive the final version. This statute was later invalidated by the Court's decision in the *Civil Rights Cases of 1883.*

the first genuine effort by the United States to extend the fundamental principle of equality under law to African Americans. Scholars disagree over whether Reconstruction actually began after the Civil War, when Confederate General Robert E. Lee surrendered his sword to Union General Ulysses S. Grant at Appomattox, or whether it commenced when President Lincoln issued the Emancipation Proclamation in January 1863. What is more certain is that Congress, increasingly led by Radical Republicans who had made abolition and black suffrage the moral basis of the Civil War, found that legislation was no match for the racial prejudice ingrained in the social and political institutions of the South. The region fiercely resisted Reconstruction.

The manner in which the Fourteenth Amendment was ratified foreshadowed the fate of Reconstruction. Originally passed by the House and Senate in June 1866, the amendment was rejected, with the exception of Tennessee, by the former Confederate states. The Southern states believed that a combination of President Andrew Johnson's indifference to the amendment and his general disdain for the policies of even the more moderate congressional Republicans—he had vetoed the Civil Rights Act of 1866, a veto Congress had overridden—would ultimately dissolve any possibility of federal protection and supervision of black civil rights. Instead, moderate and Radical Republican forces combined to pass the Military Reconstruction Act of 1867, which was also vetoed by Johnson and his veto again overriden by Congress. The law divided the South into five military districts, gave Union army officers power to oversee the provisional state governments, purged the electoral rolls of anyone who had aided the Confederate cause, and extended the vote to blacks. The 1867 law also required the former Confederate states to ratify the Fourteenth and Fifteenth Amendments for readmission into the Union, a task made much simpler by the new "purified" Southern electorate. By 1870, all the former Confederate states had been readmitted to the Union. By this time, in a truly astonishing turn of events, blacks were holding office in the South.[19]

President Ulysses Grant, elected in 1868, initially enforced the new federal civil rights measures with a vigor that Johnson had not. By the early 1870s, however, support within Congress for Reconstruction had begun to wane, due in large part to Northern frustration with the persistent and often violent resistance of Southern whites. Moreover, Republicans in Congress began to turn their attention away from the South to deal with the "Negro problem" in the North. Evidence that support for Reconstruction from moderate and even some Radical Republicans in Congress had diminished came from the beleaguered enactment of the Civil Rights Act of 1875. Originally introduced in 1870, the law's most far-reaching provision—a requirement to integrate public schools—had been removed by the time of its passage. Still the 1875 law was, by any stretch of the imagination, a radical measure, emphasizing as it did social rather than political and legal discrimination. But a pivotal decision by the Supreme Court in 1873 made clear that it would never pass constitutional muster.

In *The Slaughterhouse Cases* (1873) (see Chapter 3), a 5–4 Court ruled that the Privileges and Immunities Clause of the Fourteenth Amendment encompassed only a very narrow class of personal rights and liberties as national in scope.[20] Essentially, the Court ruled that Section 5 of the Fourteenth Amendment, the cornerstone of congressional power to enforce Reconstruction civil rights policy, did not give broad power to the federal government to enforce civil rights. Instead, the Court ruled that the Fourteenth Amendment established two levels of citizenship, one national and one state, with states still primarily responsible for determining and enforcing the rights of their citizens. In this sense, the Court's position was no different from Chief Justice Taney's opinion on citizenship in *Dred Scott*.[21]

Many Reconstruction scholars have argued that the Court's interpretation of the Fourteenth Amendment flew in the face of the intent of the Thirty-Ninth Congress that wrote it. The extent to which the congressional Republicans were willing to use their power to demand compliance from the Southern states also supports the idea that the Fourteenth Amendment's basic purpose was to bestow national citizenship on *all* persons born in the United States *and* the states in which they lived. But the Court, by 1873 composed primarily of former corporation and railroad lawyers, was just as fatigued from the battles over Reconstruction as were Congress and President Grant. The president, in fact, had signaled to the South by this time that he was prepared to compromise on the "Negro problem" to speed along regional reconciliation. In 1876, the Court, in

United States v. *Cruikshank*, lent further support to the revisionist theory of the Fourteenth Amendment established in *The Slaughterhouse Cases*. The Court held that the Ku Klux Klan Act of 1871 did not permit federal officials to protect blacks deprived of their civil rights by offenders in the states, since such acts fell under the jurisdiction of state law.[22] The 1871 law had been passed in response to the wave of violence brought by the Klan against black leaders and Republican officials in the South. *Cruikshank* underscored what had become evident to the remaining supporters of Reconstruction: No branch of the federal government, including the Supreme Court, would protect Southern blacks from the reign of terror that engulfed the region.[23]

By 1877, the eleven former Confederate states were now firmly back in the hands of conservative white Democrats, better known as the Redeemers, for the "redemption" of the social and political structure of the Old South that accompanied their return to power. The Redeemers would not be able to undo all the gains of Reconstruction. For example, states could not bar blacks from citizenship nor reinstate slavery. Nor could the Redeemers, as many had envisioned, immobilize and contain the black labor force, as the steady migration of blacks from the farms and plantations of the South to the factories of the Northern cities after the Industrial Revolution demonstrated. Moreover, a small number of blacks were able to reinstate their families, own land, form their own church and social institutions, establish businesses, and educate themselves, thus giving them a small degree of independence from white patronage.[24]

But outside of these small gains, Reconstruction's demise meant the return of African Americans to subordinate status under oppressive white rule. The Court offered an able assist in that regard when, in the *Civil Rights Cases* of 1883, it declared the Civil Rights Act of 1875 unconstitutional.[25] The last gasp of the Radical Republicans in Congress, the law prohibited discrimination on the basis of color in public accommodations. For a unanimous Court, Justice Joseph Bradley held Congress had exceeded its power under Section 5 of the Fourteenth Amendment by forbidding acts of "private" discrimination. Justice Bradley also ruled that such discrimination did not constitute a "badge of slavery," as the denial of those rights now covered by the 1866 civil rights law did. As a matter of law, the Fourteenth Amendment reached only acts of discrimination carried out by the state. Do you believe Justice Bradley's reasoning regarding the power of Congress to deal with public versus private discrimination is persuasive?

The *Civil Rights Cases*

109 U.S. 3 (1883)

The Civil Rights Act of 1875 made it a federal offense for any public accommodation to deny its services and facilities to any person on the basis of race. It was the first federal law to extend basic civil rights in public places to African Americans. The *Civil Rights Cases* brought together five cases from California, Kansas, Missouri, New Jersey, and Tennessee. African Americans in those states had been denied their lawful right to use restaurants, inns, and first-class rail cars.

After the 1875 law was struck down by the Court in the *Civil Rights Cases*, Congress would not enact a similar such comprehensive measure until the Civil Rights Act of 1964. Editorial opinion was supportive of the Court's opinion, even among journals and newspapers normally supportive of Reconstruction. *Harper's Weekly* called the Court's decision "another illustration of the wisdom of our constitutional system." The *New York Times* also endorsed the decision, noting "[t]he Court has been serving a useful purpose in thus undoing the work of Congress."

The Court's decision was 8 to 1. Justice Bradley delivered the opinion of the Court. Justice Harlan (I) dissented.

▼▲▼

MR. JUSTICE BRADLEY delivered the opinion of the Court.

Has Congress constitutional power to make such a law? Of course, no one will contend that the power to pass it was contained in the Constitution before the adoption of the last three amendments. The power is sought, first, in the Fourteenth Amendment, and the views and arguments of distinguished Senators, advanced whilst the law was under consideration, claiming authority to pass it by virtue of that amendment, are the principal arguments adduced in favor of the power. . . .

The first section of the Fourteenth Amendment (which is the one relied on) . . . [prohibits] State action of a particular character. . . . Individual invasion of individual rights is not the subject matter of the amendment. It has a deeper and broader scope. It nullifies and makes void all State legislation, and State action of every kind, which impairs the privileges and immunities of citizens of the United States or which injures them in life, liberty or property without due process of law, or which denies to any of them the equal protection of the laws. It not only does this, but, in order that the national will, thus declared, may not be a mere *brutum fulmen,* the last section of the amendment invests Congress with power to enforce it by appropriate legislation. To enforce what? To enforce the prohibition. To adopt appropriate legislation for correcting the effects of such prohibited State laws and State acts, and thus to render them effectually null, void, and innocuous. This is the legislative power conferred upon Congress, and this is the whole of it. It does not invest Congress with power to legislate upon subjects which are within the domain of State legislation, but to provide modes of relief against State legislation, or State action, of the kind referred to. It does not authorize Congress to create a code of municipal law for the regulation of private rights, but to provide modes of redress against the operation of State laws and the action of State officers executive or judicial when these are subversive of the fundamental rights specified in the amendment. Positive rights and privileges are undoubtedly secured by the Fourteenth Amendment, but they are secured by way of prohibition against State laws and State proceedings affecting those rights and privileges, and by power given to Congress to legislate for the purpose of carrying such prohibition into effect, and such legislation must necessarily be predicated upon such supposed State laws or State proceedings, and be directed to the correction of their operation and effect. . . .

An inspection of the law shows that it makes no reference whatever to any supposed or apprehended violation of the Fourteenth Amendment on the part of the States. It is not predicated on any such view. It proceeds [directly] to declare that certain acts committed by individuals shall be deemed offences, and shall be prosecuted and punished by proceedings in the courts of the United States. It does not profess to be corrective of any constitutional wrong committed by the States; it does not make its operation to depend upon any such wrong committed. It applies equally to cases arising in States which have the justest laws respecting the personal rights of citizens, and whose authorities are ever ready to enforce such laws, as to those which arise in States that may have violated the prohibition of the amendment. In other words, it steps into the domain of local jurisprudence, and lays down rules for the conduct of individuals in society towards each other, and imposes sanctions for the enforcement of those rules, without referring in any manner to any supposed action of the State or its authorities.

If this legislation is appropriate for enforcing the prohibitions of the amendment, it is difficult to see where it is to stop. Why may not Congress, with equal show of authority, enact a code of laws for the enforcement and vindication of all rights of life, liberty, and property? If it is supposable that the States may deprive persons of life, liberty, and property without due process of law (and the amendment itself does suppose this), why should not Congress proceed at once to prescribe due process of law for the protection of every one of these fundamental rights, in every possible case, as well as to prescribe equal privileges in inns, public conveyances, and theatres? The truth is that the implication of a power to legislate in this manner is based upon the assumption that, if the States are forbidden to legislate or act in a particular way on a particular subject, and power is conferred upon Congress to enforce the prohibition, this gives Congress power to legislate generally upon that subject, and not merely power to provide modes of redress against such State legislation or action. The assumption is certainly unsound. It is repugnant to the Tenth Amendment of the Constitution, which declares that powers not delegated to the United States by the Constitution, nor prohibited by it to the States, are reserved to the States respectively or to the people. . . .

[C]ivil rights, such as are guaranteed by the Constitution against State aggression, cannot be impaired by the wrongful acts of individuals, unsupported by State authority in the shape of laws, customs, or judicial or executive proceedings. The wrongful act of an individual, unsupported by any such authority, is simply a private wrong, or a crime of that individual; an invasion of the rights of the injured party, it is true, whether they affect his person, his property, or his reputation; but if not sanctioned in some way by the State, or not done under State authority, his rights remain in full force, and may presumably be vindicated by resort to the laws of the State for redress. . . . Hence, in all those cases where the Constitution seeks to protect the rights of the citizen against discriminative and unjust laws of the State by prohibiting such laws, it is not individual offences, but abrogation and denial of rights, which it denounces and for which it clothes the Congress with power to provide a remedy. . . .

[T]he power of Congress to adopt direct and primary, as distinguished from corrective, legislation on the subject in hand is sought, in the second place, from the Thirteenth Amendment, which abolishes slavery. . . .

This amendment, as well as the Fourteenth, is undoubtedly self-executing, without any ancillary legislation, so far as its terms are applicable to any existing state of circumstances. By its own unaided force and effect, it abolished slavery and established universal freedom. Still, legislation may be necessary and proper to meet all the various cases and circumstances to be affected by it, and to prescribe proper modes of redress for its violation in letter or spirit. And such legislation may be primary and direct in its character, for the amendment is not a mere prohibition of State laws establishing or upholding slavery, but an absolute declaration that slavery or involuntary servitude shall not exist in any part of the United States.

It is true that slavery cannot exist without law, any more than property in lands and goods can exist without law, and, therefore, the Thirteenth Amendment may be regarded as nullifying all State laws which establish or uphold slavery. . . . Conceding . . . that Congress has a right to enact all necessary and proper laws for the obliteration and prevention of slavery with all its badges and incidents, is the minor proposition also true, that the denial to any person of admission to the accommodations and privileges of an inn, a public conveyance, or a theatre does subject that person to any form of servitude, or tend to fasten upon him any badge of slavery? If it does not, then power to pass the law is not found in the Thirteenth Amendment. . . .

The only question under the present head, therefore, is whether the refusal to any persons of the accommodations of an inn or a public conveyance or a place of public amusement by an individual, and without any sanction or support from any State law or regulation, does inflict upon such persons any manner of servitude or form of slavery as those terms are understood in this country? Many wrongs may be obnoxious to the prohibitions of the Fourteenth Amendment which are not, in any just sense, incidents or elements of slavery. Such, for example, would be the taking of private property without due process of law, or allowing persons who have committed certain crimes (horse stealing, for example) to be seized and hung by [lynch mobs] without regular trial, or denying to any person, or class of persons, the right to pursue any peaceful avocations allowed to others. What is called class legislation would belong to this category, and would be obnoxious to the prohibitions of the Fourteenth Amendment, but would not necessarily be so to the Thirteenth, when not involving the idea of any subjection of one man to another. The Thirteenth Amendment has respect not to distinctions of race or class or color, but to slavery. The Fourteenth Amendment extends its protection to races and classes, and prohibits any State legislation which has the effect of denying to any race or class, or to any individual, the equal protection of the laws. . . .

On the whole, we are of opinion that no countenance of authority for the passage of the law in question can be found in either the Thirteenth or Fourteenth Amendment of the Constitution, and no other ground of authority for its passage being suggested, it must necessarily be declared void, at least so far as its operation in the several States is concerned.

MR. JUSTICE HARLAN, dissenting.

The opinion in these cases proceeds, it seems to me, upon grounds entirely too narrow and artificial. I cannot resist the conclusion that the substance and spirit of the recent amendments of the Constitution have been sacrificed by a subtle and ingenious verbal criticism. . . . Constitutional provisions, adopted in the interest of liberty and for the purpose of securing, through national legislation, if need be, rights inhering in a state of freedom and belonging to American citizenship have been so construed as to defeat the ends the people desired to accomplish, which they attempted to accomplish, and which they supposed they had accomplished by changes in their fundamental law. By this I do not mean that the determination of these cases should have been materially controlled by considerations of mere expediency or policy. I mean only, in this form, to express an earnest conviction that the court has departed from the familiar rule requiring, in the interpretation of constitutional provisions, that full effect be given to the intent with which they were adopted. . . .

The terms of the Thirteenth Amendment are absolute and universal. They embrace every race which then was, or might thereafter be, within the United States. No race, as such, can be excluded from the benefits or rights thereby conferred. Yet it is historically true that that amendment was suggested by the condition, in this country, of that race which had been declared by this Court to have had—according to the opinion entertained by the most civilized portion of the white race at the time of the adoption of the Constitution—"no rights which the white man was bound to respect," none of the privileges or immunities secured by that instrument to citizens of the United States. It had reference, in a peculiar sense, to a people which (although the larger part of them were in slavery) had been invited by an act of Congress to aid in saving from overthrow a government which, theretofore, by all of its departments, had treated them as an inferior race, with no legal rights or privileges except such as the white race might choose to grant them. . . .

The Thirteenth Amendment, it is conceded, did something more than to prohibit slavery as an *institution* resting upon distinctions of race and upheld by positive law. My brethren admit that it established and decreed universal *civil freedom* throughout the United States. But did the freedom thus established involve nothing more than exemption from actual slavery? Was nothing more intended than to forbid one man from owning another as property? Was it the purpose of the nation simply to destroy the institution, and then remit the race, theretofore held in bondage, to the several States for such protection, in their civil rights, necessarily growing out of freedom, as those States, in their discretion, might choose to provide? Were the States against whose protest the institution was destroyed to be left free, so far as national interference was concerned, to make or allow discriminations against that race, as such, in the enjoyment of those fundamental rights which, by universal concession, inhere in a state of freedom? Had the Thirteenth Amendment stopped with the sweeping declaration in its first section against the existence of slavery and involuntary servitude except for crime, Congress would have had the power . . . to protect the freedom established, and consequently, to secure the enjoyment of such civil rights as were fundamental in freedom. That it can exert its authority to that extent is made clear, and was intended to be made clear, by the express grant of power contained in the second section of the Amendment. . . .

I am of the opinion that such discrimination practi[c]ed by corporations and individuals in the exercise of their public or *quasi*-public functions is a badge of servitude the imposition of which Congress may prevent under its power, by appropriate legislation, to enforce the Thirteenth Amendment; and consequently, without reference to its enlarged power under the Fourteenth Amendment, the act of March 1, 1875, is not, in my judgment, repugnant to the Constitution. . . .

But what was secured to colored citizens of the United States—as between them and their respective States—by the national grant to them [by the Fourteenth Amendment] of State citizenship? With what rights, privileges, or immunities did this grant invest them? There is one, if there be no other—exemption from race discrimination in respect of any civil right belonging to citizens of the white race in the same State. That, surely, is their constitutional privilege when within the jurisdiction of other States. And such must be their constitutional right in their own State, unless the recent amendments be splendid baubles thrown out to delude those who deserved fair and generous treatment at the hands of the nation. Citizenship in this country necessarily imports at least equality of civil rights among citizens of every race in the same State. It is fundamental in American citizenship that, in respect of such rights, there shall be no discrimination by the State, or its officers, or by individuals or corporations exercising public functions or authority, against any citizen because of his race or previous condition of servitude. . . .

If, then, exemption from discrimination in respect of civil rights is a new constitutional right, secured by the grant of State citizenship to colored citizens of the United States—and I do not see how this can now be questioned—why may not the nation, by means of its own legislation of a primary direct character, guard, protect, and enforce that right? It is a right and privilege which the nation conferred. It did not come from the States in which those colored citizens reside. It has been the established doctrine of this Court during all its history, accepted as essential to the national supremacy, that Congress, in the absence of a positive delegation of power to the State legislatures, may, by its own legislation, enforce and protect any right derived from or created by the national Constitution. . . .

It was said of the case of *Dred Scott* v. *Sandford* that this Court there overruled the action of two generations, virtually inserted a new clause in the Constitution, changed its character, and made a new departure in the workings of the federal government. I may be permitted to say that, if the recent amendments are so construed that Congress may not, in its own discretion and independently of the action or nonaction of the States, provide by legislation of a direct character for the security of rights created by the national Constitution, if it be adjudged that the obligation to protect the fundamental privileges and immunities granted by the Fourteenth Amendment to citizens residing in the several States rests primarily not on the nation, but on the States, if it be further adjudged that individuals and corporations exercising public functions or wielding power under public authority may, without liability to direct primary legislation on the part of Congress, make the race of citizens the ground for denying them that equality of civil rights which the Constitution ordains as a principle of republican citizenship, then not only the foundations upon which the national supremacy has always securely rested will be materially disturbed, but we shall enter upon an era of constitutional law when the rights of freedom and American citizenship cannot receive from the nation that efficient protection which heretofore was unhesitatingly accorded to slavery and the rights of the master. . . .

Today it is the colored race which is denied, by corporations and individuals wielding public authority, rights fundamental in their freedom and citizenship. At some future time, it may be that some other race will fall under the ban of race discrimination. If the constitutional amendments be enforced according to the intent with which, as I conceive, they were adopted, there cannot be, in this republic, any class of human beings in practical subjection to another class with power in the latter to dole out to the former just such privileges as they may choose to grant. The supreme law of the land has decreed that no authority shall be exercised in this country upon the basis of discrimination, in respect of civil rights, against freemen and citizens because of their race, color, or previous condition of servitude. To that decree—for the due enforcement of which, by appropriate legislation, Congress has been invested with express power—everyone must bow, whatever may have been, or whatever now are, his individual views as to the wisdom or policy either of the recent changes in the fundamental law or of the legislation which has been enacted to give them effect.

The South understood this decision as Justice Harlan did, as an opportunity to press ahead, without constraint, with the systematic legal disenfranchisement of blacks. During Reconstruction, the Redeemers had slowly put into place a system of racial separation designed to maintain the social segregation of whites and blacks. With the exception of laws forbidding interracial marriage enacted immediately after the Civil War, this social system had no legal authority. In some communities, particularly those in which the federally backed provisional governments were still strong, blacks had a modest degree of freedom to use the same public accommodations as whites. But in most cases, especially after the withdrawal of federal troops from the South in 1877, breaches of the color line carried with it the implicit threat of violence against its trespassers.[26]

Four years after the Court's decision in the *Civil Rights Cases,* Florida enacted the nation's first post-Reconstruction Jim Crow law outside the context of marriage, mandating the separation of blacks and whites in all train cars. Segregation had been common in first-class train cars even during Reconstruction, but common-class cars had generally been exempt from the legal mandate of racial separation. In rapid succession, other former Confederate states began enacting similar laws to enforce racial segregation aboard trains. Ironically, as legal segregation became more prevalent in the late 1880s and early 1890s, editorial opinion in numerous Southern newspapers clashed with the practice. By the turn of the century, however, all the Southern states extended Jim Crow laws to every conceivable aspect of both private and public life. The *Charleston News and Courier,* once skeptical of the need for Jim Crow, commented in 1906 that outside of deportation, the most desirable solution, "separation of the races is the only radical solution of the negro problem in this country." By this time, this view had come to dominate the editorial opinion of the major Southern newspapers.[27]

The South's blueprint to settle the "negro problem" came in *Plessy* v. *Ferguson* (1896), in which the Court held that laws mandating racial separation did not violate the Fourteenth Amendment as long as the facilities in question were equal. *Plessy* provides a near-perfect example of how little public attitudes had changed toward African Americans since *Dred Scott.* Justice Henry B. Brown, writing for an 8–1 Court, held that the assumption of "the colored race" that enforced racial separation stamped blacks with a "badge of inferiority" was simply false. The Constitution could not make distinctions between the civil and political rights of the races, said the Court. But neither could it make a "socially inferior" race the equal of whites. "In the nature of things," wrote Justice Brown, the Fourteenth Amendment "could not have been intended to abolish distinctions based upon color, or to enforce social, as distinguished from political, equality, or a commingling of the two races upon terms unsatisfactory to either."[28]

Note, as you read *Plessy,* how the Court treats the "social" sphere, as opposed to the "civic" and "political" spheres. The system of Jim Crow, in the Court's view, reflects a natural condition of society, and not a system created by law. The Court seemed not even to consider that Jim Crow evolved as the legal means by which the white South could continue to subjugate African Americans after the collapse of Reconstruction. Jim Crow was anything but voluntary and indifferent to legal pressure. The system of legal segregation that came about in the 1890s and lasted into the 1960s was a deliberate creation of the political process. It was not until *Brown* v. *Board of Education* (1954) that the idea of racial segregation as something that existed independent of the system of law and politics responsible for its creation collapsed.[29] How it did so offers a remarkable lesson in the use of litigation as an instrument of reform.

Plessy v. *Ferguson*

163 U.S. 537 (1896)

Homer Plessy was arrested for violating a Louisiana law making it illegal for members of the "colored race" to ride in the same train cars as whites. Segregation on rail systems was one the originating points of "Jim Crow," the name given to the system of racial apartheid that dominated the South from the collapse of Reconstruction until the early 1960s. Ironically, Plessy had often "passed" as white in the diverse Creole community of late 1800s New Orleans. Homer Plessy's decision to defy the segregation law was a deliberate effort, supported by one of the city's leading civil liberties lawyers, Rudolph Desdunes, who headed the New Orleans branch of the American Citizens' Equal Rights Association. Desdunes had recruited Plessy to test the rail car law in large part because of his "white" features. But according to the Southern system, any person who possessed one drop of "colored" blood was considered a member of the "colored race." If not for his conscious proclamation of his mixed heritage, Homer Plessy would have continued to pass as white.

Plessy was a "test" case in every sense of the term. Indeed, Homer Plessy's trip from New Orleans to Covington, Louisiana, had no other purpose than to obtain arrest. In fact, Plessy never made it to Covington. He was arrested almost as soon as he sat down in the first-class rail car he boarded in New Orleans and taken to jail. As his case moved through the Louisiana courts, Plessy was represented by two white lawyers active in civil rights causes: Albion Tourgee, a former Union officer who had helped write North Carolina's post–Civil War constitution; and James C. Walker, a local lawyer who had worked previously with Desdunes. They lost in the Louisiana courts, and appealed to the United States Supreme Court.[30]

The Court's decision was 8 to 1. Justice Brown delivered the opinion of the Court. Justice Harlan (I) dissented.

MR. JUSTICE BROWN delivered the opinion of the Court.

The constitutionality of this act is attacked upon the ground that it conflicts both with the Thirteenth Amendment of the Constitution, abolishing slavery, and the Fourteenth Amendment, which prohibits certain restrictive legislation on the part of the States.

That it does not conflict with the Thirteenth Amendment, which abolished slavery and involuntary servitude, except as a punishment for crime, is too clear for argument. Slavery implies involuntary servitude—a state of bondage; the ownership of mankind as a chattel, or at least the control of the labor and services of one man for the benefit of another, and the absence of a legal right to the disposal of his own person, property and services. . . . It was intimated, however, in that case that this amendment was regarded by the statesmen of that day as insufficient to protect the colored race from certain laws which had been enacted in the Southern States, imposing upon the colored race onerous disabilities and burdens and curtailing their rights in the pursuit of life, liberty and property to such an extent that their freedom was of little value; and that the Fourteenth Amendment was devised to meet this exigency. . . .

A statute which implies merely a legal distinction between the white and colored races—a distinction which is founded in the color of the two races and which must always exist so long as white men are distinguished from the other race by color—has no tendency to destroy the legal equality of the two races, or reestablish a state of involuntary servitude. Indeed, we do not understand that the Thirteenth Amendment is strenuously relied upon by the plaintiff in error in this connection. . . .

The object of the amendment was undoubtedly to enforce the absolute equality of the two races before the law, but, in the nature of things, it could not have been intended to abolish distinctions based upon color, or to enforce social, as distinguished from political, equality, or a commingling of the two races upon terms unsatisfactory to either. Laws permitting, and even requiring, their separation in places where they are liable to be brought into contact do not necessarily imply the inferiority of either race to the other, and have been generally, if not universally, recognized as within the competency of the state legislatures in the exercise of their police power. The most common instance of this is connected with the establishment of separate schools for white and colored children, which has been held to be a valid exercise of the legislative power even by courts of States where the political rights of the colored race have been longest and most earnestly enforced. . . .

Laws forbidding the intermarriage of the two races may be said in a technical sense to interfere with the freedom of contract, and yet have been universally recognized as within the police power of the State.

The distinction between laws interfering with the political equality of the negro and those requiring the separation of the two races in schools, theatres and railway carriages has been frequently drawn by this Court. . . . So, where the laws of a particular locality or the charter of a particular railway corporation has provided that no person shall be excluded from the cars on account of color, we have held that this meant that persons of color should travel in the same car as white ones, and that the enactment was not satisfied by the company's providing cars assigned exclusively to people of color, though they were as good as those which they assigned exclusively to white persons. . . .

It is claimed by [Plessy] that, in any mixed community, the reputation of belonging to the dominant race, in this instance the white race, is property in the same sense that a right of action or of inheritance is property. Conceding this to be so for the purposes of this case, we are unable to see how this statute deprives him of, or in any way affects his right to, such property. If he be a white man and assigned to a colored coach, he may have his action for damages against the company for being deprived of his so-called property. Upon the other hand, if he be a colored man and be so assigned, he has been deprived of no property, since he is not lawfully entitled to the reputation of being a white man.

In this connection, it is also suggested by the learned counsel for the plaintiff in error that the same argument that will justify the state legislature in requiring railways to provide separate accommodations for the two races will also authorize them to require separate cars to be provided for people whose hair is of a certain color, or who are aliens, or who belong to certain nationalities, or to enact laws requiring colored people to walk upon one side of the street and white people upon the other, or requiring white men's houses to be painted white and colored men's black, or their vehicles or business signs to be of different colors, upon the theory that one side of the street is as good as the other, or that a house or vehicle of one color is as good as one of another color. The reply to all this is that every exercise of the police power must be reasonable, and extend only to such laws as are enacted in good faith for the promotion for the public good, and not for the annoyance or oppression of a particular class. . . .

So far, then, as a conflict with the Fourteenth Amendment is concerned, the case reduces itself to the question whether the statute of Louisiana is a reasonable regulation, and, with respect to this, there must necessarily be a large discretion on the part of the legislature. In determining the question of reasonableness, it is at liberty to act with reference to the established usages, customs, and traditions of the people, and with a view to the promotion of their comfort and the preservation of the public peace and good order. Gauged by this standard, we cannot say that a law which authorizes or even requires the separation of the two races in public conveyances is unreasonable, or more obnoxious to the Fourteenth Amendment than the acts of Congress requiring separate schools for colored children in the District of Columbia, the constitutionality of which does not seem to have been questioned, or the corresponding acts of state legislatures.

We consider the underlying fallacy of the plaintiff's argument to consist in the assumption that the enforced separation of the two races stamps the colored race with a badge of inferiority. If this be so, it is not by reason of anything found in the act, but solely because the colored race chooses to put that construction upon it. The argument necessarily assumes that if, as has been more than once the case and is not unlikely to be so again, the colored race should become the dominant power in the state legislature, and should enact a law in precisely similar terms, it would thereby relegate the white race to an inferior position. We imagine that the white race, at least, would not acquiesce in this assumption. The argument also assumes that social prejudices may be overcome by legislation, and that equal rights cannot be secured to the negro except by an enforced commingling of the two races. We cannot accept this proposition. If the two races are to meet upon terms of social equality, it must be the result of natural affinities, a mutual appreciation of each other's merits, and a voluntary consent of individuals. . . . Legislation is powerless to eradicate racial instincts or to abolish distinctions based upon physical differences, and the attempt to do so can only result in accentuating the difficulties of the present situation. If the civil and political rights of both races be equal, one cannot be inferior to the other civilly or politically. If one race be inferior to the other socially, the Constitution of the United States cannot put them upon the same plane.

It is true that the question of the proportion of colored blood necessary to constitute a colored person, as distinguished from a white person, is one upon which there is a difference of opinion in the different States, some holding that any visible admixture of black blood stamps the person as belonging to the colored race; others that it depends upon the preponderance of blood; and still others that the predominance of white blood must only be in the proportion of three-fourths. But these are questions to be determined under the laws of each State, and are not properly put in issue in this case. Under the allegations of his petition, it may undoubtedly become a question of importance whether, under the laws of Louisiana, the petitioner belongs to the white or colored race.

The judgment of the Court below is, therefore,

Affirmed.

MR. JUSTICE HARLAN, dissenting.

In respect of civil rights common to all citizens, the Constitution of the United States does not, I think, permit any public authority to know the race of those entitled to be protected in the enjoyment of such rights. Every true man has pride of race, and, under appropriate circumstances, when the rights of others, his equals before the law, are not to be affected, it is his privilege to express such pride and to take such action based upon it as to him seems proper. But I deny that any legislative body or judicial tribunal may have regard to the race of citizens when the civil rights of those citizens are involved. Indeed, such legislation as that here in question is inconsistent not only with that equality of rights which pertains to citizenship, National and State, but with the personal liberty enjoyed by everyone within the United States.

The Thirteenth Amendment does not permit the withholding or the deprivation of any right necessarily inhering in freedom. It not only struck down the institution of slavery as previously existing in the United States, but it prevents the imposition of any burdens or disabilities that constitute badges of slavery or servitude. It decreed universal civil freedom in this country. This court has so adjudged. But that amendment having been found inadequate to the protection of the rights of those who had been in slavery, it was followed by the Fourteenth Amendment, which added greatly to the dignity and glory of American citizenship and to the security of personal liberty. . . .

These two amendments, if enforced according to their true intent and meaning, will protect all the civil rights that pertain to freedom and citizenship. . . .

It is one thing for railroad carriers to furnish, or to be required by law to furnish, equal accommodations for all whom they are under a legal duty to carry. It is quite another thing for government to forbid citizens of the white and black races from traveling in the same public conveyance, and to punish officers of railroad companies for permitting persons of the two races to occupy the same passenger coach. If a State can prescribe, as a rule of civil conduct, that whites and blacks shall not travel as passengers in the same railroad coach, why may it not so regulate the use of the streets of its cities and towns as to compel white citizens to keep on one side of a street and black citizens to keep on the other? Why may it not, upon like grounds, punish whites and blacks who ride together in streetcars or in open vehicles on a public road or street? Why may it not require sheriffs to assign whites to one side of a courtroom and blacks to the other? And why may it not also prohibit the commingling of the two races in the galleries of legislative halls or in public assemblages convened for the consideration of the political questions of the day? Further, if this statute of Louisiana is consistent with the personal liberty of citizens, why may not the State require the separation in railroad coaches of native and naturalized citizens of the United States, or of Protestants and Roman Catholics?

The answer given at the argument to these questions was that regulations of the kind they suggest would be unreasonable, and could not, therefore, stand before the law. Is it meant that the determination of questions of legislative power depends upon the inquiry whether the statute whose validity is questioned is, in the judgment of the courts, a reasonable one, taking all the circumstances into consideration? A statute may be unreasonable merely because a sound public policy forbade its enactment. But I do not understand that the courts have anything to do with the policy or expediency of legislation. A statute may be valid and yet, upon grounds of public policy, may well be characterized as unreasonable. . . .

The white race deems itself to be the dominant race in this country. And so it is in prestige, in achievements, in education, in wealth and in power. So, I doubt not, it will continue to be for all time if it remains true to its great heritage and holds fast to the principles of constitutional liberty. But in view of the Constitution, in the eye of the law, there is in this country no superior, dominant, ruling class of citizens. There is no caste here. Our Constitution is color-blind, and neither knows nor tolerates classes among citizens. In respect of civil rights, all citizens are equal before the law. The humblest is the peer of the most powerful. The law regards man as man, and takes no account of his surroundings or of his color when his civil rights as guaranteed by the supreme law of the land are involved. It is therefore to be regretted that this high tribunal, the final expositor of the fundamental law of the land, has reached the conclusion that it is competent for a State to regulate the enjoyment by citizens of their civil rights solely upon the basis of race.

In my opinion, the judgment this day rendered will, in time, prove to be quite as pernicious as the decision made by this tribunal in the *Dred Scott Case*. . . .

The recent amendments of the Constitution, it was supposed, had eradicated these principles from our institutions. But it seems that we have yet, in some of the States, a dominant race—a superior class of citizens, which assumes to regulate the enjoyment of civil rights, common to all citizens, upon the basis of race. The present decision, it may well be apprehended, will not only stimulate aggressions, more or less brutal and irritating, upon the admitted rights of colored citizens, but will encourage the belief that it is possible, by means of state enactments, to defeat the beneficent purposes which the people of the United States had in view when they adopted the recent amendments of the Constitution, by one of which the blacks of this country were made citizens of the United States and of the States in which they respectively reside, and whose privileges and immunities, as citizens, the States are forbidden to abridge. Sixty millions of whites are in no danger from the presence here of eight millions of blacks. The destinies of the two races in this country are indissolubly linked together, and the interests of both require that the common government of all shall not permit the seeds of race hate to be planted under the sanction of law. What can more certainly arouse race hate, what more certainly create and perpetuate a feeling of distrust between these races, than state enactments which, in fact, proceed on the ground that colored citizens are so inferior and degraded that they cannot be allowed to sit in public coaches occupied by white citizens. That, as all will admit, is the real meaning of such legislation as was enacted in Louisiana.

The sure guarantee of the peace and security of each race is the clear, distinct, unconditional recognition by our governments, National and State, of every right that inheres in civil freedom, and of the equality before the law of all citizens of the United States, without regard to race. State enactments regulating the enjoyment of civil rights upon the basis of race, and cunningly devised to defeat legitimate results of the war under the pretence of recognizing equality of rights, can have no other result than to render permanent peace impossible and to keep alive a conflict of races the continuance of which must do harm to all concerned. This question is not met by the suggestion that social equality cannot exist between the white and black races in this country. That argument, if it can be properly regarded as one, is scarcely worthy of consideration, for social equality no more exists between two races when traveling in a passenger coach or a public highway than when members of the same races sit by each other in a street car or in the jury box, or stand or sit with each other in a political assembly, or when they use in common the street of a city or town, or when they are in the same room for the purpose of having their names placed on the registry of voters, or when they approach the ballot box in order to exercise the high privilege of voting. . . .

I am of opinion that the statute of Louisiana is inconsistent with the personal liberty of citizens, white and black, in that State, and hostile to both the spirit and letter of the Constitution of the United States. If laws of like character should be enacted in the several States of the Union, the effect would be in the highest degree mischievous. Slavery, as an institution tolerated by law would, it is true, have disappeared from our country, but there would remain a power in the States, by sinister legislation, to interfere with the full enjoyment of the blessings of freedom to regulate civil rights, common to all citizens, upon the basis of race, and to place in a condition of legal inferiority a large body of American citizens now constituting a part of the political community called the People of the United States, for whom and by whom, through representatives, our government is administered. Such a system is inconsistent with the guarantee given by the Constitution to each State of a republican form of government, and may be stricken down by Congressional action, or by the courts in the discharge of their solemn duty to maintain the supreme law of the land, anything in the constitution or laws of any State to the contrary notwithstanding.

The Stranglehold of Jim Crow

By the turn of the twentieth century, Jim Crow ruled the social and political spheres of Southern life. Separate schools and other public facilities, such as parks, bathrooms, waiting rooms in train stations and bus depots, swimming pools, and ball fields, were established for African Americans. Commercial establishments open to the public, such as restaurants, theatres, and amusement parks, were off limits to blacks as well. In some cases, grocery stores and department stores would serve blacks, but not permit them to use the front entrance, touch merchandise without the assistance of sales clerks (all of whom were white), or extend them credit. African American political power established by Reconstruction disappeared, as the Southern states developed numerous methods, such as poll taxes, property requirements, and literacy tests, to exclude blacks from the voter rolls. The Constitution and federal law banned none of these methods at the time. And whites were rarely, if ever, required to meet such qualifications to register to vote.

Legal segregation is most often remembered as the Goliath brought down by the civil rights movement of the 1950s and 1960s, but it was social segregation—quite literally, the prohibition of contact between blacks and whites—that whites found more important and were willing to defend at all costs. And the foundation of that social segregation was built around preventing black men from having sex with white women. In his classic study of race relations published in 1944, *The American Dilemma,* Gunnar Myrdal asked white Southerners how they ranked various aspects of segregation. Whether blacks voted or held good jobs did not even rank toward the top; the prohibition against intermarriage and sexual intercourse involving white women was far and away the most important.[31] Whites held various stereotypes about blacks: They were "simple and affectionate," "childlike," "on moral holiday," and saddled by "incapacity."[32] But none so aroused the fear and, subsequently, the "need" to control blacks, with force, if necessary, as their "uncontrollable" sexuality. Of life in the Mississippi Delta, one long-time white resident wrote:

> The Negro . . . is sexually completely free and untrammeled. . . . To him the expressions and manifestations of sex are as simple and as natural as the manifestations of nature in the wind and the sun and the rain, in the cycles of the seasons and the rounds of the growing crops. Sexual desire is an imperative need, raw and crude and strong. It is to be satisfied when and wherever it arises. . . . We do not give the Negro civic equality because we are fearful that this will lead in turn to demands for social equality. And social equality will tend toward what we will never grant—the right of equal marriage. As a corollary to these propositions we enforce racial separation and segregation.[33]

Such explicit acknowledgment that racial segregation was rooted in the desire to protect the social status of whites as self-proclaimed superiors to African Americans offers further testament to the myth of the "separate but equal" doctrine created by the Court in *Plessy.* The handful of white benevolent societies that formed after Reconstruction to advance black equality did not possess the resources or the political will to mount any serious challenge to the system of Jim Crow. In 1908, a series of bloody race riots in Springfield, Illinois (the birthplace of Abraham Lincoln), that culminated in the lynching of two blacks and dozens of serious injuries led a group of liberal whites and African American activists to form the National Association for the Advancement of Colored People (NAACP). The NAACP announced its formation on February 12, 1909, Lincoln's birthday, and devoted its early efforts to publicizing violence against blacks and lobbying Congress and state legislatures to enact anti-lynching laws. By the 1920s, the NAACP leadership had broadened the organization's objectives to include the elimination, by root and branch, of Jim Crow. The attack on school segregation became the primary vehicle to launch the dismantling of the "separate but equal" principle.

Litigation as an Instrument of Reform

In 1924, Charles Hamilton Houston finished his doctoral and legal studies at Harvard University and returned home to Washington, D.C., determined to improve the lives of blacks through the law. By 1929, Houston had been appointed the vice dean of Howard Law School, a part of the city's African American university. During this time Houston began to assist the NAACP with various civil rights complaints, often with the support of his students, a method he believed would accomplish one of his most important goals: to increase the number of black lawyers representing black clients. During this time, Houston also traveled the South on behalf of the NAACP with a movie camera, filming the staggeringly inferior schools that blacks in the South attended. Houston's mission received its first major funding from a white philanthropist named Charles Garland, who pledged $100,000 to the NAACP's fledgling legal campaign. The Garland Fund believed the final result of this campaign would give the "southern Negro" his "constitutional rights, his political and civil equality . . . which would inevitably tend to effect a revolution in the economic life of the country."[34]

In 1933, the NAACP published a report written by Nathan Margold, a white lawyer whom it had hired as special counsel to design a litigation strategy to advance black equality. Margold rejected the approach of such luminaries within the NAACP as W. E. B. Du Bois, who believed that litigation to achieve integration was fruitless and counterproductive to the economic interests of African Americans. Du Bois believed that white America would never abandon segregation, and encouraged blacks to build their own independent institutions to achieve greater power. Margold's report encouraged a direct, long-term challenge to the "separate but equal" doctrine, and visualized law and litigation as tools of social reform. So incensed was Du Bois with the decision to press ahead with a litigation campaign to overturn *Plessy* that he resigned from the NAACP. Wrote Du Bois: "A black man born in Boston has a right to oppose any separation of schools by color. But this black man in Boston has no right . . . to send his own helpless child into school where white children kick, cuff or abuse him, or where teachers openly and persistently neglect or hurt or dwarf its soul."[35]

Du Bois's opinion, however, did not represent the consensus that had emerged within the NAACP to move forward on the strategy outlined in the Margold Report. In 1934, Charles Houston replaced Margold as special counsel, and began to devise a long-range plan to attack segregation in the courts. Successful litigation could not proceed without vigorous support from local black communities. Houston set about recruiting African American attorneys to stimulate such support. By this point, the NAACP believed it was essential to replace many of the white attorneys who had worked on discrimination cases in the 1920s and early 1930s with black lawyers. NAACP leadership wanted its chapters to have the best representation possible in local communities, and it believed that black lawyers were the best qualified to provide it. Equally as important was the symbolism of having skilled black lawyers make the case on behalf of African American equality in courts that were, without exception, presided over by white judges.

In 1935, Houston initiated the NAACP's first major lawsuit against segregated education. It challenged the decision of the University of Maryland's all-white law school to deny admission to Donald Murray solely because he was black. Houston had decided to begin the NAACP's legal campaign by focusing on law schools because most Jim Crow states did not provide separate law schools for blacks. Following the logic of *Plessy,* the courts would either have to rule that states provide black students with their own equal schools, or admit them into white schools. Sending them out-of-state on scholarships to attend black law schools left the states in a weak position under the Fourteenth Amendment, since the state could not argue it was providing an equal education within its borders.

Houston tried Murray's case in Baltimore municipal court, which ruled that the University of Maryland had no choice but to admit his client, a decision that was upheld on appeal in the Maryland courts.[36] The decision, of course, carried no precedential weight beyond the state, but it sent a clear message to other Jim Crow states: either they would have to start laying out substantial expenditures to build separate law schools and other graduate programs for blacks who wanted to attend them, or admit them into all-white schools. Integration was then inconceivable, so Jim Crow states began providing separate such facilities for blacks. Houston knew that it would take years for black schools to come up to speed with white schools. He decided the time was right to bring a test case in the federal courts to expose the blatant inferiority of black public education.

Beyond its solid victory, the Maryland law school case marked another critical turning point for the NAACP's campaign. Murray's case had been brought to Houston's attention by one of his former students, Thurgood Marshall, who was then practicing law in Baltimore. Marshall had helped to revitalize the Baltimore chapter of the NAACP after graduating from law school in 1933. His commitment to civil rights was such that he soon found himself spending more time on his NAACP volunteer work than his private practice. Houston persuaded the NAACP to hire Marshall full time to bolster its staff resources. In 1936, Marshall left his practice, joined the NAACP, and moved to its headquarters in New York. He and Houston soon began work on the case that culminated in its first victory in the Supreme Court, *Gaines ex re. Canada* v. *Missouri* (1938).[37]

Like Maryland, the University of Missouri did not admit black students into its law school. Houston, working with NAACP activists in St. Louis, recruited Lloyd Gaines, a graduate of Missouri's all-black Lincoln University, to challenge the law school's admissions system. Missouri's response to the NAACP's challenge was identical to Maryland's: If Gaines wanted to attend law school, the state would provide him with an out-of-state scholarship. Following the logic of the Maryland case, the Court ruled that the opportunities afforded by Missouri for black students to attend law school elsewhere was "beside the point." The issue was what Missouri offered its black and white students in-state. Here, the Court, 7 to 2, ruled that the state had failed to meet its burden under *Plessy.*

Ultimately, Missouri circumvented the Court's decision by allocating $200,000 to improve graduate and law instruction at Lincoln, hoping that its commitment to equalizing black education would permit the state to continue its segregated admissions policies. When *Gaines* was retried after the Court's decision, a Missouri court ruled that Lincoln had achieved substantial parity with the University of Missouri's law school and thus permitted its Jim Crow admissions policies to remain in place. Still years away from challenging segregation as unconstitutional under any circumstance, the NAACP forced Jim Crow states to make good on the "separate but equal" guarantee that the Court had ruled they were required to meet. Success or failure in the NAACP's desegregation lawsuits during this time hinged upon whether a state could improve its facilities for African Americans before its lawyers beat them to the punch.

Still, *Gaines* demonstrated that the Court was willing to take seriously the NAACP's challenge to segregated education. After the decision, Houston returned to private practice in Washington, and Marshall, in 1940, became the NAACP's full-time chief lawyer. The change was significant. Although equally as committed as Houston to litigation to undo racial segregation, Marshall was his mirror opposite in almost every respect. He was as gregarious as Houston was serious, able to disarm a courtroom of white lawyers and judges with a joke and self-effacing manner without bowing to the racial norms expected of a black man. Houston read the law with laser-like precision and honed his strategy and tactics accordingly, whereas Marshall was the quintessential trial lawyer, able to extract information through seemingly casual conversation and approached his cases with a set of political and social skills that Houston could not match. With Houston still very much involved in the NAACP's campaign, he and Marshall became a powerful team, complementing each other in a way that made it difficult for their opponents to outmaneuver them.

During the early 1940s, the NAACP focused its efforts on equalization suits in state courts, securing victories in Tennessee, Maryland, Louisiana, and Tennessee. Here again, the NAACP's strategy was not to challenge racial segregation as unequal, but the resources allocated to African Americans under the system. Marshall and Houston's objective was to establish a line of successful precedent that could then be taken into federal court, preparing all the while to challenge segregation as inherently violative of the Fourteenth Amendment. The NAACP was also actively engaged in federal civil rights litigation outside the sphere of public education. In *Smith* v. *Allwright* (1944) (see Chapter 12), a case argued by Marshall, the Court ruled that Texas's all-white primary electoral system was unconstitutional.[38] *Allwright* was a major victory for the NAACP, and pointed the way toward the gradual reform of the electoral process nationwide. It also demonstrated that the Court was prepared to scrutinize carefully state laws that disenfranchised African Americans from any meaningful stake in the political process.

But perhaps the NAACP's most significant victory between *Gaines* and *Brown* v. *Board of Education* came four years later in *Shelley* v. *Kraemer* (1948). In *Shelley*, a unanimous Court ruled that the Equal Protection Clause prohibited state courts from enforcing racially restrictive real estate agreements. In some ways, *Shelley* is a remarkable exercise in judicial opinion writing: The Court's decision managed to skirt the distinction between discriminatory state action and private action, one that traced its origins to the *Civil Rights Cases* of 1883. Chief Justice Fred Vinson's decision was lauded by civil rights advocates, but came under severe criticism from many legal scholars, who argued the Court did not fully explain the element of state action that brought racial convenants within the orbit of the Fourteenth Amendment. Do you believe the Court's opinion in *Shelley* effectively distinguished itself from the logic of the *Civil Rights Cases*?

Shelley v. *Kraemer*

334 U.S. 1 (1948)

In August 1945, J. D. Shelley, a construction worker, and his wife, Ethel Lee, who worked in a munitions plant, moved into a predominantly white neighborhood in the Grand Prairie section of St. Louis. The Shelleys, who had six children, had been assisted in their housing search by their church pastor, Robert Bishop, who also sold real estate. After the Shelleys had settled in to their new home, they were sued for violating the neighborhood's racially restrictive covenants by Louis and Fern Kraemer, who owned a house ten blocks away on the same street. Both houses were covered by the same racially restrictive covenants, which dated back to 1911 and bound any subsequent owner of the home for fifty years.

Bishop put the Shelleys in touch with George Vaughn, a local NAACP activist, who had been working on a similar case in Chicago. Charles Houston and Thurgood Marshall had been overseeing several restrictive convenant cases that stretched from California to Washington, D.C. The Shelleys' case was not the first on the NAACP's list to take to the Court—it had other cases where the factual record had been better developed—but events propelled it ahead of the others. Houston and Marshall enlisted the support of several civil rights organizations, which agreed to file *amicus* briefs emphasizing the state action issue. The NAACP's most important support, however, came from the Department of Justice. In its *amicus* brief, the Justice Department emphasized the social stigma caused by racial discrimination and the state action arguments, a blueprint for the litigation strategies used in the school desegregation cases.

Houston, Marshall, and several other lawyers from the NAACP's national staff argued the case before the Court. But George Vaughn got his turn, and offered what Solicitor General Philip Elman called the "the most moving plea" he had ever heard in the Court: "[A]s the Negro knocks at America's door, he cries: 'Let me come in and sit by the fire. I helped build the house'." "All of a sudden," Elman said, "there was drama in the courtroom, a sense of what the case was really all about rather than the technical legal arguments."[39]

The Court's decision was unanimous. Chief Justice Vinson delivered the opinion of the Court. Justices Jackson, Reed, and Rutledge did not participate.

▼▲▼

Mr. Chief Justice Vinson delivered the opinion of the Court.

These cases present for our consideration questions relating to the validity of court enforcement of private agreements, generally described as restrictive covenants, which have as their purpose the exclusion of persons of designated race or color from the ownership or occupancy of real property. . . . Basic constitutional issues of obvious importance have been raised.

It is well, at the outset, to scrutinize the terms of the restrictive agreements involved in these cases. In the Missouri case, the covenant declares that no part of the affected property shall be "occupied by any person not of the Caucasian race, it being intended hereby to restrict the use of said property . . . against the occupancy as owners or tenants of any portion of said property for resident or other purpose by people of the Negro or Mongolian Race."

Not only does the restriction seek to proscribe use and occupancy of the affected properties by members of the excluded class, but, as construed by the Missouri courts, the agreement requires that title of any person who uses his property in violation of the restriction shall be divested. The restriction of the covenant in the Michigan case seeks to bar occupancy by persons of the excluded class. It provides that "This property shall not be used or occupied by any person or persons except those of the Caucasian race."

It should be observed that these covenants do not seek to proscribe any particular use of the affected properties. Use of the properties for residential occupancy, as such, is not forbidden. The restrictions of these agreements, rather, are directed toward a designated class of persons and seek to determine who may and who may not own or make use of the properties for residential purposes. The excluded class is defined wholly in terms of race or color; "simply that, and nothing more."

It cannot be doubted that among the civil rights intended to be protected from discriminatory state action by the Fourteenth Amendment are the rights to acquire, enjoy, own and dispose of property. Equality in the enjoyment of property rights was regarded by the framers of that Amendment as an essential pre-condition to the realization of other basic civil rights and liberties which the Amendment was intended to guarantee. . . . It is likewise clear that restrictions on the right of occupancy of the sort sought to be created by the private agreements in these cases could not be squared with the requirements of the Fourteenth Amendment if imposed by state statute or local ordinance. . . .

But the present cases . . . do not involve action by state legislatures or city councils. Here, the particular patterns of discrimination and the areas in which the restrictions are to operate are determined, in the first instance, by the terms of agreements among private individuals. Participation of the State consists in the enforcement of the restrictions so defined. The crucial issue with which we are here confronted is whether this distinction removes these cases from the operation of the prohibitory provisions of the Fourteenth Amendment.

Since the decision of this Court in the *Civil Rights Cases* (1883), the principle has become firmly embedded in our constitutional law that the action inhibited by the first section of the Fourteenth Amendment is only such action as may fairly be said to be that of the States. That

Amendment erects no shield against merely private conduct, however discriminatory or wrongful.

We conclude, therefore, that the restrictive agreements, standing alone, cannot be regarded as violative of any rights guaranteed to petitioners by the Fourteenth Amendment. So long as the purposes of those agreements are effectuated by voluntary adherence to their terms, it would appear clear that there has been no action by the State, and the provisions of the Amendment have not been violated. . . .

But here there was more. These are cases in which the purposes of the agreements were secured only by judicial enforcement by state courts of the restrictive terms of the agreements. The respondents urge that judicial enforcement of private agreements does not amount to state action, or, in any event, the participation of the State is so attenuated in character as not to amount to state action within the meaning of the Fourteenth Amendment. Finally, it is suggested, even if the States in these cases may be deemed to have acted in the constitutional sense, their action did not deprive petitioners of rights guaranteed by the Fourteenth Amendment. We move to a consideration of these matters.

That the action of state courts and judicial officers in their official capacities is to be regarded as action of the State within the meaning of the Fourteenth Amendment is a proposition which has long been established by decisions of this Court. . . . The action of state courts in imposing penalties or depriving parties of other substantive rights without providing adequate notice and opportunity to defend has, of course, long been regarded as a denial of the due process of law guaranteed by the Fourteenth Amendment. . . .

The short of the matter is that, from the time of the adoption of the Fourteenth Amendment until the present, it has been the consistent ruling of this Court that the action of the States to which the Amendment has reference includes action of state courts and state judicial officials. Although, in construing the terms of the Fourteenth Amendment, differences have from time to time been expressed as to whether particular types of state action may be said to offend the Amendment's prohibitory provisions, it has never been suggested that state court action is immunized from the operation of those provisions simply because the act is that of the judicial branch of the state government.

We hold that, in granting judicial enforcement of the restrictive agreements in these cases, the States have denied petitioners the equal protection of the laws, and that, therefore, the action of the state courts cannot stand. We have noted that freedom from discrimination by the States in the enjoyment of property rights was among the basic objectives sought to be effectuated by the framers of the Fourteenth Amendment. That such discrimination has occurred in these cases is clear. Because of the race or color of these petitioners, they have been denied rights of ownership or occupancy enjoyed as a matter of course by other citizens of different race or color.

In *Shelley,* the Court did not rule that racial covenants between private parties were unconstitutional. But, by ruling that courts could not enforce such agreements, the Court sent a powerful signal to African Americans and other minorities that one of the most effective and long-standing tools of housing discrimination was as good as dead. *Shelley* also demonstrated that the Court was prepared to rule in ways that resulted in racial integration, not just better but still separate facilities for African Americans.

Confident that the Court was now prepared to rule directly on the constitutionality of racial segregation, the NAACP pressed ahead with two separate university cases involving discrimination against African Americans. In *McLaurin* v. *Oklahoma State Regents* (1950), the Court held that the University of Oklahoma could not segregate George McLaurin, a sixty-eight-year-old college professor, from his classmates once he had been admitted to its doctoral program. McLaurin had been refused admission to the university solely on the basis of race. After a lower federal court ruled that Oklahoma had to provide him with "the education he seeks as soon as it does for applicants of any other group," McLaurin was granted admission. He was, however, restricted to his own tables in the cafeteria and the library, and forced to sit in the hall at a special desk outside the classroom. The Court unanimously ruled that such policies denied Professor McLaurin the equal education to which he was entitled under law. As in *Shelley,* the NAACP was supported by the Justice Department, which argued in its *amicus* brief that *Plessy* was wrong and the Court should overrrule it.

McLaurin was argued and later decided on the same day as *Sweatt* v. *Painter* (1950), a case involving the exclusion of Herman Sweatt, a black postal worker, from the University of Texas law school. The NAACP had several cases moving through the federal courts during this time, including one involving segregated dining car service on trains regulated by the Interstate Commerce Commission. These cases were aimed directly at *Plessy* and supported by the Justice Department. The Texas law school case, however, commanded the center of the NAACP's attention. *Sweatt's* attractiveness did not rest so much with the facts, as they were familiar from previous cases involving segregated graduate and law school education. In response to the NAACP's initial challenge, Texas agreed to create a makeshift law school for blacks, borrowing faculty, staff, books, and other resources from the University of Texas until the state established a permanent one. Sweatt's letter of denial included a promise, upon demand, to follow the equalization route. Even Thurgood Marshall conceded that by the time *Sweatt* reached the Court the resource inequality argument was weak. Marshall, of course, would press that issue, relying on *Gaines,* and there was some evidence to support that position. But the real gamble in *Sweatt* came in Marshall's decision, one reached in conjunction with Charles Houston and James M. Nabrit, another NAACP lawyer, to challenge the extracurricular and "intangible" aspects of Jim Crow legal education.

Marshall noted that the black law school did not have a law review or a moot court, that a degree from it carried no prestige, and that it lacked a network of professional contacts. The University of Texas possessed all these qualities and more. These were the differences between black and white education that Marshall emphasized in the NAACP's briefs and arguments once *Sweatt* reached the Court. The strategy was clear: Either the Court could rule on the "equalization" issues, or it could move farther down the path toward overruling *Plessy* by pursuing the sociological dimension of the NAACP's argument. The Justice Department endorsed the NAACP's approach in *Sweatt,* arguing that the "separate but equal" doctrine was an "anachronism which a half-century of history and experience has shown to be a departure from the basic constitutional principle that all Americans, regardless of their race or color or religion or national origin, stand equal and alike in the sight of the law."

The Court's unanimous opinion in *Sweatt,* written by Chief Justice Vinson, did not go as far as either the NAACP or the Justice Department wished. Rather, the Court combined "equalization" and "intangibles" arguments, holding that the benefits of a University of Texas legal education were superior for just the reasons outlined in the briefs of the NAACP and the Justice Department. Herman Sweatt's exclusion from the all-white school was thus a violation of the "separate but equal" requirement. Within the Court, sentiment was on the rise to confront *Plessy* head-on. Several justices believed that precedents building on behalf of the NAACP's position clearly put the social foundation of racial segregation on a collision course with logic. And once the Court ruled that segregation *per se* was unconstitutional in a university case, no meaningful line could be drawn between higher education and elementary and secondary education. Three weeks after the *McLaurin* and *Sweatt* decisions, Marshall convened NAACP lawyers to insist that the time had come to "map . . . the legal machinery" for an "all-out attack" on segregation "from top to bottom—from law school to kindergarten." The stage was thus set for *Brown.*

Brown v. *Board of Education:* The Demise of "Separate But Equal"

Marshall understood, as Houston had when he first committed the NAACP to attacking segregated education in the 1930s, that an assault on elementary and secondary schools raised a much more complex set of issues than the university cases. First, after the dust had settled, states forced to admit African American applicants into all-white universities were still dealing with less than a handful of people in classes where white students outnumbered them by the hundreds. Maryland, where Houston and Marshall had secured their first major desegregation victory in 1935, did not abolish its out-of-state scholarship system until 1954. Missouri, the site of the *Gaines* victory, was able to stave off black enrollment in all-white schools until the 1950s by upgrading its black institutions. Neither Marshall nor Houston was confident that the Court, which otherwise struck down discriminatory state laws as fast as the NAACP could bring its cases, was prepared to supervise a large-scale social experiment that would accompany desegregation at the elementary and high school levels.

Second, Marshall, Houston, and, as the NAACP's staff expanded in the 1940s, attorneys such as Constance Baker Motley, Spottswood Robinson, Jack Greenberg, and James Nabit, often faced considerable opposition from local black communities in pushing desegregation. It was one thing for attorneys to come down to South Carolina, Alabama, Georgia, and Louisiana and argue the merits of desegregation. It was something else entirely for African Americans who had to live in those states with the fear of white violence for daring to challenge the most coveted of the Old South's customs. The NAACP could not proceed with desegregation lawsuits it claimed were in the best interest of blacks if it could not build support at the community level. By the time it moved forward on *Brown*, the NAACP had worked with its local branches to recruit plaintiffs to secure that support.

Long before his appointment to the Supreme Court in 1967, Thurgood Marshall was a hero to many African Americans for his work with the NAACP. From the late 1930s until the early 1960s, Marshall was a key architect behind the NAACP's effort to abolish legal segregation through litigation. Marshall argued 32 cases before the Supreme Court during his years with the NAACP, and won 29 of them.

Courtesy of The African American Newspaper Company of Baltimore, Inc.

In *Brown*, the NAACP did not introduce the equalization argument as a fallback strategy, as it had in *McLaurin* and *Sweatt*. Instead, Marshall and his team of lawyers argued that racial segregation in education violated the Equal Protection Clause under any circumstance. Far from a system designed to reflect the "nature of things," as the Court had ruled in *Plessy*, racial segregation reminded blacks of their inferior position in every aspect of American society. Racial segregation damaged the self-esteem of black school children by reminding them on a daily basis that they did not belong with whites. In support of this position, the NAACP had enlisted Kenneth Clark, a prominent African American social psychologist, to conduct a series of studies on black school children using black and white dolls. In repeated tests, a majority of children told Clark that they liked the white dolls better, that they were prettier, and that they identified them with "good qualities." When asked to point to the doll that was most like them, a majority of the children identified the black doll, the one they had rejected. The NAACP believed that evidence such as this helped make its case that segregation promoted racial inferiority. Marshall insisted that the Court would find such evidence relevant.

In May 1954, a unanimous Court ruled that segregation had "no place" in the field of public education. Although the Court reached only the education issue, Chief Justice Earl Warren, who came to the Court in October 1953, wrote a simple, eleven-page opinion that made clear that racial segregation was an evil that found no protection in the Constitution. Warren's reference to Kenneth Clark's research brought the Court's opinion under fire as an exercise in sociology rather than law from quarters normally unsympathetic to racial segregation. Such criticism, however, assumes that *Plessy* was decided as a matter of "law," completely indifferent to the prevailing racial norms of the time. The Court understood that to conclude anything other than racial segregation was a product of social attitudes and the political power to turn them into law was to say that *Plessy* was right.

Brown was decided in two separate phases. In May 1954, the Court handed down its decision holding segregated schools unconstitutional; in May 1955, the Court issued an opinion ordering states in violation of *Brown* to desegregate with "all deliberate speed." This phrase was carefully inserted into the desegregation order to assure the South that the Court understood the difficulties of such a massive social and political reorganization of its school system. It quickly became clear that the South did not view the Court's gesture as a means to desegregate gradually, but to resist forcefully the integration of its schools.

Brown v. *Board of Education* (I)

347 U.S. 483 (1954)

Linda Brown's challenge to the Topeka, Kansas, law requiring racially segregated public schools was one of four suits the Court consolidated and decided as *Brown* v. *Board of Education.* The other suits came from Delaware, Virginia, and South Carolina. The same day it handed down *Brown,* the Court, in *Bolling* v. *Sharpe,* ruled that the Fifth Amendment banned Washington, D.C., from operating segregated schools. The NAACP had succeeded in persuading the Delaware courts to order integration rather than equalization after the state conceded that its schools were unequal. Thus, Delaware was appealing the judgment of its own state supreme court. In the other cases, however, the NAACP lost at the trial and appeals level.

Of the five cases, the most widely anticipated showdown came in *Briggs* v. *Clarendon County,* the South Carolina case. More so than any other state, South Carolina had launched a massive drive to equalize its schools. South Carolina also had one of the nation's most skilled Supreme Court advocates, John W. Davis, defending its segregation policies. Davis had argued over two hundred and fifty cases before the Court during his career, and that experience, the NAACP knew, would be a daunting factor.

Davis argued South Carolina's case for close to an hour, with only a few interruptions, and concluded his defense of segregation by saying:

> I am reminded—and I hope it won't be treated as a reflection on anybody—of Aseop's fable of the dog and the meat: The dog, with a fine piece of meat in his mouth, crossed a bridge and saw the shadow in the stream and plunged for it and lost both substance and shadow.
>
> Here is an equal education, not promised, not prophesied, but present. Shall it be thrown away on some fancied question of racial prestige?

Davis sat down, voice broken and tears running down his cheeks, leading one skeptical lawyer in the gallery to mention, "That sonofabitch cries in every case he argues."

But Davis had clearly met his match in Thurgood Marshall. In rebuttal, Marshall, whose own presentation to the Court was interrupted over fifty times, offered what many of his colleagues considered his finest argument ever:

> As Mr. Davis said yesterday, the only thing the Negroes are trying to get is prestige.
>
> Exactly correct. Ever since the Emancipation Proclamation, the Negro has been trying to get what was recognized [by the Fourteenth Amendment], which is the same status as anybody else regardless of race.
>
> They can't take race out of this case. From the day this case was filed until this moment, nobody has in any form or fashion, despite the fact I made it clear in the opening argument that I was relying on it, done anything to distinguish this statute from the Black Codes, which they must admit, because nobody can dispute, say anything anybody wants to say, one way or the other, the Fourteenth Amendment was intended to deprive the states of power to enforce Black Codes or anything else like it. . . .
>
> The only thing can be is an inherent determination that the people who were formerly in slavery, regardless of anything else, shall be kept as near that stage as possible, and now is the time, we submit, that this Court should make it clear that that is not what our Constitution stands for.

Marshall did not cry after he sat down, but he still managed to make his point.

The Court's decision was unanimous. Chief Justice Warren delivered the opinion of the Court.

▼▲▼

MR. CHIEF JUSTICE WARREN delivered the opinion of the Court.

In each of the cases, . . . the plaintiffs contend that segregated public schools are not "equal" and cannot be made

"equal," and that hence they are deprived of the equal protection of the laws. Because of the obvious importance of the question presented, the Court took jurisdiction. Argument was heard in the 1952 Term, and reargument was heard this Term on certain questions propounded by the Court.

Reargument was largely devoted to the circumstances surrounding the adoption of the Fourteenth Amendment in 1868. It covered exhaustively consideration of the Amendment in Congress, ratification by the states, then-existing practices in racial segregation, and the views of proponents and opponents of the Amendment. This discussion and our own investigation convince us that, although these sources cast some light, it is not enough to resolve the problem with which we are faced. At best, they are inconclusive. The most avid proponents of the post-War Amendments undoubtedly intended them to remove all legal distinctions among "all persons born or naturalized in the United States." Their opponents, just as certainly, were antagonistic to both the letter and the spirit of the Amendments and wished them to have the most limited effect. What others in Congress and the state legislatures had in mind cannot be determined with any degree of certainty.

An additional reason for the inconclusive nature of the Amendment's history with respect to segregated schools is the status of public education at that time. In the South, the movement toward free common schools, supported by general taxation, had not yet taken hold. Education of white children was largely in the hands of private groups. Education of Negroes was almost nonexistent, and practically all of the race were illiterate. In fact, any education of Negroes was forbidden by law in some states. Today, in contrast, many Negroes have achieved outstanding success in the arts and sciences, as well as in the business and professional world. It is true that public school education at the time of the Amendment had advanced further in the North, but the effect of the Amendment on Northern States was generally ignored in the congressional debates. Even in the North, the conditions of public education did not approximate those existing today. The curriculum was usually rudimentary; ungraded schools were common in rural areas; the school term was but three months a year in many states, and compulsory school attendance was virtually unknown. As a consequence, it is not surprising that there should be so little in the history of the Fourteenth Amendment relating to its intended effect on public education.

In the first cases in this Court construing the Fourteenth Amendment, decided shortly after its adoption, the Court interpreted it as proscribing all state-imposed discriminations against the Negro race. The doctrine of "separate but equal" did not make its appearance in this Court until 1896 in the case of *Plessy* v. *Ferguson* involving not education but transportation. American courts have since labored with the doctrine for over half a century. . . . Our decision cannot turn on merely a comparison of these tangible factors in the Negro and white schools involved in each of the cases. We must look instead to the effect of segregation itself on public education.

In approaching this problem, we cannot turn the clock back to 1868, when the Amendment was adopted, or even to 1896, when *Plessy* v. *Ferguson* was written. We must consider public education in the light of its full development and its present place in American life throughout the Nation. Only in this way can it be determined if segregation in public schools deprives these plaintiffs of the equal protection of the laws.

Today, education is perhaps the most important function of state and local governments. Compulsory school attendance laws and the great expenditures for education both demonstrate our recognition of the importance of education to our democratic society. It is required in the performance of our most basic public responsibilities, even service in the armed forces. It is the very foundation of good citizenship. Today it is a principal instrument in awakening the child to cultural values, in preparing him for later professional training, and in helping him to adjust normally to his environment. In these days, it is doubtful that any child may reasonably be expected to succeed in life if he is denied the opportunity of an education. Such an opportunity, where the state has undertaken to provide it, is a right which must be made available to all on equal terms.

We come then to the question presented: does segregation of children in public schools solely on the basis of race, even though the physical facilities and other "tangible" factors may be equal, deprive the children of the minority group of equal educational opportunities? We believe that it does.

In *Sweatt* v. *Painter* . . . this Court relied in large part on "those qualities which are incapable of objective measurement but which make for greatness in a law school." In *McLaurin* v. *Oklahoma State Regents,* the Court again resorted to intangible considerations: ". . . his ability to study, to engage in discussions and exchange views with other students, and, in general, to learn his profession." Such considerations apply with added force to children in grade and high schools. To separate them from others of similar age and qualifications solely because of their race generates a feeling of inferiority as to their status in the community that may affect their hearts and minds in a way unlikely ever to be undone. The effect of this separation on their educational opportunities was well stated by a finding in the Kansas case by a court which nevertheless felt compelled to rule against the Negro plaintiffs:

> Segregation of white and colored children in public schools has a detrimental effect upon the colored children. The impact is greater when it has the sanction of the law, for the policy of separating the races is usually interpreted as denoting the inferiority of the negro group. A sense of inferiority affects the motivation of a child to learn. Segregation with the sanction of law, therefore, has a tendency to [retard] the educational and mental development of negro children and to deprive them of some of the benefits they would receive in a racial[ly] integrated school system.

Whatever may have been the extent of psychological knowledge at the time of *Plessy* v. *Ferguson,* this finding is amply supported by modern authority.* Any language in *Plessy* v. *Ferguson* contrary to this finding is rejected.

We conclude that, in the field of public education, the doctrine of "separate but equal" has no place. Separate educational facilities are inherently unequal. Therefore, we hold that the plaintiffs and others similarly situated for whom the actions have been brought are, by reason of the segregation complained of, deprived of the equal protection of the laws guaranteed by the Fourteenth Amendment. This disposition makes unnecessary any discussion whether such segregation also violates the Due Process Clause of the Fourteenth Amendment.

Because these are class actions, because of the wide applicability of this decision, and because of the great variety of local conditions, the formulation of decrees in these cases presents problems of considerable complexity. On reargument, the consideration of appropriate relief was necessarily subordinated to the primary question—the constitutionality of segregation in public education. We have now announced that such segregation is a denial of the equal protection of the laws. In order that we may have the full assistance of the parties in formulating decrees, the cases will be restored to the docket, and the parties are requested to present further argument on [the appropriate remedies for these cases].

*K. B. Clark, Effect of Prejudice and Discrimination on Personality Development (Midcentury White House Conference on Children and Youth, 1950); Witmer and Kotinsky, *Personality in the Making* (1952), c. VI; Deutscher and Chein, The Psychological Effects of Enforced Segregation: A Survey of Social Science Opinion, *J. Psychol.* 26 (1948), p. 259; Chein, What Are the Psychological Effects of Segregation Under Conditions of Equal Facilities?, *Int. J. Opinion and Attitude Res.* 3 (1949), p. 229; Brameld, Educational Costs, in MacIver, ed., *Discrimination and National Welfare* (1949), pp. 44–48; Frazier, *The Negro in the United States* (1949), pp. 674–681. And see generally Myrdal, *An American Dilemma* (1944).

Brown v. *Board of Education* (II)
349 U.S. 294 (1955)

The Court ordered the parties in *Brown I* to prepare arguments on the appropriate remedies to achieve desegregation of the public schools. By any measure, the Court's ruling holding segregated schools unconstitutional was bold and historic. It did not, however, reach the question of when desegregation should begin or establish a timetable for dismantling the South's system of Jim Crow education.

The defendants in *Brown I,* along with six other Southern states, emphasized the need for delay in the Court's desegregation order. Among the grounds justifying such a delay: "sustained hostility" of Southern public opinion, the withdrawl of white children from the public schools, an increase in racial tension, the loss of jobs for black teachers and administrators, and the refusal of legislatures to fund the public schools. Virginia argued that African Americans scored lower on IQ tests than whites, and also had higher rates of tuberculosis, venereal disease, and illegitimacy. North Carolina argued, without documentation, that in some counties up to one-third of black children were retarded, and to force them into school with white children would create serious administrative and instructional difficulties.

During reargument, Topeka, Delaware, and Washington, D.C., claimed that they had taken affirmative steps to desegregate their schools. But each permitted blacks and whites to remain in schools where they constituted their respective majorities. States in the Deep South were more openly defiant. A lawyer for North Carolina, I. Beverly Lake, told the Court that a state commission on desegregation had concluded: "The mixing of the races forthwith in the public schools throughout the state cannot be accomplished and should not be attempted." Integration, Lake concluded, might well end up abolishing the public school system. Justice Frankfurter countered: "[The state] could bring up its children in ignorance if it wanted to," to which Lake responded, "It could do that too."

The *Brown II* opinion reflects the sensitive political position of the Court. An immediate and court-supervised desegregation order would put the Court in the position of enforcing its opinion by injunction, a certain recipe for disaster. But giving the South an open-ended timetable to desegregate its schools would mean endless delays. Ultimately, the Court would take a much more aggressive stand in ordering schools in violation of *Brown* to desegregate, a posture exemplified by *Swann* v. *Charlotte-Mecklenburg Board of Education* (1971) (see pp. 583–588).

The Court's decision was unanimous. Chief Justice Warren delivered the opinion of the Court.

MR. CHIEF JUSTICE WARREN delivered the opinion of the Court.

These cases were decided on May 17, 1954. The opinions of that date, declaring the fundamental principle that racial discrimination in public education is unconstitutional, are incorporated herein by reference. All provisions of federal, state, or local law requiring or permitting such discrimination must yield to this principle. There remains for consideration the manner in which relief is to be accorded. . . .

Full implementation of these constitutional principles may require solution of varied local school problems. School authorities have the primary responsibility for elucidating, assessing, and solving these problems; courts will have to consider whether the action of school authorities constitutes good faith implementation of the governing constitutional principles. Because of their proximity to local conditions and the possible need for further hearings, the courts which originally heard these cases can best perform this judicial appraisal. Accordingly, we believe it appropriate to remand the cases to those courts.

In fashioning and effectuating the decrees, the courts will be guided by equitable principles. Traditionally, equity has been characterized by a practical flexibility in shaping its remedies and by a facility for adjusting and reconciling public and private needs. These cases call for the exercise of these traditional attributes of equity power. At stake is the personal interest of the plaintiffs in admission to public schools as soon as practicable on a nondiscriminatory basis. To effectuate this interest may call for elimination of a variety of obstacles in making the transition to school systems operated in accordance with the constitutional principles set forth in our May 17, 1954, decision. Courts of equity may properly take into account the public interest in the elimination of such obstacles in a systematic and effective manner. But it should go without saying that the vitality of these constitutional principles cannot be allowed to yield simply because of disagreement with them.

While giving weight to these public and private considerations, the courts will require that the defendants make a prompt and reasonable start toward full compliance with our May 17, 1954, ruling. Once such a start has been made, the courts may find that additional time is necessary to carry out the ruling in an effective manner. The burden rests upon the defendants to establish that such time is necessary in the public interest and is consistent with good faith compliance at the earliest practicable date. To that end, the courts may consider problems related to administration, arising from the physical condition of the school plant, the school transportation system, personnel, revision of school districts and attendance areas into compact units to achieve a system of determining admission to the public schools on a nonracial basis, and revision of local laws and regulations which may be necessary in solving the foregoing problems. They will also consider the adequacy of any plans the defendants may propose to meet these problems and to effectuate a transition to a racially nondiscriminatory school system. During this period of transition, the courts will retain jurisdiction of these cases.

The judgments below, except that in the Delaware case, are accordingly reversed, and the cases are remanded to the District Courts to take such proceedings and enter such orders and decrees consistent with this opinion as are necessary and proper to admit to public schools on a racially nondiscriminatory basis with all deliberate speed the parties to these cases.

After *Brown:* Equality Redefined

By the late 1950s, the Court had used *Brown,* either explicitly or implicitly, as the basis for striking down segregation in public transportation (effectively overturning *Plessy,* which the Court had not mentioned by name in *Brown*), public parks, and recreation facilities. Several state courts, citing *Brown* as authority, issued decisions declaring segregation in public housing projects unconstitutional. Discrimination outside the boundaries of state action was still beyond the reach of *Brown,* thus leaving restaurants, hotels, retail stores, and, perhaps most significantly, private businesses free to discriminate against African Americans and other minorities. Not until a decade later, when Congress passed the Civil Rights Act of 1964, did the equal protection principles announced in *Brown* begin to make their way into the everyday aspects of American life.

But turning the promise of *Brown* into a meaningful guarantee, enforced by the lower courts and supported by public opinion, soon proved to be a much more difficult enterprise, one that is still very much a work in progress. And nowhere has the battleground over racial desegregation been more visible and confrontational than in the public schools.

Racial Discrimination in Education: Rights and Remedies

Southern resistance to *Brown* was fierce. In 1956, nineteen Senators and eighty-two Representatives—all from the eleven former Confederate states—signed and issued the "Southern Manifesto," which denounced *Brown* as an "unwarranted" decision driven by the Court's "personal political and social ideas for the established law of the land."[40] Only three Southern Senators refused to sign the manifesto: Lyndon Johnson of Texas, who, as president (1963–1969), spearheaded the passage of the Civil Rights Act of 1964 and the Voting Rights Act of 1965; Estes Kefauver, a liberal Tennessean best remembered for holding the first major Senate hearings investigating organized crime; and Albert Gore Sr., whose son, Al, ran unsuccessfully for president in 2000 after serving as a senator and as vice-president. In 1958, Southern senators came within a single vote of passing the Jenner-Butler bill, which would have stripped the Court of its jurisdiction to hear cases on appeal from state courts that raised federal constitutional issues. The issue here, of course, was school desegregation.

By 1958, lopsided majorities in Alabama, Georgia, Louisiana, Mississippi, North Carolina, South Carolina, and Virginia had passed either legislation or state constitutional amendments that prohibited integration, required or permitted the abolition of public schools, abolished compulsory school attendance laws, authorized the sale of public schools to private organizations to bypass the state action requirement, and enacted "voucher" programs to subsidize private education.[41] Most federal district courts in the South, which, under *Brown II*, were responsible for overseeing school desegregation, interpreted "all deliberate speed" as "any conceivable delay."[42] Underneath the surface of the legal maneuvering was the ever-present threat of violence against African Americans who insisted upon their right to an equal education. Such was the climate in which the Court, in *Cooper* v. *Aaron* (1958), decided the first major challenge to its authority to compel the desegregation of the nation's public schools.

Cooper v. *Aaron*

358 U.S. 1 (1958)

In September 1957, limited school desegregation had been scheduled to begin at all-white Central High School in Little Rock, Arkansas. Governor Orval Faubus refused, even in the wake of a federal court order, to comply with the desegregation plan. Faubus had developed a reputation as a populist reformer not particularly interested in fanning the flames of racial prejudice. However, in January 1956, under attack from segregationist opponents, Faubus jumped on the segregationist bandwagon. He publicly announced that Arkansas was "not ready for complete and sudden mixing of races in public schools." Faubus further commented that integration would lead to "race mixing" at social functions and permit "love scenes in class plays featuring students of different races." Faubus announced on television that he would order the Arkansas National Guard to turn away any black student who attempted to enter Central High School. One student who did not get the message was Elizabeth Eckford, who was met at the school by jeering white students shouting, "Lynch the nigger bitch," and Arkansas guardsmen holding bayonet-tipped rifles. Eckford turned and ran, reaching a local bus stop, where she was shielded by a newspaper reporter and a sympathetic white woman whose husband taught at the local black college.

President Dwight D. Eisenhower appeared on national television shortly after the events in Little Rock to calm matters. No matter "our personal opinions on the decision"—and Eisenhower never demonstrated any interest in school desegregation before or after the Little Rock crisis—it was imperative to understand that *Brown* was the law of the land and must be obeyed. Eisenhower dispatched one thousand federal paratroopers to Little Rock and federalized the Arkansas guardsmen to protect the physical safety of the black students attending Central

High. The students and the soldiers remained at Central High for the entire year.

After the troops arrived, a young reporter asked Daisy Bates, the president of the Arkansas NAACP, if she was excited to see black students receive the federal government's protection. "Excited, yes, but not happy," Bates replied. "Any time it takes eleven thousand five hundred soldiers to assure nine Negro children their constitutional right in a democratic society, I can't be happy."

The Court's decision was unanimous. Each justice signed the *Cooper* opinion, an unprecedented step undertaken—never repeated—to underscore the Court's authority and its commitment to *Brown*. Justice Frankfurter filed a concurring opinion.

▼▲▼

Opinion of the Court by THE CHIEF JUSTICE, MR. JUSTICE BLACK, MR. JUSTICE FRANKFURTER, MR. JUSTICE DOUGLAS, MR. JUSTICE BURTON, MR. JUSTICE CLARK, MR. JUSTICE HARLAN, MR. JUSTICE BRENNAN, and MR. JUSTICE WHITTAKER.

As this case reaches us, it raises questions of the highest importance to the maintenance of our federal system of government. It necessarily involves a claim by the Governor and Legislature of a State that there is no duty on state officials to obey federal court orders resting on this Court's considered interpretation of the United States Constitution. Specifically, it involves actions by the Governor and Legislature of Arkansas upon the premise that they are not bound by our holding in *Brown* v. *Board of Education* (1954). That holding was that the Fourteenth Amendment forbids States to use their governmental powers to bar children on racial grounds from attending schools where there is state participation through any arrangement, management, funds or property. We are urged to uphold a suspension of the Little Rock School Board's plan to do away with segregated public schools in Little Rock until state laws *Brown* and efforts to upset and nullify our holding in have been further challenged and tested in the courts. We reject these contentions. . . .

While the School Board was thus going forward with its preparation for desegregating the Little Rock school system, other state authorities, in contrast, were actively pursuing a program designed to perpetuate in Arkansas the system of racial segregation which this Court had held violated the Fourteenth Amendment. First came, in November, 1956, an amendment to the State Constitution flatly commanding the Arkansas General Assembly to oppose "in every Constitutional manner the Unconstitutional desegregation decisions of May 17, 1954, and May 31, 1955, of the United States Supreme Court."

Pursuant to this state constitutional command, a law relieving school children from compulsory attendance at racially mixed schools, and a law establishing a State Sovereignty Commission, were enacted by the General Assembly in February, 1957. . . .

The constitutional rights of respondents are not to be sacrificed or yielded to the violence and disorder which have followed upon the actions of the Governor and Legislature. . . . Thus, law and order are not here to be preserved by depriving the Negro children of their constitutional rights. The record before us clearly establishes that the growth of the Board's difficulties to a magnitude beyond its unaided power to control is the product of state action. Those difficulties, as counsel for the Board forthrightly conceded on the oral argument in this Court, can also be brought under control by state action.

The controlling legal principles are plain. . . . In short, the constitutional rights of children not to be discriminated against in school admission on grounds of race or color declared by this Court in the *Brown* case can neither be nullified openly and directly by state legislators or state executive or judicial officers nor nullified indirectly by them through evasive schemes for segregation whether attempted "ingeniously or ingenuously."

What has been said, in the light of the facts developed, is enough to dispose of the case. However, we should answer the premise of the actions of the Governor and Legislature that they are not bound by our holding in the *Brown* case. It is necessary only to recall some basic constitutional propositions which are settled doctrine.

Article VI of the Constitution makes the Constitution the "supreme Law of the Land." In 1803, Chief Justice Marshall, speaking for a unanimous Court, referring to the Constitution as "the fundamental and paramount law of the nation," declared in the notable case of *Marbury* v. *Madison* (1803) that "It is emphatically the province and duty of the judicial department to say what the law is." This decision declared the basic principle that the federal judiciary is supreme in the exposition of the law of the Constitution, and that principle has ever since been respected by this Court and the Country as a permanent and indispensable feature of our constitutional system. It follows that the interpretation of the Fourteenth Amendment enunciated by this Court in the *Brown* case is the supreme law of the land, and Art. VI of the Constitution makes it of binding effect on the States "any Thing in the Constitution or Laws of any State to the Contrary notwithstanding." Every state legislator and executive and judicial officer is solemnly committed by oath taken pursuant to Art. VI, cl. 3 "to support this Constitution." Chief Justice Taney, speaking for a unanimous Court in 1859, said that this requirement reflected the framers' "anxiety to preserve it [the Constitution] in full force, in all its powers, and to guard against resistance to or evasion of its authority, on the part of a State. . . ." No state legislator or executive or judicial officer can war against the Constitution without violating his undertaking to support it. . . .

It is, of course, quite true that the responsibility for public education is primarily the concern of the States, but it is equally true that such responsibilities, like all other state activity, must be exercised consistently with federal constitutional requirements as they apply to state action. The Constitution created a government dedicated to equal justice under law. The Fourteenth Amendment embodied and emphasized that ideal. State support of segregated schools through any arrangement, management, funds, or property cannot be squared with the Amendment's command that no State shall deny to any person within its jurisdiction the equal protection of the laws. The right of a student not to be segregated on racial grounds in schools so maintained is indeed so fundamental and pervasive that it is embraced in the concept of due process of law. The basic decision in *Brown* was unanimously reached by this Court only after the case had been briefed and twice argued and the issues had been given the most serious consideration. Since the first *Brown* opinion, three new Justices have come to the Court. They are at one with the Justices still on the Court who participated in that basic decision as to its correctness, and that decision is now unanimously reaffirmed. The principles announced in that decision and the obedience of the States to them, according to the command of the Constitution, are indispensable for the protection of the freedoms guaranteed by our fundamental charter for all of us. Our constitutional ideal of equal justice under law is thus made a living truth.

Concurring opinion of MR. JUSTICE FRANKFURTER.

While unreservedly participating with my brethren in our joint opinion, I deem it appropriate also to deal individually with the great issue here at stake. . . .

The use of force to further obedience to law is, in any event, a last resort, and one not congenial to the spirit of our Nation. But the tragic aspect of this disruptive tactic was that the power of the State was used not to sustain law, but as an instrument for thwarting law. The State of Arkansas is thus responsible for disabling one of its subordinate agencies, the Little Rock School Board, from peacefully carrying out the Board's and the State's constitutional duty. Accordingly, while Arkansas is not a formal party in these proceedings and a decree cannot go against the State, it is legally and morally before the Court.

We are now asked to hold that the illegal, forcible interference by the State of Arkansas with the continuance of what the Constitution commands, and the consequences in disorder that it entrained, should be recognized as justification for undoing what the School Board had formulated, what the District Court in 1955 had directed to be carried out, and what was in process of obedience. No explanation that may be offered in support of such a request can obscure the inescapable meaning that law should bow to force. To yield to such a claim would be to enthrone official lawlessness, and lawlessness, if not checked, is the precursor of anarchy. On the few tragic occasions in the history of the Nation, North and South, when law was forcibly resisted or systematically evaded, it has signaled the breakdown of constitutional processes of government on which ultimately rest the liberties of all. Violent resistance to law cannot be made a legal reason for its suspension without loosening the fabric of our society. What could this mean but to acknowledge that disorder under the aegis of a State has moral superiority over the law of the Constitution? For those in authority thus to defy the law of the land is profoundly subversive not only of our constitutional system, but of the presuppositions of a democratic society. . . .

For carrying out the decision that color alone cannot bar a child from a public school, this Court has recognized the diversity of circumstances in local school situations. But is it a reasonable hope that the necessary endeavors for such adjustment will be furthered, that racial frictions will be ameliorated, by a reversal of the process and interrupting effective measures toward the necessary goal? The progress that has been made in respecting the constitutional rights of the Negro children, according to the graduated plan sanctioned by the two lower courts, would have to be retraced, perhaps with even greater difficulty because of deference to forcible resistance. It would have to be retraced against the seemingly vindicated feeling of those who actively sought to block that progress. Is there not the strongest reason for concluding that to accede to the Board's request, on the basis of the circumstances that gave rise to it, for a suspension of the Board's nonsegregation plan, would be but the beginning of a series of delays calculated to nullify this Court's adamant decisions in the *Brown* case that the Constitution precludes compulsory segregation based on color in state-supported schools?

That the responsibility of those who exercise power in a democratic government is not to reflect inflamed public feeling, but to help form its understanding, is especially true when they are confronted with a problem like a racially discriminating public school system. This is the lesson to be drawn from the heartening experience in ending enforced racial segregation in the public schools in cities with Negro populations of large proportions. Compliance with decisions of this Court, as the constitutional organ of the supreme Law of the Land, has often, throughout our history, depended on active support by state and local authorities. It presupposes such support. To withhold it, and indeed to use political power to try to paralyze the supreme Law, precludes the maintenance of our federal system as we have known and cherished it for one hundred and seventy years.

▼▲▼

After *Brown,* Thurgood Marshall predicted that a combination of aggressive civil rights litigation and the Court's revolutionary commitment to racial equality would eliminate school segregation within five years. Marshall's optimism was soon tempered by a reality check from Virginia governor Thomas Stanley, who, after greeting *Brown* with moderate words, declared five weeks later: "I will use every legal means at my command to continue segregated schools in Virginia."[43] Buoyed by *Brown II,* Marshall told colleagues: "You can say all you want but those white cracker lawyers are going to get tired of having Negro lawyers beating 'em every day in court."[44] Even after the Court's authoritative declaration of support for school desegregation in *Cooper,* the South showed no signs of giving up its cherished traditions or giving in to federal authority. As of 1960, not one black child in Alabama, Georgia, Louisiana, Mississippi, or South Carolina was attending a public school with white children.[45]

By the early 1960s, however, minor cracks began to appear in the Southern firewall protecting Jim Crow. The Fifth Circuit Court of Appeals, which then encompassed Alabama, Florida, Georgia, Louisiana, Mississippi, and Texas, emerged as a major ally of the civil rights movement, taking lower courts to task for evading their responsibilities and demanding that local school boards implement the desegregation decree in *Brown.* Mostly Republicans appointed by President Eisenhower, the Fifth Circuit judges made clear that if the politicians did not do their jobs, the courts would step in and do it for them. Some observers of this period of the civil rights movement have commented that the Fifth Circuit was singly responsible for bringing school desegregation to the South.[46] On the national level, Congress, in passing the Civil Rights Act of 1964 and the Elementary and Secondary Education Act of 1965, had given the federal government jurisdiction to bring lawsuits against schools that failed to comply with *Brown.* Consequently, schools that would never have considered opening their doors to black children began to reconsider their position when faced with the prospect of losing massive amounts of federal funds and having to go to court, where they would inevitably lose.

The Court, too, by this time had finally exhausted its patience with Southern school districts, holding in *Green* v. *School Board of New Kent County* (1968) that it was incumbent upon school boards "to come forward with a plan that promises realistically to work . . . until it is clear that state-imposed segregation has been completely removed . . . root and branch."[47] *Green* invalidated a "freedom of choice" plan in a Virginia county that permitted black students to attend all-white schools, but proved ineffective in achieving desegregation. Writing for a unanimous Court, Justice Black remarked that since *Brown II* "there had been entirely too much deliberation and not enough speed" in desegregating the public schools. A year later, in *Alexander* v. *Holmes County Board of Education* (1969), Chief Justice Warren E. Burger, in his first term on the Court, wrote that "the obligation of every school district is to terminate dual school systems *at once* and to operate now and hereafter only unitary schools."[48]

The South had reached its last line of defense. After a decade of unprecedented federal support for racial equality from Congress and the executive branch, by the late 1960s Jim Crow was left standing at the crossroads. For the South, the only angle even remotely left to argue was that the federal courts had exceeded their authority by fashioning and imposing desegregation orders on local school districts. In *Swann* v. *Charlotte-Mecklenburg County Board of Education* (1971), the Court effectively settled the question of the scope of its power to order appropriate remedies once it had determined the violation of a constitutional right.

Civil rights activists often met violent resistance from local law enforcement when they took their grievances to the streets. Here, African Americans protesting Jim Crow laws in 1963 were blasted with water hoses by the Birmingham Fire Department after refusing to disperse from a sidewalk.

Swann v. Charlotte-Mecklenburg Board of Education

402 U.S. 1 (1971)

In September 1964, six-year-old Julius Swann was denied admission to the white school located near his house on the campus of Jonathan C. Smith University, where his father, James, taught theology. Around the same time, a young NAACP lawyer, Julius Chambers, had secured the consent of ten black families in the Charlotte-Mecklenburg school system to proceed with a lawsuit to compel the county to desegregate its schools. James Swann was chosen as the lead plaintiff because of his relatively secure position in the community as being less likely than many others to experience local retaliation from whites.

The Charlotte public schools had merged with the Mecklenburg County schools in 1960 to combine urban and rural schools into a more efficient system. By 1965, when *Swann* began, fewer than 2 percent of black students in Charlotte attended schools with whites, or about 490 out of approximately 21,000. The numbers improved slightly over the next few years, but, by the late 1960s, over two-thirds of all black students in Charlotte still attended schools that were 99 percent black. A lower court agreed with the NAACP that the school board's plan was inadequate, and appointed John A. Finger Jr., an education professor from Rhode Island College, to develop a desegregation plan. Finger's plan called for the creation of noncontiguous school districts to expand the base of black and white students eligible to attend a single school; provided free transportation for all students who were assigned to attend schools outside their neighborhood, putting ten thousand students on buses solely to promote desegregation; and offered new zoning, clustering, and pairing plans to alter attendance zones. Finger's ultimate aim was to create a racial balance in the schools that approximated the racial composition of the school district, which was 71 percent white and 29 percent black. In 1969, a federal judge, James McMillian, ordered the Finger plan implemented. A federal appeals court upheld Judge McMillian's decision in part, leading both the Charlotte-Mecklenburg school system and the NAACP to seek review in the Supreme Court.

The Court's decision was unanimous. Chief Justice Burger delivered the opinion of the Court.

▼▲▼

MR. CHIEF JUSTICE BURGER delivered the opinion of the Court.

This case and those argued with it arose in States having a long history of maintaining two sets of schools in a single school system deliberately operated to carry out a governmental policy to separate pupils in schools solely on the basis of race. That was what *Brown* v. *Board of Education* was all about. These cases present us with the problem of defining in more precise terms than heretofore the scope of the duty of school authorities and district courts in implementing *Brown I* and the mandate to eliminate dual systems and establish unitary systems at once. Meanwhile, district courts and courts of appeals have struggled in hundreds of cases with a multitude and variety of problems under this Court's general directive. Understandably, in an area of evolving remedies, those courts had to improvise and experiment without detailed or specific guidelines. This Court, in *Brown I*, appropriately dealt with the large constitutional principles; other federal courts had to grapple with the flinty, intractable realities of day-to-day implementation of those constitutional commands. Their efforts, of necessity, embraced a process of "trial and error," and our effort to formulate guidelines must take into account their experience. . . .

Nearly 17 years ago, this Court held, in explicit terms, that state-imposed segregation by race in public schools denies equal protection of the laws. At no time has the Court deviated in the slightest degree from that holding or its constitutional underpinnings. . . .

Over the 16 years since *Brown II*, many difficulties were encountered in implementation of the basic constitutional requirement that the State not discriminate between public school children on the basis of their race. Nothing in our national experience prior to 1955 prepared anyone for dealing with changes and adjustments of the magnitude and complexity encountered since then. Deliberate resistance of some to the Court's mandates has impeded the good faith efforts of others to bring school systems into compliance. The detail and nature of these dilatory tactics have been noted frequently by this Court and other courts.

By . . . 1968, very little progress had been made in many areas where dual school systems had historically been maintained by operation of state laws. . . .

The problems encountered by the district courts and courts of appeals make plain that we should now try to amplify guidelines, however incomplete and imperfect, for the assistance of school authorities and courts. The failure of local authorities to meet their constitutional obligations aggravated the massive problem of converting from the state-enforced discrimination of racially separate school systems. This process has been rendered more difficult by changes since 1954 in the structure and patterns of communities, the growth of student population, movement of families, and other changes, some of which had marked impact on school planning, sometimes neutralizing or negating remedial action before it was fully implemented. Rural areas accustomed for half a century to the consolidated school systems implemented by bus transportation could make adjustments more readily than metropolitan areas with dense and shifting population, numerous schools, congested and complex traffic patterns.

The objective today remains to eliminate from the public schools all vestiges of state-imposed segregation. Segregation was the evil struck down by *Brown I* as contrary to the equal protection guarantees of the Constitution. That was the violation sought to be corrected by the remedial measures of *Brown II*. . . .

If school authorities fail in their affirmative obligations under these holdings, judicial authority may be invoked. Once a right and a violation have been shown, the scope of a district court's equitable powers to remedy past wrongs is broad, for breadth and flexibility are inherent in equitable remedies. . . .

This allocation of responsibility once made, the Court attempted from time to time to provide some guidelines for the exercise of the district judge's discretion and for the reviewing function of the courts of appeals. However, a school desegregation case does not differ fundamentally from other cases involving the framing of equitable remedies to repair the denial of a constitutional right. The task is to correct, by a balancing of the individual and collective interests, the condition that offends the Constitution.

In seeking to define even in broad and general terms how far this remedial power extends, it is important to remember that judicial powers may be exercised only on the basis of a constitutional violation. Remedial judicial authority does not put judges automatically in the shoes of school authorities whose powers are plenary. Judicial authority enters only when local authority defaults.

School authorities are traditionally charged with broad power to formulate and implement educational policy, and might well conclude, for example, that, in order to prepare students to live in a pluralistic society, each school should have a prescribed ratio of Negro to white students reflecting the proportion for the district as a whole. To do this as an educational policy is within the broad discretionary powers of school authorities; absent a finding of a constitutional violation, however, that would not be within the authority of a federal court. As with any equity case, the nature of the violation determines the scope of the remedy. In default by the school authorities of their obligation to proffer acceptable remedies, a district court has broad power to fashion a remedy that will assure a unitary school system. . . .

We turn now to the problem of defining with more particularity the responsibilities of school authorities in desegregating a state-enforced dual school system in light of the Equal Protection Clause. Although the several related cases before us are primarily concerned with problems of student assignment, it may be helpful to begin with a brief discussion of other aspects of the process.

In *Green* [v. *School Board of New Kent County* (1968)], we pointed out that existing policy and practice with regard to faculty, staff, transportation, extracurricular activities, and facilities were among the most important indicia of a segregated system. Independent of student assignment, where it is possible to identify a "white school" or a "Negro school" simply by reference to the racial composition of teachers and staff, the quality of school buildings and equipment, or the organization of sports activities, a *prima facie* case of violation of substantive constitutional rights under the Equal Protection Clause is shown.

When a system has been dual in these respects, the first remedial responsibility of school authorities is to eliminate invidious racial distinctions. With respect to such matters as transportation, supporting personnel, and extracurricular activities, no more than this may be necessary. Similar corrective action must be taken with regard to the maintenance of buildings and the distribution of equipment. In these areas, normal administrative practice should produce schools of like quality, facilities, and staffs. Something more must be said, however, as to faculty assignment and new school construction. . . .

The construction of new schools and the closing of old ones are two of the most important functions of local school authorities and also two of the most complex. They must decide questions of location and capacity in light of population growth, finances, land values, site availability, through an almost endless list of factors to be considered. The result of this will be a decision which, when combined with one technique or another of student assignment, will determine the racial composition of the student body in each school in the system. Over the long run, the consequences of the choices will be far-reaching. People gravitate toward school facilities, just as schools are located in response to the needs of people. The location of schools may thus influence the patterns of residential development of a metropolitan area and have important impact on composition of inner-city neighborhoods.

In the past, choices in this respect have been used as a potent weapon for creating or maintaining a state-segregated school system. In addition to the classic pattern of building schools specifically intended for Negro or white students, school authorities have sometimes, since *Brown,* closed schools which appeared likely to become racially mixed through changes in neighborhood residential patterns. This was sometimes accompanied by building new schools in the areas of white suburban expansion farthest from Negro population centers in order to maintain the separation of the races with a minimum departure from the formal principles of "neighborhood zoning." Such a policy does more than simply influence the short-run composition of the student body of a new school. It may well promote segregated residential patterns which, when combined with "neighborhood zoning," further lock the school system into the mold of separation of the races. Upon a proper showing, a district court may consider this in fashioning a remedy.

In ascertaining the existence of legally imposed school segregation, the existence of a pattern of school construction and abandonment is thus a factor of great weight. In devising remedies where legally imposed segregation has been established, it is the responsibility of local authorities and district courts to see to it that future school construction and abandonment are not used and do not serve to perpetuate or reestablish the dual system. When necessary, district courts should retain jurisdiction to assure that these responsibilities are carried out.

The central issue in this case is that of student assignment, and there are essentially four problem areas:

1. to what extent racial balance or racial quotas may be used as an implement in a remedial order to correct a previously segregated system;
2. whether every all-Negro and all-white school must be eliminated as an indispensable part of a remedial process of desegregation;
3. what the limits are, if any, on the rearrangement of school districts and attendance zones, as a remedial measure; and
4. what the limits are, if any, on the use of transportation facilities to correct state-enforced racial school segregation.

1. Racial Balances or Racial Quotas

The constant theme and thrust of every holding from *Brown I* to date is that state-enforced separation of races in public schools is discrimination that violates the Equal Protection Clause. The remedy commanded was to dismantle dual school systems.

We are concerned in these cases with the elimination of the discrimination inherent in the dual school systems, not with myriad factors of human existence which can cause discrimination in a multitude of ways on racial, religious, or ethnic grounds. The target of the cases from *Brown I* to the present was the dual school system. The elimination of racial discrimination in public schools is a large task, and one that should not be retarded by efforts to achieve broader purposes lying beyond the jurisdiction of school authorities. One vehicle can carry only a limited amount of baggage. It would not serve the important objective of *Brown I* to seek to use school desegregation cases for purposes beyond their scope, although desegregation of schools ultimately will have impact on other forms of discrimination. We do not reach in this case the question whether a showing that school segregation is a consequence of other types of state action, without any discriminatory action by the school authorities, is a constitutional violation requiring remedial action by a school desegregation decree. This case does not present that question and we therefore do not decide it.

Our objective in dealing with the issues presented by these cases is to see that school authorities exclude no pupil of a racial minority from any school, directly or indirectly, on account of race; it does not and cannot embrace all the problems of racial prejudice, even when those problems contribute to disproportionate racial concentrations in some schools.

In this case, it is urged that the District Court has imposed a racial balance requirement of 71%–29% on individual schools. . . .

[T]he use made of mathematical ratios was no more than a starting point in the process of shaping a remedy, rather than an inflexible requirement. From that starting point, the District Court proceeded to frame a decree that was within its discretionary powers, as an equitable remedy for the particular circumstances. As we said in *Green*, a school authority's remedial plan or a district court's remedial decree is to be judged by its effectiveness. Awareness of the racial composition of the whole school system is likely to be a useful starting point in shaping a remedy to correct past constitutional violations. In sum, the very limited use made of mathematical ratios was within the equitable remedial discretion of the District Court.

2. One-Race Schools

The record in this case reveals the familiar phenomenon that, in metropolitan areas, minority groups are often found concentrated in one part of the city. In some circumstances, certain schools may remain all or largely of one race until new schools can be provided or neighborhood patterns change. Schools all or predominately of one race in a district of mixed population will require close scrutiny to determine that school assignments are not part of state-enforced segregation.

In light of the above, it should be clear that the existence of some small number of one-race, or virtually one-race, schools within a district is not, in and of itself, the mark of a system that still practices segregation by law. The district judge or school authorities should make every effort to achieve the greatest possible degree of actual desegregation, and will thus necessarily be concerned with the elimination of one-race schools. No *per se* rule can adequately embrace all the difficulties of reconciling the competing interests involved; but, in a system with a history of segregation, the need for remedial criteria of sufficient specificity to assure a school authority's compliance with its constitutional duty warrants a presumption against schools that are substantially disproportionate in their racial composition. Where the school authority's proposed plan for conversion from a dual to a unitary system contemplates the continued existence of some schools that are all or predominately of one race, they have the burden of showing that such school assignments are genuinely nondiscriminatory. The court should scrutinize such schools, and the burden upon the school authorities will be to satisfy the court that their racial composition is not the result of present or past discriminatory action on their part.

An optional majority-to-minority transfer provision has long been recognized as a useful part of every desegregation plan. Provision for optional transfer of those in the majority racial group of a particular school to other schools where they will be in the minority is an indispensable remedy for those students willing to transfer to other schools in order to lessen the impact on them of the state-imposed stigma of segregation. In order to be effective, such a transfer arrangement must grant the transferring student free transportation and space must be made available in the school to which he desires to move. . . .

3. Remedial Altering of Attendance Zones

Absent a constitutional violation, there would be no basis for judicially ordering assignment of students on a racial basis. All things being equal, with no history of discrimination, it might well be desirable to assign pupils to schools nearest their homes. But all things are not equal in a system that has been deliberately constructed and maintained to enforce racial segregation. The remedy for such segregation may be administratively awkward, inconvenient, and even bizarre in some situations, and may impose burdens on some; but all awkwardness and inconvenience cannot be avoided in the interim period when remedial adjustments are being made to eliminate the dual school systems.

No fixed or even substantially fixed guidelines can be established as to how far a court can go, but it must be recognized that there are limits. The objective is to dismantle the dual school system. "Racially neutral" assignment plans proposed by school authorities to a district court may be inadequate; such plans may fail to counteract the continuing effects of past school segregation resulting from discriminatory location of school sites or distortion of school size in order to achieve or maintain an artificial racial separation. When school authorities present a district court with a "loaded game board," affirmative action in the form of remedial altering of attendance zones is proper to achieve truly nondiscriminatory assignments. In short, an assignment plan is not acceptable simply because it appears to be neutral. . . .

We hold that the pairing and grouping of noncontiguous school zones is a permissible tool, and such action is to be considered in light of the objectives sought. . . . Maps do not tell the whole story, since noncontiguous school zones may be more accessible to each other in terms of the critical travel time, because of traffic patterns and good highways, than schools geographically closer together. Conditions in different localities will vary so widely that no rigid rules can be laid down to govern all situations.

4. Transportation of Students

The scope of permissible transportation of students as an implement of a remedial decree has never been defined by this Court, and, by the very nature of the problem, it cannot be defined with precision. No rigid guidelines as to student transportation can be given for application to the infinite variety of problems presented in thousands of situations. Bus transportation has been an integral part of the public education system for years, and was perhaps the single most important factor in the transition from the one-room schoolhouse to the consolidated school. Eighteen million of the Nation's public school children, approximately 39%, were transported to their schools by bus in 1969–1970 in all parts of the country.

The importance of bus transportation as a normal and accepted tool of educational policy is readily discernible in this and the companion case. The Charlotte school authorities did not purport to assign students on the basis of geographically drawn zones until 1965, and then they allowed almost unlimited transfer privileges. The District Court's conclusion that assignment of children to the school nearest their home serving their grade would not produce an effective dismantling of the dual system is supported by the record.

Thus, the remedial techniques used in the District Court's order were within that court's power to provide equitable relief; implementation of the decree is well within the capacity of the school authority. . . .

An objection to transportation of students may have validity when the time or distance of travel is so great as to either risk the health of the children or significantly impinge on the educational process. . . . It hardly needs stating that the limits on time of travel will vary with many factors, but probably with none more than the age of the students. The reconciliation of competing values in a desegregation case is, of course, a difficult task with many sensitive facets, but fundamentally no more so than remedial measures courts of equity have traditionally employed.

The Court of Appeals, searching for a term to define the equitable remedial power of the district courts, used the term "reasonableness." In *Green,* this Court used the term "feasible," and, by implication, "workable," "effective," and "realistic" in the mandate to develop "a plan that promises realistically to work, and . . . to work *now.*" On the facts of this case, we are unable to conclude that the order of the District Court is not reasonable, feasible and workable. However, in seeking to define the scope of remedial power or the limits on remedial power of courts in an area as sensitive as we deal with here, words are poor instruments to convey the sense of basic fairness inherent in equity. Substance, not semantics, must govern, and we have sought to suggest the nature of limitations without frustrating the appropriate scope of equity. . . .

It does not follow that the communities served by such systems will remain demographically stable, for, in a growing, mobile society, few will do so. Neither school authorities nor district courts are constitutionally required to make year-by-year adjustments of the racial composition of student bodies once the affirmative duty to desegregate has been accomplished and racial discrimination through official action is eliminated from the system. This does not mean that federal courts are without power to deal with future problems; but, in the absence of a showing that either the school authorities or some other agency of the State has deliberately attempted to fix or alter demographic patterns to affect the racial composition of the schools, further intervention by a district court should not be necessary.

. . . The order of the district court . . . is . . . affirmed.

Swann put school districts throughout the nation, not just in the South, on notice that they could no longer avoid desegregation, regardless of the excuses they were prepared to offer the federal courts now firmly positioned to supervise the dismantling of the old dual systems of public education. The Court said in *Swann,* more or less, that since the school districts and the legislatures that funded them had gotten themselves into this mess, they were now obligated to get themselves out of it, regardless of how "awkward, inconvenient and even bizarre in some situations" such remedies proved to be. Busing emerged as the key tool to accomplish desegregation and, as such, became a lightning rod of political controversy. Civil rights organizations argued that meaningful desegregation could not take place without busing, given the hardened nature of residential segregation in most communities. After *Swann,* local political resistance responded somewhat, as the South especially began to direct its resources to desegregation rather than litigation. By September 1973, close to 50 percent of African American children in the South were attending public schools where the majority of students were white, making the region the most desegregated in the nation.[49]

The South's gradual surrender to school desegregation in the early 1970s stood in contrast to the position President Richard Nixon (1969–1974) and his administration had taken on the matter. The Nixon administration had submitted several anti-busing and court-stripping bills to Congress, some of which passed, but none of which was effective. Several states followed President Nixon's lead, but civil rights organizations were successful in persuading the courts to maintain their supervision of the desegregation process. Around the same time, the NAACP enlisted the support of several civil rights groups to uncover what school desegregation lawyers had known for some time: that the Department of Health, Education and Welfare (now the Department of Health and Human Services) was sitting on its hands and refusing to carry out its enforcement responsibilities. Gradually, HEW began to process complaints and to withhold federal funds from school districts that had not met the terms of *Swann.* By the late 1970s, the federal government was back on board as an ally of school desegregation, a shift that also reflected the different policies of the Carter administration (1977–1981).[50]

Few expected *Swann* to settle the issue of school desegregation. In fact, the Court's decision raised more questions than it answered. Did desegregation requirements extend to school districts that did not have official policies of racial exclusion but nonetheless operated segregated schools in fact? Should desegregation plans compensate for changing population and residential housing patterns, or should the courts take a more hands-off approach in such situations? The Court has addressed many of these questions in subsequent desegregation cases.

After *Swann,* the NAACP directed the Court's attention to school desegregation outside the South. By September 1973, only about 28 percent of African American students in Northern and Western states were attending schools where white students were in the majority. In *Keyes* v. *Denver School District No. 1,* the Court, 7 to 1, ruled that school districts were not immune from the responsibility to desegregate their schools simply because they did not formally prohibit racially integrated education. The NAACP demonstrated that a predominantly white school district in Denver had taken affirmative steps to exclude blacks from white schools. The Court ruled that policies such as drawing student-attendance zones to confine blacks to predominantly black schools, constructing new schools in black communities to discourage blacks from attending established white schools, and the excessive use of mobile classrooms in black schools to prevent black students from citing overcrowded conditions as a reason to leave were indistinguishable from the explicit Jim Crow policies of the South. The result, the Court noted, was the same: African American students attended predominantly black schools and white students attended predominantly white schools. In *Keyes,* the Court offered another warning to Northern communities: School districts were obligated to eliminate racial segregation in any form, whether *de jure* (by law) or *de facto* (in fact), as long as evidence existed demonstrating that government action was responsible for such an outcome.

The Court, however, soon demonstrated that there were limits to its willingness to order school desegregation. In *Milliken* v. *Bradley* (1974), the Court, 5 to 4, overturned a lower federal court decision that ordered the Detroit city schools to merge with fifty-three suburban school districts to create a single metropolitan district. The plan affected over 750,000 students. Of the approximately 280,000 students attending public school in Detroit, 65 percent were African American. Of the approximately 500,000 students in the suburbs, 81 percent were white. The racial composition of the metropolitan Detroit area had developed in large part because of white families' decisions to leave the city rather than to have their children attend schools with African Americans. The NAACP, which brought the case, argued the only way to achieve meaningful desegregation was to combine the urban and suburban school systems. To rule otherwise was to reward "white flight" from urban areas that remained predominantly black.

Chief Justice Burger acknowledged that Detroit had engaged in practices to foster segregation, but held that school districts with no history of discriminatory educational practices should not have to take part in any remedial plan designed to compensate for the sins of their inner-city neighbors. *Milliken* also marked the first time that the Court rejected a desegregation plan offered by the NAACP since the civil rights group began attacking segregated education in the 1930s. Critics of the Court's decision insisted that the formal boundaries drawn in *Milliken* ignored the racial presumptions that went into "white flight" from Northern inner cities; without interdistrict remedies, genuine desegregation would be impossible to achieve. Opponents of busing claimed that the Court had somewhat stabilized a highly contentious debate by recognizing the importance of neighborhood schools. Either way, *Milliken* marked a significant departure point in the Court's willingness to allow the lower courts to use their remedial authority to achieve school desegregation.[51]

Still, several Southern cities with long histories of racial segregation in their school systems, such as Charlotte, Jacksonville, and Nashville, voluntarily created interdistrict arrangements to achieve desegregation. Moreover, the Court did not say in *Milliken* that inter-district remedies were prohibited when evidence of city-suburban complicity to encourage segregation was present. In cases such as these, courts were within their authority to order remedies that crossed district lines. In fact, the NAACP relitigated the *Milliken* case, and, in 1977, succeeded in persuading the Court to uphold a district court decision ordering comprehensive remedies, including, for the first time, the power of the courts to intervene in curriculum and educational content issues.[52]

The courts remained involved in the design and supervision of desegregation programs into the 1980s, despite the boundaries created by *Milliken I.* By then, however, the issue that had dominated the desegregation agenda since the late 1960s, the elimination of state-imposed racial disparities in public education, gave way to a more difficult question: What is the role of the courts when once-segregated school districts, which have complied with all judicial mandates to desegregate, return to their previous status? In *Board of Education of Oklahoma City Schools* v. *Dowell* (1991), the Court offered its first signal that it was prepared to release school districts from federal judicial supervision if "good faith" efforts to achieve desegregation could not overcome population shifts and other factors leading to residential segregation. In *Dowell* Chief Justice Rehnquist, writing for a 5–3 Court, distinguished between those "vestiges" of discrimination that were the result of state action, which the courts were still to bound to eliminate, and those independent factors that were beyond the scope of government authority.[53]

Over the next several years, the Court decided three important cases that dealt with remedies for racial segregation in elementary and high schools and, separately, colleges. In *Freeman* v. *Pitts* (1992), the Court unanimously ruled that federal courts could gradually release school districts from a desegregation order even if full compliance with it was not yet complete. This conclusion was based on a finding that the school district had ended any practices leading to segregation.[54] In *Missouri* v. *Jenkins* (1995), the Court continued the direction it chartered in *Dowell* and *Freeman*, ruling that unless a school district's return to segregated status was the product of state action, no constitutional violation was present that warranted judicial intervention.[55] By *Jenkins*, note the evolution of the Court's approach to holding school districts accountable for racial segregation: The significant question was not whether schools were racially identifiable, but *how* they got that way. Here, it appeared that Chief Justice Burger's holding in *Swann* guided the Court: "Neither school authorities nor district courts are constitutionally required to make year-by-year adjustments of the racial composition of student bodies once the affirmative duty to desegregate has been accomplished and racial discrimination through official action is eliminated from the system."[56]

But in *United States* v. *Fordice* (1992), the Court, over the partial dissent of Justice Scalia, demonstrated that it was not prepared to disengage judicial power when the "vestiges" of school segregation remained alive and well. *Fordice* culminated a battle of nearly twenty-five years between the federal government and Mississippi over the state's obligation to desegregate its colleges and universities. In holding that Mississippi had not satisfied its burden under the Equal Protection Clause, Justice White, writing for the Court, also made sure to point out that the standards applicable in *Fordice* did not extend beyond higher education. Thus, almost a half century after *Brown* v. *Board of Education*, the Court continues to debate the consequences of four centuries of slavery, Jim Crow, and racial discrimination, and how the lessons of the past will shape the future of school desegregation.

Missouri v. *Jenkins*
515 U.S. 70 (1995)

Jenkins is a case with a long and complex procedural history. In 1977, the Kansas City, Missouri, School District (KCSMD), after several feeble attempts to comply with *Brown II*, brought suit in federal court, along with several African American parents, against Missouri, seeking permission to reassign students across district lines to achieve school desegregation. The court severed the school district from the parents, and made it the defendant. Kalima Jenkins, represented by the NAACP, filed a subsequent complaint against the KCMSD, alleging that it had not made appropriate efforts to desegregate its schools. The court agreed with Jenkins that the KCMSD had not achieved desegregation, but, citing *Milliken* v. *Bradley* (1973), ruled that all relief must take place within the boundaries of the district. After nearly a decade of hearings, negotiations, and courtroom battles, the court, in 1985, ordered Missouri to shoulder the brunt of the $100 million the KCMSD estimated compliance would cost. The school district was responsible for coming up with the rest of the funding.

When it became evident that the school district did not have the funding to carry out the desegregation order, federal judge Russell Clark ordered the KCMSD to increase property taxes, issue bonds to fund construction and other capital improvements, and add a local income tax surcharge. Missouri challenged the lower court's authority to order a direct tax increase as part of its remedial authority. In 1990, the Supreme Court, in *Missouri* v. *Jenkins I*, ultimately decided that the district court abused its discretion in imposing a direct tax increase. It did rule, however, that a district court was within its equitable power to order the proper political authorities to raise taxes.

Five years and over $900 million in tax expenditures later, *Missouri* v. *Jenkins* returned to the Court. This time the issue was whether Judge Clark's order mandating continuing expenditures to make the KCMSD more attractive to white students exceeded the court's remedial authority. Under Judge Clark's plan, the school district, at great expense, built magnet schools and developed other special resources to draw white students into the city from the suburbs. Even so, over 90 percent of the students in the KCMSD were still African American. Ted Shaw, the NAACP lawyer who argued the case, emphasized the distinct racial composition of the city and suburban schools, and said that interdistrict remedies of the sort Judge Clark ordered were necessary. The United States filed a brief on behalf of the school board, claiming that the school district should now be free to concentrate on improving the schools without regard to their racial composition.

The Court's decision was 5 to 4. Chief Justice Rehnquist delivered the opinion of the Court. Justice O'Connor and Justice Thomas filed separate concurring opinions. Justice Souter, joined by Justices Breyer, Ginsburg, and Stevens, dissented. Justice Ginsburg filed a separate dissenting opinion.

▼▲▼

CHIEF JUSTICE REHNQUIST delivered the opinion of the Court.

As this school desegregation litigation enters its 18th year, we are called upon again to review the decisions of the lower courts. In this case, the State of Missouri has challenged the District Court's order of salary increases for virtually all instructional and noninstructional staff within the Kansas City, Missouri, School District (KCMSD) and the District Court's order requiring the State to continue to fund remedial "quality education" programs because student achievement levels were still "at or below national norms at many grade levels." . . .

First, the State has challenged the District Court's requirement that it fund salary increases for KCMSD instructional and noninstructional staff. The State claimed that funding for salaries was beyond the scope of the District Court's remedial authority. Second, the State has challenged the District Court's order requiring it to continue to fund the remedial quality education programs for the 1992–1993 school year. The State contended that under *Freeman* v. *Pitts* (1992), it had achieved partial unitary status with respect to the quality education programs already in place. As a result, the State argued that the District Court should have relieved it of responsibility for funding those programs.

The District Court rejected the State's arguments. It first determined that the salary increases were wanted because "[h]igh quality personnel are necessary not only to implement specialized desegregation programs intended to "improve educational opportunities and reduce racial isolation" . . . but also to "ensure that there is no diminution in the quality of its regular academic program." Its "ruling [was] grounded in remedying the vestiges of segregation by improving the desegregative attractiveness of the KCMSD." The District Court did not address the State's *Freeman* arguments; nevertheless, it ordered the State to continue to fund the quality education programs for the 1992–1993 school year. . . . The Court of Appeals for the Eighth Circuit affirmed. . . .

[W]e granted certiorari to consider the following: (1) whether the District Court exceeded its constitutional authority when it granted salary increases to virtually all instructional and noninstructional employees of the KCMSD, and (2) whether the District Court properly relied upon the fact that student achievement test scores had failed to rise to some unspecified level when it declined to find that the State had achieved partial unitary status as to the quality education programs. . . .

Almost 25 years ago, in *Swann* v. *Charlotte-Mecklenburg Bd. of Ed.* (1971), we dealt with the authority of a district court to fashion remedies for a school district that had been segregated in law in violation of the Equal Protection Clause of the Fourteenth Amendment. Although recognizing the discretion that must necessarily adhere in a district court in fashioning a remedy, we also recognized the limits on such remedial power: "[E]limination of racial discrimination in public schools is a large task, and one that should not be retarded by efforts to achieve broader purposes lying beyond the jurisdiction of the school authorities. One vehicle can carry only a limited amount of baggage. It would not serve the important objective of *Brown I* to seek to use school desegregation cases for purposes beyond their scope, although desegregation of schools ultimately will have impact on other forms of discrimination." . . .

[I]n *Milliken* v. *Bradley* (1977) (*Milliken II*), we articulated a three-part framework derived from our prior cases to guide district courts in the exercise of their remedial authority. In the first place, like other equitable remedies, the nature of the desegregation remedy is to be determined by the nature and scope of the constitutional violation. The remedy must therefore be related to "the condition alleged to offend the Constitution. . . ." Second, the decree must indeed be remedial in nature, that is, it must be designed as nearly as possible "to restore the victims of discriminatory conduct to the position they would have occupied in the absence of such conduct." Third, the federal courts in devising a remedy must take into account the interests of state and local authorities in managing their own affairs, consistent with the Constitution. We added that the principle that the nature and scope of the remedy are to be determined by the violation means simply that federal court decrees must directly address and relate to the constitutional violation itself. In applying these principles, we have identified "student assignments, . . . 'faculty, staff, transportation, extracurricular activities and facilities,'" as the most important indicia of a racially segregated school system.

Because "federal supervision of local school systems was intended as a temporary measure to remedy past discrimination," we also have considered the showing that must be made by a school district operating under a desegregation order for complete or partial relief from that order. In *Freeman*, we stated that [a]mong the factors which must inform the sound discretion of the court in ordering partial withdrawal are the following: [1] whether there has been full and satisfactory compliance with the decree in those aspects of the system where supervision is to be withdrawn; [2] whether retention of judicial control is necessary or practicable to achieve compliance with the decree in other facets of the school system; and [3] whether the school district has demonstrated, to the public and to the parents and students of the once disfavored race, its good-faith commitment to the whole of the courts' decree and to those provisions of the law and the Constitution that were the predicate for judicial intervention in the first instance. The ultimate inquiry is "whether the [constitutional violator] ha[s] complied in good faith with the desegregation decree since it was entered, and whether the vestiges of past discrimination ha[ve] been eliminated to the extent practicable."

Proper analysis of the District Court's orders challenged here, then, must rest upon their serving as proper means to the end of restoring the victims of discriminatory conduct to the position they would have occupied in the absence of that conduct and their eventual restoration of "state and local authorities to the control of a school system that is operating in compliance with the Constitution." We turn to that analysis.

Instead of seeking to remove the racial identity of the various schools within the KCMSD, the District Court has set out on a program to create a school district that was equal to or superior to the surrounding [suburban school districts]. Its remedy has focused on "desegregative attractiveness," coupled with "suburban comparability." Examination of the District Court's reliance on "desegregative attractiveness" and "suburban comparability" is instructive for our ultimate resolution of the salary order issue.

The purpose of desegregative attractiveness has been not only to remedy the system-wide reduction in student achievement, but also to attract nonminority students not presently enrolled in the KCMSD. This remedy has included an elaborate program of capital improvements, course enrichment, and extracurricular enhancement not simply in the formerly identifiable black schools, but in schools throughout the district. The District Court's remedial orders have converted every senior high school, every middle school, and one-half of the elementary schools in the KCMSD into "magnet" schools. The District Court's remedial order has all but made the KCMSD itself into a magnet district.

We previously have approved of intradistrict desegregation remedies involving magnet schools. Magnet schools have the advantage of encouraging voluntary movement of students within a school district in a pattern that aids desegregation on a voluntary basis, without requiring extensive busing and redrawing of district boundary fines. As a component in an intradistrict remedy, magnet schools also are attractive because they promote desegregation while limiting the withdrawal of white student enrollment that may result from mandatory student reassignment.

The District Court's remedial plan in this case, however, is not designed solely to redistribute the students within the KCMSD in order to eliminate racially identifiable schools within the KCMSD. Instead, its purpose is to attract nonminority students from outside the KCMSD schools. But this interdistrict goal is beyond the scope of the intradistrict violation identified by the District Court. In effect, the District Court has devised a remedy to accomplish indirectly what it admittedly lacks the remedial authority to mandate directly: the interdistrict transfer of students. . . .

Respondents argue that the District Court's reliance upon desegregative attractiveness is justified in light of the District Court's statement that segregation has "led to white flight from the KCMSD to suburban districts." The lower court's "findings" as to "white flight" are both inconsistent internally, and inconsistent with the typical supposition, bolstered here by the record evidence, that "white flight" may result from desegregation, not de jure segregation. The United States, as amicus curiae, argues that the District Court's finding that de jure segregation in the KCMSD caused white students to leave the system . . . is not inconsistent with the district court's earlier conclusion that the suburban districts did nothing to cause this white flight, and therefore could not be included in a mandatory interdistrict remedy. . . .

In *Freeman*, we stated that [t]he vestiges of segregation that are the concern of the law in a school case may be subtle and intangible, but nonetheless they must be so real that they have a causal link to the de jure violation being remedied. The record here does not support the District Court's reliance on "white flight" as a justification for a permissible expansion of its intradistrict remedial authority through its pursuit of desegregative attractiveness. . . .

The District Court's pursuit of "desegregative attractiveness" cannot be reconciled with our cases placing limitations on a district court's remedial authority. It is certainly theoretically possible that the greater the expenditure per pupil within the KCMSD, the more likely it is that some unknowable number of nonminority students not presently attending schools in the KCMSD will choose to enroll in those schools. Under this reasoning, however, every increased expenditure, whether it be for teachers, noninstructional employees, books, or buildings, will make the KCMSD in some way more attractive, and thereby perhaps induce nonminority students to enroll in its schools. But this rationale is not susceptible to any objective limitation. This case provides numerous examples demonstrating the limitless authority of the District Court operating under this rationale. In short, desegregative attractiveness has been used "as the hook on which to hang numerous policy choices about improving the quality of education in general within the KCMSD," *Missouri* v. *Jenkins I* (1990). . . .

[We] . . . conclude that the District Court's order requiring the State to continue to fund the quality education programs because student achievement levels were still "at or below national norms at many grade levels" cannot be sustained. The State does not seek from this Court a declaration of partial unitary status with respect to the quality education programs. It challenges the requirement of indefinite funding of a quality education program until national norms are met, based on the assumption that while a mandate for significant educational improvement, both in teaching and in facilities, may have been justified originally, its indefinite extension is not. . . .

On remand, the District Court must bear in mind that its end purpose is not only "to remedy the violation" to the extent practicable, but also "to restore state and local authorities to the control of a school system that is operating in compliance with the Constitution." The judgment of the Court of Appeals is reversed.

It is so ordered.

Justice Thomas, concurring.

It never ceases to amaze me that the courts are so willing to assume that anything that is predominantly black must be inferior. Instead of focusing on remedying the harm done to those black schoolchildren injured by segregation, the District Court here sought to convert the Kansas City, Missouri, School District (KCMSD) into a "magnet district" that would reverse the "white flight" caused by desegregation. In this respect, I join the Court's decision concerning the two remedial issues presented for review. I write separately, however, to add a few thoughts with respect to the overall course of this litigation. In order to evaluate the scope of the remedy, we must understand the scope of the constitutional violation and the nature of the remedial powers of the federal courts.

Two threads in our jurisprudence have produced this unfortunate situation, in which a District Court has taken it upon itself to experiment with the education of the KCMSD's black youth. First, the court has read our cases to support the theory that black students suffer an unspecified psychological harm from segregation that retards their mental and educational development. This approach not only relies upon questionable social science research, rather than constitutional principle, but it also rests on an assumption of black inferiority. Second, we have permitted the federal courts to exercise virtually unlimited equitable powers to remedy this alleged constitutional violation. The exercise of this authority has trampled upon principles of federalism and the separation of powers and has freed courts to pursue other agendas unrelated to the narrow purpose of precisely remedying a constitutional harm. . . .

When a district court holds the State liable for discrimination almost 30 years after the last official state action, it must do more than show that there are schools with high black populations or low test scores. Here, the district judge did not make clear how the high black enrollments in certain schools were fairly traceable to the State of Missouri's actions. I do not doubt that Missouri maintained the despicable system of segregation until 1954. But I question the District Court's conclusion that because the State had enforced segregation until 1954, its actions, or lack thereof, proximately caused the "racial isolation" of the predominantly black schools in 1984. In fact, where, as here, the finding of liability comes so late in the day, I would think it incumbent upon the District Court to explain how more recent social or demographic phenomena did not cause the "vestiges." This the District Court did not do. . . .

Brown I did not say that "racially isolated" schools were inherently inferior; the harm that it identified was tied purely to de jure segregation, not de facto segregation. Indeed, *Brown I* itself did not need to rely upon any psychological or social-science research in order to announce the simple, yet fundamental truth that the Government cannot discriminate among its citizens on the basis of race. As the Court's unanimous opinion indicated: "[I]n the field of public education, the doctrine of 'separate but equal' has no place. Separate educational facilities are inherently unequal. At the heart of this interpretation of the Equal Protection Clause lies the principle that the Government must treat citizens as individuals, and not as members of racial, ethnic or religious groups. It is for this reason that we must subject all racial classifications to the strictest of scrutiny, which (aside from two decisions rendered in the midst of wartime, see *Hirabayashi* v. *United States* [1943]; *Korematsu* v. *United States* [1944]) has proven automatically fatal. . . .

Segregation was not unconstitutional because it might have caused psychological feelings of inferiority. Public school systems that separated blacks and provided them with superior educational resources—making blacks "feel" superior to whites sent to lesser schools—would violate the Fourteenth Amendment whether or not the white students felt stigmatized, just as do school systems in which the positions of the races are reversed. Psychological injury or benefit is irrelevant to the question whether state actors have engaged in intentional discrimination—the critical inquiry for ascertaining violations of the Equal Protection Clause. The judiciary is fully competent to make independent determinations concerning the existence of state action without the unnecessary and misleading assistance of the social sciences.

Regardless of the relative quality of the schools, segregation violated the Constitution because the State classified students based on their race. Of course, segregation additionally harmed black students by relegating them to schools with substandard facilities and resources. But neutral policies, such as local school assignments, do not offend the Constitution when individual private choices concerning work or residence produce schools with high black populations. The Constitution does not prevent individuals from choosing to live together, to work together, or to send their children to school together, so long as the State does not interfere with their choices on the basis of race.

Given that desegregation has not produced the predicted leaps forward in black educational achievement, there is no reason to think that black students cannot learn as well when surrounded by members of their own race as when they are in an integrated environment. Indeed, it may very well be that what has been true for historically black colleges is true for black middle and high schools. Despite their origins in "the shameful history of state-enforced segregation," these institutions can be "both a source of pride to blacks who have attended them and a source of hope to black families who want the benefits of . . . learning for their children." Because of their "distinctive histories and traditions," black schools can function as the center and symbol of black communities, and provide examples of independent black leadership, success, and achievement.

Thus, even if the District Court had been on firmer ground in identifying a link between the KCMSD's pre-1954 de jure segregation and the present "racial isolation" of some of the district's schools, mere de facto segregation (unaccompanied by discriminatory inequalities in educational resources) does not constitute a continuing harm after the end of de jure segregation. "Racial isolation" itself is not a harm; only state-enforced segregation is. After all, if separation itself is a harm, and if integration therefore is the only way that blacks can receive a proper education, then there must be something inferior about blacks. Under this theory, segregation injures blacks because blacks, when left on their own, cannot achieve. To my way of thinking, that conclusion is the result of a jurisprudence based upon a theory of black inferiority.

This misconception has drawn the courts away from the important goal in desegregation. The point of the Equal Protection Clause is not to enforce strict race-mixing, but to ensure that blacks and whites are treated equally by the State without regard to their skin color. The lower courts should not be swayed by the easy answers of social science, nor should they accept the findings, and the assumptions, of sociology and psychology at the price of constitutional principle.

JUSTICE SOUTER, with whom JUSTICE STEVENS, JUSTICE GINSBURG, and JUSTICE BREYER join, dissenting.

In 1984, 30 years after our decision in *Brown* v. *Board of Education* (1954), the District Court found that the State of Missouri and the Kansas City, Missouri, School District (KCMSD) had failed to reform the segregated scheme of public school education in the KCMSD, previously mandated by the State, which had required black and white children to be taught separately according to race. After *Brown*, neither the State nor the KCMSD moved to dismantle this system of separate education "root and branch," despite their affirmative obligation to do that under the Constitution. "Instead, the [KCMSD] chose to operate some completely segregated schools and some integrated ones," using devices like optional attendance zones and liberal transfer policies to "allo[w] attendance patterns to continue on a segregated basis." Consequently, on the 20th anniversary of Brown in 1974, 39 of the 77 schools in the KCMSD had student bodies that were more than 90 percent black, and 80 percent of all black schoolchildren in the KCMSD attended those schools. Ten years later, in the 1983–1984 school year, 24 schools remained racially isolated with more than 90 percent black enrollment. Because the State and the KCMSD intentionally created this segregated system of education, and subsequently failed to correct it, the District Court concluded that the State and the district had "defaulted in their obligation to uphold the Constitution." . . .

The two discrete questions that we actually accepted for review are, then, answerable on their own terms without any need to consider whether the District Court's use of the magnet school concept in its remedial plan is itself constitutionally vulnerable. The capacity to deal thus with the questions raised, coupled with the unfairness of doing otherwise without warning, are enough to demand a dissent.

But there is more to fuel dissent. On its face, the Court's opinion projects an appealing pragmatism in seeming to cut through the details of many facts by applying a rule of law that can claim both precedential support and intuitive sense, that there is error in imposing an interdistrict remedy to cure a merely intradistrict violation. Since the District Court has consistently described the violation here as solely intradistrict, and since the object of the magnet schools under its plan includes attracting students into the district from other districts, the Court's result seems to follow with the necessity of logic, against which arguments about detail or calls for fair warning may not carry great weight.

The attractiveness of the Court's analysis disappears, however, as soon as we recognize two things. First, the District Court did not mean by an "intradistrict violation" what the Court apparently means by it today. The District Court meant that the violation within the KCMSD had not led to segregation outside of it, and that no other school districts had played a part in the violation. It did not mean that the violation had not produced effects of any sort beyond the district. Indeed, the record that we have indicates that the District Court understood that the violation here did produce effects spanning district borders and leading to greater segregation within the KCMSD, the reversal of which the District Court sought to accomplish by establishing magnet schools. Insofar as the Court assumes that this was not so in fact, there is at least enough in the record to cast serious doubt on its assumption. Second, the Court violates existing case law even on its own apparent view of the facts, that the segregation violation within the KCMSD produced no proven effects, segregative or otherwise, outside it. Assuming this to be true, the Court's decision that the rule against interdistrict remedies for intradistrict violations applies to this case, solely because the remedy here is meant to produce effects outside the district in which the violation occurred, is flatly contrary to established precedent. . . .

The unreality of the Court's categorical distinction can be illustrated by some examples. There is no dispute that, before the District Court's remedial plan was placed into effect, the schools in the unreformed segregated system were physically a shambles.

The KCMSD facilities still have numerous health and safety hazards, educational environment hazards, functional impairments, and appearance impairments. The specific problems include: inadequate lighting; peeling paint and crumbling plaster on ceilings, walls and corridors; loose tiles, torn floor coverings; odors resulting from unventilated restrooms with rotted, corroded toilet fixtures; noisy classrooms due to lack of adequate acoustical treatment; lack of off-street parking and bus loading for parents, teachers and students; lack of appropriate space for many cafeterias, libraries and classrooms; faulty and antiquated heating and electrical systems; damaged and inoperable lockers; and inadequate fire safety systems. The conditions at Paseo High School are such that even the principal stated that he would not send his own child to that facility. The cost of turning this shambles into habitable schools was enormous, as anyone would have seen long before the District Court ordered repairs. Property taxpaying parents of white children, seeing the handwriting on the wall in 1985, could well have decided that the inevitable cost of cleanup would produce an intolerable tax rate, and could have moved to escape it. The District Court's remedial orders had not yet been put in place. Was the white flight caused by segregation or desegregation? The distinction has no significance. . . .

I respectfully dissent.

JUSTICE GINSBURG, dissenting.

The Court stresses that the present remedial programs have been in place for seven years. But compared to more than two centuries of firmly entrenched official discrimination, the experience with the desegregation remedies ordered by the District Court has been evanescent.

In 1724, Louis XV of France issued the Code Noir, the first slave code for the Colony of Louisiana, an area that included Missouri. When Missouri entered the Union in 1821, it entered as a slave State.

Before the Civil War, Missouri law prohibited the creation or maintenance of schools for educating blacks: "No person shall keep or teach any school for the instruction of negroes or mulattoes, in reading or writing, in this State."

Beginning in 1865, Missouri passed a series of laws requiring separate public schools for blacks. The Missouri Constitution first permitted, then required, separate schools.

After this Court announced its decision in *Brown* v. *Board of Education* (1954), Missouri's Attorney General declared these provisions mandating segregated schools unenforceable. The statutes were repealed in 1957, and the constitutional provision was rescinded in 1976. Nonetheless, thirty years after *Brown*, the District Court found that "the inferior education indigenous of the state-compelled dual school system has lingering effects in the Kansas City, Missouri, School District." The District Court concluded that the State . . . cannot defend its failure to affirmatively act to eliminate the structure and effects of its past dual system on the basis of restrictive state law. Just ten years ago, in June, 1985, the District Court issued its first remedial order.

Today, the Court declares illegitimate the goal of attracting nonminority students to the Kansas City, Missouri, School District, and thus stops the District Court's efforts to integrate a school district that was, in the 1984/1985 school year, sorely in need and 68.3% black. Given the deep, inglorious history of segregation in Missouri, to curtail desegregation at this time and in this manner is an action at once too swift and too soon.

▼▲▼

United States v. *Fordice*

505 U.S. 717 (1992)

In 1848, the Mississippi legislature chartered the state's first public university, the University of Mississippi, located in Jackson. By 1950, Mississippi had established eight additional public universities, which, by law, operated on a strictly segregated basis. Mississippi did not admit an African American into any one of its all-white universities until 1962, when federal marshals escorted James Meredith into classes at the University of Mississippi. Meredith's admission came only after the NAACP, which represented him, and the Kennedy administration forced Mississippi's segregationist governor, Ross Barnett, to yield to this powerful combination of legal and political pressure.

Still, Mississippi engaged in no more than nominal efforts to desegregate its higher education system. In 1975, the United States and several African American students sued the state, claiming that it continued to perpetuate segregation through its admission policies. A decade of negotiation, charges, and countercharges produced nothing in the way of meaningful desegregation. In 1987, the case went back into court. By this time, 99 percent of white students were enrolled in the state's six historically all-white colleges, whereas just over 70 percent of African American students were enrolled in the state's three historically black colleges. So severe was segregation in higher education that even the Reagan administration, which opposed busing, affirmative action, and other such remedies to overcome prior discrimination, continued to press the lawsuit against Mississippi's higher education system.

The Court's decision was 8 to 1. Justice White delivered the opinion of the Court. Justice Thomas and Justice O'Connor wrote separate concurring opinions. Justice Scalia dissented.

Of note is Justice Clarence Thomas's concurring opinion. Only the second African American to serve on the Court, Thomas expressed concern that a spare-no-expenses approach to integration might well lead to the demise of historically black colleges. Thomas argued that black colleges continued to serve an important function in higher education, today as much as yesterday, even though blacks had complete mobility within the system.

JUSTICE WHITE delivered the opinion of the Court.

Since [*Brown* v. *Board of Education* I and II], the Court has had many occasions to evaluate whether a public school district has met its affirmative obligation to dismantle its prior *de jure* segregated system in elementary and secondary schools. In this case we decide what standards to apply in determining whether the State of Mississippi has met this obligation in the university context. . . .

Our decisions establish that a State does not discharge its constitutional obligations until it eradicates policies and practices traceable to its prior *de jure* dual system that continue to foster segregation. Thus, we have consistently asked whether existing racial identifiability is attributable to the State, and examined a wide range of factors to determine whether the State has perpetuated its formerly *de jure* segregation in any facet of its institutional system. . . .

It is important to state . . . that we make no effort to identify an exclusive list of unconstitutional remnants of Mississippi's prior *de jure* system. In highlighting, as we do below, certain remnants of the prior system that are readily apparent from the findings of fact made by the District

Court and affirmed by the Court of Appeals we by no means suggest that the Court of Appeals need not examine, in light of the proper standard, each of the other policies now governing the State's university system that have been challenged or that are challenged on remand in light of the standard that we articulate today. With this caveat in mind, we address four policies of the present system: admission standards, program duplication, institutional mission assignments, and continued operation of all eight public universities.

We deal first with the current admissions policies of Mississippi's public universities. As the District Court found, the three flagship historically white universities in the system—University of Mississippi, Mississippi State University, and University of Southern Mississippi—enacted policies in 1963 requiring all entrants to achieve a minimum composite score of 15 on the American College Testing Program (ACT). The court described the "discriminatory taint" of this policy, an obvious reference to the fact that, at the time, the average ACT score for white students was 18 and the average score for blacks was 7. The District Court concluded, and the en banc Court of Appeals agreed, that present admissions standards derived from policies enacted in the 1970's to redress the problem of student unpreparedness. Obviously, this mid-passage justification for perpetuating a policy enacted originally to discriminate against black students does not make the present admissions standards any less constitutionally suspect.

The present admission standards are not only traceable to the *de jure* system and were originally adopted for a discriminatory purpose, but they also have present discriminatory effects. Every Mississippi resident under 21 seeking admission to the university system must take the ACT. Any applicant who scores at least 15 qualifies for automatic admission to any of the five historically white institutions except Mississippi University for Women, which requires a score of 18 for automatic admission unless the student has a 3.0 high school grade average. Those scoring less than 15 but at least 13 automatically qualify to enter Jackson State University, Alcorn State University, and Mississippi Valley State University. Without doubt, these requirements restrict the range of choices of entering students as to which institution they may attend in a way that perpetuates segregation. Those scoring 13 or 14, with some exceptions, are excluded from the five historically white universities, and if they want a higher education, must go to one of the historically black institutions or attend junior college with the hope of transferring to a historically white institution. Proportionately more blacks than whites face this choice: in 1985, 72 percent of Mississippi's white high school seniors achieved an ACT composite score of 15 or better, while less than 30 percent of black high school seniors earned that score. It is not surprising, then, that Mississippi's universities remain predominantly identifiable by race.

The segregative effect of this automatic entrance standard is especially striking in light of the differences in minimum automatic entrance scores among the regional universities in Mississippi's system. The minimum score for automatic admission to Mississippi University for Women (MUW) is 18; it is 13 for the historically black universities. Yet MUW is assigned the same institutional mission as two other regional universities, Alcorn State and Mississippi Valley—that of providing quality undergraduate education. The effects of the policy fall disproportionately on black students who might wish to attend MUW; and though the disparate impact is not as great, the same is true of the minimum standard ACT score of 15 at Delta State University—the other "regional" university—as compared to the historically black "regional" universities, where a score of 13 suffices for automatic admission. The courts below made little if any effort to justify in educational terms those particular disparities in entrance requirements, or to inquire whether it was practicable to eliminate them.

We also find inadequately justified by the courts below or by the record before us the differential admissions requirements between universities with dissimilar programmatic missions. We do not suggest that, absent a discriminatory purpose, different programmatic missions accompanied by different admission standards would be constitutionally suspect simply because one or more schools are racially identifiable. But here the differential admission standards are remnants of the dual system, with a continuing discriminatory effect, and the mission assignments "to some degree follow the historical racial assignments." Moreover, the District Court did not justify the differing admission standards based on the different mission assignments. It observed only that, in the 1970's, the Board of Trustees justified a minimum ACT score of 15 because too many students with lower scores were not prepared for the historically white institutions, and that imposing the 15 score requirement on admissions to the historically black institutions would decimate attendance at those universities. The District Court also stated that the mission of the regional universities had the more modest function of providing quality undergraduate education. Certainly the comprehensive universities are also, among other things, educating undergraduates. But we think the 15 ACT test score for automatic admission to the comprehensive universities, as compared with a score of 13 for the regionals, requires further justification in terms of sound educational policy.

Another constitutionally problematic aspect of the State's use of the ACT test scores is its policy of denying automatic admission if an applicant fails to earn the minimum ACT score specified for the particular institution, without also resorting to the applicant's high school grades as an additional factor in predicting college performance. The United States produced evidence that the American College Testing Program (ACTP), the administering organization of the ACT, discourages use of ACT scores as the sole admissions criterion on the ground that it gives an incomplete "picture" of the student applicant's ability to perform adequately in college. One ACTP report presented into evidence suggests that "it would be foolish" to substitute a 3- or 4-hour test in place of a student's high school grades as a means of predicting college performance. The record also indicated that the disparity between black and white students' high school grade averages was much narrower than the gap between their average ACT scores, thereby suggesting that an admissions formula which included grades would increase the number of black students eligible for automatic admission to all of Mississippi's public universities. . . .

A second aspect of the present system that necessitates further inquiry is the widespread duplication of programs. . . . The District Court found that 34.6 percent of the 29 undergraduate programs at historically black institutions are "unnecessarily duplicated" by the historically white universities, and that 90 percent of the graduate programs at the historically black institutions are unnecessarily duplicated at the historically white institutions. In its conclusions of law on this point, the District Court nevertheless determined that "there is no proof" that such duplication "is directly associated with the racial identifiability of institutions," and that there is no proof that the elimination of unnecessary program duplication would be justifiable from an educational standpoint, or that its elimination would have a substantial effect on student choice."

The District Court's treatment of this issue is problematic from several different perspectives. First, the court appeared to impose the burden of proof on the plaintiffs to meet a legal standard the court itself acknowledged was not yet formulated. It can hardly be denied that such duplication was part and parcel of the prior dual system of higher education—the whole notion of "separate but equal" required duplicative programs in two sets of schools—and that the present unnecessary duplication is a continuation of that practice. *Brown* and its progeny, however, established that the burden of proof falls on the State, and not the aggrieved plaintiffs, to establish that it has dismantled its prior *de jure* segregated system. The court's holding that petitioners could not establish the constitutional defect of unnecessary duplication, therefore, improperly shifted the burden away from the State. Second, implicit in the District Court's finding of "unnecessary" duplication is the absence of any educational justification and the fact that some, if not all, duplication may be practicably eliminated. Indeed, the District Court observed that such duplication "cannot be justified economically or in terms of providing quality education." Yet by stating that "there is no proof" that elimination of unnecessary duplication would decrease institutional racial identifiability, affect student choice, and promote educationally sound policies, the court did not make clear whether it had directed the parties to develop evidence on these points, and if so, what that evidence revealed. Finally, by treating this issue in isolation, the court failed to consider the combined effects of unnecessary program duplication with other policies, such as differential admissions standards, in evaluating whether the State had met its duty to dismantle its prior *de jure* segregated system.

We next address Mississippi's scheme of institutional mission classification, and whether it perpetuates the State's formerly *de jure* dual system. The District Court found that, throughout the period of *de jure* segregation, University of Mississippi, Mississippi State University, and University of Southern Mississippi were the flagship institutions in the state system. They received the most funds, initiated the most advanced and specialized programs, and developed the widest range of curricular functions. At their inception, each was restricted for the education solely of white persons. The missions of Mississippi University for Women and Delta State University (DSU), by contrast, were more limited than their other all-white counterparts during the period of legalized segregation. MUW and DSU were each established to provide undergraduate education solely for white students in the liberal arts and such other fields as music, art, education, and home economics. When they were founded, the three exclusively black universities were more limited in their assigned academic missions than the five all-white institutions. Alcorn State, for example, was designated to serve as "an agricultural college for the education of Mississippi's black youth." Jackson State and Mississippi Valley State were established to train black teachers. Though the District Court's findings do not make this point explicit, it is reasonable to infer that state funding and curriculum decisions throughout the period of *de jure* segregation were based on the purposes for which these institutions were established.

In 1981, the State assigned certain missions to Mississippi's public universities as they then existed. It classified University of Mississippi, Mississippi State, and Southern Mississippi as "comprehensive" universities having the most varied programs and offering graduate degrees. Two of the historically white institutions, Delta State University and Mississippi University for Women, along with two of the historically black institutions, Alcorn State University and Mississippi Valley State University, were designated as "regional" universities with more limited programs and devoted primarily to undergraduate education. Jackson State University was classified as an "urban" university whose mission was defined by its urban location.

The institutional mission designations adopted in 1981 have as their antecedents the policies enacted to perpetuate racial separation during the *de jure* segregated regime. The Court of Appeals expressly disagreed with the District Court by recognizing that the inequalities among the institutions largely follow the mission designations, and the mission designations to some degree follow the historical racial assignments." It nevertheless upheld this facet of the system as constitutionally acceptable based on the existence of good faith racially neutral policies and procedures. That different missions are assigned to the universities surely limits to some extent an entering student's choice as to which university to seek admittance. . . .

We do not suggest that, absent discriminatory purpose, the assignment of different missions to various institutions in a State's higher education system would raise an equal protection issue where one or more of the institutions become or remain predominantly black or white. But here the issue is whether the State has sufficiently dismantled its prior dual system; and, when combined with the differential admission practices and unnecessary program duplication, it is likely that the mission designations interfere with student choice, and tend to perpetuate the segregated system. On remand, the court should inquire whether it would be practicable and consistent with sound educational practices to eliminate any such discriminatory effects of the State's present policy of mission assignments.

Fourth, the State attempted to bring itself into compliance with the Constitution by continuing to maintain and operate all eight higher educational institutions. The existence of eight, instead of some lesser number, was undoubtedly occasioned by State laws forbidding the mingling of the races. And as the District Court recognized, continuing to maintain all eight universities in Mississippi is wasteful and irrational. The District Court pointed especially to the facts that Delta State and Mississippi Valley are only 35 miles apart, and that only 20 miles separate Mississippi State and Mississippi University for Women. . . .

Unquestionably, a larger, rather than a smaller, number of institutions from which to choose, in itself, makes for different choices, particularly when examined in the light of other factors present in the operation of the system, such as admissions, program duplication, and institutional mission designations. Though certainly closure of one or more institutions would decrease the discriminatory effects of the present system based on the present record, we are unable to say whether such action is constitutionally required. Elimination of program duplication and revision of admissions criteria may make institutional closure unnecessary. However, on remand, this issue should be carefully explored by inquiring and determining whether retention of all eight institutions itself affects student choice and perpetuates the segregated higher education system, whether maintenance of each of the universities is educationally justifiable, and whether one or more of them can be practicably closed or merged with other existing institutions.

Because the former *de jure* segregated system of public universities in Mississippi impeded the free choice of prospective students, the State, in dismantling that system, must take the necessary steps to ensure that this choice now is truly free. The full range of policies and practices must be examined with this duty in mind. That an institution is predominantly white or black does not, in itself, make out a constitutional violation. But surely the State may not leave in place policies rooted in its prior officially segregated system that serve to maintain the racial identifiability of its universities if those policies can practicably be eliminated without eroding sound educational policies.

If we understand private petitioners to press us to order the upgrading of Jackson State, Alcorn State, and Mississippi Valley solely so that they may be publicly financed, exclusively black enclaves by private choice, we reject that request. The State provides these facilities for all its citizens, and it has not met its burden under *Brown* to take affirmative steps to dismantle its prior *de jure* system when it perpetuates a separate, but "more equal" one. Whether such an increase in funding is necessary to achieve a full dismantlement under the standards we have outlined, however, is a different question, and one that must be addressed on remand.

The decision of the Court of Appeals is vacated, and the cases are remanded for further proceedings consistent with this opinion.

It is so ordered.

JUSTICE THOMAS, concurring.

I agree with the Court that a State does not satisfy its obligation to dismantle a dual system of higher education merely by adopting race-neutral policies for the future administration of that system. . . .

From the beginning, we have recognized that desegregation remedies cannot be designed to ensure the elimination of any remnant at any price, but rather must display "a practical flexibility" and "a facility for adjusting and reconciling public and private needs." Quite obviously, one compelling need to be considered is the *educational* need of the present and future *students* in the Mississippi university system, for whose benefit the remedies will be crafted.

In particular, we do not foreclose the possibility that there exists "sound educational justification" for maintaining historically black colleges *as such*. Despite the shameful history of state-enforced segregation, these institutions have survived and flourished. Indeed, they have expanded as opportunities for blacks to enter historically white institutions have expanded. Between 1954 and 1980, for example, enrollment at historically black colleges increased from 70,000 to 200,000 students, while degrees awarded increased from 13,000 to 32,000. . . .

I think it undisputable that these institutions have succeeded in part because of their distinctive histories and traditions; for many, historically black colleges have become "a symbol of the highest attainments of black culture." Obviously, a State cannot maintain such traditions by closing particular institutions, historically white or historically black, to particular racial groups. Nonetheless, it hardly follows that a State cannot operate a diverse assortment of institutions—including historically black institutions—open to all on a race-neutral basis, but with established traditions and programs that might disproportionately appeal to one race or another. No one, I imagine, would argue that such institutional *diversity* is without "sound educational justification," or that it is even remotely akin to program *duplication*, which is designed to separate the races for the sake of separating the races. The Court at least hints at the importance of this value when it distinguishes *Green* in part on the ground that colleges and universities "are not fungible." Although I agree that a State is not constitutionally *required* to maintain its historically black institutions as such, I do not understand our opinion to hold that a State is *forbidden* from doing so. It would be ironic, to say the least, if the institutions that sustained blacks during segregation were themselves destroyed in an effort to combat its vestiges.

▼▲▼

Beyond State Action: The Civil Rights Act of 1964

The *Civil Rights Cases* of 1883 constrained the ability of Congress to use the Equal Protection Clause to enact legislation barring discrimination outside the immediate context of state action. Since Reconstruction, few states—and none in the South—had passed laws prohibiting racial discrimination by public accommodations or established fair employment standards. But the momentum of the civil rights movement after *Brown* v. *Board of Education* meant that African American demands for full and equal rights in every facet of citizenship would soon put Congress in the position of confronting what appeared to be a legal double standard: Discriminatory state action was clearly unconstitutional, but discriminatory "private" action was not. What choices did Congress have in trying to extend civil rights beyond the boundaries of state action?

In 1964, Congress combined the *dicta* of Justice Bradley's majority opinion in the *Civil Rights Cases* with Justice Harlan's (I) dissent in the same decision. Harlan's dissent had criticized the Court for ignoring what he believed the purpose of the Fourteenth Amendment had been, and that was to establish equal civil and political rights for African Americans. Harlan believed it was wrong to say that all persons were equal before the law, but, at the same time, to protect special privileges for whites only. Relying on its power to regulate interstate commerce, Congress, in the Civil Rights Act of 1964, banned discrimination in public accommodations. The law also banned discrimination by employers of fifteen persons or more and by any institution receiving federal funds. Almost immediately, the Court heard a challenge to the public accommodations provisions of the law. To the dismay of segregationists, the justices, in *Heart of Atlanta Motel* v. *United States* (1964) and *Katzenbach* v. *McClung* (1964) (see Volume I, Chapter 6), unanimously ruled that Congress had acted appropriately under its Commerce Clause power.[57]

Seven years after *Heart of Atlanta Motel* and *Katzenbach*, the Court handed down what is still considered its most important decision concerning the scope and application of the 1964 law's fair employment provision, Title VII. In *Griggs* v. *Duke Power Co.* (1971), the Court heard an NAACP challenge to a common employment practice that resulted in racial discrimination: the use of IQ tests to determine hiring and promotion in jobs that bore no real relationship to job performance. In *Griggs*, the NAACP set forth what was then a novel theory of Title VII's application. It argued that Congress intended to ban employment practices that *resulted* in discrimination, not just arbitrary barriers clearly intended to exclude persons on the basis of race. As far back as *Yick Wo* v. *Hopkins* (1886), the Court ruled that laws "neutral" on their race, which nonetheless resulted in racial discrimination, violated the Fourteenth Amendment.[58] Conceptually, *Griggs* was about the same thing, in this case, an employer's effort to shield discriminatory motives behind seemingly race-neutral employment practices.

Griggs v. *Duke Power Co.*

401 U.S. 424 (1971)

Soon after the passage of the Civil Rights Act of 1964, Duke Power, a North Carolina utility company, modified its employment practices to stop discriminating expressly against African Americans. Duke Power's history of racial discrimination followed a fairly standard formula for many employers: Blacks were prohibited from applying for more skilled, better paying jobs with opportunities for promotion. Those jobs were reserved for whites; blacks were confined to jobs involving semiskilled and unskilled labor. In 1965, Duke Power changed its hiring and promotion standards to require a high school diploma and test scores equal to that of average high school graduates on two common IQ tests. Duke Power defended the tests by claiming they demonstrated academic potential and the ability to perform certain jobs well. Fifty-eight percent of whites who took the tests passed; fewer than 6 percent of blacks achieved the same result.

The NAACP viewed Frank Griggs's case as having enormous potential payoff. Here was a black man who wanted to work as a coal handler, and who was told he could not because he had failed the IQ tests. Title VII permitted employers to use tests that were not "designed or intended or used to discriminate because of race." The NAACP researched Duke Power's decision to use the tests and concluded that its motive was to achieve the same discriminatory employment practices that were in place before Title VII's passage. Although sympathetic to the NAACP's position, the Department of Justice and the Equal Employment Opportunity Commission (EEOC), the federal agency charged with enforcing Title VII, warned the NAACP that challenging the testing issue was risky. Jack Greenberg, the NAACP's litigation director since 1961, argued that the use of testing to exclude a black man who wanted to work as a coal handler—a job traditionally reserved for whites—offered a prime opportunity to develop an "in-effect" theory of employment discrimination.

The Court's decision was unanimous. Chief Justice Burger delivered the opinion of the Court.

Mr. Chief Justice Burger delivered the opinion of the Court.

We granted the writ in this case to resolve the question whether an employer is prohibited by the Civil Rights Act of 1964, Title VII, from requiring a high school education or passing of a standardized general intelligence test as a condition of employment in or transfer to jobs when (a) neither standard is shown to be significantly related to successful job performance, (b) both requirements operate to disqualify Negroes at a substantially higher rate than white applicants, and (c) the jobs in question formerly had been filled only by white employees as part of a long-standing practice of giving preference to whites.

In 1955, [Duke Power] Company instituted a policy of requiring a high school education for initial assignment to any department except Labor, and for transfer from the Coal Handling to any "inside" department (Operations, Maintenance, or Laboratory). When the Company abandoned its policy of restricting Negroes to the Labor Department in 1965, completion of high school also was made a prerequisite to transfer from Labor to any other department. From the time the high school requirement was instituted to the time of trial, however, white employees hired before the time of the high school education requirement continued to perform satisfactorily and achieve promotions in the "operating" departments. Findings on this score are not challenged.

The Company added a further requirement for new employees on July 2, 1965, the date on which Title VII became effective. To qualify for placement in any but the Labor Department, it became necessary to register satisfactory scores on two professionally prepared aptitude tests, as well as to have a high school education. Completion of high school alone continued to render employees eligible for transfer to the four desirable departments from which Negroes had been excluded if the incumbent had been employed prior to the time of the new requirement. In

September, 1965, the Company began to permit incumbent employees who lacked a high school education to qualify for transfer from Labor or Coal Handling to an "inside" job by passing two tests—the Wonderlic Personnel Test, which purports to measure general intelligence, and the Bennett Mechanical Comprehension Test. Neither was directed or intended to measure the ability to learn to perform a particular job or category of jobs. The requisite scores used for both initial hiring and transfer approximated the national median for high school graduates. . . .

The objective of Congress in the enactment of Title VII is plain from the language of the statute. It was to achieve equality of employment opportunities and remove barriers that have operated in the past to favor an identifiable group of white employees over other employees. Under the Act, practices, procedures, or tests neutral on their face, and even neutral in terms of intent, cannot be maintained if they operate to "freeze" the *status quo* of prior discriminatory employment practices.

The Court of Appeals' opinion, and the partial dissent, agreed that, on the record in the present case, "whites register far better on the Company's alternative requirements" than Negroes. This consequence would appear to be directly traceable to race. Basic intelligence must have the means of articulation to manifest itself fairly in a testing process. Because they are Negroes, petitioners have long received inferior education in segregated schools, and this Court expressly recognized these differences in *Gaston County* v. *United States* (1969). There, because of the inferior education received by Negroes in North Carolina, this Court barred the institution of a literacy test for voter registration on the ground that the test would abridge the right to vote indirectly on account of race. Congress did not intend by Title VII, however, to guarantee a job to every person regardless of qualifications. In short, the Act does not command that any person be hired simply because he was formerly the subject of discrimination, or because he is a member of a minority group. Discriminatory preference for any group, minority or majority, is precisely and only what Congress has proscribed. What is required by Congress is the removal of artificial, arbitrary, and unnecessary barriers to employment when the barriers operate invidiously to discriminate on the basis of racial or other impermissible classification.

Congress has now provided that tests or criteria for employment or promotion may not provide equality of opportunity merely in the sense of the fabled offer of milk to the stork and the fox. On the contrary, Congress has now required that the posture and condition of the job seeker be taken into account. It has—to resort again to the fable—provided that the vessel in which the milk is proffered be one all seekers can use. The Act proscribes not only overt discrimination, but also practices that are fair in form, but discriminatory in operation. The touchstone is business necessity. If an employment practice which operates to exclude Negroes cannot be shown to be related to job performance, the practice is prohibited.

On the record before us, neither the high school completion requirement nor the general intelligence test is shown to bear a demonstrable relationship to successful performance of the jobs for which it was used. Both were adopted, as the Court of Appeals noted, without meaningful study of their relationship to job performance ability. Rather, a vice-president of the Company testified, the requirements were instituted on the Company's judgment that they generally would improve the overall quality of the workforce.

The evidence, however, shows that employees who have not completed high school or taken the tests have continued to perform satisfactorily, and make progress in departments for which the high school and test criteria are now used. The promotion record of present employees who would not be able to meet the new criteria thus suggests the possibility that the requirements may not be needed even for the limited purpose of preserving the avowed policy of advancement within the Company. In the context of this case, it is unnecessary to reach the question whether testing requirements that take into account capability for the next succeeding position or related future promotion might be utilized upon a showing that such long-range requirements fulfill a genuine business need. In the present case, the Company has made no such showing. . . .

The Company's lack of discriminatory intent is suggested by special efforts to help the undereducated employees through Company financing of two-thirds the cost of tuition for high school training. But Congress directed the thrust of the Act to the consequences of employment practices, not simply the motivation. More than that, Congress has placed on the employer the burden of showing that any given requirement must have a manifest relationship to the employment in question.

The facts of this case demonstrate the inadequacy of broad and general testing devices, as well as the infirmity of using diplomas or degrees as fixed measures of capability. History is filled with examples of men and women who rendered highly effective performance without the conventional badges of accomplishment in terms of certificates, diplomas, or degrees. Diplomas and tests are useful servants, but Congress has mandated the common sense proposition that they are not to become masters of reality. . . .

Nothing in the Act precludes the use of testing or measuring procedures; obviously they are useful. What Congress has forbidden is giving these devices and mechanisms controlling force unless they are demonstrably a reasonable measure of job performance. Congress has not commanded that the less qualified be preferred over the better qualified simply because of minority origins. Far from disparaging job qualifications as such, Congress has made such qualifications the controlling factor, so that race, religion, nationality, and sex become irrelevant. What Congress has commanded is that any tests used must measure the person for the job, and not the person in the abstract.

The judgment of the Court of Appeals is, as to that portion of the judgment appealed from, reversed.

Chief Justice Burger's opinion offered a sweeping interpretation of Title VII's application to employment discrimination. By concluding that employers had to demonstrate that tests and other employment practices resulting in racially "disparate" outcomes among job applicants and current employees were justified by a "business necessity," the Court, in *Griggs*, handed civil rights advocates a landmark victory, one that has weathered subsequent legal challenges.

Affirmative Action

In May 1965, President Lyndon Johnson stood before the graduating class of Howard University, one the nation's oldest and most prestigious historically black universities, to deliver the commencement address. Commenting on the changes taking place in American society as a result of the civil rights movement, Johnson said that "you do not take a person who, for years, has been hobbled by chains and liberate him, bring him up to the starting line and then say, 'You are free to compete with all the others,' and still justly believe that you have been completely fair." That same year, President Johnson ordered the United States Department of Labor to monitor whether contractors doing business with the federal government were hiring and retaining minorities. Companies with poor minority hiring records were notified that they would lose their contracts with the federal government unless they met certain hiring and promotion criteria. President John F. Kennedy (1961–1963) had actually first used the phrase "affirmative action" in an executive order he issued requiring federal contractors to step up their recruitment of racial minorities. Johnson's action, however, transformed affirmative action from an aggressive outreach program into minority communities to one that emphasized "goals," "timetables," and other numerical objectives to include the positive representation of minorities.[59]

Affirmative action raises questions that go to the heart of a wider debate over the meaning of equality under law. Does the Constitution prohibit the use of race-conscious remedies (later to include sex and ethnic origin) to overcome prior discrimination? Or does the equal protection guarantee require more "affirmative" measures to achieve racial diversity in education, employment, and other aspects of American life? Some of the nation's most memorable rhetoric has been plucked from Supreme Court decisions and public speeches to defend both positions, from Justice Harlan's (I) dissent in *Plessy*—"Our Constitution is color-blind, and neither knows nor tolerates classes among its citizens . . ."—to Martin Luther King Jr.'s plea that people "not be judged by the color of their skin, but by the content of their character," to Justice Harry Blackmun's concurring opinion in *Regents, University of California* v. *Bakke* (1978), the Court's first major affirmative action decision, "To get beyond race, we must first take race into account. There is no other way." In fairness, affirmative action was neither born of nor requires such a stark choice between color-blind and color-conscious remedies.

How Colorblind Is the Constitution?

In January 1865, Union general William T. Sherman, having marched from Atlanta to Savannah, assembled twenty local African American leaders and asked them whether blacks would prefer to live among whites or settle on their own land. Replied one local Baptist minister: "I would prefer to live by ourselves, for there is a prejudice against us in the South that will take years to get over." Persuaded that such sentiment captured the feeling of local blacks, General Sherman then issued Special Field Order No. 15, setting aside the Sea Islands off the Georgia coast and the low rice country just south of Charleston, South Carolina, for the exclusive settlement of blacks. Each family was eligible to receive "forty acres of land and a mule," a phrase that would soon echo throughout the African American South as

MAJOR CIVIL RIGHTS ACTS PASSED SINCE RECONSTRUCTION

The Civil Rights Act of 1957	This law was the first civil rights legislation passed by Congress since Reconstruction. The primary aim of the law was to increase federal authority to monitor and enforce voting rights. The law also established the Civil Rights Division within the Department of Justice, and created the Civil Rights Commission, a federal fact-finding body that investigates civil rights complaints, holds public hearings, and offers policy recommendations. In reality, the law did little to improve the status of African Americans and other minorities.
The Civil Rights Act of 1964	The most comprehensive and effective civil rights law ever enacted by Congress. The law eradicated legal discrimination in almost every sphere of American life. Major provisions of the law include Title II, which prohibits discrimination in public accommodations on the basis of race, color, religion, and national origin; Title VI, which prohibits discrimination on the basis of race, color, religion, and national origin by any institution receiving federal funding; and Title VII, which prohibits discrimination on the basis of race, color, religion, national origin, and sex in employment and hiring by businesses of fifteen persons or more. The 1964 law also established a Community Relations Service to mediate civil rights disputes at the local level and increased the federal government's authority to bring lawsuits to enforce the statute's major provisions. In 1972, Title IX was added to the Civil Rights Act of 1964. This provision prohibits discrimination on the basis of sex by institutions receiving federal funds. Title IX is often given credit for launching the revolution in women's athletic programs at the high school and college levels.
The Civil Rights Act of 1968	This law marked the first major congressional effort to ban discrimination on the basis of race, color, and national origin involving the financing, sale, or rental of housing. The law was amended to include sex in 1974 and physical disability in 1988. The law does not cover buildings where the owner is present and consists of fewer than four housing units.
The Civil Rights Act of 1988	This law modified a decision by the Supreme Court, *Grove City College* v. *Bell* (1984), which held that students receiving federal grants were not covered by Title VI or Title IX of the Civil Rights Act of 1964. The 1988 law made clear that any person receiving federal funds was considered to be receiving assistance no different than if the money had been directed toward the institution.
The Americans with Disabilities Act of 1990	This law marked the first comprehensive effort of the federal government to address discrimination against the physically and mentally disabled. Passed by a broad bipartisan majority in Congress and endorsed by President George Bush (I), the ADA applies to state and local governments, private employers of fifteen or more, labor unions, and employment agencies. The ADA defines "disability" as a physical or mental impairment that substantially limits one or more major life activities. A qualified individual with a disability is a person who meets legitimate skill, experience, education, or other requirements of an employment position that he or she holds or seeks and who can perform the "essential functions" of the position with or without reasonable accommodation.

MAJOR CIVIL RIGHTS ACTS PASSED SINCE RECONSTRUCTION (*continued*)

The Civil Rights Act of 1991	This law came about in response to several Supreme Court decisions handed down during 1989 that made it more difficult for individuals to bring "in-effect" discrimination claims (see *Griggs* v. *Duke Power Co.* [1971]) against their employers under Title VII of the Civil Rights Act of 1964 and that narrowed the remedies available to individuals bringing discrimination claims under the Civil Rights Act of 1866. The 1991 law clarified congressional intent on the scope of protection afforded by the major federal civil rights laws, and restored the "in-effect" standard established in *Griggs*.

the rallying cry for the economic justice owed to the former black slaves.[60]

After the Civil War, Congress enacted the Freedman's Bureau bill over two separate vetoes by President Andrew Johnson. The legislation provided land, medical care, schools, loans, and other support exclusively for African Americans, the end purpose being the assimilation of blacks into white society. Johnson's first veto message foreshadowed the rhetoric of contemporary opponents of affirmative action, writing that the bill established "for the security of the colored race safeguards which go infinitely beyond any that the General Government has ever provided for the white race. In fact, the distinction of race and color is by the bill made to operate in favor of the colored and against the white race." President Johnson was not alone in seeing the Freedman's Bureau program as a system of "special rights" for blacks. One congressional opponent of the bill had commented during debate that "[w]e used to talk about having a white man's chance. It seems to me now that a man may be very happy if he can get a negro's chance." Nonetheless, Congress enacted several laws during Reconstruction designed specifically to protect African Americans or provide them with material benefits.[61]

In the modern era, *Swann* and *Griggs* demonstrated well before *Bakke* that the Court was not adverse to the idea of race-conscious decision making if the purpose was to overcome prior discrimination. Recall that in *Swann* the Court permitted the lower courts to devise remedies that included student assignment to schools based on race. Although less explicit, the implications in *Griggs* for race-conscious decision making in employment were clear: Businesses with racial disparities in their labor forces had to defend them as necessary, something that was hard to do. After *Griggs*, many businesses began to make race-conscious efforts to hire minorities to discourage potential "disparate impact" lawsuits. The Court's position on race-conscious decision making after these two cases thus could be summarized as follows: The Constitution banned racial discrimination that harmed African Americans, but it did not prohibit the use of race-conscious tools to address the consequences of prior discrimination and, in some cases, even required the government and private employers to do so.[62]

By the time the Court decided *Bakke*, the Court had had second thoughts about the constitutionality of affirmative action. In the school desegregation cases, race was an explicit factor in the assignment of students to schools and in the remedial alteration of attendance zones. But the costs to whites did not seem as great as being denied a job or admission to a university, since all students ended up attending school under judicial supervision and no one was excluded on the basis of race. In *Bakke*, the Court confronted a different situation: In an effort to promote greater minority enrollment, the University of California at Davis, a public university, designed an admissions program for its medical school that limited the number of seats for which white students could compete. Four years before, in *DeFunis* v. *Odegaard* (1974), the Court faced a nearly identical set of issues. A white student claimed that the University of Washington law school's affirmative action program excluded him from competing for seats set aside specifically for minorities. Earlier, a state court agreed with Marco DeFunis, and ordered his admission. By the time the case reached the Supreme Court, DeFunis was in his last semester of law school. The Court, in a 5–4 decision, ruled that DeFunis's complaint was moot since he was about to graduate and thus had suffered no direct injury. Any hope, however, that the issues raised in *DeFunis* would go away were quickly dispelled by Justice Douglas's dissent:

> There is no constitutional right for any race to be preferred. The years of slavery did more than retard the progress of blacks. Even a greater wrong was done the whites by creating arrogance instead of humility and by encouraging the growth of the fiction of a superior race. There is no superior person by constitutional standards. A DeFunis who is white is entitled to no advantage by reason of that fact; nor is he subject to any disability, no matter what his race or color. Whatever his race, he had a constitutional right to have his application considered on its individual merits in a racially neutral manner.

On the issue of race-conscious admissions, Douglas wrote:

> The key to the problem is the consideration of each application in a racially neutral way. . . . The Equal Protection Clause commands the elimination of racial barriers, not their creation in order to satisfy our theory as to how society ought to be organized. The purpose of the University of Washington cannot be to produce black lawyers for blacks, Polish lawyers for Poles, Jewish lawyers for Jews, Irish lawyers for Irish. It should be to produce good lawyers for Americans and not to place First Amendment barriers against anyone. . . . A segregated admissions process creates suggestions of stigma and caste no less than a segregated classroom, and in the end it may produce that result despite its contrary intentions. One other assumption must be clearly disapproved; that blacks or browns cannot make it on their individual merit. That is a stamp of inferiority that a State is not permitted to place on any lawyer.

Shortly after *DeFunis,* the University of California at Davis rejected Allan Bakke's application for admission into its medical school for a second time. A white, thirty-three-year-old aerospace engineer who had served in the Vietnam War, Bakke had applied for admission to Davis in 1972, been rejected, then reapplied in 1973. Both times the admissions committee concluded that Bakke's academic record, while certainly competitive, was not strong enough to merit admission. Davis admitted one hundred students into its first-year class; Bakke was one of approximately 2,600 applicants in 1972 and 3,700 in 1973. By the time of his second rejection, Bakke had been turned down by a dozen other medical schools, most of which cited his age as a major factor in their decisions. At Davis, Bakke had been interviewed by an admissions officer who, impressed with his application, informed him that Davis utilized a two-tier admissions program. Sixteen of the school's one hundred spaces were set aside for designated minorities—Chicanos, African Americans, Asian Americans, and Native Americans. Although it did not formally exclude whites, as it sought applicants from disadvantaged economic backgrounds, not one white student of the two hundred who had applied to the program had ever been admitted. Students who qualified for the minority admissions program were held to much lower admissions standards than white students, who were only eligible to compete for the remaining eighty-four seats.

In 1973, Bakke had higher scores than all but one student admitted into the special program reserved for minorities. His college grade-point-average was 3.46, and on the medical school board exams he scored in the 97th, 96th, and 94th percentiles on the science, verbal, and math sections, respectively. After his second rejection, Peter Storandt, the admissions officer who had told Bakke about the special admissions program, wrote him, encouraging him to sue: "You might consider taking my other suggestion which is then to pursue your research into admissions policies based on quota-oriented minority recruiting. . . . It might be of interest to you to review carefully the current suit against the University of Washington School of Law [*DeFunis*] by a man who is now a second year student there but who was originally rejected and brought suit on the very grounds you outlined in your letter."[63]

Convinced that he would have been admitted into Davis if not for its special admissions program, Bakke sued and won in the California courts. Davis conceded that it could not "meet the burden of proving that the special admissions program did not result in Mr. Bakke's failure to be admitted." Many civil rights lawyers who had closely followed Bakke's lawsuit believed that the university had thrown the case, for no other reason than to protect itself against future such lawsuits. Davis did not challenge Bakke's assertion that it utilized a quota system, even though the medical school had not, in two of the six years since the school was founded, met the target of sixteen minority applicants. In both cases, the admissions committee determined it had not found qualified candidates. Davis also did not mention the medical school dean's intervention on behalf of well-connected applicants, a long-standing tradition in higher education.[64] Affirmative action proponents within the university and several civil rights organizations put substantial pressure on Davis to appeal the decision to the United States Supreme Court, and to replace the attorneys who had previously argued the case.[65] Davis's decision to hire Archibald Cox, one of the nation's most eminent constitutional scholars and a former solicitor general under Presidents Kennedy and Johnson, demonstrated that it had received the message loud and clear.

Regents, University of California v. Bakke

438 U.S. 265 (1978)

Allan Bakke's decision to challenge the Davis medical school's admissions program set off the first full-scale national debate over affirmative action. It also exposed a major rift between African American and Jewish civil rights organizations over the use of race-conscious measures to address discrimination and promote diversity. Jews helped found the NAACP in 1909. For years, Louis Marshall, a prominent Jewish attorney who helped found the American Jewish Committee, represented the NAACP in its early discrimination cases. After the NAACP launched its legal campaign to challenge segregation, groups such as the AJCommittee, the American Jewish Congress, and the Anti-Defamation League supported it at each and every turn, providing financial assistance and litigation aid. Jews were also major supporters of the grass-roots civil rights movement that grew outside the courtroom. Perhaps the greatest symbol of the black-Jewish alliance was the brutal murder in 1964 of three young men: two Jewish civil rights activists, Andrew Goodman and Michael Schwerner, and James Chaney, a twenty-year-old black Mississippian and civil rights worker, whose bodies were found in the underbrush of a dam near Philadelphia, Mississippi. Their offense had been to register blacks in Mississippi to vote.

In *DeFunis*, the major Jewish organizations, for the first time, openly opposed a remedy sought by black civil rights organizations, submitting briefs attacking the law school's admissions policies as unconstitutional. They believed that affirmative action measures that utilized "goals," "timetables," and "quotas" unfairly punished qualified whites and stigmatized minorities by leaving them with the impression that they were accepted because of their race, not their qualifications. In *Bakke*, the AJCommittee, AJCongress, and the ADL pressed ahead with the same arguments, which were driven largely by bitter memories of the quota systems used by elite universities until the middle 1950s to limit Jewish enrollment.

Bakke also tested the resolve of the Department of Justice, which had supported the objectives of the NAACP and other civil rights organizations in court since *Brown*. After the Court agreed to hear *Bakke*, a draft of the Solicitor General's brief was leaked, in which President Jimmy Carter's administration (1977–1981) argued for Allan Bakke's admission. The government's position created an uproar among several high-ranking African Americans in that administration and in the civil rights community. President Carter, after a considerable lobbying effort by civil rights groups, intervened and pressed the Justice Department to defend affirmative action. Ultimately, the government's brief began by stating "race may be taken into account to counteract the effects of prior discrimination," while arguing against rigid quotas.

In sum, fifty-eight *amicus* briefs were submitted in *Bakke* representing approximately two hundred different civil rights, religious, fraternal, educational, and civic organizations. Most of these briefs offered little original analysis; they did, however, show the Court how divided the nation was over affirmative action and how contentious the issue had become. In a sense, the disagreement over affirmative action was captured, with perfect pitch, by Justice Thurgood Marshall, when he responded to a point brought by Reynold Colvin, Allan Bakke's attorney: "You're arguing about keeping somebody out, and the other side is arguing about getting somebody in," said Marshall. "That's right," answered Colvin. Replied Marshall, "So it depends on which way you look at it."

The Court's decision was 4 to 1 to 4. Justices Blackmun, Brennan, Marshall, and White concurred and dissented in part, concluding that the Davis admissions program was constitutional. Justices Burger, Rehnquist, Stevens, and Stewart concurred and dissented in part, concluding that the program violated the Equal Protection Clause. Justice Powell steered a middle course and, in effect, wrote the blueprint for a generation of affirmative action programs in higher education.

▼▲▼

MR. JUSTICE POWELL announced the judgment of the Court.

Petitioner does not deny that decisions based on race or ethnic origin by faculties and administrations of state universities are reviewable under the Fourteenth Amendment. For his part, respondent does not argue that all racial or ethnic classifications are *per se* invalid. The parties do disagree as to the level of judicial scrutiny to be applied to the special admissions program. Petitioner argues that the court below erred in applying strict scrutiny, as this inexact term has been applied in our cases. That level of review, petitioner asserts, should be reserved for classifications that disadvantage "discrete and insular minorities." Respondent, on the other hand, contends that the California court correctly rejected the notion that the degree of Judicial scrutiny accorded a particular racial or ethnic classification hinges upon membership in a discrete and insular minority and duly recognized that the "rights established [by the Fourteenth Amendment] are personal rights."

En route to this crucial battle over the scope of judicial review, the parties fight a sharp preliminary action over the proper characterization of the special admissions program. Petitioner prefers to view it as establishing a "goal" of minority representation in the Medical School. Respondent, echoing the courts below, labels it a racial quota.

This semantic distinction is beside the point: the special admissions program is undeniably a classification based on race and ethnic background. To the extent that there existed a pool of at least minimally qualified minority applicants to fill the 16 special admissions seats, white applicants could compete only for the 84 seats in the entering class, rather than the 100 open to minority applicants. Whether this limitation is described as a quota or a goal, it is a line drawn on the basis of race and ethnic status.

The guarantees of the Fourteenth Amendment extend to all persons. Its language is explicit: "No State shall . . . deny to any person within its jurisdiction the equal protection of the laws." It is settled beyond question that the rights created by the first section of the Fourteenth Amendment are, by its terms, guaranteed to the individual. The rights established are personal rights. . . .

Although many of the Framers of the Fourteenth Amendment conceived of its primary function as bridging the vast distance between members of the Negro race and the white "majority," the Amendment itself was framed in universal terms, without reference to color, ethnic origin, or condition of prior servitude. . . . Indeed, it is not unlikely that, among the Framers, were many who would have applauded a reading of the Equal Protection Clause that states a principle of universal application and is responsive to the racial, ethnic, and cultural diversity of the Nation.

Over the past 30 years, this Court has embarked upon the crucial mission of interpreting the Equal Protection Clause with the view of assuring to all persons "the protection of equal laws," in a Nation confronting a legacy of slavery and racial discrimination. Because the landmark decisions in this area arose in response to the continued exclusion of Negroes from the mainstream of American society, they could be characterized as involving discrimination by the "majority" white race against the Negro minority. But they need not be read as depending upon that characterization for their results. It suffices to say that "[o]ver the years, this Court has consistently repudiated '[d]istinctions between citizens solely because of their ancestry' as being 'odious to a free people whose institutions are founded upon the doctrine of equality,'" *Loving v. Virginia* (1967).

Petitioner urges us to adopt for the first time a more restrictive view of the Equal Protection Clause, and hold that discrimination against members of the white "majority" cannot be suspect if its purpose can be characterized as "benign." The clock of our liberties, however, cannot be turned back to 1868. It is far too late to argue that the guarantee of equal protection to all persons permits the recognition of special wards entitled to a degree of protection greater than that accorded others. . . .

Once the artificial line of a "two-class theory" of the Fourteenth Amendment is put aside, the difficulties entailed in varying the level of judicial review according to a perceived "preferred" status of a particular racial or ethnic minority are intractable. The concepts of "majority" and "minority" necessarily reflect temporary arrangements and political judgments. As observed above, the white "majority" itself is composed of various minority groups, most of which can lay claim to a history of prior discrimination at the hands of the State and private individuals. Not all of these groups can receive preferential treatment and corresponding judicial tolerance of distinctions drawn in terms of race and nationality, for then the only "majority" left would be a new minority of white Anglo-Saxon Protestants. There is no principled basis for deciding which groups would merit "heightened judicial solicitude" and which would not. Courts would be asked to evaluate the extent of the prejudice and consequent harm suffered by various minority groups. Those whose societal injury is thought to exceed some arbitrary level of tolerability then would be entitled to preferential classifications at the expense of individuals belonging to other groups. Those classifications would be free from exacting judicial scrutiny. As these preferences began to have their desired effect, and the consequences of past discrimination were undone, new judicial rankings would be necessary. The kind of variable sociological and political analysis necessary to produce such rankings simply does not lie within the judicial competence—even if they otherwise were politically feasible and socially desirable. . . .

Petitioner contends that, on several occasions, this Court has approved preferential classifications without applying the most exacting scrutiny. Most of the cases upon which petitioner relies are drawn from three areas: school desegregation, employment discrimination, and sex discrimination. Each of the cases cited presented a situation materially different from the facts of this case.

The school desegregation cases are inapposite. Each involved remedies for clearly determined constitutional violations. Racial classifications thus were designed as remedies for the vindication of constitutional entitlement. Moreover, the scope of the remedies was not permitted to exceed the extent of the violations. Here, there was no judicial determination of constitutional violation as a predicate for the formulation of a remedial classification. . . .

The special admissions program purports to serve the purposes of: (i) "reducing the historic deficit of traditionally disfavored minorities in medical schools and in the medical profession," (ii) countering the effects of societal discrimination; (iii) increasing the number of physicians who will practice in communities currently underserved; and (iv) obtaining the educational benefits that flow from an ethnically diverse student body. It is necessary to decide which, if any, of these purposes is substantial enough to support the use of a suspect classification.

If petitioner's purpose is to assure within its student body some specified percentage of a particular group merely because of its race or ethnic origin, such a preferential purpose must be rejected not as insubstantial, but as facially invalid. Preferring members of any one group for no reason other than race or ethnic origin is discrimination for its own sake. This the Constitution forbids.

The State certainly has a legitimate and substantial interest in ameliorating, or eliminating where feasible, the disabling effects of identified discrimination. The line of school desegregation cases, commencing with *Brown*, attests to the importance of this state goal and the commitment of the judiciary to affirm all lawful means toward its attainment. In the school cases, the States were required by court order to redress the wrongs worked by specific instances of racial discrimination. That goal was far more focused than the remedying of the effects of "societal discrimination," an amorphous concept of injury that may be ageless in its reach into the past.

We have never approved a classification that aids persons perceived as members of relatively victimized groups at the expense of other innocent individuals in the absence of judicial, legislative, or administrative findings of constitutional or statutory violations. After such findings have been made, the governmental interest in preferring members of the injured groups at the expense of others is substantial, since the legal rights of the victims must be vindicated. In such a case, the extent of the injury and the consequent remedy will have been judicially, legislatively, or administratively defined. Also, the remedial action usually remains subject to continuing oversight to assure that it will work the least harm possible to other innocent persons competing for the benefit. Without such findings of constitutional or statutory violations, it cannot be said that the government has any greater interest in helping one individual than in refraining from harming another. Thus, the government has no compelling justification for inflicting such harm. . . .

[T]he purpose of helping certain groups whom the faculty of the Davis Medical School perceived as victims of "societal discrimination" does not justify a classification that imposes disadvantages upon persons like respondent, who bear no responsibility for whatever harm the beneficiaries of the special admissions program are thought to have suffered. To hold otherwise would be to convert a remedy heretofore reserved for violations of legal rights into a privilege that all institutions throughout the Nation could grant at their pleasure to whatever groups are perceived as victims of societal discrimination. That is a step we have never approved.

Petitioner identifies, as another purpose of its program, improving the delivery of health care services to communities currently underserved. It may be assumed that, in some situations, a State's interest in facilitating the health care of its citizens is sufficiently compelling to support the use of a suspect classification. But there is virtually no evidence in the record indicating that petitioner's special admissions program is either needed or geared to promote that goal. . . .

The fourth goal asserted by petitioner is the attainment of a diverse student body. This clearly is a constitutionally permissible goal for an institution of higher education. Academic freedom, though not a specifically enumerated constitutional right, long has been viewed as a special concern of the First Amendment. The freedom of a university to make its own judgments as to education includes the selection of its student body. . . .

[I]n arguing that its universities must be accorded the right to select those students who will contribute the most to the "robust exchange of ideas," petitioner invokes a countervailing constitutional interest, that of the First Amendment. In this light, petitioner must be viewed as seeking to achieve a goal that is of paramount importance in the fulfillment of its mission.

It may be argued that there is greater force to these views at the undergraduate level than in a medical school, where the training is centered primarily on professional competency. But even at the graduate level, our tradition and experience lend support to the view that the contribution of diversity is substantial. In *Sweatt* v. *Painter* (1950), the Court made a similar point with specific reference to legal education: "The law school, the proving ground for legal learning and practice, cannot be effective in isolation from the individuals and institutions with which the law interacts. Few students, and no one who has practiced law, would choose to study in an academic vacuum, removed from the interplay of ideas and the exchange of views with which the law is concerned."

Physicians serve a heterogeneous population. An otherwise qualified medical student with a particular background—whether it be ethnic, geographic, culturally advantaged or disadvantaged—may bring to a professional school of medicine experiences, outlooks, and ideas that enrich the training of its student body and better equip its graduates to render with understanding their vital service to humanity.

Ethnic diversity, however, is only one element in a range of factors a university properly may consider in attaining the goal of a heterogeneous student body. Although a university must have wide discretion in making the sensitive judgments as to who should be admitted, constitutional limitations protecting individual rights may not be disregarded. Respondent urges—and the courts below have held—that petitioner's dual admissions program is a racial classification that impermissibly infringes his rights under the Fourteenth Amendment. As the interest of diversity is compelling in the context of a university's admissions program, the question remains whether the program's racial classification is necessary to promote this interest. . . .

It may be assumed that the reservation of a specified number of seats in each class for individuals from the preferred ethnic groups would contribute to the attainment of considerable ethnic diversity in the student body. But petitioner's argument that this is the only effective means of serving the interest of diversity is seriously flawed. In a most fundamental sense, the argument misconceives the nature of the state interest that would justify consideration of race or ethnic background. It is not an interest in simple ethnic diversity, in which a specified percentage of the student body is in effect guaranteed to be members of selected ethnic groups, with the remaining percentage an undifferentiated aggregation of students. The diversity that furthers a compelling state interest encompasses a far broader array of qualifications and characteristics, of which racial or ethnic origin is but a single, though important, element. Petitioner's special admissions program, focused solely on ethnic diversity, would hinder, rather than further, attainment of genuine diversity. . . .

The experience of other university admissions programs, which take race into account in achieving the educational diversity valued by the First Amendment, demonstrates that the assignment of a fixed number of places to a minority group is not a necessary means toward that end. An illuminating example is found in the Harvard College program:

> In recent years, Harvard College has expanded the concept of diversity to include students from disadvantaged economic, racial and ethnic groups. Harvard College now recruits not only Californians or Louisianans but also blacks and Chicanos and other minority students. . . .
>
> In practice, this new definition of diversity has meant that race has been a factor in some admission decisions. When the Committee on Admissions reviews the large middle group of applicants who are "admissible" and deemed capable of doing good work in their courses, the race of an applicant may tip the balance in his favor just as geographic origin or a life spent on a farm may tip the balance in other candidates' cases. A farm boy from Idaho can bring something to Harvard College that a Bostonian cannot offer. Similarly, a black student can usually bring something that a white person cannot offer. . . .

> In Harvard College admissions, the Committee has not set target quotas for the number of blacks, or of musicians, football players, physicists or Californians to be admitted in a given year. . . . But that awareness [of the necessity of including more than a token number of black students] does not mean that the Committee sets a minimum number of blacks or of people from west of the Mississippi who are to be admitted. It means only that, in choosing among thousands of applicants who are not only "admissible" academically but have other strong qualities, the Committee, with a number of criteria in mind, pays some attention to distribution among many types and categories of students.

In such an admissions program, race or ethnic background may be deemed a "plus" in a particular applicant's file, yet it does not insulate the individual from comparison with all other candidates for the available seats. The file of a particular black applicant may be examined for his potential contribution to diversity without the factor of race being decisive when compared, for example, with that of an applicant identified as an Italian-American if the latter is thought to exhibit qualities more likely to promote beneficial educational pluralism. Such qualities could include exceptional personal talents, unique work or service experience, leadership potential, maturity, demonstrated compassion, a history of overcoming disadvantage, ability to communicate with the poor, or other qualifications deemed important. In short, an admissions program operated in this way is flexible enough to consider all pertinent elements of diversity in light of the particular qualifications of each applicant, and to place them on the same footing for consideration, although not necessarily according them the same weight. Indeed, the weight attributed to a particular quality may vary from year to year depending upon the "mix" both of the student body and the applicants for the incoming class.

This kind of program treats each applicant as an individual in the admissions process. The applicant who loses out on the last available seat to another candidate receiving a "plus" on the basis of ethnic background will not have been foreclosed from all consideration for that seat simply because he was not the right color or had the wrong surname. It would mean only that his combined qualifications, which may have included similar nonobjective factors, did not outweigh those of the other applicant. His qualifications would have been weighed fairly and competitively, and he would have no basis to complain of unequal treatment under the Fourteenth Amendment.

It has been suggested that an admissions program which considers race only as one factor is simply a subtle and more sophisticated—but no less effective—means of according racial preference than the Davis program. A facial intent to discriminate, however, is evident in petitioner's preference program, and not denied in this case. No such facial infirmity exists in an admissions program where race or ethnic background is simply one element—to be weighed fairly against other elements—in the selection process. . . . And a court would not assume that a university, professing to employ a facially nondiscriminatory admissions policy, would operate it as a cover for the functional equivalent of a quota system. In short, good faith would be presumed in the absence of a showing to the contrary in the manner permitted by our cases.

In summary, it is evident that the Davis special admissions program involves the use of an explicit racial classification never before countenanced by this Court. It tells applicants who are not Negro, Asian, or Chicano that they are totally excluded from a specific percentage of the seats in an entering class. No matter how strong their qualifications, quantitative and extracurricular, including their own potential for contribution to educational diversity, they are never afforded the chance to compete with applicants from the preferred groups for the special admissions seats. At the same time, the preferred applicants have the opportunity to compete for every seat in the class.

The fatal flaw in petitioner's preferential program is its disregard of individual rights as guaranteed by the Fourteenth Amendment. Such rights are not absolute. But when a State's distribution of benefits or imposition of burdens hinges on ancestry or the color of a person's skin, that individual is entitled to a demonstration that the challenged classification is necessary to promote a substantial state interest. Petitioner has failed to carry this burden. For this reason, that portion of the California court's judgment holding petitioner's special admissions program invalid under the Fourteenth Amendment must be affirmed.

In enjoining petitioner from ever considering the race of any applicant, however, the courts below failed to recognize that the State has a substantial interest that legitimately may be served by a properly devised admissions program involving the competitive consideration of race and ethnic origin. For this reason, so much of the California court's judgment as enjoins petitioner from any consideration of the race of any applicant must be reversed.

Affirmed in part and reversed in part.

TABLE 11.1 Grade Point Averages and MCAT Scores of the Entering Class at the University of California at Davis Medical School, 1973 and 1974

	SGPA	OGPA	Verbal	Quantitative	Science	General
1973						
Allan Bakke	3.44	3.46	96	94	97	72
Regular Admissions	3.51	3.49	81	76	83	69
Special Admissions	2.62	2.88	46	24	35	33
1974						
Allan Bakke	3.44	3.46	96	94	97	72
Regular Admissions	3.36	3.29	69	67	82	72
Special Admissions	2.42	2.62	34	30	37	18

Key: SGPA = Science Grade Point Average
OGPA = Overall Grade Point Average
Source: *Regents of the University of California* v. *Bakke* (1978).

Justice Powell's opinion synthesized the rationale of the Court's earlier decisions in *Griggs* and *Swann* upholding race-conscious remedies. Race was a permissible tool to promote an important social or educational objective, but there had to be some demonstrable relationship between means and ends. Powell concluded that Davis had an important interest in addressing prior discrimination at the institutional and social levels, promoting educational diversity, increasing the number of minorities in the medical profession, and improving the delivery of health care services to minority communities. These interests justified giving race heavy consideration in the admissions process. On the other hand, Justice Powell noted that Davis could not utilize a quota to achieve those goals. Instead, Davis—and all other colleges, universities, and professional schools with affirmative action programs—needed to state their minority admissions objectives in terms of "goals" and "timetables." Critics of Powell's opinion argued there was not much of a real difference between a "quota" and a "goal." In the end, though, it was Powell's approach that carried the day.

For a decade after *Bakke,* the Court upheld the use of goals, timetables, and, in some cases, even quotas to achieve racial balance in employment, increase minority participation in public contracting programs, or compensate for prior discrimination. In *Johnson* v. *Transportation Agency* (1987), the Court ruled that sex could be considered to address issues of discrimination and diversity in employment involving women, bringing affirmative action for women under the explicit protection of the Constitution.[66] On occasion, the Court struck down affirmative action programs as unworkable or unrelated to the objectives they were trying to achieve, but such cases were rare. The Court's position on affirmative action stood in contrast to the position of the Department of Justice under President Ronald Reagan (1981–1989). The Reagan Administration put the elimination of race-conscious remedies near the top of its list and had supported several plaintiffs challenging their legality. Then, in June 1989, six months after President Reagan left office, the Court rewarded his administration's persistence when, in *City of Richmond* v. *J. A. Croson,* it handed down its most important affirmative action decision since *Bakke*. *Croson* suggested that the Court was prepared to examine anew the underlying foundations of race-conscious measures to address the consequences of discrimination.

City of Richmond v. *J. A. Croson*

488 U.S. 469 (1989)

The Reagan administration opposed affirmative action on two fronts. One was political: Race-conscious remedies hurt white men the most, and white men made up the core of President Reagan's support. The second had more intellectual origins: The notion that the Fourteenth Amendment's "universal" language could be interpreted to permit the use of race, even if for positive purposes, was inconsistent with the original intent of the Reconstruction-era Congress that wrote and ratified it. The Department of Justice under President Reagan was staffed with conservative legal scholars who believed undoing affirmative action was necessary to restore the proper meaning of the Fourteenth Amendment. For eight years, an intense battle waged between civil rights groups, which argued that the Fourteenth Amendment permitted—even required—race-conscious measures to advance minority interests, and the Reagan administration, which insisted that the Constitution was colorblind and should be interpreted as such.

Croson became the vehicle to advance the Reagan administration's cause after it had determined the judicial climate had become more favorable to its position on affirmative action. In 1985, the Justice Department found itself drawn to a complaint filed by the J. A. Croson Co., a contractor that had bid on a Richmond, Virginia, public works project. The company learned it was denied a contract to provide plumbing fixtures for the local jail because it could not obtain a minority-owned business enterprise (MBE) to supply parts and materials. Moreover, the city located another minority-owned company and awarded it a contract, even though its bid came in several thousand dollars higher. This decision was based on a Richmond program that set 30 percent of its public contracts aside for MBEs. A federal district court upheld the Richmond program against Croson's complaint that it was unconstitutional. But the Fourth Circuit Court of Appeals, home to many appointees of President Reagan, reversed the lower court.

The Department of Justice filed a friend of the court brief urging the Court to strike down the Richmond program and, in future cases, prohibit any form of race-conscious affirmative action unless it was tied to a particular, individualized act of discrimination. *Croson* attracted numerous *amici*, including over a dozen states whose programs stood to fall if the Court affirmed the Fourth Circuit's ruling. These states supported Richmond.

The Court's decision was 6 to 3. Justice O'Connor delivered the opinion of the Court. Justice Blackmun, joined by Justice Brennan, dissented, as did Justice Marshall, who was joined by Justices Blackmun and Brennan.

JUSTICE O'CONNOR . . . delivered the opinion of the Court.

In this case, we confront once again the tension between the Fourteenth Amendment's guarantee of equal treatment to all citizens, and the use of race-based measures to ameliorate the effects of past discrimination on the opportunities enjoyed by members of minority groups in our society. . . .

Congress, unlike any State or political subdivision, has a specific constitutional mandate to enforce the dictates of the Fourteenth Amendment. The power to "enforce" may at times also include the power to define situations which *Congress* determines threaten principles of equality, and to adopt prophylactic rules to deal with those situations. The Civil War Amendments themselves worked a dramatic change in the balance between congressional and state power over matters of race. Speaking of the Thirteenth and Fourteenth Amendments in *Ex parte Virginia* (1880), the Court stated: "They were intended to be, what they really are, limitations of the powers of the States and enlargements of the power of Congress."

That Congress may identify and redress the effects of society-wide discrimination does not mean that . . . the States and their political subdivisions are free to decide that such remedies are appropriate. Section 1 of the Fourteenth Amendment is an explicit *constraint* on state power, and the States must undertake any remedial efforts in accordance with that provision. To hold otherwise would be to cede control over the content of the Equal Protection Clause to the 50 state legislatures and their myriad political subdivisions. The mere recitation of a benign or compensatory purpose for the use of a racial classification would essentially entitle the States to exercise the full power of Congress under § 5 of the Fourteenth Amendment and insulate any racial classification from judicial scrutiny under Section 1. We believe that such a result would be contrary to the intentions of the Framers of the Fourteenth Amendment, who desired to place clear limits on the States' use of race as a criterion for legislative action, and to have the federal courts enforce those limitations.

We do not . . . find in Section 5 of the Fourteenth Amendment some form of federal preemption in matters of race. We simply note what should be apparent to all—Section 1 of the Fourteenth Amendment stemmed from a distrust of state legislative enactments based on race; Section 5 is . . . "'a *positive* grant of legislative power'" to Congress. . . .

It would seem equally clear, however, that a state or local subdivision (if delegated the authority from the State) has the authority to eradicate the effects of private discrimination within its own legislative jurisdiction. This authority must, of course, be exercised within the constraints of Section 1 of the Fourteenth Amendment. . . .

Thus, if the city could show that it had essentially become a "passive participant" in a system of racial exclusion practiced by elements of the local construction industry, we think it clear that the city could take affirmative steps to dismantle such a system. It is beyond dispute that any public entity, state or federal, has a compelling interest in assuring that public dollars, drawn from the tax contributions of all citizens, do not serve to finance the evil of private prejudice.

The Equal Protection Clause of the Fourteenth Amendment provides that "[N]o State shall . . . deny to *any person* within its jurisdiction the equal protection of the laws." . . . The Richmond Plan denies certain citizens the opportunity to compete for a fixed percentage of public contracts based solely upon their race. To whatever racial group these citizens belong, their "personal rights" to be treated with equal dignity and respect are implicated by a rigid rule erecting race as the sole criterion in an aspect of public decision making.

Absent searching judicial inquiry into the justification for such race-based measures, there is simply no way of determining what classifications are "benign" or "remedial" and what classifications are in fact motivated by illegitimate notions of racial inferiority or simple racial politics. Indeed, the purpose of strict scrutiny is to "smoke out" illegitimate uses of race by assuring that the legislative body is pursuing a goal important enough to warrant use of a highly suspect tool. The test also ensures that the means chosen "fit" this compelling goal so closely that there is little or no possibility that the motive for the classification was illegitimate racial prejudice or stereotype.

Classifications based on race carry a danger of stigmatic harm. Unless they are strictly reserved for remedial settings, they may in fact promote notions of racial inferiority, and lead to a politics of racial hostility. We thus reaffirm the view expressed by the plurality in *Wygant* [v. *Jackson Board of Education* (1986)], that the standard of review under the Equal Protection Clause is not dependent on the race of those burdened or benefited by a particular classification. . . .

Even were we to accept a reading of the guarantee of equal protection under which the level of scrutiny varies according to the ability of different groups to defend their interests in the representative process, heightened scrutiny would still be appropriate in the circumstances of this case. One of the central arguments for applying a less exacting standard to "benign" racial classifications is that such measures essentially involve a choice made by dominant racial groups to disadvantage themselves. If one aspect of the judiciary's role under the Equal Protection Clause is to protect "discrete and insular minorities" from majoritarian prejudice or indifference, *United States* v. *Carolene Products Co.* (1938), some maintain that these concerns are not implicated when the "white majority" places burdens upon itself. *See* J. Ely, *Democracy and Distrust* (1980).

In this case, blacks comprise approximately 50% of the population of the city of Richmond. Five of the nine seats on the city council are held by blacks. The concern that a political majority will more easily act to the disadvantage of a minority based on unwarranted assumptions or incomplete facts would seem to militate for, not against, the application of heightened judicial scrutiny in this case.

In *Bakke,* the Court confronted a racial quota employed by the University of California at Davis Medical School. Under the plan, 16 out of 100 seats in each entering class at the school were reserved exclusively for certain minority groups. Among the justifications offered in support of the plan were the desire to "reduc[e] the historic deficit of traditionally disfavored minorities in medical school and the medical profession" and the need to "counte[r] the effects of societal discrimination." Five Members of the Court determined that none of these interests could justify a plan that completely eliminated nonminorities from consideration for a specified percentage of opportunities. . . .

[The city of Richmond] argues that it is attempting to remedy various forms of past discrimination that are alleged to be responsible for the small number of minority businesses in the local contracting industry. Among these, the city cites the exclusion of blacks from skilled construction trade unions and training programs. This past discrimination has prevented them "from following the traditional path from laborer to entrepreneur." The city also lists a host of nonracial factors which would seem to face a member of any racial group attempting to establish a new business enterprise, such as deficiencies in working capital, inability to meet bonding requirements, unfamiliarity with bidding procedures, and disability caused by an inadequate track record. . . .

It is sheer speculation how many minority firms there would be in Richmond absent past societal discrimination, just as it was sheer speculation how many minority medical students would have been admitted to the medical school at Davis absent past discrimination in educational opportunities. Defining these sorts of injuries as "identified discrimination" would give local governments license to create a patchwork of racial preferences based on statistical generalizations about any particular field of endeavor.

These defects are readily apparent in this case. The 30% quota cannot in any realistic sense be tied to any injury suffered by anyone. The District Court relied upon five predicate "facts" in reaching its conclusion that there was an adequate basis for the 30% quota: (1) the ordinance declares itself to be remedial; (2) several proponents of the measure stated their views that there had been past discrimination in the construction industry; (3) minority businesses received 0.67% of prime contracts from the city while minorities constituted 50% of the city's population; (4) there were very few minority contractors in local and state contractors' associations; and (5) in 1977, Congress made a determination that the effects of past discrimination had stifled minority participation in the construction industry nationally.

None of these "findings," singly or together, provide the city of Richmond with a "strong basis in evidence for its conclusion that remedial action was necessary." There is nothing approaching a *prima facie* case of a constitutional or statutory violation by anyone in the Richmond construction industry. . . . [T]he mere recitation of a "benign" or legitimate purpose for a racial classification is entitled to little or no weight. Racial classifications are suspect, and that means that simple legislative assurances of good intention cannot suffice. . . .

Reliance on the disparity between the number of prime contracts awarded to minority firms and the minority population of the city of Richmond is similarly misplaced. There is no doubt that "[w]here gross statistical disparities can be shown, they alone in a proper case may constitute *prima facie* proof of a pattern or practice of discrimination under Title VII." But it is equally clear that "[w]hen special qualifications are required to fill particular jobs, comparisons to the general population (rather than to the smaller group of individuals who possess the necessary qualifications) may have little probative value." . . .

In this case, the city does not even know how many MBE's in the relevant market are qualified to undertake prime or subcontracting work in public construction projects. Nor does the city know what percentage of total city construction dollars minority firms now receive as subcontractors on prime contracts let by the city. . . .

Finally, the city and the District Court relied on Congress' finding in connection with the set-aside approved in *Fullilove* [v. *Klutznick* (1980)] that there had been nationwide discrimination in the construction industry. The probative value of these findings for demonstrating the existence of discrimination in Richmond is extremely limited. By its inclusion of a waiver procedure in the national program addressed in *Fullilove,* Congress explicitly recognized that the scope of the problem would vary from market area to market area. . . .

In sum, none of the evidence presented by the city points to any identified discrimination in the Richmond construction industry. We therefore hold that the city has failed to demonstrate a compelling interest in apportioning public contracting opportunities on the basis of race. To accept Richmond's claim that past societal discrimination alone can serve as the basis for rigid racial preferences would be to open the door to competing claims for "remedial relief" for every disadvantaged group. The dream of a Nation of equal citizens in a society where race is irrelevant to personal opportunity and achievement would be lost in a mosaic of shifting preferences based on inherently unmeasurable claims of past wrongs. . . .

The foregoing analysis applies only to the inclusion of blacks within the Richmond set-aside program. There is *absolutely no evidence* of past discrimination against Spanish-speaking, Oriental, Indian, Eskimo, or Aleut persons in any aspect of the Richmond construction industry. The District Court took judicial notice of the fact that the vast majority of "minority" persons in Richmond were black. It may well be that Richmond has never had an Aleut or Eskimo citizen. The random inclusion of racial groups that, as a practical matter, may never have suffered from discrimination in the construction industry in Richmond suggests that perhaps the city's purpose was not in fact to remedy past discrimination. . . .

As noted by the court below, it is almost impossible to assess whether the Richmond Plan is narrowly tailored to remedy prior discrimination, since it is not linked to identified discrimination in any way. We limit ourselves to two observations in this regard.

First, there does not appear to have been any consideration of the use of race-neutral means to increase minority business participation in city contracting. Many of the barriers to minority participation in the construction industry relied upon by the city to justify a racial classification appear to be race-neutral. If MBE's disproportionately lack capital or cannot meet bonding requirements, a race-neutral program of city financing for small firms would, *a fortiori*, lead to greater minority participation. The principal opinion in *Fullilove* found that Congress had carefully examined and rejected race-neutral alternatives before enacting the MBE set-aside. There is no evidence in this record that the Richmond City Council has considered any alternatives to a race-based quota.

Second, the 30% quota cannot be said to be narrowly tailored to any goal, except perhaps outright racial balancing. It rests upon the "completely unrealistic" assumption that minorities will choose a particular trade in lockstep proportion to their representation in the local population. . . .

Under Richmond's scheme, a successful black, Hispanic, or Oriental entrepreneur from anywhere in the country enjoys an absolute preference over other citizens based solely on their race. We think it obvious that such a program is not narrowly tailored to remedy the effects of prior discrimination.

Nothing we say today precludes a state or local entity from taking action to rectify the effects of identified discrimination within its jurisdiction. If the city of Richmond had evidence before it that nonminority contractors were systematically excluding minority businesses from subcontracting opportunities, it could take action to end the discriminatory exclusion. Where there is a significant statistical disparity between the number of qualified minority contractors willing and able to perform a particular service and the number of such contractors actually engaged by the locality or the locality's prime contractors, an inference of discriminatory exclusion could arise. Under such circumstances, the city could act to dismantle the closed business system by taking appropriate measures against those who discriminate on the basis of race or other illegitimate criteria. In the extreme case, some form of narrowly tailored racial preference might be necessary to break down patterns of deliberate exclusion.

Nor is local government powerless to deal with individual instances of racially motivated refusals to employ minority contractors. Where such discrimination occurs, a city would be justified in penalizing the discriminator and providing appropriate relief to the victim of such discrimination. Moreover, evidence of a pattern of individual discriminatory acts can, if supported by appropriate statistical proof, lend support to a local government's determination that broader remedial relief is justified. . . .

Because the city of Richmond has failed to identify the need for remedial action in the awarding of its public construction contracts, its treatment of its citizens on a racial basis violates the dictates of the Equal Protection Clause. Accordingly, the judgment of the Court of Appeals for the Fourth Circuit is

Affirmed.

JUSTICE SCALIA, concurring in the judgment.

I agree with much of the Court's opinion, and, in particular, with JUSTICE O'CONNOR's conclusion that strict scrutiny must be applied to all governmental classification by race, whether or not its asserted purpose is "remedial" or "benign." I do not agree, however, with JUSTICE O'CONNOR's dictum suggesting that, despite the Fourteenth Amendment, state and local governments may in some circumstances discriminate on the basis of race in order (in a broad sense) "to ameliorate the effects of past discrimination." The benign purpose of compensating for social disadvantages, whether they have been acquired by reason of prior discrimination or otherwise, can no more be pursued by the illegitimate means of racial discrimination than can other assertedly benign purposes we have repeatedly rejected. The difficulty of overcoming the effects of past discrimination is as nothing compared with the difficulty of eradicating from our society the source of those effects, which is the tendency—fatal to a Nation such as ours—to classify and judge men and women on the basis of their country of origin or the color of their skin. . . .

In my view, there is only one circumstance in which the States may act by race to "undo the effects of past discrimination:" where that is necessary to eliminate their own maintenance of a system of unlawful racial classification. If, for example, a state agency has a discriminatory pay scale compensating black employees in all positions at 20% less than their nonblack counterparts, it may assuredly promulgate an order raising the salaries of "all black employees" to eliminate the differential. This distinction explains our school desegregation cases, in which we have made plain that States and localities sometimes have an obligation to adopt race-conscious remedies. . . .

It is plainly true that, in our society, blacks have suffered discrimination immeasurably greater than any directed at other racial groups. But those who believe that racial preferences can help to "even the score" display, and reinforce, a manner of thinking by race that was the source of the injustice and that will, if it endures within our society, be the source of more injustice still. The relevant proposition is not that it was blacks, or Jews, or Irish who were discriminated against, but that it was individual men and women, "created equal," who were discriminated against. And the relevant resolve is that that should never happen again. Racial preferences appear to "even the score" (in some small degree) only if one embraces the proposition that our society is appropriately viewed as divided into races, making it right that an injustice rendered in the past to a black man should be compensated for by discriminating against a white. Nothing is worth that embrace. Since blacks have been disproportionately disadvantaged by racial discrimination, any race-neutral remedial program aimed at the disadvantaged as such will have a disproportionately beneficial impact on blacks. Only such a program, and not one that operates on the basis of race, is in accord with the letter and the spirit of our Constitution.

Since I believe that the appellee here had a constitutional right to have its bid succeed or fail under a decision making process uninfected with racial bias, I concur in the judgment of the Court.

JUSTICE MARSHALL, with whom JUSTICE BRENNAN and JUSTICE BLACKMUN join, dissenting.

It is a welcome symbol of racial progress when the former capital of the Confederacy acts forthrightly to confront the effects of racial discrimination in its midst. . . . [But] today's decision marks a deliberate and giant step backward in this Court's affirmative action jurisprudence. Cynical of one municipality's attempt to redress the effects of racial discrimination in a particular industry, the majority launches a grapeshot attack on race-conscious remedies in general. The majority's unnecessary pronouncements will inevitably discourage or prevent governmental entities, particularly States and localities, from acting to rectify the scourge of past discrimination. This is the harsh reality of the majority's decision, but it is not the Constitution's command. . . .

However, I am compelled to add [that] . . . the majority has gone beyond the facts of this case to announce a set of principles which unnecessarily restricts the power of governmental entities to take race-conscious measures to redress the effects of prior discrimination.

Today, for the first time, a majority of this Court has adopted strict scrutiny as its standard of Equal Protection Clause review of race-conscious remedial measures. This is an unwelcome development. A profound difference separates governmental actions that themselves are racist and governmental actions that seek to remedy the effects of prior racism or to prevent neutral governmental activity from perpetuating the effects of such racism.

Racial classifications "drawn on the presumption that one race is inferior to another or because they put the weight of government behind racial hatred and separatism warrant the strictest judicial scrutiny because of the very irrelevance of these rationales." By contrast, racial classifications drawn for the purpose of remedying the effects of discrimination that itself was race-based have a highly pertinent basis: the tragic and indelible fact that discrimination against blacks and other racial minorities in this Nation has pervaded our Nation's history, and continues to scar our society. . . .

In concluding that remedial classifications warrant no different standard of review under the Constitution than the most brutal and repugnant forms of state-sponsored racism, a majority of this Court signals that it regards racial discrimination as largely a phenomenon of the past, and that government bodies need no longer preoccupy themselves with rectifying racial injustice. I, however, do not believe this Nation is anywhere close to eradicating racial discrimination or its vestiges. In constitutionalizing its wishful thinking, the majority today does a grave disservice not only to those victims of past and present racial discrimination in this Nation whom government has sought to assist, but also to this Court's long tradition of approaching issues of race with the utmost sensitivity. . . .

[I]t is too late in the day to assert seriously that the Equal Protection Clause prohibits States—or for that matter, the Federal Government, to whom the equal protection guarantee has largely been applied—from enacting race-conscious remedies. Our cases in the areas of school desegregation, voting rights, and affirmative action have demonstrated time and again that race is constitutionally germane, precisely because race remains dismayingly relevant in American life. . . .

The majority today sounds a full-scale retreat from the Court's longstanding solicitude to race-conscious remedial efforts "directed toward deliverance of the century-old promise of equality of economic opportunity." The new and restrictive tests it applies scuttle one city's effort to surmount its discriminatory past, and imperil those of dozens more localities. I, however, profoundly disagree with the cramped vision of the Equal Protection Clause which the majority offers today, and with its application of that vision to Richmond, Virginia's, laudable set-aside plan. The battle against pernicious racial discrimination or its effects is nowhere near won. I must dissent.

JUSTICE BLACKMUN, with whom JUSTICE BRENNAN joins, dissenting.

I join JUSTICE MARSHALL's perceptive and incisive opinion revealing great sensitivity toward those who have suffered the pains of economic discrimination in the construction trades for so long.

I never thought that I would live to see the day when the city of Richmond, Virginia, the cradle of the Old Confederacy, sought on its own, within a narrow confine, to lessen the stark impact of persistent discrimination. But Richmond, to its great credit, acted. Yet this Court, the supposed bastion of equality, strikes down Richmond's efforts as though discrimination had never existed or was not demonstrated in this particular litigation. JUSTICE MARSHALL convincingly discloses the fallacy and the shallowness of that approach. History is irrefutable, even though one might sympathize with those who—though possibly innocent in themselves—benefit from the wrongs of past decades.

So the Court today regresses. I am confident, however, that, given time, it one day again will do its best to fulfill the great promises of the Constitution's Preamble and of the guarantees embodied in the Bill of Rights—a fulfillment that would make this Nation very special.

"I like you, Jim, not because you're black but because you have excellent qualifications."

Justice O'Connor did not extend her analysis in *Croson* beyond the immediate facts of the case, but the implications for affirmative action in other fields were clear. In holding that minority set asides in state and local public contracting programs were permissible only when the government (1) had demonstrated a clear history of prior discrimination and (2) had crafted a remedy that was narrowly tailored to address such discrimination, O'Connor had given opponents of affirmative action their first real victory since *Bakke*. Of critical importance was O'Connor's conclusion that *all* racial classifications in the law, regardless of their motive or objective, had to satisfy "strict scrutiny," a standard once solely reserved for purposeful discrimination and its "vestiges."

Six years later, the Court applied the *Croson* standard to federal set-aside programs, holding that Congress and executive agencies responsible must also demonstrate a "compelling" government interest to defend the use of race-conscious measures. In *Adarand Constructors, Inc.* v. *Pena* (1995), the Court, as in *Croson,* did not address affirmative action outside the sphere of public contracting, but it sent another clear message on the appropriateness of race-conscious measures to address prior discrimination or promote diversity and minority representation in public policy programs.[67] *Adarand* prompted President Bill Clinton (1993–2001), a supporter of affirmative action, to order his administration to conduct a review of all such federal programs for compliance with the Court's new standards. In 1996, the Clinton administration issued a report calling for the government, private employers, and universities to work together to "mend, not end" affirmative action. In *Adarand,* the Department of Justice had filed a brief in support of the federal government's contracting program, the first time since the Carter administration that the executive branch had defended affirmative action before the Supreme Court.

Neither the constitutional status of affirmative action nor litigation to challenge existing race-conscious programs in education, employment, and public contracting is a settled matter. Since *Bakke,* several conservative public interest law firms have brought lawsuits on behalf of individuals wishing to challenge race-conscious measures. In contrast to the pre-*Bakke* era of desegregation and race-based remedies, the litigation environment is no longer dominated by liberal groups working in a judicially favorable climate. Rather, affirmative action litigation is now more plural, complex, and contentious, reflecting the social and political forces at play in this continuing controversy.

Sex Discrimination

On March 31, 1776, Abigail Adams wrote a letter to her husband, John, to discuss the "new code of laws" that would reflect the spirit of the Declaration of Independence that he and the other great *men* of the Founding generation were preparing to write. Abigail admonished her husband to "remember the ladies and be more generous and favorable to them than your ancestors. Do not put such unlimited power into the hands of the husbands." She continued, "[A]ll men would be tyrants if they could. If particular care and attention is not paid to the ladies, we are determined to foment a rebellion, and will not hold ourselves bound by any laws in which we have no voice or representation." John Adams, by any account a great man—key architect of the Constitution, future president, and respected statesman—brushed off his wife's concerns. Two weeks later, he responded, "As to your extraordinary code of laws, I cannot but laugh . . . [Y]our letter was the first intimation that another tribe, more numerous and powerful than all the rest, were grown discontented." Abigail responded: "I cannot say that I think you are very generous to the ladies; for whilst you are proclaiming peace and goodwill to men, emancipating all nations, you insist on retaining an absolute power over wives. . . . Arbitrary power is like most other things which are very hard, very liable to be broken."[68]

Abigail Adams was a bold and articulate voice on behalf of women's rights during the Revolution and in the years after ratification of the Constitution. Hers was also a lonely and unheeded voice, as women were by custom and ultimately law relegated to an entirely separate societal sphere from men, one that consisted solely of the home, family, and domestic concerns. Women who married forfeited their legal existence, as a wife became the property of her husband. This principle, known as *coverture*, was derived from British common law.[69] A husband controlled all the marital property, including the property he acquired from his wife when he married her, any wages she may have earned or continued to earn through menial employment, and the right to enter into contracts without her consent. Because of the unitary status of marriage, women could not testify against their husbands in a criminal proceeding, since that would be the equivalent of testifying against one's self. Finally, the most fundamental of democratic rights, the right to vote, was denied to women. Property ownership was a condition of suffrage in most states, and since women were divested of their property upon marriage, they were, under law, not a person with any vested interests in politics and society.[70]

By the 1830s, women had begun to make modest gains in their legal and social status. Several states enacted laws that allowed women to retain the property they brought into marriage, although no state even considered granting women the right to vote. For the first time, women formed associations and entered the public sphere—the world of business and politics was reserved for men—to advocate reform on the pressing moral issues of the day, such as improper sexual behavior, alcohol abuse, and violence against women. The most daring and overtly political cause of the early women's movement was the "sin of slavery." Between 1833, when the Female Anti-Slavery Society formed in Philadelphia, and 1861, the outbreak of the Civil War, women's groups collected hundreds of thousands of signatures and joined many male abolitionist groups to demand an end to slavery.[71]

Women's involvement in the abolitionist movement led them to demand greater attention to their own inferior legal status. In 1840, Elizabeth Cady Stanton and Lucretia Mott, two prominent women active in the abolitionist cause, attended the World Anti-Slavery Convention in London, only to learn that its male organizers would not seat women on the convention floor. Incensed, Stanton and Mott returned to the United States determined to make a bold statement about the need to revolutionize the place of women in American society. In 1848, about three hundred women's rights activists met in Seneca Falls, New York, to draft the equivalent of a Declaration of Independence for women. The Seneca Falls Declaration of Sentiments read, in part:

> When in the course of human events it becomes necessary for one portion of the family of man to assume among the peoples of the earth a position different from that they have hitherto occupied . . .
>
> We hold these truths to be self-evident: that all men and women are created equal; that they are endowed by their Creator with certain inalienable rights; that among these are life, liberty, and the pursuit of happiness . . .
>
> The History of mankind is a history of repeated injuries and usurpations on the part of man toward woman, having

> in direct object the establishment of an absolute tyranny over her . . .
>
> He has never permitted her to exercise her inalienable right to the elective franchise . . .
>
> Having deprived her of this first right of a citizen, the elective franchise, thereby leaving her without representation in the halls of legislation, he has oppressed her on all sides . . .

The Seneca Falls Convention is generally credited for launching the first concerted wave of feminist activism, a period that lasted until the Supreme Court's decision in *Minor* v. *Happersett* (1875), which held that the Fourteenth Amendment did not establish a right to vote for women. The Court, building on the interpretation it had given the Fourteenth Amendment two years before in *The Slaughterhouse Cases* (see Chapter 3), ruled that the Privileges and Immunities Clause did not confer "new" rights, but merely gave constitutional protection to those already in existence. Suffrage, ruled the Court in *Happersett,* was not one the privileges and immunities of national citizenship:

> Certainly, if the courts can consider any question settled, this is one. For nearly ninety years the people have acted upon the idea that the Constitution, when it conferred citizenship, did not necessarily confer the right of suffrage. If uniform practice long continued can settle the construction of so important an instrument as the Constitution of the United States confessedly is, most certainly it has been done here. Our province is to decide what the law is, not to declare what it should be.
>
> If the law is wrong, it ought to be changed; but the power for that is not with us.[72]

Happersett ended the first major campaign of women to gain the right to vote, a cause that had actually divided several of the fledgling movement's most visible advocates. Feminists such as Susan B. Anthony and Elizabeth Cady Stanton had actually opposed the ratification of the Fourteenth Amendment because it specifically inserted, for the first time, the word "male" into the Constitution. Section 2 described the punishment to any state that abridged the right to vote in any election of any of its *male* inhabitants—its representation "shall be reduced in the proportion which the number of such male citizens shall bear to the whole number of *male* citizens twenty-one years of age in such State." Other women's rights activists, including the abolitionist Frederick Douglass, argued that the Fourteenth Amendment "belong[ed] to the negro," leading Stanton to retort: "My question is this: Do you believe the African race is composed entirely of males?"[73]

The fundamental disagreement over support for the Fourteenth Amendment and the Fifteenth Amendment, which, in guaranteeing the right to vote without regard to color, race, or previous condition of servitude, deliberately excluded sex, created an organizational split among feminists. Stanton and Anthony formed the National Woman Suffrage Association (NWSA) to lobby on behalf of a constitutional amendment securing the right of women to vote, insisting female suffrage was a national cause that required a national remedy. The NWSA ultimately refused to support the Fifteenth Amendment after it became clear that women's suffrage was not included among its protections. Other feminist leaders, such as Lucy Stone and male supporters such as Henry Blackwell, formed the American Woman Suffrage Association (ASWA), and continued to support the Fifteenth Amendment's core purpose of black enfranchisement and to work for women's suffrage on a state-by-state basis. ASWA leaders were convinced that the Republicans would turn their attention to women's suffrage once they had secured the political rights of African Americans. Such hope quickly evaporated, as the Republicans did not place women's suffrage in their convention platform until 1916.[74]

Separate Spheres Becomes the Law

As the NWSA and ASWA battled each other and the male-dominated world of politics to improve the status of women, the Court sent a clear signal two years before *Happersett* indicating what the rights of women were under the Fourteenth Amendment—that, basically, they did not have any. In *Bradwell* v. *Illinois* (1873), the Court held that the Privileges and Immunities Clause did not entitle a woman to enter the legal profession, even if she was professionally qualified. Notice as you read Justice Bradley's concurring opinion in *Bradwell* just how powerful the doctrine of coverture was in his legal analysis.

Bradwell v. *Illinois*

83 U.S. 130 (1873)

In October 1868, Myra Colby Bradwell published the first edition of the *Chicago Legal News*, the first weekly legal periodical published in the West, and the first to be edited by a woman. Bradwell had been drawn to the law after she married James Bolesworth Bradwell, a man of humble origins who financed his legal education by doing manual labor. Myra Bradwell had begun reading the law to assist her husband in setting up a law practice. Before long, Bradwell knew as much law as her husband. Limited by the restrictions placed on the rights of women to enter the legal profession, Bradwell turned her attention to publishing. The *Chicago Legal News* was innovative in many respects: It concentrated on gathering information on new laws, judicial opinions, and other important developments of interest to the legal community. It soon became an indispensable tool for lawyers throughout Illinois.

Bradwell also used the *Chicago Legal News* as a platform to advocate the expansion of women's rights, writing a column called "The Law Relating to Women." Bradwell challenged the coverture laws, established by men to benefit men, and succeeded in leading a modest reform effort that culminated with an 1869 Illinois law that allowed a woman to keep any money she earned for work outside the household. The law also permitted women to sue to return any earnings that were rightfully theirs. That same year, Bradwell took the Chicago bar exam and passed. She was denied admission to the legal profession because she was a married woman. After a series of appeals through the Illinois courts, Bradwell appealed to the United States Supreme Court.

The Court's decision was 8 to 1. Justice Miller delivered the opinion of the Court. Justice Bradley, joined by Justices Field and Swayne, filed a concurring opinion. Chief Justice Chase dissented, but filed no written opinion.

▼▲▼

MR. JUSTICE BRADLEY, concurring.

I concur in the judgment of the court in this case, by which the judgment of the Supreme Court of Illinois is affirmed, but not for the reasons specified in the opinion just read. The claim of the plaintiff, who is a married woman, to be admitted to practice as an attorney and counsellor-at-law, is based upon the supposed right of every person, man or woman, to engage in any lawful employment for a livelihood. The Supreme Court of Illinois denied the application on the ground that, by the common law, which is the basis of the laws of Illinois, only men were admitted to the bar, and the legislature had not made any change in this respect, but had simply provided that no person should be admitted to practice as attorney or counsellor without having previously obtained a license for that purpose from two justices of the Supreme Court, and that no person should receive a license without first obtaining a certificate from the court of some county of his good moral character. In other respects it was left to the discretion of the court to establish the rules by which admission to the profession should be determined. The court, however, regarded itself as bound by at least two limitations. One was that it should establish such terms of admission as would promote the proper administration of justice, and the other that it should not admit any persons, or class of persons, not intended by the legislature to be admitted, even though not expressly excluded by statute. In view of this latter limitation the court felt compelled to deny the application of females to be admitted as members of the bar. Being contrary to the rules of the common law and the usages of Westminster Hall from time immemorial, it could not be supposed that the legislature had intended to adopt any different rule.

The claim that, under the fourteenth amendment of the Constitution, which declares that no State shall make or enforce any law which shall abridge the privileges and immunities of citizens of the United States, the statute law of Illinois, or the common law prevailing in that State, can no longer be set up as a barrier against the right of females to pursue any lawful employment for a livelihood (the practice of law included), assumes that it is one of the privileges and immunities of women as citizens to engage in any and every profession, occupation, or employment in civil life. It certainly cannot be affirmed, as an historical fact, that this has ever been established as one of the fundamental privileges and immunities of the sex. On the contrary, the civil law, as well as nature herself, has always recognized a wide difference in the respective spheres and destinies of man and woman. Man is, or should be, woman's protector and defender. The natural and proper timidity and delicacy which belongs to the female sex evidently unfits it for many of the occupations of civil life. The constitution of the family organization, which is founded in the divine ordinance, as well as in the nature of things, indicates the domestic sphere as that which properly belongs to the domain and functions of womanhood. The harmony, not to say identity, of interest and views which belong, or should belong, to the family institution is repugnant to the idea of a woman adopting a distinct and independent career from that of her husband. So firmly fixed was this sentiment in the founders of the common law that it became a maxim of that system of jurisprudence that a woman had no legal existence separate from her husband, who was regarded as her head and representative in the social state; and, notwithstanding some recent modifications of this civil status, many of the special rules of law flowing from and dependent upon this cardinal principle still exist in full force in most States. One of these is, that a married woman is incapable, without her husband's consent, of making contracts which shall be binding on her or him. This very incapacity was one circumstance which the Supreme Court of Illinois deemed important in rendering a married woman incompetent fully to perform the duties and trusts that belong to the office of an attorney and counsellor.

It is true that many women are unmarried and not affected by any of the duties, complications, and incapacities arising out of the married state, but these are exceptions to the general rule. The paramount destiny and mission of woman are to fulfil the noble and benign offices of wife and mother. This is the law of the Creator. And the rules of civil society must be adapted to the general constitution of things, and cannot be based upon exceptional cases.

The humane movements of modern society, which have for their object the multiplication of avenues for woman's advancement, and of occupations adapted to her condition and sex, have my heartiest concurrence. But I am not prepared to say that it is one of her fundamental rights and privileges to be admitted into every office and position, including those which require highly special qualifications and demanding special responsibilities. In the nature of things it is not every citizen of every age, sex, and condition that is qualified for every calling and position. It is the prerogative of the legislator to prescribe regulations founded on nature, reason, and experience for the due admission of qualified persons to professions and callings demanding special skill and confidence. This fairly belongs to the police power of the State; and, in my opinion, in view of the peculiar characteristics, destiny, and mission of woman, it is within the province of the legislature to ordain what offices, positions, and callings shall be filled and discharged by men, and shall receive the benefit of those energies and responsibilities, and that decision and firmness which are presumed to predominate in the sterner sex.

For these reasons I think that the laws of Illinois now complained of are not obnoxious to the charge of abridging any of the privileges and immunities of citizens of the United States. . . .

Justice Bradley's concurring opinion is remarkable by twenty-first-century standards, but it was well within the mainstream of how the male-dominated worlds of business, law, and politics viewed women in the nineteenth century and, it is fair to say, well into the twentieth. His opinion offered no analysis of Myra Bradwell's constitutional claim that women were entitled to the same privileges and immunities under law as men. Instead, Bradley retreated into the "separate spheres" understanding of men's and women's roles in society to justify excluding women from the Fourteenth Amendment's coverage. According to Bradley, the "natural and proper timidity and delicacy" of women left them suited to the domestic sphere while men, the sterner sex, were, by their nature, left to occupy public life and the professions. All this, said Bradley, was the law of the Creator.

Bradwell foreshadowed *Happersett*, which was brought by the NWSA to publicize the cause of woman's suffrage. Susan B. Anthony and Elizabeth Cady Stanton had no illusions about the Court's attitude toward women's rights after *Bradwell*, but they did believe that litigation could serve as a useful vehicle to publicize their cause. Although they would not live to see the passage of the Nineteenth Amendment in 1920, which secured the constitutional right of women to vote, the efforts of Anthony, Stanton, Bradwell, Stone, and many others involved in the first wave of feminist activism were responsible for encouraging society to see women as people with rights, aspirations, and equal standing in an era that viewed them as mothers, wives, and little else.[75]

For almost one hundred years after *Happersett*, the "separate spheres" approach to sex roles continued to define the Court's conception of women's rights under the Fourteenth Amendment. In *Muller* v. *Oregon* (1908) (Volume 1, Chapter 9), the Court upheld an Oregon law limiting the number of hours that female laundresses could work per day. *Muller* was a notable exception during a period in American constitutional development in which the Court routinely struck down laws designed to limit child labor, establish a minimum wage, regulate prices, and generally legislate in the public interest. Beginning in the late 1890s and continuing until the Constitutional Revolution of 1937, the Court interpreted the Fourteenth Amendment to protect a near-absolute right of "liberty of contract" that banned economic regulation, unless the state could demonstrate that such regulation served an essential public interest. The Court had recognized as far back as 1837 that government could regulate the economy in the public interest; during the forty-year period from 1897 to 1937, it raised the bar to a height nearly impossible for states and localities to scale.

Oregon was represented by the National Consumers' League, which was led by Florence Kelley, a pioneering women's rights activist who sought to expose the harsh working conditions in which women and children found themselves after the Industrial Revolution. Kelley was able to persuade Louis Brandeis, the nation's premier public interest lawyer before his appointment to the Surpeme Court in 1916, to defend the Oregon law against a "liberty of contract" challenge brought by Curt Muller, who owned a Portland laundry. Brandeis, in a direct nod to the "separate spheres" understanding of sex roles, emphasized the need for protective legislation because of the physical weaknesses of women. A unanimous Court agreed, noting that the "physical structure and a proper discharge of her maternal functions . . . justify legislation [for women] to protect her from the greed as well as passion, of man."[76] Three years before, in *Lochner* v. *New York* (1905) (Volume 1, Chapter 9), the Court struck down, on "liberty of contract" grounds, a New York maximum work hour law for bakers, in large part because the law applied only to men. In keeping with "separate spheres" thinking, men did not need the protection of the state in making and carrying out business arrangements.[77]

Even after World War II, a time when women, either fueled by patriotism or out of necessity, worked in dirty, physically demanding factory jobs once reserved for men, putting the separate spheres model to its severest test, the Court clung to the old sexual stereotypes. In *Goessart* v. *Cleary* (1948), the Court, 6 to 3, upheld a Michigan law that prohibited women from working as bartenders because of the moral and social problems allegedly associated with that occupation. Justice Felix Frankfurter, for the first time, suggested that laws encroaching upon the equal protection of its citizens, including women, must serve some sort of rational basis. "The Constitution in enjoining the equal protection of the laws upon States precludes irrational discrimination as between persons or groups of persons in the incidence of a law," wrote Frankfurter. "[But] Michigan has not violated its duty to afford equal protection of its laws" to women by denying them the right to work as "barmaids."[78]

In 1961, the Court followed a similar approach in *Hoyt* v. *Florida*, ruling that a state could automatically exempt women from jury service unless they specifically asked to serve. A Florida woman was tried and convicted before an all-male jury for killing her unfaithful husband with a baseball bat. She challenged her conviction on sex discrimination grounds, claiming that had women served on her jury she would have received greater sympathy and thus increased her chances for acquittal. Justice John Harlan (II), whose grandfather had been the sole dissenter in *Plessy* v. *Ferguson*, wrote in *Hoyt* that women, "despite [their] enlightened emancipation . . . from the restrictions and protections of bygone years . . . are still regarded as the center of home and family life."[79] In another not-so-subtle embrace of the separate spheres model, the Court ruled that states could restrict the civic obligations of women to protect the integrity of the family.

By the early 1960s, however, a growing number of women, inspired by the courage and success of the African American civil rights movement, began openly to question their roles in American society. During this time, several long-time women's rights activists persuaded President Kennedy to appoint a national commission on the status of women. Chaired by former first lady and social activist Eleanor Roosevelt, the commission's purpose was to reassess the role of women in the economy, the family, and the legal system. It drew its membership from government agencies that dealt with issues that affected women, such as the Department of Labor, labor unions, universities, and such feminist groups as the National Woman's Party, which had formed in 1914 to campaign on behalf of female suffrage. In 1963, the commission released a meticulously documented report of the social and legal hurdles facing women in society. The report described employment discrimination, few child care options, and the lingering remnants of coverture laws that rendered women legal subordinates to men. That same year, President Kennedy, for the first time, issued an executive order banning sex discrimination in federal government employment. Following suit, Congress passed the Equal Pay Act of 1963, which banned a common form of employment discrimination against women: paying them less than men to perform the same work. Building on these victories, women's rights activists persuaded Congress to include "sex" in Title VII of the Civil Rights Act of 1964, the federal law banning discrimination in employment.[80]

But the strongest impetus for the next great wave of feminist activism emerged not from seasoned social and political activists, but from an obscure, self-described housewife from the New York City suburbs. Betty Goldstein had graduated from Smith College in 1942 and moved to Manhattan to explore the world of social and political activism long before it emerged on the national stage. She found work as a journalist, specializing in labor and civil rights issues, and soon developed a reputation as bright, well-connected, and socially conscious. Whatever dreams Goldstein may have had for independent fame and fortune quickly disappeared after she met and married a World War II veteran named Carl Friedan. By the early 1950s, Betty Friedan—she took her husband's last name without a second thought—lived in the suburbs with her husband and young family. She had been fired from her reporting job after her boss learned she was pregnant with her second child, the firing an act from which there was at the time no legal protection.

As a young mother, Friedan began to question many of the articles she read in the self-styled "women's magazines" that flourished as part of the great suburban boom of the years following World War II. Friedan was familiar with their content, as she had written articles on domestic and family matters for *Cosmopolitan, Mademoiselle,* and *Parents* magazines. But she soon noticed that the magazines focused on how women could please the men and children to whom they had dedicated their lives. Friedan discovered that she was not alone in the frustration, loneliness, and anxiety that she often felt in her role as full-time wife and mother. *McCall's*, a magazine that trumpeted the "domestic bliss" secured for women by unprecedented levels of economic prosperity, canceled an article it had asked Friedan to write about her college class. Fifteen years after graduation, most of the women with whom she spoke felt unfulfilled and resentful of their husbands' professional lives. Friedan turned her *McCall's* rejection into the basis for her first book, *The Feminine Mystique,* published in 1963. In it, Friedan argued that women needed to rise up against the social expectations created for women by the mass media and the "separate spheres" model of sex roles perpetuated by employers, educators, and politicians. The solution, wrote Friedan, was for women to look outside the home for meaningful work to overcome "the problem that has no name."[81]

The Rejection of Separate Spheres

By the late 1960s, *The Feminine Mystique* had encouraged socially conscious and politically active women to organize on behalf of women's rights. Several organizations grew out of this movement—including the National Organization for Women and the Women's Equity Action League—to lobby Congress and the state legislatures to enforce civil rights law and expand the range of legal protections for women. Feminists pressed the ACLU to expand its litigation work to include sex discrimination and other issues pertaining to women's rights. Such was the social and political climate that fueled the litigation that ultimately led the Court, in *Reed* v. *Reed* (1971), to invalidate, for the first time, a state law that discriminated against women under the Fourteenth Amendment.

Reed v. *Reed*

404 U.S. 71 (1971)

Reed arose when Richard Reed, the adopted son of Sally and Cecil Reed, died in March 1967, leaving no legal heirs to his estate, which was valued at less than $1,000. The Reeds had separated before their son's death. Seven months after Richard's death, Sally had petitioned the probate court to administer Richard's estate. Shortly before the court was to hold a hearing on her request, Cecil applied to serve as his son's executor. In accord with Idaho law, a probate court judge appointed Cecil to execute his son's estate, since men received automatic preference over women in such matters.

Sally Reed challenged the Idaho law under a state civil rights law and the Equal Protection Clause, claiming that it was arbitrary and bore absolutely no relationship to the relative abilities of men and women to administer a legal estate. A lower state court agreed with Sally, but the Idaho Supreme Court reversed, claiming that the law was not "designed to discriminate" against women. The law's purpose, the court held, was intended to promote efficiency in the probate hearings process.

The ACLU viewed Sally Reed's case as a perfect vehicle to encourage the Supreme Court to bring sex discrimination within the orbit of the Equal Protection Clause. Led by Ruth Bader Ginsburg, a Rutgers University law professor, the ACLU argued that laws drawing a distinction on the basis of sex should, like laws classifying on the basis of race, be considered inherently "suspect" and entitled to strict judicial scrutiny. The ACLU also stated in plain terms that the Court should discard the separate spheres model of sex roles as a basis for upholding laws that discriminated on the basis of sex. No rational basis existed to assume that men were somehow presumptively more qualified to handle such mundane tasks as executing a small estate.

The Court's decision was unanimous. Chief Justice Burger delivered the opinion of the Court.

▼▲▼

MR. CHIEF JUSTICE BURGER delivered the opinion of the Court.

Having examined the record and considered the briefs and oral arguments of the parties, we . . . conclude that the arbitrary preference established in favor of males by § 15-314 of the Idaho Code cannot stand in the face of the Fourteenth Amendment's command that no State deny the equal protection of the laws to any person within its jurisdiction.

Idaho does not, of course, deny letters of administration to women altogether. Indeed, under § 15-312, a woman whose spouse dies intestate has a preference over a son, father, brother, or any other male relative of the decedent. Moreover, we can judicially notice that, in this country, presumably due to the greater longevity of women, a large proportion of estates, both intestate and under wills of decedents, are administered by surviving widows.

Section 15-314 is restricted in its operation to those situations where competing applications for letters of administration have been filed by both male and female members of the same entitlement class established by § 15-312. In such situations, § 15-314 provides that different treatment be accorded to the applicants on the basis of their sex; it thus establishes a classification subject to scrutiny under the Equal Protection Clause.

In applying that clause, this Court has consistently recognized that the Fourteenth Amendment does not deny to States the power to treat different classes of persons in different ways. The Equal Protection Clause of that amendment does, however, deny to States the power to legislate that different treatment be accorded to persons placed by a statute into different classes on the basis of criteria wholly unrelated to the objective of that statute. A classification must be reasonable, not arbitrary, and must rest upon some ground of difference having a fair and substantial relation to the object of the legislation, so that all persons similarly circumstanced shall be treated alike, *Royster Guano Co.* v. *Virginia* (1920). The question presented by this case, then, is whether a difference in the sex of competing applicants for letters of administration bears a rational relationship to a state objective that is sought to be advanced by the operation of §§ 15-312 and 15-314.

In upholding the latter section, the Idaho Supreme Court concluded that its objective was to eliminate one area of controversy when two or more persons, equally entitled under § 15-312, seek letters of administration, and thereby present the probate court "with the issue of which one should be named." The court also concluded that, where such persons are not of the same sex, the elimination of females from consideration is neither an illogical nor arbitrary method devised by the legislature to resolve an issue that would otherwise require a hearing as to the relative merits . . . of the two or more petitioning relatives.

Clearly the objective of reducing the workload on probate courts by eliminating one class of contests is not without some legitimacy. The crucial question, however, is whether § 15-314 advances that objective in a manner consistent with the command of the Equal Protection Clause. We hold that it does not. To give a mandatory preference to members of either sex over members of the other, merely to accomplish the elimination of hearings on the merits, is to make the very kind of arbitrary legislative choice forbidden by the Equal Protection Clause of the Fourteenth Amendment; and whatever may be said as to the positive values of avoiding intrafamily controversy, the choice in this context may not lawfully be mandated solely on the basis of sex.

We note finally that, if § 15-314 is viewed merely as a modifying appendage to § 15-312 and as aimed at the same objective, its constitutionality is not thereby saved. The

S I D E B A R

RUTH BADER GINSBURG

Breaking the Glass Ceiling

In the spring of 1960, Justice Felix Frankfurter went about securing clerks for the Supreme Court's next term in his usual way. He sent a note along to some friends on the faculty of the Harvard Law School asking for recommendations. A Harvard graduate who later served on the law school faculty before President Franklin D. Roosevelt appointed him to the Court in 1939, Frankfurter was accustomed to having the pick of his alma mater's best and brightest students. That year was no different, except in one major regard: One of the names forwarded to him was Ruth Bader Ginsburg, who had graduated from Columbia Law School in May 1959 tied for first in her class. From 1956 to 1958, Ginsburg had attended Harvard Law School along with her husband, Martin. During his third year of law school, Martin was diagnosed with cancer and unable to attend classes. Ruth attended her husband's classes in addition to her own, took notes, and helped Martin keep up with his work. After Martin recovered and finished school, he accepted a job with a New York firm, and Ruth finished her law degree at Columbia.

Despite sterling recommendations from Ginsburg's former professors and a federal court judge for whom she was clerking, Frankfurter refused even to interview her for a clerkship. Frankfurter confessed that he "simply wasn't ready" to hire a woman, especially one who was also the mother of a four-year-old daughter. Ginsburg had encountered similar reservations about her suitability for a career in law after she graduated from Columbia. She did not receive a single offer from a New York City law firm, even though her academic credentials were superior to her husband's. Indeed, Ginsburg began the clerkship she landed with Judge Edmund Palmieri as a legal secretary. As Ginsburg said of her early encounter with sex discrimination in the male-dominated world of law: "To be a woman, a Jew and a mother to boot, that combination was a bit much."

Ginsburg returned to Columbia Law School, where she worked on several research projects involving international law and procedure. In many ways, this turn of events suited Ginsburg just fine. As far back as her days as a baton-twirler while attending New York City public schools, Ginsburg had always impressed her teachers and classmates by combining her formidable intellect with an exacting discipline. While in law school, Ginsburg, who served on both the Columbia and Harvard law reviews, earned the nickname "Ruthless Ruthie" for her razor-sharp attention to detail. In 1963, Ginsburg joined the law faculty of Rutgers University, becoming only the second woman to do so. Although this might not seem impressive by contemporary standards, nationwide, fewer than twenty women were full-time law professors. This meant that Rutgers accounted for more than 10 percent of all female law professors in the United States. Still, Ginsburg, as an untenured female assistant professor, was so uncertain about keeping her position after she became pregnant with her second child that she took to wearing her mother's larger clothes to hide her pregnancy.

Her awareness of the social conditions and pervasive discrimination that women faced even if they managed to break into the fields controlled for so long by men led Ginsburg to begin, by the late 1960s, her decade-long association with the American Civil Liberties Union. Drawn to cases involving women who were fired from teaching jobs because they were pregnant, Ginsburg began working closely with the New Jersey affiliate of the ACLU to devise strategies to challenge such discriminatory employment practices. Success there and her growing national reputation as a scholar led Columbia to lure Ginsburg away from Rutgers with an offer to become its first tenured female full professor. Ginsburg accepted and joined the Columbia law school in 1972. By this time, Ginsburg had begun her work with the national ACLU and achieved her first great success as the architect behind the litigation strategy in *Reed* v. *Reed* (1971).

From 1973 to 1976, Ginsburg, as head of the ACLU's Women's Rights Project, argued six discrimination cases before the Supreme Court, winning five, and appeared as an attorney of record on fifteen *amicus* briefs filed during the same period. Although the core of Ginsburg's equal protection argument—that men and women should not be treated differently by the law simply because one group has the power to do so—was anything but radical by contemporary standards, it was, during the early 1970s, still a rather shocking proposition to many male lawyers and judges. During her final oral argument before the Court in *Weinberger* v. *Wiesenfeld* (1975), which involved an ACLU challenge to a provision of the federal social security program that bestowed a lesser death benefit to widowers than to widows, Justice Rehnquist interrupted Ginsburg's presentation to ask her: "You won't settle for putting Susan B. Anthony on the new dollar, then?" Ginsburg said nothing, but what ran through her mind she later said was, "We won't settle for tokens." For Ginsburg, gender was an issue precisely because it should not be an issue.

Indeed, Ginsburg has never accepted the position, advanced by more liberal feminists, that men and women have distinctively different ways of thinking, reasoning, and relating to other people. As she often responds when asked about her position on whether the Constitution permits the law to advantage women for educational or public policy reasons, "A wise old man and a wise old woman reach the same conclusion." Indeed, Ginsburg's enduring commitment to the "similarly situated" model of equal protection and

In 1993, Ruth Bader Ginsburg was appointed to the Supreme Court by President Bill Clinton, making her the second woman, after Sandra Day O'Connor, to serve as a justice. She was confirmed by a 96–3 Senate vote. Since coming to the Court, Ginsburg has remained true to her moderate-to-liberal leanings, and has thus often found herself dissenting in key decisions handed down by the generally conservative Rehnquist Court. But Ginsburg has managed to achieve one great personal victory during her tenure. In United States v. Virginia *(1996), Ginsburg wrote the Court's majority opinion striking down the male-only admissions policy of the Virginia Military Institute. Chief Justice William Rehnquist was in the seven-member majority, but elected to assign the opinion to Ginsburg, no doubt as a tribute to her years as a pioneering public interest lawyer on behalf of expanding women's rights.*

Collection, Supreme Court Historical Society. Photographed by Richard Strauss, Smithsonian Institution.

reluctance to embrace more expansive approaches to constitutional interpretation have drawn criticism from some liberal feminist groups. One such example is Ginsburg's position on abortion rights. Always pro-choice, Ginsburg nonetheless criticized *Roe* v. *Wade*

(1973) as somewhat poorly reasoned, arguing that the Court should have advanced an equal protection argument instead of relying on the idea that the Due Process Clause protected such a right on the basis of personal privacy. In Ginsburg's view, the fact that abortion laws affected women *only* made them constitutionally suspect, but from an equal protection, not due process clause, point of view. Ginsburg also argued that the Court should have crafted an opinion that encouraged state legislatures to adopt more liberal abortion laws rather than to mandate such sweeping rules through a judicial order. Such an approach, suggested Ginsburg, would have given abortion rights a stronger foundation in public opinion and strengthened their legitimacy.

Such independence has been a hallmark of Ginsburg's career as a jurist. Appointed to the D.C. Circuit Court of Appeals by President Jimmy Carter in 1980, she quickly earned a reputation as a meticulous, open-minded, and collegial judge. Her best friend on the court soon became Antonin Scalia, its most conservative member. After President Bill Clinton named her to the Supreme Court in 1993, Ginsburg was again reunited with Scalia, who had been elevated from the D.C. Circuit in 1986 by President Ronald Reagan. Ginsburg and Scalia are fellow devotees of the opera, and have appeared together in full period costume as extras in productions of the Washington Opera.

On the Court, however, Ginsburg does not trade friendship for votes. She remains steadfastly committed to laws and programs that she believes promote equal rights for women and minorities, and she has continued to support affirmative action programs in an era when the Court has placed tight limits on the power of government to use race, ethnicity, and gender to promote diversity aims or redress prior discrimination. Forty years after she was unable to land an interview to clerk for Justice Frankfurter, Ruth Bader Ginsburg, in a remarkable twist of fate, is now positioned as a Supreme Court justice to protect the pioneering legal victories she did so much to create.

References

The Oyez Project, Northwestern University, www.nwu.edu/justices/justices.

Ruth Bader Ginsburg, Wilson Lecture, Wellesley College, November 13, 1998. www.wellesley.edu/public affairs/Releases/1998/111098.html.

objective of § 15-312 clearly is to establish degrees of entitlement of various classes of persons in accordance with their varying degrees and kinds of relationship to the intestate. Regardless of their sex, persons within any one of the enumerated classes of that section are similarly situated with respect to that objective. By providing dissimilar treatment for men and women who are thus similarly situated, the challenged section violates the Equal Protection Clause.

The judgment of the Idaho Supreme Court is reversed, and the case remanded for further proceedings not inconsistent with this opinion.

Reversed and remanded.

▼▲▼

The Court did not find it necessary in *Reed* to decide whether sex discrimination should be treated the same as race-based discrimination under the Fourteenth Amendment. Chief Justice Burger's opinion makes clear that the Idaho law was a relic of nineteenth-century coverture doctrine. Men were given preference based on an outmoded sexual stereotype. In ruling that Idaho's law had no rational basis, the Court explicitly rejected the separate spheres model of sex roles that it had upheld, in *Hoyt,* just ten years before.

But the Court's decision not to treat sex as a suspect class in *Reed* encouraged the ACLU to establish an in-house program, the Women's Rights Project (WRP), to litigate sex discrimination issues. Overseen by Ginsburg, the WRP became an active participant in sex discrimination litigation throughout the 1970s, sponsoring several cases and participating in nearly every sex discrimination and abortion case decided by the Court during this time. Two years after *Reed,* the Court, in *Frontiero* v. *Richardson* (1973) turned to the WRP's *amicus* brief to address the question of the appropriate legal standard for sex discrimination.[82] *Frontiero* involved a challenge brought by a female Air Force lieutenant against military regulations that required her husband to prove that he was financially dependent on her. The same regulations imposed no such similar requirement on women, since it was assumed that women were dependent on their husbands for financial support. Living in Mobile, Alabama, Sharon Frontiero contacted the Southern Poverty Law Center, a non-profit civil rights law firm based in Montgomery, to take her case. Persuaded that Frontiero had raised an important civil rights claim, the SPLC agreed to represent her, with the WRP agreeing to file an *amicus* brief after the case reached the Supreme Court.

Writing for an 8–1 Court, Justice William Brennan held that the Due Process Clause of the Fifth Amendment prohibited the Air Force from subjecting men and women to different standards under its benefits policy. Three other justices, Douglas, Marshall, and White, agreed with the WRP that sex should be treated as a suspect class, a point the SPLC did not raise in its brief on behalf of Sharon Frontiero. But the remaining four justices in the majority refused to go along with Justice Brennan's opinion, thus leaving the Court without a coherent legal standard in sex discrimination cases. Still, the Court's willingness to consider sex discrimination as a serious problem deserving of vigorous constitutional protection was a milestone, as was its willingness to look for expertise among the organizations appearing before it that had developed specialties in this area, such as the WRP.[83]

Justice Powell, concurring in *Frontiero,* alluded to one of the difficulties facing the Court in its effort to define an appropriate legal standard in sex discrimination cases. In 1972, Congress passed the Equal Rights Amendment (ERA), which read, "Equality of rights under the law shall not be denied or abridged by the United States or by any State on account of sex." Wrote Powell:

> There is another, and I find compelling, reason for deferring a general categorizing of sex classifications as invoking the strictest test of judicial scrutiny. The Equal Rights Amendment, which if adopted will resolve the substance of this precise question, has been approved by the Congress and submitted for ratification by the States. If this Amendment is duly adopted, it will represent the will of the people accomplished in the manner prescribed by the Constitution. By acting prematurely and unnecessarily, as I view it, the Court has assumed a decisional responsibility at the very time when state legislatures, functioning within the traditional democratic process, are debating the proposed Amendment. It seems to me that this reaching out to preempt by judicial action a major political decision which is currently in process of resolution does not reflect appropriate respect for duly prescribed legislative processes.

By 1976, the ERA had failed to secure the necessary two-thirds majority from the states for ratification, falling short by three states. Women's rights groups successfully lobbied Congress for three separate two-year extensions to make the ERA's case. Still, they came up short, due in large part to an extremely well-organized campaign to defeat its ratification, initiated by conservative political activist Phyllis Schlafly. In 1972, after Congress passed the ERA, Schlafly formed the Eagle Forum and STOP ERA to defeat the amendment and lobby more generally against the passage of sex discrimination legislation in Congress and the states. Schlafly referred to women's rights activists as "a bunch of bitter women seeking a constitutional solution for their problems." She claimed that passage of the ERA would result in unisex public restrooms, mandatory military service for women, decriminalized rape, and promotion of lesbianism as the feminist ideal.[84] Even with support from the Carter administration and a congressional majority, ERA supporters could not overcome the fears that Schlafly tapped into among a sizable segment of American women about the perceived consequences of absolute gender equality.

Liberal feminists continued to press ahead, confident that the Court would extend the scope of the Fourteenth Amendment to protect women from laws rooted in sexual stereotypes. And in 1976, the same year the ERA went down to its first defeat, the Court, in *Craig* v. *Boren,* handed women's rights advocates their most important constitutional victory to date.

Craig v. *Boren*

429 U.S. 190 (1976)

Twenty-year-old Curtis Craig wanted a simple right: to buy beer. After all, his female contemporaries could. But, thanks to an Oklahoma law enacted in 1972, Craig would have to wait until he turned twenty-one to buy his first legal beer. That same year, Congress and the states completed the ratification of the Twenty-Sixth Amendment, which lowered the voting age from twenty-one to eighteen. In response, most states enacted laws soon afterward lowering the age at which minors entered the legal majority. And Oklahoma was one of those states, but its law establishing the age of legal adulthood carried an unusual twist: At age 18 women could buy "near beer," or beer with a lower alcohol level (3.2%) than the industry standard (5.0%), but men could not.

Carolyn Whitener owned a beer distributorship, and viewed young men like Curtis Craig as a potential lucrative customer base. She and Craig joined forces to challenge Oklahoma's law as violative of the Equal Protection Clause. In their view, Oklahoma had offered nothing more than speculative commentary rooted in sexual stereotypes to justify its "near beer" law. Men, the legislature offered, drove more, drank more beer, and got into more alcohol-fueled scrapes with the law than women did. Craig and Whitener also pointed to another peculiarity of the law: it did not prohibit men from drinking beer, just buying it.

The WRP, in an *amicus* brief written primarily by Ginsburg, argued that the Court did not have to choose between the rational basis standard of *Reed,* upon which Oklahoma relied, or the strict scrutiny approach advocated by the attorneys for Craig and Whitener. Instead, the Court could chart a middle ground that required something more than *Reed* and something less than the compelling interest standard applicable in race discrimination cases.

The Court's decision was 7 to 2. Justice Brennan delivered the opinion of the Court. Justices Powell, Stevens, Stewart, and Blackmun wrote concurring opinions. Justice Rehnquist and Chief Justice Burger wrote separate dissents.

▼▲▼

MR. JUSTICE BRENNAN delivered the opinion of the Court.

Analysis may appropriately begin with the reminder that *Reed* [v. *Reed* (1971)] emphasized that statutory classifications that distinguish between males and females are "subject to scrutiny under the Equal Protection Clause." To withstand constitutional challenge, previous cases establish that classifications by gender must serve important governmental objectives and must be substantially related to achievement of those objectives. Thus, in *Reed,* the objectives of "reducing the workload on probate courts," and "avoiding intra-family controversy," were deemed of insufficient importance to sustain use of an overt gender criterion in the appointment of administrators of intestate decedents' estates. Decisions following *Reed* similarly have rejected administrative ease and convenience as sufficiently important objectives to justify gender-based classifications. . . .

Reed v. *Reed* has also provided the underpinning for decisions that have invalidated statutes employing gender as an inaccurate proxy for other, more germane bases of classification. Hence, "archaic and overbroad" generalizations, concerning the financial position of servicewomen, and working women, could not justify use of a gender line in determining eligibility for certain governmental entitlements. Similarly, increasingly outdated misconceptions concerning the role of females in the home, rather than in the "marketplace and world of ideas," were rejected as loose-fitting characterizations incapable of supporting state statutory schemes that were premised upon their accuracy. In light of the weak congruence between gender and the characteristic or trait that gender purported to represent, it was necessary that the legislatures choose either to realign their substantive laws in a gender-neutral fashion or to adopt procedures for identifying those instances where the sex-centered generalization actually comported with fact.

In this case, too, "*Reed,* we feel, is controlling. . . ." We turn then to the question whether, under *Reed,* the difference between males and females with respect to the purchase of 3.2% beer warrants the differential in age drawn by the Oklahoma statute. We conclude that it does not.

The District Court recognized that *Reed* v. *Reed* was controlling. In applying the teachings of that case, the court found the requisite important governmental objective in the traffic safety goal proffered by the Oklahoma Attorney General. It then concluded that the statistics introduced by the appellees established that the gender-based distinction was substantially related to achievement of that goal. . . . Clearly, the protection of public health and safety represents an important function of state and local governments. However, appellees' statistics, in our view, cannot support the conclusion that the gender-based distinction closely serves to achieve that objective, and therefore the distinction cannot, under *Reed,* withstand equal protection challenge.

The appellees introduced a variety of statistical surveys. First, an analysis of arrest statistics for 1973 demonstrated that 18–20-year-old male arrests for "driving under the influence" and "drunkenness" substantially exceeded female arrests for that same age period. Similarly, youths aged 17–21 were found to be overrepresented among those killed or injured in traffic accidents, with males again numerically exceeding females in this regard. Third, a random roadside survey in Oklahoma City revealed that young males were more inclined to drive and drink beer than were their female counterparts. Fourth, Federal Bureau of Investigation nationwide statistics exhibited a notable increase in arrests for "driving under the influence." Finally, statistical evidence gathered in other jurisdictions, particularly Minnesota and Michigan, was offered to corroborate Oklahoma's experience by indicating the pervasiveness of youthful participation in motor vehicle accidents following the imbibing of alcohol. . . .

Even were this statistical evidence accepted as accurate, it nevertheless offers only a weak answer to the equal protection question presented here. The most focused and relevant of the statistical surveys, arrests of 18–20-year-olds for alcohol-related driving offenses, exemplifies the ultimate unpersuasiveness of this evidentiary record. Viewed in terms of the correlation between sex and the actual activity that Oklahoma seeks to regulate—driving while under the influence of alcohol—the statistics broadly establish that .18% of females and 2% of males in that age group were arrested for that offense. While such a disparity is not trivial in a statistical sense, it hardly can form the basis for employment of a gender line as a classifying device. Certainly if maleness is to serve as a proxy for drinking and driving, a correlation of 2% must be considered an unduly tenuous "fit." Indeed, prior cases have consistently rejected the use of sex as a decision-making factor even though the statutes in question certainly rested on far more predictive empirical relationships than this.

Moreover, the statistics exhibit a variety of other shortcomings that seriously impugn their value to equal protection analysis. . . . [T]he surveys do not adequately justify the salient features of Oklahoma's gender-based traffic safety law. None purports to measure the use and dangerousness of 3.2% beer, as opposed to alcohol generally, a detail that is of particular importance since, in light of its low alcohol level, Oklahoma apparently considers the 3.2% beverage to be "nonintoxicating." Moreover, many of the studies, while graphically documenting the unfortunate increase in driving while under the influence of alcohol, make no effort to relate their findings to age-sex differentials as involved here. Indeed, the only survey that explicitly centered its attention upon young drivers and their use of beer—albeit apparently not of the diluted 3.2% variety—reached results that hardly can be viewed as impressive in justifying either a gender or age classification.

There is no reason to belabor this line of analysis. It is unrealistic to expect either members of the judiciary or state officials to be well versed in the rigors of experimental or statistical technique. But this merely illustrates that proving broad sociological propositions by statistics is a dubious business, and one that inevitably is in tension with the normative philosophy that underlies the Equal Protection Clause. Suffice to say that the showing offered by the appellees does not satisfy us that sex represents a legitimate, accurate proxy for the regulation of drinking and driving. In fact, when it is further recognized that Oklahoma's statute prohibits only the selling of 3.2% beer to young males, and not their drinking the beverage once acquired (even after purchase by their 18–20-year-old female companions), the relationship between gender and traffic safety becomes far too tenuous to satisfy *Reed*'s requirement that the gender-based difference be substantially related to achievement of the statutory objective.

We hold, therefore, that under *Reed,* Oklahoma's 3.2% beer statute invidiously discriminates against males 18–20 years of age.

MR. JUSTICE STEVENS, concurring.

There is only one Equal Protection Clause. It requires every State to govern impartially. It does not direct the courts to apply one standard of review in some cases and a different standard in other cases. Whatever criticism may be leveled at a judicial opinion implying that there are at least three such standards applies with the same force to a double standard.

I am inclined to believe that what has become known as the two-tiered analysis of equal protection claims does not describe a completely logical method of deciding cases, but rather is a method the Court has employed to explain decisions that actually apply a single standard in a reasonably consistent fashion. I also suspect that a careful explanation of the reasons motivating particular decisions may contribute more to an identification of that standard than an attempt to articulate it in all-encompassing terms. . . .

The classification is not totally irrational. For the evidence does indicate that there are more males than females in this age bracket who drive, and also more who drink. Nevertheless, there are several reasons why I regard the justification as unacceptable. It is difficult to believe that the statute was actually intended to cope with the problem of traffic safety, since it has only a minimal effect on access to a not very intoxicating beverage, and does not prohibit its consumption. Moreover, the empirical data submitted by the State accentuate the unfairness of treating all 18–20-year-old males as inferior to their female counterparts. The legislation imposes a restraint on 100% of the males in the class allegedly because about 2% of them have probably violated one or more laws relating to the consumption of alcoholic beverages. It is unlikely that this law will have a significant deterrent effect either on that 2% or on the law-abiding 98%. But even assuming some such slight benefit, it does not seem to me that an insult to all of the young men of the State can be justified by visiting the sins of the 2% on the 98%.

MR. JUSTICE REHNQUIST, dissenting.

The Court's disposition of this case is objectionable on two grounds. First is its conclusion that *men* challenging a gender-based statute which treats them less favorably than women may invoke a more stringent standard of judicial review than pertains to most other types of classifications. Second is the Court's enunciation of this standard, without citation to any source, as being that "classifications by gender must serve *important* governmental objectives, and must be *substantially* related to achievement of those objectives." . . . I think the Oklahoma statute challenged here need pass only the "rational basis" equal protection analysis expounded in cases such as *McGowan* v. *Maryland* (1961) . . . , and I believe that it is constitutional under that analysis.

The Court does not discuss the nature of the right involved, and there is no reason to believe that it sees the purchase of 3.2% beer as implicating any important interest, let alone one that is "fundamental" in the constitutional sense of invoking strict scrutiny. Indeed, the Court's accurate observation that the statute affects the selling, but not the drinking, of 3.2% beer, further emphasizes the limited effect that it has on even those persons in the age group involved. There is, in sum, nothing about the statutory classification involved here to suggest that it affects an interest, or works against a group, which can claim under the Equal Protection Clause that it is entitled to special judicial protection.

It is true that a number of our opinions contain broadly phrased dicta implying that the same test should be applied to all classifications based on sex, whether affecting females or males. However, before today, no decision of this Court has applied an elevated level of scrutiny to invalidate a statutory discrimination harmful to males, except where the statute impaired an important personal interest protected by the Constitution. There being no such interest here, and there being no plausible argument that this is a discrimination against females, the Court's reliance on our previous sex discrimination cases is ill-founded. It treats gender classification as a talisman which—without regard to the rights involved or the persons affected—calls into effect a heavier burden of judicial review.

The Court's conclusion that a law which treats males less favorably than females "must serve important governmental objectives and must be substantially related to achievement of those objectives" apparently comes out of thin air. The Equal Protection Clause contains no such language, and none of our previous cases adopt that standard. I would think we have had enough difficulty with the two standards of review which our cases have recognized—the norm of "rational basis," and the "compelling state interest "required where a "suspect classification" is involved—so as to counsel weightily against the insertion of still another "standard" between those two. How is this Court to divine what objectives are important? How is it to determine whether a particular law is "substantially" related to the achievement of such objectives, rather than related in some other way to its achievement . . .

I would have thought that, if this Court were to leave anything to decision by the popularly elected branches of the Government, where no constitutional claim other than that of equal protection is invoked, it would be the decision as to what governmental objectives to be achieved by law are "important," and which are not. As for the second part of the Court's new test, the Judicial Branch is probably in no worse position than the Legislative or Executive Branches to determine if there is any rational relationship between a classification and the purpose which it might be thought to serve. But the introduction of the adverb "substantially" requires courts to make subjective judgments as to operational effects, for which neither their expertise nor their access to data fits them. And even if we manage to avoid both confusion and the mirroring of our own preferences in the development of this new doctrine, the thousands of judges in other courts who must interpret the Equal Protection Clause may not be so fortunate. . . .

This is not a case where the classification can only be justified on grounds of administrative convenience. There being no apparent way to single out persons likely to drink and drive, it seems plain that the legislature was faced here with the not atypical legislative problem of legislating in terms of broad categories with regard to the purchase and consumption of alcohol. I trust, especially in light of the Twenty-first Amendment, that there would be no due process violation if no one in this age group were allowed to purchase 3.2% beer. Since males drink and drive at a higher rate than the age group as a whole, I fail to see how a statutory bar with regard only to them can create any due process problem.

Note how Justice Brennan, while relying on *Reed*, took his cue from the WRP's suggestion that the Court find a middle ground on sex discrimination claims. By holding that laws using sex as a "classifying device . . . must serve important governmental objectives and must be substantially related to achievement of those objectives," Brennan built upon the rational basis standard of *Reed* without arguing that sex should be a suspect classification. Perhaps Brennan's motive was to find a compromise that would allow him—and women's rights advocates—to find a majority hospitable to greater protection for women's rights without pushing such key swing votes as Powell, Stewart, and Blackmun away. *Craig* was a case as much about judicial statesmanship and internal Court politics as it was constitutional principle.[85]

Sex Discrimination After *Craig*

Since it decided *Craig*, the Court has invalidated most laws challenged under the Equal Protection Clause involving sex discrimination and widened the scope of protection under Title VII of the Civil Rights Act to ban an array of discriminatory employment practices. In cases such as these, the Court has examined whether the challenged law or practice is rooted in antiquated sexual stereotypes. Accordingly, the Court has struck down laws prohibiting men from receiving alimony and Social Security benefits as surviving spouses, ruled that husbands may no longer dispose of jointly own property without their wives' permission, invalidated sex-specific policies in college admissions, and held that women may not be excluded from juries solely on the basis of sex.[86] The Court has also ruled that employers may not exclude women from jobs considered hazardous to their reproductive health without medical evidence.[87] Moreover, Congress has enacted several laws that have allowed women to move further into worlds once limited to men. In 1972, Congress amended the Civil Rights Act of 1964 to include Title IX, which requires colleges receiving federal funds to provide equal athletic opportunities to women. Needless to say, the impact of Title IX has been dramatic, completely reconfiguring the world of intercollegiate athletics and pushing women's athletics on all levels, from high school to the professional ranks, into the spotlight as never before.

Nonetheless, the Court has upheld laws treating the sexes differently since *Craig* when it has determined that men and women are not "similarly situated," and it is here that the difference between the intermediate and strict scrutiny standards of review is most apparent. Feminist scholar Wendy Williams has noted that cases in which the Court has upheld laws with sex-based classifications are those that highlight the physical differences between men and women, as opposed to those laws it has struck down, which have been rooted in "an outdated economic model of the family that no longer predominates."[88] Two cases decided by the Court in 1981, *Rostker* v. *Goldberg* and *Michael M.* v. *Superior Court of Sonoma County,* reflect this point. In *Rostker,* the Court, in a 6–3 decision, upheld the exclusion of women from the federal Selective Service Act, reinstituted by President Jimmy Carter in 1979. Justice Rehnquist, writing for the majority, accepted the government's argument at face value, holding that Congress possessed authority over military affairs, including administration of the draft. Since the law made men available for combat and not women, the sexes, in Justice Rehnquist's view, were not similarly situated and thus eligible for distinct treatment.[89]

In *Michael M.*, a seventeen-year-old male was arrested for having consensual sex with a sixteen-and-a-half-year-old girl. Under California law, men could be charged with statutory rape and punished for having sex with an unmarried woman under the age of eighteen. The Court, 5 to 4, ruled that the law bore a substantial relationship to an important government objective: preventing unwanted teenage pregnancies. Since women, obviously, stood to bear the immediate consequences of an unwanted pregnancy, "young men and young women are not similarly situated with respect to the problems and the risks of sexual intercourse."[90] The Court viewed the issue of societal harm and the state's paternalistic role in protecting "young women" from "young men" as paramount, whereas many women's rights groups submitting briefs in the case argued the major issue was the right of women to make their own intimate choices as long as they were consensual. In their view, the era of the state's paternalistic role in protecting women from their own sexuality had long passed. Some feminist scholars have suggested the Court's decision in *Michael M.* relied upon the separate spheres model of sex roles. Do you agree?

But the Court's most recent major decision on sex discrimination based on sexual stereotype straddled the line between traditional sex roles and inherent physical differences between men and women. In *United States* v. *Virginia* (1996), the Court was faced with a question it appeared to have settled fourteen years before in *Mississippi University for Women* v. *Hogan* (1982). In *Hogan,* the Court ruled that Mississippi could not ban men from admission into a state college established originally for women. Writing for the Court, Justice Sandra Day O'Connor held that the state's admissions policy failed both prongs of the analysis established in *Craig.* No reason existed to exclude men other than a desire to perpetuate an all-female environment. Unpersuasive as well was the state's argument that women needed special protection to succeed academically. Finally, the Court seized upon the sexual stereotype that informed the basis, in Justice O'Connor's view, for the university's discriminatory admissions policy. "MUW's policy of excluding males from admission to the School of Nursing," O'Connor wrote, "tends to perpetuate the stereotyped view of nursing as exclusively a woman's job."[91]

When Thomas Jefferson founded the University of Virginia, that institution never imagined it would one day open its doors to women. By the late 1960s, all of Virginia's public colleges, universities, and professional schools had become coeducational—except one, the Virginia Military Institute. By 1996, when the Court declared VMI's males-only admissions policy unconstitutional, only two state-supported single-sex institutions of higher education remained: VMI and The Citadel, located in Charleston, South Carolina. In 1993, Shannon Faulkner launched a two-year legal battle to enter The Citadel, having originally been accepted by deleting all references to gender on her application. However, Faulkner was ultimately turned down when the admissions committee learned she was a woman. With the assistance of the NOW Legal Defense Fund, Faulkner sued The Citadel, arguing that its admissions policy violated the Fourteenth Amendment. A federal court agreed and ordered Faulkner admitted in September 1995. After a week, most of it spent in the school infirmary, Faulkner, citing stress and physical exhaustion, dropped out of The Citadel. VMI, however, refused to bow to similar pressure to admit a female high school student who had applied for admission. Thus the single-sex education question returned to the Court, except this time with a different spin: Are men and women similarly situated to attend a coeducational military college?

United States v. *Virginia*

518 U.S. 515 (1996)

The Virginia Military Institute (VMI) was established in 1839 to train young men for positions in military and civic leadership. "Citizen-soldiers," as VMI calls them, are required to demonstrate their resolve through four years of intensive, adversarially oriented education, which emphasizes physical rigor, mental stress, absolute equality of treatment, spartan living conditions with no privacy, and indoctrination in the school's values. VMI students must wear military uniforms, eat all their meals in mess-hall style, take part in an endless stream of parades and drills, and are at all times on call to serve their superior officers. For the first seven months, first-year cadets are subjected to the "rat line," a form of treatment to remind them they resemble, in VMI's class system, "the lowest animals on earth." If a cadet survives the rat line, VMI's philosophy goes, then he is able to do anything he sets his mind to, having exceeded his own physical and psychological limits. VMI offers a full range of liberal arts, science, and engineering courses, leading to either a Bachelor of Arts or Science degree.

In 1990, the Bush administration brought suit against VMI after a female applicant complained to the Department of Justice that she had been denied admission on the basis of sex. A lower federal court ruled against the administration, holding that VMI's admissions policy did

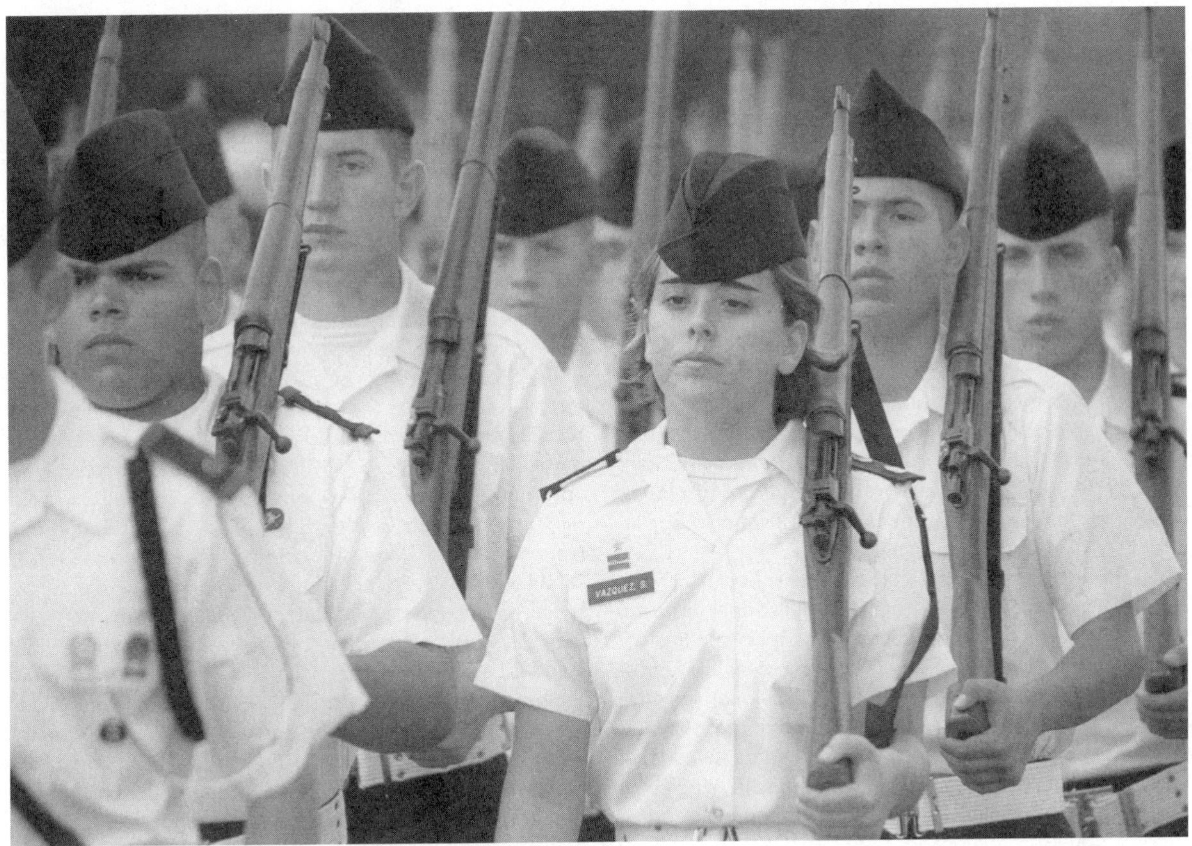

By the early 1990s, several state-sponsored military colleges found their male-only admissions policies under attack. The Supreme Court's decision in United States v. Virginia *(1996) declared that military colleges funded by the state could not discriminate on the basis of sex, allowing women to break down the door of one of the last official bastions of male supremacy.*
AP/Wide World Photos

not violate the Equal Protection Clause of the Fourteenth Amendment. VMI's mission to train "citizen-solidiers" served an important government interest and its harsh military-style educational philosophy was substantially related to achieving that interest. Alluding to the physical differences that justified upholding the male-only selective service requirements in *Rostker,* the lower court noted that the rigors of VMI might test women in a way that the single-sex restriction excluding men in *Hogan* did not. The Fourth Circuit Court of Appeals, considered by most lawyers a very conservative court, reversed, and ordered VMI to develop a satisfactory remedy.

VMI offered to develop a separate leadership program for women steeped in VMI values on the campus of Mary Baldwin, a private women's liberal arts college located about thirty-five miles away. The United States, now represented by the Clinton administration, argued that the Virginia Women's Institute for Leadership, as VMI called its program, offered nothing more than a separate and inferior education for women, and was, in many ways, similar to the responses offered by whites-only law schools that did not want to open their doors to African Americans fifty years earlier. Nonetheless, a federal district court approved VMI's plan, ruling that the "developmental and emotional differences" between men and women justified a program that it acknowledged was substantially different from a VMI education. This time, the Fourth Circuit Court of Appeals affirmed. The United States and VMI both petitioned the

Supreme Court to review the appeals court's decision—the Clinton administration continued to argue that VMI's male-only policy was unconstitutional, and VMI continued to argue its separate educational and leadership program for women was consistent with the Equal Protection Clause.

The Court's decision was 7 to 1. Justice Ginsburg delivered the opinion of the Court. Justice Scalia dissented.

Justice Thomas did not participate, as his son was attending VMI at the time the case was argued and decided.

▼▲▼

JUSTICE GINSBURG delivered the opinion of the Court.

Virginia's public institutions of higher learning include an incomparable military college, Virginia Military Institute (VMI). The United States maintains that the Constitution's equal protection guarantee precludes Virginia from reserving exclusively to men the unique educational opportunities VMI affords. We agree. . . .

[T]his case presents two ultimate issues. First, does Virginia's exclusion of women from the educational opportunities provided by VMI—extraordinary opportunities for military training and civilian leadership development—deny to women "capable of all of the individual activities required of VMI cadets," the equal protection of the laws guaranteed by the Fourteenth Amendment? Second, if VMI's "unique" situation—as Virginia's sole single-sex public institution of higher education—offends the Constitution's equal protection principle, what is the remedial requirement? . . .

In 1971, for the first time in our Nation's history, this Court ruled in favor of a woman who complained that her State had denied her the equal protection of its laws, *Reed* v. *Reed* (1971). Since *Reed*, the Court has repeatedly recognized that neither federal nor state government acts compatibly with the equal protection principle when a law or official policy denies to women, simply because they are women, full citizenship stature—equal opportunity to aspire, achieve, participate in and contribute to society based on their individual talents and capacities.

Without equating gender classifications, for all purposes, to classifications based on race or national origin, the Court, in post-*Reed* decisions, has carefully inspected official action that closes a door or denies opportunity to women (or to men). To summarize the Court's current directions for cases of official classification based on gender: focusing on the differential treatment or denial of opportunity for which relief is sought, the reviewing court must determine whether the proffered justification is "exceedingly persuasive." The burden of justification is demanding and it rests entirely on the State. . . . The justification must be genuine, not hypothesized or invented *post hoc* in response to litigation. And it must not rely on overbroad generalizations about the different talents, capacities, or preferences of males and females.

The heightened review standard our precedent establishes does not make sex a proscribed classification. Supposed "inherent differences" are no longer accepted as a ground for race or national origin classifications. Physical differences between men and women, however, are enduring. . . .

"Inherent differences" between men and women, we have come to appreciate, remain cause for celebration, but not for denigration of the members of either sex or for artificial constraints on an individual's opportunity. Sex classifications may be used to compensate women "for particular economic disabilities [they have] suffered," to "promot[e] equal employment opportunity," to advance full development of the talent and capacities of our Nation's people. But such classifications may not be used, as they once were, to create or perpetuate the legal, social, and economic inferiority of women.

Measuring the record in this case against the review standard just described, we conclude that Virginia has shown no "exceedingly persuasive justification" for excluding all women from the citizen soldier training afforded by VMI. We therefore affirm the Fourth Circuit's initial judgment, which held that Virginia had violated the Fourteenth Amendment's Equal Protection Clause. Because the remedy proffered by Virginia—the Mary Baldwin VWIL program—does not cure the constitutional violation, *i.e.*, it does not provide equal opportunity, we reverse the Fourth Circuit's final judgment in this case. . . .

Single-sex education affords pedagogical benefits to at least some students, Virginia emphasizes, and that reality is uncontested in this litigation. Similarly, it is not disputed that diversity among public educational institutions can serve the public good. But Virginia has not shown that VMI was established, or has been maintained, with a view to diversifying, by its categorical exclusion of women, educational opportunities within the State. In cases of this genre, our precedent instructs that "benign" justifications proffered in defense of categorical exclusions will not be accepted automatically; a tenable justification must describe actual state purposes, not rationalizations for actions in fact differently grounded. . . .

Neither recent nor distant history bears out Virginia's alleged pursuit of diversity through single-sex educational options. In 1839, when the State established VMI, a range of educational opportunities for men and women was scarcely contemplated. Higher education at the time was considered dangerous for women; reflecting widely held views about women's proper place, the Nation's first universities and colleges—for example, Harvard in Massachusetts, William and Mary in Virginia—admitted only men. VMI was not at all novel in this respect: in admitting no women, VMI followed the lead of the State's flagship school, the University of Virginia, founded in 1819.

"[N]o struggle for the admission of women to a state university," a historian has recounted, "was longer drawn out, or developed more bitterness, than that at the University of Virginia." In 1879, the State Senate resolved to look into the possibility of higher education for women, recognizing that Virginia "'has never at any period of her history,'" provided for the higher education of her daughters, though she "'has liberally provided for the higher education of her sons.'" Despite this recognition, no new opportunities were instantly open to women.

Virginia eventually provided for several women's seminaries and colleges. Farmville Female Seminary became a public institution in 1884. Two women's schools, Mary Washington College and James Madison University, were founded in 1908; another, Radford University, was founded in 1910. By the mid-1970s, all four schools had become coeducational. . . .

In sum, we find no persuasive evidence in this record that VMI's male-only admission policy "is in furtherance of a state policy of 'diversity.'" . . . A purpose genuinely to advance an array of educational options, as the Court of Appeals recognized, is not served by VMI's historic and constant plan—a plan to "affor[d] a unique educational benefit only to males." However "liberally" this plan serves the State's sons, it makes no provision whatever for her daughters. That is not *equal* protection.

Virginia next argues that VMI's adversative method of training provides educational benefits that cannot be made available, unmodified, to women. Alterations to accommodate women would necessarily be "radical," so "drastic," Virginia asserts, as to transform, indeed "destroy," VMI's program. Neither sex would be favored by the transformation, Virginia maintains: men would be deprived of the unique opportunity currently available to them; women would not gain that opportunity, because their participation would "eliminat[e] the very aspects of [the] program that distinguish [VMI] from . . . other institutions of higher education in Virginia." . . .

The United States does not challenge any expert witness estimation on average capacities or preferences of men and women. Instead, the United States emphasizes that time and again since this Court's turning point decision in *Reed* v. *Reed* (1971), we have cautioned reviewing courts to take a "hard look" at generalizations or "tendencies" of the kind pressed by Virginia, and relied upon by the District Court. State actors controlling gates to opportunity, we have instructed, may not exclude qualified individuals based on "fixed notions concerning the roles and abilities of males and females," *Mississippi Univ. for Women* v. *Hogan* (1982). . . .

The notion that admission of women would downgrade VMI's stature, destroy the adversative system and, with it, even the school, is a judgment hardly proved, a prediction hardly different from other "self-fulfilling prophec[ies]," once routinely used to deny rights or opportunities. When women first sought admission to the bar and access to legal education, concerns of the same order were expressed. . . .

Medical faculties similarly resisted men and women as partners in the study of medicine. More recently, women seeking careers in policing encountered resistance based on fears that their presence would "undermine male solidarity," deprive male partners of adequate assistance, and lead to sexual misconduct. Field studies did not confirm these fears.

Women's successful entry into the federal military academies, and their participation in the Nation's military forces, indicate that Virginia's fears for the future of VMI may not be solidly grounded. The State's justification for excluding all women from "citizen soldier" training for which some are qualified, in any event, cannot rank as "exceedingly persuasive," as we have explained and applied that standard. . . .

Virginia [later] presented its remedial plan—maintain VMI as a male-only college and create VWIL as a separate program for women. The plan met District Court approval. . . .

The constitutional violation in this case is the categorical exclusion of women from an extraordinary educational opportunity afforded men. A proper remedy for an unconstitutional exclusion, we have explained, aims to "eliminate [so far as possible] the discriminatory effects of the past" and to "bar like discrimination in the future," *Louisiana* v. *United States* (1965).

Virginia chose not to eliminate, but to leave untouched, VMI's exclusionary policy. For women only, however, Virginia proposed a separate program, different in kind from VMI and unequal in tangible and intangible facilities. Having violated the Constitution's equal protection requirement, Virginia was obliged to show that its remedial proposal "directly address[ed] and relate[d] to" the violation, the equal protection denied to women ready, willing, and able to benefit from educational opportunities of the kind VMI offers. Virginia described VWIL as a "parallel program," and asserted that VWIL shares VMI's mission of producing "citizen soldiers" and VMI's goals of providing "education, military training, mental and physical discipline, character . . . and leadership development." If the VWIL program could not "eliminate the discriminatory effects of the past," could it at least "bar like discrimination in the future"? A comparison of the programs said to be "parallel" informs our answer. . . .

VWIL affords women no opportunity to experience the rigorous military training for which VMI is famed. Instead, the VWIL program "deemphasize[s]" military education, and uses a "cooperative method" of education "which reinforces self-esteem."

VWIL students participate in ROTC and a "largely ceremonial" Virginia Corps of Cadets, but Virginia deliberately did not make VWIL a military institute. The VWIL House is not a military-style residence, and VWIL students need not live together throughout the 4-year program, eat meals together, or wear uniforms during the school day. VWIL students thus do not experience the "barracks" life "crucial to the VMI experience," the spartan living arrangements designed to foster an "egalitarian ethic." "[T]he most important aspects of the VMI educational experience occur in the barracks," yet Virginia deemed that core experience nonessential, indeed inappropriate, for training its female citizen soldiers.

VWIL students receive their "leadership training" in seminars, externships, and speaker series, episodes and encounters lacking the "[p]hysical rigor, mental stress, . . . minute regulation of behavior, and indoctrination in desirable values" made hallmarks of VMI's citizen soldier training. Kept away from the pressures, hazards, and psychological bonding characteristic of VMI's adversative training, VWIL students will not know the "feeling of tremendous accomplishment" commonly experienced by VMI's successful cadets. . . .

[G]eneralizations about "the way women are," estimates of what is appropriate for *most women,* no longer justify denying opportunity to women whose talent and capacity place them outside the average description. Notably, Virginia never asserted that VMI's method of education suits *most men.* It is also revealing that Virginia accounted for its failure to make the VWIL experience "the entirely militaristic experience of VMI" on the ground that VWIL "is planned for women who do not necessarily expect to pursue military careers." By that reasoning, VMI's "entirely militaristic" program would be inappropriate for men in general or *as a group,* for "[o]nly about 15% of VMI cadets enter career military service." . . .

In myriad respects other than military training, VWIL does not qualify as VMI's equal. VWIL's student body, faculty, course offerings, and facilities hardly match VMI's. Nor can the VWIL graduate anticipate the benefits associated with VMI's 157-year history, the school's prestige, and its influential alumni network. . . .

Virginia, in sum, while maintaining VMI for men only, has failed to provide any "comparable single-gender women's institution." Instead, the Commonwealth has created a VWIL program fairly appraised as a "pale shadow" of VMI in terms of the range of curricular choices and faculty stature, funding, prestige, alumni support and influence.

Virginia's VWIL solution is reminiscent of the remedy Texas proposed 50 years ago, in response to a state trial court's 1946 ruling that, given the equal protection guarantee, African Americans could not be denied a legal education at a state facility. Reluctant to admit African Americans to its flagship University of Texas Law School, the State set up a separate school for Herman Sweatt and other black law students. As originally opened, the new school had no independent faculty or library, and it lacked accreditation. Nevertheless, the state trial and appellate courts were satisfied that the new school offered Sweatt opportunities for the study of law "substantially equivalent to those offered by the State to white students at the University of Texas." . . . This Court contrasted resources at the new school with those at the school from which Sweatt had been excluded. The University of Texas Law School had a full-time faculty of 16, a student body of 850, a library containing over 65,000 volumes, scholarship funds, a law review, and moot court facilities.

More important than the tangible features, the Court emphasized, are "those qualities which are incapable of objective measurement but which make for greatness" in a school, including "reputation of the faculty, experience of the administration, position and influence of the alumni, standing in the community, traditions and prestige." Facing the marked differences reported in the *Sweatt* [v. *Painter* (1950)] opinion, the Court unanimously ruled that Texas had not shown "substantial equality in the [separate] educational opportunities" the State offered. Accordingly, the Court held, the Equal Protection Clause required Texas to admit African Americans to the University of Texas Law School. In line with *Sweatt,* we rule here that Virginia has not shown substantial equality in the separate educational opportunities the State supports at VWIL and VMI. . . .

For the reasons stated, the initial judgment of the Court of Appeals is affirmed, the final judgment of the Court of Appeals is reversed, and the case is remanded for further proceedings consistent with this opinion.

CHIEF JUSTICE REHNQUIST, concurring in the judgment.

Our cases dealing with gender discrimination also require that the proffered purpose for the challenged law be the actual purpose. It is on this ground that the Court rejects the first of two justifications Virginia offers for VMI's single-sex admissions policy, namely, the goal of diversity among its public educational institutions. While I ultimately agree that the State has not carried the day with this justification, I disagree with the Court's method of analyzing the issue. . . .

Even if diversity in educational opportunity were the State's actual objective, the State's position would still be problematic. The difficulty with its position is that the diversity benefited only one sex; there was single-sex public education available for men at VMI, but no corresponding single-sex public education available for women. When *Hogan* placed Virginia on notice that VMI's admissions policy possibly was unconstitutional, VMI could have dealt with the problem by admitting women; but its governing body felt strongly that the admission of women would have seriously harmed the institution's educational approach. Was there something else the State could have done to avoid an equal protection violation? Since the State did nothing, we do not have to definitively answer that question. . . .

The dissent criticizes me for "disregarding the four all-women's private colleges in Virginia (generously assisted by public funds)." The private women's colleges are treated by the State *exactly* as all other private schools are treated, which includes the provision of tuition-assistance grants to Virginia residents. Virginia gives no special support to the women's single-sex education. But obviously, the same is not true for men's education. Had the State provided the kind of support for the private women's schools that it provides for VMI, this may have been a very different case. For in so doing, the State would have demonstrated that its interest in providing a single-sex education for men was to some measure matched by an interest in providing the same opportunity for women.

Virginia offers a second justification for the single-sex admissions policy: maintenance of the adversative method. I agree with the Court that this justification does not serve an important governmental objective. A State does not have substantial interest in the adversative methodology unless it is pedagogically beneficial. While considerable evidence shows that a single-sex education is pedagogically beneficial for some students, and hence a State may have a valid interest in promoting that methodology, there is no similar evidence in the record that an adversative method is pedagogically beneficial or is any more likely to produce character traits than other methodologies. . . .

Accordingly, the remedy should not necessarily require either the admission of women to VMI, or the creation of a VMI clone for women. An adequate remedy in my opinion might be a demonstration by Virginia that its interest in educating men in a single-sex environment is matched by its interest in educating women in a single-sex institution. To demonstrate such, the State does not need to create two institutions with the same number of faculty PhD's, similar SAT scores, or comparable athletic fields. Nor would it necessarily require that the women's institution offer the same curriculum as the men's; one could be strong in computer science, the other could be strong in liberal arts. It would be a sufficient remedy, I think, if the two institutions offered the same quality of education and were of the same overall calibre. . . .

In the end, the women's institution Virginia proposes, VWIL, fails as a remedy, because it is distinctly inferior to the existing men's institution and will continue to be for the foreseeable future. VWIL simply is not, in any sense, the institution that VMI is. In particular, VWIL is a program appended to a private college, not a self-standing institution; and VWIL is substantially underfunded as compared to VMI. I therefore ultimately agree with the Court that Virginia has not provided an adequate remedy.

JUSTICE SCALIA, dissenting.

Today the Court shuts down an institution that has served the people of the Commonwealth of Virginia with pride and distinction for over a century and a half. To achieve that desired result, it rejects (contrary to our established practice) the factual findings of two courts below, sweeps aside the precedents of this Court, and ignores the history of our people. As to facts: it explicitly rejects the finding that there exist "gender-based developmental differences" supporting Virginia's restriction of the "adversative" method to only a men's institution, and the finding that the all-male composition of the Virginia Military Institute (VMI) is essential to that institution's character. As to precedent: it drastically revises our established standards for reviewing sex-based classifications. And as to history: it counts for nothing the long tradition, enduring down to the present, of men's military colleges supported by both States and the Federal Government.

Much of the Court's opinion is devoted to deprecating the closed-mindedness of our forebears with regard to women's education, and even with regard to the treatment of women in areas that have nothing to do with education. Closed-minded they were—as every age is, including our own, with regard to matters it cannot guess, because it simply does not consider them debatable. The virtue of a democratic system with a First Amendment is that it readily enables the people, over time, to be persuaded that what they took for granted is not so, and to change their laws accordingly. That system is destroyed if the smug assurances of each age are removed from the democratic process and written into the Constitution. So, to counterbalance the Court's criticism of our ancestors, let me say a word in their praise: they left us free to change. The same cannot be said of this most illiberal Court, which has embarked on a course of inscribing one after another of the current preferences of the society (and, in some cases, only the countermajoritarian preferences of the society's law-trained elite) into our Basic Law. Today it enshrines the notion that no substantial educational value is to be served by an all-men's military academy—so that the decision by the people of Virginia to maintain such an institution denies equal protection to women who cannot attend that institution but can attend others. Since it is entirely clear that the Constitution of the United States—the old one—takes no sides in this educational debate, I dissent. . . .

I have no problem with a system of abstract tests such as rational basis, intermediate, and strict scrutiny (though I think we can do better than applying strict scrutiny and intermediate scrutiny whenever we feel like it). Such formulas are essential to evaluating whether the new restrictions that a changing society constantly imposes upon private conduct comport with that "equal protection" our society has always accorded in the past. But, in my view, the function of this Court is to *preserve* our society's values regarding (among other things) equal protection, not to *revise* them; to prevent backsliding from the degree of restriction the Constitution imposed upon democratic government, not to prescribe, on our own authority, progressively higher degrees. For that reason, it is my view that, whatever abstract tests we may choose to devise, they cannot supersede—and indeed ought to be crafted *so as to reflect*—those constant and unbroken national traditions that embody the people's understanding of ambiguous constitutional texts. . . .

Today, however, change is forced upon Virginia, and reversion to single-sex education is prohibited nationwide not by democratic processes but by order of this Court. Even while bemoaning the sorry, bygone days of "fixed notions" concerning women's education, the Court favors current notions so fixedly that it is willing to write them into the Constitution of the United States by application of custom-built "tests." This is not the interpretation of a Constitution, but the creation of one. . . .

As is frequently true, the Court's decision today will have consequences that extend far beyond the parties to the case. What I take to be the Court's unease with these consequences, and its resulting unwillingness to acknowledge them, cannot alter the reality. . . .

In an odd sort of way, it is precisely VMI's attachment to such old-fashioned concepts as manly "honor" that has made it, and the system it represents, the target of those who today succeed in abolishing public single-sex education. The record contains a booklet that all first-year VMI students (the so-called "rats") were required to keep in their possession at all times. Near the end there appears the following period-piece, entitled "The Code of a Gentleman":

> Without a strict observance of the fundamental Code of Honor, no man, no matter how "polished," can be considered a gentleman. The honor of a gentleman demands the inviolability of his word, and the incorruptibility of his principles. He is the descendant of the knight, the crusader; he is the defender of the defenseless and the champion of justice . . . or he is not a Gentleman.
>
> A Gentleman . . .
>
> Does not discuss his family affairs in public or with acquaintances.
>
> Does not speak more than casually about his girl friend.
>
> Does not go to a lady's house if he is affected by alcohol. He is temperate in the use of alcohol.
>
> Does not lose his temper; nor exhibit anger, fear, hate, embarrassment, ardor or hilarity in public.
>
> Does not hail a lady from a club window.
>
> A gentleman never discusses the merits or demerits of a lady.
>
> Does not mention names, exactly as he avoids the mention of what things cost.
>
> Does not borrow money from a friend, except in dire need. Money borrowed is a debt of honor, and must be repaid as promptly as possible. Debts incurred by a deceased parent, brother, sister or grown child are assumed by honorable men as a debt of honor.
>
> Does not display his wealth, money or possessions.
>
> Does not put his manners on and off, whether in the club or in a ballroom. He treats people with courtesy, no matter what their social position may be.
>
> Does not slap strangers on the back nor so much as lay a finger on a lady.
>
> Does not "lick the boots of those above" nor "kick the face of those below him on the social ladder."
>
> Does not take advantage of another's helplessness or ignorance, and assumes that no gentleman will take advantage of him.

A Gentleman respects the reserves of others, but demands that others respect those which are his.

A Gentleman can become what he wills to be. . . .

I do not know whether the men of VMI lived by this Code; perhaps not. But it is powerfully impressive that a public institution of higher education still in existence sought to have them do so. I do not think any of us, women included, will be better off for its destruction.

▼▲▼

Twenty-five years after Ruth Bader Ginsburg, as an ACLU lawyer, helped bring sex discrimination under the umbrella of constitutional protection in *Reed,* she wrote the Court's opinion in *VMI.* This watershed decision may well close the gap in how the Court treats cases involving sexual stereotypes and physical differences between men and women under the Equal Protection Clause. Note that Justice Ginsburg tried—without success—to urge the Court to adopt a more stringent standard of review in sex discrimination cases. For now, it is important to note that Justice Ginsburg's opinion made clear that the "inherent differences" between men and women worth celebrating leave no room for discrimination that either denigrates or places economic restrictions on the rights of women.

Sexual Harassment

In July 1974, Mechelle Vinson stopped by a Washington, D.C., branch of the Meritor Savings Bank to inquire about employment. She filled out an application and brought it back the following morning. That afternoon, Sidney Taylor, the branch manager, called Vinson to tell her that she had been hired. Vinson began as a teller-trainee, and, over a period of four years, was soon promoted to teller, to head teller, and ultimately to assistant branch manager. In September 1978, Vinson took indefinite sick leave for undisclosed reasons. Two months later, she was fired for abusing the bank's sick leave policy. In November 1980, Vinson filed suit in federal court claiming that she had received unwanted sexual advances from Taylor, her supervisor. According to Vinson, Taylor demanded sexual favors from her soon after she began work, and repeatedly fondled her and used coarse sexual language in front of coworkers. Fearing that she would lose her job, Vinson, by her own estimate, had sex with Taylor between thirty and forty times.

Vinson lost at trial, but won on appeal. Ruling that Vinson had been subjected to an "offensive and hostile working environment," the D.C. Circuit Court of Appeals held that sexual harassment was a form of sex discrimination and thus prohibited by Title VII of the Civil Rights Act of 1964. Of note in the appeals court's ruling was its dismissal of the lower court's ruling that Taylor was not guilty of sexual harassment because his relationship with Vinson was "voluntary," since her employment status was dependent upon continuing the relationship. Meritor Savings appealed to the Supreme Court, which unanimously affirmed the appeals court's decision. "Without question," wrote Justice Rehnquist, "when a supervisor sexually harasses a subordinate because of the subordinate's sex, that supervisor discriminate[s] on the basis of sex." Moreover, wrote Rehnquist, an individual bringing a sexual harassment complaint was not required to demonstrate a tangible economic loss. It was sufficient to show that sexual harassment "create[d] a hostile or offensive work environment for one sex," and was "severe [enough] to alter the conditions of [the victim's] employment and create an abusive working environment."[92]

The Court's decision in *Meritor Savings Bank* v. *Vinson* (1986) codified the guidelines on sexual harassment released by the federal Equal Employment Opportunity Commission (EEOC) in November 1980. Those guidelines stated that Title VII's prohibition on sex discrimination is violated when:

1. Submission to unwelcome sexual advances, requests for sexual favors or other verbal or physical conduct of a sexual nature is made either explicitly or implicitly a term or condition of an individual's employment.
2. Submission to or rejection of such conduct by an individual is used as the basis for employment decisions affecting the individual.
3. Such conduct has the purpose or effect of unreasonably interfering with an individual's work performance or creating an intimidating, hostile or offensive working environment.

The EEOC's guidelines and, later, the Court's decision in *Vinson,* were based largely on a theory of sex subjugation articulated by one of Mechelle Vinson's lawyers, Catharine MacKinnon, a law professor and feminist scholar. In the early 1970s, MacKinnon argued in a series of articles for mostly academic audiences that federal civil rights law ought to include harassment based on sex among its prohibitions. Those views soon entered the mainstream of legal and political debate. As she later wrote, "[s]exual harassment, the event, was not invented by feminists; the perpetrators did that with no help from us. Sexual harassment, the legal claim—the idea that the law should see it the way its victims see it—is definitely a feminist invention."[93]

In *Harris* v. *Forklift Systems* (1993), the Court eased the legal burden for individuals bringing sexual harassment lawsuits and broadened the definition of sexual harassment. Five years later, the Court expanded the legal definition of sexual harassment by holding, in *Oncale* v. *Sundowner Offshore Services* (1998), that same-sex sexual harassment is also barred by Title VII. *Oncale* also clarified that sexual harassment may consist of derogatory comments directed to a person based on sex, and did not have to include references to sexual behavior. Taken together, *Harris* and *Oncale* represent the Court's two strongest opinions to date on the law of sexual harassment.

Harris v. Forklift Systems, Inc.

510 U.S 17 (1993)

From 1985 until 1987, Teresa Harris worked as a rental manager for a small Nashville company that sold, leased, and repaired forklift machinery. She quit after the president and chief executive officer of Forklift Systems, Charles Hardy, engaged in a continuous pattern of sexual harassment, creating a working environment so hostile that she could no longer come to work. By August 1987, Harris had experienced regular anxiety attacks and emotional trauma, was drinking heavily, and had suffered through a difficult period with her husband and children. In October, Harris resigned after Hardy—jokingly, in his own words—suggested that she promise sexual favors to a customer to secure an account. She filed suit in federal district court under Title VII alleging that Hardy and Forklift Systems had created a hostile working environment.

That comment was the breaking point for Harris. Among the comments by Hardy that were admitted as evidence during her trial were the following:

- In the presence of other employees, Hardy often told Harris, "We need a man as the rental manager."
- Hardy asked Harris to retrieve some coins from his front pants pocket in front of other female employees. He often threw coins on the ground in front of Harris and asked her to bend over and pick them up. Following this, he made sexually oriented comments about her body.
- Hardy suggested to Harris that they "go to the Holiday Inn to negotiate [her] raise."
- Hardy frequently made sexually laced comments to Harris and other female employees about their clothing.

At trial, Forklift Systems tried to portray Harris as "one of the boys." Its lawyers put on witnesses who testified that Harris and her husband had a social relationship with Hardy and his wife. Company employees testified that Harris was no prude, enjoyed drinking beer and telling off-color jokes, and cursed as much as anyone. The lower court concluded that Hardy was a "vulgar man who demeaned his female employees," but did not create a hostile working environment to interfere with Harris's ability to perform her job. A key holding of the trial court was that Harris had not demonstrated a "severe psychological injury." A federal appeals court, calling Harris's case "close," affirmed.

The Court's decision was unanimous. Justice O'Connor delivered the opinion of the Court. Appropriately enough for the woman who had done so much to create the modern law of sex discrimination, Justice Ginsburg wrote a concurring opinion in *Harris*, setting out her views on sexual harassment law.

▼▲▼

JUSTICE O'CONNOR delivered the opinion of the Court.

As we made clear in *Meritor Savings Bank* v. *Vinson* (1986), [the Civil Rights Act of 1964] is not limited to "economic" or "tangible" discrimination. The phrase "terms, conditions, or privileges of employment" evinces a congressional intent "to strike at the entire spectrum of disparate treatment of men and women" in employment, which includes requiring people to work in a discriminatorily hostile or abusive environment. When the workplace is permeated with "discriminatory intimidation, ridicule, and insult," that is "sufficiently severe or pervasive to alter the conditions of the victim's employment and create an abusive working environment," Title VII is violated.

This standard, which we reaffirm today, takes a middle path between making actionable any conduct that is merely offensive and requiring the conduct to cause a tangible psychological injury. As we pointed out in *Meritor,* "mere utterance of an . . . epithet which engenders offensive feelings in an employee," does not sufficiently affect the conditions of employment to implicate Title VII. Conduct that is not severe or pervasive enough to create an objectively hostile or abusive work environment—an environment that a reasonable person would find hostile or abusive—is beyond Title VII's purview. Likewise, if the victim does not subjectively perceive the environment to be abusive, the conduct has not actually altered the conditions of the victim's employment, and there is no Title VII violation.

But Title VII comes into play before the harassing conduct leads to a nervous breakdown. A discriminatorily abusive work environment, even one that does not seriously affect employees' psychological wellbeing, can and often will detract from employees' job performance, discourage employees from remaining on the job, or keep them from advancing in their careers. Moreover, even without regard to these tangible effects, the very fact that the discriminatory conduct was so severe or pervasive that it created a work environment abusive to employees because of their race, gender, religion, or national origin offends Title VII's broad rule of workplace equality. The appalling conduct alleged in *Meritor,* and the reference in that case to environments "'so heavily polluted with discrimination as to destroy completely the emotional and psychological stability of minority group workers,'" merely present some especially egregious examples of harassment. They do not mark the boundary of what is actionable.

We therefore believe the District Court erred in relying on whether the conduct "seriously affect[ed] plaintiff's psychological wellbeing" or led her to "suffe[r] injury." Such an inquiry may needlessly focus the factfinder's attention on concrete psychological harm, an element Title VII does not require. Certainly Title VII bars conduct that would seriously affect a reasonable person's psychological wellbeing, but the statute is not limited to such conduct. So long as the environment would reasonably be perceived, and is perceived, as hostile or abusive, there is no need for it also to be psychologically injurious.

This is not, and by its nature cannot be, a mathematically precise test. . . . But we can say that whether an environment is "hostile" or "abusive" can be determined only by looking at all the circumstances. These may include the frequency of the discriminatory conduct; its severity; whether it is physically threatening or humiliating, or a mere offensive utterance; and whether it unreasonably interferes with an employee's work performance. The effect on the employee's psychological wellbeing is, of course, relevant to determining whether the plaintiff actually found the environment abusive. But, while psychological harm, like any other relevant factor, may be taken into account, no single factor is required. . . .

We therefore reverse the judgment of the Court of Appeals, and remand the case for further proceedings consistent with this opinion.

So ordered.

JUSTICE GINSBURG, concurring.

Today the Court reaffirms the holding of *Meritor Savings Bank* v. *Vinson* (1986): "[A] plaintiff may establish a violation of Title VII by proving that discrimination based on sex has created a hostile or abusive work environment." The critical issue, Title VII's text indicates, is whether members of one sex are exposed to disadvantageous terms or conditions of employment to which members of the other sex are not exposed. As the Equal Employment Opportunity Commission emphasized, [the] inquiry should center, dominantly, on whether the discriminatory conduct has unreasonably interfered with the plaintiff's work performance. To show such interference, "the plaintiff need not prove that his or her tangible productivity has declined as a result of the harassment." It suffices to prove that a reasonable person subjected to the discriminatory conduct would find, as the plaintiff did, that the harassment so altered working conditions as to "ma[k]e it more difficult to do the job." [*Washington* v.] *Davis* [1976] concerned race-based discrimination, but that difference does not alter the analysis; except in the rare case in which a bona fide occupational qualification is shown, Title VII declares discriminatory practices based on race, gender, religion, or national origin equally unlawful.

The Court's opinion, which I join, seems to me in harmony with the view expressed in this concurring statement.

Oncale v. *Sundowner Offshore Services, Inc*

523 U.S. 75 (1998)

Joseph Oncale was a twenty-one-year-old "roustabout" for Sundowner Offshore Services, a company that provided crews to work on a Chevron U.S.A. oil platform off the coast of Louisiana. A roustabout is the name given to a semiskilled deckhand. Oncale was one of eight men assigned to work on the Chevron crew, beginning in August 1991. He earned seven dollars an hour, and reported to three supervisors, John Lyons, Danny Pippen, and Brandon Johnson.

From the moment Oncale began work, Lyons, Pippen, and Johnson repeatedly taunted him. By late October, the verbal harassment escalated into physical assaults. On one occasion, Pippen held Oncale down, while Lyons exposed himself and brushed his penis against the back of his head. A similar incident took place the next day when Johnson restrained Oncale, and Lyons against brushed his penis against Oncale's body. This time, Oncale complained to management. That night, aware that Oncale had reported their attack, Pippen and Lyons attempted to sexually assault Oncale in the shower. After Oncale reported this incident to management, the physical attacks ceased, but the verbal abuse continued. In early November, Oncale, fearful that he would be raped and possibly killed, quit his job.

Oncale was unsuccessful in persuading a federal district court to uphold a claim of same-sex sexual harassment. The Fifth Circuit Court of Appeals affirmed the lower court, despite the fact that every other federal circuit had allowed claims of same-sex sexual harassment to go forward under Title VII. Oncale appealed to the Supreme Court, where he received *amicus* support from the EEOC, with whom he had filed a complaint in December 1991, and from Catharine MacKinnon, who authored a brief on behalf of fourteen groups.

The Court's decision was unanimous. Justice Scalia delivered the opinion of the Court. Justice Thomas filed a concurring opinion.

▼▲▼

JUSTICE SCALIA delivered the opinion of the Court.

This case presents the question whether workplace harassment can violate Title VII's prohibition against "discriminat[ion] . . . because of . . . sex," when the harasser and the harassed employee are of the same sex. . . .

Title VII's prohibition of discrimination "because of . . . sex" protects men as well as women, and in the related context of racial discrimination in the workplace we have rejected any conclusive presumption that an employer will not discriminate against members of his own race. In *Johnson* v. *Transportation Agency, Santa Clara Cty.* (1987), a male employee claimed that his employer discriminated against him because of his sex when it preferred a female employee for promotion. Although we ultimately rejected the claim on other grounds, we did not consider it significant that the supervisor who made that decision was also a man. If our precedents leave any doubt on the question, we hold today that nothing in Title VII necessarily bars a claim of discrimination "because of . . . sex" merely because the plaintiff and the defendant (or the person charged with acting on behalf of the defendant) are of the same sex. Courts have had little trouble with that principle in cases like Johnson, where an employee claims to have been passed over for a job or promotion. . . .

We see no justification in the statutory language or our precedents for a categorical rule excluding same-sex harassment claims from the coverage of Title VII. As some courts have observed, male-on-male sexual harassment in the workplace was assuredly not the principal evil Congress was concerned with when it enacted Title VII. But statutory prohibitions often go beyond the principal evil to cover reasonably comparable evils, and it is ultimately the provisions of our laws rather than the principal concerns of our legislators by which we are governed. Title VII prohibits "discriminat[ion] . . . because of . . . sex" in the "terms" or "conditions" of employment. Our holding that this includes sexual harassment must extend to sexual harassment of any kind that meets the statutory requirements.

Respondents and their *amici* contend that recognizing liability for same-sex harassment will transform Title VII into a general civility code for the American workplace. But that risk is no greater for same-sex than for opposite-sex harassment, and is adequately met by careful attention to the requirements of the statute. Title VII does not prohibit all verbal or physical harassment in the workplace; it is directed only at "discriminat[ion] . . . because of . . . sex." We have never held that workplace harassment, even harassment between men and women, is automatically discrimination because of sex merely because the words used have sexual content or connotations. "The critical issue, Title VII's text indicates, is whether members of one sex are exposed to disadvantageous terms or conditions of employment to which members of the other sex are not exposed." . . .

[T]here is another requirement that prevents Title VII from expanding into a general civility code: As we emphasized in *Meritor* and *Harris,* the statute does not reach genuine but innocuous differences in the ways men and women routinely interact with members of the same sex and of the opposite sex. The prohibition of harassment on the basis of sex requires neither asexuality nor androgyny in the workplace; it forbids only behavior so objectively offensive as to alter the "conditions" of the victim's employment. "Conduct that is not severe or pervasive enough to create an objectively hostile or abusive work environment—an environment that a reasonable person would find hostile or abusive—is beyond Title VII's purview." We have always regarded that requirement as crucial, and as sufficient to ensure that courts and juries do not mistake ordinary socializing in the workplace—such as male-on-male horseplay or intersexual flirtation—for discriminatory "conditions of employment."

We have emphasized, moreover, that the objective severity of harassment should be judged from the perspective of a reasonable person in the plaintiff's position, considering "all the circumstances." In same-sex (as in all) harassment cases, that inquiry requires careful consideration of the social context in which particular behavior occurs and is experienced by its target. A professional football player's working environment is not severely or pervasively abusive, for example, if the coach smacks him on the buttocks as he heads onto the field—even if the same behavior would reasonably be experienced as abusive by the coach's secretary (male or female) back at the office. The real social impact of workplace behavior often depends on a constellation of surrounding circumstances, expectations, and relationships which are not fully captured by a simple recitation of the words used or the physical acts performed. Common sense, and an appropriate sensitivity to social context, will enable courts and juries to distinguish between simple teasing or roughhousing among members of the same sex, and conduct which a reasonable person in the plaintiff's position would find severely hostile or abusive.

▼▲▼

By holding that an individual need not demonstrate "severe psychological injury" to argue the existence of a hostile working environment, the Court indicated in *Harris* that it believed plaintiffs should have wide latitude under Title VII to proceed with sex discrimination claims. *Oncale* clarifies two additional, important rules in sexual harassment law: (1) Same-sex sexual harassment is legally actionable and (2) a coworker may not technically need to be a supervisor to engage in sexual harassment. Since *Oncale*, the Court has ruled that private employers and public school systems can be held legally accountable for sexual harassment of their employees, even if the employer was unaware that such harassment had taken place.[94] As sexual harassment law continues to develop, so too will opportunities for the Court to further refine its meaning.

Discrimination Based on Sexual Orientation

On June 28, 1969, New York City police raided a gay bar in Greenwich Village called the Stonewall Inn. This was not the first time police had targeted the club. Surprise raids of gay bars, restaurants, and nightclubs were ways for police to remind homosexuals that they had better keep quiet and remain out of public view. Such an attitude toward homosexuals was typical of the times, even in liberal New York, which had been home (albeit one that thrived underground) to a vibrant gay and lesbian community extending back to the early twentieth century. But that sweltering June night produced a response from gays that the police had never seen before: They fought back hard. For almost a week, Stonewall patrons engaged in violent battles with police, whose tactics to bring the protestors to their knees, seen on nightly television reports, recalled the brutality of Southern sheriffs against civil rights demonstrators in the early 1960s.

After intervention by Mayor John Lindsey, the Stonewall patrons and the police reached a truce, but one that decidedly favored the gay community. The police would cease their raids on known gay establishments, and the city agreed to reach out to local gay rights leaders on matters of political interest to the gay community. Born out of the Stonewall riots was the Gay Liberation Front, a group versed in late 1960s–style street activism and one of the first visible symbols of the fledgling gay rights movement. Like other social movements before it, the gay rights groups soon turned to the political arena and the courts to press their argument for civil rights protection.

Gay rights groups, however, have not found Congress or the state legislatures very receptive to civil rights protection, whether in employment, housing, or matters related to intimate and familial choices. Congress does not include sexual orientation among the classes protected by any piece of federal civil rights legislation. In a law that highlights the ambivalence of public attitudes toward homosexuals, Congress, in 1996, enacted the Defense of Marriage Act, a law designed to prevent any state or locality from permitting the right of homosexuals to marry. Impetus for this law came about when the Hawaii Supreme Court struck down its state marriage law on the grounds that it discriminated on the basis of sex by not including homosexuals among eligible parties.[95] Concerned that this development would lead other states to follow Hawaii's lead, Congress, with the support of President Clinton, who had asked for and received the support of gays and lesbians during his 1992 and 1996 campaigns, enacted the marriage law. Since the Defense of Marriage Act simply banned what no state, including Hawaii, which later rejected a state referendum to legalize same-sex marriage, permitted, some commentators have called the law nothing more than a transparent form of legal prejudice against gays and lesbians.[96]

In 1996, the same year Congress passed the Defense of Marriage Act, the Supreme Court, for the first time, ruled that state-enforced discrimination against homosexuals violated the Equal Protection Clause. In *Romer* v. *Evans* (1996), the Court invalidated a provision of the Colorado Constitution, Amendment 2, which prohibited any branch of the state government or any locality from enacting laws prohibiting discrimination against homosexuals. The ruling prompted a furious dissent from Justice Scalia. At bottom, Justice Scalia argued that the Court had taken sides in a "culture war" over the rights of homosexuals. Writing for the Court, Justice Kennedy treats *Evans* as a straightforward discrimination case, drawing parallels between Amendment 2 and the "separate but equal language" of *Plessy* v. *Ferguson*. Who, in your view, makes the better argument, Kennedy or Scalia?

Romer v. *Evans*

517 U.S. 620 (1996)

In November 1992, Colorado voters enacted Amendment 2 to their state constitution by a 53.4 percent to 46.6 percent margin. Amendment 2, which overturned several local ordinances protecting gays against discrimination, provided that

> [n]either the State of Colorado, through any of its branches or departments, nor any of its agencies, political subdivisions, municipalities, or school districts, shall enact, adopt or enforce any statute, regulation, ordinance or policy whereby homosexual, lesbian or bisexual orientation, conduct, practices or relationship shall constitute or otherwise be the basis of or entitle any person or class of persons to have or claim any minority status quota preferences, protected status or claim of discrimination. This Section of the Constitution shall be in all respects self-executing.

Richard G. Evans, a openly gay Denver municipal employee, and several local governments whose laws were jeopardized by Amendment 2 filed suit against Colorado Governor Roy Romer, claiming that the provision violated the Equal Protection Clause of the Fourteenth Amendment. After two trials and two rounds of appeals, the Colorado Supreme Court struck down Amendment 2 as unconstitutional. Romer appealed to the Supreme Court.

The Court's decision was 6 to 3. Justice Kennedy delivered the opinion of the Court. Justice Scalia, joined by Chief Justice Rehnquist and Justice Thomas, dissented.

▼▲▼

JUSTICE KENNEDY delivered the opinion of the Court.

One century ago, the first Justice Harlan admonished this Court that the Constitution "neither knows nor tolerates classes among citizens," ***Plessy*** **v.** ***Ferguson*** **(1896) (dissenting opinion). Unheeded then, those words now are understood to state a commitment to the law's neutrality where the rights of persons are at stake. The Equal Protection Clause enforces this principle and today requires us to hold invalid a provision of Colorado's Constitution. . . .**

The State's principal argument in defense of Amendment 2 is that it puts gays and lesbians in the same position as all other persons. So, the State says, the measure does no more than deny homosexuals special rights. This reading of the amendment's language is implausible. We rely not upon our own interpretation of the amendment, but upon the authoritative construction of Colorado's Supreme Court. The state court, deeming it unnecessary to determine the full extent of the amendment's reach, found it invalid even on a modest reading of its implications. The critical discussion of the amendment, set out in ***Evans I*****, is as follows:**

> The immediate objective of Amendment 2 is, at a minimum, to repeal existing statutes, regulations, ordinances, and policies of state and local entities that barred discrimination based on sexual orientation. . . .
>
> The "ultimate effect" of Amendment 2 is to prohibit any governmental entity from adopting similar, or more

protective statutes, regulations, ordinances, or policies in the future unless the state constitution is first amended to permit such measures.

Sweeping and comprehensive is the change in legal status effected by this law. So much is evident from the ordinances that the Colorado Supreme Court declared would be void by operation of Amendment 2. Homosexuals, by state decree, are put in a solitary class with respect to transactions and relations in both the private and governmental spheres. The amendment withdraws from homosexuals, but no others, specific legal protection from the injuries caused by discrimination, and it forbids reinstatement of these laws and policies.

The change that Amendment 2 works in the legal status of gays and lesbians in the private sphere is far-reaching, both on its own terms and when considered in light of the structure and operation of modern antidiscrimination laws. That structure is well illustrated by contemporary statutes and ordinances prohibiting discrimination by providers of public accommodations. . . .

Amendment 2 bars homosexuals from securing protection against the injuries that these public-accommodations laws address. That in itself is a severe consequence, but there is more. Amendment 2, in addition, nullifies specific legal protections for this targeted class in all transactions in housing, sale of real estate, insurance, health and welfare services, private education, and employment.

Not confined to the private sphere, Amendment 2 also operates to repeal and forbid all laws or policies providing specific protection for gays or lesbians from discrimination by every level of Colorado government. The State Supreme Court cited two examples of protections in the governmental sphere that are now rescinded and may not be reintroduced. The first is Colorado Executive Order D0035 (1990), which forbids employment discrimination against "'all state employees, classified and exempt' on the basis of sexual orientation." Also repealed, and now forbidden, are "various provisions prohibiting discrimination based on sexual orientation at state colleges." The repeal of these measures and the prohibition against their future reenactment demonstrates that Amendment 2 has the same force and effect in Colorado's governmental sector as it does elsewhere and that it applies to policies as well as ordinary legislation.

Amendment 2's reach may not be limited to specific laws passed for the benefit of gays and lesbians. It is a fair, if not necessary, inference from the broad language of the amendment that it deprives gays and lesbians even of the protection of general laws and policies that prohibit arbitrary discrimination in governmental and private settings. At some point in the systematic administration of these laws, an official must determine whether homosexuality is an arbitrary and thus forbidden basis for decision. Yet a decision to that effect would itself amount to a policy prohibiting discrimination on the basis of homosexuality, and so would appear to be no more valid under Amendment 2 than the specific prohibitions against discrimination the state court held invalid.

. . . [A]mendment [2] imposes a special disability upon those persons alone. Homosexuals are forbidden the safeguards that others enjoy or may seek without constraint. They can obtain specific protection against discrimination only by enlisting the citizenry of Colorado to amend the state constitution or perhaps, on the State's view, by trying to pass helpful laws of general applicability. This is so no matter how local or discrete the harm, no matter how public and widespread the injury. We find nothing special in the protections Amendment 2 withholds. These are protections taken for granted by most people either because they already have them or do not need them; these are protections against exclusion from an almost limitless number of transactions and endeavors that constitute ordinary civic life in a free society.

The Fourteenth Amendment's promise that no person shall be denied the equal protection of the laws must coexist with the practical necessity that most legislation classifies for one purpose or another, with resulting disadvantage to various groups or persons. We have attempted to reconcile the principle with the reality by stating that, if a law neither burdens a fundamental right nor targets a suspect class, we will uphold the legislative classification so long as it bears a rational relation to some legitimate end.

Amendment 2 fails, indeed defies, even this conventional inquiry. First, the amendment has the peculiar property of imposing a broad and undifferentiated disability on a single named group, an exceptional and, as we shall explain, invalid form of legislation. Second, its sheer breadth is so discontinuous with the reasons offered for it that the amendment seems inexplicable by anything but animus toward the class that it affects; it lacks a rational relationship to legitimate state interests.

Taking the first point, even in the ordinary equal protection case calling for the most deferential of standards, we insist on knowing the relation between the classification adopted and the object to be attained. The search for the link between classification and objective gives substance to the Equal Protection Clause; it provides guidance and discipline for the legislature, which is entitled to know what sorts of laws it can pass; and it marks the limits of our own authority. In the ordinary case, a law will be sustained if it can be said to advance a legitimate government interest, even if the law seems unwise or works to the disadvantage of a particular group, or if the rationale for it seems tenuous. . . . By requiring that the classification bear a rational relationship to an independent and legitimate legislative end, we ensure that classifications are not drawn for the purpose of disadvantaging the group burdened by the law.

Amendment 2 confounds this normal process of judicial review. It is at once too narrow and too broad. It identifies persons by a single trait and then denies them protection across the board. The resulting disqualification of a class of persons from the right to seek specific protection from the law is unprecedented in our jurisprudence. . . .

It is not within our constitutional tradition to enact laws of this sort. Central both to the idea of the rule of law and to our own Constitution's guarantee of equal protection is the principle that government and each of its parts remain open on impartial terms to all who seek its assistance. Respect for this principle explains why laws singling out a certain class of citizens for disfavored legal status or general hardships are rare. A law declaring that in general it shall be more difficult for one group of citizens than for all others to seek aid from the government is itself a denial of equal protection of the laws in the most literal sense. . . .

A second and related point is that laws of the kind now before us raise the inevitable inference that the disadvantage imposed is born of animosity toward the class of persons affected. . . . Even laws enacted for broad and ambitious purposes often can be explained by reference to legitimate public policies which justify the incidental disadvantages they impose on certain persons. Amendment 2, however, in making a general announcement that gays and lesbians shall not have any particular protections from the law, inflicts on them immediate, continuing, and real injuries that outrun and belie any legitimate justifications that may be claimed for it. We conclude that, in addition to the far-reaching deficiencies of Amendment 2 that we have noted, the principles it offends, in another sense, are conventional and venerable; a law must bear a rational relationship to a legitimate governmental purpose, and Amendment 2 does not.

The primary rationale the State offers for Amendment 2 is respect for other citizens' freedom of association, and in particular the liberties of landlords or employers who have personal or religious objections to homosexuality. Colorado also cites its interest in conserving resources to fight discrimination against other groups. The breadth of the Amendment is so far removed from these particular justifications that we find it impossible to credit them. We cannot say that Amendment 2 is directed to any identifiable legitimate purpose or discrete objective. It is a status-based enactment divorced from any factual context from which we could discern a relationship to legitimate state interests; it is a classification of persons undertaken for its own sake, something the Equal Protection Clause does not permit.

We must conclude that Amendment 2 classifies homosexuals not to further a proper legislative end, but to make them unequal to everyone else. This Colorado cannot do. A State cannot so deem a class of persons a stranger to its laws. Amendment 2 violates the Equal Protection Clause, and the judgment of the Supreme Court of Colorado is affirmed.

It is so ordered.

Justice Scalia, with whom The Chief Justice and Justice Thomas join, dissenting.

The Court has mistaken a Kulturkampf for a fit of spite. The constitutional amendment before us here is not the manifestation of a "'bare . . . desire to harm'" homosexuals, but is rather a modest attempt by seemingly tolerant Coloradans to preserve traditional sexual mores against the efforts of a politically powerful minority to revise those mores through use of the laws. That objective, and the means chosen to achieve it, are not only unimpeachable under any constitutional doctrine hitherto pronounced (hence the opinion's heavy reliance upon principles of righteousness, rather than judicial holdings); they have been specifically approved by the Congress of the United States and by this Court.

In holding that homosexuality cannot be singled out for disfavorable treatment, the Court contradicts a decision, unchallenged here, pronounced only 10 years ago, and places the prestige of this institution behind the proposition that opposition to homosexuality is as reprehensible as racial or religious bias. Whether it is or not is *precisely* the cultural debate that gave rise to the Colorado constitutional amendment (and to the preferential laws against which the amendment was directed). Since the Constitution of the United States says nothing about this subject, it is left to be resolved by normal democratic means, including the democratic adoption of provisions in state constitutions. This Court has no business imposing upon all Americans the resolution favored by the elite class from which the Members of this institution are selected, pronouncing that "animosity" toward homosexuality, is evil. I vigorously dissent.

Let me first discuss [the section of] the Court's opinion . . . which is devoted to rejecting the State's arguments that Amendment 2 "puts gays and lesbians in the same position as all other persons," and "does no more than deny homosexuals special rights." The Court concludes that this reading of Amendment 2's language is "implausible" under the "authoritative construction" given Amendment 2 by the Supreme Court of Colorado. . . .

The clear import of the Colorado court's conclusion that it is not affected is that "general laws and policies that prohibit arbitrary discrimination" would continue to prohibit discrimination on the basis of homosexual conduct as well. This analysis, which is fully in accord with (indeed, follows inescapably from) the text of the constitutional provision, lays to rest such horribles, raised in the course of oral argument, as the prospect that assaults upon homosexuals could not be prosecuted. The amendment prohibits *special treatment* of homosexuals, and nothing more. It would not affect, for example, a requirement of state law that pensions be paid to all retiring state employees with a certain length of service; homosexual employees, as well as others, would be entitled to that benefit. But it would prevent the State or any municipality from making death benefit payments to the "life partner" of a homosexual when it does not make such payments to the long-time roommate of a nonhomosexual employee. Or again, it does not affect the requirement of the State's general insurance laws that customers be afforded coverage without discrimination unrelated to anticipated risk. Thus, homosexuals could not be denied coverage, or charged a greater premium, with respect to auto collision insurance; but neither the State nor any municipality could require that distinctive health insurance risks associated with homosexuality (if there are any) be ignored.

Despite all of its handwringing about the potential effect of Amendment 2 on general antidiscrimination laws, the Court's opinion ultimately does not dispute all this, but assumes it to be true. The only denial of equal treatment it contends homosexuals have suffered is this: they may not obtain *preferential* treatment without amending the state constitution. That is to say, the principle underlying the Court's opinion is that one who is accorded equal treatment under the laws, but cannot as readily as others obtain *preferential* treatment under the laws, has been denied equal protection of the laws. If merely stating this alleged "equal protection" violation does not suffice to refute it, our constitutional jurisprudence has achieved terminal silliness.

The central thesis of the Court's reasoning is that any group is denied equal protection when, to obtain advantage (or, presumably, to avoid disadvantage), it must have recourse to a more general and hence more difficult level of political decisionmaking than others. The world has never heard of such a principle, which is why the Court's opinion is so long on emotive utterance and so short on relevant legal citation. And it seems to me most unlikely that any multilevel democracy can function under such a principle. For *whenever* a disadvantage is imposed, or conferral of a benefit is prohibited at one of the higher levels of democratic decision making (*i.e.,* by the state legislature, rather than local government, or by the people at large in the state constitution rather than the legislature), the affected group has (under this theory) been denied equal protection. To take the simplest of examples, consider a state law prohibiting the award of municipal contracts to relatives of mayors or city councilmen. Once such a law is passed, the group composed of such relatives must, in order to get the benefit of city contracts, persuade the state legislature—unlike all other citizens, who need only persuade the municipality. It is ridiculous to consider this a denial of equal protection, which is why the Court's theory is unheard-of. . . .

I turn next to whether there was a legitimate rational basis for the substance of the constitutional amendment—for the prohibition of special protection for homosexuals. It is unsurprising that the Court avoids discussion of this question, since the answer is so obviously yes. The case most relevant to the issue before us today is not even mentioned in the Court's opinion: In *Bowers* v. *Hardwick* (1986), we held that the Constitution does not prohibit what virtually all States had done from the founding of the Republic until very recent years—making homosexual conduct a crime. That holding is unassailable, except by those who think that the Constitution changes to suit current fashions. . . .

But assuming that, in Amendment 2, a person of homosexual "orientation" is someone who does not engage in homosexual conduct but merely has a tendency or desire to do so, *Bowers* still suffices to establish a rational basis for the provision. If it is rational to criminalize the conduct, surely it is rational to deny special favor and protection to those with a self-avowed tendency or desire to engage in the conduct. Indeed, where criminal sanctions are not involved, homosexual "orientation" is an acceptable stand-in for homosexual conduct. A State "does not violate the Equal Protection Clause merely because the classifications made by its laws are imperfect." Just as a policy barring the hiring of methadone users as transit employees does not violate equal protection simply because *some* methadone users pose no threat to passenger safety, and just as a mandatory retirement age of 50 for police officers does not violate equal protection even though it prematurely ends the careers of many policemen over 50 who still have the capacity to do the job, Amendment 2 is not constitutionally invalid simply because it could have been drawn more precisely so as to withdraw special antidiscrimination protections only from those of homosexual "orientation" who actually engage in homosexual conduct. . . .

The Court's opinion contains grim, disapproving hints that Coloradans have been guilty of "animus" or "animosity" toward homosexuality, as though that has been established as Unamerican. Of course it is our moral heritage that one should not hate any human being or class of human beings. But I had thought that one could consider certain conduct reprehensible—murder, for example, or polygamy, or cruelty to animals—and could exhibit even "animus" toward such conduct. Surely that is the only sort of "animus" at issue here: moral disapproval of homosexual conduct, the same sort of moral disapproval that produced the centuries-old criminal laws that we held constitutional in *Bowers*. The Colorado amendment does not, to speak entirely precisely, prohibit giving favored status to people who are *homosexuals;* they can be favored for many reasons—for example, because they are senior citizens or members of racial minorities. But it prohibits giving them favored status *because of their homosexual conduct*—that is, it prohibits favored status *for homosexuality*.

But though Coloradans are, as I say, *entitled* to be hostile toward homosexual conduct, the fact is that the degree of hostility reflected by Amendment 2 is the smallest conceivable. The Court's portrayal of Coloradans as a society fallen victim to pointless, hate-filled "gay-bashing" is so false as to be comical. Colorado not only is one of the 25 States that have repealed their anti-sodomy laws, but was among the first to do so. But the society that eliminates criminal punishment for homosexual acts does not necessarily abandon the view that homosexuality is morally wrong and socially harmful; often, abolition simply reflects the view that enforcement of such criminal laws involves unseemly intrusion into the intimate lives of citizens.

. . . Amendment 2 . . . sought to counter both the geographic concentration and the disproportionate political power of homosexuals by (1) resolving the controversy at the statewide level, and (2) making the election a single issue contest for both sides. It put directly, to all the citizens of the State, the question: should homosexuality be given special protection? They answered no. The Court today asserts that this most democratic of procedures is unconstitutional. Lacking any cases to establish that facially absurd proposition, it simply asserts that it *must* be unconstitutional, because it has never happened before.

As I have noted above, this is proved false every time a state law prohibiting or disfavoring certain conduct is passed, because such a law prevents the adversely affected group—whether drug addicts, or smokers, or gun owners, or motorcyclists—from changing the policy thus established in "each of [the] parts" of the State. . . .

But there is a much closer analogy, one that involves precisely the effort by the majority of citizens to preserve its view of sexual morality statewide, against the efforts of a geographically concentrated and politically powerful minority to undermine it. The constitutions of the States of Arizona, Idaho, New Mexico, Oklahoma, and Utah *to this day* contain provisions stating that polygamy is "forever prohibited." Polygamists, and those who have a polygamous "orientation," have been "singled out" by these provisions for much more severe treatment than merely denial of favored status; and that treatment can only be changed by achieving amendment of the state constitutions. The Court's disposition today suggests that these provisions are unconstitutional, and that polygamy must be permitted in these States on a state-legislated, or perhaps even local-option, basis—unless, of course, polygamists for some reason have fewer constitutional rights than homosexuals. . . .

[The] Court today . . . invent[s] a novel and extravagant constitutional doctrine to take the victory away from traditional forces. . . . To suggest, for example, that this constitutional amendment springs from nothing more than "'a bare . . . desire to harm a politically unpopular group,'" is nothing short of insulting. (It is also nothing short of preposterous to call "politically unpopular" a group which enjoys enormous influence in American media and politics, and which, as the trial court here noted, though composing no more than 4% of the population, had the support of 46% of the voters on Amendment 2). . . .

Today's opinion has no foundation in American constitutional law, and barely pretends to. The people of Colorado have adopted an entirely reasonable provision which does not even disfavor homosexuals in any substantive sense, but merely denies them preferential treatment. Amendment 2 is designed to prevent piecemeal deterioration of the sexual morality favored by a majority of Coloradans, and is not only an appropriate means to that legitimate end, but a means that Americans have employed before. Striking it down is an act not of judicial judgment, but of political will. I dissent.

▼▲▼

Note that the Court invalidates Amendment 2 under the same standard it used to strike down Idaho's law in *Reed* v. *Reed* (1971). The Colorado law, by "fencing" out gays and lesbians from using the political process to enact protective legislation, had demonstrated "animus" toward homosexuals. Such motivation was, in the Court's opinion, irrational. State and local antidiscrimination laws did not grant homosexuals special rights, as Amendment 2 supporters claimed. Instead, such laws gave them a level of protection no different from that of racial minorities, women, and other groups covered under civil rights laws. *Evans* left open the question of whether a legal classification based on sexual orientation should be considered, like race and ethnic origin, suspect, or like sex, deserving of intermediate scrutiny. How the Court chooses to treat discrimination based on sexual orientation will have a considerable impact on the development of protective legislation for gays and lesbians.

Discrimination Based on Wealth and Social Status

In 1932, President Franklin D. Roosevelt, promising Americans a "New Deal" to lift them out of the Great Depression, defeated incumbent Herbert Hoover by a landslide majority, winning all but four states and capturing almost 60 percent of the popular vote. Roosevelt's stunning victory left no aspect of the American political landscape untouched. Political scientists often point to his first election—he would be reelected three consecutive times—as one that permanently altered the prevailing conception of the relationship between government and the people. Out of the New Deal came the modern social welfare state, and more Americans than ever before found their lives touched by the federal government. A number of laws and programs that Americans today take for granted, such as Social Security, occupational safety and health regulation, the minimum wage, and federal subsidies for roads, utilities, and basic infrastructure, were born during the New Deal. Indeed, so accepted is the New Deal in post–Great Depression America that no president, despite occasional rhetoric to the contrary, has dared to launch a full-scale effort to dismantle the social welfare state created by Roosevelt.[97]

One of the most extraordinary features of the New Deal was the directness with which it addressed the nature of social and economic relations. Unlike any president before him, Roosevelt actually acknowledged that poverty was the result of an economic system created and maintained by the process of politics, rather than simply the product of a predetermined, natural state. "We must lay hold of the fact that economic laws are not made by nature," said Roosevelt in an early speech to Congress on the New Deal legislative agenda. "They are made by human beings." Economic arrangements and their social consequences, he observed, were not accidental. They were, in Roosevelt's words, the products of "this man-made world of ours."[98] The New Deal punctured the myth of *laissez-faire* as the natural economic order of the Constitution. Economic rights do not just *exist;* they are *created* by law, and it is the law that establishes who can do what to whom. Not even the purest of laissez-faire economic arrangements can avoid this basic fact of political organization. Government had the right to address the social and economic problems of the people it was entrusted to represent. It could respond, in the words of Justice Oliver Wendell Holmes, to the "felt necessities" of the time.[99]

The next major wave of government activism crested in the 1960s when President Lyndon Johnson launched the Great Society, a series of social and economic programs that marked the most ambitious effort of the federal government to address what the sociologist Michael Harrington, in his influential book *The Other America,* called the "economic underworld of American life."[100] The Great Society left virtually no area of social policy untouched, creating many new programs and greatly expanding many others established by the New Deal. Perhaps the best symbol of President Johnson's determination to eradicate poverty and establish a minimum income level was the dramatic expansion of the Aid to Families with Dependent Children (AFDC) program, established during the New Deal as part of the Social Security Act of 1935. Over time, the AFDC grew from a modest effort by the federal government to supplement state and private assistance programs into a major social welfare program. By 1969, the number of families receiving AFDC benefits was approximately 1,698,000, compared with 774,000 in 1959 and 305,000 in 1939.[101]

Since not all states provided the same level of benefits to supplement AFDC payments, migration from state to state in search of more generous social welfare assistance was not uncommon. To discourage out-of-state residents from taking advantage of their social welfare programs, many states enacted laws that required AFDC recipients to live in-state for a fixed period of time to become eligible for assistance. In *Shapiro* v. *Thompson* (1969), the Supreme Court ruled that such eligibility requirements violated the "fundamental rights" of individuals to travel under the Equal Protection Clause.[102] By making the right to travel the constitutional issue, the Court avoided what many advocates of expansive social welfare rights had wanted, which was to treat laws such as the one struck down in *Shapiro* as violative of a fundamental right to equal treatment under law without regard to wealth and social status. Social service lawyers and advocates for the poor, emboldened by *Shapiro*, pressed the courts to treat the rights established by Great Society programs as deserving of the same level of constitutional protection as discrimination based on race and ethnic origin.

The Court soon demonstrated that it was not prepared to depart from the traditional model of equal protection analysis to embrace wealth and social status as criteria that merited special constitutional protection. In *Dandridge* v. *Williams* (1971), the Court held that Maryland's AFDC program, which limited allowances to $250 per month per family regardless of its size or need, did not violate the Equal Protection Clause. Justice Potter Stewart, who concurred in *Shapiro*, wrote that "[i]n the area of economics and social welfare, a State does not violate the Equal Protection Clause merely because the classifications made by its laws are imperfect. If the classification has some 'reasonable basis,' it does not offend the Constitution simply because the classification 'is not made with mathematical nicety or because in practice it results in some inequality.'"[103] But the Court's most important decision setting out the level of protection afforded to privileges established by legislation and rights considered fundamental under the Constitution came in *San Antonio Independent School District* v. *Rodriguez* (1973). There, the Court considered one of the most controversial issues to emerge from the social activism of the 1960s: the right to an equal public education regardless of wealth and social status.

San Antonio Independent School District v. Rodriguez

411 U.S. 1 (1973)

The Edgewood School District is located about four miles west of San Antonio, a southwestern Texas city that, like Dallas and Houston, experienced an economic boom in the late 1960s. San Antonio had been given a national "Cleanest City" award in 1967 and used the good publicity to attract new business and promote tourism, including renewing interest in the Alamo, the site of the famous 1836 battle between Mexican and American troops. The twenty-five schools in the Edgewood district, which served twenty-two thousand students, 90 percent of whom were Mexican American, remained invisible in the shadows of this new-found prosperity. It was among the poorest school districts in the state, with a crumbling infrastructure, less than adequate classroom supplies, and teachers who lacked state certification.

In July 1968, Demetrio Rodriguez challenged the complex financing scheme for public schools in Texas, claiming that its system discriminated against poor school districts such as Edgewood. Texas, like most states, financed its schools through a combination of federal and state funds. Property taxes fund most of states' education budgets, and it was here that Rodriguez highlighted the inequities in Texas's system. In 1968, property values were assessed at $5,960 per pupil, and Edgewood residents were taxed at the rate of $1.05 per $100 in an assessed value. In Alamo Heights, an affluent San Antonio school district, property values were assessed at approximately $49,000 per pupil, based on a taxation rate of eighty-five cents per $100 in assessed value. Rodriguez claimed that this disparity in property values and taxation rates left poor people in an inferior position in the Texas education system, and violated their rights under the Equal Protection Clause by denying them an equal education.

A federal district court agreed with Rodriguez, holding that Texas's education system was unconstitutional because it discriminated against individuals based on wealth. Texas appealed to the Supreme Court. Because of the potential significance that *Rodriguez* held for rights claims brought under the Equal Protection Clause, numerous liberal public interest organizations filed *amicus* briefs when the case reached the Court, as did the governors of five states that had reformed their own school financing systems. Twenty-five states and several more local governments filed a joint brief supporting the Texas system.

The Court's decision was 5 to 4. Justice Powell delivered the opinion of the Court. Justice Stewart filed a concurring opinion. Justice Brennan dissented. Justice White, joined by Justices Douglas and Brennan, also dissented, as did Justice Marshall, who was joined by Justice Douglas.

▼▲▼

MR. JUSTICE POWELL delivered the opinion of the Court.

Texas virtually concedes that its historically rooted dual system of financing education could not withstand the strict judicial scrutiny that this Court has found appropriate in reviewing legislative judgments that interfere with fundamental constitutional rights or that involve suspect classifications. If, as previous decisions have indicated, strict scrutiny means that the State's system is not entitled to the usual presumption of validity, that the State rather than the complainants must carry a "heavy burden of justification," that the State must demonstrate that its educational system has been structured with "precision," and is "tailored" narrowly to serve legitimate objectives and that it has selected the "less drastic means" for effectuating its objectives, the Texas financing system and its counterpart in virtually every other State will not pass muster. The State candidly admits that "[n]o one familiar with the Texas system would contend that it has yet achieved perfection." Apart from its concession that educational financing in Texas has "defects" and "imperfections," the State defends the system's rationality with vigor and disputes the District Court's finding that it lacks a "reasonable basis."

This, then, establishes the framework for our analysis. We must decide, first, whether the Texas system of financing public education operates to the disadvantage of some suspect class or impinges upon a fundamental right explicitly or implicitly protected by the Constitution, thereby requiring strict judicial scrutiny. If so, the judgment of the District Court should be affirmed. If not, the Texas scheme must still be examined to determine whether it rationally furthers some legitimate, articulated state purpose and therefore does not constitute an invidious discrimination in violation of the Equal Protection Clause of the Fourteenth Amendment. . . .

The wealth discrimination discovered by the District Court in this case, and by several other courts that have recently struck down school-financing laws in other States, is quite unlike any of the forms of wealth discrimination heretofore reviewed by this Court. Rather than focusing on the unique features of the alleged discrimination, the courts in these cases have virtually assumed their findings of a suspect classification through a simplistic process of analysis: since, under the traditional systems of financing public schools, some poorer people receive less expensive educations than other more affluent people, these systems discriminate on the basis of wealth. This approach largely ignores the hard threshold questions, including whether it makes a difference for purposes of consideration under the Constitution that the class of disadvantaged "poor" cannot be identified or defined in customary equal protection terms, and whether the relative—rather than absolute—nature of the asserted deprivation is of significant consequence. Before a State's laws and the justifications for the classifications they create are subjected to strict judicial scrutiny, we think these threshold considerations must be analyzed more closely than they were in the court below. The case comes to us with no definitive description of the classifying facts or delineation of the disfavored class. Examination of the District Court's opinion and of appellees' complaint, briefs, and contentions at oral argument suggests, however, at least three ways in which the discrimination claimed here might be described. The Texas system of school financing might be regarded as discriminating (1) against "poor" persons whose incomes fall below some identifiable level of poverty or who might be characterized as functionally "indigent," or (2) against those who are relatively poorer than others, or (3) against all those who, irrespective of their personal incomes, happen to reside in relatively poorer school districts. Our task must be to ascertain whether, in fact, the Texas system has been shown to discriminate on any of these possible bases and, if so, whether the resulting classification may be regarded as suspect. . . .

First, in support of their charge that the system discriminates against the "poor," appellees have made no effort to demonstrate that it operates to the peculiar disadvantage of any class fairly definable as indigent, or as composed of persons whose incomes are beneath any designated poverty level. Indeed, there is reason to believe that the poorest families are not necessarily clustered in the poorest property districts. A recent and exhaustive study of school districts in Connecticut concluded that "[i]t is clearly incorrect . . . to contend that the 'poor' live in 'poor' districts. . . . Defining 'poor' families as those below the Bureau of the Census 'poverty level,'" the Connecticut study found, not surprisingly, that the poor were clustered around commercial and industrial areas—those same areas that provide the most attractive sources of property tax income for school districts. Whether a similar pattern would be discovered in Texas is not known, but there is no basis on the record in this case for assuming that the poorest people—defined by reference to any level of absolute impecunity—are concentrated in the poorest districts.

Second, neither appellees nor the District Court addressed the fact that, unlike each of the foregoing cases, lack of personal resources has not occasioned an absolute deprivation of the desired benefit. The argument here is not that the children in districts having relatively low assessable property values are receiving no public education; rather, it is that they are receiving a poorer quality education than that available to children in districts having more assessable wealth. Apart from the unsettled and disputed question whether the quality of education may be determined by the amount of money expended for it, a sufficient answer to appellees' argument is that, at least where wealth is involved, the Equal Protection Clause does not require absolute equality or precisely equal advantages. . . .

For these two reasons—the absence of any evidence that the financing system discriminates against any definable category of "poor" people or that it results in the absolute deprivation of education—the disadvantaged class is not susceptible of identification in traditional terms. . . .

[I]t is clear that [Rodriguez's] suit asks this Court to extend its most exacting scrutiny to review a system that allegedly discriminates against a large, diverse, and amorphous class, unified only by the common factor of residence in districts that happen to have less taxable wealth than other districts. The system of alleged discrimination and the class it defines have none of the traditional indicia of suspectness: the class is not saddled with such disabilities, or subjected to such a history of purposeful unequal treatment, or relegated to such a position of political powerlessness as to command extraordinary protection from the majoritarian political process. . . .

We thus conclude that the Texas system does not operate to the peculiar disadvantage of any suspect class. But in recognition of the fact that this Court has never heretofore held that wealth discrimination alone provides an adequate basis for invoking strict scrutiny, appellees have not relied solely on this contention. They also assert that the State's system impermissibly interferes with the exercise of a "fundamental" right and that accordingly the prior decisions of this Court require the application of the strict standard of judicial review. It is this question—whether education is a fundamental right, in the sense that it is among the rights and liberties protected by the Constitution—which has so consumed the attention of courts and commentators in recent years.

In *Brown* v. *Board of Education* (1954), a unanimous Court recognized that "education is perhaps the most important function of state and local governments." . . . But the importance of a service performed by the State does not determine whether it must be regarded as fundamental for purposes of examination under the Equal Protection Clause. . . .

It is not the province of this Court to create substantive constitutional rights in the name of guaranteeing equal protection of the laws. Thus, the key to discovering whether education is "fundamental" is not to be found in comparisons of the relative societal significance of education as opposed to subsistence or housing. Nor is it to be found by weighing whether education is as important as the right to travel. Rather, the answer lies in assessing whether there is a right to education explicitly or implicitly guaranteed by the Constitution.

Education, of course, is not among the rights afforded explicit protection under our Federal Constitution. Nor do we find any basis for saying it is implicitly so protected. As we have said, the undisputed importance of education will not alone cause this Court to depart from the usual standard for reviewing a State's social and economic legislation. It is appellees' contention, however, that education is distinguishable from other services and benefits provided by the State because it bears a peculiarly close relationship to other rights and liberties accorded protection under the Constitution. Specifically, they insist that education is itself a fundamental personal right because it is essential to the effective exercise of First Amendment freedoms and to intelligent utilization of the right to vote. In asserting a nexus between speech and education, appellees urge that the right to speak is meaningless unless the speaker is capable of articulating his thoughts intelligently and persuasively. The "marketplace of ideas" is an empty forum for those lacking basic communicative tools. Likewise, they argue that the corollary right to receive information becomes little more than a hollow privilege when the recipient has not been taught to read, assimilate, and utilize available knowledge.

A similar line of reasoning is pursued with respect to the right to vote. Exercise of the franchise, it is contended, cannot be divorced from the educational foundation of the voter. The electoral process, if reality is to conform to the democratic ideal, depends on an informed electorate: a voter cannot cast his ballot intelligently unless his reading skills and thought processes have been adequately developed.

We need not dispute any of these propositions. The Court has long afforded zealous protection against unjustifiable governmental interference with the individual's rights to speak and to vote. Yet we have never presumed to possess either the ability or the authority to guarantee to the citizenry the most effective speech or the most informed electoral choice. That these may be desirable goals of a system of freedom of expression and of a representative form of government is not to be doubted. These are indeed goals to be pursued by a people whose thoughts and beliefs are freed from governmental interference. But they are not values to be pursued by judicial intrusion into otherwise legitimate state activities. . . .

It must be remembered, also, that every claim arising under the Equal Protection Clause has implications for the relationship between national and state power under our federal system. Questions of federalism are always inherent in the process of determining whether a State's laws are to be accorded the traditional presumption of constitutionality, or are to be subjected instead to rigorous judicial scrutiny. While "[t]he maintenance of the principles of federalism is a foremost consideration in interpreting any of the pertinent constitutional provisions under which this Court examines state action," it would be difficult to imagine a case having a greater potential impact on our federal system than the one now before us, in which we are urged to abrogate systems of financing public education presently in existence in virtually every State. . . .

In sum, to the extent that the Texas system of school financing results in unequal expenditures between children who happen to reside in different districts, we cannot say that such disparities are the product of a system that is so irrational as to be invidiously discriminatory. Texas has acknowledged its shortcomings and has persistently endeavored—not without some success—to ameliorate the differences in levels of expenditures without sacrificing the benefits of local participation. The Texas plan is not the result of hurried, ill-conceived legislation. It certainly is not the product of purposeful discrimination against any group or class. On the contrary, it is rooted in decades of experience in Texas and elsewhere, and in major part is the product of responsible studies by qualified people. . . . One also must remember that the system here challenged is not peculiar to Texas or to any other State. In its essential characteristics, the Texas plan for financing public education reflects what many educators for a half century have thought was an enlightened approach to a problem for which there is no perfect solution. We are unwilling to assume for ourselves a level of wisdom superior to that of legislators, scholars, and educational authorities in 50 States, especially where the alternatives proposed are only recently conceived and nowhere yet tested. The constitutional standard under the Equal Protection Clause is whether the challenged state action rationally furthers a legitimate state purpose or interest. We hold that the Texas plan abundantly satisfies this standard.

MR. JUSTICE MARSHALL, with whom MR. JUSTICE DOUGLAS concurs, dissenting.

The Court today decides, in effect, that a State may constitutionally vary the quality of education which it offers its children in accordance with the amount of taxable wealth located in the school districts within which they reside. The majority's decision represents an abrupt departure from the mainstream of recent state and federal court decisions concerning the unconstitutionality of state educational financing schemes dependent upon taxable local wealth. More unfortunately, though, the majority's holding can only be seen as a retreat from our historic commitment to equality of educational opportunity and as unsupportable acquiescence in a system which deprives children in their earliest years of the chance to reach their full potential as citizens. The Court does this despite the absence of any substantial justification for a scheme which arbitrarily channels educational resources in accordance with the fortuity of the amount of taxable wealth within each district.

In my judgment, the right of every American to an equal start in life, so far as the provision of a state service as important as education is concerned, is far too vital to permit state discrimination on grounds as tenuous as those presented by this record. Nor can I accept the notion that it is sufficient to remit these appellees to the vagaries of the political process which, contrary to the majority's suggestion, has proved singularly unsuited to the task of providing a remedy for this discrimination. I, for one, am unsatisfied with the hope of an ultimate "political" solution sometime in the indefinite future while, in the meantime, countless children unjustifiably receive inferior educations that "may affect their hearts and minds in a way unlikely ever to be undone," *Brown* v. *Board of Education* (1954). I must therefore respectfully dissent. . . .

I must once more voice my disagreement with the Court's rigidified approach to equal protection analysis. The Court apparently seeks to establish today that equal protection cases fall into one of two neat categories which dictate the appropriate standard of review—strict scrutiny or mere rationality. But this Court's decisions in the field of equal protection defy such easy categorization. A principled reading of what this Court has done reveals that it has applied a spectrum of standards in reviewing discrimination allegedly violative of the Equal Protection Clause. This spectrum clearly comprehends variations in the degree of care with which the Court will scrutinize particular classifications, depending, I believe, on the constitutional and societal importance of the interest adversely affected and the recognized invidiousness of the basis upon which the particular classification is drawn. . . .

I therefore cannot accept the majority's labored efforts to demonstrate that fundamental interests, which call for strict scrutiny of the challenged classification, encompass only established rights which we are somehow bound to recognize from the text of the Constitution itself. To be sure, some interests which the Court has deemed to be fundamental for purposes of equal protection analysis are themselves constitutionally protected rights. Thus, discrimination against the guaranteed right of freedom of speech has called for strict judicial scrutiny. Further, every citizen's right to travel interstate, although nowhere expressly mentioned in the Constitution, has long been recognized as implicit in the premises underlying that document: the right "was conceived from the beginning to be a necessary concomitant of the stronger Union the Constitution created." . . . But it will not do to suggest that the "answer" to whether an interest is fundamental for purposes of equal protection analysis is always determined by whether that interest "is a right . . . explicitly or implicitly guaranteed by the Constitution."

I would like to know where the Constitution guarantees the right to procreate, or the right to vote in state elections, or the right to an appeal from a criminal conviction. These are instances in which, due to the importance of the interests at stake, the Court has displayed a strong concern with the existence of discriminatory state treatment. But the Court has never said or indicated that these are interests which independently enjoy full-blown constitutional protection. . . .

The Court seeks solace for its action today in the possibility of legislative reform. The Court's suggestions of legislative redress and experimentation will doubtless be of great comfort to the schoolchildren of Texas's disadvantaged districts, but considering the vested interests of wealthy school districts in the preservation of the status quo, they are worth little more. The possibility of legislative action is, in all events, no answer to this Court's duty under the Constitution to eliminate unjustified state discrimination. In this case we have been presented with an instance of such discrimination, in a particularly invidious form, against an individual interest of large constitutional and practical importance. To support the demonstrated discrimination in the provision of educational opportunity the State has offered a justification which, on analysis, takes on at best an ephemeral character. Thus, I believe that the wide disparities in taxable district property wealth inherent in the local property tax element of the Texas financing scheme render that scheme violative of the Equal Protection Clause.

▼▲▼

Lawyers for Rodriguez had hoped that the Court would see their argument—that wealth and social status should not serve as an impediment to an equal education—as analogous to the NAACP's position in *Brown* on school segregation. But Justice Powell, writing for the majority, ruled instead that it was "not the province of this Court to create substantive constitutional rights in the name of guaranteeing equal protection of the laws." The Court's position in *Rodriguez* recalled, in many ways, the legal formalism that dominated constitutional jurisprudence prior to the New Deal. Rather than acknowledge the legacy of the Constitutional Revolution of 1937, namely, that rights were a product of political choices, the Court retreated to the idea that certain rights were prepolitical and presocial and others were privileges established through legislation. *Rodriguez* did not close the door on the social activism on behalf of the poor, but it did send a very clear message that the Court was not prepared to embrace the Great Society vision of equality as having a basis in the Constitution.

The Court has not foreclosed the possibility of successful equal protection claims involving classifications beyond race, sex, and sexual orientation. With Justice Powell providing the crucial swing vote, the Court, in *Plyler* v. *Doe* (1982), ruled that a Texas law making the children of illegal aliens ineligible to attend public schools violated the Equal Protection Clause. Note, as you read Justice Brennan's majority opinion, how carefully he treads around the Court's holding in *Rodriguez* to treat the constitutional claim as one involving discrimination based on alienage and ethnic origin, not education.

Plyler v. *Doe*

457 U.S. 202 (1982)

Labor shortages in the southwestern United States and California during World War II led the federal government to negotiate an agreement with Mexico permitting temporary laborers into the United States to work on farms and in other low-level, poorly paid capacities. By the early 1960s, the rights of migrant labor had been swept into the emergent social movement on behalf of the poor. Congress's decision to end the Bracero Program, however, had no real effect on illegal aliens entering the United States in search of work, education, and social service benefits unavailable to them in Mexico. Illegal immigration was spread throughout the Southwest, but Texas received a disproportionate share. And in contrast to the commonly held notion of illegal immigration, not all aliens arrived in the United States below the border patrol's radar screen. Cheap Mexican farm labor was an economic boon to the region, and many companies involved in agribusiness recruited such workers and arranged for their arrivals.

In 1975, two years after *Rodriguez,* Texas, in an effort to discourage illegal immigration, amended its state education laws to bar illegal and undocumented aliens from attending its public elementary and secondary schools. Many Texas school districts opposed the plan, both because they believed it punished innocent school-age children for their parents' decision to enter the United States and because agribusinesses believed it would discourage the arrival of cheap labor on which they had come to depend. In 1977, the parents of two children with illegal alien status enrolled in the Tyler Independent School District filed suit in federal district court, claiming that the Texas law violated the Equal Protection Clause. The court ruled that the Texas law was unconstitutional under any standard of review, and did not rule on whether laws targeting illegal aliens were entitled to heightened or even strict scrutiny. A federal court agreed, setting the stage for an appeal to the Supreme Court.

The Court's decision was 5 to 4. Justice Brennan delivered the opinion of the Court. Justices Blackmun, Marshall, and Powell filed separate concurring opinions. Chief Justice Burger, joined by Justices O'Connor, Rehnquist, and White, dissented.

▼▲▼

Justice Brennan delivered the opinion of the Court.

The question presented by these cases is whether, consistent with the Equal Protection Clause of the Fourteenth Amendment, Texas may deny to undocumented school-age children the free public education that it provides to children who are citizens of the United States or legally admitted aliens. . . .

The Fourteenth Amendment provides that "[n]o State shall . . . deprive any person of life, liberty, or property, without due process of law; nor deny to any person within its jurisdiction the equal protection of the laws." Appellants argue at the outset that undocumented aliens, because of their immigration status, are not "persons within the jurisdiction" of the State of Texas, and that they therefore have no right to the equal protection of Texas law. We reject this argument. Whatever his status under the immigration laws, an alien is surely a "person" in any ordinary sense of that term. Aliens, even aliens whose presence in this country is unlawful, have long been recognized as "persons" guaranteed due process of law by the Fifth and Fourteenth Amendments. Indeed, we have clearly held that the Fifth Amendment protects aliens whose presence in this country is unlawful from invidious discrimination by the Federal Government.

In appellants' view, persons who have entered the United States illegally are not "within the jurisdiction" of a State even if they are present within a State's boundaries and subject to its laws. Neither our cases nor the logic of the Fourteenth Amendment supports that constricting construction of the phrase "within its jurisdiction." We have never suggested that the class of persons who might avail themselves of the equal protection guarantee is less than coextensive with that entitled to due process. To the contrary, we have recognized that both provisions were fashioned to protect an identical class of persons, and to reach every exercise of state authority. . . .

There is simply no support for appellants' suggestion that "due process" is somehow of greater stature than "equal protection" and therefore available to a larger class of persons. To the contrary, each aspect of the Fourteenth Amendment reflects an elementary limitation on state power. To permit a State to employ the phrase "within its jurisdiction" in order to identify subclasses of persons whom it would define as beyond its jurisdiction, thereby relieving itself of the obligation to assure that its laws are designed and applied equally to those persons, would undermine the principal purpose for which the Equal Protection Clause was incorporated in the Fourteenth Amendment. The Equal Protection Clause was intended to work nothing less than the abolition of all caste-based and invidious class-based legislation. That objective is fundamentally at odds with the power the State asserts here to classify persons subject to its laws as nonetheless excepted from its protection. . . .

Our conclusion that the illegal aliens who are plaintiffs in these cases may claim the benefit of the Fourteenth Amendment's guarantee of equal protection only begins the inquiry. The more difficult question is whether the Equal Protection Clause has been violated by the refusal of the State of Texas to reimburse local school boards for the education of children who cannot demonstrate that their presence within the United States is lawful, or by the imposition by those school boards of the burden of tuition on those children. It is to this question that we now turn.

The Equal Protection Clause directs that "all persons similarly circumstanced shall be treated alike." But so too, "[t]he Constitution does not require things which are different in fact or opinion to be treated in law as though they were the same," *Tigner* v. *Texas* (1940). The initial discretion to determine what is "different" and what is "the same" resides in the legislatures of the States. A legislature must have substantial latitude to establish classifications that roughly approximate the nature of the problem perceived, that accommodate competing concerns both public and private, and that account for limitations on the practical ability of the State to remedy every ill. In applying the Equal Protection Clause to most forms of state action, we thus seek only the assurance that the classification at issue bears some fair relationship to a legitimate public purpose. . . .

Sheer incapability or lax enforcement of the laws barring entry into this country, coupled with the failure to establish an effective bar to the employment of undocumented aliens, has resulted in the creation of a substantial "shadow population" of illegal migrants—numbering in the millions—within our borders. This situation raises the specter of a caste of undocumented resident aliens, encouraged by some to remain here as a source of cheap labor, but nevertheless denied the benefits that our society makes available to citizens and lawful residents. The existence of such an underclass presents most difficult problems for a Nation that prides itself on adherence to principles of equality under law.

The children who are plaintiffs in these cases are special members of this underclass. Persuasive arguments support the view that a State may withhold its beneficence from those whose very presence within the United States is the product of their own unlawful conduct. These arguments do not apply with the same force to classifications imposing disabilities on the minor children of such illegal entrants. At the least, those who elect to enter our territory by stealth and in violation of our law should be prepared to bear the consequences, including, but not limited to, deportation. But the children of those illegal entrants are not comparably situated. Their "parents have the ability to conform their conduct to societal norms," and presumably the ability to remove themselves from the State's jurisdiction; but the children who are plaintiffs in these cases "can affect neither their parents' conduct nor their own status." *Trimble* v. *Gordon* (1977). Even if the State found it expedient to control the conduct of adults by acting against their children, legislation directing the onus of a parent's misconduct against his children does not comport with fundamental conceptions of justice. . . .

Public education is not a "right" granted to individuals by the Constitution, *San Antonio Independent School Dist.* v. *Rodriguez* (1973). But neither is it merely some governmental "benefit" indistinguishable from other forms of social welfare legislation. Both the importance of education in maintaining our basic institutions, and the lasting impact of its deprivation on the life of the child, mark the distinction. . . . We have recognized "the public schools as a most vital civic institution for the preservation of a democratic system of government." . . . In addition, education provides the basic tools by which individuals might lead economically productive lives to the benefit of us all. In sum, education has a fundamental role in maintaining the fabric of our society. We cannot ignore the significant social costs borne by our Nation when select groups are denied the means to absorb the values and skills upon which our social order rests. . . .

If the State is to deny a discrete group of innocent children the free public education that it offers to other children residing within its borders, that denial must be justified by a showing that it furthers some substantial state interest. No such showing was made here. Accordingly, the judgment of the Court of Appeals in each of these cases is

Affirmed.

JUSTICE POWELL, concurring.

I join the opinion of the Court, and write separately to emphasize the unique character of the cases before us.

The classification in question severely disadvantages children who are the victims of a combination of circumstances. Access from Mexico into this country, across our 2,000-mile border, is readily available and virtually uncontrollable. Illegal aliens are attracted by our employment opportunities, and perhaps by other benefits as well. This is a problem of serious national proportions, as the Attorney General recently has recognized. Perhaps because of the intractability of the problem, Congress—vested by the

Constitution with the responsibility of protecting our borders and legislating with respect to aliens—has not provided effective leadership in dealing with this problem. It therefore is certain that illegal aliens will continue to enter the United States and, as the record makes clear, an unknown percentage of them will remain here. I agree with the Court that their children should not be left on the streets uneducated. . . .

In reaching this conclusion, I am not unmindful of what must be the exasperation of responsible citizens and government authorities in Texas and other States similarly situated. Their responsibility, if any, for the influx of aliens is slight compared to that imposed by the Constitution on the Federal Government. So long as the ease of entry remains inviting, and the power to deport is exercised infrequently by the Federal Government, the additional expense of admitting these children to public schools might fairly be shared by the Federal and State Governments. But it hardly can be argued rationally that anyone benefits from the creation within our borders of a subclass of illiterate persons many of whom will remain in the State, adding to the problems and costs of both State and National Governments attendant upon unemployment, welfare, and crime.

CHIEF JUSTICE BURGER, with whom JUSTICE WHITE, JUSTICE REHNQUIST, and JUSTICE O'CONNOR join, dissenting.

Were it our business to set the Nation's social policy, I would agree without hesitation that it is senseless for an enlightened society to deprive any children—including illegal aliens—of an elementary education. I fully agree that it would be folly—and wrong—to tolerate creation of a segment of society made up of illiterate persons, many having a limited or no command of our language. However, the Constitution does not constitute us as "Platonic Guardians" nor does it vest in this Court the authority to strike down laws because they do not meet our standards of desirable social policy, "wisdom," or "common sense." We trespass on the assigned function of the political branches under our structure of limited and separated powers when we assume a policymaking role as the Court does today. . . .

The Court's holding today manifests the justly criticized judicial tendency to attempt speedy and wholesale formulation of "remedies" for the failures—or simply the laggard pace—of the political processes of our system of government. The Court employs, and in my view abuses, the Fourteenth Amendment in an effort to become an omnipotent and omniscient problem solver. That the motives for doing so are noble and compassionate does not alter the fact that the Court distorts our constitutional function to make amends for the defaults of others. . . .

I have no quarrel with the conclusion that the Equal Protection Clause of the Fourteenth Amendment applies to aliens who, after their illegal entry into this country, are indeed physically "within the jurisdiction" of a state. However, as the Court concedes, this "only begins the inquiry." The Equal Protection Clause does not mandate identical treatment of different categories of persons.

The [central] issue in these cases, simply put, is whether, for purposes of allocating its finite resources, a state has a legitimate reason to differentiate between persons who are lawfully within the state and those who are unlawfully there. The distinction the State of Texas has drawn—based not only upon its own legitimate interests but on classifications established by the Federal Government in its immigration laws and policies—is not unconstitutional.

▼▲▼

By the early 1990s, the rights of illegal aliens to receive public education and other basic social services provided by state governments resurfaced as a controversial political issue. In 1994, California enacted a statewide referendum, popularly known as Proposition 187, which denied illegal aliens, including children, access to state medical services and health care, police and emergency rescue assistance, and the right to attend its public schools. California, as Texas had a decade before, argued that such legislation was necessary to deter illegal immigration. A federal district court, however, ruled that Proposition 187 was unconstitutional, and an appeals court affirmed. The Supreme Court, without comment, later let stand the lower court decisions.

As Proposition 187 made its way through the federal courts, Congress enacted the first major change to the nation's social welfare system since the Great Society—the Personal Responsibility and Work Opportunity Act of 1996. Supported by President Bill Clinton, the first Democratic president to serve two consecutive elected terms since Franklin D. Roosevelt, the law terminated the AFDC program and replaced it with a new one—Temporary Assistance for Needy Families (TANF). For the first time since 1935, the federal government no longer guaranteed welfare to the eligible poor. Under TANF, the United States Department of Health and Human Services provides block grants to the states, which are then free to develop their own welfare programs to suit their particular needs. The 1996 law also included a provision that allowed states to impose a residency requirement, which permitted a state, for the first twelve months, to apply the rules of a new resident's old state in determining benefit eligibility. Congress enacted the residency requirement based on the belief that "some families move across state lines to maximize welfare benefits" and that "[s]tates that want to pay higher benefits should not be deterred from doing so by the fear that they will attract large numbers of recipients from bordering States."[104]

Saenz v. *Roe* (1999) involved a challenge to a California law that included a one-year residency requirement in accordance with TANF. Upon first blush, the California provision recalls the requirement struck down in *Shapiro*. A closer inspection of the California law, as you will discover as you read the opinion, reveals some important differences between the Connecticut provision struck down in *Shapiro* and the one the Court ultimately invalidated in *Saenz*.

Saenz v. *Roe*

526 U.S. 489 (1999)

In a preview of the changes enacted by the federal Personal Responsibility and Work Opportunity Reconciliation Act of 1996, California amended its welfare program in 1992 to add a residency requirement of one year before new residents could receive full state benefits. A federal district court ruled that the California amendments were unconstitutional and the new law never went into effect. In 1996, California submitted a virtually identical plan to the Department of Health and Human Services, a plan that was approved and went into effect in April 1997. A federal district court declared the TANF plan submitted by California unconstitutional, and an appeals court affirmed.

California maintained that the 1996 TANF plan was not motivated by a desire to exclude the migration of welfare recipients in search of higher benefits, but by the need to control costs, an appropriate exercise of state legislative authority. Lawyers on behalf of Anna Doe and Brenda Roe argued that the California law was based on the "welfare magnet myth," or the belief that poor families migrate from state to state in search of higher benefits. Relying on an *amicus* brief submitted by a coalition of social scientists specializing in social welfare policy, Doe and Roe pointed to several long-term studies showing that less than 2 percent of the eligible AFDC population moved to states offering higher welfare benefits. They also pointed to alarming disparities in the benefits offered to established residents of California versus newcomers: In 1997, when the state law went into effect, the monthly benefit for a family of three living in California for at least one year was $565. For a family of three arriving from Arizona within the twelve-month requirement, $347; Nevada, $348; Texas, $188; and Mississippi, $120. Doe and Roe argued that the California law put poor families that could not satisfy the durational requirement at a substantial disadvantage.

The Court's decision was 7 to 2. Justice Stevens delivered the opinion of the Court. Justice Rehnquist and Justice Thomas joined each other in separately filed dissents.

▼▲▼

JUSTICE STEVENS delivered the opinion of the Court.

The word "travel" is not found in the text of the Constitution. Yet the "constitutional right to travel from one State to another" is firmly embedded in our jurisprudence. Indeed, as Justice Stewart reminded us in *Shapiro* v. *Thompson* (1969), the right is so important that it is "assertable against private interference as well as governmental action . . . a virtually unconditional personal right, guaranteed by the Constitution to us all."

In *Shapiro*, we reviewed the constitutionality of three statutory provisions that denied welfare assistance to residents of Connecticut, the District of Columbia, and Pennsylvania, who had resided within those respective jurisdictions less than one year immediately preceding their applications for assistance. Without pausing to identify the specific source of the right, we began by noting that the Court had long "recognized that the nature of our Federal Union and our constitutional concepts of personal liberty unite to require that all citizens be free to travel throughout the length and breadth of our land uninhibited by statutes, rules, or regulations which unreasonably burden or restrict this movement." We squarely held that it was "constitutionally impermissible" for a State to enact durational residency requirements for the purpose of inhibiting the migration by needy persons into the State. We further held that a classification that had the effect of imposing a penalty on the exercise of the right to travel violated the Equal Protection Clause "unless shown to be necessary to promote a *compelling* governmental interest," and that no such showing had been made. . . .

The "right to travel" discussed in our cases embraces at least three different components. It protects the right of a citizen of one State to enter and to leave another State, the right to be treated as a welcome visitor rather than an unfriendly alien when temporarily present in the second State, and, for those travelers who elect to become permanent residents, the right to be treated like other citizens of that State. . . .

Given that [the Califorinia law] imposed no obstacle to respondents' entry into California, we think the State is correct when it argues that the statute does not directly impair the exercise of the right to free interstate movement. For the purposes of this case, therefore, we need not identify the source of that particular right in the text of the Constitution.

The second component of the right to travel is, however, expressly protected by the text of the Constitution. The first sentence of Article IV, Sec. 2, provides:

> The Citizens of each State shall be entitled to all Privileges and Immunities of Citizens in the several States.

Thus, by virtue of a person's state citizenship, a citizen of one State who travels in other States, intending to return home at the end of his journey, is entitled to enjoy the "Privileges and Immunities of Citizens in the several States" that he visits. This provision removes "from the citizens of each State the disabilities of alienage in the other States." It provides important protections for nonresidents who enter a State whether to obtain employment, to procure medical services, or even to engage in commercial shrimp fishing. Those protections are not "absolute," but the Clause "does bar discrimination against citizens of other States where there is no substantial reason for the discrimination beyond the mere fact that they are citizens of other States." . . . Permissible justifications for discrimination between residents and nonresidents are simply inapplicable to a nonresident's exercise of the right to move into another State and become a resident of that State.

What is at issue in this case, then, is this third aspect of the right to travel—the right of the newly arrived citizen to the same privileges and immunities enjoyed by other citizens of the same State. That right is protected not only by the new arrival's status as a state citizen, but also by her status as a citizen of the United States. That additional source of protection is plainly identified in the opening words of the Fourteenth Amendment:

> All persons born or naturalized in the United States, and subject to the jurisdiction thereof, are citizens of the United States and of the State wherein they reside. No State shall make or enforce any law which shall abridge the privileges or immunities of citizens of the United States; . . .

Despite fundamentally differing views concerning the coverage of the Privileges or Immunities Clause of the Fourteenth Amendment, most notably expressed in the majority and dissenting opinions in the *Slaughter-House Cases* (1873), it has always been common ground that this Clause protects the third component of the right to travel. Writing for the majority in the *Slaughter-House Cases*, Justice Miller explained that one of the privileges conferred by this Clause "is that a citizen of the United States can, of his own volition, become a citizen of any State of the Union by a *bona fide* residence therein, with the same rights as other citizens of that State."

That newly arrived citizens "have two political capacities, one state and one federal," adds special force to their claim that they have the same rights as others who share their citizenship. Neither mere rationality nor some intermediate standard of review should be used to judge the constitutionality of a state rule that discriminates against some of its citizens because they have been domiciled in the State for less than a year. The appropriate standard may be more categorical than that articulated in *Shapiro* but it is surely no less strict.

Because this case involves discrimination against citizens who have completed their interstate travel, the State's argument that its welfare scheme affects the right to travel only "incidentally" is beside the point. Were we concerned solely with actual deterrence to migration, we might be persuaded that a partial withholding of benefits constitutes a lesser incursion on the right to travel than an outright denial of all benefits. But since the right to travel embraces the citizen's right to be treated equally in her new State of residence, the discriminatory classification is itself a penalty.

It is undisputed that respondents and the members of the class that they represent are citizens of California and that their need for welfare benefits is unrelated to the length of time that they have resided in California. We thus have no occasion to consider what weight might be given to a citizen's length of residence if the bona fides of her claim to state citizenship were questioned. Moreover, because whatever benefits they receive will be consumed while they remain in California, there is no danger that recognition of their claim will encourage citizens of other States to establish residency for just long enough to acquire some readily portable benefit, such as a divorce or a college education, that will be enjoyed after they return to their original domicile. . . .

Disavowing any desire to fence out the indigent, California has instead advanced an entirely fiscal justification for its multitiered scheme. The enforcement of [the law] will save the State approximately $10.9 million a year. The question is not whether such saving is a legitimate purpose but whether the State may accomplish that end by the discriminatory means it has chosen. An evenhanded, across-the-board reduction of about 72 cents per month for every beneficiary would produce the same result. But our negative answer to the question does not rest on the weakness of the State's purported fiscal justification. It rests on the fact that the Citizenship Clause of the Fourteenth Amendment expressly equates citizenship with residence: "That Clause does not provide for, and does not allow for, degrees of citizenship based on length of residence." It is equally clear that the Clause does not tolerate a hierarchy of 45 subclasses of similarly situated citizens based on the location of their prior residence. Thus [the law] is doubly vulnerable: Neither the duration of respondents' California residence, nor the identity of their prior States of residence, has any relevance to their need for benefits. Nor do those factors bear any relationship to the State's interest in making an equitable allocation of the funds to be distributed among its needy citizens. As in *Shapiro,* we reject any contributory rationale for the denial of benefits to new residents. . . .

The question that remains is whether congressional approval of durational residency requirements in the 1996 amendment to the Social Security Act somehow resuscitates the constitutionality of [the law]. That question is readily answered, for we have consistently held that Congress may not authorize the States to violate the Fourteenth Amendment. Moreover, the protection afforded to the citizen by the Citizenship Clause of that Amendment is a limitation on the powers of the National Government as well as the States. . . .

Citizens of the United States, whether rich or poor, have the right to choose to be citizens "of the State wherein they reside." The States, however, do not have any right to select their citizens. The Fourteenth Amendment, like the Constitution itself, was, as Justice Cardozo put it, "framed upon the theory that the peoples of the several states must sink or swim together, and that in the long run prosperity and salvation are in union and not division." The judgment of the Court of Appeals is affirmed.

It is so ordered.

CHIEF JUSTICE REHNQUIST, with whom JUSTICE THOMAS joins, dissenting.

The Court today breathes new life into the previously dormant Privileges or Immunities Clause of the Fourteenth Amendment—a Clause relied upon by this Court in only one other decision, *Colgate* v. *Harvey* (1935), overruled five years later by *Madden* v. *Kentucky* (1940). It uses this Clause to strike down what I believe is a reasonable measure falling under the head of a "good-faith residency requirement." Because I do not think any provision of the Constitution—and surely not a provision relied upon for only the second time since its enactment 130 years ago—requires this result, I dissent.

JUSTICE THOMAS, with whom THE CHIEF JUSTICE joins, dissenting.

In my view, the majority attributes a meaning to the Privileges or Immunities Clause that likely was unintended when the Fourteenth Amendment was enacted and ratified.

The Privileges or Immunities Clause of the Fourteenth Amendment provides that "[n]o State shall make or enforce any law which shall abridge the privileges or immunities of citizens of the United States." Unlike the Equal Protection and Due Process Clauses, which have assumed near-talismanic status in modern constitutional law, the Court all but read the Privileges or Immunities Clause out of the Constitution in the *Slaughter-House Cases* (1873). . . . The Court declined to specify the privileges or immunities that fell into this latter category, but it made clear that few did. . . .

As THE CHIEF JUSTICE points out, it comes as quite a surprise that the majority relies on the Privileges or Immunities Clause at all in this case. That is because, as I have explained, the *Slaughter-House Cases* sapped the Clause of any meaning. Although the majority appears to breathe new life into the Clause today, it fails to address its historical underpinnings or its place in our constitutional jurisprudence. Because I believe that the demise of the Privileges or Immunities Clause has contributed in no small part to the current disarray of our Fourteenth Amendment jurisprudence, I would be open to reevaluating its meaning in an appropriate case. Before invoking the Clause, however, we should endeavor to understand what the framers of the Fourteenth Amendment thought that it meant. We should also consider whether the Clause should displace, rather than augment, portions of our equal protection and substantive due process jurisprudence. The majority's failure to consider these important questions raises the specter that the Privileges or Immunities Clause will become yet another convenient tool for inventing new rights, limited solely by the "predilections of those who happen at the time to be Members of this Court," *Moore* v. *East Cleveland* (1977).

▼▲▼

As in *Shapiro* and *Plyler,* the Court treated the challenge to the California welfare law as one that involved discrimination based on a recognized fundamental right, in this case, the right to travel. Even though the Court shows great concern for the rights of new residents to receive equal benefits under California's two-tier welfare program, Justice Stevens's opinion centers the constitutional question on the right to travel from state to state—the core issue in *Shapiro.* But rather than concluding that California's law violated the Equal Protection Clause, as the Court did in *Shapiro,* Justice Stevens revived the Privileges or Immunities Clause of the Fourteenth Amendment, considered dormant since *The Slaughterhouse Cases* (1873) (see Chapter 3), to base the fundamental right to travel. Dissenting, Justice Thomas suggested that a revival of the Privileges or Immunities Clause was welcome, but argued that the majority Court had not gone about it in the right way. Is Justice Thomas's emphasis on the original meaning of the Privileges or Immunities Clause persuasive in helping the Court determine its contemporary application to constitutional claims?

Equal Protection in the Contemporary Context

The formal guarantee of equal protection under the law traces its constitutional origins to the ratification of the Fourteenth Amendment in 1868, but the debate over what constitutes equality predates the Civil War and even the ratification of the Constitution. Since the Framers debated the idea of America during the Revolutionary period and through the early years of the Republic, a period in which the Court played an instrumental role in shaping the relationship between law and politics, Americans have argued about equality and what it means under the Constitution. Slavery, racial segregation, the separate spheres assigned to men and women, and the notion that equality was merely a formal legal requirement without a basis in substance were all, at one time, considered consistent with the equal protection guarantee. As recently as 1973, the American Medical Association considered homosexuality a psychiatric disorder. After abolishing that position, the AMA began to support gay rights organizations in their effort to repeal laws that discriminated on the basis of sexual orientation. Indeed, as the Court's decisions in cases involving the rights of the poor demonstrate, the equal protection guarantee has not evolved based on the four corners of the Constitution. It has come about through deliberation rooted in a social and political vision of what American society should be, and this requires principles drawn from beyond the text of the Constitution.

When the Court decided *Brown* v. *Board Education* in 1954, the case that more than any other forced Americans to rethink the meaning of equality, few people thought that one day a social movement would emerge on behalf of the physically and mentally disabled, the aged, and those stricken with AIDS, and succeed in persuading Congress to enact legislation protecting them from discriminatory treatment. By 2000, complaints alleging age discrimination and discrimination based on disability, spurred by the passage of the Age Discrimination in Employment Act of 1967 and the Americans with Disabilities Act of 1990, comprised the majority of those filed with the EEOC. The Court is still finding its way through many of the interpretive issues raised by these federal civil rights laws, as well as cases involving the Fourteenth Amendment. How the Court determines the difference between equality rights considered fundamental and those it believes are merely privileges will have a major impact on all levels of contemporary American society and thus merits close watching.

FOR FURTHER READING

Baer, Judith A. *Women in American Law: the Struggle Toward Equality from the New Deal to the Present.* New York: Holmes and Meier, 1991.

———. *Our Lives Before the Law.* Princeton, N.J.: Princeton University Press, 1999.

Bell, Derrick. *And We Are Not Saved: The Elusive Quest for Racial Justice.* New York: Basic Books, 1987.

Bass, Jack. *Taming the Storm.* New York: Anchor Books, 1993.

Branch, Taylor. *Parting the Waters: America in the King Years, 1954–1963.* New York: Simon & Schuster, 1988.

———. *Pillar of Fire: America in the King Years, 1963–1965.* New York: Simon & Schuster, 1998.

Clark, E. Culpepper. *The Schoolhouse Door: Segregation's Last Stand at the University of Alabama.* New York: Oxford University Press, 1993.

Cortner, Richard C. *A Mob Intent on Death: The NAACP and the Arkansas Riot Cases.* Middletown, Conn.: Wesleyan University Press, 1988.

Du Bois, W. E. B. *The Education of Black People.* Herbert Aptheker, ed. New York: Monthly Review Press, 1973.

Egerton, John. *Speak Now Against the Day: The Generation Before the Civil Rights Movement in the South.* New York: Alfred A. Knopf, 1994.

Ellison, Ralph. *Invisible Man.* New York: Random House, 1952.

Foner, Eric. *Reconstruction, 1863–1877.* New York: Harper & Row, 1988.

Friedan, Betty. *The Second Stage.* Cambridge, Mass.: Harvard University Press, 1998.

Gerstmann, Evan. *The Constitutional Underclass: Gays, Lesbians, and the Failure of Class-Based Equal Protection.* Chicago: University of Chicago Press, 1999.

Halberstam, David. *The Children.* New York: Fawcett Books, 1998.

Jacoby, Tamar. *Someone Else's House: The Unfinished Struggle for Integration.* New York: Simon & Schuster, 1998.

Kahlenberg, Richard. *The Remedy: Class, Race, and Affirmative Action.* New York: Basic Books, 1996.

Kluger, Richard. *Simple Justice.* New York: Alfred A. Knopf, 1976.

MacKinnon, Catharine A. *Feminism Unmodified: Discourses on Life and Law.* Cambridge, Mass.: Harvard University Press, 1987.

Raines, Howell. *My Soul Is Rested: Movement Days in the Deep South Remembered.* New York: G. P. Putnam's Sons, 1977.

Rimmerman, Craig A., Kenneth D. Wald and Clyde Wilcox, eds. *The Politics of Gay Rights.* Chicago: University of Chicago Press, 2000.

Roiphe, Katie. *The Morning After: Sex, Fear, and Feminism.* New York: Little, Brown, 1994.

Schwartz, Bernard. *Swann's Way: The School Busing Case and the Supreme Court.* New York: Oxford University Press, 1986.

Shipler, David K. *A Country of Strangers: Blacks and Whites in America.* New York: Alfred A. Knopf, 1997.

Simpson, Andrea Y. *The Tie That Binds: Identity and Political Attitudes in the Post–Civil Rights Generation.* New York: New York University Press, 1998.

Skerry, Peter. *Mexican-Americans: The Ambivalent Minority.* Cambridge, Mass.: Harvard University Press, 1995.

Sommers, Christina Hoff. *Who Stole Feminism? How Women Have Betrayed Women.* New York: Simon & Schuster, 1995.

Soss, Joe. *Unwanted Claims: The Politics of Participation in the U.S. Welfare System.* Ann Arbor: University of Michigan Press, 2000.

Strasser, Mark. *Legally Wed: Same-Sex Marriage and the Constitution.* Ithaca, N.Y.: Cornell University Press, 1998.

Taylor, Steven. *Desegregation in Boston and Buffalo: The Influence of Local Leaders.* Albany: State University of New York Press, 1998.

Thernstrom, Stephan, and Abigail Thernstrom. *America in Black and White: One Nation, Indivisible.* New York: Touchstone Books, 1999.

Vose, Clement E. *Caucasians Only: The Supreme Court, the NAACP, and the Restrictive Covenant Cases.* Berkeley: University of California Press, 1959.

Wasby, Stephen V. *Race-Relations Litigation in an Age of Complexity.* Charlottesville: University Press of Virginia, 1995.

West, Robin. *Progressive Constitutionalism: Reconstructing the Fourteenth Amendment.* Durham, N.C.: Duke University Press, 1994.

Wilkinson, J. Harvie. *From Brown to Bakke: The Supreme Court and School Integration, 1954–1978.* New York: Oxford University Press, 1979.

Wilson, Paul. *A Time to Lose: Representing Kansas in Brown v. Board of Education.* Lawrence: University Press of Kansas, 1995.

12 Voting Rights

In June 1964, Andrew Goodman, a twenty-year-old college student from Queens, New York, boarded a bus bound for Meridian, Mississippi, for what promised to be the most exciting summer of his life. Along with hundreds of other college students and young political activists, Goodman had responded to the call for volunteers from various civil rights organizations to travel to Mississippi that summer to educate and register African American voters. Twenty-four-year-old Michael Schwerner, who had come to Meridian six months earlier to open a voter education office, made the trip with Goodman, warning his young friend that white Mississippians would resort to any measure, including violence, to discourage black voter registration. After arriving in Meridian, Goodman and Schwerner met up with James Chaney, a twenty-year-old black Mississippian and voter education worker, to discuss their agenda for "Freedom Summer," the name civil rights activists had given to their ambitious voter registration project. They understood the danger of their work, but their fears were offset by their youthful enthusiasm and idealism.

On June 22, one day after they met in Meridian, Goodman, Schwerner, and Chaney, on their way to investigate a black church burning in Lawndale, were pulled over for an alleged traffic violation in Philadelphia, Mississippi. They were taken into custody, but released later, long after darkness had settled on the small town. Freedom Summer workers back in Meridian knew something was terribly wrong after a day passed with no word from any of them. Local police, the FBI, and the United States Department of Justice were notified, as were reporters from the *New York Times*, of their disappearance. Public outrage mounted as Mississippi law enforcement professed indifference to the whereabouts of Goodman, Schwerner, and Chaney. "If they're missing," said one local sheriff, "they're just hid somewhere trying to get a lot of publicity out it, I figure." Within days, President Lyndon Johnson (1963–1969) sent teams of divers, FBI agents, military helicopters, and sailors to search the rivers, streams, lakes, and countryside in and around Philadelphia for the missing men.

On August 4, the FBI, acting on an anonymous tip, bulldozed through an earthen dam just outside of Philadelphia, where they found the dead bodies of Goodman, Schwerner, and Chaney, each of whom had been shot through the head. Chaney, being black, had come in for a particularly savage beating, suffering a fractured skull. Twenty-one men were later arrested in connection with their kidnapping and murder, including the Philadelphia deputy who had pulled Schwerner over. All twenty-one later had the charges against them dropped in the Mississippi courts. But six of the accused conspirators were then arrested under federal civil rights laws and sent to jail.

Nonetheless, the reign of terror by white racists continued against the mostly white, predominantly Jewish Northern volunteers and black Mississippians for the remainder of Freedom Summer, accounting for more than one thousand arrests, eighty documented beatings, and thirty-five burned churches. Finally, in keeping with the entrenched racism that engulfed Mississippi and, by extension, the entire South, state officials would not grant the families' wish that their slain sons be buried side-by-side: The state's segregation laws prohibited interracial cemeteries. Goodman and Schwerner were buried together, while James Chaney was laid to rest in a black cemetery.[1]

In 1960, Mississippi's population was just over 40 percent African American, giving it a higher proportion of blacks to the general population than any other state. Yet, less than 7 percent of the eligible black population in Mississippi was registered to vote, the lowest in the nation.[2] After the collapse of Reconstruction in the late 1870s, the Southern states gradually eliminated African Americans from the voting rolls, despite the enactment of the Fifteenth Amendment in 1870, which banned states from denying individuals the right to vote based on race, color, or previous condition of servitude. Initially, violence and intimidation were the most common methods used to prevent African Americans from voting. By the early 1900s, however, most Southern states had followed the practices initiated by Mississippi in the late 1880s. Poll taxes, literacy tests, and property requirements were devised to exclude African Americans from access to the ballot box. None of these laws included a specific racial component. Indeed, most of them were justified as reforms to promote "good government." But they were applied almost exclusively to blacks. Whites who were no more literate or knowledgeable about American government or the Mississippi constitution than blacks were almost always exempted through the use of "grandfather clauses," which permitted individuals registered to vote prior to the enactment of the qualification laws to waive any of the new tests. By the early 1920s, less than 1 percent of eligible African Americans in Mississippi, Alabama, South Carolina, and Louisiana were registered to vote.[3]

Between the time Goodman, Schwerner, and Chaney disappeared in June 1964 and when their bodies were found six weeks later, President Johnson signed the the Civil Rights Act of 1964, the nation's most comprehensive civil rights law to date. Still, the measure did not reach the question of political participation. As discussed in Chapter 11, the 1964 law prohibited discrimination by employers, discrimination in public accommodations, and discrimination by any institution receiving federal funding. Freedom Summer and subsequent events in the unfolding drama of the civil rights movement ultimately moved Congress the following year to enact the Voting Rights Act of 1965. This act went far beyond any previous federal law in abolishing the discriminatory barriers that stood between African Americans and their right to participate meaningfully in American electoral politics.

The right to vote is certainly among the most fundamental rights of any political system claiming a democratic foundation. But the high-gloss rhetoric of democratic theory, particularly the notion that the only legitimate government is one elected by and accountable to the people, has not always practiced in the electoral arrangements of the American political system. This chapter will focus on the constitutional evolution of voting rights in the United States, with considerable attention given to the push and pull of the political forces engaged in the struggle to define electoral fairness and accountability in American electoral politics.

Government by Consent? Suffrage in the Early Republic

The Framers' twin emphases on representative institutions and the consent of the governed was offset by rules and customs—in place by the time the Constitution was ratified—that placed firm limits on the right to vote. After the Revolution, many states changed their electoral systems to make people, not county subdivisions, the basis for determining representation in state and local governing institutions. Property owned and taxes paid, however, became the main factors that determined how many representatives were apportioned to a particular district. Counties were still the basic unit of representation, reflecting their own subsets of economic and political interests. But the gradual shift to the vested interests of property holders in fashioning a system of representation was in accord with the growing belief in late 1700s America that individuals should be the primary constituency in any governing arrangement accountable to the people.[4]

Expanding the electoral base and linking representation to people did not mean that the Framers embraced the notion of universal suffrage, as that term is understood today. Suffrage was the exclusive privilege of property-owning white males who were at least twenty-one years old. Indeed, the right to vote was intimately associated with one's perceived stake in society. Property owners, because they were thought to have a greater interest in maintaining economic and political stability, were viewed as the most deserving of the right to take part. Although attaching property qualifications to the right to vote certainly did narrow the qualifying electorate who could participate in the political process, the availability of land made property ownership much easier than is sometimes commonly thought. Historians of the early Republic estimate that roughly 75 to 90 percent of white males were qualified to vote by the late eighteenth century. As representative democracy in America took shape in the late 1700s and early 1800s, it could not have survived had the right to vote been so narrowly drawn that it resembled the European models of government that had been rejected during the Constitutional Convention.[5]

But not all white men, even if they owned property, were necessarily eligible to vote. Jews, who numbered about fourteen hundred in 1790, were not permitted to vote in eight of the nation's thirteen states, although it is hard to imagine how such a small percentage of the population could affect a nation numbering approximately 4 million people. Even those states that permitted Jews to vote would not let them hold office or enter the legal profession. Catholics were often subject to the same sorts of restrictions on suffrage and office holding as were Jews. Connecticut and New Jersey, for example, limited ballot access and the right to run for office to Protestants until the 1820s. North Carolina excluded any person who denied the "truth of the Christian Religion, or the divine authority of the Old or New Testament" from holding any government position until after the Civil War. Since the "truth of the Christian Religion" was defined in every state by the Protestant majorities holding power, such a provision often excluded Catholics, as well as Jews. Quakers, Jehovah's Witnesses, and other smaller religious denominations were also frequently excluded from political participation.[6]

White women were excluded completely from the franchise, regardless of their age, marital status, ethnic heritage, or religion. Bound by the rule of *coverture,* or the principle that wives were the property of their husbands, women had almost no voice in the affairs of business, politics, or government. The one political right women did have was the right to petition. Such notable feminist leaders of the nineteenth century as Lucy Stone, Susan B. Anthony, and Elizabeth Cady Stanton (all of whom were active in abolition societies) formed organizations to campaign on behalf of women's suffrage. After the Civil War, disputes over whether to support the Fourteenth Amendment divided women's organizations because it imposed penalties on states that denied "male inhabitants" the right to vote. The National Woman Suffrage Association (NWSA), founded by Stanton and Anthony, ultimately refused to support the Fifteenth Amendment because it did not apply to women. Stone founded the American Woman Suffrage Association (AWSA), which continued to support black enfranchisement through a constitutional amendment, and focused its effort to secure the vote for women in the state legislatures. Ultimately, the major political parties ignored the suffragette movement until 1916, when the Republican Party platform included a proposed constitutional amendment guaranteeing women the right to vote.[7] By then, only nine states recognized a woman's right to vote. Finally, in 1920, the nation ratified the Nineteenth Amendment, which extended the constitutional right to vote without regard to sex.

By the Civil War, white male suffrage was almost universal. The rise of political parties as a permanent feature of American politics, as much as any innate desire to transform the parchment promise of government by consent into a fulfilled promise, led many states to eliminate property ownership as the basis for political enfranchisement.[8] Such sweeping reform, which began in earnest under President Andrew Jackson (1829–1837), increased the voter rolls in states nationwide.[9] Certainly, many religious and ethnic minorities had to wait until after the Civil War to experience their first taste of the franchise, but that chance, as long as they were men, ultimately arrived. After the Civil War, suffrage for African Americans, saddled by a history of enslavement in the South and pervasive discrimination in the Northern states (that, ironically, had fought for their emancipation), presented a complex and different set of questions.

Reconstruction and the False Promise of African American Enfranchisement

After the end of the Civil War, many questions emerged regarding the social, political, and economic reconstruction of the United States, but the most immediate centered, not surprisingly, on the status of the nation's 4 million newly freed African slaves. Chapter 11 discusses in detail the ratification of the Fourteenth Amendment, the centerpiece of the Civil War Amendments and the high-water mark for Radical Republicans intent on establishing equal constitutional rights for blacks. Although the Fourteenth Amendment did make clear in Section 2 that states could not bar any "male inhabitant" from the right to vote, Radical Republicans in the Thirty-Ninth Congress insisted on a separate amendment setting out in clear terms a constitutional right to vote without regard to color or race. Black suffrage had posed, by far, Reconstruction's most vexing political problem. Moderate Republicans, in the short term, were less convinced than the Radicals that suffrage was a necessary component to establish citizenship for blacks. They tried to convince party leaders that granting blacks the right to vote would produce a fatal backlash among the Southern states, whose deposed white leaders would not stand for political subjugation under black political rule. Moreover, many congressional Republicans could not defend a constitutional amendment extending blacks the right to vote when only five Northern states, all in New England, had granted blacks the right to vote by 1865.[10] Seven more Northern states soon defeated popular referenda that would have added blacks to the voter rolls. By 1868, when the Fourteenth Amendment was ratified, only eight of the sixteen Northern states permitted blacks to vote.[11]

Against this backdrop, black suffrage faced a severe uphill battle. How could the Republicans demand from the South compliance with the Fourteenth Amendment if their home states continued to exclude African Americans from the voter rolls? Initially, congressional Republicans treaded lightly around the possibility of black suffrage for fear of alienating white Southerners with whom they were hoping to create a national political alliance. Former Confederate rebels already had been stripped of their voting rights by the Military Reconstruction Act of 1867—the law, as discussed in Chapter 11, that made possible the enactment of the Fourteenth Amendment. Moderate and conservative Republicans worried that imposing black suffrage would alienate further the "loyal" Southerners committed to restoring the Union. On the other hand, Republicans slowly began to break with President Andrew Johnson's (1865–1869) plan for Reconstruction, concluding that it did not go far enough in securing full equality for the recently freed slaves. Ultimately, congressional Republicans embraced the cause of black suffrage, believing that shoring up more votes and solidifying their hold on the South was more important than risking the return of untrustworthy ex-Confederates to political power in their now-conquered states or in Congress. Reconstruction policy now moved firmly into the hands of the Radical Republicans in Congress, who were firmly committed to black suffrage.[12]

A peculiar blend of hardball politics and moral principle spirited the path toward the ratification of the Fifteenth Amendment. By December 1868, President Johnson, having lost the November election, proclaimed universal amnesty for all former Confederates, including General Robert E. Lee. This was the third such pardon Johnson had issued since September 1867. Having debated several suffrage amendments throughout 1868, including one that would have barred discrimination based on "race, color, nativity, property, education, or religious beliefs," Congress approved the Fifteenth Amendment for submission to the states in February 1869. Designed to offset the growing political power of the Democratic Party, now bolstered by the return of ex-Confederates, the Fifteenth Amendment was explicitly intended to protect the gains of Reconstruction by further empowering African Americans in the South and in border states such as Kentucky, Maryland, and Delaware. Blacks in the South were already voting and holding office by the time the Fifteenth Amendment was ratified in March 1870. Nonetheless, Democrats viewed the measure as the "crowning" act of a Radical Republican conspiracy intended to promote a revolution in American politics centered around African American equality. Republicans were certainly not unaware of the political advantages of an enfranchised black population. But one should not overlook the steadfast commitment that many Republicans in Congress and their constituents at home had toward securing equal rights for blacks as ordained by the Union victory in the Civil War. In the words of the nation's most famous abolitionist, William Lloyd Garrison, "Nothing in all history [equaled] this wonderful, quiet, sudden transformation of four million human beings from . . . the auction block to the ballot-box."[13]

Ironically, the Fifteenth Amendment's ratification came just as many moderate and conservative Republicans in Congress were beginning to question the wisdom of long-term occupation of the South and continued control of the internal political arrangements of the states. But whatever reluctance congressional Republicans may have had about continuing Reconstruction soon evaporated as reports emerged from the South of violence against African Americans who decided to exercise their newly minted constitutional rights. In 1870 and 1871, Congress enacted two separate Enforcement Acts, which banned *state* officials from discriminating against voters on the basis of race and authorized the president to appoint supervisors to monitor elections in the South. An even more aggressive exercise of congressional power was on display in the Ku Klux Klan Act of 1871. For the first time, Congress designated certain crimes committed by individuals in the states as punishable under federal law. The Klan, a white supremacist organization characterized by secrecy and best known for the white hoods its members wore in public and during its ritual cross burnings, had begun terrorizing African Americans who dared to carry out their basic civic and constitutional rights. Conspiracies to deprive black citizens of the right to vote, hold office, serve on juries, and enjoy the equal protection of the laws were now crimes punishable by federal prosecutors. The 1871 anti-Klan law represented the outer limits of congressional power because it granted the federal government jurisdiction to prosecute *individuals* within states for criminal offenses, a radical departure from the previous focus on restraining discriminatory state action against private individuals.

President Grant was quite willing, at first, to enforce the Klan Act, committing federal troops to those areas in the South where Klan violence was most severe. From 1871 to 1872, hundreds of Klansmen were arrested and indicted, and thousands more threw down their robes and guns and fled before federal authorities could find them. National power had been able to achieve what Southern governments could not and, in truth, had no real interest in doing: controlling violence and intimidation toward blacks who believed that the Civil War and the Reconstruction Amendments that followed had actually made them free and equal citizens.[14]

The Klan and the other contemptible acts of the Southern states aside, however, many Northern Republicans had begun shifting their attention to national economic and business issues. They were increasingly content to let the Southern states go their own way, and that meant the return of white supremacist governments to power. By 1877, when President Grant left office, only three states—South Carolina, Florida, and Louisiana—were under the control of Republican authorities. Grant's successor, Rutherford Hayes, a business-minded former governor of Ohio, agreed to withdraw federal troops from the South, returning complete control of the region to ex-Confederates. As a matter of law, African Americans could still vote and hold office; the abandonment of Reconstruction could not change what the Fourteenth and Fifteenth Amendments had done to establish the legal and political rights of blacks. What did change was the notion that a powerful national government was prepared to defend the rights of blacks in the Southern states. "The Negro," editorialized the *Nation* magazine, "will disappear from the field of national politics. Henceforth, the nation, as a nation, will have nothing more to do with him."[15]

Early on, the United States Supreme Court had demonstrated support for various Reconstruction policies that dealt with free labor and loyalty questions. In *In re Turner* (1867), Chief Justice Salmon P. Chase, hearing a Maryland case as part of his circuit riding duties, ruled that President Lincoln's decision to emancipate the slaves in January 1863 made any person working in servitude a national citizen and thus entitled to receive compensation for his or her labor. In *Texas* v. *White* (1869), the Court ruled that Texas was entitled to recover payment for U.S. property that it had owned prior to the Civil War, reinforcing President Lincoln's position that the Southern states actually had never left the Union, but simply rebelled against its policies. By confirming the legal status of individuals and states and their connection to the Union, *Turner* and *White* lent firm support to the national government's power to enforce Reconstruction policies designed to promote African American equality.[16]

Legal scholar Michael Kent Curtis has commented that in the early 1870s, Republican federal judges began changing their views toward Reconstruction and the obligation of the national government to protect African

American freedom.[17] In an ominous sign of things to come, the Court, in the *Slaughterhouse Cases* (1873) (see Chapter 3), ruled that Section 5 of the Fourteenth Amendment, the cornerstone of federal power to enforce Reconstruction civil rights policy, did not give Congress the power to interfere with state guarantees of citizenship. Rather than embrace the Fourteenth Amendment's emphasis on national citizenship, the Court returned to the pre–Civil War conception of dual citizenship that put the powers of the states first. Three years later, the Court, in *United States* v. *Cruikshank* (1876), ruled that the Ku Klux Klan Act of 1871 did not permit federal authorities to protect blacks deprived of their civil rights by private individuals in the states, since such responsibility was a matter of state law. *Cruikshank* stemmed from a racial massacre in Colfax, Louisiana, where whites killed dozens of African Americans who had assembled in a county courthouse to protect the outcome of a recent election favorable to them. Earlier that year, the Court, in *United States* v. *Reese* (1876), dismissed the indictment of a Kentucky election official who refused to register qualified blacks to vote. In *Reese,* the Court ruled that the 1870 Enforcement Act granted too much power to the national government to "interfere" in state matters.[18] But *Cruikshank* was more disturbing, for the Court simply ignored the violence toward blacks in the South that was becoming more and more endemic.

Cruikshank, Hayes's election in 1876, and the return of the Democrats to power in each of the former Confederate states by 1877 closed the door on Reconstruction. During the 1880s, the Southern states, freed from national supervision, gradually installed an entirely new social, political, and economic system so severe that it stopped just short of returning African Americans to slavery. Blacks and whites had rarely crossed the informal boundaries that separated the races during the early days of Reconstruction. But the collapse of Reconstruction permitted the Southern states to write those customs into law. The repeal of the state anti-Klan laws demanded by congressional Republicans after the Civil War gave white supremacist political leaders a powerful enforcement tool to control any potential black uprising. As a matter of constitutional right, African Americans could still vote and run for office, but the Southern states did not consider the Fifteenth Amendment an effective bar against black disenfranchisement. For the next fifty years, the Southern states systematically purged eligible blacks from the voting rolls by requiring land ownership, mandating literacy requirements, and exacting the payment of poll taxes. One of the most effective tools developed by the Southern states was racially restrictive voting in primary elections. In the late 1930s, the National Association for the Advancement of Colored People (NAACP), which had formed in 1909 to promote the civil rights of African Americans, decided to challenge the exclusion of blacks from voting in primary elections. This decision had profound implications for African American voting rights and, more generally, the future course of civil rights litigation.

Access to the Ballot

During the 1890s, the Democratic Party in the South successfully defeated the Populist rebellion led by Tom Watson, a Georgian. The rebellion had attempted to unite disaffected white farmers, African Americans, and white Republicans in a challenge to the economic and political status quo. Watson's battle, however, was a decidedly uphill one, as the Democrats now dominated every statehouse and legislature in the South. Ultimately, the Democrats were able to persuade white Populists that interracial politics would elevate African American power at their own expense, and offered the "dark days" of Reconstruction as evidence of what the South would look like under a combination of black and white Republican rule. To expunge African Americans from the voter rolls, the Democratic Party turned to the primary election as the means to immunize white supremacists from any charges that state authorities were enforcing discriminatory voting rules. Continuing in the early 1900s, Southern states argued that primary elections were not subject to legal authority because they reflected the outcome of a "private" association of individuals who shared similar political values.[19] True, primary elections were intimately connected to the public because they preceded the general election. But the Southern states understood quite well that the Court's post-Reconstruction decisions on race evidenced no enthusiasm for federal intervention in private matters involving discrimination. In the *Civil Rights Cases* of 1883 (see Chapter 11), the Court held that Congress had no authority to prohibit discrimination in hotels, restaurants, theatres, and other such public accommodations on the grounds that these establishments were "private" in nature. And since the Court had construed the definition of state action in the *Civil Rights Cases* so narrowly, many Southern states relied upon the idea that political parties were private organizations that could create their own rules. Persuading the Court that primary elections were an integral component of the electoral process and thus entitled to constitutional supervision was a tricky course to navigate, but one that the NAACP believed was necessary to break the stranglehold on African American political participation in the South.

"Nah, You Ain't Got Enough Edjiccashun To Vote"

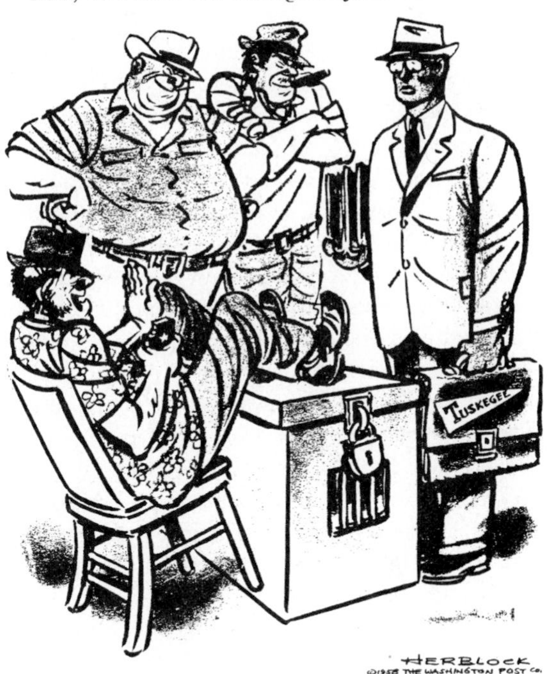

© From *Straight Herblock*, Simon & Schuster, 1972

The "White Primary" Cases

Houston and El Paso had developed sizable African American professional communities by the early 1900s, but not even business acumen and education qualified blacks to vote in the eyes of the Democratic Party of Texas. Black voter registration in Texas after Reconstruction's collapse was abysmal, as it was throughout the South. But Texas had not opted to follow Mississippi's technique of excluding black voters through literacy tests, poll taxes, and so on. Instead, in 1923 the Texas legislature modified its primary election system, in place since 1905, to exclude blacks from voting in the Democratic primary. L. A. Nixon, an African American physician from El Paso, agreed to serve as the plaintiff in a case the NAACP wanted to bring against Texas's "white primary" system. Louis Marshall, the president of the American Jewish Committee, agreed to argue the case on behalf of the NAACP when it came before the Supreme Court in 1927. The NAACP argued that Texas, by excluding blacks from the opportunity to vote in the Democratic primary election, had made race the determining factor in political participation, an act that violated the Fourteenth and Fifteenth Amendments.[20]

Writing for a unanimous Court, Justice Oliver Wendell Holmes held that Texas had indeed violated the Fourteenth Amendment by drawing an explicit color line in its primary election law. The Texas legislature responded immediately to *Nixon* v. *Herndon* (1927) by rewriting its law to allow party committees to determine voting eligibility in its primaries.[21] Without missing a beat, the NAACP challenged the 1927 Texas white primary law. In *Nixon* v. *Condon* (1932), a 5–4 majority ruled that Texas's new election law had "lodged in the [party] committee" the power to discriminate on the basis of race.[22] The Court found no evidence that the Texas Democratic Party had declared any intent to exclude African Americans from its primaries. The power to exclude blacks had been granted by the state legislature through the 1927 law, which made the ultimate objective no different from the previously invalidated 1923 law. Undaunted, white Texas Democrats called an immediate convention, where they passed a declaration making all qualified white citizens eligible to join the party and participate in its nominating elections. The NAACP went back to court, this time arguing that while the Texas Democratic convention had indeed said that whites were eligible to participate in Democratic Party politics, it had never said that blacks were ineligible. A lower court agreed, but the decision had very little real impact on black voter registration and participation in Texas politics.

At this point, the NAACP found very little enthusiasm among its Texas members for continuing to challenge the white primary system. Even though the NAACP had won two major decisions in the United States Supreme Court, Texas Democrats continued to find some way to exclude African Americans from their primary elections. In 1935, the Court dealt the NAACP a major blow when it ruled, in *Grovey* v. *Townsend,* that the Texas Democratic Party was a voluntary association and thus entitled to choose its members.[23] The justices unanimously rejected the NAACP's argument that the Texas primary election system was, in effect, the equivalent of its general election, since no Republican had been elected to any office in Texas or sent to Congress since 1859. *Grovey* led the NAACP to suspend its attack on the white primary, since local members saw no point in contributing money or serving as plaintiffs in lawsuits they stood no chance of winning.[24] The NAACP had not sponsored *Grovey,* but its future litigation plans were certainly affected by its outcome.

Six years later the Court handed the NAACP an unexpected victory when, in *United States* v. *Classic* (1941), it upheld federal indictments brought against several Louisiana election officials for manipulating vote counts and engaging in other forms of fraud during a primary election. Contradicting but not overruling *Grovey,* the Court held that primaries were, in fact, elections in every sense of the word. Chief Justice Harlan Fiske Stone described primaries as an "integral part" of the electoral process, and suggested that state action was clearly implicated because of the state's central role in the primary system. NAACP legal director Thurgood Marshall, who came to the NAACP after *Grovey,* desperately wanted to continue the white primary litigation. Buoyed by Stone's opinion, which clearly suggested that "white primaries" were unconstitutional, Marshall went to Texas in search of another plaintiff to challenge the Texas system. The result was *Smith* v. *Allwright* (1944).

Smith v. *Allwright*

321 U.S. 649 (1944)

In 1940, less than 6 percent of eligible blacks in Texas were registered to vote. Remarkably, this figure placed Texas at the high end of black voter registration in the Southern states. In Alabama, Louisiana, Mississippi, and South Carolina, less than 1 percent of eligible blacks were registered to vote. Although blacks constituted approximately 10 percent of the nation's population in 1940, only two African Americans, both from Northern states, then served in Congress. For blacks in the South, the consequences of disenfranchisement were particularly severe, since the majority of African Americans lived in the former Confederate states.

Thurgood Marshall was determined to break the white primary system in Texas, as he believed that unlocking the door to the ballot box held out the greatest hope for black equality in the United States. Marshall traveled the country is search of funding and support, wrapping himself in the American flag as he went. Foreshadowing later themes in the school desegregation cases (see Chapter 11), Marshall said America could not wage war against Hitler and white supremacy in Europe and then enforce racially exclusionary practices at home. Marshall gradually built up support for another lawsuit in Texas, recruiting a black Houston physician, Lonnie Smith, who had been denied the right to vote in a recent primary election, to serve as the plaintiff.

Once *Smith* reached the United States Supreme Court, Marshall persuaded the ACLU and the National Lawyers Guild to file *amicus* briefs in support of the NAACP's position. Marshall asked the Justice Department to support the NAACP's claim that discrimination in primary elections was no different from vote fraud, and thus consistent with *Classic.* The Justice Department begged off, claiming that Southern senators, who wielded considerable power on key committees, would find ways to punish the administration during a time when they needed their cooperation on World War II. Unofficially, however, Justice Department lawyers involved in *Classic* endorsed the NAACP's position.[25]

Marshall and William Hastie, the dean of Howard Law School, argued that *Classic* had overruled *Grovey,* and the Court should apply the same logic to the Texas white primary system.

The Court's decision was unanimous. Justice Reed delivered the opinion of the Court.

▼▲▼

Mr. Justice Reed delivered the opinion of the Court.

The State of Texas by its Constitution and statutes provides that every person, if certain other requirements are

met which are not here in issue, qualified by residence in the district or county "shall be deemed a qualified elector." Primary elections for United States Senators, Congressmen and state officers are provided for by Chapters Twelve and Thirteen of the statutes. Under these chapters, the Democratic Party was required to hold the primary which was the occasion of the alleged wrong to petitioner. . . .

When *Grovey* v. *Townsend* (1935) was written, the Court looked upon the denial of a vote in a primary as a mere refusal by a party of party membership. As the Louisiana statutes for holding primaries are similar to those of Texas, our ruling in *United States* v. *Classic* (1941) as to the unitary character of the electoral process calls for a reexamination as to whether or not the exclusion of Negroes from a Texas party primary was state action.

The statutes of Texas relating to primaries and the resolution of the Democratic party of Texas extending the privileges of membership to white citizens only are the same in substance and effect today as they were when *Grovey* v. *Townsend* was decided by a unanimous Court. The question as to whether the exclusionary action of the party was the action of the State persists as the determinative factor. In again entering upon consideration of the inference to be drawn as to state action from a substantially similar factual situation, it should be noted that *Grovey* v. *Townsend* upheld exclusion of Negroes from primaries through the denial of party membership by a party convention. A few years before, this Court refused approval of exclusion by the State Executive Committee of the party. A different result was reached on the theory that the Committee action was state authorized, and the Convention action was unfettered by statutory control. Such a variation in the result from so slight a change in form influences us to consider anew the legal validity of the distinction which has resulted in barring Negroes from participating in the nominations of candidates of the Democratic party in Texas. . . .

It may now be taken as a postulate that the right to vote in such a primary for the nomination of candidates without discrimination by the State, like the right to vote in a general election, is a right secured by the Constitution. By the terms of the Fifteenth Amendment, that right may not be abridged by any state on account of race. Under our Constitution, the great privilege of the ballot may not be denied a man by the State because of his color.

We are thus brought to an examination of the qualifications for Democratic primary electors in Texas, to determine whether state action or private action has excluded Negroes from participation. Despite Texas' decision that the exclusion is produced by private or party action, [f]ederal courts must for themselves appraise the facts leading to that conclusion. It is only by the performance of this obligation that a final and uniform interpretation can be given to the Constitution, the "supreme Law of the Land." Texas requires electors in a primary to pay a poll tax. Every person who does so pay and who has the qualifications of age and residence is an acceptable voter for the primary. As appears above in the summary of the statutory provisions set out in note 6, Texas requires by the law the election of the county officers of a party. These compose the county executive committee. The county chairmen so selected are members of the district executive committee and choose the chairman for the district. Precinct primary election officers are named by the county executive committee. Statutes provide for the election by the voters of precinct delegates to the county convention of a party and the selection of delegates to the district and state conventions by the county convention. The state convention selects the state executive committee. No convention may place in platform or resolution any demand for specific legislation without endorsement of such legislation by the voters in a primary. Texas thus directs the selection of all party officers.

Primary elections are conducted by the party under state statutory authority. The county executive committee selects precinct election officials and the county, district or state executive committees, respectively, canvass the returns. These party committees or the state convention certify the party's candidates to the appropriate officers for inclusion on the official ballot for the general election. No name which has not been so certified may appear upon the ballot for the general election as a candidate of a political party. No other name may be printed on the ballot which has not been placed in nomination by qualified voters who must take oath that they did not participate in a primary for the selection of a candidate for the office for which the nomination is made. . . .

We think that this statutory system for the selection of party nominees for inclusion on the general election ballot makes the party which is required to follow these legislative directions an agency of the state in so far as it determines the participants in a primary election. The party takes its character as a state agency from the duties imposed upon it by state statutes; the duties do not become matters of private law because they are performed by a political party. The plan of the Texas primary follows substantially that of Louisiana, with the exception that, in Louisiana, the state pays the cost of the primary, while Texas assesses the cost against candidates. In numerous instances, the Texas statutes fix or limit the fees to be charged. Whether paid directly by the state or through state requirements, it is state action which compels. When primaries become a part of the machinery for choosing officials, state and national, as they have here, the same tests to determine the character of discrimination or abridgement should be applied to the primary as are applied to the general election. . . .

The United States is a constitutional democracy. Its organic law grants to all citizens a right to participate in the choice of elected officials without restriction by any state because of race. This grant to the people of the opportunity for choice is not to be nullified by a state through casting its electoral process in a form which permits a private organization to practice racial discrimination in the election. Constitutional rights would be of little value if they could be thus indirectly denied.

The privilege of membership in a party may be . . . no concern of a state. But when, as here, that privilege is also the essential qualification for voting in a primary to select nominees for a general election, the state makes the action of the party the action of the state. In reaching this conclusion, we are not unmindful of the desirability of continuity of decision in constitutional questions. However, when convinced of former error, this Court has never felt constrained to follow precedent. In constitutional questions, where correction depends upon amendment, and not upon legislative action, this Court throughout its history has freely exercised its power to reexamine the basis of its constitutional decisions. This has long been accepted practice, and this practice has continued to this day. This is particularly true when the decision believed erroneous is the application of a constitutional principle, rather than an interpretation of the Constitution to extract the principle itself. Here, we are applying, contrary to the recent decision in *Grovey* v. *Townsend,* the well established principle of the Fifteenth Amendment, forbidding the abridgement by a state of a citizen's right to vote. *Grovey* v. *Townsend* is overruled.

Judgment reversed.

Sensitive to the impact that *Smith* would have on Southern electoral politics, Justice Stanley Reed, a Kentuckian and Southern Democrat, was assigned by Chief Justice Harlan Fiske Stone to write the opinion. Originally, Chief Justice Stone assigned the majority opinion to Justice Frankfurter, but changed his mind after reading a memo written by Justice Robert Jackson, who suggested Reed instead. "In the first place," said Jackson, "[Frankfurter] is a Jew. In the second place, he is from New England, the seat of the abolition movement. In the third place, he has not been thought of as a person particularly sympathetic with the Democratic Party in the past."[26] Jackson's implication was quite clear: The Court's opinion must come from someone viewed as the least sympathetic to African American rights. It is rather amazing to think that seventy years after the ratification of the Fifteenth Amendment the Court was having to walk on eggshells to explain why blacks, who had fought to preserve the Union during the Civil War and in every American war since then, should have a constitutional right to vote.

Thurgood Marshall considered *Smith,* even more so that *Brown* v. *Board of Education* (1954), the greatest triumph of his career as the NAACP's chief lawyer, a career that spanned the years 1938 to 1961. After *Smith,* the Southern states could no longer use the white primary system to exclude African Americans. The short-term effect in some states was an increase in black voter registration to more meaningful levels. By the early 1950s, black voter turnout had reached record levels. In Georgia, for example, where only 3 percent of eligible blacks were registered to vote in 1940, 23 percent of eligible blacks were registered to vote by 1952, and a high percentage of those were turning out to vote in state elections. In Texas, ironically, more blacks were registered to vote by 1952 than in any other state in the former Confederacy. In fact, the NAACP later supported Lyndon Johnson (who would appoint Marshall to the Supreme Court) when he ran for the United States Senate in 1948.[27]

Smith may have given impetus to black voter registration in states such as Georgia, Texas, and Tennessee, but that did not mean that blacks were always turning out to vote, as the fear of violence was omnipresent in the minds of many Southern blacks. *Smith* also stimulated the search for legal substitutes in states such as Alabama, Louisiana, and Virginia to deny African Americans access to the ballot. Literacy tests, more so than poll taxes, soon emerged as the most popular method to prevent black voter registration. Voting registrars at the state and county levels were given complete discretion to administer tests requiring applicants to interpret sections of the state constitution or describe in detail the ratification history of the state's voter education laws. Registrars were nearly always white, and the applicants

TABLE 12.1 Estimated Percentage of Voting-Age Blacks Registered in the South, 1940–1964

State	1940	1947	1952	1956	1958	1960	1962	1964
Alabama	0.4	1.2	5	11	15	13.7	13.4	23.0
Arkansas	1.5	17.3	27	36	33	37.3	34.0	49.3
Florida	5.7	15.4	33	32	31	38.9	36.8	63.8
Georgia	3.0	18.8	23	27	26	29.3	26.7	44.0
Louisiana	0.5	2.6	25	31	26	29.3	27.8	32.0
Mississippi	0.4	0.9	4	5	5	5.2	5.3	6.7
North Carolina	7.1	15.2	18	24	32	38.1	35.8	46.8
South Carolina	0.8	13.0	20	27	15	15.6	22.9	38.7
Tennessee	6.5	25.8	27	29	48	58.9	49.8	69.4
Texas	5.6	18.5	31	37	39	34.9	37.3	57.7
Virginia	4.1	13.2	16	19	21	22.8	24.0	45.7
All Southern States	3.0	12.0	20	24.9	25	29.1	29.4	43.1

Source: David J. Garrow, *Protest at Selma* (New Haven, Conn.: Yale University Press, 1978), pp. 7, 11, 19.

were nearly always black. By the early 1960s, it was still not unusual to find rural counties in the South well-populated by blacks but without a single registered black voter.[28]

The Voting Rights Act of 1965

Congress responded to stagnant black voter registration by enacting the Civil Rights Act of 1957, which permitted the attorney general to file lawsuits against states and localities that engaged in racially discriminatory practices prohibited by the Fifteenth Amendment. Later, Congress sought to strengthen the Justice Department's power in the Civil Rights Act of 1960, which authorized the attorney general to send federal officials to examine voter rolls and supervise elections in states where blacks claimed that racial discrimination had prevented them from registering to vote or from actually voting. What soon became clear to civil rights organizations and their supporters in the Congress, the Department of Justice, and the administrations of Presidents John F. Kennedy (1961–1963) and Johnson was that judicial enforcement of voting rights was not going to improve the status of black voters in the South without a meaningful federal law to support it. Comprehensive federal measures were needed to abolish the racially discriminatory barriers, albeit in the guise of literacy tests, poll taxes, and so on, still in place in the Southern states.

In *Louisiana* v. *United States* (1965), the Court unanimously struck down a Louisiana law that gave voting registrars complete discretion to determine if an applicant was sufficiently literate to register to vote.[29] Together with the ratification of the Twenty-Fourth Amendment the year before, which had abolished the poll tax in federal elections, the Court and Congress had taken major steps to remove the racially motivated barriers that existed throughout the South to African American enfranchisement. But the Court, in *Louisiana*, did not hold that literacy tests were unconstitutional per se. Rather, they were unconstitutional because of the way in which they were carried out. A year later the Court, in *Harper* v. *Virginia State Board of Elections* (1966), struck down poll taxes in *state* as well as federal elections as unconstitutional under the Fourteenth Amendment. *Harper* removed, in Thurgood Marshall's phrase, the "coin-operated turnstile" that stood in front of the voting booth. Still, the Southern states had many resources at their disposal to discourage black political participation.[30] Foremost among those resources were state and local political leaders determined to resist the demands of the blossoming civil rights movement for the right to vote.

Perhaps the key event that spurred the passage of the Voting Rights Act of 1965 was the ill-fated "Walk for Freedom" from Selma to Montgomery, Alabama, on March 7, 1965. Nearly six hundred marchers, black and white, gathered in Selma to march to the courthouse in Montgomery to register to vote. After congressional enactment of the Civil Rights Act of 1964, the civil rights movement had turned its attention to the right to vote, and had begun staging peaceful marches throughout the South. Alabama and Mississippi had become the focal points in the drive to register black voters. The events of "Bloody Sunday," as the Selma march became known, struck a chord in the nation's conscience just as the gruesome events of "Freedom Summer" had the year before. The accompanying SIDEBAR describes the impact of "Bloody Sunday" on the enactment of the Voting Rights Act of 1965.

Using its power under Section 2 of the Fifteenth Amendment, Congress banned literacy tests and other backhanded measures traditionally used to exclude black voters from access to the ballot. Building upon the 1957 and 1960 civil rights laws, the Voting Rights Act of 1965 greatly expanded the power of the federal government to supervise elections in the states covered by the law. Section 5 of the law included an even more controversial provision that required states with a demonstrated history of voting rights discrimination against racial minorities to submit their apportionment plans to the Justice Department for "preclearance" before they could go into effect. The Voting Rights Act of 1965 was also designed to eliminate a practice known as "vote dilution" (discussed later in this chapter) that was used by the Southern states to limit black political participation. The South was now down to its last line of defense. As civil rights groups and the Department of Justice expected, a Southern state, in *South Carolina* v. *Katzenbach* (1966), quickly stepped forward to challenge the constitutionality of the Voting Rights Act of 1965.

South Carolina v. *Katzenbach*

383 U.S. 301 (1966)

Katzenbach marked only the fifteenth time that the Supreme Court had assumed original jurisdiction in a case. The Court's decision to hear the case directly testified to the gravity of the issue presented by South Carolina's decision to challenge immediately the Voting Rights Act of 1965. Five states—Alabama, Georgia, Louisiana, Mississippi, and Virginia—filed *amicus* briefs in support of South Carolina's position that the law was unconstitutional. These six states had the lowest percentage of eligible blacks registered to vote in the United States. Twenty-one states—not one from the South—submitted *amicus* briefs in support of the law's constitutionality.

Attorney General Nicholas Katzenbach was the named defendant in the suit, since the Department of Justice was responsible for enforcing the landmark voting rights measure. With him on the federal government's brief, however, was Thurgood Marshall, who had been named by President Lyndon Johnson in 1965 to serve as solicitor general, the first African American to do so. Two years later, Johnson would name Marshall to the Supreme Court, where he again broke the color barrier.

The Court's decision was unanimous. Chief Justice Warren delivered the opinion of the Court.

MR. CHIEF JUSTICE WARREN delivered the opinion of the Court.

The Voting Rights Act was designed by Congress to banish the blight of racial discrimination in voting, which has infected the electoral process in parts of our country for nearly a century. The Act creates stringent new remedies for voting discrimination where it persists on a pervasive scale, and, in addition, the statute strengthens existing remedies for pockets of voting discrimination elsewhere in the country. Congress assumed the power to prescribe these remedies from Section 2 of the Fifteenth Amendment, which authorizes the National Legislature to effectuate by "appropriate" measures the constitutional prohibition against racial discrimination in voting. We hold that the sections of the Act which are properly before us, are an appropriate means for carrying out Congress' constitutional responsibilities, and are consonant with all other provisions of the Constitution. We therefore deny

S I D E B A R

THE VOTING RIGHTS ACT OF 1965

Bloody Sunday

Selma, Alabama, personified the Old South's determination to resist any effort of African Americans to register to vote. By the early 1960s, blacks made up about half the voting-age population in Dallas County, where Selma was located, but only 1 percent of voting-age blacks were registered to vote. Just 156 of Selma's approximately 15,000 voting-age blacks were on the voting rolls. In February 1963, the Student Non-Violent Coordinating Committee (SNCC), one of the civil rights movement's most important groups, began holding voter education seminars in Selma to demonstrate how to comply with the city's complex voter registration requirements. Like every other Southern city, small town, and rural outpost, Selma used literacy tests and other qualifying requirements to determine if a citizen was fit to vote. Somehow, whites were always well qualified to vote and African Americans were not.

SNCC had only modest success in encouraging local blacks to register to vote. An older generation, steeped in the region's entrenched customs of segregation, was afraid to challenge white authority for fear that registering to vote would cost them their jobs or result in physical retaliation. Ameila Platts Boynton was one of Selma's few registered blacks during that time. After escorting an elderly African American man to the voting registrar's office, Boynton noticed the clerk staring at the man's shaking hand as he tried to write his name on the voting form. "I can't write so good," the man explained. The clerk responded by ordering the man out of line. Said the black man, "I am sixty-five years old, I own one hundred acres of land that is paid for, I am a taxpayer and I have six children. All of them is teachin', workin'. . . . If what I done ain't enough to be a registered voter with all the tax I got to pay, then Lord have mercy on America."

In the early winter of 1965, SNCC, along with the Southern Christian Leadership Conference (SCLC), headed by Martin Luther King Jr., began to organize a steady stream of protests in Selma and marches to encourage voter registration. In February 1965, the SCLC organized twenty-five demonstrators to march to the Dallas County courthouse to register to vote. The march ended in violence after Sheriff Jim Clark, who had become increasingly intolerant of civil rights demonstrators, turned his forces loose on the marchers as they approached the courthouse after darkness had settled over Selma. A twenty-six-year-old demonstrator, Jimmie Lee Jackson, was beaten to death after attempting to move his eighty-two-year-old grandfather out of harm's way. Jackson's death touched a nerve deep within the African American community. After the tragedy, Martin Luther King announced that the SCLC was preparing to organize a fifty-mile march from Selma to Montgomery, the state capital, to demand the right to vote. As one local activist said, "We had decided that we were going to get killed or we was going to be free."

Governor George Wallace wasted no time in announcing that he would not permit the march because it would block highway traffic. In reality, a fuming Wallace told his staff, "I'm not gonna have a bunch of niggers walking along a highway in this state as long as I'm governor." In a stunning move, SNCC, the group with the longest history in Alabama, declined to support or take part in the march because it believed the specter of violence was too great for too little return. SNCC president John Lewis broke with his group's decision, deciding that too much was at stake for him to sit on the sidelines. As it turned out, Lewis's decision to take part in the Selma march turned out to be the most fateful day of his life.

On Sunday, March 7, 1965, John Lewis assembled with six hundred other demonstrators at Brown's Chapel in Selma to begin the march to Montgomery. By a coin flip, Lewis and Hosea Williams, a top street lieutenant in the SCLC, ended up in the front of the line. They left the church about four o'clock in the afternoon, walked the six blocks to the Edmund Pettus Bridge, and began to cross the Alabama River into East Selma. Four slow-moving ambulances, staffed with doctors and nurses, brought up the rear. As they reached the crest of the bridge, Lewis stopped dead in his tracks. Williams, without looking at Lewis, also froze. Down at the bottom of the bridge, several dozen Alabama state troopers, deputy sheriffs, and other local police, some of whom had been "deputized" that morning, stood ready for the marchers, poised in riot gear and armed with rifles and clubs that resembled oversized baseball bats. On one side of the road, a crowd of whites had gathered, many of whom were waving Confederate flags and shouting epithets. Next to them were scattered news photographers and reporters, prepared to record what became one of the most important events of the civil rights movement.

Lewis and Williams continued to lead the marchers down the bridge, while noticing that several troopers had put on gas masks. As they reached the bottom, Major John Cloud pulled out a bullhorn and faced the marchers, who stopped as if following a drum major.

"This is an unlawful assembly," Cloud bellowed. "Your march is not conducive to the public safety. You are ordered to disperse and go back to your church or to your homes."

Williams responded, "May we have a word with the major?"

"There is no word to be had," Cloud shot back. "You have two minutes to turn around and go back to your church."

Lewis thought that advancing would invite aggression, but believed they had come too far to turn around. He whispered to Williams that they should kneel and lead the group in prayer. Just as they prepared to bow down, Lewis heard Cloud shout an order to his troops:

"Troopers, advance!"

At that point, dozens of troopers burst forth simultaneously, some wielding clubs and rifle butts, others flashing bullwhips. They attacked the marchers, grabbing anyone they could find, including women and

John Lewis, chairman of the Student Non-Violent Coordinating Committee (SNCC), lower left, under assault by Alabama state troopers after leading a march across the Edmund Pettus bridge in Selma to encourage African American voter registration. Twenty-one years later, Lewis was elected to Congress.
© Bettmann/CORBIS

teenagers, and beat them indiscriminately. Marchers fell to the ground in waves; many had lost consciousness. Soon after the initial beatings, the troopers sprayed C-4 tear gas, specifically made to induce nausea. Those escaping the first wave of attacks began to flee, only to see troopers on horseback following them, brandishing their weapons and using them as soon as they got in range. One by one, the demonstrators staggered back to the Brown Chapel, private homes, and black-owned businesses to safety. From that moment on, the "Walk for Freedom" would be known as "Bloody Sunday."

President Lyndon Johnson, like millions of other Americans, watched the scene from Selma on the special news bulletins that broke into regular Sunday evening news programming. Appalled, Johnson summoned Wallace to Washington, where he told his fellow Southerner that he was not going to allow Wallace to stand in the way of a civil rights movement whose "time ha[d] come." Wallace returned to Alabama defeated, knowing full well that the crude violence had been witnessed worldwide on that fateful Sunday afternoon. Five days after "Bloody Sunday," Johnson introduced the Voting Rights Act of 1965 to a joint session of Congress. To underscore his commitment to the African American civil rights movement, Johnson ended his speech by quoting an old black spiritual that had become the anthem of the civil rights movement: "And we shall overcome."

On August 6, Johnson, flanked by prominent leaders from the civil rights movement, signed the voting rights bill into law. Just over one hundred years earlier, Abraham Lincoln had signed the Emancipation Proclamation in the same room, and the symbolism was not lost on anyone who attended the signing ceremony. An array of social and political forces had come together to make the Voting Rights Act of 1965 and the promise of African American enfranchisement reality. But few events, standing alone, were as crucial in awakening the nation's conscience as "Bloody Sunday" in Selma, Alabama.

References

Lewis, John, with Michael D'Orso. *Walking with the Wind: A Memoir of the Movement.* New York: Harcourt Brace, 1998.

Williams, Juan. *Eyes on the Prize: America's Civil Rights Years, 1954–1965.* New York: Viking Books, 1987.

South Carolina's request that enforcement of these sections of the Act be enjoined.

The constitutional propriety of the Voting Rights Act of 1965 must be judged with reference to the historical experience which it reflects. Before enacting the measure, Congress explored with great care the problem of racial discrimination in voting. The House and Senate Committees on the Judiciary each held hearings for nine days and received testimony from a total of 67 witnesses. More than three full days were consumed discussing the bill on the floor of the House, while the debate in the Senate covered 26 days in all. At the close of these deliberations, the verdict of both chambers was overwhelming. The House approved the bill by a vote of 328–74, and the measure passed the Senate by a margin of 79–18.

Two points emerge vividly from the voluminous legislative history of the Act contained in the committee hearings and floor debates. First: Congress felt itself confronted by an insidious and pervasive evil which had been perpetuated in certain parts of our country through unremitting and ingenious defiance of the Constitution. Second: Congress concluded that the unsuccessful remedies which it had prescribed in the past would have to be replaced by sterner and more elaborate measures in order to satisfy the clear commands of the Fifteenth Amendment. . . .

In recent years, Congress has repeatedly tried to cope with the problem by facilitating case-by-case litigation against voting discrimination. The Civil Rights Act of 1957 authorized the Attorney General to seek injunctions against public and private interference with the right to vote on racial grounds. Perfecting amendments in the Civil Rights Act of 1960 permitted the joinder of States as parties defendant, gave the Attorney General access to local voting records, and authorized courts to register voters in areas of systematic discrimination. . . .

Despite the earnest efforts of the Justice Department and of many federal judges, these new laws have done little to cure the problem of voting discrimination. According to estimates by the Attorney General during hearings on the Act, registration of voting-age Negroes in Alabama rose only from 14.2% to 19.4% between 1958 and 1964; in Louisiana, it barely inched ahead from 31.7% to 31.8% between 1956 and 1965, and in Mississippi it increased only from 4.4% to 6.4% between 1954 and 1964. In each instance, registration of voting-age whites ran roughly 50 percentage points or more ahead of Negro registration. . . .

The Voting Rights Act of 1965 reflects Congress' firm intention to rid the country of racial discrimination in voting. The heart of the Act is a complex scheme of stringent remedies aimed at areas where voting discrimination has been most flagrant. Section 4(a)-(d) lays down a formula defining the States and political subdivisions to which these new remedies apply. The first of the remedies, contained in § 4(a), is the suspension of literacy tests and similar voting qualifications for a period of five years from the last occurrence of substantial voting discrimination. Section 5 prescribes a second remedy, the suspension of all new voting regulations pending review by federal authorities to determine whether their use would perpetuate voting discrimination. The third remedy is the assignment of federal examiners on certification by the Attorney General to list qualified applicants who are thereafter entitled to vote in all elections.

Other provisions of the Act prescribe subsidiary cures for persistent voting discrimination. Section 8 authorizes the appointment of federal poll-watchers in places to which federal examiners have already been assigned. Section 10(d) excuses those made eligible to vote in sections of the country covered by Section 4(b) of the Act from paying accumulated past poll taxes for state and local elections. Section 12(e) provides for balloting by persons denied access to the polls in areas where federal examiners have been appointed.

The remaining remedial portions of the Act are aimed at voting discrimination in any area of the country where it may occur. Section 2 broadly prohibits the use of voting rules to abridge exercise of the franchise on racial grounds. Sections 3, 6(a), and 13(b) strengthen existing procedures for attacking voting discrimination by means of litigation. Section 4(e) excuses citizens educated in American schools conducted in a foreign language from passing English language literacy tests. Section 10(a)-(c) facilitates constitutional litigation challenging the imposition of all poll taxes for state and local elections. Sections 11 and 12(a)-(d) authorize civil and criminal sanctions against interference with the exercise of rights guaranteed by the Act. . . .

These provisions of the Voting Rights Act of 1965 are challenged on the fundamental ground that they exceed the powers of Congress and encroach on an area reserved to the States by the Constitution. . . .

The ground rules for resolving this question are clear. The language and purpose of the Fifteenth Amendment, the prior decisions construing its several provisions, and the general doctrines of constitutional interpretation all point to one fundamental principle. As against the reserved powers of the States, Congress may use any rational means to effectuate the constitutional prohibition of racial discrimination in voting. We turn now to a more detailed description of the standards which govern our review of the Act.

Section 1 of the Fifteenth Amendment declares that, "[t]he right of citizens of the United States to vote shall not be denied or abridged by the United States or by any State on account of race, color, or previous condition of servitude." This declaration has always been treated as self-executing, and has repeatedly been construed, without further legislative specification, to invalidate state voting qualifications or procedures which are discriminatory on their face or in practice. . . . The gist of the matter is that the Fifteenth Amendment supersedes contrary exertions of state power. "When a State exercises power wholly within the domain of state interest, it is insulated from federal judicial review. But such insulation is not carried over when state power is used as an instrument for circumventing a federally protected right."

South Carolina contends that . . . to allow an exercise of this authority by Congress would be to rob the courts of their rightful constitutional role. On the contrary, Section 2 of the Fifteenth Amendment expressly declares that "Congress shall have power to enforce this article by appropriate legislation." By adding this authorization, the Framers indicated that Congress was to be chiefly responsible for implementing the rights created in Section 1. "It is the power of Congress which has been enlarged. Congress is authorized to enforce the prohibitions by appropriate legislation. Some legislation is contemplated to make the [Civil War] amendments fully effective." Accordingly, in addition to the courts, Congress has full remedial powers to effectuate the constitutional prohibition against racial discrimination in voting. . . .

After enduring nearly a century of widespread resistance to the Fifteenth Amendment, Congress has marshalled an array of potent weapons against the evil, with authority in the Attorney General to employ them effectively. Many of the areas directly affected by this development have indicated their willingness to abide by any restraints legitimately imposed upon them. We here hold that the portions of the Voting Rights Act properly before us are a valid means for carrying out the commands of the Fifteenth Amendment. Hopefully, millions of non-white Americans will now be able to participate for the first time on an equal basis in the government under which they live. We may finally look forward to the day when truly, "[t]he right of citizens of the United States to vote shall not be denied or abridged by the United States or by any State on account of race, color, or previous condition of servitude."

The bill of complaint is [d]ismissed.

Later that term, the Court decided an important follow-up case to *Katzenbach* that greatly expanded the power of Congress to define and enforce constitutional rights under the Fourteenth Amendment. In *Katzenbach v. Morgan* (1966), the justices ruled that Congress had power under Section 5 of the Fourteenth Amendment to expand the "substance" of Court-created constitutional guarantees, as long as the legislation was "appropriate" and "remedial" in nature.[31] *Morgan* involved a conflict between a New York state law that required its citizens to meet a literacy requirement to register to vote and Section 4 (e) of the Voting Rights Act of 1965. Section 4 (e) stated that no person who had successfully completed the sixth grade in an accredited public or private school in Puerto Rico could be denied the right to vote in any election in the United States. The New York law, which required residents to read and write English in order to vote, effectively disenfranchised several hundred thousand Puerto Ricans who lived in New York City. Justice William Brennan, writing for the 7–2 majority, also concluded that, under the Supremacy Clause of Article VI of the Constitution, the Voting Rights Act of 1965 superseded any state law to the contrary. *Morgan* demonstrated quite clearly that the Court was willing to give broad deference to Congress to enforce the new voting rights law.

The Voting Rights Act had an immediate impact on black voter registration in the South. By 1968, Mississippi had increased black registered voters from less than 7 percent to nearly 60 percent. Black voter registration in Alabama increased to 60 percent of the eligible population from just under 25 percent in 1964. Similar improvement occurred throughout the South. Access to the ballot for African Americans was the crowning achievement of the Voting Rights Act of 1965. Beyond that, however, other questions soon emerged about black political participation. Did the Fourteenth Amendment prohibit the states from drawing their legislative districts to favor particular economic and political interests that effectively diluted black votes? Did the federal courts now have authority to intervene in legislative apportionment in the states, a matter that had always been considered a political, not a judicial, question? And, raising questions similar to the Court's later cases involving affirmative action in education, employment, and government contracting, did the Voting Rights Act require states to create "majority-minority" districts, thus increasing the likelihood that black voters could elect black candidates to office? These questions will take up the remainder of this chapter.

TABLE 12.2 Estimated Percentage of Eligible Blacks Registered to Vote in the South, 1966–1968

State	1966	1968
Alabama	51.2	56.7
Arkansas	59.7	67.5
Florida	60.9	62.1
Georgia	47.2	56.1
Louisiana	47.1	59.3
Mississippi	32.9	59.4
North Carolina	51.0	55.3
South Carolina	51.4	50.8
Tennessee	71.7	72.8
Texas	61.6	83.1
Virginia	46.9	58.4
All Southern States	52.2	62.0

Source: David J. Garrow, *Protest at Selma* (New Haven, Conn.: Yale University Press, 1978), p. 189.

Apportionment and the Right to Equal Representation

Equal access to the electoral ballot is certainly a prerequisite for any system of government that professes allegiance to the principle of consent of the governed. But once those ballots have been cast, an equally compelling question arises: What impact will those votes have on electoral outcomes? Much of the answer depends on how the states draw their legislative districts. Representation based on population has always been the dominant theme when state legislatures draw their district lines. In accord with Article IV, Section 4, of the Constitution, which guarantees to each state a republican form of government, Congress insisted early on that any state admitted into the Union require legislative representation based on population. During the 1830s, Congress enacted legislation requiring that districts in the House of Representatives have "contiguous" borders and equal populations. After the Civil War, the migration of African Americans to the North in search of greater freedom and economic opportunity, the large number of eligible black voters in Southern cities, an influx of European immigrants to the nation's major cities, and the Industrial Revolution combined to produce new population patterns in many states. These changes were in greater evidence after World War II, when the nation's cities and fast-developing suburbs exploded in population. Entrenched political interests protected themselves by persuading state legislatures not to redraw district lines to reflect population shifts from rural to urban districts. Although many state constitutions required their legislative districts to undergo reapportionment every ten years, consistent with the decennial federal census, powerful legislators routinely ignored this obligation, particularly in the South.[32]

What considerations, then, may states take into account when drawing district lines? Geography, communities of interest, traditional neighborhoods, racial and ethnic enclaves, incumbency, and the boundaries of political subdivisions (cities, towns, special taxing districts, and so on) are all factors that the Court has ruled are permissible, and in some cases, required, in creating legislative districts.[33] As you can imagine, these factors

WHAT IS GERRYMANDERING?

The term *gerrymandering* describes legislative districts that have been drawn specifically to protect incumbents, party interests, or any other explicitly partisan interest. The term *"racial" gerrymandering* is used to describe deliberate efforts to create "minority-majority" districts to bolster the power of minority voters and improve their chances of electing minority candidates. Early-eighteenth-century cartoonist Gilbert Stuart drew the salamander-like "Gerrymander" after Massachusetts Governor Elbridge Gerry, whose ability to manipulate state legislative apportionment to protect his political interests was well appreciated by his allies and resented by his enemies.

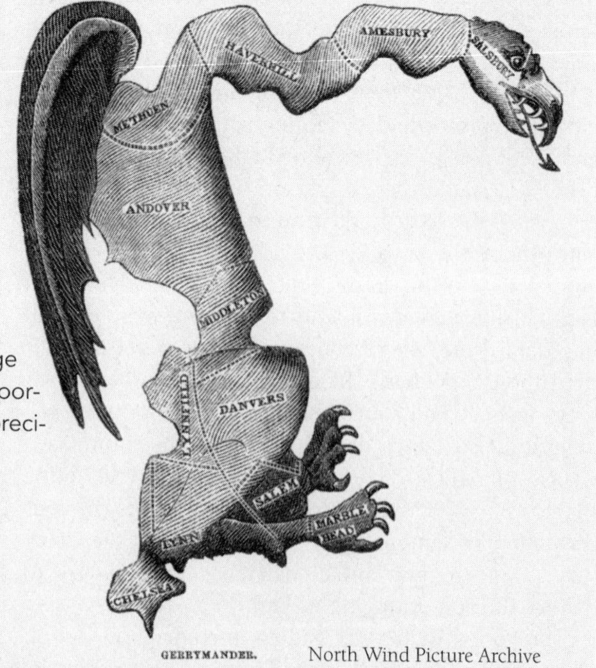

North Wind Picture Archive

give state legislatures considerable degrees of freedom when deciding to establish or reconfigure district boundaries. Not surprisingly, deciding when legislative apportionment reflects an appropriate combination of the above criteria and when it crosses the threshold from political give-and-take to intentional vote dilution based on discriminatory action has been a difficult course for the Court to chart. In *Gomillion* v. *Lightfoot* (1960), the Court dealt with just this issue.

Gomillion v. *Lightfoot*

364 U.S. 339 (1960)

In 1956, black voter registration in Alabama stood at 11 percent, but that did not stop white politicians from taking precautionary measures against any potential gains that future court decisions or federal laws might have in store for blacks. So in 1957, Tuskegee mayor Phil Lightfoot persuaded the Alabama legislature to redraw the city's electoral boundaries to strengthen further the white vote. Before then, Tuskegee's boundaries had been a square that encompassed the city. The 1957 law redrew the city's electoral boundaries so that it now had twenty-eight different sides and excluded all but four of Tuskegee's 400 registered black voters.

NAACP lawyer Robert L. Carter, who had argued the actual *Brown* case of the four cases argued together as *Brown* v. *Board of Education* (1954), represented C. G. Gomillion and several other black Tuskegee residents who had been gerrymandered out of the original boundaries. Carter's argument was simple: The right of states to determine their own electoral arrangements free from judicial intervention was balanced against the Fifteenth Amendment's ban on racially discriminatory measures in voting. Carter also pointed out that not one white voter had been placed outside the city's new electoral boundaries. The lower federal courts agreed with Tuskegee's argument that the courts had no jurisdiction to interfere with state apportionment decisions.

The Court's decision was unanimous. Justice Frankfurter delivered the opinion of the Court. Justice Whittaker filed a concurring opinion.

▼▲▼

JUSTICE FRANKFURTER delivered the opinion of the Court.

The complaint amply alleges a claim of racial discrimination. Against this claim the respondents have never suggested, either in their brief or in oral argument, any countervailing municipal function which Act 140 is designed to serve. The respondents invoke generalities expressing the State's unrestricted power—unlimited, that is, by the United States Constitution—to establish, destroy, or reorganize by contraction or expansion its political subdivisions, to wit, cities, counties, and other local units. We freely recognize the breadth and importance of this aspect of the State's political power. . . .

[T]he Court has never acknowledged that the States have power to do as they will with municipal corporations regardless of consequences. Legislative control of municipalities, no less than other state power, lies within the scope of relevant limitations imposed by the United States Constitution. . . .

If all this is so in regard to the constitutional protection of contracts, it should be equally true that, to paraphrase, such power, extensive though it is, is met and overcome by the Fifteenth Amendment to the Constitution of the United States, which forbids a State from passing any law which deprives a citizen of his vote because of his race. The opposite conclusion, urged upon us by respondents, would sanction the achievement by a State of any impairment of voting rights whatever, so long as it was cloaked in the garb of the realignment of political subdivisions. "It is inconceivable that guaranties embedded in the Constitution of the United States may thus be manipulated out of existence."

The respondents find another barrier to the trial of this case in *Colegrove* v. *Green* (1946). In that case, the Court passed on an Illinois law governing the arrangement of congressional districts within that State. The complaint rested upon the disparity of population between the different districts which rendered the effectiveness of each individual's vote in some districts far less than in others. This disparity came to pass solely through shifts in population between 1901, when Illinois organized its congressional districts, and 1946, when the complaint was lodged. During this entire period, elections were held under the districting scheme devised in 1901. The Court affirmed the dismissal of the complaint on the ground that it presented a subject not meet for adjudication. The decisive facts in this case, which at this stage must be taken as proved, are wholly different from the considerations found controlling in Colegrove.

That case involved a complaint of discriminatory apportionment of congressional districts. The appellants in *Colegrove* complained only of a dilution of the strength of their votes as a result of legislative inaction over a course of many years. The petitioners here complain that affirmative legislative action deprives them of their votes and the consequent advantages that the ballot affords. When a legislature thus singles out a readily isolated segment of a racial minority for special discriminatory treatment, it violates the Fifteenth Amendment. In no case involving unequal weight in voting distribution that has come before the Court did the decision sanction a differentiation on racial lines whereby approval was given to unequivocal withdrawal of the vote solely from colored citizens. Apart from all else, these considerations lift this controversy out of the so-called "political" arena and into the conventional sphere of constitutional litigation.

In sum, as Mr. Justice Holmes remarked when dealing with a related situation in *Nixon* v. *Herndon* (1927), "Of course the petition concerns political action," but "[t]he objection that the subject matter of the suit is political is little more than a play upon words." A statute which is alleged to have worked unconstitutional deprivations of petitioners' rights is not immune to attack simply because the mechanism employed by the legislature is a redefinition of municipal boundaries. According to the allegations here made, the Alabama Legislature has not merely redrawn the Tuskegee city limits with incidental inconvenience to the petitioners; it is more accurate to say that it has deprived the petitioners of the municipal franchise and consequent rights, and, to that end, it has incidentally changed the city's boundaries. While in form this is merely an act redefining metes and bounds, if the allegations are established, the inescapable human effect of this essay in geometry and geography is to despoil colored citizens, and only colored citizens, of their theretofore enjoyed voting rights. That was no *Colegrove* v. *Green*.

When a State exercises power wholly within the domain of state interest, it is insulated from federal judicial review. But such insulation is not carried over when state power is used as an instrument for circumventing a federally protected right. . . .

For these reasons, the principal conclusions of the District Court and the Court of Appeals are clearly erroneous, and the decision below must be reversed.

Reversed.

Appendix to the Opinion of the Court

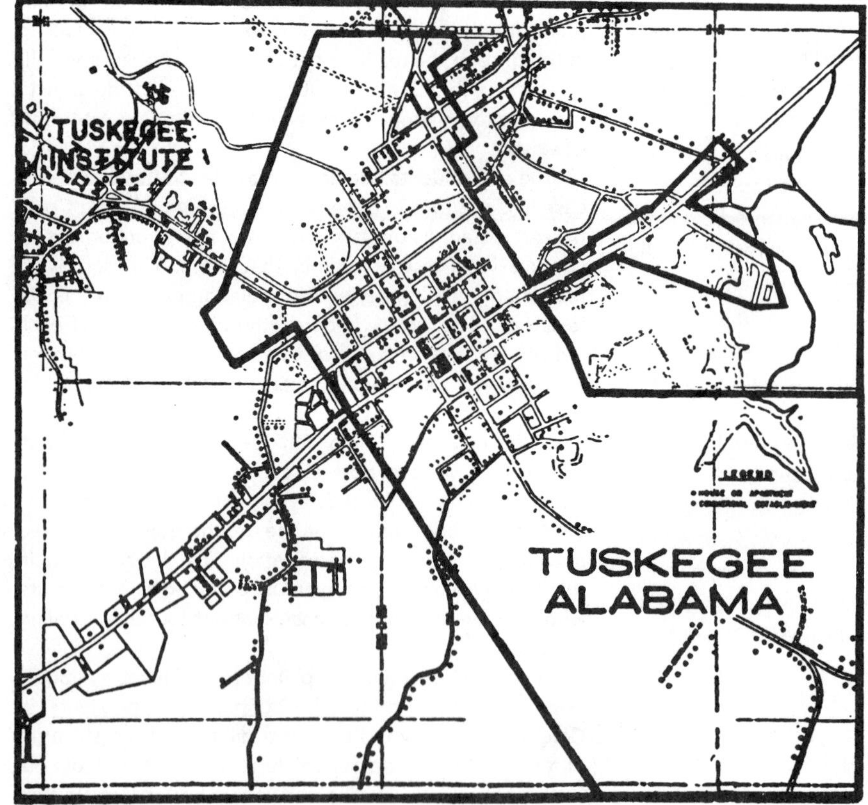

Tuskegee, Alabama, before and after Act 140. The entire area of the square comprised the city prior to Act 140. The irregular black-bordered figure within the square represents the post-enactment city.

Gomillion made clear that apportionment laws intended to dilute votes on the basis of race were unconstitutional, and that the Court would not hesitate to strike any such law down. But what did *Gomillion* mean for those states that had not bothered, for reasons of political power, to redraw their legislative districts to reflect changing population patterns? Historically, the Court had avoided interfering in state apportionment controversies, claiming that such matters were "political questions" beyond the reach of the judiciary. Any remedy in such cases had to come from the legislatures themselves. While the Court did not fully articulate and refine the "political questions" doctrine until the mid-twentieth century, Chief Justice John Marshall first alluded to the distinctions between questions of law and those questions that were political in nature in *Marbury* v. *Madison* (1803). There, Marshall wrote that "[t]he province of the court is, solely, to decide on the rights of individuals, not to inquire how the executive, or executive officers, perform duties in which they have a discretion. Questions in their nature political . . . can never be made in this court."[34]

Given the political nature of constitutional litigation, how does the Court distinguish between "legal" and "political" questions? In general, the Court will invoke the "political questions" doctrine when it believes that a legal dispute involves political or policy differences between the parties rather than questions of law. Few areas of American constitutional law illustrate the fluid nature of the Court's use of the "political questions" doctrine better than the interrelated issues of voting rights and legislative malapportionment. In *Luther* v. *Borden* (1849), the Court first invoked the "political questions" doctrine to avoid considering the substance of a constitutional claim. *Luther* involved a political scenario that is unthinkable in modern times. Unable to persuade Rhode Island to call a state constitutional convention for the purpose of reconsidering its voting-eligibility requirements, a rival political faction decided to form a separate government, complete with its own militia. Several leaders of Rhode Island's political opposition argued that the existing charter—Rhode Island had no written constitution—denied them their right to a "republican form of government" under Article IV of the Constitution. Article IV reads:

> The United States shall guarantee to every State in this Union a Republican Form of Government, and shall protect them against invasion; and on application of the Legislature, or of the Executive (when the Legislature cannot be convened) against domestic Violence.

In *Luther,* Chief Justice Taney held that responsibility for enforcing the Guarantee Clause of Article IV rested with Congress, not the courts. Writing for an 8–1 majority, Taney wrote that "Congress must necessarily decide what government is established in the State before it can determine whether is republican or not . . . [a]nd its decision is binding on every other department of the government, and could not be questioned in a judicial tribunal." Further describing the Court's limits to review "political" disputes, Taney wrote:

> Much of the argument on the part of the plaintiff turned upon political rights and political questions, upon which the court has been urged to express an opinion. We decline. . . . This tribunal . . . should be the last to overstep the boundaries which limit its own jurisdiction. And while it should always be ready to meet any question confided to it by the Constitution, it is equally its duty not to pass beyond its appropriate sphere of action.

For over one hundred years, the Court continued to invoke the "political questions" doctrine to explain its refusal to decide constitutional claims attempting to invoke the Guarantee Clause. In *Colegrove* v. *Green* (1946), Justice Felix Frankfurter, in a classic example of the "legal process" approach to constitutional interpretation, explained that the Court was powerless to intervene in cases involving legislative malapportionment. Frankfurter did not contest the evidence presented at trial demonstrating the gross inequities that existed in the electoral representation of state residents in the Illinois legislature. Nor did he suggest that the disproportionate power wielded by sparsely populated rural districts in legislative politics was desirable or even defensible, or mention that Illinois, despite population shifts from rural to urban areas, had not redrawn its legislative districts since 1901. Rather, it was the power of the Court to enter the "political thicket" that concerned him:

> We are of the opinion that the petitioners ask of this Court what is beyond its competence to grant. This is one of those demands on judicial power which cannot be met by verbal fencing about "jurisdiction." It must be resolved by considerations on the basis of which this Court, from time

> to time, has refused to intervene in controversies. It has refused to do so because due regard for the effective working of our Government revealed this issue to be of a peculiarly political nature and therefore not meet for judicial determination. . . .
>
> Nothing is clearer than that this controversy concerns matters that bring courts into immediate and active relations with party contests. From the determination of such issues this Court has traditionally held aloof. It is hostile to the democratic system to involve the judiciary in the politics of the people. And it is not less pernicious if such judicial intervention is an essentially political contest dressed up in the abstract phrases of the law.[35]

Sixteen years later, the Court retreated from its position in *Colegrove.* In *Baker* v. *Carr* (1962), the Court held that when individuals have exhausted all possible remedies available through the political process, the federal courts have the jurisdiction to decide whether a state legislative apportionment plan violates the Equal Protection Clause of the Fourteenth Amendment. Note how Justice Brennan's opinion for the Court expressly rejects Justice Frankfurter's *Colegrove* opinion. Brennan concluded that the claim brought by Tennessee voters in *Baker* did not implicate the Guarantee Clause, thus raising the issue of justiciablity. Rather, Brennan emphasized the wide disparities that existed among legislative districts in Tennessee's apportionment plan and concluded that the issue involved the right to equal participation in the political process. Framed in this manner, Brennan understood the issues to involve the Equal Protection Clause.

For Justice Frankfurter, *Baker* marked his last great exposition on the "legal process" approach to judicial review and constitutional interpretation. By the early 1960s, Frankfurter's approach to constitutional decision making placed him at odds with the Court's liberals, such as Brennan, Black, Douglas, and Warren. The liberals were more willing to strike down laws that violated their conception of fundamental fairness. Frankfurter, on the other hand, distrusted judicial intervention in matters that he believed rested properly in the hands of the legislatures, a view that stemmed from his days as a confidant to President Franklin D. Roosevelt during the formation of the New Deal. Remembering quite well the Court's willingness to strike down social and economic reform legislation in defense of corporate and business interests, Frankfurter believed the role of the courts was to make sure that legislatures had the freedom to pursue their reform impulses.

As the facts in *Baker* v. *Carr* demonstrated, however, it was hard for reformers to emerge in a legislature when their votes did not carry the same weight as those of the established powers-that-be. Which approach do you believe offers the best explanation of the Court's role in legislative malapportionment cases where racial exclusion is not the predominant factor, Brennan or Frankfurter's? Do you believe that the Court's decision in *Baker* to reconsider the "political questions" doctrine was influenced by the social and political forces of the time?

Baker v. *Carr*

369 U.S. 186 (1962)

Charles William Baker lived in the west Tennessee county of Shelby, which included Memphis and many of its adjoining suburbs. After leaving the army in 1944, Baker knocked around a bit before settling into a career in Shelby County politics. By 1954, Baker had been elected chairman of the Shelby County Court, which ran the county's fiscal affairs. With a population of approximately six hundred thousand, Shelby County was bursting at the seams in economic growth, but lacked the attendant political power. In contrast, neighboring Stewart County counted a population of nine thousand, but had the same representation in the state legislature as urban Shelby County. This pattern was consistent throughout the state. Cities watched as rural counties enacted legislation granting themselves farm subsidies and tax exemptions, while precious few tax dollars flowed into the cities. Tennessee had not redrawn its district lines since 1901, even though the state's population had long since shifted to urban areas. In 1959, Baker and dozens of other taxpayers from Tennessee's three other major cities, Chattanooga, Knoxville, and Nashville, filed suit against Secretary of State Joe C. Carr, alleging that the state's malapportioned legislative districts violated the Equal Protection Clause of the Fourteenth Amendment.

Unlike many other landmark cases decided by the Supreme Court during this time, *Baker* was not conceived of or litigated by an interest group. Instead, several ad hoc coalitions of lawyers, "good government" groups such as the League of Women Voters, and reform-minded judges worked together to finance and manage the *Baker* litigation. Although acutely aware of Frankfurter's opinion in *Colegrove*, the *Baker* lawyers believed that *Gomillion* was a better indicator of the Court's thinking on whether judicial intervention was appropriate in apportionment cases where vote dilution was clearly evident. The plaintiffs lost in the lower courts, which relied upon the "political questions" doctrine to avoid deciding the equal protection claim. One note of optimism was the lower courts' recognition that Tennessee's apportionment plan effectively denied urban communities equal representation in the legislature.

The Court's decision was 6 to 2. Justice Brennan delivered the opinion of the Court. Justices Clark, Douglas, and Stewart filed concurring opinions. Justices Frankfurter and Harlan filed dissents.

▼▲▼

MR. JUSTICE BRENNAN delivered the opinion of the Court.

Between 1901 and 1961, Tennessee . . . experienced substantial growth and redistribution of her population. In 1901, the population was 2,020,616, of whom 487,380 were eligible to vote. The 1960 Federal Census reports the State's population at 3,567,089, of whom 2,092,891 are eligible to vote. The relative standings of the counties in terms of qualified voters have changed significantly. It is primarily the continued application of the 1901 Apportionment Act to this shifted and enlarged voting population which gives rise to the present controversy.

Indeed, the complaint alleges that the 1901 statute, even as of the time of its passage, "made no apportionment of Representatives and Senators in accordance with the constitutional formula . . . but instead arbitrarily and capriciously apportioned representatives in the Senate and House without reference . . . to any logical or reasonable formula whatever." It is further alleged that, "because of the population changes since 1900, and the failure of the Legislature to reapportion itself since 1901," the 1901 statute became "unconstitutional and obsolete." Appellants also argue that, because of the composition of the legislature effected by the 1901 Apportionment Act, redress in the form of a state constitutional amendment to change the entire mechanism for reapportioning, or any other change short of that, is difficult or impossible. The complaint concludes that "these plaintiffs and others similarly situated, are denied the equal protection of the laws accorded them by the Fourteenth Amendment to the Constitution of the United States by virtue of the debasement of their votes." . . .

[W]e hold today only (a) that the court possessed jurisdiction of the subject matter; (b) that a justiciable cause of action is stated upon which appellants would be entitled to appropriate relief, and (c) because appellees raise the issue before this Court, that the appellants have standing to challenge the Tennessee apportionment statutes. Beyond noting that we have no cause at this stage to doubt the District Court will be able to fashion relief if violations of constitutional rights are found, it is improper now to consider what remedy would be most appropriate if appellants prevail at the trial.

Jurisdiction of the Subject Matter

The District Court was uncertain whether our cases withholding federal judicial relief rested upon a lack of federal jurisdiction or upon the inappropriateness of the subject matter for judicial consideration—what we have designated "nonjusticiability." The distinction between the two grounds is significant. In the instance of nonjusticiability, consideration of the cause is not wholly and immediately foreclosed; rather, the Court's inquiry necessarily proceeds to the point of deciding whether the duty asserted can be judicially identified and its breach judicially determined, and whether protection for the right asserted can be judicially molded. In the instance of lack of jurisdiction, the cause either does not "arise under" the Federal Constitution, laws or treaties (or fall within one of the other enumerated categories of Article III, Section 2); or is not a "case or controversy" within the meaning of that section; or the cause is not one described by any jurisdictional statute. Our conclusion, that this cause presents no nonjusticiable "political question" settles the only possible doubt that it is a case or controversy. . . .

The appellees refer to *Colegrove* v. *Green* (1946), as authority that the District Court lacked jurisdiction of the subject matter. Appellees misconceive the holding of that case. The holding was precisely contrary to their reading of it. Seven members of the Court participated in the decision. Unlike many other cases in this field which have assumed without discussion that there was jurisdiction, all three opinions filed in *Colegrove* discussed the question. Two of the opinions expressing the views of four of the Justices, a majority, flatly held that there was jurisdiction of the subject matter. MR. JUSTICE BLACK, joined by MR. JUSTICE DOUGLAS and MR. JUSTICE MURPHY, stated: "It is my judgment that the District Court had jurisdiction . . ." Mr. Justice Rutledge, writing separately, expressed agreement with this conclusion. Indeed, it is even questionable that the opinion of MR. JUSTICE FRANKFURTER, joined by Justices Reed and Burton, doubted jurisdiction of the subject matter. . . .

We hold that the District Court has jurisdiction of the subject matter of the federal claim asserted in the complaint. . . .

Justiciability

In holding that the subject matter of this suit was not justiciable, the District Court relied on *Colegrove,* and subsequent per curiam cases. The court stated, "From a review of these decisions, there can be no doubt that the federal rule . . . is that the federal courts . . . will not intervene in cases of this type to compel legislative reapportionment." We understand the District Court to have read the cited cases as compelling the conclusion that, since the appellants sought to have a legislative apportionment held unconstitutional, their suit presented a "political question," and was therefore nonjusticiable. We hold that this challenge to an apportionment presents no nonjusticiable "political question." . . .

Of course, the mere fact that the suit seeks protection of a political right does not mean it presents a political question. Such an objection "is little more than a play upon words." Rather, it is argued that apportionment cases, whatever the actual wording of the complaint, can involve no federal constitutional right except one resting on the guaranty of a republican form of government, and that complaints based on that clause have been held to present political questions which are nonjusticiable.

We hold that the claim pleaded here neither rests upon nor implicates the Guaranty Clause, and that its justiciability is therefore not foreclosed by our decisions of cases involving that clause. To show why we reject the argument based on the Guaranty Clause, we must examine the authorities under it. But because there appears to be some uncertainty as to why those cases did present political questions, and specifically as to whether this apportionment case is like those cases, we deem it necessary first to consider the contours of the "political question" doctrine.

Our discussion, even at the price of extending this opinion, requires review of a number of political question cases, in order to expose the attributes of the doctrine—attributes which, in various settings, diverge, combine, appear, and disappear in seeming disorderliness. Since that review is undertaken solely to demonstrate that neither singly nor collectively do these cases support a conclusion that this apportionment case is nonjusticiable, we, of course, do not explore their implications in other contexts. That review reveals that, in the Guaranty Clause cases and in the other "political question" cases, it is the relationship between the judiciary and the coordinate branches of the Federal Government, and not the federal judiciary's relationship to the States, which gives rise to the "political question."

We have said that, "In determining whether a question falls within [the political question] category, the appropriateness under our system of government of attributing finality to the action of the political departments and also the lack of satisfactory criteria for a judicial determination are dominant considerations." The nonjusticiability of a political question is primarily a function of the separation of powers. Much confusion results from the capacity of the "political question" label to obscure the need for case-by-case inquiry. Deciding whether a matter has in any measure been committed by the Constitution to another branch of government, or whether the action of that branch exceeds whatever authority has been committed, is itself a delicate exercise in constitutional interpretation, and is a responsibility of this Court as ultimate interpreter of the Constitution. To demonstrate this requires no less than to analyze representative cases and to infer from them the analytical threads that make up the political question doctrine. We shall then show that none of those threads catches this case.

Foreign Relations There are sweeping statements to the effect that all questions touching foreign relations are political questions. Not only does resolution of such issues frequently turn on standards that defy judicial application, or involve the exercise of a discretion demonstrably committed to the executive or legislature, but many such questions uniquely demand single-voiced statement of the Government's views. Yet it is error to suppose that every case or controversy which touches foreign relations lies beyond judicial cognizance. Our cases in this field seem invariably to show a discriminating analysis of the particular question posed, in terms of the history of its management by the political branches, of its susceptibility to judicial handling in the light of its nature and posture in the specific case, and of the possible consequences of judicial action. . . .

Dates of Duration of Hostilities Though it has been stated broadly that "the power which declared the necessity is the power to declare its cessation, and what the cessation requires," here too analysis reveals isolable reasons for the presence of political questions, underlying this

Court's refusal to review the political departments' determination of when or whether a war has ended. Dominant is the need for finality in the political determination, for emergency's nature demands "[a] prompt and unhesitating obedience." . . .

Validity of Enactments In *Coleman* v. *Miller* (1939), this Court held that the questions of how long a proposed amendment to the Federal Constitution remained open to ratification, and what effect a prior rejection had on a subsequent ratification, were committed to congressional resolution and involved criteria of decision that necessarily escaped the judicial grasp. Similar considerations apply to the enacting process: "[t]he respect due to coequal and independent departments," and the need for finality and certainty about the status of a statute contribute to judicial reluctance to inquire whether, as passed, it complied with all requisite formalities. But it is not true that courts will never delve into a legislature's records upon such a quest: if the enrolled statute lacks an effective date, a court will not hesitate to seek it in the legislative journals in order to preserve the enactment. The political question doctrine, a tool for maintenance of governmental order, will not be so applied as to promote only disorder. . . .

Republican Form of Government *Luther* v. *Borden* (1849), though in form simply an action for damages for trespass was, as Daniel Webster said in opening the argument for the defense, "an unusual case." The defendants, admitting an otherwise tortious breaking and entering, sought to justify their action on the ground that they were agents of the established lawful government of Rhode Island, which State was then under martial law to defend itself from active insurrection; that the plaintiff was engaged in that insurrection, and that they entered under orders to arrest the plaintiff. . . .

The plaintiff's right to recover depended upon which of the two groups was entitled to such recognition; but the lower court's refusal to receive evidence or hear argument on that issue, its charge to the jury that the earlier established or "charter" government was lawful, and the verdict for the defendants were affirmed upon appeal to this Court. . . .

Clearly, several factors were thought by the Court in *Luther* to make the question there "political": the commitment to the other branches of the decision as to which is the lawful state government; the unambiguous action by the President in recognizing the charter government as the lawful authority; the need for finality in the executive's decision, and the lack of criteria by which a court could determine which form of government was republican.

But the only significance that *Luther* could have for our immediate purposes is in its holding that the Guaranty Clause is not a repository of judicially manageable standards which a court could utilize independently in order to identify a State's lawful government. The Court has since refused to resort to the Guaranty Clause—which alone had been invoked for the purpose as the source of a constitutional standard for invalidating state action. . . .

We come, finally, to the ultimate inquiry whether our precedents as to what constitutes a nonjusticiable "political question" bring the case before us under the umbrella of that doctrine. A natural beginning is to note whether any of the common characteristics which we have been able to identify and label descriptively are present. We find none: the question here is the consistency of state action with the Federal Constitution. We have no question decided, or to be decided, by a political branch of government coequal with this Court. Nor do we risk embarrassment of our government abroad, or grave disturbance at home if we take issue with Tennessee as to the constitutionality of her action here challenged. Nor need the appellants, in order to succeed in this action, ask the Court to enter upon policy determinations for which judicially manageable standards are lacking. Judicial standards under the Equal Protection Clause are well developed and familiar, and it has been open to courts since the enactment of the Fourteenth Amendment to determine, if, on the particular facts, they must, that a discrimination reflects no policy, but simply arbitrary and capricious action.

This case does, in one sense, involve the allocation of political power within a State, and the appellants might conceivably have added a claim under the Guaranty Clause. Of course, as we have seen, any reliance on that clause would be futile. But because any reliance on the Guaranty Clause could not have succeeded, it does not follow that appellants may not be heard on the equal protection claim which, in fact, they tender. True, it must be clear that the Fourteenth Amendment claim is not so enmeshed with those political question elements which render Guaranty Clause claims nonjusticiable as actually to present a political question itself. But we have found that not to be the case here. . . .

We conclude, then, that the nonjusticiability of claims resting on the Guaranty Clause, which arises from their embodiment of questions that were thought "political," can have no bearing upon the justiciability of the equal protection claim presented in this case. Finally, we emphasize that it is the involvement in Guaranty Clause claims of the elements thought to define "political questions," and no other feature, which could render them nonjusticiable. . . .

We conclude that the complaint's allegations of a denial of equal protection present a justiciable constitutional cause of action upon which appellants are entitled to a trial and a decision. The right asserted is within the reach of judicial protection under the Fourteenth Amendment. . . .

Reversed and remanded.

MR. JUSTICE DOUGLAS, concurring.

While I join the opinion of the Court and, like the Court, do not reach the merits, a word of explanation is necessary. I put to one side the problems of "political" questions involving the distribution of power between this Court, the Congress, and the Chief Executive. We have here a phase of the recurring problem of the relation of the federal courts to state agencies. More particularly, the question is the extent to which a State may weight one person's vote more heavily than it does another's.

So far as voting rights are concerned, there are large gaps in the Constitution. Yet the right to vote is inherent in the republican form of government envisaged by Article IV, Section 4, of the Constitution. The House—and now the Senate—are chosen by the people. The time, manner, and place of elections of Senators and Representatives are left to the States subject to the regulatory power of Congress. Yet, those who vote for members of Congress do not "owe their right to vote to the State law in any sense which makes the exercise of the right to depend exclusively on the law of the State." The power of Congress to prescribe the qualifications for voters, and thus override state law, is not in issue here. It is, however, clear that, by reason of the commands of the Constitution, there are several qualifications that a State may not require.

Race, color, or previous condition of servitude is an impermissible standard by reason of the Fifteenth Amendment. . . .

Sex is another impermissible standard by reason of the Nineteenth Amendment.

There is a third barrier to a State's freedom in prescribing qualifications of voters, and that is the Equal Protection Clause of the Fourteenth Amendment, the provision invoked here. And so the question is, may a State weight the vote of one county or one district more heavily than it weights the vote in another?

The traditional test under the Equal Protection Clause has been whether a State has made "an invidious discrimination," as it does when it selects "a particular race or nationality for oppressive treatment," *Skinner* v. *Oklahoma* (1942). Universal equality is not the test; there is room for weighting. . . .

I agree with my Brother CLARK that, if the allegations in the complaint can be sustained, a case for relief is established. We are told that a single vote in Moore County, Tennessee, is worth 19 votes in Hamilton County, that one vote in Stewart or in Chester County is worth nearly eight times a single vote in Shelby or Knox County. The opportunity to prove that an "invidious discrimination" exists should therefore be given the appellants.

It is said that any decision in cases of this kind is beyond the competence of courts. Some make the same point as regards the problem of equal protection in cases involving racial segregation. Yet the legality of claims and conduct is a traditional subject for judicial determination. Adjudication is often perplexing and complicated. . . . The constitutional guide is often vague, as the decisions under the Due Process and Commerce Clauses show. The problem under the Equal Protection Clause is no more intricate. . . .

There are, of course, some questions beyond judicial competence. Where the performance of a "duty" is left to the discretion and good judgment of an executive officer, the judiciary will not compel the exercise of his discretion one way or the other for to do so would be to take over the office. . . .

With the exceptions of *Colegrove* and the decisions [it] spawned, the Court has never thought that protection of voting rights was beyond judicial cognizance. Today's treatment of those cases removes the only impediment to judicial cognizance of the claims stated in the present complaint.

MR. JUSTICE CLARK, concurring.

One emerging from the rash of opinions with their accompanying clashing of views may well find himself suffering a mental blindness. The Court holds that the appellants have alleged a cause of action. However, it refuses to award relief here—although the facts are undisputed—and fails to give the District Court any guidance whatever. One dissenting opinion, bursting with words that go through so much and conclude with so little, contemns the majority action as "a massive repudiation of the experience of our whole past." Another describes the complaint as merely asserting conclusory allegations that Tennessee's apportionment is "incorrect," "arbitrary," "obsolete," and "unconstitutional." I believe it can be shown that this case is distinguishable from earlier cases dealing with the distribution of political power by a State, that a patent violation of the Equal Protection Clause of the

United States Constitution has been shown, and that an appropriate remedy may be formulated. . . .

Although I find the Tennessee apportionment statute offends the Equal Protection Clause, I would not consider intervention by this Court into so delicate a field if there were any other relief available to the people of Tennessee. But the majority of the people of Tennessee have no "practical opportunities for exerting their political weight at the polls" to correct the existing "invidious discrimination." Tennessee has no initiative and referendum. I have searched diligently for other "practical opportunities" present under the law. I find none other than through the federal courts. The majority of the voters have been caught up in a legislative strait jacket. Tennessee has an "informed, civically militant electorate" and "an aroused popular conscience," but it does not sear "the conscience of the people's representatives." This is because the legislative policy has riveted the present seats in the Assembly to their respective constituencies, and by the votes of their incumbents a reapportionment of any kind is prevented. The people have been rebuffed at the hands of the Assembly; they have tried the constitutional convention route, but since the call must originate in the Assembly it, too, has been fruitless. They have tried Tennessee courts with the same result, and Governors have fought the tide only to flounder. It is said that there is recourse in Congress, and perhaps that may be, but, from a practical standpoint, this is without substance. To date, Congress has never undertaken such a task in any State. We therefore must conclude that the people of Tennessee are stymied, and, without judicial intervention, will be saddled with the present discrimination in the affairs of their state government. . . .

As John Rutledge (later Chief Justice) said 175 years ago in the course of the Constitutional Convention, a chief function of the Court is to secure the national rights. Its decision today supports the proposition for which our forebears fought and many died, namely that, to be fully conformable to the principle of right, the form of government must be representative. That is the keystone upon which our government was founded and lacking which no republic can survive. It is well for this Court to practice self-restraint and discipline in constitutional adjudication, but never in its history have those principles received sanction where the national rights of so many have been so clearly infringed for so long a time. National respect for the courts is more enhanced through the forthright enforcement of those rights, rather than by rendering them nugatory through the interposition of subterfuges. In my view, the ultimate decision today is in the greatest tradition of this Court.

MR. JUSTICE STEWART, concurring.

The separate writings of my dissenting and concurring Brothers stray so far from the subject of today's decision as to convey, I think, a distressingly inaccurate impression of what the Court decides. For that reason, I think it appropriate, in joining the opinion of the Court, to emphasize in a few words what the opinion does and does not say.

The Court today decides three things, and no more. "(a) that the court possessed jurisdiction of the subject matter; (b) that a justiciable cause of action is stated upon which appellants would be entitled to appropriate relief, and (c) . . . that the appellants have standing to challenge the Tennessee apportionment statutes."

MR. JUSTICE FRANKFURTER, with whom MR. JUSTICE HARLAN joins, dissenting.

The Court today reverses a uniform course of decision established by a dozen cases, including one by which the very claim now sustained was unanimously rejected only five years ago. The impressive body of rulings thus cast aside reflected the equally uniform course of our political history regarding the relationship between population and legislative representation—a wholly different matter from denial of the franchise to individuals because of race, color, religion or sex. Such a massive repudiation of the experience of our whole past in asserting destructively novel judicial power demands a detailed analysis of the role of this Court in our constitutional scheme. Disregard of inherent limits in the effective exercise of the Court's "judicial Power" not only presages the futility of judicial intervention in the essentially political conflict of forces by which the relation between population and representation has time out of mind been, and now is, determined. It may well impair the Court's position as the ultimate organ of "the supreme Law of the Land" in that vast range of legal problems, often strongly entangled in popular feeling, on which this Court must pronounce. The Court's authority—possessed of neither the purse nor the sword—ultimately rests on sustained public confidence in its moral sanction. Such feeling must be nourished by the Court's complete detachment, in fact and in appearance, from political entanglements and by abstention from injecting itself into the clash of political forces in political settlements.

A hypothetical claim resting on abstract assumptions is now for the first time made the basis for affording illusory relief for a particular evil even though it foreshadows deeper and more pervasive difficulties in consequence. The claim is hypothetical, and the assumptions are abstract, because the Court does not vouchsafe the lower courts—state and federal—guidelines for formulating specific, definite, wholly unprecedented remedies for the inevitable litigations that today's umbrageous disposition is bound to stimulate in connection with politically motivated reapportionments in so many States. In such a setting, to promulgate jurisdiction in the abstract is meaningless. It is as devoid of reality as "a brooding omnipresence in the sky," for it conveys no intimation what relief, if any, a District Court is capable of affording that would not invite legislatures to play ducks and drakes with the judiciary. For this Court to direct the District Court to enforce a claim to which the Court has over the years consistently found itself required to deny legal enforcement and, at the same time, to find it necessary to withhold any guidance to the lower court how to enforce this turnabout, new legal claim, manifests an odd—indeed an esoteric—conception of judicial propriety. One of the Court's supporting opinions, as elucidated by commentary, unwittingly affords a disheartening preview of the mathematical quagmire (apart from divers judicially inappropriate and elusive determinants) into which this Court today catapults the lower courts of the country without so much as adumbrating the basis for a legal calculus as a means of extrication. Even assuming the indispensable intellectual disinterestedness on the part of judges in such matters, they do not have accepted legal standards or criteria or even reliable analogies to draw upon for making judicial judgments. To charge courts with the task of accommodating the incommensurable factors of policy that underlie these mathematical puzzles is to attribute, however flatteringly, omnicompetence to judges. The Framers of the Constitution persistently rejected a proposal that embodied this assumption, and Thomas Jefferson never entertained it. . . .

We were soothingly told at the bar of this Court that we need not worry about the kind of remedy a court could effectively fashion once the abstract constitutional right to have courts pass on a statewide system of electoral districting is recognized as a matter of judicial rhetoric, because legislatures would heed the Court's admonition. This is not only a euphoric hope. It implies a sorry confession of judicial impotence in place of a frank acknowledgment that there is not under our Constitution a judicial remedy for every political mischief, for every undesirable exercise of legislative power. The Framers, carefully and with deliberate forethought, refused so to enthrone the judiciary. In this situation, as in others of like nature, appeal for relief does not belong here. Appeal must be to an informed, civically militant electorate. In a democratic society like ours, relief must come through an aroused popular conscience that sears the conscience of the people's representatives. In any event, there is nothing judicially more unseemly nor more self-defeating than for this Court to make *in terrorem* pronouncements, to indulge in merely empty rhetoric, sounding a word of promise to the ear sure to be disappointing to the hope. . . .

The *Colegrove* doctrine, in the form in which repeated decisions have settled it, was not an innovation. It represents long judicial thought and experience. From its earliest opinions, this Court has consistently recognized a class of controversies which do not lend themselves to judicial standards and judicial remedies. . . .

The present case involves all of the elements that have made the Guarantee Clause cases nonjusticiable. It is, in effect, a Guarantee Clause claim masquerading under a different label. But it cannot make the case more fit for judicial action that appellants invoke the Fourteenth Amendment, rather than Art. IV, § 4, where, in fact, the gist of their complaint is the same—unless it can be found that the Fourteenth Amendment speaks with greater particularity to their situation. We have been admonished to avoid "the tyranny of labels." Art. IV, § 4, is not committed by express constitutional terms to Congress. It is the nature of the controversies arising under it, nothing else, which has made it judicially unenforceable. . . .

What, then, is this question of legislative apportionment? Appellants invoke the right to vote and to have their votes counted. But they are permitted to vote, and their votes are counted. They go to the polls, they cast their ballots, they send their representatives to the state councils. Their complaint is simply that the representatives are not sufficiently numerous or powerful—in short, that Tennessee has adopted a basis of representation with which they are dissatisfied. Talk of "debasement" or "dilution" is circular talk. One cannot speak of "debasement" or "dilution" of the value of a vote until there is first defined a standard of reference as to what a vote should be worth. What is actually asked of the Court in this case is to choose among competing bases of representation—ultimately, really, among competing theories of political philosophy—in order to establish an appropriate frame of government for the State of Tennessee, and thereby for all the States of the Union.

In such a matter, abstract analogies which ignore the facts of history deal in unrealities; they betray reason. This is not a case in which a State has, through a device however oblique and sophisticated, denied Negroes or Jews or redheaded persons a vote, or given them only a third or a sixth of a vote. . . . What Tennessee illustrates is an old and still widespread method of representation—representation by local geographical division, only in part respective of population—in preference to others, others, forsooth, more appealing. Appellants contest this choice, and seek to make this Court the arbiter of the disagreement. They would make the Equal Protection Clause the charter of adjudication, asserting that the equality which it guarantees comports, if not the assurance of equal weight to every voter's vote, at least the basic conception that representation ought to be proportionate to population, a standard by reference to which the reasonableness of apportionment plans may be judged.

To find such a political conception legally enforceable in the broad and unspecific guarantee of equal protection is to rewrite the Constitution. Certainly "equal protection" is no more secure a foundation for judicial judgment of the permissibility of varying forms of representative government than is "Republican Form." Indeed, since "equal protection of the laws" can only mean an equality of persons standing in the same relation to whatever governmental action is challenged, the determination whether treatment is equal presupposes a determination concerning the nature of the relationship. . . .

The notion that representation proportioned to the geographic spread of population is so universally accepted as a necessary element of equality between man and man that it must be taken to be the standard of a political equality preserved by the Fourteenth Amendment—that it is, in appellants' words "the basic principle of representative government"—is, to put it bluntly, not true. However desirable and however desired by some among the great political thinkers and framers of our government, it has never been generally practiced, today or in the past. It was not the English system, it was not the colonial system, it was not the system chosen for the national government by the Constitution, it was not the system exclusively or even predominantly practiced by the States at the time of adoption of the Fourteenth Amendment, it is not predominantly practiced by the States today. Unless judges, the judges of this Court, are to make their private views of political wisdom the measure of the Constitution—views which, in all honesty, cannot but give the appearance, if not reflect the reality, of involvement with the business of partisan politics so inescapably a part of apportionment controversies—the Fourteenth Amendment, "itself a historical product," provides no guide for judicial oversight of the representation problem.

▼▲▼

Students of the Court are often surprised to learn that Chief Justice Earl Warren (1953–1969) considered *Baker* v. *Carr* the most important decision of his tenure. Coming from the man who presided over an era in which the Court declared an end to segregated public education, banned state-sponsored prayer and Bible reading in the public schools, revolutionized the rights of criminal defendants, and erected a near-impenetrable barrier on behalf of the news media against libel suits, this statement is remarkable. So why *Baker*? By ruling that malapportioned legislative districts presented a judicial, and not political, question, Warren viewed *Baker* as the "parent case" of the "one person, one vote" doctrine announced in three subsequent cases, *Gray* v. *Sanders* (1963), *Wesberry* v. *Sanders* (1964), and *Reynolds* v. *Sims* (1964).[36] The Court understood full well that *Baker* had opened the floodgates to litigation asking the Court to create constitutional standards for equal representation. In *Gray*, the Court invalidated Georgia's reliance on the county-unit system in state primary elections. The county-unit system allowed rural counties to carry greater weight than more densely populated urban areas because each county received roughly the same number of representatives. Justice Douglas, writing for the Court, offered the phrase that ultimately became the mantra for civil rights and reform-minded groups determined to clean up the inequities in state apportionment plans: "The conception of political equality from the Declaration of Independence, to Lincoln's Gettysburg Address, to the Fifteenth, Seventeenth, and Nineteenth Amendments can mean only one thing—one person, one vote."[37]

But the Court, in *Gray*, did not address the question left open by *Baker* of what judicial remedies were appropriate when either a congressional or state legislative district was found to violate the Equal Protection Clause. *Gray* simply announced that the "one person, one vote" standard meant that states could not draw their boundaries based on the county-unit system, but had to base them instead on population. In *Wesberry*, the Court extended the one person, one vote rule to the House of Representatives, holding that Article I, Section 2, of the Constitution required states to draw their congressional legislative districts on the basis of equal population. That same term, the Court, in *Reynolds* v. *Sims* (1964), turned its attention back to the problem of malapportionment in state legislative districts. This time the justices confronted the question of whether the Fourteenth Amendment permitted federal courts to compel state legislatures to draw their districts on the basis of the one person, one vote rule declared in *Gray* and *Wesberry*.

Reynolds v. *Sims*

377 U.S. 533 (1964)

In August 1961, M. O. Sims and thirteen other Jefferson County, Alabama, residents filed suit against B. A. Reynolds and several other election officials, claiming that the state's apportionment plan, which had gone unmodified since 1901, violated the Equal Protection Clause of the Fourteenth Amendment. Similar to Georgia and Tennessee, Alabama's population had gradually shifted from the farms to the cities, but state legislators, despite a state constitutional provision mandating reapportionment every ten years, had done nothing to bring legislative representation in line with these changes. Estimates of political power in Alabama had about 25 percent of the state's population electing a majority of state representatives and senators.

After *Baker* v. *Carr*, the Alabama legislature offered two plans to ward off potential complaints that its apportionment system was unconstitutional. The first was called the "67 Senator Amendment." This proposal gave each county one seat in each of the state's 67 districts, and distributed the rest based on population. Each county also received a seat in the state senate. But because the population was so widely distributed among Alabama counties, the less populous counties came out way ahead. In the event the "67 Amendment" was not ratified, the state legislature passed the Crawford-Webb Act, which established thirty-five senatorial districts with one member each and an open-ended plan for the house. The lower courts threw out both plans as unconstitutional.

Reynolds was argued by Alabama native Charles B. Morgan, who had drawn national attention for his open criticism of Governor George Wallace's violent treatment of civil rights demonstrators and refusal to budge on school desegregation. Long active in Birmingham civic causes, Morgan helped to open a Southern regional office of the ACLU, a daring move in the early 1960s. He had worked with the ACLU in many other constitutional cases, and persuaded it, along with the American Jewish Congress and the NAACP, to submit an *amicus* brief in *Reynolds*. Whereas the principal parties focused on the impact that Alabama's plan had in weakening the political power of urban areas, the *amicus* brief filed by the coalition of civil rights groups emphasized the consequences of malapportionment on the voting rights of racial minorities. By allowing rural voters to dominate state legislative proceedings, malapportioned districts placed majority power in the hands of a minority of residents, a principle at odds with representative government. Since the African American population in the South was becoming increasingly urban, skewed representation further weakened the already disadvantaged position of blacks in the electoral process.[38]

The Court heard *Reynolds* together with apportionment cases from five other states—Colorado, Delaware, Maryland, New York, and Virginia.

The Court's decision was 8 to 1. Chief Justice Warren delivered the opinion of the Court. Justices Clark and Stewart filed concurring opinions. Justice Harlan dissented.

▼▲▼

CHIEF JUSTICE WARREN delivered the opinion of the Court.

A predominant consideration in determining whether a State's legislative apportionment scheme constitutes an invidious discrimination violative of rights asserted under the Equal Protection Clause is that the rights allegedly impaired are individual and personal in nature. Undoubtedly, the right of suffrage is a fundamental matter in a free and democratic society. Especially since the right to exercise the franchise in a free and unimpaired manner is preservative of other basic civil and political rights, any alleged infringement of the right of citizens to vote must be carefully and meticulously scrutinized. . . .

Legislators represent people, not trees or acres. Legislators are elected by voters, not farms or cities or economic interests. As long as ours is a representative form of government, and our legislatures are those instruments of government elected directly by and directly representative of the people, the right to elect legislators in a free and unimpaired fashion is a bedrock of our political system. It could hardly be gainsaid that a constitutional claim had been asserted by an allegation that certain otherwise qualified voters had been entirely prohibited from voting for members of their state legislature. And, if a State should provide that the votes of citizens in one part of the State should be given two times, or five times, or 10 times the weight of votes of citizens in another part of the State, it could hardly be contended that the right to vote of those residing in the disfavored areas had not been effectively diluted. It would appear extraordinary to suggest that a State could be constitutionally permitted to enact a law providing that certain of the State's voters could vote two, five, or 10 times for their legislative representatives, while voters living elsewhere could vote only once. And it is inconceivable that a state law to the effect that, in counting votes for legislators, the votes of citizens in one part of the State would be multiplied by two, five, or 10, while the votes of persons in another area would be counted only at face value, could be constitutionally sustainable. Of course, the effect of state legislative districting schemes which give the same number of representatives to unequal numbers of constituents is identical. Overweighting and overvaluation of the votes of those living here has the certain effect of dilution and undervaluation of the votes of those living there. The resulting discrimination against those individual voters living in disfavored areas is easily demonstrable mathematically. Their right to vote is simply not the same right to vote as that of those living in a favored part of the State. Two, five, or 10 of them must vote before the effect of their voting is equivalent to that of their favored neighbor. Weighting the votes of citizens differently, by any method or means, merely because of where they happen to reside, hardly seems justifiable. . . .

Logically, in a society ostensibly grounded on representative government, it would seem reasonable that a majority of the people of a State could elect a majority of that State's legislators. To conclude differently, and to sanction minority control of state legislative bodies, would appear to deny majority rights in a way that far surpasses any possible denial of minority rights that might otherwise be thought to result. Since legislatures are responsible for enacting laws by which all citizens are to be governed, they should be bodies which are collectively responsive to the popular will. And the concept of equal protection has been traditionally viewed as requiring the uniform treatment of persons standing in the same relation to the governmental action questioned or challenged. With respect to the allocation of legislative representation, all voters, as citizens of a State, stand in the same relation regardless of where they live. Any suggested criteria for the differentiation of citizens are insufficient to justify any discrimination, as to the weight of their votes, unless relevant to the permissible purposes of legislative apportionment. Since the achieving of fair and effective representation for all citizens is concededly the basic aim of legislative apportionment, we conclude that the Equal Protection Clause guarantees the opportunity for equal participation by all voters in the election of state legislators. Diluting the weight of votes because of place of residence impairs basic constitutional rights under the Fourteenth Amendment just as much as invidious discriminations based upon factors such as race, or economic status. . . .

We are told that the matter of apportioning representation in a state legislature is a complex and many-faceted one. We are advised that States can rationally consider factors other than population in apportioning legislative representation. We are admonished not to restrict the power of the States to impose differing views as to political philosophy on their citizens. We are cautioned about the dangers of entering into political thickets and mathematical quagmires. Our answer is this: a denial of constitutionally protected rights demands judicial protection; our oath and our office require no less of us. . . . To the extent that a citizen's right to vote is debased, he is that much less a citizen. The fact that an individual lives here or there is not a legitimate reason for overweighting or diluting the efficacy of his vote. The complexions of societies and civilizations change, often with amazing rapidity. A nation once primarily rural in character becomes predominantly urban. Representation schemes once fair and equitable become archaic and outdated. But the basic principle of representative government remains, and must remain, unchanged—the weight of a citizen's vote cannot be made to depend on where he lives. . . .

We hold that, as a basic constitutional standard, the Equal Protection Clause requires that the seats in both houses of a bicameral state legislature must be apportioned on a population basis. Simply stated, an individual's right to vote for state legislators is unconstitutionally impaired when its weight is in a substantial fashion diluted when compared with votes of citizens living in other parts of the State. . . .

The system of representation in the two Houses of the Federal Congress is one ingrained in our Constitution, as part of the law of the land. It is one conceived out of compromise and concession indispensable to the establishment of our federal republic. Arising from unique historical circumstances, it is based on the consideration that, in establishing our type of federalism a group of formerly independent States bound themselves together under one national government. . . .

Political subdivisions of States—counties, cities, or whatever—never were and never have been considered as sovereign entities. Rather, they have been traditionally regarded as subordinate governmental instrumentalities created by the State to assist in the carrying out of state governmental functions. . . . The relationship of the States to the Federal Government could hardly be less analogous.

Thus, we conclude that the plan contained in the 67-Senator Amendment for apportioning seats in the Alabama Legislature cannot be sustained by recourse to the so-called federal analogy. Nor can any other inequitable state legislative apportionment scheme be justified on such an asserted basis. This does not necessarily mean that such a plan is irrational, or involves something other than a "republican form of government." We conclude simply that such a plan is impermissible for the States under the Equal Protection Clause, since perforce resulting, in virtually every case, in submergence of the equal population principle in at least one house of a state legislature. . . .

By holding that, as a federal constitutional requisite, both houses of a state legislature must be apportioned on a population basis, we mean that the Equal Protection Clause requires that a State make an honest and good faith effort to construct districts, in both houses of its legislature, as nearly of equal population as is practicable. We realize that it is a practical impossibility to arrange legislative districts so that each one has an identical number of residents, or citizens, or voters. Mathematical exactness or precision is hardly a workable constitutional requirement. . . .

A State may legitimately desire to maintain the integrity of various political subdivisions, insofar as possible, and provide for compact districts of contiguous territory in designing a legislative apportionment scheme. Valid considerations may underlie such aims. Indiscriminate districting, without any regard for political subdivision or natural or historical boundary lines, may be little more than an open invitation to partisan gerrymandering. Single-member districts may be the rule in one State, while another State might desire to achieve some flexibility by creating multi-member or floterial districts. Whatever the means of accomplishment, the overriding objective must be substantial equality of population among the various districts, so that the vote of any citizen is approximately equal in weight to that of any other citizen in the State.

History indicates, however, that many States have deviated, to a greater or lesser degree, from the equal population principle in the apportionment of seats in at least one house of their legislatures. So long as the divergences from a strict population standard are based on legitimate considerations incident to the effectuation of a rational state policy, some deviations from the equal population principle are constitutionally permissible with respect to the apportionment of seats in either or both of the two houses of a bicameral state legislature. But neither history alone, nor economic or other sorts of group interests, are permissible factors in attempting to justify disparities from population-based representation. Citizens, not history or economic interests, cast votes. Considerations of area alone provide an insufficient justification for deviations from the equal population principle. . . .

We do not consider here the difficult question of the proper remedial devices which federal courts should utilize in state legislative apportionment cases. Remedial techniques in this new and developing area of the law will probably often differ with the circumstances of the challenged apportionment and a variety of local conditions. It is enough to say now that, once a State's legislative apportionment scheme has been found to be unconstitutional, it would be the unusual case in which a court would be justified in not taking appropriate action to insure that no further elections are conducted under the invalid plan. . . .

We find, therefore, that the action taken by the District Court in this case, in ordering into effect a reapportionment of both houses of the Alabama Legislature for purposes of the 1962 primary and general elections, by using the best parts of the two proposed plans which it had found, as a whole, to be invalid, was an appropriate and well considered exercise of judicial power. Admittedly, the lower court's ordered plan was intended only as a temporary and provisional measure, and the District Court correctly indicated that the plan was invalid as a permanent apportionment. In retaining jurisdiction while deferring a hearing on the issuance of a final injunction in order to give the provisionally reapportioned legislature an opportunity to act effectively, the court below proceeded in a proper fashion. Since the District Court evinced its realization that its ordered reapportionment could not be sustained as the basis for conducting the 1966 election of Alabama legislators, and avowedly intends to take some further action should the reapportioned Alabama Legislature fail to enact a constitutionally valid, permanent apportionment scheme in the interim, we affirm the judgment below and remand the cases for further proceedings consistent with the views stated in this opinion. . . .

Affirmed and remanded.

MR. JUSTICE HARLAN, dissenting.

In these cases, the Court holds that seats in the legislatures of six States are apportioned in ways that violate the Federal Constitution. Under the Court's ruling, it is bound to follow that the legislatures in all but a few of the other 44 States will meet the same fate. These decisions, with *Wesberry* v. *Sanders* (1964) involving congressional districting by the States, and *Gray* v. *Sanders* (1963) relating to elections for statewide office, have the effect of placing basic aspects of state political systems under the pervasive overlordship of the federal judiciary. Once again, I must register my protest.

Generalities cannot obscure the cold truth that cases of this type are not amenable to the development of judicial standards. No set of standards can guide a court which has to decide how many legislative districts a State shall have, or what the shape of the districts shall be, or where to draw a particular district line. No judicially manageable standard can determine whether a State should have single member districts or multi-member districts or some combination of both. No such standard can control the balance between keeping up with population shifts and having stable districts. In all these respects, the courts will be called upon to make particular decisions with respect to which a principle of equally populated districts will be of no assistance whatsoever. Quite obviously, there are limitless possibilities for districting consistent with such a principle. Nor can these problems be avoided by judicial reliance on legislative judgments so far as possible. Reshaping or combining one or two districts, or modifying just a few district lines, is no less a matter of choosing among many possible solutions, with varying political consequences, than reapportionment broadside.

The Court ignores all this, saying only that "what is marginally permissible in one State may be unsatisfactory in another, depending on the particular circumstances of the case." It is well to remember that the product of today's decisions will not be readjustment of a few districts in a few States which most glaringly depart from the principle of equally populated districts. It will be a redetermination, extensive in many cases, of legislative districts in all but a few States.

Although the Court—necessarily, as I believe—provides only generalities in elaboration of its main thesis, its opinion nevertheless fully demonstrates how far removed these problems are from fields of judicial competence. Recognizing that "indiscriminate districting" is an invitation to "partisan gerrymandering," the Court nevertheless excludes virtually every basis for the formation of electoral districts other than "indiscriminate districting." . . .

Finally, these decisions [*Baker* v. *Carr, Gray* v. *Sanders, Wesberry* v. *Sanders,* and *Sims*] give support to a current mistaken view of the Constitution and the constitutional function of this Court. This view, in a nutshell, is that every major social ill in this country can find its cure in some constitutional "principle," and that this Court should "take the lead" in promoting reform when other branches of government fail to act. The Constitution is not a panacea for every blot upon the public welfare, nor should this Court, ordained as a judicial body, be thought of as a general haven for reform movements. The Constitution is an instrument of government, fundamental to which is the premise that in a diffusion of governmental authority lies the greatest promise that this Nation will realize liberty for all its citizens. This Court, limited in function in accordance with that premise, does not serve its high purpose when it exceeds its authority, even to satisfy justified impatience with the slow workings of the political process. For when, in the name of constitutional interpretation, the Court adds something to the Constitution that was deliberately excluded from it, the Court, in reality, substitutes its view of what should be so for the amending process.

Together, the apportionment cases had a tremendous impact on representation in Congress and the state legislatures. After *Reynolds*, forty-eight states, all but Alaska and Hawaii, were required under the Court's new one person, one vote standard to redraw their congressional and state legislative boundaries. And the Court was quite serious about the states following their new directives on legislative apportionment. States that refused to follow *Wesberry* and *Reynolds* were subject to the mercy of the federal courts, which now had the power to draw district lines and demand compliance. By the late 1960s, the states made major strides in improving the fairness of representation based on population. Few states, by this time, had the political tenacity to evade the Court's tough new standards set down in the apportionment cases.[39]

Nonetheless, serious problems continued to hinder the promise of the one person, one vote principle. Although legislatures were now required to create apportionment plans in which congressional and state districts were roughly equal to each other in population, that mandate did not necessarily prohibit states from weakening potentially powerful new voters by drawing lines that divided communities of interest. Some states drew lines that divided cities into several districts, rather than making them the focal point of a new district. Well-established political machines that dominated many state legislatures were not about to give up the advantages of incumbency by transferring political power into newly potent urban populations. Bound by *Baker, Wesberry,* and *Reynolds,* the states could no longer ignore the census counts or the one person, one vote principle. Did these decisions, however, mean that states were banned from engaging in partisan gerrymandering to establish politically safe districts? For many states, the answer was clearly no. Crude efforts to eliminate black voters by, quite literally, drawing them out of cities in which they constituted a majority of the eligible voting population had been rejected out of hand by the Court in *Gomillion*. But using political power to protect political power had long been considered one of the standard fruits of electoral victory. In *Davis* v. *Bandemer* (1986), the Court considered whether a reapportionment plan drawn to establish safe seats on the basis of political party violated the Equal Protection Clause.

Davis v. *Bandemer*

478 U.S. 109 (1986)

Following the 1980 census, the Indiana legislature rewrote its legislative apportionment plan to reflect changes in the state's population. Republican majorities existed in both the state senate, which consisted of fifty members, and the house of representatives, which consisted of one hundred members. The state's governor was also a Republican. The new plan, adopted in early 1981, called for fifty single-member seats in the senate and seven triple-member, nine double-member, and sixty-one single-member seats in the house. The multimember districts were concentrated in Marion and Allen counties, where African Americans made up a substantial part of the population. (In Indiana, over 90 percent of African Americans were then registered Democrats.)

Irwin Bandemer and several other registered Democrats filed suit in 1982 contesting the reapportionment plan on the grounds that it intentionally sealed districts into safe Democratic and Republican seats, with neither political party having much of a chance to make inroads into the other's territory. Under the plan, Democrats were ensured some seats, but appeared to have almost no chance of ever taking majority control in the legislature. The 1982 elections, which took place while Bandemer's suit was still pending, appeared to bear out his argument. Democrats won 51.6 percent of the popular vote in the house elections, but won only forty-three seats. In Marion and Allen counties, Democrats won 46.6 percent of the vote, but won only three of the twenty-one seats. In the senate races, Democrats won 53.1 percent of the votes, but won only thirteen of the twenty-five seats up for reelection. The Indiana NAACP also filed suit against the state's 1981 redistricting plan, claiming that the newly drawn multimember districts intentionally fragmented concentrations of African American voters. Said one Indiana Democrat, "People who live near the line are going to need an Indian guide and a compass to figure out which district they're in."

A federal district court agreed with the state Democrats that the redistricting plan was unconstitutional, but rejected the NAACP's claim that the plan intentionally diluted African American votes. The NAACP decided not to appeal the district court's verdict, but it filed a brief on behalf of Bandemer after the state decided to challenge the decision; claiming that the redistricting plan discriminated against African Americans as disproportionate members of the Democratic Party

The Court's decision was 7 to 2. Justice White delivered the judgment of the Court, as the only voting majority was for Part II of the opinion. Chief Justice Burger and Justice O'Connor wrote concurring opinions. Justice Powell, joined by Justice Stevens, concurred in part and dissented in part.

JUSTICE WHITE announced the judgment of the Court and delivered the opinion of the Court as to Part II and an opinion as to Parts I, III, and IV, in which JUSTICE BRENNAN, JUSTICE MARSHALL, and JUSTICE BLACKMUN join.

I

[Omitted]

II

We address first the question whether this case presents a justiciable controversy or a nonjusticiable political question. . . . The appellants contend that we have affirmed on

the merits decisions of lower courts finding such claims to be nonjusticiable.

Since *Baker* v. *Carr* (1962), we have consistently adjudicated equal protection claims in the legislative districting context regarding inequalities in population between districts. In the course of these cases, we have developed and enforced the "one person, one vote" principle. . . .

The issue here is . . . different from that adjudicated in *Reynolds*. It does not concern districts of unequal size. Not only does everyone have the right to vote and to have his vote counted, but each elector may vote for and be represented by the same number of lawmakers. Rather, the claim is that each political group in a State should have the same chance to elect representatives of its choice as any other political group. Nevertheless, the issue is one of representation, and we decline to hold that such claims are never justiciable.

Our [previous] racial gerrymander cases . . . indicate as much. In those cases, there was no population variation among the districts, and no one was precluded from voting. The claim instead was that an identifiable racial or ethnic group had an insufficient chance to elect a representative of its choice, and that district lines should be redrawn to remedy this alleged defect. In both cases, we adjudicated the merits of such claims. . . .

[Previous] decisions support a conclusion that this case is justiciable. . . . [T]hat . . . a claim is submitted by a political group, rather than a racial group, does not distinguish it in terms of justiciability. That the characteristics of the complaining group are not immutable, or that the group has not been subject to the same historical stigma, may be relevant to the manner in which the case is adjudicated, but these differences do not justify a refusal to entertain such a case. . . .

III

Having determined that the political gerrymandering claim in this case is justiciable, we turn to the question whether the District Court erred in holding that the appellees had alleged and proved a violation of the Equal Protection Clause. . . .

We do not accept . . . the District Court's legal and factual bases for concluding that the 1981 Act visited a sufficiently adverse effect on the appellees' constitutionally protected rights to make out a violation of the Equal Protection Clause. The District Court held that, because any apportionment scheme that purposely prevents proportional representation is unconstitutional, Democratic voters need only show that their proportionate voting influence has been adversely affected. Our cases, however, clearly foreclose any claim that the Constitution requires proportional representation, or that legislatures in reapportioning must draw district lines to come as near as possible to allocating seats to the contending parties in proportion to what their anticipated statewide vote will be.

The typical election for legislative seats in the United States is conducted in described geographical districts, with the candidate receiving the most votes in each district winning the seat allocated to that district. If all or most of the districts are competitive—defined by the District Court in this case as districts in which the anticipated split in the party vote is within the range of 45% to 55%—even a narrow statewide preference for either party would produce an overwhelming majority for the winning party in the state legislature. This consequence, however, is inherent in winner-take-all, district-based elections, and we cannot hold that such a reapportionment law would violate the Equal Protection Clause because the voters in the losing party do not have representation in the legislature in proportion to the statewide vote received by their party candidates. As we have said: "[W]e are unprepared to hold that district-based elections decided by plurality vote are unconstitutional in either single- or multimember districts simply because the supporters of losing candidates have no legislative seats assigned to them." This is true of a racial, as well as a political, group. It is also true of a statewide claim as well as an individual district claim. . . .

To draw district lines to maximize the representation of each major party would require creating as many safe seats for each party as the demographic and predicted political characteristics of the State would permit. This, in turn, would leave the minority in each safe district without a representative of its choice. We upheld this "political fairness" approach in *Gaffney* v. *Cummings* (1973), despite its tendency to deny safe district minorities any realistic chance to elect their own representatives. But *Gaffney* in no way suggested that the Constitution requires the approach that Connecticut had adopted in that case.

In cases involving individual multimember districts, we have required a substantially greater showing of adverse effects than a mere lack of proportional representation to support a finding of unconstitutional vote dilution. Only where there is evidence that excluded groups have "less opportunity to participate in the political processes and to elect candidates of their choice" have we refused to approve the use of multimember districts. In these cases, we have also noted the lack of responsiveness by those elected to the concerns of the relevant groups.

These holdings rest on a conviction that the mere fact that a particular apportionment scheme makes it more difficult for a particular group in a particular district to elect the representatives of its choice does not render that scheme constitutionally infirm. This conviction, in turn, stems from a perception that the power to influence the political process is not limited to winning elections. An individual or a group of individuals who votes for a losing candidate is usually deemed to be adequately represented by the winning candidate, and to have as much opportunity to influence that candidate as other voters in the district. We cannot presume in such a situation, without actual proof to the contrary, that the candidate elected will entirely ignore the interests of those voters. This is true even in a safe district where the losing group loses election after election. Thus, a group's electoral power is not unconstitutionally diminished by the simple fact of an apportionment scheme that makes winning elections more difficult, and a failure of proportional representation alone does not constitute impermissible discrimination under the Equal Protection Clause.

As with individual districts, where unconstitutional vote dilution is alleged in the form of statewide political gerrymandering, the mere lack of proportional representation will not be sufficient to prove unconstitutional discrimination. Again, without specific supporting evidence, a court cannot presume in such a case that those who are elected will disregard the disproportionately underrepresented group. Rather, unconstitutional discrimination occurs only when the electoral system is arranged in a manner that will consistently degrade a voter's or a group of voters' influence on the political process as a whole.

Although this is a somewhat different formulation than we have previously used in describing unconstitutional vote dilution in an individual district, the focus of both of these inquiries is essentially the same. In both contexts, the question is whether a particular group has been unconstitutionally denied its chance to effectively influence the political process. In a challenge to an individual district, this inquiry focuses on the opportunity of members of the group to participate in party deliberations in the slating and nomination of candidates, their opportunity to register and vote, and hence their chance to directly influence the election returns and to secure the attention of the winning candidate. Statewide, however, the inquiry centers on the voters' direct or indirect influence on the elections of the state legislature as a whole. And, as in individual district cases, an equal protection violation may be found only where the electoral system substantially disadvantages certain voters in their opportunity to influence the political process effectively. In this context, such a finding of unconstitutionality must be supported by evidence of continued frustration of the will of a majority of the voters or effective denial to a minority of voters of a fair chance to influence the political process.

Based on these views, we would reject the District Court's apparent holding that *any* interference with an opportunity to elect a representative of one's choice would be sufficient to allege or make out an equal protection violation, unless justified by some acceptable state interest that the State would be required to demonstrate. In addition to being contrary to the above-described conception of an unconstitutional political gerrymander, such a low threshold for legal action would invite attack on all or almost all reapportionment statutes. District-based elections hardly ever produce a perfect fit between votes and representation. The one person, one vote imperative often mandates departure from this result, as does the no-retrogression rule required by § 5 of the Voting Rights Act. Inviting attack on minor departures from some supposed norm would too much embroil the judiciary in second-guessing what has consistently been referred to as a political task for the legislature, a task that should not be monitored too closely unless the express or tacit goal is to effect its removal from legislative halls. We decline to take a major step toward that end which would be so much at odds with our history and experience. . . .

In sum, we hold that political gerrymandering cases are properly justiciable under the Equal Protection Clause. We also conclude, however, that a threshold showing of discriminatory vote dilution is required for a *prima facie* case of an equal protection violation. In this case, the findings made by the District Court of an adverse effect on the appellees do not surmount the threshold requirement. Consequently, the judgment of the District Court is

Reversed.

Justice O'Connor, with whom The Chief Justice and Justice Rehnquist join, concurring in the judgment.

I would hold that the partisan gerrymandering claims of major political parties raise a nonjusticiable political question that the judiciary should leave to the legislative branch, as the Framers of the Constitution unquestionably intended. Accordingly, I would reverse the District Court's judgment on the grounds that appellees' claim is nonjusticiable.

There can be little doubt that the emergence of a strong and stable two-party system in this country has contributed enormously to sound and effective government. The preservation and health of our political institutions, state and federal, depends to no small extent on the continued vitality of our two-party system, which permits both stability and measured change. The opportunity to control the drawing of electoral boundaries through the legislative process of apportionment is a critical and traditional part of politics in the United States, and one that plays no small role in fostering active participation in the political parties at every level. Thus, the legislative business of apportionment is fundamentally a political affair, and challenges to the manner in which an apportionment has been carried out—by the very parties that are responsible for this process—present a political question in the truest sense of the term.

To turn these matters over to the federal judiciary is to inject the courts into the most heated partisan issues. It is predictable that the courts will respond by moving away from the nebulous standard a plurality of the Court fashions today and toward some form of rough proportional representation for all political groups. The consequences of this shift will be as immense as they are unfortunate. I do not believe, and the Court offers not a shred of evidence to suggest, that the Framers of the Constitution intended the judicial power to encompass the making of such fundamental choices about how this Nation is to be governed. Nor do I believe that the proportional representation towards which the Court's expansion of equal protection doctrine will lead is consistent with our history, our traditions, or our political institutions. . . .

In my view, where a racial minority group is characterized by "the traditional indicia of suspectness" and is vulnerable to exclusion from the political process, individual voters who belong to that group enjoy some measure of protection against intentional dilution of their group voting strength by means of racial gerrymandering. As a matter of past history and present reality, there is a direct and immediate relationship between the racial minority's group voting strength in a particular community and the individual rights of its members to vote and to participate in the political process. In these circumstances, the stronger nexus between individual rights and group interests, and the greater warrant the Equal Protection Clause gives the federal courts to intervene for protection against racial discrimination, suffice to render racial gerrymandering claims justiciable. Even so, the individual's right is infringed only if the racial minority group can prove that it has "essentially been shut out of the political process."

Clearly, members of the Democratic and Republican Parties cannot claim that they are a discrete and insular group vulnerable to exclusion from the political process by some dominant group: these political parties are the dominant groups, and the Court has offered no reason to believe that they are incapable of fending for themselves through the political process. Indeed, there is good reason to think that political gerrymandering is a self-limiting enterprise. In order to gerrymander, the legislative majority must weaken some of its safe seats, thus exposing its own incumbents to greater risks of defeat—risks they may refuse to accept past a certain point. Similarly, an overambitious gerrymander can lead to disaster for the legislative majority: because it has created more seats in which it hopes to win relatively narrow victories, the same swing in overall voting strength will tend to cost the legislative majority more and more seats as the gerrymander becomes more ambitious. More generally, each major party presumably has ample weapons at its disposal to conduct the partisan struggle that often leads to a partisan apportionment, but also often leads to a bipartisan one. There is no proof before us that political gerrymandering is an evil that cannot be checked or cured by the people or by the parties themselves. Absent such proof, I see no basis for concluding that there is a need, let alone a constitutional basis, for judicial intervention.

JUSTICE POWELL, with whom JUSTICE STEVENS joins, concurring in part and dissenting in part.

This case presents the question whether a state legislature violates the Equal Protection Clause by adopting a redistricting plan designed solely to preserve the power of the dominant political party, when the plan follows the doctrine of "one person, one vote" but ignores all other neutral factors relevant to the fairness of redistricting.

In answering this question, the plurality expresses the view, with which I agree, that a partisan political gerrymander violates the Equal Protection Clause only on proof of "both intentional discrimination against an identifiable political group and an actual discriminatory effect on that group." The plurality acknowledges that the record in this case supports a finding that the challenged redistricting plan was adopted for the purpose of discriminating against Democratic voters. The plurality argues, however, that appellees failed to establish that their voting strength was diluted statewide despite uncontradicted proof that certain key districts were grotesquely gerrymandered to enhance the election prospects of Republican candidates. This argument appears to rest solely on the ground that the legislature accomplished its gerrymander consistent with "one person, one vote," in the sense that the legislature designed voting districts of approximately equal population and erected no direct barriers to Democratic voters' exercise of the franchise. Since the essence of a gerrymandering claim is that the members of a political party as a group have been denied their right to "fair and effective representation," I believe that the claim cannot be tested solely by reference to "one person, one vote." Rather, a number of other relevant neutral factors must be considered. Because the plurality ignores such factors and fails to enunciate standards by which to determine whether a legislature has enacted an unconstitutional gerrymander, I dissent.

By concluding that political gerrymandering presented a justiciable question, the Court, in *Bandemer,* broadened beyond racial discrimination the type of voting rights claims entitled to their day in federal court. However, the Court created exceedingly difficult standards for plaintiffs to meet in trying to make a successful partisan gerrymandering claim under the Equal Protection Claim under the Fourteenth Amendment. An additional interesting note about *Bandemer* was the unusual assortment of groups that filed *amicus* briefs opposing the constitutionality of Indiana's redistricting plan. The ACLU, the national NAACP, and Common Cause, a Washington, D.C.–based campaign finance and electoral reform group, filed briefs urging the Court to invalidate the redistricting plan. Joining these groups was the Republican National Committee. On its face, this seemed to make little sense since the state Republican Party stood to benefit from the Indiana redistricting plan. Moreover, less than 10 percent of African Americans nationwide were registered Republicans in 1980. In fact, only 14 percent of African Americans voted for Ronald Reagan, the successful Republican presidential candidate in 1980.[40]

Although the Court did not address the racial discrimination claim by the Indiana NAACP in *Bandemer,* racial equity in representation was never very far below the surface of this case. Certainly, the apportionment cases of the early 1960s and the enactment of the Voting Rights Act of 1965 had advanced the cause of African American voter registration. For example, black voter registration in Mississippi, which stood at 6.7 percent in 1964, rose to 62.2 percent by 1972.[41] Nonetheless, African Americans still found it difficult to elect black candidates to public office, especially in the South. After Reconstruction's demise, Southern legislatures, now dominated by the Democratic Party, redrew their districts to favor white majorities across the board, making it impossible for black majorities to elect black candidates. Between the earliest days of Reconstruction and 1900, twenty-one African Americans won forty-one congressional elections, but not a single black representative was elected from a district with a white majority. Thirty-six of those black victories occurred in districts where the percentage of blacks was greater than 55 percent of the eligible voting population. The other five black victories came in districts that were composed of a bare African American majority.[42]

Political scientist David Canon points out that African Americans were not concentrated in large enough numbers outside the South and were thus unable to elect blacks to Congress, since whites outside the region had not demonstrated that they were willing to support black candidates. From 1901 to 1928, no African American served in the House of Representatives. From 1929 to 1969, no more than six African Americans served in the House at any one time, all of whom were elected outside the South from districts that had a black majority. Not another African American was elected to Congress from the South until 1972, when a Texas district with a black majority sent Democrat Barbara Jordan to the House of Representatives.[43]

On this score, the Voting Rights Act of 1965, as originally drafted, did not address the question of whether fairness in districting included drawing districts where blacks constituted a majority, thus increasing the likelihood of electing a black candidate. With African American voices marginalized in Congress and the state legislatures well into the 1970s, racial fairness in representation, and what that meant, emerged as the other major unresolved issue of the reapportionment revolution.

Race, Remedies, and Representation

Civil rights and civil liberties organizations such as the NAACP and the ACLU, which had been primarily responsibile for enforcing the Voting Rights Act throughout the South, continued to maintain that African Americans were woefully underrepresented in American electoral politics. In response, Congress amended the Voting Rights Act in 1982 to strengthen Section 2, which bans states from engaging in discriminatory voting practices on the basis of race or color, and Section 5, which requires any covered jurisdiction with a history of prior discrimination to "preclear" any redistricting plan with the Department of Justice or the U.S. District Court for the District of Columbia before it can go into effect. Most states preclear their apportionment plans through the Justice Department because the courts pose a far more expensive option.

The Section 2 changes were far more significant for future battles over minority representation in the political process. Triggering the 1982 amendments had been the Court's decision two years before in *City of Mobile* v. *Borden* (1980). There, the Court ruled that racially disparate outcomes in elections were not enough to demonstrate a voting discrimination claim. Instead, minorities had to demonstrate that district lines were *intentionally* drawn to disadvantage minorities. Since the enactment of the Voting Rights Act of 1965, vote dilution had been the one major fallback strategy that had worked for Southern legislatures. Letting blacks register to vote was one thing, but permitting those registered voters to exercise political power was quite another. By splitting black votes into different districts with equal populations, many state legislatures could meet the one person, one vote requirement without conceding any real political strength.

Section 2 was changed to void *Borden* by permitting minorities to challenge as illegal voting practices *resulting* in a denial or abridgement of their right, not merely those that *intentionally* diluted minority voting power. Senate supporters claimed the original purpose of the 1965 law had been to ban discrimination in any form from the voting process, not simply intentionally discriminatory barriers such as literacy tests and qualifications tests. Critics of the changes to Section 2 argued that the original law had been about allowing African Americans the equal opportunity to walk into the voting booth and cast their ballot just like white Americans. The 1982 amendment, in their view, would now require states to draw legislative districts to ensure that blacks could nominate and elect black candidates, a form of racial gerrymandering that was inconsistent with the Constitution. However, in releasing the report on the final version of the legislation, the Senate Judiciary Committee wrote that "contrary to any assertion made [about proportional representation of minorities in Congress], this provision is both clear and straightforward. It puts to rest any concerns that have been voiced about racial quotas."[44]

The Court's first brush with the amended voting rights law came in *Thornburg* v. *Gingles* (1986), where the justices applied the "discriminatory effects" analysis of the new Section 2 language to strike down portions of North Carolina's 1984 redistricting plan. Although the Court produced four opinions and varied widely on appropriate standards and practices in voting rights cases, five justices agreed that race played a major role in allowing voters to elect the "candidate of their choice." Three major criteria to determine racial fairness in voting came out of *Gingles:*

- A minority group must be able to demonstrate that it is sufficiently large and geographically compact to constitute a majority in a single-member district.
- A minority group must be able to claim it is politically cohesive.
- White majorities vote in blocs that render almost impossible the minority group's chance to elect its preferred candidate.[45]

Translated, this meant that racial bloc voting was alive and well in the South, and that the only way to elect black members to Congress was to create districts that constituted a majority of African American voters. Ironically, the Court decided *Bandemer,* which gave plaintiffs little room to challenge apportionment plans rooted in established patterns of political partisanship, the same term as *Gingles,* which seemed to invite challenges to apportionment plans based on districts whose racial boundaries disadvantaged blacks.

Southern legislatures understood the implications of *Gingles* quite clearly: either create majority-black districts or invite litigation demanding to know why state regions with high concentrations of black voters were not sending black representatives to Congress. After the 1990 census, fourteen states revamped their apportionment plans to include additional new majority-minority seats. In the South, these districts were drawn to maximize African American voters; in the Southwest, Latinos were the primary beneficiaries of racially gerrymandered districts. By the 1992 elections, *Gingles*'s impact was evident. North Carolina, which had received an additional seat in Congress, elected two African American representatives to the House of Representatives from the two newly created black districts. This marked the first time that North Carolina had elected an African American to the House since the late 1890s. Not everyone thought this was a good idea, including several white North Carolina voters who decided to form a coalition to challenge the validity of the redistricting plan. The result was *Shaw* v. *Reno* (1993).

Shaw v. *Reno*

509 U.S 630 (1993)

After Reconstruction collapsed in the late 1870s, the newly installed "Redeemer" governments of the South redrew their legislative districts to dilute black voting strength. Mississippi created a "shoestring" district that ran up and down the Mississippi River and through the Delta region where most blacks lived, leaving the state's five remaining white districts in white hands. Alabama placed blacks in six separate districts to dilute their vote. Other Southern states followed suit, leaving blacks powerless to affect state and local politics. Racially gerrymandered districts were followed by other mechanisms to disenfranchise blacks—literacy tests, poll taxes, and so on—that carried over into the 1960s.

North Carolina brought its last black representative back from Congress in 1901. In 1990, before it was awarded another seat and encouraged by *Gingles* to redraw its districts to encourage the election of black representatives, North Carolina did not have a single majority-black district, although African Americans made up over 20 percent of the state's population. In accord with the Voting Rights Act of 1965, forty counties were still under supervision by the Justice Department. The range of voting-eligible blacks in North Carolina's eleven congressional districts ranged from a high of 40 percent in the Second District to 5 percent in the Eleventh District. After North Carolina redrew its electoral map in 1992, two new majority-black districts had been created, the First (57 percent black) and the Twelfth (57 percent black), while the remaining ten districts were solidly white. No other district outside the First and Twelfth had African American populations beyond 23 percent. In 1992, North Carolina elected two African American black representatives, Eva Clayton and Melvin Watt, both Democrats, to the House of Representatives.

Ruth Shaw and other white North Carolina voters challenged North Carolina's reapportioned electoral map. They did not allege a vote dilution claim under Section 2 of the Voting Rights Act. Rather, the plaintiffs argued the state had segregated voters on the basis of race in violation of the Equal Protection Clause of the Fourteenth Amendment. A three-judge federal court dismissed Shaw's claim, ruling that an earlier decision of the Court, *United Jewish Organizations, Inc.* v. *Carey* (1977), permitted states to create majority-black districts as long as they did not dilute white votes. In *United Jewish Organizations,* Hasidic Jews in Brooklyn, New York, challenged a redistricting plan favorable to blacks as weakening their voting power by dividing them into different districts. Although the Court has recognized that protecting "ethnic enclaves" is a permissible factor in legislative apportionment, the justices ruled that Hasidic Jews did not have interests separate from other white voters.

The Court's decision was 5 to 4. Justice O'Connor delivered the opinion of the Court. Justice White, joined by Justices Blackmun and Stevens, dissented. Justices Blackmun, Stevens, and Souter wrote separate dissenting opinions.

JUSTICE O'CONNOR delivered the opinion of the Court.

This case involves two of the most complex and sensitive issues this Court has faced in recent years: the meaning of the constitutional "right" to vote, and the propriety of race-based state legislation designed to benefit members of historically disadvantaged racial minority groups. . . .

An understanding of the nature of appellants' claim is critical to our resolution of the case. In their complaint, appellants did not claim that the General Assembly's reapportionment plan unconstitutionally "diluted" white voting strength. They did not even claim to be white. Rather, appellants' complaint alleged that the deliberate segregation of voters into separate districts on the basis of race violated their constitutional right to participate in a "color-blind" electoral process.

Despite their invocation of the ideal of a "color-blind" Constitution, see *Plessy* v. *Ferguson* (1896) (Harlan, J., dissenting), appellants appear to concede that race-conscious redistricting is not always unconstitutional. That conces-

sion is wise: this Court never has held that race-conscious state decision making is impermissible in all circumstances. What appellants object to is redistricting legislation that is so extremely irregular on its face that it rationally can be viewed only as an effort to segregate the races for purposes of voting, without regard for traditional districting principles and without sufficiently compelling justification. For the reasons that follow, we conclude that appellants have stated a claim upon which relief can be granted under the Equal Protection Clause. . . .

Appellants contend that redistricting legislation that is so bizarre on its face that it is "unexplainable on grounds other than race," demands the same close scrutiny that we give other state laws that classify citizens by race. Our voting rights precedents support that conclusion.

In *Guinn* v. *United States* (1915), the Court invalidated under the Fifteenth Amendment a statute that imposed a literacy requirement on voters but contained a "grandfather clause" applicable to individuals and their lineal descendants entitled to vote "on [or prior to] January 1, 1866." The determinative consideration for the Court was that the law, though ostensibly race neutral, on its face "embod[ied] no exercise of judgment and rest[ed] upon no discernible reason" other than to circumvent the prohibitions of the Fifteenth Amendment. In other words, the statute was invalid because, on its face, it could not be explained on grounds other than race.

The Court applied the same reasoning to the "uncouth twenty-eight-sided" municipal boundary line at issue in *Gomillion.* Although the statute that redrew the city limits of Tuskegee was race neutral on its face, plaintiffs alleged that its effect was impermissibly to remove from the city virtually all black voters and no white voters. . . .

The difficulty of proof, of course, does not mean that a racial gerrymander, once established, should receive less scrutiny under the Equal Protection Clause than other state legislation classifying citizens by race. Moreover, it seems clear to us that proof sometimes will not be difficult at all. In some exceptional cases, a reapportionment plan may be so highly irregular that, on its face, it rationally cannot be understood as anything other than an effort to "segregat[e] . . . voters" on the basis of race. *Gomillion,* in which a tortured municipal boundary line was drawn to exclude black voters, was such a case. So, too, would be a case in which a State concentrated a dispersed minority population in a single district by disregarding traditional districting principles such as compactness, contiguity, and respect for political subdivisions. We emphasize that these criteria are important not because they are constitutionally required—they are not—but because they are objective factors that may serve to defeat a claim that a district has been gerrymandered on racial lines.

Put differently, we believe that reapportionment is one area in which appearances do matter. A reapportionment plan that includes in one district individuals who belong to the same race, but who are otherwise widely separated by geographical and political boundaries, and who may have little in common with one another but the color of their skin, bears an uncomfortable resemblance to political apartheid. It reinforces the perception that members of the same racial group—regardless of their age, education, economic status, or the community in which they live—think alike, share the same political interests, and will prefer the same candidates at the polls. We have rejected such perceptions elsewhere as impermissible racial stereotypes. By perpetuating such notions, a racial gerrymander may exacerbate the very patterns of racial bloc voting that majority-minority districting is sometimes said to counteract.

The message that such districting sends to elected representatives is equally pernicious. When a district obviously is created solely to effectuate the perceived common interests of one racial group, elected officials are more likely to believe that their primary obligation is to represent only the members of that group, rather than their constituency as a whole. This is altogether antithetical to our system of representative democracy. . . .

For these reasons, we conclude that a plaintiff challenging a reapportionment statute under the Equal Protection Clause may state a claim by alleging that the legislation, though race neutral on its face, rationally cannot be understood as anything other than an effort to separate voters into different districts on the basis of race, and that the separation lacks sufficient justification. It is unnecessary for us to decide whether or how a reapportionment plan that, on its face, can be explained in nonracial terms successfully could be challenged. Thus, we express no view as to whether "the intentional creation of majority-minority districts, without more," always gives rise to an equal protection claim. We hold only that, on the facts of this case, appellants have stated a claim sufficient to defeat the state appellees' motion to dismiss.

Racial classifications of any sort pose the risk of lasting harm to our society. They reinforce the belief, held by too many for too much of our history, that individuals should be judged by the color of their skin. Racial classifications with respect to voting carry particular dangers. Racial gerrymandering, even for remedial purposes, may balkanize us into competing racial factions; it threatens to carry us further from the goal of a political system in which race no longer matters—a goal that the Fourteenth and Fifteenth Amendments embody, and to which the Nation continues to aspire. It is for these reasons that race-based districting by our state legislatures demands close judicial scrutiny. . . .

Today we hold only that appellants have stated a claim under the Equal Protection Clause by alleging that the North Carolina General Assembly adopted a reapportionment scheme so irrational on its face that it can be understood only as an effort to segregate voters into separate voting districts because of their race, and that the separation lacks sufficient justification.

JUSTICE WHITE, with whom JUSTICE BLACKMUN and JUSTICE STEVENS join, dissenting.

The facts of this case mirror those presented in *United Jewish Organizations of Williamsburgh, Inc.* v. *Carey* (1977), where the Court rejected a claim that creation of a majority-minority district violated the Constitution, either as a per se matter or in light of the circumstances leading to the creation of such a district. Of particular relevance, five of the Justices reasoned that members of the white majority could not plausibly argue that their influence over the political process had been unfairly canceled. Accordingly, they held that plaintiffs were not entitled to relief under the Constitution's Equal Protection Clause. On the same reasoning, I would affirm the District Court's dismissal of appellants' claim in this instance.

The Court today chooses not to overrule, but rather to sidestep, *UJO*. It does so by glossing over the striking similarities, focusing on surface differences, most notably the (admittedly unusual) shape of the newly created district, and imagining an entirely new cause of action. Because the holding is limited to such anomalous circumstances, it perhaps will not substantially hamper a State's legitimate efforts to redistrict in favor of racial minorities. Nonetheless, the notion that North Carolina's plan, under which whites remain a voting majority in a disproportionate number of congressional districts, and pursuant to which the State has sent its first black representatives since Reconstruction to the United States Congress, might have violated appellants' constitutional rights is both a fiction and a departure from settled equal protection principles. Seeing no good reason to engage in either, I dissent. . . .

JUSTICE SOUTER, dissenting.

Today, the Court recognizes a new cause of action under which a State's electoral redistricting plan that includes a configuration "so bizarre," that it "rationally cannot be understood as anything other than an effort to separate voters into different districts on the basis of race [without] sufficient justification," will be subjected to strict scrutiny. In my view, there is no justification for the Court's determination to depart from our prior decisions by carving out this narrow group of cases for strict scrutiny in place of the review customarily applied in cases dealing with discrimination in electoral districting on the basis of race.

Until today, the Court has analyzed equal protection claims involving race in electoral districting differently from equal protection claims involving other forms of governmental conduct, and before turning to the different regimes of analysis, it will be useful to set out the relevant respects in which such districting differs from the characteristic circumstances in which a State might otherwise consciously consider race. Unlike other contexts in which we have addressed the State's conscious use of race, electoral districting calls for decisions that nearly always require some consideration of race for legitimate reasons where there is a racially mixed population. As long as members of racial groups have the commonality of interest implicit in our ability to talk about concepts like "minority voting strength," and "dilution of minority votes," and as long as racial bloc voting takes place, legislators will have to take race into account in order to avoid dilution of minority voting strength in the districting plans they adopt. One need look no further than the Voting Rights Act to understand that this may be required, and we have held that race may constitutionally be taken into account in order to comply with that Act.

A second distinction between districting and most other governmental decisions in which race has figured is that those other decisions using racial criteria characteristically occur in circumstances in which the use of race to the advantage of one person is necessarily at the obvious expense of a member of a different race. Thus, for example, awarding government contracts on a racial basis excludes certain firms from competition on racial grounds. And when race is used to supplant seniority in layoffs, someone is laid off who would not be otherwise. The same principle pertains in nondistricting aspects of voting law, where race-based discrimination places the disfavored voters at the disadvantage of exclusion from the franchise without any alternative benefit.

In districting, by contrast, the mere placement of an individual in one district instead of another denies no one a right or benefit provided to others. All citizens may register, vote, and be represented. In whatever district, the individual voter has a right to vote in each election, and the election will result in the voter's representation. As we have held, one's constitutional rights are not violated merely because the candidate one supports loses the election or because a group (including a racial group) to which one belongs winds up with a representative from outside that group. It is true, of course, that one's vote may be more or less effective depending on the interests of the other individuals who are in one's district, and our cases recognize the reality that members of the same race often have shared interests. "Dilution" thus refers to the effects of districting decisions not on an individual's political power viewed in isolation, but on the political power of a group. This is the reason that the placement of given voters in a given district, even on the basis of race, does not, without more, diminish the effectiveness of the individual as a voter. . . .

There is thus no theoretical inconsistency in having two distinct approaches to equal protection analysis, one for cases of electoral districting and one for most other types of state governmental decisions. Nor, because of the distinctions between the two categories, is there any risk that Fourteenth Amendment districting law as such will be taken to imply anything for purposes of general Fourteenth Amendment scrutiny about "benign" racial discrimination, or about group entitlement as distinct from individual protection, or about the appropriateness of strict or other heightened scrutiny. . . .

The Court offers no adequate justification for treating the narrow category of bizarrely shaped district claims differently from other districting claims. The only justification I can imagine would be the preservation of "sound districting principles," such as compactness and contiguity. But as JUSTICE WHITE points out, and as the Court acknowledges, we have held that such principles are not constitutionally required, with the consequence that their absence cannot justify the distinct constitutional regime put in place by the Court today. Since there is no justification for the departure here from the principles that continue to govern electoral districting cases generally in accordance with our prior decisions, I would not respond to the seeming egregiousness of the redistricting now before us by untethering the concept of racial gerrymander in such a case from the concept of harm exemplified by dilution. In the absence of an allegation of such harm, I would affirm the judgment of the District Court. I respectfully dissent.

▼▲▼

Shaw completely upset the pattern of legislative redistricting taking place in states still covered by the Voting Rights Act. Although the Court did not rule that North Carolina's First and Twelfth Districts were unconstitutional, white voters heeded Justice O'Connor's emphasis on the "bizarrely" configured lines and her likening of racially gerrymandered districts to favor minorities as "political apartheid" and began challenging redistricting plans in other states covered by the Voting Rights Act. In 1993, sixteen states, nine more than in 1965, were still covered by the law in whole or in part. By the late 1980s, state legislatures were using computer software packages designed to identify concentrated areas of minority population so they could draw district lines to create majority-minority districts. Although states attempted to defend their majority-minority districts as politically, rather than racially, gerrymandered, the ongoing relationship with the Justice Department to achieve preclearance suggested to the Court that race, not politics, was the driving consideration.[46]

Two years later, the consequences of *Shaw* came to fruition in *Miller* v. *Johnson* (1995). The 1990 census required Georgia to reapportion its population because of growing urbanization during the 1980s. Unlike North Carolina, Georgia did not receive an additional seat, since its population did not grow enough to warrant one. Rather, the Georgia state legislature was required to work with the existing population distribution to create majority-black districts. Whereas the Court ruled in *Shaw* only that racially gerrymandered districts presented a justiciable claim under the Equal Protection Clause of the Fourteenth Amendment, *Miller* went the next step and declared unconstitutional districts in which race is the *predominant* factor in line drawing.

Miller v. *Johnson*

512 U.S. 622 (1995)

In 1992, voters from the newly configured majority-black Eleventh District in Georgia elected Cynthia McKinney, a liberal African American Democrat, to the House of Representatives. Georgia's two other majority-black districts (the Fifth and Second) also had elected African Americans to the House, one of whom was John Lewis, the former SNCC leader who was badly beaten during the "Bloody Sunday" voting rights march in Selma, Alabama, in March 1965. Lewis had first been elected to Congress in 1986, making him the first African American to represent the Fifth District since it was redrawn in 1982 to make it majority black.

After McKinney was reelected in 1994, Davida Johnson and four other white voters sued Georgia governor Zell Miller, a Democrat, claiming that the predominant use of race to reapportion the state's congressional districts violated the Equal Protection Clause of the Fourteenth Amendment.

Additional facts and background of this case are set out in the accompanying SIDEBAR.

The Court's decision was 5 to 4. Justice Kennedy delivered the opinion of the Court. Justice O'Connor wrote a concurring opinion. Justice Stevens dissented. Justice Ginsburg, joined by Justices Breyer, Souter, and Stevens, also dissented.

▼▲▼

JUSTICE KENNEDY delivered the opinion of the Court.

In *Shaw* v. *Reno* (1993), we held that a plaintiff states a claim under the Equal Protection Clause by alleging that a state redistricting plan, on its face, has no rational explanation save as an effort to separate voters on the basis of race. The question we now decide is whether Georgia's new Eleventh District gives rise to a valid equal protection claim under the principles announced in *Shaw,* and, if so, whether it can be sustained nonetheless as narrowly tailored to serve a compelling governmental interest.

The Equal Protection Clause of the Fourteenth Amendment provides that no State shall "deny to any person within its jurisdiction the equal protection of the laws." Its central mandate is racial neutrality in governmental decision making. Though application of this imperative raises difficult questions, the basic principle is straightforward: "Racial and ethnic distinctions of any sort are inherently suspect, and thus call for the most exacting judicial examination. . . . This perception of racial and ethnic distinctions is rooted in our Nation's constitutional and demographic history." This rule obtains with equal force regardless of "the race of those burdened or benefited by a particular classification." Laws classifying citizens on the basis of race cannot be upheld unless they are narrowly tailored to achieving a compelling state interest.

In *Shaw* [I] we recognized that these equal protection principles govern a State's drawing of congressional districts, though, as our cautious approach there discloses, application of these principles to electoral districting is a most delicate task. . . .

This case requires us to apply the principles articulated in Shaw to the most recent congressional redistricting plan enacted by the State of Georgia. . . .

Appellants . . . contend that evidence of a legislature's deliberate classification of voters on the basis of race cannot alone suffice to state a claim under *Shaw.* They argue that, regardless of the legislature's purposes, a plaintiff must demonstrate that a district's shape is so bizarre that it is unexplainable other than on the basis of race, and that appellees failed to make that showing here. Appellants' conception of the constitutional violation misapprehends our holding in *Shaw* and the Equal Protection precedent upon which *Shaw* relied.

Shaw recognized a claim "analytically distinct" from a vote dilution claim. Whereas a vote dilution claim alleges that the State has enacted a particular voting scheme as a purposeful device "to minimize or cancel out the voting potential of racial or ethnic minorities," *Mobile* v. *Bolden* (1980), an action disadvantaging voters of a particular race, the essence of the equal protection claim recognized in *Shaw* is that the State has used race as a basis for separating voters into districts. Just as the State may not, absent extraordinary justification, segregate citizens on the basis of race in its public parks, so did we recognize in *Shaw* that it may not separate its citizens into different voting districts on the basis of race. . . . When the State assigns voters on the basis of race, it engages in the offensive and demeaning assumption that voters of a particular race, because of their race, "think alike, share the same political interests, and will prefer the same candidates at the polls." Race-based assignments embody stereotypes that treat individuals as the product of their race, evaluating their thoughts and efforts—their very worth as citizens—according to a criterion barred to the Government by history and the Constitution. They also cause society serious harm. . . .

Our observation in *Shaw* of the consequences of racial stereotyping was not meant to suggest that a district must be bizarre on its face before there is a constitutional violation. Nor was our conclusion in *Shaw* that in certain instances a district's appearance (or, to be more precise, its appearance in combination with certain demographic evidence) can give rise to an equal protection claim, a holding that bizarreness was a threshold showing, as appellants believe it to be. Our circumspect approach and narrow holding in *Shaw* did not erect an artificial rule barring accepted equal protection analysis in other redistricting cases. Shape is relevant not because bizarreness is a necessary element of the constitutional wrong or a threshold requirement of proof, but because it may be persuasive circumstantial evidence that race for its own sake, and not other districting principles, was the legislature's dominant and controlling rationale in drawing its district lines.

The logical implication, as courts applying *Shaw* have recognized, is that parties may rely on evidence other than bizarreness to establish race-based districting.

Our reasoning in *Shaw* compels this conclusion. We recognized in *Shaw* that, outside the districting context, statutes are subject to strict scrutiny under the Equal Protection Clause not just when they contain express racial classifications, but also when, though race neutral on their face, they are motivated by a racial purpose or object. In the rare case, where the effect of government action is a pattern "'unexplainable on grounds other than race,'" . . . "[t]he evidentiary inquiry . . . is relatively easy." [I]n *Gomillion* v. *Lightfoot* (1960), the Court concluded that the redrawing of Tuskegee, Alabama's municipal boundaries left no doubt that the plan was designed to exclude blacks. Even in those cases, however, it was the presumed racial purpose of state action, not its stark manifestation, that was the constitutional violation. Patterns of discrimination as conspicuous as these are rare, and are not a necessary predicate to a violation of the Equal Protection Clause. . . .

Appellants and some of their amici argue that the Equal Protection Clause's general proscription on race-based decision making does not obtain in the districting context because redistricting by definition involves racial considerations. Underlying their argument are the very stereotypical assumptions the Equal Protection Clause forbids. It is true that redistricting in most cases will implicate a political calculus in which various interests compete for recognition, but it does not follow from this that individuals of the same race share a single political interest. The view that they do is based on the demeaning notion that members of the defined racial groups ascribe to certain "minority views" that must be different from those of other citizens, the precise use of race as a proxy the Constitution prohibits. . . .

In sum, we make clear that parties alleging that a State has assigned voters on the basis of race are neither confined in their proof to evidence regarding the district's geometry and makeup nor required to make a threshold showing of bizarreness. Today's case requires us further to consider the requirements of the proof necessary to sustain this equal protection challenge.

. . . The courts, in assessing the sufficiency of a challenge to a districting plan, must be sensitive to the complex interplay of forces that enter a legislature's redistricting calculus. Redistricting legislatures will, for example, almost always be aware of racial demographics; but it does not follow that race predominates in the redistricting process. The distinction between being aware of racial considerations and being motivated by them may be difficult to make. This evidentiary difficulty, together with the sensitive nature of redistricting and the presumption of good faith that must be accorded legislative enactments, requires courts to exercise extraordinary caution in adjudicating claims that a state has drawn district lines on the basis of race. The plaintiff's burden is to show, either through circumstantial evidence of a district's shape and demographics or more direct evidence going to legislative purpose, that race was the predominant factor motivating the legislature's decision to place a significant number of voters within or without a particular district. To make this showing, a plaintiff must prove that the legislature subordinated traditional race-neutral districting principles, including but not limited to compactness, contiguity, respect for political subdivisions or communities defined by actual shared interests, to racial considerations. Where these or other race-neutral considerations are the basis for redistricting legislation, and are not subordinated to race, a state can "defeat a claim that a district has been gerrymandered on racial lines." . . .

In our view, the District Court applied the correct analysis, and its finding that race was the predominant factor motivating the drawing of the Eleventh District was not clearly erroneous. The court found it was "exceedingly obvious" from the shape of the Eleventh District, together with the relevant racial demographics, that the drawing of narrow land bridges to incorporate within the District outlying appendages containing nearly 80% of the district's total black population was a deliberate attempt to bring black populations into the district. Although by comparison with other districts the geometric shape of the Eleventh District may not seem bizarre on its face, when its shape is considered in conjunction with its racial and population densities, the story of racial gerrymandering seen by the District Court becomes much clearer. . . .

Race was, as the District Court found, the predominant, overriding factor explaining the General Assembly's decision to attach to the Eleventh District various appendages containing dense majority-black populations. As a result, Georgia's congressional redistricting plan cannot be upheld unless it satisfies strict scrutiny, our most rigorous and exacting standard of constitutional review. . . . To satisfy strict scrutiny, the State must demonstrate that its districting legislation is narrowly tailored to achieve a compelling interest. . . .

We do not accept the contention that the State has a compelling interest in complying with whatever preclearance mandates the Justice Department issues. When a state governmental entity seeks to justify race-based remedies to cure the effects of past discrimination, we do not accept the government's mere assertion that the remedial action is required. Rather, we insist on a strong basis in evidence of the harm being remedied. The history of racial classifications in this country suggests that blind judicial deference to legislative or executive pronouncements of necessity has no place in equal protection analysis. Our presumptive skepticism of all racial classifications prohibits us as well from accepting on its face the Justice Department's conclusion that racial districting is necessary under the Voting Rights Act. Where a State relies on the Department's determination that race-based districting is necessary to comply with the Voting Rights Act, the judiciary retains an independent obligation in adjudicating consequent equal protection challenges to ensure that the State's actions are narrowly tailored to achieve a compelling interest. Were we to accept the Justice Department's objection itself as a compelling interest adequate to insulate racial districting from constitutional review, we would be surrendering to the Executive Branch our role in enforcing the constitutional limits on race-based official action. We may not do so. . . .

The Voting Rights Act [of 1965], and its grant of authority to the federal courts to uncover official efforts to abridge minorities' right to vote, has been of vital importance in eradicating invidious discrimination from the electoral process and enhancing the legitimacy of our political institutions. Only if our political system and our society cleanse themselves of that discrimination will all members of the polity share an equal opportunity to gain public office regardless of race. As a Nation we share both the obligation and the aspiration of working toward this end. The end is neither assured nor well served, however, by carving electorates into racial blocs. If our society is to continue to progress as a multiracial democracy, it must recognize that the automatic invocation of race stereotypes retards that progress and causes continued hurt and injury. It takes a shortsighted and unauthorized view of the Voting Rights Act to invoke that statute, which has played a decisive role in redressing some of our worst forms of discrimination, to demand the very racial stereotyping the Fourteenth Amendment forbids.

The judgment of the District Court is affirmed, and the case is remanded for further proceedings consistent with this decision.

It is so ordered.

JUSTICE O'CONNOR, concurring.

To invoke strict scrutiny, a plaintiff must show that the State has relied on race in substantial disregard of customary and traditional districting practices. Those practices provide a crucial frame of reference and therefore constitute a significant governing principle in cases of this kind. The standard would be no different if a legislature had drawn the boundaries to favor some other ethnic group; certainly the standard does not treat efforts to create majority-minority districts less favorably than similar efforts on behalf of other groups. Indeed, the driving force behind the adoption of the Fourteenth Amendment was the desire to end legal discrimination against blacks.

Application of the Court's standard does not throw into doubt the vast majority of the Nation's 435 congressional districts, where presumably the States have drawn the boundaries in accordance with their customary districting principles. That is so even though race may well have been considered in the redistricting process. But application of the Court's standard helps achieve *Shaw*'s basic objective of making extreme instances of gerrymandering subject to meaningful judicial review. I therefore join the Court's opinion.

JUSTICE STEVENS, dissenting.

I add these comments because I believe the respondents in these cases have not suffered any legally cognizable injury. . . .

In particular instances, of course, members of one race may vote by an overwhelming margin for one candidate, and in some cases that candidate will be of the same race. "Racially polarized voting" is one of the circumstances plaintiffs must prove to advance a vote dilution claim, *Thornburg* v. *Gingles* (1986). Such a claim allows voters to allege that gerrymandered district lines have impaired their ability to elect a candidate of their own race. The Court emphasizes, however, that a so-called Shaw claim is "'analytically distinct' from a vote dilution claim." . . . [I]n *Shaw* . . . the Court [did not] answer . . . the question its analytic distinction raises: If the *Shaw* injury does not flow from an increased probability that white candidates will lose, then how can the increased probability that black candidates will win cause white voters, such as respondents, cognizable harm?

The Court attempts an explanation in these cases by equating the injury it imagines respondents have suffered with the injuries African Americans suffered under segregation. The heart of respondents' claim, by the Court's account, is that "a State's assignment of voters on the basis of race" violates the Equal Protection Clause for the same reason a State may not segregate citizens on the basis of race in its public parks, golf courses, beaches, and schools. This equation, however, fails to elucidate the elusive *Shaw* injury. Our desegregation cases redressed the exclusion of black citizens from public facilities reserved for whites. In this case, in contrast, any voter, black or white, may live in the Eleventh District. What respondents contest is the inclusion of too many black voters in the District as drawn. In my view, if respondents allege no vote dilution, that inclusion can cause them no conceivable injury.

The Court's equation of *Shaw* claims with our desegregation decisions is inappropriate for another reason. In each of those cases, legal segregation frustrated the public interest in diversity and tolerance by barring African Americans from joining whites in the activities at issue. The districting plan here, in contrast, serves the interest in diversity and tolerance by increasing the likelihood that a meaningful number of black representatives will add their voices to legislative debates. There is no moral or constitutional equivalence between a policy that is designed to perpetuate a caste system and one that seeks to eradicate racial subordination. . . .

Equally distressing is the Court's equation of traditional gerrymanders, designed to maintain or enhance a dominant group's power, with a dominant group's decision to share its power with a previously underrepresented group. In my view, districting plans violate the Equal Protection Clause when they serve no purpose other than to favor one segment—whether racial, ethnic, religious, economic, or political—that may occupy a position of strength at a particular point in time, or to disadvantage a politically weak segment of the community. In contrast, I do not see how a districting plan that favors a politically weak group can violate equal protection. . . .

The Court's refusal to distinguish an enactment that helps a minority group from enactments that cause it harm is especially unfortunate at the intersection of race and voting, given that African Americans and other disadvantaged groups have struggled so long and so hard for inclusion in that most central exercise of our democracy. I have long believed that treating racial groups differently from other identifiable groups of voters, as the Court does today, is itself an invidious racial classification. Racial minorities should receive neither more nor less protection than other groups against gerrymanders. . . . [R]acial minorities should not be less eligible than other groups to benefit from districting plans the majority designs to aid them.

JUSTICE GINSBURG, with whom JUSTICES STEVENS and BREYER join, and with whom JUSTICE SOUTER joins except as to Part III-B, dissenting.

Legislative districting is highly political business. This Court has generally respected the competence of state legislatures to attend to the task. When race is the issue, however, we have recognized the need for judicial intervention to prevent dilution of minority voting strength. Generations of rank discrimination against African Americans, as citizens and voters, account for that surveillance. . . .

Today the Court . . . announc[es] that federal courts are to undertake searching review of any district with contours "predominantly motivated" by race: "strict scrutiny" will be triggered not only when traditional districting practices are abandoned, but also when those practices are "subordinated to"—given less weight than—race. Applying this new "race as predominant factor" standard, the Court invalidates Georgia's districting plan even though Georgia's Eleventh District, the focus of today's dispute, bears the imprint of familiar districting practices. Because I do not endorse the Court's new standard and would not upset Georgia's plan, I dissent. . . .

I

[Omitted]

II

Before *Shaw* v. *Reno* (1993), this Court invoked the Equal Protection Clause to justify intervention in the quintessentially political task of legislative districting in two circumstances: to enforce the "one person one vote" requirement, and to prevent dilution of a minority group's voting strength. . . .

In *Shaw*, the Court recognized a third basis for an equal protection challenge to a State's apportionment plan. The Court wrote cautiously, emphasizing that judicial intervention is exceptional: "[S]trict [judicial] scrutiny" is in order, the Court declared, if a district is "so extremely irregular on its face that it rationally can be viewed only as an effort to segregate the races for purposes of voting."

The record before us does not show that race similarly overwhelmed traditional districting practices in Georgia. Although the Georgia General Assembly prominently considered race in shaping the Eleventh District, race did not crowd out all other factors, as the Court found it did in North Carolina's delineation of the *Shaw* district.

In contrast to the snake-like North Carolina district inspected in *Shaw*, Georgia's Eleventh District is hardly "bizarre," "extremely irregular," or "irrational on its face." Instead, the Eleventh District's design reflects significant consideration of traditional districting factors (such as keeping political subdivisions intact) and the usual political process of compromise and trades for a variety of nonracial reasons. . . .

Georgia's Eleventh District . . . is not an outlier district shaped without reference to familiar districting techniques. Tellingly, the District that the Court's decision today unsettles is not among those on a statistically calculated list of the 28 most bizarre districts in the United States, a study prepared in the wake of our decision in *Shaw*.

Along with attention to size, shape, and political subdivisions, the Court recognizes as an appropriate districting principle, "respect for . . . communities defined by actual shared interests." The Court finds no community here, however, because a report in the record showed "fractured political, social, and economic interests within the Eleventh District's black population."

But ethnicity itself can tie people together, as volumes of social science literature have documented—even people with divergent economic interests. For this reason, ethnicity is a significant force in political life. As stated in a classic study of ethnicity in one city of immigrants: "[M]any elements—history, family and feeling, interest, formal organizational life—operate to keep much of New York life channeled within the bounds of the ethnic group. . . . The political realm . . . is least willing to consider [ethnicity] a purely private affair. . . . [P]olitical life itself emphasizes the ethnic character of the city, with its balanced tickets and its special appeals," Nathan Glazer & Daniel Patrick Moynihan, *Beyond the Melting Pot* (1963).

To accommodate the reality of ethnic bonds, legislatures have long drawn voting districts along ethnic lines. Our Nation's cities are full of districts identified by their ethnic character—Chinese, Irish, Italian, Jewish, Polish, Russian, for example. The creation of ethnic districts reflecting felt identity is not ordinarily viewed as offensive or demeaning to those included in the delineation. . . .

III

To separate permissible and impermissible use of race in legislative apportionment, the Court orders strict scrutiny for districting plans "predominantly motivated" by race. No longer can a State avoid judicial oversight by giving—as in this case—genuine and measurable consideration to traditional districting practices. Instead, a federal case can be mounted whenever plaintiffs plausibly allege that other factors carried less weight than race. This invitation to litigate against the State seems to me neither necessary nor proper. . . .

B

State legislatures like Georgia's today operate under federal constraints imposed by the Voting Rights Act—constraints justified by history and designed by Congress to make once-subordinated people free and equal citizens. But these federal constraints do not leave majority voters in need of extraordinary judicial solicitude. The Attorney General, who administers the Voting Rights Act's preclearance requirements, is herself a political actor. She has a duty to enforce the law Congress passed, and she is no doubt aware of the political cost of venturing too far to the detriment of majority voters. Majority voters, furthermore, can press the State to seek judicial review if the Attorney General refuses to preclear a plan that the voters favor. Finally, the Act is itself a political measure, subject to modification in the political process.

The Court's disposition renders redistricting perilous work for state legislatures. Statutory mandates and political realities may require States to consider race when drawing district lines. But today's decision is a counterforce; it opens the way for federal litigation if "traditional . . . districting principles" arguably were accorded less weight than race. Genuine attention to traditional districting practices and avoidance of bizarre configurations seemed, under *Shaw*, to provide a safe harbor. In view of today's decision, that is no longer the case.

Only after litigation—under either the Voting Rights Act, the Court's new *Miller* standard, or both—will States now be assured that plans conscious of race are safe. Federal judges in large numbers may be drawn into the fray. This enlargement of the judicial role is unwarranted. The reapportionment plan that resulted from Georgia's political process merited this Court's approbation, not its condemnation. Accordingly, I dissent.

After *Miller*, the Court returned to North Carolina. This time, in *Shaw* v. *Hunt* (1996), the justices struck down the First and Twelfth Districts challenged in *Shaw* v. *Reno* as unconstitutional under the Equal Protection Clause. In *Shaw I*, the plaintiffs had sued U.S. Attorney General Janet Reno in her capacity as head of the Department of Justice, which oversees enforcement of the Voting Rights Act. In *Shaw II*, the plaintiffs sued Democratic governor Jim Hunt, following O'Connor's opinion in *Shaw I* that federal courts were permitted to hear equal protection challenges brought against racially gerrymandered districts under the Fourteenth Amendment. The Court decided another important majority-minority redistricting case, in 1996, *Bush* v. *Vera*, in which white voters challenged Texas's redistricting plan based on the 1990 census. *Vera* differed from

S I D E B A R

SHAW V. RENO
MILLER V. JOHNSON

Racial Gerrymandering and the Law of Unintended Consequences

In 1991, the North Carolina General Assembly created its first majority-black congressional district since Reconstruction by linking together several African American communities in the state's northeastern region. Few state legislators anticipated what happened next. The Department of Justice, which was required by Section 5 of the Voting Rights Act of 1965 to approve any changes to North Carolina's electoral map, rejected the General Assembly's plan. Assistant Attorney General for Civil Rights John Dunne, in a letter to the General Assembly, scolded legislators for what he sensed was their lack of sincerity in creating districts for African Americans to elect the candidates of their choice:

> [The General Assembly] was well aware of significant interest on the part of the minority community in creating a second majority-minority congressional district in North Carolina. For the south-central to Southeast area, there were several plans drawn providing for a second majority-minority congressional district, including at least one alternative presented to the legislature. . . .
>
> These alternatives, and other variations identified in our analysis, appear to provide the minority community with an opportunity to elect a second member of Congress of their choice to office, but, despite this fact, such configuration for a second majority-minority congressional district was dismissed for what appears to be pretextual reasons.

Underneath the Department of Justice's concern that black North Carolinians were not getting a fair shake from their state legislature was a compelling political subtext. The North Carolina legislature was controlled by Democrats, with African Americans their most loyal voting constituency. The Department of Justice, for the third consecutive term, was under the political sway of a Republican president firmly on record as opposed to race-based remedies to increase minority representation in university admissions, employment, public contracting, and so on. In no mood for any additional grief from the Department of Justice or potential lawsuits under the *Gingles* rules, the North Carolina General Assembly, following Dunne's letter, created two majority-black districts. The First District was taken largely from the seat of retiring white Democrat Walter Jones, and cut up from north-to-south near the eastern part of the state. The Twelfth District, on the other hand, looked like the work of a small child playing with crayons at the dinner table. Following I-85 through the central portion of the state, the Twelfth District, in linking up the black populations of Gastonia, Charlotte, Winston-Salem, Greensboro, and Durham, ignored city boundaries and county seats. Commented state representative Mickey Michaux after observing the General Assembly's handiwork: "If you drove down the interstate with both car doors open, you'd kill most of the people in the district." The Justice Department cleared North Carolina's plan without objection.

Why would Republicans embrace such an explicitly race-conscious government directive when they opposed such policies in nearly every other context? The respectable answer is that the Justice Department simply wanted to avoid litigation on the 1982 amendments to the Voting Rights Act and give black voters what they were entitled to under federal law. But under President Reagan, the Justice Department opposed race-conscious redistricting, submitting a brief in *Gingles* arguing for a very narrow interpretation of the amended language of Section 2 of the Voting Rights Act. The Reagan administration also had refused to endorse changes to Section 2 during the 1982 congressional hearings held to renew the 1965 law. Did the Justice Department under President George Bush see majority-minority districts as part of an effort to pursue more moderate policies on race relations? Or, as some commentators have suggested, did the Bush administration finally see the flip side of creating "majority-minority" districts? By demanding that states make congressional districts safe for black voters to elect black representatives wherever possible, white Republicans, who were emerging as the South's new political majority, were making majority-white districts equally safe to elect the candidate of *their* choice. Since 1980, no Republican presidential nominee had received more than 14 percent of the African American vote. And in the 2000 presidential election, just 9 percent of African American voters supported the successful Republican nominee, George W. Bush. Moreover, of the thirty-seven African Americans elected or reelected to the House of Representatives in November 2000, only one was a Republican.

This shrewd political calculus was even more evident in the political redistricting battle that resulted in Georgia after the 1990 census, one that led directly to *Miller* v. *Johnson*. The state legislature permitted third parties to comment on the redistricting plans being considered. One such group was the American Civil Liberties Union, which ended up working very closely with the Black Caucus of the Georgia General Assembly and the Bush Justice Department. The ACLU and the Black Caucus developed a plan, dubbed the "Max-Black" plan, that provided for two majority-black districts, the Second, concentrated in the state's southwestern region, and the Fifth, encompassing Atlanta, which had a majority-black voting age population. The ACLU aggressively pushed for districts that swept in well-populated black cities and towns. During the Georgia redistricting process, the ACLU acted as the Georgia Black Caucus's informal law firm. The ACLU provided advice on maximizing black political power to the legislature's mapmakers, and then persuaded

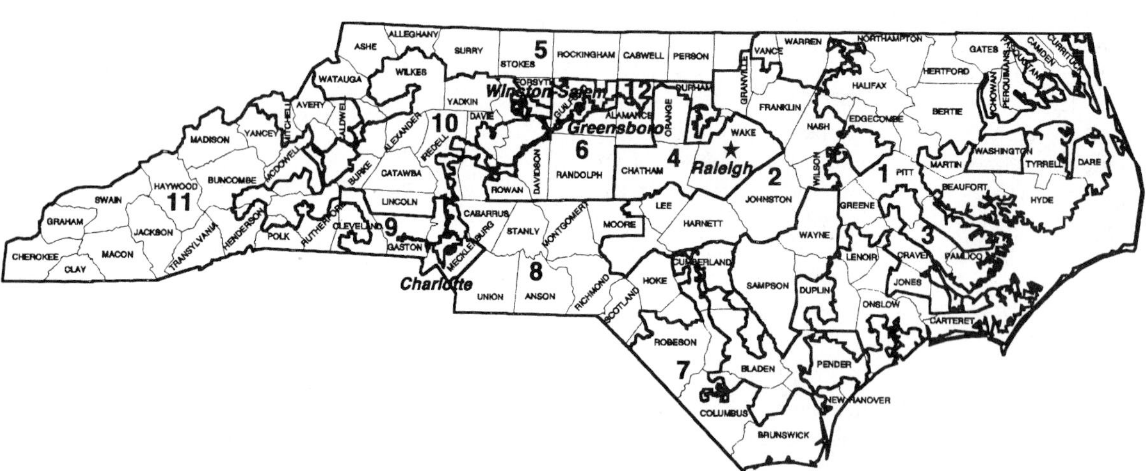

The First District, which ran from the southeastern corner of North Carolina north to the Virginia border, and the Twelfth District, whose "smoke-like" boundaries included part of Charlotte, Winston-Salem, and Greensboro, were created as majority-black districts by the North Carolina legislature.

Reprinted with the permission of Election Data Services, Inc. www.electiondataservices.com.

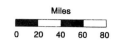

the Justice Department to adopt the majority-black districts.

Nonetheless, the Justice Department rejected the Georgia plan, claiming that enough black voters existed to warrant a third majority-black district. The Justice Department's letter noted that Section 5 does not require a majority-black district to resemble any particular configuration. If there was any doubt about flexibility in drawing district lines to include African American voters, North Carolina's Twelfth District settled that concern.

Using other elements of the "Max-Black" plan, the ACLU and the Black Caucus went back to work to create a third majority-black district. Ultimately, the General Assembly bent to the demands of the Department of Justice and found another majority-black district, the Eleventh, which extended 260 miles eastward from Atlanta through Augusta to Savannah, crisscrossing rivers and land bridges to link major concentrations of eligible black voters. During the final negotiation stage, ACLU lawyers and Black Caucus members worked in one room with an open telephone line to the Justice Department, while other General Assembly members worked in another room with a separate line to the Justice Department. So pervasive was the ACLU's involvement in the Georgia redistricting process that the Department of Justice notified its lawyers of the first plan's rejection before informing the leadership of the General Assembly. This incident only exacerbated the already tense environment that engulfed the negotiations over creating black-majority districts.

Georgia General Assembly Speaker of the House Tom Murphy, a legendary backroom, cigar-chomping politician of the old school, gave the ACLU and the Black Caucus the one vote it needed to send the final plan for Justice Department approval. Said Murphy: "I held my nose and shut my eyes and put one elbow in one ear and voted for it and passed it to get something to keep the courts from doing it." After *Shaw, Miller,* and *Bush* v. *Vera* (1996), state legislators in the future will not have to worry about such "stinky" votes, as Murphy described his own. Racially gerrymandered minority districts are now under close judicial scrutiny, and few have any real chance of surviving. What has not only survived but also prospered since the Court's racial redistricting decisions of the 1990s are majority-white districts, many of which were deliberately created as a tradeoff with black Democrats. Whether minority voters will step forward to challenge these majority-white districts as unconstitutional is not beyond the realm of possibility.

References

Cook, Rhoda, and Ken Foskett. "Governor Signs Redistricting Bills; Feds Might Not Give Approval Till May," *Atlanta Journal-Constitution,* September 19, 1991.

———. "State to Appeal 11th District Ruling, Bowers Will Ask High Court to Allow November Elections," *Atlanta Journal-Constitution,* September 13, 1994.

Coyle, Marcia. "Politics, Law Clash in Racial Redistricting; Bizarre District," *National Law Journal,* October 31, 1994.

Pomper, Gerald. *The Election of 1996.* Chatham, N.J.: Chatham House, 1997.

Shaw I, Shaw II, and *Miller* in two key respects. First, the Republican plaintiffs in *Vera* challenged twenty-four of the state's thirty House seats as unconstitutional under the Fourteenth Amendment. Second, the Texas redistricting plan created majority districts for African American and Latino voters, adding another element of minority representation into the mix.

Bush v. *Vera*

517 U.S. 952 (1996)

In 1978, Al Vera, a schoolteacher at Jefferson Davis High School in Houston, ran for Congress as a Republican in Texas's Eighteenth District. Since 1972, Barbara Jordan, a prominent black lawyer and nationally known liberal Democrat, had held the seat. Vera did not win. But his defeat led him to investigate how Texas drew its legislative districts. Although he encountered discrimination growing up Hispanic in Texas, Vera later commented, "I don't think any of us [speaking of his family] allowed discrimination to interfere with what we wanted to do. One of the things my mom and dad always told me is that you are an American first and then you have a Hispanic background."

In 1994, Vera and six other Republican voters formed the Coalition for a Color Blind Texas and challenged Texas's post-1990 census redistricting plan. A three-judge federal court declared three of the twenty-four challenged districts unconstitutional. On appeal, the United States supported Texas's redistricting plan before the Supreme Court.

The Court's decision was 5 to 4. Justice O'Connor delivered the judgment of the Court, but there was no majority opinion. Only Chief Justice Rehnquist and Justice Kennedy joined O'Connor's opinion. Justices Scalia and Thomas filed concurring opinions. Justices Stevens and Souter filed dissenting opinions, which were joined by Justices Breyer and Ginsburg.

▼▲▼

JUSTICE O'CONNOR announced the judgment of the Court and delivered an opinion, in which THE CHIEF JUSTICE and JUSTICE KENNEDY join.

The present case is a mixed motive case. The appellants concede that one of Texas' goals in creating the three districts at issue was to produce majority minority districts, but they also cite evidence that other goals, particularly incumbency protection (including protection of "functional incumbents," i.e., sitting members of the Texas Legislature who had declared an intention to run for open congressional seats), also played a role in the drawing of the district lines. The record does not reflect a history of "purely race based" districting revisions. . . .

The means that Texas used to make its redistricting decisions provides further evidence of the importance of race. The primary tool used in drawing district lines was a computer program called "REDAPPL." REDAPPL permitted redistricters to manipulate district lines on computer maps, on which racial and other socioeconomic data were superimposed. At each change in configuration of the district lines being drafted, REDAPPL displayed updated racial composition statistics for the district as drawn. REDAPPL contained racial data at the block by block level, whereas other data, such as party registration and past voting statistics, were only available at the level of voter tabulation districts (which approximate election precincts). The availability and use of block by block racial data was unprecedented; before the 1990 census, data were not broken down beyond the census tract level. By providing uniquely detailed racial data, REDAPPL enabled districters to make more intricate refinements on the basis of race than on the basis of other demographic information. . . .

These findings—that the State substantially neglected traditional districting criteria such as compactness, that it was committed from the outset to creating majority minority districts, and that it manipulated district lines to exploit unprecedentedly detailed racial data—together weigh in favor of the application of strict scrutiny. We do not hold that any one of these factors is independently sufficient to require strict scrutiny. The Constitution does not mandate regularity of district shape, and the neglect of traditional districting criteria is merely necessary, not sufficient. For strict scrutiny to apply, traditional districting criteria must be subordinated to race. Nor, as we have emphasized, is the decision to create a majority minority district objectionable in and of itself. The direct evidence of that decision is not, as Justice Stevens suggests, "the real key" to our decision; it is merely one of several essential ingredients. Nor do we "condemn state legislation merely because it was based on accurate information." The use of sophisticated technology and detailed information in the drawing of majority minority districts is no more objectionable than it is in the drawing of majority majority districts. . . .

Several factors other than race were at work in the drawing of the districts. Traditional districting criteria were not entirely neglected: Districts 18 and 29 maintain the integrity of county lines; each of the three districts takes its character from a principal city and the surrounding urban area; and none of the districts is as widely dispersed as the North Carolina district held unconstitutional in *Shaw II*. (These characteristics are, however, unremarkable in the context of large, densely populated urban counties.) . . .

The population of District 30 is 50% African American and 17.1% Hispanic. Fifty percent of the district's population is located in a compact, albeit irregularly shaped, core in south Dallas, which is 69% African American. But the remainder of the district consists of narrow and bizarrely shaped tentacles—the State identifies seven "segments"—extending primarily to the north and west. Over 98% of the district's population is within Dallas County, but it crosses two county lines at its western and northern extremities. Its western excursion into Tarrant County grabs a small community that is 61.9% African American, its northern excursion into Collin County occupies a hook like shape mapping exactly onto the only area in the southern half of that county with a combined African American and Hispanic percentage population in excess of 50%. . . .

In some circumstances, incumbency protection might explain as well as, or better than, race a State's decision to depart from other traditional districting principles, such as compactness, in the drawing of bizarre district lines. And the fact that, "[a]s it happens, . . . many of the voters being fought over [by the neighboring Democratic incumbents] were African American," would not, in and of itself, convert a political gerrymander into a racial gerrymander, no matter how conscious redistricters were of the correlation between race and party affiliation. If district lines merely correlate with race because they are drawn on the basis of political affiliation, which correlates with race, there is no racial classification to justify, just as racial disproportions in the level of prosecutions for a particular crime may be unobjectionable if they merely reflect racial disproportions in the commission of that crime. . . .

If the promise of the Reconstruction Amendments, that our Nation is to be free of state sponsored discrimination, is to be upheld, we cannot pick and choose between the basic forms of political participation in our efforts to eliminate unjustified racial stereotyping by government actors. . . .

Finally, and most significantly, the objective evidence provided by the district plans and demographic maps suggests strongly the predominance of race. Given that the districting software used by the State provided only racial data at the block by block level, the fact that District 30, unlike Johnson's original proposal, splits voter tabulation districts and even individual streets in many places, suggests that racial criteria predominated over other districting criteria in determining the district's boundaries. And, despite the strong correlation between race and political affiliation, the maps reveal that political considerations were subordinated to racial classification in the drawing of many of the most extreme and bizarre district lines. For example, the northernmost hook of the district, where it ventures into Collin County, is tailored perfectly to maximize minority population . . . whereas it is far from the shape that would be necessary to maximize the Democratic vote in that area.

The combination of these factors compels us to agree with the District Court that "the contours of Congressional District 30 are unexplainable in terms other than race." It is true that District 30 does not evince a consistent, single minded effort to "segregate" voters on the basis of race, and does not represent "apartheid." But the fact that racial data were used in complex ways, and for multiple objectives, does not mean that race did not predominate over other considerations. The record discloses intensive and pervasive use of race both as a proxy to protect the political fortunes of adjacent incumbents, and for its own sake in maximizing the minority population of District 30 regardless of traditional districting principles. District 30's combination of a bizarre, noncompact shape and overwhelming evidence that that shape was essentially dictated by racial considerations of one form or another is exceptional; Texas Congressional District 6, for example, which Justice Stevens discusses in detail, has only the former characteristic. That combination of characteristics leads us to conclude that District 30 is subject to strict scrutiny.

The United States and the State next contend that the district lines at issue are justified by the State's compelling interest in "ameliorating the effects of racially polarized voting attributable to past and present racial discrimination." In support of that contention, they cite Texas' long history of discrimination against minorities in electoral processes, stretching from the Reconstruction to modern times, including violations of the Constitution and of the VRA. Appellants attempt to link that history to evidence that in recent elections in majority minority districts, "Anglos usually bloc voted against" Hispanic and African American candidates.

A State's interest in remedying discrimination is compelling when two conditions are satisfied. First, the discrimination that the State seeks to remedy must be specific, "identified discrimination"; second, the State "must have had a 'strong basis in evidence' to conclude that remedial action was necessary, 'before it embarks on an affirmative action program.'" *Shaw II*. Here, the only current problem that appellants cite as in need of remediation is alleged vote dilution as a consequence of racial bloc voting . . . which we have assumed to be valid for purposes of this opinion. We have indicated that such problems will not justify race based districting unless "the State employ[s] sound districting principles, and . . . the affected racial group's residential patterns afford the opportunity of creating districts in which they will be in the majority." . . .

This Court has now rendered decisions after plenary consideration in five cases applying the *Shaw I* doctrine (*Shaw I*, *Miller*, *Hays*, *Shaw II*, and this case). The dissenters would have us abandon those precedents, suggesting that fundamental concerns relating to the judicial role are at stake. . . . While we agree that those concerns are implicated here, we believe they point the other way. Our legitimacy requires, above all, that we adhere to stare decisis, especially in such sensitive political contexts as the present, where partisan controversy abounds. Legislators and district courts nationwide have modified their practices—or, rather, reembraced the traditional districting practices that were almost universally followed before the 1990 census—in response to *Shaw I*. Those practices and our precedents, which acknowledge voters as more than mere racial statistics, play an important role in defining the political identity of the American voter. Our Fourteenth Amendment jurisprudence evinces a commitment to eliminate unnecessary and excessive governmental use and reinforcement of racial stereotypes. We decline to retreat from that commitment today. . . .

JUSTICE O'CONNOR, concurring.

I write separately to express my view on two points. First, compliance with the results test of § 2 of the Voting Rights Act (VRA) is a compelling state interest. Second, that test can co exist in principle and in practice with *Shaw v. Reno* (1993), and its progeny, as elaborated in today's opinions. . . .

The results test is violated if, "based on the totality of circumstances, it is shown that the political processes leading to nomination or election in the State or political subdivision are not equally open to participation by members of [e.g., a racial minority group] in that its members have less opportunity than other members of the electorate to participate in the political process and to elect representatives of their choice."

In the 14 years since the enactment of § 2(b), we have interpreted and enforced the obligations that it places on States in a succession of cases, assuming but never directly addressing its constitutionality. Meanwhile, lower courts have unanimously affirmed its constitutionality.

Against this background, it would be irresponsible for a State to disregard the § 2 results test. The Supremacy Clause obliges the States to comply with all constitutional exercises of Congress' power. Statutes are presumed constitutional, and that presumption appears strong here in light of the weight of authority affirming the results test's constitutionality. In addition, fundamental concerns of federalism mandate that States be given some leeway so that they are not "trapped between the competing hazards of liability." We should allow States to assume the constitutionality of § 2 of the Voting Rights Act, including the 1982 amendments. . . .

This conclusion is bolstered by concerns of respect for the authority of Congress under the Reconstruction Amendments. The results test of § 2 is an important part of the apparatus chosen by Congress to effectuate this Nation's commitment "to confront its conscience and fulfill the guarantee of the Constitution" with respect to equality in voting. Congress considered the test "necessary and appropriate to ensure full protection of the Fourteenth and Fifteenth Amendments rights." It believed that without the results test, nothing could be done about "overwhelming evidence of unequal access to the electoral system," or about "voting practices and procedures [that] perpetuate the effects of past purposeful discrimination." And it founded those beliefs on the sad reality that "there still are some communities in our Nation where racial politics do dominate the electoral process." Respect for those legislative conclusions mandates that the § 2 results test be accepted and applied unless and until current lower court precedent is reversed and it is held unconstitutional.

In my view, therefore, the States have a compelling interest in complying with the results test as this Court has interpreted it.

Although I agree with the dissenters about § 2's role as part of our national commitment to racial equality, I differ from them in my belief that that commitment can and must be reconciled with the complementary commitment of our Fourteenth Amendment jurisprudence to eliminate the unjustified use of racial stereotypes. At the same time that we combat the symptoms of racial polarization in politics, we must strive to eliminate unnecessary race based state action that appears to endorse the disease.

JUSTICE THOMAS, with whom JUSTICE SCALIA joins, concurring in the judgment.

In my view, application of strict scrutiny in this case was never a close question. . . .

Strict scrutiny applies to all governmental classifications based on race, and we have expressly held that there is no exception for race based redistricting. While we have recognized the evidentiary difficulty of proving that a redistricting plan is, in fact, a racial gerrymander, we have never suggested that a racial gerrymander is subject to anything less than strict scrutiny. . . .

JUSTICE STEVENS, with whom JUSTICE GINSBURG and JUSTICE BREYER join, dissenting.

Today, the Court strikes down three of Texas' majority minority districts, concluding . . . that their odd shapes reveal that the State impermissibly relied on predominantly racial reasons when it drew the districts as it did. For two reasons, I believe that the Court errs in striking down those districts.

First, I believe that the Court has misapplied its own tests for racial gerrymandering, both by applying strict scrutiny to all three of these districts, and then by concluding that none can meet that scrutiny. In asking whether strict scrutiny should apply, the Court improperly ignores the "complex interplay" of political and geographical considerations that went into the creation of Texas' new congressional districts, and focuses exclusively on the role that race played in the State's decisions to adjust the shape of its districts. A quick comparison of the unconstitutional majority minority districts with three equally bizarre majority Anglo districts . . . demonstrates that race was not necessarily the predominant factor contorting the district lines. I would follow the fair implications of the District Court's findings, and conclude that Texas' entire map is a political, not a racial, gerrymander.

Even if strict scrutiny applies, I would find these districts constitutional, for each considers race only to the extent necessary to comply with the State's responsibilities under the Voting Rights Act while achieving other race neutral political and geographical requirements. The plurality's finding to the contrary unnecessarily restricts the ability of States to conform their behavior to the Voting Rights Act while simultaneously complying with other race neutral goals.

Second, even if I concluded that these districts failed an appropriate application of this still developing law to appropriately read facts, I would not uphold the District Court decision. The decisions issued today serve merely to reinforce my conviction that the Court has, with its "analytically distinct" jurisprudence of racial gerrymandering, struck out into a jurisprudential wilderness that lacks a definable constitutional core and threatens to create harms more significant than any suffered by the individual plaintiffs challenging these districts. Though we travel ever farther from it with each passing decision, I would return to the well traveled path that we left in *Shaw I*.

▼▲▼

The Court's decisions in the racial gerrymandering cases of the 1990s have left little room for state legislatures to draw majority-minority districts in which race is the predominant factor. Justices O'Connor and Kennedy, who have written the Court's opinions in the racial gerrymandering cases since *Shaw I*, did not foreclose the possibility that such districts could survive a challenge under the Equal Protection Clause, holding that when compelling circumstances exist states may emphasize race to improve black electoral representation. In reality, the upshot has been the elimination of many majority-minority districts across the nation, including areas outside the South. Georgia, for example, lost two of its three majority-black districts after *Miller*. But successful federal court challenges have also been brought against minority districts in New York City. There, districts bounded by the rivers and bridges of the city's outer boroughs connecting pockets of African American and Latino voters, often placing them in separate districts, were drawn to maximize minority representation. This trend is certain to continue as long as the Court's decisions in cases from *Shaw I* through *Vera* remain good law.

Beyond legislative mapmaking and line drawing, what has been the fallout from the upheaval in voting rights law in the 1990s? The 1996 congressional elections were closely watched to see whether African American and Latino representatives ousted from their majority-minority districts could win reelection in districts that were now majority-white. The results confounded the expectations of many civil rights groups, which were harshly critical of the Court's racial districting decisions. Every minority incumbent that ran for reelection in districts that were now majority-white was victorious. In suburban Indianapolis, Indiana, which had been affected by the redistricting plan challenged in *Bandemer*, Julia Carson, an African American woman, won an open contest for a congressional seat in a majority-white district, defeating her white male challenger by sixteen percentage points. Minority incumbents have continued to fare well in congressional reelections involving majority-white districts. In 1996, thirty-nine African Americans served in the House of Representatives; through 2000, that figure has remained even. Two black representatives who lost their majority-minority districts after *Miller* retired rather than run for re-election. In both cases, white candidates were victorious. In 2000, no black representative running for re-election lost, regardless of the racial make-up of the district.[47]

These results have led some scholars to question whether majority-minority districts are required to elect minority lawmakers to Congress, or whether the United States has truly arrived as an interracial democracy in which racial bloc voting has diminished to the point where it is no longer a major factor in electoral politics. Political scientists have produced several compelling studies that suggest the solution is somewhere in between. Minorities, especially African Americans, have historically had little success running as challengers in white districts. Once elected, however, their success in getting reelected is not much different from that of white representatives, suggesting that continued electoral success is heavily weighted toward the advantages that incumbency brings.[48] Another interesting note is the absence, in 2000, of a single African American in the U.S. Senate, suggesting that white voters are still reluctant to cross over to vote for minority candidates. Operating within a new set of constitutional constraints, the success of African Americans, Latinos, and other minorities in congressional elections without the support structure of majority-minority districting will remain a closely watched feature of American politics.

The Presidential Election of 2000

In December 2000, the United States Supreme Court was asked to intervene directly in an electoral dispute involving the outcome of the November presidential election, one of the closest and most controversial in American history. The election pitted Republican candidate George W. Bush, the governor of Texas, against Democratic candidate Al Gore, the incumbent vice president, with a third candidate, Ralph Nader, running on the Green Party ticket. Shortly before 8 P.M. on election day, Tuesday, November 7, all the major television networks, which had already begun their reporting of state-by-state outcomes based on exit polls of voters, awarded Florida to Gore. This news stunned many campaign and election analysts, who had widely expected Bush to win Florida. Based on the reported and predicted results from the other states, Gore's win in Florida appeared to assure him of the 270 electoral votes he needed to win the presidency. But as results continued to come in from Florida's panhandle, the state's most solidly Republican region, it soon became clear that the earlier prediction of Gore's victory might not hold. By 10 P.M., the networks had retracted their prediction and decided that Florida was "too close to call."

Midnight passed with still no presidential victor. By around 2:15 A.M., the networks decided, based on the exit polling from around the state, to award Florida to Bush. Told that he would probably lose Florida by around fifty thousand votes, Gore phoned Bush and conceded the election. But forty-five minutes later, as Gore was preparing to deliver his public concession speech before a rally of supporters in Nashville, Tennessee, campaign aides delivered some unexpected and good news: Bush's lead in Florida was now down, at most, to a few thousand votes. Gore then called Bush to tell him he was not prepared to give up. "Let me make sure I understand," Bush said. "You're calling me back to retract your concession." The Texas governor then told Gore that his brother, Florida governor Jeb Bush, had assured him that he had won Florida. "Your younger brother is not the ultimate authority on this," Gore replied.[49]

By 4:15 A.M., the networks had retracted their call of just a few hours earlier that Bush had won Florida. By late the next afternoon, the Florida Division of Elections reported that Bush had received 2,909,135 votes to Gore's 2,907, 351, a margin of 1,784 for the Texas governor. Under Florida law, an automatic machine recount takes place in any election where the margin of victory is less than one half of a percent. On November 10, the automated recount showed that Bush's margin of victory had dropped to 327 votes. Gore pressed ahead for a manual hand recount in four counties, Volusia, Palm Beach, Broward, and Miami-Dade, where he believed thousands of ballots had been improperly "disqualified" by local election officials. Gore campaign officials cited Palm Beach's "butterfly ballot," which lists the names of candidates on the left and right, with holes placed in the middle to make a selection, as one major source of confusion for the county's substantial elderly population. In Miami-Dade, where Democratic turnout had been high, Gore claimed that thousands of ballots had been "undercounted"—that is, marked but not punched all the way through—that were meant for him.

Lawyers for Gore and Bush soon took their dispute to the Florida courts, with the Gore campaign asking for manual hand counts to begin in selected counties where voting "irregularities" appeared most evident. Bush attorneys filed suit in federal district court seeking to have the manual recounts, which had begun in several counties, stopped. After a protracted round of legal battles in the county, state, and federal courts, the Florida Supreme Court, on December 8, handed Gore a major victory by ordering hand counts to begin in selected counties with significant numbers of presidential "undervotes." But the next day, the United States Supreme Court, responding to an emergency appeal by Bush, ordered the hand counts stopped. In his appeal, Governor Bush claimed that the Florida Supreme Court's order for manual recounts had proceeded without any clear standard to tally the votes, a decision which violated the Equal Protection and Due Process Clauses of the Fourteenth Amendment.

The Court's decision to hear the case set off much speculation about its motives. Since the mid-1990s, the Court's conservative majority, consisting of Chief Justice Rehnquist and Justices Kennedy, O'Connor, Scalia, and Thomas, had won several important victories that had reinvigorated the power and independence of the states in the federal system. In three key cases, *United States* v. *Lopez* (1995) (invalidating a federal gun possession law applicable to local school zones) (see Volume I, Chapter 6), *Printz* v. *United States* (1997) (invalidating the "background check" requirement on gun purchases mandated by the Brady Bill) (see Volume I, Chapter 7), and *United States* v. *Morrison* (2000) (striking down a provision of the Violence Against Women Act of 1994 permitting victims of sex crimes to sue their attackers in federal court) (see Volume 1, Chapter 6), the Court, by 5–4 majorities, had struck down congressional legislation requiring states to comply with federal mandates. Together, these three cases marked the most dramatic curtailment of congressional power to legislate in the public interest since the Constitutional Revolution of 1937 (see Chapter 2). Would Kennedy, O'Connor, Rehnquist, Scalia, and Thomas continue along this path and respect the decision of the Florida Supreme Court on a matter of state election law?

All five members of the *Lopez, Printz,* and *Morrison* majorities were appointed by Republican presidents. And since the Court, by agreeing to intervene directly in a presidential election, was entering uncharted waters in American constitutional law, some observers believed that the Court's conservatives were determined to bring the post-election escapades to a conclusion by halting the Florida recount, as George W. Bush had asked. Indeed, Justice Scalia had written in the Court's decision to vacate the Florida Supreme Court's order to continue the recount, "It suffices to say that the issuance of th[is decision] . . . suggests that a majority of the Court, while not deciding the issues presented, believe that the petitioner has a substantial probability of success."[50] Dissenting, Justice Stevens, joined by Breyer, Ginsburg, and Souter, wrote:

> To stop the counting of legal votes, the majority today departs from three venerable rules of judicial restraint that have guided the Court throughout its history. On questions of state law, we have consistently respected the opinions of the highest courts of the States. On questions whose resolution is committed at least in large measure to another branch of the Federal Government, we have construed our own jurisdiction narrowly and exercised it cautiously. On federal constitutional questions that were not fairly presented to the court whose judgment is being reviewed, we have prudently declined to express an opinion. The majority has acted unwisely.[51]

On Monday, December 11, nearly five weeks after Americans had gone to the polls to vote for the next president of the United States, lawyers for George Bush and Al Gore stood before the Supreme Court to argue the case of *Bush* v. *Gore* (2000).

Bush v. *Gore*

531 U.S. 98 (2000)

Governor Bush argued there were two major constitutional questions before the Court in *Bush* v. *Gore*:

1. Did the manual recounts ordered by the Florida Supreme Court establish new standards for resolving presidential election contests that conflicted with existing state law? Governor Bush relied on Article II, Section 1, Clause 2, of the United States Constitution, which provides that each state shall appoint electors "in such manner as the Legislature thereof may direct" to make this argument. Bush alleged that the Florida Supreme Court had changed state election law by ordering hand counts to proceed and by moving the date that the Florida Secretary of State was required to certify the election results.
2. Did the manual recounts ordered by the Florida Supreme Court proceed without a uniform standard across counties and within counties in Florida and thus violate the Equal Protection or Due Process Clauses of the Fourteenth Amendment?

In response, Vice President Gore argued that the Florida Supreme Court's decision raised no federal constitutional question under Article II or the Fourteenth Amendment:

1. The Florida courts retained the primary responsibility to interpret state election law under the Florida Constitution, and nothing in Article II of the United States Constitution authorized the federal courts to intervene.
2. The equal protection issue in the Florida recount, to the extent there was one, involved the right of each Florida voter to have his or her legal vote counted. By refusing to count votes even where voter intent was clear had the effect of disenfranchising thousands of Florida voters.

The Court's decision was 5 to 4. Seven justices agreed in an unsigned *per curiam* opinion that equal protection problems existed with the Florida Supreme Court's order to undertake manual recounts in the counties with serious reports of undervoting. But only five justices, Kennedy, O'Connor, Rehnquist, Stevens, and Thomas, concluded that the constitutional problems were so severe that they warranted halting the recount. Justices Stevens, Souter, Ginsburg, and Breyer all dissented on this point.

PER CURIAM.

The petition presents the following questions: whether the Florida Supreme Court established new standards for resolving Presidential election contests, thereby violating Art. II, § 1, cl. 2, of the United States Constitution . . . and whether the use of standardless manual recounts violates the Equal Protection and Due Process Clauses. With respect to the equal protection question, we find a violation of the Equal Protection Clause.

The closeness of this election, and the multitude of legal challenges which have followed in its wake, have brought into sharp focus a common, if heretofore unnoticed, phenomenon. Nationwide statistics reveal that an estimated 2% of ballots cast do not register a vote for President for whatever reason, including deliberately choosing no candidate at all or some voter error, such as voting for two candidates or insufficiently marking a ballot. In certifying election results, the votes eligible for inclusion in the certification are the votes meeting the properly established legal requirements.

This case has shown that punch card balloting machines can produce an unfortunate number of ballots which are not punched in a clean, complete way by the voter. After the current counting, it is likely legislative bodies nationwide will examine ways to improve the mechanisms and machinery for voting. . . .

The right to vote is protected in more than the initial allocation of the franchise. Equal protection applies as well to the manner of its exercise. Having once granted the right to vote on equal terms, the State may not, by later arbitrary and disparate treatment, value one person's vote over that of another. It must be remembered that "the right of suffrage can be denied by a debasement or dilution of the weight of a citizen's vote just as effectively as by wholly prohibiting the free exercise of the franchise," *Reynolds* v. *Sims* (1964).

There is no difference between the two sides of the present controversy on these basic propositions. Respondents say that the very purpose of vindicating the right to vote justifies the recount procedures now at issue. The question before us, however, is whether the recount procedures the Florida Supreme Court has adopted are consistent with its obligation to avoid arbitrary and disparate treatment of the members of its electorate. . . .

Much of the controversy seems to revolve around ballot cards designed to be perforated by a stylus but which, either through error or deliberate omission, have not been perforated with sufficient precision for a machine to count them. In some cases a piece of the card—a chad—is hanging, say by two corners. In other cases there is no separation at all, just an indentation.

The Florida Supreme Court has ordered that the intent of the voter be discerned from such ballots. For purposes of resolving the equal protection challenge, it is not necessary to decide whether the Florida Supreme Court had the authority under the legislative scheme for resolving election disputes to define what a legal vote is and to mandate a manual recount implementing that definition. The recount mechanisms implemented in response to the decisions of the Florida Supreme Court do not satisfy the minimum requirement for non-arbitrary treatment of voters necessary to secure the fundamental right. Florida's basic command for the count of legally cast votes is to consider the "intent of the voter." This is unobjectionable as an abstract proposition and a starting principle. The problem inheres in the absence of specific standards to ensure its equal application. The formulation of uniform rules to determine intent based on these recurring circumstances is practicable and, we conclude, necessary. . . .

The want of those rules here has led to unequal evaluation of ballots in various respects. As seems to have been acknowledged at oral argument, the standards for accepting or rejecting contested ballots might vary not only from county to county but indeed within a single county from one recount team to another. . . .

An early case in our one person, one vote jurisprudence arose when a State accorded arbitrary and disparate treatment to voters in its different counties, *Gray* v. *Sanders* (1963). The Court found a constitutional violation. We relied on these principles in the context of the Presidential selection process in *Moore* v. *Ogilvie* (1969), where we invalidated a county-based procedure that diluted the influence of citizens in larger counties in the nominating process. There we observed that "[t]he idea that one group can be granted greater voting strength than another is hostile to the one man, one vote basis of our representative government." . . .

The State Supreme Court ratified this uneven treatment. It mandated that the recount totals from two counties, Miami-Dade and Palm Beach, be included in the certified total. The court also appeared to hold *sub silentio* that the recount totals from Broward County, which were not completed until after the original November 14 certification by the Secretary of State, were to be considered part of the new certified vote totals even though the county certification was not contested by Vice President Gore. Yet each of the counties used varying standards to determine what was a legal vote. Broward County used a more forgiving standard than Palm Beach County, and uncovered almost three times as many new votes, a result markedly disproportionate to the difference in population between the counties.

In addition, the recounts in . . . [Miami-Dade, Palm Beach, and Broward Counties] were not limited to so-called undervotes but extended to all of the ballots. The distinction has real consequences. A manual recount of all ballots identifies not only those ballots which show no vote but also those which contain more than one, the so-called overvotes. Neither category will be counted by the machine. This is not a trivial concern. At oral argument, respondents estimated there are as many as 110,000 overvotes statewide. As a result, the citizen whose ballot was not read by a machine because he failed to vote for a candidate in a way readable by a machine may still have his vote counted in a manual recount; on the other hand, the citizen who marks two candidates in a way discernable by the machine will not have the same opportunity to have his vote count, even if a manual examination of the ballot would reveal the requisite indicia of intent. Furthermore, the citizen who marks two candidates, only one of which is discernable by the machine, will have his vote counted even though it should have been read as an invalid ballot. The State Supreme Court's inclusion of vote counts based on these variant standards exemplifies concerns with the remedial processes that were under way.

That brings the analysis to yet a further equal protection problem. The votes certified by the court included a partial total from one county, Miami-Dade. The Florida Supreme Court's decision thus gives no assurance that the recounts included in a final certification must be complete. Indeed, it is respondent's submission that it would be consistent with the rules of the recount procedures to include whatever partial counts are done by the time of final certification, and we interpret the Florida Supreme Court's decision to permit this. This accommodation no doubt results from the truncated contest period established by the Florida Supreme Court in *Bush* [v. *Gore*] *I*, at respondents' own urging. The press of time does not diminish the constitutional concern. A desire for speed is not a general excuse for ignoring equal protection guarantees.

In addition to these difficulties the actual process by which the votes were to be counted under the Florida Supreme Court's decision raises further concerns. That order did not specify who would recount the ballots. The county canvassing boards were forced to pull together ad hoc teams comprised of judges from various Circuits who had no previous training in handling and interpreting ballots. Furthermore, while others were permitted to observe, they were prohibited from objecting during the recount. . . .

The question before the Court is not whether local entities, in the exercise of their expertise, may develop different systems for implementing elections. Instead, we are presented with a situation where a state court with the power to assure uniformity has ordered a statewide recount with minimal procedural safeguards. When a court orders a statewide remedy, there must be at least some assurance that the rudimentary requirements of equal treatment and fundamental fairness are satisfied.

Given the Court's assessment that the recount process underway was probably being conducted in an unconstitutional manner, the Court stayed the order directing the recount so it could hear this case and render an expedited decision. The contest provision, as it was mandated by the State Supreme Court, is not well calculated to sustain the confidence that all citizens must have in the outcome of elections. The State has not shown that its procedures include the necessary safeguards. The problem, for instance, of the estimated 110,000 overvotes has not been addressed, although Chief Justice Wells called attention to the concern in his dissenting opinion.

Upon due consideration of the difficulties identified to this point, it is obvious that the recount cannot be conducted in compliance with the requirements of equal protection and due process without substantial additional work. It would require not only the adoption (after opportunity for argument) of adequate statewide standards for determining what is a legal vote, and practicable procedures to implement them, but also orderly judicial review of any disputed matters that might arise. In addition, the Secretary of State has advised that the recount of only a portion of the ballots requires that the vote tabulation equipment be used to screen out undervotes, a function for which the machines were not designed. If a recount of overvotes were also required, perhaps even a second screening would be necessary. Use of the equipment for this purpose, and any new software developed for it, would have to be evaluated for accuracy by the Secretary of State. . . .

[Florida law] . . . requires that any controversy or contest that is designed to lead to a conclusive selection of electors be completed by December 12. That date is upon us, and there is no recount procedure in place under the State Supreme Court's order that comports with minimal constitutional standards. Because it is evident that any recount seeking to meet the December 12 date will be unconstitutional for the reasons we have discussed, we reverse the judgment of the Supreme Court of Florida ordering a recount to proceed.

Seven Justices of the Court agree that there are constitutional problems with the recount ordered by the Florida Supreme Court that demand a remedy. (SOUTER, J., dissenting); (BREYER, J., dissenting). The only disagreement is as to the remedy. . . .

. . .

None are more conscious of the vital limits on judicial authority than are the members of this Court, and none stand more in admiration of the Constitution's design to leave the selection of the President to the people, through their legislatures, and to the political sphere. When contending parties invoke the process of the courts, however, it becomes our unsought responsibility to resolve the federal and constitutional issues the judicial system has been forced to confront.

The judgment of the Supreme Court of Florida is reversed, and the case is remanded for further proceedings not inconsistent with this opinion. . . .

It is so ordered.

CHIEF JUSTICE REHNQUIST, with whom JUSTICE SCALIA and JUSTICE THOMAS join, concurring.

In most cases, . . . respect for federalism compels us to defer to the decisions of state courts on issues of state law. That practice reflects our understanding that the decisions of state courts are definitive pronouncements of the will of the States as sovereigns. Of course, in ordinary cases, the distribution of powers among the branches of a State's government raises no questions of federal constitutional law, subject to the requirement that the government be republican in character. But there are a few exceptional cases in which the Constitution imposes a duty or confers a power on a particular branch of a State's government. This is one of them. Article II, § 1, cl. 2, provides that "[e]ach State shall appoint, in such Manner as the Legislature thereof may direct," electors for President and Vice President. Thus, the text of the election law itself, and not just its interpretation by the courts of the States, takes on independent significance. . . .

In Florida, the legislature has chosen to hold statewide elections to appoint the State's 25 electors. Importantly, the legislature has delegated the authority to run the elections and to oversee election disputes to the Secretary of State (Secretary), Fla. Isolated sections of the code may well admit of more than one interpretation, but the general coherence of the legislative scheme may not be altered by judicial interpretation so as to wholly change the statutorily provided apportionment of responsibility among these various bodies. In any election but a Presidential election, the Florida Supreme Court can give as little or as much deference to Florida's executives as it chooses, so far as Article II is concerned, and this Court will have no cause to question the court's actions. But, with respect to a Presidential election, the court must be both mindful of the legislature's role under Article II in choosing the manner of appointing electors and deferential to those bodies expressly empowered by the legislature to carry out its constitutional mandate.

JUSTICE STEVENS, with whom JUSTICE GINSBURG and JUSTICE BREYER join, dissenting.

The Constitution assigns to the States the primary responsibility for determining the manner of selecting the Presidential electors. When questions arise about the meaning of state laws, including election laws, it is our settled practice to accept the opinions of the highest courts of the States as providing the final answers. On rare occasions, however, either federal statutes or the Federal Constitution may require federal judicial intervention in state elections. This is not such an occasion.

The federal questions that ultimately emerged in this case are not substantial. Article II provides that "[e]ach State shall appoint, in such Manner as the Legislature thereof may direct, a Number of Electors." It does not create state legislatures out of whole cloth, but rather takes them as they come—as creatures born of, and constrained by, their state constitutions. Lest there be any doubt, we stated over 100 years ago in *McPherson* v. *Blacker* (1892), that "[w]hat is forbidden or required to be done by a State" in the Article II context "is forbidden or required of the legislative power under state constitutions as they exist." In the same vein, we also observed that "[t]he [State's] legislative power is the supreme authority except as limited by the constitution of the State." The legislative power in Florida is subject to judicial review pursuant to Article V of the Florida Constitution, and nothing in Article II of the Federal Constitution frees the state legislature from the constraints in the state constitution that created it. Moreover, the Florida Legislature's own decision to employ a unitary code for all elections indicates that it intended the Florida Supreme Court to play the same role in Presidential elections that it has historically played in resolving electoral disputes. The Florida Supreme Court's exercise of appellate jurisdiction therefore was wholly consistent with, and indeed contemplated by, the grant of authority in Article II.

It hardly needs stating that Congress, pursuant to 3 U.S.C. § 5, did not impose any affirmative duties upon the States that their governmental branches could "violate." Rather, § 5 provides a safe harbor for States to select electors in contested elections "by judicial or other methods" established by laws prior to the election day. Section 5, like Article II, assumes the involvement of the state judiciary in interpreting state election laws and resolving election disputes under those laws. Neither § 5 nor Article II grants federal judges any special authority to substitute their views for those of the state judiciary on matters of state law. . . .

Admittedly, the use of differing substandards for determining voter intent in different counties employing similar voting systems may raise serious concerns. Those concerns are alleviated—if not eliminated—by the fact that a single impartial magistrate will ultimately adjudicate all objections arising from the recount process. Of course, as a general matter, "[t]he interpretation of constitutional principles must not be too literal. We must remember that the machinery of government would not work if it were not allowed a little play in its joints." If it were otherwise, Florida's decision to leave to each county the determination of what balloting system to employ—despite enormous differences in accuracy—might run afoul of equal protection. So, too, might the similar decisions of the vast majority of state legislatures to delegate to local authorities certain decisions with respect to voting systems and ballot design. . . .

What must underlie petitioners' entire federal assault on the Florida election procedures is an unstated lack of confidence in the impartiality and capacity of the state judges who would make the critical decisions if the vote count were to proceed. Otherwise, their position is wholly without merit. The endorsement of that position by the majority of this Court can only lend credence to the most cynical appraisal of the work of judges throughout the land. It is confidence in the men and women who administer the judicial system that is the true backbone of the rule of law. Time will one day heal the wound to that confidence that will be inflicted by today's decision. One thing, however, is certain. Although we may never know with complete certainty the identity of the winner of this year's Presidential election, the identity of the loser is perfectly clear. It is the Nation's confidence in the judge as an impartial guardian of the rule of law.

I respectfully dissent.

JUSTICE SOUTER, with whom JUSTICE BREYER joins and with whom JUSTICE STEVENS and JUSTICE GINSBURG join with regard to all but Part C, dissenting.

The Court should not have reviewed either *Bush* v. *Palm Beach County Canvassing Bd.* or this case, and should not have stopped Florida's attempt to recount all undervote ballots, by issuing a stay of the Florida Supreme Court's orders during the period of this review. If this Court had allowed the State to follow the course indicated by the opinions of its own Supreme Court, it is entirely possible that there would ultimately have been no issue requiring our review, and political tension could have worked itself out in the Congress following the procedure provided in 3 U.S.C. § 15. The case being before us, however, its resolution by the majority is another erroneous decision. . . .

C

In deciding what to do about this, we should take account of the fact that electoral votes are due to be cast in six days. I would therefore remand the case to the courts of Florida with instructions to establish uniform standards for evaluating the several types of ballots that have prompted differing treatments, to be applied within and among counties when passing on such identical ballots in any further recounting (or successive recounting) that the courts might order.

Unlike the majority, I see no warrant for this Court to assume that Florida could not possibly comply with this requirement before the date set for the meeting of electors, December 18. Although one of the dissenting justices of the State Supreme Court estimated that disparate standards potentially affected 170,000 votes, the number at issue is significantly smaller. The 170,000 figure apparently represents all uncounted votes, both undervotes (those for which no Presidential choice was recorded by a machine) and overvotes (those rejected because of votes for more than one candidate. But as JUSTICE BREYER has pointed out, no showing has been made of legal overvotes uncounted, and counsel for Gore made an uncontradicted representation to the Court that the statewide total of undervotes is about 60,000. To recount these manually would be a tall order, but before this Court stayed the effort to do that the courts of Florida were ready to do their best to get that job done. There is no justification for denying the State the opportunity to try to count all disputed ballots now.

I respectfully dissent.

JUSTICE GINSBURG, with whom JUSTICE STEVENS joins, and with whom JUSTICE SOUTER and JUSTICE BREYER join as to Part I, dissenting.

I

The CHIEF JUSTICE acknowledges that provisions of Florida's Election Code "may well admit of more than one interpretation." But instead of respecting the state high court's province to say what the State's Election Code means, THE CHIEF JUSTICE maintains that Florida's Supreme Court has veered so far from the ordinary practice of judicial review that what it did cannot properly be called judging. My colleagues have offered a reasonable construction of Florida's law. Their construction coincides with the view of one of Florida's seven Supreme Court justices. I might join THE CHIEF JUSTICE were it my commission to interpret Florida law. But disagreement with the Florida court's interpretation of its own State's law does not warrant the conclusion that the justices of that court have legislated. There is no cause here to believe that the members of Florida's high court have done less than "their mortal best to discharge their oath of office," and no cause to upset their reasoned interpretation of Florida law. . . .

In deferring to state courts on matters of state law, we appropriately recognize that this Court acts as an "'outside[r]' lacking the common exposure to local law which comes from sitting in the jurisdiction." That recognition has sometimes prompted us to resolve doubts about the meaning of state law by certifying issues to a State's highest court, even when federal rights are at stake. Notwithstanding our authority to decide issues of state law underlying federal claims, we have used the certification devise to afford state high courts an opportunity to inform us on matters of their own State's law because such restraint "helps build a cooperative judicial federalism." . . .

The extraordinary setting of this case has obscured the ordinary principle that dictates its proper resolution: Federal courts defer to state high courts' interpretations of their state's own law. This principle reflects the core of federalism, on which all agree. "The Framers split the atom of sovereignty. It was the genius of their idea that our citizens would have two political capacities, one state and one federal, each protected from incursion by the other." The CHIEF JUSTICE's solicitude for the Florida Legislature comes at the expense of the more fundamental solicitude we owe to the legislature's sovereign. U.S. Const., Art. II, § 1, cl. 2. Were the other members of this Court as mindful as they generally are of our system of dual sovereignty, they would affirm the judgment of the Florida Supreme Court.

II

I agree with JUSTICE STEVENS that petitioners have not presented a substantial equal protection claim. Ideally, perfection would be the appropriate standard for judging the recount. But we live in an imperfect world, one in which thousands of votes have not been counted. I cannot agree that the recount adopted by the Florida court, flawed as it may be, would yield a result any less fair or precise than the certification that preceded that recount. Even if there were an equal protection violation, I would agree with JUSTICE STEVENS, JUSTICE SOUTER, and JUSTICE BREYER that the Court's concern about "the December 12 deadline," is misplaced. Time is short in part because of the Court's entry of a stay on December 9, several hours after an able circuit judge in Leon County had begun to superintend the recount process. More fundamentally, the Court's reluctance to let the recount go forward—despite its suggestion that "[t]he search for intent can be confined by specific rules designed to ensure uniform treatment," ultimately turns on its own judgment about the practical realities of implementing a recount, not the judgment of those much closer to the process. . . .

The Court assumes that time will not permit "orderly judicial review of any disputed matters that might arise." But no one has doubted the good faith and diligence with which Florida election officials, attorneys for all sides of this controversy, and the courts of law have performed their duties. Notably, the Florida Supreme Court has produced two substantial opinions within 29 hours of oral argument. In sum, the Court's conclusion that a constitutionally adequate recount is impractical is a prophecy the

Court's own judgment will not allow to be tested. Such an untested prophecy should not decide the Presidency of the United States.

I dissent.

JUSTICE BREYER, with whom JUSTICE STEVENS and JUSTICE GINSBURG join except as to Part I-A-1, and with whom JUSTICE SOUTER joins as to Part I, dissenting.

The Court was wrong to take this case. It was wrong to grant a stay. It should now vacate that stay and permit the Florida Supreme Court to decide whether the recount should resume.

I

The political implications of this case for the country are momentous. But the federal legal questions presented, with one exception, are insubstantial.

A

1

The majority raises three Equal Protection problems with the Florida Supreme Court's recount order: first, the failure to include overvotes in the manual recount; second, the fact that all ballots, rather than simply the undervotes, were recounted in some, but not all, counties; and third, the absence of a uniform, specific standard to guide the recounts. As far as the first issue is concerned, petitioners presented no evidence, to this Court or to any Florida court, that a manual recount of overvotes would identify additional legal votes. The same is true of the second, and, in addition, the majority's reasoning would seem to invalidate any state provision for a manual recount of individual counties in a statewide election.

The majority's third concern does implicate principles of fundamental fairness. The majority concludes that the Equal Protection Clause requires that a manual recount be governed not only by the uniform general standard of the "clear intent of the voter," but also by uniform subsidiary standards (for example, a uniform determination whether indented, but not perforated, "undervotes" should count). The opinion points out that the Florida Supreme Court ordered the inclusion of Broward County's undercounted "legal votes" even though those votes included ballots that were not perforated but simply "dimpled," while newly recounted ballots from other counties will likely include only votes determined to be "legal" on the basis of a stricter standard. In light of our previous remand, the Florida Supreme Court may have been reluctant to adopt a more specific standard than that provided for by the legislature for fear of exceeding its authority under Article II. However, since the use of different standards could favor one or the other of the candidates, since time was, and is, too short to permit the lower courts to iron out significant differences through ordinary judicial review, and since the relevant distinction was embodied in the order of the State's highest court, I agree that, in these very special circumstances, basic principles of fairness may well have counseled the adoption of a uniform standard to address the problem. In light of the majority's disposition, I need not decide whether, or the extent to which, as a remedial matter, the Constitution would place limits upon the content of the uniform standard. . . .

Of course, the selection of the President is of fundamental national importance. But that importance is political, not legal. And this Court should resist the temptation unnecessarily to resolve tangential legal disputes, where doing so threatens to determine the outcome of the election.

The Constitution and federal statutes themselves make clear that restraint is appropriate. They set forth a road map of how to resolve disputes about electors, even after an election as close as this one. That road map foresees resolution of electoral disputes by state courts. But it nowhere provides for involvement by the United States Supreme Court.

To the contrary, the Twelfth Amendment commits to Congress the authority and responsibility to count electoral votes. A federal statute, the Electoral Count Act, enacted after the close 1876 Hayes-Tilden Presidential election, specifies that, after States have tried to resolve disputes (through "judicial" or other means), Congress is the body primarily authorized to resolve remaining disputes. . . .

The decision by both the Constitution's Framers and the 1886 Congress to minimize this Court's role in resolving close federal presidential elections is as wise as it is clear. However awkward or difficult it may be for Congress to resolve difficult electoral disputes, Congress, being a political body, expresses the people's will far more accurately than does an unelected Court. And the people's will is what elections are about. . . .

[T]he Court is not acting to vindicate a fundamental constitutional principle, such as the need to protect a basic human liberty. No other strong reason to act is present. Congressional statutes tend to obviate the need. And, above all, in this highly politicized matter, the appearance of a split decision runs the risk of undermining the public's confidence in the Court itself. That confidence is a public treasure. It has been built slowly over many years, some of which were marked by a Civil War and the tragedy of segregation. It is a vitally necessary ingredient of any successful effort to protect basic liberty and, indeed, the rule of law itself. We run no risk of returning to the days when a President (responding to this Court's efforts to protect the Cherokee Indians) might have said, "John Marshall has made his decision; now let him enforce it!" But we do risk a self-inflicted wound—a wound that may harm not just the Court, but the Nation.

I fear that in order to bring this agonizingly long election process to a definitive conclusion, we have not adequately attended to that necessary "check upon our own exercise of power," "our own sense of self-restraint." Justice Brandeis once said of the Court, "The most important thing we do is not doing." What it does today, the Court should have left undone. I would repair the damage done as best we now can, by permitting the Florida recount to continue under uniform standards.

I respectfully dissent.

Note the stark contrast between the concurring opinion of Chief Justice Rehnquist, who believed that the dispute over the Florida vote recount presented a clear set of federal constitutional questions, and the dissenting opinions of Justices Stevens, Ginsburg, and Breyer, who all argued that the federal courts had no proper jurisdiction over what they believed was a matter of state law. Breyer and Souter were the two justices in the minority who agreed with the Court's *per curiam* opinion that equal protection problems existed with the Florida recount as ordered by the Florida Supreme Court. They each believed, however, that the case should have been remanded to the Florida Supreme Court with instructions to provide a more uniform standard for recounting all the undercounted votes in Florida, including those from Broward, Volusia, Palm Beach, and Miami-Dade counties.

Of the four dissenting justices in *Bush* v. *Gore,* two, Stevens (by Ford, 1975) and Souter (by George H. W. Bush, 1990), were appointed by Republican presidents. Ginsburg and Breyer were appointed by Democrat Bill Clinton in 1993 and 1994, respectively. The Court, then, did not divide along party lines. But the decision of the *Bush* majority to set aside the Florida Supreme Court's ruling on a matter of law traditionally the responsibility of state courts to decide led some critics to charge that it had intervened to stop the recount and deliver the election to Governor Bush. Read carefully, the opinions of the dissenting justices in *Bush* suggest that the Court's decision carried clear partisan overtones. The majority, on the other hand, argued that its intervention was appropriate because the Florida Supreme Court had allowed a recount to proceed with no clear standards, violating the right of Florida voters of the "rudimentary requirements of equal treatment and fundamental fairness."

Although the Bush majority claimed that its decision was narrow and applicable only to Florida election law, Justice Stevens suggested that applying equal protection standards to ballot recounting might mean that the federal courts were now authorized to oversee the voting systems and ballot designs of "the vast majority of state legislatures." Whether *Bush* stands as an exception to or expansion of the role of the federal courts in state electoral processes remains to be seen. Either way, *Bush* was a momentous decision that demonstrated the many intersections, some subtle and some not, that exist between law and politics under the Constitution.

FOR FURTHER READING

Ayers, Edward. *The Promise of the New South.* New York: Oxford University Press, 1992.

Black, Earl, and Merle Black. *Politics and Society in the South.* Cambridge, Mass.: Harvard University Press, 1987.

Canon, David T. *Race, Redistricting, and Representation: The Unintended Consequences of Black Majority Districts.* Chicago: University of Chicago Press, 1999.

Cortner, Richard C. *The Apportionment Cases.* Knoxville: University of Tennessee Press, 1970.

Davidson, Chandler, and Bernard Grofman, eds. *Quiet Revolution in the South: The Impact of the Voting Rights Act, 1965–1990.* Princeton, N.J.: Princeton University Press, 1994.

Foner, Eric. *Reconstruction, 1863–1877: America's Unfinished Revolution.* New York: Harper & Row, 1988.

Garrow, David J. *Protest at Selma*. New Haven, Conn.: Yale University Press, 1978.

Guiner, Lani. *The Tyranny of the Majority: Fundamental Fairness and Representative Democracy.* New York: Free Press, 1994.

Kinder, Donald R., and Lynn M. Sanders. *Divided by Color: Racial Politics and Democratic Ideals.* Chicago: University of Chicago Press, 1997.

Kousser, J. Morgan. *Colorblind Injustice: Minority Voting Rights and the Undoing of the Second Reconstruction.* Chapel Hill: University of North Carolina Press, 1999.

Lublin, David. *The Paradox of Representation*. Princeton, N.J.: Princeton University Press, 1997.

Parker, Frank R. *Black Votes Count: Political Power in Mississippi After 1965.* Chapel Hill: University of North Carolina Press, 1990.

Swain, Carol. *Black Faces, Black Interests: The Representation of African Americans in Congress.* Cambridge, Mass.: Harvard University Press, 1993.

Scher, Richard K., Jon L. Mills, and John J. Hotaling. *Voting Rights and Democracy: The Law and Politics of Districting.* Chicago: Nelson-Hall Publishers, 1997.

Thernstrom, Abigail. *Whose Votes Count?* Cambridge, Mass.: Harvard University Press, 1987.

Appendix 1

The Constitution of the United States

We the People of the United States, in Order to form a more perfect Union, establish Justice, insure domestic Tranquility, provide for the common defence, promote the general Welfare, and secure the Blessings of Liberty to ourselves and our Posterity, do ordain and establish this Constitution for the United States of America.

Article I.

Section 1. All legislative Powers herein granted shall be vested in a Congress of the United States, which shall consist of a Senate and House of Representatives.

Section 2. The House of Representatives shall be composed of Members chosen every second Year by the People of the several States, and the Electors in each State shall have the Qualifications requisite for Electors of the most numerous Branch of the State Legislature.

No person shall be a Representative who shall not have attained to the age of twenty five Years, and been seven Years a Citizen of the United States, and who shall not, when elected, be an Inhabitant of that State in which he shall be chosen.

Representatives and direct Taxes shall be apportioned among the several States which may be included within this Union, according to their respective Numbers, which shall be determined by adding to the whole Number of free Persons, including those bound to Service for a Term of Years, and excluding Indians not taxed, three fifths of all other Persons.[1] The actual Enumeration shall be made within three Years after the first Meeting of the Congress of the United States, and within every subsequent Term of ten Years, in such Manner as they shall by Law direct. The Number of Representatives shall not exceed one for every thirty Thousand, but each State shall have at Least one Representative; and until such enumeration shall be made, the State of New Hampshire shall be entitled to chuse three, Massachusetts eight, Rhode-Island and Providence Plantations one, Connecticut five, New-York six, New Jersey four, Pennsylvania eight, Delaware one, Maryland six, Virginia ten, North Carolina five, South Carolina five, and Georgia three.

When vacancies happen in the Representation from any State, the Executive Authority thereof shall issue Writs of Election to fill such Vacancies.

The House of Representatives shall chuse their Speaker and other Officers; and shall have the sole Power of Impeachment.

Section 3. The Senate of the United States shall be composed of two Senators from each State, *chosen by the Legislature thereof,*[2] for six Years; and each Senator shall have one Vote.

Immediately after they shall be assembled in Consequence of the first Election, they shall be divided as equally as may be into three Classes. The Seats of the Senators of the first class shall be vacated at the Expiration of the second Year, of the second Class at the Expiration of the fourth Year, and of the third Class at the Expiration of the sixth Year, so that one third may be chosen every second Year; *and if Vacancies happen by Resignation, or otherwise, during the Recess of the Legislature of any State, the Executive thereof may make temporary Appointments until the next Meeting of the Legislature, which shall then fill such Vacancies.*[3]

No Person shall be a Senator who shall not have attained to the Age of thirty Years, and been nine Years a Citizen of the United States, and who shall not, when elected, be an Inhabitant of that State for which he shall be chosen.

The Vice President of the United States shall be President of the Senate, but shall have no Vote, unless they be equally divided.

The Senate shall chuse their other Officers, and also a President pro tempore, in the Absence of the Vice President, or when he shall exercise the Office of President of the United States.

The Senate shall have the sold Power to try all Impeachments. When sitting for that Purpose, they shall

Note: Those portions set in italic type have been superseded or changed by later amendments.

[1] Changed by the Fourteenth Amendment, Section 2.

[2] Changed by the Seventeenth Amendment.

[3] Changed by the Seventeenth Amendment.

be on Oath or Affirmation. When the President of the United States is tried the Chief Justice shall preside: And no Person shall be convicted without the Concurrence of two thirds of the Members present.

Judgment in Cases of Impeachment shall not extend further than to removal from Office, and disqualification to hold and enjoy any Office of honor, Trust or Profit under the United States: but the Party convicted shall nevertheless be liable and subject to Indictment, Trial, Judgment and Punishment, according to Law.

Section 4. The Times, Places and Manner of holding Elections for Senators and Representatives, shall be prescribed in each State by the Legislature thereof; but the Congress may at any time by Law make or alter such Regulations, except as to the Places of chusing Senators.

The Congress shall assemble at least once in every Year, and such Meeting shall be on the *first Monday in December, unless they shall by Law appoint a different Day.*[4]

Section 5. Each House shall be the Judge of the Elections, Returns and Qualifications of its own Members, and a Majority of each shall constitute a Quorum to do Business; but a smaller number may adjourn from day to day, and may be authorized to compel the Attendance of absent Members, in such Manner, and under such Penalties as each House may provide.

Each House may determine the Rules of its Proceedings, punish its Members for disorderly Behaviour, and, with the Concurrence of two thirds, expel a Member.

Each House shall keep a Journal of its Proceedings, and from time to time publish the same, excepting such Parts as may in their Judgment require Secrecy; and the Yeas and Nays of the Members of either House on any question shall, at the Desire of one fifth of those Present, be entered on the Journal.

Neither House, during the Session of Congress, shall, without the Consent of the other, adjourn for more than three days, nor to any other Place than that in which the two Houses shall be sitting.

Section 6. The Senators and Representatives shall receive a Compensation for their Services, to be ascertained by Law, and paid out of the Treasury of the United States. They shall in all Cases, except Treason, Felony and Breach of the Peace, be privileged from Arrest during their Attendance at the Session of their respective Houses, and in going to and returning from the same; and for any Speech or Debate in either House, they shall not be questioned in any other Place.

[4] Changed by the Twentieth Amendment, Section 2.

No Senator or Representative shall, during the Time for which he was elected, be appointed to any civil Office under the Authority of the United States, which shall have been created, or the Emoluments whereof shall have been encreased during such time; and no Person holding any Office under the United States, shall be a Member of either House during his Continuance in Office.

Section 7. All Bills for raising Revenue shall originate in the House of Representatives; but the Senate may propose or concur with Amendments as on other Bills.

Every Bill which shall have passed the House of Representatives and the Senate, shall, before it become a Law, be presented to the President of the United States; If he approve he shall sign it, but if not he shall return it, with Objections to that House in which it shall have originated, who shall enter the Objections at large on their Journal, and proceed to reconsider it. If after such Reconsideration two thirds of that House shall agree to pass the Bill, it shall be sent, together with the Objections, to the other House, by which it shall likewise be reconsidered, and if approved by two thirds of that House, it shall become a Law. But in all such Cases the Votes of both Houses shall be determined by yeas and Nays, and the Names of the Persons voting for and against the Bill shall be entered on the Journal of each House respectively. If any Bill shall not be returned by the President within ten days (Sundays excepted) after it shall have been presented to him, the Same shall be a Law, in like Manner, as if he had signed it, unless the Congress by their Adjournment prevent its Return, in which Case it shall not be a Law.

Every Order, Resolution, or Vote to which the Concurrence of the Senate and House of Representatives may be necessary (except on a question of Adjournment) shall be presented to the President of the United States; and before the Same shall take Effect, shall be approved by him, or being disapproved by him, shall be repassed by two thirds of the Senate and House of Representatives, according to the Rules and Limitations prescribed in the Case of a Bill.

Section 8. The Congress shall have Power To lay and Collect Taxes, Duties, Imposts and Excises, to pay the Debts and provide for the common Defence and general Welfare of the United States; but all Duties, Imposts and Excises shall be uniform throughout the United States.

To borrow Money on the credit of the United States;

To regulate Commerce with foreign Nations, and among the several States, and with the Indian Tribes;

To establish an uniform Rule of Naturalization, and uniform Laws on the subject of Bankruptcies throughout the United States;

To coin Money, regulate the Value thereof, and of foreign Coin, and fix the Standard of Weights and Measures;

To provide for the Punishment of counterfeiting the Securities and current Coin of the United States;

To establish Post Offices and post Roads;

To promote the Progress of Science and useful Arts, by securing for limited Times to Authors and Inventors the exclusive Right to their respective Writings and Discoveries;

To constitute Tribunals inferior to the Supreme Court;

To define and punish Piracies and Felonies committed on the high Seas, and Offences against the Law of Nations;

To declare War, grant Letters of Marque and Reprisal, and make Rules concerning Captures on Land and Water;

To raise and support Armies, but no Appropriation of Money to that Use shall be for a longer Term than two Years;

To provide and maintain a Navy;

To make Rules for the Government and Regulation of the land and naval Forces;

To provide for calling forth the Militia to execute the Laws of the Union, suppress Insurrections and repel Invasions;

To provide for organizing, arming, and disciplining, the Militia, and for governing such Part of them as may be employed in the Service of the United States, reserving to the States respectively, the Appointment of the Officers, and the Authority of training the Militia according to the discipline prescribed by Congress;

To exercise exclusive Legislation in all Cases whatsoever, over such District (not exceeding ten Miles square) as may, by Cession of Particular States, and the Acceptance of Congress, become the Seat of the Government of the United States, and to exercise like Authority over all Places purchased by the Consent of the Legislature of the State in which the Same shall be, for the Erection of Forts, Magazines, Arsenals, dock-Yards and other needful Buildings;—And

To make all Laws which shall be necessary and proper for carrying into Execution the foregoing Powers, and all other Powers vested by this Constitution in the Government of the United States, or in any Department or Officer thereof.

Section 9. The Migration or Importation of such Persons as any of the States now existing shall think proper to admit, shall not be prohibited by the Congress prior to the Year one thousand eight hundred and eight, but a Tax or duty may be imposed on such Importation, not exceeding ten dollars for each Person.

The Privilege of the Writ of Habeas Corpus shall not be suspended, unless when in Cases of Rebellion or Invasion the public Safety may require it.

No bill of Attainder or ex post facto Law shall be passed.

No Capitation, or other direct, Tax shall be laid, *unless in Proportion to the Census or Enumeration herein before directed to be taken.*[5]

No Tax or Duty shall be laid on Articles exported from any State.

No Preference shall be given by any Regulation of Commerce or Revenue to the Ports of one State over those of another; nor shall Vessels bound to, or from, one State, be obliged to enter, clear or pay Duties in another.

No Money shall be drawn from the Treasury, but in Consequence of Appropriations made by Law; and a regular Statement and Account of the Receipts and Expenditures of all public Money shall be published from time to time.

No Title of Nobility shall be granted by the United States: And no Person holding any Office of Profit or Trust under them, shall, without the Consent of the Congress, accept of any present, Emolument, Office, or Title, of any kind whatever, from any King, Prince, or foreign State.

Section 10. No State shall enter into any Treaty, Alliance, or Confederation; grant Letters of Marque and Reprisal; coin Money; emit Bills of Credit; make any Thing but gold and silver Coin a Tender in Payment of Debts; pass any Bill of Attainder, ex post facto Law, or Law impairing the Obligation of Contracts, or grant any Title of Nobility.

No State shall, without the Consent of Congress, lay any Imposts or Duties on Imports or Exports, except what may be absolutely necessary for executing its inspection Laws; and the net Produce of all Duties and Imposts, laid by any State on Imports or Exports, shall be for the Use of the Treasury of the United States; and all such Laws shall be subject to the Revision and Controul of the Congress.

No State shall, without the Consent of Congress, lay any Duty of Tonnage, keep Troops, or Ships of War in time of Peace, enter into any Agreement or Compact

[5] Changed by the Sixteenth Amendment.

with another State, or with a foreign Power, or engage in War, unless actually invaded, or in such imminent Danger as will not admit of delay.

Article II.

Section 1. The executive Power shall be vested in a President of the United States of America. He shall hold his Office during the Term of four Years, and, together with the Vice President, chosen for the same Term, be elected, as follows

Each State shall appoint, in such Manner as the Legislature thereof may direct, a Number of Electors, equal to the whole Number of Senators and Representatives to which the State may be entitled in the Congress: but no Senator or Representative, or Person holding an Office of Trust or Profit under the United States, shall be appointed an Elector.

The Electors shall meet in their respective States, and vote by Ballot for two Persons, of whom one at least shall not be an Inhabitant of the same State with themselves. And they shall make a List of all the Persons voted for, and of the Number of Votes for each; which List they shall sign and certify, and transmit sealed to the Seat of the Government of the United States, directed to the President of the Senate. The President of the Senate shall, in the Presence of the Senate and House of Representatives, open all the Certificates, and the Votes shall then be counted. The Person having the greatest Number of Votes shall be the President, if such Number be a Majority of the whole Number of Electors appointed; and if there be more than one who have such Majority, and have an equal Number of Votes, then the House of Representatives shall immediately chuse by Ballot one of them for President; and if no Person have a Majority, then from the five highest on the List said House shall in like Manner chuse the President. But in chusing the President, the Votes shall be taken by States, the Representation from each State having one Vote; a quorum for this Purpose shall consist of a Member or Members from two thirds of the States, and a Majority of all the States shall be necessary to a Choice. In every Case, after the Choice of the President, the Person having the greatest Number of Votes of the Electors shall be the Vice President. But if there should remain two or more who have equal Votes, the Senate shall chuse from them by Ballot the Vice President.[6]

The Congress may determine the Time of chusing the Electors, and the Day on which they shall give their Votes, which Day shall be the same throughout the United States.

No Person except a natural born Citizen, or a Citizen of the United States, at the time of the Adoption of this Constitution, shall be eligible to the Office of President; neither shall any person be eligible to that Office who shall not have attained to the Age of thirty five Years, and been fourteen Years a Resident within the United States.

In Case of the Removal of the President from Office, or of his Death, Resignation, or Inability to discharge the Powers and Duties of the said Office, the Same shall devolve on the Vice President, and the Congress may by Law provide for the Case of Removal, Death, Resignation or Inability, both of the President and Vice President, declaring what Officer shall then act as President, and such Officer shall act accordingly, until the Disability be removed, or a President shall be elected.[7]

The President shall, at stated Times, receive for his Services, a Compensation, which shall neither be increased nor diminished during the Period for which he shall have been elected, and he shall not receive within that Period any other Emolument from the United States, or any of them.

Before he enter on the Execution of his Office, he shall take the following Oath or Affirmation:—"I do solemnly swear (or affirm) that I will faithfully execute the Office of President of the United States, and will to the best of my Ability preserve, protect and defend the Constitution of the United States."

Section 2. The President shall be Commander in Chief of the Army and Navy of the United States, and of the Militia of the several States, when called into the actual Service of the United States; he may require the Opinion, in writing, of the principal Officer in each of the executive Departments, upon any Subject relating to the Duties of their respective Offices, and he shall have Power to grant Reprieves and Pardons for Offences against the United States, except in Cases of Impeachment.

He shall have Power, by and with the Advice and Consent of the Senate, to make Treaties, provided two thirds of the Senators present concur; and he shall nominate, and by and with the Advice and Consent of the Senate, shall appoint Ambassadors, other public Ministers and Consuls, Judges of the supreme Court, and all other Officers of the United States, whose Appoint-

[6] Superseded by the Twelfth Amendment.

[7] Modified by the Twenty-fifth Amendment.

ments are not herein otherwise provided for, and which shall be established by Law: but the Congress may by Law vest the Appointment of such inferior Officers, as they think proper, in the President alone, in the Courts of Law, or in the Heads of Departments.

The President shall have Power to fill up all Vacancies that may happen during the Recess of the Senate, by granting Commissions which shall expire at the End of their new Session.

Section 3. He shall from time to time give to the Congress Information of the State of the Union, and recommend to their Consideration such Measures as he shall judge necessary and expedient; he may, on extraordinary Occasions, convene both Houses, or either of them, and in Case of Disagreement between them, with Respect to the Time of Adjournment, he may adjourn them to such Time as he shall think proper; he shall receive Ambassadors and other public Ministers; he shall take Care that the Laws be faithfully executed, and shall Commission all the Officers of the United States.

Section 4. The President, Vice President and all civil Officers of the United States, shall be removed from Office on Impeachment for, and Conviction of, Treason, Bribery, or other high Crimes and Misdemeanors.

Article III.

Section 1. The judicial Power of the United States, shall be vested in one supreme Court, and in such inferior Courts as the Congress may from time to time ordain and establish. The Judges, both of the supreme and inferior Courts, shall hold their Offices during good Behaviour, and shall, at stated Times, receive for their Services, a Compensation, which shall not be diminished during their Continuance in Office.

Section 2. The judicial Power shall extend to all Cases, in Law and Equity, arising under this Constitution, the Laws of the United States, and Treaties made, or which shall be made, under their Authority;—to all Cases affecting Ambassadors, other public Ministers and Consuls;—to all Cases of admiralty and maritime Jurisdiction;—to Controversies to which the United States shall be a Party;—to Controversies between two or more States;—*between a State and Citizens of another State;*[8]—between Citizens of different States;—between Citizens of the same State claiming Lands under Grants of different States, and between a State, or the Citizens thereof, and foreign States, Citizens or Subjects.

In all Cases affecting Ambassadors, other public Ministers and Consuls, and those in which a State shall be Party, the supreme Court shall have original Jurisdiction. In all the other Cases before mentioned, the supreme Court shall have appellate Jurisdiction, both as to Law and Fact, with such Exceptions, and under such Regulations as the Congress shall make.

The Trial of all Crimes, except in Cases of Impeachment, shall be by Jury; and such Trial shall be held in the State where the said Crimes shall have been committed; but when not committed within any State, the Trial shall be at such Place or Places as the Congress may by Law have directed.

Section 3. Treason against the United States, shall consist only in levying War against them, or in adhering to their Enemies, giving them Aid and Comfort. No Person shall be convicted of Treason unless on the Testimony of two Witnesses to the same overt Act, or on Confession in open Court.

The Congress shall have Power to declare the Punishment of Treason, but no Attainder of Treason shall work Corruption of Blood, or Forfeiture except during the Life of the Person attainted.

Article IV.

Section 1. Full Faith and Credit shall be given in each State to the public Acts, Records, and judicial Proceedings of every other State. And the Congress may by general Laws prescribe the Manner in which such Acts, Records and Proceedings shall be proved, and the Effect thereof.

Section 2. The Citizens of each State shall be entitled to all Privileges and Immunities of Citizens in the several States.

A person charged in any State with Treason, Felony, or other Crime, who shall flee from Justice, and be found in another State, shall on Demand of the executive Authority of the State from which he fled, be delivered up, to be removed to the State having Jurisdiction of the Crime.

No Person held to Service or Labour in one State, under the Laws thereof, escaping into another, shall, in Consequence of any Law or Regulation therein, be discharged from

[8] Modified by the Eleventh Amendment.

such Service or Labour, but shall be delivered up on Claim of the Party to whom such Service or Labour may be due.[9]

Section 3. New States may be admitted by the Congress into this Union; but no new State shall be formed or erected within the Jurisdiction of any other State; nor any State be formed by the Junction of two or more States, or Parts of States, without the Consent of the Legislatures of the States concerned as well as of the Congress.

The Congress shall have Power to dispose of and make all needful Rules and Regulations respecting the Territory or other Property belonging to the United States; and nothing in this Constitution shall be so construed as to Prejudice any Claims of the United States, or of any particular State.

Section 4. The United States shall guarantee to every State in this Union a Republican Form of Government, and shall protect each of them against Invasion; and on Application of the Legislature, or of the Executive (when the Legislature cannot be convened) against domestic Violence.

Article V.

The Congress, whenever two thirds of both Houses shall deem it necessary, shall propose Amendments to this Constitution, or, on the Application of the Legislatures of two thirds of the several States, shall call a Convention for proposing Amendments, which, in either Case, shall be valid to all Intents and Purposes, as Part of this Constitution, when ratified by the Legislatures of three fourths of the several States, or by Conventions in three fourths thereof, as the one or the other Mode of Ratification may be proposed by the Congress; Provided that no Amendment which may be made prior to the Year One thousand eight hundred and eight shall in any Manner after the first and fourth Clauses in the Ninth Section of the first Article; and that no State, without its Consent, shall be deprived of its equal Suffrage in the Senate.

Article VI.

All Debts contracted and Engagements entered into, before the Adoption of this Constitution, shall be as valid against the United States under this Constitution, as under the Confederation.

[9]Changed by the Thirteenth Amendment.

This Constitution, and the Laws of the United States which shall be made in Pursuance thereof; and all Treaties made, or which shall be made, under the Authority of the United States, shall be the Supreme Law of the Land; and the Judges in every State shall be bound thereby, any Thing in the Constitution or Laws of any State to the Contrary notwithstanding.

The Senators and Representatives before mentioned, and the Members of the several State Legislatures, and all executive and judicial Officers, both of the United States and of the several States, shall be bound by Oath or Affirmation, to support this Constitution; but no religious Test shall ever be required as a Qualification to any Office or public Trust under the United States.

Article VII.

The Ratification of the Conventions of nine States, shall be sufficient for the Establishment of this Constitution between the States so ratifying the Same.

Done in Convention by the Unanimous Consent of the States present the Seventeenth Day of September in the Year of our Lord one thousand seven hundred and Eighty seven and of the Independence of the United States of America the Twelfth In witness whereof We have hereunto subscribed our Names,

G°. WASHINGTON—*Presid.*[t]
and deputy from Virginia

New Hampshire — JOHN LANGDON, NICHOLAS GILMAN

Massachusetts — NATHANIEL GORHAM, RUFUS KING

New Jersey — WIL: LIVINGSTON, DAVID BREARLEY, W.M PATERSON, JONA: DAYTON

Pennsylvania — B FRANKLIN, THOMAS MIFFLIN, ROB.T MORRIS, GEO. CLYMER, THO.S FITZSIMONS, JARED INGERSOLL, JAMES WILSON, GOUV MORRIS

Connecticut	Wm. Saml. Johnson Roger Sherman
New York	Alexander Hamilton
Maryland	James McHenry Dan of St Thos. Jenifer Danl Carroll
Virginia	John Blair— James Madison Jr.
North Carolina	Wm. Blount Richd. Dobbs Spaight Hu Williamson
South Carolina	J. Rutledge Charles Cotesworthy Pinckney Charles Pinckney Pierce Butler
Delaware	Geo: Read Gunning Bedford jun John Dickinson Richard Bassett Jaco: Broom
Georgia	William Few Abr Baldwin

[The first ten amendments, known as the "Bill of Rights," were ratified in 1791.]

Amendment I (1791)

Congress shall make no law respecting an establishment of religion, or prohibiting the free exercise thereof, or abridging the freedom of speech, or of the press; or the right of the people peaceably to assemble, and to petition the Government for a redress of grievances.

Amendment II (1791)

A well regulated Militia, being necessary to the security of a free State, the right of the people to keep and bear Arms, shall not be infringed.

Amendment III (1791)

No Soldier shall, in time of peace be quartered in any house without the consent of the Owner, nor in time of war, but in a manner to be prescribed by law.

Amendment IV (1791)

The right of the people to be secure in their persons, houses, papers, and effects, against unreasonable searches and seizures, shall not be violated, and no Warrants shall issue, but upon probable cause, supported by Oath or affirmation, and particularly describing the place to be searched, and the persons or things to be seized.

Amendment V (1791)

No person shall be held to answer for a capital, or otherwise infamous crime, unless on a presentment or indictment of a Grand Jury, except in cases arising in the land or naval forces, or in the Militia, when in actual service in time of War or public danger; nor shall any person be subject for the same offence to be twice put in jeopardy of life or limb; nor shall be compelled in any criminal case to be a witness against himself, nor be deprived of life, liberty, or property, without due process of law, nor shall private property be taken for public use, without just compensation.

Amendment VI (1791)

In all criminal prosecutions, the accused shall enjoy the right to a speedy and public trial, by an impartial jury of the State and district wherein the crime shall have been committed, which district shall have been previously ascertained by law, and to be informed of the nature and cause of the accusation; to be confronted with the witnesses against him; to have compulsory process for obtaining witnesses in his favor, and to have the Assistance of Counsel for his defence.

Amendment VII (1791)

In Suits at common law, where the value in controversy shall exceed twenty dollars, the right of trial by jury shall be preserved, and no fact tried by a jury, shall be otherwise reexamined in any Court of the United States, than according to the rules of the common law.

Amendment VIII (1791)

Excessive bail shall not be required, nor excessive fines imposed, nor cruel and unusual punishments inflicted.

Amendment IX (1791)

The enumeration in the Constitution, of certain rights, shall not be construed to deny or disparage others retained by the people.

Amendment X (1791)

The powers not delegated to the United States by the Constitution, nor prohibited by it to the States, are reserved to the States respectively, or to the people.

Amendment XI (1795)

The Judicial power of the United States shall not be construed to extend to any suit in law or equity, commenced or prosecuted against one of the United States by Citizens of another state, or by Citizens or Subjects of any Foreign State.

Amendment XII (1804)

The Electors shall meet in their respective states and vote by ballot for President and Vice President, one of whom, at least, shall not be an inhabitant of the same state with themselves; they shall name in their ballots the person voted for as President, and in distinct ballots the person voted for as Vice President, and they shall make distinct lists of all persons voted for as President, and of all persons voted for as Vice President, and of the number of votes for each, which lists they shall sign and certify, and transmit sealed to the seat of government of the United States, directed to the President of the Senate;—The President of the Senate shall, in the presence of the Senate and House of Representatives, open all the certificates and the votes shall then be counted;—The person having the greatest number of votes for President, shall be the President, if such number be a majority of the whole number of Electors appointed; and if no person have such majority, then from the persons having the highest numbers not exceeding three on the list of those voted for as President, the House of Representatives shall choose immediately, by ballot, the President. But in choosing the President, the votes shall be taken by states, the representation from each state having one vote; a quorum for this purpose shall consist of a member or members from two-thirds of the states, and a majority of all the states shall be necessary to a choice. *And if the House of Representatives shall not choose a President whenever the right of choice shall devolve upon them, before the fourth day of March next following, then the Vice President shall act as President, as in the case of the death or other constitutional disability of the President.*—[10] The person having the greatest number of votes as Vice President, shall be the Vice President, if such number be a majority of the whole number of Electors appointed, and if no person have a majority, then from the two highest numbers on the list, the Senate shall choose the Vice President; a quorum for the purpose shall consist of two-thirds of the whole number of Senators, and a majority of the whole number shall be necessary to a choice. But no person constitutionally ineligible to the office of President shall be eligible to that of Vice President of the United States.

Amendment XIII (1865)

Section 1. Neither slavery nor involuntary servitude, except as a punishment for crime whereof the party shall have been duly convicted, shall exist within the United States, or any place subject to their jurisdiction.

Section 2. Congress shall have power to enforce this article by appropriate legislation.

Amendment XIV (1868)

Section 1. All persons born or naturalized in the United States and subject to the jurisdiction thereof, are citizens of the United States and of the State wherein they reside. No State shall make or enforce any law which shall abridge the privileges or immunities of citizens of the United States; nor shall any State deprive any person of life, liberty, or property, without due process of law; nor deny to any person within its jurisdiction the equal protection of the laws.

Section 2. Representatives shall be apportioned among the several States according to their respective numbers, counting the whole number of persons in each State, excluding Indians not taxed. But when the right to vote at any election for the choice of electors for

[10] Changed by the Twentieth Amendment, Section 3.

President and Vice President of the United States, Representatives in Congress, the Executive and Judicial officers of a State, or the members of the Legislature thereof, is denied to any of the male inhabitants of such State, being *twenty-one*[11] years of age and citizens of the United States, or in any way abridged, except for participation in rebellion, or other crime, the basis of representation therein shall be reduced in the proportion which the number of such male citizens shall bear to the whole number of male citizens twenty-one years of age in such State.

Section 3. No person shall be a Senator or Representative in Congress, or elector of President and Vice President, or hold any office, civil or military, under the United States, or under any State, who, having previously taken an oath, as a member of Congress, or as an officer of the United States, or as a member of any State legislature, or as an executive or judicial officer of any State, to support the Constitution of the United States, shall have engaged in insurrection or rebellion against the same, or given aid or comfort to the enemies thereof. But Congress may by a vote of two-thirds of each House, remove such disability.

Section 4. The validity of the public debt of the United States, authorized by law, including debts incurred for payment of pensions and bounties for services in suppressing insurrection or rebellion, shall not be questioned. But neither the United States nor any State shall assume or pay any debt or obligation incurred in aid of insurrection or rebellion against the United States, or any claim for the loss or emancipation of any slave; but all such debts, obligations and claims shall be held illegal and void.

Section 5. The Congress shall have power to enforce, by appropriate legislation, the provisions of this article.

Amendment XV (1870)

Section 1. The right of citizens of the United States to vote shall not be denied or abridged by the United States or by any State on account of race, color, or previous condition of servitude.

Section 2. The Congress shall have power to enforce this article by appropriate legislation.

[11] Changed by the Twenty-sixth Amendment.

Amendment XVI (1913)

The Congress shall have power to lay and collect taxes on incomes, from whatever source derived, without apportionment among the several States, and without regard to any census or enumeration.

Amendment XVII (1913)

The Senate of the United States shall be composed of two Senators from each State, elected by the people thereof, for six years; and each Senator shall have one vote. The electors in each State shall have the qualifications requisite for electors of the most numerous branch of the State legislatures.

When vacancies happen in the representation of any State in the Senate, the executive authority of such State shall issue writs of election to fill such vacancies: Provided, That the legislature of any State may empower the executive thereof to make temporary appointments until the people fill the vacancies by election as the legislature may direct.

This amendment shall not be so construed as to affect the election or term of any Senator chosen before it becomes valid as part of the Constitution.

Amendment XVIII (1919)

Section 1. *After one year from the ratification of this article the manufacture, sale, or transportation of intoxicating liquors within, the importation thereof into, or the exportation thereof from the United States and all territory subject to the jurisdiction thereof for beverage purposes is hereby prohibited.*

Section 2. *The Congress and the several States shall have concurrent power to enforce this article by appropriate legislation.*

Section 3. *This article shall be inoperative unless it shall have been ratified as an amendment to the Constitution by the legislatures of the several States, as provided in the Constitution, within seven years from the date of the submission hereof to the States by the Congress.*[12]

Amendment XIX (1920)

The right of citizens of the United States to vote shall not be denied or abridged by the United States or by any State on account of sex.

[12] Repealed by the Twenty-first Amendment.

Congress shall have power to enforce this article by appropriate legislation.

Amendment XX (1933)

Section 1. The terms of the President and Vice President shall end at noon on the 20th day of January, and the terms of Senators and Representatives at noon on the 3d day of January, of the years in which such terms would have ended if this article had not been ratified; and the terms of their successors shall then begin.

Section 2. The Congress shall assemble at least once in every year, and such meeting shall begin at noon on the 3d day of January, unless they shall by law appoint a different day.

Section 3. If, at the time fixed for the beginning of the term of the President, the President elect shall have died, the Vice President elect shall become President. If a President shall not have been chosen before the time fixed for the beginning of his term, or if the President elect shall have failed to qualify, then the Vice President elect shall act as President until a President shall have qualified; and the Congress may by law provide for the case wherein neither a President elect nor a Vice President elect shall have qualified, declaring who shall then act as President, or the manner in which one who is to act shall be selected, and such person shall act accordingly until a President or Vice President shall have qualified.

Section 4. The Congress may by law provide for the case of the death of any of the persons from whom the House of Representatives may choose a President whenever the right of choice shall have devolved upon them, and for the case of the death of any of the persons from whom the Senate may choose a Vice President whenever the right of choice shall have devolved upon them.

Section 5. Sections 1 and 2 shall take effect on the 15th day of October following the ratification of this article.

Section 6. This article shall be inoperative unless it shall have been ratified as an amendment to the Constitution by the legislatures of three-fourths of the several States within seven years from the date of its submission.

Amendment XXI (1933)

Section 1. The eighteenth article of amendment to the Constitution of the United States is hereby repealed.

Section 2. The transportation or importation into any State, Territory, or possession of the United States for delivery or use therein of intoxicating liquors, in violation of the laws thereof, is hereby prohibited.

Section 3. This article shall be inoperative unless it shall have been ratified as an amendment to the Constitution by conventions in the several States, as provided in the Constitution, within seven years from the date of submission hereof to the States by the Congress.

Amendment XXII (1951)

Section 1. No person shall be elected to the office of the President more than twice, and no person who has held the office of President, or acted as President, for more than two years of a term to which some other person was elected President shall be elected to the office of President more than once. But this Article shall not apply to any person holding the office of President when this Article was proposed by the Congress, and shall not prevent any person who may be holding the office of President, or acting as President, during the term within which this Article becomes operative from holding the office of President or acting as President during the remainder of such term.

Section 2. This Article shall be inoperative unless it shall have been ratified as an amendment to the Constitution by the legislatures of three-fourths of the several States within seven years from the date of its submission to the States by the Congress.

Amendment XXIII (1961)

Section 1. The District constituting the seat of Government of the United States shall appoint in such manner as the Congress may direct:

A number of electors of President and Vice President equal to the whole number of Senators and Representatives in Congress to which the District would be entitled if it were a State, but in no event more than the least populous State; they shall be in addition to those appointed by the States, but they shall be considered, for the purposes of the election of President and Vice President, to be electors appointed by a State; and they shall meet in the District and perform such duties as provided by the twelfth article of amendment.

Section 2. The Congress shall have power to enforce this article by appropriate legislation.

Amendment XXIV (1964)

Section 1. The right of citizens of the United States to vote in any primary or other election for President or Vice President, for electors for President or Vice President, or for Senator or Representative in Congress, shall not be denied or abridged by the United States or any State by reason of failure to pay any poll tax or other tax.

Section 2. The Congress shall have the power to enforce this article by appropriate legislation.

Amendment XXV (1967)

Section 1. In case of the removal of the President from office or of his death or resignation, the Vice President shall become President.

Section 2. Whenever there is a vacancy in the office of the Vice President, the President shall nominate a Vice President who shall take office upon confirmation by a majority vote of both Houses of Congress.

Section 3. Whenever the President transmits to the President pro tempore of the Senate and the Speaker of the House of Representatives his written declaration that he is unable to discharge the powers and duties of his office, and until he transmits to them a written declaration to the contrary, such powers and duties shall be discharged by the Vice President as Acting President.

Section 4. Whenever the Vice President and a majority of either the principal officers of the executive departments or of such other body as Congress may by law provide, transmit to the President pro tempore of the Senate and the Speaker of the House of Representatives their written declaration that the President is unable to discharge the powers and duties of his office, the Vice President shall immediately assume the powers and duties of the office as Acting President.

Thereafter, when the President transmits to the President pro tempore of the Senate and the Speaker of the House of Representatives his written declaration that no inability exists, he shall resume the powers and duties of his office unless the Vice President and a majority of either the principal officers of the executive department[s] or of such other body as Congress may by law provide, transmit within four days to the President pro tempore of the Senate and the Speaker of the House of Representatives their written declaration that the President is unable to discharge the powers and duties of his office. Thereupon Congress shall decide the issue, assembling within forty-eight hours for that purpose if not in session. If the Congress, within twenty-one days after receipt of the latter written declaration, or, if Congress is not in session, within twenty-one days after Congress is required to assemble, determines by two-thirds vote of both Houses that the President is unable to discharge the powers and duties of his office, the Vice President shall continue to discharge the same as Acting President; otherwise, the President shall resume the powers and duties of his office.

Amendment XXVI (1971)

Section 1. The right of citizens of the United States, who are eighteen years of age or older, to vote shall not be denied or abridged by the United States or by any State on account of age.

Section 2. The Congress shall have power to enforce this article by appropriate legislation.

Amendment XXVII (1992)

No law varying the compensation for the services of the Senators and Representatives shall take effect, until an election of Representatives shall have intervened.

Appendix 2

How to Brief a Supreme Court Case

A case brief is a simple summary of the facts, questions, resolution, and holding of a Supreme Court decision. In many ways a brief serves a function similar to an outline of a short story or a book—it provides you with the essentials of the cast of characters, the story line, what happened along the way, the significance of the outcome, and how it fits into the larger picture. I encourage my students to brief the cases for three reasons:

1. It allows them to organize their notes and materials for class discussion in a much more effective way than thumbing through pages of notes and highlighted case opinions, saving time and encouraging better student preparation and participation.
2. It gives students the chance to build a filing system that will serve them well at exam time.
3. It permits the instructor to point out to students the important parts of the case they may have missed, underemphasized, or overstated.

An Example:

Lochner v. *People of State of New York*
198 U.S. 45 (1905)

Facts: In 1897 the New York legislature passed a law setting the maximum hours that bakers could work at ten per day and sixty per week. Joseph Lochner, who owned and operated the Lochner Bakery in Utica, located in upstate New York, was fined $50 for breaking the law. He challenged the New York Bakeshop Act as a violation of his "liberty of contract" rights under the Due Process Clause of the Fourteenth Amendment. He was unsuccessful in the New York courts and appealed to the United States Supreme Court.

Legal Question: Did the New York Bakeshop Act represent a valid exercise of police power to regulate the health and welfare of bakers?

Decision: By a 5-4 vote, the Court struck down the law.

Majority Opinion: Justice Peckham:

1. The New York law interferes with the right of contract between employers and employees concerning the number of hours bakers may work. The Court previously held in *Allgeyer* v. *Louisiana* (1897) that the right to liberty and property under the Fourteenth Amendment is absolute and may not be abridged except for the most compelling public health, safety, and welfare reasons.
2. No significant safety, moral, welfare, or public interest is affected by the New York law. Clean and wholesome bread does not depend on the number of hours per day or week a baker works. Any law infringing on the contract rights between employer and employee must have a more direct relationship to the public interest or the status of the employee.
3. The mere assertion of a public health interest does not necessarily render a law valid. Documentation must accompany any such legislation.

Dissenting Opinion: Justice Harlan:

1. Even recognizing the right to liberty of contract, the New York law represents valid public welfare legislation and should be upheld as such.

Dissenting Opinion: Justice Holmes:

1. The Constitution does not embody a particular economic theory. The New York law was a valid exercise of state police power to protect the health and welfare of bakers, not a violation of a fundamental liberty of contract right.
2. A judge's personal views on proper economic theory have nothing to do with the right of the majority to embody its opinions in law. The word *liberty* is perverted when the Fourteenth Amendment is interpreted to prevent the natural outcome of dominant opinion in a way that a rational person would consider fair and reasonable.
3. The New York law represents a reasonable measure to regulate health. Reasonable people can also inter-

pret the law as a proper means to regulate more generally the hours and conditions of work.

General Significance:

- *Lochner* became synonymous with the period of American constitutional development between the early 1900s and the late 1930s. During this time the Court used the liberty of contract theory to invalidate state efforts to enact wage, hour, workplace, and public health legislation.
- Justice Holmes's dissent is considered his greatest, both for its contribution to legal theory and the role of the courts in the American constitutional system.

Appendix 3

Internet Guide to Legal Research

Several excellent law and law-related research sites are available on the Internet. The sites listed offer great variety and are easy to locate. Two notes of caution:

1. Do not confuse pulling material off the Web with "real" research. Research is what you extract and find from the materials you have located. Cutting and pasting material without understanding its significance and how it supports your research inquiry is not research.
2. There is no substitute for actually reading—several times, if necessary—the case(s) you are trying to learn more about. Technology is a great asset in the learning process but cannot do the hard thinking for you.

The author welcomes additional suggestions for research sites and other Internet resources not mentioned here. Please contact the author at either: ivers@american.edu or through the *American Constitutional Law* Web site (www.college.hmco.com).

General

http://www.supremecourtus.gov
The official site of the Supreme Court of the United States.

http://www.findlaw.com/casecode/supreme.html
Search by citation, party name, or full text for U.S. Supreme Court cases since 1983. Also provides links to a wealth of legal databases.

http://supct.law.cornell.edu/supct/
The Legal Information Institute offers all Supreme Court opinions issued since May 1990. In addition, this site has more than 580 of the Court's most important decisions dating back to 1793. This site also provides the Court calendar, the schedule of oral arguments, and a glossary of legal terms.

http://www.fedworld.gov/supcourt/index.htm
The site contains the full text of U.S. Supreme Court decisions from 1937 to 1975. You can search each case by using a keyword.

http://www.washingtonpost.com/wp-srv/national/longterm/supcourt/supcourt.htm
Use this site to access the Supreme Court docket, as well as the history and summary of major cases in the past few years.

http://www.supremecourthistory.org
The Supreme Court Historical Society is devoted to expanding public awareness of the Supreme Court's history and heritage.

http://oyez.nwu.edu
Oyez, Oyez, Oyez multimedia database: A searchable database of solicited cases, including summaries of both written decisions and oral arguments in audio biographies of every Supreme Court justice with links to their opinions and a virtual tour of the Supreme Court.

http://www.courttv.com/legaldocs
Court TV Law Center Library: This site has Supreme Court news and decisions, biographies of Supreme Court justices, a legal glossary, and a guide to the federal courts. This site categorizes cases according to topic such as business cases, civil rights cases, cyber law, government documents, and miscellaneous cases.

http://www.americanlawyer.com
The *American Lawyer* is a monthly journal that covers topics of general interest to practicing lawyers. The journal also offers criticism, book reviews, Supreme Court coverage, and first-person essays by lawyers on the work they do.

http://www.legaltimes.com
The *Legal Times* is a weekly newspaper offering general coverage of the legal profession, including important litigation, legal developments, personality profiles and many other features. The Web site offers daily coverage of breaking news stories of interest to lawyers and students on a state-by-state basis.

http://www.cato.org
The Cato Institute's Center for Constitutional Studies publishes daily articles on legal issues from a libertarian perspective.

http://www.lawhost.com/suprctsrch.html
A search engine for full text display of Supreme Court cases going back to 1893. Browse by year, U.S. Reports, or volume number or search by citation or case title.

http://www.clubs.psu.edu/SCTSociety/links.htm
This site not only includes important links to Supreme Court cases but also provides the link to state supreme courts as well as international courts. Furthermore, use this site to find out more about current constitutional issues.

http://www.usc.edu/dept/law-lib/legal/topiclst.html
This menu provides links to a variety of legal resources available on the Internet including federal and state statutes and case law, government information, and publications. Resources have been arranged by subject. This index is a service of the USC Law Library.

http://www.westgroup.com/products/westlaw/
Westlaw is an online legal research service that provides legal and business information drawn from more than 10,000 databases. You can access federal and state statutes and court cases, federal regulations, citation information, public records, news, business, and financial information.

http://www.jmls.edu/Library/Journals.html
A full text search of law journals on the Internet. Many links as well as individual journals regarding various aspects of the law. Look here for journals on gender issues, constitutional law, and civil law.

Constitutional Law

http://www.lectlaw.com/tcon.htm
This site provides specific articles and issues related to the Bill of Rights and various other constitutional issues.

http://www.law.indiana.edu/law/v-lib/
Search a variety of articles written on constitutional law issues. This site also provides articles in other areas of the law such as civil, business, and criminal law.

http://www.law.cornell.edu/topics/first_amendment.html
First Amendment Law—Overview of First Amendment, which includes historic and more recent decisions. View U.S. court of appeals decisions regarding freedom of religion, press, and speech.

http://www.fedlaw.gsa.gov/legal31.htm
This site links you to the circuit appeals courts and searchable databases of their opinions.

http://jurist.law.pitt.edu/ol_artcl.htm
Online articles about constitutional law that give the current status of constitutional law today.

Civil Rights Law

http://www.ljx.com/practice/civilrights/index.html
This site has news, case law, legal memos, statutes, and resources on civil rights issues from *Law Journal Extra!*

http://www.law.cornell.edu/topics/civil_rights.html
Overview of federal civil rights and discrimination law. Includes recent court decisions and text of civil rights statutes.

http://www.eeoc.gov/qs-employees.html
Outlines employee rights, equal opportunity laws, sexual harassment, discrimination, and the federal complaint process.

http://fedlaw.gsa.gov:80/legal6.htm
Fedlaw highlights civil liberties, civil rights, equal opportunity, and discrimination laws compiled by the General Services Administration.

http://www.usdoj.gov/crt/crt-home.html
This site is put together by the Civil Rights division of the Department of Justice and displays recent articles, speeches, special issues, and particular cases on the topic.

U.S. Code

http://www4.law.cornell.edu/uscode
This legal information institute allows you to access parts of U.S. Code. You can search by title or refer to the table of popular names. If you know the title and section of the code you are looking for, you can search that way as well.

Civil Rights and Liberties: Gender Issues

http://www.law.cam.ac.uk/ESSAYS/SCHOL.HTM
Legal essays indexed by subject. The list of subjects includes gender and the law, civil liberties, and procedures and constitutional law.

http://www.aclu.org:80/issues/women/hmwo.html
The American Civil Liberties Union provides recent developments in women's rights and links to other useful sites.

http://dol.gov:80/dol/wb/
U.S. Labor Department Women's Bureau publications. Includes statistics and data applicable to gender issues, searchable by region. Link to other sites and learn about recent developments.

http://now.org:80/issues/economic/eratext.html
The National Organization for Women provides information on the history of the Equal Protection Amendment and related articles.

http://www.feminist.org/
The Feminist Majority provides an updated account of current issues that are affecting women.

Directory of Law Libraries Across the Country

http://library.wcl.american.edu
American University—Washington College of Law—includes information about the library and the entire catalog online.

http://pappas-ntl.bu.edu/pappas.htm
Boston University—Pappas Law Library

http://lawwww.cwru.edu/cwrulaw/library/libinfo.html
Case Western Reserve University Law Library

http://clelaw.lib.oh.us/
Cleveland Law Library Association—contains the law library catalog, Cuyahoga County, Ohio, court and agency information, research guides, and legal information services.

http://users.ccnet.com/~cccllib/
Contra Costa County Law Library

http://www.lawschool.cornell.edu/lawlibrary/
Cornell Law Library

http://www.bcpl.gov.bc.ca/ell/
Electronic Law Library—British Columbia, Canada—links to online legal information for British Columbians.

http://www.law.emory.edu/LAW/law.html
Emory University—Hugh F. MacMillan Law Library

http://www.gmu.edu/departments/law/library/index.html
George Mason University School of Law Library

http://www.ll.georgetown.edu/
Georgetown University Law Library—extensive source of legal information on the Internet.

http://www.co.hennepin.mn.us/lawlibrary/lawlib.htm
Hennepin County Law Library—library information and links to legal information.

http://www.jenkinslaw.org/
Jenkins Law Library—the county law library for the city and county of Philadelphia.

http://lcweb2.loc.gov/glin/lawhome.html
Law Library of Congress

http://lawsocnsw.asn.au/resources/library/
Law Society of New South Wales Library

http://lalaw.lib.ca.us/
Los Angeles County Law Library

http://www.maricopa.gov/lawlibrary/
Maricopa County Superior Court Law Library

http://www.lawlib.state.md.us/
Maryland State Law Library

http://library.law.mercer.edu/
Mercer University—Furman Smith Law Library

http://www.osu.edu/units/law/law3.htm
Michael E. Moritz Law Library—Ohio State University College of Law

http://www.courts.state.mn.us/library/
Minnesota State Law Library—includes an archive of Minnesota appellate court opinions, library information, and other legal research content and links.

http://www.library.nwu.edu/law/
Northwestern University Law Library

http://wwwl.sdcll.org
San Diego County Public Law Library—provides legal research and reference books for attorneys, lawyers, judges, and citizens. Automated legal research and access services available.

http://pw1.netcom.com/~smcll/smcll.htm
San Mateo County Law Library

http://www.socialaw.com/
Social Law Library—Boston, Massachusetts—private, not-for-profit institution serving the research needs of the practicing and the judiciary in Massachusetts,

http://www.aallnet.org/chapter/scall/
Southern California Association of Law Libraries (SCALL)

http://www.siu.edu/offices/lawlib/
Southern Illinois University School of Law Library

http://www.stanford.edu/group/law/library/index.html
Stanford University—Robert Crown Law Library

http://www.lawlibrary.state.mt.us
State Law Library of Montana

http://www.sclqld.org.au
Supreme Court Library of Queensland—contains information on legal research.

http://www.sll.courts.state.tx.us/
Texas State Law Library—provides access to basic sources of legal information for citizens and state entities.

http://www.law.berkeley.edu/library/index.shtml
University of California at Berkeley—Boalt Hall Library

http://lawlibrary.ucdavis.edu/
University of California at Davis

http://www.lib.uchicago.edu/LibInfo/Law/
University of Chicago—D'Angelo Law Library

http://stripe.colorado.edu/~lawlib/Home.html
University of Colorado Law Library

http://www.lawlib.uh.edu/Libraries/
University of Houston Law Libraries

http://www.law.miami.edu/library/
University of Miami Law School Library

http://www.olemiss.edu/depts/law_library_school/libndex.html
University of Mississippi—Law Library

http://library.usask.ca/law/
University of Saskatchewan Law Library—with links to internal resources and to electronic legal material in numerous Canadian, American, and international legal sites.

http://www.usc.edu/dept/law-lib/
University of Southern California—Law Center and Law Library

http://www.law.usyd.edu.au/~library/
University of Sydney Law Library

http://www.law.utexas.edu/
University of Texas at Austin—Tarlton Law Library

http://lib.law.washington.edu
University of Washington Gallagher Law Library

http://www.vermontlaw.edu/library/library.htm
Vermont Law School—Cornell Library

http://www.droit.umontreal.ca/doc/biblio/en/index.html
Virtual Canadian Law Library

http://198.187.0.226/courts/lawlib/home.htm
Washington State Law Library

http://elsinore.cis.yale.edu/lawweb/lawlib.htm
Yale Law School—Lillian Goldman Library

Notes

Chapter 1

1. Kermit L. Hall, *The Magic Mirror: Law in American History* (New York: Oxford University Press, 1989), pp. 4–8.
2. Alexander Hamilton, John Jay, and James Madison, *The Federalist Papers,* Clinton Rossiter, ed. (New York: Mentor Books, 1961), p. 301. (All references from here on are taken from this edition.)
3. Ibid.
4. Ibid., p. 322.
5. *Federalist* 1, p. 33 (emphasis added).
6. Quoted in Hall, *The Magic Mirror,* p. 67.
7. Michael Kammen, *A Machine That Would Go of Itself: The Constitution in American Culture* (New York: Vintage Books, 1987), pp. 1–39.
8. "Essays of 'Brutus' to the Citizens of the State of New-York," in Michael Kammen, ed. *Origins of the American Constitution* (New York: Penguin Books, 1986), pp. 304–305.
9. Herbert J. Storing, *What the Anti-Federalists Were For* (Chicago: University of Chicago Press, 1981), p. 24.
10. *Federalist* 23, p. 157.
11. Storing, *What the Anti-Federalists Were For,* p. 29.
12. Ibid.
13. *Federalist* 44, p. 284.
14. Ibid., p. 47.
15. David F. Epstein, *The Political Theory of the Federalist* (Chicago: University of Chicago Press, 1984).
16. *Federalist* 47, p. 301 (emphasis added).
17. Epstein, *Political Theory of the Federalist,* p. 127.
18. John Locke, *Second Treatise of Government,* chapter 11, section 136, pp. 405–406.
19. Epstein, *Political Theory of the Federalist,* pp. 126–130.
20. *Federalist* 51, p. 322 (emphasis added).
21. Quoted in Storing, *What the Anti-Federalists Were For,* p. 34.
22. *Federalist* 39, p. 246.
23. Ibid., pp. 244–245.
24. *Federalist* 51, p. 322.
25. Catherine Drinker Bowen, *Miracle at Philadelphia* (New York: Little, Brown, 1986), p. 243.
26. Quoted in Storing, *What the Anti-Federalists Were For,* pp. 64–65.
27. Ibid., p. 66.
28. *Federalist* 84, p. 515.
29. Quoted in Storing, *What the Anti-Federalists Were For,* p. 66.
30. In Chapter 2 I discuss in greater depth what "natural law" is and the place that some legal and political theorists see for natural law in constitutional interpretation.
31. Quoted in Storing, *What the Anti-Federalists Were For,* p. 70.
32. Thomas Jefferson, *The Papers of Thomas Jefferson,* vol. 12, Julian Boyd, ed. (Princeton, N.J.: Princeton University Press, 1950), p. 440.
33. Richard C. Cortner, "Strategies and Tactics in Litigants in Constitutional Cases," *Journal of Public Law* 17 (1968), pp. 287–307.
34. George L. Watson and John A. Stookey, *Shaping America: The Politics of Supreme Court Appointments* (New York: HarperCollins, 1995).
35. *NAACP* v. *Button,* 371 U.S. 415 (1963), at 429–430.

Chapter 2

1. Mark Hertsgaard, *A Day in the Life: The Music and Artistry of the Beatles* (New York: Delacorte Press, 1995), p. 58.
2. Jack N. Rakove, *Original Meanings: Politics and Ideas in the Making of the Constitution* (New York: Alfred A. Knopf, 1997), pp. 3–22.
3. Thomas L. Pangle, *The Spirit of Modern Republicanism* (Chicago: University of Chicago Press, 1988), pp. 1–12.
4. Thomas L. Pangle, "The Philosophic Understandings of Human Nature Informing the Constitution," in *Confronting the Constitution,* Allan Bloom, ed. (Washington, D.C.: American Enterprise Institute, 1990), p. 9.
5. Harry H. Wellington, *Interpreting the Constitution* (New Haven, Conn.: Yale University Press, 1990), pp. 54–55.
6. For an effective discussion of this literature, see Lee Epstein and Jack Knight, *The Choices Justices Make* (Washington, D.C.: Congressional Quarterly, 1997); Jeffrey A. Segal and Harold J. Spaeth, *The Supreme Court and the Attitudinal Model* (New York: Cambridge University Press, 1993); and the pioneering work in this area, C. Herman Pritchett, "Divisions of Opinion Among Justices of the U.S. Supreme Court, 1939–41," *American Political Science Review* 35 (1941), pp. 890–898.
7. Cass R. Sunstein, *The Partial Constitution* (Cambridge, Mass.: Harvard University Press, 1993), p. 119.
8. Robert H. Bork, *The Tempting of America: The Political Seduction of the Law* (New York: The Free Press, 1990).
9. For a rich and even-handed treatment of the Bork nomination, see Ethan Bronner, *Battle for Justice* (New York: W. W. Norton, 1989).
10. George L. Watson and John A. Stookey, *Shaping America, The Politics of Supreme Court Appointments* (New York: HarperCollins, 1995); John Anthony Maltese, *The Selling of Supreme Court Nominees* (Baltimore: Johns Hopkins University Press, 1998).
11. Edwin Meese III, "Address Before the American Bar Association," Washington, D.C., July 12, 1985.
12. William J. Brennan, "Address to the Text and Teaching Symposium," Georgetown University, Washington, D.C., October 12, 1985 (emphasis added).
13. Judge Bork took Justice Brennan directly to task as one of the offenders of "liberal constitutional revisionism" in *The Tempting of America,* pp. 219–220.
14. Maltese, *Selling of Supreme Court Nominees,* pp. 137–138.
15. For a discussion of Judge Bork's difficulties before the Senate Judiciary Committee with *Brown* and *Roe,* see Bronner, *Battle for Justice,* pp. 231–232, 292–293. Judge Bork's criticism of *Roe* was much harsher than his criticism of *Brown,* which he called a "great and correct decision, but . . . in all candor . . . supported by a very weak opinion." See Bork, *The Tempting of America,* pp. 74–84. *Roe,* on the other hand, was "itself,

an unconstitutional decision, a serious and wholly unjustifiable judicial usurpation of state legislative authority." Testimony of Robert H. Bork, *Hearings on a Bill to Provide That Human Life Shall Be Deemed to Exist from Conception,* J-97-16, April, May, June 1981, p. 310.
16. Bork, *The Tempting of America,* pp. 159–166.
17. Ibid., pp. 147, 165, 166.
18. Michael Kammen, *The Origins of the American Constitution* (New York: Penguin Books, 1986), pp. 90–93.
19. James H. Hutson, "The Creation of the Constitution: The Integrity of the Documentary Record," *Texas Law Review* 65 (1986): 1–39, p. 2.
20. Bork, *The Tempting of America,* p. 176.
21. Sunstein, *The Partial Constitution,* p. 99.
22. H. Jefferson Powell, "The Original Understanding of Original Intent," *Harvard Law Review* 98 (1985): 885–948, p. 948.
23. Sunstein, *The Partial Constitution,* p. 107.
24. *Ferguson* v. *Skrupa,* 372 U.S. 726 (1963), at 732.
25. Tinsley E. Yarbrough, *Mr. Justice Black and His Critics* (Durham, N.C.: Duke University Press, 1988), pp. 39–40.
26. *Youngstown Sheet & Tube Co.* v. *Sawyer,* 343 U.S. 579, 587-89 (1952).
27. Leonard W. Levy, *The Emergence of a Free Press* (New York: Oxford University Press, 1985). When this book was published under its original title, *Legacy of Suppression: Freedom of Speech and Press in Early American History* (Cambridge, Mass.: Harvard University Press), in 1960, Justice Black remarked that "it raised disquieting questions about the constitutional future of the United States. [It] seems to be part of a well organized, carefully planned advocacy of a philosophy which reduces all of the Constitution's affirmations and prohibitions to a rather lowly standard of reasonableness as determined by judges. Whether this is good for a country or not, I am unable to persuade myself up to now that it is what our Constitution meant." The latter quote is taken from Roger K. Newman, *Hugo Black* (New York: Pantheon Books, 1994), p. 498.
28. Hugo L. Black, *A Constitutional Faith* (New York: Alfred A. Knopf, 1969), pp. 45–46.
29. Bork, *The Tempting of America,* pp. 333–336.
30. Robert Hale, "Coercion and Distribution in a Supposedly Non-Coercive State," *Political Science Quarterly* 38 (1923), pp. 470–494; Morris Cohen, "Property and Sovereignty," *Cornell Law Quarterly* 13 (1927), pp. 8–30.
31. Oliver Wendell Holmes Jr., *The Common Law,* 2d. ed., Mark DeWolfe Howe, ed. (Cambridge, Mass.: Harvard University Press, 1963).
32. Ibid., p. 5.
33. "The Place of Justice Holmes in American Legal Thought," in Robert W. Gordon, ed., *The Legacy of Oliver Wendell Holmes, Jr.* (Stanford, Calif.: Stanford University Press, 1992), p. 63.
34. Philippa Strum, *Louis D. Brandeis: Justice for the People* (New York: Schoken, 1984), p. 337.
35. 208 U.S. 412 (1908).
36. Herbert Wechsler, "Toward Neutral Principles of Constitutional Law," *Harvard Law Review* 73 (1959), pp. 1–35.
37. Richard Kluger, *Simple Justice* (New York: Alfred A. Knopf, 1976).
38. Ronald Kahn, *The Supreme Court and Constitutional Theory, 1953–1993* (Lawrence: University Press of Kansas, 1994), pp. 87–89.
39. John Hart Ely, *Democracy and Distrust* (Cambridge, Mass.: Harvard University Press, 1980), pp. 181, 11–41.
40. Wellington, *Interpreting the Constitution,* p. 67.
41. Ely, *Democracy and Distrust,* pp. 11–14.
42. Sunstein, *The Partial Constitution,* pp. 104–105.
43. See, for example, Laurence Tribe, "The Puzzling Persistence of Process Based Constitutional Theories," *Yale Law Journal* 89 (1980), pp. 1063–1080; Tribe, *American Constitutional Law,* 2d ed. (Mineola, Minn.: Foundation Press, 1988); Ronald Dworkin, *Law's Empire* (Cambridge, Mass.: Harvard University Press, 1986); and Ronald Dworkin, *Taking Rights Seriously* (Cambridge, Mass.: Harvard University Press, 1977).
44. Ronald Dworkin, *A Matter of Principle* (Cambridge, Mass.: Harvard University Press, 1985).
45. John H. Garvey, *What Are Freedoms For?* (Cambridge, Mass.: Harvard University Press, 1996).
46. Sunstein, *The Partial Constitution,* pp. 25–37.
47. Forrest McDonald, *Novus Ordo Seclorum: The Intellectual Origins of the Constitution* (Lawrence: University Press of Kansas, 1985), pp. 57–60.
48. Edward S. Corwin, "The 'Higher Law' Background of American Constitutional Law," *Harvard Law Review* 42 (1928), pp. 149–185, 365–409.
49. Benjamin F. Wright, *American Interpretations of Natural Law* (Cambridge, Mass.: Harvard University Press, 1931), pp. 339–340.
50. 60 U.S. 393 (1857).
51. 83 U.S. 130 (1872), at 141.
52. 163 U.S. 537 (1896), at 544.
53. Garry Wills, *Inventing America* (Garden City, N.Y.: Doubleday, 1978), p. xiii.
54. These are discussed and criticized in Bork, *The Tempting of America,* pp. 209–210. Bork opposes the use of natural law theories in constitutional interpretation.
55. Ely, *Democracy and Distrust,* p. 49.
56. Erwin Chemerinsky, "Foreword: The Vanishing Constitution," *Harvard Law Review* 103 (1989): 43–104, p. 104.

Chapter 3

1. The narrative of Roger Keith Coleman's arrest, trial, conviction, and unsuccessful appeal is drawn from John C. Tucker's superb journalistic account of the murder of Wanda Thompson McCoy, *May God Have Mercy* (New York: W. W. Norton, 1997).
2. *Coleman* v. *Thompson,* 501 U.S. 722 (1991).
3. *Federalist* 84, p. 513.
4. Letter, James Madison in New York to Thomas Jefferson in Paris, October 17, 1788, in William Lee Miller, *The Business of May Next: James Madison and the Founding* (Charlottesville: University Press of Virginia, 1992), pp. 239–240.
5. Ibid., pp. 235–236.
6. Ibid., p. 236.
7. Bernard Schwartz, *The Bill of Rights: A Documentary History* (New York: Chelsea House, 1971). Madison' s comments came in a speech dated June 8, 1789.

8. Akhil Reed Amar, *The Bill of Rights: Creation and Reconstruction* (New Haven, Conn.: Yale University Press, 1998); Michael Kent Curtis, *No State Shall Abridge: The Fourteenth Amendment and the Bill of Rights* (Durham, N.C.: Duke University Press, 1986).
9. Curtis, *No State Shall Abridge,* pp. 22–23.
10. Alfred H. Kelly, Winifred A. Harbison, and Herman Belz, *The American Constitution: Its Origins and Development,* Vol. 1 (New York: W. W. Norton, 1991), pp. 263–290.
11. Curtis, *No State Shall Abridge,* pp. 47–56.
12. Quoted in ibid., pp. 85–86.
13. Quoted in ibid., p. 87.
14. Quoted in Amar, *The Bill of Rights,* p. 183.
15. Ibid., pp. 186–187.
16. Curtis, *No State Shall Abridge,* p. 91. See also David E. Kyvig, *Explicit and Authentic Acts: Amending the U.S. Constitution, 1776–1995* (Lawrence: University of Kansas Press, 1995), pp. 163–176.
17. 26 F. Cas. 79 (C. C. S. D. Ala 1871), at 81–82.
18. Amar, *The Bill of Rights,* pp. 209–210.
19. Curtis, *No State Shall Abridge,* pp. 172–173.
20. *Slaughterhouse Cases,* 83 U.S. 36 (1873).
21. Curtis, *No State Shall Abridge,* pp. 175–176.
22. *Slaughterhouse Cases,* 83 U.S. at 96.
23. Eric Foner, *Reconstruction: America's Unfinished Revolution* (New York: Harper & Row, 1989), pp. 529–530.
24. 92 U.S. 542 (1876).
25. *Slaughterhouse Cases,* 83 U.S. at 123.
26. *The Civil Rights Cases,* 109 U.S. 3 (1883), at 17.
27. Foner, *Reconstruction,* pp. 528–529.
28. John Hope Franklin, *Reconstruction after the Civil War* (Chicago: University of Chicago Press, 1994), pp. 211–219.
29. Quoted in Foner, *Reconstruction,* p. 582.
30. 166 U.S. 226 (1908).
31. Amar, *The Bill of Rights,* pp. 206–214; Curtis, *No State Shall Abridge,* pp. 212–220.
32. This point is raised but not endorsed by Joseph B. James, *The Ratification of the Fourteenth Amendment* (Macon, Ga.: Mercer University Press, 1984), pp. 6–7.
33. This view receives the fullest explanation in Raoul Berger, *Government by Judiciary: The Transformation of the Fourteenth Amendment* (Cambridge, Mass.: Harvard University Press, 1977); and Charles Fairman, "Does the Fourteenth Amendment Incorporate the Bill of Rights?" *Stanford Law Review* 2 (1949), p. 5.
34. This narrow view of the Fourteenth Amendment and, specifically, the Privileges and Immunities Clause, is endorsed by Berger, *Government by Judiciary,* and Fairman, "Does the Fourteenth Amendment Incorporate the Bill of Rights?" Legal historian Michael Nelson, who offers a much more expansive interpretation of the Fourteenth Amendment than do Berger and Fairman but stops short of the total incorporation position, notes that passage of the Fourteenth Amendment was an essential part of the Republican plan to secure the Northern victory and the abolition of slavery. See Michael Nelson, *The Fourteenth Amendment: From Political Principle to Judicial Doctrine* (Cambridge, Mass.: Harvard University Press, 1988).
35. See, generally, Berger, *Government by Judiciary*; Fairman, "Does the Fourteenth Amendment Incorporate the Bill of Rights?"
36. 176 U.S. 581 (1900), at 82.
37. Ibid., at 615–616.
38. 211 U.S. 78 (1908), at 117–118.
39. For more on this point, see Amar, *The Bill of Rights,* pp. 229–230.
40. Richard C. Cortner, *The Supreme Court and the Second Bill of Rights* (Madison: University of Wisconsin Press, 1981), p. 54; Samuel C. Walker, *In Defense of American Liberties: A History of the American Civil Liberties Union* (New York: Oxford University Press, 1990), pp. 46–47, 61–62.
41. Description of the facts in *Gitlow,* including quotations, is taken from Cortner, *Second Bill of Rights,* pp. 51–52.
42. 263 U.S. 652 (1925), at 669–670.
43. 283 U.S. 697 (1931).
44. 283 U.S. 359 (1931).
45. 287 U.S. 45 (1932).
46. The other is Footnote 11 in *Brown* v. *Board of Education* (see Chapter 11).
47. 304 U.S. 144 (1938), at 154 (emphasis added).
48. 310 U.S. 296 (1940).
49. 334 U.S. 1 (1948).
50. 347 U.S. 483 (1954).
51. The rivalry between Black and Frankfurter is one of the great stories in the Court's history. But, like many great songwriting partnerships featuring opposite talents of equal strengths, they brought out the best in each other. See James F. Simon, *The Antagonists* (New York: Simon & Schuster, 1989).
52. Description of the facts in *Adamson,* including quotations, is taken from Cortner, *Second Bill of Rights,* pp. 139–142.
53. Amar, *The Bill of Rights,* pp. 179–180.
54. Cass R. Sunstein, *After the Rights Revolution: Reconceiving the Regulatory State* (Cambridge, Mass.: Harvard University Press, 1990), pp. 12–13.
55. For a good discussion of the rise of conservative interest group litigation, see Lee Epstein, *Conservatives in Court* (Knoxville: University of Tennessee Press, 1985). See also Gregg Ivers, "Please God, Save This Honorable Court: The Emergence of the Conservative Religious Bar," in Paul Herrnson, Ronald G. Shaiko, and Clyde Wilcox, eds., *The Interest Group Connection: Electioneering, Lobbying, and Policymaking in Washington* (Chatham, N.J.: Chatham House, 1998), pp. 289–301.

Chapter 4

1. Stanley Karnow, *Vietnam: A History* (New York: Viking Press, 1983), p. 9.
2. This paragraph and the subsequent account of *Tinker* v. *Des Moines* (1969) are drawn from John W. Johnson, *The Struggle for Student Rights: Tinker v. Des Moines and the 1960s* (Lawrence: University Press of Kansas, 1997), pp. 1–15.
3. 393 U.S. 503 (1969), at 505.
4. Quoted in Johnson, *Struggle for Student Rights,* p. 199.
5. Leonard W. Levy, *Emergence of a Free Press* (New York: Oxford University Press, 1985), pp. 3–15.
6. Akhil Reed Amar, *The Bill of Rights* (New Haven, Conn.: Yale University Press, 1998), pp. 20–26. See also Michael Kent Curtis, *Freedom of Speech: The "People's Darling Privilege"* (Durham, N.C.: Duke University Press, 2000).

7. Leonard W. Levy, *Jefferson and Civil Liberties: The Darker Side* (Cambridge, Mass.: Harvard University Press, 1963), pp, 48–55.
8. Letter from Thomas Jefferson to Abigail Adams, September 4, quoted in Levy, *Emergence of a Free Press,* p. 307.
9. Cass Sunstein, *Democracy and the Problem of Free Speech* (New York: Free Press, 1995).
10. Mark A. Graber, *Transforming Free Speech: The Ambiguous Legacy of Civil Libertarianism* (Berkeley: University of California Press, 1991), pp. 17–44.
11. Zechariah Chafee Jr., *Freedom of Speech* (New York: Harcourt, Brace and Howe, 1920).
12. John Keegan, *The First World War* (New York: Alfred A. Knopf, 1999), pp. 351–355.
13. Robert Justin Goldstein, *Political Repression in Modern America: From 1870 to the Present* (Boston: G. K. Hall, 1978), pp. 105–108.
14. Quotes and factual background are drawn from Peter Irons, *A People's History of the Supreme Court* (New York: Viking Press, 1999), pp. 268–270.
15. Rodney K. Smolla, *Free Speech in an Open Society* (New York: Oxford University Press, 1992), pp. 98–99.
16. 249 U.S. 204 (1919), at 206.
17. 249 U.S. 211 (1919).
18. 158 U.S. 564 (1895).
19. David Ray Papke, *The Pullman Case: The Clash of Labor and Capital in Industrial America* (Lawrence: University Press of Kansas, 1999).
20. 249 U.S. 211 (1919), at 214-215.
21. President Wilson issued an executive order in 1921 commuting Debs's prison sentence to time served. However, his citizenship was never restored.
22. David Rabban, "The Emergence of Modern American First Amendment Doctrine," *University of Chicago Law Review* 50 (1984), p. 1205.
23. Smolla, *Free Speech in an Open Society,* p. 101.
24. Quotes and factual background are drawn from Irons, *A People's History of the Supreme Court,* pp. 276–278.
25. 268 U.S. 652 (1925), at 673.
26. Ross Evans Paulson, *Liberty, Equality and Justice: Civil Rights, Women's Rights, and the Regulation of Business, 1865–1932* (Durham, N.C.: Duke University Press, 1997), pp. 178–203.
27. Walter Goodman, *The Committee: The Extraordinary Career of the House Committee on Un-American Activities* (New York: Farrar, Straus & Giroux, 1968), pp. 6–8.
28. William L. O'Neill, *American High: The Years of Confidence, 1945–1960* (New York: The Free Press, 1986), pp. 141–142.
29. Ellen W. Schrecker, *No Ivory Tower: McCarthyism and the Universities* (New York: Oxford University Press, 1986), p. 9.
30. Richard H. Rovere, *Senator Joe McCarthy* (New York: Harper Books, 1959), pp. 125–126.
31. O'Neill, *American High,* p. 159.
32. Ibid., pp. 160–162.
33. *Dennis* v. *United States,* 341 U.S. 494 (1951).
34. Samual C. Walker, *In Defense of American Liberties: A History of the American Civil Liberties Union* (Madison: University of Wisconsin Press, 1990), pp. 185–191.
35. Rovere, *Senator Joe McCarthy,* pp. 205–229.
36. 354 U.S. 178 (1957), at 200.
37. 354 U.S. 298 (1957).
38. 357 U.S. 545 (1958).
39. Ibid., at 137.
40. R. Kent Rasmussen and Shelley Fisher Fishkin, *The Quotable Mark Twain: His Essential Aphorisms, Witticisms and Concise Opinions* (New York: Contemporary Books, 1998).
41. Walker, *In Defense of American Liberties,* p. 280.
42. 394 U.S. 576 (1969), at 578–579.
43. 418 U.S. 405 (1974).
44. See *www.aclu.org.* for a complete discussion of reported flag burning incidents since 1990.
45. Karen O'Connor, *No Neutral Ground* (Boulder. Colo.: Westview Press, 1996), pp. 158–167.
46. For a provocative discussion of the limits of formal understandings of free speech, see Stanley Fish, *There's No Such Thing As Free Speech* (New York: Oxford University Press, 1994), pp. 102–119.
47. 403 U.S. 15 (1971), at 25.
48. Facts and background on Walter Chaplinsky are drawn from Shawn Francis Peters, *Judging Jehovah's Witnesses: Religious Persecution and the Dawn of the Rights Revolution* (Lawrence: University Press of Kansas, 2000), pp. 203–229.
49. Two fine books discuss the Nazis in the Skokie case. One is by the attorney who defended the Nazis' right to march, Aryeh Neier, *Defending My Enemy* (New York: Dutton, 1979); the other is by Philippa Strum, *When the Nazis Came to Skokie: Freedom for Speech We Hate* (Lawrence: University Press of Kansas, 1999).
50. Donald Alexander Downs, *Nazis in Skokie: Freedom, Community and the First Amendment* (South Bend, Ind.: University of Notre Dame Press, 1985).
51. The impact of the Comstock Law on the birth control movement is discussed in Chapter 10.
52. Edward De Grazia, *Girls Lean Back Everywhere* (New York: Random House, 1992), p. 4.
53. Ibid., p. 12.
54. Margaret A. Blanchard, "The American Urge to Censor: Freedom of Expression versus the Desire to Sanitize Society—From Anthony Comstock to 2 Live Crew," *William and Mary Law Review* 33 (1992), p. 741.
55. Ibid., p. 758; De Grazia, *Girls Lean Back Everywhere,* pp. 72–73.
56. *United States* v. *One Book Named Ulysses by James Joyce,* 72 F. 2d 433 (2nd Cir. 1934).
57. Facts and background on Samuel Roth's life and career are drawn from Jay A. Gertzman, *Bookleggers and Smuthounds: The Trade in Erotica, 1920–1940* (Philadelphia: University of Pennsylvania Press, 1999), pp. 227–228, 275–278; De Grazia, *Girls Lean Back Everywhere,* p. 276.
58. Nadine Strossen, *Defending Pornography* (New York: Scribner, 1995), pp. 56–58.
59. 394 U.S. 557 (1969), at 565.
60. Walker, *In Defense of American Liberties,* pp. 235–236.
61. Strossen, *Defending Pornography,* pp. 37–59.
62. 413 U.S. 49 (1973).
63. *Rowan* v. *U.S. Post Office Department,* 397 U.S. 728 (1970); *California* v. *LaRue,* 409 U.S. 109 (1972); *FW/PBS, Inc.* v. *City of Dallas,* 493 U.S. 215 (1990).

64. For a fuller description of Dworkin and MacKinnon's feminist-based argument against pornography, see Andrea Dworkin, *Pornography: Men Possessing Women* (New York: E. P. Dutton, 1979); Catherine MacKinnon, *Only Words* (Cambridge, Mass.: Harvard University Press, 1993).
65. *American Booksellers* v. *Hudnut*, 771 F. 2d 323 (7th Cir. 1985).
66. Attorney General's Commission on Pornography, Final Report (1986), p. 728.
67. Ibid., p. 649.
68. 529 U.S. 803 (2000).
69. Data on Internet growth obtained from *www.mit.edu/people/mkgray/net/web-growth-summary.html.*
70. 492 U.S. 155 (1989).
71. The discussion of the WPA's arts program and that which follows is drawn from T. H. Watkins, *The Great Depression* (Boston: Back Bay Books, 1993), pp. 250–255.
72. Alexis de Tocqueville, *Democracy in America* (New York: Doubleday, 1969), pp. 513–517, 522.
73. An excellent overview of the different forms and values of associational freedom can be found in Amy Gutmann, *Freedom of Association* (Princeton, N.J.: Princeton University Press, 1998), pp. 1–32.
74. *NAACP* v. *Button*, 357 U.S. 449 (1958).
75. 468 U.S. 609 (1984).
76. 487 U.S. 1 (1988).

Chapter 5

1. This account of *United States* v. *Progressive, Inc.*, 467 F. Supp 990 (1979), is drawn from Rodney A. Smolla, *Free Speech in an Open Society* (New York: Alfred A. Knopf, 1992), pp. 265–269.
2. Leonard W. Levy, *Constitutional Opinions: Aspects of the Bill of Rights* (New York: Oxford University Press, 1986), p. 72.
3. John P. Roche, "American Liberty: An Examination of the 'Tradition' of Freedom," in *Aspects of Liberty*, M. R. Konvitz and Clinton Rossiter, eds. (Ithaca, N.Y.: Cornell University Press, 1958), p. 137.
4. Anthony Lewis, *Make No Law: The Sullivan Case and the First Amendment* (New York: Random House, 1991), pp. 51–52.
5. Quoted in Edward W. Knappman, *Great American Trials: From Salem Witchcraft to Rodney King* (Detroit: Visible Ink Press, 1994), p. 27.
6. Levy, *Constitutional Opinions*, pp. 162–163.
7. William Blackstone, *Commentaries on the Laws of England*, Vol. 4 (Chicago: University of Chicago Press, 1979), pp. 151–152.
8. Lewis, *Make No Law*, p. 54.
9. Levy, *Constitutional Opinions*, pp. 164–165.
10. Peter Irons, *A People's History of the Supreme Court* (New York: Viking Press, 1999), pp. 98–100.
11. Quoted in Levy, *Constitutional Opinions*, p. 168.
12. George Hay, *An Essay on the Liberty of the Press* (New York: DaCapo Press, 1970), p. 29.
13. The most comprehensive account of the evolution of freedom of the press in the United States is Leonard W. Levy, *The Emergence of a Free Press* (New York: Oxford University Press, 1985).
14. Harry Kalven, Jr., *A Worthy Tradition: Freedom of Speech in America* (New York: Harper & Row, 1988), pp. 64–66.
15. Fred W. Friendly, *Minnesota Rag: The Dramatic Story of the Landmark Supreme Court Case That Gave New Meaning to Freedom of the Press* (New York: Random House, 1981).
16. *Grosjean* v. *American Press Co.*, 297 U.S. 233 (1936); *Lovell* v. *Griffin*, 303 U.S. 444 (1938); *Scheider* v. *Irvington*, 308 U.S. 147 (1938); *Talley* v. *California*, 362 U.S. 60 (1960).
17. Louis Fisher, *Presidential War Power* (Lawrence: University Press of Kansas, 1995), pp. 123–128.
18. Sanford J. Ungar, *The Papers and the Papers* (New York: Columbia University Press, 1972), pp. 36–37.
19. Ibid., pp. 83–84.
20. 403 U.S. 713 (1971).
21. In *Snepp* v. *U.S.* (1980), the Court held that a Central Intelligence Agency rule, derived in part from congressional requirements, prohibiting former officers from publishing information about its operations without prior permission, was a valid exercise of government power to safeguard national security interests.
22. The material that follows is drawn from Fred W. Friendly, *The Constitution: That Delicate Balance* (New York: Random House, 1984), pp. 50–66, and David Halberstam, *The Powers That Be* (New York: Alfred A. Knopf, 1979).
23. George C. Herring, *America's Longest War: The United States and Vietnam, 1950–1975* (New York: John Wiley & Sons, 1979), pp. 252–256.
24. 484 U.S. 260 (1988).
25. Mark A. Uhlig, "From Hazelwood to the High Court," *New York Times Magazine*, September 13, 1987, p. 102.
26. Quoted in Herbert J. Storing, *What the Anti-Federalists Were For* (Chicago: University of Chicago Press, 1981), p. 19.
27. 381 U.S. 532 (1965).
28. Eliot E. Slotnick and Jennifer A. Segal make a persuasive case for opening the Court's proceedings to the public in *Television News and the Supreme Court: All the News That's Fit to Air* (New York: Cambridge University Press, 1998).
29. Details from the Sheppard trial and related events are drawn from Knappman, *Great American Trials*, pp. 471–474.
30. Bailey later represented the "Boston Strangler" in 1974, Patty Hearst in 1976, and O. J. Simpson from 1994–1996.
31. Details from the Simants trial and related events are drawn from Friendly, *The Constitution: That Delicate Balance*, pp. 144–158.
32. Quotations taken from Bernard Schwartz, *The Ascent of Pragmatism: The Burger Court in Action* (Reading, Mass.: Addison-Wesley, 1990), pp. 171–173.
33. *Cox Broadcasting Corp.* v. *Cohn*, 420 U.S. 469 (1975); *The Florida Star* v. *B. J. F.*, 491 U.S. 524 (1989).
34. Quotations taken from Schwartz, *The Ascent of Pragmatism*, pp. 163–164.
35. An excellent overview of federal and state laws granting the public the right to retrieve once-confidential records can be found in Thomas L. Tedford, *Freedom of Speech in the United States*, 3d ed. (State College, Penn.: Strata Press, 1997).
36. Levy, *Constitutional Opinions*, p. 168.
37. Kalven, *A Worthy Tradition*, pp. 60–61.
38. 343 U.S. 254 (1952), at 286–287.
39. Lewis, *Make No Law*, pp. 13–14.
40. Taylor E. Branch, *Parting the Waters: America During the King Years, 1954–63* (New York: Simon & Schuster, 1988), p. 580.
41. 388 U.S. 130 (1967).

42. Ibid., at 158.
43. Peter Irons, *The Courage of Their Convictions* (New York: Free Press, 1988), pp. 333–335.
44. 424 U.S. 448 (1976), at 455.
45. Smolla, *Free Speech in an Open Society,* pp. 147–148.
46. Samuel G. Warren and Louis D. Brandeis, "The Right to Privacy," *Harvard Law Review* 4 (1890): 193–220.
47. The above account of the *Falwell* v. *Flynt* trial is drawn from Knappman, *Great American Trials,* pp. 741–743, and Rodney A. Smolla, *Jerry Falwell* v. *Larry Flynt* (New York: St. Martin's Press, 1988).
48. Smolla, *Free Speech in an Open Society,* p. 148.
49. 497 U.S. 1 (1990), at 18.

Chapter 6

1. Quoted in Ray Ginger, *Six Days or Forever? Tennessee* v. *John Thomas Scopes* (New York: Oxford University Press, 1958), p. 90.
2. Ibid, p. 134.
3. Peter Irons, *The Courage of Their Convictions* (New York: The Free Press, 1990), pp. 211–212.
4. 393 U.S. 97 (1968); *Edwards* v. *Aguillard,* 482 U.S. 578 (1987).
5. 143 U.S. 457 (1892), at 463.
6. Thomas J. Curry, *The First Freedoms: Church and State in America to the Passage of the First Amendment* (New York: Oxford University Press, 1986).
7. Leonard W. Levy, *Constitutional Opinions: Aspects of the Bill of Rights* (New York: Oxford University Press, 1986), pp. 135–161.
8. Curry, *The First Freedoms,* pp. 193–222.
9. Stephen M. Feldman, *Please Don't Wish Me a Merry Christmas: A Critical History of the Separation of Church and State* (New York: New York University Press, 1997), pp. 166–167.
10. R. Laurence Moore, *Religious Outsiders and the Making of Americans* (New York: Oxford University Press, 1986), pp. 3–21.
11. Feldman, *Please Don't Wish Me a Merry Christmas,* p. 167.
12. Patricia U. Bonomi, *Under the Cope of Heaven: Religion, Society and Politics in Colonial America* (New York: Oxford University Press, 1986).
13. *Federalist* 51, p. 322.
14. Levy, *Constitutional Opinions,* pp. 152–156.
15. Leonard W. Levy, *The Establishment Clause: Religion and the First Amendment* (New York: Macmillan, 1986), pp. 25–62.
16. Garry Wills, *Under God: Religion and American Politics* (New York: Simon & Schuster, 1990), p. 363.
17. Roger Williams, *The Bloody Tenant of Persecution* (1644), quoted in Bonomi, *Under the Cope of Heaven,* p. 34.
18. Robert S. Alley, *The Constitution and Religion: Leading Supreme Court Cases on Church and State* (Amherst, N.Y.: Prometheus Books, 1999), pp. 15–20.
19. Wills, *Under God,* pp. 373–380.
20. Anson Stokes Phelps, *Church and State in the United States, Vols. 1–3* (New York: Harper & Bros., 1950); James M. O'Neill, *Religion and Education under the Constitution* (Harper & Bros., 1949); Walter Berns, *The First Amendment and the Future of American Democracy* (New York: Basic Books, 1977); and Garrett Ward Sheldon and Daniel L. Dreisbach, eds., *Religion and Political Culture in Jefferson's Virginia* (Lanham, Md.: Rowman and Littlefield, 2000).
21. Levy, *Constitutional Opinions,* p. 142.
22. A. James Reichley, *Religion in American Public Life* (Washington, D.C.: The Brookings Institution, 1985); Daniel L. Dreisbach, ed. *Religion and Politics in the Early Republic: Jasper Adams and the Church-State Debate* (Lexington: University Press of Kentucky, 1996).
23. Feldman, *Please Don't Wish Me a Merry Christmas,* p. 167.
24. Steven D. Smith, *Foreordained Failure: The Quest for a Constitutional Principle of Religious Freedom* (New York: Oxford University Press, 1995), pp. 37–38.
25. Morris U. Schappes, ed., *A Documentary History of the Jews in the United States, 1654-1875* (New York: Schocken Books, 1950), p. 80.
26. Quoted in Curry, *The First Freedoms,* p. 219.
27. Bette Novit Evans, *Interpreting the Free Exercise of Religion: The Constitution and American Pluralism* (Chapel Hill, N.C.: University of North Carolina Press, 1997).
28. Akhil Reed Amar, "The Bill of Rights as a Constitution," *Yale Law Journal* 100 (1991), p. 1131; Michael W. McConnell, "The Origins and Historical Understanding of the Free Exercise of Religion," *Harvard Law Review* 103 (1990), p. 1409; Stephen L. Carter, *The Culture of Disbelief* (New York: Basic Books, 1993).
29. Eric Michael Mazur, *The Americanization of Religious Minorities: Confronting the Constitutional Order* (Baltimore: Johns Hopkins University Press, 1999).
30. Alexis de Tocqueville, *Democracy in America,* Vol. 1, Francis Bowen, ed. (New York: Alfred A. Knopf, 1945), pp. 302–303.
31. 281 U. S. 370 (1930).
32. 175 U.S. 291 (1899).
33. "Supreme Court Decision on Bus Transportation," *America,* February 22, 1947, p. 561.
34. "High Court Backs State Right to Run Parochial School Buses," *New York Times,* February 11, 1947, p. 1.
35. Gregg Ivers, *To Build a Wall: American Jews and the Separation of Church and State* (Charlottesville: University Press of Virginia, 1995), pp. 26–27.
36. Transcript, "Sectarianism in the Public Schools," Leo Pfeffer Papers, Box 1.
37. Memorandum, Leo Pfeffer to Will Maslow, October 14, 1946, Leo Pfeffer Papers, Box 19.
38. Author interview with Will Maslow, former general counsel of the American Jewish Congress, August 5, 1992, New York.
39. Samuel Walker, *In Defense of American Liberties: A History of the ACLU* (New York: Oxford University Press, 1990), p. 221; Ivers, *To Build a Wall,* pp. 70–84.
40. Irving Kane, "Impact on the Jewish Community," *Congress Weekly,* p. 5.
41. Ivers, *To Build a Wall,* pp. 83–89.
42. Ibid., pp. 83–93.
43. 343 U.S. 306 (1952), at 313–314, 316.
44. Ibid., at 324, 325.
45. Walker, *In Defense of American Liberties,* pp. 222–223.
46. Quoted in Ivers, *To Build a Wall,* p. 116.
47. Ibid., pp. 117–119; see also Frank J. Sorauf, *The Wall of Separation: The Constitutional Politics of Church and State* (Princeton, N.J.: Princeton University Press, 1976).

48. 367 U.S. 488 (1961), 495–496 (emphasis added).
49. 374 U.S. 487 (1963).
50. *The Gallup Poll* 3 (1935–1971), p. 1857; General Social Survey, National Opinion Research Center, University of Chicago, various years.
51. *Washington Post,* July 7, 1962; *New York Times,* July 1, 1962; quoted in Walker, *In Defense of American Liberties,* p. 225.
52. Edward Keynes and Randall K. Miller, *The Court vs. Congress: Prayer, Busing and Abortion* (Durham, N.C.: Duke University Press, 1989).
53. Sorauf, *The Wall of Separation,* pp. 313–314; Walker, *In Defense of Liberties,* pp. 225–226; Ivers, *To Build a Wall,* pp. 140–144.
54. Keynes and Miller, *The Court vs. Congress,* pp. 174–202.
55. 463 U.S. 783 (1983).
56. 465 U.S. 668 (1984).
57. Gregg Ivers, "Please God, Save This Honorable Court: The Emergence of the Conservative Religious Bar," in Paul Herrnson, Ronald G. Shaiko, and Clyde Wilcox, *The Interest Group Connection: Electioneering, Lobbying, and Policymaking in Washington* (Chatham, N.J.: Chatham House, 1998), pp. 289–301.
58. Quoted in Walker, *In Defense of American Liberties,* p. 344.
59. Leo Pfeffer, *Church, State and the Burger Court* (Buffalo, N.Y.: Prometheus Books, 1984), p. 100.
60. 515 U.S. 753 (1995).
61. Ivers, "Please God, Save This Honorable Court," pp. 300–301.
62. 392 U.S. 236 (1968).
63. Ibid., at 252.
64. Ibid., at 251.
65. 473 U.S. 373 (1985); 473 U.S. 402 (1985).
66. Ivers, *To Build a Wall,* pp. 183–188.
67. 473 U.S. 402 (1985), at 430.
68. Michael J. Sandel, "Freedom of Conscience or Freedom of Choice," in *Articles of Faith, Articles of Peace: The Religious Liberty Clauses and the American Public Philosophy,* James Davison Hunter and Os Guinness, eds. (Washington, D.C.: The Brookings Institution, 1990), pp. 74–92.
69. Shawn Francis Peters, *Judging Jehovah's Witnesses: Religious Persecution and the Dawn of the Rights Revolution* (Lawrence: University Press of Kansas, 2000), pp. 28–29.
70. Ibid., pp. 30–31.
71. Ibid., pp. 31–32.
72. David Manwaring, *Render Unto Caesar: The Flag Salute Controversy* (Chicago: University of Chicago Press, 1962); Richard C. Cortner, *The Supreme Court and the Second Bill of Rights* (Madison: University of Wisconsin Press, 1982), pp. 279–291.
73. Peters, *Judging Jehovah's Witnesses,* pp. 178-181.
74. Merlin Owen Newton, *Armed With the Constitution: Jehovah's Witnesses in Alabama and the U.S. Supreme Court* (Tuscaloosa: University of Alabama Press, 1995), p. 8.
75. Quoted in Peters, *Judging Jehovah's Witnesses,* p. 186.
76. Evans, *Interpreting the Free Exercise of Religion,* pp. 192–193.
77. 322 U.S. 78 (1944), at 86, 87.
78. The subsequent discussion of the Mormons' confrontation with antipolygamy laws is drawn from Mazur, *The Americanization of Religious Minorities,* pp. 62–93.
79. 98 U.S. 145 (1878); 113 U.S. 333 (1890).
80. 98 U.S 145 (1878), at 166.
81. *United States* v. *Lee,* 455 U.S. 252 (1981); *Heffron* v. *International Society for Krishna Consciousness,* 452 U.S. 460 (1981); *Goldman* v. *Weinberger,* 475 U.S. 503 (1986); and *Lyng* v. *Northwest Indian Cemetery Protective Association,* 485 U.S. 439 (1986).
82. *Thomas* v. *Review Board of Indiana Employment Security Division,* 450 U.S. 707 (1981); *Hobbie* v. *Unemployment Appeals Commission of Florida,* 480 U.S. 136 (1987); *Frazee* v. *Illinois Department of Employment Security,* 489 U.S. 829 (1989).
83. *Wooley* v. *Maynard,* 430 U.S. 705 (1977).
84. *McDaniel* v. *Paty,* 435 U.S. 618 (1977).
85. 58 U.S.L.W 3676 (1990).
86. *First Covenant Church* v. *City of Seattle,* 111 S. Ct. 1097 (1991); *St. Bartholomew's Church* v. *City of New York,* 111 S. Ct. 1103 (1991); *Minnesota* v. *Hershberger,* 495 U.S. 901 (1990).
87. Current through June 2000.
88. Joan Biskupic, "Supreme Court Overturns Religious Practice Statute," *Washington Post,* June 26, 1997, p. 1. The quotation is from Douglas Laycock, a University of Texas law professor who was instrumental in the drafting and passage of the Religious Freedom Restoration Act of 1993.

Chapter 7

1. Paul Valentine, "For Fugitives, End of Freedom Dawns Suddenly," *Washington Post,* May 1, 1992, p. D1; Joan Biskupic, "High Court to Review Reporter Ride-Alongs," *Washington Post,* March 21, 1999, p. A2.
2. Legal arguments are drawn from Brief of the Petitioners (the Wilsons), *Wilson* v. *Layne,* 1998 U.S. Briefs 83, December 28, 1998; Brief for the Federal Respondents (the Marshals Service), ibid.; Brief for the Montgomery County Sheriff's Office, ibid.
3. 119 S. Ct. 1692 (1999).
4. Louis Brandeis and Samuel Warren, "The Right of Privacy," *Harvard Law Review* 4 (1893), p. 193.
5. Nelson B. Lasson, *The History and Development of the Fourth Amendment to the United States Constitution* (New York: AMS Press, 1988).
6. M. H. Smith, *The Writs of Assistance Case* (Berkeley: University of California Press, 1978), pp. 250–254.
7. Akhil Reed Amar, "Of Sovereignty and Federalism, 96 *Yale Law Journal* (1987), p. 1245.
8. 116 U.S. 616 (1886).
9. Akhil Reed Amar, *The Bill of Rights: Creation and Reconstruction* (New Haven, Conn.: Yale University Press, 1998), p. 71.
10. *Katz* v. *United States,* 389 U.S. 347 (1967), at 357.
11. Amar, *The Bill of Rights,* p. 70; William E. Nelson, *The Americanization of the Common Law* (Athens: University of Georgia Press, 1975).
12. *Beck* v. *Ohio,* 362 U.S. 725 (1960).
13. Samuel Walker, *In Defense of American Liberties* (New York: Oxford University Press, 1990), pp. 51–52, 68.
14. 308 U.S. 338 (1939).
15. 316 U.S. 129 (1942).
16. Richard Gid Powers, *Secrecy and the Power* (New York: Free Press, 1987), pp. 234–239.

17. Ibid., pp. 370–373.
18. David J. Garrow, *Bearing the Cross: Martin Luther King, Jr. and the Southern Christian Leadership Conference* (New York: William Morrow, 1986), pp. 360–377.
19. Quote and background on the shift in wiretapping policies under J. Edgar Hoover is drawn from Powers, *Secrecy and Power,* pp. 400–403.
20. For more background on Carnivore, see John Schwartz, "FBI Makes Case for Net Wiretaps," *Washington Post,* July 25, 2000, p. E1. Barry Steinhardt, associate director of the American Civil Liberties Union, said in testimony before Congress on the FBI's eavesdropping software: "Carnivore is roughly equivalent to a wiretap capable of accessing the contents of the conversations of all the phone company's customers, with the 'assurance' that the FBI will record only conversations of the specified target."
21. Yale Kamisar, "The Warren Court (Was It Really So Defense-Minded?), The Burger Court (Is It Really So Prosecution-Oriented?), and Police Investigatory Practices," in Vincent Blasi, ed., *The Burger Court: The Counterrevolution That Wasn't* (New Haven, Conn.: Yale University Press, 1983), p. 64.
22. 508 U.S. 366 (1993).
23. *Cupp* v. *Murphy,* 412 U.S. 291 (1973); *Chimel* v. *California,* 395 U.S. 752 (1969); *Arizona* v. *Hicks,* 480 U.S. 321 (1987); *Warden* v. *Hayden,* 387 U.S. 294 (1967); and *Oliver* v. *United States,* 466 U.S. 170 (1984). A comprehensive discussion of the Court-created exceptions to the warrant requirement can be found in Akhil Reed Amar, *The Constitution and Criminal Procedure: First Principles* (New Haven, Conn.: Yale University Press, 1998), pp. 1–45.
24. Background on the ACLU and the AELE is drawn from Gregg Ivers and Karen O'Connor, "Friends as Foes: The Amicus Curiae Participation and Effectiveness of the American Civil Liberties Union and the Americans for Effective Law Enforcement in Criminal Cases, 1969–1982," 9 *Law and Policy* (1987): 161–178; Lee Epstein, *Conservatives in Court* (Knoxville: University of Tennessee Press, 1985); and Yale Kamisar, *Police Interrogations and Confessions* (Ann Arbor: University of Michigan Press, 1980), 95–112.
25. Charles Kaiser, *1968 in America* (New York: Weidenfeld & Nicholson, 1988), pp. 141–142.
26. See *www.aclu.org/profiling/report/*; See also Jeffrey Goldberg, "The Color of Suspicion," *New York Times Magazine,* June 20, 1999, p. 85 (reporting that in a two-year period, New York City Police Department Street Crimes Unit made 45,000 stops, only 9,500, or 20 percent, of which resulted in arrest); Casimir, (reporting that in 1997, New York City's Street Crimes Unit conducted 27,061 stop-and-frisks, only 4,647 of which, 17%, resulted in arrest).
27. 232 U.S. 383 (1914), at 393.
28. *United States* v. *La Jeune Eugenie,* 26 F. Cas. 832 (C. C. D. 1822), at 842–843.
29. Amar, *The Constitution and Criminal Procedure,* pp. 21–31.
30. 273 U.S. 28 (1927); 275 U.S. 310 (1927).
31. 364 U.S. 206 (1960).
32. Richard C. Cortner, *The Supreme Court and the Second Bill of Rights* (Madison: University of Wisconsin Press), p. 290.
33. Background on Dolly Mapp is drawn from Cortner, *The Supreme Court and the Second Bill of Rights,* pp. 179–180.
34. Ibid., p. 183.
35. Quoted in Bernard Schwartz, *The Ascent of Pragmatism: The Burger Court in Action* (Reading, Mass.: Addison-Wesley, 1990), p. 358.
36. Bernard Schwartz, *Super Chief* (New York: New York University Press, 1983), pp. 391–398.
37. 428 U.S. 465 (1976), at 494.
38. 467 U.S. 431 (1984).

Chapter 8

1. Facts and background of *Brewer* v. *Williams,* the "Christian burial speech" case, are drawn from Yale Kamisar, *Police Interrogation and Confessions* (Ann Arbor: University of Michigan Press, 1980), pp. 113–137, 139–224.
2. 430 U.S. 387 (1977).
3. 467 U.S. 431 (1984).
4. 468 U.S. 902 (1984); 468 U.S. 981 (1984).
5. Wayne LaFave, ed., *Criminal Justice and the Supreme Court* (New York: Macmillan, 1990), pp. 227–228.
6. Facts and background of *Powell* are drawn from James Goodman, *Stories of Scottsboro* (New York: Pantheon, 1994), pp. 3–5.
7. 304 U.S. 458 (1938).
8. 316 U.S. 455 (1942).
9. Facts and background of Gideon's arrest and appeal are drawn from Richard C. Cortner, *The Supreme Court and the Second Bill of Rights* (Madison: University of Wisconsin Press, 1981), pp. 193–195.
10. Quoted in Peter Irons and Stephanie Guitton, eds., *May It Please the Court* (New York: The New Press, 1993), p. 187.
11. 407 U.S. 25 (1972).
12. 417 U.S. 600 (1974).
13. *Glasser* v. *United States,* 315 U.S. 60 (1942); *United States* v. *Chronic,* 466 U.S. 648 (1984).
14. Leonard Levy, *Origins of the Fifth Amendment* (New York: Oxford University Press, 1968), pp. 405–432.
15. Akhil Reed Amar, *The Constitution and Criminal Procedure: First Principles* (New Haven, Conn.: Yale University Press, 1997), pp. 46–88.
16. Ibid., pp. 68–69.
17. *Bram* v. *United States,* 168 U.S. 532 (1897).
18. Levy, *Origins of the Fifth Amendment,* p. 432.
19. 297 U.S. 278 (1936); 322 U.S. 143 (1936); 360 U.S. 315 (1959).
20. 378 U.S. 1 (1964).
21. Ibid., at 8.
22. 378 U.S. 478 (1964), at 491.
23. Ibid., at 490.
24. Richard C. Medalie, *From Escobedo to Miranda: The Anatomy of a Supreme Court Decision* (Washington, D.C.: Lerner Law Books, 1966), p. xvii.
25. Samuel Walker, *In Defense of American Liberties: A History of the ACLU* (New York: Oxford University Press, 1990), pp. 248–249.
26. Liva Baker, *Miranda: Crime, Law and Politics* (Boston: Atheneum, 1983), pp. 176–185.
27. Lee Epstein, *Conservatives in Court* (Knoxville: University of Tennessee Press, 1985).
28. Quoted in Baker, *Miranda,* pp. 114–115.
29. *Oregon* v. *Mathiason,* 429 U.S. 492 (1977).

30. *Harris* v. *New York,* 401 U.S. 222 (1971).
31. *Edwards* v. *Arizona,* 451 U.S. 477 (1981).
32. Tom C. Clark, "Criminal Justice in America," *Texas Law Review* 46 (1968): 742.
33. Charles Fried, *Order and Law* (New York: Simon & Schuster, 1991), p. 48.
34. George C. Thomas III, "Plain Talk About the Miranda Empirical Debate: A Steady-State Theory of Confessions," *U.C.L.A. Law Review* 43 (1996), p. 933; Stephen J. Schulhofer, "Miranda's Practical Effect: Substantial Benefits and Vanishingly Small Social Costs," *Northwestern University Law Review* 90 (1996), p. 500; Stephen J. Schulhofer, "Reconsidering Miranda," *University of Chicago Law Review* 54 (1987), p. 435.
35. *New York Times Magazine,* September 26, 1999, pp. 84, 87.
36. See, for example, *Arizona* v. *Fulminante,* 499 U.S. 279 (1991) (ruling that the admission of "coerced confessions" into evidence was a "harmless error"); *New York* v. *Harris,* 495 U.S. 14 (1990) (ruling that confession given after a suspect had been read his *Miranda* warnings was permissible even though the police had entered his home illegally).
37. 386 U.S. 18 (1967).
38. 521 U.S. 507 (1997).
39. Amar, *The Constitution and Criminal Procedure,* pp. 161–162.
40. Levy, *Constitutional Opinions,* pp. 72–87.
41. 368 U.S. 57 (1961).
42. 419 U.S. 522 (1975).
43. Amar, *The Constitution and Criminal Procedure,* pp. 170–171.
44. For more on the NAACP's involvement in jury cases concerning racial discrimination, see Jack Greenberg, *Crusaders in the Courts: How a Dedicated Band of Lawyers Fought for the Civil Rights Revolution* (New York: Basic Books, 1994).
45. See, generally, Stuart Svonkin, *Jews Against Prejudice: American Jews and the Fight for Civil Liberties* (New York: Columbia University Press, 1997).
46. *Georgia* v. *McCollum,* 505 U.S. 42 (1992).
47. *Illinois* v. *Allen,* 397 U.S.337 (1970).

Chapter 9

1. The facts and background of the Willie Francis cases are drawn from Fred W. Friendly and Martha J. H. Elliott, *The Constitution: That Delicate Balance* (New York: Random House, 1984), p. 164; Arthur S. Miller and Jeffrey S. Bowmann, "Slow Dance on the Killing Ground: The Willie Francis Case Revisited," *DePaul Law Review* 32 (1983), p. 1.
2. 329 U.S. 459 (1947).
3. Ibid., at 468.
4. Ibid., quoting *Snyder* v. *Commonwealth of Massachusetts* 291 U.S. 97 (1934).
5. Lawrence M. Friedman, *A History of American Law* (New York: Touchstone, 1985), pp. 280–283.
6. Michigan continued to permit execution for treason (a provision it never enforced) until 1963. See Franklin E. Zimring and Gordon Hawkins, *Capital Punishment and the American Agenda* (London: Cambridge University Press, 1986), p. 29.
7. Edward L. Ayers, *Vengeance and Justice: Crime and Punishment in the Nineteenth-Century American South* (New York: Oxford University Press, 1984).
8. Michael Meltsner, *Cruel and Unusual Punishment: The Supreme Court and Capital Punishment* (New York: Random House, 1973); Jack Greenberg, *Crusaders in the Courts: How a Dedicated Band of Lawyers Fought for the Civil Rights Revolution* (New York: Basic Books, 1994).
9. 356 U.S. 86 (1958), at 101.
10. 375 U.S. 889 (1963), at 889–891.
11. Meltsner, *Cruel and Unusual Punishment,* pp. 29–34.
12. Greenberg, *Crusaders in the Courts,* pp. 440–441.
13. Meltsner, *Cruel and Unusual Punishment,* pp. 106–167, 286–316.
14. Mark Tushnet, *Making Constitutional Law: Thurgood Marshall and the Supreme Court, 1961–1991* (New York: Oxford University Press, 1997), pp. 147–148.
15. 391 U.S. 510 (1968), at 522.
16. *Maxwell* v. *Bishop,* 398 U.S. 262 (1970).
17. *McGautha* v. *California,* 402 U.S. 183 (1971); *Crampton* v. *Ohio* 402 U.S. 183 (1971).
18. Greenberg, *Crusaders in the Courts,* pp. 446–447.
19. Jack Greenberg, "Capital Punishment as a System," *Yale Law Journal* 91 (1982), pp. 908–928.
20. *Woodson* v. *North Carolina,* 428 U.S. 280 (1976); *Roberts* v. *Louisiana,* 428 U.S. 325 (1976).
21. Excerpts of the exchange between Amsterdam and Stewart are drawn from Peter Irons, *May It Please the Court,* Peter Irons and Stephanie Guitton, eds. (New York: New Press, 1993).
22. But this has not kept political scientists from trying. See Lee Epstein and Joseph F. Kobylka, *The Supreme Court and Legal Change: Abortion and the Death Penalty* (Chapel Hill: University of North Carolina Press, 1992).
23. Comprehensive statistics on the death penalty are available from the Death Penalty Information Center, a Washington, D.C.–based information clearinghouse on capital punishment. Go to *www.deathpenaltyinfo.org.*
24. 433 U.S. 587 (1977).
25. 438 U.S. 586 (1978).
26. *Ford* v. *Wainwright,* 477 U.S. 399 (1986); *Edmund* v. *Florida,* 458 U.S. 782 (1982).
27. See *www.deathpenaltyinfo.org/dpicrace.html.*
28. Tushnet, *Making Constitutional Law,* pp. 160–161.
29. John C. Jeffries Jr., *Justice Lewis F. Powell, Jr.: A Biography* (New York: Scribner, 1994), p. 451.
30. See *www.deathpenaltyinfo.org/juvexec.html.*
31. 455 U.S. 104 (1982).
32. 487 U.S. 815 (1985).
33. See *www.deathpenaltyinfo.org/juvexec.html.*
34. 482 U.S. 496 (1987); 490 U.S. 805 (1989).
35. 499 U.S. 467 (1991).
36. 501 U.S. 722 (1991).
37. 510 U.S. 1141 (1994).
38. See *www.deathpenaltyinfo.org,* for execution rates in the states during this time.
39. 392 U.S. 914 (1968).
40. 445 U.S. 263 (1980); 463 U.S. 277 (1983).
41. 503 U.S. 1 (1992).

Chapter 10

1. *Buck* v. *Bell,* 274 U.S. 200 (1927), at 207–208.
2. 198 U.S. 45 (1905).
3. Ibid., at 75.
4. Quoted in Peter Irons, *A People's History of the Supreme Court* (New York: Viking Press, 1999), pp. 251–252.
5. The background of *Buck* v. *Bell* is drawn from the following sources: Henry J. Abraham and Barbara A. Perry, *Freedom*

and the Court, 7th ed. (New York: Oxford University Press, 1998), pp. 96–100; Peter Irons, *A People's History of the Supreme Court* (New York: Viking Press, 1999), pp. 252–253; Paul A. Lombardo, "Three Generations of Imbeciles: New Light on *Buck* v. *Bell*," *New York University Law Review* 60 (1985), pp. 1–62.

6. Richard A. Posner, ed., *The Essential Holmes: Selections from the Letters, Speeches, Judicial Opinions and Other Writings of Oliver Wendell Holmes, Jr.* (Chicago: University of Chicago Press, 1992), pp. xii–xiii.
7. 262 U.S. 390 (1923), at 398, 401.
8. 268 U.S. 510 (1925), at 535.
9. Robert S. Alley, *The Constitution and Religion* (Buffalo, N.Y.: Prometheus Books, 2000).
10. Thomas M. Cooley, *Torts*, 2d ed. (Boston: Little, Brown, 1888), p. 29.
11. Samuel D. Warren and Louis D. Brandeis, "The Right to Privacy," *Harvard Law Review* 4 (1890): 193–220, p. 193, pp. 215–216, pp. 206–207.
12. David J. Garrow, *Liberty and Sexuality: The Right to Privacy and the Making of Roe v. Wade* (New York: Macmillan, 1994), pp. 260–262.
13. 277 U.S. 438 (1928), at 478.
14. David M. Kennedy, *Birth Control in America: The Career of Margaret Sanger* (New Haven, Conn.: Yale University Press, 1970), p. 218; Karen O'Connor, *No Neutral Ground: Abortion Politics in an Age of Absolutes* (Boulder, Colo.: Westview Press, 1996), pp. 20–22.
15. Garrow, *Liberty and Sexuality*, pp. 10–15; O'Connor, *No Neutral Ground*, pp. 23–25.
16. Garrow, *Liberty and Sexuality*, pp. 40–45.
17. Ibid., pp. 91–104.
18. 318 U.S. 44 (1943).
19. 367 U.S. 497 (1961), at 550.
20. Ibid., at 554, 552, 531–534.
21. 300 U.S. 379 (1937), at 391–392.
22. Irons, *A People's History of the Supreme Court*, pp. 429–430.
23. *Ferguson* v. *Skrupa*, 372 U.S. 726 (1963).
24. The factual background and oral argument transcripts in *Loving* are drawn from Peter Irons, *May It Please the Court* (New York: New Press, 1993), pp. 277–283.
25. 405 U.S. 438 (1972), at 453 (emphasis in original).
26. Quotes and commentary are drawn from Garrow, *Liberty and Sexuality*, pp. 542–545.
27. O'Connor, *No Neutral Ground*, pp. 42–53.
28. Garrow, *Liberty and Sexuality*, pp. 548–560.
29. Ibid., pp. 557–658.
30. Ibid., pp. 605–606.
31. Ruth Bader Ginsburg, "Some Thoughts on Autonomy and Equality in Relation to *Roe* v. *Wade*," *North Carolina Law Review* 63 (January 1985), pp. 375, 381.
32. Quoted in Garrow, *Liberty and Sexuality*, p. 599.
33. Christopher Z. Mooney and Mei-Hsien Lee, "Legislating Morality in the American States: The Case of Pre-Roe Abortion Regulation Reform," *American Journal of Political Science* 39 (1995), pp. 599–627.
34. Neal Devins, *Shaping Constitutional Values: Elected Government, the Supreme Court and the Abortion Debate* (Baltimore. Md.: Johns Hopkins University Press, 1995), 4–5.
35. O'Connor, *No Neutral Ground*, pp. 57–67; Devins, *Shaping Constitutional Values*, pp. 60–62; Edward Keynes and Randall K. Miller, *The Court* v. *Congress: Prayer, Busing, and Abortion* (Durham, N.C.: Duke University Press, 1989), pp. 174–312.
36. Debra W. Stewart and Jeanne Bell Nicholson, "Abortion Policy in 1978: A Follow-up Analysis," *Publius* 9 (1979), p. 161.
37. 476 U.S. 747 (1986); 492 U.S. 490 (1989).
38. Anne Kornhauser, "Amicus Scurry; Pro-Choice Legal Barrage," *Legal Times*, January 30, 1989, p. 1.
39. Eric Harrison, "Missouri Law: Catchall for Abortion Foes," *Los Angeles Times*, June 26, 1989, p. 16.
40. Charles Fried, *Order and Law : Arguing the Reagan Revolution* (New York: Simon & Schuster, 1991), pp. 71–88. Charles Fried also served as a clerk for Justice John Harlan during the term in which *Griswold* was argued and decided, and worked closely with him in developing the argument declaring the Connecticut anti–birth control law unconstitutional. See Garrow, *Liberty and Sexuality*, pp. 174–175, 190–191.
41. Quoted in Devins, *Shaping Constitutional Values*, p. 66.
42. 492 U.S. 490 at 535.
43. O'Connor, *No Neutral Ground*, pp.132–133; Barbara Hinkson Craig and David M. O'Brien, *Abortion and American Politics* (Chatham, N.J.: Chatham House, 1993), pp. 245–277.
44. 497 U.S. 502 (1990); 497 U.S. 417 (1990).
45. Garrow, *Liberty and Sexuality*, pp. 471–472; O'Connor, *No Neutral Ground*, p. 139.
46. Quoted in John C. Jeffries, Jr., *Justice Lewis F. Powell, Jr.* (New York: Scribners, 1994), p. 530.
47. 355 A.2d 647 (1976).
48. 497 U.S. 261 (1990).
49. 521 U.S. 702 (1997).
50. Cass R. Sunstein, *One Case at a Time: Judicial Minimalism and the Supreme Court* (Cambridge, Mass.: Harvard University Press, 1999), pp. 84–88.

Chapter 11

1. Quotes and narrative taken from Juan Williams, *Eyes on the Prize* (New York: Viking, 1987), pp. 36–57.
2. Gerald Rosenberg, *The Hollow Hope: Can Courts Bring About Social Change?* (Chicago: University of Chicago Press, 1991).
3. David M. Oshinsky, *Worse Than Slavery: Parchman Farm and the Ordeal of Jim Crow Justice* (New York: The Free Press, 1996).
4. Don E. Fehrenbacher, *Slavery, Law & Politics: The Dred Scott Case in Historical Perspective* (New York: Oxford University Press, 1981), p. 7.
5. Ibid., pp. 7–10.
6. William Lee Miller, *Arguing About Slavery: John Quincy Adams and the Great Battle in the United States Congress* (New York: Vintage Books, 1998), pp. 16–19; Fehrenbacher, *Slavery, Law & Politics*, pp. 8–9.
7. Miller, *Arguing About Slavery*, p. 21.
8. Fehrenbacher, *Slavery, Law & Politics*, pp. 14–15.
9. Ibid., p. 15.
10. Ibid., p. 17.
11. James D. Anderson, *The Education of Blacks in the South, 1860–1935* (Chapel Hill: University of North Carolina Press, 1988), pp. 1–3.
12. Alfred H. Kelly, Winfred A. Harbison, and Herman Belz, *The American Constitution: Its Origins and Development, Vol. 1* (New York: Norton, 1991), pp. 242–246.

13. Ibid., pp. 259–262.
14. Ibid., pp. 265–268.
15. Kelly, Harbison, and Belz, *The American Constitution,* pp. 157–159.
16. Peter Irons, *A People's History of the Supreme Court* (New York: Viking Press, 1999), pp. 164–170.
17. Kelly, Harbison, and Belz, *The American Constitution,* pp. 274–275.
18. Eric Foner, *Reconstruction, 1863–1877: America's Unfinished Revolution* (New York: Harper & Row, 1988), pp. 445–446.
19. John Hope Franklin, *Reconstruction After the Civil War* (Chicago: University of Chicago Press, 1995), pp. 69–83; Kelly, Harbison, and Belz, *The American Constitution,* pp. 336–340.
20. 83 U.S. 36 (1873).
21. Michael Kent Curtis, *No State Shall Abridge: The Fourteenth Amendment and the Bill of Rights* (Durham, N.C.: Duke University Press, 1990), pp. 174–178.
22. 92 U.S. 542 (1876).
23. Irons, *A People's History of the Constitution,* pp. 203–206.
24. Foner, *Reconstruction,* pp. 602–603.
25. 109 U.S. 3 (1883).
26. C. Vann Woodward, *The Strange Career of Jim Crow* (New York: Oxford University Press, 1974), pp. 11–29.
27. Ibid, p. 96.
28. 163 U.S. 537 (1896), at 544.
29. Cass R. Sunstein, *The Partial Constitution* (Cambridge, Mass.: Harvard University Press, 1993), pp. 42–45.
30. Irons, *A People's History of the Supreme Court,* pp. 222–227.
31. Gunnar Myrdal, *The American Dilemma: The Negro Problem and Modern Democracy* (New York: Harper & Row, 1944), pp. 587–588.
32. Quoted in Nicholas Lemann, *The Promised Land: The Great Black Migration and How It Changed America* (New York: Alfred A. Knopf, 1991), pp. 24–28. Lemann is quoting David L. Cohn, *Where I Was Born and Raised* (South Bend, Ind.: University of Notre Dame Press, 1967).
33. Ibid., pp. 26–27.
34. The above narrative and that which follows on the NAACP litigation campaign are drawn largely from Clement E. Vose, *Caucasians Only* (Berkeley: University of California Press, 1959); Richard Kluger, *Simple Justice* (New York: Alfred A. Knopf, 1976); Juan Williams, *Eyes on the Prize* (New York: Viking, 1987); Mark V. Tushnet, *The NAACP's Legal Campaign Against Segregated Education, 1925–1950* (Chapel Hill: University of North Carolina Press, 1987); Jack Greenberg, *Crusaders in the Courts: How a Dedicated Band of Lawyers Fought for the Civil Rights Revolution* (New York: Basic Books, 1994); Mark V. Tushnet, *Making Civil Rights Law: Thurgood Marshall and the Supreme Court, 1936–1961* (New York: Oxford University Press, 1994); Juan Williams, *Thurgood Marshall: American Revolutionary* (New York: Times Books, 1998).
35. W. E. B. Du Bois, "Separation and Self-Respect," *The Crisis* 41 (March 1934), p. 85.
36. *Pearson* v. *Murray,* 169 Md. 478, 182 A. 590 (1936).
37. 305 U.S. 337 (1938).
38. 321 U.S. 649 (1944).
39. Tushnet, *Making Civil Rights Law,* pp. 89–92.
40. Quoted in Kluger, *Simple Justice,* p. 752.
41. Greenberg, *Crusaders in the Courts,* pp. 214–217.
42. Kluger, *Simple Justice,* pp. 752–753.
43. Ibid., p. 714.
44. Quoted in Irons, *A People's History of the Supreme Court,* p. 400.
45. Greenberg, *Crusaders in the Courts,* pp. 254–255.
46. For more on the Fifth Circuit's role in the civil rights revolution, see Jack Bass, *Unlikely Heroes* (New York: Touchstone, 1981). The Fifth Circuit was later divided in 1981 as part of a massive reorganization of the federal appeals courts.
47. 391 U.S. 430 (1968).
48. 396 U.S. 19 (1969).
49. Kluger, *Simple Justice,* p. 768.
50. Greenberg, *Crusaders in the Courts,* pp. 392–397; see also, David R. Goldfield, *Black, White and Southern: Race Relations and Southern Culture, 1940 to the Present* (Baton Rouge: Louisiana State University Press, 1990).
51. J. Harvie Wilkinson, *From Brown to Bakke* (New York: Oxford University Press, 1979).
52. *Milliken* v. *Bradley,* 433 U.S. 717 (1977).
53. 498 U.S. 237 (1991).
54. 503 U.S. 467 (1992).
55. 515 U.S. 70 (1995).
56. *Swann,* 402 U.S. 1, at 32.
57. 379 U.S. 241 (1964); 379 U.S. 294 (1964).
58. 118 U.S. 356 (1886).
59. See, for example, Herman Belz, *Equality Transformed: A Quarter Century of Affirmative Action* (New Brunswick, N.J.: Transaction Books, 1990).
60. Eric Foner, *Reconstruction,* pp. 70–71.
61. Greenberg, *Crusaders in the Courts,* pp. 464–465.
62. Mark V. Tushnet, *Making Constitutional Law: Thurgood Marshall and the Supreme Court, 1961–1991* (New York: Oxford University Press, 1997), pp. 120–121.
63. Greenberg, *Crusaders in the Courts,* pp. 464–465; Irons, *A People's History of the Supreme Court,* pp. 450–453.
64. Greenberg, *Crusaders in the Courts,* p. 464.
65. Greenberg, *Crusaders in the Courts,* p. 465; Joel Dreyfuss and Charles Lawrence III, *The Bakke Case: The Politics of Inequality* (New York: Harcourt Brace Jovanovich, 1979), pp. 17–30.
66. 480 U.S. 616 (1987).
67. 515 U.S. 200 (1995).
68. Quoted in Susan Gluck Mezey, *In Pursuit of Equality: Women, Public Policy and the Federal Courts* (New York: St. Martin's Press, 1992), pp. 8–9. The Adamses' letters are drawn from *Familiar Letters of John Adams and His Wife, Abigail Adams During the Revolution* (1876).
69. William Blackstone, *Commentaries on the Laws of England,* Book I.
70. Linda K. Kerber, *Women of the Republic* (Chapel Hill: University of North Carolina Press, 1980), pp. 119–121.
71. Sara M. Evans, *Born for Liberty: A History of Women in America* (New York: The Free Press, 1989), 74–77.
72. 21 Wallace 162 (1875).
73. Quoted in Evans, *Born for Liberty,* pp. 122–123.
74. Albie Sachs and Joan Hoff Wilson, *Sexism and the Law* (New York: The Free Press, 1978), pp. 81–83; Evans, *Born for Liberty,* pp. 123–124.
75. Karen O'Connor, *Women's Organizations' Use of the Courts* (Lexington, Mass.: Lexington Books, 1980), pp. 33–64.
76. 208 U.S. 412 (1908), at 422.
77. 198 U.S. 45 (1905).

78. 335 U.S. 464 (1948), at 466.
79. 368 U.S. 57 (1961), at 59.
80. Evans, *Born for Liberty,* 273–276.
81. David Halberstam, *The Fifties* (New York: Ballantine Books, 1994), pp. 592–598.
82. 411 U.S. 677 (1973).
83. O'Connor, *Women's Organizations' Use of the Court,* pp. 112–114.
84. Quoted in Jane J. Mansbridge, *Why We Lost the ERA* (Chicago: University of Chicago Press, 1986), pp. 102–104.
85. Bernard Schwartz, *The Ascent of Pragmatism* (Reading, Mass.: Addison-Wesley, 1990), pp. 226–232.
86. *Orr* v. *Orr,* 440 U.S. 268 (1979); *Califano* v. *Goldfarb,* 430 U.S. 199 (1977); and *Kirchberg* v. *Fennstra,* 450 U.S. 455 (1981); *Mississippi University for Women* v. *Hogan,* 458 U.S. 718 (1982); *J.E.B.* v. *Alabama ex rel. T.B.,* 511 U.S. 127 (1994).
87. *International Union, American Workers, Aerospace, Agricultural Implement Workers of America, UAW* v. *Johnson Controls,* 499 U.S. 187 (1991).
88. Wendy Williams, "The Equality Crisis: Some Reflections on Culture, Courts, and Feminism," *Women's Rights Law Reporter* 7 (1982), p. 181.
89. 453 U.S. 57 (1981).
90. 450 U.S. 464 (1981).
91. 458 U.S. 718 (1982).
92. *Meritor Savings Bank* v. *Vinson,* 477 U.S. 57 (1986).
93. Catharine MacKinnon, *Feminism Unmodified: Discourses on Life and Law* (Cambridge, Mass.: Harvard University Press, 1986), p. 103.
94. *Burlington Industries, Inc.* v. *Ellerth,* 524 U.S. 742 (1998); *Davis* v. *Monroe County Board of Education,* 526 U.S. 629 (1999).
95. *Baehr* v. *Lewin,* 875 P. 2d 225 (1993).
96. Mark Strasser, *Legally Wed: Same Sex Marriage and the Constitution* (Ithaca, N.Y.: Cornell University Press, 1997).
97. For an excellent discussion of the New Deal and post-Depression challenges to the social welfare state, see Alonzo Hamby, *Liberalism and Its Challengers* (New York: Oxford University Press, 1992).
98. Quoted in Cass Sunstein, *The Partial Constitution* (Cambridge, Mass.: Harvard University Press, 1993), p. 58.
99. Oliver Wendell Holmes Jr., *The Common Law,* Mark DeWolfe Howe, ed. (Boston: Back Bay Books, 1963), p. 37.
100. Michael Harrington, *The Other America* (New York: Collier Books, 1997).
101. The figures for all years (by families and by individuals) can be found at *http://www.acf.dhhs.gov/news/stats/3697.htm,* the Web site of the Aid to Children and Families program, United States Department of Health and Human Services.
102. 394 U.S. 618 (1969).
103. 397 U.S. 471 (1970), at 485.
104. H. R. Rep. No. 104-651 (1996), p. 1137.

Chapter 12

1. Juan Williams, *Eyes on the Prize: America's Civil Rights Years, 1954–1965* (New York: Viking Press, 1987); Allen J. Matusow, *The Unraveling of America* (New York: Harper, 1984), pp. 348–349.
2. Frank J. Parker, *Black Votes Count: Political Empowerment in Mississippi after 1965* (Chapel Hill: University of North Carolina Press, 1990), p. 2.
3. Mark V. Tushnet, *Making Civil Rights Law: Thurgood Marshall and the Supreme Court, 1936–1961* (New York: Oxford University Press, 1994), pp. 99–100.
4. Alfred H. Kelly, Winfred A. Harbison, and Herman Belz, *The American Constitution: Its Origins and Development,* Vol. 1 (New York: W. W. Norton, 1991), pp. 74–75.
5. Kermit L. Hall, *The Magic Mirror: Law in American History* (New York: Oxford University Press, 1989), pp. 16–17.
6. Leonard Dinnerstein, *Anti-Semitism in America* (New York: Oxford University Press, 1994), pp. 14–15; Shawn Peters, *Judging Jehovah's Witnesses: Religious Persecution at the Dawn of the Rights Revolution* (Lawrence: University Press of Kansas, 2000).
7. Sara M. Evans, *Born for Liberty: A History of Women in America* (New York: Free Press, 1989), pp. 122–124.
8. Richard Hofstadter, *The Idea of a Party System: The Rise of Legitimate Opposition in the United States, 1780–1840.* Berkeley: University of California Press, 1969.
9. Bruce Ackerman, *We the People: Foundations* (Cambridge, Mass.: Harvard University Press, 1991), pp. 75–77.
10. Eric Foner, *Reconstruction: America's Unfinished Revolution, 1863–1877* (New York: Harper & Row, 1988), p. 222.
11. Bruce Ackerman, *We the People: Transformations* (Cambridge, Mass.: Harvard University Press, 1998), pp. 106–107.
12. Foner, *Reconstruction,* pp. 216–227.
13. John Hope Franklin, *Reconstruction after the Civil War* (Chicago: University of Chicago Press, 1994), pp. 82–83; Foner, *Reconstruction,* pp. 446–448.
14. Foner, *Reconstruction,* pp. 457–459.
15. Ibid., p. 582.
16. Harold M. Hyman, *The Reconstruction Justice of Salmon P. Chase* (Lawrence: University Press of Kansas, 1997).
17. Michael Kent Curtis, *No State Shall Abridge: The Fourteenth Amendment and the Bill of Rights* (Durham, N.C.: Duke University Press, 1990), pp. 174–178.
18. *United States* v. *Reese,* 92 U.S. 214 (1876).
19. Patricia Sullivan, *Days of Hope: Race and Democracy in the New Deal Era* (Chapel Hill: University of North Carolina Press, 1996), pp. 12–15; C. Vann Woodward, *Tom Watson: Agrarian Rebel* (New York: Oxford University Press, 1987).
20. Tushnet, *Making Civil Rights Law,* pp. 100–101.
21. 273 U.S. 536 (1927).
22. 286 U.S. 73 (1932).
23. 295 U.S. 45 (1935).
24. Tushnet, *Making Civil Rights Law,* pp. 102–103.
25. Juan Williams, *Thurgood Marshall: American Revolutionary* (New York: Times Books, 1998), pp. 107–112.
26. Quoted in Jack Greenberg, *Crusaders in the Courts: How a Dedicated Band of Lawyers Fought for the Civil Rights Revolution* (New York: Basic Books, 1994), p. 109.
27. Williams, *Thurgood Marshall,* pp. 112, 313.
28. David Garrow, *Protest at Selma* (New Haven, Conn.: Yale University Press, 1978), pp. 7–30.
29. 380 U.S. 145 (1965).
30. 383 U.S. 663 (1966).
31. 384 U.S. 641 (1966).
32. Richard K. Scher, Jon L. Mills, and John J. Hotaling, *Voting Rights and Democracy: The Law and Politics of Districting* (Chicago: Nelson-Hall, 1997), pp. 21–22.

33. *Thornburg* v. *Gingles,* 478 U.S. 30 (1986).
34. *Marbury* v. *Madison,* 1 Cranch 137 (1803), at 170.
35. 328 U.S. 549 (1946), at 553–554.
36. 372 U.S. 368 (1963); 376 U.S. 1 (1964); 377 U.S. 533 (1964).
37. 372 U.S. 368 (1963), at 381.
38. Richard C. Cortner, *The Apportionment Cases* (Knoxville: University of Tennessee Press, 1970), p. 207; Samuel Walker, *In Defense of American Liberties: A History of the ACLU* (New York: Oxford University Press, 1990), pp. 256–257.
39. Scher, Mills, and Hotaling. *Voting Rights and Democracy,* pp. 25–27.
40. Gerald R. Pomper, ed. *The Election of 1980* (Chatham, N.J.: Chatham House, 1981), p. 71.
41. Parker, *Black Votes Count,* p. 31.
42. David Lublin, *The Paradox of Representation* (Princeton, N.J.: Princeton University Press, 1997), pp. 124–125.
43. David T. Canon, *Race, Redistricting and Representation: The Unintended Consequences of Black Majority Districts* (Chicago: University of Chicago Press, 1999), pp. 61–62.
44. Quoted in ibid., pp. 69–70.
45. 478 U.S. 30 (1986).
46. Lublin, *The Paradox of Representation,* pp. 124–125.
47. On this point, see especially Canon, *Race, Redistricting and Representation,* pp. 69–70; and Lublin, *The Paradox of Representation,* pp. 120–133.
48. See *www.fairvote.org; www.jointctr.org.*
49. This account is drawn from *www.cnn.com/allpolitics,* accessed December 13, 2000.
50. *Bush* v. *Gore I,* 531 U.S. 98 (2000).
51. Ibid.

Glossary

a fortiori By even greater force of logic; even more so <if a 14-year-old child cannot sign a binding contract, then, *a fortiori*, a 13 year old cannot>.

ad hoc Formed for a particular purpose <the board created an ad hoc committee to discuss funding for the new arena>.

adjudicate To rule upon judicially.

advisory opinion A nonbinding statement by a court of its interpretation of the law on a matter submitted for that purpose.

affirm 1. To confirm (a judgment) on appeal. 2. To solemnly declare, rather than swear under oath.

amicus curiae (Latin "friend of the court") A person who is not a party to a lawsuit but who petitions the court or is requested by the court to file a brief in the action because that person has a strong interest in the subject matter.

appeal To seek review (from a lower court's decision) by a higher court <petitioner appeals the conviction>.

appellant A party who appeals a lower court's decision, usually seeking reversal of that decision.

appellee A party against whom an appeal is taken and whose role is to respond to that appeal, usually seeking affirmance of that lower court's decision.

arguendo (Latin "in arguing") 1. For the sake of argument (assuming *arguendo* that discovery procedures were correctly followed, the court still cannot grant the defendant's motion to dismiss). 2. During the course of argument.

bill of attainder A legislative act that inflicts punishment on named individuals or members of an easily ascertainable group without a judicial trial. The U.S. Constitution forbids Congress and the states from passing bills of attainder.

Black Codes 1. Antebellum state laws enacted to regulate the institution of slavery. 2. Laws enacted shortly after the Civil War in the former Confederate states to restrict the liberties of the newly freed slaves as a way to ensure a supply of inexpensive agricultural labor and to maintain white supremacy.

brief A written statement setting out the legal contentions of a party in litigation, especially on appeal; a document prepared by council as the basis for arguing a case, consisting of legal and factual arguments and the authorities in support of them.

case A proceeding, action, suit, or controversy at law or in equity.

***certiorari,* writ of** (Latin "to be more fully informed") An extraordinary writ issued by an appellate court, at its discretion, directing a lower court to deliver the record in the case for review.

civil law The law of civil or private rights, as opposed to criminal law or administrative law.

class action A lawsuit in which a single person or a small group of people represents the interests of a larger group. Requirements under federal law for maintaining a class action are (1) the class must be so large that individual suits would be impracticable, (2) there must be legal or factual questions common to the class, (3) the claims or defenses of the representative parties must be typical of those of the class, and (4) the representative parties must adequately protect the interests of the class.

color of law The appearance or semblance, without the substance, of legal right. The term usually implies a misuse of power made possible because the wrongdoer is clothed with the authority of the state. State action is synonymous with color of law in the context of federal civil rights statutes or criminal law.

comity Courtesy among political entities (as nations, states, or courts of different jurisdiction), involving especially mutual recognition of legislative, executive, and judicial acts.

common law The body of law derived from judicial decisions, rather than from statutes or constitutions.

concurring opinion A separate written opinion explaining such a vote.

consent decree A court decree that all parties agree to. Also termed consent order.

contempt Conduct that defies the authority or dignity of a court or legislature. Such conduct interferes with the administration of justice and is punishable, usually by fine or imprisonment.

criminal law The body of law defining offenses against the community at large, regulating how suspects are investigated, charged, and tried, and establishing punishment for convicted offenders.

declaratory judgment A court's final determination of the rights and obligations of the parties in a case.

de facto (Latin "in point of fact") 1. Actual; existing in fact; having effect, even though not formally or legally recognized.

de jure (Latin "as a matter of law") Existing by right or according to law.

dicta A statement of opinion or belief considered authoritative because of the dignity of the person making it.

dissenting opinion A judicial opinion disagreeing with that of the majority of the same court, given by one or more members of the court.

docket A brief entry describing the proceedings and filings in a court case.

due process The conduct of legal proceedings according to established rules and principles for the protection and enforcement of private rights, including notice and the right to a fair hearing before a tribunal with the power to decide the case.

enjoin 1. To legally prohibit or restrain by injunction (the company was enjoined from selling its stock). 2. To prescribe, mandate, or strongly encourage.

equity The recourse to principles of justice to correct or supplement the law as applied to particular circumstances.

error, writ of A writ issued by an appellate court directing a lower court to deliver the record in the case for review.

ex parte On or from one party only, usually without notice to or argument from the adverse party (the judge conducted the hearing *ex parte*).

grand jury A body of people who are chosen to sit permanently for at least a month—sometimes a year—and who, in *ex parte* proceedings, decide whether to issue indictments. If the grand jury decides that evidence is strong enough to hold a suspect for trial, it returns a bill of indictment charging the suspect with a specific crime.

habeas corpus (Latin "that you have the body") A writ employed to bring a person before a court, most frequently to ensure that the party's imprisonment or detention is not illegal.

immunity An exemption from a duty, liability, or service of process; especially, such as exemption granted to a public official.

in camera 1. In the judge's private chambers. 2. In the courtroom with all spectators excluded. 3. (Of judicial action) taken when court is not in session. Also termed in reference to the opinion of one judge.

in forma pauperis (Latin "in the manner of a pauper") In the manner of an indigent who is permitted to disregard filing fees and court costs <when suing, a poor person is generally entitled to proceed *in forma pauperis*>.

infra (Latin "below") Later in this text. *Infra* is used as a citational signal to refer to a later-cited authority. In medieval Latin, *infra* also acquired the sense "within."

inter alia Among other things.

ipso facto (Latin "by the fact itself") By the very nature of the situation.

litigant A party to a lawsuit.

mandamus, writ of (Latin "we command") A writ issued by a superior court to compel a lower court or a government officer to perform mandatory or purely ministerial duties correctly.

moot Having no practical significance; hypothetical or academic.

motion A written or oral application requesting a court to make a specified ruling or order.

obiter dicta (see dicta) (Latin "something said on passing") A judicial comment made during the course of delivering a judicial opinion, but one that is unnecessary to the decision in the case and therefore not precedential.

per curiam By the court as a whole.

per se 1. Of, in, or by itself; standing alone, without reference to additional facts. 2. As a matter of law.

petit jury A jury (usually consisting of twelve persons) summoned and empaneled in the trial of a specific case.

petitioner A party who presents a petition to a court or other official body, especially when seeking relief on appeal.

plaintiff The party who brings a civil suit in a court of law.

plenary Full; complete; to be attended by all members or participants.

plurality opinion An appellate opinion without enough judges' votes to constitute a majority, but having received the greatest number of votes of any of the opinions filed.

recuse To remove (oneself) as a judge in a particular case because of prejudice or conflict of interest.

remand To send (a case or claim) back to the court or tribunal from which it came for some further action <the appellate court reversed the trial court's opinion and remanded the case for new trial>.

respondent The party against whom an appeal is taken.

reverse An appellate court's overturning of a lower court's decision.

seriatim One after another; in a series; successively.

stare decisis (Latin "to stand by things decided") The doctrine of precedent, under which it is necessary for a court to follow earlier judicial decisions when the same points arise again in litigation.

state action Official government action, especially, in constitutional law, an intrusion on a person's rights (especially civil rights) either by a governmental entity or by a private requirement that can be enforced only by governmental action.

statute A law passed by a legislative body.

stay The postponement or halting of a proceeding, judgment, or the like.

sub silento Under silence; without notice being taken; without being expressly mentioned.

subpoena (Latin "under penalty") A writ commanding a person to appear before a court or other tribunal, subject to a penalty for failing to comply.

subpoena *duces tecum* A subpoena ordering the witness to appear and to bring specified documents or records.

summary judgment A judgment granted on a claim about which there is no genuine issue of material fact and upon which the movant is entitled to prevail as a matter of law. This procedural device allows the speedy disposition of a controversy without the need for trial.

supra (Latin "above") Earlier in this text; used as a citational signal to refer to a previously cited authority.

tort A civil wrong for which a remedy may be obtained, usually in the form of damages; as breach of a duty that the law imposes on everyone in the same relation to one another as those involved in a given transaction.

trespass An unlawful act committed against the person or property of another.

vacate To nullify or cancel; make void; invalidate.

writ A written court order, in the name of a state or other competent legal authority, commanding the addressee to do or refrain from doing some specified act.

Subject Index

Case Index

Note: cases in boldface type are excerpted in this text.